Lecture Notes in Computer Science 14000

Formal Methods

Subline of Lecture Notes in Computer Science

More information about this series at https://link.springer.com/bookseries/558

Marsha Chechik · Joost-Pieter Katoen ·
Martin Leucker
Editors

Formal Methods

25th International Symposium, FM 2023
Lübeck, Germany, March 6–10, 2023
Proceedings

Springer

Editors
Marsha Chechik
University of Toronto
Toronto, ON, Canada

Joost-Pieter Katoen
RWTH Aachen University
Aachen, Germany

Martin Leucker
University of Lübeck
Lübeck, Germany

ISSN 0302-9743 ISSN 1611-3349 (electronic)
Lecture Notes in Computer Science
ISBN 978-3-031-27480-0 ISBN 978-3-031-27481-7 (eBook)
https://doi.org/10.1007/978-3-031-27481-7

This Springer imprint is published by the registered company Springer Nature Switzerland AG
The registered company address is: Gewerbestrasse 11, 6330 Cham, Switzerland

Preface

This volume contains the papers presented at the 25th Symposium on Formal Methods (FM 2023), organized by the Institute for Software Engineering and Programming Languages, University of Lübeck, and held at the University of Lübeck, Germany during March 6–10, 2023. In addition, these proceedings contain 7 papers selected by the Program Committee of the Industry Day (I-Day@FM 2023). FM 2023 was organized under the auspices of Formal Methods Europe (FME), an independent association whose aim is to stimulate the use of, and research on, formal methods for software development. It has been over 35 years since the first VDM symposium in 1987 brought together researchers with the common goal of creating methods to produce high-quality software based on rigor and reason. Since then the diversity and complexity of computer technology has changed enormously and the formal methods community has stepped up to the challenges those changes brought by adapting, generalizing, and improving the models and analysis techniques that were the focus of that first symposium. The papers in this proceedings reflect this progress, and demonstrate how formal methods have been successfully applied in many different application areas and domains including software, cyber-physical systems and integrated computer-based systems.

To establish the program of FM 2023, we assembled a Program Committee (PC) which included 43 internationally renowned scientists. We sought submissions in five categories: regular papers, long tool papers, case study papers, short papers and tool demonstration papers. And, for the first time for FM, we ran a double-blind review process. We received 95 paper submissions from authors in 29 different countries: 75 regular paper submissions, 8 long tool paper submissions and four each of case study, short and tool demo submissions. Each submission went through a rigorous review process in which the papers were reviewed by at least three PC members. Following a two-week discussion phase, we selected 28 papers for presentation during the symposium and inclusion into these proceedings: 18 regular, 5 long tool, 3 case study, 1 short and 1 tool demo, with the overall acceptance rate of 29%. Accepted papers were invited for review by the Artifact Evaluation committee, chaired by Matthias Volk, which gave out reproducibility and availability badges. This year, FM 2023 featured a special session on “Formal Methods Meets AI” which focused on formal and rigorous modeling and analysis techniques to ensure the safety, robustness and trustworthiness of AI-based systems. We thank Benedikt Bollig, Daniel Neider, and Özgür Özcep for chairing this track. This year, FME awarded the 3rd Lucas Prize for a Highly Influential Paper published in an FM symposium.

The symposium featured an FM luminary talk by Jeannette Wing (Columbia University, Data Science Institute, USA) and three keynotes by Laura Kovács (Vienna University of Technology, Institute of Logic and Computation, Austria), Harald Ruess (fortiss GmbH, Germany) and Nils Jansen (Radboud University Nijmegen, Department of Software Science, The Netherlands). We hereby thank these invited speakers for having accepted our invitation. The program also featured three workshops, four tutorials and presentation of four journal-first papers. We are grateful to all involved in FM 2023, in particular, the FME board members for their constant support, the PC members and sub-reviewers for their accurate and timely reviewing, all authors for their submissions, and all attendees of the symposium for their participation. We also thank all the other committees (I-Day, Doctoral Symposium, Journal First Track, Workshops, and Tutorials), listed on the following pages, and the excellent local organization and publicity teams. We are very grateful to our sponsors: AWS, Dräger, Huawei, fortiss, UniTransferKlinik Lübeck and Universität zu Lübeck. Finally, we thank Springer for publishing these proceedings in their FM subline and we acknowledge the support from EasyChair in assisting us in managing the complete process from submissions to these proceedings to the program.

January 2023

Marsha Chechik
Joost-Pieter Katoen
Martin Leucker

Organization

Program Committee

Dalal Alrajeh	Imperial College London, UK
Luís Soares Barbosa	University of Minho, Portugal
Ezio Bartocci	TU Wien, Austria
Nikolaj Bjørner	Microsoft Research, USA
Sandrine Blazy	University of Rennes 1 - IRISA, France
Benedikt Bollig	LSV, ENS Cachan, CNRS, France
Borzoo Bonakdarpour	Michigan State University, USA
Pablo Castro	National University of Río Cuarto, Argentina
Ana Cavalcanti	University of York, UK
Milan Ceska	Brno University of Technology, Czech Republic
Marsha Chechik	University of Toronto, Canada
Nancy Day	University of Waterloo, Canada
Bernd Fischer	Stellenbosch University, South Africa
Adrian Francalanza	University of Malta, Malta
Arie Gurfinkel	University of Waterloo, Canada
Ichiro Hasuo	National Institute of Informatics, Japan
Keijo Heljanko	University of Helsinki, Finland
Holger Hermanns	Saarland University, Germany
Marieke Huisman	University of Twente, The Netherlands
Reiner Hähnle	TU Darmstadt, Germany
Peter Höfner	Australian National University, Australia
Einar Broch Johnsen	University of Oslo, Norway
Sebastian Junges	Radboud University, The Netherlands
Joost-Pieter Katoen	RWTH Aachen University, Germany
Martin Leucker	University of Lübeck, Germany
Yi Li	Nanyang Technological University, Singapore
Lei Ma	University of Alberta, Canada
Mieke Massink	CNR-ISTI, Italy
Christoph Matheja	Technical University of Denmark (DTU), Denmark
Annabelle McIver	Macquarie University, Australia
Claudio Menghi	McMaster University, Canada
Daniel Neider	TU Dortmund, Germany
Jan Peleska	University of Bremen, Germany
André Platzer	Karlsruhe Institute of Technology, Germany
Baishakhi Ray	Columbia University, USA
Jan Oliver	Ringert Bauhaus University Weimar, Germany
Cristina Seceleanu	Mälardalen University, Sweden
Marjan Sirjani	Mälardalen University, Sweden

Paola Spoletini	Kennesaw State University, USA
Jun Sun	Singapore University, Singapore
Emilio Tuosto	Gran Sasso Science Institute, Italy
Matthias Volk	University of Twente, The Netherlands
Ou Wei	Thales, Canada
Mike Whalen	Amazon Web Services, USA
Naijun Zhan	Chinese Academy of Sciences, China
Özgür Özcep	University of Lübeck, Germany

FME Board

Ana Cavalcanti (Chair)	University of York, UK
Nico Plat (Treasurer)	University of Twente, The Netherlands
Lars-Henrik Eriksson (Secretary)	Uppsala University, Sweden
Maurice ter Beek (Conferences)	CNR-ISTI, Italy
Einar Broch Johnsen (Communication)	University of Oslo, Norway

Organization Committee

General Chair

Martin Leucker	University of Lübeck, Germany

PC Chairs

Marsha Chechik	University of Toronto, Canada
Joost-Pieter Katoen	RWTH Aachen University, Germany

AE Chair

Matthias Volk	University of Twente, The Netherlands

Workshop Chairs

Esfandiar Mohammadi	University of Lübeck, Germany
Volker Stolz	Western Norway, University of Applied Science, Norway

Tutorial Chairs

Martin Sachenbacher	University of Lübeck, Germany
Cesar Sanchez	IMDEA Software Institute, Spain

Publicity Chair

Violet Ka I Pun	Western Norway, University of Applied Science, Norway

Exhibition Chairs

Marieke Huisman	University of Twente, The Netherlands
Einar Broch Johnsen	University of Oslo, Norway
Tim Suthau	University of Lübeck, Germany

Industry Day Chairs

Chih-Hong Cheng	Fraunhofer IKS, Germany
Ralf Huuck	Logilica, Australia
Grigore Rosu	University of Illinois, USA
Tim Suthau	University of Lübeck, Germany
Oksana Tkachuk	Amazon Web Services, USA
Alexander Weiss	Accemic, Germany

Financial Chair

Maria Ernst	University of Lübeck, Germany

Local Organization Chair

Martin Mildner	University of Lübeck, Germany

Doctoral Symposium Chairs

Wolfgang Ahrendt	Chalmers University of Technology, Sweden
Ralf Möller	University of Lübeck, Germany

FM Meets AI Track Chairs

Benedikt Bollig	ENS Paris-Saclay, France
Daniel Neider	MPI SWS, Germany
Özgür Özcep	University of Lübeck, Germany

Journal First Committee

Maurice ter Beek	CNR-ISTI, Italy
Eerke Boiten	De Montfort University, UK
Manfred Broy	Technical University of Munich, Germany
Cliff Jones	Newcastle University, UK

Artifact Evaluation Committee

Roman Andriushchenko	Brno University of Technology, Czech Republic
César Cornejo	Universidad Nacional de Rio Cuarto, Argentina
Federico Formica	McMaster University, Canada
Ritam Ganguly	Michigan State University, USA
Lutz Klinkenberg	RWTH Aachen University, Germany
Anik Momtaz	Michigan State University, USA
Luciano Putruele	Universidad Nacional de Rio Cuarto, Argentina

Marco Scaletta	Technische Universität Darmstadt, Germany
Soaibuzzaman Soaibuzzaman	Bauhaus University Weimar, Germany
Gerard Tabone	University of Malta, Malta
Matthias Volk	University of Twente, The Netherlands
Yiming Xu	Australia National University, Australia

Journal-First Presentations

1. Debbi, H.: A debugging game for probabilistic models. Formal Aspects Comput. **34** (2022). https://doi.org/10.1145/3536429
2. Ferrando, A., et al.: Bridging the gap between single- and multi-model predictive runtime verification. Formal Methods Syst. Des. **59** (2022). https://doi.org/10.1007/s10703-022-00395-7
3. Coughlin, N., Smith, G.: Compositional noninterference on hardware weak memory models. Sci. Comput. Program. **217** (2022). https://doi.org/10.1016/j.scico.2022.102779
4. Gleirscher, M., et al.: Verified synthesis of optimal safety controllers for human-robot collaboration. Sci. Comput. Program. **218** (2022). https://doi.org/10.1016/j.scico.2022.102809

Additional Reviewers

An, Jie
Andriushchenko, Roman
Attala, Ziggy
Backeman, Peter
Badings, Thom
Balu, Balahari Vignesh
Bartolo Burlò, Christian
Basile, Davide
Baxter, James
Bengolea, Valeria
Betarte, Gustavo
Brieger, Marvin
Brix, Christopher
Bubel, Richard
Cai, Simin
Cassano, Valentin
Ciancia, Vincenzo
Cordwell, Katherine
Coto, Alex
Demasi, Ramiro
Dillmann, Stefan
Doan, Nguyen Anh Vu
Eberhart, Clovis
Enea, Constantin
Farzan, Azadeh
Fesefeldt, Ira
Filipovikj, Predrag
Foster, Simon
Ganguly, Ritam
Gleirscher, Mario
Grätz, Lukas
Gu, Rong
Herd, Benjamin
Heydari Tabar, Asmae
Hsu, Tzu-Han
Inverso, Omar
Kabra, Aditi
Kamburjan, Eduard
Klinkenberg, Lutz
Kobayashi, Tsutomu
Latella, Diego
Laurent, Jonathan
Le, Nham
Leander, Björn

Leemhuis, Mena
Lengal, Ondrej
Lluch Lafuente, Alberto
Lopez Pombo, Carlos Gustavo
Lopez-Miguel, Ignacio D.
Luo, Weilin
Marksteiner, Stefan
Mauro, Jacopo
Mitsch, Stefan
Moezkarimi, Zahra
Momtaz, Anik
Moradi, Fereidoun
Morgan, Carroll
Nesterini, Eleonora
Neufeld, Emery
Noah Abou El Wafa
Noll, Thomas
Pontiggia, Francesco
Putruele, Luciano
Qi, Xiaodong
Quatmann, Tim
Regis, Germán
Sachtleben, Robert
Sakar, Ömer
Sales, Emerson
Salimi, Maghsood
Scalas, Alceste
Scaletta, Marco
Schlatte, Rudolf
Schmidtke, Hedda Rahel
Schmitt, Anna
Schupp, Stefan
Seferis, Emmanouil
Stolz, Volker
Su, Yusen
Suilen, Marnix
Tabone, Gerard
Theodorou, Konstantinos
Tokas, Shukun
Vaandrager, Frits
Vandin, Andrea
Vazquez, Gricel
Visconti, Ennio
Waga, Masaki
Wang, Shuling
Windsor, Matt
Wu, Xiuheng
Xuereb, Jasmine
Yadav, Drishti
Yan, Rongjie
Zhang, Zhenya
Zhao, Hengjun

Contents

Keynotes

SAT/SMT

Verification I

Industry Day

Keynotes

Symbolic Computation in Automated Program Reasoning

Laura Kovács(✉)

TU Wien, Vienna, Austria
laura.kovacs@tuwien.ac.at

Abstract. We describe applications of symbolic computation towards automating the formal analysis of while-programs implementing polynomial arithmetic. We combine methods from static analysis, symbolic summation and computer algebra to derive polynomial loop invariants, yielding a finite representation of all polynomial equations that are valid before and after each loop execution. While deriving polynomial invariants is in general undecidable, we identify classes of loops for which we automatically can solve the problem of invariant synthesis. We further generalize our work to the analysis of probabilistic program loops. Doing so, we compute higher-order statistical moments over (random) program variables, inferring this way quantitative invariants of probabilistic program loops. Our results yield computer-aided solutions in support of formal software verification, compiler optimization, and probabilistic reasoning.

Keywords: Symbolic computation · Formal methods · Loop analysis · Algebraic recurrences · Probabilistic reasoning

1 Introduction

The long list of software failures over the past years calls for serious concerns in our digital society, imposing bad reputations and huge economic burdens on organizations, industries and governments. Improving software reliability is not enough anymore, ensuring software reliability is mandatory. The area of formal methods, in particular automated reasoning, addresses this demand, by providing rigorous mathematical arguments proving that the software has no errors. Yet, there are theoretical results showing that there is no "one" formal approach that can be used for every software error, in every technology. Existing solutions therefore exploit combinations of domain-specific software challenges by means of various kinds of reasoning based on deductive verification [9,10], model checking [5,23], abstract interpretation [8], theorem proving [21], and related areas, bringing technology breakthroughs in formal verification [2,7]. During the recent years, automated reasoning has become the back-bone of formal verification [6,20].

In this invited article, we focus on symbolic computation approaches easing automated reasoning about computer programs implementing loops with polynomial arithmetic and possibly probabilistic updates. The key ingredient of these approaches comes with novel combinations of computer mathematics and computational logic, enabling

M. Chechik et al. (Eds.): FM 2023, LNCS 14000, pp. 3–9, 2023.
https://doi.org/10.1007/978-3-031-27481-7_1

the design of new techniques towards *precisely capturing the meaning of program loops*. We advocate the *confluence of computer algebra and automated deduction* towards loop analysis, by developing and joining the best practices in (i) recurrence equations, symbolic summation and polynomial ideal theory from computer algebra with (ii) program structure detection, decision procedures and probabilistic reasoning from automated deduction. We believe a tight confluence between computer algebra and automated deduction turns symbolic computation into a powerful approach for automating reasoning about program loops, closely relating our intentions to the definition of symbolic computation as "the algorithmic solution of problems dealing with symbolic objects" [4].

The algorithmic solutions described in this invited article establish interactions between computer algebra and automated deduction for automating reasoning about program correctness. Importantly,

- we enhance automated deduction techniques with computer algebra insights, for example to derive loop properties that summarize/explain the functional behaviour of program loops (Sect. 2);
- we extend computer algebra methods by automated deduction approaches, for example by detecting and eliminating algebraic operations in program loops that cannot be handled by symbolic summation methods (Sect. 3);
- we design hybrid approaches complementing computer algebra and automated deduction, for example using statistical moments to enable exact inferences in probabilistic programs (Sect. 4);
- we develop cross-fertilizing techniques combining the computational power of computer algebra and automated deduction, yielding efficient reasoning engines in support of formal analysis an verification of program loops (Sects. 2–4).

2 Symbolic Computation in Inductive Invariant Synthesis

We first present our work advancing the state-of-the-art in *synthesizing program properties, such as loop invariants*. Such properties imply the absence of program errors at intermediate program steps and are thus critical in ensuring software reliability.

We motivate and illustrate our work for invariant synthesis using the C-like imperative program of Fig. 1 over integer-valued program variables x, y, z. The expected behaviour of Fig. 1 is specified using program assertions in the first-order fragment of non-linear (polynomial) arithmetic: pre-condition in line 1 using the `assume` construct, and post-condition in line 7 using `assert`. Figure 1 satisfies its requirements. Yet, formally proving its correctness is challenging: it requires "summarizing" the behavior of the program lines 2–6 by formulating program properties, such as loop invariants, that hold at an arbitrary loop iteration. While it is relatively easy to argue that $x \leq z$ is a loop invariant of Fig. 1, this property is a necessary but

```
1 assume
  (∃k)(k > 1 ∧ z = 2^k)
2 x := 1; y := 0;
3 while (x < z) do
4   x := 2 * x;
5   y := 1/2 * y + 1;
6 end do
7 assert
  (y − 2) * z + 2 = 0
```

Fig. 1. Invariant synthesis for polynomial loops.

not sufficient condition to establish correctness of Fig. 1. In addition to $x \leq z$, one also need loop invariants relating the values of x and y at arbitrary loop iterations. In our work [12,18], *we instrument automated deduction in program analysis with algebraic solutions* and infer inductive loop invariants as polynomial relations among loop variables. For example, in the case of Fig. 1, our work derives $x * y - 2 * x + 2 = 0$ as an inductive loop invariant. With this additional loop invariant at hand, correctness of Fig. 1 can formally be proven.

The main steps of our work towards polynomial invariant synthesis are summarized as follows:

I1 We consider the loop language $\mathcal{L}$ as the language defined by the symbols used in the program loop under analysis;

I2 We extend $\mathcal{L}$ with a fresh new variable n, denoting the loop counter. As such, we have $n \geq 0$;

I3 We translate loop updates into algebraic recurrence equations over n, by considering loop variables as algebraic sequences over n. As such, the loop semantics is precisely captured by a system of algebraic recurrences over n;

I4 We apply symbolic summation to derive closed form solutions of loop variables as functions of n and some initial values. These closed forms hold at an arbitrary loop iteration n, and hence are valid loop invariants over $\mathcal{L}$ extended with n;

I5 We eliminate n from the derived closed form solutions, obtaining this way inductive invariants in the original loop language $\mathcal{L}$.

While steps (I1)–(I5) yield a general, *recurrence-based approach towards precisely capturing loop semantics*, its genericity comes with the costs of being undecidable. For example, even when considering loops with only polynomial updates, the recurrences in step (I4) yield linear recurrences with polynomial coefficients, called P-finite recurrences, which do not always yield closed form solutions [16]. In fact, it turns out that deriving (strongest) polynomial invariants of loops with arbitrary polynomial updates is in general undecidable [11]. To circumvent undecidability issues, we impose structural constraints over the loops we consider in steps (I1)–(I5). Namely, we define so-called *P-solvable loops* [18] which are polynomial program loops whose arithmetic can be described by linear recurrences with constant coefficients, i.e. C-finite recurrences. As a result, closed form solutions of loop variables can always be computed in step (I4). Moreover, whenever the resulting closed form solutions are algebraically dependent, in step (I5) we derive a finite representation of all polynomial invariant equalities of the loop. To this end, in step (I5) we use Gröbner basis computation tailored to P-solvable loop analysis and derive Gröbner bases of polynomial invariant ideals of P-solvable loops [18,22].

In summary, we provide an algorithmic solution towards deriving all polynomial invariants of P-solvable loops, by *strengthening automated deduction in loop analysis with C-finite recurrence solving and Gröbner basis computation*. A crucial step in our work comes with the *structural analysis of loops*: we define the class of P-solvable loops for which generating all polynomial invariants is decidable [14]. Our framework is automated in the Aligator software package [13,17] and generalized to restricted classes of P-finite recurrences [14].

3 Symbolic Computation in Unsolvable Loops

While enhancing automated deduction with computer algebra methods yields algorithmic solutions towards invariant synthesis, our approach in Sect. 2 is limited to P-solvable loops. Addressing the syntactic restrictions of C-finite recurrences, in our recent work [1] we *extend algebra-based loop analysis by automated deduction approaches based on program transformations*, allowing us to derive loop invariants of loops that are not P-solvable. We refer to loops that are not P-solvable simply as *unsolvable loops*. The crux in handling unsolvable loops comes with applying program analysis to compute the set of loop variables whose loop updates do not yield C-finite recurrences in the loop counters. We call these variables defective. Intuitively speaking, defective variables are loop variables violating the structural constraints of P-solvable loops. Defective variables do not generally admit closed-form solutions, hindering thus the application of step (I4) in Sect. 2.

In a nutshell, we proceed as follows. Given an unsolvable loop, we complement step (I4) from Sect. 2 with a polynomial-time algorithm to derive the set of defective loop variables. We synthesize polynomial transformations among defective loop variables in order to eliminate reasoning about defective loop variables and translate, whenever possible, an unsolvable loop into a P-solvable loop whose invariants can be computed. While an unsolvable loop and its P-solvable loop version are not equivalent in terms of operational semantics, loop invariants of the derived P-solvable loop are also loop invariants of the original unsolvable loops. As such, our polynomial transformations over unsolvable loops yield an *algorithmic solution towards inferring invariants of unsolvable loops*.

We illustrate the benefit of our approach on the unsolvable loop of Fig. 2[1]. While the polynomial update of y yields a C-finite recurrence as in Fig. 1, note that the variable b depends on itself in a non-linear manner (i.e. dependency upon b^2). As such, the sequence capturing the values of b at arbitrary loop iterations is not a C-finite sequence, implying also that the update of a in Fig. 2 does not yield a C-finite recurrence.

```
a := −2; b :=3; y := 0;
while (true) do
    a := 2 ∗ a + b²;
    b := 2 ∗ b − b²;
    y := 1/2 ∗ y + 1;
end do
```

Fig. 2. Invariants of unsolvable loops.

Hence, variables a and b are defective variables as they are "responsible" for Fig. 2 being unsolvable. Nevertheless, by considering the polynomial relation $a + b$, note that $a(n+1)+b(n+1) = 2*a(n)+2*b(n)$, where $a(n), b(n)$ respectively denote the values of a, b at loop iteration n. We therefore introduce a new loop variable x to denote $a + b$, yielding thus the C-finite sequence $x(n + 1) = 2 * x(n)$ which gives a valid polynomial relation among the values of variables a and b at arbitrary loop iterations n. With such a transformation, the unsolvable loop body of Fig. 2 is translated into the P-solvable loop body of Fig. 1, where the initial values of x and y are respectively 1 and 0, as in Fig. 1. Hence, we reduced the problem of inferring invariants of the unsolvable loop of Fig. 2 into the problem of deriving invariants for Fig. 1 and the approach of Sect. 2 can further be applied. As a result, by substituting $a + b$ for x in the inductive

[1] As we focus now only on invariant synthesis, we set $true$ to be the loop condition of Fig. 2.

```
x := 0;
while (true) do
    x := x − 1 [1/2] x + 1;
end do
```

(a)

```
x := 0;
while (true) do
    x := 2 ∗ x − 1 [1/2] 2 ∗ x + 1;
end do
```

(b)

Fig. 3. Probabilistic polynomial programs.

loop invariant $x * y - 2 * x + 2 = 0$ of Fig. 1, we obtain the inductive loop invariant $(a + b) * y - 2 * (a + b) + 2 = 0$ for Fig. 2.

In summary and as illustrated above, polynomial transformations over defective variables enlarge the class of loops for which inductive loop invariants can be derived by means of algebraic recurrence solving. Based on the structural analysis of unsolvable loops with defective variables, in [1] we give an algorithmic solutions for computing all polynomial combinations (up to an a priori given polynomial degree) of defective variables, such that the derived polynomial combinations satisfy C-finite recurrences. With such polynomial transformations, unsolvable loops can be translated into P-solvable ones, from which polynomial loop invariants can be inferred as discussed in Sect. 2. With our work being implemented in the Polar tool [1,19], we thus *strengthen computer algebra methods with polynomial program transformations* over defective variables. Our approach may automate compiler optimization steps, by translating complex unsolvable loops into simpler P-solvable ones.

4 Symbolic Computation in Probabilistic Reasoning

We finally argue that synergies between computer algebra and automated deduction yield further interesting applications of symbolic computation in emerging fields of automated reasoning. In particular, in this section we focus on the analysis of probabilistic programs that allow drawing random values from predefined probability distribution. As such, instead of treating program variables as having a certain value, program variables in probabilistic programs need to be treated as probabilistic distributions. Compared to the results of Sects. 2–3, this means that, in the presence of probabilistic program loops, we cannot consider values of program variables at arbitrary loop iterations, but need to reason about the probabilistic value distributions of variables at arbitrary loop iterations.

Despite the intrinsic hardness of reasoning about general probabilistic programs [15], we believe that symbolic computation is a powerful workhorse for analysing quantitative aspects of probabilistic programs. In particular, in the setting of probabilistic program loops, we advocate the use of so-called *moment-based recurrences* to lift algebraic recurrences over statistical moments of probabilistic loop variables [3,19]. By exploiting closure properties of statistical moments, moment-based recurrences express probabilistic loop semantics as algebraic recurrences over higher-order moments of the value distribution of program variables, allowing us, for example, to reason about expected values of (blocks of) program variables at arbitrary iteration.

By combining the P-solvable loop constraints of Sect. 2 with moment-based reasoning, we define the class of so-called *Prob-solvable loops*. Figure 3 lists two examples of Prob-solvable loops, where the updates to variable x are probabilistic updates. For example, in Fig. 3(a), the variable x is updated by $x - 1$ with probability 1/2 and by $x+1$ with probability 1-1/2, that is with probability 1/2. Essentially, Prob-solvable loops admit C-finite recurrences over the statistical moments of loop variables, and thus the resulting moment-based recurrences always admit closed-form solutions representing (moment-based) loop invariants.

Given the probabilistic nature of Prob-solvable loop variables, reasoning about higher-order moments is essential. Essentially, the more we know about the higher-order statistical moments of random variables, the better can we characterize the functional behaviour of Prob-solvable loop. For example, the expected values of the random variable x in both Fig. 3(a) and Fig. 3(b) are 0. Yet, Fig. 3(a) and Fig. 3(b) are clearly implementing different stochastic processes. This difference is already witnessed when computing, for example, the second-order moments of x, yielding the statistical variances of x. Namely, the variance of x at an arbitrary loop iteration n of Fig. 3(a) is given by the closed-form expression $\frac{4^n}{3}$, whereas the variance of x at an arbitrary loop iteration n of Fig. 3(b) is n. Hence, probability distributions of x in Fig. 3(a) and Fig. 3(b) are different, and this difference can be detected fully automatically by comparing the higher-order moments of x.

Our results from [3, 19] prove that higher-order moments of Prob-solvable loop variables always exits. Our work is fully automated in the Polar tool, providing an *algorithmic solutions towards probabilistic loop reasoning* by means of statistical analysis, recurrence solving and moment-based invariant inference.

Acknowledgments. The work described in this talk is based on joint works with a number of authors, including Daneshvar Amrollahi (TU Wien alumni), Ezio Bartocci (TU Wien), Andreas Humenberger (TU Wien alumni), Maximillian Jaroschek (TU Wien alumni), Tudor Jebelean (RISC-Linz), George Kenison (TU Wien), Marcel Moosbrugger (TU Wien), and Miroslav Stankovic (TU Wien).

The author acknowledges funding and support from the ERC Consolidator Grant 2020 ARTIST 101002685, the ProbInG grant of the Vienna Science and Technology Fund (WWTF) [10.47379/ICT19018], the Austrian FWF project W1255-N23, and the SecInt Doctoral College funded by TU Wien.

References

1. Amrollahi, D., Bartocci, E., Kenison, G., Kovács, L., Moosbrugger, M., Stankovic, M.: Solving invariant generation for unsolvable loops. In: Singh, G., Urban, C. (eds.) SAS 2022. LNCS, vol. 13790, pp. 19–43. Springer, Cham (2022). https://doi.org/10.1007/978-3-031-22308-2_3
2. Ball, T., Rajamani, S.: The SLAM project: debugging system software via static analysis. In: POPL, pp. 1–3 (2002)
3. Bartocci, E., Kovács, L., Stankovič, M.: Automatic generation of moment-based invariants for prob-solvable loops. In: Chen, Y.-F., Cheng, C.-H., Esparza, J. (eds.) ATVA 2019. LNCS, vol. 11781, pp. 255–276. Springer, Cham (2019). https://doi.org/10.1007/978-3-030-31784-3_15

4. Buchberger, B.: Symbolic computation (an editorial). J. Symbolic Comput. **1**(1), 1–6 (1985)
5. Clarke, E.M., Emerson, E.A.: Design and synthesis of synchronization skeletons using branching-time temporal logic. In: Logic of Programs, pp. 52–71 (1981)
6. Cook, B.: Formal reasoning about the security of amazon web services. In: Chockler, H., Weissenbacher, G. (eds.) CAV 2018. LNCS, vol. 10981, pp. 38–47. Springer, Cham (2018). https://doi.org/10.1007/978-3-319-96145-3_3
7. Cook, B., Podelski, A., Rybalchenko, A.: Terminator: beyond safety. In: CAV, pp. 415–418 (2006)
8. Cousot, P., Cousot, R.: Abstract interpretation: a unified lattice model for static analysis of programs by construction or approximation of fixpoints. In: POPL, pp. 238–252 (1977)
9. Floyd, R.W.: Assigning meanings to programs. J. Math. Aspects Comput. Sci. **19**, 19–37 (1967)
10. Hoare, C.A.R.: An axiomatic basis for computer programming. Commun. ACM **12**(10), 576–580 (1969)
11. Hrushovski, E., Ouaknine, J., Pouly, A., Worrell, J.: On strongest algebraic program invariants. J. ACM (2019). To appear
12. Humenberger, A., Jaroschek, M., Kovács, L.: Automated generation of non-linear loop invariants utilizing hypergeometric sequences. In: ISSAC, pp. 221–228 (2017)
13. Humenberger, A., Jaroschek, M., Kovács, L.: Aligator.jl – a julia package for loop invariant generation. In: Rabe, F., Farmer, W.M., Passmore, G.O., Youssef, A. (eds.) CICM 2018. LNCS (LNAI), vol. 11006, pp. 111–117. Springer, Cham (2018). https://doi.org/10.1007/978-3-319-96812-4_10
14. Humenberger, A., Jaroschek, M., Kovács, L.: Invariant generation for multi-path loops with polynomial assignments. In: VMCAI 2018. LNCS, vol. 10747, pp. 226–246. Springer, Cham (2018). https://doi.org/10.1007/978-3-319-73721-8_11
15. Kaminski, B.L., Katoen, J.P., Matheja, C.: On the hardness of analyzing probabilistic programs. Acta Informatica **56**(3), 255–285 (2019). https://doi.org/10.1007/s00236-018-0321-1
16. Kauers, M., Zimmermann, B.: Computing the algebraic relations of c-finite sequences and multisequences. J. Symbolic Comput. **43**(11), 787–803 (2008)
17. Kovács, L.: Aligator: a mathematica package for invariant generation (system description). In: Armando, A., Baumgartner, P., Dowek, G. (eds.) IJCAR 2008. LNCS (LNAI), vol. 5195, pp. 275–282. Springer, Heidelberg (2008). https://doi.org/10.1007/978-3-540-71070-7_22
18. Kovács, L.: Reasoning algebraically about p-solvable loops. In: Ramakrishnan, C.R., Rehof, J. (eds.) TACAS 2008. LNCS, vol. 4963, pp. 249–264. Springer, Heidelberg (2008). https://doi.org/10.1007/978-3-540-78800-3_18
19. Moosbrugger, M., Stankovic, M., Bartocci, E., Kovács, L.: This is the moment for probabilistic loops. ACM Program. Lang. **6**(OOPSLA2), 1497–1525 (2022)
20. O'Hearn, P.W.: Continuous reasoning: scaling the impact of formal methods. In: LICS, pp. 13–25 (2018)
21. Robinson, J.A., Voronkov A. (eds.): Handbook of Automated Reasoning (in 2 volumes). Elsevier, MIT Press; Amsterdam, Cambridge (2001)
22. Rodríguez-Carbonell, E., Kapur, D: Automatic generation of polynomial loop invariants: algebraic foundations. In: ISSAC, pp. 266–273 (2004)
23. Sifakis, J.: A unified approach for studying the properties of transition systems. Theor. Comput. Sci. **18**, 227–258 (1982)

The Next Big Thing: From Embedded Systems to Embodied Actors

Harald Ruess(✉)

fortiss - Research Institute of the Free State of Bavaria, Munich, Germany
ruess@fortiss.org

Abstract. Traditional engineering is coming to a junction from *embedded systems* to *embodied actors*, and with assuring the beneficial and robust behavior of dynamic federations of situation-aware, intent-driven, explorative, ever-evolving, and increasingly autonomous actors in uncertain and largely unpredictable real-world contexts. In our quest for a meaningful deployment of embodied actors in our societal fabric we are deriving central design challenges. A particular emphasis thereby is put on the role of formal methods for designing embodied systems in which we actually may put our trust.

Keywords: Formal methods · Advanced systems engineering · AI

1 Introduction

A new generation of increasingly autonomous and self-learning systems is about to be deployed into all kinds of aspects of everyday life. This machinery, which we call *embodied actors*, is used beyond mere automation and assistance to humans, as manufacturing robots make way for autonomous machine workers, business and administrative services are performed by autonomous virtual organizations, and processes and value chains in both material and virtual worlds are executed by federations of autonomous machine actors. A main driver for the development of *embodied actors* lies in their ubiquitous disruptive potential, as autonomic and unsupervised learning capabilities are widely believed to be the key technological base for initiating and driving the next economic and societal phase shift.

Embodied actors are not a distant AI-ish fiction, as purpose-built technical machinery might be *hand-crafted* with currently available software technology. But only at very high cost and sometimes with unknown risks, as we do not yet have a mature science and technology to support the engineering of embodied

This research has been supported by the BMWK-funded project *Embodied Intelligence - The Next Big Thing*, and by the Bavarian Ministry of Economics in the context of the fortiss AI Center. It also draws on the results, extensive discussions and constructive feedback to earlier versions by Manfred Broy (TU Munich), John Rushby (SRI), Natarajan Shankar (SRI), Henrik Putzer (fortiss), and Chihhong Cheng (fortissian).

M. Chechik et al. (Eds.): FM 2023, LNCS 14000, pp. 10–25, 2023.
https://doi.org/10.1007/978-3-031-27481-7_2

systems in which we may put our trust. Failing to deploy embodied actors in a meaningful manner, therefore, can all too easily and quickly turn dystopian.

We clearly face serious social, economic, legislative, jurisdictional, and engineering challenges when deploying embodied actors to the real world, and sound sociopolitical and legal conditions and frameworks must be created for embodying autonomously acting machines in essential real-world processes and structures.

1. How can we assure that increasingly autonomous embodied actors behave *beneficially*? That is, they function as intended and they behave, by-and-large, in accordance with widely accepted higher-level societal goals and norms.
2. How can we assure that self-evolving embodied actors are *robust* across their whole life cycle? That is, they are dependable, safe, and predictable (up to quantified tolerances) in uncertain and largely unpredictable environments.

Traditionally, the field of systems engineering tackles these kinds of questions for assuring purposeful and acceptable technical systems. Engineering of software-intensive systems, however, has so far mainly been concerned with relatively small-scale, centralized, determinate, non-evolving, automated, and task-specific *embedded* and *cyber-physical systems*, which are operating in well-defined and largely predictable operating environments.

In Sect. 2 we review recent developments on assurance-driven embedded systems, and in Sect. 3 we take a look at some of the current challenges and approaches for assuring embedded systems with learning-enabled components. Then, in Sect. 4 we characterize the new generation of *embodied actors* as the basis for deriving, in Sect. 5, essential rigorous design challenges for a meaningful deployment of these increasingly autonomous and self-learning machines into our societal fabric. We conclude with some final remarks in Sect. 6.

It is our hope that this high-level description of embodied actors together with urgent design challenges can stimulate researchers from the formal methods community to develop and evaluate rigorous methods for constructing, analyzing, and assuring embodied actors, and, possibly, also better understand machine intelligence.

2 Embedded Systems

Ensuring dependable and safe control of embedded and cyber-physical systems involves a rather complex interaction of uncertain sensing, discrete/probabilistic computation, physical motion, and real-time combination with other systems (including humans) [30,41]. Model-based engineering (MBE), in particular, is a systematic and widely used approach for tackling these embedded systems challenges in industrial engineering [51]. Formal methods are used, on a case-by-case basis, in every phase of MBE for supporting requirement specification,

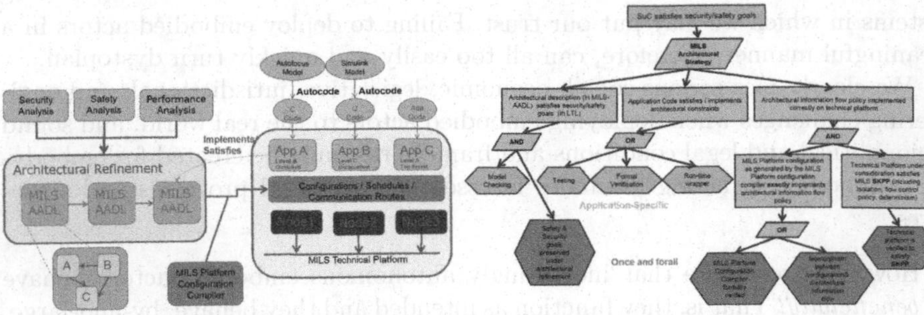

Fig. 1. MILS architectural design strategy and assurance case pattern. (Color figure online)

design, validation, and verification. Stylized requirements language for embedded systems such as EARS [44,45] are successfully used, coverage-based *test case generation* is supported by automated theorem proving, and *autocoding*, that is, the generation of production-quality code from executable models, is common practice in developing industrial embedded systems. Likewise, *correct-by-construction* synthesis of programmable logic control code (in IEC 61131-3) from declarative, real-time specifications has been integrated into an industrial design process for embedded control systems [13].

Consider, for example, the MILS architectural design strategy in Fig. 1.[1] The objective of MILS [7,54] is to provide an environment for the design, analysis, verification, compositional implementation and certification of scalable, interoperable, and affordable trustworthy security architectures based on formal methods for specifying safety, security, and performance requirements, for the architectural design, for autocoding components from models, and for configuring and faithfully implementing the model-based communication structure on a (distributed) separation kernel for resource sharing. The design steps depicted in Fig. 1 heavily rely on constraint solving based on SMT [23] or EFSMT [9,24], the extension of SMT to *exists-forall* quantified constraints. Transformational architectural patterns, for example, support automated safety and security co-design [19,20,35], autocoding from executable models in Autofocus [1] or any industrial MBE tool chain such as Matlab or Lustre, code synthesis from temporal specifications [10], optimized design space exploration, configuration and deployment compilation [25,26], and, say, verifying partitioning properties for an integrated modular avionics kernel [32].

The explicit assurance case (see, for example, [59]) pattern in Fig. 1 for the MILS architectural design strategy is constructed in a compositional manner from assurance cases of individual components such as the configuration compiler, which needs to implement given policies such as topological separation of high-security components, and the separation kernel, which needs to satisfy the given protection profile (SKPP) [42]. This kind of assurance needs to be

[1] See also: www.d-mils.org.

provided, modulo possible instantiation, only once for each component (green). Moreover, the assurance argument for the MILS design strategy (blue) encodes design knowledge that may also be reused across different applications. Thus, when using the MILS design strategy for building a specific secure application one may concentrate (orange) on providing safety, security, and performance requirements, a logical architecture, which is detailed enough for enabling autocoding or component synthesis, and evidence as generated from formal verification, both static and dynamic, as well as traditional testing methods.

Finally, the modular creation of assurance cases [4,8] is coordinated through the Evidential Toolbus [18], which supports rigorous workflows, including the generation of claims along with supporting evidence, and the maintenance of claims and evidence in the face of change. In this way, verification supports the evolutionary nature of design, where new requirements are added, old ones are revised, and designs themselves are improved, modified, and adapted.

3 Embedded Systems with AI/ML

Embedded systems increasingly contain learning-enabled components. In automated driving scenarios, for instance, *artificial neural networks* (ANN) are often used for perception and for constructing a faithful model of the operating environment, and behavior generation may be based on, say, techniques of *reinforcement learning*. The inherent multitude of sources of entangled uncertainty for these kinds of learning-enabled components is particularly challenging [57], and the consequences of accumulated uncertainties are profound. For instance, ANNs are usually not robust with unseen inputs, as there is also quite some uncertainty in their behavior for even small input changes [16]. The main question therefore is if learning-enabled technologies such as ANNs can be engineered in a rigorous manner as to be able to be integrated in safety-related embedded systems applications.

Our initial response at fortiss to this challenge has been the *neural network dependability kit* (NNDK) [12].[2] It is based on a novel set of dependability metrics for ANNs [14,15], establishing maximum resilience bounds [16], and the runtime monitoring of neuron activation patterns for determining the trustworthiness of some ANN functional behavior [17]. Figure 2 demonstrates how these techniques are combined in a structured design approach for arguing given safety requirements for ANN components. NNDK has been applied in a number of real-world use cases, including Level-3 autonomous driving components [11], the detection of diabetic retinopathy, and monitoring of traffic flows in tunnels [61]. NNDK, however, is restricted to the analysis of ANN components only, and as such it needs to be integrated into a larger safety engineering framework for supporting more complex systems with learning-enabled components.

We first notice that the basic assumptions of traditional safety engineering, as outlined in Sect. 2, no longer pertain to AI-based systems. First, with increased

[2] https://www.fortiss.org/ergebnisse/software/nndk.

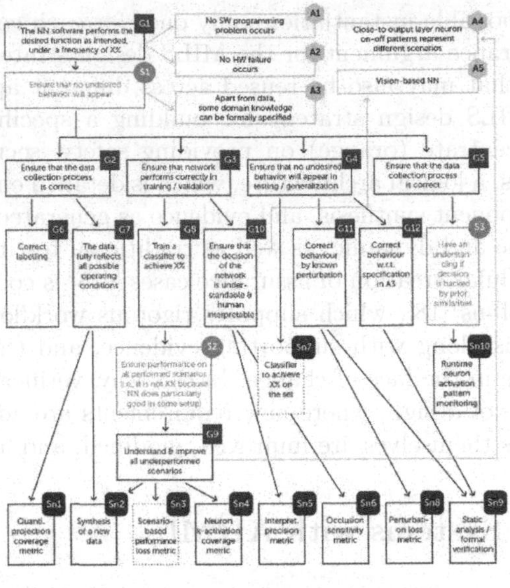

Fig. 2. Neural network dependability kit.

autonomy, a fallback mechanism to a human is often not possible anymore. Consider, for example, an emergency braking system which needs to perform without any human intervention, as the required reaction times is well below the capabilities of human beings. Second, AI systems make their own knowledge-based judgments and decisions. While added flexibility, resilience, elasticity, and robustness of AI systems are clearly important, the gains in these dimensions come at the loss of testability due to the admittance of nondeterminism due to uncertainty (below a measure of 1). This disadvantage is costly because systematic testing and simulation are still the single most used technique for verifying the correct functioning of software-intensive systems. Third, AI-based systems increasingly need to cope with operating environments in which comprehensive monitoring and controlling is impossible and in which unpredictable events may occur. In fact, AI systems are mainly used for situations where the full details of the operating context can not be known in advance. Risk estimation is therefore difficult to perform for AI systems using conventional techniques. Fourth, it is very hard, if not impossible, to correctly and completely specify the intended behavior of an AI-enabled, and possibly continually changing, system [60].

For all these reasons, well-established and successful safety standards for software-intensive systems, including DO 178C and ISO 26262, cannot readily be applied to AI systems (see [57] for an in-depth discussion). Indeed, these safety standards barely heed autonomy and the particularly advanced software technologies for system autonomy.

The recent VDE-AR-E 2842-61 takes up the challenge of dependable and safe embedded systems with at least some autonomous/cognitive functionality [53]. These guidelines are based on a model-centered structured approach and lifecycle. One of the distinguishing features of the VDE-AR-E 2842-61 is that it recognizes the many sources of uncertainty of AI-enabled systems and the need for quantifying and managing related uncertainties below acceptable levels. Other recent developments for assuring systems with learning-enabled components include, say, requirements for explicit safety cases [36], AMLAS [33] for integrating safety case patterns, VerifAI [66], a toolkit for the formal design and analysis of systems that include AI/ML components, and model-centered assurance techniques for autonomous systems based on safety monitors [34].

4 Embodied Actors

We illustrate the main characteristics of embodied actors by means of a robotic co-pilot whom we envision to act as a companion to a pilot in a single-pilot cockpit.[3] Such a robotic co-pilot needs to be more like a human co-pilot than a conventional flight management system or functionally automated autopilot. In particular, the robot companion needs to perform heterogeneous and complementary tasks, including radio communications, interpreting weather data and making route adjustments, pilot monitoring tasks, shared tasks (flaps, gear), ground taxi, and communication with the cabin-crew (emergency evacuation). The robotic co-pilot also needs to integrate these tasks to accomplish a safe flight, it needs to base its decisions and actions on an overall situational assessment. In case something goes wrong, the robot companion needs to find effective explanations based on fault diagnosis, and it needs to engage in an effective resolution process with the (human) pilot, based on a model of the pilot's beliefs. In extreme situations, for instance, if there is smoke in the cockpit, the robotic co-pilot might need to take over control.[4] In these rare cases, the robotic co-pilot must now also cope with inconsistencies (for example, in sensor readings) based on flight laws, training procedures, models of the physical environment, and unforeseen situations without the possibility of a structured hand-over to the human pilot.

The envisioned robotic co-pilot is a particular instance of a larger class of *embodied actors*. Personal companions for supporting and taking over tedious household chores and for assisting with tax declarations, including the communication with tax authorities, and suggesting new possibilities based on our intents are an old dream. Embodied companions are also designated to assist, say, truck drivers, ship captains, caregivers, investors, administrators, managers, workers, farmers, lawyers, medical doctors, and, in fact, everybody. Potential benefits include increased safety, reliability, efficiency, affordability, and previously unattainable capabilities.

---

[3] This use case draws on J. Rushby's presentation at the FoMLAS workshop at ETAPS 2018.

[4] http://understandingaf447.com/extras/18-4_minutes__23_seconds_EN.pdf..

	Embedded Systems	Embodied Actors
Architecture	centralized	federated
Behavior	determinate	largely unpredictable
Context	well-defined	uncertain/unknown
Maintenance	managed update	self-learning
Requirement	dependability	trustworthiness
Human control	yes	increasingly no

Fig. 3. Embedded systems vs. embodied actors.

Characteristics. Embodied systems, in general, are comprised of federations of collaborating actors, they operate in largely unpredictable environments, physical or not, and they recognize their operating environment through sensors. Moreover, they are informed about the intentions of other actors in their respective and immediate operating environments; they take non-trivial decisions based on reasoning, they influence their environment, including other actors, via actuators; they interact and cooperate with the elements of their operating environment, they influence elements in their environment to better meet own goals; and they show a certain behavior based on skills; and they learn new and improved behavior during operation and through interactions. In summary, embodied actors are characterized as being:

1. *Cognitive*, in that actions are based on situational awareness, model-building, and planning.
2. *Intent-driven*, in that actions are based on capturing actors' intents, tasks, and goals.
3. *Federated*, in that actions of decentralized actors are coordinated in a collaborative manner between stakeholders and on an intentional level to accomplish joint tasks or missions.
4. *Autonomous*, in that actions are increasingly determined by an actor's, or federations of actors', own knowledge, beliefs, intents, preferences, and choices.
5. *Self-learning*, in that actions are adapted and improved through experience, exploration, and reasoning, both inductive and deductive, of a situated actor.

Based on these characteristics, Fig. 3 illustrates characteristic differences between traditional embedded systems (with or without AI/ML components) and embodied actors.

Trustworthiness. We might be willing to put our *trust* into embodied actors which are, as a necessary condition, demonstrably beneficial and robust (see Sect. 1). That is, we might be willing to be vulnerable to the actions of such machine actors on the basis of the expectation that it will perform a particular action important to the us, irrespective of our ability to monitor or control the machine (see also [46]).

Assuring the trustworthiness of embodied actors, however, is quite a challenge, as embodied actors learn continually and they adapt and optimize their behavior based on experience and targeted exploration; they need to be robust, possibly employing a *never-give-up* strategy, in the presence of inaccuracies, uncertainty, and errors in their world models ("known unknown") and also in the presence of non-modeled phenomena ("unknown unknown"); they increasingly lack the fallback to a responsible human being; they offer a variety of new attack surfaces due to data-driven programming; they exhibit largely unpredictable and emergent behavior due to data-driven programming; and they can not be certified as current certification regimes require the system's behavior and its intended operating context to be fully specified and verified prior to commissioning.

5 Design Challenges

Based on the characteristics of embodied actors as outlined in the Sect. 4 we are now deriving all-important and inter-woven design challenges for developing, deploying, and operating beneficial and robust embodied actors (see Fig. 4; an in-depth discussion is included in [56]).

5.1 Robust AI/ML

Despite technological advances that have led to the proliferation of machine learning (ML) algorithms there still is the question of the level of trust that we can put on these systems. More *robust machine learning* techniques are needed (cmp. [64]) which work in uncertain and largely unpredictable environments, which can make timely and confident decisions, whose results are understandable and explainable to a human operator, which are resilient to erroneous inputs and targeted attacks, which can process ever-increasing amounts of data from decentralized and heterogeneous data sources, but which can also extract useful insights from small amounts of data and sparse rewards without significant compromises in confidentiality and privacy in federated multi-actor settings.

There is, of course, a flurry of developments on a new generation of robust AI/ML algorithms, including, say, integrated logical neural networks [55] with logic and neural structures as projections, resource-efficient *neuromorphic* computation, and privacy-preserving machine learning based on federated machine learning. Verification of (the results of) machine learning algorithms, in particular, has been a field day for formal verification [62]. Symbolic approaches, however, usually do not scale sufficiently, are often restricted to static (non-learning) networks, and there usually is a certain lack of useful requirements for learning-enabled components in support of safety assurance cases.

5.2 Human-Centered AI/ML

The overarching goal is in achieving a sufficient mutual understanding of state and intent of both humans and machine as to optimally blend their competences in jointly acting towards overarching objectives, while respecting privacy [43,60].

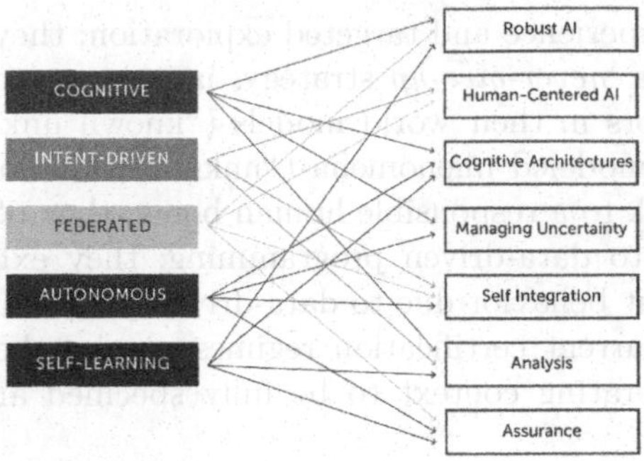

Fig. 4. Tracing characteristics to design challenges.

The challenge here is to model human behavior interactions and to provide the appropriate uncertainty characteristics related to the largely unpredictable behavior of humans under unforeseen circumstances. Moreover, as individual spheres of control may overlap arbitrarily, there is a pronounced need for orchestrating these processes such that they jointly serve, say, not only a single human, but can best-possibly multi-task in serving arbitrarily large groups at the same time despite uncorrelated requests and uncoordinated missions.

5.3 Cognitive Architectures

Cognitive architectures [49] create programs for realizing all kinds of cognitive functionality [37,47,48]. Soar [39], for instance is a modular cognitive architecture for integrating (System 1) *fast*, sub-symbolic capabilities for performing intuitive, automated tasks that we as humans can do instinctively with (System 2) *slow*, logic-based capabilities for performing tasks that require conscious decision in the face of incomplete and uncertain knowledge [6]. With a similar motivation in mind, *neurosymbolic programming* proposes integrated frameworks which have neural, logical, and probabilistic methods as special cases. *Probabilistic programming* provides yet another framework in which basic components of cognitive architectures are represented in a *unified and elegant fashion* [40,52]. If knowledge is expressed as programs, learning is expressed as programming [58] Moreover, knowledge encoded as probabilistic programs is directly amenable to well-defined formal concepts of program induction, construction, and analysis [3].

An obvious question is if and how structural principles of cognitive architectures are aiding in the design of embodied systems and their assurance? Cognitive architectures and theories from psychology, such as *cue theory* [5,38], may serve as the basis and inspiration for designing novel control regimes for embodied actors capable of coping with epistemic uncertainty by cautiously exploring and navigating the *unknown unknown.* In this way, careful terrain exploration is approached by *minimizing surprises* based on active inference — that is, maintaining a model and its predictions through action to change the sensory inputs to minimize prediction error indirectly — and the *free energy* principle [28] or, alternatively, by maximizing *predictive information* [2].

5.4 Uncertainty Quantification

There is *aleatoric* and *epistemic* uncertainty all around AI-ish systems [22,57]. Now, the challenge of *uncertainty quantification* is to systematically and continually reduce uncertainty to acceptable level, as the basis for trustworthy and (up to tolerable quantities) predictable embodied systems. This is accomplished by (for details see [57]) (1) identifying all relevant sources of uncertainty, (2) adequately quantifying and estimating uncertainty, (3) understanding how uncertainty propagates, forward and inverse, along chains of computations, (4) reducing overall uncertainty below acceptable levels, and (5) managing incremental change of uncertainty. The problem of (forward) *uncertainty propagation*, for instance, is to characterise the distribution of $y = F(x)$ for a system model F and an input distribution for x, where distributions may, as usually, be represented by its moments or in terms of polynomial chaos (Wiener) expansion. In this way one may explore the design space, optimize the system under performance, assess its robustness with respect to uncertainty and its reliability, and perform sensitivity analysis [65]. Uncertainty quantification approaches in engineering have been designed, for example, to demonstrate that, with high probability, a real-valued response function of a given physical system does not exceed a given safety threshold [50]. What seems to be completely missing, however, is a comprehensive set of formal techniques for the rigorous and compositional design of systems based on uncertainty quantification.

5.5 Self-integration

Intent-driven formation of purposeful federations of embodied actors requires individual actors to be open to collaborate with others, while still operating as self-sufficient individually purposeful systems. Formation of these federations therefore is based on *self-integration*, which seeks out other systems to support to meet their local and global intents and goals, which cannot be accomplished on their own.

The formation of intent-driven and trustworthy federations of actors is a challenging endeavor indeed, as trust certainly is not modular. We therefore need to come up with suitable architectural principles and composition operators for constructing assured (systems of) embodied actors from a set of heterogeneous, and possibly untrusted, constituent actors.

Since embodied systems are acting in the real world with their wickerwork of societal norms, rules and laws, smart, that is software-based, contracts are a central concept towards intent-driven dynamic federations of embodfied actors. In this way, trustworthy self-integration of federations of embodied actors might be approached by means of smart contracts based on collections of identified intents, goals, and plans. These considerations on smart contracts and self-integration point to a multitude of serious formal specification and verification challenges: How do we formally specify smart contracts based on recognized intents and goals? What is the right framework for negotiating contracts? In particular, can we use basic principles of *mechanism design* for synthesizing goal-oriented contracts? How can we formally verify smart contracts? How can we provide checkable evidence of the conclusion or breach of contract? How to incentivize/penalize embodied actors as to ensure beneficial behavior? It is also open to discussion if such federations can/should be deployed in social contexts without an orchestrating higher instance.

5.6 Analysis

Analysis of embodied actors is particularly challenging for their openness, adaptivity, situatedness, and largely unpredictable behavior. Embodied actors also have the possibility of autonomously acting in regulated sectors such as healthcare, finance, insurance, accounting, or retail. As such they need to comply with applicable regulations and national law. These compliance checks need to be automated, but only what is formalized can be automated. It is therefore crucial, and non-trivial, to formalize applicable regulations in formal policy languages. Embodied actors are also expected to be resilient to common and possibly also new kinds of breakdowns and malicious attacks, the risk of unintended harm to humans, machinery and the environment is demonstrably below acceptable levels, and identified confidentiality, integrity, and availability requirements are satisfied. Other requirements include transparency demonstrable fairness of decisions, inverse privacy, and contextual integrity.

Non-determinate systems are usually considered to be *untestable*, because of the overwhelming and open-ended number of cases to be considered, and formal verification of a static snapshot of such a system seems to be largely useless in such a dynamic environment, unless verification results can continually be kept in sync with the evolution of the system. *Runtime analysis* [66] therefore is an essential element for analyzing embodied actors, as it may handle the multitude of sources for uncertainty, stringent real-time requirements, and continually changing conditions. Runtime analysis is also an essential element of the *never-give-up* failure detection, isolation, and recovery (FDIR) cycle of embodied actors.

Architectural design principles for monitoring increasingly autonomous systems are needed to ensure that monitoring does not perturb the system (at least, not too much) [21,31]. Run-time monitoring may also be used for measuring uncertainties of, say, input-output behavior of learning-enabled components [17]. Moreover, there is not yet a systematic understanding of what kind of analysis can be achieved at design time, how the design process can contribute to safe and correct operation of the embodied system at run time, and how the design-time and run-time analysis techniques can inter-operate effectively.

The distributed and dynamic nature of federations of embodied actors and their goals is particularly challenging for run-time analysis. A run-time monitoring framework for embodied actors must also support reasoning under uncertainty, and also partially observable systems with nondeterministic and probabilistic behavior. Run-time monitoring of typical hyper-properties [27], including information flow, transparency, and privacy are of particular interest.

5.7 Assurance

How can we be assured that an embodied actor indeed is worth of the trust we may put in it? We hypothesize that rigorous and continual assurance arguments and their interweaving with system evolvement play a key rôle in satisfactorily answering this question. This kind of *assurance-driven design* is based on constructing and maintaining explicit assurance cases, which are compelling, comprehensive, evidence-based defensible, and valid justification of compliance [29,59,63].

We have already seen such an assurance case for the MILS architectural design pattern in Fig. 1. The challenge now is to construct convincing assurance patterns for embodied actors and their underlying cognitive architectures (see Sect. 5.3); for example, for blackboard architectures for integrating slow and fast cognitive capabilities. Now, evidence is obtained both from static analysis (testing, model checking, theorem proving) but also during operation from runtime analysis (see Sect. 5.6).

Major assurance challenges for embodied actors include (1) rigorous assurance case patterns with efficient, easily verifiable arguments for capturing trustworthiness requirements (2) rigorous and compositional operators on assurance cases, (3) generation of semantically coherent evidence, for example, based on runtime analysis, and validation throughout the lifecycle, (4) rigorous mechanisms of *continual assurance* for synchronizing assurance cases with system evolvement (5) and measures of confidence in assurance arguments as the basis for, say, suggesting stronger arguments.

Explicit assurance cases, in particular, open new possibilities of *assurance-driven operation* for dependable and safe exploration of embodied actors in largely unknown operating contexts based on relevant information from an assurance case. If there is only weak evidence on the fact that the traffic light in front of the ego car is green, for example, then the ego car might want to increase her assurance by strengthen this case, say, by means of moving closing and initiating additional sensor activity. In this way, rigorous assurance cases can be instrumental in online behavioral self-adaptation and for determining safe behavior when operating in uncertain contexts.

6 Conclusion

We have been arguing that traditional safety and dependability engineering is coming to a climacteric from embedded systems to embodied actors, and with assuring the trustworthiness of a new generation of dynamic federations of situationally aware, intent-driven, explorative, ever-evolving, largely non-predictable, and increasingly autonomous embodied systems in uncertain, complex, and unpredictable real-world contexts. Solving the corresponding design challenges for assured embodied actors will require synergistic innovations in formal methods and model-based engineering, architectures for autonomously acting systems, and core AI/ML algorithms.

In particular, we have been emphasizing that the presented design challenges are yet another great opportunity for formal methods themselves, because the assurance of embodied actors needs to be largely automated, and rigorous models are a prerequisite to automation. Embedding (embodying?) formal methods into automated engineering and change cycles should also create *virtuous cycles* for immediately judging the effectiveness of applied formal methods and as a playground for accelerating their future development.

We should also be prepared for future embodied actors which are equipped with substantial self-engineering capabilities, including experience-driven functional updates, zero-touch repair and maintenance capabilities, and the possibility of by-need-augmentation of sensing, cognitive, and acting capabilities. Moreover, future embodied actors may also perform their own risk analysis and define their own mitigation strategies based on their own understanding of socially acceptable behavior.

References

1. Aravantinos, V., Voss, S., Teufl, S., Hölzl, F., Schätz, B.: AutoFOCUS3: tooling concepts for seamless, model-based development of embedded systems. MoDELS **1508**, 19–26 (2015)
2. Ay, N., Bertschinger, N., Der, R., Güttler, F., Olbrich, E.: Predictive information and explorative behavior of autonomous robots. Eur. Phys. J. B **63**(3), 329–339 (2008). https://doi.org/10.1140/epjb/e2008-00175-0
3. Barthe, G., Katoen, J.P., Silva, A.: Foundations of Probabilistic Programming. Cambridge University Press, Cambridge (2020)
4. Beyene, T.A., Carlan, C.: CyberGSN: a semi-formal language for specifying safety cases. In: 2021 51st Annual IEEE/IFIP International Conference on Dependable Systems and Networks Workshops (DSN-W), pp. 63–66. IEEE (2021)
5. Björkman, M.: Internal cue theory: calibration and resolution of confidence in general knowledge. Organ. Behav. Hum. Decis. Process. **58**(3), 386–405 (1994)
6. Booch, G., et al.: Thinking fast and slow in AI. In: Proceedings of the AAAI Conference on Artificial Intelligence, vol. 35, pp. 15042–15046 (2021)
7. Bytschkow, D., Quilbeuf, J., Igna, G., Ruess, H.: Distributed MILS architectural approach for secure smart grids. In: Cuellar, J. (ed.) SmartGridSec 2014. LNCS, vol. 8448, pp. 16–29. Springer, Cham (2014). https://doi.org/10.1007/978-3-319-10329-7_2
8. Cârlan, C., Beyene, T.A., Ruess, H.: Integrated formal methods for constructing assurance cases. In: 2016 IEEE International Symposium on Software Reliability Engineering Workshops (ISSREW), pp. 221–228. IEEE (2016)
9. Cheng, C.H., Bensalem, S., Ruess, H., Shankar, N., Tiwari, A.: EFSMT: a logical framework for the design of cyber-physical systems. Cyber-Phys. Syst. Architectures Design Methodologies (CPSArch) (2014)

10. Cheng, C.-H., Hamza, Y., Ruess, H.: Structural synthesis for GXW specifications. In: Chaudhuri, S., Farzan, A. (eds.) CAV 2016. LNCS, vol. 9779, pp. 95–117. Springer, Cham (2016). https://doi.org/10.1007/978-3-319-41528-4_6
11. Cheng, C.H., Huang, C.H., Brunner, T., Hashemi, V.: Towards safety verification of direct perception neural networks. In: 2020 Design, Automation & Test in Europe Conference & Exhibition (DATE), pp. 1640–1643. IEEE (2020)
12. Cheng, C.H., Huang, C.H., Nührenberg, G.: NN-Dependability-Kit: engineering neural networks for safety-critical autonomous driving systems. In: 2019 IEEE/ACM International Conference on Computer-Aided Design (ICCAD), pp. 1–6. IEEE (2019)
13. Cheng, C.-H., Huang, C.-H., Ruess, H., Stattelmann, S.: G4LTL-ST: automatic generation of PLC programs. In: Biere, A., Bloem, R. (eds.) CAV 2014. LNCS, vol. 8559, pp. 541–549. Springer, Cham (2014). https://doi.org/10.1007/978-3-319-08867-9_36
14. Cheng, C.H., Huang, C.H., Ruess, H., Yasuoka, H., et al.: Towards dependability metrics for neural networks. In: 2018 16th ACM/IEEE International Conference on Formal Methods and Models for System Design (MEMOCODE), pp. 1–4. IEEE (2018)
15. Cheng, C.-H., Huang, C.-H., Yasuoka, H.: Quantitative projection coverage for testing ML-enabled autonomous systems. In: Lahiri, S.K., Wang, C. (eds.) ATVA 2018. LNCS, vol. 11138, pp. 126–142. Springer, Cham (2018). https://doi.org/10.1007/978-3-030-01090-4_8
16. Cheng, C.-H., Nührenberg, G., Ruess, H.: Maximum resilience of artificial neural networks. In: D'Souza, D., Narayan Kumar, K. (eds.) ATVA 2017. LNCS, vol. 10482, pp. 251–268. Springer, Cham (2017). https://doi.org/10.1007/978-3-319-68167-2_18
17. Cheng, C.H., Nührenberg, G., Yasuoka, H.: Runtime monitoring neuron activation patterns. In: 2019 Design, Automation & Test in Europe Conference & Exhibition (DATE), pp. 300–303. IEEE (2019)
18. Cruanes, S., Hamon, G., Owre, S., Shankar, N.: Tool integration with the evidential tool bus. In: Giacobazzi, R., Berdine, J., Mastroeni, I. (eds.) VMCAI 2013. LNCS, vol. 7737, pp. 275–294. Springer, Heidelberg (2013). https://doi.org/10.1007/978-3-642-35873-9_18
19. Dantas, Y.G., Nigam, V.: Automating safety and security co-design through semantically-rich architectural patterns. arXiv preprint arXiv:2201.10563 (2022)
20. Dantas, Y.G., Nigam, V., Ruess, H.: Security engineering for ISO 21434. arXiv preprint arXiv:2012.15080 (2020)
21. Desai, A., Ghosh, S., Seshia, S.A., Shankar, N., Tiwari, A.: SOTER: a runtime assurance framework for programming safe robotics systems. In: 2019 49th Annual IEEE/IFIP International Conference on Dependable Systems and Networks (DSN), pp. 138–150. IEEE (2019)
22. Dietterich, T.G.: Steps toward robust artificial intelligence. AI Mag. **38**(3), 3–24 (2017)
23. Dutertre, B.: Yices 2.2. In: Biere, A., Bloem, R. (eds.) CAV 2014. LNCS, vol. 8559, pp. 737–744. Springer, Cham (2014). https://doi.org/10.1007/978-3-319-08867-9_49
24. Dutertre, B.: Solving exists/forall problems with Yices. In: Workshop on satisfiability modulo theories (2015)
25. Eder, J., Bahya, A., Voss, S., Ipatiov, A., Khalil, M.: From deployment to platform exploration: automatic synthesis of distributed automotive hardware architectures.

In: Proceedings of the 21th ACM/IEEE International Conference on Model Driven Engineering Languages and Systems, pp. 438–446 (2018)
26. Eder, J., Voss, S.: Usable design space exploration in AutoFOCUS3. In: EduSymp/OSS4MDE@ MoDELS, pp. 51–58 (2016)
27. Finkbeiner, B., Hahn, C., Stenger, M., Tentrup, L.: Monitoring hyperproperties. Formal Methods Syst. Des. **54**(3), 336–363 (2019)
28. Friston, K.: The free-energy principle: a unified brain theory? Nat. Rev. Neurosci. **11**(2), 127–138 (2010)
29. Gade, D., Deshpande, D.S.: A literature review on assurance driven software design. Int. J. Adv. Res. Comput. Commun. Eng. **4**(9) (2015)
30. Geisberger, E., Broy, M.: AgendaCPS: Integrierte Forschungsagenda Cyber-Physical Systems, vol. 1. Springer-Verlag, Cham (2012)
31. Goodloe, A.E., Pike, L.: Monitoring distributed real-time systems: a survey and future directions. Technical report (2010)
32. Ha, V., Rangarajan, M., Cofer, D., Rue, H., Duterte, B.: Feature-based decomposition of inductive proofs applied to real-time avionics software: an experience report. In: Proceedings of the 26th International Conference on Software Engineering, pp. 304–313. IEEE (2004)
33. Hawkins, R., Paterson, C., Picardi, C., Jia, Y., Calinescu, R., Habli, I.: Guidance on the assurance of machine learning in autonomous systems (amlas). arXiv preprint arXiv:2102.01564 (2021)
34. Jha, S., Rushby, J., Shankar, N.: Model-centered assurance for autonomous systems. In: Casimiro, A., Ortmeier, F., Bitsch, F., Ferreira, P. (eds.) SAFECOMP 2020. LNCS, vol. 12234, pp. 228–243. Springer, Cham (2020). https://doi.org/10.1007/978-3-030-54549-9_15
35. Kondeva, A., Nigam, V., Ruess, H., Carlan, C.: On computer-aided techniques for supporting safety and security co-engineering. In: 2019 IEEE International Symposium on Software Reliability Engineering Workshops (ISSREW), pp. 346–353. IEEE (2019)
36. Koopman, P.: Key ideas: UL 4600 safety standard for autonomous vehicles (2022)
37. Kotseruba, I., Gonzalez, O.J.A., Tsotsos, J.K.: A review of 40 years of cognitive architecture research: focus on perception, attention, learning and applications. arXiv preprint arXiv:1610.08602 pp. 1–74 (2016)
38. Laibson, D.: A cue-theory of consumption. Q. J. Econ. **116**(1), 81–119 (2001)
39. Laird, J.E.: The Soar Cognitive Architecture. MIT Press, Cambridge (2019)
40. Lake, B.M., Salakhutdinov, R., Tenenbaum, J.B.: Human-level concept learning through probabilistic program induction. Science **350**(6266), 1332–1338 (2015)
41. Lee, E.A., Seshia, S.A.: Introduction to Embedded Systems: A Cyber-Physical Systems Approach. MIT Press, Cambridge (2016)
42. Levin, T.E., Nguyen, T.D., Irvine, C.E.: Separation kernel protection profile revisited: choices and rationale. Technical report Naval Postgraduate School, Monterey, CA (2010)
43. Liu, Y., Shen, H.: Human centric machine learning: A human machine collaboration. Technical Report, ISSN Print: 2699–1217, ISSN: 2700–2977, fortiss Whitepaper (2021)
44. Lúcio, L., Rahman, S., Cheng, C.-H., Mavin, A.: Just formal enough? automated analysis of EARS requirements. In: Barrett, C., Davies, M., Kahsai, T. (eds.) NFM 2017. LNCS, vol. 10227, pp. 427–434. Springer, Cham (2017). https://doi.org/10.1007/978-3-319-57288-8_31

45. Mavin, A., Wilkinson, P., Harwood, A., Novak, M.: Easy approach to requirements syntax (ears). In: 2009 17th IEEE International Requirements Engineering Conference, pp. 317–322. IEEE (2009)
46. Mayer, R.C., Davis, J.H., Schoorman, F.D.: An integrative model of organizational trust. Acad. Manag. Rev. **20**(3), 709–734 (1995)
47. Metzler, T., Shea, K., et al.: Taxonomy of cognitive functions. In: DS 68-7: Proceedings of the 18th International Conference on Engineering Design (ICED 11), Impacting Society through Engineering Design, Vol. 7: Human Behaviour in Design, Lyngby/Copenhagen, Denmark, 15.-19.08. 2011, pp. 330–341 (2011)
48. Nancy, A., Balamurugan, D.M., Vijaykumar, S.: A comparative analysis of cognitive architecture. Int. J. Adv. Res. Trends Eng. Technol. (IJARTET) **3**, 152–155 (2016)
49. Newell, A.: Unified Theories of Cognition. Harvard University Press, Cambridge (1994)
50. Owhadi, H., Scovel, C., Sullivan, T.J., McKerns, M., Ortiz, M.: Optimal uncertainty quantification. Siam Rev. **55**(2), 271–345 (2013)
51. Pohl, K., Hönninger, H., Achatz, R., Broy, M.: Model-Based Engineering of Embedded Systems: The SPES 2020 Methodology. Springer, Cham (2012)
52. Potapov, A.: A step from probabilistic programming to cognitive architectures. arXiv preprint arXiv:1605.01180 (2016)
53. Putzer, H.J., Rueß, H., Koch, J.: Trustworthy AI-based systems with VDE-AR-E 2842-61 (2021)
54. Quilbeuf, J., Igna, G., Bytschkow, D., Ruess, H.: Security policies for distributed systems. arXiv preprint arXiv:1310.3723 (2013)
55. Riegel, R., et al.: Logical neural networks. arXiv preprint arXiv:2006.13155 (2020)
56. Ruess, H.: Systems challenges for trustworthy embodied systems. arXiv preprint arXiv:2201.03413 (2022)
57. Rueß, H., Burton, S.: Safe AI- How is this possible? arXiv preprint arXiv:2201.10436 (2022)
58. Rule, J.S.: The child as hacker: building more human-like models of learning. Ph.D. thesis, Massachusetts Institute of Technology (2020)
59. Rushby, J., Bloomfield, R.: Assessing confidence with assurance 2.0. arXiv preprint arXiv:2205.04522 (2022)
60. Russell, S.: Artificial intelligence and the problem of control. Perspect. Digit. Humanism, p. 19 (2022)
61. Sahu, A., Vállez, N., Rodríguez-Bobada, R., Alhaddad, M., Moured, O., Neugschwandtner, G.: Applications of the neural network dependability kit in real-world environments. arXiv preprint arXiv:2012.09602 (2020)
62. Seshia, S.A., Sadigh, D., Sastry, S.S.: Toward verified artificial intelligence. Commun. ACM **65**(7), 46–55 (2022)
63. Shankar, N., et al.: Descert: design for certification. arXiv preprint arXiv:2203.15178 (2022)
64. Stoica, I., et al.: A berkeley view of systems challenges for AI. arXiv preprint arXiv:1712.05855 (2017)
65. Sudret, B.: Global sensitivity analysis using polynomial chaos expansions. Reliab. Eng. Syst. Saf. **93**(7), 964–979 (2008)
66. Torfah, H., Junges, S., Fremont, D.J., Seshia, S.A.: Formal analysis of AI-based autonomy: from modeling to runtime assurance. In: Feng, L., Fisman, D. (eds.) RV 2021. LNCS, vol. 12974, pp. 311–330. Springer, Cham (2021). https://doi.org/10.1007/978-3-030-88494-9_19

Intelligent and Dependable Decision-Making Under Uncertainty

Nils Jansen(✉)

Radboud University Nijmegen, Nijmegen, The Netherlands
nilsjansen123@gmail.com

Abstract. This talk highlights our vision of foundational and application-driven research toward safety, dependability, and correctness in artificial intelligence (AI). We take a broad stance on AI that combines formal methods, machine learning, and control theory. As part of this research line, we study problems inspired by autonomous systems, planning in robotics, and industrial applications. We consider reinforcement learning (RL) as a specific machine learning technique for decision-making under uncertainty. RL generally learns to behave optimally via trial and error. Consequently, and despite its massive success in the past years, RL lacks mechanisms to ensure safe and correct behavior. Formal methods, in particular formal verification, is a research area that provides formal guarantees of a system's correctness and safety based on rigorous methods and precise specifications. Yet, fundamental challenges have obstructed the effective application of verification to reinforcement learning. Our main objective is to devise novel, data-driven verification methods that tightly integrate with RL. In particular, we develop techniques that address real-world challenges to the safety of AI systems in general: Scalability, expressiveness, and robustness against the uncertainty that occurs when operating in the real world. The overall goal is to advance the real-world deployment of reinforcement learning.

1 Synopsis: Robust and Dependable Artificial Intelligence

Artificial intelligence (AI) is a disruptive force. Most major technology companies employ or develop AI, and with growing applications in fields like healthcare [37], transportation [48,68], game playing [51], finance [9], or robotics in general [44], it is entering our everyday lives. We can expect that our societal and technological involvement with AI will only intensify in the future. Such tight interaction with AI requires serious safety and correctness considerations. Recently, the field of safety in AI has triggered a vast amount of research with several seminal works defining their view on this area [4,25,58,61].

Can Formal Verification Help to Ensure AI Safety? The area of formal methods offers structured and rigorous ways to reason about the correctness

N. Jansen—This work was supported by the ERC Starting Grant 101077178 (DEUCE).

M. Chechik et al. (Eds.): FM 2023, LNCS 14000, pp. 26–36, 2023.
https://doi.org/10.1007/978-3-031-27481-7_3

of a system. Techniques range from model learning [66], over testing [36], to formal verification [24]. As an example for the application of verification in AI, solving techniques like SAT or SMT [11] help to assess the robustness of neural networks [30,33,41]. A specific verification technique is *model checking* [10,19]. For a fixed system model, a plethora of methods assert the system's correctness regarding *formal specifications*. The rigor of model checking suggests it is natural to employ model checking to prove the correctness of AI systems.

We focus on a specific branch of AI, namely *decision-making under uncertainty* [45]. Intelligent AI agents typically operate in unknown or unpredictable environments, coping with contextual changes at runtime or incompleteness of information. This unpredictability leads to the problem that the outcome of decisions made by an agent is *uncertain*. *Reinforcement learning* (RL) [64] agents make decisions under uncertainty via the exploration of potentially unknown environments. The area of *safe RL* [2,27] aims to restrict the behavior of an agent with respect to safety, or with respect to more general correctness constraints.

Several shortcomings towards the potential deployment of RL in critical environments remain. Specifically, we identify the following three main challenges to the state-of-the-art in formal verification and its application for safe RL:

- Scalability to **high-dimensional problems**,
- Providing correctness guarantees in **continuous spaces**, and
- effective handling of **uncertainty**.

Indeed, common approaches and case studies for safe RL employ idealized settings with a low number of dimensions that contribute to a problem. Most approaches assume discretized state spaces instead of realistic continuous settings. Currently employed simplistic notions of uncertainty may lead to incorrect behavior, and RL agents are often trained without any notion of safe behavior under uncertainty [72]. Finally, standard safety notions cannot express sophisticated task or correctness specifications.

The state-of-the-art leaves the aforementioned three challenges largely unaddressed. Our approaches to fundamentally overcome these restrictions employ a particularly tight integration of verification and learning. We see the data-driven nature not as a threat to effective and rigorous verification, but embrace the inherent access to state-of-the-art machine learning and exploit its flexibility.

Finally, to demonstrate the practical applicability of our work, we use the QComp [31] and Arch-Comp [1] competitions, and for more AI-related benchmarks, the OpenAI gym [53] and Google Deepmind's AI Safety Gridworlds [47]. Towards industrial demonstrators, we use, for instance, case studies from predictive maintenance, such as [42].

How to Make Intelligent Decisions Under Uncertainty? Various types and applications of uncertainty play a central role in our research. Uncertainty has been "largely related to the lack of predictability of some major events or stakes, or a lack of data" [5]. To name a few, there is uncertainty (1) in technological, social, environmental, or financial factors in the *business literature* [60],

(2) about sensor imprecisions and lossy communication channels in *robotics* [65], and (3) about the expected responses of a *human* operator in decision support systems [45]. The level of uncertainty affects the capabilities of AI systems that have to make decisions [3,45]. In particular, for strict safety requirements, decisions must be *verifiably robust* against uncertainty. Such considerations require precise knowledge about the nature of uncertainty.

Model checking for AI systems necessitates dedicated models. Markov decision processes (MDPs) capture sequential decision-making problems for agents operating in uncertain environments [57]. Sensor limitations may lead to partial observability of the system's current state, giving rise to partially observable Markov decision processes (POMDPs) [40]. While mature model checking tools like PRISM [46], Storm [22], or Uppaal [21] provide efficient synthesis or verification methods for MDPs, the situation is different for POMDPs. Policy synthesis for POMDPs is a hard problem, both from the theoretical and the practical perspective [50]. For infinite- or indefinite-horizon problems, computing an optimal policy is undecidable [49]. Optimal action choices depend on the whole observation history, requiring an infinite amount of memory.

If precise probabilities are not known, *uncertainty models* employ so-called uncertainty sets of probabilities. Uncertain MDPs (uMDPs) use, for example, *probability intervals* or *likelihood functions* [23,28,52,56,69–71,73]. Similar extensions exist for uPOMDPs, where uncertainty also affects the observation model [12,13,20,34,62].

A Motivating Example: Spacecraft Motion Planning. Consider a spacecraft motion planning system which serves as decision support for a human operator [26,32]. This system delivers advice on switching to a different orbit or avoiding close encounters with other objects in space. The spacecraft orbits the earth along a set of predefined natural motion trajectories (NMTs) [43]. While the spacecraft follows its current NMT, it does not consume fuel. We introduced the underlying uncertain POMDP model in [20]. The figure to the right depicts three models that differ only in the level of uncertainty (low, medium, high). Black spheres are the objects, and the colored lines depict NMTs. The thick red line indicates a trajectory of the spacecraft including orbit switches along the NMTs. A policy requires *robustness* against uncertainty, and *memory* to predict

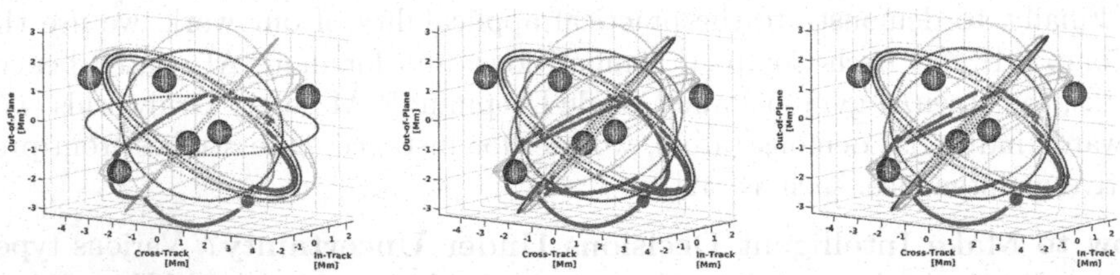

(a) Low uncertainty (b) Med uncertainty (c) High uncertainty

Fig. 1. Robust spacecraft motion planning.

the location of the spacecraft based on its past trajectory (Fig. 1). The figure shows that *more uncertainty causes less-informed decisions*, as policies need to be more conservative.

2 Research Highlights

In the following, we discuss a number of results that are in line with the aforementioned research challenges to combining formal verification, AI systems, and reinforcement learning.

2.1 Reliable Neural Network Controllers for Autonomous Agents

Summary. These results are part of the publications [16–18]. Machine learning methods typically train recurrent neural networks (RNN) to effectively represent POMDP policies that can efficiently process sequential data. However, it is hard to verify whether the POMDP driven by such RNN-based policies satisfies safety constraints, for instance, given by temporal logic specifications. We propose a novel method that combines techniques from machine learning with the field of formal methods: training an RNN-based policy and automatically extracting a so-called finite-state controller (FSC) from the RNN. Such FSCs offer a convenient way to verify temporal logic constraints. Implemented on a POMDP, they induce a Markov chain. Probabilistic verification methods can efficiently check whether this induced Markov chain satisfies a temporal logic specification. Our method exploits this diagnostic information from verification to either adjust the complexity of the extracted FSC or improve the policy by performing focused retraining of the RNN. We synthesize policies that satisfy temporal logic specifications for POMDPs with up to millions of states, three orders of magnitude larger than comparable approaches.

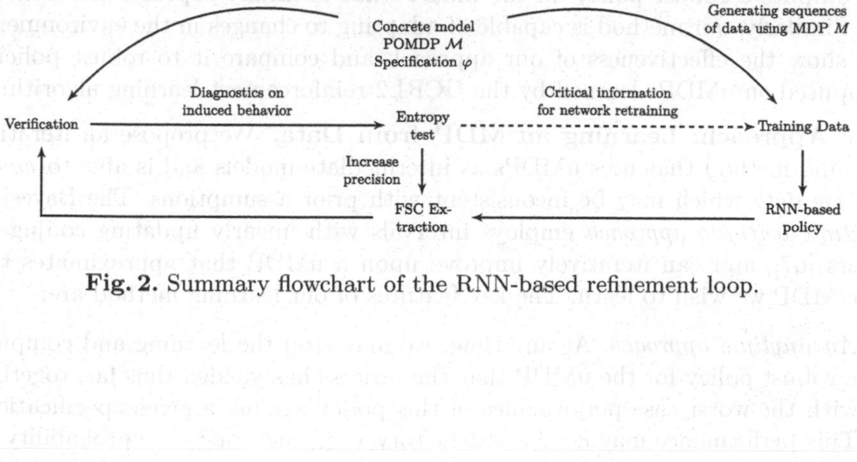

Fig. 2. Summary flowchart of the RNN-based refinement loop.

Our Approach: Learning and Verification. We combine the effectiveness of RNN-based representations from machine learning with the provable guarantees that are at the heart of formal verification. In a nutshell, we train RNN-based policy representations from sequences of data, to find candidate policies that might ensure an agent satisfies a temporal logic specification.

The central technical problem is: How to close the loop between training an RNN-based policy and efficiently verifying for a candidate policy? First, FSCs [39,54] encode memory in a finite automata-style fashion. For an FSC and a POMDP, formal verification methods like model checking are able to efficiently compute the probability of satisfying a specification [10]. We tightly integrate formal verification and machine learning towards three key steps: (1) extracting an FSC from an RNN-based policy, (2) verifying this candidate FSC for the POMDP against a temporal logic specification, and (3) if needed, either refining the FSC or generating more training data for the RNN. For an overview, see Fig. 2.

2.2 Learning Uncertainty Models

Summary. This result is part of the publication [63]. In data-driven applications, deriving precise probabilities from (limited) data introduces statistical errors that may lead to unexpected or undesirable outcomes. Consequently, we aim to learn uncertain MDPs (uMDPs) that use so-called uncertainty sets in the transitions, accounting for such limited data. Efficient implementations in tools like PRISM compute robust policies for uMDPs that provably adhere to formal specifications, like safety constraints, under the worst-case instance in the uncertainty set. We continuously learn the transition probabilities of an MDP in a robust anytime-learning approach that combines a dedicated Bayesian inference scheme with the computation of robust policies. In particular, our method (1) approximates probabilities as intervals, (2) adapts to new data that may be inconsistent with an intermediate model, and (3) may be stopped at any time to compute a robust policy on the uMDP that faithfully captures the data so far. Similarly, our method is capable of adapting to changes in the environment. We show the effectiveness of our approach and compare it to robust policies computed on uMDPs learned by the UCRL2 reinforcement learning algorithm.

Our Approach: Learning an MDP from Data. We propose an iterative learning method that uses uMDPs as intermediate models and is able to *adapt to new data* which may be inconsistent with prior assumptions. The Bayesian *anytime-learning approach* employs intervals with linearly updating conjugate priors [67], and can iteratively improve upon a uMDP that approximates the true MDP we wish to learn. The key features of our learning method are:

- *An anytime approach.* At any time, we may stop the learning and compute a robust policy for the uMDP that the process has yielded thus far, together with the worst-case performance of this policy against a given specification. This performance may not be satisfactory, e. g., the worst-case probability to reach a set of critical states may be below a certain threshold. We continue

learning towards a new uMDP that more faithfully captures the true MDP due to the inclusion of further data. Thereby, we ensure that the robust policy gradually gets closer to the optimal policy for the true MDP.
- *Specification-driven.* Our method features the possibility to learn in a task-aware fashion, that is, to learn transitions that matter for a given specification. In particular, for reachability or expected reward (temporal logic) specifications that require a certain set of target states to be reached, we only learn and update transitions along paths toward these states. Transitions outside those paths do not affect the satisfaction of the specification.
- *Adaptive to changing environment dynamics.* When using linearly updating intervals, our approach is adaptive to changing environment dynamics. That is, if during the learning process the probability distributions of the underlying MDP change, our method can easily adapt and learns these new distributions.

2.3 Robust Control for Dynamical Systems Under Uncertainty

Summary. These results are part of the publications in [6–8]. We provide probably correct controllers for dynamical systems that operate in noisy environments, where the uncertainty can be both aleatoric and epistemic. In particular, we consider environments where stochastic disturbances in the environment are not necessarily Gaussian, and external uncertainty may be caused by factors such as uncertain system parameters. In our work, no explicit representation of a noise distribution is necessary, but we only assume sampling access to the environment. Using the so-called scenario approach, we provide probabilistic guarantees on reach-avoid properties, that is, safely reaching a target while avoiding unsafe regions of the state space. At the heart of our approach is an abstraction of the dynamical system into an uncertain MDP. We show that a robust policy for this finite-state model carries guarantees on the performance of the analogous controller in the dynamical system.

Our Approach: Probabilities Are Not Enough. We consider stochastic dynamical models with continuous state and action spaces, under aleatoric and epistemic uncertainty. More precisely, aleatoric uncertainty captures natural randomness (i.e., stochasticity) in the outcome of transitions, while epistemic uncertainty is in particular modeled by parameters that are not precisely known [59].

- *PAC guarantees on abstractions.* We show that both probabilities and nondeterminism can be captured in the probability intervals of an uncertain MDP. We use sampling methods from scenario optimization [14] and show that, with a predefined confidence probability, the uncertain MDP correctly captures both aleatoric and epistemic uncertainty.
- *Correct-by-construction.* For the uncertain MDP, we compute a *robust optimal policy* that maximizes the worst-case probability of satisfying the reach-avoid specification. This policy is automatically translated to a *provably-correct feedback controller* for the original, continuous model 'on the fly'. This means that, by construction, the PAC guarantees on the uncertain MDP carry over

to the satisfaction of the specification for the continuous model, thus solving the problem stated above.
- *Contributions.* We develop the first abstraction-based, formal controller synthesis method that simultaneously captures epistemic and aleatoric uncertainty for continuous-state/action models. We provide results on the PAC-correctness of obtained uncertain MDP abstractions, and guarantees on the synthesized controllers for a reach-avoid specification.

2.4 Safe Deep Reinforcement Learning

Summary. These results are part of the publications in [15,29,35,38,55]. A common approach to safe reinforcement learning is to employ a so-called shield that forces an RL agent to select only safe actions. However, for adoption in various applications, one must look beyond enforcing safety and also ensure the applicability of RL with good performance. We extend the applicability of shields via tight integration with state-of-the-art deep RL, and provide an extensive, empirical study in challenging, sparse-reward environments under partial observability. We show that a carefully integrated shield ensures safety and can improve the convergence rate and final performance of RL agents. We furthermore show that a shield can be used to bootstrap state-of-the-art RL agents: they remain safe after initial learning in a shielded setting, allowing us to disable a potentially too-conservative shield eventually.

Our Approach: Shielding in Deep Reinforcement Learning. Our study demonstrates the following effects of shielding in a partially observable setting.

- *Shield construction:* We discuss several approaches to effectively construct and compute a shield in environments that exhibit various sources of uncertainty.
- *Safety during learning:* Exploration is only safe when the RL agent is provided with a shield. Without the shield, the agent makes unsafe choices even if it has access to the state estimation. Even an unshielded *trained agent* still behaves unsafe sometimes.
- *RL convergence rate:* A shield not only ensures safety, but may also significantly improve the convergence rate of modern RL agents by avoiding spending time to learn unsafe actions. Other knowledge interfaces like state estimators do help to a lesser extent.
- *Bootstrapping:* Due to the improved convergence rate, shields are a way to bootstrap RL algorithms, even if they are overly restrictive. RL agents can learn to mimic the shield by slowly disabling the shield.
- *Tool support:* We provide an open source tool called COOL-MC[1] that features a tied integration between state-of-the-art RL in OpenAI gym [53] and the Storm model checker [22].

[1] Available at https://github.com/LAVA-LAB/COOL-MC.

Acknowledgements. The approaches presented in this talk are the results of fruitful and enjoyable collaborations with a number of co-authors, in particular: Alessandro Abate, Thom S. Badings, Bernd Becker, Roderick Bloem, Steven Carr, Murat Cubuktepe, Dennis Gross, Sebastian Junges, Joost-Pieter Katoen, Bettina Könighofer, David Parker, Guillermo A. Pérez, Hasan A. Poonawala, Licio Romao, Sanjit Seshia, Alex Serban, Thiago D. Simão, Mariëlle Stoelinga, Marnix Suilen, Ufuk Topcu, and Ralf Wimmer.

References

1. Abate, A., et al.: ARCH-COMP18 category report: stochastic modelling. In: ARCH@ADHS. EPiC Series in Computing, vol. 54, pp. 71–103. EasyChair (2018)
2. Alshiekh, M., Bloem, R., Ehlers, R., Könighofer, B., Niekum, S., Topcu, U.: Safe reinforcement learning via shielding. In: AAAI. AAAI Press (2018)
3. Amato, C.: Decision-making under uncertainty in multi-agent and multi-robot systems: planning and learning. In: IJCAI, pp. 5662–5666. ijcai.org (2018)
4. Amodei, D., Olah, C., Steinhardt, J., Christiano, P., Schulman, J., Mané, D.: Concrete problems in AI safety. CoRR abs/1606.06565 (2016)
5. Argote, L.: Input uncertainty and organizational coordination in hospital emergency units. Adm. Sci. Q., 420–434 (1982)
6. Badings, T.S., Abate, A., Jansen, N., Parker, D., Poonawala, H.A., Stoelinga, M.: Sampling-based robust control of autonomous systems with non-Gaussian noise. In: AAAI (2022). To appear
7. Badings, T.S., Romano, L., Abate, A., Jansen, N.: Probabilities are not enough: Formal controller synthesis for stochastic dynamical models with epistemic uncertainty. In: AAAI (2023)
8. Badings, T.S., et al.: Robust control for dynamical systems with non-gaussian noise via formal abstractions. J. Artif. Intell. Res. (2023)
9. Bahrammirzaee, A.: A comparative survey of artificial intelligence applications in finance: artificial neural networks, expert system and hybrid intelligent systems. Neural Comput. Appl. **19**(8), 1165–1195 (2010). https://doi.org/10.1007/s00521-010-0362-z
10. Baier, C., Katoen, J.P.: Principles of Model Checking. The MIT Press, Cambridge (2008)
11. Biere, A., Heule, M., van Maaren, H., Walsh, T. (eds.): Handbook of Satisfiability Frontiers in Artificial Intelligence and Applications, vol. 185. IOS Press, Amsterdam (2009)
12. Bry, A., Roy, N.: Rapidly-exploring random belief trees for motion planning under uncertainty. In: ICRA, pp. 723–730. IEEE (2011)
13. Burns, B., Brock, O.: Sampling-based motion planning with sensing uncertainty. In: ICRA, pp. 3313–3318. IEEE (2007)
14. Campi, M.C., Garatti, S.: Introduction to the scenario approach. SIAM (2018)
15. Carr, S., Jansen, N., Junges, S., Topcu, U.: Safe reinforcement learning via shielding under partial observability. In: AAAI (2023)
16. Carr, S., Jansen, N., Topcu, U.: Verifiable RNN-based policies for POMDPs under temporal logic constraints. In: IJCAI, pp. 4121–4127. ijcai.org (2020)
17. Carr, S., Jansen, N., Topcu, U.: Task-aware verifiable RNN-based policies for partially observable Markov decision processes. J. Artif. Intell. Res. **72**, 819–847 (2021)

18. Carr, S., Jansen, N., Wimmer, R., Serban, A.C., Becker, B., Topcu, U.: Counterexample-guided strategy improvement for POMDPs using recurrent neural networks. In: IJCAI, pp. 5532–5539. ijcai.org (2019)
19. Clarke, E.M., Henzinger, T.A., Veith, H., Bloem, R.: Handbook of Model Checking, vol. 10. Springer, Cham (2018)
20. Cubuktepe, M., Jansen, N., Junges, S., Marandi, A., Suilen, M., Topcu, U.: Robust finite-state controllers for uncertain POMDPs. In: AAAI, pp. 11792–11800. AAAI Press (2021)
21. David, A., Jensen, P.G., Larsen, K.G., Mikučionis, M., Taankvist, J.H.: UPPAAL STRATEGO. In: Baier, C., Tinelli, C. (eds.) TACAS 2015. LNCS, vol. 9035, pp. 206–211. Springer, Heidelberg (2015). https://doi.org/10.1007/978-3-662-46681-0_16
22. Dehnert, C., Junges, S., Katoen, J.P., Volk, M.: A **storm** is coming: a modern probabilistic model checker. In: Majumdar, R., Kuncak, V. (eds.) CAV 2017. LNCS, Springer, Cham (2017). https://doi.org/10.1007/978-3-319-63390-9_31
23. Delahaye, B., Larsen, K.G., Legay, A., Pedersen, M.L., Wasowski, A.: Decision problems for interval Markov chains. In: Dediu, A.-H., Inenaga, S., Martín-Vide, C. (eds.) LATA 2011. LNCS, vol. 6638, pp. 274–285. Springer, Heidelberg (2011). https://doi.org/10.1007/978-3-642-21254-3_21
24. Drechsler, R.: Advanced Formal Verification. Kluwer Academic Publishers, Dordrecht (2004)
25. Freedman, R.G., Zilberstein, S.: Safety in AI-HRI: challenges complementing user experience quality. In: AAAI Fall Symposium Series (2016)
26. Frey, G.R., Petersen, C.D., Leve, F.A., Kolmanovsky, I.V., Girard, A.R.: Constrained spacecraft relative motion planning exploiting periodic natural motion trajectories and invariance. J. Guid. Control. Dyn. **40**(12), 3100–3115 (2017)
27. Garcıa, J., Fernández, F.: A comprehensive survey on safe reinforcement learning. J. Mach. Learn. Res. **16**(1), 1437–1480 (2015)
28. Givan, R., Leach, S., Dean, T.: Bounded-parameter Markov decision processes. Artif. Intell. **122**(1–2), 71–109 (2000)
29. Gross, D., Jansen, N., Junges, S., Pérez, G.A.: COOL-MC: a comprehensive tool for reinforcement learning and model checking. In: Dong, W., Talpin, J.P. (eds.) SETTA 2022. LNCS, vol. 13649, pp. 41–49. Springer, Cham (2022)
30. Gross, D., Jansen, N., Pérez, G.A., Raaijmakers, S.: Robustness verification for classifier ensembles. In: Hung, D.V., Sokolsky, O. (eds.) ATVA 2020. LNCS, vol. 12302, pp. 271–287. Springer, Cham (2020). https://doi.org/10.1007/978-3-030-59152-6_15
31. Hahn, E.M., et al.: The 2019 comparison of tools for the analysis of quantitative formal models. In: Beyer, D., Huisman, M., Kordon, F., Steffen, B. (eds.) TACAS 2019. LNCS, vol. 11429, pp. 69–92. Springer, Cham (2019). https://doi.org/10.1007/978-3-030-17502-3_5
32. Hobbs, K.L., Feron, E.M.: A taxonomy for aerospace collision avoidance with implications for automation in space traffic management. In: AIAA Scitech 2020 Forum, p. 0877 (2020)
33. Huang, X., Kwiatkowska, M., Wang, S., Wu, M.: Safety verification of deep neural networks. In: Majumdar, R., Kunčak, V. (eds.) CAV 2017. LNCS, vol. 10426, pp. 3–29. Springer, Cham (2017). https://doi.org/10.1007/978-3-319-63387-9_1
34. Itoh, H., Nakamura, K.: Partially observable Markov decision processes with imprecise parameters. Artif. Intell. **171**(8), 453–490 (2007)

35. Jansen, N., Könighofer, B., Junges, S., Serban, A., Bloem, R.: Safe reinforcement learning using probabilistic shields (invited paper). In: CONCUR. LIPIcs, vol. 171, pp. 1–16. Schloss Dagstuhl - Leibniz-Zentrum für Informatik (2020)
36. Jia, Y., Harman, M.: An analysis and survey of the development of mutation testing. IEEE Trans. Software Eng. **37**(5), 649–678 (2011)
37. Jiang, F., et al.: Artificial intelligence in healthcare: past, present and future. Stroke Vasc. Neurol. **2**(4) (2017)
38. Junges, S., Jansen, N., Seshia, S.A.: Enforcing almost-sure reachability in POMDPs. In: Silva, A., Leino, K.R.M. (eds.) CAV 2021. LNCS, vol. 12760, pp. 602–625. Springer, Cham (2021). https://doi.org/10.1007/978-3-030-81688-9_28
39. Junges, S., et al.: Finite-state controllers of POMDPs using parameter synthesis. In: UAI, pp. 519–529. AUAI Press (2018)
40. Kaelbling, L.P., Littman, M.L., Cassandra, A.R.: Planning and acting in partially observable stochastic domains. Artif. Intell. **101**(1), 99–134 (1998)
41. Katz, G., Barrett, C., Dill, D.L., Julian, K., Kochenderfer, M.J.: Reluplex: an efficient SMT solver for verifying deep neural networks. In: Majumdar, R., Kunčak, V. (eds.) CAV 2017. LNCS, vol. 10426, pp. 97–117. Springer, Cham (2017). https://doi.org/10.1007/978-3-319-63387-9_5
42. Kerkkamp, D., Bukhsh, Z.A., Zhang, Y., Jansen, N.: Grouping of maintenance actions with deep reinforcement learning and graph convolutional networks. In: ICAART (2022). To Appear
43. Kim, S.C., Shepperd, S.W., Norris, H.L., Goldberg, H.R., Wallace, M.S.: Mission design and trajectory analysis for inspection of a host spacecraft by a microsatellite. In: 2007 IEEE Aerospace Conference, pp. 1–23. IEEE (2007)
44. Klingspor, V., Demiris, J., Kaiser, M.: Human-robot communication and machine learning. Appl. Artif. Intell. **11**(7), 719–746 (1997)
45. Kochenderfer, M.J.: Decision Making Under Uncertainty: Theory and Application. MIT press, Cambridge (2015)
46. Kwiatkowska, M., Norman, G., Parker, D.: PRISM 4.0: verification of probabilistic real-time systems. In: Gopalakrishnan, G., Qadeer, S. (eds.) CAV 2011. LNCS, vol. 6806, pp. 585–591. Springer, Heidelberg (2011). https://doi.org/10.1007/978-3-642-22110-1_47
47. Leike, J., et al.: AI safety gridworlds. arXiv preprint arXiv:1711.09883 (2017)
48. Levinson, J., et al.: Towards fully autonomous driving: Systems and algorithms. In: Intelligent Vehicles Symposium, pp. 163–168. IEEE (2011)
49. Madani, O., Hanks, S., Condon, A.: On the undecidability of probabilistic planning and infinite-horizon partially observable Markov decision problems. In: AAAI. pp. 541–548. AAAI Press (1999)
50. Meuleau, N., Peshkin, L., Kim, K.E., Kaelbling, L.P.: Learning finite-state controllers for partially observable environments. In: UAI, pp. 427–436. Morgan Kaufmann (1999)
51. Mnih, V., et al.: Playing atari with deep reinforcement learning. CoRR abs/1312.5602 (2013)
52. Nilim, A., El Ghaoui, L.: Robust control of Markov decision processes with uncertain transition matrices. Oper. Res. **53**(5), 780–798 (2005)
53. OpenAI Gym: (2018). http://gymlibrary.dev/
54. Poupart, P., Boutilier, C.: Bounded finite state controllers. In: Advances in Neural Information Processing Systems, pp. 823–830 (2004)
55. Pranger, S., Könighofer, B., Tappler, M., Deixelberger, M., Jansen, N., Bloem, R.: Adaptive shielding under uncertainty. In: ACC, pp. 3467–3474. IEEE (2021)

56. Puggelli, A., Li, W., Sangiovanni-Vincentelli, A.L., Seshia, S.A.: Polynomial-time verification of PCTL properties of MDPs with convex uncertainties. In: Sharygina, N., Veith, H. (eds.) CAV 2013. LNCS, vol. 8044, pp. 527–542. Springer, Heidelberg (2013). https://doi.org/10.1007/978-3-642-39799-8_35
57. Puterman, M.L.: Markov Decision Processes: Discrete Stochastic Dynamic Programming. John Wiley and Sons, Hoboken (1994)
58. Russell, S.J., Dewey, D., Tegmark, M.: Research priorities for robust and beneficial artificial intelligence. CoRR abs/1602.03506 (2016)
59. Smith, R.C.: Uncertainty Quantification: Theory, Implementation, and Applications, vol. 12. Siam, New Delhi (2013)
60. Sniazhko, S.: Uncertainty in decision-making: a review of the international business literature. Cogent Bus. Manage. **6**(1), 1650692 (2019)
61. Stoica, I., et al.: A Berkeley view of systems challenges for AI. CoRR abs/1712.05855 (2017)
62. Suilen, M., Jansen, N., Cubuktepe, M., Topcu, U.: Robust policy synthesis for uncertain POMDPs via convex optimization. In: IJCAI, pp. 4113–4120. ijcai.org (2020)
63. Suilen, M., Simão, T.D., Parker, D., Jansen, N.: Robust anytime learning of Markov decision processes. In: NeurIPS (2022)
64. Sutton, R.S., Barto, A.G.: Reinforcement Learning: An Introduction. MIT Press, Cambridge (1998)
65. Thrun, S., Burgard, W., Fox, D.: Probabilistic Robotics. The MIT Press, Cambridge (2005)
66. Vaandrager, F.W.: Model learning. Commun. ACM **60**(2), 86–95 (2017)
67. Walter, G., Augustin, T.: Imprecision and prior-data conflict in generalized Bayesian inference. J. Stat. Theor. Pract. **3**(1), 255–271 (2009)
68. Wang, F.: Toward a revolution in transportation operations: AI for complex systems. IEEE Intell. Syst. **23**(6), 8–13 (2008)
69. Wiesemann, W., Kuhn, D., Rustem, B.: Robust Markov decision processes. Math. Oper. Res. **38**(1), 153–183 (2013)
70. Wolff, E.M., Topcu, U., Murray, R.M.: Robust control of uncertain Markov decision processes with temporal logic specifications. In: CDC, pp. 3372–3379. IEEE (2012)
71. Xu, H., Mannor, S.: Distributionally robust Markov decision processes. Math. Oper. Res. **37**(2), 288–300 (2012)
72. Zhang, J., Cheung, B., Finn, C., Levine, S., Jayaraman, D.: Cautious adaptation for reinforcement learning in safety-critical settings. In: ICML. Proceedings of Machine Learning Research, vol. 119, pp. 11055–11065. PMLR (2020)
73. Zhao, X., Calinescu, R., Gerasimou, S., Robu, V., Flynn, D.: Interval change-point detection for runtime probabilistic model checking. In: 35th IEEE/ACM International Conference on Automated Software Engineering. York (2020)

SAT/SMT

A Coq Formalization of Lebesgue Induction Principle and Tonelli's Theorem

Sylvie Boldo[1(✉)], François Clément[2,3], Vincent Martin[4], Micaela Mayero[5], and Houda Mouhcine[1,2,3,5]

[1] Université Paris-Saclay, CNRS, ENS Paris-Saclay, Inria, Laboratoire Méthodes Formelles, 91190 Gif-sur-Yvette, France
sylvie.boldo@inria.fr
[2] Inria, 2 rue Simone Iff, 75589 Paris, France
[3] CERMICS, École des Ponts, 77455 Marne-la-Vallée, France
[4] Université de technologie de Compiègne, LMAC, 60203 Compiègne, France
[5] LIPN, Université Paris 13 - USPN, CNRS UMR 7030, 93430 Villetaneuse, France

Abstract. Lebesgue integration is a well-known mathematical tool, used for instance in probability theory, real analysis, and numerical mathematics. Thus, its formalization in a proof assistant is to be designed to fit different goals and projects. Once the Lebesgue integral is formally defined and the first lemmas are proved, the question of the convenience of the formalization naturally arises. To check it, a useful extension is Tonelli's theorem, stating that the (double) integral of a nonnegative measurable function of two variables can be computed by iterated integrals, and allowing to switch the order of integration. This article describes the formal definition and proof in Coq of product sigma-algebras, product measures and their uniqueness, the construction of iterated integrals, up to Tonelli's theorem. We also advertise the *Lebesgue induction principle* provided by an inductive type for nonnegative measurable functions.

Keywords: Formal proof · Coq · Measure theory · Lebesgue integration · Tonelli's theorem

1 Introduction

This work deals with the Coq[1] formalization of the Lebesgue induction principle and Tonelli's theorem as a direct continuation of previous work [2]. Our long-term objective is to formally prove in Coq scientific computing programs and the correctness of parts of a C++ library, such as FreeFEM++[2] or XLiFE++,[3]

[1] https://coq.inria.fr/.
[2] https://freefem.org/.
[3] https://uma.ensta-paris.fr/soft/XLiFE++/.

This work was partly supported by the European Research Council (ERC) under the European Union's Horizon 2020 Research and Innovation Programme - Grant Agreement n°810367.

M. Chechik et al. (Eds.): FM 2023, LNCS 14000, pp. 39–55, 2023.
https://doi.org/10.1007/978-3-031-27481-7_4

that implements the Finite Element Method (FEM), a widely used method for numerically solving Partial Differential Equations (PDEs) arising in different domains like engineering and mathematical modeling. With this work, we carry on with our goal of providing a Coq library usable by scientific computing people. It started with the first development of a real numbers library [18], and then with the first complete formalization and proof of a numerical program [3] (a C program for the approximated resolution of the wave equation). More recently, the Lax–Milgram theorem [1] (for the resolution of a class of PDEs), then Lebesgue integration of nonnegative measurable functions [2], and Bochner integration [4] (a generalization for functions taking their values in a Banach space).

The proof of Tonelli's theorem is the natural next step. And, as a side result, it also allows us to validate our previous developments and in particular our formalization choices for the definitions and results about the Lebesgue integral. For example, as we work in Coq, the question arises of whether to use classical or intuitionistic real analysis. Following [2], we decided to be completely classical.

The Lebesgue induction principle is a proof technique for properties about nonnegative measurable functions, and usually involves the integral. It reflects the three construction steps followed by Henri Lebesgue to build his integral [15]. The property is first established for indicator functions, then for nonnegative simple functions by checking that the property is compatible with positive linear operations, and finally for all nonnegative measurable functions by checking that it is compatible with the supremum. This is an important asset for the proof of Tonelli's theorem, and we provide it as a byproduct of an inductive type.

Tonelli's theorem provides a convenient way to ease the computation of multiple integrals by stating their equality with iterated integrals, each in a single dimension. Tonelli's theorem applies to nonnegative measurable functions. A similar result, Fubini's theorem, applies to integrable functions with an arbitrary sign, or even taking their values in a Banach space when using the Bochner integral. This article focuses on the case of nonnegative functions, and we only address the case of functions of two variables, as it is common in mathematics.

We aim to the construction of the full formal proof in Coq of Tonelli's theorem, stating that the (double) integral of a nonnegative measurable function of two variables can be computed by iterated integrals, and allowing to switch the order of integration. It can be expressed in a mathematical setting as follows.

Theorem 1: Tonelli

Let (X_1, Σ_1, μ_1) and (X_2, Σ_2, μ_2) be measure spaces. Assume that μ_1 and μ_2 are σ-finite. Let $f \in \mathcal{M}_+(X_1 \times X_2, \Sigma_1 \otimes \Sigma_2)$. Then, we have

$$(\forall x_1 \in X_1,\ f_{x_1} \in \mathcal{M}_+(X_2, \Sigma_2)) \quad \wedge \quad \int_{X_2} f_{x_1}\, d\mu_2 \in \mathcal{M}_+(X_1, \Sigma_1), \tag{1}$$

$$(\forall x_2 \in X_2,\ f^{x_2} \in \mathcal{M}_+(X_1, \Sigma_1)) \quad \wedge \quad \int_{X_1} f^{x_2}\, d\mu_1 \in \mathcal{M}_+(X_2, \Sigma_2), \tag{2}$$

$$\int_{X_1 \times X_2} f\, d(\mu_1 \otimes \mu_2) = \int_{X_1} \left(\int_{X_2} f_{x_1}\, d\mu_2 \right) d\mu_1 = \int_{X_2} \left(\int_{X_1} f^{x_2}\, d\mu_1 \right) d\mu_2.$$

The notations are specified in the remainder of this paper. Just note that many measures, including the Lebesgue measure, are σ-finite (defined in Sect. 4), $\mathcal{M}_+$ denotes the set of nonnegative measurable functions (see Sect. 2.2), and f_{x_1} and f^{x_2} are partial applications of f (see Sect. 5.1). Notice also that the properties (1) and (2) ensure the existence of all simple integrals, while the existence of the double integral is granted by the assumption on the function f.

The mathematical definitions and proofs are taken from textbooks [8,12,17]. The Coq code is available at (mainly in files `Tonelli.v`, `LInt_p.v` and `Mp.v`)

https://lipn.univ-paris13.fr/coq-num-analysis/tree/Tonelli.1.0/Lebesgue

where the tag `Tonelli.1.0` corresponds to the code of this article. An Opam package, coq-num-analysis, is also available.[4]

Tonelli's theorem is known enough and useful enough to have been formalized before our work in several proof assistants. It has been done in PVS in the PVS-NASA library[5] by Lester, probably as a follow-up of [16]. Some Fubini-like results are available in HOL Light [13]. More recently, Tonelli's theorem was formalized in Mizar by Endou [11]. The formalizations nearest to ours are in Isabelle/HOL and Lean. Hölzl and Heller defined binary and iterated product measure before Fubini's theorem [14]. It relies on Isabelle type classes and locales. A more recent work[6] extends it to the Bochner integral. In Lean, van Doorn defines the product of measures and properties of the product space towards Tonelli and Fubini's theorems in a way similar to ours, but for the Bochner integral [20]. He also provides a similar Lebesgue induction principle, but to our knowledge, our approach of getting it from an inductive type is new. A recent work in Coq has been developed for probability theory.[7] Many definitions are similar to ours, but in a simpler setting where measures are finite. Fubini's theorem also appeared in math-comp/analysis[8] after the submission of this article. This formalization relies on the math-comp/analysis hierarchy of classes. First, this hierarchy is not compatible with the canonical structures of Coquelicot we used to prove the Lax–Milgram theorem [1]. Second, the depth of this hierarchy involves many abstractions for the unfamiliar user to process.

For a comparison of the Lebesgue integral in various proof assistants, we refer the reader to [2,20], and we refer to [6] for a wider comparison of real analysis in proof assistants.

We think Coq is the most suitable tool for our goal: to prove properties on the FEM algorithm and program, including floating point errors. Coq indeed provides both libraries and results for the mathematical part [1,2] and the Flocq library for floating-point arithmetic [7]. We are not aware of another proof assistant able to address these two issues together.

---

4 https://coq.inria.fr/opam/www/.

5 https://github.com/nasa/pvslib/blob/master/measure_integration/fubini_tonelli.pvs.

6 https://isabelle.in.tum.de/library/HOL/HOL-Analysis/Bochner_Integration.html.

7 https://github.com/jtassarotti/coq-proba/.

8 https://github.com/math-comp/analysis/blob/master/theories/lebesgue_integral.v.

This paper is organized as follows. Section 2 summarizes the prerequisites and the main concepts of measure and integration theories developed in previous works. The formalization of the Lebesgue induction principle is detailed in Sect. 3. Section 4 describes the building of the product measure, and Sect. 5 is devoted to the building of the iterated integrals and the full proof of Tonelli's theorem. Finally, Sect. 6 concludes and provides directions for future work.

2 Prerequisites

Our formalizations and proofs are conducted in Coq. In this section, we present the necessary prerequisites and libraries for our developments.

2.1 The Coquelicot Library, $\overline{\mathbb{R}}$ and Logic

The Coquelicot[9] library [5] is a conservative extension of the standard Coq library of real numbers [10,18] supplying basic results in real analysis. It is a classical library, and a salient feature is that it provides total functions, e.g. for limit, derivative, and (Riemann) integral. This is consistent with classical logic, and it means a natural way to write mathematical formulas and theorem statements. The library also provides a formalization of the extended real numbers $\overline{\mathbb{R}} := \mathbb{R} \cup \{-\infty, +\infty\}$ equipped, among other operations, with `Rbar_lub` for the least-upper bound of subsets, and `Sup_seq` for the supremum of sequences.

As in the Coquelicot library, we use the full classical logic: total order on real numbers, propositional and functional extensionality axioms, excluded middle and choice axioms. We rely on the same axioms detailed in [2, Section 2].

2.2 Lebesgue Integration Theory

The theory of integration is commonly built upon measure theory (e.g. see [9]): first, the measurability of subsets is defined, and then a measure associates a nonnegative number in $\overline{\mathbb{R}}_+$ to each measurable subset; second, the measurability of functions is defined, and then the integral associates a nonnegative number in $\overline{\mathbb{R}}_+$ to each nonnegative measurable function. The following summarizes what we need from [2].

Measurable Subsets. A measurable space (X, Σ) consists of a set X, and a *σ-algebra Σ* collecting all measurable subsets. A σ-algebra is closed under most set operations, such as complement, (countable) union and intersection. It can be *generated* as the closure of a collection of subsets with respect to some of the set operations. In our Coq developments, the generators on `X : Type` are typically denoted `genX : (X → Prop) → Prop`, and a subset `A : X → Prop` belongs to the σ-algebra generated by `genX` when the inductive property `measurable genX A` holds.

When the set X has a topological structure, it is convenient to use its *Borel σ-algebra* that is generated by all the open subsets. The Borel σ-algebra of $\overline{\mathbb{R}}$ can also be generated by the right closed rays ($[a, \infty]$), denoted in Coq by `gen_Rbar`.

[9] https://gitlab.inria.fr/coquelicot/coquelicot/.

Given two measurable spaces (X_1, Σ_1) and (X_2, Σ_2), the *product σ-algebra on* $X_1 \times X_2$ is the one generated by the products of measurable subsets of X_1 and X_2. Some details are provided in Sect. 4 where it is a major ingredient.

Measure. A measure space (X, Σ, μ) contains an additional *measure* μ: a function $\Sigma \to \overline{\mathbb{R}}$ that is nonnegative, homogeneous ($\mu(\varnothing) = 0$), and σ-additive. In Coq, a measure is a record collecting the function μ and its three properties. In Sect. 4, we rely on the properties of *continuity from below* and *from above*. For all sequences $(A_n)_{n\in\mathbb{N}} \in \Sigma$, they respectively state for any measure μ that when the sequence is nondecreasing, $\mu\left(\bigcup_{n\in\mathbb{N}} A_n\right) = \lim_{n\to\infty} \mu(A_n) = \sup_{n\in\mathbb{N}} \mu(A_n)$, and when it is nonincreasing and one of the subsets is of finite measure, then we have $\mu\left(\bigcap_{n\in\mathbb{N}} A_n\right) = \inf_{n\in\mathbb{N}} \mu(A_n)$. Note also that the monotonicity of measures allows to replace the limit of a nondecreasing sequence by its supremum.

Measurable Functions. Given two measurable spaces (X, Σ) and $(Y, \mathcal{T})$, a function $f : X \to Y$ is said *measurable* when the preimage of every measurable subset is measurable:[10]

```
Definition measurable_fun (f : X → Y) : Prop :=
  ∀ B, measurable genY B → measurable genX (fun x ⇒ B (f x)).
```

When $Y := \overline{\mathbb{R}}$, and usually $\mathcal{T}$ is its Borel σ-algebra, we simply say that the function is *Σ-measurable*, and we use the predicate `measurable_fun_Rbar` corresponding to `genY := gen_Rbar`. We denote the *set of nonnegative measurable functions* $\mathcal{M}_+(X, \Sigma)$. The "(X, Σ)" annotation may be dropped when there is no possible confusion. Among other operations, $\mathcal{M}_+$ is closed under nonnegative scalar multiplication, addition, and supremum. In Coq, we use the predicate `Mplus genX : (X → R̄) → Prop` that gathers nonnegativity and measurability, and `Mplus_seq genX : (ℕ → X → R̄) → Prop` for sequences of functions in $\mathcal{M}_+$.

Simple functions are functions whose image has finite cardinality. The *set of nonnegative measurable simple functions* is denoted $\mathcal{SF}_+(X, \Sigma)$. In Coq, simple functions are *canonically* represented by their strictly sorted list of values, and we use the predicate `SFplus genX : (X → R̄) → Prop`. Given $f \in \mathcal{M}_+$, `mk_adapted_seq` provides an *adapted sequence for* f, i.e. a nondecreasing sequence $(\varphi_n)_{n\in\mathbb{N}}$ in $\mathcal{SF}_+$ such that $f = \lim_{n\to\infty} \varphi_n = \sup_{n\in\mathbb{N}} \varphi_n$.

The *set of measurable indicator functions* is denoted $\mathcal{IF}(X, \Sigma)$. Note that an indicator function $\mathbb{1}_A$ is measurable whenever its support subset A belongs to Σ. Simple functions in $\mathcal{SF}_+$ are nonnegative linear combinations of indicator functions.

Lebesgue Integral. The construction of the Lebesgue integral in $\mathcal{M}_+$ operates in three steps. The first stage is to integrate indicator functions in $\mathcal{IF}$ by taking the measure of their support. Then, the second stage extends the integral to simple functions in $\mathcal{SF}_+$ by positive linearity. And finally, the third stage extends it again to measurable functions in $\mathcal{M}_+$ by taking the supremum. In the end,

[10] Note that we often rely on the Section mechanism of Coq for "hiding" some arguments, here `genX` and `genY` (see https://coq.inria.fr/refman/language/core/sections.html).

the *integral of a function* $f \in \mathcal{M}_+$ is defined as the supremum of the integrals of all simple functions in $\mathcal{SF}_+$ smaller than f and formalized in [2] by

```
Definition LInt_p (f : X → R̄ ) : R̄ :=
  Rbar_lub (fun z ⇒ ∃(phi : X → R) (Hphi : SF genX phi),
    nonneg phi ∧ (∀ x, phi x ≤_R̄ f x) ∧ LInt_SFp mu phi Hphi = z).
```

The proof of Tonelli's theorem relies on several properties of the integral in $\mathcal{M}_+$, such as monotonicity, positive linearity, σ-additivity, and the Beppo Levi (monotone convergence) theorem. The latter states the compatibility with the supremum: for all nondecreasing sequences $(f_n)_{n\in\mathbb{N}} \in \mathcal{M}_+$, the limit $\lim_{n\to\infty} f_n$ (which actually equals $\sup_{n\in\mathbb{N}} f_n$) is also in $\mathcal{M}_+$, and the integral-limit exchange formula holds, $\int \sup_{n\in\mathbb{N}} f_n \, d\mu = \sup_{n\in\mathbb{N}} \int f_n \, d\mu$ (see [2, Section 7.2]).

3 Lebesgue Induction Principle

Let (X, Σ) be a measurable space. The properties of the function spaces $\mathcal{M}_+$, $\mathcal{SF}_+$ and $\mathcal{IF}$ recalled in Sect. 2.2 suggest to represent nonnegative measurable functions by an inductive type. Indeed, functions in $\mathcal{M}_+$ are the supremum of simple functions in $\mathcal{SF}_+$, which are themselves positive linear combinations of indicator functions in $\mathcal{IF}$. Moreover, the associated structural induction principle is a common proof technique for several results in Lebesgue integration theory, among which is Tonelli's theorem as noted in [20].

In addition to Mplus recalled in Sect. 2.2, we now define the inductive type

```
Inductive Mp : (X → R̄ ) → Prop :=
 | Mp_charac : ∀A, measurable genX A → Mp (charac A)
 | Mp_scal : ∀ a f, 0 ≤ a → Mp f → Mp (fun x ⇒ a *_R̄ f x)
 | Mp_plus : ∀ f g, Mp f → Mp g → Mp (fun x ⇒ f x +_R̄ g x)
 | Mp_sup : ∀ f, incr_fun_seq f → (∀n, Mp (f n)) →
        Mp (fun x ⇒ Sup_seq (fun n ⇒ f n x)).
```

where `charac A` stands for the characteristic function of A (denoted $\mathbb{1}_A$), and `incr_fun_seq f` stands for the property `∀ x n, Rbar_le (f n x) (f (S n) x)`. In other words, `Mp` is the closure of measurable characteristic functions under positive linear combination and increasing supremum.

We also have an inductive type for $\mathcal{SF}_+$ denoted by `SFp`, whose constructors are essentially the same as the first three of `Mp`. Several inductive types equivalent to `Mp` are defined in order to split the proof steps, for instance one is built over `SFp`. They are not given here for the sake of simplicity and brevity.

The important point is then the correctness of this definition, compared to the existing one. The only delicate part is to obtain the correctness result for simple functions, stated as `Lemma SFp_correct : ∀f, SFp f ↔ SFplus gen f`.

For that, from a simple function represented by a list of values of size $n + 1$, we need to construct a smaller simple function associated to a sublist of size n. The tricky needed result is the following:

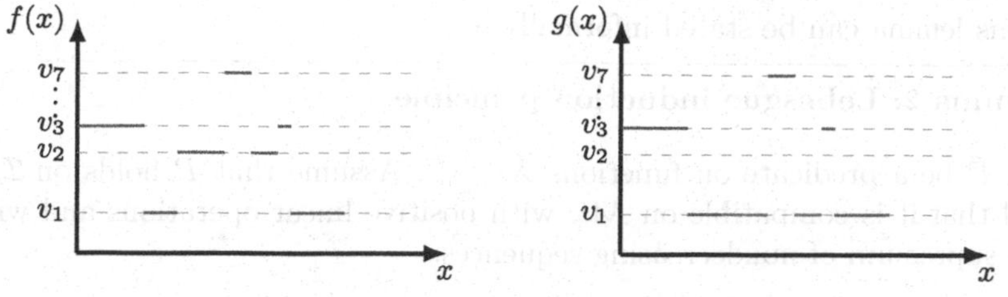

Fig. 1. Illustration of Lemma SF_aux_cons. The value v_2 taken by the simple function f (on the left) is replaced in g (on the right) by the value v_1 (in red). (Color figure online)

```
Lemma SF_aux_cons :
  ∀ (f : X → ℝ) v1 v2 l, nonneg f → SF_aux genX f (v1 :: v2 :: l) →
    let g x := f x + (v1 − v2) ∗ charac (fun t ⇒ f t = v2) x in
    nonneg g ∧ SF_aux genX g (v1 :: l).
```

Given $f \in \mathcal{SF}_+$ and its associated canonical list ℓ, the lemma builds a new g in $\mathcal{SF}_+$ canonically associated with the list ℓ deprived of some item v_2. This means that on the nonempty subset $f^{-1}(\{v_2\})$, g must take one of the remaining values, v_1 as shown in Fig. 1, which also provides the property $g \leqslant f$.

More precisely, let us assume that f is of the form $\sum_{v \in \{v_1, v_2\} \cup \ell} v \times \mathbb{1}_{f^{-1}(\{v\})}$ with $v_1 < v_2$ and $v_1, v_2 \notin \ell$. Then, by setting $g := f + (v_1 - v_2) \times \mathbb{1}_{f^{-1}(\{v_2\})}$, one has $g = \sum_{v \in \{v_1\} \cup \ell} v \times \mathbb{1}_{f^{-1}(\{v\})}$. Thus, g belongs to $\mathcal{SF}_+$ with a smaller list of values, and $f = g + (v_2 - v_1) \times \mathbb{1}_{f^{-1}(\{v_2\})}$ with $v_2 - v_1 \geq 0$. This is tricky for two reasons. First, we cannot set g to zero on $f^{-1}(\{v_2\})$ (as zero may be a new value, defeating the point of reducing the size of the value list); thus, the initial list must contain at least two values. Second, by proceeding the other way around and setting g to v_2 on $f^{-1}(\{v_1\})$, we cannot write f as the sum of g and a *nonnegative* value times an indicator function, as needed by the constructor SFp_scal, similar to Mp_scal.

Now, we have all the ingredients to check that the definition of Mp is satisfactory, that is to say that Mp represents $\mathcal{M}_+$ as Mplus already does:

```
Lemma Mp_correct : ∀f, Mp f ↔ Mplus genX f.
```

The proof is mainly based on inductions, the construction of adapted sequences mk_adapted_seq (see Sect. 2.2), and the previous lemma.

This gives us for free the following induction lemma corresponding to Mp:

```
Mp_ind : ∀ P : (E → R̄) → Prop,
  (∀ A, measurable gen A → P (charac A)) →
  (∀ a f, 0 ⩽ a → Mp f → P f → P (fun x ⇒ a ∗R̄ f x)) →
  (∀ f g, Mp f → P f → Mp g → P g → P (fun x ⇒ f x +R̄ g x)) →
  (∀ f, incr_fun_seq f → (∀ n, Mp (f n)) →
    (∀ n, P (f n)) → P (fun x ⇒ Sup_seq (fun n ⇒ f n x))) →
  ∀ f, Mp f → P f.
```

This lemma can be stated informally as

Lemma 2: Lebesgue induction principle

Let P be a predicate on functions $X \to \overline{\mathbb{R}}$. Assume that P holds on $\mathcal{IF}$, and that it is compatible on $\mathcal{M}_+$ with positive linear operations and with the supremum of nondecreasing sequences:

$$\forall A, \quad A \in \Sigma \Rightarrow P(\mathbb{1}_A), \tag{3}$$

$$\forall a \in \mathbb{R}_+, \forall f \in \mathcal{M}_+, \quad P(f) \Rightarrow P(af), \tag{4}$$

$$\forall f, g \in \mathcal{M}_+, \quad P(f) \wedge P(g) \Rightarrow P(f+g), \tag{5}$$

$$\forall (f_n)_{n\in\mathbb{N}} \in \mathcal{M}_+, \quad (\forall n \in \mathbb{N},\, f_n \leqslant f_{n+1} \wedge P(f_n)) \Rightarrow P\left(\sup_{n\in\mathbb{N}} f_n\right). \tag{6}$$

Then, P holds on $\mathcal{M}_+$.

There are a few alternative statements of the Lebesgue induction principle. For instance, we choose to have a in $\mathbb{R}$ and not in $\overline{\mathbb{R}}$ in (4), as it makes an equivalent, but simpler to use lemma. Moreover, as noted in the Lean source code,[11] it is possible to sharpen the premises of the constructors. For instance, it may be sufficient to have in (5) simple functions that do not share the same image value, except 0, or with disjoint supports.

4 Product Measure on a Product Space

In this section, we build the product measure for the measurable subsets of a product space. This allows us to integrate on such a product space in Sect. 5.

Given two measure spaces (X_1, Σ_1, μ_1) and (X_2, Σ_2, μ_2), a *product measure on* $(X_1 \times X_2, \Sigma_1 \otimes \Sigma_2)$ *induced by* μ_1 *and* μ_2 is a measure μ defined on the product σ-algebra $\Sigma_1 \otimes \Sigma_2$ (defined in Sect. 4.1) satisfying the *box property*:

$$\forall A_1 \in \Sigma_1, \forall A_2 \in \Sigma_2, \quad \mu(A_1 \times A_2) = \mu_1(A_1)\,\mu_2(A_2). \tag{7}$$

To ensure the existence and uniqueness of such a product measure, we assume that μ_1 and μ_2 are σ-*finite*, i.e. that the full sets X_1 and X_2 are nondecreasing unions of subsets of finite measure (see a detailed definition in Sect. 4.3).

A candidate product measure is first built in three steps, see Fig. 2. Firstly, X_1-*sections* (or *"vertical" cuttings*) of subsets are proved to be Σ_2-measurable. Then, the measure of sections is proved to be Σ_1-measurable. The candidate is the integral of the measure of sections. Then, this candidate is proved to be a product measure, and the product measure is guaranteed to be unique. The main argument for this construction is the monotone class theorem, whose intricate proof is not detailed here (e.g. see [9, Sec 1.6], and Sect. 4.3 for a quick presentation). It is used twice: for the measurability of the measure of sections, and for the uniqueness of the product measure.

---

[11] https://leanprover-community.github.io/mathlib_docs/measure_theory/integral/lebesgue.html#measurable.ennreal_induction.

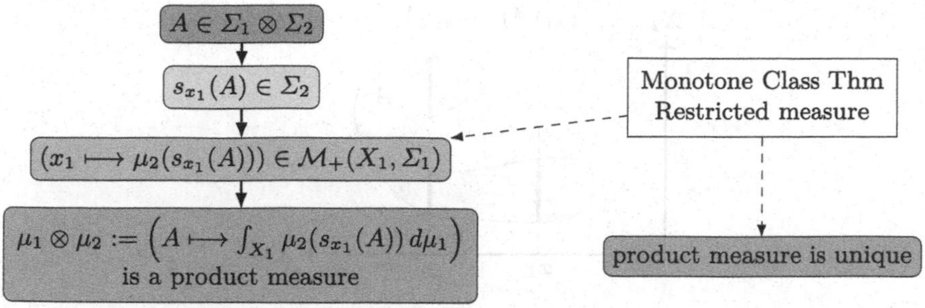

Fig. 2. Flowchart for the construction of the product measure. The fill colors refer to sections: 4.1 in brown, 4.2 in yellow, 4.3 in green, and 4.4 in blue. Dashed lines denote the use of the listed proof arguments, that were developed for the present work. (Color figure online)

The definition of the product σ-algebra is first reviewed in Sect. 4.1. Then, Sect. 4.2 is dedicated to sections, and Sect. 4.3 to the measure of sections. Finally, the existence and uniqueness of the product measure is in Sect. 4.4.

4.1 Product σ-Algebra

Let us detail the notion of product σ-algebra that was introduced in [2]. Given two measurable spaces (X_1, Σ_1) and (X_2, Σ_2), the *product σ-algebra on $X_1 \times X_2$* is the σ-algebra $\Sigma_1 \otimes \Sigma_2$ generated by the products of measurable subsets:

$$\Sigma_1 \otimes \Sigma_2 := \sigma\text{-algebra generated by } \Sigma_1 \overline{\times} \Sigma_2 := \{A_1 \times A_2 \mid A_1 \in \Sigma_1 \wedge A_2 \in \Sigma_2\}.$$

Given generators `genX1` and `genX2` for Σ_1 and Σ_2, the generator $\Sigma_1 \overline{\times} \Sigma_2$ is denoted in Coq by `Product_Sigma_algebra genX1 genX2`. It is proved in [2, Sect. 4.3] that $\Sigma_1 \otimes \Sigma_2$ is also the σ-algebra generated by $\text{gen}(\Sigma_1) \cup \{X_1\} \overline{\times} \text{gen}(\Sigma_2) \cup \{X_2\}$. This generator is denoted in Coq by `Gen_Product genX1 genX2`, and simply by `genX1xX2` in the sequel. Symmetrically, `genX2xX1` represents `Gen_Product genX2 genX1`.

4.2 Section of Subset

The notion of *section* consists in keeping one of the variables fixed (see Fig. 3). Given a subset A of $X_1 \times X_2$ and a point $x_1 \in X_1$, the *X_1-section of A at x_1* is the subset of X_2 defined by $s_{x_1}(A) := \{x_2 \in X_2 \mid (x_1, x_2) \in A\}$.

```
Definition section (x1 : X1) (A : X1 * X2 → Prop) (x2 : X2) : Prop := A (x1, x2).
```

Sections commute with most set operations. For example, they are compatible with the empty set ($s_{x_1}(\varnothing) = \varnothing$), the complement ($s_{x_1}(A^c) = s_{x_1}(A)^c$), countable union and intersection, and are monotone. Sections also satisfy the following box property: for all subsets $A_1 \subseteq X_1$, $A_2 \subseteq X_2$, and point $x_1 \in X_1$,

$$x_1 \in A_1 \Rightarrow s_{x_1}(A_1 \times A_2) = A_2 \quad \text{and} \quad x_1 \notin A_1 \Rightarrow s_{x_1}(A_1 \times A_2) = \varnothing. \tag{8}$$

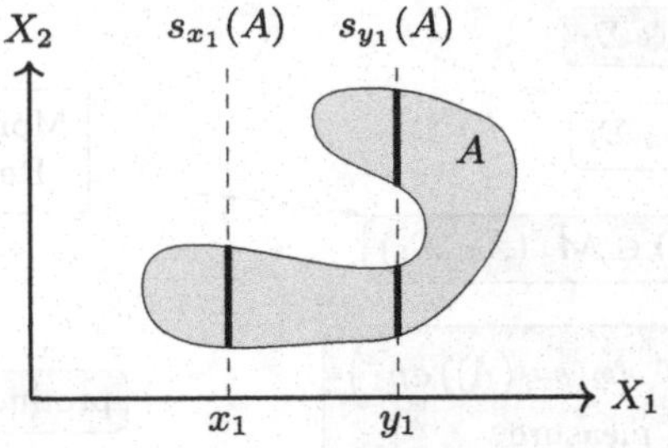

Fig. 3. X_1-sections of a subset A of $X_1 \times X_2$ at points x_1 and y_1.

Then, we prove that, if a subset A is $\Sigma_1 \otimes \Sigma_2$-measurable, then its X_1-sections at any point in X_1 are Σ_2-measurable. As measurability is an inductive type, the proof is a simple induction on the hypothesis.

```
Lemma section_measurable :
  ∀ A x1, measurable genX1xX2 A → measurable genX2 (section x1 A).
```

4.3 Measurability of Measure of Section

As sections are measurable (see Sect. 4.2), one can take their measure. In Sect. 4.4, the product measure is defined as the integral of the measure of sections, but before that, we have to prove nonnegativity and measurability of these functions. More precisely, that for all $\Sigma_1 \otimes \Sigma_2$-measurable subsets A, the function $(x_1 \mapsto \mu_2(s_{x_1}(A)))$ belongs to $\mathcal{M}_+(X_1, \Sigma_1)$.

The nonnegativity property directly follows from that of measures. The proof of measurability goes in two stages: firstly when the measure μ_2 is assumed to be *finite* (i.e. when $\mu_2(X_2)$ is finite), and then in the more general σ-finite case. The first stage is quite high-level; it relies on the monotone class theorem. The second stage extends the first one by means of restricted measures.

The measure of sections is represented in Coq by the total function

```
Definition meas_section (A : X1 * X2 → Prop) (x1 : X1) : R̄ :=
muX2 (section x1 A).
```

Then, the first stage of the proof is stated in Coq as

```
Lemma meas_section_Mplus_finite : ∀A, is_finite_measure muX2 →
  measurable genX1xX2 A → Mplus genX1 (meas_section A).
```

Let $\mathcal{S}$ be the set of measurable subsets satisfying the property to prove,

$$\mathcal{S} := \left\{ A \in \Sigma_1 \otimes \Sigma_2 \,|\, (x_1 \longmapsto \mu_2(s_{x_1}(A))) \in \mathcal{M}_+(X_1, \Sigma_1) \right\}.$$

It suffices to show that $\Sigma_1 \otimes \Sigma_2 \subseteq \mathcal{S}$. Firstly, $\mathcal{S}$ is proved to contain the generator $\overline{\Sigma} := \Sigma_1 \overline{\times} \Sigma_2$ of $\Sigma_1 \otimes \Sigma_2$ (see Sect. 4.1). Then, it is proved to contain the algebra of sets generated by $\overline{\Sigma}$ (i.e. the closure of $\overline{\Sigma}$ under complement and finite union). Then, $\mathcal{S}$ is also proved to be a monotone class, i.e. closed under monotone countable union and intersection. This step uses the finiteness assumption on μ_2, and continuity from below and from above (see Sect. 2.2). And finally, we conclude by applying the following corollary of the monotone class theorem (with `X := X1 * X2`, `P :=` $\mathcal{S}$, and `genX :=` $\overline{\Sigma}$) which states that if a monotone class contains the smallest algebra of sets containing `genX`, then it also contains the smallest σ-algebra containing `genX`.

```
Theorem monotone_class_Prop :
  ∀ P : (X → Prop) → Prop, is_Monotone_class P →
    Incl (Algebra genX) P → Incl (Sigma_algebra genX) P.
```

Note that `Incl` denotes the inclusion of subsets of the power set of X.

In the second stage, the measure μ_2 is supposed to be σ-finite. Thus, there exists a nondecreasing sequence $(B_n)_{n\in\mathbb{N}} \in \Sigma_2$ such that $X_2 = \bigcup_{n\in\mathbb{N}} B_n$, and $\mu_2(B_n)$ is finite for all $n \in \mathbb{N}$. Then, for each $n \in \mathbb{N}$, the *restricted measure* $\mu_2^n := (A_2 \in \Sigma_2 \longmapsto \mu_2(A_2 \cap B_n) \in \overline{\mathbb{R}}_+)$ is proved to be a finite measure. Thus, the previous result applies,

$$\forall A \in \Sigma_1 \otimes \Sigma_2, \quad (x_1 \longmapsto \mu_2^n(s_{x_1}(A))) \in \mathcal{M}_+(X_1, \Sigma_1).$$

Moreover, from the properties of sections (see Sect. 4.2) and from the continuity from below of μ_2, for all $A \in \Sigma_1 \otimes \Sigma_2$ and $x_1 \in X_1$, we have

$$\mu_2(s_{x_1}(A)) = \mu_2\left(\bigcup_{n\in\mathbb{N}} s_{x_1}(A) \cap B_n\right) = \sup_{n\in\mathbb{N}} \mu_2^n(s_{x_1}(A)).$$

Finally, the closedness of $\mathcal{M}_+(X_1, \Sigma_1)$ under supremum (see Sect. 2.2) concludes the proof. Thus, the lemma in the σ-finite case holds,

```
Lemma meas_section_Mplus_sigma_finite :
  ∀ A, is_sigma_finite_measure muX2 →
    measurable genX1xX2 A → Mplus genX1 (meas_section A).
```

Note that from (8), the measure of the section of a box reads

$$\forall A_1 \in \Sigma_1, \forall A_2 \in \Sigma_2, \quad (x_1 \longmapsto \mu_2(s_{x_1}(A_1 \times A_2))) = \mu_2(A_2)\, \mathbb{1}_{A_1}. \tag{9}$$

4.4 Existence and Uniqueness of the Product Measure

As the measures of sections belong to $\mathcal{M}_+$ (see Sect. 4.3), one can take their integral. The candidate product measure is the function defined on the product σ-algebra $\Sigma_1 \otimes \Sigma_2$ (see Sect. 4.1) by $(\mu_1 \otimes \mu_2)(A) := \int_{X_1} \mu_2(s_{x_1}(A))\, d\mu_1$,

```
Definition meas_prod_meas (A : X1 * X2 → Prop) : R̄ :=
  LInt_p muX1 (meas_section muX2 A).
```

We easily deduce that this candidate function is both nonnegative and equal to zero on the empty set. The σ-additivity property is obtained by means of the σ-additivity of the integral (see Sect. 2.2), and of the measure μ_2. This proves that the candidate is a measure, and that we can instantiate the record defining the product measure `meas_prod` as an object of type measure (see Sect. 2.2), so all the proved results on measures are available.

Moreover, Eq. (9), and the positive linearity of the integral ensure the box property (7), thus making `meas_prod` a product measure.

Product measures are proved to keep the finiteness, or σ-finiteness, property of the initial measures μ_1 and μ_2. Then, the proof of the uniqueness of the product measure follows exactly the same path as for the measurability of the measure of sections (see Sect. 4.3). Firstly, when the measures μ_1 and μ_2 are finite, we introduce two (finite) product measures m and $\tilde{m}$ induced by μ_1 and μ_2, i.e. both satisfying (7). The set $\mathcal{S} \stackrel{\text{def.}}{=} \{A \in \Sigma_1 \otimes \Sigma_2 \,|\, m(A) = \tilde{m}(A)\}$ is proved to contain $\Sigma_1 \otimes \Sigma_2$ using `monotone_class_Prop`, which shows uniqueness. Then, the result is extended to σ-finite measures by means of restricted measures.

5 Tonelli's Theorem

With the product measure built in Sect. 4, we can now consider integration on a product space. As in Sect. 4, we assume that the measures are σ-finite, which ensures the existence and uniqueness of the product measure.

This section addresses the proof of Tonelli's theorem that allows to compute a double integral on a product space by integrating successively with respect to each variable, either way. Besides the following formulas, the theorem also states measurability properties that ensure the legitimacy of all integrals (see Theorem 1):

$$\int_{X_1 \times X_2} f \, d(\mu_1 \otimes \mu_2) = \int_{X_1} \left(\int_{X_2} f \, d\mu_2 \right) d\mu_1 \tag{10}$$

$$= \int_{X_2} \left(\int_{X_1} f \, d\mu_1 \right) d\mu_2. \tag{11}$$

Similarly to the process used in Sect. 4, the iterated integral (right-hand side of (10)) is built in three steps, see Fig. 4. Firstly, X_1-sections of functions are proved to be Σ_2-measurable. Then, the integral (in X_2) of sections of functions is proved to be Σ_1-measurable. And the iterated integral is the integral (in X_1) of the integral (in X_2) of the sections of functions. Finally, Formula (10) is proved, and then (11) is deduced from the latter by a swap of variables relying both on a change of measure and on the uniqueness of the product measure. The main argument for this proof is the Lebesgue induction principle (see Sect. 3). It is used twice: for the measurability of the integral of sections of functions together with the first Tonelli formula, and for the change-of-measure formula.

Section 5.1 is dedicated to sections of functions, and Sect. 5.2 to the iterated integral and the proof of the first formula of Tonelli's theorem. Finally, the full proof of Tonelli's theorem is obtained in Sect. 5.3.

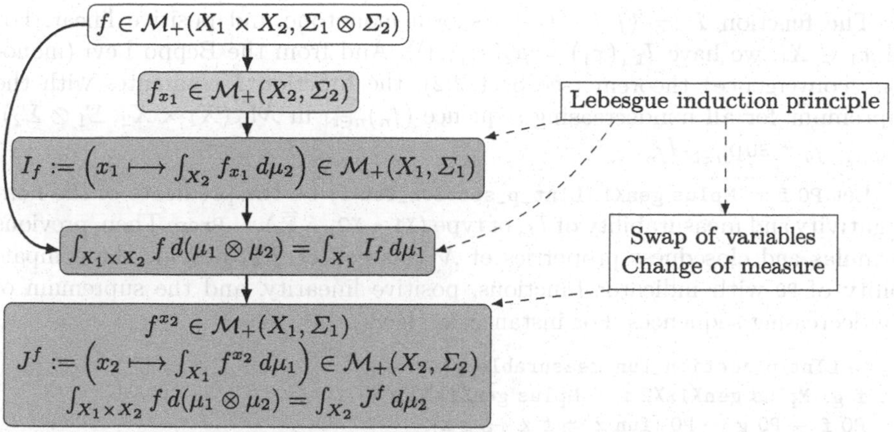

Fig. 4. Flowchart for the construction of the iterated integrals on a product space. The fill colors refer to sections: 5.1 in yellow , 5.2 in green , and 5.3 in blue . Dashed lines denote the use of the listed proof arguments, that were developed for the present work. (Color figure online)

5.1 Section of Function

Similarly to Sect. 4.2, given a numeric function $f : X_1 \times X_2 \to \overline{\mathbb{R}}$ and $x_1 \in X_1$, the X_1*-section of* f *at* x_1 is the partial application $f_{x_1} := (x_2 \mapsto f(x_1, x_2))$.

```
Definition section_fun (x1 : X1) (f : X1 * X2 → R̄) (x2 : X2) : R̄ := f (x1, x2).
```

From the measurability of sections of subsets, we deduce that, if f belongs to $\mathcal{M}_+(X_1 \times X_2, \Sigma_1 \otimes \Sigma_2)$, then its X_1-sections are in $\mathcal{M}_+(X_2, \Sigma_2)$.

```
Lemma section_fun_Mplus :
  ∀ f x1, Mplus genX1xX2 f → Mplus genX2 (section_fun x1 f).
```

Symmetrically, for all $x_2 \in X_2$, we introduce the X_2*-section of* f *at* x_2, the partial application with respect to the second variable, $f^{x_2} := (x_1 \mapsto f(x_1, x_2))$.

5.2 Iterated Integral and the First Formula of Tonelli's Theorem

As sections of functions are nonnegative and Σ_2-measurable (see Sect. 5.1), one can take their integral (in X_2). For all functions $f \in \mathcal{M}_+(X_1 \times X_2, \Sigma_1 \otimes \Sigma_2)$, we define $I_f := \left(x_1 \longmapsto \int_{X_2} f_{x_1}\, d\mu_2\right)$,

```
Definition LInt_p_section_fun (f : X1 * X2 → R̄) x1 : R̄ :=
  LInt_p muX2 (section_fun x1 f).
```

The iterated integral corresponds to integrating once more (in X_1), but one must first establish that $I_f \in \mathcal{M}_+(X_1, \Sigma_1)$. The nonnegativity result directly follows from the monotonicity of the integral (see Sect. 2.2). The general measurability result and the first Tonelli formula (10), are proved by means of the Lebesgue induction principle of Sect. 3.

The function $I := (f \mapsto I_f)$ is shown monotone and positive linear. For all $x_1 \in X_1$, we have $I_{\mathbb{1}_A}(x_1) = \mu_2(s_{x_1}(A))$. And from the Beppo Levi (monotone convergence) theorem (see Sect. 2.2), the function I commutes with the supremum: for all nondecreasing sequence $(f_n)_{n\in\mathbb{N}}$ in $\mathcal{M}_+(X_1 \times X_2, \Sigma_1 \otimes \Sigma_2)$, $I_{\sup_{n\in\mathbb{N}} f_n} = \sup_{n\in\mathbb{N}} I_{f_n}$.

Let `P0 f := Mplus genX1 (LInt_p_section_fun f)` be the predicate of the nonnegativity and measurability of I_f, of type `(X1 * X2 →` $\overline{\mathbb{R}}$ `) → Prop`. Then, previous formulas and closedness properties of $\mathcal{M}_+$ (see Sect. 2.2) provide the compatibility of `P0` with indicator functions, positive linearity, and the supremum of nondecreasing sequences. For instance, we have

```
Lemma LInt_p_section_fun_measurable_plus :
  ∀ f g, Mplus genX1xX2 f → Mplus genX1xX2 g →
    P0 f → P0 g → P0 (fun x ⇒ f x +R̄ g x).
```

Let us now define the predicate `P` of the existence of the iterated integral (granted by `P0`) and the validity of the first Tonelli formula of (10):

```
Let P (f : X1 * X2 → R̄) : Prop :=
  P0 f ∧ LInt_p meas_prod f = LInt_p muX1 (LInt_p_section_fun f).
```

where `meas_prod` is the product measure defined in Sect. 4.4. Again, the compatibility of `P` with indicator functions, positive linearity, and the supremum is easily obtained from the previous results. For instance, we have

```
Lemma LInt_p_section_fun_meas_prod_Sup_seq :
  ∀ f, incr_fun_seq f → Mplus_seq genX1xX2 f →
    (∀ n, P (f n)) → P (fun x ⇒ Sup_seq (fun n ⇒ f n x)).
```

Now, the first part of Tonelli's theorem (10) can be stated in Coq as

```
Lemma Tonelli_aux1 : ∀f, Mplus genX1xX2 f →
  Mplus genX1 (LInt_p_section_fun f) ∧
  LInt_p meas_prod f = LInt_p muX1 (LInt_p_section_fun f).
```

Its proof is a direct application of the Lebesgue induction principle (see Sect. 3) with the predicate `P`, as all the premises are already shown.

5.3 Change of Measure, Second Formula, and Tonelli's Theorem

There is no doubt that the second formula (11) can be proved using the same path as the first claim: use sections with respect to the second variable, define J^f (see Fig. 4), prove $J^f \in \mathcal{M}_+$ and the equality by the Lebesgue induction principle. This would be easy, but pretty long and redundant. Instead, we have exploited the "symmetry" between the right-hand sides of both formulas. The first idea is a simple exchange of the roles of the two variables that expresses the previous result for functions of type `X2 * X1 →` $\overline{\mathbb{R}}$. And then, the difficult part is a change of measure that brings back to the target type `X1 * X2 →` $\overline{\mathbb{R}}$.

The change of measure is an application of the concept of *image measure* (e.g. see [9, Sect. 2.6]), also called *pushforward measure* as the measure is transported between σ-algebras, here from $\Sigma_2 \otimes \Sigma_1$ to $\Sigma_1 \otimes \Sigma_2$.

Change of Measure. Let (X, Σ) and $(Y, \mathcal{T})$ be measurable spaces. Let $h : X \to Y$ be a function and `Mh` be a proof of its measurability. Let μ be a measure on (X, Σ). The *image measure of* μ *by* h is the measure on $(Y, \mathcal{T})$ defined by $h\#\mu := \mu \circ h^{-1}$, and denoted in Coq by `meas_image h Mh mu`. The proof that it is indeed a measure directly follows from the measure properties of μ, and `Mh`.

Now, given $g \in \mathcal{M}_+(Y, \mathcal{T})$, the compatibility of measurability with the composition of functions provides $g \circ h \in \mathcal{M}_+(X, \Sigma)$, and one has the change-of-measure formula: $\int_Y g \, d(h\#\mu) = \int_X g \circ h \, d\mu$.

```
Lemma LInt_p_change_meas : ∀g, Mplus genY g →
  LInt_p (meas_image h Mh mu) g = LInt_p mu (fun x ⇒ g (h x)).
```

The proof follows the Lebesgue induction principle with the predicate `P` corresponding to the formula. Again, the compatibility of `P` with indicator functions, positive linearity, and the supremum follows from properties of the integral, such as positive linearity and the Beppo Levi (monotone convergence) theorem.

Swap and Second Formula. Using Sect. 4.4, let $\mu_{12} := \mu_1 \otimes \mu_2$ be the product measure on the product space $(X_1 \times X_2, \Sigma_1 \otimes \Sigma_2)$ induced by μ_1 and μ_2. In Coq, `muX1xX2 := meas_prod muX1 muX2`. Symmetrically, let $\mu_{21} := \mu_2 \otimes \mu_1$ be the product measure on $(X_2 \times X_1, \Sigma_2 \otimes \Sigma_1)$. In Coq, `muX2xX1 := meas_prod muX2 muX1`. Let $h := (x_2, x_1) \mapsto (x_1, x_2)$ be the swap of variables. The image measure $h\#\mu_{21}$ is also proved to be a product measure on $(X_1 \times X_2, \Sigma_1 \otimes \Sigma_2)$ induced by μ_1 and μ_2. In Coq, `meas_prod_swap := meas_image h Mh muX2xX1`.

Now, let $f \in \mathcal{M}_+(X_1 \times X_2, \Sigma_1 \otimes \Sigma_2)$. One has $f \circ h \in \mathcal{M}_+(X_2 \times X_1, \Sigma_2 \otimes \Sigma_1)$, and using the section with respect to the second variable (see Sect. 5.1),

$$\forall x_2 \in X_2, \quad f^{x_2} := (x_1 \longmapsto f(x_1, x_2)) = (x_1 \longmapsto f \circ h(x_2, x_1)) = (f \circ h)_{x_2}. \quad (12)$$

We then deduce

$$\int_{X_1 \times X_2} f \, d\mu_{12} \overset{(a)}{=} \int_{X_1 \times X_2} f \, d(h\#\mu_{21}) \overset{(b)}{=} \int_{X_2 \times X_1} f \circ h \, d\mu_{21}$$
$$\overset{(c)}{=} \int_{X_2} \left(\int_{X_1} (f \circ h)_{x_2} \, d\mu_1 \right) d\mu_2 \overset{(d)}{=} \int_{X_2} \left(\int_{X_1} f^{x_2} \, d\mu_1 \right) d\mu_2.$$

The uniqueness of the product measure of Sect. 4.4 yields $h\#\mu_{21} = \mu_{12}$, thus gives (a). The above change-of-measure formula gives (b). The first formula of Tonelli's theorem (10) applied to $X_2 \times X_1$ gives (c), and Eq. (12) gives (d). With `swap f` denoting $f \circ h$, the second part of Tonelli's theorem (11) is

```
Lemma Tonelli_aux2 : ∀f, Mplus genX1xX2 f →
  Mplus genX2 (LInt_p_section_fun muX1 (swap f)) ∧
  LInt_p meas_prod_swap f = LInt_p muX2 (LInt_p_section_fun muX1 (swap f)).
```

Statement of Tonelli's Theorem. Finally, assuming that X_1 and X_2 are non-empty and that μ_1 and μ_2 are σ-finite measures, we have (a more comprehensive theorem legitimating of all integrals is also provided as `Theorem Tonelli`):

```
Lemma Tonelli_formulas : ∀f, Mplus genX1xX2 f →
  LInt_p muX1xX2 f = LInt_p muX1 (LInt_p_section_fun muX2 f) ∧
  LInt_p muX1xX2 f = LInt_p muX2 (LInt_p_section_fun muX1 (swap f)).
```

6 Conclusion and Perspectives

This paper is devoted to the full formal proof of Tonelli's theorem. An original point is the definition of nonnegative measurable functions as an inductive type. It is proved equivalent to the usual mathematical definition, and leads to a useful induction scheme. Although the Lebesgue induction principle is present in other works such as [20], we have not seen its construction from an inductive type in the literature.

To achieve this proof, we have also formalized in Coq generic results and constructions such as the monotone class theorem, restricted measures, image measures, and a change-of-measure formula for the integral. The latter, combined with a swap of variables, has prevented redundancies in our proofs.

This work confirms that the library we are developing, in line with the choices of the Coquelicot library, is rather comprehensive and usable. First, this work has resulted in few additions in the core of the library, except for the inductive definition for $\mathcal{M}_+$ (related to the needed Lebesgue induction principle). Second, both Coq and the library seem easy to learn, as one author was a Coq novice at the beginning of this work.

After Tonelli's theorem on nonnegative measurable functions, the natural extension is to prove Fubini's theorem. It provides the same formulas for integrable functions with an arbitrary sign, or taking their values in a Banach space when using the Bochner integral [4]. We can also take inspiration from [20], in particular for the "marginal integral" to handle finitary Cartesian products.

Our long-term purpose is to formally prove the correctness of parts of a library implementing the Finite Element Method, which is used to compute approximated solutions of Partial Differential Equations (PDEs). We already formalized the Lax–Milgram theorem [1], one of the key ingredients to numerically solve PDEs, and we need to build suitable Hilbert functional spaces on which to apply it. The target candidates are the Sobolev spaces, such as H^1, which represents square-integrable functions with square-integrable first derivatives. Of course, this will involve the formalization of the L^p Lebesgue spaces as complete normed vector spaces, and parts of the distribution theory [19].

References

1. Boldo, S., Clément, F., Faissole, F., Martin, V., Mayero, M.: A Coq formal proof of the Lax–Milgram theorem. In: Proceedings of the 6th ACM SIGPLAN International Conference on Certified Programs and Proofs (CPP 2017), pp. 79–89. Association for Computing Machinery, New York (2017). https://hal.inria.fr/hal-01391578/
2. Boldo, S., Clément, F., Faissole, F., Martin, V., Mayero, M.: A Coq formalization of Lebesgue integration of nonnegative functions. J. Autom. Reason. **66**(2), 175–213 (2021). https://hal.inria.fr/hal-03471095/

3. Boldo, S., Clément, F., Filliâtre, J.-C., Mayero, M., Melquiond, G., Weis, P.: Wave equation numerical resolution: a comprehensive mechanized proof of a C program. J. Autom. Reason. **50**(4), 423–456 (2013). https://hal.inria.fr/hal-00649240/
4. Boldo, S., Clément, F., Leclerc, L.: A Coq formalization of the Bochner integral (2022). https://hal.inria.fr/hal-03516749/
5. Boldo, S., Lelay, C., Melquiond, G.: Coquelicot: a user-friendly library of real analysis for Coq. Math. Comput. Sci. **9**(1), 41–62 (2015). https://hal.inria.fr/hal-00860648/
6. Boldo, S., Lelay, C., Melquiond, G.: Formalization of real analysis: a survey of proof assistants and libraries. Math. Struct. Comput. Sci. **26**(7), 1196–1233 (2016). https://hal.inria.fr/hal-00806920/
7. Boldo, S., Melquiond, G.: Flocq: a unified library for proving floating-point algorithms in Coq. In: Proceedings of the IEEE 20th Symposium on Computer Arithmetic (ARITH-20), pp. 243–252. IEEE (2011). https://doi.org/10.1109/ARITH.2011.40
8. Clément, F., Martin, V.: Lebesgue integration. Detailed proofs to be formalized in Coq. Research Report RR-9386, Inria, Paris (2021). Version 2. https://hal.inria.fr/hal-03105815v2
9. Cohn, D.L.: Measure Theory, 2nd edn. Birkhäuser, New York (2013). https://doi.org/10.1007/978-1-4614-6956-8
10. The Coq reference manual. https://coq.inria.fr/refman/
11. Endou, N.: Fubini's theorem. Formaliz. Math. **27**(1), 67–74 (2019). https://doi.org/10.2478/forma-2019-0007
12. Gallouët, T., Herbin, R.: Mesure, intégration, probabilités. Ellipses Edition Marketing (2013). https://hal.science/hal-01283567/. In French
13. Harrison, J.: The HOL light theory of Euclidean space. J. Autom. Reason. **50**(2), 173–190 (2013). https://doi.org/10.1007/s10817-012-9250-9
14. Hölzl, J., Heller, A.: Three chapters of measure theory in Isabelle/HOL. In: van Eekelen, M., Geuvers, H., Schmaltz, J., Wiedijk, F. (eds.) ITP 2011. LNCS, vol. 6898, pp. 135–151. Springer, Heidelberg (2011). https://doi.org/10.1007/978-3-642-22863-6_12
15. Lebesgue, H.L.: Leçons sur l'intégration et la recherche des fonctions primitives professées au Collège de France. Cambridge University Press, Cambridge (2009). Reprint of the 1904 original [Gauthier-Villars, Paris]. https://doi.org/10.1017/CBO9780511701825. In French
16. Lester, D.R.: Topology in PVS: continuous mathematics with applications. In: Proceedings of the 2nd Workshop on Automated Formal Methods (AFM 2007), pp. 11–20 (2007). https://doi.org/10.1145/1345169.1345171
17. Maisonneuve, F.: Mathématiques 2 : Intégration, transformations, intégrales et applications - Cours et exercices. Presses de l'École des Mines (2014). In French
18. Mayero, M.: Formalisation et automatisation de preuves en analyses réelle et numérique. Université Paris VI, Thèse de doctorat (2001). https://www-lipn.univ-paris13.fr/~mayero/publis/these-mayero.ps.gz. In French
19. Schwartz, L.: Théorie des Distributions, 2nd edn. Hermann, Paris (1966). 1st edition in 1950–1951. In French
20. van Doorn, F.: Formalized Haar measure. In: Cohen, L., Kaliszyk, C. (eds.) Proceedings of the 12th International Conference on Interactive Theorem Proving. LIPIcs, vol. 193, pp. 18:1–18:17. Schloss Dagstuhl – Leibniz-Zentrum für Informatik (2021). https://doi.org/10.4230/LIPIcs.ITP.2021.18

Railway Scheduling Using Boolean Satisfiability Modulo Simulations

Tomáš Kolárik[1(✉)] and Stefan Ratschan[2]

[1] Faculty of Information Technology, Czech Technical University in Prague, Prague, Czechia
kolarto5@fit.cvut.cz

[2] Institute of Computer Science, The Czech Academy of Sciences, Prague, Czechia
stefan.ratschan@cs.cas.cz

FM Artifact Evaluation ★ Available

Abstract. Railway scheduling is a problem that exhibits both non-trivial discrete and continuous behavior. In this paper, we model this problem using a combination of SAT and ordinary differential equations (SAT modulo ODE). In addition, we adapt our existing method for solving such problems in such a way that the resulting solver is competitive with methods based on dedicated railway simulators while being more general and extensible.

1 Introduction

Existing benchmark problems for SAT modulo ODE [5, 6] do not exhibit complex discrete state space. In this paper, we develop a benchmark problem that combines a non-trivial propositional part with differential equations. Moreover, we apply and improve a corresponding algorithm [9] that tightly integrates SAT and numeric simulations of differential equations. The resulting tool is available online [11].

The benchmark problem comes from the domain of railway scheduling, and is inspired by an approach to railway design capacity analysis [13], that combines a SAT solver with a railway simulator. The authors of that approach, referring to SAT modulo non-linear real arithmetic, "found these solvers insufficiently scalable for real-world problem sizes". Our experiments show that it indeed *is* possible to realistically handle continuous dynamics in the railway domain directly by SAT modulo theory solvers. A major difficulty lies in modeling the fact that trains sometimes have to switch to a deceleration phase to obey velocity limits. Here, it is non-trivial to predict when such a switch must happen when modeling dynamics based on differential equations.

We are not aware of any other approach to railway scheduling based on SAT modulo theories with realistic modeling of continuous dynamics. The mentioned approach [13] solves the problem of design capacity analysis, a different, but related problem. The main differences are:

M. Chechik et al. (Eds.): FM 2023, LNCS 14000, pp. 56–73, 2023.
https://doi.org/10.1007/978-3-031-27481-7_5

- Instead of an ad-hoc combination of SAT and a simulator, we model the problem in a precisely defined Satisfiability Modulo Theories language [9]. As a result, numeric (e.g. timing) constraints can appear throughout a formula.
- Our model allows rich timing constraints, including their Boolean combinations. Consequently, trains are allowed to keep waiting in stations, or before entering the network, even in cases when their routes do not collide with the other trains. Hence, our model may exhibit more nondeterminism which makes the scheduling problem more difficult.
- The dynamics of trains is an integral, but modifiable part of the model, instead of being hidden in a simulator.

Both approaches have different strong and weak aspects of the run-time performance.

As in the case of any formal model of real-world problems, also here, we abstract from certain aspects of the problem domain. Our model does not take into account railway policies, signaling principles, and the like, as Luteberget et al. [13] do. Especially we do not claim ETCS (European Train Control System) compatibility of our model, meaning that it may be less suitable for railway systems based on signal interlocking. However, not all railways use such a mechanism, for example urban railways may leave the responsibility to the driver.

Railway route planning can also be viewed as a multi-agent path finding problem [16], where trains are viewed as agents. However, in this area, usually much simpler models of continuous behavior are used [1]. On the other hand, the resulting plans are often minimized wrt. a given parameter, for example, sum of lengths of the agents' paths, while we do not optimize at all.

Of course, many other approaches dedicated to railway scheduling exist. Some support only limited precision, or work only under certain assumptions, for example, fixed routes, or not taking into account limited track capacity. Some use networks that were transformed from a microscopic level to an aggregated, macroscopic level [17]. Also, probabilistic methods exist [18, 8].

There are approaches that are quite accurate, but still ignore some constraints that we take into account. For example, not all combinations of possible train paths are considered [19], or bi-directional tracks are replaced by pairs of one-directional tracks, and simpler train dynamics is used [7].

The paper is structured as follows. We start with an explanation of the problem area in Sect. 2. We briefly describe the used theory in Sect. 3, and present encoding of the problem as a formula of that theory in Sect. 4. The algorithm we use to solve the problem follows in Sect. 5. Finally, in Sect. 6, we analyze the behavior of our approach and of [13] on selected case studies. Some parts of the study are omitted due to lack of space, but are available in an extended version of the paper [10].

2 Problem Overview

This section describes the overall problem and introduces related keywords. We start with an illustrative example.

2.1 Example

In Fig. 1, one can see a model of a rail network with three trains. We distinguish the model itself and the required constraints on trains.

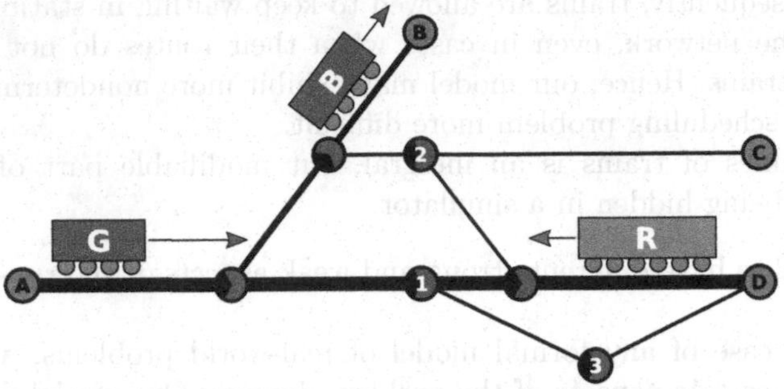

Fig. 1. An example of a rail network graph with trains (Color figure online)

The model consists of a graph of the network, and of abstracted trains. Each train is described by its physical properties, for example length, velocity limit, etc. The red train is a freight train, longer and slower than the other, passenger trains. For illustrative reasons, the boundary nodes of the graph are distinguished from the others. The thicker an edge is, the faster railroad it represents. Nodes that model stations are labeled with a number. To support modeling of railway junctions, nodes of the graph have two sides, illustrated by black and blue colors in the figure. In order to avoid physically impossible (e.g. too sharp) turns, a train has to visit both sides when transferring via such a double-sided node.

Constraints. Examples of constraints, that the trains in the figure might be required to satisfy, are:

- The blue train must start from the boundary A, and has no further requirements on visiting nodes.
- The green train must start from A, and is in addition required to visit node 3, where it will stop. Eventually, the train must continue to node D afterwards.
- The red train must start at D and exit at A, with no other required visits.
- Possible orderings of the trains: the blue train must start before the green train; the red train starts before the green train approaches node 1.
- Possible timings of the trains: the red train must arrive at A within 10 min after entering; the green train must wait at node 3 for at least 2 min.

The result of the search is a plan that demonstrates how the trains can move through the network while satisfying the given constraints and with no collisions of trains.

2.2 General Problem Statement

The task is to find a plan for a given set of trains and a railway network (viewed as a graph) such that all specified places are visited, meeting all timing and ordering constraints, and with no collisions of trains.

We assume that each train can only enter the network at a boundary, and that at the beginning of the whole search, there are no trains present in the network. Also, trains are not allowed to reverse their direction.

2.3 Railway Model

Infrastructure. An infrastructure (or a network) is modeled using a graph of vertices called *nodes* and edges called *segments*. Each segment has a length and a velocity limit. Only a single train is allowed inside a segment and the chosen next segment where the train currently aims to. A node that is not boundary either may or may not allow stopping, where nodes that allow stopping model stations. The fact that a train shall stop at a node is not modeled explicitly, but by temporarily setting the velocity limit of the train's chosen next segment (which the other trains are not allowed to enter) to zero. After stopping, trains may wait in stations for a limited time, or may not.

As explained in the example (Sect. 2.1), the graph is a *double-vertex* graph [14], which is commonly used for modeling railways with junctions [17].

We assume that each segment is at least as long as the longest train (Fig. 1 violates this property). The model directly supports infrastructures with cycles and looping of trains, in contrast with [13] where this needs an extra effort.

Train. A train T has an acceleration and a deceleration rate, a velocity limit, and a length. The dynamics of trains is deterministic—each train drives at the maximum possible speed, which, however, depends on discrete decisions—the choice of segments on the train's way, and where to stop. Such a model already allows meaningful experiments, but can be easily extended.

2.4 Constraints

Connection Constraints. A *connection* is a mapping of a train to a non-empty list of nodes that must be visited in the given order. For instance, $T_{green} \mapsto (A, 3)$ is the connection of the green train from the example. The user must specify exactly one connection for each train. The list can contain boundary nodes too, but only as the first or the last element. The first element of the list indeed must be a boundary node. Trains always stop at the listed nodes that model stations, and never stop at any other stations.

The *starting* node is the first node in the list. A connection may have several *ending* nodes—any boundary node terminating a path following the given connection. For example, in Fig. 1, given a connection list $(A, 2)$, A is the starting node and C, D are two possible ending nodes, but for connection list $(A, 2, D)$, D is the only ending node. We call segments incident with the starting node *starting segments*, and segments incident with an ending node *ending segments*.

Schedule Constraints. Schedule constraints are optional constraints that compare the time when a train either arrives at or departs from a node. In the following, we will denote by *arrival*(T, N) (or *departure*(T, N)) the time when train T arrives at (or departs from) node N. To allow both variants in a formula, we will write *visit*(T, N), possibly distinguishing several occurrences by indices ($visit_1(T_1, N_1)$, $visit_2(T_2, N_2)$, etc.). Schedule constraints assume that all mentioned visits are the consequence of some connection constraint.

We allow two types of schedule constraints, ordering, and timing constraints. An *ordering* enforces two visits to happen in a given order. It has the form

$$visit_1(T_1, N_1) \circ visit_2(T_2, N_2), \tag{1}$$

where $\circ$ is one of $\{<, \leq\}$. A *relative timing* enforces a time constraint on a transfer, that is, on the time from one visit to another. It has the form

$$transfer(visit_1(T_1, N_1), visit_2(T_2, N_2)) \circ \xi, \tag{2}$$

where $transfer(v_1, v_2) := v_2 - v_1$, $\circ \in \{<, \leq, >, \geq\}$, and $\xi \in \mathbb{Q}_{\geq 0}$. We support absolute timings, as well, but they are omitted here. In the case of [13], the only supported timing constraints are $transfer(arrival(T_1, N_1), arrival(T_2, N_2)) < \xi$.

3 Theory Description

For encoding our problem, we use a Satisfiability Modulo Theories (SMT) [15] language. For this, we use a theory for reasoning about ordinary differential equations (ODEs) that we introduced earlier [9]. In this section, we provide an informal summary of this theory.

In addition to variables ranging over the real numbers, together with the usual operations on them, the theory allows variables ranging over real functions $[0, \tau] \to \mathbb{R}$, that we call *functional variables.* Here $\tau \in \mathbb{R}^{\geq 0}$. Functional variables can be constrained by *differential constraints* of the form $\dot{x} = \eta$ with x being a functional variable and η a term containing functional and real variables; by *invariants* that have to hold over the whole interval $[0, \tau]$, and by real-valued constraints that restrict the initial value *init* or final value *final* of a functional variable. For example, the formula $init(x) = 0 \wedge \dot{x} = x \wedge x \leq 10$ restricts the initial value of the functional variable x to zero, restricts its evolution over time by the differential equation $\dot{x} = x$, and restricts x to functions for which the upper bound τ of the time interval is such that the invariant $x \leq 10$ holds over the whole interval.

Since this theory is undecidable [3], we also introduced an alternative semantics that approximates the mathematical semantics using floating-point numbers [4] and simulations of ODEs (i.e. numeric integrations). Using this semantics, the theory is not only decidable in the theoretical sense, but also efficiently decidable for formulas of the type occurring in this paper. We will use this semantics in the algorithm in Sect. 5 and in all our experiments in Sect. 6.

In contrast to the original semantics [9], where simulations could be terminated before violation of an invariant, here we always continue simulations until an invariant is violated. As a consequence the length of each interval $[0, \tau]$ is completely determined and all nondeterminism in the model described below will stem from discrete decisions.

4 Encoding and Formalization

In this section, we present an encoding of the planning problem from Sect. 2 as a formula in the theory described in Sect. 3. All of the presented formulas are generated automatically, from user input in the form of a preprocessing language [12]. The user input consists of specification of an infrastructure and of trains, and of connections and schedule constraints.

We unroll the planning problem in a similar way as in bounded model checking (BMC) [2]. Unrolling ranges over discrete steps $0, 1, \ldots, J$. A variable x specific to a discrete step j has the form $x^{[j]}$. All trains are modeled *synchronously*, meaning that every discrete step j corresponds to the same global moment in time. Functional variables specific to one and the same discrete step will have the same length $\tau^{[j]}$ of integration, from which we get global time by defining real variables $t^{[j]}$ s.t. $t^{[0]} = 0$ and for all $j > 0$, $t^{[j]} = t^{[j-1]} + \tau^{[j-1]}$. In the case of [13], the planner considers longer units for unrolling where a step may consist of movements over several segments, and within such a step all deterministic discrete constraints are handled by the simulator.

We use one-hot encoding for some Boolean variables for increased readability. Moreover, we improve readability by using an abbreviation ITE (*cond*, *a*, *b*) for $((cond \Rightarrow a) \wedge (\neg cond \Rightarrow b))$.

4.1 Railway Model

We only present the most significant constraints that are necessary for understanding the principles of the model. See the extended version of the paper [10] for more details.

Train. A train $T \in \mathcal{T}$ is defined by fixed constants $T.A$, $T.B$, $T.V_{max}$, and $T.L$ that represent the properties of the train (acceleration, deceleration, velocity limit and length); T is just a prefix of the constant names, representing an identifier of the train. In a similar way, the state of each train is described by a set of variables, distinguished by a discrete step j. The most important variables are:

- *Booleans*: $T.mode^{[j]}$, $mode \in \mathcal{M} = \{idle, steady, acc, brake\}$ (*steady* means the train does not accelerate, but in mode *idle*, in addition, it has zero velocity); $T.away^{[j]}$, $T.enter^{[j]}$ and $T.finished^{[j]}$ (whether the train is currently outside the graph, whether it is entering, and whether it already finished); and $T.pos\_S^{[j]}$, $pos \in \mathcal{P} = \{back, front, next\}$, for a segment $S \in \mathcal{S}$ (the train's back and front being in S; whether S is selected as the next segment).
- *Reals*: $T.a^{[j]}$ (acceleration/deceleration rate); $T.d_{max}{}^{[j]}$ (remaining distance to the end of the current segments, either with the back or the front of the train, i.e., for segments S where $T.back\_S^{[j]}$ or $T.front\_S^{[j]}$ holds); $T.v_{max}{}^{[j]}$

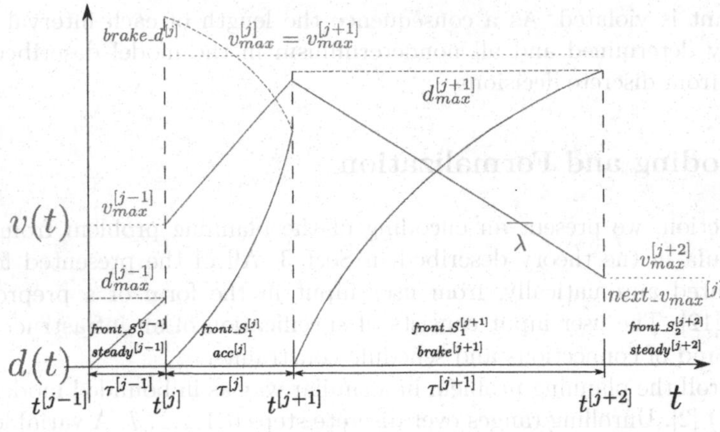

Fig. 2. Possible train trajectories and their limits

(velocity limit of the current segments and the train itself); and $T.next\_v_{max}{}^{[j]}$ (velocity limit of the selected next segment S, for which $T.next\_S^{[j]}$ holds).
- *Functional variables*: $T.d^{[j]}$, $init(T.d^{[j]}) = 0$ (relative distance traveled from the start of unrolling step j), and $T.v^{[j]}$ (current velocity). The functional variables range over $[0, \tau^{[j]}]$, where a timeout $\tau^{[j]} < \rho$, with the constant ρ user-defined, must hold. This allows decisions on when to enter the network or when to leave the current station to happen in certain intervals—if the timeout is too short, the number of necessary discrete steps may be too high; if it is too long, a plan where trains stay idle for too long may be returned.

Result. The resulting plan is represented by the global variables $t^{[j]}$ and the variables $T.idle^{[j]}$, $T.front\_S^{[j]}$ and $T.finished^{[j]}$, for all trains T, segments S and discrete steps j. All other variables are either auxiliary or are completely determined by the plan and the model described in this subsection.

Dynamic Phenomena

Mode conditions. Unlike in capacity analysis [13], where behavior is deterministic, as soon as routes have been chosen, here continuous dynamics depends on each train's mode, where a train can choose to stay idle in stations, or before entering the network. Each train T is always in exactly one dynamic mode, and according to this mode, an appropriate (constant) acceleration rate is set:

$$\begin{aligned}&((T.idle^{[j]} \vee T.steady^{[j]}) \Leftrightarrow T.a^{[j]} = 0)\\ &\quad \wedge (T.acc^{[j]} \Leftrightarrow T.a^{[j]} = T.A) \wedge (T.brake^{[j]} \Leftrightarrow T.a^{[j]} = -T.B).\end{aligned} \tag{3}$$

There are also other restrictions, like that braking is not possible if the velocity is already zero, or that *steady* mode is not allowed if acceleration is possible.

Dynamics. We model the dynamics of trains using the basic laws of motion, but it is possible to extend the model such that it exhibits more complex phenomena. Figure 2 illustrates how the resulting trajectories of functional variables can look like (T is omitted from the variable names). Both functions v and d are limited by a corresponding dashed line, a constant $v_{max}{}^{[\cdot]}$ in the case of the function v, and a distance limit in the case of d, either in the form of a straight line, representing $d_{max}{}^{[\cdot]}$, or a curve, that stands for the function $brake\_d^{[\cdot]}$ that is about to be discussed further. The limit $v_{max}{}^{[j+2]}$ is equivalent to $next\_v_{max}{}^{[j]}$.

Since trains are modeled synchronously, the dynamics of the trains is represented mainly by one system of ODEs—for each train T, and discrete step j:

$$\begin{aligned} T.\dot{d}^{[j]} = T.v^{[j]} \quad &\wedge \quad T.\dot{v}^{[j]} = T.a^{[j]} \\ \wedge \quad T.d^{[j]} \leq T.d_{max}{}^{[j]} \quad &\wedge \quad T.v^{[j]} \in \left[0, T.v_{max}{}^{[j]}\right]. \end{aligned} \tag{4}$$

The first row of the formula shows particular ODEs, and the second the invariants. Thus, each integration ends when a distance limit or a velocity limit is exceeded, or when the timeout is reached, which was explained in the description of functional variables.

For the definition of the variables $T.\alpha_{max}{}^{[j]}$, $\alpha \in \{d, v\}$, we use auxiliary variables $T.pos\_\alpha_{max}{}^{[j]}$, $pos \in \mathcal{P}$ which correspond to the limits of the current and the next segments, as mentioned in the description of the real variables. Moreover, $T.min\_\alpha_{max}{}^{[j]} := \min\{T.back\_\alpha_{max}{}^{[j]}, T.front\_\alpha_{max}{}^{[j]}\}$. Then, the distance limit is defined by $T.d_{max}{}^{[j]} = T.min\_d_{max}{}^{[j]}$ and the velocity limit as

$$\begin{aligned} &\text{ITE}\big(init(T.v^{[j]}) \geq T.next\_v_{max}{}^{[j]}, \\ &\quad T.v_{max}{}^{[j]} = \min\{T.V_{max}, T.min\_v_{max}{}^{[j]}\}, \\ &\quad T.v_{max}{}^{[j]} = \min\{T.V_{max}, T.min\_v_{max}{}^{[j]}, T.next\_v_{max}{}^{[j]}\}\big), \end{aligned} \tag{5}$$

where $T.next\_v_{max}{}^{[j]}$ is used to ensure correctness of braking prediction.

Braking prediction. In Fig. 2, within stage j, one can see that the function d is limited by a yet unexplained function $brake\_d^{[j]}$. Such a function is necessary for prediction of the moment when a train has to start braking to obey the velocity limit of the next segment—in cases when $T.v^{[j]} > T.next\_v_{max}{}^{[j]}$ (if the train is not already braking). The main idea is to compute the braking trajectory backward from the point where the train enters the next segment, synchronously with the actual forward dynamics. Details follow.

The prediction depends on the relation $init(T.v^{[j]}) \circ T.next\_v_{max}{}^{[j]}$, where $\circ \in \{=, >\}$. First, let us assume that $init(T.v^{[j]}) = T.next\_v_{max}{}^{[j]}$. To make $T.v^{[j]} > T.next\_v_{max}{}^{[j]}$ happen eventually, $T.acc^{[j]}$ must hold. Such a case would correspond to Fig. 2, if $next\_v_{max}{}^{[j]}$ was in the place of the separator λ. Since $T.a^{[j]}$ from Formula 4 is a constant (due to Formula 3), the ratio between the length (in time) of the acceleration phase and the braking phase is fixed. Since the temporal relationship between the two phases is not yet clear, we use independent time axes, writing

$$\frac{dv_A}{dt_A} = T.A, \frac{dv_B}{dt_B} = -T.B, \tag{6}$$

where v_A and v_B corresponds to $T.v^{[j]}$ and $T.v^{[j+1]}$, resp., and t_A and t_B corresponds to $\tau^{[j]}$ and $\tau^{[j+1]}$, resp. To determine the time to switch from acceleration to braking, it would be possible to compute the braking trajectory backward in time starting at the position corresponding to $T.\mathit{front\_d_{max}}^{[j]}$, and with the velocity corresponding to $T.\mathit{next\_v_{max}}^{[j]}$. However, it is not clear how far backward such a backward braking trajectory has to be computed, and moreover, even after its computation, it is non-trivial to ensure that at the switching time, *both* position and velocity of the train are identical to a corresponding point on the backward braking trajectory. To get around these complications, we not only reverse, but also scale the time axis of the braking process using the relationship

$$t_B = -\frac{T.A}{T.B} \cdot t_A. \tag{7}$$

As a result, we have a common time axis t_A, along which the derivative of the velocity of the braking train is identical to the derivative of the velocity of the accelerating train:

$$\frac{dv_B}{dt_A} = \frac{dv_B}{dt_B}\frac{dt_B}{dt_A} = -\frac{dv_B}{dt_B}\frac{T.A}{T.B} = T.B \cdot \frac{T.A}{T.B} = \frac{dv_A}{dt_A}. \tag{8}$$

As a consequence, both velocities will be identical at all time if starting from the same initial value. Under this assumption, we can compute both the acceleration phase and the backward braking trajectory synchronously along the same time axis, ensuring identical speed at all times. Such an approach can be generalized for more complicated systems of ODEs (e.g. with $T.v^{[j]}$ other than a linear function), if such a relationship between the time axes is available.

Based on Formula 8, it suffices to switch from acceleration to braking at the point when the corresponding positions are identical. This results in a synchronous braking prediction with ODEs and an invariant of the form

$$\begin{aligned}\text{ITE}(T.\mathit{acc}^{[j]},\ T.\dot{\mathit{brake\_d}}^{[j]} &= -\frac{T.A}{T.B} \cdot T.v^{[j]},\ T.\dot{\mathit{brake\_d}}^{[j]} = 0)\\ \wedge\ \ (\neg T.\mathit{brake}^{[j]} &\Rightarrow T.d^{[j]} \le T.\mathit{brake\_d}^{[j]})\end{aligned} \tag{9}$$

where the coefficient $-\frac{T.A}{T.B}$ implements the mentioned scaling also for the prediction of the position of the train.

If $\mathit{init}(T.v^{[j]}) > T.\mathit{next\_v_{max}}^{[j]}$, the part of the braking phase with $T.v^{[j+1]} \in [T.\mathit{next\_v_{max}}^{[j]}, \mathit{init}(T.v^{[j]})]$ must be precomputed asynchronously. In the figure, this corresponds to the part from the end of stage $j+1$ to the separator λ (backwards). Such an asynchronous prediction uses the functional variables *back_d* and *back_v*, starting from

$$\mathit{init}(T.\mathit{back\_d}^{[j]}) = T.\mathit{front\_d_{max}}^{[j]} \wedge \mathit{init}(T.\mathit{back\_v}^{[j]}) = T.\mathit{next\_v_{max}}^{[j]}, \tag{10}$$

with a flow defined by the following ODEs and invariants:

$$\begin{aligned}T.\dot{\mathit{back\_d}}^{[j]} &= -T.\mathit{back\_v}^{[j]} \quad \wedge \quad T.\dot{\mathit{back\_v}}^{[j]} = T.B\\ \wedge\ \ T.\mathit{back\_d}^{[j]} &\ge 0 \quad \wedge \quad T.\mathit{back\_v}^{[j]} \le \mathit{init}(T.v^{[j]}).\end{aligned} \tag{11}$$

These functional variables are the only ones that may have a different length τ of integration than the other variables (which are synchronous). The reached position serves for the consecutive synchronous part:

$$\mathit{init}(T.\mathit{brake\_d}^{[j]}) = \mathit{final}(T.\mathit{back\_d}^{[j]}), \tag{12}$$

and Formula 9 becomes computable then. This works even in cases when $T.\mathit{steady}^{[j]}$ holds, where $T.\mathit{brake\_d}^{[j]}$ just serves as a constant upper bound on $T.d^{[j]}$, based on the value from Formula 12.

If $T.{v_{max}}^{[j]}$ had been reached before the start of the braking phase, there just would be an additional phase in the steady mode between the phases j and $j+1$ in the figure.

Positional Constraints. In the following, we use train $T \in \mathcal{T}$ and the relation $S_1 \rightarrow_T S_2$ for segments $S_1, S_2 \in \mathcal{S}$ to denote that segment S_2 is adjacent to segment S_1 on a path that obeys the connection constraints of train T. In fact, this relation enforces the connection constraints completely if $T.\mathit{finished}^{[J]}$ (at the final step J) holds. The relation is used only within the preprocessing stage when generating the formula.

For each segment S_1, the possible next segments are defined s.t.

$$\neg T.\mathit{idle}^{[j]} \Rightarrow (T.\mathit{front\_}S_1^{[j]} \Rightarrow \bigvee_{S_2 \in \mathcal{S}, S_1 \rightarrow_T S_2} T.\mathit{next\_}S_2^{[j]}). \tag{13}$$

Away conditions distinguish the cases when a train already entered the network, or is outside of it. The decision variable *enter* triggers a starting segment:

$$T.\mathit{enter}^{[j]} \Rightarrow \bigvee_{S \in T.\mathit{Start}} (\neg T.\mathit{back\_}S^{[j]} \wedge T.\mathit{front\_}S^{[j]}), \tag{14}$$

where $T.\mathit{Start}$ is the set of starting segments of the train T. To denote that a train is entirely outside the network, we use

$$T.\mathit{away}^{[j]} \Leftrightarrow \neg\Big(\bigvee_{S \in \mathcal{S}} T.\mathit{back\_}S^{[j]} \vee \bigvee_{S \in \mathcal{S}} T.\mathit{front\_}S^{[j]}\Big). \tag{15}$$

The variable *finished* is triggered within the transfer constraints when reaching a boundary in Formula 18 below. Once the variable is activated, it implies that at least the front of the train is already outside of the network:

$$T.\mathit{finished}^{[j]} \Rightarrow \neg \bigvee_{S \in \mathcal{S}} T.\mathit{front\_}S^{[j]}. \tag{16}$$

Trains that are leaving the network remain in the steady mode, until they get away entirely and become idle.

Transfer constraints control transferring of a train to a next segment when the end of one of the current segments is reached (even when stopping). We denote

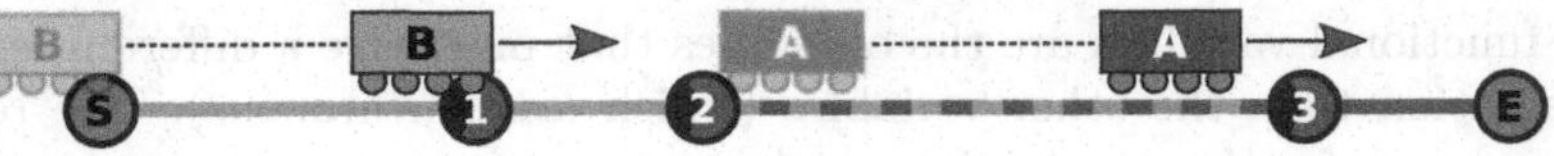

Fig. 3. A conflicting plan of two consecutive trains with no stops

the fact that the back or front of train T reaches the end of segment $S_1 \in \mathcal{S}$ by $T.pos\_exceed\_S_1^{[j]}$, $pos \in \{back, front\}$, which allows the train to move into S_2:

$$\neg T.idle^{[j]} \Rightarrow \bigwedge_{S_2 \in \mathcal{S}, S_1 \to_T S_2} ((T.pos_1\_S_1^{[j]} \wedge T.pos_2\_S_2^{[j]}) \Rightarrow \text{ITE}(T.pos_1\_exceed\_S_1^{[j]}, T.pos_1\_S_2^{[j+1]}, T.pos_1\_S_1^{[j+1]})) \quad (17)$$

where $pos_1 \in \{back, front\}$, $pos_2 = \Delta(pos_1)$, $\Delta = \{back \mapsto front, front \mapsto next\}$.

When a train exceeds a segment $S \in \mathcal{S}$ that is boundary, the train is claimed as finished based on the front of the train:

$$T.front\_S^{[j]} \Rightarrow \text{ITE}(T.front\_exceed\_S^{[j]}, T.finished^{[j+1]}, T.front\_S^{[j+1]}), \quad (18)$$

and it is claimed as away based on its back:

$$T.back\_S^{[j]} \Rightarrow \text{ITE}(T.back\_exceed\_S^{[j]}, T.away^{[j+1]}, T.back\_S^{[j+1]}). \quad (19)$$

Mutual exclusion conditions prevent trains from collisions. For each train T_1 and for all segments S, all the mutual exclusion conditions are jointly defined as

$$\bigwedge_{pos_1, pos_2 \in \mathcal{P}} \bigwedge_{T_2 \in \mathcal{T}, T_2 \neq T_1} \neg(T_1.pos_1\_S^{[j]} \wedge T_2.pos_2\_S^{[j]}). \quad (20)$$

Thus, we require the segments adjacent to the current front segment to be free (because $next \in \mathcal{P}$)—while it is whole sections in the case of [13], as a consequence of signal interlocking. As a result, tighter plans are possible in our case, but the algorithm may also be forced to resolve more violations of mutual exclusion conditions. Figure 3 illustrates a situation where train A is followed by train B that enters as soon as train A leaves node 2. Since the segment 2–3 is long, train B will reach node 1 sooner than train A leaves node 3, resulting in a conflict at segment 2–3 that is claimed by train B as the next segment.

Initial Conditions. At the beginning, each train stands still, either is away or starts its journey, and is not finished. And some train has to enter:

$$\bigwedge_{T \in \mathcal{T}} (init(T.v^{[0]}) = 0 \ \wedge \ (T.enter^{[0]} \vee T.away^{[0]}) \ \wedge \ \neg T.finished^{[0]}) \wedge \bigvee_{T \in \mathcal{T}} T.enter^{[0]}. \quad (21)$$

Final Conditions. In order to satisfy the connection constraints of trains completely, we require the trains to have finished moving through the network at the final unrolling step J:

$$\bigwedge_{T \in \mathcal{T}} (T.\mathit{finished}^{[J]} \wedge T.\mathit{away}^{[J]}). \tag{22}$$

4.2 Schedule Constraints

Schedule formulas enforce schedule constraints and their Boolean combinations. Orderings and timings described in Sect. 2.4 are translated into particular constraints related to visiting nodes at discrete steps. To encode such a visit related to train $T \in \mathcal{T}$, node $N \in \mathcal{N}$, where $\mathcal{N}$ represents the set of nodes of the network, and discrete step j, we use auxiliary Boolean variables $T.\mathit{visit\_N}^{[j]}$, $\mathit{visit} \in \{\mathit{arrive}, \mathit{depart}\}$, defined s.t.

$$\begin{aligned}
T.\mathit{arrive_N}^{[j]} &\Leftrightarrow \begin{cases} \bot, & \text{if } j = 0, \text{else} \\ \bigvee_{S, S \to_T N} T.\mathit{front_S}^{[j-1]} & \\ \quad \wedge\, T.\mathit{finished}^{[j]}, & \text{if } N \in T.\mathit{End}, \text{ otherwise} \\ \bigvee_{S, N \to_T S} \left(\neg T.\mathit{front_S}^{[j-1]} \wedge T.\mathit{front_S}^{[j]}\right) & \\ \quad \wedge\, \neg T.\mathit{enter}^{[j]}; & \end{cases} \\
T.\mathit{depart_N}^{[j]} &\Leftrightarrow \begin{cases} T.\mathit{enter}^{[j]}, & \text{if } N = T.\mathit{Start}, \text{else} \\ \bot, & \text{if } j = 0 \vee N \in T.\mathit{End}, \text{ otherwise} \\ \bigvee_{S, N \to_T S} T.\mathit{front_S}^{[j]} \wedge T.\mathit{acc}^{[j]} \wedge \mathit{init}(T.v^{[j]}) = 0, & \end{cases}
\end{aligned} \tag{23}$$

where $N \to_T S$ and $S \to_T N$ means incidence of the node N and segment $S \in \mathcal{S}$ within the train T's connection, in the corresponding direction; $T.\mathit{Start}$ is the starting node of train T, and $T.\mathit{End}$ is the set of the train's ending nodes.

Ordering. Formula 1 enforces visit_1 to happen before visit_2 ($\circ \in \{<, \leq\}$). This requires to forbid visit_2 to take place before visit_1, *and* to make sure that visit_2 implies that visit_1 already happened:

$$\begin{aligned}
&\bigwedge_{k=0}^{J} \left(T_1.\mathit{visit}_1_N_1^{[k]} \Rightarrow \bigwedge_{l=0}^{K(k)} \neg T_2.\mathit{visit}_2_N_2^{[l]} \right) \\
\wedge &\bigwedge_{l=0}^{J} \left(T_2.\mathit{visit}_2_N_2^{[l]} \Rightarrow \bigvee_{k=0}^{L(l)} T_1.\mathit{visit}_1_N_1^{[k]} \right),
\end{aligned} \tag{24}$$

where $K(k) = k$, $L(l) = l - 1$ if $\circ$ is $<$, and $K(k) = k - 1$, $L(l) = l$ if $\circ$ is $\leq$.

Relative Timing. In the first place, it is necessary to guarantee that the corresponding time condition holds in cases when all the corresponding visits are active. In cases where $\circ \in \{<, \leq\}$, similarly to orderings, we also make sure that violation of the timing implies that the corresponding visits did already happen. So Formula 2 translates to

$$\bigwedge_{j=0}^{J}\Big(T_1.visit_1\_N_1^{[j]} \Rightarrow \Big(\psi_j \wedge \bigwedge_{k=j}^{J}(T_2.visit_2\_N_2^{[k]} \Rightarrow (t^{[k]} - t^{[j]}) \circ \xi)\Big)\Big); \quad (25)$$

$$\psi_j \Leftrightarrow \begin{cases} \top, & \text{if } \circ \in \{>, \geq\}; \\ \bigwedge_{k=j}^{J}\Big(\neg((t^{[k]} - t^{[j]}) \circ \xi) \Rightarrow \bigvee_{l=j}^{k-1} T_2.visit_2\_N_2^{[l]}\Big), & \text{if } \circ \in \{<, \leq\}. \end{cases} \quad (26)$$

Since timings support both lower and upper bounds, and since Boolean combinations are allowed, it is possible to define interval boundaries, and more.

Recall that the variables $t^{[j]}$ only depend on the lengths $\tau^{[j]}$ of integrations, so the timing constraints are checked at the end of each integration.

5 Algorithm

We solve the benchmark problem using an improvement of an SMT solver we introduced earlier [9]. The solver is based on DPLL with conflict-driven clause learning (CDCL), but improves the original naive lazy offline approach to a lazy online approach with exhaustive theory propagation [15] to support efficient handling of both Boolean and theory constraints. The rest of this section requires basic knowledge of SAT and SMT solving [15, 10] .

Our theory solver is based on the floating-point simulation semantics of the theory described in Sect. 3. It uses equalities with only a single variable on one of their two sides and differential constraints as *inference rules* [9] that may assign values to the corresponding isolated variables. For example, if the values of $t^{[j-1]}$ and $\tau^{[j-1]}$ in $t^{[j]} = t^{[j-1]} + \tau^{[j-1]}$ are already fixed, then we can infer the value of $t^{[j]}$. In a similar way, if the initial value of $T.v^{[j]}$ and the value of $T.a^{[j]}$ is fixed, then we can use $T.\dot{v}^{[j]} = T.a^{[j]}$ to infer the value of the functional variable $T.v^{[j]}$. All other constraints are numerically evaluated as soon as all their variables have assigned values. This is not complete in general, but suffices to eventually decide the problems necessary for solving the planning problems described in this article.

Atomic predicates form vertices of a directed *dependency graph*, where an edge means that the source vertex is an inference rule that may assign a value to a floating-point variable that is shared with the target vertex. Inference rules corresponding to vertices with no input edges are *initial* inference rules.

Theory propagation. We perform exhaustive theory propagation, along with consistency checks, because all inference rules are based on floating-point arithmetic, which is cheap[1]. Constraints that are currently not evaluable cannot be propagated nor checked for consistency, though.

[1] Simulations of ODEs are actually not that cheap, but we currently do not have evidence that postponing them within theory propagation would be beneficial.

Decision heuristics. In the case of formulas with a structure similar to a BMC unrolling, each consecutive step depends on the values from the previous one. Thus, a suitable strategy, called BMC strategy, is to first decide Booleans that correspond to the lower steps.

In our case, it is often useful to prefer deciding inference rules that can be used, for example, initial inference rules, or those that depend on the already evaluated ones, based on the dependency graph. Then, the inference rule allows theory propagation, which may then enable consistency checks. Thus, within the same discrete step, we prefer initial inference rules, then the other inference rules, then other predicates, and lastly pure Booleans.

In the case of railway scheduling, we designed a strategy that is specific to the given task. We modified the BMC strategy s.t. the Booleans $T.enter^{[j]}$, $T.idle^{[j]}$, and $T.next\_S^{[j]}$ are additionally set to the highest decision priority within each step j, in the listed order. Here we first set $T.enter^{[j]}$ to $\top$ and $T.idle^{[j]}$ to $\bot$ to prefer that the trains finish as soon as possible. We first set $T.next\_S^{[j]}$ to $\bot$ to avoid activation of a segment before being unit-propagated using Formula 13.

6 Experimental Part

In Sects. 1, 2 and 4, we mentioned differences of our model and algorithm compared to an approach that is based on dedicated railway simulations [13]. Although we support a richer set of schedule constraints, here we stick to case studies that can be handled by both approaches. Still, we omit numerical comparisons (e.g. the absolute run-times) here, since the respective tools solve different problems and a thorough discussion is needed—details can be found in the extended version of the paper [10]. Especially, our model is not based on signal interlocking and exhibits more nondeterminism (e.g., we allow the trains to wait in stations and before entering the network). Hence, we focus on a qualitative analysis of the behavior of the tools.

We use our model from Sect. 4 and our implementation [11] of the algorithm from Sect. 5, and the *railperfcheck* tool [13]. We focus on case studies where it is not trivial to decide whether a plan that meets both ordering and timing constraints exists. For this, we generalized the experiments named *Gen* in [13], where all the other experiments, in contrast, exhibit easily satisfiable schedule constraints, which should not be challenging for approaches that are based on SAT solving.

Specification. We use a serial-parallel network for our experiments—a track with N_S serially connected groups of N_P identical parallel tracks with a station. See an example in Fig. 4. For our experiments, we will assume $N_S = N_P$. We use trains $\mathcal{T} = \{T_1, \ldots, T_{N_T}\}$ with acceleration rate $A = 2$, deceleration rate $B = 1$, velocity limit $V_{max} = 40$ and length $L = 50$. Each train is assigned to connection list (*start*, *end*), which only contains the boundary nodes. As a result, multiple paths are possible ($N_P^{N_S}$, at most) for each train. Also, the trains are not allowed to stop at any station, but just drive through, once they enter the network. In

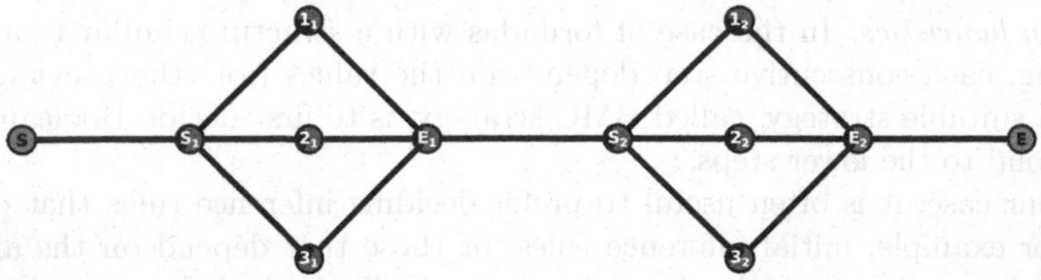

Fig. 4. An example of a serial-parallel infrastructure, with $N_S = 2$ and $N_P = 3$

the case of [13], it is not possible to force the trains not to stop at stations *and* to make them drive consecutively after each other, due to signal interlocking [10]. However, this fact does not affect the analysis provided in this section.

In our case, we selected the number of unrollings J manually for each particular experiment—high enough to allow all the trains to finish (i.e., to satisfy Formula 22). Such a parameter is not needed in the case of *railperfcheck*.

We present two scenarios, *last* and *all*, that are defined as follows:

- *last*: the last train T_{N_T} must satisfy a relative timing, and the other trains T_i just enter in a given order:

$$timing(T_{N_T}, bnd) \wedge \bigwedge_{i<N_T} \left(enter_{before}(T_i, T_{i+1}) \wedge early_{after}(T_{i+1}, T_i)\right), \tag{27}$$

- *all*: each particular train T_i must satisfy a relative timing:

$$\bigwedge_i \Big(timing(T_i, bnd) \wedge \Big(enter_{first}(T_i) \vee \bigvee_{j \neq i} \left(enter_{before}(T_j, T_i) \wedge early_{after}(T_i, T_j)\right)\Big)\Big), \tag{28}$$

where $T_i, T_j \in \mathcal{T}$, and with

- $timing(T, bnd) \Leftrightarrow transfer(departure(T, start), arrival(T, end)) < bnd$,
- $enter_{before}(T_1, T_2) \Leftrightarrow departure(T_1, start) < departure(T_2, start)$,
- $early_{after}(T_1, T_2) \Leftrightarrow departure(T_1, start) \leq arrival(T_2, end_1)$, and
- $enter_{first}(T) \Leftrightarrow departure(T, start) = 0$,

where end_1 is the joint node E_1 in the figure. The purpose of $early_{after}$ along with $enter_{before}$ is to avoid long gaps between two consecutive trains, to reduce the amount of nondeterminism of waiting of the trains. In the case of *railperfcheck*, this is not necessary since waiting is deterministic. Note that in scenario *last*, trains are fully ordered, while in scenario *all*, they are not ordered at all.

Each case study is parametrized by a scenario, variables $N_T, N_S \in \{1, 2, 3, 4\}$, and a timing upper bound $bnd \in \{10^1, 10^2, 10^3\}$. In our case, additionally, $\rho = 30$ (timeout for functional variables in Sect. 4.1), and $J = \Gamma(N_T)$, with $\Gamma = \{1 \mapsto 45, 2 \mapsto 80, 3 \mapsto 115, 4 \mapsto 150\}$. In the case of [13], J is incrementally increased up to $2 \cdot N_T$.

Both scenarios *last* and *all* are equivalent in cases with only one train ($N_T = 1$). These are the cases named *Gen* in [13].

Results. The results of all the specified case studies are as follows:

- `unsat` when $bnd \leq 10^2$: cases with lower timing upper bound are unsatisfiable, that is, it is impossible for the trains to finish within this time bound,
- `sat` when $bnd = 10^3$: plans with high timing upper bound do exist.

To give a basic idea on the run-times of particular experiments in the case of our approach, the satisfiable cases do not exceed 4 min and the unsatisfiable cases usually do not exceed 2 h.

Discussion. First, we compare the scenarios *last* and *all*. In the satisfiable cases, run-times of both scenarios are similar. In the unsatisfiable cases, the run-time of scenario *all* is generally longer than that of *last*, because the trains are unordered and all their permutations are tried, a significant effort with multiple trains. On the other hand, to detect that the relative timing of the last train in scenario *last* is unfeasible, all the preceding trains have to be simulated first, regardless the timing. Depending on the value of *bnd*, it is not certain which part will dominate the run-time—simulations of the preceding trains, or of the last train.

Next, we investigate the behavior of our tool and the tool *railperfcheck* [13]. We start with *railperfcheck*. Recall that it handles mutual exclusion conditions using signal interlocking, which is efficient for networks that do use signals. Moreover, they do simulations in lazy offline fashion, that is, only after a full propositional assignment was found. This is especially efficient in the presented satisfiable cases. However, within the unsatisfiable cases, it is entirely insensitive to the value of *bnd*, because only the overall simulation is checked, independently from whether it satisfies the timing or not. In this way, early detection of unsatisfiability is not possible, and all $N_P^{N_S}$ choices of paths are always examined.

In our case, the value of *bnd* has significant impact on pruning the searched state space—Formula 26 ensures termination of all search attempts where it is already obvious that the timing cannot be satisfied. As a result, with growing size of the network and the set of trains, unsatisfiability is detected more efficiently by our more sophisticated algorithm. Consequently, if the timing upper bound is low ($bnd = 10^1$), scenario *all* is always faster than scenario *last* in our case, because the unfeasible timing of the train that enters first in the case of scenario *all* can be detected sooner than that in the case of scenario *last*, where the train that must satisfy the timing is the last one (as discussed above). For example, the run-time of our tool in the cases with $N_T = N_S = 3$, $bnd = 10^1$ was 1 s and 38 s in the case of scenario *all* and *last*, respectively, while with $bnd = 10^2$, it was approximately 15 min in both cases.

When multiple trains drive consecutively, our method suffers from a number of mutual exclusion conflicts (Formula 20). For example, in the case of the conflict captured in Fig. 3, we resolve it by backtracking the whole situation and seeking another plan where train B enters later. The tool *railperfcheck* prevents such a conflict implicitly within the simulator—by stopping train B at node 1 (if there is a signal) until the conflicting section becomes free. If the signal was not there, such a plan of two consecutive trains would not even be considered.

7 Conclusion

We presented a formalization of a low-level railway scheduling problem, where the dynamics of trains is described by differential equations, and where rich timing and ordering constraints are supported. We analyzed the behavior of our approach compared to an existing method on selected case studies, and identified strong and weak aspects of the run-time performance. We demonstrated that despite the complexity of our model, the resulting problems can be solved successfully within a SAT modulo theory framework. This opens the possibility of applying such techniques to further application domains with similar complexity.

Acknowledgements. The work of Stefan Ratschan was supported by the project GA21-09458S of the Czech Science Foundation GA ČR and institutional support RVO:67985807. The work of Tomáš Kolárik was supported by CTU project SGS20/211/OHK3/3T/18.

References

1. Andreychuk, A., Yakovlev, K., Surynek, P., Atzmon, D., Stern, R.: Multi-agent pathfinding with continuous time. Artif. Intell. **305**, 103662 (2022). https://doi.org/10.1016/j.artint.2022.103662
2. Biere, A.: Bounded model checking. In: Biere, A., Heule, M., van Maaren, H., Walsh, T. (eds.) Handbook of Satisfiability, chap. 14, pp. 457–481. IOS Press (2009). https://doi.org/10.3233/978-1-58603-929-5-457
3. Bournez, O., Campagnolo, M.L.: A survey on continuous time computations. In: Cooper, S., Löwe, B., Sorbi, A. (eds.) New Computational Paradigms, pp. 383–423. Springer, New York (2008). https://doi.org/10.1007/978-0-387-68546-5_17
4. Brain, M., Tinelli, C., Rümmer, P., Wahl, T.: An automatable formal semantics for IEEE-754 floating-point arithmetic. In: 22nd IEEE Symposium on Computer Arithmetic, pp. 160–167. IEEE (2015), https://doi.org/10.1109/ARITH.2015.26
5. Eggers, A., Ramdani, N., Nedialkov, N., Fränzle, M.: Improving SAT Modulo ODE for hybrid systems analysis by combining different enclosure methods. In: Barthe, G., Pardo, A., Schneider, G. (eds.) SEFM 2011. LNCS, vol. 7041, pp. 172–187. Springer, Heidelberg (2011). https://doi.org/10.1007/978-3-642-24690-6_13
6. Gao, S., Kong, S., Clarke, E.M.: dReal: an SMT solver for nonlinear theories over the reals. In: Bonacina, M.P. (ed.) CADE 2013. LNCS (LNAI), vol. 7898, pp. 208–214. Springer, Heidelberg (2013). https://doi.org/10.1007/978-3-642-38574-2_14
7. Haehn, R., Ábrahám, E., Nießen, N.: Freight train scheduling in railway systems. In: Hermanns, H. (ed.) MMB 2020. LNCS, vol. 12040, pp. 225–241. Springer, Cham (2020). https://doi.org/10.1007/978-3-030-43024-5_14
8. Haehn, R., Ábrahám, E., Nießen, N.: Symbolic simulation of railway timetables under consideration of stochastic dependencies. In: Abate, A., Marin, A. (eds.) QEST 2021. LNCS, vol. 12846, pp. 257–275. Springer, Cham (2021). https://doi.org/10.1007/978-3-030-85172-9_14
9. Kolárik, T., Ratschan, S.: SAT modulo differential equation simulations. In: Ahrendt, W., Wehrheim, H. (eds.) TAP 2020. LNCS, vol. 12165, pp. 80–99. Springer, Cham (2020). https://doi.org/10.1007/978-3-030-50995-8_5

10. Kolárik, T., Ratschan, S.: Railway scheduling using Boolean satisfiability modulo simulations (2022). https://arxiv.org/abs/2212.05382. Extended version of the paper
11. Kolárik, T.: UN/SOT (UN/SAT modulo ODES Not SOT) (2020). https://gitlab.com/Tomaqa/unsot
12. Kolárik, T.: UN/SOT preprocessing language (2022). https://gitlab.com/Tomaqa/unsot/-/blob/master/doc/lang/preprocess.pdf
13. Luteberget, B., Claessen, K., Johansen, C., Steffen, M.: SAT modulo discrete event simulation applied to railway design capacity analysis. Formal Methods Syst. Design **57**(2), 211–245 (2021). https://doi.org/10.1007/s10703-021-00368-2
14. Montigel, M.: Formal representation of track topologies by double vertex graphs. In: Proceedings of Railcomp 92 held in Washington DC, Computers in Railways 3, vol. 2. Computational Mechanics Publications (1992)
15. Nieuwenhuis, R., Oliveras, A., Tinelli, C.: Solving SAT and SAT modulo theories: from an abstract Davis-Putnam-Logemann-Loveland procedure to DPLL(T). J. ACM (JACM) **53**(6), 937–977 (2006). https://doi.org/10.1145/1217856.1217859
16. Salerno, M., E-Martín, Y., Fuentetaja, R., Gragera, A., Pozanco, A., Borrajo, D.: Train route planning as a multi-agent path finding problem. In: Alba, E., et al. (eds.) CAEPIA 2021. LNCS (LNAI), vol. 12882, pp. 237–246. Springer, Cham (2021). https://doi.org/10.1007/978-3-030-85713-4_23
17. Schlechte, T., Borndörfer, R., Erol, B., Graffagnino, T., Swarat, E.: Micro-macro transformation of railway networks. J. Rail Transp. Plann. Manage. **1**(1), 38–48 (2011). https://doi.org/10.1016/j.jrtpm.2011.09.001
18. Schwanhäußer, W.: Die Bemessung der Pufferzeiten im Fahrplangefüge der Eisenbahn. Ph.D. thesis (1974). https://www.via.rwth-aachen.de/downloads/Dissertation_Schwanhaeusser_2te_Auflage_Text.pdf
19. Weiß, R., Opitz, J., Nachtigall, K.: A novel approach to strategic planning of rail freight transport. In: Helber, S., et al. (eds.) Operations Research Proceedings 2012. ORP, pp. 463–468. Springer, Cham (2014). https://doi.org/10.1007/978-3-319-00795-3_69

SMT Sampling via Model-Guided Approximation

Matan I. Peled, Bat-Chen Rothenberg(✉), and Shachar Itzhaky

Technion—Israel Institute of Technology, Haifa, Israel
{mip,batg,shachari}@cs.technion.ac.il

Abstract. We investigate the domain of satisfiable formulas in satisfiability modulo theories (SMT), in particular, automatic generation of a multitude of satisfying assignments to such formulas. Despite the long and successful history of SMT in model checking and formal verification, this aspect is relatively under-explored. Prior work exists for generating such assignments, or *samples*, for Boolean formulas and for quantifier-free first-order formulas involving bit-vectors, arrays, and uninterpreted functions (QF_AUFBV). We propose a new approach that is suitable for a theory T of integer arithmetic and to T with arrays and uninterpreted functions. The approach involves reducing the general sampling problem to a simpler instance of sampling from a set of independent intervals, which can be done efficiently. Such reduction is carried out by expanding a single model—a *seed*—using top-down propagation of constraints along the original first-order formula.

Keywords: SMT sampling · Under-approximation · SMT · Satisfiability modulo theories · Model-guided approximation

1 Introduction

Satisfiability Modulo Theories (SMT) formulas are the centerpiece of many modern-day algorithms for the testing and verification of hardware and software systems. In constrained-random verification (CRV) [34]—one of the most popular methods for hardware testing in the industry—the functional model and verification scenarios of a hardware design are translated into an SMT formula. In software verification [12, 22, 24], SMT formulas are used to express safety requirements extracted from the code.

The problem of SMT solving has been widely investigated, and many solvers are available [3, 11, 14, 32]. These tools can determine satisfiability and return a (single) model if it exists. However, there are use cases in which multiple, sometimes multitudes of, such models are needed. For example, in CRV, solutions of the formula represent stimuli for the design under test, and multiple and

This work is supported by the Israeli Science Foundation Grant No. 243/19 and the Binational Science Foundation (NSF-BSF) Grant No. 2018675.

M. Chechik et al. (Eds.): FM 2023, LNCS 14000, pp. 74–91, 2023.
https://doi.org/10.1007/978-3-031-27481-7_6

diverse solutions increase the likelihood of discovering bugs [34]. In the context of software verification, a solution of the formula often represents an input causing a safety violation, along with the buggy execution of the program for that input [12,24]. Obtaining multiple such solutions provides additional insight into the bug in question, which may help guide the debugging process.

This paper is concerned with the *SMT sampling* problem, *i.e.*, efficiently generating multiple random solutions for an SMT formula with good coverage of the solution space. The naïve solution of enumerating models using a solver often becomes too expensive in practice, and most solvers tend to return similar models in successive invocations. Notably, while the problem of *SAT* sampling has been successfully established with techniques such as Markov Chain Monte-Carlo (MCMC) [26,27] and universal hashing [18,30,31], the history of the same problem applied to SMT formulas is shorter [15,16]. When considering propositional formulas or formulas over bit-vector theories, a reduction from SMT sampling to SAT sampling is possible. However, it was shown in [15] that such an approach is significantly less efficient than sampling at the SMT level directly. Furthermore, when considering formulas over infinite domains, such as the integers or the reals, a reduction to SAT is not even an option.

This paper presents a novel algorithm for sampling SMT formulas in the theory of linear integer arithmetic enhanced with (possibly non-linear) multiplication, denoted T_{MIA}. We also present an extension to integer arrays and uninterpreted functions. The extended theory is denoted T_{AUFMIA}. Our approach is *epoch-based* [15]: it operates in a series of rounds, called *epochs*, where in each epoch a *seed* m, which is a random model of the formula, is generated using an off-the-shelf solver. This model is then extended to a large set of models of similar nature, in a cost-effective manner.

The novelty of our approach lies in the algorithm for extending the model m and in the representation of the set of models returned in each epoch. This algorithm relies on the novel notion of *model-guided approximation* (MGA), which we introduce. MGA uses a model m of a formula φ to derive a simpler formula, φ', s.t. $m \models \varphi'$ and φ' *underapproximates* φ. The rationale is that using m during the underapproximation process can help guide it towards solutions that are similar to m, and avoid parts of the search space which are devoid of solutions.

Our sampling algorithm uses MGA in every epoch to convert a T_{MIA}-formula φ into a fomrula φ' in a theory of intervals, T_{IC}. In T_{IC}, formulae are restricted to a conjunction of constraints of the form $x \geq c$ or $x \leq c$, where x is a variable and c is a constant. The underapproximation is done using a rule-based approach, which propagates constraints in a top-down fashion along the abstract syntax tree (AST) of the formula. Obtaining a set of concrete solutions from φ' is straightforward: by repeatedly sampling all variables from within their boundaries. Note that the underapproximation property of MGA ensures that every point within these intervals is necessarily a model of φ.

The ability of our algorithm to represent the set of solutions at each epoch symbolically in the form of an interval formula φ' has several advantages. First, it allows blocking all previously seen solutions by conjoining φ with $\neg\varphi'$. Such blocking is often feasible since the size of φ' is proportional to the number of variables (rather than the size of the solution set, which can be large or even infinite). On top of that, the interval formula itself can be returned instead of a concrete set of solutions, which can give added value to the user. For example, in the scenario where solutions of the formula represent inputs that cause a bug in a program, knowing that every x in a certain range causes the bug can be helpful for debugging.

Our algorithm does not aim to provide formal guarantees regarding uniform sampling nor coverage. This is in contrast to some prior work on SAT sampling [9, 18, 31], but similar to prior work on SMT sampling [15, 16]. We believe that the ability to adjust the sampling method towards an application-specific goal, as opposed to a universal metric, is more important than approximating a uniform distribution, since the purpose of sampling varies by use case. Our algorithm therefore allows to control the sampling heuristic via two parameters: the choice of the initial seed, and the sampling of each interval formula. Here, too, the use of intervals have the advantage of being a convenient representation, in which it is easy to apply diverse sampling heuristics such as uniform or even exhaustive sampling (if the space is finite).

We have implemented our algorithm in an open-source tool, MeGASampler[1]. In order to compare it with state-of-the-art sampler SMTSampler [15], we have also implemented an adaptation of their algorithm (originally designed for the theory of bit-vectors with arrays and uninterpreted functions) to integers. We provide an experimental evaluation of their method and ours on a large set of benchmarks from SMT-LIB. Our results show that MeGASampler significantly improves state-of-the-art in terms of both the number of solutions and their quality, as measured in [15].

To sum up, our main contributions are:

1. Define the problem of Model-Guided Approximation (MGA) for pairs of first-order theories T and T'.
2. Present an algorithm for computing MGA of an integer theory onto the theory of intervals, with support for arrays and uninterpreted functions. On top of this, we implement an epoch-based procedure for sampling formulas in the source theory.
3. Implement the algorithm in an open-source sampling tool, MeGASampler, and evaluate it against an integer-based variant of the state-of-the-art sampling tool, SMTSampler, on a large set of SMT-LIB benchmarks.

1.1 Motivating Example

As an introductory example, consider the integer formula:

$$\varphi\colon (x - 5y \leq 7) \wedge (x \geq 0)$$

MeGASampler begins its first epoch by consulting an off-the-shelf SMT solver; let us assume that the solver returned that $m = \{x \mapsto 12, y \mapsto 2\}$

[1] Available at: https://github.com/chaosite/MeGASampler.

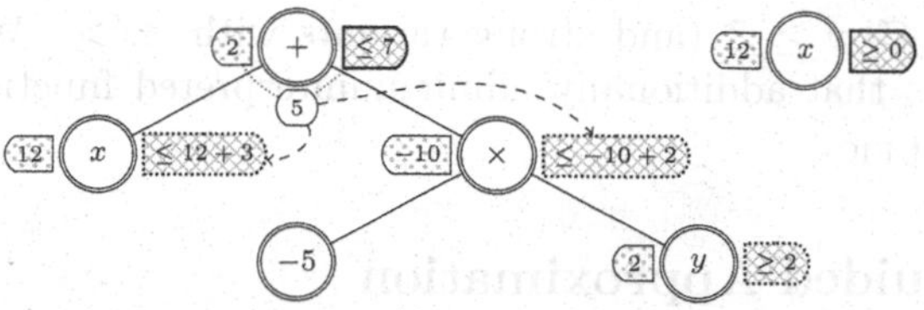

Fig. 1. Annotated syntax tree of $(x - 5y \leq 7) \wedge (x \geq 0)$ with model $\{x \mapsto 12, y \mapsto 2\}$

is a valid solution to φ. To get more solutions from this seed solution, we can under-approximate φ with an interval formula φ', which is easier to sample. In Fig. 1, we see how this is done.

Figure 1 shows an annotated syntax tree of φ: to the left side of each node is its value per the model m; to the right, we show the bound for this term. Solid outlines indicate that the inequalities are taken directly from the formula, as is the case for the root nodes. Bounds with dotted outlines are an inferred under-approximation. Bounds are propagated in a top-down manner until the leaf nodes (integer variables) are reached. For example, the value "5" written below the addition node represents the amount of "slack" to be distributed among child nodes, as illustrated by the dashed arrows. By gathering the constraints on the leaves (shown with thick borders) we obtain $\varphi' = x \leq 15 \wedge y \geq 2 \wedge x \geq 0$, which represents the set of intervals $\{x \in [0, 15], y \in [2, \infty]\}$. Note that, any solution that satisfies φ' also satisfies φ. Sampling these intervals is then straight-forward: we can choose any value for x and y in the intervals and it will be a valid solution to φ. This example is discussed in further detail in Sect. 4.1.

2 Preliminaries

A first-order theory T consists of: a set of variables, each mapped to a concrete domain; a set of logical symbols (such as $\wedge$, $\neg$); a set of non-logical symbols (such as $+$, $-$, $<$), each with an *arity* and a *sort*, called the *signature* of T, denoted $\Sigma(T)$; a grammar $G(T)$; a fixed interpretation for the symbols of the signature. In addition, a theory may admit *uninterpreted* function and predicate symbols, which appear in $G(T)$ but do not have fixed interpretations. These symbols are not considered to be part of $\Sigma(T)$.

The set of logical symbols is a subset of $\{\wedge, \vee, \neg\}$ and their interpretation is fixed across all theories to be the standard one. Note that, the interpretation of the non-logical symbols of the signature is also fixed, but depends on the theory.

A *structure* m consists of a domain, an interpretation of the symbols in the signature and an assignment of domain elements to all variables of the formula.

In the following sections, we will use T_{LIA}—the standard theory of linear integer arithmetic; T_{MIA}, which extends T_{LIA} by allowing variable multiplication (but not division); and T_{IC}, which restricts T_{LIA} to conjunctions of inequalities of the form $v \leq \mathcal{Z}$, $v \geq \mathcal{Z}$ (and strong variants with $<$, $>$). We also consider extended theories that additionally admit uninterpreted functions and arrays, T_{AUFMIA} and T_{AUFIC}.

3 Model-Guided Approximation

In this section, we define the problem of *model-guided approximation* (MGA). Consider a formula φ in a theory T, and a model m of φ. φ can be seen as a representation of the set of structures satisfying it, $\text{Models}(\varphi) \triangleq \{m \mid m \models \varphi\}$. Model-guided approximation aims to find a subset $M \subseteq \text{Models}(\varphi)$, which contains m, and can be represented using a formula φ' that is better than φ for some criteria. For example, for the purpose of sampling discussed in this paper, φ' should be easier to sample than φ. Alternatively, one can think of other goals, such as making φ' human-readable or easier to solve than φ.

To make sure φ' is more suitable than φ in the criteria, φ' is limited to a theory T'. The theory T' can be chosen a-priori based on the criteria, and can be considered to be a part of the problem. Intuitively, T' restricts T by adding syntactic limitations to the way formulas are built, but does not change the semantics of operations. Formally, the restriction relation is defined as follows:

Definition 1 (Theory restriction). *A theory T' restricts T, denoted $T' \preceq T$, if:*

- *The language of the grammar of T' is a subset of the language of the grammar of T. That is, every T'-formula is also a T-formula. Note that this requires, in particular, that $\Sigma(T') \subseteq \Sigma(T)$.*
- *The set of variables and uninterpreted function symbols (if any) as well as their mapped domains are identical in T and T'.*
- *Every symbol $\sigma \in \Sigma(T')$ (which also belongs to $\Sigma(T)$) has the same fixed interpretation in both theories.*

Example 1. The theory T_{IC}, described in Sect. 2, restricts both theories T_{LIA} and T_{MIA}, which are also described there. The common interpreted symbols, $<, \leq, >, \geq$, and all integer concepts, have the same interpretations, and any T_{IC}-formula is also a T_{LIA}-formula, as well as a T_{MIA}-formula.

Definition 2 (Entailment). *Semantic entailment is defined as a binary relation $\Rightarrow$ over formulas such that $\varphi \Rightarrow \psi$ iff for every structure m, if $m \models \varphi$ then $m \models \psi$.*

That is all well and good when referring to formulas of the same theory. In the presence of multiple theories, the situation is a bit more subtle. Let φ be a T'-formula, ψ a T-formula, and $T' \preceq T$. For a T'-structure m, we denote m^T its *extension* to T, naturally obtained by filling in any symbols that are not assigned in m with their fixed interpretations according to T (all uninterpreted symbols are already assigned interpretations in m, as follows from the previous definitions). This allows for a slightly adjusted definition of $\Rightarrow$, namely:

Definition 3 ($\preceq$-Entailment). *For φ,ψ as above, $\varphi \Rightarrow \psi$ iff for every T'-structure m, if $m \models \varphi$ then $m^T \models \psi$.*

To formally define model-guided approximation, we begin with the notion of *m-approximation*:

Definition 4. *Let φ be a formula in a theory T and m be a model of φ. A formula φ' is called an m-*approximation of φ (in T') *if φ' belongs to a theory T' s.t. $T' \preceq T$, $m \models \varphi'$ and $\varphi' \Rightarrow \varphi$.*

An m-approximation has the following properties, which will be of use for us later on:

Proposition 1 (m-approximation transitivity). *If φ'' is an m-approximation of φ' in T'' and φ' is an m-approximation of φ in T', then φ'' is an m-approximation of φ in T''.*

Proposition 2 (m-approximation conjunction closure). *If φ_1' is an m-approximation of φ_1 in T' and φ_2' is an m-approximation of φ_2 in T', then $\varphi_1' \wedge \varphi_2'$ is an m-approximation of $\varphi_1 \wedge \varphi_2$ in T'.*

The problem of *model-guided approximation* (MGA) with respect to two theories T, T' s.t. $T' \preceq T$ is now defined as: given a formula φ in T and a model m of φ, find an m-approximation of φ in T'. In the sequel, we will often use the abbreviated phrase "model approximation" instead of the full "model-guided approximation", which is a mouthful.

4 Solving the MGA Problem

In this section, we focus on how to solve the model approximation problem with respect to T and T'. For the remainder of this section, we fix φ and m to be the inputs of the problem (φ is a formula in T, m is a model of φ).

A useful first step in solving this problem is via a reduction to the special case where φ is a product term, *i.e.*, a conjunction of literals. We refer to this case as the *product model-guided approximation* (PMGA) problem. Such a reduction is useful since it simplifies the problem without depending on the particular T and T' in question.

In the literature, a product term P s.t. $P \Rightarrow \varphi$ is called an *implicant* of φ. For our purposes, we add the notion of an *m-implicant* of φ, which is an implicant of φ that is satisfied by m. Thus, by definition, an m-implicant of φ is an m-approximation of φ in T, which is a product term. Since m-approximation is transitive (Proposition 1), reducing the MGA problem of φ and m to a PMGA problem can be done by simply replacing φ with one of its m-implicants. We explain how to extract an m-implicant of φ in the appendix [36].

In the following, we focus on two instances of the PMGA problem and present specialized algorithms for them.

$$\frac{t_i \leq [\![t_i]\!] + \text{Portion}\left(c - \sum_i [\![t_i]\!], k, i\right) \quad i = 1\,..\,k}{t_1 + \cdots + t_k \leq c} \quad (1) \qquad \frac{\prod_i [\![t_i]\!] < 0 \quad \text{sign}\left([\![t_i]\!]\right) \cdot t_i \geq |[\![t_i]\!]| \quad i = 1\,..\,k}{t_1 \cdots t_k \leq c} \quad (2)$$

$$\frac{\text{sign}(a) \cdot t_1 \leq \text{sign}(a) \cdot (c//a)}{a \cdot t_1 \leq c} \quad (3) \qquad \frac{\prod_i [\![t_i]\!] \geq 0 \quad 0 \leq \text{sign}\left([\![t_i]\!]\right) \cdot t_i \leq |[\![t_i]\!]| \quad i = 1\,..\,k}{t_1 \cdots t_k \leq c} \quad (4)$$

Auxiliary notation: $\text{Portion}(n, k, i) \triangleq \lfloor \frac{n}{k} \rfloor + \begin{cases} 1, & i \leq n \mod k \\ 0, & \text{otherwise} \end{cases} \qquad x//y \triangleq \begin{cases} \lfloor x/y \rfloor, & y > 0 \\ \lceil x/y \rceil, & y < 0 \end{cases}$

Fig. 2. Rules for strengthening (transforming) integer terms to interval terms

4.1 Approximating the Theory of Linear Integer Arithmetic with Non-Linear Multiplication Using the Theory of Intervals

The first instance we present a solution for is computing the PMGA problem for $T = T_{\text{MIA}}$ and $T' = T_{\text{IC}}$. That is, given a product term P in T_{MIA} and a model m of P, our goal is to find a formula φ' in T_{IC} s.t. φ' is an m-approximation of P. To do that, for each literal l in P, we find an m-approximation of l, denoted ξ' (note that ξ' is not necessarily a literal). Then, we conjoin all ξ's back together to form the formula φ'. From Proposition 2, φ' that is created this way is indeed an m-approximation of P.

In order to find an m-approximation for a T_{MIA} literal l, we use a rule-based approach. Figure 2 shows inference rules to transform T_{MIA} literals into T_{IC} formulas. We assume, without loss of generality, that literals have the form $t \leq c$ where c is a constant and t has no constant terms (addends). Integer inequalities can always be normalized to this form. In rule 1, addition is modeled by proportionally dividing the "slack" between the value of the constant and the value of the left-hand side in m among the variables. For example, given $x_1 + x_2 + x_3 \leq 11$ and a model $m = \{x_1 \mapsto 1, x_2 \mapsto 2, x_3 \mapsto 3\}$, we are distributing $11 - 6$ amongst three variables, and can approximate that $x_1 \leq 1+2$, $x_2 \leq 2+2$, and $x_3 \leq 3+1$. Multiplication by a constant (rule 3) is fairly simple, and is done by dividing the right-hand side of the constraint by the constant, only taking care to adjust for negative constants correctly. With multiplication of variables, we only use the calculated sign of the result to provide a range in which the sign is consistent with the model, shown in rules 2 and 4. If the product is positive, then factors are allowed to expand toward zero, and if it is negative—away from zero. For example, if we have a constraint $x_1 \cdot x_2 \leq -42$ and a model $m = \{x_1 \mapsto 5, x_2 \mapsto -9\}$, then from rule 4 we get $x_1 \geq 5$, $x_2 \leq -9$.

The rules as shown in Fig. 2 follow some conventions to aid readability. All formulas are assumed to be in canonical form: all the variables are on the left-hand side with only a constant, c, on the right-hand side, and inequalities are normalized into less-than forms, *i.e.*, $x \geq c \Rightarrow -x \leq -c$. t_i denotes terms in the formula (not always literals). $[\![t_i]\!]$ is the matching values per the model m. $\text{sign}(x)$ gives the sign of x, *i.e.*, $\frac{x}{|x|}$.

Example 2. As a demonstration of the application of these rules, recall Fig. 1. In the addition node, we demonstrate the usage of rule 1. The amount of "slack"

$$\begin{array}{rl}\varphi ::= & \neg\varphi \mid \varphi \wedge \varphi \mid \varphi \vee \varphi \mid \mathit{Atom} \\ \mathit{Atom} ::= & t < t \mid t \leq t \mid t > t \mid t \geq t \mid t = t \mid t \neq t \\ \mid & s = s \mid s \neq s \\ t ::= & \mathcal{Z} \mid v \mid t + t \mid t - t \mid t \cdot t \mid f_i(t) \mid \mathit{select}(s,t) \\ s ::= & a \mid \mathit{store}(s,t,t)\end{array}$$

(a) T_{AUFMIA}

$$\begin{array}{rl}\varphi ::= & \varphi \wedge \varphi \mid \mathit{Atom} \\ \mathit{Atom} ::= & \psi < \mathcal{Z} \mid \psi \leq \mathcal{Z} \mid \psi > \mathcal{Z} \mid \psi \geq \mathcal{Z} \\ \psi ::= & v \mid \mathit{select}(a,t) \mid f_i(t) \\ t ::= & \mathcal{Z} \mid v \mid t + t \mid t - t \mid \mathcal{Z} \cdot t \mid f_i(t) \mid \mathit{select}(a,t) \\ s ::= & a \mid \mathit{store}(s,t,t)\end{array}$$

(b) T_{AUFIC}

Fig. 3. Grammars for theories used

to be shared between the child nodes is $c - \sum_i [\![t_i]\!] = 7 - 12 + 10 = 5$, as noted in the value below the node. 5 cannot be evenly divided into two parts, therefore Portion assigns 3 to the first child and 2 to the other. This gives $x \leq 15$ and $-5y \leq -8$. The multiplication node in this example represents multiplication by constant -5, therefore rule 3 is applied. The constant is negative, so the operator is reversed, and since $\lceil 8/5 \rceil$ is 2, we obtain $y \geq 2$.

4.2 Adding Arrays and Uninterpreted Functions

In this section, we solve the PMGA problem of P and m with respect to two integer theories with arrays and uninterpreted functions, T_{AUFMIA} and T_{AUFIC}. The theory of arrays, uninterpreted functions, and linear integer arithmetic with multiplication, T_{AUFMIA}, is defined via the grammar shown in Fig. 3a, where $\mathcal{Z}$ is an integer constant, v is an int variable symbol, a is an array variable symbol, and f_i are uninterpreted function symbols $\notin \Sigma(T_{\mathrm{MIA}})$.[2]

Integer variables are mapped to the $\mathbb{Z}$ domain, array variables are mapped to the $\mathbb{Z} \to \mathbb{Z}$ domain (both the indices and the values are integers), and function symbols are also mapped to the $\mathbb{Z} \to \mathbb{Z}$ domain (both the argument and the return value are integers). Except for the variable and function symbols, all symbols are interpreted using the standard interpretation. Specifically, the interpretation of $\mathit{select}(s, i)$ intuitively means querying the value of array s in index i, and the interpretation of $\mathit{store}(s, i, e)$ intuitively means returning a fresh array which results from cloning s and then storing the value of e in index i. We refer to terms of the form $f_i(\_)$, $\mathit{select}(\_,\_)$, and $\mathit{store}(\_,\_,\_)$ as *function application*, *select*, and *store terms*, resp.

To under-approximate formulas in T_{AUFMIA}, we use the theory T_{AUFIC} as shown in Fig. 3b, which allows for intervals over integer variables, function call terms, and select terms where the first argument is an array variable.

For now, let us ignore the presence of literals of the form $s = s$ or $s \neq s$ in T (that is, assume the input formula contains no array comparison). This is done for simplification of presentation; later we will show how to lift this restriction. For similar reasons, since a function application term $f(i)$ is handled similarly to the select term $\mathit{select}(f, i)$, we assume, without loss of generality, that only the former are present. We consider the exact identification of such terms to be an implementation detail.

[2] The arity of functions is restricted to 1 for simplicity of presentation; an extension of our algorithm to functions with arbitrary arity is straightforward.

The derivation of an m-approximation for P (a product term in T_{AUFMIA}) in T_{AUFIC} now proceeds in multiple stages (explained below): – Elimination of *select-store*; – Atomic grounding; – Applying the PMGA procedure for T_{MIA} and T_{IC} (Sect. 4.1); – Un-grounding the resulting formula.

To ease the presentation of the rest of the section, we introduce a few notations. Since several stages make use of syntactic replacement, we use $t \sqsubseteq \varphi$ to denote that the term t appears syntactically as a sub-term in the formula φ; and $\varphi[\![t \hookleftarrow t']\!]$ for the formula obtained by syntactically replacing every occurrence $t \sqsubseteq \varphi$ with t'.

The first stage is a preprocessing step in which we use the model m to remove all *select-store* sub-terms (*i.e.*, terms of the form $\mathit{select}(\mathit{store}(\_), \_)$) from P: For every literal $l \in P$ s.t. there exists $t = \mathit{select}(\mathit{store}(s, t_i, t_e), t_j) \sqsubseteq l$, we remove l from P, construct an equivalent formula φ_l without *select-store* sub-terms (as shown below), find an m-implicant P_l of φ_l using the method described in the appendix [36], and conjoin P with P_l. The formula φ_l is constructed recursively. Initially φ_l is:

$$\big((t_i = t_j) \wedge l[\![t \hookleftarrow t_e]\!]\big) \vee \big((t_i \neq t_j) \wedge l[\![t \hookleftarrow \mathit{select}(s, t_j)]\!]\big)$$

Then, the term $\mathit{select}(s, t_j)$ is recursively replaced likewise, as long as s is a *store*. The second stage is the grounding procedure, whose purpose is to connect the semantics of T_{AUFMIA} formulas with that of T_{MIA}, with the aim of reducing the problem.

We define an injective *grounding function* $t \mapsto v_t$ over terms of T_{AUFMIA} that assigns to any term t of sort S a unique variable symbol v_t of sort S. Given a formula $\varphi \in T_{\text{AUFMIA}}$, we define its *atomic grounding* $\widetilde{\varphi}$ that is obtained from φ by (syntactically) replacing every select-term $t \sqsubseteq \varphi$ with v_t.

Similarly, we define *atomic grounding on structures*, for structures of T_{AUFMIA}. A structure $\widetilde{m}$ is obtained from a T_{AUFMIA}-structure m by elision of all array interpretations and introduction of appropriate interpretations $\widetilde{m}[v_t] = m[t]$. Clearly, doing that for every possible t will lead to infinite structures; therefore, atomic grounding of structures is always done with respect to some set S of terms, such that v_t is assigned only for $t \in S$. We denote this by $m \overset{S}{\mapsto} \widetilde{m}$. In particular, having received an input formula φ, we fix S to be the set of all select-terms occurring in φ.

It is worth noting that the mapping $\varphi \mapsto \widetilde{\varphi}$ is readily invertible, while $m \mapsto \widetilde{m}$—not necessarily. For example, the model $\widetilde{m}^\star = \langle i \mapsto 0, j \mapsto 0, v_{\mathit{select}(a,i)} \mapsto 1, v_{\mathit{select}(a,j)} \mapsto 2\rangle$ has no model m such that $\widetilde{m} = \widetilde{m}^\star$; because any $\widetilde{m}$ that maps i and j to the same value must also map $v_{\mathit{select}(a,i)}$ and $v_{\mathit{select}(a,j)}$ to the same value.

The process of generating an m-approximation of $\varphi \in T_{\text{AUFMIA}}$ is as follows: first, construct $\widetilde{\varphi}$ and $\widetilde{m}$. Subject to the language restrictions above, $\widetilde{\varphi} \in T_{\text{MIA}}$. Then, generate an $\widetilde{m}$-approximation of $\widetilde{\varphi}$ as a new formula $\widetilde{\varphi}' \in T_{\text{IC}}$. Finally, construct the corresponding $\varphi' \in T_{\text{AUFIC}}$ of which $\widetilde{\varphi}'$ is an atomic grounding. We will now show that φ' is indeed an m-approximation of the original φ.

Lemma 1 (grounding fidelity). *Given φ, m over a theory with arrays, $m \overset{S}{\mapsto} \widetilde{m}$, for some S that contains (at least) all select-terms occurring in φ. Then $m \models \varphi \iff \widetilde{m} \models \widetilde{\varphi}$.*

Proof. In the appendix [36].

Based on the lemma and the correctness of the T_{MIA} model-based approximation procedure of Sect. 4.1, we can now establish a correct approximation of T_{AUFMIA}, based on the stages above. From the lemma, $\widetilde{m} \models \widetilde{\varphi}$, and since $\widetilde{\varphi}'$ is an $\widetilde{m}$-approximation of $\widetilde{\varphi}$, it follows that $\widetilde{m} \models \widetilde{\varphi}'$. Recall that the variables of $\widetilde{\varphi}'$ are (a subset of) the variables of $\widetilde{\varphi}$ and as a consequence, the select-terms occurring in φ' also occur in φ, hence are contained in S. We can therefore apply the lemma in the opposite direction, and obtain $m \models \varphi'$.

The second property that φ' must satisfy is that $\varphi' \Rightarrow \varphi$. The proof is very similar: let $m' \models \varphi'$ be some model of it, and construct $\widetilde{m}'$. From the lemma, $\widetilde{m}' \models \widetilde{\varphi}'$. Again, $\widetilde{\varphi}'$ under-approximates $\widetilde{\varphi}$, hence $\widetilde{m}' \models \widetilde{\varphi}$; thus from the lemma, $m' \models \varphi$.

The astute reader may observe that the procedure above, while fulfilling the requirements for being a model-based approximation in T_{AUFIC}, is somewhat unsatisfying because T_{AUFIC} formulas are not as easy to sample as T_{IC}. Sampling the individual array elements independently from their corresponding intervals may lead to clashes; *e.g.*, if i, j, $\mathit{select}(a, i)$, and $\mathit{select}(a, j)$ are all constrained to some interval $[c, d]$, then an assignment of $i = j$ and $\mathit{select}(a, i) \neq \mathit{select}(a, j)$ is inconsistent and does not yield a valid structure. One possible course of action is to detect clashes as soon as they occur and restart the sampling procedure. But this may lead to a large number of false flags and wasted computations, which was the whole point of a sampling algorithm to avoid in the first place. A better alternative would be to adjust the construction of $\varphi \in T_{\text{AUFIC}}$ in a way that avoids these clashes.

To do that, we first create two sets of literals, $L_=$ and $L_{\neq}$, which constrain the indices to a fixed aliasing configuration, namely the one exhibited by m.

$$L_{\neq} = \{t_1 \neq t_2 \mid \exists a.\, \mathit{select}(a, t_1), \mathit{select}(a, t_2) \sqsubseteq P \ \wedge\ m[t_1] \neq m[t_2]\}$$
$$L_{=} = \{t_1 = t_2, \mathit{select}(a, t_1) = \mathit{select}(a, t_2) \mid \exists a.\mathit{select}(a, t_1), \mathit{select}(a, t_2) \sqsubseteq P \ \wedge\ m[t_1] = m[t_2]\}$$

Adding these literals to P will make sure that the same array accesses that are aliased in m are aliased in any model of φ', and no others.

Finally, we handle array equality $a_1 = a_2$ (and its negation) via a similar preprocessing. Since the details are somewhat technical, they are deferred to the appendix [36].

5 Sampling Using Model-Guided Approximation

In this section, we present an algorithm, `MeGASample`, for sampling T_{MIA} and T_{AUFMIA} formulas, using model-guided approximation to the theories T_{IC} and

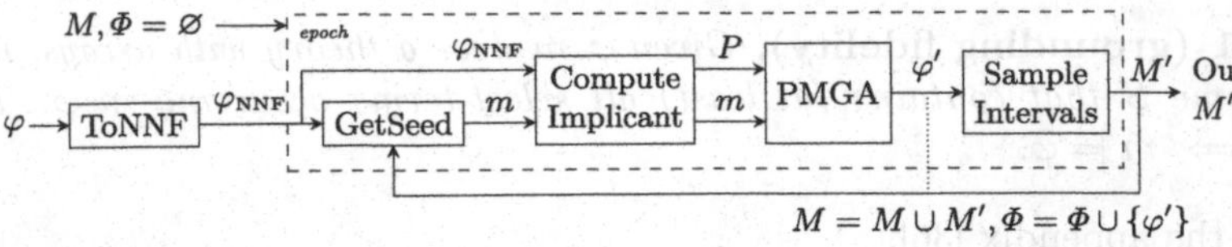

Fig. 4. Workflow of the `MeGASample` sampling procedure

T_{AUFIC}, respectively. An outline of the algorithm is presented in Fig. 4. Similar to [15], the sampling process is *epoch-based*: it obtains an initial model with the help of a solver, and then utilizes it to create a set of distinct models in an efficient manner. This process is repeated iteratively, where each such iteration is called *an epoch*. The initial model of each epoch is called the *seed* of the epoch.

As a preliminary step, the input formula φ is transformed into negation normal form (NNF). Then, the epoch loop begins, collecting models in the set M (initialized to $\varnothing$). First, the seed of the epoch, m, is obtained using a `GetSeed` procedure. Then, model-guided approximation takes place. As discussed in Sect. 4, the first step is to find a product term P that is an m-implicant of φ_{NNF} (and φ) in `ComputeImplicant`. Then, the procedure `PMGA` that is appropriate to the current theory is used to obtain φ', an m-approximation of P (and φ). Finally, in `Sample intervals`, the interval formula φ' (which is either in T_{IC} or T_{AUFIC}) is repeatedly sampled, and samples are saved in M'. Note that, the m-approximation property guarantees that every model of φ' is also a model of φ. Therefore, all models in M' are output if they were not seen before (*i.e.*, not in M), and the set M is updated accordingly. In addition, the m-approximations φ' are accumulated for future use by `GetSeed`.

We suggest two variants for the `GetSeed` procedure. The first, following [15], picks a random assignment and chooses the model of φ that is closest to it using a MAX-SMT query. The second, avoids a costly MAX-SMT query and uses SMT instead, but only after discrading all models of φ' by adding $\neg\varphi'$ to the formula. Unlike the random-based variant, constraints are accumulated between different calls to the solver, to enable blocking based on the entire history of epochs. Both variants aim at increasing the diversity of the seeds and covering new areas of the solution space.

With regard to `Sample Intervals`, for $T' = T_{\text{IC}}$ this procedure can be realized by repeatedly drawing a value at random from within the lower and higher bounds of each variable. For $T' = T_{\text{AUFIC}}$, things get a little more complicated since we need to also sample array elements constrained by an interval. As already mentioned in Sect. 4.2, clashes may occur between terms that are not syntactically identical but refer to the same array element (are aliased). However, we have already shown that with the addition of equality and inequality constraints we can eliminate aliasing a-priori. We therefore use the T_{IC} sampling procedure also for T_{AUFIC}.

The suggested implementations for `GetSeed` and `Sample Intervals` are suitable for the general case, where we have no information as to the form of the solution space nor the goal of sampling. However, we believe that for a particular application such additional insight will be available and can be incorporated into these procedures in order to guide the search towards the more useful solutions. We leave this to future work.

6 Evaluation

We have developed MeGASampler as an open-source sampling tool based on the Z3 solver [32]. In this section, we empirically evaluate MeGASampler with either blocking or random initial assignments, and compare it against a variant of state-of-the-art sampler SMTSampler [15] which was ported from bit-vector logic to integer logic. The latter was constructed by modifying the original implementation as follows. SMTSampler is built upon three operations: transforming a seed into a set of satisfying conditions, finding similar solutions by negating one of these conditions, and combining the resulting solutions to generate solution candidates. Porting to a different logic requires translating these operations to fit that logic. For bit-vectors, SMTSampler used conditions of the form "bit i in vector v is set", and combined solutions by applying a bitwise or operation to mutated values. For the integer domain, we treated the entire assignment as a condition, *i.e.*, "integer x is equal to value n", and used addition as the integer analogue for combining mutations.

We performed tests on benchmarks from SMT-LIB [4], using the problems in logics QF_LIA, QF_NIA[3], and QF_ALIA. Some of the benchmarks represent real-world problems, including formulas used for software verification, *e.g.*, from the AProVE [20] and VeryMax [6] termination analysis tools. Other benchmarks are synthetic, designed to stress SMT solvers.

Benchmarks deemed inappropriate for the evaluation were discarded, including those marked as unsatisfiable or unknown and benchmarks for which at least 100 samples were not gathered by any tested technique. As we are not evaluating SMT solvers, benchmarks for which finding a single solution took over one minute were also discarded. After applying these criteria, we followed the methodology of [15] and randomly selected 15 benchmark files as a representative sample of each directory, in order to keep the experiments tractable. We consider this reasonable as benchmarks from the same directory tend to be similar in nature. In total, our evaluation set consisted of 28 benchmark directories (420 files), 4 in QF_NIA, 1 in QF_ALIA, and the rest in QF_LIA.

As noted in previous work [15], the number of unique solutions generated is an incomplete metric, which may not represent the samples' coverage of the solution space. The authors proposed an alternative metric, which measures coverage statistics of the internal nodes of the abstract syntax tree (AST) of the (bit-vector) formula: each node of sort Bool represents 1 bit, and each node of sort bit-vector represents 64 bits. Each such bit is considered covered if it has received both 1 and 0 among the set of samples. The coverage metric is then the ratio of covered bits to total bits. The intuition being that if one were to synthesize

[3] The "interesting" operation in T_{NIA} is multiplication; most benchmarks in this directory are actually in T_{MIA}, which is supported by MeGASampler.

Table 1. Results (averaged) over the benchmarks

Benchmarks	vars	depth	Coverage (%)			Epochs			#SMT	Unique solutions		
			MEGA	MEGA^b	SMTint	MEGA	MEGA^b	SMTint	SMTint	MEGA	MEGA^b	SMTint
QF_ALIA/qlock2	484	233	**87.90**	20.40	26.25	**3**	2	2	23	12332	**14877**	20
QF_LIA/CAV2009-slacked	55	5	**98.36**	66.11	89.87	143	**646**	247	6746	1647400	**1915995**	633047
QF_LIA/CAV2009	26	5	67.38	**95.08**	79.98	184	996	**1585**	20793	2201716	**3788132**	1075097
QF_LIA/bofill-sched-random	780	6	**99.84**	83.95	76.00	628	**927**	4	196	627	**927**	112
QF_LIA/bofill-sched-real	576	6	**99.94**	91.95	81.74	689	**1159**	3	580	688	**1158**	249
QF_LIA/convert	768	1339	30.61	27.71	**80.24**	**7**	6	2	65	**90635**	76671	53
QF_LIA/dillig	31	25	42.20	**97.70**	53.57	133	**1164**	769	10551	1729099	**3983851**	455503
QF_LIA/pb2010	5842	5	**75.64**	71.85	51.37	30099	107	**42907**	128875	53	**214**	27
QF_LIA/prime-cone	10	5	96.89	63.86	**97.00**	2705	9313	**39360**	155484	**13658385**	3906854	613784
QF_LIA/slacks	61	5	**99.11**	69.50	85.75	135	205	**383**	11005	1923319	**2245506**	335504
QF_NIA/20170427-VeryMax	181	13	**86.09**	54.47	53.99	13	**506**	2	30	81822	**1563188**	18698
QF_NIA/AProVE	40	6	**97.87**	71.57	77.17	714	6016	**10053**	73190	6478901	**6982253**	1394814
QF_NIA/leipzig	92	2	59.55	**74.50**	54.22	20	**1305**	3	64	96843	**1189523**	1207

a circuit that takes as inputs assignments to the variables of the formula and produces a Boolean output of *True* or *False* indicating whether the formula is satisfied, then the coverage metric would be equivalent to the coverage of internal wires in this circuit, when exercised by the generated solutions. Therefore, this metric serves as a good proxy to coverage for formulas that encode hardware systems, *e.g.*, in CRV [34], and a good proxy to path coverage for formulas that encode software systems, *e.g.*, in bounded model checking [12].

We have ported this metric from bit-vector logic to integer logic by considering only the lower 64 bits of each arbitrary-size integer. Note that the maximum score using this metric is not necessarily 100%, because, naturally, some bits are restricted by the input formula and can only take one of the values. Therefore, we have normalized it and calculated it instead as the ratio of covered bits to total bits covered by at least one of the methods in the evaluation.

All experiments were run on a 64-core (128-thread) AMD EPYC 7742 based server with 512GiB of memory. Each execution utilized a single core, until either a time limit of 15 min was reached, or 25M unique samples were generated.

6.1 Results

Table 1 shows the results of the executions, broken down by origin directory. For each directory of benchmarks, the columns, averaged over the benchmarks in that directory, are as follows: Number of variables, depth of the formula AST, the computed coverage metric, number of epochs, number of calls to the solver (only shown for SMTint, for MEGA and MEGA^b it is exactly the number of epochs), and number of unique solutions. Columns titled MEGA report measurements for the random-based MEGASAMPLER, MEGA^b the blocking MEGASAMPLER, and SMTint is SMTSAMPLER retrofitted for the integer domain. Bold indicates the highest value in each rubric. Results are aggregated per top-level directory; for a more detailed breakdown, see the appendix [36].

MEGASAMPLER consistently produces more samples than SMTint. Moreover, the blocking technique is shown to be overall effective for increasing the number of unique solutions. Blocking does incur some overhead, which is why in

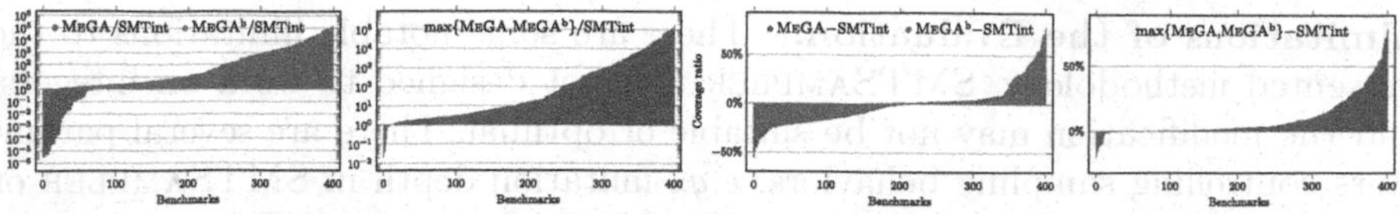

Fig. 5. A comparison of the number of samples and coverage generated by MEGASAMPLER, relative to those from SMTSAMPLER. The plots show ratios per single benchmark, in ascending order, comparing each of two variants of MEGASAMPLER to SMTSAMPLER.

some cases the non-blocking variant was able to produce more samples within the time frame. MEGASAMPLER also improves the coverage when considering the averages per collection of 15 benchmarks. Here, blocking produces lower coverage even when it produces more samples, because, while producing intervals that are disjoint in successive epochs, it utilizes less randomization than the MAX-SMT-based version.

The benchmarks in the `qlock2` and `convert` categories were difficult to solve (possibly due to the large AST depth), reflected in the low number of epochs for all methods shown. Remarkably, MEGA manages to extract tens of thousands of samples from a single-digit number of seeds for these benchmarks, compared to tens of SMTint. Surprisingly, for `convert` it is SMTint that manages to achieve the greatest coverage, despite a low number of unique solutions, suggesting that it moved further away from the seed using mutations.

For the two `bofill` categories, we see that for both MEGA variants the number of samples is about the number of epochs, meaning that MGA failed to generalize the seeds obtained from the solver. In SMTint the number of epochs is very small and the number of solutions obtained is lower than the number of calls made to the solver, *i.e.*, its seed expansion attempts were mostly unsuccessful. One takeaway is that there are examples where generalization does not work well but solving the formula isn't difficult, so maximizing the number of epochs is a good strategy. There were several categories where the number of epochs was significantly larger in MEGA^{b} compared to the other two; we ascribe this result to the cost of MAX-SMT calls, which aren't utilized by MEGA^{b}.

For a deeper look into the performance of the method, we perform a case-by-case comparison between both variants of MEGASAMPLER and SMTSAMPLER. We compute the ratio between the number of samples generated by MEGA or MEGA^{b} on each benchmark to SMTint; then plot the results in descending order on a logarithmic scale, on the same axis, as shown in Fig. 5. We show the same for a "virtual best" where the maximal value is compared with the baseline. The same process is repeated for the coverage metric that was described earlier. Since coverage is a percentage metric, we plot the difference on a linear scale.

In number of samples, the result of MEGA^{b} are similar to those of the virtual best and support the previous conclusion that blocking is good for increasing the sample volume. We also see that for coverage, the race is largely inconclusive, but that the virtual best still offers significant improvement over the baseline.

Limitations of the Evaluation. There are some notable limitations to the presented methodology. SMTSampler was not designed to work on integers, and the modification may not be suitable or optimal. There are several parameters controlling sampling behaviors, *e.g.*, mutation depth in SMTSampler or maximum number of samples per epoch in MeGASampler. Different selections for these parameters, as well as other experimental parameters such as time limit and inputs, may impact the results.

There may be other coverage metrics for estimating quality of samples, or other metrics that better characterize good sampling for particular uses. However, we do not believe that there is any single metric that would be good for all applications. As future work, we plan to design an MGA-based goal-aware sampling algorithm that guides the exploration towards better solutions for a specific purpose.

7 Related Work

There is a rich line of work on Markov-Chain Monte-Carlo (MCMC) sampling techniques in the statistics and operations research community [5,21,23,29, 35,37,38,40]. These techniques were used for sampling propositional formulas in [26,27]. Additional algorithms for sampling propositional formulas are based on syntactic mutations [17], random walks [41], recursive search [19], knowledge compilation [39], adaptation of SAT solvers and model counters [1,2,33], and universal hashing [9,18,30,31].

The problem of sampling for arbitrary SMT formulae was, however, much less explored. A prominent exception is SMTSampler [15], which samples formulas at the SMT level. Like MeGASampler, SMTSampler is epoch-based. However, their way of extending a single model to a set of models relies on syntactic mutations and their combination. Another difference is that SMT-Sampler was designed for formulas in the theory of bit-vectors with arrays and uninterpreted functions. In our experiments, we implemented a version of their algorithm for the T_{MIA} and T_{AUFMIA} theories and compared it empirically against MeGASampler. A follow-up work on SMT sampling is GuidedSampler [16], which is a variant of [15] that allows providing a problem-specific coverage metric and aims to optimize it.

The theory of intervals, T_{IC}, has been used for approximation in abstract interpretation since the very beginning [13]. However, the use of intervals in that context is for over-approximation, while ours is for under-approximation. Intervals have also been used in [25] to improve the efficiency of solving bit-vector formulas, and in [10], to approximate path constraints for concolic testing. The work of [7] uses fuzzing techniques on SMT formulas to increase their efficiency for fuzzing-related instances, and also makes use of intervals. Other methods of approximation were used to improve SMT solving [8,42]. However, to the best of our knowledge, this is the first work to use approximation for SMT sampling.

The notion of Model-Based Projection (MBP) [28] has some common ground with the notion of Model-Guided Approximation (MGA) (Sect. 3), but there are also some significant differences between the two; see discussion in the appendix [36].

8 Conclusion

We have shed some new light on the intriguing problem of sampling from the set of satisfying assignments for an SMT formula, by offering an alternative to the existing stochastic mutation-based approach. The reduction to an intermediate theory, such as the interval theories $T_{\text{IC}}, T_{\text{AUFIC}}$ that we used in our proof of concept and evaluation, sidesteps the need for intensive generate-and-test cycles, as model-guided approximation is guaranteed to be an underapproximation of the input formula from which we can freely sample without having to check, and possibly discard, some of the generated assignments. In a sense, model-guided approximation "squeezes the most" out of each seed. Our evaluation shows that the new approach indeed improves the performance of SMT sampling in practice.

Acknowledgements. The authors would like to thank Profs. Orna Grumberg and Ofer Strichman for their valuable input and contributions to this work. We would additionally like to thank the anonymous reviewers for their time and effort.

References

1. Achlioptas, D., Hammoudeh, Z.S., Theodoropoulos, P.: Fast sampling of perfectly uniform satisfying assignments. In: Beyersdorff, O., Wintersteiger, C.M. (eds.) SAT 2018. LNCS, vol. 10929, pp. 135–147. Springer, Cham (2018). https://doi.org/10.1007/978-3-319-94144-8_9
2. Agbaria, S., Carmi, D., Cohen, O., Korchemny, D., Lifshits, M., Nadel, A.: SAT-based semiformal verification of hardware. In: Formal Methods in Computer Aided Design, pp. 25–32 (2010)
3. Barrett, C., et al.: CVC4. In: Gopalakrishnan, G., Qadeer, S. (eds.) CAV 2011. LNCS, vol. 6806, pp. 171–177. Springer, Heidelberg (2011). https://doi.org/10.1007/978-3-642-22110-1_14
4. Barrett, C.W., Fontaine, P., Tinelli, C.: The satisfiability modulo theories library (SMT-LIB) (2021). https://smtlib.cs.uiowa.edu
5. Baumert, S., Ghate, A., Kiatsupaibul, S., Shen, Y., Smith, R.L., Zabinsky, Z.B.: Discrete hit-and-run for sampling points from arbitrary distributions over subsets of integer hyperrectangles. Oper. Res. **57**(3), 727–739 (2009)
6. Borralleras, C., Brockschmidt, M., Larraz, D., Oliveras, A., Rodríguez-Carbonell, E., Rubio, A.: Proving termination through conditional termination. In: Legay, A., Margaria, T. (eds.) Tools and Algorithms for the Construction and Analysis of Systems, pp. 99–117. Springer, Berlin, Heidelberg (2017)
7. Borzacchiello, L., Coppa, E., Demetrescu, C.: Fuzzing symbolic expressions. In: 2021 IEEE/ACM 43rd International Conference on Software Engineering (ICSE) (2021). https://doi.org/10.1109/icse43902.2021.00071
8. Bryant, R.E., Kroening, D., Ouaknine, J., Seshia, S.A., Strichman, O., Brady, B.: Deciding bit-vector arithmetic with abstraction. In: Grumberg, O., Huth, M. (eds.) TACAS 2007. LNCS, vol. 4424, pp. 358–372. Springer, Heidelberg (2007). https://doi.org/10.1007/978-3-540-71209-1_28

9. Chakraborty, S., Meel, K.S., Vardi, M.Y.: A scalable and nearly uniform generator of SAT witnesses. In: Sharygina, N., Veith, H. (eds.) CAV 2013. LNCS, vol. 8044, pp. 608–623. Springer, Heidelberg (2013). https://doi.org/10.1007/978-3-642-39799-8_40
10. Choi, J., Jang, J., Han, C., Cha, S.K.: Grey-box concolic testing on binary code. In: 2019 IEEE/ACM 41st International Conference on Software Engineering (ICSE), pp. 736–747. IEEE (2019)
11. Cimatti, A., Griggio, A., Schaafsma, B.J., Sebastiani, R.: The MathSAT5 SMT solver. In: Piterman, N., Smolka, S.A. (eds.) Tools and Algorithms for the Construction and Analysis of Systems. Lecture Notes in Computer Science, pp. 93–107. Springer, Cham (2013)
12. Clarke, E., Kroening, D., Yorav, K.: Behavioral consistency of C and Verilog programs using bounded model checking. In: Proceedings of the Design Automation Conference, pp. 368–371. IEEE (2003)
13. Cousot, P., Cousot, R.: Static determination of dynamic properties of programs. In: Proceedings of the Second International Symposium on Programming, pp. 106–130. Dunod, Paris, France (1976)
14. Dutertre, B.: Yices 2.2. In: Biere, A., Bloem, R. (eds.) CAV 2014. LNCS, vol. 8559, pp. 737–744. Springer, Cham (2014). https://doi.org/10.1007/978-3-319-08867-9_49
15. Dutra, R., Bachrach, J., Sen, K.: SMTSampler: efficient stimulus generation from complex SMT constraints. In: 2018 IEEE/ACM International Conference on Computer-Aided Design (ICCAD), pp. 1–8 (2018). https://doi.org/10.1145/3240765.3240848
16. Dutra, R., Bachrach, J., Sen, K.: Guidedsampler: coverage-guided sampling of SMT solutions. In: 2019 Formal Methods in Computer Aided Design (FMCAD), pp. 203–211 (2019). https://doi.org/10.23919/FMCAD.2019.8894251
17. Dutra, R., Laeufer, K., Bachrach, J., Sen, K.: Efficient sampling of SAT solutions for testing. In: Chaudron, M., Crnkovic, I., Chechik, M., Harman, M. (eds.) Proceedings of the 40th International Conference on Software Engineering, ICSE 2018, Gothenburg, Sweden, 27 May–03 June 2018, pp. 549–559. ACM (2018). https://doi.org/10.1145/3180155.3180248
18. Ermon, S., Gomes, C.P., Sabharwal, A., Selman, B.: Embed and project: discrete sampling with universal hashing. In: NIPS, pp. 2085–2093 (2013)
19. Ermon, S., Gomes, C.P., Selman, B.: Uniform solution sampling using a constraint solver as an oracle. arXiv preprint arXiv:1210.4861 (2012)
20. Giesl, J., Thiemann, R., Schneider-Kamp, P., Falke, S.: Automated termination proofs with AProVE. In: van Oostrom, V. (ed.) RTA 2004. LNCS, vol. 3091, pp. 210–220. Springer, Heidelberg (2004). https://doi.org/10.1007/978-3-540-25979-4_15
21. Glynn, P.W., Iglehart, D.L.: Importance sampling for stochastic simulations. Manag. Sci. **35**(11), 1367–1392 (1989)
22. Gurfinkel, A., Kahsai, T., Komuravelli, A., Navas, J.A.: The seahorn verification framework. In: CAV (2015)
23. Hastings, W.K.: Monte carlo sampling methods using markov chains and their applications. Biometrika **57**(1), 97–109 (1970)
24. Heizmann, M., Hoenicke, J., Podelski, A.: Software model checking for people who love automata. In: Sharygina, N., Veith, H. (eds.) CAV 2013. LNCS, vol. 8044, pp. 36–52. Springer, Heidelberg (2013). https://doi.org/10.1007/978-3-642-39799-8_2

25. Huang, H., Yao, P., Wu, R., Shi, Q., Zhang, C.: Pangolin: incremental hybrid fuzzing with polyhedral path abstraction. In: 2020 IEEE Symposium on Security and Privacy (SP), pp. 1613–1627. IEEE (2020)
26. Kitchen, N.: Markov Chain Monte Carlo Stimulus Generation for Constrained Random Simulation. Ph.D. thesis, University of California, Berkeley, USA (2010). http://www.escholarship.org/uc/item/6gp3z1t0
27. Kitchen, N., Kuehlmann, A.: Stimulus generation for constrained random simulation. In: Gielen, G.G.E. (ed.) 2007 International Conference on Computer-Aided Design, ICCAD 2007, San Jose, CA, USA, 5–8 November 2007, pp. 258–265. IEEE Computer Society (2007). https://doi.org/10.1109/ICCAD.2007.4397275
28. Komuravelli, A., Gurfinkel, A., Chaki, S.: SMT-based model checking for recursive programs. Formal Methods Syst. Des. **48**(3), 175–205 (2016)
29. Liu, J.S.: Metropolized independent sampling with comparisons to rejection sampling and importance sampling. Stat. Comput. **6**(2), 113–119 (1996)
30. Meel, K.S.: Sampling techniques for Boolean satisfiability. CoRR abs/1404.6682 (2014). http://arxiv.org/abs/1404.6682
31. Meel, K.S., et al.: Constrained sampling and counting: Universal hashing meets sat solving. In: Workshops at the Thirtieth AAAI Conference on Artificial Intelligence (2016)
32. de Moura, L., Bjørner, N.: Z3: an efficient SMT solver. In: Ramakrishnan, C.R., Rehof, J. (eds.) TACAS 2008. LNCS, vol. 4963, pp. 337–340. Springer, Heidelberg (2008). https://doi.org/10.1007/978-3-540-78800-3_24
33. Nadel, A.: Generating diverse solutions in SAT. In: Sakallah, K.A., Simon, L. (eds.) SAT 2011. LNCS, vol. 6695, pp. 287–301. Springer, Heidelberg (2011). https://doi.org/10.1007/978-3-642-21581-0_23
34. Naveh, Y., et al.: Constraint-based random stimuli generation for hardware verification. AI Mag. **28**(33), 13–13 (2007)
35. Ozols, M., Roetteler, M., Roland, J.: Quantum rejection sampling. ACM Trans. Comput. Theory **5**(3), 11:1–11:33 (2013)
36. Peled, M., Rothenberg, B.C., Itzhaky, S.: SMT sampling via model-guided approximation. CoRR (arXiv) (2022)
37. van Ravenzwaaij, D., Cassey, P., Brown, S.D.: A simple introduction to Markov chain monte-Carlo sampling. Psychon. Bull. Rev. **25**(1), 143–154 (2018)
38. Shapiro, A.: Monte Carlo sampling methods, stochastic programming, vol. 10, pp. 353–425. Elsevier (2003)
39. Sharma, S., Gupta, R., Roy, S., Meel, K.S.: Knowledge compilation meets uniform sampling. In: LPAR, pp. 620–636 (2018)
40. Tokdar, S.T., Kass, R.E.: Importance sampling: a review. WIREs Comput. Stat. **2**(1), 54–60 (2010)
41. Wei, W., Erenrich, J., Selman, B.: Towards efficient sampling: exploiting random walk strategies. In: AAAI, Vol. 4, pp. 670–676 (2004)
42. Yao, P., Shi, Q., Huang, H., Zhang, C.: Fast bit-vector satisfiability. In: Proceedings of the 29th ACM SIGSOFT International Symposium on Software Testing and Analysis, pp. 38–50 (2020)

Efficient SMT-Based Network Fault Tolerance Verification

Yu Liu[1], Pavle Subotic[2], Emmanuel Letier[3], Sergey Mechtaev[3](✉), and Abhik Roychoudhury[1]

[1] National University of Singapore, Queenstown, Singapore
{liuyu,abhik}@comp.nus.edu.sg

[2] Microsoft, Beograd, Serbia
pavlesubotic@microsoft.com

[3] University College London, London, UK
{e.letier,s.mechtaev}@ucl.ac.uk

Abstract. Network control planes are highly sophisticated, resulting in networks that are difficult and error-prone to configure. Although several network verification tools have been developed to assist network operators, they are limited and inefficient in handling fault-tolerance policies. In this paper, we propose a novel SMT encoding to speed up control plane fault tolerance verification by pruning failed topologies. This encoding exploits the observation that the verifier has to check failures only for the links lying on a set of best paths which can be computed by a recursive algorithm. We implemented our technique in Minesweeper, a state-of-the-art SMT-based verifier. Our evaluation shows that the new encoding speeds up verification by the factor of 3.1–26.9X.

1 Introduction

Correctly configuring modern computer networks is hard due to their size and complexity. The total lines of the low-level network configuration code may reach millions [6]. To alleviate network operators' burden, automatic control plane verifiers [1,4,16] have been proposed. These tools take network configurations as input and analyze them to gauge the possible routing behaviours. Then, they answer questions such as whether router A computes a route to router B, *i.e.* reachability policy, or whether router A computes a route to router B regardless of any number of failed links, *i.e.* fault-tolerance reachability policy.

SMT-based network verifiers have been successfully employed on large scale industrial networks [8,9]. These tools encode the network verification problem in logic and rely on the SMT solver to check the encoded property. For these verifiers, fault-tolerant policies are particularly challenging. SMT-based verifiers are inefficient in checking fault-tolerance policies, because their algorithms do not scale to the number of possible failed topologies, which combinatorially grows with the number of failed links. For example, a widely-used verifier Minesweeper [4] encodes all possible failed topologies using SMT constraints.

To address the combinatorial explosion of the failed topologies, we propose an SMT encoding that prunes the space of topologies by eliminating those that

M. Chechik et al. (Eds.): FM 2023, LNCS 14000, pp. 92–100, 2023.
https://doi.org/10.1007/978-3-031-27481-7_7

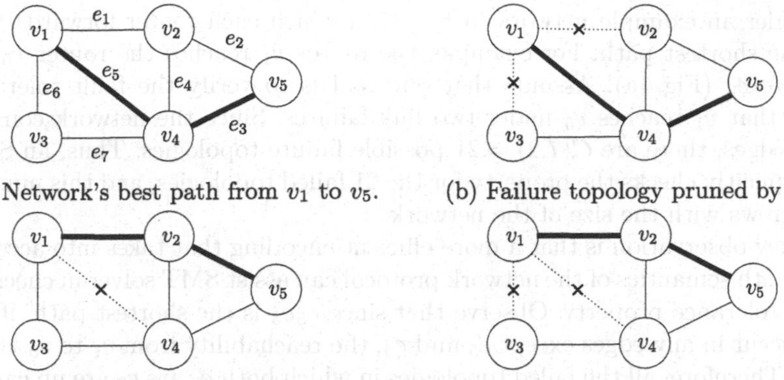

(a) Network's best path from v_1 to v_5. (b) Failure topology pruned by RBP.

(c) New best path after the link e_5 fails. (d) Extra failure topology pruned by RBP.

Fig. 1. Topologies pruned by recursive best path optimization.

are guaranteed not to change the verification result. We refer to this encoding as *recursive best path optimization (RBP)*. Our SMT encoding represents information about best paths using logical constraints, and applies cardinality constraints to control the number of network failures. This proposed encoding significantly improves performance of fault tolerance verification in similar tools [4].

We have implemented our proposed approach as the open source tool[1] Trailblazer, a variant of Minesweeper with the RBP encoding. We have evaluated Trailblazer on three benchmarks from the zoo topology [14] and a network from Rocketfuel [17]. The results show that Trailblazer is 3.1–26.9X faster than Minesweeper, while being able to verify the same policies. Our contributions are listed as the following:

- A novel SMT encoding for optimising network fault tolerance verification.
- A comprehensive evaluation of Trailblazer on widely-used benchmarks.

2 Motivation

Let V be the nodes of a network, and $E \subseteq V \times V$ be its edges. The SMT-based verifier Minesweeper encodes the network fault-tolerance verification problem under k link failures into the formula $\psi \wedge \xi_k \wedge \neg\pi$, where ψ encodes network behaviour, π is the property of interest, and ξ_k encodes that the number of failed links, controlled by the pseudo-boolean variables $failed_e$, is bound by k:

$$\xi_k \triangleq \Sigma_{e \in E} failed_e \leq k \tag{1}$$

If an SMT solver determines that the formula is unsatisfiable, the policy holds on all possible network topologies with at most k link failures.

[1] https://github.com/rainLiuplus/trailblazer.

Consider an example network in Fig. 1, in which each router forwards traffic via the shortest path. For example, the router v_1 reaches the router v_5 via the path e_5e_3 (Fig. 1a). Assume that our goal is to verify the fault tolerance property that v_1 reaches v_5 under two link failures. Since the network consists of seven edges, there are $C(7,2) = 21$ possible failure topologies. Thus, an SMT solver implicitly checks the property for the 21 failed topologies, and this number quickly grows with the size of the network.

Our key observation is that a more efficient encoding that takes into account the best path semantics of the network protocol can assist SMT solver in checking the fault tolerance property. Observe that since e_5e_3 is the shortest path, if the failures occur in any edges except e_5 and e_3, the reachability from v_1 to v_5 is not affected. Therefore, all the failed topologies in which both e_5 are e_3 are up can be pruned. An example of such a topology is given Fig. 1b. Moreover, significantly more topologies can be pruned if we analyze the new best paths that appear after an edge on the previous best paths fails. Assume that e_5 fails. Then, e_5e_3 no longer exists, and the network computes a new best path from v_1 to v_5, *e.g.* e_1e_2 (Fig. 1c). Then, we need to only consider all single-edge failures for this failed topology. Similar to the previous case, the topologies whose dropped links are not in $\{e_1, e_2\}$ can be pruned. Thus, the topologies whose two dropped links are in $\{(e_5, e_6), (e_5, e_7), (e_5, e_3), (e_5, e_4)\}$ can be pruned. An example is given in Fig. 1d. The link e_2 can be handled similarly. Totally, this optimisation prunes 17 of 21 topologies. We refer to this optimisation as RBP.

We apply RBP by adding stronger constraints ξ_k. Instead of the formula 1, we encode network semantics under link failures it as

$$\xi_k \triangleq \mathit{failed}_{e_5} \rightarrow \mathit{AtLeast}(1, \{\mathit{failed}_{e_1}, \mathit{failed}_{e_2}\}) \wedge ...$$

where $\mathit{failed}_{e_5} \rightarrow \mathit{AtLeast}(1, \{\mathit{failed}_{e_1}, \mathit{failed}_{e_2}\})$ states that if e_5 fails, the second failed link should be on the new best path (Fig. 1d). This is repeated recursively for all edges on the best paths up to a configurable depth d. This encoding significantly optimises constraint solving as shown in Sect. 4.

3 Trailblazer

In this section, we first provide background on network verification, then discuss the details of Trailblazer.

3.1 Background

For a node v and a destination node dst, a network protocol computes the *forwarding path(s)* FP_v, a set of sequences of edges for forwarding traffic to dst. We denote the set of forwarding paths of all nodes to dst as $\mathcal{FP} \triangleq \{FP_v | v \in V\}$. A network policy is a predicate ϕ over $\mathcal{FP}$. For example, $\mathit{Reachability}_v(\mathcal{FP})$ states that FP_v is not empty. To verify a policy is to check if $\phi(\mathcal{FP})$ holds. A failed link in the network topology changes the forwarding paths. So, to verify a policy ϕ under k failed links, we need to check ϕ on $C(|E|, k)$ failed topologies.

Table 1. Common network policies

Predicate (ϕ)	Policy	Description
$Reachability_v$	$FP_v \neq \emptyset$	Traffic $v \rightarrow dst$ can reach dst
$Waypoint_{(v,w)}$	$w \in nodes(FP_v)$	Traffic $v \rightarrow dst$ traverses node w
$Isolation_v$	$FP_v = \emptyset$	Traffic $v \rightarrow dst$ cannot reach dst
$Balance_v$	$\lvert FP_v \rvert \geq 2$	Mutiple paths for traffic $v \rightarrow dst$

Four common network policies are reachability, waypoint, isolation and balance shown in Table 1. Note that the balance policy is the only one that deals with sets of best paths.

Minesweeper is an SMT-based network verifier, which reduces the verification problem to an SMT problem. Minesweeper's encoding given in Sect. 2 is described in more details in Sects. 3–5 of their paper [4].

3.2 Our Approach

Trailblazer improves the SMT encoding of Minesweeper using additional constraints that capture network semantics under failures, and optimises the encoding using cardinality constraints. The key intuition of our optimisation is that failed links outside of the best path do not affect the network semantics. To capture this intuition, we add extra constraint λ_L to restrict the failure model:

$$\lambda_L \triangleq \Sigma_{e \in L} failed_e \geq 1 \tag{2}$$

where L is the set of links in the best path. The encoding of the failure model now becomes:

$$\xi_k \triangleq \Sigma_{e \in E} failed_e \leq k \wedge \lambda_L \tag{3}$$

We first acquire the best paths corresponding to all failure topologies by leveraging Batfish [9]. After obtaining this mapping, we encode them to SMT formulas. RBP works by recursively dropping a link in the best path, then treating the current network with one failed link as new network and compute the new best path on it. We encode these recursive best paths as formulas. For example, if the dropped link is e' and the corresponding best path is L', then they should be encoded as $failed_{e'} \rightarrow \lambda_{L'}$. Similarly, if another edge e'' fails in L' and the new best path is L'', the encoding should be $failed_{e'} \rightarrow failed_{e''} \rightarrow \lambda_{L''}$. The encoding could be interpreted as: if e' is broken and e'' is broken, the remained broken links can only be in L''. Let E_f be the set of failed links and L be the corresponding best path of the topology with E_f dropped. The constraint for restricting the failure model under E_f and L is:

$$\bigwedge_{e \in E_f} failed_e \rightarrow \lambda_L \tag{4}$$

This constraint states that if all links in E_f are down, then there is at least one link should be dropped in its corresponding best path L.

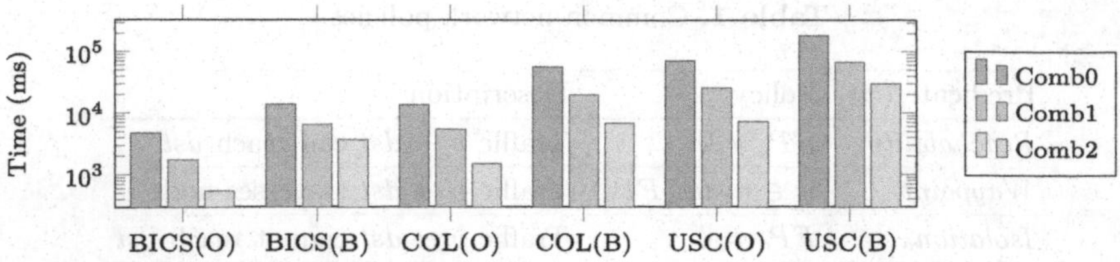

Fig. 2. Verification time of Minesweeper and Trailblazer for k=2, d=1.

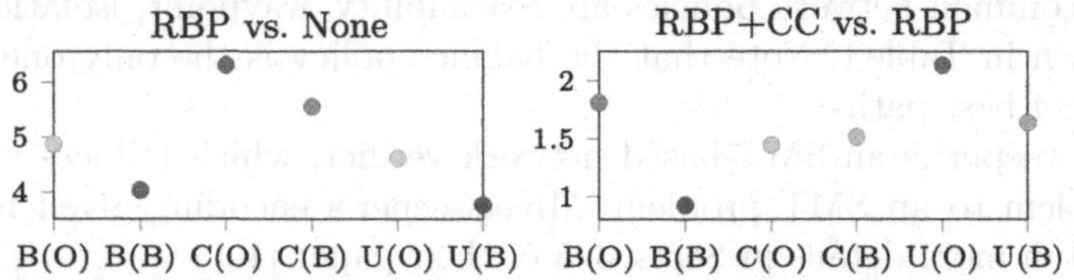

(a) Recursive best path optimization. **(b)** Cardinality constraints.

Fig. 3. Speedup for the two optimisations in isolation.

To efficiently encode the failure model, we applied cardinality constraints [2] instead of the integer inequalities used by Minesweeper. Cardinality constraints efficiently place a bound on the number of literals within a given set that can be assigned True. So, given the constraints in Eq. (1) and Eq. (2) where $failed_e$ is replaced with a boolean binary variable, they are naturally meet the semantics of AtMost and AtLeast constraints, respectively.

4 Evaluation

We conducted experiments on three networks selected from topology zoo [14]: Bics, Columbus and USCarrier, and the network AS1755 from Rocketfuel [17]. Bics consists of 33 routers and 48 links; Columbus has 70 routers and 85 links; USCarrier includes 158 routers and 189 links; AS1755 has 87 routers and 322 links. Each network from topology zoo has two types of network configuration, OSPF and BGP. We collect test policies by using Config2Spec's sampler [7], which infers policies from a data plane. We inferred four kinds of policies: reachability, waypoint, isolation and balance (see Sect. 3.1 for details). The policies that never hold were filtered out using the trimmer of Config2Spec. We considered four failure models where $k \in [1..4]$, representing there are at most 1, 2, 3 or 4 failed links respectively. We ran experiments on a machine with 64 GB RAM and 56 virtual cores with 2.00 GHz. We cross-checked the verification outputs of Trailblazer and Minesweeper; their verification results were all consistent.

To compare Trailblazer with the vanilla Minesweeper and identify how the proposed techniques contribute to its results, we compared three configurations of Trailblazer: **Comb0** with no optimization (original Minesweeper), **Comb1** with recursive best path optimization, and **Comb2** with recursive best path

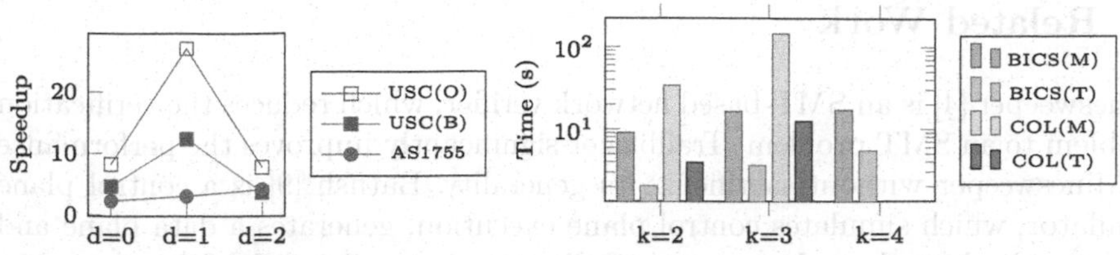

(a) Trailblazer's speedup with $d \in$ [0..2]; k=3 for USC; k=4 for AS1755.

(b) Time of Minesweeper (M) and Trailblazer (T) with k=2,3,4 and d=1.

Fig. 4. Trailblazer's performance depending on failed links and recursion depth.

optimization + cardinality constraints (Sect. 3.2). We run the three combinations on BICS, Columbus and USCarrier under the failure model k=2 with the recursion depth d=1. Comb0 and Comb2 in Fig. 2 shows the verification time of Minesweeper and Trailblazer. The time is averaged over all policies. The 'O' and 'B' inside brackets denote OSPF and BGP respectively. The average verification time of Minesweeper for OSPF networks is ranged from 4.71 s to 71.63 s, for BGP networks is 13.65 s–185.53 s. Trailblazer takes 0.53 s–7.25 s for OSPF networks and 3.64 s–29.91 s for BGP networks. Overall, Trailblazer is faster than Minesweeper by the factor of 3.75–9.88X.

To evaluate the effectiveness of RBP and cardinality constraints in isolation, we compared Comb0 with Comb1 and Comb1 with Comb2. The results are shown in Fig. 3, where B,C,U represents BICS, Columbus, USCarrier respectively; O and B denote OSPF and BGP. RBP results in speedup from 3.78X to 6.31X. By using cardinality constraints, the verifier is accelerated by 0.92X–2.14X as shown in Fig. 3(b).

To investigate how Trailblazer's performance vary with number of failed links and recursion depth, we conducted two sets of experiments. First, we set the tested failure models as k=2,3,4 and recursion depth d=1. The results of an experiment with Columbus and Bics are shown in Fig. 4b. All sampled Columbus' policies are pre-pruned when k=4. The speedup ranges from 3.14X to 15.92X. Verification is accelerated the most when k=3, while it is improved the least when k=4. We speculate that when k is large, the policy tends not to hold, and thus it is easier for the solver to find a solution, thus it will benefit less from the pruned search space. Second, we set the failure model to k=3,4 and recursion depths to d=0,1,2. We use USCarrier and AS1755 as the experimental networks. The results shown in Fig. 4a demonstrate that d=1 is the optimal recursion depth in USCarrier networks, with the highest speedup reaching 26.94x, while AS1755 has the best performance at d=2. We speculate that the performance will not keep increasing as *d* increases, since increasing the depth also increases the overhead for computing the best paths.

5 Related Work

Minesweeper [4] is an SMT-based network verifier, which reduces the verification problem to an SMT problem. Trailblazer significantly improves the performance of Minesweeper without sacrificing its generality. Batfish [9] is a control plane simulator, which simulates control plane execution, generates a data plane and analyses the data plane. In respect to fault-tolerance policies, Batfish enumerates every failed topology, an approach that doesn't scale in practice. Plankton [16] models different routing protocols by simple path vector protocol [12]. It uses an explicit model checker, Spin [13], to thoroughly explore the possible network states to check whether there exists a state that violates the queried policy. For fault-tolerance, it checks the policies by naive enumeration, which negatively affects its performance. Plankton implementation is not publicly available. ARC [10] models the network as a graph. It performs verification by standard graph algorithms which are ensured to be polynomial. As a result scales for fault-tolerance policies. However, it is incapable of representing some common network features, including BGP local preferences and communities. Tiramisu [1] is an improved version of ARC. It can support richer network features. However, it trades the scope of its application for verification efficiency e.g. it does not verify properties such as the loop freedom and cannot compute counter-examples. Netdice [18] is a probabilistic verifier which can prune the failed topologies when verifying iBGP networks. Our technique performs similar pruning decisions via an SMT encoding, and it is more general e.g., supports eBGP networks. Surgeries [15] and Bonsai [5] both exploits structural symmetry of network to accelerate verification for network. They achieve good performance when networks are highly symmetrical, but none of them can verify properties pertaining to when network failures may occur. Origami [11] targets on fault-tolerance verification, but it focuses on symmetrical networks and only reasons about reachability policies. MonoSAT [3] is an SMT solver that is efficient at solving problems involving monotonic theories. The reachability policy is monotonic with respect to links since removing a link can decrease the network's reachability but cannot increase it. The same applies to the isolation policy. However, other policies like waypoint and balance are not monotonic, so MonoSAT is unable to verify them efficiently.

6 Conclusion

In this paper, we proposed an SMT encoding that significantly accelerates the verification of network fault tolerance properties by pruning the space of topologies that are guaranteed not to change the verification result. We implemented this new encoding in the open source tool Trailblazer, a variant of the state-of-the-art verifier Minesweeper with the optimised encoding. Our evaluation shows that Trailblazer significantly improves verification performance compared to Minesweeper, with the highest speedups reaching 26.9X.

References

1. Abhashkumar, A., Gember-Jacobson, A., Akella, A.: Tiramisu: fast multilayer network verification. In: 17th USENIX Symposium on Networked Systems Design and Implementation (NSDI 2020), pp. 201–219 (2020)
2. Abío, I., Nieuwenhuis, R., Oliveras, A., Rodríguez-Carbonell, E.: A Parametric approach for smaller and better encodings of cardinality constraints. In: Schulte, C. (ed.) CP 2013. LNCS, vol. 8124, pp. 80–96. Springer, Heidelberg (2013). https://doi.org/10.1007/978-3-642-40627-0_9
3. Bayless, S., Bayless, N., Hoos, H., Hu, A.: SAT modulo monotonic theories. In: Proceedings of the AAAI Conference on Artificial Intelligence, vol. 29 (2015)
4. Beckett, R., Gupta, A., Mahajan, R., Walker, D.: A general approach to network configuration verification. In: Proceedings of the Conference of the ACM Special Interest Group on Data Communication, pp. 155–168 (2017)
5. Beckett, R., Gupta, A., Mahajan, R., Walker, D.: Control plane compression. In: Proceedings of the 2018 Conference of the ACM Special Interest Group on Data Communication, pp. 476–489 (2018)
6. Beckett, R., Gupta, A., Mahajan, R., Walker, D.: Abstract interpretation of distributed network control planes. Proc. ACM Program. Lang. **4**(POPL), 1–27 (2019)
7. Birkner, R., Drachsler-Cohen, D., Vanbever, L., Vechev, M.: Config2spec: mining network specifications from network configurations. In: 17th {USENIX} Symposium on Networked Systems Design and Implementation ({NSDI} 20), pp. 969–984 (2020)
8. Backes, J., et al.: Reachability analysis for AWS-based networks. In: Dillig, I., Tasiran, S. (eds.) CAV 2019. LNCS, vol. 11562, pp. 231–241. Springer, Cham (2019). https://doi.org/10.1007/978-3-030-25543-5_14
9. Fogel, A., et al.: A general approach to network configuration analysis. In: 12th {USENIX} Symposium on Networked Systems Design and Implementation ({NSDI} 15), pp. 469–483 (2015)
10. Gember-Jacobson, A., Viswanathan, R., Akella, A., Mahajan, R.: Fast control plane analysis using an abstract representation. In: Proceedings of the 2016 ACM SIGCOMM Conference, pp. 300–313 (2016)
11. Giannarakis, N., Beckett, R., Mahajan, R., Walker, D.: Efficient verification of network fault tolerance via counterexample-guided refinement. In: Dillig, I., Tasiran, S. (eds.) CAV 2019. LNCS, vol. 11562, pp. 305–323. Springer, Cham (2019). https://doi.org/10.1007/978-3-030-25543-5_18
12. Griffin, T.G., Shepherd, F.B., Wilfong, G.: The stable paths problem and interdomain routing. IEEE/ACM Trans. Netw. **10**(2), 232–243 (2002)
13. Holzmann, G.J.: The model checker spin. IEEE Trans. Softw. Eng. **23**(5), 279–295 (1997)
14. Knight, S., Nguyen, H.X., Falkner, N., Bowden, R., Roughan, M.: The internet topology zoo. IEEE J. Sel. Areas Commun. **29**(9), 1765–1775 (2011)
15. Plotkin, G.D., Bjørner, N., Lopes, N.P., Rybalchenko, A., Varghese, G.: Scaling network verification using symmetry and surgery. ACM SIGPLAN Not. **51**(1), 69–83 (2016)
16. Prabhu, S., Chou, K.Y., Kheradmand, A., Godfrey, B., Caesar, M.: Plankton: scalable network configuration verification through model checking. In: 17th {USENIX} Symposium on Networked Systems Design and Implementation ({NSDI} 20), pp. 953–967 (2020)

17. Spring, N., Mahajan, R., Wetherall, D.: Measuring ISP topologies with Rocketfuel. ACM SIGCOMM Comput. Commun. Rev. **32**(4), 133–145 (2002)
18. Steffen, S., Gehr, T., Tsankov, P., Vanbever, L., Vechev, M.: Probabilistic verification of network configurations. In: Proceedings of the Annual conference of the ACM Special Interest Group on Data Communication on the Applications, Technologies, Architectures, and Protocols for Computer Communication, pp. 750–764 (2020)

Verification I

Formalising the Prevention of Microarchitectural Timing Channels by Operating Systems

Robert Sison[1,2](✉), Scott Buckley[2], Toby Murray[1], Gerwin Klein[2,3], and Gernot Heiser[2]

[1] The University of Melbourne, Melbourne, Australia
{robert.sison,toby.murray}@unimelb.edu.au
[2] UNSW Sydney, Sydney, Australia
{s.buckley,kleing,gernot}@unsw.edu.au
[3] Proofcraft, Sydney, Australia

FM Artifact Evaluation ★ Available

FM Artifact Evaluation ★★ Reproducible

Abstract. Microarchitectural timing channels are a well-known mechanism for information leakage. *Time protection* has recently been demonstrated as an operating-system mechanism able to prevent them. However, established theories of information-flow security are insufficient for verifying time protection, which must distinguish between (legal) overt and (illegal) covert flows. We provide a machine-checked formalisation of time protection via a dynamic, observer-relative, intransitive nonleakage property over a careful model of the state elements that cause timing channels. We instantiate and prove our property over a generic model of OS interaction with its users, demonstrating for the first time the feasibility of proving time protection for OS implementations.

1 Introduction

Microarchitectural timing channels present a major attack vector on information security [12], with the Spectre attacks demonstrating that even seemingly innocuous code can be subverted into a Trojan that leaks secrets via such channels [20]. Ge et al. recently introduced *time protection* mechanisms to prevent microarchitectural channels, experimentally demonstrating their effectiveness [11] on a modified version of the seL4 operating system (OS) microkernel [19].

While seL4 comes with an extensive body of formal proofs, including information-flow enforcement and freedom from storage channels [24], these proofs do not consider properties about timing channels; the same is true for other OS security proofs [2,8,21]. Work that does consider timing does not extend to the full OS [4] or assumes mechanisms that are too expensive in practice [3].

Reasoning about timing channels is challenging, as timing is a non-functional property and hardware details that affect timing are intentionally unspecified to enable optimisations. While the correctness of time protection can, in principle, be reduced to functional properties [15], to date there is not even a precise formulation of the security property it is meant to enforce.

M. Chechik et al. (Eds.): FM 2023, LNCS 14000, pp. 103–121, 2023.
https://doi.org/10.1007/978-3-031-27481-7_8

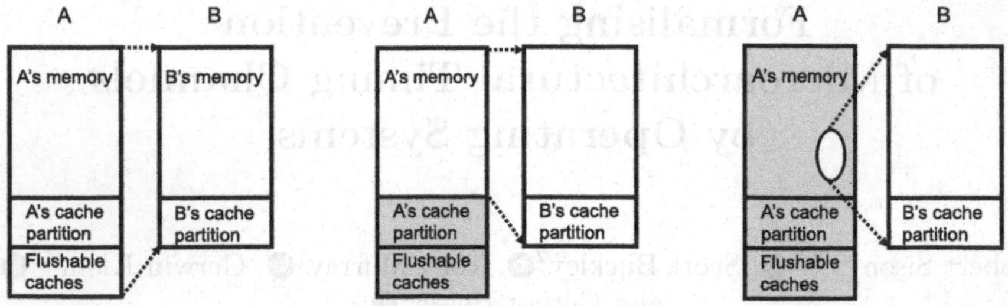

(a) Channels that would be allowed by the property of Murray et al. [24, 25] at all times that A is running.

(b) *Time protection* excludes channels via microarchitectural state used by A when it is running.

(c) *Policy channels* our property can enforce to be open only when A makes a specific system call.

Fig. 1. Restriction of information flow allowed from domain A to B to occur only via the channel indicated by the dotted lines, i.e. not from any shaded regions.

Stating and verifying such a property faces two core challenges. Firstly, the complexity of microarchitectural state requires abstraction to make formal reasoning feasible, while retaining sufficient precision to allow proving a meaningful isolation property. Secondly, time protection is, by its nature, an *asymmetric* property: A (trusted) security domain, e.g. a downgrader, may have the right to communicate with another domain, but this *overt information flow* must happen in the absence of any *covert information flow* (through timing channels). This point is explained later in Sect. 4.1.

To address the first challenge we formalise (Sect. 3) an abstraction of the state elements related to temporal flows and their interaction with time, which distinguishes overt memory state from covert microarchitectural state. The abstraction separates that covert state according to the applicable elimination mechanisms (spatial or temporal partitioning), as proposed by Heiser et al. [15,16] and based on a minimally-augmented *hardware–software contract* [13].

We address the second challenge (Sect. 4) by formalising a *dynamic* and *observer-relative* intransitive nonleakage property. This property generalises the one used for seL4 by Murray et al. [24,25] (Fig. 1a), to enforce elimination of flows via microarchitectural state (Fig. 1b). We find that this requires a form of *policy channel specification*, which allows arbitrary *spatial* precision, i.e. to specify *from where* flows can occur. The natural formalisation of such specifications also supports arbitrary *temporal* precision, i.e. dynamic policy on *when* flows can occur, as depicted by Fig. 1c. The observation relation specifying policy channels from a running domain A, as well as the granularity of steps between observation points, are then both relative to the observer domain B.

Finally, we instantiate and prove (Sect. 5) our property over a generic model of OS interaction with a formalisation of the threat scenario presented in Sect. 2. In doing so, we demonstrate the first formal approach to capture a precise, fine-grained, time-protection property, even in the presence of the greater spatial and temporal precision of the policy channel specifications it enables.

All our results are formalised and machine checked using the Isabelle/HOL interactive proof assistant [26] and are provided as supplement material [5].

2 Threat Scenario

We adopt the threat scenario of Heiser et al. [15]: A *spy* in one security domain attempts to obtain information from a *sender* in a different domain in violation of the system's security policy. We assume the defender's worst-case scenario where the sender is a Trojan that deliberately attempts to leak information, i.e. a *covert channel*. If we can prevent this information flow, we implicitly rule out inadvertent leaks (i.e. *side channels*).

Specifically we are looking at leakage through *microarchitectural timing channels* [12]. These result from microarchitectural state, i.e. hardware state hidden by the hardware–software contract (i.e. *instruction-set architecture*) but affected by program execution. This includes caches and other hardware features whose state depends on execution history, such as branch predictors and prefetchers.

We assume that the spy has access to an independent time source. The spy observes the speed of its own progress, looking for variance in execution speed that cannot be explained by any information to which it already has access (i.e. its own state). This includes the latency of memory accesses [14,27,28,36], the latency of system calls operating on deterministic user state [11], or preemption periods resulting from interrupts [11].

Such latency variations can be the result of the sender's manipulation of microarchitectural state, which can happen through accessing memory in specific patterns, executing system calls with specific arguments, or initiating input-output (I/O) operations that result in interrupts at a time chosen by the sender.

Importantly, covert channels must be precluded even where overt channels are permitted. For example, consider an off-the-shelf web browser consisting of hundreds of thousands of lines of code; it handles secret information (e.g. passwords supplied by the user) but cannot be trusted to keep it secret. The web browser runs in security domain H. It communicates with the outside world via an untrusted network interface, running in domain L. The system's security policy requires that H can only communicate with L (and thus the outside world) via a trusted encryption/filter server, acting as a *downgrader*, running in domain D. While there is an overt channel $H \rightsquigarrow D \rightsquigarrow L$, the system must prevent H from using a timing channel that bypasses D. In addition, the system should prevent covert channels between H and D, even when an overt channel is permitted, and likewise between D and L, as otherwise D might unwittingly act as a courier for covert channel information between H and L.[1]

We use the term *policy channel* to refer to information flow that is explicitly permitted by the system's security policy and represented by OS *protection*

[1] Ensuring that it does not act as a courier requires very sophisticated reasoning about D, e.g. proving that it obeys constant-time programming discipline [1,6].

state, such as access control lists, or capabilities [10]; for example, seL4 uses the latter. *Time protection* then becomes the requirement that a confidentiality property is enforced, which prevents any information flow other than through policy channels. We propose such a policy in Sect. 4.

Reasoning about time protection requires a system model that makes timing channels explicit, by including microarchitectural state. The challenge is to keep this model sufficiently abstract to apply to a wide class of real processors, yet precise enough to allow reasoning about timing channels and their prevention. We present such a model in Sect. 3. In Sect. 5 we present an OS security model, parameterised over OS-specific features and processor-specific implementation details, using our model of microarchitectural state to prove enforcement of a time protection property; we hope it will serve as a roadmap for proving the effectiveness of time protection implementations (e.g. Ge et al. [11] for seL4).

3 Modelling Channels by Elimination Strategy

As observed in Sect. 2, we need a model of microarchitectural state. This must be sufficiently precise to support reasoning about the absence of channels that exploit it, while abstracting away as many implementation details as possible, so it can apply to a large class of real processors. We defer to Sect. 5 a description of our full state model, depicted in Fig. 3b; here, we explain the philosophy behind its microarchitectural and other timing-affecting elements.

Heiser et al. [15] observe that, to implement time protection, the OS only needs to know how microarchitectural state can be partitioned between security domains. Partitioning can either be *spatial*, where the OS can force a domain to only access a specific part of the state, or *temporal*, where state is exclusively owned by one partition at a time, and reset to a defined state when the OS hands ownership to another partition. Implementing time protection is possible if the hardware–software contract ensures that microarchitectural state can be partitioned either spatially or temporally, where the latter comes down to the OS being given a mechanism to reset (flush) that state.

For simplicity, we refer to state that can be spatially partitioned as *partitionable*, while state that can be temporally partitioned we call *flushable*.

To reason about how usermode execution may affect such state, we assume that this happens exclusively through referencing memory (data or instruction) addresses. This matches typical real hardware, for which any state directly accessed by programs is architected and explicitly context-switched by the OS; for such hardware, microarchitectural state can only be accessed indirectly via addresses. Note that programs (including the OS) can only issue *virtual addresses*.

3.1 Flushable Microarchitectural State

For our purposes it is not necessary to distinguish between different parts of flushable state (e.g. caches vs. branch-predictor state vs. prefetcher state), even if the hardware provides different mechanisms for flushing different parts of it.

We only need to deal with the complete collection of such state, and treat the sum of flushing mechanisms as a single operation.

Furthermore, it does not matter whether issuing distinct addresses affects different parts of microarchitectural state (as with caches) or causes different changes in the same state (as with state machines used in prefetchers). All that matters is capturing *which* state might be affected; for that we can make the worst-case assumption that each address in a domain maps to potentially different state, but some address in a different domain may map to the same state.

Thus we model *flushable state* (flst) as a simple function from address to boolean, representing whether a state referred by a particular address is currently affected – the entire flst is considered observable to the currently executing program. We model OS and user operations to modify flst in an under-defined way, assuming that secrets of the currently running domain can be stored in flst.

In the absence of flushing, our confidentiality property will not hold for this configuration, as secrets are being transmitted through flst. We therefore need to show that the OS performs the flush when switching domains, but also that any changes made to flst during the domain switch (during which the OS must issue addresses) have a deterministic effect on flst: After the flush, the OS must only issue addresses in a sequence that is not affected by user secrets.

3.2 Partitionable Microarchitectural State

Partitionable state generally exists outside the processor core (typically caches other than the on-core first-level cache). Such state is accessed by *physical address*, meaning it has undergone address translation by the memory-management unit (MMU). Partitioning may use explicit hardware mechanisms, or may be achieved by the OS restricting the address mapping so that addresses from different partitions access disjoint cache state (this is referred to as *page colouring* [11,17,22]). This assumes that the OS understands how collisions may occur, which is realistic for contemporary hardware.

We model *partitionable state* (pst) as a function from address to boolean, similarly to flst. We do not explicitly model how cache collisions occur between addresses, instead we assume that the OS has set up the memory map to prevent collisions between partitions. By modeling both user and OS operations to only access memory visible to the present domain, we can show that no secrets are imprinted on the pst in a way that is visible to another domain.

However, the above assumptions break down if the OS accesses the same memory locations while operating on behalf of different user domains. This is unavoidable, as the OS must access memory while performing a domain switch, meaning that it is impossible to completely partition the OS's memory accesses. We call such non-partitionable memory *shared OS memory*, and its accesses may potentially leak secrets via their corresponding pst impacts.

We model this leak by parameterising our model over the set of all addresses in the shared OS memory in union with all addresses that collide with them. We then allow a user domain to affect the pst of that set, alongside pst corresponding to its own memory. This forces, at the time of domain switch, a flush of the pst for the shared OS addresses and their collisions, to ensure that they convey no secrets from the previously executing domain to the next one. The mechanism used, and cost incurred, for this flush depends on what the architecture offers.

3.3 Interrupts and Other Directly Observed Impacts on Time

We have thus far encoded the spy's ability to make time-related observations via variations in memory access latency as direct user observations of flst and pst, as these are the primary channels through which execution time can vary. However, some leaks can happen through observation of the real-time clock, which are not directly related to shared microarchitecture.

Interrupts are inherently non-deterministic (their arrival depends on the environment beyond the control of the OS). This can be used as a channel [11]: a domain initiates an I/O operation such that the interrupt indicating completion arrives while another domain is executing. The time the OS takes to handle the interrupt can be observed as a gap in execution by the preempted domain.

Time protection prevents this channel by partitioning interrupts between domains, masking off any interrupts not belonging to the current domain. The preemption-timer interrupt, which causes a domain switch, is not subject to this masking; the rest we call *user interrupts*. We will model hardware masking of user interrupts by asserting that they can only arise during user execution depending on the state of devices belonging to the current domain (Sect. 5.2).

Our model enforces the following timing properties of interrupt arrivals:

- Timer interrupts arrive at a fixed interval, aside from delays described below.
- User execution will continue until halted either by the timer interrupt arriving at its fixed-interval time, or by a user interrupt arriving before that.
- There is a worst-case execution time (WCET) for handling an interrupt. Handling a user interrupt may then delay the arrival of a timer interrupt by an amount of time up to that WCET after its fixed-interval time.

As interrupt-related leaks are always via accurate observation of the *time*, we now turn to how we model time to be treated as observable by our property.

We model time as a numeric field of the state, tm, which we consider to be observable only by the currently-running domain; others are only able to observe at what point in the schedule the OS resides currently, but not tm directly.

Rather than modelling any automatic progression of time, we bake it in manually as the following assumptions to our under-defined user and OS operations:

- Flushing the flst will take some amount of time that depends only on the original flst state, up to some predefined WCET.
- Partially flushing the pst (for shared OS memory) takes an amount of time that depends only on the part of pst being flushed, up to a predefined WCET.
- Interrupt-handling OS operations obey a predefined WCET (as just noted).
- The OS can perform a *padding* operation that will progress time to a specified value, without changing any other state (by decrementing a register-held counter in a tight loop, or possibly using hardware support [34]).

Our domain-switch operation performs the following tasks:

1. a partial flush of OS shared memory addresses in pst;
2. a full flush of the flst;
3. changing the currently running domain over to the next domain, according to the deterministic schedule (see Sect. 4);
4. padding to the end of the allocated time.

We know that the padding at the end of this operation will always get us to a predetermined time, as we calculate the end-of-switch time to account for the WCETs for flst and pst flushes, as well as accounting for a potentially late start due to the handling of a user interrupt before domain-switch. At the start of such a domain-switch, as well as at many points in the middle of these operations, the tm field contains secrets from the domain who just executed. However, these secrets are removed when we pad time to a predetermined value.

The actual amount of time allocated to each domain, as well as the sequence of domains scheduled to execute, is completely predetermined; it is not possible to influence how long each timeslice will be, or which domain will execute next. This is implemented via an appropriately adapted *scheduler oracle* [24], whose details we relegate to the Isabelle/HOL supplement material [5].

4 Formalising Time Protection

What does time protection mean formally, and why are previous security definitions [25], used to state absence of storage channels in OSes, insufficient to express it? In this section we answer these questions by formalising a new dynamic and observer-relative intransitive nonleakage property.

Let *domain* be the set of *security domains* ranged over by u, v, w, etc. Following Murray et al. [24,25], we distinguish *user domains*, which include one or more user-mode processes, from the *scheduler domain*, which represents the parts of the OS responsible for scheduling the execution of user-mode processes. Therefore let $\mathsf{sched} \in$ *domain* be the distinguished *scheduling domain*. At any time, a single domain is running, called the *current domain*: execution proceeds in a sequence of *steps* in which sched is interleaved between other domains (to choose the next domain that is to execute after the arrival of a timer interrupt).

Let *state* be the type of system states, s, t, etc. Then $\mathsf{dom}\ s$ denotes the current domain in state s. The part of the system state observable to domain u in state s is defined by an equivalence relation $\overset{u}{\sim}$, such that this part of the state is equal between states s and t iff $s \overset{u}{\sim} t$. The state of the scheduling domain includes which domain is currently running, hence: $s \overset{\mathsf{sched}}{\sim} t \implies \mathsf{dom}\ s = \mathsf{dom}\ t$ [25].

Information-flow security requires that for all domains u, for each step of execution, u only learns information it is supposed to. If time protection holds, what information is domain u allowed to learn? As in prior work [24,25] we prove deterministic scheduling. Therefore, at all times, all domains are assumed to know which domain is the current domain, i.e. all information given by $\overset{\mathsf{sched}}{\sim}$. Domain u is also allowed to learn everything it can observe (equivalently, already knows), i.e. all information given by $\overset{u}{\sim}$. Finally, it is also allowed to learn certain information communicated to it by the current domain in that execution step.

4.1 State-Dependent Policy Channels

One of our key insights is that according to time protection, what constitutes this "certain information" depends on whether u is the current domain, i.e. time protection is an *asymmetric* property. Specifically, when u is not the current domain, time protection says that at most it is allowed to learn the information communicated by the current domain via *overt* channels (those allowed by the current protection state); but none via *covert* channels (including microarchitectural state). This is strictly *less* than all information observable by the current domain, given by $\overset{\mathsf{dom}\ s}{\sim}$ where s is the state from which the step occurred, because $\overset{\mathsf{dom}\ s}{\sim}$ necessarily includes microarchitectural state visible to the current domain (e.g. its caches influencing its execution speed as captured in our model by tm).

Thus, departing from prior nonleakage properties, for two domains v and u let $\overset{|v \rightsquigarrow u|}{\sim}$ be a state equivalence relation that defines the part of the state whose contents domain v is allowed to send to domain u on an execution step. If v is allowed to send no information to u, then $\overset{|v \rightsquigarrow u|}{\sim}$ is the trivial relation that holds for all states. As we demonstrate later in Sect. 5, this formulation is sufficiently general to specify dynamic policies, since the part of the state via which domain v is allowed to communicate with u can depend on the state itself. We call $\overset{|v \rightsquigarrow u|}{\sim}$ a *policy channel*, as it defines the allowed channel from v to u.

With these definitions we can define our top-level security property as follows. For now, the argument u to each of $\mathsf{obs\text{-}reachable}\ u\ s$ and $\mathsf{obs\text{-}Step}\ u$ can be ignored (we will explain its meaning directly, in Sect. 4.2); the former can be read as saying that state s is reachable via a finite number of steps of the latter.

Definition 1 (Observer-relative big-step confidentiality).

$$\begin{array}{l} \mathsf{obs\text{-}confidentiality}\ u \triangleq \\ \forall s\ t.\ \mathsf{obs\text{-}reachable}\ u\ s \wedge \mathsf{obs\text{-}reachable}\ u\ t \longrightarrow \\ \quad s \overset{\mathsf{sched}}{\sim} t \longrightarrow s \overset{|\mathsf{dom}\ s \rightsquigarrow u|}{\sim} t \longrightarrow s \overset{u}{\sim} t \longrightarrow \\ \quad (\forall s'\ t'.\ (s, s') \in \mathsf{obs\text{-}Step}\ u \wedge (t, t') \in \mathsf{obs\text{-}Step}\ u \longrightarrow s' \overset{u}{\sim} t') \end{array}$$

This definition says that an arbitrary observer domain u, on an execution step, is allowed to learn the scheduler state ($\overset{\mathsf{sched}}{\sim}$), the information that the current domain is allowed to send it via the policy channel ($\overset{|\mathsf{dom}\ s \rightsquigarrow u|}{\sim}$), and anything it knew or could have observed already ($\overset{u}{\sim}$), by saying that if two initial, reachable states s and t agree on this information, then u's view of the states s' and t' reached after a single step must be identical: $s' \overset{u}{\sim} t'$.

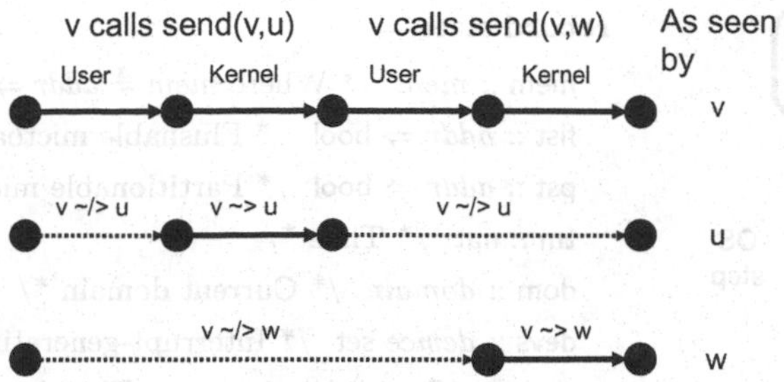

Fig. 2. Observer-relative state transition system model.

4.2 Policy-Dependent State Observability

What constitutes an execution step? Our second major observation is that, for time protection, the answer depends on which domain is observing the execution.

Figure 2 provides an illustration of this phenomenon. It depicts (top row) a single timeslice of domain v (the current domain), in which it performs two consecutive system calls. First it makes a system call to communicate with domain u, and then subsequently to communicate with domain w. For each system call, a user-mode step occurs in which v first computes the data it wishes to communicate (e.g. the system call arguments), followed by an OS step in which the OS carries out the system call (i.e. puts into effect the communication). For simplicity, assume the protection state authorises both system calls.

Let us consider what each domain u and w is allowed to observe and when. From u's point of view (middle row of Fig. 2), since v communicates with it, it implicitly learns that this communication has occurred. Thus it observes the occurrence of the second step (the first OS step) that v makes. However what v does before that step occurs should remain opaque: e.g. the precise number of user-mode state changes required to compute the system call arguments should not be revealed to u (though it can of course infer what the system call arguments must have been, and so those are observable to it).

From w's point of view (bottom row of Fig. 2), all of this activity is opaque: the precise number of execution steps that v performs prior to the OS step that carries out the communication from v to w should remain hidden to w. Indeed from w's point of view, v performs a single execution step from the beginning of its timeslice up to the OS step that performs the v-to-w communication.

Thus execution steps are very much in the eye of the beholder. Our time protection formalisation captures this idea as follows. We require the existence of an underlying *small-step* transition system that defines the system's behaviour. From this we construct for each domain u its *observer-relative, big-step* transition system that defines u's view of the system's execution by coalescing together consecutive small-steps between states that are unobservable to u. Which states are observable to u is naturally captured in the policy channel specification $\overset{|v \rightsquigarrow u|}{\sim}$:

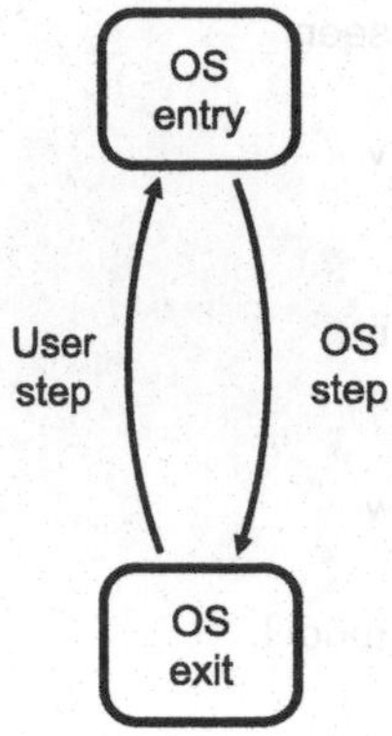

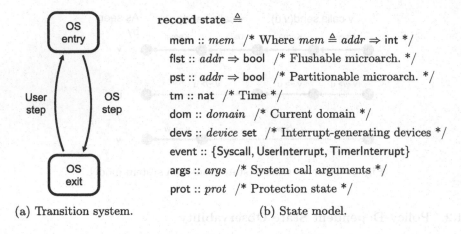

(a) Transition system.

record state ≜

mem :: *mem* /* Where *mem* ≜ *addr* ⇒ int */

flst :: *addr* ⇒ bool /* Flushable microarch. */

pst :: *addr* ⇒ bool /* Partitionable microarch. */

tm :: nat /* Time */

dom :: *domain* /* Current domain */

devs :: *device* set /* Interrupt-generating devices */

event :: {Syscall, UserInterrupt, TimerInterrupt}

args :: *args* /* System call arguments */

prot :: *prot* /* Protection state */

(b) State model.

Fig. 3. Generic OS on which we model enforcement of time protection.

When $s \overset{|\mathsf{dom}\ s \rightsquigarrow u|}{\sim} t$ such that this relation is non-trivial (i.e. the current domain is allowed to communicate with u), then state s is observable to domain u.

This explains why Definition 1 takes the observer domain u as an argument. This definition is defined against a set of big-step transition systems, one for each domain u, that defines u's view of the underlying system's small-step transition system. The state reachability predicate is also parameterised by the observing domain u: obs-reachable u s means that state s is reachable in u's big-step transition system. Similarly for the step relation: obs-Step u is the set of state transitions in the big-step transition system that represents u's view.

Our confidentiality property (Definition 1) is a generalisation of the one used for the seL4 microkernel [24,25], which is an intransitive nonleakage property that confines the allowed information flows to those according to a static (possibly intransitive) information flow policy "$\rightsquigarrow$": $v \rightsquigarrow u$ holds iff the policy permits information to flow directly from domain v (while v is the current domain) to domain u. Our property generalises theirs in that (1) fixing our policy channel relation $\overset{|\mathsf{dom}\ s \rightsquigarrow u|}{\sim}$ to be $\overset{\mathsf{dom}\ s}{\sim}$ whenever dom $s \rightsquigarrow u$ and the universal set otherwise, and (2) fixing all big-step transition systems to be the same for all observers u, results in their property (confidentiality-u, p9 of Murray et al. [24]).

5 System Model of OS-Enforced Time Protection

We have thus far presented an explanation of how to model covert state (Sect. 3) and a confidentiality property capable of distinguishing between overt and covert state (Sect. 4), both as needed to express and model time protection.

Here we apply these principles to demonstrate that, regardless of the set of system calls supported by the OS and the architecture that it runs on, an OS designer now has the means to prove formally that an OS implementation for any given architecture enforces time protection, as long as the designer: (1) can prove that each of its system call handling routines permits only information flow via policy channels that exclude microarchitecture, (2) has proved or can reliably assume the functionality of certain architectural features key to time protection, and (3) has reliably measured and bounded the WCETs of the above.

5.1 Model Overview and Property

We achieve this level of generality with a model (Fig. 3) that abstracts the essential elements of OS-enforced time protection over the following parameters:

1. an OS-specific set of system calls, their implementations, and specifications of their policy channels that can depend on arguments and protection state;
2. architecture-specific implementations of
   (a) an interrupt handling routine and
   (b) a domain switch routine that occurs on timer interrupt;
3. the WCETs of all of the above; and
4. the types of memory addresses *addr*, domain IDs *domain*, IRQ-generating device state *device*, syscall arguments *args*, and protection state *prot*.

Over this model, we instantiate our property so that Definition 1 expresses that the OS enforces time protection, in the sense that information only ever flows to a given user domain from the current domain's overt state elements (like a system call's arguments and relevant memory) as specified by some policy channel, and not ever via any covert state elements (like microarchitecture and user-configured device interrupts) that impact timing. Importantly, time (tm) and microarchitectural state that could influence memory access time (the entire flst, and the relevant pst partition) are always considered observable to the current domain, so our property ensures the absence of timing channels as directly observed after domain switch, and from subsequent variations in memory access latency, respectively. Formally, we then prove that Definition 1 holds at all times as seen by every possible user domain:

Theorem 1 (OS model enforces confidentiality with time protection).

$$\forall u.\ \mathsf{obs\text{-}confidentiality}\ u$$

Our model and its proofs are mechanised in about 7.9K lines of Isabelle/HOL proof script, of which about 2.1K lines are the adaptations described in Sect. 4 of prior mechanised theory [24,25,29] – all are provided as supplement material [5], whose documentation includes a detailed guide between their features as described in this paper and their corresponding proof script formalisations. The mechanisation also includes an instantiation of our generic model, for a pair of system calls with tightly specified policy channels, to ensure it is nontrivial.

We now describe the requirements our generic model imposes on an OS and its configuration that make it possible to prove that it enforces time protection. In particular, we believe that any OS that implements time protection, such as that of Ge et al. [11] for seL4, can satisfy all these requirements.

5.2 User Steps

The user-step model captures requirements on the memory subsystem and device hardware and their adequate configuration by the OS to ensure the partitioning between domains of (i) memory, through address *mappings*; (ii) caches, through *colouring*; and (iii) user-configured interrupts, through *masking*.

It also captures assumptions about the spy and sender: They can choose when to make a syscall and with which argument values, but cannot directly modify the OS protection state; furthermore, they can program their devices to cause interrupts. Thus, we model the reason for OS entry, system call arguments, and device state in the state fields event, args, and devs respectively (see Fig. 3b) and specify the user step as free to choose them in a manner dependent on the state accessible to the currently running domain. In contrast, we model protection state with field prot but disallow the user step from modifying it.

Memory and Cache Partitioning. We partition both memory and pst by security *domain*, assuming a mapping addr-domain :: $addr \Rightarrow domain$. We consider the parts of mem that belong to some domain u to be the input addresses where addr-domain $a = u$, and the same for pst.

User steps are restricted to those that do not read from or write to any part of mem that does not belong to the executing domain u. A similar restriction is enforced for pst, except that we do allow user steps to modify parts of the pst outside of u's domain if they are in the shared OS address set. While in reality OS memory will only be affected by system calls, allowing user modification of shared OS memory is a sound over-approximation that simplifies our model.

We implement these restrictions by "quarantining" a transition: we mask off any state that should not be accessed, perform the transition on this modified state, and then return the masked-off data to the output state. A transition that does not read or write outside of its domain will not be modified by quarantining. This process is similar to prior models of OS memory protection [9].

In reality, this kind of memory protection is implemented by the OS correctly configuring the MMU and is covered by typical integrity proofs [32]. Cache partitioning might be implemented via *colouring*. Shared OS memory is, by definition, not partitioned.

Interrupt and Device Partitioning. We partition interrupts by domain, via partitioning *devices* by domain. The state field devs abstracts the states of a set of devices, each assigned to some domain by a parameter device-domain :: $device \Rightarrow domain$. Note it is this assignment of ownership, and not the *device* type we abstract over, that matters for our model; furthermore, we assume that separate devices do not communicate with each other.

We abstract interactions with devices via mostly-arbitrary modifications to the devs field, specifying that user steps (as well as interrupt-handling and syscall steps) can only access or modify the device subset belonging to the currently executing domain. Further, we model the user as being able to choose the event indicating the reason for entry into the OS to be set to UserInterrupt or TimerInterrupt in a manner dependent on that device subset. This model allows us to reason about users interacting with devices outside of the observability points between transitions, and allows for interrupts to be raised at any point during a user's execution, and for their details and timing to be influenceable only by that user.

- If a TimerInterrupt has caused the end of execution, then the time must be at some ideal timer interrupt point, or possibly delayed by up to the interrupt-handling WCET. At this point we will perform a domain-switch.
- If execution was ended by a user interrupt or a syscall, the time must be strictly *before* the ideal timer interrupt point. At this point we will perform the syscall or handle the user interrupt.

In a real-world OS, we expect the interrupt partitioning abstraction to be implemented via the *masking* of interrupts associated with non-running domains, where any two partitions have a disjoint set of unmasked interrupts, with the OS switching the mask when switching partitions. The timing constraints result from the timer inevitably arriving, resulting in a domain switch.

5.3 OS Steps

The OS-step model captures requirements on domain switch (triggered by a deterministic timer interrupt), syscall handling, and handling of unmasked user interrupts, each indicated by the event field of the state taking the value TimerInterrupt, Syscall, or UserInterrupt respectively at OS entry.

Domain Switch. The domain-switch step contains the most concretely defined semantics of any step in our model. Once the appropriate interrupt has arrived, the domain-switch step will pass execution on to another security domain, and will execute some security measures to prevent leaks through microarchitectural state. The specific semantics of this step are as follows.

1. Partially flush the pst: flush all addresses conflicting with shared OS memory; time bounded by w_1.
2. Flush the flst: set the entire flst to a predefined value; time bounded by w_2.
3. Change the domain: update the *dom* field of the state according to the schedule oracle; time bounded by w_3.
4. Pad the execution time to make the overall latency constant.

If T_0 is the ideal time for the timer interrupt to occur, w_0 the WCET of handling another interrupt (i.e. the maximum time by which the timer interrupt may be delayed), and w_3 includes any operations for handling the timer interrupt that are not related to time protection (such as saving processor state), then Step (4) defers further execution until time $T_0 + w_0 + w_1 + w_2 + w_3$.

The result of this padding is that nothing a domain can influence will change the exact time when execution is passed to the next domain. The new domain will also begin execution with an empty flst, and a pst partition that is unchanged apart from the shared OS addresses and its collisions, which have been flushed.

These same operations can be performed in a real-world OS, using mostly hardware-provided primitives to perform flushing (e.g. the RISC-V temporal fence instruction `fence.t` developed by Wistoff et al. [34,35]) and a busy loop for padding, as was done by Ge et al. for seL4 [11], if no time padding primitive is provided by the hardware (e.g. the `fence.t` of the latter work by Wistoff et al. [35], which delays until a configurable cspad number of cycles after the timer interrupt arrival). Confidence in WCET bounds for OS functionality can be gained by conducting analyses such as those done for seL4 by Sewell et al. [30,31].

Syscall Handling and Policy Channels. We model system call handling as consisting of (1) a decode phase that determines whether the requested operation is permitted by the protection state, and if so, (2) a commit of the requested operation. Moreover, policy channels (the allowed information to be transmitted) for system calls are specified via a parameter commit-channels of the form *mem* rel, thereby excluding any covert parts of the state by construction. Whether a system call transmits information to domain u, and what information it may transmit, depend on which system call was made (i.e. the system call arguments args), and whether it is authorised (i.e. the protection state prot). These together form the *policy-determining state fields* that, with commit-channels, are used to define $\overset{|\mathsf{dom}\ s \rightsquigarrow u|}{\sim}$. Specifically $\overset{|\mathsf{dom}\ s \rightsquigarrow u|}{\sim}$ is defined so that (a) the commit-channels information is revealed to u only when args and prot imply that u is the recipient of the system call and the system call is authorised, and (b) args and prot themselves are allowed to be revealed to u only under these same conditions.

Thus when a domain makes a system call, other domains can learn about it only when that system call is authorised, in which case only the recipient of the syscall gets to learn about its occurrence, and all they can learn is the intended information transmitted by the syscall.

To prove this, we impose on the user-supplied parameters the proof obligations: (1) an integrity property enforcing the decode phase should only inspect, not change, any of policy-determining state fields; and (2) a confidentiality property on the commit phase enforcing it obeys the policy induced by these fields, i.e. that any changes to state accessible to the observing domain u flow only via locations specified by $\overset{|\mathsf{dom}\ s \rightsquigarrow u|}{\sim}$.

We provide an example instantiation of the parameters that we prove meets these obligations: a simple model of capability-based access control over a broadcast/subscribe pair of system calls for one-way messaging between domains.

User Interrupt Handling. We underspecify interrupt-handling operations in our model: We model the timer interrupt, but no specific operations in response to user interrupts. We assume that in response to a user interrupt, the OS will perform some action that may modify parts of the user state – this matches microkernels, like seL4, that relegate interrupt handling to user domains.

Consequently, we model the user interrupt very similarly to the user step operation: We specify that only the appropriate parts of mem and pst can be read or modified, limit modifications to devs to those belonging to the currently domain, and do not allow modifications to the prot state.

5.4 Proof Approach

Bringing all of this together, we define a small-step transition system alternating (Fig. 3a) between user steps restricted as described in Sect. 5.2 and OS steps as described in Sect. 5.3; this forms the basis for the observer-relative big-step systems upon which our security property is stated (Theorem 1).

For each of these big steps, our proof approach depends on whether the policy permits information to flow from the current domain to the observer u. Consider u's observation of each of its big-step transitions, as in Definition 1.

If u is the current domain or the policy allows a flow from the current domain to u, then it has visibility via $s \overset{u}{\sim} t$ or $s \overset{|\mathsf{dom}\ s \rightsquigarrow u|}{\sim} t$ (resp.) to all of the parts of the state that influence the details of this transition. In these cases, we have enough information to prove that the same transition function f is used, giving:

$$s' = f s \wedge t' = f t$$

For big steps produced by f like these we prove that the confidentiality property expressed by Theorem 1 holds directly using bisimulation: we can prove that a version of the relation at each point $s_n \overset{u}{\sim} t_n$ is preserved to $s_{n+1} \overset{u}{\sim} t_{n+1}$ by any of the small steps of f or their constituent parts (excepting instances where equivalence is broken temporarily but later restored, e.g. tm made deterministic by padding) and therefore that the goal $s' \overset{u}{\sim} t'$ holds.

However, when u is not the current domain and the policy does not allow a flow from the current domain to u, because $s \overset{u}{\sim} t$ and $s \overset{|\mathsf{dom}\ s \rightsquigarrow u|}{\sim} t$ do not give enough information about the operations performed, we may have two potentially different transition functions f and f'. Moreover, it may not be possible to prove a bisimulation over the small steps because f and f' may be made up of differing numbers of these steps. Thus, for the small steps that make up f and f' and their constituent parts we prove instead an integrity property: that they can change nothing observable to u. This allows us to proceed by showing at each point that $s_n \overset{u}{\sim} s_{n+1}$ holds. Eventually, through transitivity of the equivalence relation, we show $s \overset{u}{\sim} s'$ and $t \overset{u}{\sim} t'$. Since we already have $s \overset{u}{\sim} t$, we are able to obtain $s' \overset{u}{\sim} t'$ by using transitivity and symmetry of the equivalence.

6 Related Work

Prior proofs of confidentiality for OSes [8,21,24] have generally focused only on covert flows via storage channels (memory and registers), ignoring time and microarchitectural state.

Barthe et al. presented formal proofs of the elimination of cache channels by flushing the complete cache hierarchy on a context switch [3], an expensive approach that also does not deal with other microarchitectural state.

The same group verified *stealth memory* [18], where the OS reserves some pages and all their cache aliases for cryptographic applications [4]; this protects against side-channel attacks but cannot prevent a Trojan leaking through non-stealth memory. To our knowledge, no prior formalisation of OS security concurrently deals with both partitionable and flushable state, as required by time protection.

Liu et al. [23] prove a property they call *temporal isolation* for an extension of the mCertiKOS kernel with real-time scheduling. Despite its name, their property does not rule out timing channels between domains. Rather it focuses on the scheduler, proving that the behaviour of one domain cannot interfere with the scheduling of another (e.g. by preventing it from missing a deadline). This work might be combined with our approach in future to extend ours beyond the confines of simple deterministic domain scheduling.

Our security property (Definition 1) allows for specifying dynamic policies, in which the information allowed to be released on a step depends on the current state. The state-dependent specification of allowed information release is also present in prior information flow models [25,33] and proofs [8,21,24] for OSes and we expect policies from prior work, including the recent work of Li et al. [21], should be expressible in our framework. Unlike our property, however, none of these prior works allow for defining certain states as being observable to some observers but not others, which we argued in Sect. 4.2 is crucial for a precise statement of time protection with dynamic policies.

The use of two distinct phases to model system call handling, first establishing preconditions that then guarantee that the call can succeed, was used in EROS [7] and adopted by seL4 [19].

7 Conclusions

We have presented a fully machine-checked formalisation of time protection and its enforcement by an operating system that is generic enough to be adapted to any individual OS implementation on any architecture that provides the necessary hardware support. By proving our time protection property relative to the requirements formalised by our OS model, we provide a roadmap for such future OS verification efforts.

This work demonstrates for the first time the feasibility of formal proof of the elimination of microarchitectural timing channels between users by the operating system they are running on. We hope this work helps to raise the level of assurance and responsibility taken by OSes to protect the confidentiality of their users, while serving to clarify what must be asked of the architectures that will make their implementation possible.

Acknowledgements. We thank our anonymous reviewers, as well as Johannes Åman Pohjola for his feedback on our manuscript. This paper describes research that was co-funded by the Australian Research Council (ARC Project ID DP190103743).

References

1. Almeida, J.B., Barbosa, M., Barthe, G., Dupressoir, F., Emmi, M.: Verifying constant-time implementations. In: USENIX Security Symposium, pp. 53–70 (2016)
2. Barthe, G., Betarte, G., Campo, J.D., Luna, C.: Formally verifying isolation and availability in an idealized model of virtualization. In: Butler, M., Schulte, W. (eds.) FM 2011. LNCS, vol. 6664, pp. 231–245. Springer, Heidelberg (2011). https://doi.org/10.1007/978-3-642-21437-0_19
3. Barthe, G., Betarte, G., Campo, J.D., Luna, C.: Cache-leakage resilient OS isolation in an idealized model of virtualization. In: Proceedings of the 25th IEEE Computer Security Foundations Symposium, pp. 186–197. IEEE (2012)
4. Barthe, G., Betarte, G., Campo, J.D., Luna, C.D., Pichardie, D.: System-level non-interference for constant-time cryptography. In: Proceedings of the 2014 ACM SIGSAC Conference on Computer and Communications Security, Scottsdale, AZ, USA, 3–7 November 2014, pp. 1267–1279. ACM (2014). https://doi.org/10.1145/2660267.2660283
5. Buckley, S., Sison, R., Klein, G.: An Isabelle/HOL formalisation of microarchitectural timing channel prevention by operating systems - VM artifact and proof release (2022). https://zenodo.org/record/7340166
6. Cauligi, S., et al.: Constant-time foundations for the new spectre era. In: Proceedings of the 41st ACM SIGPLAN International Conference on Programming Language Design and Implementation, PLDI 2020, London, UK, 15–20 June 2020, pp. 913–926. ACM (2020). https://doi.org/10.1145/3385412.3385970
7. Chen, H., Shapiro, J.S.: Using build-integrated static checking to preserve correctness invariants. In: Proceedings of the 11th ACM Conference on Computer and Communications Security, CCS 2004, Washington, DC, USA, 25–29 October 2004, pp. 288–297. ACM (2004). https://doi.org/10.1145/1030083.1030122
8. Costanzo, D., Shao, Z., Gu, R.: End-to-end verification of information-flow security for C and assembly programs. In: ACM SIGPLAN Conference on Programming Language Design and Implementation, pp. 648–664 (2016)
9. Daum, M., Billing, N., Klein, G.: Concerned with the unprivileged: user programs in kernel refinement. Formal Aspects Comput. **26**(6), 1205–1229 (2014). https://trustworthy.systems/publications/nicta_full_text/7114.pdf
10. Dennis, J.B., Van Horn, E.C.: Programming semantics for multiprogrammed computations. Commun. ACM **9**, 143–155 (1966)
11. Ge, Q., Yarom, Y., Chothia, T., Heiser, G.: Time protection: the missing OS abstraction. In: EuroSys Conference. ACM, Dresden (2019). https://trustworthy.systems/publications/full_text/Ge_YCH_19.pdf
12. Ge, Q., Yarom, Y., Cock, D., Heiser, G.: A survey of microarchitectural timing attacks and countermeasures on contemporary hardware. J. Cryptogr. Eng. **8**, 1–27 (2018). https://trustworthy.systems/publications/full_text/Ge_YCH_18.pdf
13. Ge, Q., Yarom, Y., Heiser, G.: No security without time protection: we need a new hardware-software contract. In: Asia-Pacific Workshop on Systems (APSys). ACM SIGOPS, Korea (2018). https://trustworthy.systems/publications/full_text/Ge_YH_18.pdf
14. Gullasch, D., Bangerter, E., Krenn, S.: Cache games - bringing access-based cache attacks on AES to practice. In: Proceedings of the IEEE Symposium on Security and Privacy, pp. 490–505. IEEE, Oakland (2011)

15. Heiser, G., Klein, G., Murray, T.: Can we prove time protection? In: Workshop on Hot Topics in Operating Systems (HotOS), pp. 23–29. ACM, Bertinoro (2019). https://trustworthy.systems/publications/full_text/Heiser_KM_19.pdf
16. Heiser, G., Murray, T., Klein, G.: Towards provable timing-channel prevention. ACM Oper. Syst. Rev. **54**, 1–7 (2020). https://trustworthy.systems/publications/full_text/Heiser_MK_20.pdf
17. Kessler, R.E., Hill, M.D.: Page placement algorithms for large real-indexed caches. ACM Trans. Comput. Syst. **10**, 338–359 (1992)
18. Kim, T., Peinado, M., Mainar-Ruiz, G.: StealthMem: system-level protection against cache-based side channel attacks in the cloud. In: Proceedings of the 21st USENIX Security Symposium, pp. 189–204. USENIX, Bellevue (2012)
19. Klein, G., et al.: seL4: Formal verification of an OS kernel. In: ACM Symposium on Operating Systems Principles, pp. 207–220. ACM, Big Sky (2009). https://trustworthy.systems/publications/nicta_full_text/1852.pdf
20. Kocher, P., et al.: Spectre attacks: exploiting speculative execution [abridged version]. Commun. ACM **63**, 93–101 (2020)
21. Li, S.W., Li, X., Gu, R., Nieh, J., Hui, J.Z.: A secure and formally verified Linux KVM hypervisor. In: IEEE Security and Privacy (2021)
22. Liedtke, J., Härtig, H., Hohmuth, M.: OS-controlled cache predictability for real-time systems. In: IEEE Real-Time and Embedded Technology and Applications Symposium (RTAS), pp. 213–223. IEEE, Montreal (1997)
23. Liu, M., et al.: Virtual timeline: a formal abstraction for verifying preemptive schedulers with temporal isolation. Proc. ACM Program. Lang. **4**(POPL), 1–31 (2019)
24. Murray, T., et al.: seL4: from general purpose to a proof of information flow enforcement. In: IEEE Symposium on Security and Privacy, pp. 415–429. IEEE, San Francisco (2013). https://trustworthy.systems/publications/nicta_full_text/6464.pdf
25. Murray, T., Matichuk, D., Brassil, M., Gammie, P., Klein, G.: Noninterference for operating system kernels. In: Hawblitzel, C., Miller, D. (eds.) CPP 2012. LNCS, vol. 7679, pp. 126–142. Springer, Heidelberg (2012). https://doi.org/10.1007/978-3-642-35308-6_12, https://trustworthy.systems/publications/nicta_full_text/6004.pdf
26. Nipkow, T., Paulson, L., Wenzel, M.: Isabelle/HOL - A Proof Assistant for Higher-Order Logic. Lecture Notes in Computer Science, vol. 2283. Springer, Heidelberg (2002). https://doi.org/10.1007/3-540-45949-9
27. Osvik, D.A., Shamir, A., Tromer, E.: Cache attacks and countermeasures: the case of AES. In: Pointcheval, D. (ed.) CT-RSA 2006. LNCS, vol. 3860, pp. 1–20. Springer, Heidelberg (2006). https://doi.org/10.1007/11605805_1
28. Percival, C.: Cache missing for fun and profit. In: BSDCan 2005, Ottawa, CA (2005). http://css.csail.mit.edu/6.858/2014/readings/ht-cache.pdf
29. seL4 microkernel code and proofs. https://github.com/seL4/
30. Sewell, T., Kam, F., Heiser, G.: Complete, high-assurance determination of loop bounds and infeasible paths for WCET analysis. In: IEEE Real-Time and Embedded Technology and Applications Symposium (RTAS), Vienna, Austria (2016). https://trustworthy.systems/publications/nicta_full_text/9118.pdf
31. Sewell, T., Kam, F., Heiser, G.: High-assurance timing analysis for a high-assurance real-time OS. Real-Time Syst. **53**, 812–853 (2017). https://trustworthy.systems/publications/full_text/Sewell_KH_17.pdf
32. Sewell, T., Winwood, S., Gammie, P., Murray, T., Andronick, J., Klein, G.: seL4 enforces integrity. In: van Eekelen, M., Geuvers, H., Schmaltz, J.,

Wiedijk, F. (eds.) ITP 2011. LNCS, vol. 6898, pp. 325–340. Springer, Heidelberg (2011). https://doi.org/10.1007/978-3-642-22863-6_24, https://trustworthy.systems/publications/nicta_full_text/4709.pdf
33. Sun, J., Long, X., Zhao, Y.: A verified capability-based model for information flow security with dynamic policies. IEEE Access **6**, 16395–16407 (2018)
34. Wistoff, N., Schneider, M., Gürkaynak, F., Benini, L., Heiser, G.: Microarchitectural timing channels and their prevention on an open-source 64-bit RISC-V core. In: Design, Automation and Test in Europe (DATE). IEEE, Virtual (2021). https://trustworthy.systems/publications/full_text/Wistoff_SGBH_21.pdf
35. Wistoff, N., Schneider, M., Gürkaynak, F., Heiser, G., Benini, L.: Systematic prevention of on-core timing channels by full temporal partitioning. IEEE Trans. Comput. (2023, to appear). https://trustworthy.systems/publications/papers/Wistoff_SGHB_23.pdf
36. Yarom, Y., Falkner, K.: FLUSH+RELOAD: a high resolution, low noise, L3 cache side-channel attack. In: Proceedings of the 23rd USENIX Security Symposium, pp. 719–732. USENIX, San Diego (2014)

Can We Communicate? Using Dynamic Logic to Verify Team Automata

Maurice H. ter Beek[1](✉), Guillermina Cledou[2], Rolf Hennicker[3], and José Proença[4](✉)

[1] ISTI-CNR, Pisa, Italy
maurice.terbeek@isti.cnr.it

[2] INESC TEC & Univ. Minho, Braga, Portugal
mgc@inesctec.pt

[3] Ludwig-Maximilians-Universität München, Munich, Germany

[4] Polytechnic Institute of Porto, Porto, Portugal
pro@isep.ipp.pt

FM Artifact Evaluation ★ Available

FM Artifact Evaluation ★★ Reproducible

Abstract. Team automata describe networks of automata with input and output actions, extended with synchronisation policies guiding how many interacting components can synchronise on a shared input/output action. Given such a team automaton, we can reason over communication properties such as *receptiveness* (sent messages must be received) and *responsiveness* (pending receives must be satisfied). Previous work focused on how to *identify* these communication properties. However, automatically verifying these properties is non-trivial, as it may involve traversing networks of interacting automata with large state spaces. This paper investigates (1) how to *characterise* communication properties for team automata (and subsumed models) using test-free propositional dynamic logic, and (2) how to use this characterisation to *verify* communication properties by model checking. A prototype tool supports the theory, using a transformation to interact with the mCRL2 tool for model checking.

1 Introduction

In automata-based models of Systems of Systems (SoS) that communicate via shared actions, it is of paramount importance to guarantee safe communication, i.e. absence of failures such as message loss (typically of output not received as input, thus violating so called *receptiveness*) or indefinite waiting (typically for input that never arrives, thus violating so called *responsiveness*). This requires knowledge of the adopted communication policy that defines when and which actions are executed (synchronously) and by how many system components. Team automata, originally introduced as an extension of I/O automata [15,39] in the context of computer supported cooperative work (CSCW) to model groupware systems [30], were formalised as a theoretical framework for studying synchronisation policies in system models [12,14]. They proved useful also for capturing access control and other security protocols [11,17]. Their distinguishing feature is the variety of synchronisation policies which, in principle, allow any

M. Chechik et al. (Eds.): FM 2023, LNCS 14000, pp. 122–141, 2023.
https://doi.org/10.1007/978-3-031-27481-7_9

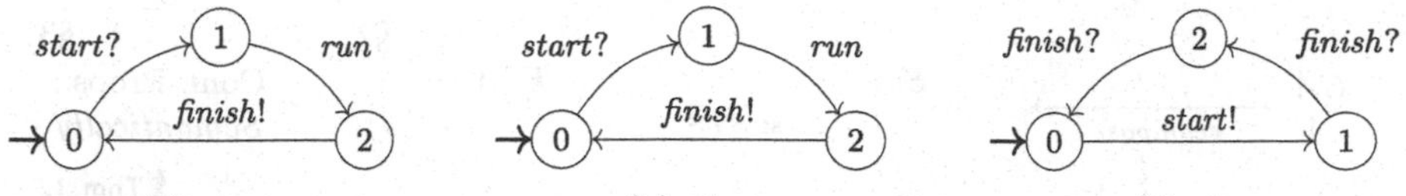

(a) $\mathcal{A}_{\mathsf{R1}}$ (b) $\mathcal{A}_{\mathsf{R2}}$ (c) $\mathcal{A}_{\mathsf{Ctrl}}$

Fig. 1. The three component automata constituting the Race system

number of interacting (component) automata to participate in the synchronised execution of a shared communicating action, either as a sender or as a receiver.

Emblematic synchronisation types were defined to systematise the synchronisation policies realisable in team automata [8] (e.g. multi-cast, broadcast, master-worker) in terms of explicit intervals for the number of sending and receiving components that can participate in a synchronisation. In extended team automata (ETA) [13], synchronisation type specifications (STS) separately assign a synchronisation type to each communicating action. STS uniquely determine a team and induce communication requirements that the team should satisfy. Generic procedures to derive requirements for receptiveness and responsiveness for each synchronisation type were developed, and communication-safety of ETA was defined in terms of compliance with such requirements. A team automaton is called compliant with a set of communication requirements if in each of its reachable states, the requirements are met (i.e. communication is safe); if the required communication cannot occur immediately, but only after some arbitrary other actions have been executed, the team automaton is called weakly compliant (akin to weak compatibility [7,34] or agreement of lazy request actions [5]).

Motivating Example. We illustrate the state-of-the-art as schematised in the upper row of Fig. 2. Consider a system ($\mathcal{S}$), called Race, to model competitions of two runner components R1 and R2 under the control of a third component Ctrl. The behaviour of the components is modelled by the component automata (CA) $\mathcal{A}_{\mathsf{R1}}$, $\mathcal{A}_{\mathsf{R2}}$, and $\mathcal{A}_{\mathsf{Ctrl}}$ in Fig. 1. Both runners have the same behaviour: $\mathcal{A}_{\mathsf{R1}} = \mathcal{A}_{\mathsf{R2}}$. Each runner starts in the initial state 0, indicated by →, in which she is able to receive a *start* signal (input?). Upon reception, she performs the (internal) action *run* and when she reaches the finish line she sends the *finish* signal (output!), after which she is ready for another competition. The controller's task is to start the runners and receive their finish signals. We want to combine these CA in a team such that the controller starts both runners at once, but each runner separately sends her *finish* signal to the controller upon reaching the finish line.

To this aim, ETA use *synchronisation type specifications* (st) to determine the number of senders and receivers allowed to participate in a communication, thus restricting the behaviour of system Race (given by a labelled transition system **lts**($\mathcal{S}$) which contains arbitrary synchronisations of shared actions of the three CA). We specify $([1,1],[2,2])$ for action *start* and $([1,1],[1,1])$ for *finish* such that *start* occurs only as a synchronisation involving exactly *one* component for which it is an output action and exactly *two* for which it is an input action, while *finish* occurs in a *one-to-one* fashion.

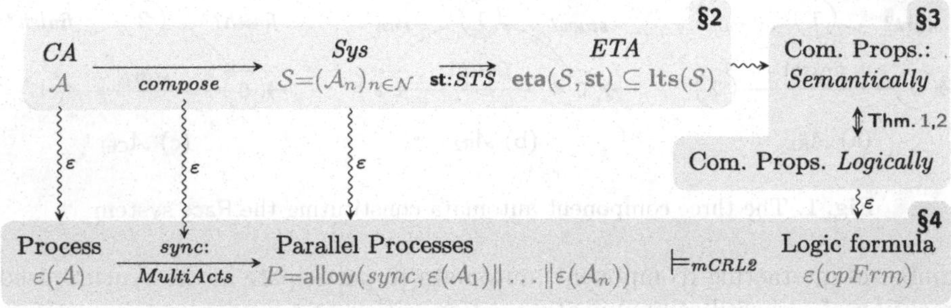

Fig. 2. Overview of this paper; the top row concerns previous work [8,13]

In the team's initial state (0, 0, 0), the controller is in its local state 0 where it can only make progress if its *start* signal is received by a runner. This induces a receptiveness requirement. The ETA **eta**($\mathcal{S}$, **st**) generated over $\mathcal{S}$ by the STS **st** is *compliant* with this requirement if other team component(s) synchronise by receiving *start* as input in accordance with the synchronisation type of *start*, which is the case. There are other receptiveness and also responsiveness requirements. Requirements and compliance of ETA are called *weak* if the other component(s) may perform intermediate actions before the requirement is satisfied.

Related Work and Challenges. Communication safety (mainly receptiveness) and related notions of compatibility have been widely studied to (*semantically*) characterise communication properties [2,8,9,13,20,21,23–26,28,29,35–38], in particular for automata-based system models, but typically limited to pairs of automata or networks with binary, peer-to-peer communication [6,23,28,35–38]. An extension to multi-component communications was first investigated in [24] and then in [8,9,13], where the notion of responsiveness was introduced. Only a few approaches come with tool support [1,3,7,9,18,27], based on algorithms following the semantic compatibility definitions. The purely semantic nature of communication properties is a serious burden in practice, making it challenging to prove properties in concrete cases: one has to go through all reachable states of a team automaton and check compliance for all requirements at each state.

Contribution. In this paper, we pursue a different approach by providing a *logical* characterisation of communication properties, which we believe is interesting by itself, and which has the advantage that it can be checked using available model-checking tools. Our results complete Fig. 2 with three main contributions.

First, after presenting the necessary background on team automata and dynamic logic in Sect. 2, we demonstrate in Sect. 3 that (weak) receptiveness and (weak) responsiveness can be characterised (*logically*) by dynamic logic formulas (w)*rcpFrm* and (w)*rspFrm*, resp., summarised as *cpFrm*. These results, formulated in Theorems 1 and 2, pave the way for automatically checking these communication properties with tooling available for dynamic logic. Proofs of these results are included in a companion paper [10]. To the best of our knowledge, we are the first to provide a logical characterisation of the communication properties of receptiveness and responsiveness.

Second, in Sect. 4, we present a transformation (ε) of component automata, systems and ETA into mCRL2 [22] processes and of the characterising dynamic logic formulas *cpFrm* into μ-calculus formulas. The latter is straightforward, whereas the former makes use of mCRL2's allow operator to suitably restrict the number of multi-action synchronisations such that the semantics of systems of component automata is preserved (up to renaming).

Third, Sect. 4 introduces the open-source prototype tool we developed to perform the transformation into mCRL2 processes and to automatically check communication properties with the model-checking facilities offered by mCRL2, which outputs the result of the formula as well as a witness or counterexample.

2 Background on Team Automata and Dynamic Logic

This section summarises the basic notions of (extended) team automata (ETA) following [13], but additionally considering internal actions, and of dynamic logic.

2.1 Component Automata and Systems

A *labelled transition system* (LTS) is a tuple $\mathcal{L}=(Q,q_0,\Sigma,E)$ such that Q is a finite set of states, $q_0 \in Q$ is the initial state, Σ is a finite set of labels, and $E \subseteq Q \times \Sigma \times Q$ is a transition relation.

Notation. Given an LTS $\mathcal{L}$, we write $q \xrightarrow{a}_{\mathcal{L}} q'$, or shortly $q \xrightarrow{a} q'$, to denote $(q,a,q') \in E$. Similarly, we write $q \xrightarrow{a}_{\mathcal{L}}$ to denote that a is *enabled* in $\mathcal{L}$ at state q, i.e. there exists $q' \in Q$ such that $q \xrightarrow{a} q'$. For $\Gamma \subseteq \Sigma$, we write $q \xrightarrow{\Gamma}{}^{*} q'$ if there exist $q \xrightarrow{a_1} q_1 \xrightarrow{a_2} \cdots \xrightarrow{a_n} q'$ for some $n \geq 0$ and $a_1,\ldots,a_n \in \Gamma$. A state $q \in Q$ is *reachable by* Γ if $q_0 \xrightarrow{\Gamma}{}^{*} q$, it is *reachable* if $q_0 \xrightarrow{\Sigma}{}^{*} q$. The set of reachable states of $\mathcal{L}$ is denoted by $\mathcal{R}(\mathcal{L})$.

A *component automaton* (CA) is an LTS $\mathcal{A}=(Q,q_0,\Sigma,E)$ such that $\Sigma = \Sigma^? \uplus \Sigma^! \uplus \Sigma^\tau$ is a set of *action labels* split into disjoint sets $\Sigma^?$ of *input actions*, $\Sigma^!$ of *output actions*, and Σ^τ of *internal actions*. For easier readability, in graphical representations input actions will be shown with suffix "?", output actions with suffix "!", and internal actions just by their name.

Example 1. Examples of component automata are shown in Fig. 1 of Sect. 1. For $i=1,2$, the action labels of $\mathcal{A}_{\mathsf{Ri}}$ are $\Sigma_{\mathsf{Ri}} = \Sigma^?_{\mathsf{Ri}} \uplus \Sigma^!_{\mathsf{Ri}} \uplus \Sigma^\tau_{\mathsf{Ri}}$, where $\Sigma^?_{\mathsf{Ri}} = \{\mathit{start}\}$, $\Sigma^!_{\mathsf{Ri}} = \{\mathit{finish}\}$, $\Sigma^\tau_{\mathsf{Ri}} = \{\mathit{run}\}$. The action labels of $\mathcal{A}_{\mathsf{Ctrl}}$ are $\Sigma_{\mathsf{Ctrl}} = \Sigma^?_{\mathsf{Ctrl}} \uplus \Sigma^!_{\mathsf{Ctrl}} \uplus \Sigma^\tau_{\mathsf{Ctrl}}$ where $\Sigma^?_{\mathsf{Ctrl}} = \{\mathit{finish}\}$, $\Sigma^!_{\mathsf{Ctrl}} = \{\mathit{start}\}$, $\Sigma^\tau_{\mathsf{Ctrl}} = \varnothing$. ▷

A *system* is a pair $\mathcal{S}=(\mathcal{N},(\mathcal{A}_n)_{n\in\mathcal{N}})$, with $\mathcal{N}$ a finite, nonempty set of component names and $(\mathcal{A}_n)_{n\in\mathcal{N}}$ an $\mathcal{N}$-indexed family of CA $\mathcal{A}_n = (Q_n, q_{0,n}, \Sigma_n, E_n)$.

Example 2. The race system of Sect. 1 is $\mathsf{Race} = (\mathcal{N}_{\mathsf{Race}},(\mathcal{A}_n)_{n\in\mathcal{N}_{\mathsf{Race}}})$, with $\mathcal{N}_{\mathsf{Race}} = \{\mathsf{R1},\mathsf{R2},\mathsf{Ctrl}\}$ and the CA $\mathcal{A}_{\mathsf{R1}}$, $\mathcal{A}_{\mathsf{R2}}$, and $\mathcal{A}_{\mathsf{Ctrl}}$ from Example 1. ▷

Any system $\mathcal{S}=(\mathcal{N},(\mathcal{A}_n)_{n\in\mathcal{N}})$ induces an LTS defined by $\mathbf{lts}(\mathcal{S}) = (Q, q_0, \Lambda(\mathcal{S}), E(\mathcal{S}))$, where $Q = \prod_{n\in\mathcal{N}} Q_n$ is the set of *system states*, $q_0 = (q_{0,n})_{n\in\mathcal{N}}$ is the *initial system state*, $\Lambda(\mathcal{S})$ is the set of *system labels*, and $E(\mathcal{S})$ is the set of *system transitions*. Each system state $q \in Q$ is an $\mathcal{N}$-indexed family $(q_n)_{n\in\mathcal{N}}$ of local component states $q_n \in Q_n$. The definitions of $\Lambda(\mathcal{S})$ and $E(\mathcal{S})$ follow below, after the intermediate notion of *system action*.

System Actions Σ. The set of *system actions* $\Sigma = \bigcup_{n\in\mathcal{N}} \Sigma_n$ determines actions that will be part of system labels. Within Σ we identify $\Sigma^\bullet = \bigcup_{n\in\mathcal{N}} \Sigma^?_n \cap \bigcup_{n\in\mathcal{N}} \Sigma^!_n$ as the set of *communicating actions*. Hence, an action $a \in \Sigma$ is communicating if it occurs in (at least) one set Σ_n of action labels as an input action and in (at least) one set Σ_m of action labels as an output action. The system is *closed* if all non-communicating actions are internal component actions. For ease of presentation, we assume in this paper that systems are closed.

Example 3. The system actions of the race system are $\Sigma_{\mathsf{Race}} = \{\mathit{start}, \mathit{finish}, \mathit{run}\}$ and its communicating actions are $\Sigma^\bullet_{\mathsf{Race}} = \{\mathit{start}, \mathit{finish}\}$. ▷

System Labels $\Lambda(\mathcal{S})$. We use *system labels* to indicate which components participate (simultaneously) in the execution of a system action. There are two kinds of system labels. In a system label of the form $(\mathsf{out}, a, \mathsf{in})$, out represents the set of senders of *outputs* and in the set of receivers of *inputs* that synchronise on the action $a \in \Sigma^\bullet$. Either out or in can be empty, but not both. A system label of the form (n, a) indicates that component n executes an internal action $a \in \Sigma^\tau_n$. Formally, the set $\Lambda(\mathcal{S})$ of system labels of $\mathcal{S}$ is defined as follows:

$$\Lambda(\mathcal{S}) = \{\, (\mathsf{out}, a, \mathsf{in}) \mid \varnothing \neq (\mathsf{out} \cup \mathsf{in}) \subseteq \mathcal{N},\ \forall_{n\in\mathsf{out}} \cdot a \in \Sigma^!_n,\ \forall_{n\in\mathsf{in}} \cdot a \in \Sigma^?_n \,\}$$
$$\cup \{\, (n, a) \mid n \in \mathcal{N},\ a \in \Sigma^\tau_n \,\}$$

Note that $\Lambda(\mathcal{S})$ depends only on $\mathcal{N}$ and the sets Σ_n of action labels for each $n \in \mathcal{N}$. As a notational convention, if $\mathsf{out} = \{n\}$ is a singleton, we write (n, a, in) instead of $(\{n\}, a, \mathsf{in})$, and similarly for singleton sets in.

Example 4. The set of system labels of the race system is given by

$$\begin{aligned}\Lambda(\mathsf{Race}) = {} & \{(\mathsf{out}, \mathit{start}, \mathsf{in}) \mid \varnothing \neq (\mathsf{out} \cup \mathsf{in}),\ \mathsf{out} \subseteq \{\mathsf{Ctrl}\}, \mathsf{in} \subseteq \{\mathsf{R1}, \mathsf{R2}\}\},\\ & \cup \{(\mathsf{out}, \mathit{finish}, \mathsf{in}) \mid \varnothing \neq (\mathsf{out} \cup \mathsf{in}),\ \mathsf{out} \subseteq \{\mathsf{R1}, \mathsf{R2}\}, \mathsf{in} \subseteq \{\mathsf{Ctrl}\}\},\\ & \cup \{(\mathsf{R1}, \mathit{run}), (\mathsf{R2}, \mathit{run})\}.\end{aligned}$$

▷

System Transitions $E(\mathcal{S})$. System labels provide an appropriate means to describe which components in a system execute, possibly together, a computation step, i.e. a system transition. Formally, a *system transition* $t \in E(\mathcal{S})$ has the form $(q_n)_{n\in\mathcal{N}} \xrightarrow{\lambda}_{\mathsf{lts}(\mathcal{S})} (q'_n)_{n\in\mathcal{N}}$ such that $\lambda \in \Lambda(\mathcal{S})$ and

- either $\lambda = (\mathsf{out}, a, \mathsf{in})$ and:
  - $q_n \xrightarrow{a}_{\mathcal{A}_n} q'_n$ for all $n \in \mathsf{out} \cup \mathsf{in}$ and
  - $q_m = q'_m$ for all $m \in \mathcal{N} \backslash (\mathsf{out} \cup \mathsf{in})$;

- or $\lambda = (n, a)$, $a \in \Sigma_n^\tau$ is an internal action of some component $n \in \mathcal{N}$, and:
  - $q_n \xrightarrow{a}_{\mathcal{A}_n} q_n'$ and
  - $q_m = q_m'$ for all $m \in \mathcal{N} \backslash \{n\}$.

We write Λ and E instead of $\Lambda(\mathcal{S})$ and $E(\mathcal{S})$, resp., if $\mathcal{S}$ is clear from the context. Surely, at most those components that are in a local state in which action a is locally enabled can participate in a system transition for a. Since, by definition of system labels, $(\mathsf{out} \cup \mathsf{in}) \neq \varnothing$, at least one component participates in any system transition. Given a system transition $t = q \xrightarrow{\lambda}_{\mathsf{lts}(\mathcal{S})} q'$, we write $t.\lambda$ for λ.

Example 5. Examples of system transitions of the race system are
$(0,0,0) \xrightarrow{(\mathsf{Ctrl}, start, \varnothing)} (0,0,1)$, $(0,0,0) \xrightarrow{(\mathsf{Ctrl}, start, \{\mathsf{R1},\mathsf{R2}\})} (1,1,1)$,
$(2,2,1) \xrightarrow{(\{\mathsf{R1},\mathsf{R2}\}, finish, \mathsf{Ctrl})} (0,0,2)$, $(2,2,1) \xrightarrow{(\mathsf{R1}, finish, \mathsf{Ctrl})} (0,2,2)$, and
$(1,1,1) \xrightarrow{(\mathsf{R1}, run)} (2,1,1)$.

The LTS of the race system, denoted by **lts**(Race), contains all possible system transitions. It can be computed by our tool as shown in Sect. 4.

Note that not all system transitions are really meaningful. For instance, the first transition should not happen, since the controller is supposed to start both runners simultaneously. We also want to reject the third transition, since in our application runners should finish individually. These transitions will be discarded based on synchronisation restrictions for teams considered in the following. ▷

2.2 Team Automata

Synchronisation types specify which synchronisations between components are admissible in a particular system $\mathcal{S}$. A *synchronisation type* $(O, I) \in \mathsf{Intv} \times \mathsf{Intv}$ is a pair of intervals O and I which determine the number of outputs and inputs that can participate in a communication. Each interval has the form $[min, max]$ with $min \in \mathbb{N}$ and $max \in \mathbb{N} \cup \{*\}$ where $*$ denotes 0 or more participants. We write $x \in [min, max]$ if $min \leq x \leq max$ and $x \in [min, *]$ if $x \geq min$.

A *synchronisation type specification* (STS) over $\mathcal{S}$ is a function $\mathbf{st} : \Sigma^\bullet \to \mathsf{Intv} \times \mathsf{Intv}$ that assigns to any communicating action a an individual synchronisation type $\mathbf{st}(a)$. We say that a system label $\lambda = (\mathsf{out}, a, \mathsf{in})$ *satisfies* $\mathbf{st}(a) = (O, I)$, written $\lambda \models \mathbf{st}(a)$, if $|\mathsf{out}| \in O \wedge |\mathsf{in}| \in I$. Each synchronisation type specification $\mathbf{st}$ generates the following subsets $\Lambda(\mathcal{S}, \mathbf{st})$ of system labels and $E(\mathcal{S}, \mathbf{st})$ of corresponding system transitions.

$$\Lambda(\mathcal{S}, \mathbf{st}) = \{\, \lambda \in \Lambda \mid \lambda = (\mathsf{out}, a, \mathsf{in}) \Rightarrow \lambda \models \mathbf{st}(a) \,\}$$
$$E(\mathcal{S}, \mathbf{st}) = \{\, t \in E \mid t.\lambda \in \Lambda(\mathcal{S}, \mathbf{st}) \,\}$$

Thus, for communicating actions, the set of system transitions is restricted to those transitions whose labels respect the synchronisation type of their communicating action. For internal actions no restriction is applied, since an internal action of a component can always be executed when it is locally enabled.

Components interacting in accordance with an STS **st** over a system $\mathcal{S}$ are seen as a team whose behaviour is represented by the *(extended) team automaton* (ETA) $\mathbf{eta}(\mathcal{S}, \mathbf{st})$ generated over $\mathcal{S}$ by **st** and defined by the LTS

$$\mathbf{eta}(\mathcal{S}, \mathbf{st}) = (Q, q_0, \Lambda(\mathcal{S}, \mathbf{st}), E(\mathcal{S}, \mathbf{st})).$$

We write $\Lambda(\mathbf{st})$ and $E(\mathbf{st})$ instead of $\Lambda(\mathcal{S}, \mathbf{st})$ and $E(\mathcal{S}, \mathbf{st})$, resp., if $\mathcal{S}$ is clear from the context, and assume $\Lambda(\mathbf{st}) \neq \varnothing$. Labels in $\Lambda(\mathbf{st})$ are called *team labels* and transitions in $E(\mathbf{st})$ are called *team transitions.*

Example 6. Recall the race system and its system labels and transitions. We require both runners to *start* simultaneously and to *finish* individually by using the STS $\mathbf{st}_{\mathsf{Race}}$ defined by $start \mapsto ([1,1],[2,2])$ and $finish \mapsto ([1,1],[1,1])$. Then the team labels of the ETA $\mathbf{eta}(\mathsf{Race}, \mathbf{st}_{\mathsf{Race}})$ are given by $\Lambda(\mathbf{st}_{\mathsf{Race}}) = \{ (\mathsf{Ctrl}, start, \{\mathsf{R1}, \mathsf{R2}\}), (\mathsf{R1}, finish, \mathsf{Ctrl}), (\mathsf{R2}, finish, \mathsf{Ctrl}), (\mathsf{R1}, run), (\mathsf{R2}, run) \}$. Example transitions are

$$(0,0,0) \xrightarrow{(\mathsf{Ctrl}, start, \{\mathsf{R1},\mathsf{R2}\})} (1,1,1) \xrightarrow{(\mathsf{R1}, run)} (2,1,1) \xrightarrow{(\mathsf{R1}, finish, \mathsf{Ctrl})} (0,1,2).$$

The full team automaton is computed by our tool, cf. [10, Appendix A]. ▷

2.3 Dynamic Logic

We use a (test-free) propositional dynamic logic over a finite set $A \neq \varnothing$ of atomic actions [32]. The set $Act(A)$ of *structured actions* over A is given by the grammar

$$\alpha \ := \ a \mid \alpha;\alpha \mid \alpha + \alpha \mid \alpha^* \qquad \text{(actions)}$$

with $a \in A$, sequential composition ;, nondeterministic choice +, and iteration ∗.

Abbreviations. If $A = \{a_1, \dots, a_n\}$, we write *some* for the structured action $a_1 + \cdots + a_n$. Given a nonempty subset of A denoted by B with elements $\{b_1, \dots, b_m\}$, we write B for the structured action $b_1 + \cdots + b_m$.

The set $Frm(A)$ of *formulas* over A is defined by the grammar

$$\varphi \ := \ true \mid \neg\varphi \mid \varphi \vee \varphi \mid \langle\alpha\rangle\,\varphi \qquad \text{(formulas)}$$

where $\alpha \in Act(A)$. Formula $\langle\alpha\rangle\,\varphi$ expresses that at the current state it is possible to execute α such that φ holds in the next state. The difference to Hennessy–Milner logic [33] is that actions used as modalities in modal operators can be structured actions, including iteration. This additional power will be crucial to express our communication requirements later on in terms of logic formulas.

Abbreviations. We use the usual abbreviations like *false*, $\varphi \wedge \varphi'$, $\varphi \to \varphi'$, and the modal box operator $[\alpha]\,\varphi$ which stands for $\neg\langle\alpha\rangle\neg\varphi$ and expresses that whenever in the current state α is executed, then φ holds afterwards. For a finite index set I, we write $\bigvee_{i \in I}$ to denote the generalised '∨', where $\bigvee_{i \in \varnothing} \psi_i = false$ (likewise $\bigwedge_{i \in \varnothing} \psi_i = true$).

Given a set A of atomic actions, we use LTS over A for the semantic interpretation of formulas. Let $\mathcal{L} = (Q, q_0, A, E)$ be an LTS. First we extend the transition relation of $\mathcal{L}$ to structured actions in $Act(A)$ defined inductively by:

$q \xrightarrow{\alpha_1+\alpha_2}_{\mathcal{L}} q'$ if $q \xrightarrow{\alpha_1}_{\mathcal{L}} q'$ or $q \xrightarrow{\alpha_2}_{\mathcal{L}} q'$,
$q \xrightarrow{\alpha_1;\alpha_2}_{\mathcal{L}} q'$ if there exists $\hat{q} \in Q$ such that $q \xrightarrow{\alpha_1}_{\mathcal{L}} \hat{q}$ and $\hat{q} \xrightarrow{\alpha_2}_{\mathcal{L}} q'$,
$q \xrightarrow{\alpha^*}_{\mathcal{L}} q'$ if $q = q'$ or there exists $\hat{q} \in Q$ such that $q \xrightarrow{\alpha}_{\mathcal{L}} \hat{q}$ and $\hat{q} \xrightarrow{\alpha^*}_{\mathcal{L}} q'$.

We write $q \xrightarrow{\alpha}_{\mathcal{L}}$ if there exists q' such that $q \xrightarrow{\alpha}_{\mathcal{L}} q'$.

The *satisfaction* of a formula $\varphi \in Frm(A)$ by an LTS $\mathcal{L} = (Q, q_0, A, E)$ at a state $q \in Q$, written $\mathcal{L}, q \models \varphi$, is inductively defined as follows:

$\mathcal{L}, q \models true$,
$\mathcal{L}, q \models \neg\varphi$ if not $\mathcal{L}, q \models \varphi$,
$\mathcal{L}, q \models \varphi_1 \vee \varphi_2$ if $\mathcal{L}, q \models \varphi_1$ or $\mathcal{L}, q \models \varphi_2$,
$\mathcal{L}, q \models \langle\alpha\rangle\, \varphi$ if there exists $q' \in Q$ such that $q \xrightarrow{\alpha}_{\mathcal{L}} q'$ and $\mathcal{L}, q' \models \varphi$.

For instance, enabledness $q \xrightarrow{\alpha}_{\mathcal{L}}$ is expressed by $\mathcal{L}, q \models \langle\alpha\rangle\, true$.

$\mathcal{L}$ *satisfies* a formula $\varphi \in Frm(A)$, written $\mathcal{L} \models \varphi$, if $\mathcal{L}, q_0 \models \varphi$. Hence, for the satisfaction of a formula by an LTS the non-reachable states are irrelevant.

We deviate from the classical semantics [32], since we use LTS with initial states as models to interpret satisfaction of formulas. This is because we are interested in the formulation of properties of (concurrently running) components, i.e. of process structures. In particular, we can express safety properties (e.g. $[some^*]\,\varphi$) and some kinds of liveness properties (e.g. $[some^*]\,\langle some^*; a\rangle\,\varphi$).

3 Logical Characterisations of Communication Properties

In this section, we first focus on the property of *receptiveness* for team automata, which has been studied before for other automata formalisms mainly in the context of peer-to-peer communication; cf. Introduction. In Sect. 3.1, we summarise the concepts of receptiveness and weak receptiveness and in Sect. 3.2 we show that both notions can be characterised by dynamic logic formulas. Then we turn to (weak) responsiveness, summarising the underlying ideas in Sect. 3.3 and providing logical characterisations in Sect. 3.4. The results form the theoretical basis for automatic checks of communication properties in Sect. 4.

We assume a given system $\mathcal{S} = (\mathcal{N}, (\mathcal{A}_n)_{n\in\mathcal{N}})$ of CA with $\mathsf{lts}(\mathcal{S}) = (Q, q_0, \Lambda, E)$, an STS st, and the generated ETA $\mathsf{eta}(\mathcal{S}, \mathsf{st}) = (Q, q_0, \Lambda(\mathcal{S}, \mathsf{st}), E(\mathcal{S}, \mathsf{st}))$.

3.1 Team Receptiveness

The idea of receptiveness for $\mathsf{eta}(\mathcal{S}, \mathsf{st})$ is as follows. Whenever, in a reachable state q of $\mathsf{eta}(\mathcal{S}, \mathsf{st})$, a group $\{\mathcal{A}_n \mid n \in \mathsf{out}\}$ of CA with $\varnothing \neq \mathsf{out} \subseteq \mathcal{N}$ is (locally) enabled to perform an output action a, i.e. $\forall_{n\in\mathsf{out}} \cdot a \in \Sigma_n^!$ and $q_n \xrightarrow{a}_{\mathcal{A}_n}$, so that (1) the number of CA in out fits the number of allowed senders according to the synchronisation type $\mathbf{st}(a) = (O, I)$, i.e. $|\mathsf{out}| \in O$, and (2) the CA need at least one receiver to join the communication, i.e. $0 \notin I$, we get a *receptiveness requirement*, denoted by $\mathbf{rcp}(\mathsf{out}, a)@q$. If $\mathsf{out} = \{n\}$, we write $\mathbf{rcp}(n, a)@q$ for $\mathbf{rcp}(\{n\}, a)@q$.

Example 7. In the initial state $(0, 0, 0)$ of the race team, there is a receptiveness requirement of the controller who wants to start the competition, expressed by $\mathbf{rcp}(\mathsf{Ctrl}, \mathit{start})@(0, 0, 0)$. Later on, when the first runner is in state 2, it wants to send *finish* which leads to three receptiveness requirements:

$$\mathbf{rcp}(\mathsf{R1}, \mathit{finish})@(2, 1, 1),\ \mathbf{rcp}(\mathsf{R1}, \mathit{finish})@(2, 2, 1),\ \mathbf{rcp}(\mathsf{R1}, \mathit{finish})@(2, 0, 2).$$

Similarly, when the second runner is in state 2, we get:

$$\mathbf{rcp}(\mathsf{R2}, \mathit{finish})@(1, 2, 1),\ \mathbf{rcp}(\mathsf{R2}, \mathit{finish})@(2, 2, 1),\ \mathbf{rcp}(\mathsf{R2}, \mathit{finish})@(0, 2, 2).\ \triangleright$$

ETA $\mathbf{eta}(\mathcal{S}, \mathbf{st})$ is compliant with a receptiveness requirement $\mathbf{rcp}(\mathsf{out}, a)@q$ if the group of components (with names in out) can find partners in the team which synchronise with the group by taking (receiving) a as input. If reception is immediate, we talk about receptiveness; if the other components may still perform some intermediate actions before accepting a, we talk about weak receptiveness. Formally, (weak) compliance and (weak) receptiveness are defined as follows: The ETA $\mathbf{eta}(\mathcal{S}, \mathbf{st})$ is *compliant* with $\mathbf{rcp}(\mathsf{out}, a)@q$ if

$$\exists_{\mathsf{in}} \cdot q \xrightarrow{(\mathsf{out}, a, \mathsf{in})}_{\mathbf{eta}(\mathcal{S}, \mathbf{st})}$$

The ETA $\mathbf{eta}(\mathcal{S}, \mathbf{st})$ is *weakly compliant* with $\mathbf{rcp}(\mathsf{out}, a)@q$ if

$$\exists_{\mathsf{in}} \cdot q \xrightarrow{(\Lambda(\mathbf{st})_{\backslash \mathsf{out}})^* \,;\, (\mathsf{out}, a, \mathsf{in})}_{\mathbf{eta}(\mathcal{S}, \mathbf{st})}$$

where $\Lambda(\mathbf{st})_{\backslash \mathsf{out}}$ denotes the set of team labels in which no component of out participates. Formally, $\Lambda(\mathbf{st})_{\backslash \mathsf{out}} = \{(\mathsf{out}', a, \mathsf{in}) \in \Lambda(\mathbf{st}) \mid (\mathsf{out}' \cup \mathsf{in}) \cap \mathsf{out} = \emptyset\} \cup \{(n, a) \in \Lambda(\mathbf{st}) \mid n \notin \mathsf{out}\}$. Obviously, compliance implies weak compliance.

Definition 1 ((weak) receptiveness). *The ETA* $\mathbf{eta}(\mathcal{S}, \mathbf{st})$ *is* (weakly) receptive *if for all reachable states* $q \in \mathcal{R}(\mathbf{eta}(\mathcal{S}, \mathbf{st}))$, *the ETA* $\mathbf{eta}(\mathcal{S}, \mathbf{st})$ *is (weakly) compliant with* all *receptiveness requirements* $\mathbf{rcp}(\mathsf{out}, a)@q$ *established for* q.

3.2 Logical Characterisations of Receptiveness

Receptiveness notions are of purely semantic nature. To prove receptiveness in concrete cases may be rather cumbersome since one has to go through all reachable states q of a team automaton and check compliance for all receptiveness requirements at q. Therefore we are interested in a syntactic, logical characterisation of receptiveness such that checks can be automated. It turns out that our version of dynamic logic is well suited to express receptiveness.

Example 8. Recall the receptiveness requirement $\mathbf{rcp}(\mathsf{Ctrl}, \mathit{start})@(0,0,0)$ from Example 7. Being a receptiveness requirement implies that the output action *start* is enabled at the local state 0 of the controller, i.e. $0 \xrightarrow{start}_{\mathcal{A}_{\mathsf{Ctrl}}}$. This is equivalent to the fact that in $\mathbf{lts}(\mathsf{Race})$ (cf. Example 5) the *system label* $(\mathsf{Ctrl}, \mathit{start}, \varnothing)$ is enabled at system state $(0,0,0)$, i.e. $(0,0,0) \xrightarrow{start}_{\mathbf{lts}(\mathsf{Race})}$. *Logically,* this is equivalent to $\mathbf{lts}(\mathsf{Race}), (0,0,0) \models \langle(\mathsf{Ctrl}, \mathit{start}, \varnothing)\rangle\, \mathit{true}$. Under this condition, we must prove there is a team transition in the ETA $\mathbf{eta}(\mathsf{Race}, \mathbf{st}_{\mathsf{Race}})$ of the form $(0,0,0) \xrightarrow{(\mathsf{Ctrl},\mathit{start},\mathsf{in})}_{\mathbf{eta}(\mathsf{Race},\mathbf{st}_{\mathsf{Race}})} q'$. This means there is an in so that $(\mathsf{Ctrl}, \mathit{start}, \mathsf{in})$ is a *team label* and $\mathbf{eta}(\mathsf{Race}, \mathbf{st}_{\mathsf{Race}}), (0,0,0) \models \langle(\mathsf{Ctrl}, \mathit{start}, \mathsf{in})\rangle\, \mathit{true}$. The latter is equivalent to $\mathbf{lts}(\mathsf{Race}), (0,0,0) \models \langle(\mathsf{Ctrl}, \mathit{start}, \mathsf{in})\rangle\, \mathit{true}$ since, for team labels, system transitions and team transitions coincide. To check that $\mathbf{eta}(\mathsf{Race}, \mathbf{st}_{\mathsf{Race}})$ satisfies the (only) receptiveness requirement at state $(0,0,0)$ it thus suffices (and it is also necessary) to show that there is an in with $(\mathsf{Ctrl}, \mathit{start}, \mathsf{in})$ being a team label such that the following holds (which is true for $\mathsf{in} = \{\mathsf{R1}, \mathsf{R2}\}$): $\mathbf{lts}(\mathsf{Race}), (0,0,0) \models \langle(\mathsf{Ctrl}, \mathit{start}, \varnothing)\rangle\, \mathit{true} \to \langle(\mathsf{Ctrl}, \mathit{start}, \mathsf{in})\rangle\, \mathit{true}$. ▷

This example illustrates a key insight in our approach: we cannot capture requests for communication on team level but must consider system transitions with *system labels* which are not team labels, e.g. $(\mathsf{Ctrl}, \mathit{start}, \varnothing)$.

Our general approach to characterise receptiveness properties is as follows. Given system labels $\Lambda(\mathcal{S})$ and synchronisation type specification $\mathbf{st}$ the *"receptiveness formula" rcpFrm* $\in \mathit{Frm}(\Lambda)$ defined below expresses that all receptiveness requirements are fulfilled in any reachable state of the team $\mathbf{eta}(\mathcal{S}, \mathbf{st})$:

$$\mathit{rcpReq} = \{(\mathsf{out}, a, \varnothing) \in \Lambda \mid |\mathsf{out}| \in O, 0 \notin I \text{ for } \mathbf{st}(a) = (O, I)\}$$

$$\mathit{InCom}(\mathsf{out}, a) = \{\mathsf{in} \subseteq \mathcal{N} \mid (\mathsf{out}, a, \mathsf{in}) \in \Lambda(\mathbf{st})\}$$

$$\mathit{rcpFrm} = [\Lambda(\mathbf{st})^*] \textstyle\bigwedge_{(\mathsf{out},a,\varnothing)\in \mathit{rcpReq}} \Big(\langle(\mathsf{out}, a, \varnothing)\rangle\, \mathit{true} \to \textstyle\bigvee_{\mathsf{in}\in \mathit{InCom}(\mathsf{out},a)} \langle(\mathsf{out}, a, \mathsf{in})\rangle\, \mathit{true}\Big)$$

Here *rcpReq* is the set of system labels which correspond to receptiveness requirements (when enabled in a reachable state of the ETA, cf. Lemma 1); and $\mathit{InCom}(\mathsf{out}, a)$ is the set of subsets $\mathsf{in} \subseteq \mathcal{N}$ of component names which complement a given $\mathsf{out} \subseteq \mathcal{N}$ and $a \in \Sigma^\bullet$ to a team label in $\Lambda(\mathbf{st})$ (for potential communication). Observe that (1) $\mathit{rcpReq} \cap \Lambda(\mathbf{st}) = \varnothing$ since $0 \notin I$ for any $\mathbf{st}(a) = (O, I)$; (2) $[\Lambda(\mathbf{st})^*]$ ranges over all reachable states of the team $\mathbf{eta}(\mathcal{S}, \mathbf{st})$, since $\Lambda(\mathbf{st})$ is the finite set of team labels that denote the non-deterministic choice of these actions; and (3) the implication in *rcpFrm* is in $\mathit{Frm}(\Lambda)$ and not in $\mathit{Frm}(\Lambda(\mathbf{st}))$ since $\mathit{rcpReq} \cap \Lambda(\mathbf{st}) = \varnothing$ and $(\mathsf{out}, a, \varnothing) \in \mathit{rcpReq}$.

Similarly, a *"weak receptiveness formula" wrcpFrm* $\in \mathit{Frm}(\Lambda)$ is defined as:

$$\mathit{wrcpFrm} = [\Lambda(\mathbf{st})^*] \textstyle\bigwedge_{(\mathsf{out},a,\varnothing)\in \mathit{rcpReq}} \Big(\langle(\mathsf{out}, a, \varnothing)\rangle\, \mathit{true} \to \textstyle\bigvee_{\mathsf{in}\in \mathit{InCom}(\mathsf{out},a)} \langle(\Lambda(\mathbf{st})_{\setminus\mathsf{out}})^*; (\mathsf{out}, a, \mathsf{in})\rangle\, \mathit{true}\Big)$$

Example 9. For Race, $rcpReq = \{(\mathsf{Ctrl}, start, \varnothing), (\mathsf{R1}, finish, \varnothing), (\mathsf{R2}, finish, \varnothing)\}$, $InCom(\mathsf{Ctrl}, start) = \{\{\mathsf{R1}, \mathsf{R2}\}\}$, $InCom(\mathsf{Ri}, finish) = \{\{\mathsf{Ctrl}\}\}$, for $i = 1, 2$, and

$$rcpFrm = [\Lambda(\mathbf{st}_{\mathsf{Race}})^*]\ (\ \langle(\mathsf{Ctrl}, start, \varnothing)\rangle\, true \rightarrow \langle(\mathsf{Ctrl}, start, \{\mathsf{R1}, \mathsf{R2}\})\rangle\, true \\ \wedge \langle(\mathsf{R1}, finish, \varnothing)\rangle\, true \rightarrow \langle(\mathsf{R1}, finish, \mathsf{Ctrl})\rangle\, true \\ \wedge \langle(\mathsf{R2}, finish, \varnothing)\rangle\, true \rightarrow \langle(\mathsf{R2}, finish, \mathsf{Ctrl})\rangle\, true\ ).$$

This receptiveness formula is satisfied by the LTS of the Race system. For the check we use the tool described in Sect. 4. Together with Theorem 1 below this implies that the ETA $\mathbf{eta}(\mathsf{Race}, \mathbf{st}_{\mathsf{Race}})$ is receptive. ▷

The next lemma provides a characterisation of receptiveness requirements in terms of the set *rcpReq* and logical satisfaction (used for the proof of Theorem 1).

Lemma 1. *For all* $q \in \mathcal{R}(\mathbf{eta}(\mathcal{S}, \mathbf{st}))$ *it holds:* $\mathbf{rcp}(\mathsf{out}, a)@q$ *is a receptiveness requirement iff* $(\mathsf{out}, a, \varnothing) \in rcpReq$ *and* $\mathbf{lts}(\mathcal{S}), q \models \langle(\mathsf{out}, a, \varnothing)\rangle\, true$.

The proof of Theorem 1 uses also the facts stated in the following two lemmas.

Lemma 2. *For all* $\varphi \in Frm(\Lambda)$:

$$\{\mathbf{lts}(\mathcal{S}) \models [\Lambda(\mathbf{st})^*]\varphi\} \textit{ iff } \{\mathbf{lts}(\mathcal{S}), q \models \varphi \textit{ for all } q \in \mathcal{R}(\mathbf{eta}(\mathcal{S}, \mathbf{st}))\}.$$

Lemma 3. *For all* $q \in \mathcal{R}(\mathbf{eta}(\mathcal{S}, \mathbf{st}))$ *and* $\alpha \in Act(\Lambda(\mathbf{st}))$:

$$q \xrightarrow{\alpha}_{\mathbf{lts}(\mathcal{S})} \textit{ iff } q \xrightarrow{\alpha}_{\mathbf{eta}(\mathcal{S}, \mathbf{st})}.$$ [1]

Theorem 1. *(1)* $\mathbf{eta}(\mathcal{S}, \mathbf{st})$ *is receptive iff* $\mathbf{lts}(\mathcal{S}) \models rcpFrm$ *and*
(2) $\mathbf{eta}(\mathcal{S}, \mathbf{st})$ *is weakly receptive iff* $\mathbf{lts}(\mathcal{S}) \models wrcpFrm$.

Remark 1. Checks of $\mathbf{lts}(\mathcal{S}) \models rcpFrm$ ($wrcpFrm$, resp.) can be optimised if we use instead of the full LTS of $\mathcal{S}$ the usually much smaller sub-LTS $\mathbf{lts}(\mathcal{S})^{opt} \subseteq \mathbf{lts}(\mathcal{S})$ constructed as follows: the set of transitions of $\mathbf{lts}(\mathcal{S})^{opt}$ consists of the transitions of $\mathbf{eta}(\mathcal{S}, \mathbf{st})$ to which we add all transitions $q \xrightarrow{(\mathsf{out}, a, \varnothing)}_{\mathbf{lts}(\mathcal{S})} q'$ with $(\mathsf{out}, a, \varnothing) \in rcpReq$. These transitions, which do not belong to $\mathbf{eta}(\mathcal{S}, \mathbf{st})$, are needed to capture receptiveness requirements. ▷

3.3 Team Responsiveness

For input actions, one can formulate responsiveness requirements with the intuition that enabled inputs should be served by appropriate outputs. The expression $\mathbf{rsp}(\mathsf{in}, a)@q$ is a *responsiveness requirement* if $q \in \mathcal{R}(\mathbf{eta}(\mathcal{S}, \mathbf{st}))$, for all $n \in \mathsf{in}$ we have $a \in \Sigma^?_n$ and $q_n \xrightarrow{a}_{\mathcal{A}_n}$, and $|\mathsf{in}| \in I, 0 \notin O$ for $\mathbf{st}(a) = (O, I)$. The ETA $\mathbf{eta}(\mathcal{S}, \mathbf{st})$ is *compliant* with $\mathbf{rsp}(\mathsf{in}, a)@q$ if $\exists_{\mathsf{out}} \cdot q \xrightarrow{(\mathsf{out}, a, \mathsf{in})}_{\mathbf{eta}(\mathcal{S}, \mathbf{st})}$. It is *weakly compliant* with $\mathbf{rsp}(\mathsf{in}, a)@q$ if $\exists_{\mathsf{out}} \cdot q \xrightarrow{\Lambda(\mathbf{st})_{\setminus \mathsf{in}}^*\, ;\, (\mathsf{out}, a, \mathsf{in})}_{\mathbf{eta}(\mathcal{S}, \mathbf{st})}$, where $\mathbf{st}(\Lambda)_{\setminus \mathsf{in}} = \{(\mathsf{out}, a, \mathsf{in}') \in \mathbf{st}(\Lambda) \mid (\mathsf{out} \cup \mathsf{in}') \cap \mathsf{in} = \varnothing\} \cup \{(n, a) \in \mathbf{st}(\Lambda) \mid n \notin \mathsf{in}\}$ denotes the set of team labels in which no component of in participates.

---

[1] This follows because for team labels system transitions and team transitions coincide.

Unlike output actions, the selection of an input action of a component is not controlled by the component but by the environment, i.e. there is an external choice. If, for a choice of enabled inputs $\{a_1, \ldots, a_n\}$, *only one of them* can be supplied with a corresponding output of the environment this suffices to guarantee progress of components waiting for input.

Definition 2 ((weak) responsiveness). *The ETA* $\mathbf{eta}(\mathcal{S}, \mathbf{st})$ *is* (weakly) responsive *if for all reachable states* $q \in \mathcal{R}(\mathbf{eta}(\mathcal{S}, \mathbf{st}))$*, either there is no responsiveness requirement at* q *or there is a responsiveness requirement* $\mathsf{rsp}(\mathsf{in}, a)@q$ *established for* q *such that the ETA* $\mathbf{eta}(\mathcal{S}, \mathbf{st})$ *is (weakly) compliant with it.*

Example 10. In the initial state $(0, 0, 0)$ of the race team, there is a responsiveness requirement of the two runners who want to be started, expressed by $\mathbf{rsp}(\{\mathsf{R1}, \mathsf{R2}\}, \mathit{start})@(0, 0, 0)$. The ETA $\mathbf{eta}(\mathsf{Race}, \mathbf{st}_{\mathsf{Race}})$ is compliant with this requirement. When the controller is in state 1, there are responsiveness requirements $\mathbf{rsp}(\mathsf{Ctrl}, \mathit{finish})@(q1,q2,1)$ for any q1, q2 $\in \{1, 2\}$. Only in state $(2, 2, 1)$ this requirement is immediately fulfilled; in all other cases, at least one *run* must happen before a *finish* is sent. Then $\mathbf{eta}(\mathsf{Race}, \mathbf{st}_{\mathsf{Race}})$ is weakly compliant. There are four more responsiveness requirements when the controller is in state 2. ▷

3.4 Logical Characterisations of Responsiveness

We now define a logical characterisation of responsiveness by the *"responsiveness formula" rspFrm* $\in \mathit{Frm}(\Lambda)$ below, for a given $\Lambda(\mathcal{S})$ and STS $\mathbf{st}$ as above.

$$\mathit{rspReq} = \{(\varnothing, a, \mathsf{in}) \in \Lambda \mid |\mathsf{in}| \in I, 0 \notin O \text{ for } \mathbf{st}(a) = (O, I)\}$$

$$\mathit{OutCom}(a, \mathsf{in}) = \{\mathsf{out} \subseteq \mathcal{N} \mid (\mathsf{out}, a, \mathsf{in}) \in \Lambda(\mathbf{st})\}$$

$$\mathit{rspFrm} = [\Lambda(\mathbf{st})^*]\Big(\big(\textstyle\bigvee_{(\varnothing,a,\mathsf{in})\in \mathit{rspReq}} \langle(\varnothing, a, \mathsf{in})\rangle\, \mathit{true}\big) \rightarrow \big(\textstyle\bigvee_{(\varnothing,a,\mathsf{in})\in \mathit{rspReq}} \bigvee_{\mathsf{out}\in \mathit{OutCom}(a,\mathsf{in})} \langle(\mathsf{out}, a, \mathsf{in})\rangle\, \mathit{true}\big)\Big)$$

where *rspReq* is the set of system labels which correspond to responsiveness requirements (when enabled in a reachable state of the ETA $\mathbf{eta}(\mathcal{S}, \mathbf{st})$); and $\mathit{OutCom}(a, \mathsf{in})$ is the set of subsets $\mathsf{out} \subseteq \mathcal{N}$ of component names which complement a given $\mathsf{in} \subseteq \mathcal{N}$ and $a \in \Sigma^\bullet$ to a team label in $\Lambda(\mathbf{st})$ (for potential communication). Note that the left side of the implication in *rspFrm* is true iff there is a responsiveness requirement for a, in at the current state q. Otherwise *rspFrm* holds anyway at q in accordance with the notion of responsiveness.

Similarly, a *"weak responsiveness formula" wrspFrm* $\in \mathit{Frm}(\Lambda)$ is defined as:

$$\mathit{wrspFrm} = [\Lambda(\mathbf{st})^*]\Big(\big(\textstyle\bigvee_{(\varnothing,a,\mathsf{in})\in \mathit{rspReq}} \langle(\varnothing, a, \mathsf{in})\rangle\, \mathit{true}\big) \rightarrow \big(\textstyle\bigvee_{(\varnothing,a,\mathsf{in})\in \mathit{rspReq}} \bigvee_{\mathsf{out}\in \mathit{OutCom}(a,\mathsf{in})} \langle \mathbf{st}(\Lambda)_{\backslash \mathsf{in}})^*; (\mathsf{out}, a, \mathsf{in})\rangle\, \mathit{true}\big)\Big)$$

Example 11. For Race, $rspReq = \{(\varnothing, start, \{\mathsf{R1}, \mathsf{R2}\}), (\varnothing, finish, \mathsf{Ctrl})\}$, $OutCom(start, \{\mathsf{R1}, \mathsf{R2}\}) = \{\{\mathsf{Ctrl}\}\}$, $OutCom(finish, \mathsf{Ctrl}) = \{\{\mathsf{R1}\}, \{\mathsf{R2}\}\}$, and

$$wrspFrm = [\Lambda(\mathbf{st}_{\mathsf{Race}})^*](\langle(\varnothing, start, \{\mathsf{R1}, \mathsf{R2}\})\rangle\, true \vee \langle(\varnothing, finish, \mathsf{Ctrl})\rangle\, true) \rightarrow \\ (\langle(\mathsf{Ctrl}, start, \{\mathsf{R1}, \mathsf{R2}\})\rangle\, true \vee \\ \langle((\mathsf{R1}, run) + (\mathsf{R2}, run))^*; (\mathsf{R1}, finish, \mathsf{Ctrl})\rangle\, true \vee \\ \langle((\mathsf{R1}, run) + (\mathsf{R2}, run))^*; (\mathsf{R2}, finish, \mathsf{Ctrl})\rangle\, true\ )$$

Note that $\Lambda(\mathbf{st}_{\mathsf{Race}})_{\backslash\{\mathsf{R1},\mathsf{R2}\}} = \varnothing$ and $\Lambda(\mathbf{st}_{\mathsf{Race}})_{\backslash \mathsf{Ctrl}} = \{(\mathsf{R1}, run), (\mathsf{R2}, run)\}$.

The weak responsiveness formula is satisfied by the LTS of the Race system. For the check we use the tool described in Sect. 4. Together with Theorem 2, this implies that the $\mathbf{eta}(\mathsf{Race}, \mathbf{st}_{\mathsf{Race}})$ is weakly responsive. ▷

Lemma 4. *For all $q \in \mathcal{R}(\mathbf{eta}(\mathcal{S}, \mathbf{st}))$ it holds: $\mathbf{rsp}(\mathsf{in}, a)@q$ is a responsiveness requirement iff $(\varnothing, a, \mathsf{in}) \in rspReq$ and $\mathbf{lts}(\mathcal{S}), q \models \langle(\varnothing, a, \mathsf{in})\rangle\, true$.*

Theorem 2. *(1) $\mathbf{eta}(\mathcal{S}, \mathbf{st})$ is responsive iff $\mathbf{lts}(\mathcal{S}) \models rspFrm$ and*
(2) $\mathbf{eta}(\mathcal{S}, \mathbf{st})$ is weakly responsive iff $\mathbf{lts}(\mathcal{S}) \models wrspFrm$.

4 Model Checking Communication Properties

In this section we show, underpinned by our running example, how to transform CA, systems and ETA into mCRL2 processes as well as dynamic logic formulas, characterising communication properties, into μ-calculus formulas. We also justify briefly the correctness of these transformations and the soundness and completeness of our verification approach. Then we present the tool support that we developed (1) to perform the transformations and (2) to automatically check communication properties through the model-checking facilities offered by the mCRL2 toolset (https://www.mcrl2.org/) [22], similarly to how mCRL2 was used earlier to verify automata composed hierarchically [40].

An mCRL2 model is expressed in an elementary process language, where actions (and possibly data types) as well as processes are defined, and (for our purpose) the initial process is given in the following standard concurrent form:

```
allow( { a, a_1|...|a_n, ... }, proc_1 || ... || proc_n );
```

This is a parallel composition of sequential processes `proc_i`, with interleaving and multi-party synchronisation specified explicitly by `allow`. This restriction operator forbids some actions, to constrain interaction and prune the state space, by listing those allowed to occur in `allow`: so action a is interleaved and, similar to synchronisation of actions a and $\bar{a}$ yielding τ in CCS, actions `a_i` are synchronised, resulting in a multi-action `a_1|...|a_n`; all other actions are blocked.

To explain our transformation, along the lines of Fig. 2, we assume given a system $\mathcal{S} = (\mathcal{N}, (\mathcal{A}_n)_{n \in \mathcal{N}})$ and a synchronisation type specification $\mathbf{st}$.

Transformation of CA. First, we transform each CA $\mathcal{A}_n$ into an mCRL2 process $\epsilon(\mathcal{A}_n)$, cf. Fig. 1(a). The transformation is defined and implemented in a straightforward way based on the idea that an LTS $\mathcal{L}$ can be represented by a process expression P, i.e. the LTS semantics of P is $\mathcal{L}$. In our context, the representation of the $\mathcal{A}_n$ is a bit more involved since we want to represent shared actions of different CA by different actions of their mCRL2 processes (later to be synchronised by multi-actions). Therefore we apply a renaming ρ which renames each action a of each $\mathcal{A}_n$ to the mCRL2 action `n_a` of $\epsilon(\mathcal{A}_n)$. Then the LTS semantics of mCRL2 processes (defined by SOS rules in [31, Def. 15.2.10]) applied to $\epsilon(\mathcal{A}_n)$ provides an LTS $\textsf{lts}(\epsilon(\mathcal{A}_n))$. (We ignore aspects of data and time included in mCRL2). Next we note that $\textsf{lts}(\epsilon(\mathcal{A}_n))$ is a reachable LTS which is, up to renaming w.r.t. ρ, isomorphic to the reachable part of $\mathcal{A}_n$, i.e. to the LTS obtained by restricting the state space of $\mathcal{A}_n$ to reachable states. For instance, the CA $\mathcal{A}_{\mathsf{R1}}$ from Fig. 1(a) is transformed into the mCRL2 process ***proc*** **R1**`(s:Int)` below. Its ***act***ions are `R1_start`, `R1_run`, and `R1_finish`, a parameter `s` (an integer) holds the state, summation (`+`) represents non-deterministic choice, and **R1**`(0)` is its ***init***ial state. The actions are renamed as explained above.

```
act R1_start, R1_run, R1_finish;
proc R1(s:Int) =
      ( s == 0 ) → ( R1_start . R1(1) ) +
      ( s == 1 ) → ( R1_run . R1(2) ) +
      ( s == 2 ) → ( R1_finish . R1(0) );
init R1(0);
```

Transformation of System $\mathcal{S}$. System $\mathcal{S}$ is transformed into an mCRL2 process $\epsilon(\mathcal{S})$ as follows. Any system label $(\mathsf{out}, a, \mathsf{in})$ is represented by the multi-action which synchronises all mCRL2 actions `o_a` with `o`$\in\mathsf{out}$ with all mCRL2 actions `i_a` with `i`$\in\mathsf{in}$. Any system label (n, a) for internal actions is represented by `n_a`. Then we construct the parallel composition of all mCRL2 processes $\epsilon(A_n)$ restricted to (multi-)actions that represent system labels. The restriction is realised by mCRL2's ***allow*** operator. By this construction the LTS semantics $\textsf{lts}(\epsilon(\mathcal{S}))$ is, up to the renaming of system labels, isomorphic to the reachable part of $\textsf{lts}(\mathcal{S})$. As non-reachable states are irrelevant for the satisfaction of formulas, this provides the basis for verifying our communication properties with mCRL2. For instance, the Race system is represented by this mCRL2 process:

```
act R1_start, R2_start, Ctrl_start, R1_run, R2_run, Ctrl_run, ...;
proc R1(s:Int) = ...;
     R2(s:Int) = ...;
     Ctrl(s:Int) = ...;
init allow ({R1_start, R1_finish, R1_run, R2_start, R2_finish, R2_run
     Ctrl_start, Ctrl_finish, Ctrl_start|R1_start, Ctrl_start|R2_start,
     R1_start|R2_start, Ctrl_start|R1_start|R2_start, ...},
     R1(0) || R2(0) || Ctrl(0)).
```

Thus we block multi-actions, like `R1_start|Ctrl_finish` and `R1_run|R2_run`, which do not correspond to system labels, by using the ***allow*** operator. In total there are 16 allowed multi-actions. The system's LTS can be computed by our tool.

We can also represent the ETA generated by the STS **st** over $\mathcal{S}$ if we further restrict the allowed actions to those whose corresponding system labels satisfy **st**. In our example, this would mean that we allow only the mCRL2 actions `Ctrl_start|R1_start|R2_start`, `R1_finish|Ctrl_finish`, `R2_finish|Ctrl_finish`, `R1_run`, and `R2_run`. Note that the representation of ETA is not used for verification of communication properties (see below). It is, however, useful for the graphical animation of ETA.

Transformation of Communication Formulas. We characterised (weak) receptiveness and (weak) responsiveness in Sects. 3.4 and 3.2 by formulas (w)*rcpFrm* and (w)*rspFrm*, resp. To automatically verify these formulas, we transform them into mCRL2's μ-calculus by the renaming of system labels explained above and by syntactic conversion of operators, e.g. $\wedge$ to `&&`, $\vee$ to `||`, and *some* to `true`. We write `<a+b+c>`ψ instead of `<a>`ψ`||<b>`ψ`||<c>`ψ for compactness. The receptiveness formula *rcpFrm* of our example is transformed into:

```
[(Ctrl_start|R1_start|R2_start + R1_finish|Ctrl_finish +
  R2_finish|Ctrl_finish + R2_run + R1_run)*]
 (((<R1_finish> true) => (<R1_finish|Ctrl_finish> true)) &&
  ((<R2_finish> true) => (<R2_finish|Ctrl_finish> true)) &&
  ((<Ctrl_start> true) => (<Ctrl_start|R1_start|R2_start> true)))
```

Note that for the transformation of communication properties the given STS **st** is crucial. Indeed, the structured action used in the modal box operator refers exactly to those actions which correspond to the system labels satisfying the synchronisation type and hence to the team labels.

Verifying Communication Properties in mCRL2. As shown in Theorems 1 and 2 the validity of the logic formulas *cpFrm* characterising communication properties must be checked over the LTS of system $\mathcal{S}$. According to our semantics preserving transformation of system $\mathcal{S}$ into the process $\epsilon(\mathcal{S})$, checking validity of *cpFrm* in $\mathsf{lts}(\mathcal{S})$ is equivalent to checking the transformed version $\epsilon(\mathit{cpFrm})$ over $\mathsf{lts}(\epsilon(\mathcal{S}))$. But the latter is exactly how satisfaction of formulas is defined for mCRL2 processes and therefore our verification approach is sound and complete.

Implementation. An open-source prototype was implemented, which can be executed online at https://github.com/arcalab/team-a. It is written in Scala, compiled into JavaScript via *Scala.js*, and uses Scala and JavaScript libraries and external tools like the mCRL2 model checker. Most final code is in JavaScript running in an Internet browser (client-side), while the external tools are executed remotely (server-side). It is also possible to compile and run the server locally.

The screenshot in Fig. 3 depicts some of the available widgets, using our running Race example. More complete screenshots can be found in [10, Appendix A]. The input team automaton is specified in widget ①, where `S` defines the system composed of 2 runners and 1 controller, and `STS` specifies the synchronisation types. The remaining widgets provide analysis of the ETA: ③ outputs the encoded mCRL2 model and formulas being evaluated; ② outputs both the result of the formula and a counterexample or a witness — in this case stating that this

ETA is not responsive with a counterexample; and ④ and ⑤ depict the composed ETA and the individual component automata, resp. Note that widget ② also reports that Race is weakly responsive, as described in Sect. 3.4, producing a witness that matches the ETA diagram (cf. Fig. 5 in [10, Appendix A]).

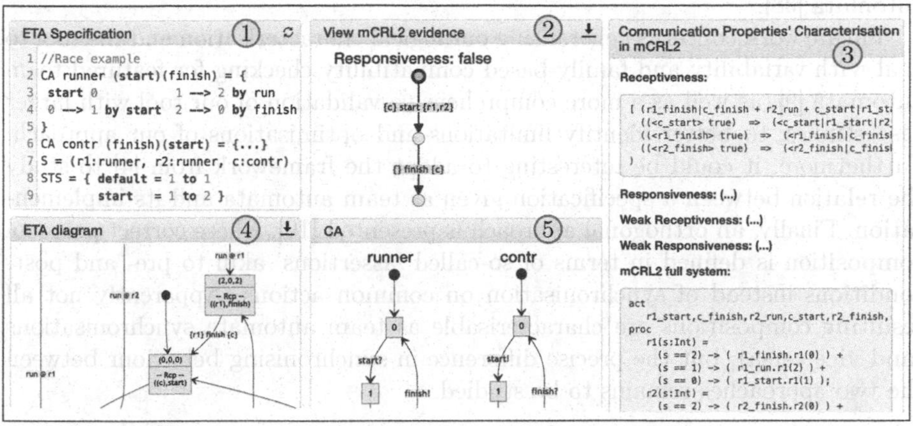

Fig. 3. Screenshot of some of the widgets in the ETA tools available online

A Note on Optimisation. Our approach can be further optimised to reduce the model's size. For example, as mentioned in Remark 1, the mCRL2 process representing system $\mathcal{S}$ can be replaced by one that allows a smaller set of multi-actions corresponding to team labels from the ETA ($\mathbf{eta}(\mathcal{S}, \mathbf{st})$) only, but enriched with $(\mathsf{out}, a, \varnothing)$ labels (when proving (weak) receptiveness) or with $(\varnothing, a, \mathsf{in})$ (when proving (weak) responsiveness). Furthermore, all internal actions could be replaced by a single non-synchronising action (e.g. τ), which may, however, lead to less readable counterexamples. Using these optimisations, one could check for receptiveness or responsiveness of our Race example using a model that allows only 7 multi-actions instead of 16. In general, this reduction depends on (1) the number of shared actions, (2) the degree of flexibility of the synchronisation policies, and (3) the number of internal actions.

5 Conclusions and Future Work

We provide the first logical characterisation of communication properties of team automata in the form of (weak) receptiveness and (weak) responsiveness. I.e., we logically characterise whether all messages that can be sent can also be received, and that components waiting to receive some input message will get one. This provides the basis for an automated verification approach of communication properties of team automata. A prototype tool, available at https://github.com/arcalab/team-a, realises this automated verification, performed by mCRL2 [22].

Our results also apply to related automata-based models that interact through shared input and output actions, since many such models are subsumed by team automata, like I/O automata [15] but also a special type of Petri nets [16]. Moreover, we believe that our results can be adjusted to capture variants of compatibility like the "optimistic" approach proposed for interface automata [38].

Future work concerns generalising our logical characterisation and the tool to deal with variability and family-based compatibility checking for featured team automata [9], as well as a more comprehensive validation of our tool with larger case studies, to better identify limitations and optimisations of our approach. Furthermore, it could be interesting to adapt the framework from [4] to study the relation between a specification given as team automata and its implementation. Finally, an orthogonal approach is presented [19], where correct protocol composition is defined in terms of so-called 'assertions' akin to pre- and post-conditions instead of synchronisation on common actions. Apparently not all resulting compositions are characterisable as team automata synchronisations (and vice versa), but the precise difference in synchronising behaviour between the two approaches remains to be studied.

Acknowledgments. Ter Beek received funding from the MIUR PRIN 2017FTXR7S project IT MaTTerS (Methods and Tools for Trustworthy Smart Systems) and PRIN 2020TL3X8X project T-LADIES (Typeful Language Adaptation for Dynamic, Interacting and Evolving Systems). Proença was partially supported by National Funds through FCT/MCTES (Portuguese Foundation for Science and Technology), within the CISTER Unit (UIDP/UIDB/04234/2020) and the IBEX project (PTDC/CCI-COM/4280/2021); also by national funds through FCT and European funds through EU ECSEL JU, within project VALU3S (ECSEL/0016/2019 - JU grant nr. 876852) – The JU receives support from the EU's Horizon 2020 research and innovation programme and Austria, Czech Republic, Germany, Ireland, Italy, Portugal, Spain, Sweden, Turkey. Disclaimer: This document reflects only the authors' view and the Commission is not responsible for any use that may be made of the information it contains.

References

1. Adler, B.T., et al.: TICC: a tool for interface compatibility and composition. In: Ball, T., Jones, R.B. (eds.) CAV 2006. LNCS, vol. 4144, pp. 59–62. Springer, Heidelberg (2006). https://doi.org/10.1007/11817963_8
2. Bartoletti, M., Cimoli, T., Zunino, R.: Compliance in behavioural contracts: a brief survey. In: Bodei, C., Ferrari, G.-L., Priami, C. (eds.) Programming Languages with Applications to Biology and Security. LNCS, vol. 9465, pp. 103–121. Springer, Cham (2015). https://doi.org/10.1007/978-3-319-25527-9_9
3. Basile, D., ter Beek, M.H.: Contract automata library. Sci. Comput. Program. **221** (2022). https://doi.org/10.1016/j.scico.2022.102841
4. Basile, D., ter Beek, M.H.: A runtime environment for contract automata. In: Chechik, M., et al. (eds.) FM 2023. LNCS, vol. 14000, pp. 550–567. Springer, Cham (2023). https://doi.org/10.1007/978-3-031-27481-7_31

5. Basile, D., et al.: Controller synthesis of service contracts with variability. Sci. Comput. Program. **187** (2020). https://doi.org/10.1016/j.scico.2019.102344
6. Basile, D., Degano, P., Ferrari, G.L.: Automata for specifying and orchestrating service contracts. Logical Methods Comput. Sci. **12**(4:6), 1–51 (2016). https://doi.org/10.2168/LMCS-12(4:6)2016
7. Bauer, S.S., Mayer, P., Schroeder, A., Hennicker, R.: On weak modal compatibility, refinement, and the MIO workbench. In: Esparza, J., Majumdar, R. (eds.) TACAS 2010. LNCS, vol. 6015, pp. 175–189. Springer, Heidelberg (2010). https://doi.org/10.1007/978-3-642-12002-2_15
8. ter Beek, M.H., Carmona, J., Hennicker, R., Kleijn, J.: Communication requirements for team automata. In: Jacquet, J.-M., Massink, M. (eds.) COORDINATION 2017. LNCS, vol. 10319, pp. 256–277. Springer, Cham (2017). https://doi.org/10.1007/978-3-319-59746-1_14
9. ter Beek, M.H., Cledou, G., Hennicker, R., Proença, J.: Featured team automata. In: Huisman, M., Păsăreanu, C., Zhan, N. (eds.) FM 2021. LNCS, vol. 13047, pp. 483–502. Springer, Cham (2021). https://doi.org/10.1007/978-3-030-90870-6_26
10. ter Beek, M.H., Cledou, G., Hennicker, R., Proença, J.: Can we Communicate? Using dynamic logic to verify team automata (extended version). Technical report, Zenodo (2022). https://doi.org/10.5281/zenodo.7418074
11. ter Beek, M.H., Ellis, C.A., Kleijn, J., Rozenberg, G.: Team automata for spatial access control. In: Prinz, W., Jarke, M., Rogers, Y., Schmidt, K., Wulf, V. (eds.) ECSCW 2001, pp. 59–78. Springer, Dordrecht (2001). https://doi.org/10.1007/0-306-48019-0_4
12. ter Beek, M.H., Ellis, C.A., Kleijn, J., Rozenberg, G.: Synchronizations in team automata for groupware systems. Comput. Support. Coop. Work **12**(1), 21–69 (2003). https://doi.org/10.1023/A:1022407907596
13. ter Beek, M.H., Hennicker, R., Kleijn, J.: Compositionality of safe communication in systems of team automata. In: Pun, V.K.I., Stolz, V., Simao, A. (eds.) ICTAC 2020. LNCS, vol. 12545, pp. 200–220. Springer, Cham (2020). https://doi.org/10.1007/978-3-030-64276-1_11
14. ter Beek, M.H., Kleijn, J.: Team automata satisfying compositionality. In: Araki, K., Gnesi, S., Mandrioli, D. (eds.) FME 2003. LNCS, vol. 2805, pp. 381–400. Springer, Heidelberg (2003). https://doi.org/10.1007/978-3-540-45236-2_22
15. ter Beek, M.H., Kleijn, J.: Modularity for teams of I/O automata. Inf. Process. Lett. **95**(5), 487–495 (2005). https://doi.org/10.1016/j.ipl.2005.05.012
16. ter Beek, M.H., Kleijn, J.: Vector team automata. Theor. Comput. Sci. **429**, 21–29 (2012). https://doi.org/10.1016/j.tcs.2011.12.020
17. ter Beek, M.H., Lenzini, G., Petrocchi, M.: Team automata for security: a survey. Electron. Notes Theor. Comput. Sci. **128**(5), 105–119 (2005). https://doi.org/10.1016/j.entcs.2004.11.044
18. Beyer, D., et al.: CHIC: Checking Interface Compatibility (2007). https://ptolemy.berkeley.edu/projects/embedded/research/chic
19. Bocchi, L., Orchard, D., Voinea, A.L.: A theory of composing protocols. Art Sci. Eng. Program. **7**(2), 6:1–6:76 (2023). https://doi.org/10.22152/programming-journal.org/2023/7/6
20. Bordeaux, L., Salaün, G., Berardi, D., Mecella, M.: When are two web services compatible? In: Shan, M.-C., Dayal, U., Hsu, M. (eds.) TES 2004. LNCS, vol. 3324, pp. 15–28. Springer, Heidelberg (2005). https://doi.org/10.1007/978-3-540-31811-8_2
21. Brand, D., Zafiropulo, P.: On communicating finite-state machines. J. ACM **30**(2), 323–342 (1983). https://doi.org/10.1145/322374.322380

22. Bunte, O., et al.: The mCRL2 toolset for analysing concurrent systems. In: Vojnar, T., Zhang, L. (eds.) TACAS 2019. LNCS, vol. 11428, pp. 21–39. Springer, Cham (2019). https://doi.org/10.1007/978-3-030-17465-1_2
23. Carmona, J., Cortadella, J.: Input/output compatibility of reactive systems. In: Aagaard, M.D., O'Leary, J.W. (eds.) FMCAD 2002. LNCS, vol. 2517, pp. 360–377. Springer, Heidelberg (2002). https://doi.org/10.1007/3-540-36126-X_22
24. Carmona, J., Kleijn, J.: Compatibility in a multi-component environment. Theor. Comput. Sci. **484**, 1–15 (2013). https://doi.org/10.1016/j.tcs.2013.03.006
25. Carrez, C., Fantechi, A., Najm, E.: Behavioural contracts for a sound assembly of components. In: König, H., Heiner, M., Wolisz, A. (eds.) FORTE 2003. LNCS, vol. 2767, pp. 111–126. Springer, Heidelberg (2003). https://doi.org/10.1007/978-3-540-39979-7_8
26. Castagna, G., Gesbert, N., Padovani, L.: A theory of contracts for web services. ACM Trans. Program. Lang. Syst. **31**(5), 19:1–19:61 (2009). https://doi.org/10.1145/1538917.1538920
27. Chakrabarti, A., de Alfaro, L., Henzinger, T.A., Jurdziński, M., Mang, F.Y.C.: Interface compatibility checking for software modules. In: Brinksma, E., Larsen, K.G. (eds.) CAV 2002. LNCS, vol. 2404, pp. 428–441. Springer, Heidelberg (2002). https://doi.org/10.1007/3-540-45657-0_35
28. de Alfaro, L., Henzinger, T.A.: Interface automata. In: Proceedings of the 8th European Software Engineering Conference Held Jointly with 9th ACM SIGSOFT International Symposium on Foundations of Software Engineering (ESEC/FSE), pp. 109–120. ACM (2001). https://doi.org/10.1145/503209.503226
29. Durán, F., Ouederni, M., Salaün, G.: A generic framework for n-protocol compatibility checking. Sci. Comput. Program. **77**(7–8), 870–886 (2012). https://doi.org/10.1016/j.scico.2011.03.009
30. Ellis, C.A.: Team automata for groupware systems. In: Proceedings of the 1st International ACM SIGGROUP Conference on Supporting Group Work (GROUP), pp. 415–424. ACM (1997). https://doi.org/10.1145/266838.267363
31. Groote, J.F., Mousavi, M.R.: Modeling and Analysis of Communicating Systems. MIT Press, Cambridge (2014)
32. Harel, D., Kozen, D., Tiuryn, J.: Dynamic Logic. Foundations of Computing. MIT Press, Cambridge (2000). https://doi.org/10.7551/mitpress/2516.001.0001
33. Hennessy, M., Milner, R.: On observing nondeterminism and concurrency. In: de Bakker, J., van Leeuwen, J. (eds.) ICALP 1980. LNCS, vol. 85, pp. 299–309. Springer, Heidelberg (1980). https://doi.org/10.1007/3-540-10003-2_79
34. Hennicker, R., Bidoit, M.: Compatibility properties of synchronously and asynchronously communicating components. Logical Methods Comput. Sci. **14**(1), 1–31 (2018). https://doi.org/10.23638/LMCS-14(1:1)2018
35. Hennicker, R., Bidoit, M., Dang, T.-S.: On synchronous and asynchronous compatibility of communicating components. In: Lluch Lafuente, A., Proença, J. (eds.) COORDINATION 2016. LNCS, vol. 9686, pp. 138–156. Springer, Cham (2016). https://doi.org/10.1007/978-3-319-39519-7_9
36. Hennicker, R., Knapp, A.: Moving from interface theories to assembly theories. Acta Inf. **52**(2–3), 235–268 (2015). https://doi.org/10.1007/s00236-015-0220-7
37. Larsen, K.G., Nyman, U., Wąsowski, A.: Modal I/O automata for interface and product line theories. In: De Nicola, R. (ed.) ESOP 2007. LNCS, vol. 4421, pp. 64–79. Springer, Heidelberg (2007). https://doi.org/10.1007/978-3-540-71316-6_6
38. Lüttgen, G., Vogler, W., Fendrich, S.: Richer interface automata with optimistic and pessimistic compatibility. Acta Inf. **52**(4–5), 305–336 (2015). https://doi.org/10.1007/s00236-014-0211-0

39. Lynch, N.A., Tuttle, M.R.: An introduction to input/output automata. CWI Q. **2**(3), 219–246 (1989). https://ir.cwi.nl/pub/18164
40. Proença, J., Madeira, A.: Taming hierarchical connectors. In: Hojjat, H., Massink, M. (eds.) FSEN 2019. LNCS, vol. 11761, pp. 186–193. Springer, Cham (2019). https://doi.org/10.1007/978-3-030-31517-7_13

The ScalaFix Equation Solver

Gianluca Amato and Francesca Scozzari(✉)

Laboratory of Computational Logic and AI,
Department of Economic Studies,
University of Chieti–Pescara,
Pescara, Italy
{gianluca.amato,francesca.scozzari}@unich.it

Abstract. We present ScalaFix, a modular library for solving equation systems by iterative methods. ScalaFix implements several solvers, involving iteration strategies from plain Kleene's iteration to more complex ones based on a hierarchical ordering of the unknowns. It works with finite and infinite equation systems and supports widening, narrowing and warrowing operators. It also allows intertwining ascending and descending chains and other advanced techniques such as localized widening.

Keywords: Static analysis · Equation systems · Iterative methods · Widening · Narrowing

1 Introduction

One of the most common approaches for performing static analysis of software, used for both simple data-flow analysis and more complex analysis based on abstract interpretation, is to setup a set of equations over some partially ordered set. The solutions of this equation system form the result of the analysis.

These equation systems are generally solved by iterative methods, based on some variant of the Knaster-Tarski theorem. This is immediate when the partial order on the values of the unknowns has a small finite height, but becomes difficult when the height is large or, worse, the partial order does not satisfy the ascending chain condition. In this case, some way of accelerating iterations is needed, such as a *widening/narrowing* [13] or *warrowing* [8].

The ScalaFix library strives to be a general solver for these kind of equation system, in the spirit of modularization of static analyzers presented in [19]. It implements several iterative algorithms for solving equations (both with a finite or infinite number of unknowns) and it has a convenient interface which is designed for the Scala programming language. Scala combines functional and object-oriented programming in a single high-level language which runs on the Java Virtual Machine (JVM). The library may also be used, with some difficulties, from other languages which run on the JVM, such as Java itself. A better interface for other languages is planned for a later version. The source code of ScalaFix is available on https://github.com/jandom-devel/ScalaFix

M. Chechik et al. (Eds.): FM 2023, LNCS 14000, pp. 142–159, 2023.
https://doi.org/10.1007/978-3-031-27481-7_10

(in this paper we present the release 0.10), while the compiled code is on the Sonatype OSSRH (OSS Repository Hosting) https://oss.sonatype.org/ with group `it.unich.scalafix` and artifact `scalafix`.

In this paper we present the structure of the ScalaFix library and we show some examples of its use. The main application target for such a library is to be a backend for a static analyzer (it is currently in use by the Jandom static analyzer [2]).

In all the code fragments appearing in this paper we assume the following import statements:

```
import it.unich.scalafix.{finite, infinite, *}
import it.unich.scalafix.finite.*
import it.unich.scalafix.graphs.*
import it.unich.scalafix.highlevel.*
import it.unich.scalafix.utils.Relation
```

In many examples we will also use the PPL (Parma Polyhedra Library) [10] trough the JPPL bindings. These are simpler and more natural to use than the default Java bindings provided by the PPL. The source code for JPPL is available on https://github.com/jandom-devel/JPPL, while the compiled code is on the Sonatype repository https://s01.oss.sonatype.org/ with group `it.unich.jppl` and artifact `jppl`.

All the examples in this paper are available with full code in the GitHub repository https://github.com/jandom-devel/ScalaFixExamples.

2 Equation Systems

The main concept of ScalaFix is the *equation system*. It comes in two flavors: either with a finite number of unknowns or with a possibly infinite number of unknowns. The main difference between the two flavors is that, in the first case, we are generally interested in solving the system for all the unknowns, while in the second case we are only interested in solving for a single unknown.

Each equation system is characterized by a type `U` for the unknowns and a type `V` for the values assumed by the unknowns. As *assignment* is a function from unknowns to values. The different solvers of ScalaFix take an assignment as the input, perform several iterative steps, and produce a new assignment as the solution of the equation system. The *body* of an equation system is the cornerstone of all the iterative algorithms: it takes an initial assignment and returns a new assignment obtained by computing all the right hand sides of the equation system. In the Scala language, we have:

```
type Assignment[-U, +V] = U => V
type Body[U, V] = Assignment[U, V] => Assignment[U, V]
```

where `[-U, +V]` means that the assignment type is covariant in `V` and contravariant in `U`.

It is important not to be misled by the type of `Body`. Given the variables `body: Body[U, V]` and `rho: Assignment[U, V]`, we have that `body(rho)` is a function, hence no real computation starts until this is applied to a specific unknown `u: U`, as in `body(rho)(u)`.

2.1 Infinite Equation Systems

For example, consider the following equations defining the Fibonacci sequence:

$$x_0 = x_1 = 1 \qquad\qquad x_{i+2} = x_i + x_{i+1}$$

This may be encoded in ScalaFix as follows:

```
val body: Body[Int, BigInt] =
  (rho: Assignment[Int, BigInt]) =>
    (u: Int) =>
      if u <= 1 then 1 else rho(u-1) + rho(u-2)
```

Note that, although many type declarations might be avoided thanks to the Scala type inference, we have decided here to be more verbose since we think it is helpful to the reader.

The body must be packed into an `EquationSystem` before being handed over to a solver:

```
val eqs = EquationSystem(body)
```

Since the number of unknowns is infinite, we use the `infinite.WorkListSolver` for computing a solution. The worklist solver needs three parameters: an equation system, an initial assignment and the set of the unknowns for which we want to get a partial solution. For example, if we want to known the sixth Fibonacci number we use:

```
infinite.WorkListSolver(eqs)(Assignment(1), Set(6))
```

where `Assignment(1)` is the assignment which maps every unknown to 1 and `Set(6)` is the singleton set $\{6\}$.

The output is an assignment which maps 6 to the 6th Fibonacci number. Morevoer, since in order to determine x_6 we also need to solve for the unknowns from x_0 to x_5, the resulting assignment also contains the values for these unknowns:

```
[ 0 -> 1, 1 -> 1, 2 -> 2, 3 -> 3, 4 -> 5, 5 -> 8, 6 -> 13 ]
```

Another solver for infinite equation systems implemented in ScalaFix is the `PriorityWorkListSolver`, where the unknown to be updated is chosen, among those in the worklist, according to priorities which are dynamically generated.

In the general case there is no guarantee of convergence: this should be assured from the specific theory used to analyze the equation system under consideration.

2.2 Finite Equation Systems

The solvers in the `infinite` package work for equation systems with a possibly infinite number of unknowns. If the number of unknowns is finite, it is possible to use a `FiniteEquationSystem` instead, which allows to use different solvers specifically tailored for this case.

A finite equation system is characterized, besides its body, also by:

- the set of all the unknowns;
- the *influence* relation between the unknowns;
- a subset of all the unknowns, called the *input unknowns*.

While the set of all the unknowns is an obvious information, the other two parameters deserve an explanation. The influence relation determines the dependencies between unknowns. If the unknown x is used in the right hand side of the equation defining y, then we say that x influences y. When x is recomputed and its value changes, all the unknowns influenced by x should be recomputed as well.

Note that not all the solvers actually need the influence relation. For example, it is not used by `KleeneSolver`, which performs a parallel update of all the unknowns, and by `RoundRobinSolver`, which repeatedly updates all the unknowns one at a time. On the contrary, it is used by those solvers which avoid to recompute an unknown when it is not strictly necessary, such as `WorkListSolver`. In the case of infinite equation systems, the influence relation is computed dynamically during the evaluation of the body when needed, while for finite equation systems we require the influence relation to be provided statically.

The set of input unknowns is used to compute a depth-first ordering of the unknowns in the equation system. This allows to determine the set of unknowns where widening should be applied to ensure convergence and the default hierarchical ordering [11] for the `HierachicalOrderingSolver`.

We may turn the Fibonacci example into a finite equation system by restricting the number of unknowns, as follows:

```
val eqs = FiniteEquationSystem(
          body,
          infl = Relation( (i: Int) => Set(i-1, i-2) ),
          unknowns = 0 to 10,
          inputUnknowns = Set(0, 1) )
```

Then we may solve the equation system, for example with:

```
finite.WorkListSolver(eqs)(Assignment(1))
```

Here we do not need to specify the set of wanted unknowns, since we assume we are interested in solving the entire equation system and find the fixpoint for all the unknowns.

2.3 A Use Case for Static Analysis

We show a use case involving the Parma Polyhedra Library trough the Java binding provided by JPPL. Consider the example program `loop` and its corresponding equation system over the interval domain in Fig. 1. We first define the body of the equation system using the interval abstract domain `DoubleBox` from PPL as follows:

```
    i = 0
[0] while [1] (i<=10) {
[2]     i = i+1
[3] }
```

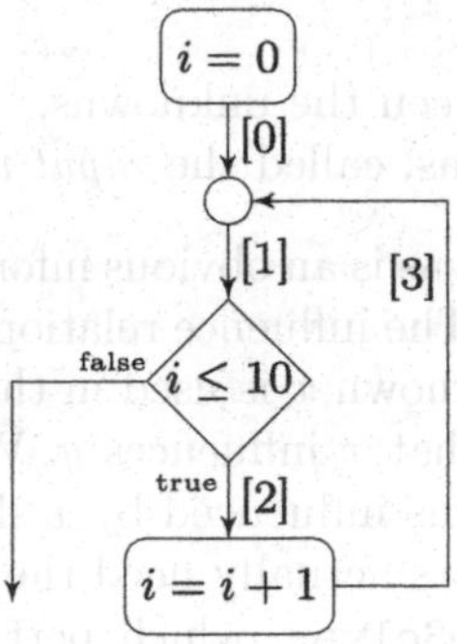

$x_0 = [0, 0]$
$x_1 = x_0 \vee x_3$
$x_2 = x_1 \wedge [-\infty, 10]$
$x_3 = x_2 + [1, 1]$

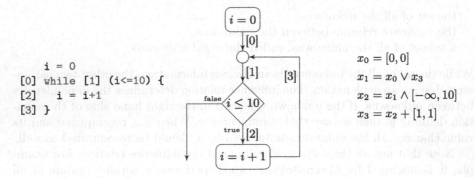

Fig. 1. The example program `loop`. The symbols $\vee$, $\wedge$ and $+$ are respectively the lub, the glb and the sum on the domain of intervals.

```
val body = (rho: Int => DoubleBox) => {
  case 0 => DoubleBox.from(/* constraint system {i=0} */)
  case 1 => rho(0).clone().upperBound(rho(3))
  case 2 => rho(1).clone().refineWith(/* constraint i<=10 */)
  case 3 => rho(2).clone().affineImage(0, /* expression i+1 */)
}
```

We can now construct a finite equation system as follows:

```
val eqs = FiniteEquationSystem[Int, DoubleBox](
    body,
    inputUnknowns = Set(0),
    unknowns = 0 to 3,
    infl = Relation(0 -> 1, 1 -> 2, 2 -> 3, 3 -> 1) )
```

where `unknowns` correspond to the program points 0, 1, 2, 3 in Fig. 1 and `infl` defines the dependency relations between the equations. For instance, `0 -> 1` means that any change in the value of x_0 requires recomputation of x_1. We can now solve the equation system with:

```
finite.WorkListSolver(eqs)(Assignment(DoubleBox.empty(1)))
```

whose solution is:

```
[0 -> i in 0, 1 -> i in [0, 11], 2 -> i in [0, 10], 3 -> i in [1, 11]]
```

where `2 -> i in [0, 10]` means that in the program point 2 the value of i is in the interval $[0, 10]$.

2.4 Infinite Equation Systems and Static Analysis

While finite equation systems are well-suited for intra-procedural analysis, infinite equation systems may be used for inter-procedural analysis, by including an abstraction of the call-stack as part of the unknowns.

Consider, for example, the following code:

```
function incr(a) {
[1]    b = a+1
[2]    return b
[3]
}

       i = j = 0
[4]    j = incr(i)
[5]    i = incr(j)
[6]
```

A possible approach for the analysis of this program consists in defining an equation system whose unknowns are pairs (p, c) where p is a program point and c is an abstraction of the call-stack, such as (but not limited to) an abstract representation of the values of the formal parameters.

Assuming to work with the interval domain, this is an excerpt of the equation system which describes the `incr` function:

```
val body: Body[(Int, DoubleBox), DoubleBox] = (rho) =>
  case (1, c) => c.clone().addSpaceDimensionAndEmbed(1)
  case (2, c) => rho((1, c)).clone()
                   .affineImage(1, /* expression a+1 */)
  case (3, c) => rho((2, c))
```

When the function `incr` is called in the context c, the value of the variables at program point 1 is obtained by enlarging the input, provided in c, with a new unconstrained dimension representing the variable b. The equation for the return statement, i.e., the unknown $(3, c)$, is a no-op: in the general case, we might decide to remove those dimensions corresponding to the local variables not returned by the function.

The following are the equations for the main program:

```
  case (4, c) => DoubleBox.from(/* constraints {i=j=0} */)
  case (5, c) =>
    val call_context = rho((4, c)).clone()
                         .removeSpaceDimensions(Array(1))
    val return_context = rho((3, call_context))
    val result = /* combine rho((4, c)) and return_context */
    result
  case (6, c) =>
    /* similar to code for (5, c) */
```

The interesting point is the equation for the program point $(5, c)$. Here we:

1. determine the abstract calling context by projecting the abstract value of the program point 4 on the actual parameters of the function call (variable i in this case);
2. take the abstract return context of the function `incr`, when invoked with the previously computed calling context;

3. combine the information at program point 4 and the return context to get the final best possible approximation of the value of variables at program point 5.

A theoretical discussion on the last step, as well as on alternative abstractions of the call-stack, is available in [21].

The reason why infinite equation systems are useful for inter-procedural analysis is that we cannot know in advance the contexts we will use for evaluating the `incr` function. In this example ScalaFix uses the intervals $[0, 0]$ and $[1, 1]$. Note that, in more complex cases, some kind of widening operator should be applied on calling contexts to avoid generating an infinite number of them.

3 Widening, Narrowing and Warrowing

ScalaFix supports the use of widenings, narrowings [14] and warrowings [8]. These operators are commonly used to combine the values of the last two iterations into a new value, in order to accelerate or ensure the convergence. In this paper, and in the ScalaFix jargon, they are generally called *combos*. Combos are implemented at the level of an equation system, and therefore work with every fixpoint solver. Mathematically, a combo over a set V is a binary function $\Box : V \times V \to V$. In ScalaFix we have that:

```
type Combo[V] = (V, V) => V
```

Applying a combo $\Box$ to an unknown x_i means replacing the equation $x_i = e$ with $x_i = x_i \Box e$. Typically, a combo is applied to a selection of unknowns, generally the loop heads in the graph generated by the unknowns and their influence relation. Potentially, we might want to use different combos for different unknowns. Therefore, when using combos in ScalaFix, we need to specify a `ComboAssignment`, i.e., a partial function which maps each unknown to the combo we want to use for it (if any). Continuing the example in Sect. 2.3, we may define a combo using the standard widening for intervals [12]:

```
val widening = Combo[DoubleBox]( (x: DoubleBox, y: DoubleBox) =>
                   y.clone().upperBound(x).widening(x) )
val comboAssignment = ComboAssignment(widening).restrict(Set(1))
```

where `restrict(Set(1))` means that we apply the widening to the unknown 1 only. We now equip the equation system with the widening:

```
val eqsWithWidening = eqs.withCombos(comboAssignment)
```

The equation system can be solved as before:

```
finite.WorkListSolver(eqsWithWidening)(Assignment(DoubleBox.empty(1)))
```

ScalaFix also implements general techniques enhancing widenings and narrowings such as delayed widening.

3.1 Automatic Determination of Combo Points

Instead of manually specifying the set of unknowns where combos should be applied, we may let ScalaFix determine this set automatically. Each finite equation system induces a dependency graph whose nodes are the unknowns and such that there is an edge (x, y) iff x influences y. We may build a depth-first ordering of this graph using

```
val ordering = DFOrdering(eqs)
```

whose result for the example program `loop` is:

```
UnknownOrdering( 0 (1) 2 3 )
```

Here the parenthesis denotes loop head nodes, i.e., nodes which are the target of retreating edges. In order to ensure convergence, it is enough to apply widenings to these nodes. This may be done with the `restrict` method used above, using the graph ordering as a parameter:

```
val comboAssignment = ComboAssignment(widening).restrict(ordering)
```

Then, everything proceeds as in the previous example.

4 Equation Systems Based on Hyper-Graphs

In the equation system shown above, the right-hand side of equations are black boxes. This is generally fine, but in some cases exposing some structure allows optimizations which are not possible otherwise. This is especially true for unknowns such as x_1 in Fig. 1 which correspond to join nodes of a flow chart.

ScalaFix allows to define a body for an equation system in a way that makes manifest the individual contributions of the edges of the flow chart. Consider again the equations in Fig. 1. For the sake of clarity, in Fig. 2 we depict the control-flow graph of the program. Note that the edge `i=0` has no source: this is fine since ScalaFix supports hyper-graphs, where each edge may have many (possibly none) sources and a single target. Hyper-graphs are needed for inter-procedural analysis [19]. Edges `enter` and `loop` correspond to the two edges entering the join node in Fig. 1, i.e., to the contributions x_0 and x_3 in the equation $x_1 = x_0 \vee x_3$.

We need to associate to each edge an action, i.e., a function that takes an assignment and returns the contribution of that edge to the new value of the target unknown.

```
type EdgeAction[U, V, E] = Assignment[U, V] => E => V
```

For our example equation system we have:

```
val edgeAction = (rho: Assignment[Int, DoubleBox]) => {
  case "i=0" => DoubleBox.from(/* constraint system {i=0} */)
  case "enter" => rho(0)
  case "i<=10" => rho(1).clone().refineWith(/* constraint i<=10 */)
  case "i=i+1" => rho(2).clone().affineImage(0, /* expression i+1 */)
  case "loop" => rho(3)
}
```

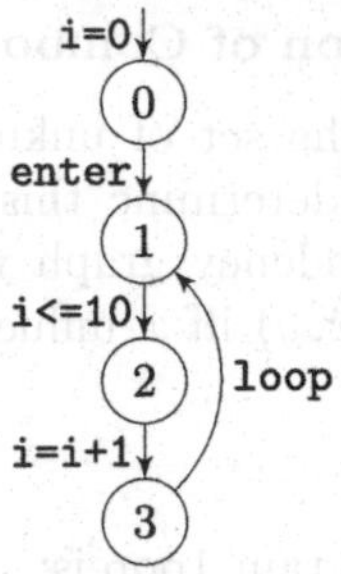

Fig. 2. The graph corresponding to the equation system in Fig. 1.

The actions for the edges should be packed together with fields describing the structure of the graph into a GraphBody:

```
val graphBody = GraphBody[Int, P, String](
  sources = Relation(
    "enter" -> 0, "i<=10" -> 1, "i=i+1" -> 2, "loop" -> 3),
  target = Map(
    "i=0" -> 0, "enter" -> 1, "i<=10" -> 2, "i=i+1" -> 3, "loop" -> 1),
  ingoing = Relation(
    0 -> "i=0",  1 -> "enter", 1 -> "loop", 2 -> "i<=10", 3 -> "i=i+1"),
  outgoing = Relation(
    0 -> "enter", 1 -> "i<=10", 2 -> "i=i+1", 3 -> "loop"),
  edgeAction = edgeAction,
  combiner = (x, y) => x.clone().upperBound(y),
  unknowns = 0 to 3 )
```

The body is automatically reconstructed in ScalaFix by combining all the contributions from the incoming edges with the specified operation `combiner`, which in our example is simply the upper bound operator of the abstract domain. Finally, the body is used to build a graph-based equation system:

```
val eqs = GraphEquationSystem(
  initialGraph = graphBody,
  inputUnknowns = Set(0) )
```

Since a `GraphEquationSystem` is a subclass of `FiniteEquationSystem`, we may use `eqs` exactly as the equation systems in the previous sections.

Note that the way we provide to `GraphBody` the structure of the graph is not particularly elegant: there is a lot of redundancy among the parameters `sources`, `target`, `ingoing` and `outgoing`. However, ScalaFix has been principally designed to be used as a backend for a static analyzer. In this context, it is likely that the analyzer has already built the control-flow graph internally. Since the four parameters above are just functions from edges (or nodes) to set of nodes (or edges), it is easy for a static analyzer to build a very thin layer providing these parameters.

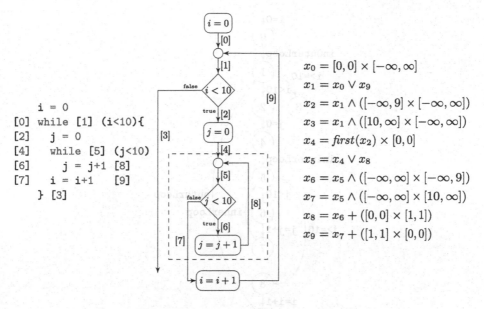

```
    i = 0
[0] while [1] (i<10){
[2]   j = 0
[4]   while [5] (j<10)
[6]     j = j+1 [8]
[7]   i = i+1     [9]
    } [3]
```

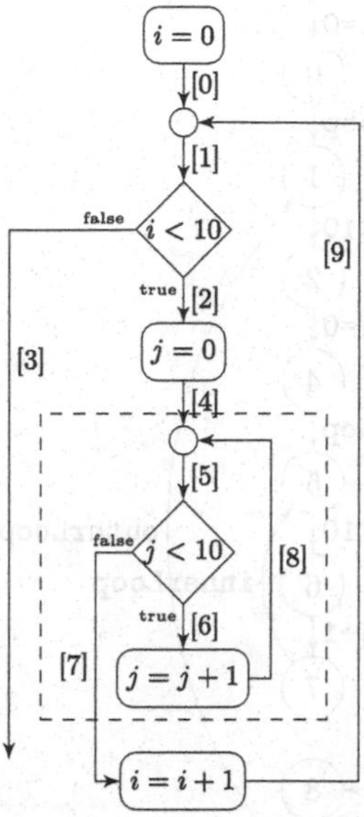

$$x_0 = [0,0] \times [-\infty, \infty]$$
$$x_1 = x_0 \vee x_9$$
$$x_2 = x_1 \wedge ([-\infty, 9] \times [-\infty, \infty])$$
$$x_3 = x_1 \wedge ([10, \infty] \times [-\infty, \infty])$$
$$x_4 = \mathit{first}(x_2) \times [0,0]$$
$$x_5 = x_4 \vee x_8$$
$$x_6 = x_5 \wedge ([-\infty, \infty] \times [-\infty, 9])$$
$$x_7 = x_5 \wedge ([-\infty, \infty] \times [10, \infty])$$
$$x_8 = x_6 + ([0,0] \times [1,1])$$
$$x_9 = x_7 + ([1,1] \times [0,0])$$

Fig. 3. The example program `nested`.

The ScalaFix library also provide a different API for building graphs (the `GraphBodyBuilder` class) which is easier to use for simple experiments but is not described in this paper.

4.1 Localized Widening

The definition of an equation system based on hyper-graphs allows us to use localized widening [7]. Consider the program `nested` in Fig. 3 and the corresponding system of equations. Let `graphBody` be the description of the graph in Fig. 3, as depicted in Fig. 4. We can build, as in the previous section, a graph equation system as follows:

```
val eqs = GraphEquationSystem(
  initialGraph = graphBody,
  inputUnknowns = Set(0) )
```

and define the widening:

```
val widening = Combo[DoubleBox]((x: DoubleBox, y: DoubleBox) =>
                 y.clone().upperBound(x).widening(x))
```

Now using `DFOrdering` we can recover the depth-first ordering of the set of unknowns:

```
val ordering = DFOrdering(eqs)
```

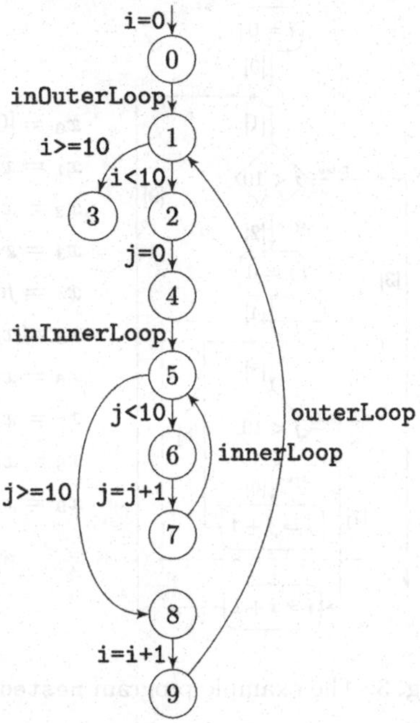

Fig. 4. The graph corresponding to the equation system in Fig. 3.

which is (0 (1) 3 2 4 (5) 8 9 6 7), where (1) and (5) are the loop head nodes. We can apply localized widening to these nodes as follows:

```
val widenings = ComboAssignment(widening).restrict(ordering)
val eqsWithWidening = eqs.withLocalizedCombos(widenings, ordering)
val solutionAscending =
    WorkListSolver(eqsWithWidening)(Assignment(DoubleBox.empty(2)))
```

where the last line computes the solution for the ascending chain. We can now start a descending phase using the narrowing defined in [12]:

```
val narrowing = Combo[DoubleBox]((x: DoubleBox, y: DoubleBox) =>
                  y.clone().intersection(x).CC76Narrowing(x))
val narrowings = ComboAssignment(narrowing).restrict(ordering)
val eqsWithNarrowing = eqs.withCombos(narrowings)
WorkListSolver(eqsWithNarrowing)(solutionAscending)
```

In the solution for the program point 3 we have that i in [10, 11), which cannot be computed without the localized widening.

5 A High-Level Interface

The interface shown above, where the user builds an equation system, decides where to apply widening/narrowing and calls the solver with appropriate parameters, is rather low-level. For example, if one wants to solve an equation system using the classical approach based on an ascending chain with widening followed by a descending chain with narrowing, this procedure must be repeated for both phases, as done in the previous section.

Albeit this allows an extreme flexibility, if we just want to solve an equation system following a standard approach, ScalaFix provides a high-level API which simplifies this task. It is enough to call the generic `FiniteFixpointSolver` with a bunch of parameters which specify how we want to solve the equation system. For example, the analysis shown in Sect. 4.1 may be implemented more easily as follows:

```
val params = Parameters[Int, DoubleBox](
  solver = Solver.WorkListSolver,
  start = Assignment(DoubleBox.empty(2)),
  comboLocation = ComboLocation.Loop,
  comboScope = ComboScope.Localized,
  comboStrategy = ComboStrategy.TwoPhases,
  restartStrategy = RestartStrategy.None,
  widenings = ComboAssignment(widening),
  narrowings = ComboAssignment(narrowing) )
FiniteFixpointSolver(eqs, params)
```

The possible choices for the above parameters are:

- `solver`: one of the following fixpoint solvers:
  - `KleeneSolver`: updates all the unknowns in parallel;
  - `RoundRobinSolver`: updates one unknown at a time, following a fixed ordering;
  - `WorkListSolver`: updates one unknown at a time, taken from a queue containing only the unknowns which might produce a different result w.r.t. the previous iteration;
  - `PriorityWorkListSolver`: it is similar to the `WorkListSolver`, but the order in which unknowns are extracted from the queue depends on an ordering of the unknowns;
  - `HierarchicalOrderingSolver`: updates the unknowns following a hierarchical ordering (see [11]).

  For the `PriorityWorkListSolver` and `HierarchicalOrderingSolver`, the ordering is based on the depth first traversal of the equation system.
- `comboLocation`: `None` does not use combos; `All` puts combos at each unknown; `Loop` places combos only at loop heads (which are automatically computed).
- `comboScope`: `Standard` or `Localized`, for standard or localized widening respectively.
- `comboStrategy`: `OnlyWidening` uses widening operators with no descending phase; `TwoPhases` uses the standard two phases widening/narrowing approach; `Warrowing` strictly intertwines ascending and descending steps in a single warrowing operator;

– **restartStrategy**: either `None` or `Restarting` for disabling or enabling the restarting policy which replaces part of the current assignment with the initial assignment, in order to improve precision [8] (only useful for the `PriorityWorklistSolver`).

The high level API also needs some extra information on the analysis domain. This may be provided to ScalaFix in the form of a *given instance* (the Scala equivalent of a type class) of the type `Domain`. This instance implicitly provides the partial ordering relation and the upper bound operator for a given type. This is a fragment of the `Domain` instance for `DoubleBox`:

```
given DoubleBoxDomain: Domain[DoubleBox] with
  def lteq(x: DoubleBox, y: DoubleBox): Boolean = y.contains(x)
  def upperBound(x: DoubleBox, y: DoubleBox): DoubleBox =
      x.clone().upperBound(y)
```

6 Performance

In this section we present some benchmarks showing the performance of the ScalaFix library. Obviously, different equation solvers will have different performances, but comparing different methods for solving equation systems is not in the scope of this paper. What we want to show is the overhead which is caused by using the ScalaFix library instead of an ad-hoc equation solver.

6.1 A Simple Benchmark Using the PPL

Consider the equation system E given by the following equations on $\mathcal{P}(\mathbb{Z})$:

$$\begin{aligned} x_0 &= (x_{N-1} \cap \{v \mid v \leq l\}) \cup \{0\} \\ x_{i+1} &= \{v+1 \mid v \in x_i\} \end{aligned} \tag{1}$$

We solve E with $N = 100$ and $l = 2{,}000$ using the following methods:

1. an ad-hoc implementation of the round-robin solver, using arrays as the data structure for assignments (`array`);
2. an ad-hoc implementation of the round-robin solver, using hash tables as the data structure for assignments (`hash`);
3. the round-robin solver of ScalaFix (`scalafix`).

For each method, we used both the `DoubleBox` and `CPolyedron` domains of the PPL, with or without widening at each unknown. In ScalaFix widenings are added to E using the `.withCombos` method, while in the custom solvers they are inlined inside the solvers.

Benchmarking programs running on the JVM is not an easy task, since a lot of factors may impact the execution speed, such as just in time compilation and garbage collection. We have used the JMH (Java Microbenchmark Harness) to perform the benchmarks, using 5 forks, each fork composed of 5 iterations for

Table 1. Benchmarks results (operations/s) with 99% confidence intervals.

Benchmarks	Array	Hash	Scalafix
Box without combos	54.364 ± 6.725	55.180 ± 6.318	54.941 ± 7.395
Box with combos	246.072 ± 36.047	261.492 ± 36.443	261.707 ± 35.318
Polyhedra without combos	14.334 ± 2.232	14.994 ± 1.759	15.081 ± 1.515
Polyhedra with combos	85.590 ± 17.383	90.507 ± 13.428	85.638 ± 16.541
Reaching definitions	15946.052 ± 64.141	15298.415 ± 134.841	15301.827 ± 59.145

warming up the JVM and 5 iterations for collecting the results. On top of this, we have tried to reduce the effect of automatic CPU performance scaling by disabling Turbo Boost and setting a fixed clock for the CPU, low enough not to overheat the processor. In particular, the results have been obtained on a Intel Core i2500K clocked at 1.6 GHz.

The results are shown in Table 1, and are expressed in operations per second (i.e., the number of times the equation system is solved per second) with a 99% confidence interval.

The benchmarks show that the difference between the three solvers is negligible, since the cost of executing the `DoubleBox` and `CPolyhedron` operations is much larger than the overhead of the fixpoint solvers.

6.2 Reaching Definitions

The second benchmark contains different implementations of an equation system for reaching definition analysis of a three-address code program from [1, p. 626], whose code is in Fig. 5. As before, we have executed the benchmark comparing the ScalaFix solver to an ad-hoc implementation of the round-robin solver, using arrays and hash tables. The results show that even in this case the difference between the solvers is negligible.

The experiments suggest that the overhead of using ScalaFix is very limited, almost zero.

7 Related Work

Most available static analyzers, both for industrial or academic applications, implement their custom procedure for solving equation systems. We believe that the use of ScalaFix could help developers in experimenting with different and state-of-the-art solvers. Also, they could contribute, by implementing new techniques that would be immediately reusable by the community. Moreover, the developers would benefit from all the experiments and development efforts behind the library. Actually, one of the major difficulty in the development of ScalaFix has been to choose the correct abstractions to put widening, narrowing, warrowing, localized techniques, equation systems, assignments, solvers, etc... inside a common API.

```
i = m-1       [d1]
j = n         [d2]
a = u1        [d3]
do
  i = i+1     [d4]
  j = j-1     [d5]
  if (e1)
    a = u2    [d6]
  else
    i = u3    [d7]
while (e2)
```

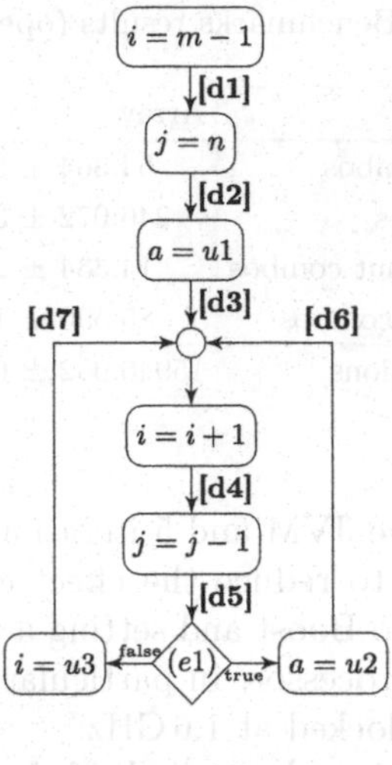

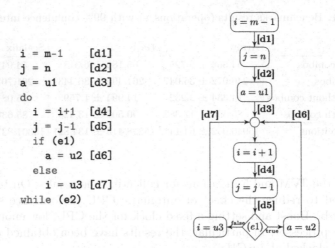

Fig. 5. Reaching definition benchmark.

To the best of our knowledge, ScalaFix is the only general purpose library for solving equation systems for static analysis which is currently available.

We are aware of only another proposal in the past with the library Fixpoint [20]. This library is unmaintained for more than nine years now and the subversion repository for the source code is not accessible. In general, while Fixpoint and ScalaFix share the same general goal, there are many differences:

- Fixpoint was written in OCaml, while ScalaFix is written in Scala for the Java Virtual Machine.
- The structure of Fixpoint was more monolithic than that of ScalaFix: the `Fixpoint.manager` type encapsulates almost all the information needed to solve an equation system, from the position of widenings to the action of the hyper-edges. In ScalaFix we give different responsibilities to different classes.
- Fixpoint had additional modules implementing some techniques for solving fixpoint equations, namely, guided static analysis [17] and widening with threshold [23]. Implementation of these techniques is a planned improvements for ScalaFix.
- ScalaFix implements many state-of-the-art techniques recently proposed, such as localized widening, warrowing and restarting.
- ScalaFix implements general solvers for infinite equation systems, suitable for the analysis of inter-procedural programs.

Since the source code of Fixpoint is no more available, neither a more detailed comparison nor a performance evaluation has been possible.

Another library for solving fixpoint equations, with a different purpose, is Killdall (https://compcert.org/doc-1.6/html/Kildall.html), written for the Coq proof assistant, and part of the CompCert project [22]. Killdall implements the same algorithm as the `PriorityWorklistSolver` for finite equation systems in ScalaFix, using the depth-first ordering of the equation system for deciding priorities. However, Killdall does not implement any of the additional features of ScalaFix such as combos (Kildall does not have any support for widening or narrowing), infinite equation systems or alternative solvers. But here the goal is to provide a mechanized verification of program analyses, which can be used to equip the CompCert C compiler, being a challenge to implement and reason upon data structures in a purely functional setting such as Coq.

Finally, FPSolve [15] is a library for solving systems of polynomial equations over a semi-ring. While in particular cases it is possible to recast data-flow equations as equations over a semi-ring, this does not hold in general. Therefore the applicability of FPSolve as a general procedure for solving data-flow equations is limited.

8 Conclusion

We have shown some features of the ScalaFix library. There are other features of ScalaFix which are not presented here, such as:

- support for observing the behaviour of the solvers with the listener class `FixpointSolverTracer` which can be used for debugging and computing metrics, and also for fine-tuning the analysis domain using statistical approaches (see for instance [3,6]);
- support for *restarting*: a policy which, under certain conditions, replaces part of the current assignment with the initial assignment, in order to improve precision [8];
- implementation of other equation solvers from the literature, such as solvers based on hierarchical ordering and priority worklists.

ScalaFix is the only general purpose library implementing advanced techniques such as localized widening and restarting. In the near future, we plan to enhance ScalaFix along several directions:

- develop a thin interface layer to make ScalaFix easier to use by other JVM based languages;
- implement more techniques such as guided abstract interpretation [17], lookahead widening [16] or the improved handling of descending chains in [18];
- implement equation systems with side-effects [9] and for different paradigms [4,5].

We have shown in Sect. 6 that the overhead of using ScalaFix instead of re-implementing an ad-hoc solver is negligible. A big effort has been provided to design the ScalaFix API to be as flexible as possible for the need of very different analyzers, and in the choice of the data structures both for equation systems and graphs to allow the implementation of many speed-up features, depending on the kind of equation systems used.

References

1. Aho, A.V., Sethi, R., Ullman, J.: Compilers: Principles, Techniques and Tools, 1st edn. Addison Wesley, Boston (1986)
2. Amato, G., Di Nardo Di Maio, S., Scozzari, F.: Numerical static analysis with Soot. In: Proceedings of the ACM SIGPLAN International Workshop on State of the Art in Java Program Analysis, SOAP 2013. ACM, New York (2013). https://doi.org/10.1145/2487568.2487571
3. Amato, G., Parton, M., Scozzari, F.: A tool which mines partial execution traces to improve static analysis. In: Barringer, H., et al. (eds.) RV 2010. LNCS, vol. 6418, pp. 475–479. Springer, Heidelberg (2010). https://doi.org/10.1007/978-3-642-16612-9_37
4. Amato, G., Scozzari, F.: Optimality in goal-dependent analysis of sharing. Theory Pract. Logic Program. **9**(5), 617–689 (2009). https://doi.org/10.1017/S1471068409990111
5. Amato, G., Scozzari, F.: Observational completeness on abstract interpretation. Fund. Inform. **106**(2–4), 149–173 (2011). https://doi.org/10.3233/FI-2011-381
6. Amato, G., Scozzari, F.: Random: R-based analyzer for numerical domains. In: Bjørner, N., Voronkov, A. (eds.) LPAR 2012. LNCS, vol. 7180, pp. 375–382. Springer, Heidelberg (2012). https://doi.org/10.1007/978-3-642-28717-6_29
7. Amato, G., Scozzari, F.: Localizing widening and narrowing. In: Logozzo, F., Fähndrich, M. (eds.) SAS 2013. LNCS, vol. 7935, pp. 25–42. Springer, Heidelberg (2013). https://doi.org/10.1007/978-3-642-38856-9_4
8. Amato, G., Scozzari, F., Seidl, H., Apinis, K., Vojdani, V.: Efficiently intertwining widening and narrowing. Sci. Comput. Program. **120**, 1–24 (2016). https://doi.org/10.1016/j.scico.2015.12.005
9. Apinis, K., Seidl, H., Vojdani, V.: Side-effecting constraint systems: a swiss army knife for program analysis. In: Jhala, R., Igarashi, A. (eds.) APLAS 2012. LNCS, vol. 7705, pp. 157–172. Springer, Heidelberg (2012). https://doi.org/10.1007/978-3-642-35182-2_12
10. Bagnara, R., Hill, P.M., Zaffanella, E.: The Parma Polyhedra Library: toward a complete set of numerical abstractions for the analysis and verification of hardware and software systems. Sci. Comput. Program. **72**(1–2), 3–21 (2008). https://doi.org/10.1016/j.scico.2007.08.001
11. Bourdoncle, F.: Efficient chaotic iteration strategies with widenings. In: Bjørner, D., Broy, M., Pottosin, I.V. (eds.) FMP&TA 1993. LNCS, vol. 735, pp. 128–141. Springer, Heidelberg (1993). https://doi.org/10.1007/BFb0039704
12. Cousot, P., Cousot, R.: Static determination of dynamic properties of programs. In: Proceedings of the Second International Symposium on Programming, Dunod, Paris, France, pp. 106–130 (1976)
13. Cousot, P., Cousot, R.: Abstract interpretation: a unified lattice model for static analysis of programs by construction or approximation of fixpoints. In: Proceedings of the 4th ACM SIGACT-SIGPLAN Symposium on Principles of Programming Languages, POPL 1977, pp. 238–252. ACM Press, New York (1977). https://doi.org/10.1145/512950.512973
14. Cousot, P., Cousot, R.: Comparing the Galois connection and widening/narrowing approaches to abstract interpretation. In: Bruynooghe, M., Wirsing, M. (eds.) PLILP 1992. LNCS, vol. 631, pp. 269–295. Springer, Heidelberg (1992). https://doi.org/10.1007/3-540-55844-6_142

15. Esparza, J., Luttenberger, M., Schlund, M.: FPsolve: a generic solver for fixpoint equations over semirings. In: Holzer, M., Kutrib, M. (eds.) CIAA 2014. LNCS, vol. 8587, pp. 1–15. Springer, Cham (2014). https://doi.org/10.1007/978-3-319-08846-4_1
16. Gopan, D., Reps, T.: Lookahead widening. In: Ball, T., Jones, R.B. (eds.) CAV 2006. LNCS, vol. 4144, pp. 452–466. Springer, Heidelberg (2006). https://doi.org/10.1007/11817963_41
17. Gopan, D., Reps, T.: Guided static analysis. In: Nielson, H.R., Filé, G. (eds.) SAS 2007. LNCS, vol. 4634, pp. 349–365. Springer, Heidelberg (2007). https://doi.org/10.1007/978-3-540-74061-2_22
18. Halbwachs, N., Henry, J.: When the decreasing sequence fails. In: Miné, A., Schmidt, D. (eds.) SAS 2012. LNCS, vol. 7460, pp. 198–213. Springer, Heidelberg (2012). https://doi.org/10.1007/978-3-642-33125-1_15
19. Jeannet, B.: Some experience on the software engineering of abstract interpretation tools. Electron. Notes Theor. Comput. Sci. **267**(2), 29–42 (2010). https://doi.org/10.1016/j.entcs.2010.09.016. https://www.sciencedirect.com/science/article/pii/. S1571066110001453, Proceedings of the Tools for Automatic Program AnalysiS (TAPAS)
20. Jeannet, B.: Fixpoint (2012). http://pop-art.inrialpes.fr/people/bjeannet/bjeannet-forge/fixpoint/
21. Jeannet, B., Serwe, W.: Abstracting call-stacks for interprocedural verification of imperative programs. In: Rattray, C., Maharaj, S., Shankland, C. (eds.) AMAST 2004. LNCS, vol. 3116, pp. 258–273. Springer, Heidelberg (2004). https://doi.org/10.1007/978-3-540-27815-3_22
22. Kästner, D., Leroy, X., Blazy, S., Schommer, B., Schmidt, M., Ferdinand, C.: Closing the gap - the formally verified optimizing compiler CompCert. In: Developments in System Safety Engineering: Proceedings of the Twenty-fifth Safety-Critical Systems Symposium, SSS 2017, pp. 163–180. Safety-Critical Systems Club (2017)
23. Lakhdar-Chaouch, L., Jeannet, B., Girault, A.: Widening with thresholds for programs with complex control graphs. In: Bultan, T., Hsiung, P.-A. (eds.) ATVA 2011. LNCS, vol. 6996, pp. 492–502. Springer, Heidelberg (2011). https://doi.org/10.1007/978-3-642-24372-1_38

HHLPy: Practical Verification of Hybrid Systems Using Hoare Logic

Huanhuan Sheng[1,2], Alexander Bentkamp[1], and Bohua Zhan[1,2](✉)

[1] State Key Laboratory of Computer Science, Institute of Software, Chinese Academy of Sciences, Beijing, China
{shenghh,bentkamp,bzhan}@ios.ac.cn
[2] University of Chinese Academy of Sciences, Beijing, China

Abstract. We present a tool for verification of hybrid systems expressed in the sequential fragment of HCSP (Hybrid Communicating Sequential Processes). The tool permits annotating HCSP programs with pre- and postconditions, invariants, and proof rules for reasoning about ordinary differential equations. Verification conditions are generated from the annotations following the rules of a Hoare logic for hybrid systems. We designed labeling and highlighting mechanisms to distinguish and visualize different verification conditions. The tool is implemented in Python and has a web-based user interface. We evaluated the effectiveness of the tool on translations of Simulink/Stateflow models and on KeYmaera X benchmarks.

Keywords: Hybrid systems · Hoare logic · Formal verification

1 Introduction

Hybrid systems refer to systems that have both continuous and discrete behaviors. They occur in diverse areas of science and engineering, ranging from transportation and spaceflight, to robots and medical devices. Hence, verifying that hybrid systems meet certain specifications is an important problem. Apart from methods such as monitoring and model checking, theorem proving is one of the major approaches to verifying hybrid systems.

There is a substantial amount of previous work on verification of hybrid systems based on theorem proving. One major framework is Platzer's differential dynamic logic ($\mathsf{d}\mathcal{L}$) [23,25], and the associated KeYmaera/KeYmaera X prover [9,26]. Recently, a Hoare logic has been introduced for $\mathsf{d}\mathcal{L}$ and implemented within the Isabelle proof assistant [21]. We review these works in detail in Sect. 8 of this paper.

Another approach is to model hybrid systems using HCSP (Hybrid CSP) [13,33], an extension of CSP (Communicating Sequential Processes) to include continuous evolution. Its semantics of continuous evolution is deterministic, so it can be used naturally for capturing Simulink/Stateflow models. A hybrid Hoare logic has been developed for HCSP, and is implemented in Isabelle [29]. However, practical application of the tool is complicated by its steep learning curve. To use

M. Chechik et al. (Eds.): FM 2023, LNCS 14000, pp. 160–178, 2023.
https://doi.org/10.1007/978-3-031-27481-7_11

this tool, the user need to be familiar with the Isabelle proof assistant, as well as manually applying a set of Hoare logic rules which are themselves very complex. This is in stark contrast to KeYmaera X, which allows users to verify hybrid programs by choosing menu actions and offers highly specialized automation.

This paper introduces HHLPy[1], a tool for verification of the sequential part of HCSP with a friendly graphical user interface. Compared to [29], we simplify the Hoare logic rules, and add more rules for reasoning about the behavior of differential equations. These latter rules are closely related to that in d$\mathcal{L}$, but due to the semantic differences of HCSP, we adapted some of the rules and proved our rules to be sound (Sect. 3).

Our Hoare logic rules are in a sufficiently simple form that automatic verification condition generation is possible. We design such a procedure to compute verification conditions (VCs) from a given annotated HCSP program (Sect. 4). We express VCs as a set of conditions, splitting up VCs that are conjunctions as much as possible. We use labels to distinguish between different VCs, so that users can choose solvers (currently either Z3 [19] or Wolfram Engine [30]) for each VC individually and such choices are maintained through minor changes on the code (Sect. 5).

To visualize to the user where each VC originates from, a highlighting mechanism highlights the set of code fragments in the annotated program that contributed to generating the VC (Sect. 6).

We implemented the tool using Python and JavaScript and evaluated it on Simulink/Stateflow models and on KeYmaera X benchmarks (Sect. 7). We translated two Simulink/Stateflow models using the toolchain developed by Zou et al. [34,35] and verified them in our tool. Due to differences in the semantics of d$\mathcal{L}$ and HCSP, we translated each KeYmaera X benchmark by hand, trying to maintain semantic equivalence as much as possible. In this way, we succeeded to use our tool to solve most of the verification problems in the basic and nonlinear KeYmaera X benchmarks.

2 Preliminaries

In this section, we present the sequential fragment of HCSP, with an informal explanation of its semantics. We further give an overview of the existing toolchain on translation of Simulink/Stateflow models into HCSP.

2.1 Sequential Fragment of HCSP

Hybrid CSP (HCSP), introduced in [13,33], is an extension of Hoare's Communicating Sequential Processes to include continuous evolution. It can model communicating processes running in parallel, where each process may have both continuous and discrete behavior. In this paper, we focus on the sequential fragment of HCSP, consisting of the following commands:

[1] The tool is available at https://github.com/bzhan/mars/tree/master/hhlpy.

$$S, T ::= \texttt{skip} \mid x := e \mid x := *(B) \mid S; T \mid \texttt{if}\ B\ \texttt{then}\ S\ \texttt{else}\ T \mid S \mathrel{++} T \mid S* \\ \mid \langle \dot{\boldsymbol{x}} = \boldsymbol{e} \,\&\, D \rangle$$

The program state is a mapping from variables to reals. `skip` leaves the state unchanged. $x := e$ assigns the value of expression e to variable x. $x := *(B)$ is nondeterministic assignment of some value satisfying condition B to x. $S; T$ and **if** B **then** S **else** T are regular sequential composition and conditional. $S \mathrel{++} T$ is a nondeterministic choice between S and T. $S*$ runs S a nondeterministic number of times (including zero).

The ordinary differential equation (ODE) command $\langle \dot{\boldsymbol{x}} = \boldsymbol{e} \,\&\, D \rangle$ specifies continuous evolution in HCSP. It makes the vector of variables $\boldsymbol{x}$ evolve according to ODE $\dot{\boldsymbol{x}} = \boldsymbol{e}$ until the domain D becomes false. If D is false from the start, the ODE is skipped. In contrast to d$\mathcal{L}$, where continuous evolution may stop at any point within the specified domain, in HCSP it always deterministically continues up to the boundary. In this paper, we assume D is given by a polynomial inequality of the form $p(\boldsymbol{x}) < 0$, so it represents an open set in $\mathbb{R}^n$.

We assume in this paper that all expressions appearing in an HCSP program (as well as in annotations to be discussed later) are polynomials, and hence continuity conditions are trivially satisfied.

For a formal treatment of semantics of HCSP (including communication and parallel composition), we refer to Zhan et al. [32, Chapter 6].

2.2 Translation from Simulink/Stateflow

The HCSP language is located at the center of a toolchain that also includes translation from Simulink/Stateflow models, simulation and code generation [2]. The original translation algorithms from Simulink [35] and Stateflow [34] produce HCSP programs that involve communication between parallel processes. However, more recent methods by Xu et al. [31] and Guo et al. [11] produce sequential HCSP programs. We use these translation methods for verification of Simulink/Stateflow models in Sect. 7.

3 Proof Rules of Hoare Logic for Hybrid Systems

In this section, we present the Hoare logic that forms the basis of our verification tool. The Hoare triple for partial correctness, written as $\{P\}c\{Q\}$, means starting from a state satisfying assertion P, any terminating execution of c reaches a state satisfying assertion Q. The Hoare rules for ordinary commands (except ODEs) are standard and are presented in the Appendix of the full version of the paper [28].

Hence, we focus on the Hoare rules for ODEs. These rules are mostly adapted from rules for d$\mathcal{L}$, as given in [25,27]. Due to the difference in semantics between HCSP and d$\mathcal{L}$, several of the rules take on different forms. We do not aim to present a minimal set of rules, instead providing users a wide range of choices.

3.1 Proof Rules Based on Invariants

In order to state proof rules based on invariants of ODEs, we require an additional kind of judgments, called invariant triples.

Definition 1 (Invariant Triple). *Let P and Q be predicates on the variables of an ODE $\dot{\boldsymbol{x}} = \boldsymbol{e}$. Let $\gamma : [0, T] \to \mathbb{R}^n$ be a solution of the ODE such that $\gamma(t)$ satisfies P for all $t \in [0, T]$ and such that $\gamma(0)$ satisfies Q. If for all such solutions γ, $\gamma(t)$ satisfies Q for all $t \in [0, T]$, then we say that Q is an invariant of ODE $\dot{\boldsymbol{x}} = \boldsymbol{e}$ under domain P, written as*

$$[\![P]\!]\langle \dot{\boldsymbol{x}} = \boldsymbol{e} \rangle [\![Q]\!]$$

Differential Weakening. The differential weakening rule (dW) reduces a Hoare triple goal to an invariant triple, incorporating the domain condition.

$$\frac{[\![\overline{D}]\!]\langle \dot{\boldsymbol{x}} = \boldsymbol{e} \rangle [\![I]\!] \quad \partial D \wedge I \to Q}{\{(D \to I) \wedge (\neg D \to Q)\}\langle \dot{\boldsymbol{x}} = \boldsymbol{e}\,\&\, D \rangle \{Q\}}\,\mathrm{dW}$$

Here, $\overline{D}$ is the closure of D, and ∂D is the boundary set of D. Note that the rule is in the form that allows us to derive a precondition from any postcondition. The precondition $(D \to I) \wedge (\neg D \to Q)$ corresponds to the two cases for the state before ODE: if the state satisfies domain D, then it should satisfy the invariant. Otherwise it should satisfy the postcondition Q directly. Two special cases of the rule, for I set to true and false, provide further intuition. They correspond to cases where no invariant is needed, and where the starting state is known to satisfy $\neg D$.

$$\frac{\partial D \to Q}{\{\neg D \to Q\}\langle \dot{\boldsymbol{x}} = \boldsymbol{e}\,\&\, D \rangle \{Q\}}\,\mathrm{dWT} \qquad \frac{}{\{\neg D \wedge Q\}\langle \dot{\boldsymbol{x}} = \boldsymbol{e}\,\&\, D \rangle \{Q\}}\,\mathrm{dWF}$$

Proof (of the (dW) rule). Given starting state $\boldsymbol{x}$, we divide into two cases based on whether $\boldsymbol{x}$ satisfies domain D. If $\boldsymbol{x}$ satisfies D, then there exists a solution $\gamma : [0, T] \to \mathbb{R}^n$, such that $\gamma(t)$ satisfies D for $t \in [0, T)$ and $\gamma(T)$ satisfies $\neg D$, and we wish to show that $\gamma(T)$ satisfies Q. By the continuity of γ, we get that $\gamma(t)$ satisfies $\overline{D}$ for $t \in [0, T]$. Moreover, since $D \to I$ holds in the precondition, we get that $\gamma(0)$ satisfies I as well. Then from $[\![\overline{D}]\!]\langle \dot{\boldsymbol{x}} = \boldsymbol{e} \rangle [\![I]\!]$, we get that $\gamma(t)$ satisfies I for $t \in [0, T]$. From $\partial D \wedge I \to Q$ and the fact that $\gamma(T)$ satisfies I and ∂D, we get that $\gamma(T)$ satisfies Q, as desired.

If $\boldsymbol{x}$ does not satisfy D, then the ODE is not executed, and we wish to show that $\boldsymbol{x}$ satisfies Q. Since $\neg D \to Q$ holds in the precondition, we get that $\boldsymbol{x}$ satisfies Q, as desired.

Differential Invariant. The differential invariant rule (dI) is essentially the same as that in d$\mathcal{L}$. It concludes invariants from computation of Lie derivatives.

$$\frac{P \to \dot{f} = 0}{[\![P]\!]\langle \dot{\boldsymbol{x}} = \boldsymbol{e} \rangle [\![f = 0]\!]}\,\mathrm{dI}_{=}$$

Here $\dot{f}$ denotes the Lie derivative of f under the differential equation $\dot{\boldsymbol{x}} = \boldsymbol{e}$. The corresponding rules for inequality and disequality are as follows, where $\succcurlyeq$ denotes either $>$ or $\geq$.

$$\frac{P \to \dot{f} \geq 0}{[\![P]\!]\langle\dot{\boldsymbol{x}} = \boldsymbol{e}\rangle[\![f \succcurlyeq 0]\!]}\,\mathrm{dI}_{\succcurlyeq} \qquad \frac{P \to \dot{f} = 0}{[\![P]\!]\langle\dot{\boldsymbol{x}} = \boldsymbol{e}\rangle[\![f \neq 0]\!]}\,\mathrm{dI}_{\neq}$$

Differential Cut. The differential cut rule (dC) inserts an intermediate invariant to be proved, and afterwards permits the use of this invariant to show further invariants. In contrast to d$\mathcal{L}$, it is not possible to record previously proved invariants as conjuncts in the domain of ODE commands. Instead we place them in the premise of the invariant triple. Indeed this is the primary motivation for introducing the concept of invariant triples.

$$\frac{[\![P]\!]\langle\dot{\boldsymbol{x}} = \boldsymbol{e}\rangle[\![Q_1]\!] \quad [\![P \wedge Q_1]\!]\langle\dot{\boldsymbol{x}} = \boldsymbol{e}\rangle[\![Q_2]\!]}{[\![P]\!]\langle\dot{\boldsymbol{x}} = \boldsymbol{e}\rangle[\![Q_1 \wedge Q_2]\!]}\,\mathrm{dC}$$

The (dC) rule can be used multiple times to show conjunction of more than two invariants. For example, if we wish to show three invariants Q_1, Q_2, Q_3 in that order, first apply the (dC) rule with Q_1 and Q_2 to obtain $[\![P]\!]\langle\dot{\boldsymbol{x}} = \boldsymbol{e}\rangle[\![Q_1 \wedge Q_2]\!]$, then apply the (dC) rule again to obtain the conclusion.

Differential Ghost. The differential ghost rule (dG) adds new variables satisfying some differential equations to help prove the Hoare triple of the original differential equations.

$$\frac{[\![\overline{D}]\!]\langle\dot{\boldsymbol{x}} = \boldsymbol{e}, \dot{\boldsymbol{y}} = \boldsymbol{f}(\boldsymbol{x}, \boldsymbol{y})\rangle[\![I]\!] \quad \partial D \wedge I \to Q}{\{(D \to \exists \boldsymbol{y}.\, I) \wedge (\neg D \to Q)\}\langle\dot{\boldsymbol{x}} = \boldsymbol{e} \,\&\, D\rangle\{Q\}}\,\mathrm{dG}$$

Here, $\boldsymbol{y}$ are fresh variables that do not occur in $\langle\dot{\boldsymbol{x}} = \boldsymbol{e} \,\&\, D\rangle$ or Q, and $\boldsymbol{f}(\boldsymbol{x}, \boldsymbol{y})$ satisfies the Lipschitz condition.

Barrier Certificate. The barrier certificate rule (bc) concludes invariants from the definition of barrier certificate.

$$\frac{P \wedge f = 0 \to \dot{f} > 0}{[\![P]\!]\langle\dot{\boldsymbol{x}} = \boldsymbol{e}\rangle[\![f \succcurlyeq 0]\!]}\,\mathrm{bc}$$

Darboux. The Darboux rule (dbx) exploits properties of Darboux invariants, which are inspired by Darboux polynomials. Darboux equality and inequality rules are as follows.

$$\frac{P \to \dot{f} = gf}{[\![P]\!]\langle\dot{\boldsymbol{x}} = \boldsymbol{e}\rangle[\![f = 0]\!]}\,\mathrm{dbx}_{=} \qquad \frac{P \to \dot{f} \geq gf}{[\![P]\!]\langle\dot{\boldsymbol{x}} = \boldsymbol{e}\rangle[\![f \succcurlyeq 0]\!]}\,\mathrm{dbx}_{\succcurlyeq}$$

3.2 Solution Rule

The solution rule offers another way to conclude Hoare triples directly, independent of using the (dW) or (dG) rule followed by proving invariants. In the rule below, $\boldsymbol{e}$ is linear in $\boldsymbol{x}$, and $\boldsymbol{u}(t, \boldsymbol{x})$ is the unique solution to the differential equation $\dot{\boldsymbol{x}} = \boldsymbol{e}$ with symbolic initial value $\boldsymbol{x}$ (that is, $\frac{du(t,\boldsymbol{x})}{dt} = \boldsymbol{e}(\boldsymbol{u}(t,\boldsymbol{x}))$ and $\boldsymbol{u}(0,\boldsymbol{x}) = \boldsymbol{x}$). Let $P'(\boldsymbol{x})$ denote the following predicate on the starting state $\boldsymbol{x}$:

$$\forall t > 0. (\forall 0 \le \tau < t. D(\boldsymbol{u}(\tau,\boldsymbol{x}))) \wedge \neg D(\boldsymbol{u}(t,\boldsymbol{x})) \to Q(\boldsymbol{u}(t,\boldsymbol{x})).$$

The solution rule for Hoare triples (sln) is:

$$\frac{}{\{(D \to P') \wedge (\neg D \to Q)\}\langle \dot{\boldsymbol{x}} = \boldsymbol{e} \,\&\, D\rangle\{Q\}}\,\text{sln}$$

4 Verification Condition Generation

The VC generation procedure operates on annotated sequential HCSP programs. For ODEs, there are two kinds of annotations: ghost variable (gvar) and invariant annotations (ode_inv):

$$\begin{aligned} \mathsf{gvar} &::= \text{ghost } z\ (\dot{z} = f(\boldsymbol{x}, z)) \\ \mathsf{ode\_inv} &::= [I] \mid [I]\ \{\text{dbx } g\} \mid [I]\ \{\text{bc}\} \end{aligned}$$

Here, 'ghost z ($\dot{z} = f(\boldsymbol{x}, z)$)' denotes a ghost variable z following the ODE $\dot{z} = f(\boldsymbol{x}, z)$, where f must be linear in z to ensure global Lipschitz condition. The annotation $[I]$ denotes showing invariant I using the (dI) rule. The annotation $[I]$ {dbx g} denotes showing an invariant using the (dbx) rule, with g being the optional cofactor. The annotation $[I]$ {bc} denotes using the (bc) rule.

The syntax for annotated sequential HCSP programs is:

$$\begin{aligned} \mathcal{S}, \mathcal{T} ::= &\ \texttt{skip} \mid x := e \mid x := *(B) \mid \mathcal{S}; \mathcal{T} \mid \texttt{if } B \texttt{ then } \mathcal{S} \texttt{ else } \mathcal{T} \mid \\ &\ \mathcal{S} \mathbin{++} \mathcal{T} \mid \mathcal{S}* \text{ invariant } [I_1] \ldots [I_n] \mid \\ &\ \langle \dot{\boldsymbol{x}} = \boldsymbol{e} \,\&\, D\rangle \text{ invariant } \mathsf{gvar}_1 \ldots \mathsf{gvar}_k, \mathsf{ode\_inv}_1 \ldots \mathsf{ode\_inv}_n \mid \\ &\ \langle \dot{\boldsymbol{x}} = \boldsymbol{e} \,\&\, D\rangle \text{ solution} \end{aligned}$$

The only addition to the syntax of HCSP is that each loop is followed by a list of invariants $I_1, \ldots, I_n$, and each ODE is either followed by a list of ghost variable declarations and a list of invariant annotations, each of which specify an invariant to be proved using one of (dI), (dbx), or (bc) rules, or followed by the annotation "solution" to indicate that the (sln) rule is to be used.

To generate the necessary VCs for a given Hoare triple, we devised a procedure using weakest preconditions [3,4]. To be able to refer to preconditions and VCs individually, we consider sets of conditions instead of composing predicates by $\wedge$.

Given a Hoare triple $\{P_1 \wedge \cdots \wedge P_m\}\mathcal{S}\{Q_1 \wedge \cdots \wedge Q_n\}$ to verify, we define the set of all VCs to be

$$\begin{aligned} &\mathrm{VC}(\{P_1 \wedge \cdots \wedge P_m\}\mathcal{S}\{Q_1 \wedge \cdots \wedge Q_n\}) = \\ &\quad \{P_1 \wedge \cdots \wedge P_m \to R \mid R \in \mathrm{pre}(\mathcal{S}, \{Q_1, \ldots, Q_n\})\} \cup \qquad \textsf{(pre)} \\ &\quad \{\tilde{P}_1 \wedge \cdots \wedge \tilde{P}_{\tilde{m}} \to R \mid R \in \mathrm{vc}(\mathcal{S}, \{Q_1, \ldots, Q_n\})\} \qquad \textsf{(vc)} \end{aligned}$$

where $\tilde{P}_1, \ldots, \tilde{P}_{\tilde{m}}$ is the subset of the preconditions $P_1, \ldots, P_m$ whose variables are never reassigned in $\mathcal{S}$, and the functions pre and vc are defined below.

Given an annotated program $\mathcal{S}$ and a set $\{Q_1, \ldots, Q_n\}$ of postconditions, we denote the set of derived preconditions as $\text{pre}(\mathcal{S}, \{Q_1, \ldots, Q_n\})$, defined as follows.

$\text{pre}(\mathcal{S}, \{Q_1, \ldots, Q_n\}) = \text{pre}(\mathcal{S}, Q_1) \cup \cdots \cup \text{pre}(\mathcal{S}, Q_n)$ (pre-multi)
$\text{pre}(\texttt{skip}, Q) = Q$ (pre-skip)
$\text{pre}(x := e, Q) = Q[e/x]$ (pre-assn)
$\text{pre}(\mathcal{S}; \mathcal{T}, Q) = \text{pre}(\mathcal{S}, \text{pre}(\mathcal{T}, Q))$ (pre-seq)
$\text{pre}(\texttt{if } B_1 \texttt{ then } \mathcal{S}_1 \texttt{ else } \cdots \texttt{ if } B_{n-1} \texttt{ then } \mathcal{S}_{n-1} \texttt{ else } \mathcal{S}_n, Q) =$
$\quad \{\neg(B_1 \vee \cdots \vee B_{i-1}) \wedge B_i \to P \mid P \in \text{pre}(\mathcal{S}_i, Q), 1 \le i \le n-1\} \cup$ (pre-if)
$\quad \{\neg(B_1 \vee \cdots \vee B_{n-1}) \to P \mid P \in \text{pre}(\mathcal{S}_n, Q)\}$ (pre-else)
$\text{pre}(\mathcal{S}_1 \texttt{++} \cdots \texttt{++} \mathcal{S}_n, Q) = \text{pre}(\mathcal{S}_1, Q) \cup \cdots \cup \text{pre}(\mathcal{S}_n, Q)$ (pre-choice)
$\text{pre}(x := *\,(B), Q) = B[y/x] \to Q[y/x]$ for a fresh variable y (pre-nassn)
$\text{pre}(\mathcal{S}* \text{ invariant } [I_1] \ldots [I_n], Q) = \{I_j \mid 1 \le j \le n\}$ (pre-loop)
$\text{pre}(\langle \dot{\boldsymbol{x}} = \boldsymbol{e} \,\&\, D \rangle \text{ invariant } \mathsf{gvar}_1 \ldots \mathsf{gvar}_k, \mathsf{ode\_inv}_1 \ldots \mathsf{ode\_inv}_n, Q) =$
$\quad P_{\text{skip}} \cup P_{\text{init}}$
$\text{pre}(\langle \dot{\boldsymbol{x}} = \boldsymbol{e} \,\&\, D \rangle \text{ solution}) = P_{\text{skip}} \cup P_{\text{sln}}$

where

$P_{\text{skip}} = \{\neg D \to Q\}$ (pre-dWG-skip)
$P_{\text{init}} = \{D \to \exists z_1, \ldots, z_k.\, I_1 \wedge \cdots \wedge I_n\}$ if $k > 0$ (pre-dG-init)
$P_{\text{init}} = \{D \to I_j, \mid 1 \le j \le n\}$ otherwise (pre-dW-init)
$P_{\text{sln}} = \{D \to (\forall t > 0.\, (\forall 0 \le \tau < t.\, D(\boldsymbol{u}(\tau, \boldsymbol{x}))) \wedge$
$\qquad \neg D(\boldsymbol{u}(t, \boldsymbol{x})) \to Q(\boldsymbol{u}(t, \boldsymbol{x})))\}$ (pre-sln)

where $z_1, \ldots, z_k$ are the ghost variables provided in $\mathsf{gvar}_1 \ldots \mathsf{gvar}_k$, and $I_1, \ldots, I_n$ are the invariants provided in $\mathsf{ode\_inv}_1, \ldots, \mathsf{ode\_inv}_n$. If the user chooses the (sln) rule, we verify that $\boldsymbol{e}$ is linear in $\boldsymbol{x}$ and compute the unique solution $\boldsymbol{u}(\tau, \boldsymbol{x})$ to the ODE with symbolic initial value $\boldsymbol{x}$.

Given an annotated program $\mathcal{S}$ and a set $\{Q_1 \ldots, Q_n\}$ of postconditions, we denote the set of internal VCs as $\text{vc}(\mathcal{S}, \{Q_1, \ldots, Q_n\})$, defined as follows.

$\text{vc}(\mathcal{S}, \{Q_1, \ldots, Q_n\}) = \text{vc}(\mathcal{S}, Q_1) \cup \cdots \cup \text{vc}(\mathcal{S}, Q_n)$ (vc-multi)
$\text{vc}(\texttt{skip}, Q) = \emptyset$ (vc-skip)
$\text{vc}(x := e, Q) = \emptyset$ (vc-assn)
$\text{vc}(\mathcal{S}; \mathcal{T}, Q) = \text{vc}(\mathcal{S}, \text{pre}(\mathcal{T}, Q)) \cup \text{vc}(\mathcal{T}, Q)$ (vc-seq)
$\text{vc}(\texttt{if } B_1 \texttt{ then } \mathcal{S}_1 \texttt{ else if } \cdots \texttt{ else if } B_{n-1} \texttt{ then } \mathcal{S}_{n-1} \texttt{ else } \mathcal{S}_n, Q) =$
$\quad \text{vc}(\mathcal{S}_1, Q) \cup \cdots \cup \text{vc}(\mathcal{S}_n, Q)$ (vc-ite)
$\text{vc}(\mathcal{S}_1 \texttt{++} \cdots \texttt{++} \mathcal{S}_n, Q) = \text{vc}(\mathcal{S}_1, Q) \cup \cdots \cup \text{vc}(\mathcal{S}_n, Q)$ (vc-choice)
$\text{vc}(x := *\,(B), Q) = \emptyset$ (vc-nassn)
$\text{vc}(\mathcal{S}* \text{ invariant } [I_1] \ldots [I_n], Q) =$
$\quad \text{vc}(\mathcal{S}, \{I_1, \ldots, I_n\}) \cup$ (vc-loop-body)
$\quad \{(I_1 \wedge \cdots \wedge I_n) \to Q\} \cup$ (vc-loop-exit)
$\quad \{(I_1 \wedge \cdots \wedge I_n) \to P \mid P \in \text{pre}(\mathcal{S}, \{I_1, \ldots, I_n\})\}$ (vc-loop-maintain)
$\text{vc}(\langle \dot{\boldsymbol{x}} = \boldsymbol{e} \,\&\, D \rangle \text{ invariant } \mathsf{gvar}_1 \ldots \mathsf{gvar}_m, \mathsf{ode\_inv}_1 \ldots \mathsf{ode\_inv}_n, Q) = C_{\text{exec}} \cup C_{\text{dC}}$
$\text{vc}(\langle \dot{\boldsymbol{x}} = \boldsymbol{e} \,\&\, D \rangle \text{ solution}, Q) = \emptyset$

where we set $C_{\text{exec}} = \emptyset$ if the only invariant is false, or else

$$C_{\text{exec}} = \{I_1 \wedge \cdots \wedge I_n \wedge \partial D \rightarrow Q\} \quad \text{(vc-dWG-exec)}$$

$$C_{\text{dC}} = \{I_1 \wedge \cdots \wedge I_{j-1} \rightarrow R \mid R \in \text{vc}(\langle \dot{\boldsymbol{x}} = \boldsymbol{e} \,\&\, D\rangle, \mathsf{ode\_inv}_j, Q), \; 1 \leq j \leq n\} \quad \text{(vc-dC)}$$

Here, $I_1, \ldots, I_n$ are the invariants provided in $\mathsf{ode\_inv}_1, \ldots, \mathsf{ode\_inv}_n$. If no invariants are specified, we set a single invariant $I_1 = \mathsf{true}$ by default. We write $\text{vc}(\langle \dot{\boldsymbol{x}} = \boldsymbol{e} \,\&\, D\rangle, \mathsf{ode\_inv}_j, Q)$ for the VC generated from annotation $\mathsf{ode\_inv}_j$, defined as follows.

$$\text{vc}(\langle \dot{\boldsymbol{x}} = \boldsymbol{e} \,\&\, D\rangle, [\mathsf{true}], Q) = \emptyset \quad \text{(vc-true)}$$
$$\text{vc}(\langle \dot{\boldsymbol{x}} = \boldsymbol{e} \,\&\, D\rangle, [\mathsf{false}], Q) = \emptyset \quad \text{(vc-false)}$$
$$\text{vc}(\langle \dot{\boldsymbol{x}} = \boldsymbol{e} \,\&\, D\rangle, [f = 0], Q) = \{\overline{D} \rightarrow \dot{f} = 0\} \quad \text{(vc-dI1)}$$
$$\text{vc}(\langle \dot{\boldsymbol{x}} = \boldsymbol{e} \,\&\, D\rangle, [f \succcurlyeq 0], Q) = \{\overline{D} \rightarrow \dot{f} \geq 0\} \quad \text{(vc-dI2)}$$
$$\text{vc}(\langle \dot{\boldsymbol{x}} = \boldsymbol{e} \,\&\, D\rangle, [f \neq 0], Q) = \{\overline{D} \rightarrow \dot{f} = 0\} \quad \text{(vc-dI3)}$$
$$\text{vc}(\langle \dot{\boldsymbol{x}} = \boldsymbol{e} \,\&\, D\rangle, [f = 0]\{\text{dbx } g\}, Q) = \{\overline{D} \rightarrow \dot{f} = gf\} \quad \text{(vc-dbx1)}$$
$$\text{vc}(\langle \dot{\boldsymbol{x}} = \boldsymbol{e} \,\&\, D\rangle, [f \succcurlyeq 0]\{\text{dbx } g\}, Q) = \{\overline{D} \rightarrow \dot{f} \geq gf\} \quad \text{(vc-dbx2)}$$
$$\text{vc}(\langle \dot{\boldsymbol{x}} = \boldsymbol{e} \,\&\, D\rangle, [f \succcurlyeq 0]\{\text{bc}\}, Q) = \{\overline{D} \wedge f = 0 \rightarrow \dot{f} > 0\} \quad \text{(vc-bc)}$$

All Lie derivatives are computed with respect to $\dot{\boldsymbol{x}} = \boldsymbol{e}$ and the equations given in $\mathsf{gvar}_1 \ldots \mathsf{gvar}_m$. For the (dbx) rule, if no cofactor g is provided, we attempt to compute the cofactor automatically. Specifically, in the case of an equality invariant, this reduces to simplifying $\dot{f}/f$ into polynomial form. In the case of an inequality invariant, we attempt to find a polynomial quotient of $\dot{f}$ and f with a non-negative remainder.

Theorem 1. *A Hoare triple* $\{P_1 \wedge \cdots \wedge P_m\} \mathcal{T} \{Q_1 \wedge \cdots \wedge Q_n\}$ *holds if all conditions in* $\text{VC}(\{P_1 \wedge \cdots \wedge P_m\} \mathcal{T} \{Q_1 \wedge \cdots \wedge Q_n\})$ *hold.*

Proof. We give the full proof in [28, Appendix B]. In short, we proceed by structural induction on $\mathcal{T}$. The difficult case is when $\mathcal{T}$ is an ODE. If the ODE is annotated to use the solution rule, we use the VC stemming from the precondition (pre-sln). Otherwise, we employ the (dG) rule or the (dW) rule depending on if ghost variables are specified. The VCs stemming from (pre-dWG-skip) and (pre-dW-init) or (pre-dG-init) show that the rule (dW) or (dG) is applicable. The condition (vc-dWG-exec) discharges the right premise of the (dW) or (dG) rule.

For the left premise $[\![\overline{D}]\!]\langle \dot{\boldsymbol{x}} = \boldsymbol{e}, \dot{\boldsymbol{y}} = \boldsymbol{f}(\boldsymbol{x}, \boldsymbol{y})\rangle [\![I_1 \wedge \cdots \wedge I_k]\!]$, (without $\boldsymbol{y}$ if using the (dW) rule), we repeatedly apply the (dC) rule to isolate each invariant I_i. For each step $[\![\overline{D} \wedge I_1 \wedge \cdots \wedge I_{i-1}]\!]\langle \dot{\boldsymbol{x}} = \boldsymbol{e}, \dot{\boldsymbol{y}} = \boldsymbol{f}(\boldsymbol{x}, \boldsymbol{y})\rangle [\![I_i]\!]$, depending on the rule specified in the annotation, we apply the (dI) rule, (dbx) rule or (bc) rule, using the corresponding VCs as premises. □

5 Labels

VCs generated by the procedure in Sect. 4 will be proved using Z3 or Wolfram Engine. In this section, we introduce a labeling mechanism to store which solver is used for each VC, in a way that is robust to minor modifications of the program or its annotations.

As indicated in Sect. 4, the generation of a VC starts from a postcondition or invariant and proceeds bottom up through the program. We call the postcondition or invariant at the beginning of this process the conclusion assertion of the VC. We associate each VC to its conclusion assertion. Labels are used to distinguish between multiple VCs from the same conclusion assertion. They can arise for the following reasons:

- Loop and ODE invariants produce VCs for showing that they initially hold and for showing that they are maintained by the loop or ODE.
- If-then-else and nondeterministic choice produce multiple preconditions, at least one for each branch.[2]
- Each ODE produces preconditions for both the case when the domain D holds initially, and for when D does not hold.

A label consists of two parts: a category label and a branch label. The category label is either empty or one of "init", "maintain", "init_all". The branch label is a list, separated by ".", of either "skip", "exec", or $n(b)$ where n is a positive integer and b is a branch label itself. We write n instead of $n()$ when the inner branch label is empty.

Category Labels. Category labels use "init" ("init_all") and "maintain" to distinguish between VCs with loop or ODE invariants as conclusion assertions. For loops, the VCs for showing the invariant holds initially are labeled "init", and the VCs that result from showing the invariant is maintained by the loop are labeled "maintain" (when there are nested loops or ODEs in the loop body, multiple VCs are computed in the loop body, this applies only to those with the invariant as conclusion assertion).

For an ODE, the VC coming from (pre-dW-init) (resp. (pre-dG-init)) are labeled "init" (resp. "init_all"). The VCs coming from (vc-dC), for showing each invariant is maintained during evolution, are labeled "maintain".

The category label is empty in all other cases.

Branch Labels. Branch labels help to distinguish VCs generated by executing different branches of programs.

The positive integer n handles branches created by '`if` B `then` $\mathcal{S}_1$ `else` $\mathcal{S}_2$' or '$\mathcal{S}_1$ ++ $\mathcal{S}_2$'. Each value of n (starting from 1) corresponds to one branch. Sequence labels $b.b$ are used for sequences of such commands. For example, the branches for '$\mathcal{S}_1$ ++ $\mathcal{S}_2$; $\mathcal{S}_3$ ++ $\mathcal{S}_4$' have labels 1.1, 1.2, 2.1 and 2.2. Nested labels $n(b)$ are used for nested commands. For example, the branches for `if` B `then` $\mathcal{S}_1$ ++ $\mathcal{S}_2$ `else` $\mathcal{S}_3$ have labels 1(1), 1(2) and 2, corresponding to $\mathcal{S}_1$, $\mathcal{S}_2$ and $\mathcal{S}_3$, respectively.

[2] A large program consisting of multiple if-then-else commands can lead to an undesired blow up of the number of VCs. For example, a program constructed by ten if-then-else commands as sequential components results in more than 2^{10} VCs.

The labels "skip" and "exec" are used for branches of the ODE. The branch where the initial state does not satisfy domain D is labeled "skip". The other branch, where the ODE is executed, is labeled "exec". They come from applying the rules (vc-dWG-skip) and (vc-dWG-exec), respectively.

Example 1. This example illustrates assignments, nondeterministic choice, and loops.

$$\begin{array}{l} \{x \le 0\} \\ \quad x := -x; \\ \quad (x := x+1 \mathbin{++} x := x+2)* \\ \qquad \text{invariant } [x \ge 0]; \\ \quad x := x+1 \\ \{x \ge 1\} \end{array}$$

The computation starts at postcondition $x \ge 1$. Applying (pre-assn) and (vc-loop-exit), we get the VC $x \ge 0 \to x+1 \ge 1$. Applying (pre-loop), the loop's precondition is $x \ge 0$. The whole program's precondition is $-x \ge 0$ by applying (pre-assn) again. The loop body yields the preconditions $x+1 \ge 0$ and $x+2 \ge 0$ by (pre-choice) and (pre-assn). Then we get $x \ge 0 \to x+1 \ge 0$ and $x \ge 0 \to x+2 \ge 0$ by applying (vc-loop-maintain). The overall VCs and their labels are:

VC	Conclusion assertion	Label
$x \le 0 \to -x \ge 0$	$x \ge 0$ (inv)	init
$x \ge 0 \to x+1 \ge 1$	$x \ge 1$ (post)	ϵ
$x \ge 0 \to x+1 \ge 0$	$x \ge 0$ (inv)	maintain 1
$x \ge 0 \to x+2 \ge 0$	$x \ge 0$ (inv)	maintain 2

With conclusion assertions and labels, we can store the solver (default Z3) for each VC and reuse the solver despite of minor modifications of code. For example, if we choose Wolfram Engine to prove $x \le 0 \to -x \ge 0$, "init: wolfram" will be annotated after the invariant $x \ge 0$. If we then change the second line from $x := -x$ into $x := -2 * x$, resulting in a different VC $x \le 0 \to -2 * x \ge 0$, the solver of the VC is still Wolfram Engine.

Example 2. This example illustrates non-deterministic assignments and ODEs (#4 of KeYmaera X's basic benchmarks):

$$\begin{array}{l} \{x \ge 0\} \\ \quad x := x+1; t := *\,(t \ge 0); \\ \quad \langle \dot{t} = -1, \dot{x} = 2 \,\&\, t > 0\rangle \text{ invariant } [x \ge 1] \\ \{x \ge 1\} \end{array}$$

The computation of pre starts at postcondition $x \ge 1$. By (pre-dWG-skip) and (pre-dW-init), the ODE's preconditions are $\neg t > 0 \to x \ge 1$ and $t > 0 \to x \ge 1$. By (pre-nassn) and (pre-assn), the whole program's preconditions are

$t_1 \geq 0 \to t_1 > 0 \to x \geq 1$ and $t_1 \geq 0 \to \neg t_1 > 0 \to x+1 \geq 1$. The VCs $x \geq 1 \wedge t = 0 \to x \geq 1$ and $t \geq 0 \to 2 \geq 0$ come from (vc-dWG-exec) and (vc-dI2), respectively. The overall list of VCs is:

VC	Conclusion assertion	Label
$x \geq 0 \to t_1 \geq 0 \to t_1 > 0 \to x+1 \geq 1$	$x \geq 1$ (inv)	init
$x \geq 0 \to t_1 \geq 0 \to \neg t_1 > 0 \to x+1 \geq 1$	$x \geq 1$ (post)	skip
$x \geq 1 \wedge t = 0 \to x \geq 1$	$x \geq 1$ (post)	exec
$t \geq 0 \to 2 \geq 0$	$x \geq 1$ (inv)	maintain

Example 3. Finally, we consider an example with multiple ghost variables (#18 of KeYmaera X's basic benchmarks):

$$\begin{array}{l} \{x \geq 0\} \\ \quad t := *\,(t \geq 0);\ \langle \dot{x} = x, \dot{t} = -1\ \&\ t > 0 \rangle \\ \quad \text{invariant ghost } y\ (\dot{y} = -y) \text{ ghost } z\ (\dot{z} = z/2) \\ \qquad [xy \geq 0]\ [yz^2 = 1] \\ \{x \geq 0\} \end{array}$$

VC	Conclusion assertion	Label
$x \geq 0 \to t_1 \geq 0 \to t_1 > 0 \to \exists y\, z.\, xy \geq 0 \wedge yz^2 = 1$	invariants	init_all
$x \geq 0 \to t_1 \geq 0 \to \neg t_1 > 0 \to x \geq 0$	$x \geq 0$ (post)	skip
$xy \geq 0 \wedge yz^2 = 1 \wedge t = 0 \to x \geq 0$	$x \geq 0$ (post)	exec
$t \geq 0 \to x \cdot (-y) + xy \geq 0$	$xy \geq 0$ (inv)	maintain
$xy \geq 0 \to t \geq 0 \to yz(z/2) + (y(z/2) + (-y)z)z = 0$	$yz^2 = 1$ (inv)	maintain

The first VC comes from (pre-dG-init). The remaining VCs are similar to Example 2, except that there is one VC for maintaining each invariant. When verifying the second invariant, the (dC) rule allows us to assume the first invariant.

6 Highlighting

In this section, we explain the highlighting mechanism we devised to help the user understand how each VC is derived from the program. Essentially, when the user hovers over a VC, we highlight all parts of the program that contribute to the computation of the VC, including commands, assertions and domain constraints.

We highlight any assertion that contributes to the VC. In particular, invariants of an ODE that are already proved will be highlighted when proving the next invariant because they are added as assumptions in (vc-dC). Preconditions

$\{x \leq 0\}$
  $x := -x;$
  $(x := x + 1 \mathbin{++} x := x + 2)*$
    invariant $[x \geq 0]$;
  $x := x + 1$
$\{x \geq 1\}$

(a) VC labeled 'init'

$\{x \leq 0\}$
  $x := -x;$
  $(x := x + 1 \mathbin{++} x := x + 2)*$
    invariant $[x \geq 0]$;
  $x := x + 1$
$\{x \geq 1\}$

(b) VC for the postcondition (no label)

$\{x \leq 0\}$
  $x := -x;$
  $(x := x + 1 \mathbin{++} x := x + 2)*$
    invariant $[x \geq 0]$;
  $x := x + 1$
$\{x \geq 1\}$

(c) VC labeled 'maintain 1'

$\{x \leq 0\}$
  $x := -x;$
  $(x := x + 1 \mathbin{++} x := x + 2)*$
    invariant $[x \geq 0]$;
  $x := x + 1$
$\{x \geq 1\}$

(d) VC labeled 'maintain 2'

Fig. 1. Highlighting for the four VCs in Example 1

$\{x \geq 0\}$
  $x := x + 1;\ t := *(t \geq 0);$
  $\langle \dot{t} = -1, \dot{x} = 2 \,\&\, t > 0\rangle$
    invariant $[x \geq 1]$
$\{x \geq 1\}$

(a) VC labeled 'skip'

$\{x \geq 0\}$
  $x := x + 1;\ t := *(t \geq 0);$
  $\langle \dot{t} = -1, \dot{x} = 2 \,\&\, t > 0\rangle$
    invariant $[x \geq 1]$
$\{x \geq 1\}$

(b) VC labeled 'maintain'

Fig. 2. Highlighting for the two of the VCs in Example 2

whose variables are never reassigned will be highlighted because they are added as assumptions in (vc).

Domain constraints of ODEs will be highlighted if they are used in the VC (e.g. the domain constraint D in the VC generated by (vc-dWG-exec)).

Atomic commands are highlighted if they are traversed during VC generation. ODE commands are highlighted for VCs computed by (vc-dC) or (pre-sln). For if-then-else and nondeterministic choice, only the branch that is actually traversed during VC generation will be considered for highlighting.

Figure 1 and 2 show the highlighting for some the VCs from Examples 1 and 2.

7 Implementation and Evaluation

In this section, we present the implementation of HHLPy and evaluate it on Simulink/Stateflow models and on KeYmaera X benchmarks. All verified examples are available online, coming with the tool.

7.1 Implementation

Figure 3 shows the architecture of the tool. The user inputs HCSP programs and annotations in the editor (the HCSP programs can also come from translation of Simulink/Stateflow models). The core HHLPy engine then parses the input and generates VCs. The user interface displays the VCs and allows users to choose a solver for each VC. The solver will be invoked, with the results displayed to the user interface. The backend of HHLPy is implemented in Python, and the graphical user interface is implemented using JavaScript. A screenshot of the user interface is shown in Fig. 4.

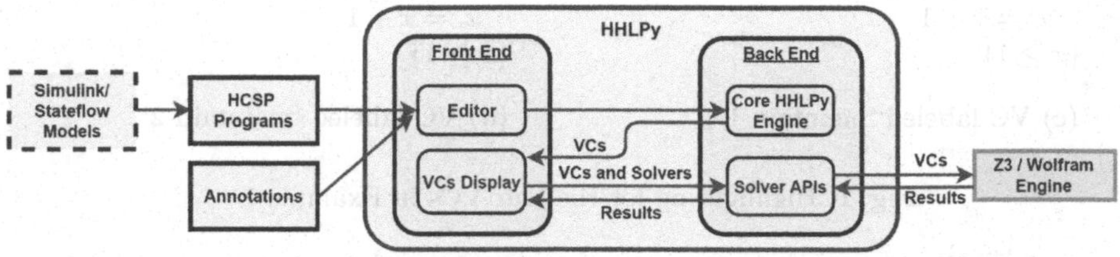

Fig. 3. Architecture of HHLPy

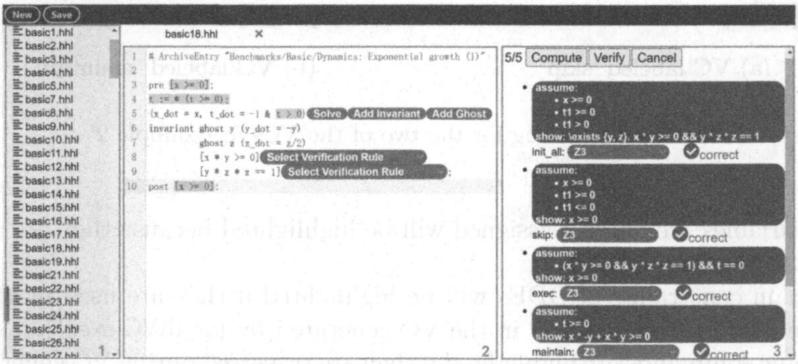

Fig. 4. Screenshot of user interface. The left panel (1) shows a list of example files. The middle panel (2) is the editor area, where user can edit the program and add annotations either directly as text or by clicking on buttons. The right panel (3) shows the VCs. When hovering over each VC, the relevant part of the code is highlighted.

7.2 Evaluation on Simulink/Stateflow Models

To illustrate the use of our tool as part of an existing toolchain to verify correctness of Simulink/Stateflow models, we show two example models, one from Simulink and one from Stateflow.

Cruise Control System. The first example is a cruise control system of an automotive vehicle [14]. The system stabilizes the speed of a vehicle around some desired speed (15 m/s in our case) using a PI controller. The PI controller adjusts the control force according to the difference between actual speed and desired speed as well as its integral. The vehicle follows its physical dynamics. The Simulink models are presented in [28, Appendix C].

We first applied the approach by Xu et al. [31] to translate the Simulink models into an HCSP program. In the program, the controller and vehicle dynamics are combined into a single ODE. Given the initial speed $v = 14$ and initial integral value $I = 700$ of the controller, which are close to the stable point $(v = 15, I = 750)$, we want to verify that the speed remains in the interval $[13.5, 16.5]$.

To verify the Hoare triple, we annotated the ODE and loop with the invariant $1.3 * (I - 750)^2 - 198 * (I - 750) * (v - 15) + 12192 * (v - 15)^2 \leq 5542$, and used (dI) rule to prove the ODE invariant. The invariant was derived following the standard theory for analyzing linear dynamical systems. The annotated HCSP program is illustrated below. The tool generated seven VCs, and Z3 can prove all of them.

```
pre [v == 14][I == 700];

t := 0;
_tick := 0;
tt := 0;

{
  {tt_dot = 1, I_dot = (15 - v) * 40, v_dot = ((15 - v) * 600 + I - v * 50) * 0.001 & tt < 1}
      invariant [1.3*(I-750)^2 - 198 * (I-750)*(v-15)+12192*(v-15)^2<=5542];
  t := t + tt;
  _tick := _tick + 1;
  tt := 0;
}*
  invariant [1.3*(I-750)^2 - 198 * (I-750)*(v-15)+12192*(v-15)^2<=5542];
post [v >= 13.5][v <= 16.5];
```

Sawtooth Wave. The sawtooth wave is a Stateflow model generating a signal that alternates between increasing from 0 to 1 and decreasing from 1 to 0. It illustrates functionality in Stateflow such as hierarchical states and specifying ODEs in a state. The Stateflow model is presented in [28, Appendix C]. The signal x follows the ODE $\dot{x} = y$, with y switching between 1 and -1 per unit time. We want to verify that every time y switches, x is still between 0 and 1.

We translated the Stateflow model into an HCSP program with the approach by Guo et al. [11] (code shown in [28, Appendix C]). To verify the program, the loop is annotated with four invariants (mostly having to do with the relationship between Stateflow locations and value of variable x), and the ODE is annotated with "solution". A total of 62 VCs are generated and proved to be true by Z3.

7.3 Evaluation on Benchmarks from KeYmaera X

We also evaluated our tool on the basic and nonlinear benchmarks[3] from KeYmaera X. We first translated the examples from d$\mathcal{L}$ to HCSP manually, trying to maintain semantic equivalence as much as possible. Due to the differences between d$\mathcal{L}$ and HCSP, some examples can not be translated into HCSP programs. We annotated the programs with invariants and proof rules, mostly following the existing proofs in KeYmaera X.

Given the annotations, HHLPy can verify 50 out of 60 examples in the basic benchmarks. In comparison, KeYmaera X solves 58 examples in the scripted mode (with detailed proof scripts), and 55 examples in the hints mode (with invariants annotated in the model) [17]. Of the ten unsolved examples, we are unable to translate eight of them to HCSP due to use of d$\mathcal{L}$-specific constructs; one is non-polynomial; and the last one makes use of invariants containing old versions of variables. For the nonlinear benchmarks, HHLPy can verify 103 out of 141 examples (compared to 108 in the scripted mode and 95 in the hints mode for KeYmaera X [17]). Most of the unsolved ones are because we are unable to find the invariants or their VCs cannot be proved in reasonable time by Z3 or Wolfram Engine. Specifically, HHLPy can verify 9 examples which KeYmaera X cannot verify in hints mode, while KeYmaera X can verify one example in hints mode that HHLPy cannot verify. For this one example, we have not found the invariants or specific rules, while KeYmaera X verifies it using a general `ODE` rule.

In the 153 examples solvable by HHLPy, the user only needs to add annotations including loop/ODE invariants and ODE rules; just a couple of annotations are needed per problem. For some problems, it is necessary to switch the backend solver from the default Z3 to Wolfram Engine. After this, HHLPy can finish the proof automatically. These experiments show that our tool can be used to solve a wide range of examples from existing benchmarks with little manual effort. Moreover, from the evaluation on the benchmarks we note that there are some VCs that Z3 can solve but Wolfram Engine cannot, and vice versa, showing the two solvers have complementary advantages. Generally speaking, Z3 handles complex boolean structures better, while Wolfram Engine has advantages in expressions containing many decimal numbers.

8 Related Work

Differential dynamic logic (d$\mathcal{L}$) [23,25] models hybrid systems by extending dynamic logic with continuous evolution. Reasoning rules about continuous evolution include differential invariants, differential weakening, differential cut, and differential ghosts. The rules are stated in the form of a uniform substitution calculus [24], and they are complete [27]. Differential dynamic logic has been

[3] The benchmarks are available at https://github.com/LS-Lab/KeYmaeraX-projects/tree/master/benchmarks.

implemented in KeYmaera [26] and KeYmaera X [9], whose user interfaces display current subgoals in sequent calculus form and allow users to point and click to construct proofs. The Bellerophon language allows users to perform proofs using a tactic language [8]. The KeYmaera X tool produces proofs that can be independently checked in Isabelle and Coq [1]. Liebrenz et al. developed a method to translate Simulink models to d$\mathcal{L}$ and to verify them in KeYmaera X [16].

Huerta y Munive and Struth represented d$\mathcal{L}$ programs using Kleene algebras, and built verification components for hybrid systems in Isabelle/HOL [21,22]. Foster et al. proposed Hoare logic rules and refinement calculi for hybrid programs [7] and extended the verification components in Isabelle/HOL [6], e.g., with syntax translation to obtain more user-friendly modeling and specification languages and with proof automation using Eisbach. Huerta y Munive and Struth also described formalization of solutions to affine and linear systems of ODEs, with applications to verifying correctness of such systems [20].

Both of the above series of works focused on hybrid programs modeled using d$\mathcal{L}$. As discussed in Sect. 2 and 3, the semantics of continuous evolution is different from that in d$\mathcal{L}$; hence the proof rules need to be adapted, resulting in particular to significant changes to differential weakening and differential cut rules. In addition, compared to KeYmaera X in scripted mode, HHLPy can finish the verification automatically once programs are annotated with loop/ODE invariants and ODE rules. Compared to KeYmaera X in hints mode, HHLPy shows the VCs that cannot be proved, and highlights the set of code fragments that contribute to generating the VCs, which help users to debug programs and annotations.

Goncharov and Neves introduced the HybCore language for hybrid computation [10]. Similarly to HCSP, HybCore defines deterministic semantics for domain constraints of ODE. The connection with Moggi's work on computational effects [18] potentially aids reasoning and verification in HybCore. However, concrete verification methods remain future work.

Compared to the previous version of hybrid Hoare logic [29], we focus only on the sequential fragment of HCSP, resulting in much simpler rules that permits automatic VC generation. On the other hand, we consider a full set of reasoning rules for ODEs in parallel with d$\mathcal{L}$, rather than only the invariant rule in [29].

The design of our tool is similar to many other (semi-)automatic program verification tools, such as Dafny [15], VeriFast [12], and Why3 [5], in that annotations are inserted into the program code. Our work differs from these tools firstly in being able to handle hybrid programs. Moreover, we designed detailed labeling and highlighting mechanisms to improve robustness of the annotations and help visualization. These improvements are not limited to hybrid programs, and can potentially be incorporated into other program verification tools as well.

9 Conclusion

We presented HHLPy, a tool for verification of hybrid programs written in the sequential fragment of HCSP. The backend of the tool implements a Hoare logic that includes rules for reasoning about continuous evolution adapted from d$\mathcal{L}$. We also designed labeling and highlighting mechanisms to improve user interaction. We demonstrated the capabilities of the tool on HCSP programs translated from Simulink/Stateflow models and on KeYmaera X benchmarks.

We leave extension of the deduction system to handle communication, interrupts, and parallel composition to future work. On the side of implementation and applications, we intend to further extend the tool to be able to handle non-polynomial ODEs and invariants and permit interactive proofs of VCs.

Acknowledgments. This work is supported by the National Natural Science Foundation of China under grant No. 62032024, 62002351, and a Chinese Academy of Sciences President's International Fellowship for Postdoctoral Researchers under grant No. 2021PT0015.

References

1. Bohrer, R., Rahli, V., Vukotic, I., Völp, M., Platzer, A.: Formally verified differential dynamic logic. In: Bertot, Y., Vafeiadis, V. (eds.) Conference on Certified Programs and Proofs (CPP 2017), pp. 208–221. ACM (2017)
2. Chen, M., et al.: MARS: a toolchain for modelling, analysis and verification of hybrid systems. In: Hinchey, M.G., Bowen, J.P., Olderog, E.-R. (eds.) Provably Correct Systems. NMSSE, pp. 39–58. Springer, Cham (2017). https://doi.org/10.1007/978-3-319-48628-4_3
3. Dijkstra, E.W.: Guarded commands, nondeterminacy and formal derivation of programs. Commun. ACM **18**(8), 453–457 (1975)
4. Dijkstra, E.W.: A Discipline of Programming. Prentice-Hall (1976)
5. Filliâtre, J.-C., Paskevich, A.: Why3—where programs meet provers. In: Felleisen, M., Gardner, P. (eds.) ESOP 2013. LNCS, vol. 7792, pp. 125–128. Springer, Heidelberg (2013). https://doi.org/10.1007/978-3-642-37036-6_8
6. Foster, S., Huerta y Munive, J.J., Gleirscher, M., Struth, G.: Hybrid systems verification with Isabelle/HOL: simpler syntax, better models, faster proofs. In: Huisman, M., Păsăreanu, C., Zhan, N. (eds.) FM 2021. LNCS, vol. 13047, pp. 367–386. Springer, Cham (2021). https://doi.org/10.1007/978-3-030-90870-6_20
7. Foster, S., Huerta y Munive, J.J., Struth, G.: Differential Hoare logics and refinement calculi for hybrid systems with Isabelle/HOL. In: Fahrenberg, U., Jipsen, P., Winter, M. (eds.) RAMiCS 2020. LNCS, vol. 12062, pp. 169–186. Springer, Cham (2020). https://doi.org/10.1007/978-3-030-43520-2_11
8. Fulton, N., Mitsch, S., Bohrer, B., Platzer, A.: Bellerophon: tactical theorem proving for hybrid systems. In: Ayala-Rincón, M., Muñoz, C.A. (eds.) ITP 2017. LNCS, vol. 10499, pp. 207–224. Springer, Cham (2017). https://doi.org/10.1007/978-3-319-66107-0_14
9. Fulton, N., Mitsch, S., Quesel, J.-D., Völp, M., Platzer, A.: KeYmaera X: an axiomatic tactical theorem prover for hybrid systems. In: Felty, A.P., Middeldorp, A. (eds.) CADE 2015. LNCS (LNAI), vol. 9195, pp. 527–538. Springer, Cham (2015). https://doi.org/10.1007/978-3-319-21401-6_36
10. Goncharov, S., Neves, R.: An adequate while-language for hybrid computation. In: Komendantskaya, E. (ed.) International Symposium on Principles and Practice of Programming Languages (PPDP 2019), pp. 11:1–11:15. ACM (2019)

11. Guo, P., Zhan, B., Xu, X., Wang, S., Sun, W.: Translating a large subset of Stateflow to hybrid CSP with code optimization. J. Syst. Archit. **130**, 102665 (2022)
12. Jacobs, B., Smans, J., Philippaerts, P., Vogels, F., Penninckx, W., Piessens, F.: VeriFast: a powerful, sound, predictable, fast verifier for C and Java. In: Bobaru, M., Havelund, K., Holzmann, G.J., Joshi, R. (eds.) NFM 2011. LNCS, vol. 6617, pp. 41–55. Springer, Heidelberg (2011). https://doi.org/10.1007/978-3-642-20398-5_4
13. Jifeng, H.: From CSP to hybrid systems, pp. 171–189. Prentice Hall International (UK) Ltd., GBR (1994)
14. Kekatos, N.: Verifying a cruise control system using Simulink and SpaceEx. CoRR abs/2101.00102 (2021)
15. Leino, K.R.M.: Dafny: an automatic program verifier for functional correctness. In: Clarke, E.M., Voronkov, A. (eds.) LPAR 2010. LNCS (LNAI), vol. 6355, pp. 348–370. Springer, Heidelberg (2010). https://doi.org/10.1007/978-3-642-17511-4_20
16. Liebrenz, T., Herber, P., Glesner, S.: Deductive verification of hybrid control systems modeled in Simulink with KeYmaera X. In: Sun, J., Sun, M. (eds.) ICFEM 2018. LNCS, vol. 11232, pp. 89–105. Springer, Cham (2018). https://doi.org/10.1007/978-3-030-02450-5_6
17. Mitsch, S., Jin, X., Zhan, B., Wang, S., Zhan, N.: ARCH-COMP21 category report: hybrid systems theorem proving. In: Frehse, G., Althoff, M. (eds.) International Workshop on Applied Verification of Continuous and Hybrid Systems (ARCH 2021). EPiC Series in Computing, vol. 80, pp. 120–132. EasyChair (2021)
18. Moggi, E.: Notions of computation and monads. Inf. Comput. **93**(1), 55–92 (1991)
19. de Moura, L., Bjørner, N.: Z3: an efficient SMT solver. In: Ramakrishnan, C.R., Rehof, J. (eds.) TACAS 2008. LNCS, vol. 4963, pp. 337–340. Springer, Heidelberg (2008). https://doi.org/10.1007/978-3-540-78800-3_24
20. Huerta y Munive, J.J.: Affine systems of ODEs in Isabelle/HOL for hybrid-program verification. In: de Boer, F., Cerone, A. (eds.) SEFM 2020. LNCS, vol. 12310, pp. 77–92. Springer, Cham (2020). https://doi.org/10.1007/978-3-030-58768-0_5
21. Huerta y Munive, J.J., Struth, G.: Verifying hybrid systems with modal Kleene algebra. In: Desharnais, J., Guttmann, W., Joosten, S. (eds.) RAMiCS 2018. LNCS, vol. 11194, pp. 225–243. Springer, Cham (2018). https://doi.org/10.1007/978-3-030-02149-8_14
22. Huerta y Munive, J.J., Struth, G.: Predicate transformer semantics for hybrid systems. J. Autom. Reason. **66**(1), 93–139 (2021). https://doi.org/10.1007/s10817-021-09607-x
23. Platzer, A.: Differential dynamic logic for hybrid systems. J. Autom. Reason. **41**(2), 143–189 (2008)
24. Platzer, A.: A complete uniform substitution calculus for differential dynamic logic. J. Autom. Reason. **59**(2), 219–265 (2017). https://doi.org/10.1007/s10817-016-9385-1
25. Platzer, A.: Logical Foundations of Cyber-Physical Systems. Springer, Cham (2018). https://doi.org/10.1007/978-3-319-63588-0
26. Platzer, A., Quesel, J.-D.: KeYmaera: a hybrid theorem prover for hybrid systems (system description). In: Armando, A., Baumgartner, P., Dowek, G. (eds.) IJCAR 2008. LNCS (LNAI), vol. 5195, pp. 171–178. Springer, Heidelberg (2008). https://doi.org/10.1007/978-3-540-71070-7_15
27. Platzer, A., Tan, Y.K.: Differential equation invariance axiomatization. J. ACM **67**(1), 6:1–6:66 (2020)

28. Sheng, H., Bentkamp, A., Zhan, B.: HHLPy: practical verification of hybrid systems using Hoare logic (full paper). CoRR abs/2210.17163 (2022). https://doi.org/10.48550/arXiv.2210.17163
29. Wang, S., Zhan, N., Zou, L.: An improved HHL prover: an interactive theorem prover for hybrid systems. In: Butler, M., Conchon, S., Zaïdi, F. (eds.) ICFEM 2015. LNCS, vol. 9407, pp. 382–399. Springer, Cham (2015). https://doi.org/10.1007/978-3-319-25423-4_25
30. Wolfram Research Inc.: Wolfram Engine, Version 13.1, Champaign, IL (2022). https://www.wolfram.com/engine
31. Xu, X., Zhan, B., Wang, S., Talpin, J.P., Zhan, N.: A denotational semantics of Simulink with higher-order UTP. J. Log. Algebraic Methods Program. **130**, 100809 (2023)
32. Zhan, N., Wang, S., Zhao, H.: Formal Verification of Simulink/Stateflow Diagrams. Springer, Cham (2017). https://doi.org/10.1007/978-3-319-47016-0
33. Chaochen, Z., Ji, W., Ravn, A.P.: A formal description of hybrid systems. In: Alur, R., Henzinger, T.A., Sontag, E.D. (eds.) HS 1995. LNCS, vol. 1066, pp. 511–530. Springer, Heidelberg (1996). https://doi.org/10.1007/BFb0020972
34. Zou, L., Zhan, N., Wang, S., Fränzle, M.: Formal verification of Simulink/Stateflow diagrams. In: Finkbeiner, B., Pu, G., Zhang, L. (eds.) ATVA 2015. LNCS, vol. 9364, pp. 464–481. Springer, Cham (2015). https://doi.org/10.1007/978-3-319-24953-7_33
35. Zou, L., Zhan, N., Wang, S., Fränzle, M., Qin, S.: Verifying Simulink diagrams via a hybrid Hoare logic prover. In: Ernst, R., Sokolsky, O. (eds.) International Conference on Embedded Software, (EMSOFT 2013), pp. 9:1–9:10. IEEE (2013)

Quantitative Verification

symQV: Automated Symbolic Verification of Quantum Programs

Fabian Bauer-Marquart[1(✉)], Stefan Leue[1], and Christian Schilling[2]

[1] University of Konstanz, Konstanz, Germany
fabian@bauer-marquart.com, stefan.leue@uni-konstanz.de
[2] Aalborg University, Aalborg, Denmark
christianms@cs.aau.dk

Abstract. We present symQV, a symbolic execution framework for writing and verifying quantum computations in the quantum circuit model. symQV can automatically verify that a quantum program complies with a first-order specification. We formally introduce a symbolic quantum program model. This allows to encode the verification problem in an SMT formula, which can then be checked with a δ-complete decision procedure. We also propose an abstraction technique to speed up the verification process. Experimental results show that the abstraction improves symQV's scalability by an order of magnitude to quantum programs with 24 qubits (a 2^{24}-dimensional state space).

Keywords: Quantum computing · Formal verification · Symbolic execution · Abstraction

1 Introduction

Quantum computing bears great potential in increasing the scalability of problem solving in many areas such as optimization [15,25], database search [19], cryptography [36], quantum dynamics simulation [10], satisfiability problems [8], and machine learning [23]. Recently, quantum computing has gained momentum with applications in safety-critical domains such as traffic flow [18], aircraft load [38], logistics [2], and medical diagnostics [21]. Furthermore, quantum simulation [1,11,37] and quantum computers in the cloud [22] are now available.

As with classical programs, detecting bugs in quantum programs is a crucial problem. For classical programs, there exist powerful formal verification techniques to automatically verify that the programs comply with a formal specification [12]. State-of-the-art verifiers, e.g., for C programs [6,7,27] perform verification *symbolically*: The developer marks specific program inputs as symbolic so that the verifier knows to use these as the "search space." The verifier then proves that all possible inputs to the program comply with the specification.

F. Bauer-Marquart—The work was done while the first author was employed at the University of Konstanz.

M. Chechik et al. (Eds.): FM 2023, LNCS 14000, pp. 181–198, 2023.
https://doi.org/10.1007/978-3-031-27481-7_12

For quantum programs, this level of automation is not yet available. In this work, we aim to bridge this gap. Existing approaches to quantum program analysis can be categorized in three directions:

Interactive Proof Assistants: Several approaches [9,20,29,30,33] propose using interactive proof assistants to verify quantum programs. These works provide a large set of deductions but require familiarity with proof assistants such as Coq [5] or Isabelle/HOL [32], competence in proof-writing, and many hours of manual programming work to conduct the verification. These techniques are not fully automatic, which would be crucial for keeping pace with the development of quantum algorithms [24].

Automated Quantum Compiler Verification: Amy [3] proposes an efficient path-sum framework that performs fully automated equivalence checking of a quantum program against a simpler version of the same program, as well as against path-sums that the author uses as specification. The approach is applicable to quantum programs written with quantum gates from the Clifford+T group. Shi et al. [35] use an SMT (satisfiability modulo theories) solver to verify a quantum compiler via equivalence checking. These approaches do not handle general formal specifications.

Quantum Assertion Checking: Li et al. [28] verify assertions during quantum program run-time via projections. Yu and Palsberg [39] use an abstraction to verify assertions on quantum programs with up to 300 qubits, but the approach is restricted to programs where inputs are fixed to a specific value. This is a severe drawback, as essential quantum algorithms such as teleportation, the quantum Fourier transform [31], or Grover's diffusion operator [19] require arbitrarily-valued inputs.

In summary, despite the significance of ensuring specification compliance in quantum software engineering, there is still a lack of practical, automated tools for the purpose of symbolic quantum verification of general formal specifications. Existing tools either:

- require a high amount of manual programming,
- restrict the type of quantum program, e.g., support only a subset of quantum gates or only measurement-free quantum programs,
- do not work symbolically, requiring to fix the inputs to the program, or
- do not support the checking of formal specifications written in first-order logic, which is the standard for classical software verification.

In this paper, we introduce symQV, a framework for writing and verifying quantum programs in the quantum circuit model. To the best of our knowledge, symQV is the first tool that allows automated "push-button" verification of quantum programs where the programs are executed symbolically. In *symbolic execution*, a program is not executed with a predetermined input value. Instead, it is executed with the complete range of possible input values. In contrast to the classical case, where the number of possible input values is bounded by the RAM architecture, the range of input values to a quantum program is infinite.

symQV's automation and high-level workflow are similar to classical verification frameworks such as CPAchecker [6]: quantum developers only need to write a quantum program (using a Cirq-like [11] syntax) and a first-order logic specification that expresses the desired program output. Then, compliance with this specification is automatically verified based on SMT technology. If the quantum program does not satisfy the specification, the user obtains a counterexample that aids in locating errors in the program.

A major obstacle in practice is that quantum program simulators require exponential memory in the number of qubits. This is because simulators running on classical computers need to utilize a matrix to represent the state of a quantum mechanical system. This matrix doubles in size with every qubit that is added to the computation [31], which naturally carries over to verifying quantum programs. We show that in many practical cases this exponential matrix representation can be avoided. In addition, we propose an *abstraction* (or *over-approximation*) [13] that makes our technique more scalable without harming verification soundness.

We evaluate our approach symQV on essential quantum algorithms and subroutines. These include teleportation, QFT, [31], Grover's diffusion operator [19], and quantum phase estimation [36]. We demonstrate that symQV efficiently verifies quantum programs with up to 24 symbolic input qubits (a 2^{24}-dimensional state space), showing its potential to be used as a general-purpose verifier by developers of quantum programs. To put this number into perspective: state-of-the-art quantum computers currently offer one error-corrected qubit [26].

The main contributions of this paper can be summarized as follows. **First**, we introduce a symbolic quantum program model to express quantum programs and safety specifications in our verification framework. **Second**, we provide an encoding of the quantum program model in SMT and show that this encoding is sound and complete. We use this encoding to automatically verify formal specifications written in first-order logic. **Third**, we introduce a sound abstraction technique, which improves the verification time by one order of magnitude. **Finally**, we evaluate our implementation symQV on several quantum programs with up to 24 qubits.

2 Background

This section briefly introduces the concepts of quantum computing used in this paper. For detailed explanations, we refer to Nielsen and Chuang [31].

The *qubit* is the basic unit of quantum information. A single qubit can be in the *ground state* $|0\rangle$ ("ket zero") or in the *excited state* $|1\rangle$ ("ket one"). In general, however, a qubit is in a superposition of both *computational basis states*, written as $|q\rangle = \alpha |0\rangle + \beta |1\rangle$. The *amplitudes* $\alpha, \beta \in \mathbb{C}$ characterize a qubit, with $|\alpha|^2$ and $|\beta|^2$ being the probability of the qubit to be in either state. Therefore, their values are restricted such that $|\alpha|^2 + |\beta|^2 = 1$. Qubits are often written as two-dimensional vectors:

$$|0\rangle \equiv \begin{bmatrix}1\\0\end{bmatrix}, \qquad |1\rangle \equiv \begin{bmatrix}0\\1\end{bmatrix}, \qquad |q\rangle \equiv \begin{bmatrix}\alpha\\\beta\end{bmatrix}.$$

The qubit states span a two-dimensional Hilbert space $\mathcal{H}_2 = \{\alpha\,|0\rangle + \beta\,|1\rangle\}$, a complete complex vector space where the inner product is defined. When we combine n qubits, the system's state vector $|\psi\rangle$ spans the *tensor product* of Hilbert spaces $\mathcal{H}_{2^n} = \bigotimes_{i=1}^{n} \mathcal{H}_2^{(i)}$, and $|\psi\rangle$ is a 2^n-dimensional vector.

Quantum logic gates are the building blocks of quantum programs and transform a quantum state into a new quantum state. They are characterized by unitary matrices U that transform quantum state vectors. Common quantum gates, shown in Fig. 1, include X (Not), Z (phase-flip), H (Hadamard), U_{CX} (controlled-Not), and U_{CZ} (controlled phase-flip).

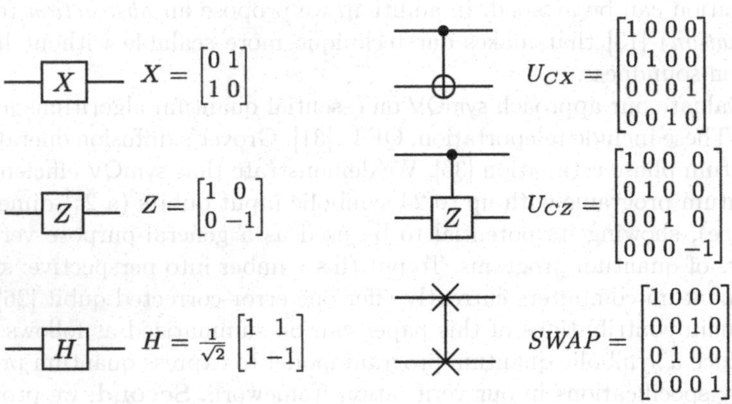

$$X = \begin{bmatrix}0&1\\1&0\end{bmatrix} \qquad U_{CX} = \begin{bmatrix}1&0&0&0\\0&1&0&0\\0&0&0&1\\0&0&1&0\end{bmatrix}$$

$$Z = \begin{bmatrix}1&0\\0&-1\end{bmatrix} \qquad U_{CZ} = \begin{bmatrix}1&0&0&0\\0&1&0&0\\0&0&1&0\\0&0&0&-1\end{bmatrix}$$

$$H = \frac{1}{\sqrt{2}}\begin{bmatrix}1&1\\1&-1\end{bmatrix} \qquad SWAP = \begin{bmatrix}1&0&0&0\\0&0&1&0\\0&1&0&0\\0&0&0&1\end{bmatrix}$$

Fig. 1. Circuit diagrams and matrices of some common quantum gates. For the controlled gates U_{CX} and U_{CZ}, the dot (•) marks the control qubit.

The state of a qubit can alternatively be described with polar coordinates,

$$|q\rangle = \cos\frac{\theta}{2}\,|0\rangle + e^{i\phi}\sin\frac{\theta}{2}\,|1\rangle\,,$$

where ϕ and θ correspond to angles that describe a point on the unit sphere, known as the *Bloch sphere* (see Fig. 2), with $|0\rangle$ being the north pole and $|1\rangle$ being the south pole. For instance, the gates X and Z perform a 180° rotation around the x and z axes, respectively, while H maps ground state $|0\rangle$ to $|+\rangle = \frac{1}{\sqrt{2}}(|0\rangle + |1\rangle)$ at the equator.

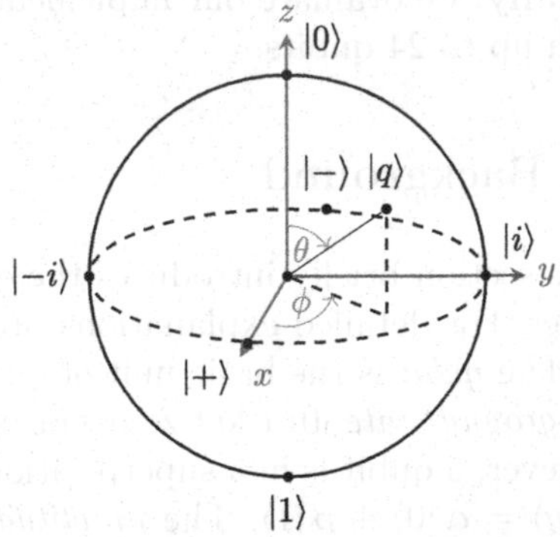

Fig. 2. A qubit $|q\rangle$ visualized on the Bloch sphere.

2.1 Entanglement

Quantum entanglement is an important concept of quantum mechanics. It occurs if the state of one qubit cannot be characterized independently of the state of another qubit, including when the qubits are separated over a large distance. Two-qubit states with perfect correlation are called the *Bell states.* An example for such a state is $|\phi^+\rangle = \frac{1}{\sqrt{2}}(|0\rangle \otimes |0\rangle + |1\rangle \otimes |1\rangle)$, where the first and second qubit are always guaranteed to be either both 0 or both 1 after measurement.

2.2 Quantum Measurement

Measuring a single qubit $|\psi\rangle = \alpha|0\rangle + \beta|1\rangle$ converts it into a classical bit: 0 with probability $|\alpha|^2$ and 1 with probability $|\beta|^2$. In circuit notation, a measurement is denoted as 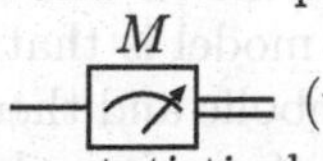 (the double stroke indicates a *classical* wire). Because there are two statistical outcomes, 0 and 1, there exists one measurement operator (a non-unitary matrix) for each: $M_0 = \begin{bmatrix} 1 & 0 \\ 0 & 0 \end{bmatrix}$ and $M_1 = \begin{bmatrix} 0 & 0 \\ 0 & 1 \end{bmatrix}$. The measurement operators irreversibly change the quantum state, which influences subsequent computations. Because of the statistical nature of quantum measurement, simulation tools (and also symQV) need to branch out into two execution paths, with a probability value associated with each of the paths.

2.3 Running Example: Teleportation

Quantum teleportation (TP) is an example of a quantum program with *symbolic* inputs; here, Alice wants to send a qubit $|\psi\rangle$ to Bob. There exists no quantum communication channel in this problem setting, but Alice and Bob each have one qubit of an entangled qubit pair $|\phi^+\rangle$. This is used to send (teleport) Alice's qubit to Bob: First, Alice uses a $CNOT$ and H gate to entangle her two qubits with each other. Then, after measuring both, she sends the measurement results via a classical communication channel to Bob, who finally retrieves $|\psi\rangle$ using two controlled gates, U_{CX} and U_{CZ}. The circuit diagram is shown in Fig. 3.

This example motivates the importance of *symbolic verification*: we want to verify that teleportation is successful for *any* quantum state and, hence, need to represent the input state symbolically.

3 The symQV Quantum Program Model

We introduce the *quantum program model* M_Q as an SMT-compatible symbolic representation of the general quantum circuit model [31]. The quantum program model, unlike the standard state-vector representation used in simulators, can represent operations on qubits as direct mappings in SMT instead of matrices. Only when necessary, for example when qubits become entangled, do we construct the state vector for this specific subset of qubits.

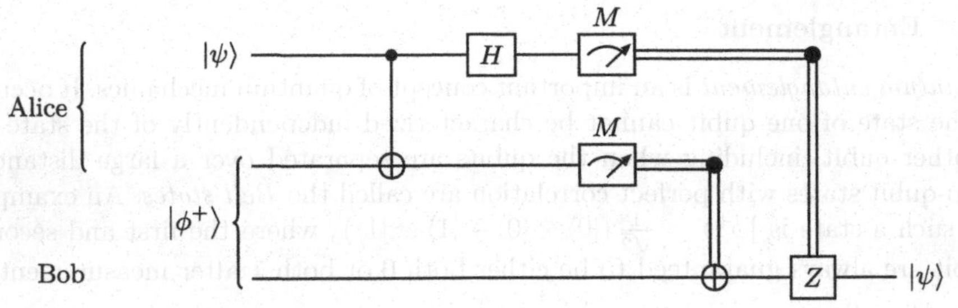

Fig. 3. Quantum teleportation circuit, adapted from [31]. The double line indicates a classical wire. Here, it simulates a communication channel.

The main benefit of the quantum program model is that it allows reasoning about quantum programs whose inputs are symbolic and therefore not fixed to a certain value. Thus we can use the model to perform formal verification against all possible inputs, i.e., the entire infinite Hilbert space. Furthermore, the quantum program model allows us to handle quantum programs with parametrized gates, which add another (infinite) dimension to the problem.

We give a high-level, bottom-up presentation of the quantum program model. At the end of the presentation we exemplify the encoding of the quantum teleportation program in Sect. 3.1 (the complete SMT formula is shown in Sect. A.4 of the supplementary material [4]). First, we need symbolic encodings for qubits, computations, and measurements. For convenience, we encode both the amplitudes and the phases into the qubit's SMT representation, allowing computations to work on either.

Encoding 1 (Qubit). *We encode a complex number as a pair $z := (z_R, z_I)$ with $z_R, z_I \in \mathbb{R}$. Using this representation, we encode a qubit as a 4-tuple*[1]

$$|q\rangle := (\alpha, \beta, \phi, \theta), \qquad \alpha, \phi, \theta \in \mathbb{R},\ \beta \in \mathbb{C}.$$

We combine both the amplitude and phase representation because we need to restrict the valuations of the variables using the following constraints:

$$\alpha = \cos\frac{\theta}{2} \ \wedge\ \beta_R = \cos\phi \cdot \sin\frac{\theta}{2} \ \wedge\ \beta_I = \sin\phi \cdot \sin\frac{\theta}{2}, \tag{1}$$

which constrains the qubit's degrees of freedom to $|\alpha|^2 + |\beta|^2 = 1$, and

$$0 \le \theta \le \pi \wedge 0 \le \phi < 2\pi \quad \wedge \quad \theta = 0 \Rightarrow \phi = 0 \quad \wedge \quad \theta = \pi \Rightarrow \phi = 0, \tag{2}$$

which constrains the angles' values to their respective periods.

Encoding 1 constrains a qubit's degree of freedom via its phases (Eq. (2)). This is because directly encoding the sphere equation $|\alpha|^2 + |\beta|^2 = 1$ requires two

[1] We choose α to be real because the global phase [31] has no observable consequences.

nested square operations, which are challenging for state-of-the-art SMT solvers (we evaluated Z3 [14] and dReal [17]).

The main motivation for our quantum program model is that we are often not required to build the whole (2^n-dimensional) state vector. Standard (unitary) quantum gates can be conveniently realized by a direct mapping on the SMT level, which we first define in an abstract way and instantiate later:

Definition 1 (Direct mapping). *We encode a unitary gate as a bijection* $U : \mathcal{H}_2^k \rightarrow \mathcal{H}_2^k$ *called* direct mapping, *where* k *is the number of modified qubits.*

Direct mappings allow us to express the effect of a quantum gate without explicitly constructing the matrix representation, unlike in standard quantum simulators. We concretize the notion of the direct mapping (Definition 1) with the following encodings of the most common quantum logic gates [31]:

Encoding 2.1 (Basic single-qubit gates). *The identity,* X*,* Z*, and* H *gates are encoded as the following mappings:*

$$I\left(\begin{bmatrix}\alpha\\\beta\end{bmatrix}\right) := \begin{bmatrix}\alpha\\\beta\end{bmatrix}, X\left(\begin{bmatrix}\alpha\\\beta\end{bmatrix}\right) := \begin{bmatrix}\beta\\\alpha\end{bmatrix}, Z\left(\begin{bmatrix}\alpha\\\beta\end{bmatrix}\right) := \begin{bmatrix}\alpha\\-\beta\end{bmatrix}, H\left(\begin{bmatrix}\alpha\\\beta\end{bmatrix}\right) := \begin{bmatrix}\frac{\alpha+\beta}{\sqrt{2}}\\\frac{\alpha-\beta}{\sqrt{2}}\end{bmatrix}.$$

We extend the encoding of the identity gate to take a variable number of arguments, such that $I(|q_0\rangle, \ldots, |q_k\rangle) = (|q_0\rangle, \ldots, |q_k\rangle)$ *for any* k*.*

The gates in Encoding 2.1 are used to modify the amplitudes of a qubit. The next encoding includes gates that modify a qubit's phases without directly affecting its amplitudes.

Encoding 2.2 (Phase gates). *The phase gates* R_X *and* R_Z *perform parametrized rotations around the* x *and* z *axes, respectively. The mappings use the phase angles:*

$$R_X(\theta')(\phi, \theta) := (\phi, \theta + \theta'), \quad R_Z(\phi')(\phi, \theta) := (\phi + \phi', \theta).$$

Encoding 2.3 (*SWAP* gate). *The mapping of the* $SWAP$ *gate applied to qubits* $|q_0\rangle$ *and* $|q_1\rangle$ *is*

$$SWAP(|q_0\rangle, |q_1\rangle) := (|q_1\rangle, |q_0\rangle).$$

In cases where it is not possible to express a quantum gate as a unitary mapping, such as entangling gates, we resort to the standard matrix representation. The matrix is then applied to a quantum state vector via matrix multiplication.

Encoding 3 (Gate matrix). *We encode a quantum gate as a* $2^k \times 2^k$ *(complex) matrix* U*, where* k *is the number of modified qubits. We further require that* U *is reversible (cf. Sect. 2).*

Encoding 4 (Matrix multiplication). *For an* $m \times n$ *matrix* A *and an* $n \times p$ *matrix* B*, the result of the matrix multiplication* $A \cdot B$*, an* $m \times p$ *matrix* C*, is encoded via the identities* $\bigwedge_{i=1}^{m} \bigwedge_{j=1}^{p} c_{i,j} = \sum_{k=1}^{n} a_{i,k} b_{k,j}$*.*

There are benefits when encoding a gate via a direct mapping instead of a matrix, which we now illustrate with an example:

Example 1. Recall that the *SWAP* gate can be encoded via a direct mapping (Encoding 2.3), i.e., we can compute

$$SWAP(|q_0\rangle, |q_1\rangle) = (|q_1\rangle, |q_0\rangle)$$

in one step. This is *not* the case for the matrix encoding:

$$\begin{aligned} SWAP(|q_0\rangle \otimes |q_1\rangle) &= \begin{bmatrix} 1&0&0&0\\ 0&0&1&0\\ 0&1&0&0\\ 0&0&0&1 \end{bmatrix} \begin{bmatrix} \alpha_0 \\ \beta_0 \end{bmatrix} \otimes \begin{bmatrix} \alpha_1 \\ \beta_1 \end{bmatrix} = \begin{bmatrix} 1&0&0&0\\ 0&0&1&0\\ 0&1&0&0\\ 0&0&0&1 \end{bmatrix} \begin{bmatrix} \alpha_0\alpha_1 \\ \alpha_0\beta_1 \\ \beta_0\alpha_1 \\ \beta_0\beta_1 \end{bmatrix} = \begin{bmatrix} \alpha_0\alpha_1 \\ \beta_0\alpha_1 \\ \alpha_0\beta_1 \\ \beta_0\beta_1 \end{bmatrix} \\ &= |q_1\rangle \otimes |q_0\rangle\,. \end{aligned}$$

Here we observe that the matrix representation is verbose. It needs 4 multiplications per tensor product and 16 multiplications only for computing the result of the matrix multiplication. Note that the number of operations increases exponentially with the number of qubits, illustrating the benefit of the direct mapping. We give a further example of a direct mapping in Sect. A.1 of the supplementary material [4].

Measurement, the only non-reversible operation in our encodings, assigns 0 or 1 to a qubit with a certain probability. For a state s consisting of a single qubit $|q\rangle = \alpha\,|0\rangle + \beta\,|1\rangle$, there are two possible subsequent states: $s'(0) = |0\rangle$ and $s'(1) = |1\rangle$. The probabilities $p(x)$ that state x occurs are

$$p(0) = |\alpha|^2,\ p(1) = |\beta|^2.$$

Therefore, for every quantum measurement taking place in M_Q, in the case of non-zero probabilities $p(0)$ and $p(1)$, there are two possible successor states, one per measurement outcome.

Encoding 5 (Quantum measurement). *We encode the measurement operators by applying the standard measurement matrices (cf. Sect. 2) to Encodings 3 to 4.*

For entangled quantum states, qubits can no longer be characterized individually [31]. Therefore, our encoding cannot use the direct-mapping strategy from Definition 1 and we fall back to a vector representation of the quantum state.

Definition 2 (Modeling a quantum state). *We define a vector data structure to represent an n-qubit quantum state $|\psi\rangle$. This structure holds (cf. Sect. 2) 2^n (symbolic) complex numbers*

$$|\psi\rangle := (\alpha_1, \alpha_2, \cdots, \alpha_{2^n}).$$

Encoding 6 (Tensor product of matrices). *For an $m \times n$ matrix A and a $p \times q$ matrix B, the tensor product $A \otimes B$, an $(mp) \times (nq)$ matrix C, is encoded via equalities $\bigwedge_{i=1}^{m} \bigwedge_{k=1}^{p} \bigwedge_{j=1}^{n} \bigwedge_{l=1}^{q} c_{ik,jl} = a_{i,j} \cdot b_{k,l}$.*

The following encoding is needed for gate matrices that only apply to a subset of the qubits in the system. This is achieved by taking a tensor product with the identity matrix I.

Encoding 7 (Applying gates to a subset of qubits). *For a quantum state $|\psi\rangle$ over $n+1$ qubits and a quantum gate U over qubits $|q_i\rangle$ to $|q_j\rangle$ where $0 \leq i < j \leq n$, the next state is*

$$|\psi'\rangle = \begin{cases} I^{\otimes i-1} \otimes U \otimes I^{\otimes n-j} |\psi\rangle & \text{if } 0 < i, j < n, \\ U \otimes I^{\otimes n-j} |\psi\rangle & \text{if } 0 = i, j < n, \\ I^{\otimes i-1} \otimes U |\psi\rangle & \text{if } 0 < i, j = n, \\ U |\psi\rangle & \text{if } 0 = i, j = n. \end{cases}$$

Having assigned a logic representation to qubits, quantum gates, and quantum measurement, we can combine them to define the *quantum program model.*

Definition 3 (Quantum program model). *A* quantum program model *is a 5-tuple*

$$M_{\mathcal{Q}} := (\mathcal{Q}, S, \rightarrow, \Theta, V_0) \tag{3}$$

where

- *$\mathcal{Q}$ is a set of n (symbolic) qubits $\{|q_0\rangle, \ldots, |q_{n-1}\rangle\}$,*
- *S is a sequence of m (symbolic) states $(s_0, \ldots, s_{m-1})$,*
- *$\rightarrow$ is a sequence of $m-1$ state operations $(\rightarrow_1, \ldots, \rightarrow_{m-1})$,*
- *Θ is a set of (symbolic) parameters, and*
- *V_0 is the qubit initializer sequence.*

The qubits of $\mathcal{Q}$ are symbolic unless an initial valuation (assignment of a subset of qubits with concrete values) is provided in V_0. The initial state is $s_0 = (|q_{0,0}\rangle, \ldots, |q_{0,n-1}\rangle)$ and all following states $s_i \in S$ $(0 < i < m)$ again consist of symbolic qubits $(|q_{i,0}\rangle, \ldots, |q_{i,n-1}\rangle)$. Every state operation $\rightarrow_i$ is either

- a direct mapping (Definition 1); or
- a unitary matrix (Encoding 3); or
- a quantum measurement (Encoding 5).

We define the shorthand

$$s_{i-1} \rightarrow_i s_i = \begin{cases} \rightarrow_i (s_{i-1}) = s_i & \rightarrow_i \text{ is a direct mapping,} \\ \rightarrow_i \cdot \bigotimes_{j=0}^{n-1} |q_{(i-1,j)}\rangle = \bigotimes_{j=0}^{n-1} |q_{(i,j)}\rangle & \rightarrow_i \text{ is a matrix,} \end{cases}$$

and tie the states and operations together via $\bigwedge_{i=1}^{m-1} s_{i-1} \rightarrow_i s_i$.

A state operation can also be a quantum measurement M. When state s_{i-1} is measured, two possible subsequent states are created: $s_i(0)$ and $s_i(1)$ (Sect. 2.2). Additionally, we allow measurement of k qubits at the same time for a bit vector $x \in \{0,1\}^k$ such that M_x is the combined measurement.

The set Θ contains symbolic, real-valued variables that are used to parameterize state operations, e.g., rotations. The sequence $V_0 = (\Psi_0, \ldots, \Psi_{n-1})$ contains sets of initial valuations $\Psi_i \subseteq \mathcal{H}_2$ (possibly singleton sets in case of a concrete valuation). The initial valuations are asserted to the initial qubits via $\bigwedge_{i=0}^{n-1} |q_i\rangle \in \Psi_i$.

Before we give an example, we note that the quantum program model $M_\mathcal{Q}$ is equivalent to the traditional presentation of quantum computing.

Theorem 1 (Equivalence). *The quantum program model $M_\mathcal{Q}$ (Definition 3) and the quantum circuit model [31] are equivalent.*

The proof for Theorem 1 is given in Sect. A.4 of the supplementary material [4].

3.1 Running Example: Quantum Program Model of Teleportation

Now that we have defined the quantum program model, we formalize our running example, teleportation, as $M_\mathcal{Q} = (\mathcal{Q}, S, \rightarrow, \varnothing, V_0)$, where

$$\begin{aligned}
\mathcal{Q} &= \{|q_0\rangle, |q_1\rangle, |q_2\rangle\},\\
S &= (s_0, s_1, s_2, s_3, s_4),\\
\rightarrow &= (U_{CX}(|q_0\rangle, |q_1\rangle), H(|q_0\rangle), \mathcal{M}(|q_0\rangle, |q_1\rangle), U_{CX}(|q_1\rangle, |q_2\rangle), U_{CZ}(|q_0\rangle, |q_2\rangle)),\\
V_0 &= (\mathcal{H}_2, \{|\phi^+\rangle\}).
\end{aligned}$$

Note that valuations V_0 are symbolic, so each input qubit can assume any state in the Hilbert space.

Next we provide a high-level encoding of this quantum program model in SMT. The complete SMT formula is shown in Sect. A of the supplementary material [4].

We begin by encoding the first state s_0, which contains the three input qubits $|q_{0,0}\rangle, |q_{0,1}\rangle, |q_{0,2}\rangle$. The first operation $s_0 \rightarrow_1 s_1$ is encoded as $|q_{1,0}\rangle \otimes |q_{1,1}\rangle = U_{CX}\, |q_{0,0}\rangle \otimes |q_{0,1}\rangle$, with s_1 containing the qubits $|q_{1,0}\rangle, |q_{1,1}\rangle, |q_{1,2}\rangle$ that encode the result of this operation. The remaining states and state operations are encoded as follows (we have omitted identity operations for the sake of brevity), with all entries connected with a conjunction:

We observe that the measurement step from s_2 to s_3 results in the creation of 4 possible execution paths, one per measurement outcome (00, 01, 10, 11). Also, recall that all the symbols and operators used in the encoding above, such as the tensor product ($\otimes$), gates (H, U_{CX}, U_{CZ}), measurements (M_0, M_1), and Hilbert space ($\mathcal{H}_2$), carry the meanings we assigned to them in Encodings 1 to 7.

State	Operation
$s_2 = (\|q_{2,0}\rangle, \|q_{2,1}\rangle, \|q_{2,2}\rangle)$	$\|q_{2,0}\rangle = H\,\|q_{1,0}\rangle$
$s_3(00) = (\|q_{3,0}(00)\rangle, \|q_{3,1}(00)\rangle, \|q_{3,2}(00)\rangle)$	$\|q_{3,0}(00)\rangle = M_0\,\|q_{2,0}\rangle,\ \|q_{3,1}(00)\rangle = M_0\,\|q_{2,1}\rangle$
$s_3(01) = (\|q_{3,0}(01)\rangle, \|q_{3,1}(01)\rangle, \|q_{3,2}(01)\rangle)$	$\|q_{3,0}(01)\rangle = M_0\,\|q_{2,0}\rangle,\ \|q_{3,1}(01)\rangle = M_1\,\|q_{2,1}\rangle$
$s_3(10) = (\|q_{3,0}(10)\rangle, \|q_{3,1}(10)\rangle, \|q_{3,2}(10)\rangle)$	$\|q_{3,0}(10)\rangle = M_1\,\|q_{2,0}\rangle,\ \|q_{3,1}(10)\rangle = M_0\,\|q_{2,1}\rangle$
$s_3(11) = (\|q_{3,0}(11)\rangle, \|q_{3,1}(11)\rangle, \|q_{3,2}(11)\rangle)$	$\|q_{3,0}(11)\rangle = M_1\,\|q_{2,0}\rangle,\ \|q_{3,1}(11)\rangle = M_1\,\|q_{2,1}\rangle$
$s_4(x) = (\|q_{4,0}(x)\rangle, \|q_{4,1}(x)\rangle, \|q_{4,2}(x)\rangle)$ $(x \in \{00, 01, 10, 11\})$	$\|q_{4,1}(x)\rangle \otimes \|q_{4,2}(x)\rangle = U_{CX}\,\|q_{3,1}(x)\rangle \otimes \|q_{3,2}(x)\rangle$
$s_5(x) = (\|q_{5,0}(x)\rangle, \|q_{5,1}(x)\rangle, \|q_{5,2}(x)\rangle)$	$\|q_{5,0}(x)\rangle \otimes \|q_{5,2}(x)\rangle = U_{CZ}\,\|q_{4,0}(x)\rangle \otimes \|q_{4,2}(x)\rangle$
Initial valuation	$\|q_{0,0}\rangle \in \mathcal{H}_2,\ \|q_{0,1}\rangle \otimes \|q_{0,2}\rangle \in \{\|\phi^+\rangle\}$

4 The symQV Verification Algorithm

Our symQV algorithm takes as input a quantum program model M_Q defined in Sect. 3 and a formal specification in the form of a first-order formula φ. From that, symQV generates an SMT encoding (which we also write M_Q with a slight abuse of notation) as described in the previous section. Finally, this encoding together with the negated specification is asserted in a query to an SMT solver.

Theorem 2 (Soundness and completeness of the encoding). *Given a quantum program model with encoding M_Q and a specification φ, we have that the program satisfies φ if and only if $M_Q \wedge \neg\varphi$ is unsatisfiable.*

Proof. This follows from the one-to-one correspondence of the quantum program model M_Q and the standard quantum circuit model [31] shown in Theorem 1. The formula is satisfiable if and only if there is an execution that violates the specification.

The formula M_Q falls into the theory of nonlinear real arithmetic with trigonometric expressions, for which checking satisfiability is undecidable [34]. Yet, the δ-relaxation of this problem is decidable [16]. That is why we use the δ-satisfiability framework from [17], which is implemented in dReal[2]. If the combined formula $M_Q \wedge \neg\varphi$ is found to be δ-SAT, either it is indeed satisfiable (i.e., a counterexample has been found), or it is unsatisfiable (i.e., the program complies with the specification) but a δ-perturbation on its numerical terms would satisfy the formula. The parameter δ is user-controllable, and we show in the evaluation that the δ-SAT case for correct programs does not occur in practice for reasonable values of δ.

While the δ-relaxation must sacrifice completeness, it preserves soundness: If the formula is found to be unsatisfiable (UNSAT), then the quantum program is indeed correct with respect to φ.

Theorem 3 (Soundness preservation). *Let M_Q be the encoding of a quantum program model and φ be a specification. Assume that a δ-satisfiability solver returns* UNSAT *for the formula $M_Q \wedge \neg\varphi$. Then the quantum program is correct.*

[2] Available at https://github.com/dreal/dreal4.

Proof. This follows from Theorem 2 and [17].

4.1 Running Example: Verification of Teleportation

Coming up with the right specifications for quantum programs is not trivial. Conveniently, as symQV maps all building blocks of quantum programs into an SMT representation, we have access to the full set of logic operators.

We want our specification to express that teleportation has been successful, i.e., qubit $|q_0\rangle$ has moved to where qubit $|q_2\rangle$ was at the beginning (compare the right-hand side of Fig. 3).

$$(|q_{5,2}\rangle = |q_{0,0}\rangle)$$

This, however, is not the full specification. We need to disallow operations crossing the line between the first two qubits and the last one, which only becomes possible after measurement, where the classical communication channel can be used (cf. Sect. 2.3). Therefore, we add an additional constraint that forbids state operations where these qubits appear together:

$$\varphi = (|q_{5,2}\rangle = |q_{0,0}\rangle) \wedge \neg\exists 0 \leq i \leq 2\colon \rightarrow_i (|q_{i,0}\rangle, |q_{i,2}\rangle) \vee \rightarrow_i (|q_{i,1}\rangle, |q_{i,2}\rangle)$$

Performing the verification is "push-button," i.e., only requires writing the quantum program model and the specification. The corresponding Python code given in Sect. A.3 of the supplementary material [4] demonstrates that a user does not have to provide any proof steps as in previous works based on proof assistants.

4.2 The symQV Over-Approximation

Encoding 1 puts trigonometric functions into the SMT formula, which are computationally expensive. This can also be later seen in the evaluation. Therefore, we introduce an over-approximation of the Hilbert space to make the verification task more efficient. This is achieved via relaxing the qubit's degrees of freedom from the unit sphere to the unit box, visualized in Fig. 4.

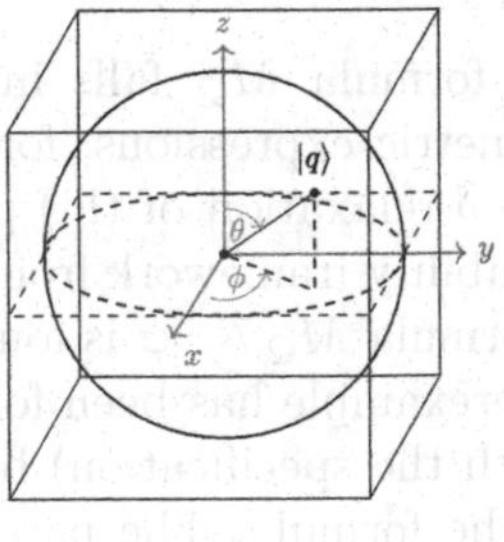

Fig. 4. The over-approximation visualized for a single qubit.

Encoding 8 (Over-approximation). *We remove the constraints in Eq.* (2) *from Encoding 1 and add the following constraint over the qubit's degrees of freedom:*

$$-1 \leq \alpha \leq 1 \;\wedge\; -1 \leq \beta_R \leq 1 \;\wedge\; -1 \leq \beta_I \leq 1. \tag{4}$$

Table 1. Benchmark quantum programs for evaluating our verification procedure. "Input" describes the input space to the quantum programs and "Parametrized" expresses whether there are parametrized gates in the quantum program.

Program	Description	Depth	Input	Parametrized
Toffoli	Toffoli Gate	5	Bit vector	No
TP	Quantum Teleportation Circuit	6	Infinite	No
ADD-8	8-bit Quantum Adder	48	Bit vector	No
QFT-n	n-Qubit Quantum Fourier Transform	$\mathcal{O}(n^2)$	Bit vector	No
QPE-n	n-Bit Quantum Phase Estimation	$\mathcal{O}(n^2)$	Concrete	Yes
GDO-n	n-Qubit Grover Diffusion Operator	$\mathcal{O}(n)$	Infinite	No

5 Evaluation

This section presents our experimental evaluation, demonstrating symQV's effectiveness in verifying several (correct) quantum programs that have symbolic inputs or symbolically parametrized quantum gates.

5.1 Implementation

symQV[3] is implemented as a Python library interfacing with dReal [17] using about 5000 lines of code. The symQV Python API allows users to specify the quantum program using a syntax inspired by Cirq [11]. The specification can be written using one of two formats:

- *State vector:* One can specify assertions on any of the 2^n vector entries.
- *Qubits:* One can specify assertions on any of the n qubits.

The logic assertions use an SMT-LIB2-compatible Python API and support specifications expressing relationships between program inputs and outputs as well as intermediate states.

5.2 Benchmark Problems and Setup

An overview of the benchmark problems is given in Table 1. Further descriptions, including the specifications, are given in Sect. A.3 of the supplementary material [4].

We compare our tool ("symQV") against quantum simulation ("Simulation"), basic SMT solving based on linear algebra ("Basic SMT"), and symQV without over-approximation ("symQV (exact)").

- *Simulation* is implemented in Qiskit [1]. The technique enumerates all possible inputs to the quantum program and then compares the outputs with the

[3] Available for download at https://doi.org/10.5281/zenodo.7400321.

specification. We can only use this technique for a finite input space, i.e., for concrete and bit-vector inputs, but neither for symbolic qubits with the entire Hilbert space $\mathcal{H}_2$ as input space, nor for parametrized gates.

- *Basic SMT* is basic SMT solving using vectors and matrices, but not using direct mappings (Definition 1).
- symQV (exact) is a modification of symQV where all over-approximation capabilities are removed, ending up with a technique that performs exact modeling, even when unnecessary (see Sect. 4.2).

We do not compare against the proof-assistant approaches [9,20,29,30,33] (cf. Sect. 1) because a comparison of run-times between an automated method, as implemented in symQV, and a semi-automated method relying on manual input is not meaningful. We also do not compare against [3] because it neither supports the full gate set nor formal logic specifications.

The experiments use the value $\delta = 10^{-4}$. We also compare the run-time of symQV for different precision levels δ.

All experiments are carried out on a workstation with an AMD Ryzen ThreadRipper 3960X @ 3.8 GHz × 24 cores processor and 256 GB RAM. The machine runs Ubuntu 20.04.3 LTS and each result is the average of 10 runs.

5.3 Results

We summarize our results in Table 2. symQV (exact) is best for quantum programs with concrete inputs or a small qubit count (TP and ADD-8); the over-approximation of symQV yields no speed-up for these instances. *Simulation* performs best for verifying combinatorial problems, i.e., for the quantum Fourier transform (QFT). Here, it can still feasibly enumerate a 12-qubit state space. Interestingly, Basic SMT scales best among the SMT-based procedures here; this is explained by the high amount of controlled operations, for which the mapping-based approach of symQV is inferior.

symQV offers a dramatic performance increase for quantum programs with symbolic inputs, i.e., quantum phase estimation (QPE) and Grover's diffusion operator (GDO). This highlights the advantage of over-approximation for this family of quantum programs. Recall that simulation is not possible for both QPE and GDO, as that would require enumerating infinitely many inputs.

The precision value $\delta = 10^{-4}$ was sufficient for all benchmarks in our evaluation. To investigate scalability in this parameter, Table 3 compares the run-times for different values for GDO with 12, 15, and 18 qubits, respectively. For the higher qubit counts, the run-time increases significantly when we lower δ to 10^{-6}, but then remains relatively stable when further tightening precision.

Overall, symQV is the strongest for quantum programs with infinite input space, i.e., programs where the (symbolic) input qubits can span the complete Hilbert space. Likewise, for programs that use parametrized quantum gates dependent on a symbolic parameter, symQV is the most effective.

Table 2. Runtime comparison results for the benchmark problems described in Table 1. "Simulation" stands for simulation and enumeration of all cases. "Basic SMT" is SMT solving with full state and matrix construction. "symQV (exact)" is symQV where over-approximations have been removed. "symQV" (this work) utilizes a sound over-approximation. "N/A" instances cannot be solved by simulation due to infinite state space. "`out of memory`" cases exceeded the available memory, and "`timeout`" cases exceed the 12-h time limit.

Benchmark	Simulation	Basic SMT	symQV (exact)	symQV
Toffoli	**0.02 s**	11.1 s	1.3 s	0.4 s
TP	N/A	44.8 s	**21.6 s**	31.0 s
ADD-8	6.1 h	`out of memory`	**7.6 s**	7.8 s
QFT-3	**0.005 s**	12.8 s	5.8 s	1.0 s
QFT-5	**0.03 s**	17.6 min	2.6 min	26.4 s
QFT-10	**1.5 s**	1.2 h	10.9 h	1.6 h
QFT-12	**14.0 s**	4.0 h	`timeout`	7.4 h
QPE-3	N/A	19.2 s	34.0 s	**8.7 s**
QPE-5	N/A	18.2 min	42.3 min	**3.9 min**
GDO-5	N/A	`timeout`	9.2 s	**1.3 s**
GDO-10	N/A	`timeout`	3.2 min	**17.0 s**
GDO-12	N/A	`timeout`	14.2 min	**20.2 s**
GDO-15	N/A	`timeout`	2.9 h	**1.0 min**
GDO-18	N/A	`timeout`	`timeout`	**4.9 min**
GDO-20	N/A	`timeout`	`timeout`	**17.1 min**
GDO-22	N/A	`timeout`	`timeout`	**1.1 h**
GDO-24	N/A	`timeout`	`timeout`	**4.2 h**

6 Discussion

Symbolic execution and formal verification scale exponentially for the quantum case, as is the case for classical software. That is to be expected: firstly, the simulation of quantum programs on classical hardware already takes exponential time and space due to the matrix representation of quantum mechanics, and secondly because the state space grows with every input variable added to the program. Nonetheless, we have shown how to keep this exponential blow-up under control by introducing mappings and over-approximations. In our evaluation, we symbolically executed quantum programs with up to 24 qubits. In comparison, even (concrete) quantum simulation for concrete inputs stops being feasible at around 30 qubits, requiring petabytes of main memory. In conclusion, symQV is most effective for unknown inputs to the quantum programs or unknown parameters of quantum gates that therefore cannot be tested.

Table 3. symQV run-time results for different precision values δ.

Delta	GDO-12	GDO-15	GDO-18
10^{-4}	20.2 s	1.0 min	4.9 min
10^{-6}	20.5 s	28.0 min	33.1 min
10^{-8}	20.8 s	49.4 min	58.7 min
10^{-10}	21.1 s	52.3 min	1.2 h

7 Conclusion

We introduced symQV, a symbolic verification technique that leverages over-approximation to make automated verification of quantum programs feasible. We formalized quantum program semantics in SMT and proposed a sound over-approximation that allows scaling to realistic program sizes. Thanks to the symbolic nature of our approach, we can analyze quantum programs with infinite input space, which is beyond the capabilities of quantum simulation. We demonstrate these achievements by formally verifying multiple quantum programs against their specifications within a modest time frame.

In this paper, we focused on formalizing the mathematical foundations to model quantum programs, define specifications, and prove their specification compliance. We intend this to be the first step in a larger, fully automated quantum verification framework, including counterexample-guided refinement. In the future, we will investigate strategies that allow us to verify hybrid programs that perform classical and quantum computations.

Acknowledgments. This research was partly supported by DIREC - Digital Research Centre Denmark and the Villum Investigator Grant S4OS.

References

1. Abraham, F.N., et al.: Qiskit: an open-source framework for quantum computing (2017). https://github.com/Qiskit
2. Ajagekar, A., Humble, T., You, F.: Quantum computing based hybrid solution strategies for large-scale discrete-continuous optimization problems. Comput. Chem. Eng. **132** (2020). https://doi.org/10.1016/j.compchemeng.2019.106630
3. Amy, M.: Towards large-scale functional verification of universal quantum circuits. In: QPL. EPTCS, vol. 287, pp. 1–21 (2018). https://doi.org/10.4204/EPTCS.287.1
4. Bauer-Marquart, F., Leue, S., Schilling, C.: symQV: automated symbolic verification of quantum programs. CoRR, abs/2212.02267 (2022). https://doi.org/10.48550/arXiv.2212.02267
5. Bertot, Y., Castéran, P.: Interactive Theorem Proving and Program Development - Coq'Art: The Calculus of Inductive Constructions. TTCS. Springer, Heidelberg (2004). https://doi.org/10.1007/978-3-662-07964-5
6. Beyer, D., Keremoglu, M.E.: CPAchecker: a tool for configurable software verification. In: Gopalakrishnan, G., Qadeer, S. (eds.) CAV 2011. LNCS, vol. 6806, pp.

184–190. Springer, Heidelberg (2011). https://doi.org/10.1007/978-3-642-22110-1_16

7. Cadar, C., Dunbar, D., Engler, D.R.: KLEE: unassisted and automatic generation of high-coverage tests for complex systems programs. In: OSDI, vol. 8, pp. 209–224. USENIX Association (2008). http://www.usenix.org/events/osdi08/tech/full_papers/cadar/cadar.pdf
8. Centrone, F., Kumar, N., Diamanti, E., Kerenidis, I.: Experimental demonstration of quantum advantage for NP verification with limited information. Nat. Commun. **12**(1), 850 (2021). https://doi.org/10.1038/s41467-021-21119-1
9. Chareton, C., Bardin, S., Bobot, F., Perrelle, V., Valiron, B.: An automated deductive verification framework for circuit-building quantum programs. In: Yoshida, N. (ed.) ESOP 2021. LNCS, vol. 12648, pp. 148–177. Springer, Cham (2021). https://doi.org/10.1007/978-3-030-72019-3_6
10. Childs, A.M., Maslov, D., Nam, Y.S., Ross, N.J., Su, Y.: Toward the first quantum simulation with quantum speedup. Proc. Natl. Acad. Sci. U.S.A. **115**(38), 9456–9461 (2018). https://doi.org/10.1073/pnas.1801723115
11. Cirq Developers. Cirq (2021). See full list of authors on Github: https://github.com/quantumlib/Cirq/graphs/contributors
12. Clarke, E.M., Henzinger, T.A., Veith, H., Bloem, R. (eds.): Handbook of Model Checking. Springer, Heidelberg (2018). https://doi.org/10.1007/978-3-319-10575-8
13. Cousot, P., Cousot, R.: Abstract interpretation: a unified lattice model for static analysis of programs by construction or approximation of fixpoints. In: POPL, pp. 238–252. ACM (1977). https://doi.org/10.1145/512950.512973
14. de Moura, L., Bjørner, N.: Z3: an efficient SMT solver. In: Ramakrishnan, C.R., Rehof, J. (eds.) TACAS 2008. LNCS, vol. 4963, pp. 337–340. Springer, Heidelberg (2008). https://doi.org/10.1007/978-3-540-78800-3_24
15. Farhi, E., Goldstone, J., Gutmann, S.: A quantum approximate optimization algorithm. arXiv preprint (2014). https://doi.org/10.48550/arXiv.1411.4028
16. Gao, S., Avigad, J., Clarke, E.M.: δ-complete decision procedures for satisfiability over the reals. In: Gramlich, B., Miller, D., Sattler, U. (eds.) IJCAR 2012. LNCS (LNAI), vol. 7364, pp. 286–300. Springer, Heidelberg (2012). https://doi.org/10.1007/978-3-642-31365-3_23
17. Gao, S., Kong, S., Clarke, E.M.: dReal: an SMT solver for nonlinear theories over the reals. In: Bonacina, M.P. (ed.) CADE 2013. LNCS (LNAI), vol. 7898, pp. 208–214. Springer, Heidelberg (2013). https://doi.org/10.1007/978-3-642-38574-2_14
18. Goddard, P., Mniszewski, S., Neukart, F., Pakin, S., Reinhardt, S.: How will early quantum computing benefit computational methods? In: Proceedings of the SIAM Annual Meeting (2017). https://sinews.siam.org/Details-Page/how-will-early-quantum-computing-benefit-computational-methods
19. Grover, L.K.: A fast quantum mechanical algorithm for database search. In: STOC, pp. 212–219. ACM (1996). https://doi.org/10.1145/237814.237866
20. Hietala, K., Rand, R., Hung, S., Li, L., Hicks, M.: Proving quantum programs correct. In: ITP, Dagstuhl, Germany. LIPIcs, vol. 193, pp. 21:1–21:19. Schloss Dagstuhl - Leibniz-Zentrum für Informatik (2021). https://doi.org/10.4230/LIPIcs.ITP.2021.21
21. Houssein, E.H., Abohashima, Z., Elhoseny, M., Mohamed, W.M.: Hybrid quantum convolutional neural networks model for COVID-19 prediction using chest X-ray images. CoRR (2021). https://arxiv.org/abs/2102.06535
22. IBM. IBM's roadmap for scaling quantum technology (2020). https://research.ibm.com/blog/ibm-quantum-roadmap

23. Jerbi, S., Fiderer, L.J., Nautrup, H.P., Kübler, J.M., Briegel, H.J., Dunjko, V.: Quantum machine learning beyond kernel methods. CoRR (2021). https://arxiv.org/abs/2110.13162
24. Jordan, S.: Quantum algorithm zoo (2021). https://quantumalgorithmzoo.org
25. Kadowaki, T., Nishimori, H.: Quantum annealing in the transverse Ising model. Phys. Rev. E **58**(5) (1998). https://doi.org/10.1103/PhysRevE.58.5355
26. Krinner, S., et al.: Realizing repeated quantum error correction in a distance-three surface code. Nature **605**(7911), 669–674 (2022). https://doi.org/10.1038/s41586-022-04566-8
27. Kroening, D., Tautschnig, M.: CBMC – C bounded model checker. In: Ábrahám, E., Havelund, K. (eds.) TACAS 2014. LNCS, vol. 8413, pp. 389–391. Springer, Heidelberg (2014). https://doi.org/10.1007/978-3-642-54862-8_26
28. Li, G., Zhou, L., Yu, N., Ding, Y., Ying, M., Xie, Y.: Projection-based runtime assertions for testing and debugging quantum programs. Proc. ACM Program. Lang. **4**(OOPSLA), 150:1–150:29 (2020). https://doi.org/10.1145/3428218
29. Liu, J., et al.: Formal verification of quantum algorithms using quantum Hoare logic. In: Dillig, I., Tasiran, S. (eds.) CAV 2019. LNCS, vol. 11562, pp. 187–207. Springer, Cham (2019). https://doi.org/10.1007/978-3-030-25543-5_12
30. Liu, S., et al.: $Q|SI\rangle$: a quantum programming environment. In: Jones, C., Wang, J., Zhan, N. (eds.) Symposium on Real-Time and Hybrid Systems. LNCS, vol. 11180, pp. 133–164. Springer, Cham (2018). https://doi.org/10.1007/978-3-030-01461-2_8
31. Nielsen, M.A., Chuang, I.L.: Quantum Computation and Quantum Information (10th Anniversary edition). Cambridge University Press (2016). https://doi.org/10.1017/CBO9780511976667. ISBN 978-1-10-700217-3
32. Nipkow, T., Wenzel, M., Paulson, L.C. (eds.): Isabelle/HOL - A Proof Assistant for Higher-Order Logic. LNCS, vol. 2283. Springer, Heidelberg (2002). https://doi.org/10.1007/3-540-45949-9
33. Rand, R., Paykin, J., Zdancewic, S.: QWIRE practice: formal verification of quantum circuits in Coq. In: QPL. EPTCS, vol. 266, pp. 119–132 (2017). https://doi.org/10.4204/EPTCS.266.8
34. Richardson, D.: Some undecidable problems involving elementary functions of a real variable. J. Symb. Log. **33**(4), 514–520 (1968). https://doi.org/10.2307/2271358
35. Shi, Y., et al.: CertiQ: a mostly-automated verification of a realistic quantum compiler. arXiv preprint (2019). https://doi.org/10.48550/arXiv.1908.08963
36. Shor, P.W.: Polynomial-time algorithms for prime factorization and discrete logarithms on a quantum computer. SIAM J. Comput. **26**(5), 1484–1509 (1997). https://doi.org/10.1137/S0097539795293172
37. Svore, K.M., et al.: Q#: enabling scalable quantum computing and development with a high-level DSL. In: RWDSL, pp. 7:1–7:10. ACM (2018). https://doi.org/10.1145/3183895.3183901
38. Traversa, F.L.: Aircraft loading optimization: MemComputing the 5th Airbus problem. CoRR, abs/1903.08189 (2019). http://arxiv.org/abs/1903.08189
39. Yu, N., Palsberg, J.: Quantum abstract interpretation. In: PLDI, pp. 542–558. ACM (2021). https://doi.org/10.1145/3453483.3454061

PFL: A Probabilistic Logic for Fault Trees

Stefano M. Nicoletti[1(✉)], Milan Lopuhaä-Zwakenberg[1], E. Moritz Hahn[1], and Mariëlle Stoelinga[1,2]

[1] Formal Methods and Tools, University of Twente, Enschede, The Netherlands
{s.m.nicoletti,m.a.lopuhaa,e.m.hahn,m.i.a.stoelinga}@utwente.nl
[2] Department of Software Science, Radboud University, Nijmegen, The Netherlands

Abstract. Safety-critical infrastructures must operate in a safe and reliable way. Fault tree analysis is a widespread method used for risk assessment of these systems: fault trees (FTs) are required by, e.g., the Federal Aviation Administration and the Nuclear Regulatory Commission. In spite of their popularity, little work has been done on formulating structural queries about FTs and analyzing these, e.g., when evaluating potential scenarios, and to give practitioners instruments to formulate queries on FTs in an understandable yet powerful way. In this paper, we aim to fill this gap by extending *BFL* [37], a logic that reasons about Boolean FTs. To do so, we introduce a Probabilistic Fault tree Logic (PFL). PFL is a simple, yet expressive logic that supports easier formulation of complex scenarios and specification of FT properties that comprise probabilities. Alongside PFL, we present LangPFL, a domain specific language to further ease property specification. We showcase PFL and LangPFL by applying them to a COVID-19 related FT and to a FT for an oil/gas pipeline. Finally, we present theory and model checking algorithms based on binary decision diagrams (BDDs).

1 Introduction

Our self-driving cars, power plants, oil/gas refineries and transportation systems must operate in a safe and reliable way. Risk assessment is a key activity to identify, analyze and prioritize the risk in a system, and come up with (cost-)effective countermeasures. Fault tree analysis (FTA) [43,45] is a widespread formalism to support risk assessment. FTA is applied to many safety-critical systems and the use of fault trees is required, e.g., by the Federal Aviation Administration (FAA), the Nuclear Regulatory Commission (NRC), in the ISO 26262 standard [28] for autonomous driving and for software development in aerospace systems. A fault tree (FT) models how component failures arise and propagate through the system, eventually leading to system level failures. Leaves in a FT represent

This work was partially funded by the NWO grant NWA.1160.18.238 (PrimaVera), and the European Union's Horizon 2020 research and innovation programme under the Marie Skłodowska-Curie grant agreement No 101008233, and the ERC Consolidator Grant 864075 (*CAESAR*).

M. Chechik et al. (Eds.): FM 2023, LNCS 14000, pp. 199–221, 2023.
https://doi.org/10.1007/978-3-031-27481-7_13

basic events (BEs), i.e. elements of the tree that do not need further refinement. Once these fail, the failure is propagated through the *intermediate events* (IEs) via *gates*, to eventually reach the *top level event* (TLE), which symbolizes system failure. In the (sub)tree represented in Fig. 1, the TLE—*Medium Corrosion*—is refined by an AND-gate (*MeC*). For *MeC* to fail, water must be present, i.e., the *With Water* (*WW*) BE must fail, and there must be at least one acid medium in the pipes, i.e., *Acid Medium* (*AcM*) has to happen. This last OR-gate is further refined with three BEs: for it to fail, at least one of its three children needs to fail. This means that either *Hydrogen sulfide* (H_2S) or *Oxygen* (O_2) or *Carbon dioxide* (CO_2) must be present. Fault tree analysis supports qualitative and quantitative analysis. Qualitative analysis aims at pointing out root causes and critical paths in the system. One can identify the *minimal cut sets* (MCSs) of a FT, i.e. minimal sets of BEs that, when failed, cause the system to fail. One can also identify *minimal path sets* (MPSs), i.e. minimal sets of BEs that - when operational - guarantee that the system will remain operational. Quantitative analysis allows to compute relevant dependability metrics, such as the system reliability, availability and mean time to failure. A formal background on FTs is given in Sect. 2.

Medium Corrosion:	
Medium Corrosion	MeC
With Water	WW
Acid Medium	AcM
H_2S	H_2S
O_2	O_2
CO_2	CO_2

Fig. 1. FT excerpt from Fig. 3.

Probabilistic Fault Tree Logic. In spite of their popularity, little work has been done on formulating structural queries about FTs and analyzing these, e.g., when evaluating potential scenarios, and to give practitioners instruments to formulate queries on FTs in an understandable yet powerful way. Usually, FTs are translated to stochastic models and existing logics specify properties on these, rather than on elements of FTs. Our previous work [37] presents a logic to reason about static FTs when BEs have Boolean values. The present work aims to extend that framework by devising a probabilistic logic for FTs, called PFL, where one could easily reason about FTs also taking probabilities into account. To further meet the need for usability - that we uncovered through interviews with a domain expert [36] - we present a domain specific language for PFL, LangPFL, and showcase property specification with both on two case studies, one with a COVID-19 FT, and one with an oil/gas pipeline FT.

Model Checking. In this paper, we provide model checking algorithms that extend our work in [37]. While we build from algorithms from [37], we require extensions for formulae in which probabilities come into play. We introduce novel algorithms which can decide 1. whether a single probability assignment to all BEs of a FT satisfies a formula; 2. whether a formula is satisfied for all possible probability assignments to BEs and 3. in which regions of the parameter space the considered formula holds. Building on our previous work, all three algorithms are based on construction and manipulation of binary decision diagrams (BDDs). This translation to BDDs constitutes a formal ground to address these procedures in a uniform way, while integrating novel work presented in this paper with previous algorithms.

Related Work. Numerous logics describe properties of state-transition systems, such as labelled transition systems (LTSs) and Markov models, e.g., CTL [14], LTL [40], and their variants for Markov models, PCTL [26] and PLTL [38]. State-transition systems are usually not written by hand, but are the result of the semantics of high-level description mechanisms, such as AADL [9], the hardware description language VHDL [19] or model description languages such as JANI [11] or PRISM [33]. Consequently, these logics are not used to reason about the structure of such models (e.g. the placement of circuit elements in a VHDL model or the structure of modules in a PRISM model), but on the temporal behaviour of the underlying state-transition system. Similarly, related work on model checking on FTs [6,8,46,47] exhibits significant differences: these works perform model checking by referring to states in the underlying stochastic models, and properties are formulated in terms of these stochastic logics, not in terms of events in the given FT. In [48], the author provides a formulation of *Pandora*, a logic for the qualitative analysis of temporal FTs. In spite of the use of logic to capture properties of FTs, [48] focuses on the analysis of time, introducing gates that are different from the ones considered in this work: the Priority-AND-gate (PAND), the Simultaneous-AND-gate (SAND), and the Priority-OR gate (POR). In PFL we do not (yet) consider time and we focus on AND, OR and VOT-gates. Furthermore, [48] focuses more on the algorithmic part of FTA while leaving out any formalization of FTs or the logic defined upon. In [25] the authors investigate how FTA results can be linked to software safety requirements by proposing the same system model for both. They introduce a duration calculus based on discrete time interval logic (ITL) [34] to give FTs formal semantics. Our work, on the other hand, adopts standard semantics for FTs and develops a logic to specify probabilistic properties on FTs. Furthermore, we do not address timed behaviours while [25] disregards probabilistic analysis on FTs. In previous work [37] we presented *BFL*, a logic on FTs that however reasons about FTs only in Boolean terms. We take this framework and develop a logic that extends *BFL* with probabilities. Literature related to FTs, property specification languages, BDDs and parametric model checking is referenced and contextualized in Sect. 2, Sect. 5, Sect. 6.1 and Sect. 6.5.

Contributions. To summarize, in this work:

1. We develop PFL, a probabilistic logic to reason about FTs.
2. We present a domain specific language for PFL, LangPFL, to further ease property specification.
3. We showcase the potential of PFL and LangPFL by applying them to a medium-sized COVID-19 related example and to a large-sized case study of an oil/gas pipeline.
4. We provide model checking algorithms to check properties defined in PFL.
5. We provide the theory and an algorithm to solve problems where the probabilities of BEs are parametric.

Structure of the Paper. Section 2 covers background on FTs, Sect. 3 describes PFL, Sect. 4 shows the application of PFL to case studies, Sect. 5 introduces LangPFL, Sect. 6 presents algorithms and Sect. 7 concludes our work.

2 Fault Trees: Background

Developed in the early '60s [21], FTs are directed acyclic graphs (DAGs) that model how low-level failures can propagate and cause a system-level failure. The overall failure of a system is captured by a *top level event* (TLE), that is refined through the use of *gates*. FTs come with different gate types. For the purposes of our paper and in order to create a modular and functional framework, we will focus on *static* fault trees, featuring OR-gates, AND-gates and VOT*(k/N)*-gates: we foresee support for dynamic gates as a possible future extension (see Sect. 7). For a low-level failure to propagate, at least one child of an OR-gate has to fail, all the children of an AND-gate must fail, and at least k out of N children must fail for a VOT(k/N)-gate to fail. When gates can no longer be refined, we reach the *basic events* (BEs) which are the leaves of the tree. FTs enable both qualitative and quantitative analyses. On the qualitative side, *minimal cut sets* (MCSs) and *minimal path sets* (MPSs) highlight root causes of failures and critical paths in the system. MCSs are minimal sets of events that - when failed - cause the failure of the TLE. MPSs are minimal sets of events that - when remaining operational - guarantee that the TLE will remain operational.

Definition 1 (*Fault Tree*). *A* Fault Tree *is a tuple* $T = (\mathtt{E}, A, t)$ *where* $(\mathtt{E}, A)$ *is a rooted directed acyclic graph (*$\mathtt{E}$ *are the vertices, called* events*) and* t *is a map* $\mathtt{E} \rightarrow \{\mathtt{AND}, \mathtt{OR}, \mathtt{BE}\}$ *such that* $t(e) = \mathtt{BE}$ *iff* e *is a leaf.*

We denote the top event by e_{top}, and the set of children of an event e by $ch(e) = \{e' \mid (e, e') \in A\}$. Slightly abusing notation, we denote the set of *basic events*, e with $t(e) = \mathtt{BE}$, as $\mathtt{BE}$, whose elements we enumerate $\mathtt{BE} = \{e_1, \ldots, e_n\}$. We also define the set of intermediate events $\mathtt{IE} = \mathtt{E} \backslash \mathtt{BE}$. The behaviour of a FT T can be rigorously expressed through its *structure function* [43] - Φ_T: if we assume the convention that a BE has value 1 if failed and 0 if operational, the structure function indicates the status of the TLE given the status of all the n BEs of T, given by a Boolean vector $\overline{b} = (b_1, \ldots, b_n)$. Such a boolean vector can also be regarded as a subset of BE, allowing us to interpret statements such as $\overline{b'} \subset \overline{b}$.

Definition 2 (*Structure Function*). *The structure function of an FT* T *is a function* $\Phi_T \colon \mathbb{B}^n \times \mathtt{E} \rightarrow \mathbb{B}$ *defined recursively by*

$$\Phi_T(\overline{b}, e) = \begin{cases} b_i & \text{if } e = e_i \in \mathtt{BE} \\ \bigvee_{e' \in ch(e)} \Phi_T(\overline{b}, e') & \text{if } t(e) = \mathtt{OR} \\ \bigwedge_{e' \in ch(e)} \Phi_T(\overline{b}, e') & \text{if } t(e) = \mathtt{AND} \end{cases}$$

Thus, for each set of BEs we can identify its characteristic vector $\overline{b}$. One can extend Definition 2 by allowing gates derived from AND- and OR-gates, e.g., voting gates, where a gate with $t(e) = \mathtt{VOT}(k/N)$ fails if at least k of its children fail, i.e.

$$\sum_{e' \in ch(e)} \Phi_T(\overline{b}, e') \geq k$$

We can also define the classical notions of minimal cut sets and minimal path sets [43]. A cut set is any set of basic events that causes the TLE to occur, i.e., for which the structure function evaluates to 1. A path set is any set of basic events that does not cause the TLE to occur, i.e., for which the structure function evaluates to 0.

Definition 3. *A status vector* $\overline{b}$ *is a* cut set (CS) *for* $e \in \mathtt{E}$ *of a given tree* T *iff* $\Phi_T(\overline{b}, e) = 1$. *A* minimal cut set (MCS) *is a cut set of which no subset is a cut set:* $\overline{b}$ *is a MCS for* $e \in \mathtt{E}$ *of* T *if* $\Phi_T(\overline{b}, e) = 1 \wedge \forall \overline{b'} \subset \overline{b}, \Phi_T(\overline{b}, e) = 0$.

Definition 4. *A status vector* $\overline{b}$ *is a* path set (PS) *for* $e \in \mathtt{E}$ *of a given tree* T *iff* $\Phi_T(\overline{b}, e) = 0$. *A* minimal path set (MPS) *is a path set of which no subset is a path set:* $\overline{b}$ *is a MPS for* $e \in \mathtt{E}$ *of* T *if* $\Phi_T(\overline{b}, e) = 0 \wedge \forall \overline{b'} \subset \overline{b}, \Phi_T(\overline{b}, e) = 1$.

3 A Probabilistic Logic to Reason About FTs

3.1 Syntax

Our logic PFL consists of three syntactical layers represented by ϕ, ψ and ξ respectively. To refer to layer-two or layer-three formulae indistinctly we write θ and χ is a generic formula in PFL. Layer-one is Boolean and we indicate atomic formulae with the letter e. Each atomic formula represent an element of a given FT, it being an IE or a BE. Furthermore, in layer-one we have the possibility to arbitrarily set the value of one atom e in complex formulae either to 0 or to 1 by writing $\phi[e \mapsto 0]$ and $\phi[e \mapsto 1]$. Note that $\phi[e \mapsto 0]$ is not equivalent to $\phi \wedge \neg e$: for $\phi = \neg e$, we have $(\neg e)[e \mapsto 0] = \mathit{true}$ while $(\neg e) \wedge \neg e$ does not necessarily equal *true*. Moreover, we have operators to check for MPSs and MCSs for a given layer-one formula. The second layer allows us to reason about probabilities and their bounds. We can check whether the probability of a given layer-one formula (potentially conditioned by another one) respects a certain threshold. We can set the value of one atom e in complex formulae to an arbitrary probability value p. We can also check if two layer-one formulae (e.g., two intermediate events) are stochastically independent. Formulae in ϕ and ψ can be rewritten with the usual negation and conjunction. Finally, the third layer allows us to return the probability value for a given layer-one formula, possibly mapping atoms to an arbitrary probability value p. Note that, for all three layers, we usually assign values to $e \in \mathtt{BE}$. We can however assign values to IEs if 1. e is a module [20], i.e., all paths between descendants of e and the rest of the FT pass through e 2. and none of the descendants of e are present in the formula. If so, we prune that (sub)FT and treat occurring IEs as BEs.

$$\phi ::= e \mid \neg\phi \mid \phi \wedge \phi \mid \phi[e \mapsto 0] \mid \phi[e \mapsto 1] \mid \mathrm{MCS}(\phi)$$
$$\psi ::= \neg\psi \mid \psi \wedge \psi \mid \Pr_{\bowtie p}(\phi \mid \phi) \mid \psi[e \mapsto q] \mid \mathrm{IDP}(\phi, \phi)$$
$$\xi ::= \Pr(\phi \mid \phi) \mid \xi[e \mapsto q]$$

where $\bowtie \in \{<, \leq, =, \geq, >\}$.

Syntactic sugar. We let X_n be the set of layer-n formulae and we define the following derived operators, where formulae θ are in the set of layer-one or layer-two formulae, i.e., such that $\theta \in X_1 \cup X_2$:

$$\theta_1 \vee \theta_2 ::= \neg(\neg\theta_1 \wedge \neg\theta_2) \qquad \theta_1 \not\Leftrightarrow \theta_2 ::= \neg(\theta_1 \Leftrightarrow \theta_2)$$
$$\theta_1 \Rightarrow \theta_2 ::= \neg(\theta_1 \wedge \neg\theta_2) \qquad \mathrm{MPS}(\phi) ::= \mathrm{MCS}(\neg\phi)$$
$$\theta_1 \Leftrightarrow \theta_2 ::= (\theta_1 \Rightarrow \theta_2) \wedge (\theta_2 \Rightarrow \theta_1) \qquad \mathrm{SUP}(e) ::= \mathrm{IDP}(e, e_{top})$$

$$\underset{\bowtie k}{\mathrm{Vot}}(\phi_1, \ldots, \phi_N) ::= \bigvee_{\substack{U \subseteq \{1,\ldots,N\} \\ |U| \bowtie k}} \left(\bigwedge_{u \in U} \phi_u \right) \wedge \left(\bigwedge_{u \in \{1,\ldots,N\} \setminus U} \neg\phi_u \right) \text{ with } k \leq N$$

where MPS checks for minimal path sets of a given formula and SUP checks if an element e is superfluous, i.e., if it is independent w.r.t. the TLE.

3.2 Semantics

The semantics for our logic is structured according to the three syntactic layers. For the first layer of PFL, formulae are evaluated on a Boolean status vector $\overline{b}$ and on a tree T. Atomic formulae e are satisfied by $\overline{b}$ and T if the structure function in Definition 2 returns 1 with these $\overline{b}$ and e as input. Formally:

$$\begin{aligned}
&\overline{b}, T \models e && \text{iff } \Phi_T(\overline{b}, e) = 1 \\
&\overline{b}, T \models \neg\phi && \text{iff } \overline{b}, T \not\models \phi \\
&\overline{b}, T \models \phi \wedge \phi' && \text{iff } \overline{b}, T \models \phi \text{ and } \overline{b}, T \models \phi' \\
&\overline{b}, T \models \phi[e_i \mapsto 0] && \text{iff } \overline{b'}, T \models \phi \text{ with } \overline{b'} = (b'_1, \ldots, b'_n) \text{ where} \\
& && \quad b'_i = 0 \text{ and for } j \neq i \text{ we have } b'_j = b_j \\
&\overline{b}, T \models \phi[e_i \mapsto 1] && \text{iff } \overline{b'}, T \models \phi \text{ with } \overline{b'} = (b'_1, \ldots, b'_n) \text{ where} \\
& && \quad b'_i = 1 \text{ and } b'_j = b_j \text{ for } j \neq i \\
&\overline{b}, T \models \mathrm{MCS}(\phi) && \text{iff } \overline{b}, T \models \phi \wedge (\neg\exists \overline{b'}.\ \overline{b'} \subset \overline{b} \wedge \overline{b'}, T \models \phi)
\end{aligned}$$

With $[\![\phi]\!]_T$ we denote the *satisfaction set* of vectors for ϕ, i.e., the set of all $\overline{b}$ that satisfy ϕ given T. Semantics for the second and third layer require the introduction of probabilities. If we consider the function $\Phi_T\colon \mathbb{B}^n \times \mathtt{E} \to \mathbb{B}$, we can devise an extension such that $\Phi_T\colon \mathbb{B}^n \times X_1 \to \mathbb{B}$, where X_1 is the set of layer-one formulae (note that $\mathtt{E} \subseteq X_1$). With a slight abuse of notation, Φ_T will now return 1 whenever the input Boolean vector satisfies the input layer-one formula. With $\phi \in X_1$, we lift the structure function to $\Phi^*_T\colon \mathit{Dist}(\mathbb{B}^n) \times X_1 \to [0,1]$, where *Dist* expresses a set of probability distributions, in a standard fashion, i.e.,

$$\Phi^*_T(\mu, \phi) = \sum \{\mu(\overline{b}) \mid \overline{b} \in \mathbb{B}^n \text{ for which } \Phi_T(\overline{b}, \phi) = 1\}$$

We further convert each probabilistic status vector $\overline{\rho} \in [0,1]^n$ to a distribution $\mu_{\overline{\rho}} \in \mathit{Dist}(\mathbb{B}^n)$:

$$\mu_{\overline{\rho}}(b_1, \ldots, b_k) = \prod_{i=1}^{k} (b_i \times \rho_i + (1 - b_i) \times (1 - \rho_i))$$

We can then define semantics for the second syntactic layer as follows[1]:

$$\begin{aligned}
&\overline{\rho}, T \models \neg\psi && \text{iff } \overline{\rho}, T \not\models \psi\\
&\overline{\rho}, T \models \psi \wedge \psi' && \text{iff } \overline{\rho}, T \models \psi \text{ and } \overline{\rho}, T \models \psi'\\
&\overline{\rho}, T \models \Pr_{\bowtie p}(\phi \mid \phi') && \text{iff } \Phi^*_T(\mu_{\overline{\rho}}, \phi \wedge \phi')/\Phi^*_T(\mu_{\overline{\rho}}, \phi') \bowtie p\\
&\overline{\rho}, T \models \psi[e_i \mapsto q] && \text{iff } \overline{\rho}[\rho_i \mapsto q], T \models \psi\\
&\overline{\rho}, T \models \mathrm{IDP}(\phi, \phi') && \text{iff } \Phi^*_T(\mu_{\overline{\rho}}, \phi \wedge \phi') = \Phi^*_T(\mu_{\overline{\rho}}, \phi) \cdot \Phi^*_T(\mu_{\overline{\rho}}, \phi')
\end{aligned}$$

Finally, to define semantics for the third layer we let $\mathsf{Val}_{\overline{\rho},T}\colon X_3 \to [0,1]$ define an evaluation function of layer-three formulae in X_3:

$$\begin{aligned}
\mathsf{Val}_{\overline{\rho},T}(\Pr(\phi \mid \phi')) &= \Phi^*_T(\mu_{\overline{\rho}}, \phi \wedge \phi')/\Phi^*_T(\mu_{\overline{\rho}}, \phi')\\
\mathsf{Val}_{\overline{\rho},T}(\xi[e_i \mapsto q]) &= \mathsf{Val}_{\overline{\rho}[\rho_i \mapsto q],T}(\xi)
\end{aligned}$$

Furthermore we write $T \models \theta$, meaning $\forall \overline{\rho} \,.\, \overline{\rho}, T \models \theta$.

4 Case Study: Examples

We showcase the potential of our logic by presenting two case studies: a COVID-19 related FT [3,37] and the FT for an oil/gas pipeline [50].

4.1 COVID-19 FT

The TLE represents a COVID-19 infected worker on site, abbreviated *IWoS*. As shown in Fig. 2, the FT considers events in several categories: COVID-19 pathogens and reservoirs (i.e., germs and objects carrying the virus); their mode of transmissions; the presence of susceptible hosts, infected objects and workers; physical contacts as well as human errors. Note that Fig. 2 contains several repeated basic events (marked with a dashed border): *IT*, *PP*, *H1* and *IW*. This

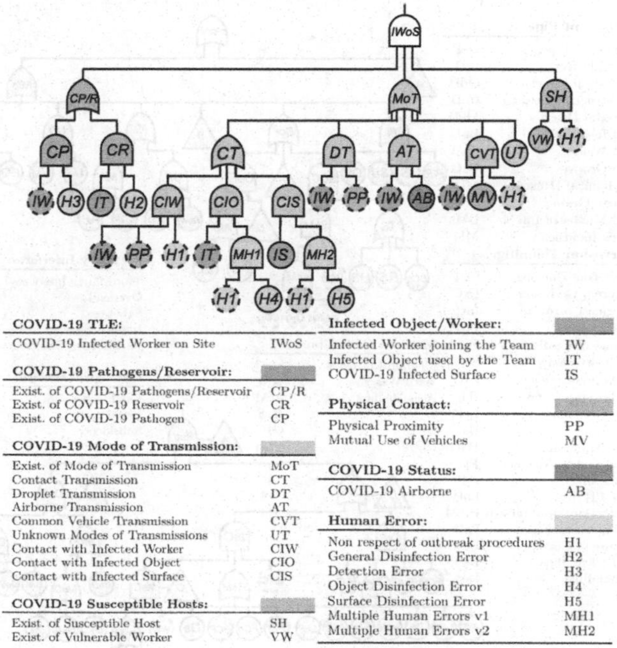
IWoS
CP/R
MoT
SH
CP
CR
CT
DT
AT
CVT
UT
VW
H1
IW
H3
IT
H2
CIW
CIO
CIS
PP
AB
MV
MH1
IS
MH2
H4
H5
COVID-19 TLE:
COVID-19 Infected Worker on Site IWoS
COVID-19 Pathogens/Reservoir:
Exist. of COVID-19 Pathogens/Reservoir CP/R
Exist. of COVID-19 Reservoir CR
Exist. of COVID-19 Pathogen CP
COVID-19 Mode of Transmission:
Exist. of Mode of Transmission MoT
Contact Transmission CT
Droplet Transmission DT
Airborne Transmission AT
Common Vehicle Transmission CVT
Unknown Modes of Transmissions UT
Contact with Infected Worker CIW
Contact with Infected Object CIO
Contact with Infected Surface CIS
COVID-19 Susceptible Hosts:
Exist. of Susceptible Host SH
Exist. of Vulnerable Worker VW
Infected Object/Worker:
Infected Worker joining the Team IW
Infected Object used by the Team IT
COVID-19 Infected Surface IS
Physical Contact:
Physical Proximity PP
Mutual Use of Vehicles MV
COVID-19 Status:
COVID-19 Airborne AB
Human Error:
Non respect of outbreak procedures H1
General Disinfection Error H2
Detection Error H3
Object Disinfection Error H4
Surface Disinfection Error H5
Multiple Human Errors v1 MH1
Multiple Human Errors v2 MH2

Fig. 2. COVID-19 FT.

[1] When considering conditional probabilities in layer-two and layer-three formulae, we disregard the case in which $\Phi^*_T(\mu_{\overline{\rho}}, \phi') = 0$.

TLE *IWoS* is refined via an AND-gate with three children. Thus, for the TLE to occur the following must happen: COVID pathogens/COVID infected objects must exist, there has to be a susceptible host and COVID pathogens must be transmitted in some way to this host. These events are captured by corresponding subtrees: the purple OR-gate CP/R refines the existence of COVID pathogens/-COVID infected objects, the OR-gate MoT in teal refines modes of transmission and the AND-gate SH in orange details the presence of a susceptible host.

Properties. Following, we specify some properties using natural language and present the corresponding PFL formulae:

1) What are all the MCSs for the modes of transmission that include errors in objects and surfaces disinfection? $[\![\mathrm{MCS}(MoT) \wedge H4 \wedge H5]\!]_T$;
2) Is the probability of TLE smaller than 0.03, if physical proximity occurred? $\mathrm{Pr}_{\leq 0.03}(IWoS)[PP \mapsto 1]$;
3) Assume that the probability of an infected worker on the team equals 0.25. How does that affect the probability of TLE? $\mathrm{Pr}(IWoS)[IW \mapsto 0.25]$;
4) Assume that both COVID-19 pathogens and a vulnerable worker exist. Does this imply that $P(IWoS) \geq 0.15$? $\mathrm{Pr}_{=1}(CP) \wedge \mathrm{Pr}_{=1}(VW) \Rightarrow \mathrm{Pr}_{\geq 0.15}(IWoS)$.

4.2 Oil/Gas Pipeline FT

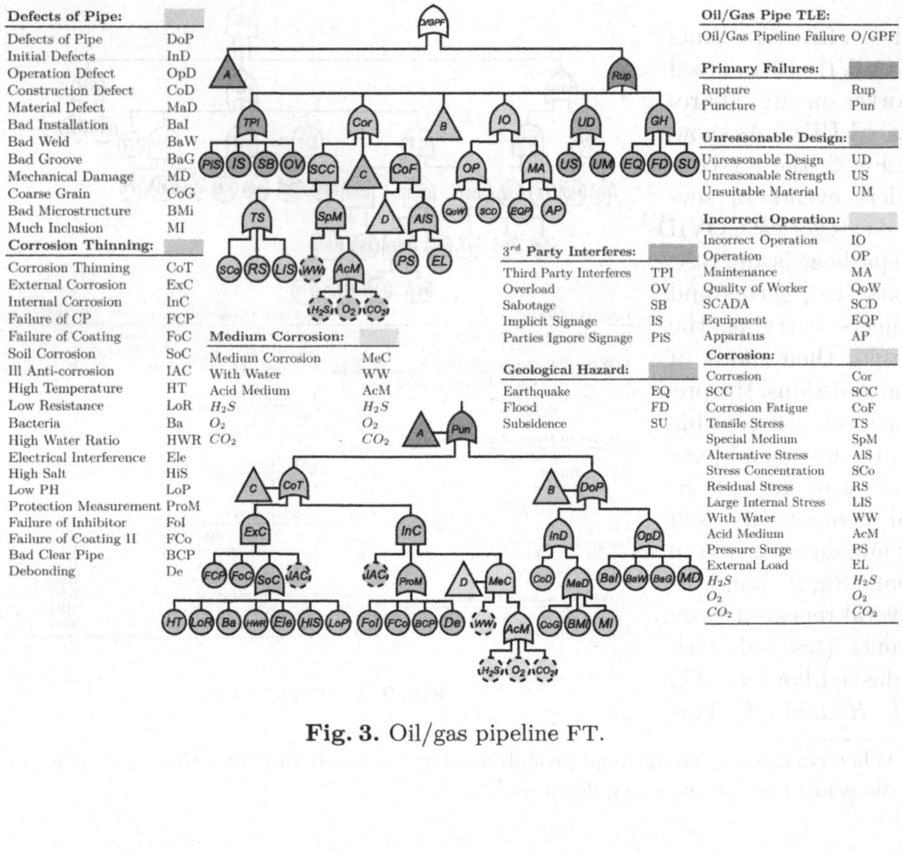

Fig. 3. Oil/gas pipeline FT.

The TLE represents the failure of an oil/gas pipeline, abbreviated O/GPF. As shown in Fig. 3, the FT considers events in several categories: failures like ruptures and punctures; third party interference; different kinds of corrosion; incorrect performance of some operations (e.g., maintenance); unreasonable design choices; as well as defects on pipes. Figure 3 contains several repeated basic events (again, marked with a dashed border): WW, H_2S, O_2, CO_2 and IAC. Furthermore, multiple sub-trees are referenced/repeated in different places: those are marked using labelled triangles. The TLE O/GPF is refined via an OR-gate with two children, in **blue**. Thus, for the TLE to occur either a rupture or a puncture must happen. These two events are captured by corresponding subtrees. The **rupture** subtree (top-right of Fig. 3) is refined by an OR-gate with six children: the **green** OR-gate TPI refines possible interference by third parties; the **violet** OR-gate Cor refines modes of pipes corrosion; the **yellow** subtree B refines modes in which pipes could be defective; the **dove gray** OR-gate IO details possible incorrect operations; the **lime green** OR-gate UD details unreasonable design choices; and the **pink** OR-gate GH refines possible geological hazards. Similarly, the **puncture** subtree (bottom of Fig. 3) is refined by an OR-gate with two children: the **orange** OR-gate CoT refines modes in which corrosion can make pipes thinner—with a detailed subtree in **light blue** refining medium corrosion; and the OR-gate DoP in **yellow** that refines modes in which pipes could be defective.

Properties. We specify some properties using natural language and present the corresponding PFL formulae:

1) What are all the MPSs for pipes rupture that include the absence of water as a corrosive medium, H_2S, O_2 and CO_2? $[\![\mathrm{MPS}(Rup) \wedge \neg WW \wedge \neg H_2S \wedge \neg O_2 \wedge \neg CO_2]\!]_T$;
2) Assume that H_2S shows up in the pipes with 0.25% probability. What is the probability of pipes corrosion, if corrosion happens with water with 2% probability and that pressure surges with 1% probability? $\Pr(Cor)[H_2S \mapsto 0.0025, WW \mapsto 0.02, PS \mapsto 0.01]$;
3) Assume that the probability of pipes corrosion with acid is equal to 0.005. Assume also that pipes present defects in their construction material with 0.2% probability. Is the probability of TLE happening lower than 1.2%? $\Pr_{\leq 0.012}(O/GPF)[AcM \mapsto 0.005, MaD \mapsto 0.02]$.

5 LangPFL: A Domain Specific Language for PFL

Design of LangPFL. To ease usability of PFL, we present LangPFL, a Domain Specific Language (DSL) to specify properties in PFL. The need for a simple way to specify properties involving probability on FT was uncovered via interviews with a domain expert from industry [36]. Defining languages and tools for properties and requirements specification is common practice: in [17] the authors capture high-level requirements for a steam boiler system in a human readable

Table 1. Properties in natural language, PFL and LangPFL.

Natural Language	Property in PFL	LangPFL
What are all the MCSs for the modes of transmission that include errors in objects and surfaces disinfection?	$[\![\mathrm{MCS}(MoT) \land H4 \land H5]\!]_T$	**assume:** **computeall:** MCS[MoT] and H4 and H5
Is the probability of TLE smaller than 0.03, if physical proximity occurred?	$\mathrm{Pr}_{\leq 0.03}(IWoS)[PP \mapsto 1]$	**assume:** setp PP = 1 **check:** P[IWoS] ≤ 0.03
Assume that the probability of an infected worker on the team equals 0.25. How does that affect the probability of TLE?	$\mathrm{Pr}(IWoS)[IW \mapsto 0.25]$	**assume:** setp IW = 0.25 **compute:** P[IWoS]
Assume that both COVID-19 pathogens and a vulnerable worker exist. Does this imply that $P(IWoS) \geq 0.15$?	$\mathrm{Pr}_{=1}(CP) \land \mathrm{Pr}_{=1}(VW) \Rightarrow \mathrm{Pr}_{\geq 0.15}(IWoS)$	**assume:** setp CP = 1 setp VW = 1 **check:** P[IWoS] ≥ 0.15
What are all the MPSs for pipes rupture that include the absence of water as a corrosive medium, H_2S, O_2 and CO_2?	$[\![\mathrm{MPS}(Rup) \land \neg WW \land \neg H_2S \land \neg O_2 \land \neg CO_2]\!]_T$	**assume:** **computeall:** MPS [Rup] and not WW and not H_2S and not O_2 and not CO_2
Assume that H_2S shows up in the pipes with 0.25% probability. What is the probability of pipes corrosion, if corrosion happens with water with 2% probability and that pressure surges with 1% probability?	$\mathrm{Pr}(Cor)[H_2S \mapsto 0.0025, WW \mapsto 0.02, PS \mapsto 0.01]$	**assume:** setp H_2S = 0.0025 setp WW = 0.02 setp PS = 0.01 **compute:** P[Cor]
Assume that the probability of pipes corrosion with acid is equal to 0.005. Assume also that pipes present defects in their construction material with 0.2% probability. Is the probability of TLE lower than 1.2%?	$\mathrm{Pr}_{\leq 0.012}(O/GPF)[AcM \mapsto 0.005, MaD \mapsto 0.02]$	**assume:** setp AcM = 0.005 setp MaD = 0.02 **check:** P[O/GPF]≤0.012

form by presenting SADL, a controlled English requirements capturing language, alongside its tool suite ASSERT. Other controlled natural languages for knowledge representation include Processable English (PENG) [49], Controlled English to Logic Translation (CELT) [39] and Computer Processable Language (CPL) [13]. LangPFL is inspired by these languages for their ease of use and close proximity to natural language. Finally, another notable example is FRETish [15], a structured natural language capturing Linear Temporal Logic (LTL). FRETish was developed at NASA and is supported by the FRET tool [23]. Other than for its usability, FRETish inspired us with the clear way in which the scope, conditions and component of specified properties are clearly separated from desired behaviours on timing and responses. LangPFL expresses only a fragment of PFL:

most notably, nesting of formulae is disallowed. By doing so, we retain most of the expressiveness of PFL while making property specification easier. In LangPFL, FT elements are referred to with their label and each operator in PFL has a counterpart in the DSL: Boolean operators, not, and, or, impl...; setting the value of FT elements to Boolean or probability values, set, setp; MCSs and MPSs, MCS[...], MPS[...]; operators to check (conditional) probability thresholds/compute (conditional) probability values, P[... | ...] $\bowtie$ ..., P[... | ...]; and to check for independence between FT elements IDP[..., ...].

LangPFL Templates. Properties can be specified in LangPFL by utilizing operators inside structured templates. Assumptions on the status of FT elements can be specified under the **assume** keyword. These assumptions will be automatically integrated in the translated formula accordingly, e.g., set or setp will be translated with the according operators to set evidence, while other assumptions will be the antecedent of an implication. A second keyword separates specified formulae from the assumptions and dictates the desired result: **compute** and **computeall** compute and return desired values, i.e., probability values and lists of MCSs/MPSs respectively, while **check** establishes if a specified property holds.

Case studies. In Table 1 we showcase the properties specified in Sect. 4 and their respective translation in LangPFL.

6 Model Checking Algorithms

Layer-One Formulae. With PFL extending previous work [37], algorithms to compute satisfiability of layer-one formulae remain unchanged. In particular, it is possible to model check PFL over a FT and a Boolean vector $\overline{b}$ when considering layer-one formulae. Furthermore, we can collect all Boolean vectors $\overline{b}$ such that $\overline{b}, T \models \phi$. As noted in [37], checking if $\overline{b}, T \models \phi$ holds is trivial if ϕ is a layer-one formula that does not contain an MCS or MPS operator. In that case, we can simply substitute the values of $\overline{b}$ in ϕ and see if the Boolean expression evaluates to true. This also works to check whether $\overline{\rho}, T \models \theta$ holds for a probabilistic vector $\overline{\rho}$, a tree-shaped FT and a layer-two/three formula θ without operators for MCS or MPS. In this case, values can be computed following usual probability laws. For the other cases, the computation becomes more complex, and procedures involving binary decision diagrams (BDDs) are necessary. Algorithms for the Boolean scenarios are described in Appendix A.3 and Appendix A.4 respectively.

Layer-Two/Three Formulae. When reasoning about satisfiability of second layer formulae, algorithms present differences. As such, we present three novel algorithms for PFL: 1. Given a vector $\overline{\rho}$, a FT T and a formula ψ, check if $\overline{\rho}, T \models \psi$ (Sect. 6.4), 2. Given T and ψ, compute regions of the parameter space where $T \models \psi$ (Sect. 6.5), 3. Given a FT T and a formula ψ, check whether $T \models \psi$ for all $\overline{\rho}$ (Sect. 6.6). In continuity with previous work, all three algorithms are based on BDDs: first, FT elements that appear in a given layer-one formula are identified. Then, BDDs for these elements are selectively constructed (see

Algorithm 5) and stored to reduce computation time. Finally, these BDDs are manipulated and equipped with probabilities (see Algorithm 1) to reflect the semantics of the operators in PFL. Probability values in layer-three formulae are computed with slight variations on layer-two algorithms (see Sect. 6.4). As in standard FTA [43], we assume that BEs fail independently. A brief overview of each algorithm is given in Sect. 6.4, Sect. 6.5 and Sect. 6.6 respectively.

6.1 (Reduced Ordered) Binary Decision Diagrams

BDDs are directed acyclic graphs (DAGs) that compactly represent Boolean functions [2] by reducing redundancy. Depending on variable's ordering, BDD's size can grow linearly in the number of variables and at worst exponentially. In practice, BDDs are heavily used, including in FT analysis [4,42] and in their security-related counterpart, attack trees (ATs) [12]. Formally, a BDD is a rooted DAG $\mathbf{B}_f$ that represents a Boolean function $f\colon \mathbb{B}^n \to \mathbb{B}$ over variables $\mathit{Vars} = \{x_i\}_{i=1}^n$. Each nonleaf w has two outgoing arrows, labeled 0 and 1, and a label $\mathit{Lab}(w) \in \mathit{Vars}$; furthermore, each leaf has a label 0 or 1. Given a b in $\mathbb{B}^n$, the BDD is used to compute $f(b)$ as follows: starting from the top, upon arriving at a node w with $\mathit{Lab}(w) = x_i$, one takes the 0-edge if $b_i = 0$ and the 1-edge if $b_i = 1$. The label of the leaf one ends up in, is then equal to $f(b)$. A function f can be represented by multiple BDDs, but has a unique *reduced ordered* representative, or ROBDD [5,10], where the x_i occur in ascending order, and the BDD is reduced as much as possible by removing irrelevant nodes and merging duplicates. This is formally defined below; we let $\mathit{Low}(w)$ (resp. $\mathit{High}(w)$) be the endpoint of w's 0-edge (resp. 1-edge) and let $R_{\mathbf{B}}$ be the BDD root.

Definition 5 (*Reduced Ordered Binary Decision Diagram ((RO)BDD)*). *Let Vars be a set. A* BDD *over Vars is a tuple* $\mathbf{B} = (W, A, \mathit{Lab}, u)$ *where* (W, A) *is a rooted directed acyclic graph, and* $\mathit{Lab}\colon W \to \mathit{Vars} \sqcup \{0, 1\}, u\colon A \to \{0, 1\}$ *are maps such that: 1. Every nonleaf* w *has exactly two outgoing edges* a, a' *with* $u(a) \neq u(a')$, *and* $\mathit{Lab}(w) \in \mathit{Vars}$; *2. Every leaf* w *has* $\mathit{Lab}(w) \in \{0, 1\}$. *3. Vars are equipped with a total order,* $\mathbf{B}_f$ *is thus defined over a pair* $\langle \mathit{Vars}, < \rangle$; *4. the variable of a node is of lower order than its children, that is:* $\forall\, w \in W_n.\, \mathit{Lab}(w) < \mathit{Lab}(\mathit{Low}(w)), \mathit{Lab}(\mathit{High}(w))$; *5. the children of nonleaf nodes are distinct nodes; 6. nodes are uniquely determined by their label, low child and high child.*

6.2 Translating FTs/Formulae to BDDs

Translations. We shortly sketch the idea of translating a layer-one formula and a (sub)tree to BDDs. As mentioned, to translate formulae to BDDs, FT elements that appear in a given formula are identified. Then, BDDs representing these elements are selectively constructed and stored to reduce computation time. Finally, operations on these BDDs are performed to reflect semantics of the operators in PFL.

Translating FTs to BDDs. As a first step, a translation from FTs to BDDs is needed [37]. These BDDs represent exactly the structure function of (sub)trees. In the following, we assume $Vars = \mathtt{V} \dot\cup \mathtt{V}'$, where the set of variables $\mathtt{V} = \mathtt{BE}$ and the set of primed variables $\mathtt{V}' = \{e' | e \in \mathtt{BE}\}$ (used for the BDD translation of the MCS operator, see Appendix A.2). Furthermore, we keep $Var_{\mathbf{B}} \colon \mathtt{BDD} \rightarrow Vars$ to be a function that returns variables occurring in a BDD [37]. Then, our translation function $\Psi_{FT} \colon \mathtt{E} \rightarrow \mathtt{BDD}$ takes elements of a FT as input and maps them to BDDs. For an exact definition of Ψ_{FT} see Appendix A.1.

Translating Formulae. With BDDs for FTs, the next step consists in manipulating them to mirror PFL operators in layer-one. I.e., given Ψ_{FT} and a FT T, for every PFL formula ϕ in the set of PFL layer-one formulae X_1 there exists a translation to BDDs $\underline{\mathbf{B}}_T \colon X_1 \rightarrow \mathtt{BDD}$ in Algorithm 5 (see Appendix A.2). The implementation of this procedure abides the dynamic programming standards: by caching, we would reuse the translation of (sub)trees and (sub)formulae between different analyses without recomputing them each time anew.

6.3 Equipping BDDs with Probabilities

Once we obtain BDDs for FTs/ϕ-formulae, we can construct a function $\Phi^*_T(\mu_{\overline{x}}, \phi)$ from $[0,1]^n$ to $[0,1]$ that computes the probability value of ϕ given probability values in $\overline{x}$, where $\overline{x}$ can be substituted with any $\overline{\rho}$. Algorithm 1 shows this procedure: first, we compute $\underline{\mathbf{B}}_T(\phi)$ via Algorithm 5, we then obtain a polynomial $poly(\underline{\mathbf{B}}_T(\phi))$ representing $\underline{\mathbf{B}}_T(\phi)$ via $\mathsf{value}(R_{\underline{\mathbf{B}}_T(\phi)})$, where $\mathsf{value}(w_i \notin W_t) = (1 - x_i) \cdot \mathsf{value}(Low(w_i)) + x_i \cdot \mathsf{value}(High(w_i))$, $\mathsf{value}(\top) = 1$ and $\mathsf{value}(\bot) = 0$. $x_1, \ldots, x_n \in \overline{x}$ are parameters of the constructed function and can be substituted in $poly(\underline{\mathbf{B}}_T(\phi))$ with values from an arbitrary $\overline{\rho}$ to compute the overall probability value of the BDD for FT/ϕ-formula.

Algorithm 1. Obtain $\Phi^*_T(\mu_{\overline{x}}, \phi)$ for $\underline{\mathbf{B}}_T(\phi)$.

Input: FT T, formula ϕ
Output: function $\Phi^*_T(\mu_{\overline{x}}, \phi) \colon [0,1]^n \rightarrow [0,1]$ where $x_1, \ldots, x_n \in \overline{x}$ are function parameters
Method:
$\underline{\mathbf{B}}_T(\phi) \leftarrow$ Algorithm 5(T, ϕ)
$poly(\underline{\mathbf{B}}_T(\phi)) \leftarrow \mathsf{value}(R_{\underline{\mathbf{B}}_T(\phi)})$, where:
- $\mathsf{value}(w_i \notin W_t) = (1 - x_i) \cdot \mathsf{value}(Low(w_i))$ $+ x_i \cdot \mathsf{value}(High(w_i))$
- $\mathsf{value}(\top) = 1$ and $\mathsf{value}(\bot) = 0$

return $poly(\underline{\mathbf{B}}_T(\phi))$

6.4 Algorithm 2: Model Checking PFL over a FT and a $\overline{\rho}$

Overview. Given a specific vector $\overline{\rho}$, a FT T and a PFL layer-two formula ψ, we want to check if $\overline{\rho}, T \models \psi$. To do so, if we come across a layer-one formula ϕ we translate it to a BDD, we equip the resulting BDD with probabilities obtained from $\overline{\rho}$ and we compute whether the resulting value respects the threshold set in the given layer-two formula ψ. Boolean connectives are resolved as usual and independence is checked according to probability laws once the value for the respective BDD is computed. For the corresponding layer-three formulae ξ, we would simply return the value computed from the BDD instead of comparing it to the given layer-two threshold.

Algorithm 2. This algorithm shows a procedure to check if $\overline{\rho}, T \models \psi$, given $\overline{\rho}$, T and ψ. Boolean connectives are handled as usual via case distinction. In the same way, probability values in $\overline{\rho}$ are replaced by mappings in ψ, if any. For $\mathrm{Pr}_{\bowtie p}(\phi \mid \phi')$, we compute the BDD $\underline{\mathbf{B}}_T(\phi_n)$ for each ϕ_n of the respective layer-one formulae via Algorithm 1. Finally, we compute the conditional probability $P(\phi \mid \phi')$. If the returned value respects the threshold set in ψ we return *True*, *False* otherwise. For IDP we follow an analogous procedure: we compute probability values of needed layer-one inner formulae and we return *True* if they are stochastically independent. An algorithm for layer-three formulae ξ would simply return the conditional probability value for $\mathrm{Pr}(\phi \mid \phi')$, after potentially modifying $\overline{\rho}$ and computing $P(\underline{\mathbf{B}}_T(\phi_n))$.

Example. Let us consider the subtree in Fig. 1 and a vector with probability values for WW, H_2S, O_2 and CO_2 respectively: $\overline{\rho} = (0.002, 0.001, 0.0015, 0.002)$. Suppose we want to know if $P(MeC)$ is lower or equal to 0.0001, assuming the scenario where $P(H_2S) = 0.0023$ and $P(WW) = 0.015$, i.e., formally with $\psi = \mathrm{Pr}_{\leq 0.0001}(MeC)[H_2S \mapsto 0.0023, WW \mapsto 0.015]$. First, $\overline{\rho}$ would be modified as per the new assignments in ψ: $\overline{\rho} = (0.015, 0.0023, 0.0015, 0.002)$. Then, Algorithm 2 is called again with the modified $\overline{\rho}$ and the BDD $\underline{\mathbf{B}}_T(MeC)$ for MeC is constructed (see Fig. 4). The value for the BDD is computed via Algorithm 1. The result (0.000087) is lower than the threshold in ψ, the formula is satisfied and the algorithm returns *True*.

Algorithm 2. Check if $\overline{\rho}, T \models \psi$, given $\overline{\rho}$, T and ψ.

Input: prob. vector $\overline{\rho}$, FT T, formula ψ
Output: *True* iff $\overline{\rho}, T \models \psi$, *False* otherwise.
Method:
if $\psi = \neg\psi'$ **then return not**(Algorithm 2($\overline{\rho}, T, \psi'$))
else if $\psi = \psi' \wedge \psi''$ **then return** Algorithm 2($\overline{\rho}, T, \psi'$) **and** Algorithm 2($\overline{\rho}, T, \psi''$)
else if $\psi = \mathrm{Pr}_{\bowtie p}(\phi \mid \phi')$ **then**
  $P(\underline{\mathbf{B}}_T(\phi)), P(\underline{\mathbf{B}}_T(\phi')) \leftarrow$ Algorithm 1$(T, \phi)(\overline{\rho})$, Algorithm 1$(T, \phi')(\overline{\rho})$
  $P(\phi \mid \phi') = \frac{P(\underline{\mathbf{B}}_T(\phi)) \cdot P(\underline{\mathbf{B}}_T(\phi'))}{P(\underline{\mathbf{B}}_T(\phi'))}$
  return $P(\phi \mid \phi') \bowtie p$
else if $\psi = \psi'[e_i \mapsto q]$ **then return** Algorithm 2($\overline{\rho}[\rho_i \mapsto q], T, \psi'$)
else if $\psi = \mathrm{IDP}(\phi, \phi')$ **then**
  $P(\underline{\mathbf{B}}_T(\phi)), P(\underline{\mathbf{B}}_T(\phi')), P(\underline{\mathbf{B}}_T(\phi \wedge \phi')) \leftarrow$ Algorithm 1$(T, \phi)(\overline{\rho})$, Algorithm 1$(T, \phi')(\overline{\rho})$, Algorithm 1$(T, \phi \wedge \phi')(\overline{\rho})$
  return $P(\underline{\mathbf{B}}_T(\phi)) \cdot P(\underline{\mathbf{B}}_T(\phi')) = P(\underline{\mathbf{B}}_T(\phi \wedge \phi'))$
end if

6.5 Algorithm 3: Computing regions where ψ-formulae are satisfied

Overview. Given a FT T and a layer-two formula ψ, we want to find the region S_{yes} in $[0,1]^n$ of all $\overline{\rho}$ that satisfy ψ. Typically, such a region is defined by large polynomials, and therefore difficult to describe analytically. Instead, we provide an algorithm that approximates this region up to a given level of precision. Such an approximation is given in the definition below: it consists of a region S_{yes} where ψ is known to hold, a region S_{no} where ψ does not hold, and the remainder S_{maybe} is of limited volume.

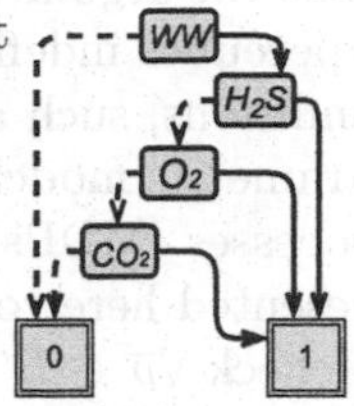

Fig. 4. BDD for Fig. 1.

Definition 6. *Let T be a FT, let $\varepsilon \in (0,1]$, and let ψ be a layer-two formula. A* ε-partition *for ψ is a partition $(S_{yes}, S_{no}, S_{maybe})$ of $[0,1]^n$ such that: 1. $\overline{\rho}, T \models \psi$ for all $\overline{\rho} \in S_{yes}$; 2. $\overline{\rho}, T \not\models \psi$ for all $\overline{\rho} \in S_{no}$; 3.* $\text{Vol}(S_{maybe}) \leq \varepsilon$, *where* Vol *denotes n-dimensional volume.*

Algorithm 3. Given T, find ε-partition for $\Pr_{\geq p}(\phi|\phi')$.

Input: FT T, formulae ϕ, ϕ', reals $p, \varepsilon \in (0,1]$.
Output: ε-partition $(S_{\text{yes}}, S_{\text{no}}, S_{\text{maybe}})$ for $\Pr_{\geq p}(\phi|\phi')$.
Method:
$\mathscr{B}_{\text{maybe}} \leftarrow \{[0,1]^n\}$; $V_{\text{maybe}} \leftarrow 1$; $S_{\text{yes}}, S_{\text{no}} \leftarrow \varnothing$
while $V_{\text{maybe}} > \varepsilon$ **do**
  Pick $B = \prod_{i=1}^n [l_i, u_i]$ from $\mathscr{B}_{\text{maybe}}$ with maximal volume
  $\mathscr{B}_{\text{maybe}} \leftarrow \mathscr{B}_{\text{maybe}} \setminus \{B\}$
  $V_{\text{maybe}} \leftarrow V_{\text{maybe}} - \text{Vol}(B)$
  $\mathscr{B}_{\text{test}} \leftarrow \left\{\prod_{i=1}^n I_i \;\middle|\; \forall i. I_i \in \{[l_i, \frac{l_i+u_i}{2}], [\frac{l_i+u_i}{2}, u_i]\}\right\}$
  for each $B' = \prod_{i=1}^n [l'_i, u'_i] \in \mathscr{B}_{\text{test}}$ **do**
    $A \leftarrow \{\overline{\rho} \in [0,1]^n \mid \forall i. \rho_i \in \{l'_i, u'_i\}\}$
    $p_{\min} \leftarrow \min_{\overline{\rho} \in A} \frac{\text{Algorithm 1}(T, \phi \wedge \phi')(\overline{\rho})}{\text{Algorithm 1}(T, \phi)(\overline{\rho})}$
    $p_{\max} \leftarrow \max_{\overline{\rho} \in A} \frac{\text{Algorithm 1}(T, \phi \wedge \phi')(\overline{\rho})}{\text{Algorithm 1}(T, \phi)(\overline{\rho})}$
    if $p \leq p_{\min}$ **then** $S_{\text{yes}} \leftarrow S_{\text{yes}} \cup B'$
    else if $p > p_{\max}$ **then** $S_{\text{no}} \leftarrow S_{\text{no}} \cup B'$
    else $\mathscr{B}_{\text{maybe}} \leftarrow \mathscr{B}_{\text{maybe}} \cup \{B'\}$; $V_{\text{maybe}} = V_{\text{maybe}} + \text{Vol}(B')$
    end if
  end for
end while
$S_{\text{maybe}} \leftarrow \bigcup \mathscr{B}_{\text{maybe}}$
return $(S_{\text{yes}}, S_{\text{no}}, S_{\text{maybe}})$

Algorithm 3. An algorithm finding a ε-partition for formulae of the form $\psi = \Pr_{\geq p}(\phi|\phi')$ is given in Algorithm 3; it works as follows. We have a set $\mathscr{B}_{\text{maybe}}$ of candidate hypercubes, which starts as the singleton $\{[0,1]^n\}$. One by one, we take hypercubes B from $\mathscr{B}_{\text{maybe}}$, and divide them into 2^n smaller hypercubes. For each of the smaller hypercubes B', we check whether $\overline{\rho}, T \models \psi$ for all $\psi \in B'$; if so, we add B' to S_{yes}. If $\overline{\rho}, T \not\models \psi$ for all $\psi \in B'$, we add B' to S_{no}. If neither is true, then we add B' to $\mathscr{B}_{\text{maybe}}$, so that later it is split up again. The algorithm stops when the joint volume of all hypercubes in $\mathscr{B}_{\text{maybe}}$ is at most ε. Algorithm 3 has the argument ε to ensure that it terminates, as one can go on partitioning hypercubes indefinitely. The algorithm can easily be adapted to other stopping conditions, such as a maximal number of hypercubes. Literature in the area of parametric model checking explored this technique, also w.r.t. Markov decision processes (MDPs) [18,22,24,30,31]. However, we leverage the specific situation presented here to devise a less generic but more convenient algorithm. In fact, to check $\forall \overline{p} \in B'.\overline{p}, T \models \psi$, we use Theorem 1 (proof in Appendix B.1), which says that the minimum of $\frac{\Phi_T^*(\overline{p},\phi\wedge\phi')}{\Phi_T^*(\overline{p},\phi')}$ $\left(\text{computed as } \frac{\text{Algorithm 1}(T,\phi\wedge\phi')(\overline{p})}{\text{Algorithm 1}(T,\phi)(\overline{p})}\right)$ on B' is attained at one of its vertices. This means that we only need to check whether $\overline{p}, T \models \psi$ for the set A of vertices of B'. The same holds for checking $\forall \overline{p} \in B'.\overline{p}, T \not\models \psi$.

Theorem 1. *Let ϕ, ϕ' be layer-one formulae, and let $B \subseteq [0,1]^n$ be a hyperrectangle. Then $\frac{\Phi_T^*(\overline{p},\phi\wedge\phi')}{\Phi_T^*(\overline{p},\phi')}$ attains its minimum and maximum (as a function of $\overline{p}$) at one of the vertices of B.*

So far, we have assumed $\psi = \Pr_{\geq p}(\phi|\phi')$. Formulae of the form $\Pr_{=p}(\phi|\phi')$ and $\text{IDP}(\phi, \phi')$ generally define hypersurfaces in $[0,1]^n$ rather than regions; these can be approximated by considering the set S_{maybe} of a ε-partition, which forms an open neighborhood of the actual hypersurface. Furthermore, one finds regions for $\neg\psi$ and $\psi \wedge \psi'$ by considering complements and intersections, respectively.

6.6 Algorithm 4: Checking PFL ψ-formulae over a FT for all $\overline{p}$

Overview. Given a FT T a layer-two formula ψ, we want to check if $T \models \psi$ for all $\overline{p}$. In this section we discuss two different approaches to answer this question, one derived from Algorithm 3 and one employing SAT solving.

Algorithm 4. Leveraging Algorithm 3, one could check whether $T \models \psi$ for all $\overline{p}$ by checking the parameter space in order to show that the negated formula $\neg\psi$ is unsatisfiable. If, on the other hand, we manage to find a candidate hypercube B' from $\mathscr{B}_{\text{maybe}}$ such that $\forall \overline{p} \in B'.\overline{p}, T \models \neg\psi$ then we can exhibit a region that serves as a counterexample for our initial question. This procedure would be bound to approximate to a given level of precision, as previously discussed.

The second possibility is to resort to SMT solving. Again, our aim is to check if the negation of the given formula is unsatisfiable. First, we translate each of the inner ϕ_n layer-one formulae (e.g., inside $\Pr_{\bowtie p}(\phi \mid \phi')$ or $\text{IDP}(\phi, \phi')$ operators) to BDDs, to then obtain representations of these BDDs as polynomials (see Algorithm 1). By comparing these to bounds set in $\Pr_{\bowtie p}(\phi \mid \phi')$ operators or to the semantics of $\text{IDP}(\phi, \phi')$, one can represent the original negated formula $\neg\psi$ via (in)equalities between polynomials. We then use already available SMT solvers - such as SMT-RAT [16] - as a black box to handle such an encoding. If the input representation is satisfiable, the SMT solver returns an assignment of variables to values, i.e., a counterexample probability vector for our original question.

7 Conclusion and Future Work

Conclusion. We presented PFL, a probabilistic logic for FTs that enables the construction of complex queries that capture many relevant scenarios. Furthermore, we introduced LangPFL, a domain specific language for PFL to ease property specification. We showcased their usefulness with an application of PFL and LangPFL to a COVID19-related FT and to a FT for an oil/gas pipeline. Specified properties can then be checked via the model checking algorithms, that we presented alongside relevant theorems.

Future Work. Our work opens several relevant perspectives for future research. First, it would be interesting to extend PFL to consider timed behaviours to further extend quantitative analysis capabilities. Secondly, it would be possible to extend PFL in order to consider dynamic gates in FTs. This further validates our first point: to handle dynamic gates in dynamic FTs it would be very natural to have a logic that can express temporal properties, moving more in the direction of LTL [40] or CTL [14] or their timed variants TLTL [41] and TCTL [1]. Moreover, it is foreseeable to extend the proposed framework to security variants of FTs, attack trees (ATs) [7,12,27,44], and to their combinations, e.g., attack-fault trees (AFTs) [32]. Another relevant area is concerned with automatic inference of FTs: further research could explore inference on PFL formulae, e.g. based on genetic algorithms [29] or dedicated methods [35]. Lastly, developing an implementation of this logic could further propel usability of PFL and LangPFL by providing hands-on feedback from domain experts acquainted with FTA.

A Appendix: Algorithms and Additional Definitions for Layer One Formulae

Following, operations between BDDs are represented by **bold** operands e.g., $\boldsymbol{\wedge}, \boldsymbol{\vee}$. Algorithms to conduct these operations on BDDs can be found in [2,5]. Given a set of variables $\mathtt{V} = \{v_1, \dots, v_n\}$, existential quantification (needed to translate part of the semantics of MCS operator) can be defined as follows: $\exists v.\mathbf{B} = \textsc{Restrict}(\mathbf{B}, v, 0) \boldsymbol{\vee} \textsc{Restrict}(\mathbf{B}, v, 1)$; $\exists V.\mathbf{B} = \exists v_1.\exists v_2. \dots \exists v_n.\mathbf{B}$.

A.1 Translating FTs to BDDs

Ψ_{FT} is defined as follows:

Definition 7. *The translation function of a FT T is a function $\Psi_{FT_T}\colon \mathtt{E} \to \mathtt{BDD}$ that takes as input an element $e \in \mathtt{E}$. With $e' \in ch(e)$, we can define Ψ_{FT_T}:*

$$\Psi_{FT_T}(e) = \begin{cases} \overline{\mathbf{B}}(e) & \text{if } e \in \mathtt{BE} \\ \bigvee \Psi_{FT_T}(e') & \text{if } e \in \mathtt{IE} \text{ and } t(e) = \mathtt{OR} \\ \bigwedge \Psi_{FT_T}(e') & \text{if } e \in \mathtt{IE} \text{ and } t(e) = \mathtt{AND} \\ \bigvee\limits_{\substack{n_1,\dots,n_k \\ n_1<\dots<n_k}} \bigwedge\limits_{i=1}^{k} \Psi_{FT_T}(e'_{n_i}) & \text{if } e \in \mathtt{IE} \text{ and } t(e)=\mathtt{VOT}(k/N) \end{cases}$$

where $\overline{\mathbf{B}}(v)$ is a BDD with a single node in which $Low(v) = \mathsf{0}$ and $High(v) = \mathsf{1}$.

A.2 Algorithm 5: Translating FTs/Formulae to BDDs

Following, the recursion scheme taken from [37] to translate FTs and layer one formulae is presented.

Algorithm 5. Given ϕ and T, compute $\underline{\mathbf{B}}_T(\phi)$

Input: FT T, formula ϕ
Output: $\underline{\mathbf{B}}_T(\phi)$
Method: Compute $\underline{\mathbf{B}}_T(\phi)$ according to the recursion scheme below. Store intermediate results $\underline{\mathbf{B}}_T(\cdots)$ and $\Psi_{FT_T}(\cdots)$ in a cache in case they are used several times.

Recursion scheme:

$$
\begin{aligned}
\underline{\mathbf{B}}_T(e): &\quad \Psi_{FT_T}(e)\\
\underline{\mathbf{B}}_T(\neg\phi): &\quad \neg(\underline{\mathbf{B}}_T(\phi))\\
\underline{\mathbf{B}}_T(\phi \wedge \phi'): &\quad \underline{\mathbf{B}}_T(\phi) \wedge \underline{\mathbf{B}}_T(\phi')\\
\underline{\mathbf{B}}_T(\phi[e_i \mapsto 0]): &\quad \textsc{Restrict}(\underline{\mathbf{B}}_T(\phi), e_i, 0)\\
\underline{\mathbf{B}}_T(\phi[e_i \mapsto 1]): &\quad \textsc{Restrict}(\underline{\mathbf{B}}_T(\phi), e_i, 1)\\
\underline{\mathbf{B}}_T(\mathrm{MCS}(\phi)): &\quad \underline{\mathbf{B}}_T(\phi) \wedge (\neg\exists \mathtt{V}'.\underline{\mathbf{B}}_T(\mathtt{V}' \subset \mathtt{V}) \wedge\\
&\quad \underline{\mathbf{B}}_T(\phi)[\mathtt{V} \curvearrowright \mathtt{V}']) \text{ where:}\\
&\quad \underline{\mathbf{B}}_T(\mathtt{V}' \subset \mathtt{V}) \equiv \underline{\mathbf{B}}_T(\bigwedge_k v'_k \Rightarrow v_k) \wedge\\
&\quad \underline{\mathbf{B}}_T(\bigvee_k v'_k \neq v_k)
\end{aligned}
$$

---

where $\underline{\mathbf{B}}_T(\phi)[\mathtt{V} \curvearrowright \mathtt{V}']$ indicates the BDD $\underline{\mathbf{B}}_T(\phi)$ in which every variable $v_k \in \mathtt{V}$ is renamed to its primed $v'_k \in \mathtt{V}'$.

A.3 Algorithm 6: Model Checking PFL over a FT and a $\overline{b}$

Overview. As per [37], given a specific vector $\overline{b}$, a FT T and a layer one formula ϕ, this algorithm showcases how to check if $\overline{b}, T \models \phi$. To do so, we translate the given formula to a BDD and then we walk down the BDD from the root node following truth assignments given in the specific vector $\overline{b}$.

Algorithm 6. Algorithm 6 shows an algorithm to check whether $\overline{b}, T \models \phi$, given a status vector $\overline{b}$, a FT T and a formula ϕ. A BDD for the formula ϕ is computed with regard to the structure function of the given FT T i.e., we compute $\underline{\mathbf{B}}_T(\phi)$ as per Algorithm 5. Subsequently, the algorithm walks down the BDD following the Boolean assignments given in $\overline{b}$: if the i-th element of $\overline{b}$ is set to 0 then the next node in the path will be given by $Low(w_i)$, if it is set to 1 then the next node will be $High(w_i)$. When the algorithm reaches a terminal node it returns *True* if its value is one - i.e., if $\overline{b}, T \models \phi$ - and *False* otherwise.

Algorithm 6. Check if $\overline{b}, T \models \phi$, given $\overline{b}$, T and ϕ.

Input: boolean vector $\overline{b}$, FT T and a formula ϕ
Output: *True* iff $\overline{b}, T \models \phi$, *False* otherwise.
Method: compute $\underline{\mathbf{B}}_T(\phi)$
Starting from BDD root,
while current node w_i of $\underline{\mathbf{B}}_T(\phi) \notin W_t$ **do:**
  if $b_i \in \overline{b} = 0$ **then:**
    $w_i = Low(w_i)$
  else if $b_i \in \overline{b} = 1$ **then:**
    $w_i = High(w_i)$
  end if
end while
if $w_i = 0$ **then:**
  return False
else if $w_i = 1$ **then:**
  return True
end if

A.4 Algorithm 7: Computing all Satisfying Vectors

Overview. Given a FT T and a formula ϕ, we now want to compute all vectors $\overline{b}$ such that $\overline{b}, T \models \phi$. In this scenario no Boolean vector is given. Thus, we need to construct the BDD for the given formula and then collect every path that leads to the terminal 1 to compute all satisfying vectors $[\![\overline{b}]\!]_T$ for the given formula.

Algorithm 7. To achieve the desired outcome we will construct the BDD $\underline{\mathbf{B}}_T(\phi)$ for the given formula following Algorithm 5. Then, the algorithm will walk down the BDD and store all the paths that lead to the terminal node 1. These paths represent all the status vectors that satisfy our formula ϕ. The value for the elements of each vector is set to 0 or 1 if the stored path follows respectively the low or high edge of the collected elements of the BDD. After computing the BDD for a given ϕ, ALLSAT [2] will achieve the desired outcome. This algorithm returns exactly all the satisfying assignments for a given BDD, i.e., in our case, all the Boolean vectors that satisfy our formula.

B Appendix: Proofs

B.1 Proof for Theorem 1

Proof. For a layer one formula ϕ and $\overline{\rho} \in B$, one can express

$$\varPhi^*_T(\mu_{\overline{\rho}}, \phi) = \sum_{\substack{b \in \mathbb{B}^n: \\ \varPhi_T(b,\phi)=1}} \prod_{i=1}^{n} \rho_i^{b_i}(1-\rho_i)^{1-b_i}. \tag{1}$$

This is a polynomial in the n variables ρ_i. Each summand has degree 1 in each ρ_i, hence $\Phi^*_T(\mu_{\overline{\rho}}, \phi)$ can be written as

$$\Phi^*_T(\mu_{\overline{\rho}}, \phi) = \sum_{w\in\{0,1\}^n} c^h_w \prod_{i=1}^{n} \rho_i^{w_i} \qquad (2)$$

for some constants $c^h_w \in \mathbb{R}$. Now fix an i, and let ϕ, ϕ' be two Boolean formulae; then we can write $\frac{\Phi^*_T(\mu_{\overline{\rho}},\phi\wedge\phi')}{\Phi^*_T(\mu_{\overline{\rho}},\phi')} = \frac{A\rho_i+B}{C\rho_i+D}$ for some polynomials A, B, C, D in the variables $\rho_1, \ldots, \rho_{i-1}, \rho_{i+1}, \ldots, \rho_n$. In particular, we have

$$\frac{\partial}{\partial\rho_i}\frac{\Phi^*_T(\mu_{\overline{\rho}}, \phi\wedge\phi')}{\Phi^*_T(\mu_{\overline{\rho}}, \phi')} = \frac{AD - BC}{(C\rho_i + D)^2}. \qquad (3)$$

The sign of this partial derivative does not depend on the value of ρ_i. In particular, when all other $\rho_{i'}$ are fixed, this expression is maximized on an interval when ρ_i is at one of the boundary points of that interval.

Now let us return to the setting of the Theorem; we will prove it for the maximum only as the minimum is proved analogously. Let Let $B = \prod_i [l_i, u_i]$ and let $\overline{\rho} \in \prod_i [l_i^{-1}, l_i^{+}]$; our aim is to find a vertex $\overline{\rho}'$ such that $\frac{\Phi^*_T(\mu_{\overline{\rho}},\phi\wedge\phi')}{\Phi^*_T(\mu_{\overline{\rho}},\phi')} \leq \frac{\Phi^*_T(\mu_{\overline{\rho}'},\phi\wedge\phi')}{\Phi^*_T(\mu_{\overline{\rho}'},\phi')}$. To do so, we construct a sequence $\overline{\rho}_0, \overline{\rho}_1, \ldots, \overline{\rho}_n$ with the following properties:

1. $\overline{\rho}_0 = \overline{\rho}$;
2. $\frac{\Phi^*_T(\mu_{\overline{\rho}_i},\phi\wedge\phi')}{\Phi^*_T(\mu_{\overline{\rho}_i},\phi')} \leq \frac{\Phi^*_T(\mu_{\overline{\rho}_{i+1}},\phi\wedge\phi')}{\Phi^*_T(\mu_{\overline{\rho}_{i+1}},\phi')}$ for $i < n$;
3. $\rho_{i,i'} \in \{l_{i'}, u_{i'}\}$ for $i' \leq i \leq n$.

This ensures that $\overline{\rho}' := \overline{\rho}_n$ has the required property. We define each $\overline{\rho}_i$ from $\overline{\rho}_{i-1}$ as follows: define $\overline{\rho}_i^-, \overline{\rho}_i^+ \in [l_i, u_i]$ by

$$\overline{\rho}^{\bullet}_{i,i'} = \begin{cases} l_i, & \text{if } \bullet = - \text{ and } i' = i,\\ u_i, & \text{if } \bullet = + \text{ and } i' = i,\\ \rho_{i-1,i'}, & \text{if } i' \neq i. \end{cases}$$

By the discussion following (3), one has $\frac{\Phi^*_T(\mu_{\overline{\rho}_i},\phi\wedge\phi')}{\Phi^*_T(\mu_{\overline{\rho}_i},\phi')} \leq \max \left\{\frac{\Phi^*_T(\mu_{\overline{\rho}^-_{i+1}},\phi\wedge\phi')}{\Phi^*_T(\mu_{\overline{\rho}^-_{i+1}},\phi')}, \frac{\Phi^*_T(\mu_{\overline{\rho}^+_{i+1}},\phi\wedge\phi')}{\Phi^*_T(\mu_{\overline{\rho}^+_{i+1}},\phi')}\right\}$. Take $\overline{\rho}_{i+1} \in \{\overline{\rho}^-_{i+1}, \overline{\rho}^+_{i+1}\}$ to maximize $\frac{\Phi^*_T(\mu_{\overline{\rho}_{i+1}},\phi\wedge\phi')}{\Phi^*_T(\mu_{\overline{\rho}_{i+1}},\phi')}$, then this satisfies conditions 1–3 above.

References

1. Alur, R., Courcoubetis, C., Dill, D.: Model-checking in dense real-time. Inf. Comput. **104**(1), 2–34 (1993)

2. Andersen, H.R.: An introduction to binary decision diagrams. Lecture notes, available online, IT University of Copenhagen, p. 5 (1997)
3. Bakeli, T., Hafidi, A.A., et al.: COVID-19 infection risk management during construction activities: an approach based on fault tree analysis (FTA). J. Emerg. Manage. **18**(7), 161–176 (2020)
4. Basgöze, D., Volk, M., Katoen, J., Khan, S., Stoelinga, M.: BDDs strike back - efficient analysis of static and dynamic fault trees. In: Deshmukh, J.V., Havelund, K., Perez, I. (eds.) NFM 2022. LNCS, vol. 13260, pp. 713–732. Springer, Cham (2022). https://doi.org/10.1007/978-3-031-06773-0_38
5. Ben-Ari, M.: Mathematical Logic for Computer Science. Springer, Heidelberg (2012). https://doi.org/10.1007/978-1-4471-4129-7
6. Bieber, P., Castel, C., Seguin, C.: Combination of fault tree analysis and model checking for safety assessment of complex system. In: Bondavalli, A., Thevenod-Fosse, P. (eds.) EDCC 2002. LNCS, vol. 2485, pp. 19–31. Springer, Heidelberg (2002). https://doi.org/10.1007/3-540-36080-8_3
7. Bobbio, A., Egidi, L., Terruggia, R.: A methodology for qualitative/quantitative analysis of weighted attack trees. IFAC Proc. Vol. **46**(22), 133–138 (2013). https://doi.org/10.3182/20130904-3-UK-4041.00007
8. Boudali, H., Crouzen, P., Stoelinga, M.: Dynamic fault tree analysis using input/output interactive Markov chains. In: DSN, pp. 708–717. IEEE Computer Society (2007). https://doi.org/10.1109/DSN.2007.37
9. Bozzano, M., Cimatti, A., Katoen, J., Nguyen, V.Y., Noll, T., Roveri, M.: Safety, dependability and performance analysis of extended AADL models. Comput. J. **54**(5), 754–775 (2011). https://doi.org/10.1093/comjnl/bxq024
10. Brace, K., Rudell, R., Bryant, R.: Efficient implementation of a BDD package. In: 27th ACM/IEEE Design Automation Conference, pp. 40–45 (1990). https://doi.org/10.1109/DAC.1990.114826
11. Budde, C.E., Dehnert, C., Hahn, E.M., Hartmanns, A., Junges, S., Turrini, A.: JANI: quantitative model and tool interaction. In: Legay, A., Margaria, T. (eds.) TACAS 2017. LNCS, vol. 10206, pp. 151–168. Springer, Heidelberg (2017). https://doi.org/10.1007/978-3-662-54580-5_9
12. Budde, C.E., Stoelinga, M.: Efficient algorithms for quantitative attack tree analysis. In: 2021 IEEE 34th Computer Security Foundations Symposium (CSF), pp. 1–15 (2021). https://doi.org/10.1109/CSF51468.2021.00041
13. Clark, P., Harrison, P., Jenkins, T., Thompson, J.A., Wojcik, R.H., et al.: Acquiring and using world knowledge using a restricted subset of English. In: Flairs Conference, pp. 506–511 (2005)
14. Clarke, E.M., Emerson, E.A.: Design and synthesis of synchronization skeletons using branching time temporal logic. In: Kozen, D. (ed.) Logic of Programs 1981. LNCS, vol. 131, pp. 52–71. Springer, Heidelberg (1982). https://doi.org/10.1007/BFb0025774
15. Conrad, E., Titolo, L., Giannakopoulou, D., Pressburger, T., Dutle, A.: A compositional proof framework for FRETish requirements. In: Proceedings of the 11th ACM SIGPLAN International Conference on Certified Programs and Proofs, pp. 68–81 (2022)
16. Corzilius, F., Kremer, G., Junges, S., Schupp, S., Ábrahám, E.: `SMT-RAT`: an open source `C++` toolbox for strategic and parallel SMT solving. In: Heule, M., Weaver, S. (eds.) SAT 2015. LNCS, vol. 9340, pp. 360–368. Springer, Cham (2015). https://doi.org/10.1007/978-3-319-24318-4_26

17. Crapo, A., Moitra, A., McMillan, C., Russell, D.: Requirements capture and analysis in ASSERT (TM). In: 2017 IEEE 25th International Requirements Engineering Conference (RE), pp. 283–291. IEEE (2017)
18. Cubuktepe, M., Jansen, N., Junges, S., Katoen, J.P., Topcu, U.: Convex optimization for parameter synthesis in MDPs. IEEE Trans. Autom. Control **67**, 6333–6348 (2021)
19. Déharbe, D., Shankar, S., Clarke, E.M.: Model checking VHDL with CV. In: Gopalakrishnan, G., Windley, P. (eds.) FMCAD 1998. LNCS, vol. 1522, pp. 508–514. Springer, Heidelberg (1998). https://doi.org/10.1007/3-540-49519-3_33
20. Dutuit, Y., Rauzy, A.: A linear-time algorithm to find modules of fault trees. IEEE Trans. Reliab. **45**(3), 422–425 (1996)
21. Ericson, C.A.: Fault tree analysis. In: System Safety Conference, vol. 1, pp. 1–9 (1999)
22. Gainer, P., Hahn, E.M., Schewe, S.: Accelerated model checking of parametric Markov chains. In: Lahiri, S.K., Wang, C. (eds.) ATVA 2018. LNCS, vol. 11138, pp. 300–316. Springer, Cham (2018). https://doi.org/10.1007/978-3-030-01090-4_18
23. Giannakopoulou, D., Mavridou, A., Rhein, J., Pressburger, T., Schumann, J., Shi, N.: Formal requirements elicitation with FRET. In: International Working Conference on Requirements Engineering: Foundation for Software Quality (REFSQ-2020). No. ARC-E-DAA-TN77785 (2020)
24. Hahn, E.M., Han, T., Zhang, L.: Synthesis for PCTL in parametric Markov decision processes. In: Bobaru, M., Havelund, K., Holzmann, G.J., Joshi, R. (eds.) NFM 2011. LNCS, vol. 6617, pp. 146–161. Springer, Heidelberg (2011). https://doi.org/10.1007/978-3-642-20398-5_12
25. Hansen, K.M., Ravn, A.P., Stavridou, V.: From safety analysis to software requirements. IEEE Trans. Software Eng. **24**(7), 573–584 (1998)
26. Hansson, H., Jonsson, B.: A logic for reasoning about time and reliability. Formal Aspects Comput. **6**(5), 512–535 (1994). https://doi.org/10.1007/BF01211866
27. Hermanns, H., Krämer, J., Krčál, J., Stoelinga, M.: The value of attack-defence diagrams. In: Piessens, F., Viganò, L. (eds.) POST 2016. LNCS, vol. 9635, pp. 163–185. Springer, Heidelberg (2016). https://doi.org/10.1007/978-3-662-49635-0_9
28. International Standardization Organization: ISO/DIS 26262: Road vehicles, functional safety (2018). https://www.iso.org/standard/68383.html
29. Jimenez-Roa, L., Heskes, T., Tinga, T., Stoelinga, M.: Automatic inference of fault tree models via multi-objective evolutionary algorithms. IEEE Trans. Dependable Secure Comput., 1–12 (2021). https://doi.org/10.1109/TDSC.2022.3203805
30. Junges, S., et al.: Parameter synthesis for Markov models. arXiv preprint arXiv:1903.07993 (2019)
31. Katoen, J.P.: The probabilistic model checking landscape. In: Proceedings of the 31st Annual ACM/IEEE Symposium on Logic in Computer Science, pp. 31–45 (2016)
32. Kumar, R., Stoelinga, M.: Quantitative security and safety analysis with attack-fault trees. In: Proceedings of the 18th IEEE International Symposium on High Assurance Systems Engineering (HASE 2017), pp. 25–32. HASE, IEEE, USA (2017). https://doi.org/10.1109/HASE.2017.12
33. Kwiatkowska, M., Norman, G., Parker, D.: PRISM 4.0: verification of probabilistic real-time systems. In: Gopalakrishnan, G., Qadeer, S. (eds.) CAV 2011. LNCS, vol. 6806, pp. 585–591. Springer, Heidelberg (2011). https://doi.org/10.1007/978-3-642-22110-1_47

34. Moszkowski, B.: A temporal logic for multi-level reasoning about hardware. Technical report, STANFORD UNIV CA (1982)
35. Nauta, M., Bucur, D., Stoelinga, M.: LIFT: learning fault trees from observational data. In: McIver, A., Horvath, A. (eds.) QEST 2018. LNCS, vol. 11024, pp. 306–322. Springer, Cham (2018). https://doi.org/10.1007/978-3-319-99154-2_19
36. Nicoletti, S., Hahn, E., Stoelinga, M.: A logic to reason about fault trees. Interview Report. https://www.utwente.nl/en/eemcs/fmt/research/files/ft-logic-interview-domain-expert.pdf
37. Nicoletti, S., Hahn, E., Stoelinga, M.: BFL: a logic to reason about fault trees. In: (DSN), pp. 441–452. IEEE/EUCA (2022). https://doi.org/10.1109/DSN53405.2022.00051
38. Ognjanovic, Z.: Discrete linear-time probabilistic logics: completeness, decidability and complexity. J. Log. Comput. **16**(2), 257–285 (2006). https://doi.org/10.1093/logcom/exi077
39. Pease, A., Murray, W.: An English to logic translator for ontology-based knowledge representation languages. In: 2003 Proceedings of the International Conference on Natural Language Processing and Knowledge Engineering, pp. 777–783. IEEE (2003)
40. Pnueli, A.: The temporal logic of programs. In: 18th Annual Symposium on Foundations of Computer Science, Providence, Rhode Island, USA, 31 October–1 November 1977, pp. 46–57. IEEE Computer Society (1977). https://doi.org/10.1109/SFCS.1977.32
41. Raskin, J.F.: Logics, automata and classical theories for deciding real time. Ph.D. thesis, Facultés universitaires Notre-Dame de la Paix, Namur (1999)
42. Rauzy, A.: New algorithms for fault trees analysis. Reliab. Eng. Syst. Saf. **40**(3), 203–211 (1993). https://doi.org/10.1016/0951-8320(93)90060-C
43. Ruijters, E., Stoelinga, M.: Fault tree analysis: a survey of the state-of-the-art in modeling, analysis and tools. Comput. Sci. Rev. **15–16**, 29–62 (2015). https://doi.org/10.1016/j.cosrev.2015.03.001
44. Schneier, B.: Attack trees. Dr. Dobb's J. **24**(12), 21–29 (1999)
45. Stamatelatos, M., Vesely, W., Dugan, J., Fragola, J., Minarick, J., Railsback, J.: Fault tree handbook with aerospace applications. Prepared for NASA Office of Safety and Mission Assurance (2002)
46. Thums, A., Schellhorn, G.: Model checking FTA. In: Araki, K., Gnesi, S., Mandrioli, D. (eds.) FME 2003. LNCS, vol. 2805, pp. 739–757. Springer, Heidelberg (2003). https://doi.org/10.1007/978-3-540-45236-2_40
47. Volk, M., Junges, S., Katoen, J.: Fast dynamic fault tree analysis by model checking techniques. IEEE Trans. Ind. Inform. **14**(1), 370–379 (2018). https://doi.org/10.1109/TII.2017.2710316
48. Walker, M.D.: Pandora: a logic for the qualitative analysis of temporal fault trees. Ph.D. thesis, The University of Hull (2009)
49. White, C., Schwitter, R.: An update on PENG light. In: Proceedings of the Australasian Language Technology Association Workshop 2009, pp. 80–88 (2009)
50. Yuhua, D., Datao, Y.: Estimation of failure probability of oil and gas transmission pipelines by fuzzy fault tree analysis. J. Loss Prev. Process Ind. **18**(2), 83–88 (2005)

Energy Büchi Problems

Sven Dziadek, Uli Fahrenberg(✉), and Philipp Schlehuber-Caissier

EPITA Research Laboratory (LRE), Paris, France
uli@lrde.epita.fr

Abstract. We show how to efficiently solve energy Büchi problems in finite weighted automata and in one-clock weighted timed automata. Solving the former problem is our main contribution and is handled by a modified version of Bellman-Ford interleaved with Couvreur's algorithm. The latter problem is handled via a reduction to the former relying on the corner-point abstraction. All our algorithms are freely available and implemented in a tool based on the open-source platforms TChecker and Spot.

Keywords: Weighted timed automaton · Weighted automaton · Energy problem · Generalized Büchi acceptance · Energy constraints

1 Introduction

Energy problems in weighted (timed) automata pose the question whether there exist infinite runs in which the accumulated weights always stay positive. Since their introduction in [7], much research has gone into different variants of these problems, for example energy games [12,16,27], energy parity games [11], robust energy problems [2], etc., and into their application in embedded systems [17, 19], satellite control [5,25], and other areas. Nevertheless, many basic questions remain open and implementations are somewhat lacking.

The above results discuss *looping* automata [28], *i.e.,* ω-automata in which all states are accepting. In practice, looping automata do not suffice because they cannot express all liveness properties. For model checking, formal properties (*e.g.,* in LTL) are commonly translated into (generalized) Büchi automata [9] that provide a simple model for the larger class of ω-regular languages.

In this work, we extend energy problems with transition-based generalized Büchi conditions and treat them for weighted automata as well as weighted timed automata with precisely one clock. On weighted automata we show that they are effectively decidable using a combination of a modified Bellman-Ford algorithm with Couvreur's algorithm. For weighted timed automata we show that one can use the corner-point abstraction to translate the problem to weighted (untimed) automata.

Partially funded by ANR project Ticktac (ANR-18-CE40-0015).

M. Chechik et al. (Eds.): FM 2023, LNCS 14000, pp. 222–239, 2023.
https://doi.org/10.1007/978-3-031-27481-7_14

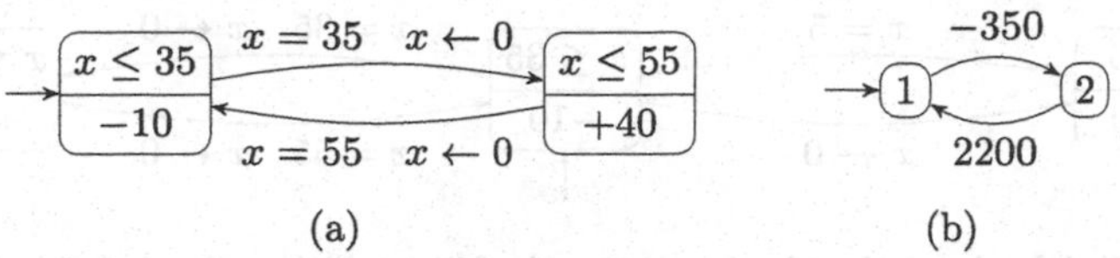

Fig. 1. Satellite example: two representations of the base circuit. (a) as weighted timed automaton A; (b) as a (finite) weighted automaton.

For looping automata, the above problems have been solved in [7]. (This paper also treats energy games and so-called universal energy problems, both of which are of no concern to us here.) While we can re-use some of the methods of [7] for our Büchi-enriched case, our extension is by no means trivial. First, in the setting of [7] it suffices to find *any* reachable and energy positive loop; now, our algorithm must consider that such loops might not be accepting in themselves but give access to new parts of the automaton which are. Secondly, [7] mostly treat the energy problem with unlimited upper bound, whereas we consider that energy has a ("weak") upper bound beyond which it cannot increase. [7] claim that the weak-upper-bound problem can be solved by slight modifications to their solution of the unbounded problem; but this is not the case. For example, the typical Bellman-Ford detection of positive cycles might not work when the energy levels attained in the previous step are already equal to the upper bound.

As a second contribution, we have implemented all of our algorithms in a tool based on the open-source platforms TChecker[1] [22] and Spot[2] [13] to solve generalized energy Büchi problems for one-clock weighted timed automata. We first employ TChecker to compute the zone graph and then use this to construct the corner-point abstraction. This in turn is a weighted (untimed) generalized Büchi automaton, in which we also may apply a variant of Alur and Dill's Zeno-exclusion technique [1]. Finally, our main algorithm to solve generalized energy Büchi problems on weighted finite automata is implemented using a fork of Spot. Our software is available at https://github.com/PhilippSchlehuberCaissier/wspot.

In our approach to solve the latter problem, we do not fully separate the energy and Büchi conditions (contrary to, for example, [11] who reduce energy parity games to energy games). We first determine the strongly connected components (SCCs) of the unweighted automaton. Then we degeneralize each Büchi accepting SCC one by one, using the standard counting construction [20]. Finally, we apply a modified Bellman-Ford algorithm to search for energy feasible lassos that start on the main graph and loop in the SCC traversing the remaining Büchi condition.

Running example 1. To clarify notation and put the concepts into context, we introduce a small running example. A satellite in low-earth orbit has a rotation

[1] See https://github.com/ticktac-project/tchecker.
[2] See https://spot.lrde.epita.fr/.

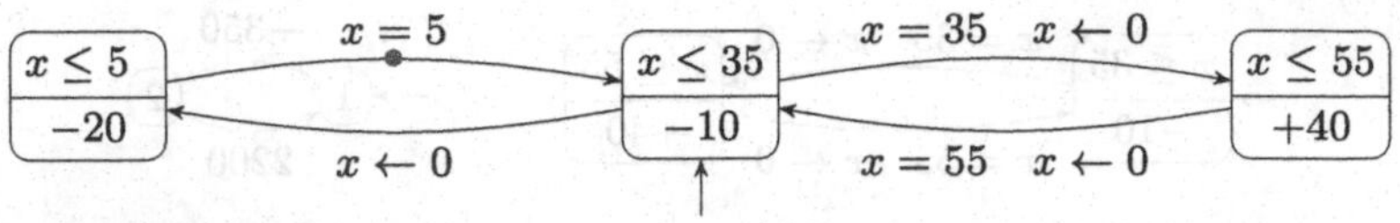

Fig. 2. Weighted timed automaton A_1 for satellite with work module.

time of about 90 min, 40% of which are spent in earth shadow. Measuring time in minutes and (electrical) energy in unspecified "energy units", we may thus model its simplified base electrical system as shown in Fig. 1a.

This is a weighted timed automaton (the formalism will be introduced in Sect. 3) with one clock, x, and two locations. The clock is used to model time, which progresses with a constant rate but can be reset on transitions. The initial location on the left (modeling earth shadow) is only active as long as $x \le 35$, and given that x is initially zero, this means that the model may stay here for at most 35 min. Staying in this location consumes 10 energy units per minute, corresponding to the satellite's base consumption.

After 35 min the model transitions to the "sun" location on the right, where it can stay for at most 55 min and the solar panels produce 50 energy units per minute, from which the base consumption has to be subtracted. Note that the transitions can only be taken if the clock shows exactly 35 (resp. 55) minutes; the clock is reset to zero after the transition, as denoted by $x \leftarrow 0$. This ensures that the satellite stays exactly 35 min in the shadow and 55 min in the sun, roughly consistent with the "physical" model.

Figure 1b shows a translation of the automaton of Fig. 1a to a weighted untimed automaton. State 1 corresponds to the "shadow" location, transitions are annotated with the corresponding weights, the rate of the location multiplied by the time spent in it. In Sect. 3 we will show how to obtain a weighted automaton from a weighted timed automaton with precisely one clock.

One may now pose the following question: for a given battery capacity b and an initial charge c, is it possible for the satellite to function indefinitely without ever running out of energy? It is clear that for $c < 350$ or $b < 350$, the answer is no: the satellite will run out of battery before ever leaving Earth's shadow; for $b \ge 350$ and $c \ge 350$, it will indeed never run out of energy.

Now assume that the satellite also has some work to do: once in a while it must, for example, send some collected data to earth. Given that we can only handle weighted automata with precisely one clock (see Sect. 3), we model the combined system as in Fig. 2. That is, work (modeled by the leftmost location) takes 5 min and costs an extra 10 energy units per minute. The dot on the outgoing transition of the work state marks a (transition-based) Büchi condition which forces us to see the transition infinitely often in order for the run to be accepted. As a consequence, all accepting runs also visit the "work" state indefinitely often, consistent with the demand to send data once in a while. In order to model the system within the constraints of our modeling formalism, we must make two simplifying assumptions, both unrealistic but conservative:

- work occurs during earth shadow;
- work prolongs earth shadow time.

The reason for the second property is that the clock x is reset to 0 when entering the work state; otherwise we would not be able to model that it lasts 5 min without introducing a second clock. It is clear how further work modules may be added in a similar way, each with their own accepting color.

We will come back to this example later and, in particular, argue that the above assumptions are indeed conservative in the sense that any behavior admitted in our model is also present in a more realistic model which we will introduce.

2 Energy Büchi Problems in Finite Weighted Automata

We now define energy Büchi problems in finite weighted automata and show how they may be solved. The similar setting for weighted *timed* automata will be introduced in Sect. 3.

Definition 1 (WBA). *A* weighted *(transition-based, generalized)* Büchi automaton *(WBA) is a structure $A = (\mathcal{M}, S, s_0, T)$ consisting of a finite set of colors $\mathcal{M}$, a set of states S with initial state $s_0 \in S$, and a set of transitions $T \subseteq S \times 2^{\mathcal{M}} \times \mathbb{R} \times S$.*

A transition $t = (s, M, w, s') \in T$ in a WBA is thus annotated by a set of colors M and a real weight w, denoted by $s \xrightarrow{w}_M s'$; to save ink, we may omit any or all of w and M from transitions and $\mathcal{M}$ from WBAs. The automaton A is *finite* if S and $T \subseteq S \times 2^{\mathcal{M}} \times \mathbb{Z} \times S$ are finite (thus finite implies integer-weighted).

A *run* in a WBA is a finite or infinite sequence $\rho = s_1 \to s_2 \to \cdots$. We write $\mathsf{first}(\rho) = s_1$ for its starting state and, if ρ is finite, $\mathsf{last}(\rho)$ for its final state. *Concatenation* $\rho_1\rho_2$ of runs is the usual partial operation defined if ρ_1 is finite and $\mathsf{last}(\rho_1) = \mathsf{first}(\rho_2)$. Also *iteration* ρ^n of finite runs is defined as usual, for $\mathsf{first}(\rho) = \mathsf{last}(\rho)$, and $\rho^\omega = \operatorname{inj\,lim}_{n\to\infty} \rho^n$ denotes infinite iteration.

For $c, b \in \mathbb{N}^3$ and a run $\rho = s_1 \xrightarrow{w_1} s_2 \xrightarrow{w_2} \cdots$, the *$(c, b)$-accumulated weights* of ρ are the elements of the finite or infinite sequence $\mathsf{weights}_{c\downarrow b}(\rho) = (e_1, e_2, \dots)$ defined by $e_1 = \min(b, c)$ and $e_{i+1} = \min(b, e_i + w_i)$. Hence the transition weights are accumulated, starting with c, but only up to the maximum bound b; increases above b are discarded. We call c the *initial credit* and b the *weak upper bound.*

Running example 2. In Fig. 1b, and choosing $c = 360$ and $b = 750$, we have a single infinite run $\rho = 1 \xrightarrow{-350} 2 \xrightarrow{2200} 1 \xrightarrow{-350} 2 \xrightarrow{2200} 1 \xrightarrow{-350} \cdots$, with $\mathsf{weights}_{c\downarrow b}(\rho) = (360, 10, 750, 400, 750, \dots)$.

A run ρ as above is said to be *(c, b)-feasible* if $\mathsf{weights}_{c\downarrow b}(\rho)_i \geq 0$ for all indices i, that is, the accumulated weights of all prefixes are non-negative. (This is the case for the example run above.)

[3] Natural numbers include 0.

An infinite run $\rho = s_1 \rightarrow_{M_1} s_2 \rightarrow_{M_2} \cdots$ is *Büchi accepted* if all colors in $\mathcal{M}$ are seen infinitely often along ρ, that is, for all $m \in \mathcal{M}$ and any index $i \in \mathbb{N}$, there exists $j > i$ such that $m \in M_j$.

We fix a weak upper bound $b \in \mathbb{N}$ for the rest of the paper and write c-feasible instead of (c, b)-feasible.

Definition 2. *The* energy Büchi problem *for a finite WBA A and initial credit $c \in \mathbb{N}$ is to ask whether there exists a Büchi accepted c-feasible run in A.*

Energy problems for finite weighted automata without Büchi conditions, asking for the existence of any c-feasible run, have been introduced in [7] and extended to multiple weight dimensions in [16] where they are related to vector addition systems and Petri nets. We extend them to (transition-based generalized) Büchi conditions here but do not consider an extension to multiple weight dimensions.

Degeneralization. As a first step to solving energy problems for finite WBAs, we show that the standard counting construction which transforms generalized Büchi automata into simple Büchi automata with only one color, see for example [20], also applies in our weighted setting. To see that, let $A = (\mathcal{M}, S, s_0, T)$ be a (generalized) WBA, write $\mathcal{M} = \{m_1, \dots, m_k\}$, and define another WBA $\bar{A} = (\bar{\mathcal{M}}, \bar{S}, \bar{s}_0, \bar{T})$ as follows:

$$\bar{\mathcal{M}} = \{m_a\} \qquad \bar{S} = S \times \{1, \dots, k\} \qquad \bar{s}_0 = (s_0, 1)$$

$$\begin{aligned}\bar{T} = {} & \big\{((s,i), \emptyset, w, (s',i)) \bigm| (s, M, w, s') \in T, m_i \notin M\big\} \\ & \cup \big\{((s,i), \emptyset, w, (s', i+1)) \bigm| i \neq k, (s, M, w, s') \in T, m_i \in M\big\} \\ & \cup \big\{((s,k), \{m_a\}, w, (s',1)) \bigm| (s, M, w, s') \in T, m_k \in M\big\}\end{aligned}$$

That is, we split the states of A into levels $\{1, \dots, k\}$. At level i, the same transitions exist as in A, except those colored with m_i; seeing such a transition puts us into level $i+1$, or 1 if $i = k$. In the latter case, the transition in $\bar{A}$ is colored by its only color m_a. Intuitively, this preserves the language as we are sure that all colors of the original automaton A have been seen:

Lemma 3. *For any $c \in \mathbb{N}$, A admits a Büchi accepted c-feasible run iff $\bar{A}$ does.*

Reduction to Lassos. An infinite run ρ in A is a *lasso* if $\rho = \gamma_1 \gamma_2^\omega$ for finite runs γ_1 and γ_2. The following lemma shows that it suffices to search for lassos in order to solve energy Büchi problems.

Lemma 4. *For any $c \in \mathbb{N}$, A admits a Büchi accepted c-feasible infinite run iff it admits a Büchi accepted c-feasible lasso.*

Hence our energy Büchi problem may be solved by searching for Büchi accepted c-feasible lassos. We detail how to do this in Sect. 4, here we just sum up the complexity result which we prove at the end of Sect. 4.

Theorem 5. *Energy Büchi problems for finite WBA are decidable in polynomial time.*

3 Energy Büchi Problems for Weighted Timed Automata

We now extend our setting to weighted timed automata. Let X be a finite set of clocks. We denote by $\Phi(X)$ the set of *clock constraints* φ on X, defined by the grammar $\varphi ::= x \bowtie k \mid \varphi_1 \wedge \varphi_2$ with $x \in X$, $k \in \mathbb{N}$, and $\bowtie \in \{\leq, <, \geq, >, =\}$. A *clock valuation* on X is a function $v : X \to \mathbb{R}_{\geq 0}$. The clock valuation v_0 is given by $v_0(x) = 0$ for all $x \in X$, and for $v : X \to \mathbb{R}_{\geq 0}$, $d \in \mathbb{R}_{\geq 0}$, and $R : X \to (\mathbb{N} \cup \{\perp\})$, we define the delay $v + d$ and reset $v[R]$ by

$$(v+d)(x) = v(x) + d, \qquad v[R](x) = \begin{cases} v(x) & \text{if } R(x) = \perp, \\ R(x) & \text{otherwise.} \end{cases}$$

Note that in $v[R]$ we allow clocks to be reset to arbitrary non-negative integers instead of only 0 which is assumed in most of the literature. It is known [24] that this does not change expressivity, but it adds notational convenience. A clock valuation v *satisfies* clock constraint φ, denoted $v \models \varphi$, if φ evaluates to true with x replaced by $v(x)$ for all $x \in X$.

Definition 6 (WTBA). *A* weighted timed *(transition-based, generalized) Büchi automaton (WTBA) is a structure $A = (\mathcal{M}, Q, q_0, X, I, E, r)$ consisting of a finite set of colors $\mathcal{M}$, a finite set of locations Q with initial location $q_0 \in Q$, a finite set of clocks X, location invariants $I : Q \to \Phi(X)$, a finite set of edges $E \subseteq Q \times 2^{\mathcal{M}} \times \Phi(X) \times (\mathbb{N} \cup \{\perp\})^X \times Q$, and location weight-rates $r : Q \to \mathbb{Z}$.*

As before, we may omit $\mathcal{M}$ from the signature and colors from edges if they are not necessary in the context. Note that the edges carry no weights here, which would correspond to discrete weight updates. In a WTBA, only locations are weighted by a rate. Even without Büchi conditions, the approach laid out here would not work for weighted edges. This was already noted in [7]; instead it requires different methods which are developed in [6] (see also [14,15]). There, one-clock weighted timed automata (with edge weights) are translated to finite automata weighted with so-called *energy functions* instead of integers. We believe that our extension to Büchi conditions should also work in this extended setting, but leave the details to future work.

The *semantics* of a WTBA A as above is the (infinite) WBA $[\![A]\!] = (\mathcal{M}, S, s_0, T)$ given by $S = \{(q, v) \in Q \times \mathbb{R}^X_{\geq 0} \mid v \models I(q)\}$ and $s_0 = (q_0, v_0)$. Transitions in T are of the following two types:

- *delays* $(q, v) \xrightarrow{w}{}^{d}_{\emptyset} (q, v+d)$ for all $(q, v) \in S$ and $d \in \mathbb{R}_{\geq 0}$ for which $v + d' \models I(q)$ for all $d' \in [0, d]$, with $w = r(q)d$;[4]
- *switches* $(q, v) \xrightarrow{0}{}^{0}_{M} (q', v')$ for all $e = (q, M, g, R, q') \in E$ for which $v \models g$, $v' = v[R]$ and $v' \models I(q')$.

Each state in $[\![A]\!]$ corresponds to a tuple containing a location in A and a clock valuation $X \to \mathbb{R}_{\geq 0}$. This allows to keep track of the discrete state as well

[4] Here we annotate transitions with the time d which passes; we only need this to exclude Zeno runs below and will otherwise omit the annotation.

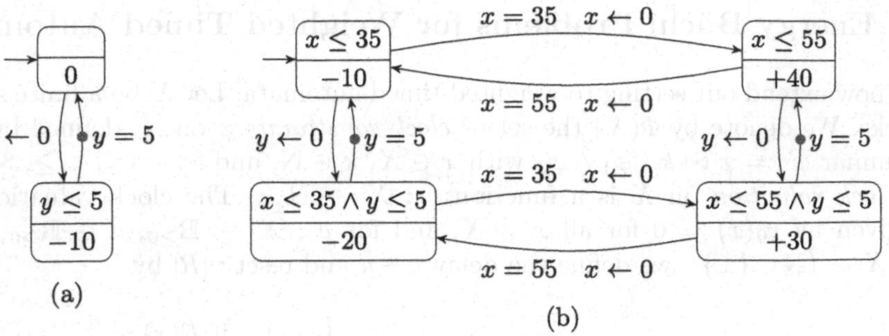

Fig. 3. Satellite example. (a) work module W; (b) product $B_1 = A \parallel W$

as the evolution of the clocks. By abuse of notation, we will sometimes write $(q, v) \in [\![A]\!]$ instead of $(q, v) \in S$, for S as defined above.

We may now pose energy Büchi problems also for WTBAs, but we wish to exclude infinite runs in which time is bounded, so-called Zeno runs. Formally an infinite run $(q_0, v_0) \to^{d_1} (q_1, v_1) \to^{d_2} \cdots$ is *Zeno* if $\sum d_i$ is finite: Zeno runs admit infinitely many steps in finite time and are hence considered unrealistic from a modeling point of view [1,21].

Definition 7. *The* energy Büchi problem *for a WTBA A and initial credit $c \in \mathbb{N}$ is to ask if there exists a Büchi accepted c-feasible non-Zeno run in* $[\![A]\!]$.

We continue our running example; but to do so properly, we need to introduce products of WTBAs. Let $A_i = (\mathcal{M}_i, Q_i, q_0^i, X_i, I_i, E_i, r_i)$, for $i \in \{1, 2\}$, be WTBAs. Their *product* is the WTBA $A_1 \parallel A_2 = (\mathcal{M}, Q, q_0, X, I, E, r)$ with

$$\mathcal{M} = \mathcal{M}_1 \cup \mathcal{M}_2, \qquad Q = Q_1 \times Q_2, \qquad q_0 = (q_0^1, q_0^2), \qquad X = X_1 \cup X_2,$$
$$I((q_1, q_2)) = I(q_1) \wedge I(q_2), \qquad r((q_1, q_2)) = r(q_1) + r(q_2),$$
$$E = \big\{((q_1, q_2), M, g, R, (q_1', q_2)) \mid (q_1, M, g, R, q_1') \in E_1\big\}$$
$$\cup \big\{((q_1, q_2), M, g, R, (q_1, q_2')) \mid (q_2, M, g, R, q_2') \in E_2\big\}.$$

Running example 3. Let A be the basic WTBA of Fig. 1a and A_1 the combination of A with the work module of Fig. 2. Now, instead of building A_1 as we have done, a principled way of constructing a model for the satellite-with-work-module would be to first model the work module W and then form the product $A \parallel W$. We show such a work module and the resulting product B_1 in Fig. 3.

As expected, W expresses that work takes 5 min and costs 10 energy units per minute, and the Büchi condition enforces that work is executed infinitely often. The product B_1 models the shadow-sun cycle together with the fact that work may be executed at any time, and contrary to our "unrealistic" model A_1 of Fig. 2, work does not prolong earth shadow time.

Now B_1 has *two* clocks, and we will see below that our constructions can handle only one. This is the reason for our "unrealistic" model A_1, and we can now state precisely in which sense it is conservative: if $[\![A_1]\!]$ admits a Büchi accepted c-feasible non-Zeno run, then so does $[\![B_1]\!]$. For a proof of this fact, one notes that any infinite run ρ in $[\![A_1]\!]$ may be translated to an infinite run $\bar{\rho}$ in $[\![B_1]\!]$ by adjusting the clock valuation by 5 whenever the work module is visited.

Bounding Clocks. As a first step to solve energy Büchi problems for WTBAs, we show that we may assume that the clocks in any WTBA A are bounded above by some $N \in \mathbb{N}$, *i.e.*, such that $v(x) \leq N$ for all $(q, v) \in [\![A]\!]$ and $x \in X$. This is shown for reachability in [3]; the following lemma extends it to Büchi acceptance.

Lemma 8. *Let* $A = (\mathcal{M}, Q, q_0, X, I, E, r)$ *be a WTBA and* $c \in \mathbb{N}$. *Let* N *the maximum constant appearing in any invariant* $I(q)$, *for* $q \in Q$, *or in any guard* g, *for* $(q, M, g, R, q') \in E$. *There is a WTBA* $\bar{A} = (\mathcal{M}, Q, q_0, X, \bar{I}, \bar{E}, r)$ *such that*

1. $v(x) \leq N + 2$ *for all* $x \in X$ *and* $(q, v) \in [\![\bar{A}]\!]$, *and*
2. *there exists a c-feasible Büchi accepted run in* $[\![A]\!]$ *iff such exists in* $[\![\bar{A}]\!]$.

Corner-Point Abstraction. We now restrict to WTBAs with only *one* clock and show how to translate these into finite untimed WBAs using the corner-point abstraction. This abstraction may be defined for any number of clocks, but it is shown in [8] that the energy problem is undecidable for weighted timed automata with four clocks or more; for two or three clocks the problem is open.

Let $A = (\mathcal{M}, Q, q_0, X, I, E, r)$ be a WTBA with $X = \{x\}$ a singleton. Using Lemma 8 we may assume that x is bounded by some $N \in \mathbb{N}$, *i.e.*, such that $v(x) \leq N$ for all $(q, v) \in [\![A]\!]$.

Let $\mathfrak{C}$ be the set of all constants which occur in invariants $I(q)$ or guards g or resets R of edges (q, M, g, R, q') in A, and write $\mathfrak{C} \cup \{N\} = \{a_1, \ldots, a_{n+1}\}$ with ordering $0 \leq a_1 < \cdots < a_{n+1}$. The *corner-point regions* [3,23] of A are the subsets $\{a_i\}$, for $i = 1, \ldots, n+1$, $[a_i, a_{i+1}[$, and $]a_i, a_{i+1}]$, for $i = 1, \ldots, n$, of $\mathbb{R}_{\geq 0}$; that is, points, left-open, and right-open intervals on $\{a_1, \ldots, a_{n+1}\}$.

These are equivalent to clock constraints $x = a_i$, $a_i \leq x < a_{i+1}$, and $a_i < x \leq a_{i+1}$, respectively, defining a notion of implication $\mathfrak{r} \Rightarrow \varphi$ for $\mathfrak{r}$ a corner-point region and $\varphi \in \Phi(\{x\})$.

The corner-point abstraction of A is the finite WBA $\mathsf{cpa}(A) = (\mathcal{M} \cup \{m_z\}, S, s_0, T)$, where $m_z \notin \mathcal{M}$ is a new color, $S = \{(q, \mathfrak{r}) \mid q \in Q, \mathfrak{r}$ corner-point region of $A, \mathfrak{r} \Rightarrow I(q)\}$, $s_0 = (q_0, \{0\})$, and transitions in T are of the following types:

- *delays* $(q, \{a_i\}) \xrightarrow{0}_{\emptyset} (q, [a_i, a_{i+1}[)$, $(q, [a_i, a_{i+1}[) \xrightarrow{w}_{\{m_z\}} (q,]a_i, a_{i+1}])$ with $w = r(q)(a_{i+1} - a_i)$, and $(q,]a_i, a_{i+1}]) \xrightarrow{0}_{\emptyset} (q, a_{i+1})$;
- *switches* $(q, \mathfrak{r}) \xrightarrow{0}_{M} (q', \mathfrak{r})$ for $e = (q, M, g, (x \mapsto \bot), q') \in E$ with $\mathfrak{r} \Rightarrow g$ and $(q, \mathfrak{r}) \xrightarrow{0}_{M} (q', \{k\})$ for $e = (q, M, g, (x \mapsto k), q') \in E$ with $\mathfrak{r} \Rightarrow g$.

The new color m_z is used to rule out Zeno runs, see [1] for a similar construction: any Büchi accepted infinite run in $\mathsf{cpa}(A)$ must have infinitely many time-increasing delay transitions $(q, [a_i, a_{i+1}[) \xrightarrow{w}_{\{m_z\}} (q,]a_i, a_{i+1}])$.

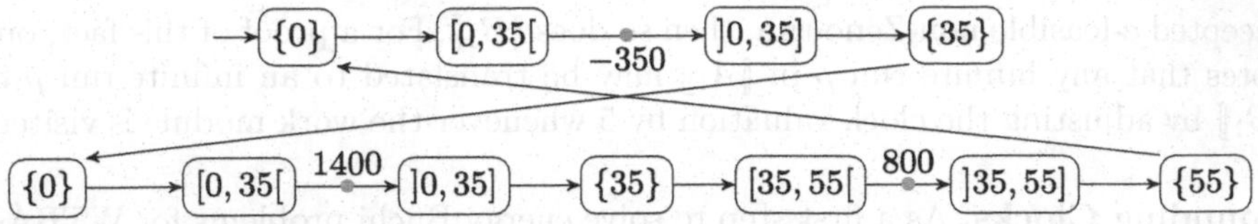

Fig. 4. Corner-point abstraction of base module of Fig. 1a.

Theorem 9. *Let A be a one-clock WTBA and $c \in \mathbb{N}$.*

1. *If there is a non-Zeno Büchi accepted c-feasible run in* $[\![A]\!]$, *then there is a Büchi accepted c-feasible run in* $\mathsf{cpa}(A)$.
2. *If there is a Büchi accepted c-feasible run in* $\mathsf{cpa}(A)$, *then there is a non-Zeno Büchi accepted* $(c+\varepsilon)$*-feasible run in* $[\![A]\!]$ *for any* $\varepsilon > 0$.

The so-called *infimum energy condition* [7] in the second part above, replacing c with $c+\varepsilon$, is necessary in the presence of *strict* constraints $x < c$ or $x > c$ in A. The proof maps runs in A to runs in $\mathsf{cpa}(A)$ by pushing delays to endpoints of corner-point regions, ignoring strictness of constraints, and this has to be repaired by introducing the infimum condition.

Running example 4. We construct the corner-point abstraction of the base module A of Fig. 1a. Its constants are $\{0, 35, 55\}$, yielding the following corner point regions:

$$\{0\}, \quad [0,35[, \quad]0,35], \quad \{35\}, \quad [35,55[, \quad]35,55], \quad \{55\}$$

The corner-point abstraction of A now looks as in Fig. 4, with the states corresponding to the "shadow" location in the top row; the colored transitions correspond to the ones in which time elapses. Note that this WBA is equivalent to the one in Fig. 1b.

Using the corner-point abstraction, we may now solve energy Büchi problems for one-clock WTBAs by translating them into finite WBAs and applying the algorithms of Sect. 2 and the forthcoming Sect. 4.

4 Implementation

We now describe our algorithm to solve energy Büchi problems for finite WBA; all of this has been implemented and is available at https://github.com/PhilippSchlehuberCaissier/wspot.

We have seen in Sect. 2 that this problem is equivalent to the search for Büchi accepted c-feasible lassos. By definition, a lasso $\rho = \gamma_1\gamma_2^\omega$ consists of two parts, the lasso prefix γ_1 (possibly empty, only traversed once) and the lasso cycle γ_2 (repeated indefinitely). In order for ρ to be Büchi accepted and c-feasible, both the prefix γ_1 and the cycle γ_2 must be c-feasible, however only the cycle needs to be Büchi accepted.

Algorithm 1 Algorithm to find Büchi accepted lassos in WBA

Input: weak upper bound b

```
 1: function BüchiEnergy(graph G, initial credit c)
 2:     E ← FindMaxE(G, G.initial_state, c)  // E: S → ℕ, mapping states to energy
 3:     SCCs ← Couvreur(G)                                     // Find all SCCs
 4:     for all scc ∈ SCCs do
 5:         GS, backedges ← degeneralize(scc)
 6:         for all t = src --w--> dst ∈ backedges do
 7:             E' ← FindMaxE(GS, dst, E[dst])            // t.dst is in G and GS...
 8:             e' ← min(b, E'[src] + w)                      // ...(see Fig. 5b)
 9:             if E[dst] ≤ e' then
10:                 return ReportLoop()
11:             else                               // Second iteration (see Fig. 5a)
12:                 E'' ← FindMaxE(GS, dst, e')
13:                 if e' ≤ min(b, E''[src] + w) then
14:                     return ReportLoop()
15:     return ReportNoLoop()
```

Finding Lassos. The overall procedure to find lassos is described in Algorithum 1. It is based on two steps. In step one we compute all energy-optimal paths starting at the initial state of the automaton with initial credit c. This step is done on the original WBA, and we do not take into account the colors. Optimal paths found in this step will serve as lasso prefixes.

The second step is done individually for each Büchi accepting SCC. The Couvreur algorithm ignores the weights, and we can use the version distributed by Spot. We then degeneralize the accepting SCCs one by one, as described in Sect. 2; recall that this creates one copy of the SCC, which we call a level, per color. The first level roots the degeneralization in the original automaton; transitions leading back from the last to the first level are called back-edges. These back-edges play a crucial role as they are the only colored transitions in the degeneralized SCC and represent the accepting transitions.

Hence any Büchi accepting cycle in the degeneralization needs to contain at least one such back-edge, and we can therefore focus our attention on these. We proceed to check for each back-edge whether we can embed it in a c-feasible cycle within the degeneralized SCC. To this end, we compute the energy-optimal paths starting at the destination of the current back-edge (by construction a state in the first level) with an initial credit corresponding to its maximal prefix energy (as found in the first step). By comparing the energy of the source state of the back-edge e while taking into account its weight, one can determine whether there exists a c-feasible cycle containing e. If this is the case, then we have found a c-feasible lasso cycle, and by concatenating it with the prefix found in the first step, we can construct a lasso. Note that we might have to check the loop a second time (using the energy level calculated in the first iteration as initial credit), see Example 10. If the answer is negative, we continue with the next back-edge in the SCC or with the next SCC once all back-edges exhausted.

Example 10. Figure 5a shows an automaton where we have to compute maximal energy levels twice (lines 11–14 in Algorithum 1): with $b = 30$ and $c = 0$, the

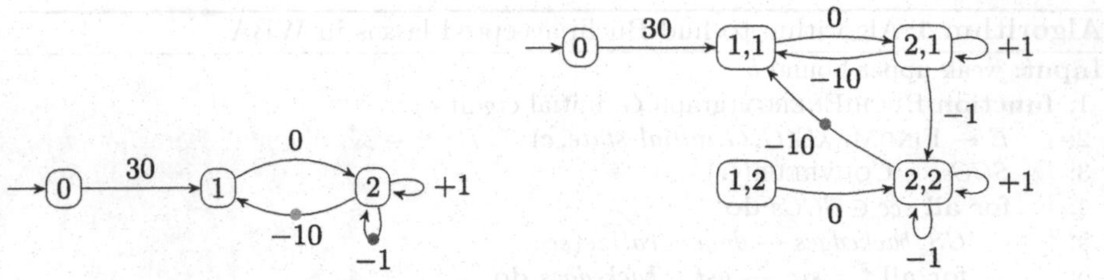

(a) Original WBA

(b) Degeneralizing SCC {1, 2} with level 1 rooted in the original WBA. Back-edges colored red.

Fig. 5. Left: WBA (also used in Example 10); right: degeneralization of one SCC (states named *originalstate*, *level*).

prefix energy of state 1 is 30, while its optimal energy on the cycle is 20, despite it being part of a energy-positive loop. Hence we cannot conclude that we have found an accepting lasso after the first iteration, but need to run the algorithm once more with an initial credit of 20.

Finding Energy Optimal Paths. We now discuss how to find energy optimal paths. The problem is equivalent (but inverse) to finding shortest paths in weighted graphs. This may be done using the well-known Bellman-Ford algorithm [4,18], which breaks with an error if it finds negative loops. In our inverted problem, we are seeking to maximize energy, so positive loops are accepted and even desired. To take into account this particularity, we modify the Bellman-Ford algorithm to invert the weight handling and to be able to handle positive loops. The modified Bellman-Ford algorithm is given in Algorithum 2.

The standard algorithm computes shortest paths by relaxing the distance approximation until the solution is found. One round relaxes all edges and the algorithm makes as many rounds as there are nodes. Inverting the algorithm is easy: the relaxation is done if the new weight is higher than the old weight; additionally the new weight has to be higher than 0 and is bounded from above by the weak upper bound.

The second modification to Bellman-Ford is the handling of positive loops. This part is a bit more involved, especially if one strives for an efficient algorithm. We could run Bellman-Ford until it reaches a fixed point, however this can significantly impact performance as shown in the following example.

Example 11. Consider the automaton shown in Fig. 6. Here one round of Bellman-Ford only increases the energy level by 1 at the rightmost state already reached and possibly reaches the state to its right once the weak upper bound attained. This means that we need to run $(N + 1) \cdot b$ rounds of Bellman-Ford to reach a fixed point. Ideally we would like the upper bound to have no influence on the runtime. To this end we introduce the function PumpAll, which sets the energy level of all states on positive loops detected by the last round of

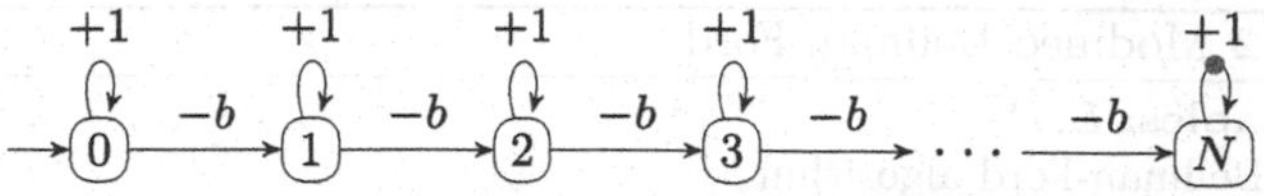

Fig. 6. WBA for Example 11

Bellman-Ford to the achievable maximum. This way, instead of needing b rounds of Bellman-Ford to attain the maximal energy, we only need one plus a call to PUMPALL.

Before continuing, we make the following observation. This stage will be called from Algorithm 1 that recognizes loops necessary to fulfill the Büchi condition. Here, we only need to check reachability. Therefore, the only reason to form a loop is to gain energy, implying that we are only interested in *simple* energy positive loops, *i.e.*, loops where every state appears at most once. If we set the optimal reachable weight in simple loops, then nested loops are updated by Bellman-Ford in the usual way afterwards.

To improve the runtime of our algorithm, we exploit that Bellman-Ford can detect positive cycles and handle these cycles specifically. Note however that contrary to a statement in [7], we cannot simply set all energy levels on a positive loop to b: in the example of Fig. 5a, starting in state 2 with an initial credit of 10, the energy level in state 1 will increase with every round of Bellman-Ford but never above $20 = b - 10$.

In order to have an algorithm whose complexity is independent of b, we instead compute the fixed point from above. We first make the following observation.

Lemma 12. *In energy positive loops, there exists at least one state on the loop that can attain the maximal energy b.*

Proof. Since the loop is energy positive we can increase the energy level at any specific node by cycling through the loop. This can be repeated until a fixed point is reached. This fixed point is only reached when at one of the states the accumulated weight reaches b (or surpasses b but is restricted to b). As the increase of energy with every cycle is a strictly monotone operation, the fixed point will be reached and no alternation is possible. □

If we knew the precise state that attains maximal energy, we could set its energy to b and loop through the cycle once while propagating the energy, causing every state on the loop to obtain its maximal energy. However, not knowing which state will effectively attain b, we start with any state on the loop, set its energy to b and propagate the energy along the loop until a fixed point is reached. This is the case after traversing the loop at most twice. This is done by the function PUMPLOOP.

Algorithm 2 Modified Bellman-Ford

```
Shared Variables: E, P
  Modified Bellman-Ford algorithm
function MODBF(weighted graph G)
    for n ∈ {1, ..., |S|} do
        for all t = s −w→ s′ ∈ T do
            e′ ← min(E(s) + w, b)
            if E[s′] < e′ and e′ ≥ 0 then
                E[s′] ← e′
                P[s′] ← t  // P: S → T, mapping states to best incoming transition

  Helper function assigning the optimal energy to all states on the energy positive
  loop containing state s
function PUMPLOOP(weighted graph G, state s)
    for all s′ ∈ LOOP(s) do          // LOOP returns the states on the loop of s ...
        E[s′] ← −1                   // Special value to detect fixed point
    E[P[s].src] ← b
    while ⊤ do                        // Loops at most twice
        for all s′ ∈ LOOP(s) do       // ... in forward order
            t ← P[s′]
            e′ ← min(b, E[t.src] + t.w)
            if e′ = E[t.dst] then
                Mark loop (and postfix) as done
                return                // fixed point reached
            E[t.dst] ← e′

  Helper function, pumping all energy positive loops induced by P
function PUMPALL(weighted graph G)
    for all states s that changed their weight do
        t = P[s]
        if min(b, E[t.src] + t.w) > E[s] then
            s′ ← s                    // s can be either on the cycle or in a postfix of one
            repeat                    // Go through it backwards to find a state on the cycle
                s′.mark ← ⊤
                s′ ← t.src
            until s′ already marked
            PUMPLOOP(G, s′)           // Pump it

  Function computing the optimal energy for each state
function FINDMAXE(graph G, start state s0, initial credit c)
    Init(s0, c)                       // initialize values in E to −∞ and E(s0) = c
    while not fixedpoint(E) do        // Iteratively search for loops, then pump them
        MODBF(G)
        PUMPALL(G)
    return copyOf(E)
```

Lemma 13. PUMPLOOP *calculates the desired fixed point after at most two cycles through the loop.*

Proof. In Algorithum 2, lines 9 and 10 ensure that the fixed point check in line 16 does not detect false positives. After setting an arbitrary state's energy to b, the algorithm cycles through the states in the loop in forward order.

Consider w.l.o.g. the positive cycle $\gamma = s_1 \xrightarrow{w_1} s_2 \xrightarrow{w_2} \cdots \xrightarrow{w_{N-1}} s_N$ with $s_1 = s_N$. By Lemma 12 we know that there exists at least one state s_j with $0 \leq j < N$ whose maximal energy equals b. Before the first energy propagating traversal of the cycle we set the energy of s_1 to b. Two cases present themselves. If $j = 0$, then energy is correctly propagated and we reach a fixed point after one traversal. In the second case, the energy attainable by s_1 is strictly smaller than b. Propagating from this energy level will over-approximate the energies reached by the states s_0 through s_{j-1} on the cycle, but only until state s_j is reached which actually attains b. As energy is bounded, the energy levels of state s_j and its successors $s_{j+1}, \ldots, s_N$ are correctly calculated. This means that after traversing the cycle $s_j \xrightarrow{w_j} \cdots \xrightarrow{w_{N-1}} s_N \xrightarrow{w_1} s_2 \xrightarrow{w_2} \cdots \xrightarrow{w_{j-1}} s_j$, all energy levels on the cycle are correctly calculated and this is guaranteed to happen before traversing the original cycle twice.

The corresponding fixed point condition is detected by line 16 which will stop the iteration. Note that we actually need to check for *changes* in the energy level on line 16, and not whether some state attained energy b, as we at this point cannot know whether this energy was reached due to over-approximation. □

Note that the pseudocode shown here is a simplification, as our implementation contains some further optimizations. Namely, we implement an early exit in MODBF if we detect that a fixed point is reached, and we keep track of states which have seen an update to their energy, as this allows to perform certain operations selectively.

Algorithm Complexity. We are now able to conclude our discussion from Sect. 2 and show that energy Büchi problems for finite WBA are decidable in polynomial time.

Proof (of Theorem 5). For our decision procedure, the search for strongly connected components can be done in polynomial time. Our modified Bellman-Ford algorithm also has polynomial complexity. It is called once at the beginning and once for every back-edge of every strongly connected component. Given that the number of such back-edges is bounded by the number of edges, we conclude that our overall algorithm has polynomial complexity. □

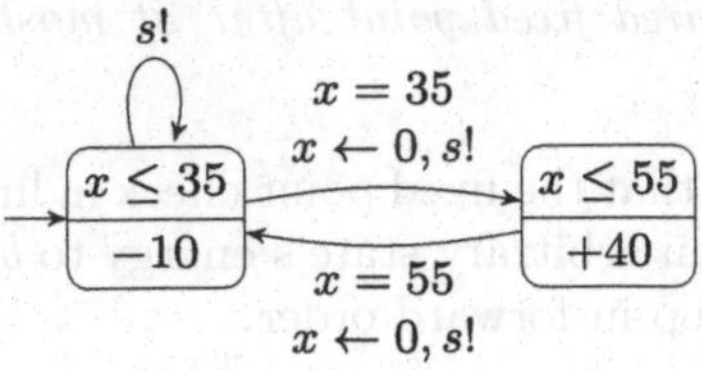

Fig. 7. Base circuit

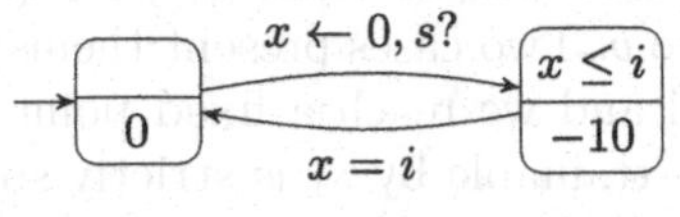

Fig. 8. Work module $\#i$

Table 1. Benchmark results. From left to right: Number of work modules, Number of states in cpa, time needed to compute cpa, time needed to solve energy Büchi problem. Benchmarks done on an ASUS G14, Ryzen 4800H CPU with 16 Gb RAM.

#mod	#states	to cpa [s]	sol [s]
1	25	0.01	0.00
3	90	0.03	0.02
5	293	0.06	0.24
7	1012	0.19	3.24
9	3759	0.89	59.52
10	7377	1.87	261.38
11	14582	4.37	1194.81

5 Benchmarks

We employ our running example to build a scalable benchmark case. For modeling convenience we use products of WTBAs as introduced above extended with standard sender/receiver synchronization via channels. The additional labels $s!$ and $s?$ are used for synchronization. Edges with $s!$ can always be taken and emit the signal s; edges with $s?$ can only be taken if a signal s is currently emitted. This modeling allows multiple work modules to start working at the same time.

As before, we use a base circuit with two states, see Fig. 7. Work module $\#i$, see Fig. 8, uses 10 energy units while working and spends exactly i time units in the work state. We then combine these models with the specification that time must pass and that every work module is activated infinitely often. All the presented instances are schedulable. Table 1 presents the results of our benchmark, showing that the presented approach scales fairly well. We note that most of the time for solving the energy Büchi problem (last column) is spent in our Python implementation of our modified Bellman-Ford algorithm. In fact the total runtime is (at least for $\#\text{mod} \geq 5$) directly proportional to the number of times lines 4 to 7 of ModBF in Algorithum 2 are executed. Therefore, the implementation could greatly benefit from a direct integration into Spot and using its C++ engine.

6 Conclusion

We have shown how to efficiently solve energy Büchi problems, both in finite weighted (transition-based generalized) Büchi automata and in one-clock weighted timed Büchi automata. We have implemented all our algorithms in a tool based on TChecker and Spot. Solving the latter problem is done by using the corner-point abstraction to translate the weighted timed Büchi automaton to a finite weighted Büchi automaton; the former problem is handled by interleaving a modified version of the Bellman-Ford algorithm with Couvreur's algorithm.

Our tool is able to handle some interesting examples, but the restriction to one-clock weighted timed Büchi automata without weights on edges does impose some constraints on modeling. We believe that trying to lift the one-clock restriction is unrealistic; but weighted edges (without Büchi conditions) have been treated in [6], and we suspect that their approach should also be viable here. (See [10] for a related approach.) In passing we should like to argue that, as shown by our running example, the modeling constraints imposed by only having one clock may be somewhat circumvented by careful modeling.

Also adopting our approach to the unlimited energy problem, without weak upper bound, should not pose any problems. In fact, setting $b = \infty$ will facilitate the algorithm, as maximal energy levels of nodes on positive loops can directly be set to ∞ (making PUMPLOOP obsolete), and also the second iteration in Algorithm 1 can be dropped.

Further, we strongly believe that our idea of investigating whether a back-edge can be embedded in an energy positive cycle is not restricted to (generalized) Büchi acceptance. In fact, the same methods should be applicable to, for example, parity acceptance conditions without losing the polynomial runtime.

As a last remark, it is known that multiple clocks, multiple weight dimensions, and even turning the weak upper bound into a strict one which may not be exceeded, rapidly leads to undecidability results, see [7,8,16,26], and we are wondering whether some of these may be sharpened when using Büchi conditions.

Acknowledgments. We are grateful to Alexandre Duret-Lutz, Nicolas Markey and Ocan Sankur for fruitful discussions on the subjects of this paper.

References

1. Alur, R., Dill, D.L.: A theory of timed automata. Theor. Comput. Sci. **126**(2), 183–235 (1994). https://doi.org/10.1007/BFb0031987
2. Bacci, G., Bouyer, P., Fahrenberg, U., Larsen, K.G., Markey, N., Reynier, P.-A.: Optimal and robust controller synthesis using energy timed automata with uncertainty. Form. Asp. Comput. **33**(1), 3–25 (2020). https://doi.org/10.1007/s00165-020-00521-4
3. Behrmann, G., et al.: Minimum-cost reachability for priced time automata. In: Di Benedetto, M.D., Sangiovanni-Vincentelli, A. (eds.) HSCC 2001. LNCS, vol. 2034, pp. 147–161. Springer, Heidelberg (2001). https://doi.org/10.1007/3-540-45351-2_15
4. Bellman, R.: On a routing problem. Quart. Appl. Math. **16**(1), 87–90 (1958). https://doi.org/10.1090/qam/102435
5. Bisgaard, M., Gerhardt, D., Hermanns, H., Krčál, J., Nies, G., Stenger, M.: Battery-aware scheduling in low orbit: the GomX–3 case. In: Fitzgerald, J.S., Heitmeyer, C.L., Gnesi, S., Philippou, A. (eds.) FM, vol. 9995, pp. 559–576. LNCS, Springer, Cham (2016). https://doi.org/10.1007/978-3-319-48989-6_34

6. Bouyer, P., Fahrenberg, U., Larsen, K.G., Markey, N.: Timed automata with observers under energy constraints. In: Proceedings of the 13th ACM International Conference on Hybrid Systems: Computation and Control, pp. 61–70 (2010). https://doi.org/10.1145/1755952.1755963
7. Bouyer, P., Fahrenberg, U., Larsen, K.G., Markey, N., Srba, J.: Infinite runs in weighted timed automata with energy constraints. In: Cassez, F., Jard, C. (eds.) FORMATS 2008. LNCS, vol. 5215, pp. 33–47. Springer, Heidelberg (2008). https://doi.org/10.1007/978-3-540-85778-5_4
8. Bouyer, P., Larsen, K.G., Markey, N.: Lower-bound-constrained runs in weighted timed automata. Perform. Eval. **73**, 91–109 (2014). https://doi.org/10.1016/j.peva.2013.11.002
9. Büchi, J.R.: Symposium on decision problems: on a decision method in restricted second order arithmetic. In: Studies in Logic and the Foundations of Mathematics, vol. 44, pp. 1–11. Elsevier (1966). https://doi.org/10.1016/S0049-237X(09)70564-6
10. Cachera, D., Fahrenberg, U., Legay, A.: An ω-algebra for real-time energy problems. Log. Methods Comput. Sci. **15**(2) (2019). https://lmcs.episciences.org/5507
11. Chatterjee, K., Doyen, L.: Energy parity games. Theor. Comput. Sci. **458**, 49–60 (2012). https://doi.org/10.1016/j.tcs.2012.07.038
12. Chatterjee, K., Doyen, L., Henzinger, T.A., Raskin, J.F.: Generalized mean-payoff and energy games. In: Lodaya, K., Mahajan, M. (eds.), FSTTCS, vol. 8, pp. 505–516. LIPIcs (2010). https://doi.org/10.4230/LIPIcs.FSTTCS.2010.505
13. Duret-Lutz, A., Lewkowicz, A., Fauchille, A., Michaud, T., Renault, É., Xu, L.: Spot 2.0 — a framework for LTL and ω-automata manipulation. In: Artho, C., Legay, A., Peled, D. (eds.) ATVA 2016. LNCS, vol. 9938, pp. 122–129. Springer, Cham (2016). https://doi.org/10.1007/978-3-319-46520-3_8
14. Ésik, Z., Fahrenberg, U., Legay, A., Quaas, K.: An algebraic approach to energy problems I: *-continuous Kleene ω-algebras. Acta Cyb. **23**(1), 203–228 (2017). https://doi.org/10.14232/actacyb.23.1.2017.13
15. Ésik, Z., Fahrenberg, U., Legay, A., Quaas, K.: An algebraic approach to energy problems II: the algebra of energy functions. Acta Cyb. **23**(1), 229–268 (2017). https://doi.org/10.14232/actacyb.23.1.2017.14
16. Fahrenberg, U., Juhl, L., Larsen, K.G., Srba, J.: Energy games in multiweighted automata. In: Cerone, A., Pihlajasaari, P. (eds.) ICTAC 2011. LNCS, vol. 6916, pp. 95–115. Springer, Heidelberg (2011). https://doi.org/10.1007/978-3-642-23283-1_9
17. Falk, H., Hammond, K., Larsen, K.G., Lisper, B., Petters, S.M.: Code-level timing analysis of embedded software: emsoft'12 invited talk session outline. In: Proceedings of the Tenth ACM International Conference on Embedded Software, pp. 163–164 (2012). https://doi.org/10.1145/2380356.2380386
18. Ford, L.R.: Network Flow Theory. RAND Corporation, Santa Monica, CA (1956)
19. Frehse, G., Larsen, K.G., Mikučionis, M., Nielsen, B.: Monitoring dynamical signals while testing timed aspects of a system. In: Wolff, B., Zaïdi, F. (eds.) ICTSS 2011. LNCS, vol. 7019, pp. 115–130. Springer, Heidelberg (2011). https://doi.org/10.1007/978-3-642-24580-0_9
20. Gastin, P., Oddoux, D.: Fast LTL to Büchi automata translation. In: Berry, G., Comon, H., Finkel, A. (eds.) CAV 2001. LNCS, vol. 2102, pp. 53–65. Springer, Heidelberg (2001). https://doi.org/10.1007/3-540-44585-4_6
21. Srivathsan, B., Herbreteau, F.: Coarse abstractions make Zeno behaviours difficult to detect. Log. Methods Comput. Sci. **9**(1) (2013). https://lmcs.episciences.org/882

22. Herbreteau, F., Srivathsan, B., Walukiewicz, I.: Better abstractions for timed automata. Inf. Comput. **251**, 67–90 (2016). https://doi.org/10.1016/j.ic.2016.07.004
23. Laroussinie, F., Markey, N., Schnoebelen, P.: Model checking timed automata with one or two clocks. In: Gardner, P., Yoshida, N. (eds.) CONCUR 2004. LNCS, vol. 3170, pp. 387–401. Springer, Heidelberg (2004). https://doi.org/10.1007/978-3-540-28644-8_25
24. Larsen, K.G., Pettersson, P., Yi, W.: UPPAAL in a nutshell. Int. J. Softw. Tools Technol. Trans. **1**(1–2), 134–152 (1997). https://doi.org/10.1007/s100090050010
25. Mikučionis, M., et al.: Schedulability analysis using Uppaal: Herschel-Planck case study. In: Margaria, T., Steffen, B. (eds.) ISoLA 2010. LNCS, vol. 6416, pp. 175–190. Springer, Heidelberg (2010). https://doi.org/10.1007/978-3-642-16561-0_21
26. Quaas, K.: On the interval-bound problem for weighted timed automata. In: Dediu, A.-H., Inenaga, S., Martín-Vide, C. (eds.) LATA 2011. LNCS, vol. 6638, pp. 452–464. Springer, Heidelberg (2011). https://doi.org/10.1007/978-3-642-21254-3_36
27. Velner, Y., Chatterjee, K., Doyen, L., Henzinger, T.A., Rabinovich, A., Raskin, J.F.: The complexity of multi-mean-payoff and multi-energy games. Inf. Comput. **241**, 177–196 (2015). https://doi.org/10.1016/j.ic.2015.03.001
28. Wolper, P., Vardi, M.Y., Sistla, A.P.: Reasoning about infinite computation paths. In: FOCS, pp. 185–194. IEEE Computer Society (1983). https://doi.org/10.1109/SFCS.1983.51

QMaude: Quantitative Specification and Verification in Rewriting Logic

Rubén Rubio(✉), Narciso Martí-Oliet, Isabel Pita, and Alberto Verdejo

Facultad de Informática,
Universidad Complutense de Madrid, Madrid, Spain
{rubenrub,narciso,ipandreu,jalberto}@ucm.es

Abstract. In formal verification, qualitative and quantitative aspects are both relevant, and high-level formalisms are convenient to naturally specify the systems under study and their properties. In this paper, we present a framework for describing probabilistic models on top of nondeterministic specifications in the highly-expressive language Maude, based on rewriting logic. Quantitative properties can be checked and calculated on them using both probabilistic and statistical methods with external tools like PRISM, Storm, MultiVeSta, and custom implementations as backends. At the same time, the underlying nondeterministic system can be verified using the qualitative model-checking and deductive tools already available in Maude.

1 Introduction

Quantitative aspects like probability, time, and cost are relevant in the formal verification of computational systems in addition to purely qualitative correctness properties. High-level specification languages are convenient to construct natural, modular and easily-understandable models describing both aspects of the systems behavior. However, broad spectrum tools combining high-level specification with quantitative and qualitative verification are rare.

Maude [13,14] is a highly-expressive specification and programming language and high-performance [23] rewriting engine based on rewriting logic [35], already used for many interesting applications [21,24,33,36,40,52]. Specifications in Maude describe the states of the target system by terms in an equational theory, while change is represented by the nondeterministic application of local rewrite rules. Nondeterminism can be controlled, if desired, with a strategy language recently introduced in Maude 3 [19,44]. These specifications are executable and several verification and analysis tools are available like a builtin LTL model checker [20], an interactive theorem prover [15], a declarative debugger [39], and several others [3,18,49]. In previous works, we have extended the Maude model checker to strategy-controlled models [46] and to additional logics like CTL, CTL*, and μ-calculus through external tools [48]. This work follows the same interoperability-based approach.

M. Chechik et al. (Eds.): FM 2023, LNCS 14000, pp. 240–259, 2023.
https://doi.org/10.1007/978-3-031-27481-7_15

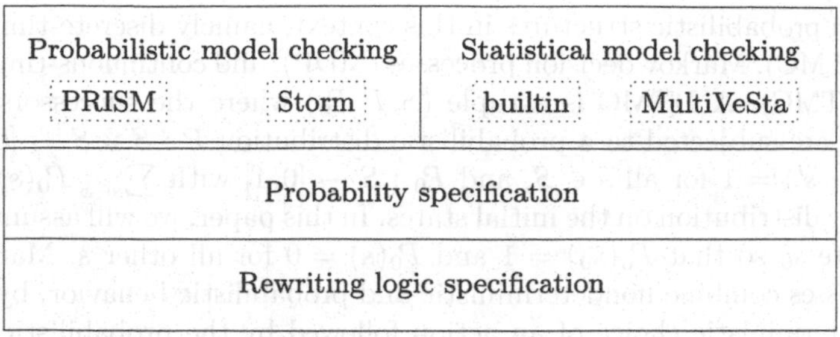

Fig. 1. Schema of the layered specification and verification approach.

In this paper, we present a framework for extending Maude specifications with probabilities and turn them into probabilistic models, which can be model checked and simulated using standard probabilistic and statistical techniques through the `umaudemc` tool [45]. Several alternative methods are offered for specifying probabilities, from selecting successors uniformly at random to programming arbitrarily-complex memoryful strategies in a probabilistic extension of the Maude strategy language. On these specifications, the `pcheck` command of `umaudemc` allows calculating transient and steady-state probabilities, checking and calculating the probabilities of LTL, PCTL*, and TCTL formulas, and computing expccted values of arbitrary functions on the states. PRISM [31] and Storm [16] are used as silent backends to perform the quantitative analysis on the models generated from the rewriting and probabilistic specifications. On these same specifications, the `scheck` command of `umaudemc` allows estimating quantitative temporal queries by Monte Carlo simulations. While `scheck` is a self-contained statistical model checker, its simulators can alternatively be used with MultiVeSta [51] via the `mvmaude` interface [42]. Moreover, the functionality of `umaudemc` is exposed as a Python library so that the quantitative models can be explored and verified programatically. Figure 1 summarizes the architecture of the proposed framework: probabilistic models are constructed by adding probabilities on top of a rewriting logic specification, and both probabilistic and statistical methods can be used to analyze them.

The paper is organized as follows. After the preliminaries in Sect. 2, the specification of probabilities on Maude models is explained in Sect. 3, and Sects. 4 and 5 respectively describe the support for probabilistic and statistical model checking on them. Section 6 discusses the implementation and Sect. 7 briefly explains two case studies. Finally, Sects. 8 and 9 discuss performance and related work, and Sect. 10 concludes the paper. Source code, documentation, and examples can be found at maude.ucm.es/qmaude and GitHub [42,45].

2 Preliminaries

We assume that the reader is familiar with the basic terminology of model checking, probability theory, and statistics. However, we recall the definition of the three main probabilistic structures in this context, namely discrete-time Markov chains (DTMC), Markov decision processes (MDP), and continuous-time Markov chains (CTMC). A DTMC is a tuple (S, P, P_0) where the successors of every state in S are subjected to a probabilistic distribution $P : S \times S \to [0, 1]$, with $\sum_{s' \in S} P(s, s') = 1$ for all $s \in S$, and $P_0 : S \to [0, 1]$ with $\sum_{s \in S} P_0(s) = 1$ is a probability distribution on the initial states. In this paper, we will assume a single initial state s_0 so that $P_0(s_0) = 1$ and $P_0(s) = 0$ for all other s. Markov decision processes combine nondeterministic and probabilistic behavior, by allowing the nondeterministic choice of an action followed by the probabilistic determination of its outcome. Formally, an MDP is a tuple (S, A, P, P_0) where P is now $P : S \times A \times S \to [0, 1]$ such that $\sum_{s' \in S} P(s, a, s') = 1$ for all $s \in S$ and $a \in A$. A CTMC is a tuple (S, R, P_0) where the transitions between states are fired at delays modeled by exponential distributions of rates $R : S \times S \to [0, \infty)$. In practice, they can be seen as DTMCs with $P(s, s') = R(s, s') \,/\, \sum_{r \in S} R(s, r)$ that stay $1 \,/\, \sum_{r \in S} R(s, r)$ units of time in s.

Probabilistic model checking [8,9,30] is a bunch of analytical methods on these structures for calculating probabilities, expected values of functions, and checking properties expressed in classical and probabilistic temporal logics like PCTL [26]. On the other hand, statistical model checking [1] estimates quantitative values of the models using Monte Carlo simulations. PRISM [31] and Storm [16] are well-known model checkers taking DTMC, MDP, and CTMC specifications as input, whereas MultiVeSta [51] is a statistical model checker that operates on user-defined simulators.

Rewriting Logic and Maude. As mentioned in the introduction, rewriting logic [35] is a high-level formalism based on term rewriting for the specification of concurrent and nondeterministic systems. Maude [13,14] is its reference implementation and includes multiple features to execute and analyze its programs. Specifications in Maude are organized in modules: *functional modules* for describing the state terms in an equational logic, *system modules* for adding nondeterministic rewrite rules on top of them, and *strategy modules* to describe strategies that control their application. For example, the following functional module `INTERVAL` specifies intervals of integer numbers $[n, m] = \{k \in \mathbb{Z} : n \leq k \leq m\}$, lists of those, and two auxiliary operations.

```
fmod INTERVAL is
  protecting INT . *** builtin module
  sorts Interval List . subsort Interval < List .
  op [_,_] : Int Int -> Interval [ctor] . *** constructor
  op __ : List List -> List [ctor assoc frozen] .
  op mid : Int Int -> Int . op even : Int Int -> Bool .
  vars N M : Int . eq mid(M,N) = (N + M) quo 2 .
  eq even(M, N) = 2 divides (N - M + 1) .
endfm
```

Operators are introduced with `op`, variables with `var`, and equations with `eq`. Operators may take attributes, like `assoc` to tell that they are associative or `frozen` to prevent rules for being applied on proper subterms.

On top of this functional module, in the KNUTH-YAO system module below, we add some rules to specify a nondeterministic version of the well-known Knuth-Yao procedure for simulating a fair dice with a fair coin [29]. Rules and conditional rules start with `rl` and `crl`, respectively.

```
mod KNUTH-YAO is
  including INTERVAL .
  vars N M : Nat . vars I J : Interval . var L : List .

  crl [head] : [M,N] => [M,mid(M,N)] if M < N .
  crl [tail] : [M,N] => [mid(M,N) + 1,N]
   if M < N /\ even(M,N) .
  crl [tail] : [M,N] => [M,N] [mid(M,N) + 1,N]
   if M < N /\ not even(M,N) .

  rl [head] : I J => J . rl [tail] : I J => I . *** go back
endm
```

The first `head`-labeled rule discards the upper half of the interval, whose midpoint is calculated by the auxiliary function `mid`. The first two rules labeled with `tail` do the same with the lower half. However, if the length of the interval is odd, this *half* will be actually larger, so the original interval is kept to allow undoing the unfair division with the last `head` and `tail` rules. We will specify probabilities on top of this model in the following sections.

Moreover, to control the nondeterministic application of rules at will, strategies can be specified using the Maude strategy language. Section 3 describes it along with the probabilistic extension proposed in this paper to quantify and not only restrict this nondeterminism.

Maude specifications can be executed with several commands like `rewrite` and `search`, and a builtin model checker is available for LTL properties [20]. Atomic propositions are defined as terms of sort `Prop` and their satisfaction is established by equations on a predefined operator `|=`. For example, the following lines declare a proposition `result` that holds on singleton intervals.

```
op result : -> Prop [ctor] .
eq [N,N] |= result = true .
eq L     |= result = false [owise] .  *** otherwise
```

Formally, the associated Kripke structure is $\mathcal{K} = (T_{\Sigma/E}, \to_R^1, t_0, T_{\Sigma,\mathtt{Prop}}, L_\Pi)$, where $T_{\Sigma/E}$ is the initial algebra of the equational theory, $\to_R^1$ is the one-step rule application relation, $t_0 \in T_{\Sigma/E}$ is an initial state, the atomic propositions are ground terms of sort `Prop`, and L_Π is induced by the equational evaluation of `|=` terms.[1] More information about Maude can be found in its manual [13].

In recent works, we have added model-checking support via external tools for CTL, CTL*, and μ-calculus, and for strategy-controlled systems [48]. These external backends are internally used by a unified interface `umaudemc` that we have extended here for probabilistic models.

[1] When the system is controlled by a strategy, the Kripke structure is refined as explained in [46,48].

3 Quantitative Specification on Top of Maude

Rewriting logic specifications are essentially nondeterministic, but probabilistic models can be obtained by quantifying this nondeterminism. Following the separation of concerns principle, we present a framework for specifying probabilities on top of the rewriting logic specification. Multiple alternative methods are provided to turn the original rewrite graph into a DTMC, an MDP, a CTMC, or a simulable random process. The probability assignment methods are the following, enunciated in terms of labeled transition systems $S = (S, A, R)$ since they can be applied to both strategy-free and strategy-controlled Maude specifications. Each method is given a name and may take some arguments between parentheses. The prefixes `mdp-` and `ctmc-` can be added to a method identifier to derive the corresponding structures, when applicable.

In the simplest case, weight-based local probability assigners specify a weight function $W : S \times A \times S \to [0, \infty)$ on the transitions of the model. Probabilities are computed by normalizing the weights, either globally or by action for MDPs,

$$P(s,s') = \frac{\sum_{a \in A} W(s,a,s')}{\sum_{(s,a,r) \in R} W(s,a,r)} \qquad P(s,a,s') = \frac{W(s,a,s')}{\sum_{(s,a,r) \in R} W(s,a,r)}$$

For deriving continuous-time Markov chains, we identify weights and firing rates, i.e. $R(s,s') = \sum_{a \in A} W(s,a,s')$. The weight function W can be specified with the following alternative methods:

- `uniform` assigns the same weight to every successor of a state by taking W as the constant function of value 1.
- `metadata` reads the weights of transitions from annotations in the source file, since rule statements can take a free-text `metadata "`w`"` attribute. These annotations can be numeric literals or Maude terms depending on the variables of the rule.
- `term(`e`)` evaluates a Maude term e of sort `Nat` or `Float` on every transition to compute the value of W. Every occurrence of the variables `L` and `R` will be instantiated with the left and right-hand side of the transition, respectively. The variable `A` will be substituted by the label of the applied rule.

Similarly, the `uaction(`a_1`=`w_1`, ..., `a_n`=`w_n`)` method takes a mapping of weights for every action of the model (omitted actions are given weight 1), but proceeds in two stages. First, the probability is distributed among the actions according to their weights, and then probabilities are shared equally among the successors of every action. Fixed probabilities can be assigned instead of weights with a`.p=`w instead of a`=`w. No `mdp-uaction` method makes sense in this case.

Finally, non-local assignments can be specified with the `strategy` method using a probabilistic extension of the Maude strategy language [19]. The main building block of the standard strategy language is the selective application of a rule, which can be invoked by its label with some optional constraints like an initial substitution for its variables. Moreover, tests `match` P `s.t.` C let equational conditions be checked on the term being rewritten, and strategies are combined with several operators like concatenation $\alpha\,;\beta$, nondeterministic choice $\alpha\,|\,\beta$, iteration $\alpha*$, conditionals $\alpha\,?\,\beta : \gamma$, subterm selection operators, and recursive definitions. More on the standard strategy language, its syntax and semantics can be found at [13,19,47]. Our probabilistic extension provides three additional operators:

- `choice(`w_1 `:` α_1`, ...,` w_n `:` α_n`)` is a quantified version of the nondeterministic choice $\alpha_1 | \cdots | \alpha_n$. Strategies are selected according to their weights w_k, which are Maude terms of sort `Nat` or `Float` that may contain variables.
- `sample X :=` π`(`t_1`, ...,` t_n`) in` α samples a probability distribution with parameters t_1 to t_n into the variable `X` of sort `Float` that can be used in α. Like with the weights in `choice`, the parameters are instantiated in the current variable context and reduced to obtain numbers.
- `matchrew` P `s.t.` C `with weight` w `by` x_1 `using` α_1`, ...,` x_n `using` α_n chooses one of the matches of the pattern P in the current term satisfying the condition C according to their weights w, instantiated with the matching variables. Then, the subterms bound to $x_1, \ldots, x_n$ are rewritten with strategies $\alpha_1, \ldots, \alpha_n$, respectively. This is a quantified version of the `matchrew` operator of the standard strategy language.

The `sample` operator is usually applied on continuous distributions for simulating delays, clocks, etc. Hence, discrete models cannot be derived from strategies containing this operator, which is intended for statistical simulation. On the contrary, strategies with `choice` and the quantified `matchrew` can yield either DTMCs or MDPs depending on whether all nondeterministic choices are quantified or not. Because of this automated detection of nondeterminism, there is no `mdp-strategy` method, but `ctmc-strategy` can be used to derive CTMC from suitable strategies.

4 Probabilistic Model Checking

Probabilistic Maude models specified as in the previous section can be analyzed using probabilistic model-checking techniques through the **`pcheck`** command of our **`umaudemc`** tool, which uses the PRISM [31] and Storm [16] model checkers as alternative backends.

`umaudemc pcheck` ⟨Maude file⟩ ⟨initial term⟩ ⟨formula⟩ [⟨strategy⟩] [**`--assign`** ⟨method⟩] [**`--steps`**] [**`--reward`** ⟨term⟩]

In addition to the input data of the rewriting model, the **`pcheck`** subcommand should also be given a probabilistic assignment method among those described in Sect. 3 with the **`--assign`** option. The **`uniform`** method will be used if this option is omitted. The strategy argument is compulsory when the **`strategy`** assignment method is used, but optional when other methods are selected. For these other methods, the strategy should be a standard strategy to control rewriting and probabilities are then assigned on the strategy-controlled graph.

The input formula should be an LTL, CTL, TCTL, or PCTL* property, or one of `@steady` and `@transient(`n`)` to calculate steady-state and transient probabilities, respectively. The syntax of temporal formulae is an extension of the `LTL` module of the standard Maude LTL model checker with the path quantifiers `A` and `E` of CTL, optional step or time bounds from TCTL, and the probabilistic operator `P` of PCTL.

$$\varphi ::= p \mid \texttt{True} \mid \texttt{False} \mid \texttt{\~{}}\,\varphi \mid \varphi \mathbin{\texttt{/\textbackslash}} \varphi \mid \varphi \mathbin{\texttt{\textbackslash/}} \varphi \mid \texttt{<>}\,b?\,\varphi \mid \texttt{[]}\,b?\,\varphi \mid \varphi\,\texttt{U}\,b?\,\varphi \mid \texttt{A}\,\varphi \mid \texttt{E}\,\varphi \mid \texttt{P}\,b\,\varphi$$

$$b ::= \texttt{[}n\texttt{,}\ n\texttt{]} \mid \texttt{>}\,n \mid \texttt{>=}\,n \mid \texttt{<}\,n \mid \texttt{<=}\,n \qquad\qquad b? ::= \varepsilon \mid b$$

The formula should meet the syntactic constraints of the corresponding logic.

Let us illustrate the specification of probabilistic models in Maude and the usage of the tool with the Knuth-Yao procedure [29] for simulating a fair dice with a fair coin, already introduced in Sect. 2. Remember that the state is modeled by an integer interval `[`m`, `n`]` that we iteratively reduce to its lower half if heads are obtained or the upper half if tails are obtained, as specified by the `head` and `tail` rules. In case the division is not fair, the part that is given more probability is marked with its parent to allow backtracking for balancing the probabilities. Even though this specification can be applied to any interval `[`m`, `n`]`, it only computes a uniform distribution when the interval size is 3, 6, a power of 2, or other combinations, but it can be adapted to work in general.

Since exactly two rules can be applied on any term, uniform probabilities are enough to model a fair coin. This can be checked by inspecting the corresponding DTMC produced by the `graph` subcommand of `umaudemc`. The algorithm stops when a singleton interval is reached, so we can compute steady-state probabilities to obtain those of the results. The outcome is the expected one.

```
$ umaudemc pcheck knuthYao6 [1,6] @steady --fraction
  1/6           [1,1]
  ...
  1/6           [6,6]
```

We can change the probabilities and consider an unfair coin that gives a head 60% of the times by passing `uaction(head=3, tail=2)` to the `--assign` option. And by using the probabilistic strategy language we can model more complex probabilities. For example, we can describe a coin that gets *damaged* on every throw and loses a 10% of the probability of obtaining a head until it drops below 25%. This is described by the following recursive strategy `bias` that uses the `choice` operator to select `head` or `tail`, and then calls itself recursively with the new value of the probability for heads. Strategy definitions are introduced with `sd` in strategy modules.

```
smod KNUTH-YAO-STRAT is
  protecting KNUTH-YAO .
  var F : Float .
  sd bias(F) := choice(F : head, 1.0 - F : tail)
       ? bias(if F > 0.25 then 0.9 * F else F fi) : idle .
endsm
```

If neither `head` nor `tail` can be applied, the execution jumps to the negative branch of the conditional (`idle`) and finishes. Steady-state probabilities are calculated in the same way.

```
$ umaudemc pcheck knuthYao6 [1,6] @steady \
    'bias(0.5)' --assign strategy
 0.2047221502318105 [2,2] ...
```

Moreover, by defining atomic propositions we can also check temporal properties on this specification. Remember that we have defined an atomic proposition `result` that holds on singleton intervals. The formula $\diamond$ `result` does not hold in absolute terms due to backtraking, as we can see with the qualitative `check` command of `umaudemc` (the counterexample is omitted).

```
$ umaudemc check knuthYao6 [1,6] '<> result'
The property is not satisfied in the initial state ...
```

However, the formula has probability 1 with `uniform` probabilities, and we can also calculate the expected number of steps until this proposition holds with the `--steps` option.

```
$ umaudemc pcheck knuthYao6 [1,6] '<> result'
Result: 1.0
$ umaudemc pcheck knuthYao6 [1,6] '<> result' --steps
Result: 3.666666667
```

For any reachability formula, the expected value of a reward on the states can be calculated with the `--reward` option followed by a Maude term of numerical sort with a single variable to be replaced by the state term. The flag `--steps` is equivalent to `--reward 1`. For further details, see maude.ucm.es/qmaude or [45].

5 Statistical Model Checking

In addition to the probabilistic techniques in the previous section, Maude specifications can be simulated to estimate their quantitative properties using the Monte Carlo method. This approach is necessary when dealing with infinite-state systems or real-valued variables, and in particular, when using the `sample` strategy operator that samples continuous probability distributions.

The `scheck` command of the `umaudemc` tool implements a statistical model checker for the previously described probabilistic models:

umaudemc scheck ⟨Maude file⟩ ⟨initial term⟩ ⟨QuaTEx file⟩ [⟨strategy⟩] [**--assign** ⟨method⟩]

This command receives the same input data as `pcheck`, except that the formula is replaced by the path of a QuaTEx or MultiQuaTEx file. These files specify *quantitative temporal expressions* that conduct the simulation to obtain a numerical result. They may contain expressions of the form `s.rval(`s`)` with s being `"steps"` for the number of elapsed steps, `"time"` for the elapsed time calculated as in a CTMC, or any other string representing a numerical or Boolean

Maude term with a single variable to be instantiated with the current term. For example, the following query calculates the expected number of steps until a result is obtained, by returning `steps` when `result` first holds and recurring with the next symbol `#` when it does not.

```
ResultSteps() = if (s.rval("S |= result") == 1)
                then s.rval("steps") else #ResultTime() fi ;
eval E[ ResultSteps() ] ;
```

Given a confidence level α, values are estimated by sequentially running batches of simulations until the radius of the confidence interval derived from the accumulated sample becomes smaller than a given upper bound δ. This is sometimes called *Chow-Robbins test* in the literature [38]. The example above can be evaluated with the following command, where `-d 0.05` fixes the maximum radius δ. Several other parameters are available to configure the simulation, like the confidence level α (`-a`) or the number of parallel simulation threads (`-j`).

```
$ umaudemc scheck knuthYao6 [1,6] knuthYao6.quatex -d 0.05
Number of simulations = 2640
  μ = 3.665151515151515        σ = 1.3052483817864313
  r = 0.04981252104845361
```

The result is a confidence interval $[\mu - r, \mu + r]$ that includes the value obtained by probabilistic model checking in Sect. 4. More complex queries can be specified, as explained in the manual of the `umaudemc` tool [45].

The probability assignment methods supported by the simulator are those of Sects. 3 and 4, except the `mdp-` variants since MDPs do not make sense in this case. The `ctmc-` prefix is without effect since the `time` observation is always computed as in a CTMC for weight-based methods. In addition, a few other assignment methods are supported:

- `step`, which identifies the steps of the simulation with complete executions of a given probabilistic strategy, which is repeated forever.
- `strategy-fast`, where steps are the rewrites within the strategy execution, like in the `strategy` method. However, `strategy-fast` is executed in a more efficient local way by assuming that the strategy never fails, because failures may discard past steps according to the semantics of the strategy language.
- `pmaude`, a legacy method for simulating PMaude specifications [2].

Alternatively, a custom simulator is available for the statistical model checker MultiVeSta [51] with support for the same probability assignment methods [42]. Moreover, probabilistic strategies can be simulated with the `srewrite` method of the `maude` Python library [43].

6 Implementation

The `umaudemc` tool [45] is a Python-based interface to multiple external and builtin verification backends for Maude specifications, introduced in [48] for model checking qualitative branching-time properties. This tool obtains the rewrite graphs for the input model through the `maude` Python library [41,43], which provides all the resources for evaluating weights, rewards, atomic propositions, and so on. The new quantitative commands `pcheck` and `scheck` share great part of the infrastructure with the qualitative tools and between them. The probabilistic `pcheck` command proceeds by obtaining the rewrite graph for the given initial term from Maude, applying the selected probability assignment method on it to obtain a DTMC, MDP, or CTMC, and passing this low-level model to the external backend to obtain the desired result. When using Storm through its Python bindings, StormPy, the model is directly built in memory and the communication is done through that library. Otherwise, `umaudemc` writes a PRISM module file, executes PRISM or Storm, and parses their answers. Most assignment methods simply decorate the graphs obtained from the `maude` Python library with the probabilities computed according to their definitions. However, other methods like `metadata` require information not exposed by the `maude` library like matching substitutions, so the probabilistic model is built from scratch in Python. In the case of the non-local `strategy` assignment method, the strategy is first compiled to an intermediate language and then executed with a custom implementation for constructing the probabilistic model. For other methods, strategies are directly passed to Maude to restrict rewriting in the standard way. Temporal formulae are input in a Maude-based syntax that is translated to the PRISM property language, and their atomic propositions are evaluated on the states. Reward terms are also instantiated on every state and reduced equationally to obtain a number. The intermediate PRISM file can be obtained with the `graph` subcommand of `umaudemc` by passing `--format prism`. Output in the JANI format [12] is also available with `--format jani` for interoperability with other tools. Visual graphs in the GraphViz's DOT format can be generated too.

The implementation of `scheck` is partitioned into a generic statistical model-checking engine and a collection of simulators adapted to the different assignment methods. These simulators are defined as Python classes exposing a simple interface that allows starting the simulation, performing a single step, and calculating observations on the current state. Simulators share most of their implementation with the `pcheck` component, but probabilities are assigned here on the fly, without expanding the whole state space. Observations on states are strings representing Maude terms with a single variable, which are parsed with the `maude` Python library, instantiated with the current state, and reduced to obtain a numerical or Boolean result. Since each observation term is usually evaluated multiple times, they are cached for efficiency once parsed.

The generic component of the statistical model checker estimates quantitative temporal expressions by running several executions of the chosen simulator. Every single simulation yields a value for each `eval` statement in the QuaTEx source file, which are separately aggregated into a sum and a sum of squares for easily computing the mean and standard deviation of the samples obtained so far. QuaTEx expressions are translated to Python and statically compiled to bytecode, and they drive the simulation process that executes new steps as required by their # operators until they compute a final value. When a block of simulations is completed, scheck computes the current confidence level with the Student's t-distribution to decide whether more simulations are needed. Multiple processes can be used to parallelize the executions in a block. The size of this block, the target confidence level, the radius of the confidence interval, the number of parallel jobs, and other simulation parameters are configurable. The mvmaude bridge to MultiVeSta shares the simulators with scheck, but this second part is done within that tool. The functionality of the pcheck and scheck commands can also be accessed programatically by using umaudemc as a Python library.

7 Case Studies

The framework presented in this paper has been used to specify several examples, like the probabilistic programming language Prob, population protocols and chemical reaction networks, and the Bounded Retransmission Protocol [22]. Here we briefly describe two of them to illustrate the approach and tools.

7.1 The Probabilistic Language Prob

With this example we aim to show the flexibility of Maude for describing high-level specifications that can be easily extended with probabilities. Prob [25] is a probabilistic programming language including, along with the typical imperative programming constructs, statements like $x \sim \pi$ where a variable x is said to follow a probabilistic distribution π. Programs are described in Maude with syntax that closely mimics the original language:

```
op _return_ : ProbStmt FTuple -> ProbProgram [ctor] .
op _:=_ : FVar FExpr -> ProbStmt [ctor prec 20] .
op _~_ : FVar FDistribution -> ProbStmt [ctor prec 20] .
op _;_ : ProbStmt ProbStmt -> ProbStmt [ctor assoc] .
op while_do_done : BoolExpr ProbStmt -> ProbStmt [ctor] .
```

Their semantics are expressed using small-step operational semantics rules, in an execution context $< p \mid \sigma >$ combining a program p and a variable context σ.

```
rl [step] : < FV := F ; S return R | VM > =>
            < S return R | VM[FV / instantiate(F, VM)] > .
```

The operational rule for the probabilistic assignment is defined with a free variable F for the sampled value, which makes the rule not (directly) executable,

```
rl [sample] : < FV ~ FD ; S return R | VM > =>
              < S return R | VM[FV / F] > [nonexec] .
```

that a strategy will fill according to the probabilistic distribution of choice.

```
csd sample(bernoulli(F), VM) := choice(
  FC : sample[B <- true], (1.0 - FC)  : sample[B <- false])
 if FC := instantiate(F, VM) .
sd sample(exponential(F), VM) :=
    sample FC := exp(instantiate(F, VM)) in sample[F <- FC] .
```

Notice that we use choice instead of sample for the Bernoulli distribution in order not to lose the ability of using probabilistic model checking when only this distribution appears. Finally, the step of the operational semantics is defined by the strategy sstep that either executes a classical statement with the step rule or a probabilistic one with the matchrew.

```
sd sstep := step | matchrew X s.t. < FV ~ D ; S return R
                 | VM > := X by X using sample(D, VM) .
```

Let us illustrate the specification with a very simple example from [25] that returns a pair of variables following a Bernoulli distribution.

```
c1 ~ bernoulli(0.5) ; c2 ~ bernoulli(0.5) return (c1 ; c2)
```

Using the pcheck command of umaudemc, since only discrete distributions are present, we can calculate the steady-state probabilities of this program and hence its possible outcomes.

```
$ umaudemc pcheck prob-lang-examples 'start(ex1a)' \
              @steady run --assign strategy
  0.25              solution(1.0 ; 1.0)
  0.25              solution(1.0 ; 0.0)
  0.25              solution(0.0 ; 1.0)
  0.25              solution(0.0 ; 0.0)
```

where ex1a is the program above, start turns it into an execution pair with an empty variable context, and run is a strategy that repeatedly calls sstep. This example becomes more interesting if the statement observe(c1 or c2) is inserted after the assignments, since the observe operator of Prob discards all executions that do not satisfy the given Boolean expression. We handle discarded executions by rewriting them to the special state discarded that allows recovering the conditional probabilities of the legitimate values. In the case of the extended example, the steady-state probabilities will coincide with the command above except that solution(0.0 ; 0.0) will be replaced by discarded. A simple automated calculation yields that the first three solutions have probability 1/3 each. Prob programs can also be simulated with the scheck command, even when continuous distributions are sampled. The complete source code for the example with further explanations is available at [22].

7.2 Head-of-Line Blocking and HTTP/3

The Hypertext Transfer Protocol is the well-known application layer protocol of the World Wide Web. Its first version was standardized in 1996 and superseded one year later by HTTP/1.1, which introduced the possibility to reuse a connection for downloading multiple resources sequentially, avoiding the expensive establishment of additional TCP connections. This performance improvement has been further developed with the new standards HTTP/2 [27] in 2015 and HTTP/3 [28] in 2022. HTTP/2 added stream multiplexing for delivering multiple resources concurrently using the same connection. However, it suffers from

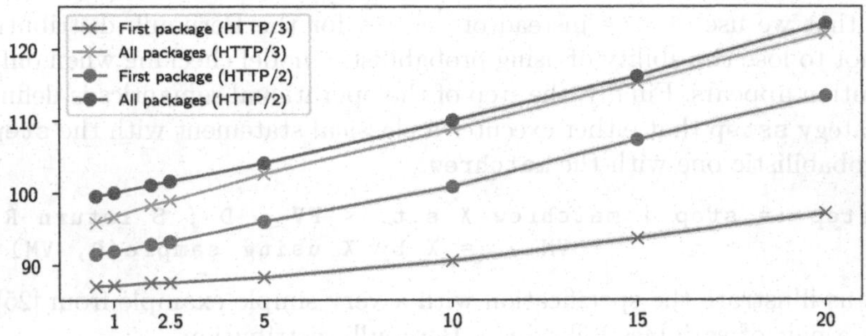

Fig. 2. Number of packages until the first and last packages have been received.

the *head-of-line blocking* problem, i.e. a delay in the transmission of one of the streams will affect all other resources due to the ordered delivery of messages of the TCP protocol. For that reason, HTTP/3 replaces TCP by an alternative transport protocol named QUIC on top of the more lightweight UDP that lets each data stream progress independently.

We have written abstract simplified specifications of both HTTP/2 and HTTP/3 to estimate and compare the mean delay for the arrival of the first and last package in a connection with multiple streams between a server and a client. Using Maude's support for object-oriented specifications, we have described the communication nodes, channels, and logical streams as objects that exchange messages. In particular, the transmission through the channel is governed by two rules `channel-ok` and `channel-loss` that give way or lose a package through it. We have then used the assignment method `uaction(channel-loss.p=`p`)` to indicate that the probability of losing a package is p. Finally, we have run the `scheck` command of `umaudemc` to calculate the expected value of two QuaTEx expressions that evaluate the number of package trips when the first and last stream have been fully transmitted. The result for both protocol versions in a fixed setting with 5 streams consisting of 10 chunks each and different loss probabilities is shown in Fig. 2. We can see that the complete delivery of the first package is faster with HTTP/3, as expected since streams can progress independently, while there is no significant difference for the last package. The complete example is at [22].

8 Evaluation

For evaluating the performance of the `pcheck` command, we have measured how much of the execution time corresponds to the generation of the rule-based model by Maude, the assignment of probabilities, and the algorithms of the model-checking backends. Since Maude is a Turing-complete programming language, its quota essentially depends on the particular specification, and then the generation of the probabilistic model takes linear time on the number of transitions. The Python profiler on the `pcheck` commands of the example collection shows that `umaudemc` introduces a constant delay of 100–150 ms plus the

Table 1. Execution time and number of simulations for multiple examples.

	scheck		mvmaude		MultiVeSta	
	Time	Runs	Time	Runs	Time	Runs
Hancke-Kuhn [5]	3 m 29 s	64530	2 m 47 s*	46350*	40 m 16 s*	46380*
RANDAO [6]	16 h 58 m	27900	17 h 3 m	28080	17 h 52 m	28080
Dice (`pmaude`)	1.06 s	2524	8.23 s	2556	71.83 s	2470
Dice (`uniform`)	947.7 ms	2468	8 s	2470	–	–
Dice (`step`)	961.52 ms	2468	7.85 s	2470	–	–

rewriting model execution. In the whole test suite, the percentage of time spent in the external backend is 97.58% when using PRISM (in client mode with Nailgun), 62.65% when using the command-line connection to Storm, and 42.52% when calling Storm through StormPy. However, in the latter case, the generation of the probabilistic graph from the Maude model does not take the remaining percentage but the 18.93% of the execution time, the rest being fixed startup delays. Moreover, by comparing global execution times, the best performance is obtained with the Storm backend connected through its Python bindings. The command-line connection to Storm is only 13.56% slower, while PRISM is 14.31 times slower. These differences increase with the size of the problem.[2]

For evaluating the `scheck` command, we consider multiple published PMaude specifications. Even though the `pmaude` assignment method is not the original contribution of this paper, we leverage on it to do a fair comparison with the statistical model checker MultiVeSta [51].[3] Since `mvmaude` [42] uses MultiVeSta with the statistical simulators of `scheck`, the comparison of its execution times with those of the `scheck` command informs about the performance of the statistical model-checking engine of `scheck`, while the comparison with MultiVeSta using its builtin PMaude simulator gives information about the performance of the simulators themselves. Moreover, we have translated the simple dice roll example included in the MultiVeSta distribution to the genuine QMaude assignment methods `uniform` and `step`, using in the latter case a strategy with a `choice` combinator giving the same probability to every outcome. Table 1 shows the execution time and number of simulations under the different tools.

We observe that our simulator for the `pmaude` method is significantly more efficient than the one in MultiVeSta. The difference is less noticeable in the RANRAO example where the execution of the model within Maude takes almost the whole simulation time. The most likely reason is that our simulators are connected to Maude through the `maude` Python library while MultiVeSta spawns a new Maude process for each simulation run and communicates with it via text

[2] The results and the scripts to reproduce them are available at maude.ucm.es/qmaude.

[3] PVesta is not included in the comparison because its actual convergence criterion differs from the one explained in its paper [2] and used by MultiVeSta and `scheck`.

input/output. Moreover, in those results marked with an asterisk, MultiVeSta does not reach the requested confidence level and stops prematurely due to an integer overflow bug. Looking at the dice example with the `uniform` and `step` methods, we see that their performance is similar or slightly better than `pmaude`. `mvmaude` takes more time than the `scheck` command, so the generic model-checking engine of `umaudemc` seems to be more efficient.

9 Related Work

The closest to our proposal is PMaude [2], a probabilistic extension of Maude based on the notion of probabilistic rewrite theory. Its rules are extended with additional variables that are sampled from probabilistic distributions, whose parameters may depend on the matching substitution. However, unquantified nondeterminism still remains in the choice of the rule and the position where it is applied, so the Monte Carlo method cannot be directly used. Users need to check that a single rewrite is possible at each step, for which a restricted actor-based framework with sampled message delays was originally proposed. The authors of PMaude also introduced the QuaTEx language and the statistical model checker VeStA, which was continued to the more general tools PVesta [4] and MultiVeSta [51]. Our approach differs in several aspects from PMaude: (1) PMaude only supports statistical simulation while we can derive discrete structures for probabilistic model checking as in Sect. 4, (2) our probability assignment methods are applied on top of a nondeterministic specification that can directly be verified with the standard qualitative tools, but rules and probabilities are entangled in PMaude and a manual transformation is required for qualitative verification, and (3) unquantified nondeterminism is avoided by construction or detected with most of our probability assignment methods and tools are offered to examine the resulting models, though in PMaude the user must manually reason about the absence of nondeterminism. Moreover, we think that our methods for specifying probabilities are simpler and more intuitive.

Strategies have already been used for quantifying nondeterminism in PSMaude [10], an extension of PMaude that provides specific syntax to quantify the choice of rules, matching positions, and substitutions, and allows checking PCTL properties. Our probabilistic strategy language pursues the same idea, although it is more expressive and able to describe memoryful probabilistic assignments. Moreover, our `choice` operator already appeared in an extension of the pioneer strategy language ELAN [11] and in the graph-rewriting strategy language Porgy [7]. Real-Time Maude [37] is also a related rewriting-logic-based tool for the formal specification and analysis of real-time systems.

Various tools allow specifying probabilistic models as low-level discrete structures or simulators, like PRISM [31], Storm [16], MATLAB [34], and R's `markovchain` package [53]. Probabilistic programming languages like Prob [25], Stan [32], and PyMC [50] combine probabilistic distributions with the typical constructs of programming languages, and are mainly focused on statistical inference.

10 Conclusions

We have presented a toolset for specifying probabilistic models on top of rewriting logic and verifying them using both probabilistic and statistical techniques via our own implementations and external tools like PRISM [31], Storm [16], and MultiVeSta [51]. Probabilities, rewards, and observations complement nondeterministic models written in the Maude language, whose qualitative properties can still be checked with a mature repertory of verification tools. In particular, nondeterminism can be quantified by a probabilistic extension of the Maude strategy language, in which complex assignments can be described with multiple operators and recursive definitions.

The main advantage of our tool is the layered specification approach that facilitates checking quantitative and qualitative properties respecting the separation of concerns principle [17]. Moreover, both analytic probabilistic and statistical model-checking techniques can be applied on the same specifications. There are great tools supporting the quantitative analysis of low-level specification of probabilistic models or simulators, like those we are using as backends. However, we have not found any general-purpose tool where specifications can be given at such a high level.

As future work, we consider other methods for assigning probabilities, and connecting to other verification and visualization tools.

Acknowledgments. Research partially supported by the Spanish AEI through project ProCode (PID2019-108528RB-C22/AEI/10.13039/501100011033). Rubén Rubio was partially supported by the Spanish Ministry of Universities through grants FPU17/02319 and EST21/00536.

References

1. Agha, G., Palmskog, K.: A survey of statistical model checking. ACM Trans. Model. Comput. Simul. **28**(1), 6:1-6:39 (2018). https://doi.org/10.1145/3158668
2. Agha, G.A., Meseguer, J., Sen, K.: PMaude: rewrite-based specification language for probabilistic object systems. In: Cerone, A., Wiklicky, H. (eds.) Proceedings of the Third Workshop on Quantitative Aspects of Programming Languages, QAPL 2005, Edinburgh, UK, 2–3 April 2005. Electronic Notes in Theoretical Computer Science, vol. 153, no. 2, pp. 213–239. Elsevier (2006). https://doi.org/10.1016/j.entcs.2005.10.040
3. Alpuente, M., Ballis, D., Sapiña, J.: Static correction of Maude programs with assertions. J. Syst. Softw. **153**, 64–85 (2019). https://doi.org/10.1016/j.jss.2019.03.061
4. AlTurki, M., Meseguer, J.: PVeStA: a parallel statistical model checking and quantitative analysis tool. In: Corradini, A., Klin, B., Cîrstea, C. (eds.) CALCO 2011. LNCS, vol. 6859, pp. 386–392. Springer, Heidelberg (2011). https://doi.org/10.1007/978-3-642-22944-2_28
5. Alturki, M.A., Kanovich, M.I., Kirigin, T.B., Nigam, V., Scedrov, A., Talcott, C.L.: Statistical model checking of distance fraud attacks on the Hancke-Kuhn family of protocols. In: Lie, D., Mannan, M. (eds.) CPS-SPC 2018, pp. 60–71. ACM (2018). https://doi.org/10.1145/3264888.3264895

6. Alturki, M.A., Roşu, G.: Statistical model checking of RANDAO's resilience to pre-computed reveal strategies. In: Sekerinski, E., et al. (eds.) FM 2019. LNCS, vol. 12232, pp. 337–349. Springer, Cham (2020). https://doi.org/10.1007/978-3-030-54994-7_25
7. Andrei, O., Fernández, M., Kirchner, H., Melançon, G., Namet, O., Pinaud, B.: PORGY: strategy-driven interactive transformation of graphs. In: Echahed, R. (ed.) Proceedings 6th International Workshop on Computing with Terms and Graphs, TERMGRAPH 2011, Saarbrücken, Germany, 2nd April 2011. EPTCS, vol. 48, pp. 54–68 (2011). https://doi.org/10.4204/EPTCS.48.7
8. Baier, C., de Alfaro, L., Forejt, V., Kwiatkowska, M.: Model checking probabilistic systems. In: Handbook of Model Checking, pp. 963–999. Springer, Cham (2018). https://doi.org/10.1007/978-3-319-10575-8_28
9. Baier, C., Katoen, J.: Principles of Model Checking. MIT Press, Cambridge (2008)
10. Bentea, L., Ölveczky, P.C.: A probabilistic strategy language for probabilistic rewrite theories and its application to cloud computing. In: Martí-Oliet, N., Palomino, M. (eds.) WADT 2012. LNCS, vol. 7841, pp. 77–94. Springer, Heidelberg (2013). https://doi.org/10.1007/978-3-642-37635-1_5
11. Bournez, O., Kirchner, C.: Probabilistic rewrite strategies. applications to ELAN. In: Tison, S. (ed.) RTA 2002. LNCS, vol. 2378, pp. 252–266. Springer, Heidelberg (2002). https://doi.org/10.1007/3-540-45610-4_18
12. Budde, C.E., Dehnert, C., Hahn, E.M., Hartmanns, A., Junges, S., Turrini, A.: JANI: quantitative model and tool interaction. In: Legay, A., Margaria, T. (eds.) TACAS 2017. LNCS, vol. 10206, pp. 151–168 (2017). https://doi.org/10.1007/978-3-662-54580-5_9
13. Clavel, M., et al.: Maude Manual v3.2.1 (2022). http://maude.lcc.uma.es/maude321-manual-html/maude-manual.html
14. Clavel, M., et al.: All About Maude - A High-Performance Logical Framework. LNCS, vol. 4350. Springer, Heidelberg (2007). https://doi.org/10.1007/978-3-540-71999-1
15. Clavel, M., Palomino, M., Riesco, A.: Introducing the ITP tool: a tutorial. J. Univers. Comput. Sci. **12**(11), 1618–1650 (2006). https://doi.org/10.3217/jucs-012-11-1618
16. Dehnert, C., Junges, S., Katoen, J.-P., Volk, M.: A storm is coming: a modern probabilistic model checker. In: Majumdar, R., Kunčak, V. (eds.) CAV 2017. LNCS, vol. 10427, pp. 592–600. Springer, Cham (2017). https://doi.org/10.1007/978-3-319-63390-9_31
17. Dijkstra, E.W.: On the Role of Scientific Thought, pp. 60–66. Texts and Monographs in Computer Science, Springer (1982). https://doi.org/10.1007/978-1-4612-5695-3_12
18. Durán, F., Rocha, C., Álvarez, J.M.: Tool interoperability in the Maude formal environment. In: Corradini, A., Klin, B., Cîrstea, C. (eds.) CALCO 2011. LNCS, vol. 6859, pp. 400–406. Springer, Heidelberg (2011). https://doi.org/10.1007/978-3-642-22944-2_30
19. Durán, F., et al.: Programming and symbolic computation in Maude. J. Log. Algebraic Methods Program. **110**, 100497 (2020). https://doi.org/10.1016/j.jlamp.2019.100497
20. Eker, S., Meseguer, J., Sridharanarayanan, A.: The Maude LTL model checker. In: Gadducci, F., Montanari, U. (eds.) Proceedings of the Fourth International Workshop on Rewriting Logic and its Applications, WRLA 2002, Pisa, Italy, 19–21 September 2002. Electronic Notes in Theoretical Computer Science, vol. 71, pp. 162–187. Elsevier (2004). https://doi.org/10.1016/S1571-0661(05)82534-4

21. Ellison, C., Rosu, G.: An executable formal semantics of C with applications. In: Field, J., Hicks, M. (eds.) Proceedings of the 39th ACM SIGPLAN-SIGACT Symposium on Principles of Programming Languages, POPL 2012, Philadelphia, Pennsylvania, USA, 22–28 January 2012, pp. 533–544. ACM (2012). https://doi.org/10.1145/2103656.2103719
22. FaDoSS: Examples of the Maude strategy language (2022). https://fadoss.github.io/strat-examples
23. Garavel, H., Tabikh, M.-A., Arrada, I.-S.: Benchmarking implementations of term rewriting and pattern matching in algebraic, functional, and object-oriented languages. In: Rusu, V. (ed.) WRLA 2018. LNCS, vol. 11152, pp. 1–25. Springer, Cham (2018). https://doi.org/10.1007/978-3-319-99840-4_1
24. González-Burgueño, A., Aparicio-Sánchez, D., Escobar, S., Meadows, C.A., Meseguer, J.: Formal verification of the YubiKey and YubiHSM APIs in Maude-NPA. In: Barthe, G., Sutcliffe, G., Veanes, M. (eds.) LPAR-22. 22nd International Conference on Logic for Programming, Artificial Intelligence and Reasoning, Awassa, Ethiopia, 16–21 November 2018. EPiC Series in Computing, vol. 57, pp. 400–417. EasyChair (2018). https://doi.org/10.29007/c4xk
25. Gordon, A.D., Henzinger, T.A., Nori, A.V., Rajamani, S.K.: Probabilistic programming. In: Herbsleb, J.D., Dwyer, M.B. (eds.) FOSE 2014, pp. 167–181. ACM (2014). https://doi.org/10.1145/2593882.2593900
26. Hansson, H., Jonsson, B.: A logic for reasoning about time and reliability. Formal Aspects Comput. **6**(5), 512–535 (1994). https://doi.org/10.1007/BF01211866
27. IETF: Hypertext Transfer Protocol version 2 (HTTP/2). RFC 7540, RFC Editor (2015). https://www.rfc-editor.org/rfc/rfc7540.txt
28. IETF: HTTP/3. RFC 9114, RFC Editor (2022). https://www.rfc-editor.org/rfc/rfc9114.txt
29. Knuth, D.E., Yao, A.C.: The complexity of nonuniform random number generation. In: Traub, J.F. (ed.) Algorithms and Complexity: New Directions and Recent Results, pp. 357–428. Academic Press (1976)
30. Kwiatkowska, M., Norman, G., Parker, D.: Stochastic model checking. In: Bernardo, M., Hillston, J. (eds.) SFM 2007. LNCS, vol. 4486, pp. 220–270. Springer, Heidelberg (2007). https://doi.org/10.1007/978-3-540-72522-0_6
31. Kwiatkowska, M., Norman, G., Parker, D.: PRISM 4.0: verification of probabilistic real-time systems. In: Gopalakrishnan, G., Qadeer, S. (eds.) CAV 2011. LNCS, vol. 6806, pp. 585–591. Springer, Heidelberg (2011). https://doi.org/10.1007/978-3-642-22110-1_47
32. Lee, D., Carpenter, B., Li, P., et al.: Stan (2017). https://doi.org/10.5281/zenodo.1101116
33. Liu, S., Ölveczky, P.C., Zhang, M., Wang, Q., Meseguer, J.: Automatic analysis of consistency properties of distributed transaction systems in Maude. In: Vojnar, T., Zhang, L. (eds.) TACAS 2019. LNCS, vol. 11428, pp. 40–57. Springer, Cham (2019). https://doi.org/10.1007/978-3-030-17465-1_3
34. MathWorks: MATLAB R2022a. The MathWorks Inc., Natick, Massachusetts (2022)
35. Meseguer, J.: Twenty years of rewriting logic. J. Log. Algebr. Program. **81**(7–8), 721–781 (2012). https://doi.org/10.1016/j.jlap.2012.06.003
36. Meseguer, J., Sasse, R., Wang, H.J., Wang, Y.: A systematic approach to uncover security flaws in GUI logic. In: 2007 IEEE Symposium on Security and Privacy (S&P 2007), Oakland, California, USA, 20–23 May 2007, pp. 71–85. IEEE Computer Society (2007). https://doi.org/10.1109/SP.2007.6

37. Ölveczky, P.C.: Real-time Maude and its applications. In: Escobar, S. (ed.) WRLA 2014. LNCS, vol. 8663, pp. 42–79. Springer, Cham (2014). https://doi.org/10.1007/978-3-319-12904-4_3
38. Pappagallo, A., Massini, A., Tronci, E.: Monte Carlo based statistical model checking of cyber-physical systems: a review. Information **11**(12), 588 (2020). https://doi.org/10.3390/info11120588
39. Riesco, A., Verdejo, A., Martí-Oliet, N., Caballero, R.: Declarative debugging of rewriting logic specifications. J. Log. Algebraic Methods Program. **81**(7–8), 851–897 (2012). https://doi.org/10.1016/j.jlap.2011.06.004
40. Rocha, C., Cadavid, H., Muñoz, C., Siminiceanu, R.: A formal interactive verification environment for the plan execution interchange language. In: Derrick, J., Gnesi, S., Latella, D., Treharne, H. (eds.) IFM 2012. LNCS, vol. 7321, pp. 343–357. Springer, Heidelberg (2012). https://doi.org/10.1007/978-3-642-30729-4_24
41. Rubio, R.: Language bindings for Maude (2021). https://fadoss.github.io/maude-bindings
42. Rubio, R.: Maude simulator for MultiVeSta (2021). https://github.com/fadoss/multivesta-maude
43. Rubio, R.: Maude as a library: an efficient all-purpose programming interface. In: Bae, K. (ed.) WRLA 2022. LNCS, vol. 13252, pp. 274–294. Springer, Cham (2022). https://doi.org/10.1007/978-3-031-12441-9_14
44. Rubio, R.: An overview of the Maude strategy language and its applications. In: Bae, K. (ed.) WRLA 2022. LNCS, vol. 13252, pp. 65–84. Springer, Cham (2022). https://doi.org/10.1007/978-3-031-12441-9_4
45. Rubio, R.: Unified Maude model-checking tool (2022). https://github.com/fadoss/umaudemc
46. Rubio, R., Martí-Oliet, N., Pita, I., Verdejo, A.: Model checking strategy-controlled systems in rewriting logic. Autom. Softw. Eng. **29**(1), 1–62 (2021). https://doi.org/10.1007/s10515-021-00307-9
47. Rubio, R., Martí-Oliet, N., Pita, I., Verdejo, A.: The semantics of the Maude strategy language. Tech. rep. 01/21, Departamento de Sistemas Informáticos y Computación, Universidad Complutense de Madrid (2021).https://eprints.ucm.es/67449/
48. Rubio, R., Martí-Oliet, N., Pita, I., Verdejo, A.: Strategies, model checking and branching-time properties in Maude. J. Log. Algebr. Methods Program. **123**, 100700 (2021). https://doi.org/10.1016/j.jlamp.2021.100700
49. Rubio, R., Riesco, A.: Theorem proving for Maude specifications using Lean. In: Zhang, M., Riesco, A. (eds.) Formal Methods and Software Engineering. ICFEM 2022. LNCS, vol. 13478, pp. 263–280. Springer, Cham (2022). https://doi.org/10.1007/978-3-031-17244-1_16
50. Salvatier, J., Wiecki, T.V., Fonnesbeck, C.: Probabilistic programming in Python using PyMC3. PeerJ Comput. Sci. **2**, e55 (2016). https://doi.org/10.7717/peerj-cs.55
51. Sebastio, S., Vandin, A.: MultiVeStA: statistical model checking for discrete event simulators. In: Horváth, A., Buchholz, P., Cortellessa, V., Muscariello, L., Squillante, M.S. (eds.) 7th International Conference on Performance Evaluation Methodologies and Tools, ValueTools 2013, Torino, Italy, 10–12 December 2013, pp. 310–315. ICST/ACM (2013). https://doi.org/10.4108/icst.valuetools.2013.254377

52. Shankesi, R., AlTurki, M., Sasse, R., Gunter, C.A., Meseguer, J.: Model-checking DoS amplification for VoIP session initiation. In: Backes, M., Ning, P. (eds.) ESORICS 2009. LNCS, vol. 5789, pp. 390–405. Springer, Heidelberg (2009). https://doi.org/10.1007/978-3-642-04444-1_24
53. Spedicato, G.A.: Discrete time Markov chains with R. R J. **9**(2), 84 (2017). https://doi.org/10.32614/rj-2017-036

Concurrency and Memory Models

Minimisation of Spatial Models Using Branching Bisimilarity

Vincenzo Ciancia[1], Jan Friso Groote[2], Diego Latella[1], Mieke Massink[1(✉)], and Erik P. de Vink[2]

[1] CNR-ISTI, Pisa, Italy
{Vincenzo.Ciancia,Diego.Latella,Mieke.Massink}@cnr.it
[2] Eindhoven University of Technology, Eindhoven, The Netherlands
j.f.groote@TUE.nl, evink@win.tue.nl

Abstract. Spatial logic and spatial model checking have great potential for traditional computer science domains and beyond. Reasoning about space involves two different conditional reachability modalities: a forward reachability, similar to that used in temporal logic, and a backward modality representing that a point can be reached from another point, under certain conditions. Since spatial models can be huge, suitable model minimisation techniques are crucial for efficient model checking. An effective minimisation method for the recent notion of spatial Compatible Path (CoPa)-bisimilarity is proposed, and shown to be correct. The core of our method is the encoding of Closure Models as Labelled Transition Systems, enabling minimisation algorithms for branching bisimulation to compute CoPa equivalence classes. Initial validation via benchmark examples demonstrates a promising speed-up in model checking of spatial properties for models of realistic size.

Keywords: Spatial minimisation · Closure spaces · Spatial logics · Spatial bisimilarity · Branching bisimilarity · Spatial model checking

1 Introduction

Spatial and spatio-temporal model checking have recently been successfully employed in a variety of application areas, ranging from Collective Adaptive Systems [14,20] to signals [30], images [5,18,25] and polyhedra [9], just to mention a few. These methods for spatial analysis are enjoying an increasing interest in computer science and beyond, also in unexpected domains such as medical imaging [6,8]. Medical images are obtained from diagnostic instruments such as magnetic resonance images (MRI), computer tomography scans, positron emission tomography or dermoscopic images. Such images usually consist of millions of pixels, in 2D, or voxels (volumetric pixels) in 3D images.

Research partially funded by the Italian MUR Projects PRIN 2017FTXR7S, "IT- MaTTerS", PRIN 2020TL3X8X "T-LADIES", and Next Generation EU - MUR Project PNRR PRI ECS00000017 "THE - Tuscany Health Ecosystem". The authors are listed in alphabetical order; they contributed to this work equally.

M. Chechik et al. (Eds.): FM 2023, LNCS 14000, pp. 263–281, 2023.
https://doi.org/10.1007/978-3-031-27481-7_16

Spatial model checking consists in the automatic verification of properties, expressed in a suitable spatial logic, on each point of a suitable spatial model. In [17] the Spatial Logic for Closure Spaces (SLCS) was introduced and further developed in [18]. Closure spaces, or Čech closure spaces [33], are a generalisation of topological spaces suitable to model many kinds of spatial objects, ranging from topological objects in continuous spaces, such as Euclidean spaces, to discrete spatial objects, such as general and regular graphs and adjacency spaces. The latter are particularly useful to represent images. Closure spaces (CS) and the sub-class of quasi-discrete closure spaces, QdCSs for short, form a convenient theoretical framework because of their generality and relative simplicity. A practical demonstration of this is the tool `VoxLogicA`, the recently developed spatial model checker [6–8] that can efficiently check SLCS properties of large images represented as *symmetric* quasi-discrete closure models—QdCMs, i.e. models with QdCSs as underlying spaces.

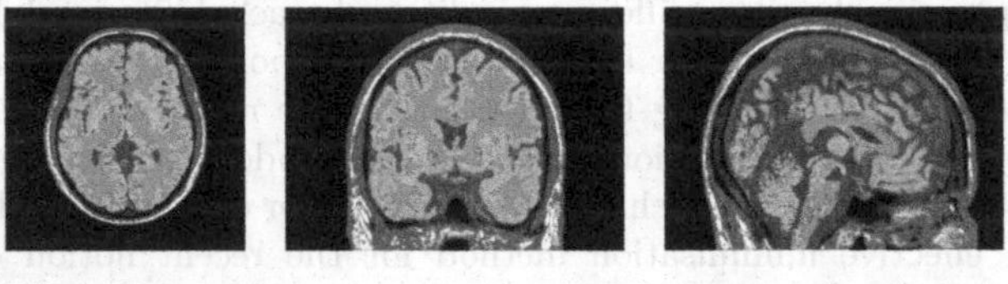

Fig. 1. Cross section of a dataset element of BrainWeb [4] pat04 MRI at slice $(x, y, z) = (129, 147, 78)$, (fLTR: axial, coronal, sagittal view): `VoxLogicA` analysis of the segmentation of white matter, shown as a green overlay on top of a red overlay representing the ground truth.

For example, the 3D MRI image of a healthy brain shown in Fig. 1 consists of circa 12 M voxels (i.e. $256 \times 256 \times 181$) requiring approximately 10 s to analyse using `VoxLogicA` on a desktop computer [7].[1] Note that `VoxLogicA` checks such logical specifications for *every* point in the model exploiting parallel execution, memoization, and state-of-the-art imaging libraries [8].

A way to increase the time efficiency of spatial model checking is to exploit suitable model minimisation algorithms based on *spatial* bisimilarity. To that purpose several spatial bisimilarities have been proposed in [13]. In particular, CoPa-bisimilarity, based on a notion of "path-compatibility" is promising. The notion of path compatibility essentially requires that two paths, in order to be compatible, have to be both composed of a (non-empty) sequence of an equal number of non-empty adjacent "zones", such that each point in one zone of one path must be related, by the bisimulation relation, to every point in the corresponding zone of the other path (see the illustration in Fig. 3b).

In [13], a logical characterisation of CoPa-bisimilarity has been given. More precisely, Infinitary Compatible Reachability Logic (ICRL) has been defined that is a modal logic with infinitary conjunction and two modalities, $\vec{\zeta}$ and $\overleftarrow{\zeta}$, expressing conditional forward and backward reachability, respectively. Given two ICRL

[1] Intel Core I9 9900K processor (with 8 cores) and 32 GB of RAM.

formulas Φ_1 and Φ_2, a point x satisfies $\vec{\zeta}\Phi_1[\Phi_2]$ if it satisfies Φ_1 or there is a path from x to a point y along the path satisfying Φ_1 and all points from x (included) to y satisfy Φ_2. Similarly for $\overleftarrow{\zeta}\Phi_1[\Phi_2]$, which is satisfied by x if it satisfies Φ_1 or there is a path *from* a point y satisfying Φ_1 to x and all points on the path *from* y to x (included) satisfy Φ_2.[2]

This paper includes two original contributions, one of more theoretical nature and another more practical one.

Theoretical Contribution. Definition and correctness proof of an encoding of finite Closure Models (CM) in Labelled Transition Systems (LTS), that preserves CoPa-bisimilarity. More precisely, two points in the input CM are CoPa-bisimilar if and only if the states they are mapped onto by the encoding are branching bisimilar [23,24,26]. Thus, given a finite CM, the encoding makes it possible to effectively compute the minimal model with respect to CoPa-bisimilarity via the composition of the encoding and a very efficient minimisation algorithm for branching bisimulation, proposed in [24,26].

Practical Contribution. For a feasibility study and validation of the approach, we developed a prototype implementation of the encoding, and assembled a toolchain involving `mCRL2` [10], `VoxLogicA` and `GraphLogicA`, a prototype spatial model checker. The latter is a variant of `VoxLogicA` handling general graphs. We applied our toolchain to a set of images at various resolutions, in order to gather insight on the potential gain in computational efficiency of spatial model checking. We observed a considerable speed-up, especially at larger resolutions, which suggests interesting directions for future research and applications.

Related Work. Qualitative reasoning about spatial entities [21] has been, and still is, a very active area of research in which the theory of topology and closure spaces play a important role. Prominent examples of that area are the region connection calculi, such as RCC8D. An embedding of the latter in the collective variant of `SLCS` was presented recently in [19]. Our work is also inspired by spatial logics (see [3] for an extensive overview), with seminal work dating back by Tarski and McKinsey in the forties of the previous century. The work on *spatial model checking* for logics with reachability originated in [18], which includes a comparison to the work of Aiello on spatial *until* operators (see e.g. [1]). In [2], Aiello envisaged practical applications of topological logics with *until* to minimisation of images. The present paper builds on and extends that vision. Bisimilarity for spatial logics with reachability is a relatively new subject. In [27], a bisimulation relation that is correct with respect to `SLCS` has been presented. Such definition has not yet been proved complete, and is aimed at characterising

[2] Note that, different from the context of classical temporal logics, in the context of space, and in particular when dealing with notions of directionality (e.g. one way roads, public area gates), it is important to be able to distinguish between the concept of "reaching" and that of "being reached". The interested reader is referred to [13] for a discussion on the issue.

the logic including the *near* operator, therefore, not quotienting up-to reachability, as done in the present paper. The papers [9] and [28] introduce bisimulation relations that characterise spatial logics with reachability in polyhedral models and in simplicial complexes, respectively. It will be interesting future work to apply the minimisation techniques we present to such relevant classes of models.

In the Computer Science literature, other kinds of spatial logics have been proposed that typically describe situations in which modal operators are interpreted *syntactically* against the structure of agents in a process calculus. We refer to [11,12] for some classical examples. Along the same lines, a recent example is given in [32], concerning model checking of security aspects in cyber-physical systems, in a spatial context based on the idea of bigraphical reactive systems introduced by Milner [29]. A bigraph consists of two graphs: A place graph, i.e. a forest defined over a set of nodes which is intended to represent entities and their locality in terms of a containment structure, and a link graph, a hypergraph composed over the same set of nodes representing arbitrary linking among those entities. The QdCS models that are the topic of the present paper, instead, address space from a topological point of view rather than as a containment structure for spatial entities.

The structure of the paper is as follows. Section 2 recalls relevant concepts and introduces notation. Section 3 recalls CoPa-bisimilarity for QdCMs. In Sect. 4 the encoding of finite QdCMs into LTSs is presented, together with the correctness results. Section 5 briefly describes a feasibility study of the application of the encoding and related toolchain to a series of examples. All detailed proofs can be found in [15].

2 Preliminaries

We first introduce some relevant concepts and notation, in particular recalling an LTS, branching bisimilarity [23,24,26], (quasi-discrete) closure spaces and closure models and paths therein.

Given a set X, $\mathcal{P}(X)$ denotes the powerset of X. For a function $f : X \to Y$, $A \subseteq X$ and $B \subseteq Y$, we let $f(A)$ and $f^{-1}(B)$ be defined as $\{f(a) \,|\, a \in A\}$ and $\{a \,|\, f(a) \in B\}$, respectively. For binary relation $R \subseteq X \times X$, we let R^{-1} denote the *converse* of R and $R^{=}$ denote the *reflexive* closure of R. The set of natural numbers is denoted by $\mathbb{N}$. For $n, m \in \mathbb{N}$ we often use the interval notation $[m, n]$ denoting the set $\{\iota \in \mathbb{N} \,|\, m \leq \iota \leq n\}$, $[m, n)$ denoting the set $\{\iota \in \mathbb{N} \,|\, m \leq \iota < n\}$, and similarly for $(m, n]$ and (m, n).

In the sequel, branching bisimilarity [23,24,26] of states of LTSs plays a central role. Below we recall the relevant definitions.

Definition 1 (Labelled Transition System - LTS). *A* Labelled Transition System, *LTS for short, is a tuple* $(S, \mathtt{Act}, \rightarrow)$ *where* S *and* $\mathtt{Act}$ *are non-empty sets of* states, *and* action labels *respectively and relation* $\rightarrow \subseteq S \times \mathtt{Act} \times S$ *is the* transition relation.

As usual, we distinguish an action $\tau \in \texttt{Act}$ that models a "silent move" of the LTS. Moreover, we call the elements of $\rightarrow$ *transitions*, and we write $s \xrightarrow{\alpha} s'$ whenever $(s, \alpha, s') \in \rightarrow$. A (non-empty, finite) *trace* in the LTS is a sequence $s_0\alpha_1 s_1 \ldots s_{n-1}\alpha_n s_n$ of states and actions such that $n > 0$ and $s_{i-1} \xrightarrow{\alpha_i} s_i$ for $i = 1, \ldots, n$. For such traces, we use the notation $s_0 \xrightarrow{\alpha_1} s_1 \cdots s_{n-1} \xrightarrow{\alpha_n} s_n$. In such a situation, if $s = s_0$, $w = \alpha_1 \cdots \alpha_n$, and $s' = s_n$, we have occassion to write $s \xrightarrow{w} s'$, as in the definition of branching bisimilarity which follows.

Definition 2 (Branching bisimilarity – $\leftrightarrows_b$). *Given an LTS $\mathcal{S} = (S, \texttt{Act}, \rightarrow)$, a symmetric relation $B \subseteq S \times S$ is a* branching bisimulation for $\mathcal{S}$ *iff, for $s, t, s' \in S$ and $\alpha \in \texttt{Act}$, whenever $s\,B\,t$ and $s \xrightarrow{\alpha} s'$, it holds that: (i) $s'\,B\,t$ and $\alpha = \tau$, or (ii) $s\,B\,\bar{t}$, $s'\,B\,t'$ and $t \xrightarrow{\tau^*} \bar{t}$, $\bar{t} \xrightarrow{\alpha} t'$ for some $\bar{t}, t' \in S$.*

Two states $s, t \in S$ are called branching bisimilar *in $\mathcal{S}$ if $s\,B\,t$ for some branching bisimulation B for $\mathcal{S}$. Notation, $s \leftrightarrows_b^{\mathcal{S}} t$.*

From now on, for readability, we omit the superscript $\mathcal{S}$ in $\leftrightarrows_b^{\mathcal{S}}$, when this does not cause confusion. Our framework for modelling space is based on the notion of *Čech closure space* [33], CS for short, that provides a convenient common framework for the study of several different kinds of spatial models, including models of both discrete and continuous space [31]. We briefly recall definitions and results on CSs, that are relevant for this paper — most of which are borrowed from [22] (see also [13,18]).

Definition 3 (Closure Space – CS). *A* closure space *is a pair $(X, \mathcal{C})$ where X is a set (of* points*) and $\mathcal{C} : \mathcal{P}(X) \rightarrow \mathcal{P}(X)$ is the* closure operator, *i.e. a function satisfying the following axioms: (i) $\mathcal{C}(\emptyset) = \emptyset$; (ii) $A \subseteq \mathcal{C}(A)$ for all $A \subseteq X$; and (iii) $\mathcal{C}(A_1 \cup A_2) = \mathcal{C}(A_1) \cup \mathcal{C}(A_2)$ for all $A_1, A_2 \subseteq X$.*

It is worth pointing out that CSs are a generalisation of topological spaces. In fact, the latter coincide with CSs that satisfy the *idempotence* axiom, i.e. $\mathcal{C}(\mathcal{C}(A)) = \mathcal{C}(A)$ for all $A \subseteq X$.

Definition 4 (Quasi-discrete CS – QdCS). *A* quasi-discrete closure space *is a CS $(X, \mathcal{C})$ such that for each $A \subseteq X$ it holds that $\mathcal{C}(A) = \bigcup_{x \in A} \mathcal{C}(\{x\})$.*

Given a relation $R \subseteq X \times X$, define the function $\mathcal{C}_R : \mathcal{P}(X) \rightarrow \mathcal{P}(X)$ as follows: for all $A \subseteq X$, $\mathcal{C}_R(A) = A \cup \{x \in X \mid \exists a \in A \text{ s.t. } a\,R\,x\}$. It is easy to see that, for any R, $\mathcal{C}_R$ satisfies all the axioms of Definition 3 and so $(X, \mathcal{C}_R)$ is a CS. The following theorem is a standard result in the theory of CSs [22].

Theorem 1. *A CS $(X, \mathcal{C})$ is quasi-discrete if and only if there is a relation $R \subseteq X \times X$ such that $\mathcal{C} = \mathcal{C}_R$.*

The above theorem implies that graphs coincide with QdCSs. We prefer to treat graphs as QdCSs since in this way we can formulate key definitions at the level of closure spaces leading to a uniform treatment for graphs and other kinds of models for space (e.g. topological spaces) [31]. Furthermore, if X is finite, any closure space $(X, \mathcal{C})$ is quasi-discrete. In the sequel, we consider only *finite* CSs and often refrain from explicitly writing the subscript R in $\mathcal{C}_R$, when this does not cause confusion. Finally, we say that $(X, \mathcal{C}_R)$ is *symmetric* iff R is a symmetric relation. An example of the result of applying the closure operator $\mathcal{C}$ induced by a relation R to a set A is shown in Fig. 2.

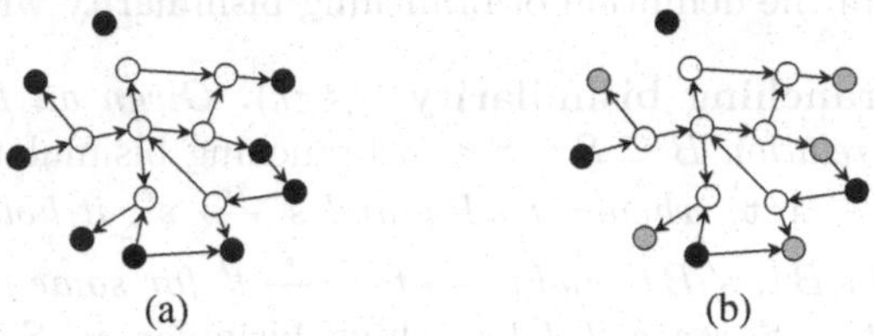

Fig. 2. a: a finite QdCS $(X, \mathcal{C})$; the arrows represent the relation underlying $\mathcal{C}$. The points of the set $A \subseteq X$ are shown in white, remaining points are shown in black. b: additional points in $\mathcal{C}(A)$ are shown in grey.

In the context of the present paper, *paths* over CSs play an important role. Following the tradition in topology, in the theory of CSs paths are defined as continuous functions from an appropriate index space to the CS at hand. For finite CSs, it is sufficient to consider bounded, finite, paths.

Definition 5 (Finite path). *A finite path in a finite CS $(X, \mathcal{C})$ is a continuous function $\pi : [0, \ell] \rightarrow X$, for some $\ell \in \mathbb{N}$, such that $\pi(i+1) \in \mathcal{C}(\{\pi(i)\})$ for $i = 0, \dots, \ell - 1$. We call ℓ the* length *of π and we denote it by* $\texttt{len}(\pi)$.

For $x \in X$, $\texttt{FPaths}^{\texttt{F}}(x)$ denotes the set of all finite paths π in $(X, \mathcal{C})$ such that $\pi(0) = x$ (paths From x). Similarly, $\texttt{FPaths}^{\texttt{T}}(x)$ denotes the set of all finite paths π in $(X, \mathcal{C})$ such that $\pi(\texttt{len}(\pi)) = x$ (paths To x). In the sequel, whenever we write "path" we mean "finite path".

Remark 1. It is worth pointing out that the notion of path in a QdCS is similar to that of a path in a graph or of a trace in an LTS, but it is *not* the same. In particular, due to axiom (ii) of closure operator $\mathcal{C}$ and the requirement $\pi(i+1) \in \mathcal{C}(\pi(i))$, paths in CSs allow *stuttering*; in other words, for QdCS $(X, \mathcal{C})$, $x \in X$, and path π, it may happen that $\pi(i) = \pi(i+1) = x$, for $i < \pi(\texttt{len}(\pi))$ *even when* (x, x) is *not* an element of the relation $R \subseteq X \times X$ underlying $\mathcal{C}$. This is different for a path $\dots n_1 n_2 \dots$ in a graph (N, E), where in order for nodes n_1 and n_2 in N to be adjacent, it is required that (n_1, n_2) is an element of the edge relation E. A similar issue arises when comparing paths in QdCSs with traces in LTSs. In fact, for LTS $(S, \texttt{Act}, \rightarrow)$, two states s_1 and s_2 can be adjacent in a trace $\cdots s_1 \xrightarrow{\alpha} s_2 \cdots$ *only* if $(s_1, \alpha, s_2) \in \rightarrow$, and this holds also if $s_2 = s_1$.

We assume a set $\texttt{AP}$ of *atomic proposition letters* is given and introduce the notion of closure *model* (CM for short).

Definition 6 (Closure model – CM). *A closure model is a tuple* $\mathcal{M} = (X, \mathcal{C}, \mathcal{V})$, *with* $(X, \mathcal{C})$ *a CS, and* $\mathcal{V} : \mathtt{AP} \to \mathcal{P}(X)$ *the* valuation function, *assigning to each* $p \in \mathtt{AP}$ *the set of points where* p *holds.*

All definitions for CSs also apply to CMs; thus, a *quasi-discrete closure model* (QdCM for short) is a CM $\mathcal{M} = (X, \mathcal{C}, \mathcal{V})$ where $(X, \mathcal{C})$ is a QdCS. For a closure model $\mathcal{M} = (X, \mathcal{C}, \mathcal{V})$ we often write $x \in \mathcal{M}$ when $x \in X$. Similarly, we speak of paths in $\mathcal{M}$ meaning paths in $(X, \mathcal{C})$.

In the sequel, for a logic $\mathcal{L}$, a formula $\Phi \in \mathcal{L}$, and a model $\mathcal{M} = (X, \mathcal{C}, \mathcal{V})$ we let $[\![\Phi]\!]^{\mathcal{M}}_{\mathcal{L}}$ denote the set $\{x \in X \mid \mathcal{M}, x \models_{\mathcal{L}} \Phi\}$ of all the points in $\mathcal{M}$ that satisfy Φ, where $\models_{\mathcal{L}}$ is the satisfaction relation for $\mathcal{L}$. For the sake of readability, we refrain from writing the subscript $\mathcal{L}$ when this does not cause confusion.

3 CoPa-Bisimilarity for QdCM

In [13] several notions of spatial bisimilarity for closure models have been investigated. In particular, CM-bisimilarity, and its refinement for QdCMs CMC-bisimilarity, are a fundamental starting point for the study of spatial bisimilarity due to their strong links to topo-bisimilarity. On the other hand, they are rather fine-grained relations for reasoning about general properties of space, since they are based directly on the closure operator.[3] For instance, with reference to the model of Fig. 3a, where all black points satisfy only atomic proposition b while the grey ones satisfy only g, the point at the center of the model is *not* CMC-bisimilar to any other black point. This is because CMC-bisimilarity is based on the fact that points reachable "in one step"—i.e. contained in the closure—are taken into consideration. This, in turn, gives bisimilarity a sort of "counting" power, that goes against the idea that, for instance, all black points in the model could be considered spatially equivalent. In fact, they are all black and all can reach black or grey points. Furthermore, they could be considered equivalent to the black point of a smaller model consisting of just one black and one grey point mutually connected—that would, in fact, be a minimal representation of the closure model.

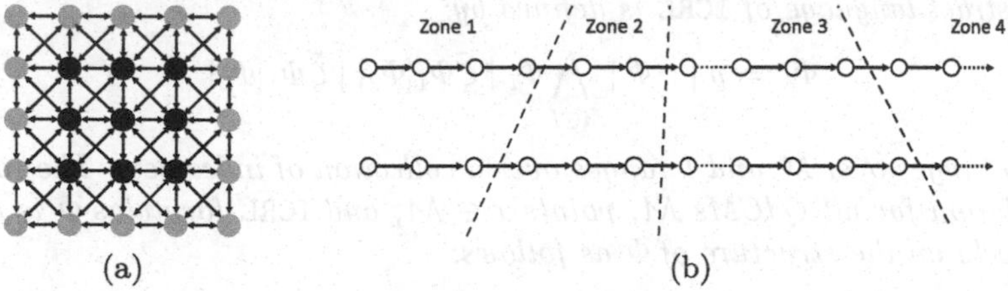

Fig. 3. A model (a); zones in paths (b).

In order to relax "counting" capability of bisimilarity as mentioned, a weaker notion of bisimulation has been introduced in [13] that is based on paths,

[3] Or its dual operator called 'interior'.

instead of single closure steps, and on a notion of "compatibility" between relevant paths that essentially requires each of them be composed of a non-empty sequence of non-empty, adjacent "zones". More precisely, both paths under consideration in a transfer condition should share the same structure, as follows (see Fig. 3b):

- both paths are composed by a sequence of (non-empty) "zones";
- the number of zones should be the same in both paths, *but*
- the length of "corresponding" zones can be different, *as well as* the length of the two paths;
- *each* point in one zone of a path should be related by the bisimulation to *every* point in the corresponding zone of the other path.

This notion of compatibility gives rise to *Compatible Path bisimulation*, CoPa-bisimulation, recalled below for QdCMs.

Definition 7 (CoPa-bisimilarity - $\rightleftharpoons^{\mathcal{M}}_{\mathtt{CoPa}}$). *Given QdCS $\mathcal{M} = (X, \mathcal{C}, \mathcal{V})$, a symmetric relation $B \subseteq X \times X$ is a CoPa-*bisimulation for $\mathcal{M}$ *if, whenever $x_1 \, B \, x_2$, the following holds:*

1. *for all $p \in \mathtt{AP}$ we have $x_1 \in \mathcal{V}(p)$ if and only if $x_2 \in \mathcal{V}(p)$;*
2. *for all $\pi_1 \in \mathtt{FPaths}^{\mathtt{F}}(x_1)$ such that $\pi_1(i_1) \, B \, x_2$ for all $i_1 \in [0, \mathtt{len}(\pi_1))$ there is $\pi_2 \in \mathtt{FPaths}^{\mathtt{F}}(x_2)$ such that the following holds: $x_1 \, B \, \pi_2(i_2)$ for all $i_2 \in [0, \mathtt{len}(\pi_2))$, and $\pi_1(\mathtt{len}(\pi_1)) \, B \, \pi_2(\mathtt{len}(\pi_2))$;*
3. *for all $\pi_1 \in \mathtt{FPaths}^{\mathtt{T}}(x_1)$ such that $\pi_1(i_1) \, B \, x_2$ for all $i_1 \in (0, \mathtt{len}(\pi_1)]$ there is $\pi_2 \in \mathtt{FPaths}^{\mathtt{T}}(x_2)$ such that the following holds: $x_1 \, B \, \pi_2(i_2)$ for all $i_2 \in (0, \mathtt{len}(\pi_2)]$, and $\pi_1(0) \, B \, \pi_2(0)$.*

Two points $x_1, x_2 \in X$ are called CoPa-bisimilar *in $\mathcal{M}$ if $x_1 \, B \, x_2$ for some CoPa-bisimulation B for $\mathcal{M}$. Notation, $x_1 \rightleftharpoons^{\mathcal{M}}_{\mathtt{CoPa}} x_2$.*

It is easy to see that $\rightleftharpoons_{\mathtt{CMC}}$ is strictly stronger than $\rightleftharpoons_{\mathtt{CoPa}}$; the interested reader is referred to [13] for details.

We recall the definition of the *Infinitary Compatible Reachability Logic* (ICRL) proposed in [13] that provides a logical characterisation of CoPa-bisimilarity.

Definition 8 (Infinitary Compatible Reachability Logic - ICRL). *The abstract language of* ICRL *is defined by:*

$$\Phi ::= p \mid \neg \Phi \mid \bigwedge_{i \in I} \Phi_i \mid \vec{\zeta} \, \Phi_1[\Phi_2] \mid \overleftarrow{\zeta} \, \Phi_1[\Phi_2]$$

where p ranges over AP *and I ranges over a collection of index sets. The satisfaction relation for all QdCMs $\mathcal{M}$, points $x \in \mathcal{M}$, and* ICRL *formulas Φ is defined recursively on the structure of Φ as follows:*

$$\begin{array}{lcl}
\mathcal{M}, x \models_{\mathtt{ICRL}} p & \Leftrightarrow & x \in \mathcal{V}(p) \\
\mathcal{M}, x \models_{\mathtt{ICRL}} \neg \Phi & \Leftrightarrow & \mathcal{M}, x \models_{\mathtt{ICRL}} \Phi \textit{ does not hold} \\
\mathcal{M}, x \models_{\mathtt{ICRL}} \bigwedge_{i \in I} \Phi_i & \Leftrightarrow & \mathcal{M}, x \models_{\mathtt{IRL}} \Phi_i \textit{ for all } i \in I \\
\mathcal{M}, x \models_{\mathtt{ICRL}} \vec{\zeta} \, \Phi_1[\Phi_2] & \Leftrightarrow & \textit{path } \pi \textit{ and index } \ell \textit{ exist such that } \pi(0) = x, \\
& & \mathcal{M}, \pi(\ell) \models_{\mathtt{ICRL}} \Phi_1, \textit{ and } \mathcal{M}, \pi(j) \models_{\mathtt{ICRL}} \Phi_2 \textit{ for } j \in [0, \ell) \\
\mathcal{M}, x \models_{\mathtt{ICRL}} \overleftarrow{\zeta} \, \Phi_1[\Phi_2] & \Leftrightarrow & \textit{path } \pi \textit{ and index } \ell \textit{ exist such that } \pi(\ell) = x, \\
& & \mathcal{M}, \pi(0) \models_{\mathtt{ICRL}} \Phi_1, \textit{ and } \mathcal{M}, \pi(j) \models_{\mathtt{ICRL}} \Phi_2 \textit{ for } j \in (0, \ell].
\end{array}$$

Logical equivalence with respect to ICRL is defined as expected.

Definition 9 (ICRL-equivalence - $\simeq^{\mathcal{M}}_{\mathtt{ICRL}}$). *For CM $\mathcal{M} = (X, \mathcal{C}, \mathcal{V})$, the equivalence relation $\simeq^{\mathcal{M}}_{\mathtt{ICRL}} \subseteq X \times X$ is defined as: $x_1 \simeq^{\mathcal{M}}_{\mathtt{ICRL}} x_2$ if and only if for all* ICRL *formulas Φ, it holds that $\mathcal{M}, x_1 \models_{\mathtt{ICRL}} \Phi$ if and only if $\mathcal{M}, x_2 \models_{\mathtt{ICRL}} \Phi$.*

The following result establishes the relationship between CoPa-bisimilarity and ICRL-equivalence [13].

Theorem 2. *For every QdCM $\mathcal{M}$ it holds that* ICRL*-equivalence $\simeq^{\mathcal{M}}_{\mathtt{ICRL}}$ coincides with CoPa-bisimilarity $\rightleftharpoons^{\mathcal{M}}_{\mathtt{CoPa}}$.*

In the remainder of the paper, since we are concerned with *finite* models only, we confine to the finitary fragment of ICRL, i.e. the fraction where I ranges over a collection of finite index sets. Furthermore, we will refrain from writing the superscript $\mathcal{M}$ in $\rightleftharpoons^{\mathcal{M}}_{\mathtt{CoPa}}$ and $\simeq^{\mathcal{M}}_{\mathtt{ICRL}}$, when this will not cause confusion.

In this work, given a QdCM $\mathcal{M} = (X, \mathcal{C}_R, \mathcal{V})$, we aim at running the model checking algorithm of [18] on the quotient of X with respect to $\simeq_{\mathtt{ICRL}}$. The remainder of this paper is devoted to explain how to compute such set. It is a natural question at this point, whether the minimal model exists in the class of QdCMs. In other words, one needs to show that the set of equivalence classes of $\simeq_{\mathtt{ICRL}}$ *can* be endowed with a quasi-discrete closure operator, in such a way that logical truth is preserved and reflected. We do so in Proposition 1 below.

Proposition 1. *Given a QdCM $\mathcal{M} = (X, \mathcal{C}_R, \mathcal{V})$, let $X_{\min}$ be the set of equivalence classes of X modulo $\simeq_{\mathtt{ICRL}}$. Let R' be the relation $\{(x, y) \in X \times X \mid y \in \mathcal{C}_R(\{x\})\}$. Let $R_{\min}$ be the relation $\{(\alpha, \beta) \in X_{\min} \times X_{\min} \mid \exists x \in \alpha. \exists y \in \beta. (x, y) \in R'\}$. For each atomic proposition p, let $\mathcal{V}_{\min}(p) = \{\alpha \in X_{\min} \mid \exists x \in \alpha. x \in \mathcal{V}(p)\}$. Let $\mathcal{M}_{\min} = (X_{\min}, \mathcal{C}_{R_{min}}, \mathcal{V}_{\min})$. Then for each x in X and for each formula Φ, we have $\mathcal{M}, x \models \Phi \iff \mathcal{M}_{\min}, [x] \models \Phi$, where $[x]$ is the equivalence class of x modulo $\simeq_{\mathtt{ICRL}}$.*

4 From QdCMs to Labelled Transition Systems

In this section we show how a finite QdCM can be encoded as an LTS in such a way that the images of points that are CoPa-bisimilar in the QdCM are mapped to branching bisimilar states in the LTS and viceversa. A simplification of the encoding is possible for the special case of QdCMs where the relation underlying the closure operator is symmetric.

4.1 General Encoding for Finite CMs

The encoding takes a finite QdCM as input and produces an LTS as output. To illustrate the various steps in the encoding, we use the QdCM in Fig. 4 and its LTS encoding in Fig. 5 as a running example. Let $\mathcal{M} = (X, \mathcal{C}, \mathcal{V})$ be a QdCM and R the binary relation on X that underlies the closure operator $\mathcal{C}$. The output

$\mathtt{LTS}(\mathcal{M}) = (S, \mathtt{Act}, \rightarrow)$ of the encoding of $\mathcal{M}$ is an LTS where we can identify two parts, the *direct* part and the *converse* part. Roughly speaking, the direct part corresponds to R, whereas the converse part corresponds to the converse of R, i.e. R^{-1}. Both parts consist of the same number of states as the number of points in X.

More specifically, the set of states of the direct part is the set $\{\vec{x} \mid x \in X\} \subset S$, i.e. for each point in X there is a state in S in $\mathtt{LTS}(\mathcal{M})$. We decorate it with an arrow from left to right to emphasise that it belongs to the direct part. Moreover, for all $x, x' \in X$, whenever $x' \in \mathcal{C}(\{x\})$ — i.e. $x\, R^{=}\, x'$ — and $x' \neq x$, there is a transition from $\vec{x}$ to $\vec{x}\,'$ in $\mathtt{LTS}(\mathcal{M})$. In particular, if x and x' satisfy the *same* set of atomic proposition letters, i.e. $\mathcal{V}^{-1}(\{x\}) = \mathcal{V}^{-1}(\{x'\})$, then an internal transition $\vec{x} \xrightarrow{\tau} \vec{x}\,'$, is generated. If, instead, there is a change in the set of atomic proposition letters satisfied by x' with respect to those satisfied by x, then the transition $\vec{x} \xrightarrow{\mathtt{ch}} \vec{x}\,'$ is generated, where $\mathtt{ch}$ signals such a change. In addition, for each $x \in X$, the actual proposition letters p satisfied by x are encoded as self-loops $\vec{x} \xrightarrow{p} \vec{x}$.

The set of states of the converse part is the set $\{\overleftarrow{x} \mid x \in X\} \subset S$ and the right-to-left arrows witness it. Moreover, for all $x, x' \in X$, whenever $x \in \mathcal{C}(\{x'\})$ — i.e. $x\,(R^{=})^{-1}\, x'$ — and $x' \neq x$, there is a transition from $\overleftarrow{x}\,'$ to $\overleftarrow{x}$ in $\mathtt{LTS}(\mathcal{M})$. For what concerns the labels of such transitions in the converse part the same rules apply as those for the direct part. The encoding of satisfaction of atomic propositions by self-loops does not need to be repeated in the converse part.

Finally, from each state $\vec{x}$ in the direct part there is a transition, labelled by $\mathtt{cv}$, leading to the corresponding state $\overleftarrow{x}$ in the converse part, i.e. $\vec{x} \xrightarrow{\mathtt{cv}} \overleftarrow{x}$ and, similarly, from each state $\overleftarrow{x}$ in the converse part there is a transition, labelled by $\mathtt{dr}$, leading to the corresponding state $\vec{x}$ in the direct part, i.e. $\overleftarrow{x} \xrightarrow{\mathtt{dr}} \vec{x}$. The translation is formalised in Definition 10.

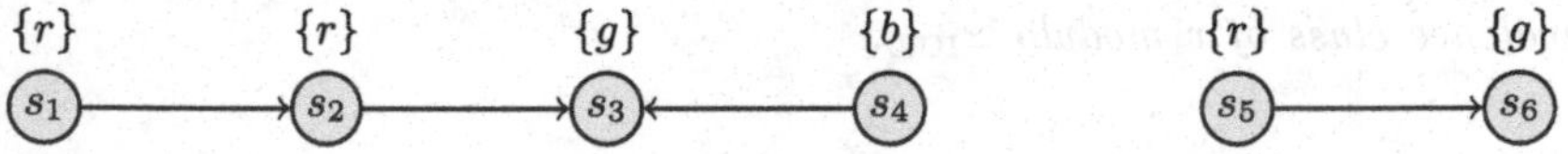

Fig. 4. A finite QdCM

Definition 10 (Encoding Finite CMs into LTSs). *Let* $\mathcal{M} = (X, \mathcal{C}, \mathcal{V})$ *be a finite CM. Define labelled transition system* $\mathtt{LTS}(\mathcal{M})$ *as follows.* $\mathtt{LTS}(\mathcal{M}) = (S, \mathtt{Act}, \rightarrow)$ *where: (i)* $S = \{\vec{s} \mid s \in X\} \cup \{\overleftarrow{s} \mid s \in X\}$*; (ii)* $\mathtt{Act} = \mathtt{AP} \cup \{\tau, \mathtt{dr}, \mathtt{cv}, \mathtt{ch}\}$*, where* $\{\tau, \mathtt{dr}, \mathtt{cv}, \mathtt{ch}\} \cap \mathtt{AP} = \emptyset$*; (iii) the transition relation* $\rightarrow$ *contains exactly the following transitions:*

$$
\begin{array}{ll}
\vec{s} \xrightarrow{p} \vec{s} & \textit{for all } p \in \mathtt{AP} \textit{ and } s \in \mathcal{V}(p) \\
\vec{s} \xrightarrow{\mathtt{cv}} \overleftarrow{s} & \textit{for all } s \in X \\
\overleftarrow{s} \xrightarrow{\mathtt{dr}} \vec{s} & \textit{for all } s \in X \\
\vec{s} \xrightarrow{\tau} \vec{s}\,', \overleftarrow{s}\,' \xrightarrow{\tau} \overleftarrow{s} & \textit{if } s' \in \mathcal{C}(\{s\}) \setminus \{s\} \textit{ and } \mathcal{V}^{-1}(\{s\}) = \mathcal{V}^{-1}(\{s'\}) \\
\vec{s} \xrightarrow{\mathtt{ch}} \vec{s}\,', \overleftarrow{s}\,' \xrightarrow{\mathtt{ch}} \overleftarrow{s} & \textit{if } s' \in \mathcal{C}(\{s\}) \setminus \{s\} \textit{ and } \mathcal{V}^{-1}(\{s\}) \neq \mathcal{V}^{-1}(\{s'\}).
\end{array}
$$

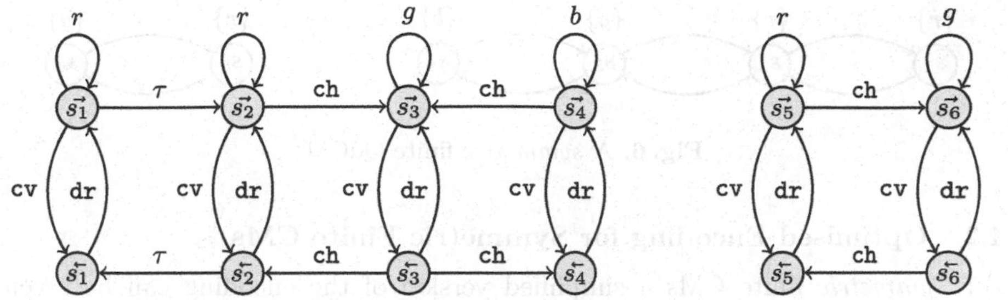

Fig. 5. LTS resulting from the application of the encoding defined in Definition 10 to the QdCM of Fig. 4.

The following lemma states an interesting property of the output of the encoding. Such a property turns out to be useful for the proof of the main result, asserting correctness of the encoding with respect to CoPa-bisimilarity.

Lemma 1. *Let $\mathcal{M} = (X, \mathcal{C}, \mathcal{V})$ be a finite CM. It holds that*

$$\vec{s} \leftrightarrows_b \vec{t} \text{ if and only if } \overleftarrow{s} \leftrightarrows_b \overleftarrow{t} \text{ for all } s, t \in X.$$

The proof of Lemma 1 builds on the following technical result.

Lemma 2. *Let $\mathcal{M} = (X, \mathcal{C}, \mathcal{V})$ be a finite CM. It holds that*

$$\text{if } \vec{s} \xrightarrow{\tau} \vec{s}\,' \text{ and } \vec{s} \leftrightarrows_b \vec{s}\,', \text{ then } \overleftarrow{s}\,' \xrightarrow{\tau} \overleftarrow{s} \text{ and } \overleftarrow{s} \leftrightarrows_b \overleftarrow{s}\,'.$$

The proof of Lemma 2 goes by induction on the *depth* of a direct state. In general, for an LTS, silent transitions $\xrightarrow{\tau^*}$ split the state space in τ-strongly connected components (τ-SCCs): states s and s' are in the same τ-SCC if both $s \xrightarrow{\tau^*} s'$ and $s' \xrightarrow{\tau^*} s$. Moreover, in the case of a finite LTS, τ-SCCs are well-ordered; a τ-SCC C is less than τ-SCC C' if $s' \xrightarrow{\tau^*} s$ for some $s' \in C'$, $s \in C$, but not the other way around. The depth of a state is then defined as the number of τ-SCCs a path of τ-transitions passes through to reach a so-called bottom τ-SCC.

Below we formulate the main theorem, showing that two points s and t in the QdCM are CoPa-bisimilar if and only if the corresponding states $\vec{s}$ and $\vec{t}$ are branching bisimilar, where the LTS is obtained by applying the encoding defined in Definition 10.

Theorem 3. *Let $\mathcal{M} = (X, \mathcal{C}, \mathcal{V})$ be a finite CM. Then, for all $s, t \in X$ we have*

$$s \rightleftharpoons_{\texttt{CoPa}} t \text{ if and only if } \vec{s} \leftrightarrows_b \vec{t}.$$

For a proof from left to right one defines a CoPa-bisimulation on $\mathcal{M}$ obtained from branching bisimulation in $\texttt{LTS}(\mathcal{M})$: put $s\,B\,t$ if $\vec{s} \leftrightarrows_b \vec{t}$ for points $s, t \in X$. Lemma 2 is used to reduce the proof of obligation for requirement 3 of Definition 7 to the case of its requirement 2. A proof right to left is more direct; a branching bisimulation R defined by having $\vec{s}\,R\,\vec{t}$ and $\overleftarrow{s}\,R\,\overleftarrow{t}$ in case $s \rightleftharpoons_{\texttt{CoPa}} t$.

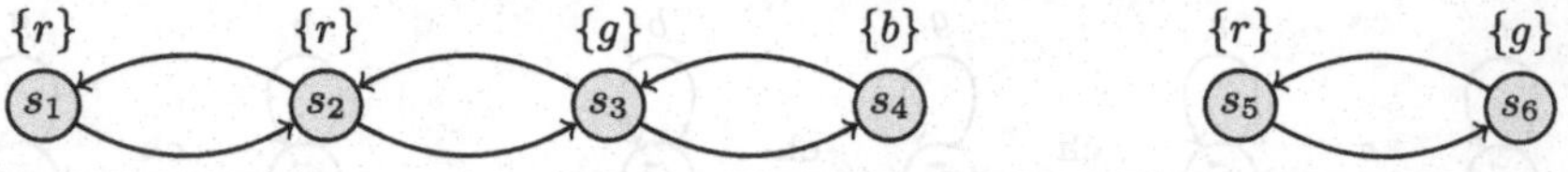

Fig. 6. A *symmetric* finite QdCM

4.2 Optimised Encoding for Symmetric Finite CMs

For *symmetric* finite CMs a simplified version of the encoding can be given. Symmetric QdCMs naturally emerge as representations of digital images where points are related via an adjacency relation as discussed in Sect. 1.

Definition 11 (Encoding Symmetric Finite CMs into LTSs). *Let* $\mathcal{M} = (X, \mathcal{C}, \mathcal{V})$ *be a symmetric finite CM. Define* $\mathtt{LTS}_{\mathrm{sym}}(\mathcal{M}) = (S, \mathtt{Act}, \rightarrow)$ *where: (i)* $S = \{\overleftrightarrow{s} \mid s \in X\}$*; (ii)* $\mathtt{Act} = \mathtt{AP} \cup \{\tau, \mathtt{ch}\}$*; (iii) the transition relation* $\rightarrow$ *contains exactly the following transitions:*

$$\overleftrightarrow{s} \xrightarrow{p} \overleftrightarrow{s} \text{ for all } p \in \mathtt{AP} \text{ and } s \in \mathcal{V}(p)$$
$$\overleftrightarrow{s} \xrightarrow{\tau} \overleftrightarrow{s}' \text{ if } s' \in \mathcal{C}(\{s\}) \setminus \{s\} \text{ and } \mathcal{V}^{-1}(\{s\}) = \mathcal{V}^{-1}(\{s'\})$$
$$\overleftrightarrow{s} \xrightarrow{\mathtt{ch}} \overleftrightarrow{s}' \text{ if } s' \in \mathcal{C}(\{s\}) \text{ and } \mathcal{V}^{-1}(\{s\}) \neq \mathcal{V}^{-1}(\{s'\}).$$

As an example, consider the symmetric finite QdCM of Fig. 6 and its LTS encoding in Fig. 7, obtained with the encoding given in Definition 11. It is easy to see that a symmetric QdCM with n nodes and t transitions leads to an LTS with n nodes and $t + n$ transitions.

Theorem 4. *Let* $\mathcal{M} = (X, \mathcal{C}, \mathcal{V})$ *be a symmetric finite CM. Then, for all* $s, t \in X$ *we have:* $s \rightleftharpoons_{\mathtt{CoPa}} t$ *if and only if* $\overleftrightarrow{s} \leftrightarroweq_b \overleftrightarrow{t}$.

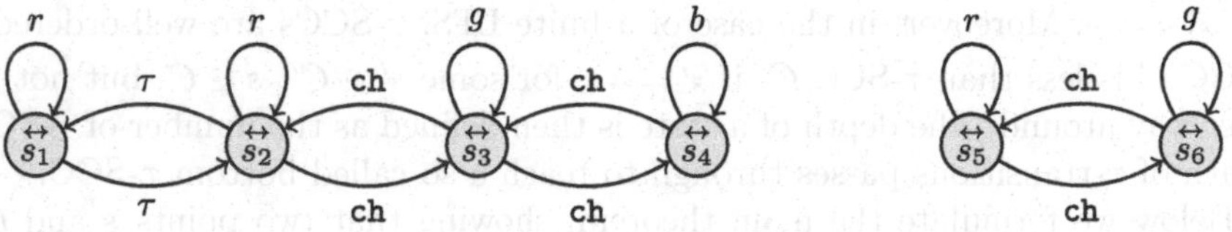

Fig. 7. LTS resulting from the application of the encoding in Definition 11 to the symmetric QdCM of Fig. 6.

The 2D maze in Fig. 9a, part of our feasibility study, exemplifies the significance of CoPa-minimization on images. Each node of the graph represents an area of interest in the image: exit (green), walls (black), walking areas (white) and starting points (blue). The three white nodes, as an example, represent three different kinds of white walking areas: the ones from which neither an exit nor a starting point can be reached (without crossing walls), the ones from which a starting point can be reached (but not the exit), and the ones from which a starting point and the exit can be reached.

5 Feasibility Study

In this section we provide an experimental validation of the theory presented in the previous sections. In particular, a prototype implementation of the encoding of Sect. 4 is introduced and applied to two representative benchmark examples.

5.1 Implementation

The encoding of Sect. 4.1 has been implemented as Free and Open Source Software, derived from the sources of the spatial model checker `GraphLogicA`, handling general finite QdCMs, in order to reuse its model loading functionality.

Procedure. The tool converts a spatial model — either an image (e.g. png), or a general graph written in a simple json format — to an LTS in the aut file format, which is one of the LTS formats accepted by the `mCRL2` tool suite [10]. For images, the optimised encoding described in Sect. 4.2 is used. The resulting LTS is minimised using the efficient branching bisimulation minimisation algorithm [24] implemented in `mCRL2`. This last step results in a minimised LTS in aut format which can be used for spatial model checking with `GraphLogicA`, after a simple conversion back to the json format. For measuring the model checking speed-up, in our toolchain, we use `GraphLogicA` for checking the minimal model, and `VoxLogicA` to check the full model[4].

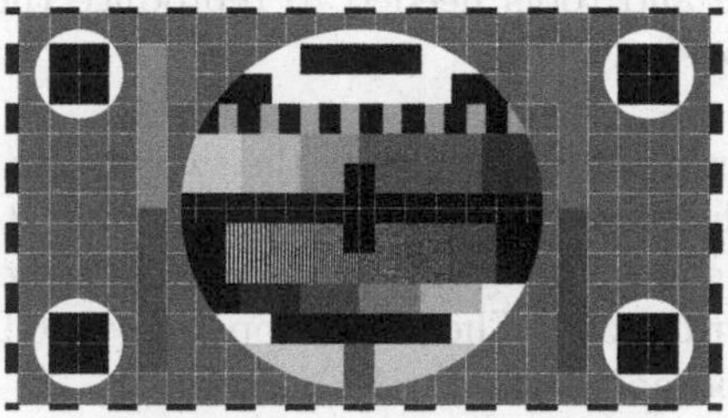

Fig. 8. Monoscope test pattern Philips PM5544

5.2 Experimental Setup

The procedure described above was used to produce the minimised LTSs shown in Fig. 9b, of the image of a maze of Fig. 9a, and to minimise the classical *Philips 5544* monoscope test pattern, shown in Fig. 8. Our tests have been run on a workstation equipped with an Intel Core™ i9 9900 K and 32 gb of RAM.

[4] Note that `VoxLogicA` is inherently much faster than `GraphLogicA` as it is specialised for images, exploiting state-of-the-art imaging libraries and automatic parallelisation. This poses a further challenge to the speed-up via minimisation and is the reason why we use `VoxLogicA` instead of `GraphLogicA` for the full model.

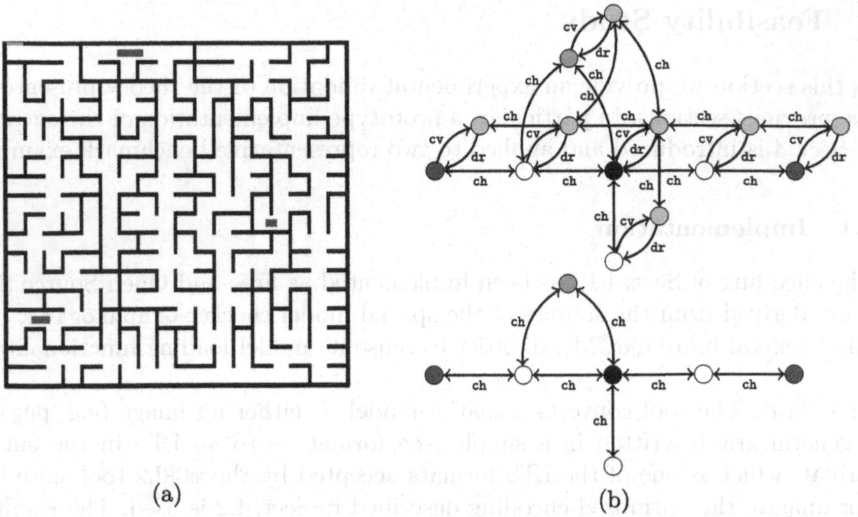

Fig. 9. An image of a 2D maze (9a), its minimal LTS using the general encoding of Definition 10 (9b - top), and that obtained using the optimised encoding of Definition 11 (9b - bottom). For readability, self-loops labelled by atomic propositions are not shown; the corresponding states are shown in the colour represented by the omitted label; symmetric transition pairs are drawn as doubly-headed arrows.

Full data, source code and tools needed to reproduce the experiments can be found in a Zenodo repository [16].

Test Images. For experimental evaluation, the two images have been rescaled at various resolutions. The "name" column of Table 1 indicates the vertical resolution of each image. The maze image is square, therefore the horizontal resolution coincides with the vertical one. The monoscope has a 16:9 ratio, thus, e.g., the horizontal resolution of mono-1080 is 1920 pixels.

Logical Specifications. For the maze image, the model checking specification consists of the computation of three reachability-based formulas, identifying: 1) the white points from which both a blue point and a green point can be reached (roughly, the white paths connecting blue points to the exit), via the formula $\vec{\zeta}\, blue[white] \wedge \vec{\zeta}\, green[white]$; 2) the blue points from which there is no white path to the exit (via a similar formula); 3) the blue points from which, instead, an exit can be reached (again, using reachability). For the monoscope pattern, the logical specification is more artificial, as it has been designed to be more demanding in terms of computation time (both model checkers have linear complexity in the number of sub-formulas). A single property Φ has been designed, characterising the points from which very specific paths start, crossing a number of different colours in a specific order, using 16 nested reachability constraints, in the shape $\vec{\zeta}'(\vec{\zeta}'(\vec{\zeta}'(\ldots)[green])[cyan])[yellow]$, where $\vec{\zeta}'\,\phi_1[\phi_2]$ is defined as $\neg\phi_1 \wedge \vec{\zeta}\,\phi_1[\phi_2]$.

5.3 Results and Discussion

Table 1 reports the results for each test image, for the logical properties specified in Sect. 5.2. Even though some models are equivalent (for instance, all the minimised versions of the maze), we have re-run all the phases of our experiment for each image, including model checking of the minimal model, as we do not test for equality of models for each pair of images in our experiment (which would yield a quadratic number of tests).

The obtained speed-up is noteworthy, especially for large images, as shown in the right-most column in Table 1. The longer formula used in the monoscope test demonstrates that minimisation clearly pays off when multiple formulas are checked on the same model, which is common in formal verification. For the larger images, the model checking time for the full model is substantially longer than the sum of the conversion, minimisation, backwards conversion, and model checking of the minimal model. For the maze example, the minimal model has the same size (actually, it is byte-by-byte the same file) for each resolution. The monoscope test, on the other hand, is designed to highlight artifacts in images. The original image is the one of 1080 pixel height and when downsampled at various resolutions, some lines disappear (specifically, belonging to the vertical bars close to the middle of the image), yielding different reachability properties, and therefore a more varied setup for our tests. We report the times both excluding and including input/output, for completeness. The intermediate file size for the `aut` files may be very large, thus saving and parsing times mask the effective computation. In perspective, the computation time is more relevant, as in the future intermediate files will be avoided altogether, by constructing `mCRL2` models directly in memory, using its programming interfaces.

As expected, with larger image sizes, the speed-up obtained in model checking becomes more prominent (again with reference to Table 1 the speed-up of model checking for the largest image is 22). Large images are particularly relevant in 3D medical imaging, which will be the subject of future work exploring the potential impact of bisimulation-based techniques to this novel application domain.

Ongoing work, also taking into account the results presented in [34], is devoted to translating spatial-logic properties to the language of `mCRL2` in order to use its state-of-the-art model checking techniques to verify spatial properties of directed graphs, in order to leverage the obtained speed-up even further.

Table 1. Results. All times are in seconds, rounded to two decimals. In order: conversion time from png to aut, without and with I/O; number of states, transitions, and aut file size of full model; minimisation time, without and with I/O; number of states and transitions of minimal model; time to convert the minimal model back to json; time for model checking the full model with `VoxLogicA`, and the minimal model with `GraphLogicA`; model checking speed-up.

Name	Conversion		Full model			Minimisation					Model checking		
	Time	t.w.IO	States	Transitions	Aut file size	Time	t.w.IO	States	Trans.	t.blck	ch. full	ch. min	Speedup
maze-128	0.34	0.34	16.00 K	142.50 K	2.47 MiB	0.00	0.03	7	21	0.36	0.49	0.39	1.25
maze-256	0.41	0.43	64.00 K	573.00 K	10.35 MiB	0.02	0.12	7	21	0.29	0.46	0.44	1.06
maze-512	0.34	0.78	256.00 K	2.24 M	44.55 MiB	0.08	0.49	7	21	0.30	0.45	0.47	0.97
maze-1024	0.39	1.28	1.00 M	8.99 M	184.34 MiB	0.32	2.06	7	21	0.31	0.51	0.38	1.34
maze-2048	0.46	4.12	4.00 M	35.98 M	793.73 MiB	1.31	8.10	7	21	0.34	0.82	0.41	1.98
maze-4096	0.87	21.91	16.00 M	143.95 M	3.27 GiB	5.37	33.32	7	21	0.33	1.81	0.45	4.01
maze-8192	2.20	173.55	64.00 M	575.91 M	13.63 GiB	21.53	135.45	7	21	0.29	5.34	0.42	12.77
mono-130	0.32	0.38	30.47 K	272.05 K	4.83 MiB	0.01	0.06	155	899	0.29	0.52	0.44	1.17
mono-260	0.31	0.62	121.88 K	1.07 M	20.27 MiB	0.03	0.26	315	1841	0.32	0.54	0.49	1.09
mono-540	0.35	0.90	506.25 K	4.44 M	90.33 MiB	0.16	1.01	460	2766	0.30	0.78	0.51	1.52
mono-1080	0.40	5.00	1.98 M	17.78 M	384.28 MiB	0.62	4.08	945	6965	0.32	1.57	0.57	2.75
mono-2160	0.57	43.87	7.91 M	71.16 M	1.55 GiB	2.45	16.74	945	6965	0.33	4.14	0.64	6.48
mono-4320	1.58	30.72	31.64 M	284.70 M	6.65 GiB	9.88	67.52	945	6965	0.72	14.96	0.65	22.87

6 Conclusions and Future Work

A practical minimisation method has been proposed for CoPa-bisimilarity for finite quasi-discrete closure models. The latter are a convenient theoretical foundation for spatial model checking. The method relies on an encoding of closure models onto LTSs such that an existing efficient algorithm for branching bisimilarity can be used to obtain a minimal model. The encoding has been proven correct, in the sense that two points in the CM are CoPa-bisimilar if and only if the states they are mapped into by the encoding are branching bisimilar. Spatial model checking can be performed exploiting the logical characterisation of CoPa-bisimilarity by the `ICRL` logic. A feasibility study has been performed to provide insight in the potential of the minimisation method for its use in the analysis of, possibly large, 2D images, in preparation of its envisioned use in spatial model checking in the medical domain. First results confirm that a very promising speed-up of spatial model checking can be obtained for single formulas, also for images of huge, but realistic, size. Minimisation also clearly pays off when multiple formulas are checked on the same model, which is common in formal verification. In such scenario, the model checking time for the full model is substantially longer than the sum of the conversion, minimisation, backwards conversion, and model checking of the minimal model, even in the current prototype setting.

Future work aims at further optimisations of the representations of the models, an integration of the toolchain and the visualisation of the results of checking the minimised model by mapping them back to the original image. The basic ingredients for such a mapping, i.e. the sets of states in the equivalence classes of the bisimulation, are readily available using the `mCRL2` tool suite [10].

Acknowledgements. We thank the anonymous reviewers for their valuable suggestions for improvement of this work.

References

1. Aiello, M.: Spatial Reasoning: Theory and Practice. Ph.D. thesis, Institute of Logic, Language and Computation, University of Amsterdam (2002)
2. Aiello, M.: The topo-approach to spatial representation and reasoning. AIIA NOTIZIE (4) (2003)
3. Aiello, M., Pratt-Hartmann, I., van Benthem, J. (eds.): Handbook of Spatial Logics. Springer, Berlin, Heidelberg (2007). https://doi.org/10.1007/978-1-4020-5587-4
4. Aubert-Broche, B., Griffin, M., Pike, G., Evans, A., Collins, D.: Twenty new digital brain phantoms for creation of validation image data bases. IEEE Trans. Med. Imaging **25**(11), 1410–1416 (2006). https://doi.org/10.1109/TMI.2006.883453
5. Banci Buonamici, F., Belmonte, G., Ciancia, V., Latella, D., Massink, M.: Spatial logics and model checking for medical imaging. Int. J. Softw. Tools Technol. Transf. **22**(2), 195–217 (2020). https://doi.org/10.1007/s10009-019-00511-9
6. Belmonte, G., Broccia, G., Ciancia, V., Latella, D., Massink, M.: Feasibility of spatial model checking for nevus segmentation. In: Bliudze, S., Gnesi, S., Plat, N., Semini, L. (eds.) 9th IEEE/ACM International Conference on Formal Methods in Software Engineering, FormaliSE@ICSE 2021, Madrid, Spain, 17–21 May 2021, pp. 1–12. IEEE (2021). https://doi.org/10.1109/FormaliSE52586.2021.00007
7. Belmonte, G., Ciancia, V., Latella, D., Massink, M.: Innovating medical image analysis via spatial logics. In: ter Beek, M.H., Fantechi, A., Semini, L. (eds.) From Software Engineering to Formal Methods and Tools, and Back. LNCS, vol. 11865, pp. 85–109. Springer, Cham (2019). https://doi.org/10.1007/978-3-030-30985-5_7
8. Belmonte, G., Ciancia, V., Latella, D., Massink, M.: VoxLogicA: a spatial model checker for declarative image analysis. In: Vojnar, T., Zhang, L. (eds.) TACAS 2019. LNCS, vol. 11427, pp. 281–298. Springer, Cham (2019). https://doi.org/10.1007/978-3-030-17462-0_16
9. Bezhanishvili, N., Ciancia, V., Gabelaia, D., Grilletti, G., Latella, D., Massink, M.: Geometric model checking of continuous space. Log. Methods Comput. Sci. **18**(4) (2022). (4:7)2022. https://doi.org/10.46298/lmcs-18, https://lmcs.episciences.org/10348
10. Bunte, O., Groote, J.F., Keiren, J.J.A., Laveaux, M., Neele, T., de Vink, E.P., Wesselink, W., Wijs, A., Willemse, T.A.C.: The mCRL2 toolset for analysing concurrent systems. In: Vojnar, T., Zhang, L. (eds.) TACAS 2019. LNCS, vol. 11428, pp. 21–39. Springer, Cham (2019). https://doi.org/10.1007/978-3-030-17465-1_2
11. Caires, L., Cardelli, L.: A spatial logic for concurrency (Part I). Inf. Comput. **186**(2), 194–235 (2003). https://doi.org/10.1016/S0890-5401(03)00137-8
12. Cardelli, L., Gordon, A.D.: Anytime, anywhere: modal logics for mobile ambients. In: Wegman, M.N., Reps, T.W. (eds.) POPL 2000, Proceedings of the 27th ACM SIGPLAN-SIGACT Symposium on Principles of Programming Languages, Boston, Massachusetts, USA, 19–21 January 2000, pp. 365–377. ACM (2000). https://doi.org/10.1145/325694.325742
13. Ciancia, V., Latella, D., Massink, M., de Vink, E.P.: Back-and-forth in space: on logics and bisimilarity in closure spaces. In: Jansen, N., Stoelinga, M., van den Bos, P. (eds.) A Journey from Process Algebra via Timed Automata to Model Learning. LNCS, vol. 13560, pp. 98–115. Springer, Cham (2022). https://doi.org/10.1007/978-3-031-15629-8_6

14. Ciancia, V., Gilmore, S., Grilletti, G., Latella, D., Loreti, M., Massink, M.: Spatio-temporal model checking of vehicular movement in public transport systems. Int. J. Softw. Tools Technol. Transf. **20**(3), 289–311 (2018). https://doi.org/10.1007/s10009-018-0483-8
15. Ciancia, V., Groote, J.F., Latella, D., Massink, M., de Vink, E.P.: Minimisation of spatial models using branching bisimilarity (Extended Version) (2022). https://doi.org/10.32079/ISTI-TR-2022/027, CNR-ISTI Technical report TR-2022-027
16. Ciancia, V., Groote, J.F., Latella, D., Massink, M., de Vink, E.P.: Minimisation of Spatial Models using Branching Bisimilarity - Validation code and data (2022)
17. Ciancia, V., Latella, D., Loreti, M., Massink, M.: Specifying and verifying properties of space. In: Diaz, J., Lanese, I., Sangiorgi, D. (eds.) TCS 2014. LNCS, vol. 8705, pp. 222–235. Springer, Heidelberg (2014). https://doi.org/10.1007/978-3-662-44602-7_18
18. Ciancia, V., Latella, D., Loreti, M., Massink, M.: Model checking spatial logics for closure spaces. Log. Methods Comput. Sci. **12**(4) (2016). https://doi.org/10.2168/LMCS-12(4:2)2016
19. Ciancia, V., Latella, D., Massink, M.: Embedding RCC8D in the collective spatial logic CSLCS. In: Boreale, M., Corradini, F., Loreti, M., Pugliese, R. (eds.) Models, Languages, and Tools for Concurrent and Distributed Programming. LNCS, vol. 11665, pp. 260–277. Springer, Cham (2019). https://doi.org/10.1007/978-3-030-21485-2_15
20. Ciancia, V., Latella, D., Massink, M., Paškauskas, R., Vandin, A.: A tool-chain for statistical spatio-temporal model checking of bike sharing systems. In: Margaria, T., Steffen, B. (eds.) ISoLA 2016. LNCS, vol. 9952, pp. 657–673. Springer, Cham (2016). https://doi.org/10.1007/978-3-319-47166-2_46
21. Cohn, A.G., Renz, J.: Qualitative spatial representation and reasoning. In: van Harmelen, F., Lifschitz, V., Porter, B.W. (eds.) Handbook of Knowledge Representation, Foundations of Artificial Intelligence, vol. 3, pp. 551–596. Elsevier (2008). https://doi.org/10.1016/S1574-6526(07)03013-1
22. Galton, A.: A generalized topological view of motion in discrete space. Theor. Comput. Sci. **305**(1–3), 111–134 (2003). Elsevier. https://doi.org/10.1016/S0304-3975(02)00701-6
23. van Glabbeek, R.J., Weijland, W.P.: Branching time and abstraction in bisimulation semantics. J. ACM **43**(3), 555–600 (1996). https://doi.org/10.1145/233551.233556
24. Groote, J.F., Jansen, D.N., Keiren, J.J.A., Wijs, A.: An O(mlogn) algorithm for computing stuttering equivalence and branching bisimulation. ACM Trans. Comput. Log. **18**(2), 13:1–13:34 (2017). https://doi.org/10.1145/3060140
25. Haghighi, I., Jones, A., Kong, Z., Bartocci, E., Grosu, R., Belta, C.: Spatel: a novel spatial-temporal logic and its applications to networked systems. In: Girard, A., Sankaranarayanan, S. (eds.) Proceedings of the 18th International Conference on Hybrid Systems: Computation and Control, HSCC 2015, Seattle, WA, USA, 14–16 April 2015, pp. 189–198. ACM (2015). https://doi.org/10.1145/2728606.2728633
26. Jansen, D.N., Groote, J.F., Keiren, J.J.A., Wijs, A.: An $O(m \log n)$ algorithm for branching bisimilarity on labelled transition systems. In: TACAS 2020. LNCS, vol. 12079, pp. 3–20. Springer, Cham (2020). https://doi.org/10.1007/978-3-030-45237-7_1

27. Linker, S., Papacchini, F., Sevegnani, M.: Analysing spatial properties on neighbourhood spaces. In: Esparza, J., Král', D. (eds.) 45th International Symposium on Mathematical Foundations of Computer Science, MFCS 2020, 24–28 August 2020, Prague, Czech Republic. LIPIcs, vol. 170, pp. 66:1–66:14. Schloss Dagstuhl - Leibniz-Zentrum für Informatik (2020). https://doi.org/10.4230/LIPIcs.MFCS.2020.66
28. Loreti, M., Quadrini, M.: A spatial logic for a simplicial complex model. CoRR abs/2105.08708 (2021). https://arxiv.org/abs/2105.08708
29. Milner, R.: The Space and Motion of Communicating Agents. Cambridge University Press, Cambridge (2009)
30. Nenzi, L., Bortolussi, L., Ciancia, V., Loreti, M., Massink, M.: Qualitative and quantitative monitoring of spatio-temporal properties with SSTL. Log. Methods Comput. Sci. **14**(4) (2018). https://doi.org/10.23638/LMCS-14(4:2)2018
31. Smyth, M.B., Webster, J.: Discrete Spatial Models. In: Aiello, M., Pratt-Hartmann, I., van Benthem, J. (eds.) Handbook of Spatial Logics, pp. 713–798. Springer, Dordrecht (2007). https://doi.org/10.1007/978-1-4020-5587-4_12
32. Tsigkanos, C., Pasquale, L., Ghezzi, C., Nuseibeh, B.: Ariadne: topology aware adaptive security for cyber-physical systems. In: Bertolino, A., Canfora, G., Elbaum, S.G. (eds.) 37th IEEE/ACM International Conference on Software Engineering, ICSE 2015, Florence, Italy, 16–24 May 2015, vol. 2, pp. 729–732. IEEE Computer Society (2015). https://doi.org/10.1109/ICSE.2015.234
33. Čech, E.: Topological Spaces. In: Pták, V. (ed.) Topological Spaces, chap. III, pp. 233–394. Publishing House of the Czechoslovak Academy of Sciences/Interscience Publishers, John Wiley & Sons, Prague/London-New York-Sydney (1966)
34. Zeven, F.: Spatial Model Checking with mCRL2. Master's thesis, Eindhoven University of Technology (2022)

Reasoning About Promises in Weak Memory Models with Event Structures

Heike Wehrheim[1], Lara Bargmann[1], and Brijesh Dongol[2(✉)]

[1] University of Oldenburg, Oldenburg, Germany
[2] University of Surrey, Guildford, UK
b.dongol@surrey.ac.uk

Abstract. Modern processors such as ARMv8 and RISC-V allow executions in which independent instructions within a process may be reordered. To cope with such phenomena, so called *promising* semantics have been developed, which permit threads to read values that have not yet been written. Each promise is a speculative update that is later validated (fulfilled) by an actual write. Promising semantics are operational, providing a pathway for developing proof calculi. In this paper, we develop an incorrectness-style logic, resulting in a framework for reasoning about state reachability. Like incorrectness logic, our assertions are *underapproximating*, since the set of all valid promises are not known at the start of execution. Our logic uses *event structures* as assertions to compactly represent the ordering among events such as promised and fulfilled writes. We prove soundness and completeness of our proof calculus and demonstrate its applicability by proving reachability properties of standard weak memory litmus tests.

Keywords: Weak memory models · Promises · Event structures · Incorrectness logic

1 Introduction

In recent years, numerous works have looked into semantics for weak memory models for various hardware architectures or languages, e.g. for x86-TSO [34], C11 [2,25], Power [33] or ARM [15]. Such semantics typically can be classified as either being declarative (aka axiomatic) or operational. Operational semantics furthermore can be divided into those following a microarchitectural style (providing formalizations of the actual hardware architecture) and those trying to abstract from architectures. Most notably, *view-based* semantics [13,20,29] avoid modelling specific hardware components and instead define the semantics in terms of *views* of thread on the shared state. *Promises* [21,23] are employed in operational semantics as a way of capturing out-of-order writes while still

Wehrheim and Bargmann are supported by DFG-WE2290/14-1. Dongol is supported by EPSRC grants EP/V038915/1, EP/R032556/1, EP/R025134/2, VeTSS and ARC Discovery Grant DP190102142.

M. Chechik et al. (Eds.): FM 2023, LNCS 14000, pp. 282–300, 2023.
https://doi.org/10.1007/978-3-031-27481-7_17

executing operations in thread order. A promise (w.r.t. a value κ and a shared location x) of a thread τ states that τ will eventually write value κ onto location x. All promised writes then need to be *fulfilled* (i.e., justified) in the future of a program run, but other threads can read from promises before they are fulfilled.

Our interest here is the development and use of Hoare-style [17] structural proof calculi (and their extensions to concurrency by Owicki and Gries [27]) for weak memory models. Owicki-Gries-like proof calculi have been proposed by a number of researchers [10,11,22,40], and have also recently been given for non-volatile memory [3,31]. Svendsen et al. [35] have developed a separation logic for promises for the C11 memory model. Wright et al. [40] have developed an Owicki-Gries proof system for out-of-order writes (as allowed by promises), but rely on pre-processing via the denotational MRD framework [28].

All of these proposals follow Hoare's principle of providing *safety* proofs. In particular, a Hoare triple $\{p\}S\{q\}$ describes the fact that an execution of program S starting in a state satisfying p is either non-terminating, or terminates in a state satisfying q (over-approximating the final states). However, for weak memory models, we often want to prove *reachability*, i.e. under-approximate the set of final states, like in the recent proposal of O'Hearn's incorrectness logic [26]. Here, a triple $[p]\, S\, [q]$ describes the possibility of program S reaching all states satisfying q when started in a state satisfying p. A verification technique supporting these *reachability* triples enables one to reason about executions that deviate from the expected sequentially consistent behaviour of concurrent programs.

Contributions. In this paper, we present a reachability proof calculus for concurrent programs where the semantics of the weak memory model is based on promises. The specific challenges therein lay in (i) capturing the meaning of promises as writes which will only happen in the future but can nevertheless already be read from, and (ii) appropriately describing the required ordering (and concurrency) between promises and fulfills as fixed by the concurrent program under consideration. We address these challenges via the following contributions. (1) We develop a program logic based on assertions which are (flow) *event structures* [5,16,39], employing parallel composition of event structure and synchronization as a means of determining whether all promises read from have eventually been fulfilled. (2) We extend the theory of flow event structures with the notion of a flow label to capture the behaviours observed in weak memory models. (3) We develop the first *compositional* proof rule for a concurrent reachability (incorrectness) logic. (4) We prove soundness and completeness of this novel event-structure based proof calculus. (5) Finally, we demonstrate its applicability on a number of litmus tests.

Overview. In Sect. 2, we provide a concrete overview via a motivating example and in Sect. 3, we present the memory model that we use. Our model is a simplified (strengthened) version of the ARMv8/RISC-V semantics of Pulte et al [29]. In Sect. 4, we present an extended theory for event structures (specifically an extension of flow event structures) that has been designed to enable reasoning about relaxed memory models. We describe our reasoning methodology and provide examples verifying common litmus tests in Sect. 5.

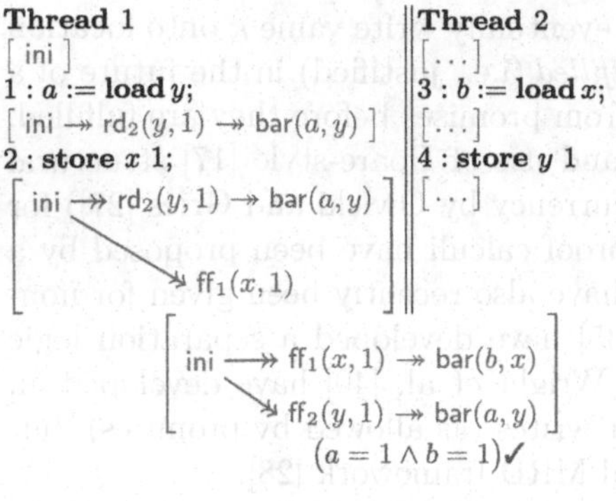

Fig. 1. Reachability for load buffering

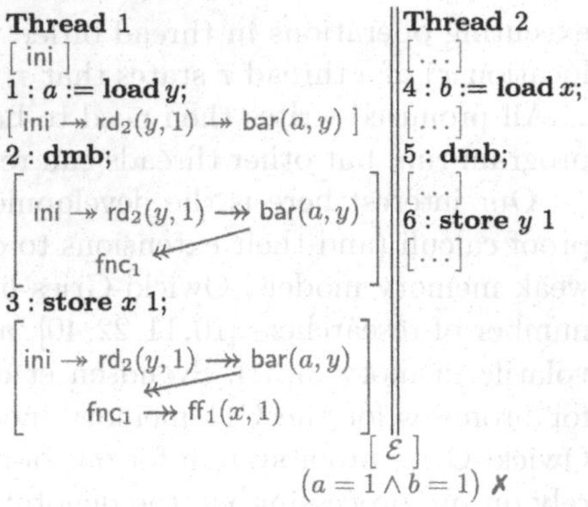

Fig. 2. Load buffering with barriers

2 Motivating Examples

Consider the program in Fig. 1, which describes the load buffering litmus test. Thread 1 (similarly thread 2) loads the value of y (sim. x) into register a (sim. b), then updates x (sim. y) to 1. Since there are no dependencies between lines 1 and 2, and similarly between lines 3 and 4, architectures such as ARMv8 and RISC-V allow the stores in both threads to be reordered with the loads. Thus the program allows the final outcome $a = 1 \wedge b = 1$.

This phenomenon is captured by promising semantics by allowing each thread to "promise" their respective stores, then later fulfilling them. In the meantime, other threads may read from promised writes. Our assertions within a thread reflect this semantics via assertions $\mathcal{E}$ which are *flow event structures* [39]. The events and their partial order reflect program executions, and in particular describe the various *views* which threads have on shared state.

The proof outlines (i.e., program texts with assertions) of individual threads may first of all contain read events for arbitrary promises, i.e. describe the reading of arbitrary values. In Thread 1 of Fig. 1, the pre-assertion of the load only contains an event for initial writes (labelled ini), yet the load may read the value 1 for y from a promised write, described by the event labelled $\mathsf{rd}_2(y, 1)$ in the post assertion. The semantics generates dependencies if the same register is used (perhaps indirectly) by a read and a later write. This is captured in our assertions using the event labelled $\mathsf{bar}(a, y)$, causally ordered after $\mathsf{rd}_2(y, 1)$, which states that the view of register a is at least that of the read of y. Execution of line 2 then adds a fulfill event with label $\mathsf{ff}_1(x, 1)$ to the assertion, which is not ordered with any other event except ini. Symmetric assertions can be generated for Thread 2. To obtain an assertion describing the combined execution, we compose the final event structures of both threads to obtain a "postcondition" of the program. For this, we use parallel composition of event structures, synchronising read with their corresponding fulfill events. In Fig. 1, both reads are valid since the promises that these reads rely on can be fulfilled in the composition without creating cyclic dependencies.

Figure 2 presents a variation of the program in Fig. 1, which includes additional barriers **dmb** (fences) between the load and store in each thread, preventing their reordering. Again we build a proof outline for an execution in which Thread 1 loads 1 into a, obtaining the assertions shown. Note that here the event structure contains an additional fence event, fnc, that is ordered after $\mathsf{bar}(a, y)$ and before $\mathsf{ff}_1(x, 1)$. Similarly, for Thread 2 loading 1 into b, we would obtain a symmetric set of assertions. Here, the parallel composition of local assertions is however not *interference free* (see below): the promises that threads 1 and 2 have read from cannot be fulfilled in this concurrent program. More detailedly, let $\mathcal{E}_1$ and $\mathcal{E}_2$ below be the (final) event structures of threads 1 and 2, respectively, where $\twoheadrightarrow$ arrow denotes ordering and we now give event names together with labels.

$$\mathcal{E}_1\text{:}\;\; e_{\mathsf{ini}} : \mathsf{ini} \twoheadrightarrow e_1 : \mathsf{rd}_2(y, 1) \twoheadrightarrow e_2 : \mathsf{bar}(a, y) \twoheadrightarrow e_3 : \mathsf{fnc}_1 \twoheadrightarrow e_4 : \mathsf{ff}_1(x, 1)$$

$$\mathcal{E}_2\text{:}\;\; f_{\mathsf{ini}} : \mathsf{ini} \twoheadrightarrow f_1 : \mathsf{rd}_1(x, 1) \twoheadrightarrow f_2 : \mathsf{bar}(b, x) \twoheadrightarrow f_3 : \mathsf{fnc}_2 \twoheadrightarrow f_4 : \mathsf{ff}_2(y, 1)$$

To reason about the set of reachable final states of the concurrent program, we again construct the parallel composition of $\mathcal{E}_1$ and $\mathcal{E}_2$ (denoted $\mathcal{E}_1 \| \mathcal{E}_2$):

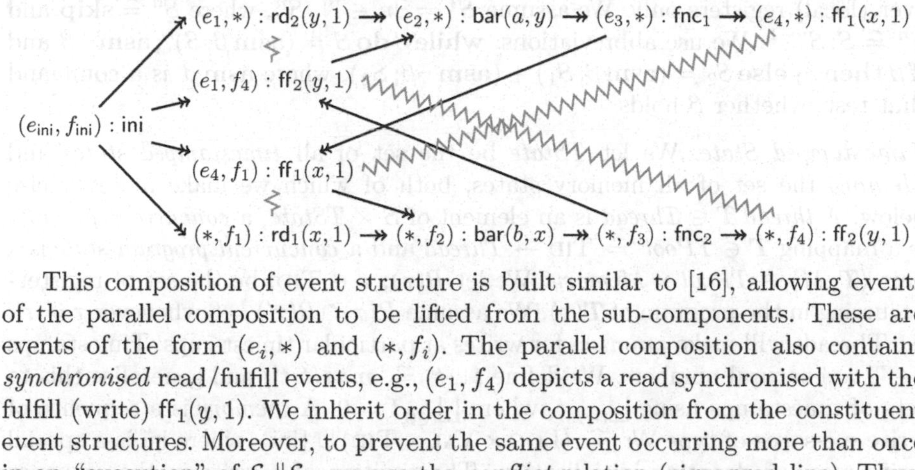

This composition of event structure is built similar to [16], allowing events of the parallel composition to be lifted from the sub-components. These are events of the form $(e_i, *)$ and $(*, f_i)$. The parallel composition also contains *synchronised* read/fulfill events, e.g., (e_1, f_4) depicts a read synchronised with the fulfill (write) $\mathsf{ff}_1(y, 1)$. We inherit order in the composition from the constituent event structures. Moreover, to prevent the same event occurring more than once in an "execution" of $\mathcal{E}_1 \| \mathcal{E}_2$, we use the *conflict* relation (zigzagged line). Thus, the synchronised event (e_1, f_4) conflicts with both $(e_1, *)$ and $(*, f_4)$.

The final step in proving is the generation of a valid interference free *configuration* of the parallel composition, which is a subset of the event structure satisfying certain conditions, including acyclicity of $\twoheadrightarrow$, absence of conflicts and absence of unsynchronised reads (ensuring the fulfillment of all promises read from). It turns out that for the event structure above, it is impossible to generate such a configuration. The event $(e_1, *)$ cannot be included since it is an unsynchronised read. Therefore, (e_1, f_4) must be included. However, by the definition of a configuration, this also means that the downclosure of (e_1, f_4) must be included, which results in a cycle: $(e_1, f_4) \twoheadrightarrow (e_2, *) \twoheadrightarrow (e_3, *) \twoheadrightarrow (e_4, f_1) \twoheadrightarrow (*, f_2) \twoheadrightarrow (*, f_3) \twoheadrightarrow (e_1, f_4)$. Since $\mathcal{E}_1 \| \mathcal{E}_2$ has no interference free configurations, the proof outline is not valid and in fact, a final state with $a = 1 \wedge b = 1$ is unreachable here.

3 A Weak Memory Semantics with Promises

We develop a promising semantics inspired by the recent view-based operational semantics by Pulte et al. [29]. We have reduced architecture-specific details, allowing us to focus on the interaction between promises and thread views. Our notion of a *promise* coincides with earlier works [21,23,29]. Threads can promise to write certain values on shared locations and other threads can read from this promise even before the actual write has occurred. All promises however need to be fulfilled at the end of the program execution.

Syntax. Let $x, y \in \text{Loc}$ be the set of *shared locations*, $\kappa \in \text{Val}$ the set of *values*, $\tau \in \text{Tid}$ the set of *thread identifiers* and $a, b \in \text{Reg}$ *local registers*. Our sequential language encompasses the following constructs:

$$rv ::= \kappa \mid a \qquad st ::= \textbf{skip} \mid a := \textbf{load}\, x \mid \textbf{store}\, x\ rv \mid a := \eta \mid \textbf{dmb}$$
$$S ::= st \mid S; S \mid \textbf{asm}\, \beta \mid S + S \mid S^*$$

where $\eta \in \text{Exp}$ is an arithmetic and $\beta \in \text{BExp}$ is a boolean expressions, both over (local) registers only. We assume $S^* = \exists n \in \mathbb{N}.\ S^n$, where $S^0 \mathrel{\widehat{=}} \textbf{skip}$ and $S^n \mathrel{\widehat{=}} S; S^{n-1}$. We use abbreviations: $\textbf{while}\, \beta\, \textbf{do}\, S = (\textbf{asm}\, \beta; S)^*; \textbf{asm}\, \neg\beta$ and $\textbf{if}\, \beta\, \textbf{then}\, S_1\, \textbf{else}\, S_2 = (\textbf{asm}\, \beta; S_1) + (\textbf{asm}\, \neg\beta; S_2)$, where $\textbf{asm}\, \beta$ is a command that tests whether β holds.

Timestamped State. We let *TState* be the set of all *timestamped states* and *Memory* the set of all memory states, both of which we make more precise below. A *thread* $T \in \mathit{Thread}$ is an element of $S \times \mathit{TState}$, a *concurrent program* is a mapping $\boldsymbol{T} \in \mathit{TPool} \mathrel{\widehat{=}} \text{Tid} \rightarrow \mathit{Thread}$ and a *concurrent program state* is a pair $\langle \boldsymbol{T}, M\rangle \in \mathit{TPool} \times \mathit{Memory}$. We let $R(\tau)$, $\tau \in \text{Tid}$, be the set of registers occurring in the program of $\boldsymbol{T}(\tau)$. We assume $R(\tau) \cap R(\tau') = \emptyset$ whenever $\tau \neq \tau'$.

Threads will make *promises* for writes at particular timestamps. Timestamps $t \in \mathbb{T}$ are natural numbers. We define $t \sqcup t' \mathrel{\widehat{=}} \mathit{max}(t, t')$ and generalise this to sets of timestamps using $\bigsqcup_{t \in T} t$, where $\bigsqcup_{t \in \emptyset} t = 0$. A *memory* is a sequence of write messages of type $\mathsf{Wr} \mathrel{\widehat{=}} (\text{Loc} \times \text{Val} \times \text{Tid}) \cup \{\mathsf{ini}\}$, where ini is a special write message denoting initialisation. The position of a write in the sequence fixes its timestamp. We assume all variables are initialised with value 0.

We denote a write $w \mathrel{\widehat{=}} (x, \kappa, \tau)$ using $\langle x := \kappa \rangle_\tau$ and let $w.\mathit{loc} = x$, $w.\mathit{val} = \kappa$ and $w.\mathit{tid} = \tau$. For a memory M and thread $\tau \in \text{Tid}$, we let $M_\tau \subseteq \mathbb{T}$ be the set of timestamps of entries of τ in M, i.e. $\{t \in \mathbb{T} \mid M(t).\mathit{tid} = \tau\}$. M_τ is used to determine the promise set of each τ. We write $\mathit{tids}(M)$ to denote the set of threads with entries in M. New messages w are appended at the end of the memory, which we write as $M \mathbin{+\!\!+} w$.

A thread state $ts \in \mathit{TState}$ consists of the following components: a set of (non-fulfilled) *promises* $\mathit{prom} \in 2^{\mathbb{T}}$, a *coherence* view of each location, $\mathit{coh} : \text{Loc} \rightarrow \mathbb{T}$, the value and view of each register, $\mathit{regs} : \text{Reg} \rightarrow \text{Val} \times \mathbb{T}$, a read view $v_{\mathit{read}} : \mathbb{T}$, two write views $v_{\mathit{wOld}}, v_{\mathit{wNew}} : \mathbb{T}$ and a condition view $v_C : \mathbb{T}$. We write $\mathit{regs}(a)$ as $\kappa @ v$ and also let v_a be this view v of register a. Finally, the evaluation of an expression η with respect to a register assignment *regs*, $[\![\eta]\!]_{regs} \in \text{VAL} \times \mathbb{T}$, is defined as follows:

$$[\![\kappa]\!]_{regs} \mathrel{\widehat{=}} \kappa@0 \text{ for } \kappa \in \text{VAL}, \qquad [\![a]\!]_{regs} \mathrel{\widehat{=}} regs(a) \text{ for } a \in \text{REG},$$
$$[\![\eta_1 op \eta_2]\!]_{regs} \mathrel{\widehat{=}} (\kappa_1 [\![op]\!] \kappa_2)@(v_1 \sqcup v_2) \text{ with } [\![\eta_1]\!]_{regs} = \kappa_1@v_1, [\![\eta_2]\!]_{regs} = \kappa_2@v_2$$

Note that this evaluation is with respect to the register function *regs* and this calculates both the value of the expression and the maximal view of the registers within the expression.

To define the initial state of a program, we let

$$M_{\mathsf{ini}} \mathrel{\widehat{=}} \langle \mathsf{ini} \rangle \qquad ts_{\mathsf{ini}} \mathrel{\widehat{=}} \begin{bmatrix} prom = \{\}, v_{read} = v_{wNew} = v_{wOld} = v_C = 0, \\ coh = (\lambda x.\ 0), regs = (\lambda a.\ 0@0) \end{bmatrix}$$

where ts_{ini} is a record initialising the promises to the empty set, each view to 0, the coherence function to a map from locations to timestamp 0, and the register function to a map from registers to value 0 with timestamp 0. We say that a program $\boldsymbol{T}$ is locally in its initial state iff for each thread τ, we have $\pi_2(\boldsymbol{T}(\tau)) = ts_{\mathsf{ini}}$, where π_i projects the ith component of a tuple. Given that $\boldsymbol{T}$ is in its initial state, the initial concurrent program state is given by $\langle \boldsymbol{T}, M_{\mathsf{ini}} \rangle$.

The rules of the operational semantics (except for standard rules for program constructs) are given in Fig. 3. The two key rules are the READ and FULFILL rule. READ identifies a timestamp t to read a value for x from such that in between t and the maximum of read view and coherence of x, there are no further promises to x in memory M. It updates read view, coherence of x and the view of the register involved in the load as to ensure preservation of dependencies. FULFILL fulfills an already made promise (to write κ to x) of a thread at timestamp t, and to this end has to ensure that views $v_{wNew}, v_C, coh(x)$ as well as that of the value/register are less than t. It removes t from the thread's promise set and updates $coh(x)$ and v_{wOld} (as to ensure dependencies with fences). Rule PROMISE simply adds an arbitrary new promise at the end of memory. FENCE ensures views v_{read} and v_{wNew} are updated. This rule for instance guarantees that store operations separated by barriers **dmb** can only be fulfilled in that order, i.e. the write of the first store cannot be promised to happen later than the write of the second store (more precisely, such promises cannot be fulfilled).

Finally, we say that $\langle T, M \rangle$ is *certifiable* (used in PROGRAM STEP) if there is some T', M' such that $\langle T, M \rangle \rightarrow_\tau^* \langle T', M' \rangle$ and $T'.prom = \emptyset$. Certifiability ensures that a concurrent program can only make steps when all promises can eventually be fulfilled. Like [29], in our semantics, all promise steps can be done at the beginning without losing any of the reachable states.

4 Event Structures

Event structures [4,5,16,39] are models of concurrent systems which compactly represent (concurrent) executions. Here, we use flow event structures because of their ease in defining a compositional parallel composition [16].

$$\textsc{Promise}\quad \frac{w.tid = \tau \quad w.loc = x \quad w.val = \kappa \qquad t = |M|+1 \qquad ts' = ts[prom \mapsto ts.prom \cup \{t\}]}{\langle\langle S, ts\rangle, M\rangle \xrightarrow{prm(x,\kappa)}_\tau \langle\langle S, ts'\rangle, M +\!\!+ w\rangle}$$

$$\textsc{Fence}\quad \frac{v = ts.v_{read} \sqcup ts.v_{wOld} \qquad ts' = ts\begin{bmatrix} v_{read} \mapsto v \\ v_{wNew} \mapsto v\end{bmatrix}}{\langle\langle \mathbf{dmb}, ts\rangle, M\rangle \xrightarrow{\mathsf{fnc}}_\tau \langle\langle \mathbf{skip}, ts'\rangle, M\rangle}$$

$$\textsc{Read}\quad \frac{\begin{array}{c} M(t).loc = x \qquad M(t).val = \kappa \\ \forall t'.\ t < t' \leq (ts.v_{read} \sqcup ts.coh(x)) \Rightarrow M(t').loc \neq x \\ v_{post} = ts.v_{read} \sqcup t \\ ts' = ts\begin{bmatrix} regs(a) \mapsto \kappa@v_{post}, \\ coh(x) \mapsto ts.coh(x) \sqcup v_{post}, \\ v_{read} \mapsto v_{post}\end{bmatrix}\end{array}}{\langle\langle a := \mathbf{load}\, x, ts\rangle, M\rangle \xrightarrow{rd(x,\kappa)}_\tau \langle\langle \mathbf{skip}, ts'\rangle, M\rangle}$$

$$\textsc{Fulfill}\quad \frac{\begin{array}{c} t \in ts.prom \qquad [\![rv]\!]_{ts.regs} = \kappa@v_{rv} \\ M(t) = \langle x := \kappa\rangle_\tau \\ ts.v_{wNew} \sqcup ts.v_C \sqcup ts.coh(x) \sqcup v_{rv} < t \\ ts' = ts\begin{bmatrix} prom \mapsto ts.prom \setminus \{t\}, \\ coh(x) \mapsto t, \\ v_{wOld} \mapsto v_{wOld} \sqcup t\end{bmatrix}\end{array}}{\langle\langle \mathbf{store}\ x\ rv, ts\rangle, M\rangle \xrightarrow{ff(x,\kappa)}_\tau \langle\langle \mathbf{skip}, ts'\rangle, M\rangle}$$

$$\textsc{Register}\quad \frac{regs(a) = \kappa_a@u \qquad [\![\eta]\!]_{ts.regs} = \kappa@v \qquad ts' = ts\,[regs(a) \mapsto \kappa@(u \sqcup v)]}{\langle\langle a := \eta, ts\rangle, M\rangle \xrightarrow{lst(a,\eta)}_\tau \langle\langle \mathbf{skip}, ts'\rangle, M\rangle}$$

$$\textsc{Assume}\quad \frac{[\![\beta]\!]_{ts.regs} = \mathsf{true}@v \qquad ts' = ts[v_C \mapsto ts.v_C \sqcup v]}{\langle\langle \mathbf{asm}\,\beta, ts\rangle, M\rangle \xrightarrow{asm(\beta)}_\tau \langle\langle \mathbf{skip}, ts'\rangle, M\rangle}$$

$$\textsc{Program Step}\quad \frac{\langle \boldsymbol{T}(\tau), M\rangle \xrightarrow{op}_\tau \langle T', M\rangle \qquad \langle T', M\rangle \text{ certifiable}}{\langle \boldsymbol{T}, M\rangle \xrightarrow{op}_\tau \langle \boldsymbol{T}[\tau \mapsto T'], M'\rangle}$$

Fig. 3. Operational semantics (Atomic statement rules)

Notation. Event structures consist of sets of *events* $d, e, f \in E$. Events will be labelled with *actions* which are here specific to our usage and give us information about program executions:

$$Act^x \mathrel{\hat{=}} \bigcup_{\tau\in\textsc{Tid},\kappa\in\textsc{Val}} \{\mathsf{rd}_\tau(x,\kappa), \mathsf{ff}_\tau(x,\kappa)\} \cup \{\mathsf{ini}\} \qquad Act^{\mathsf{fnc}} \mathrel{\hat{=}} \bigcup_{\tau\in\textsc{Tid}} \{\mathsf{fnc}_\tau\}$$

$$Act^a \mathrel{\hat{=}} \bigcup_{x\in\textsc{Loc},\eta\in\textsc{Exp}} \{\mathsf{bar}(a,x), \mathsf{bar}(a,\eta)\} \qquad Act^{\mathsf{tst}} \mathrel{\hat{=}} \bigcup_{\tau\in\textsc{Tid},\beta\in\textsc{BExp}} \{\mathsf{tst}_\tau(\beta)\}$$

Actions on a location x can be *read* actions $\mathsf{rd}_\tau(\cdot,\cdot)$, *fulfill* actions $\mathsf{ff}_\tau(\cdot,\cdot)$ or the initialization ini. Note that the thread identifier τ in read actions is the id of the thread having made the promise and in fulfill actions it is the thread executing the fulfill (and having made the corresponding promise). We let Act^{rd} denote all read and Act^{ff} all fulfill actions. To record loading into register a, we use so called *bar* actions $\mathsf{bar}(a,\cdot)$. The action fnc occurs when a **dmb** statement is executed and $\mathsf{tst}.(\cdot)$ describes the execution of some **asm** statement.

We often lift notations to sets of locations $L \subseteq \textsc{Loc}$ or sets of registers $R \subseteq \textsc{Reg}$. For example, $Act^L = \bigcup_{x\in L} Act^x$. The overall set of actions is $Act = Act^{\textsc{Loc}} \cup Act^{\textsc{Reg}} \cup Act^{\mathsf{fnc}} \cup Act^{\mathsf{tst}}$.

Definition 1. *A* location-coloured flow event structure *(short: event structure)* $\mathcal{E} = (E, \twoheadrightarrow, \#, \Lambda, \ell)$ *labelled over a set of actions Act consists of a finite set of events E, an irreflexive* flow relation $\twoheadrightarrow \subseteq E \times E$, *a* location restriction *function* $\Lambda : E \times E \to 2^{\text{Loc}}$, *a symmetric* conflict relation $\# \subseteq E \times E$, *and a* labelling function $\ell : E \to Act$.

For $L \subseteq \text{Loc}$, we write $e \overset{L}{\twoheadrightarrow} f$ to denote $e \twoheadrightarrow f$ and $\Lambda(e, f) = L$. The location restrictions are employed to reflect the application condition of rule READ within the event structure: it tells us that there is no write to $x \in L$ in between e and f, where e and f will eventually be mapped to timestamps in memory.

We let Ini be the event structure $(\{e_{\mathsf{ini}}\}, \emptyset, \emptyset, \emptyset, \ell)$ with $\ell(e_{\mathsf{ini}}) = \mathsf{ini}$. Given an event structure $\mathcal{E} = (E, \twoheadrightarrow, \#, \Lambda, \ell)$, we – similarly to actions – define its set of events labelled with specific actions as $\mathsf{Rd}(\mathcal{E})$, $\mathsf{Rd}_\tau(\mathcal{E})$, $\mathsf{Rd}^x_\tau(\mathcal{E})$, $\mathsf{Ff}(\mathcal{E})$, $\mathsf{Ff}_\tau(\mathcal{E})$ and $\mathsf{Ff}^x_\tau(\mathcal{E})$ via the labelling function ℓ. For an event e labelled with an action in $Act^x \setminus \{\mathsf{ini}\}$, we let $e.loc = x$. We slightly abuse notation so that $e_{\mathsf{ini}}.loc = x$ for all x. We furthermore define $last_\alpha(\mathcal{E})$, $\alpha \in Act$, to be the last event in flow order labelled α, i.e., $last_\alpha(\mathcal{E}) = e$ if $\ell(e) = \alpha$ and for all e' such that $e' \neq e$ and $\ell(e') = \alpha$, we have $e' \twoheadrightarrow^+ e$. Moreover, $last_\alpha(\mathcal{E}) = \bot$ if no event labelled α exists. We lift $last$ to sets of actions by $last_A(\mathcal{E}) = \{last_\alpha(\mathcal{E}) \mid \alpha \in Act\}$. An event structure $\mathcal{E}$ is *sequential* if all events are flow-ordered: $\forall e, e' \in E, e \neq e' : e \twoheadrightarrow^+ e' \vee e' \twoheadrightarrow^+ e$. We let $\mathcal{S}$ be the set of sequential event structures.

An event structure describes (several) concurrent executions in compact form. One execution is therein given as a configuration.

Definition 2. *A* configuration $C \subseteq E$ *of an event structure* $\mathcal{E} = (E, \twoheadrightarrow, \#, \Lambda, \ell)$ *satisfies the following properties: (1) C is cycle-free:* $(\twoheadrightarrow \cap (C \times C))^+$ *is irreflexive, (2) C is conflict-free:* $\# \cap (C \times C) = \emptyset$, *(3) C is left-closed up to conflicts:* $\forall d, e \in E$, *if* $e \in C$, $d \twoheadrightarrow e$ *and* $d \notin C$, *then there exists* $f \in C$ *such that* $d \# f$ *and* $f \twoheadrightarrow e$.

We let $Conf(\mathcal{E})$ be the set of configurations of $\mathcal{E}$. We identify a configuration with the (conflict-free) event structure $\mathcal{E}_C$ which is $\mathcal{E}$ restricted to events of C.

Our intention is to use event structures to record information about the local history of each thread, in particular the promises of other threads which they have read from. Eventually (i.e., when combining local event structures) all promises read from need to be fulfilled. This is captured by our notion of parallel composition which requires fulfills (of a thread τ) to *synchronize* with reads from promises of τ. Similary to CCS [24], we model this synchronisation via *complementary* actions where $\overline{\mathsf{rd}_\tau(x, \kappa)} = \mathsf{ff}_\tau(x, \kappa)$ and vice versa, and $\overline{\overline{a}} = a$. Contrary to CCS, the synchronisation does not create internal actions, but keeps the fulfill labels (as to still see what promise a fulfill belonged to).

We first define the *synchronising events* of n event structures $\mathcal{E}_1, \ldots, \mathcal{E}_n$, as follows, where E_{i*} denotes $E_i \cup \{*\}$.

$$sync(\mathcal{E}_1, \ldots, \mathcal{E}_n) \mathrel{\widehat{=}} \left\{ \begin{array}{l} (e_1, e_2, \ldots, e_n) \in E_{1*} \times E_{2*} \times \cdots \times E_{n*} \mid \\ \exists i.\ \ell_i(e_i) \in Act^{\mathsf{ff}} \wedge (\forall j \neq i.\ e_j \neq * \Rightarrow \overline{\ell_i(e_i)} = \ell_j(e_j)) \wedge \\ \qquad (\exists j \neq i.\ e_j \neq *) \end{array} \right\}$$
$$\cup \{(e^1_{\mathsf{ini}}, e^2_{\mathsf{ini}}, \ldots, e^n_{\mathsf{ini}})\}$$

An event e might also occur unsynchronized in a parallel composition (which is then written as $(*, \ldots, *, e, *, \ldots, *)$.

Note that since we aim to reason about reachability of states (underapproximation), we just need parallel composition for *conflict-free* event structures, i.e. for event structures describing a single execution. Thus the Δ-axiom of Castellani and Zhang [6] which they impose in order to get compositionality is trivially fulfilled for our application. Next, we still first of all define parallel composition of arbitrary event structures.

We let $\times_i S$ denote the product $S \times S \times \ldots S$ generating a tuple of length i. If $i \leq 0$, we let $\times_i S = \bot$. Finally, we let $\bot \times S = S \times \bot = S$.

Definition 3 (Parallel composition). *Let $\mathcal{E}_1, \mathcal{E}_2, \ldots, \mathcal{E}_n$ be event structures for threads $\tau_1, \tau_2, \ldots, \tau_n$, respectively. The* parallel composition $\mathcal{E} = \mathcal{E}_1 || \mathcal{E}_2 || \ldots || \mathcal{E}_n$ *is the event structure $(E, \twoheadrightarrow, \#, \Lambda, \ell)$ with*

- $E = sync(\mathcal{E}_1, \mathcal{E}_2, \ldots \mathcal{E}_n) \cup \left(\bigcup_i (\times_{i-1}\{*\}) \times (E_i \setminus \{e^i_{\mathsf{ini}}\}) \times (\times_{n-i}\{*\})\right)$
- $(e_1, e_2, \ldots, e_n) \twoheadrightarrow (d_1, d_2, \ldots, d_n)$ *iff* $\exists i.\ e_i \twoheadrightarrow_i d_i$,
- $\Lambda((e_1, e_2, \ldots, e_n), (d_1, d_2, \ldots, d_n)) = \bigcup_i \Lambda(e_i, d_i)$,
- $(e_1, e_2, \ldots, e_n) \# (d_1, d_2, \ldots, d_n)$ *iff*
  - $\exists i.\ e_i \#_i d_i$, *or* *(inherit conflicts)*
  - $\exists i, j.\ e_i = d_i \wedge e_i \neq * \wedge e_j \neq d_j$ *(conflicts on differently paired events),*
- *Labels:*

$$\ell(e_1, e_2, \ldots e_n) = \begin{cases} \mathsf{ini} & \text{if } (e_1, e_2, \ldots e_n) = (e^1_{\mathsf{ini}}, e^2_{\mathsf{ini}}, \ldots e^n_{\mathsf{ini}}) \\ \ell(e_i) & \text{if } (e_1, e_2, \ldots e_n) \in sync(\mathcal{E}_1, \mathcal{E}_2, \ldots \mathcal{E}_n) \wedge \ell(e_i) = \mathsf{ff}.(\cdot, \cdot) \\ \ell(e_i) & \text{if } (e_1, e_2, \ldots e_n) \notin sync(\mathcal{E}_1, \mathcal{E}_2, \ldots \mathcal{E}_n) \wedge e_i \neq * \end{cases}$$

Parallel composition of event structures is used to combine local proof outlines of threads. This combination is only possible if enough synchronization partners are available. Event structures $\mathcal{E}_1$ to $\mathcal{E}_n$ are *synchronizable* if $\pi_i(sync(\mathcal{E}_1, \ldots, \mathcal{E}_n)) \supseteq \mathsf{Rd}(E_i)$, $i \in \{1, \ldots, n\}$ (all the reads have a synchronization with a fulfill). The configuration (describing an execution of the parallel composition of threads) which we extract from $Conf(\mathcal{E}_1 || \ldots || \mathcal{E}_n)$ furthermore has to guarantee that no events from the local proof outlines are lost and that the local assertions make no contradictory assumptions about the contents of memory.

Definition 4. *The event structure $\mathcal{E}_C = (E_C, \twoheadrightarrow_C, \emptyset, \Lambda_C, \ell_C)$ corresponding to a configuration $C \in Conf(\mathcal{E}_1 || \ldots || \mathcal{E}_n)$ is* interference free *if*

1. *C is* thread-covering*: $\forall i \in \{1, \ldots, n\} : \pi_i(E_C) = E_i$,*
2. *C is* memory-consistent linearizable*: there exists a total order $\prec \subseteq Act^x(E_C) \times Act^x(E_C)$ among reads, fulfills and the* ini *event such that*
   - $\twoheadrightarrow_C^+ \cap (Act^x(E_C) \times Act^x(E_C)) \subseteq \prec$ *and*
   - $\forall d, e, f \in E_C \colon d \overset{L}{\twoheadrightarrow} f \wedge d \prec e \prec f \implies e.loc \notin L$,
3. *C contains* no unsynchronised reads*: there is no event in E_C of the form $(*, *, \ldots, *, e_i, * \ldots, *)$, where $e_i \in \mathsf{Rd}(\mathcal{E}_i)$.*

Example 1. Consider the two event structures given next (which belong to a message passing program with barriers, see Sect. 5).

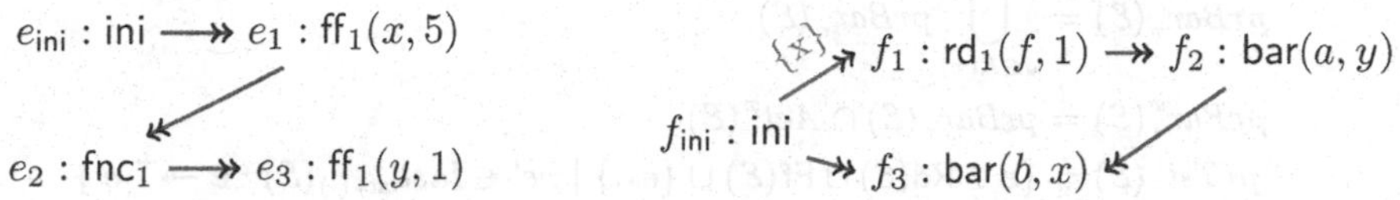

Their parallel composition gives the following event structure:

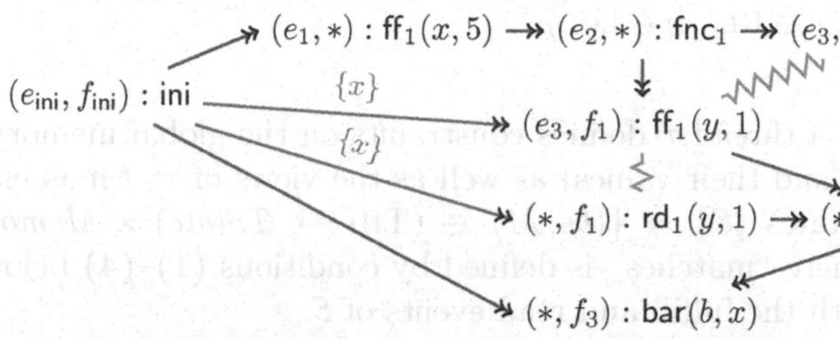

This event structure has no interference-free configuration. To satisfy the conditions "thread-covering" and "no unsynchronised reads", we must include event (e_3, f_1). This means the only possible configuration must also include the down-closure $(e_1,*)$ and $(e_2,*)$. However, together with the location restriction $\{x\}$ on the edge $((e_{ini}, f_{ini}), (e_3, f_1))$, the resulting event structure is not memory-consistent linearizable, since it contains a sequence $(e_{ini}, f_{ini}) \twoheadrightarrow (e_1,*) \twoheadrightarrow (e_2,*) \twoheadrightarrow (e_3, f_1)$, where $(e_1,*)$ corresponds to a fulfilled write on x that is forbidden by the edge $((e_{ini}, f_{ini}) \overset{\{x\}}{\twoheadrightarrow} (e_3, f_1))$. Conceptually, this means that we cannot find a memory M which matches the constraints on its contents given in the event structure.

5 Reasoning

Our overall objective is the design of a proof calculus for reasoning about the *reachability* of certain final states of concurrent programs. A concurrent program state describes the values of registers and shared variables, the contents of memory and the views of threads. During reasoning, we employ event structures as *assertions* in proof outlines. They abstract from the concrete state in neither giving the exact contents of memory nor the timestamps of thread views.

5.1 Semantics of Assertions

Local assertions in the proof outlines of single threads take the form $\mathcal{E}$, where $\mathcal{E}$ is a conflict-free event structure (i.e., $\# = \emptyset$). The event structure is conflict-free because it describes a *single* execution of the thread (reachability logic). An assertion for a thread τ can have fence and fulfill events of τ, read events reading from (promises of) threads $\tau' \neq \tau$ as well as bar and test events over registers of $R(\tau)$. The events in $\mathcal{E}$ – together with some memory M – allow us to compute the current views of threads. Figure 4 gives some definitions for calculating views.

$$prFnc_\tau(\mathcal{E}) = \{e \in \mathsf{Rd}(\mathcal{E}) \cup \mathsf{Ff}(\mathcal{E}) \cup \{e_{\mathsf{ini}}\} \mid \exists e' \in last_{\mathsf{fnc}_\tau}(\mathcal{E}) : e \twoheadrightarrow^+ e'\}$$
$$prBar_a(\mathcal{E}) = \{e \in \mathsf{Rd}(\mathcal{E}) \cup \mathsf{Ff}(\mathcal{E}) \cup \{e_{\mathsf{ini}}\} \mid \exists e' \in last_{\mathsf{bar}(a,\cdot)}(\mathcal{E}) : e \twoheadrightarrow^+ e'\}$$
$$prBar_\tau(\mathcal{E}) = \bigcup_{a \in R(\tau)} prBar_a(\mathcal{E})$$
$$prBar^x_\tau(\mathcal{E}) = prBar_\tau(\mathcal{E}) \cap Act^x(\mathcal{E})$$
$$prTst_\tau(\mathcal{E}) = \{e \in \mathsf{Rd}(\mathcal{E}) \cup \mathsf{Ff}(\mathcal{E}) \cup \{e_{\mathsf{ini}}\} \mid \exists e' \in last_{\mathsf{tst}_\tau(\cdot)}(\mathcal{E}) : e \twoheadrightarrow^+ e'\}$$

Fig. 4. Determining the decisive reads and writes prior to an event ($\mathcal{E} = (E, \twoheadrightarrow, \#, \Lambda, \ell)$ event structure, $\tau \in \text{TID}$, $a \in \text{REG}$, $x \in \text{LOC}$)

A local assertion of a thread τ defines constraints on the global memory M (the ordering of writes and their values) as well as the views of τ: An assertion $\mathcal{E}$ describes a set of states $[\![\mathcal{E}]\!] = \{\langle \boldsymbol{ts}, M\rangle \in (\text{TID} \to \mathit{TState}) \times \mathit{Memory} \mid \langle \boldsymbol{ts}, M\rangle$ matches $\mathcal{E}\}$ where "matches" is defined by conditions **(1)**–**(4)** below.

(1) M is consistent with the fulfill and read events of $\mathcal{E}$.

There exists a total mapping $\psi : \mathsf{Ff}(\mathcal{E}) \cup \mathsf{Rd}(\mathcal{E}) \cup \{e_{\mathsf{ini}}\} \to dom(M)$ which

1. *initializes at zero*: the one event e_{ini} labelled ini is mapped to 0,
2. is *consecutive* for every thread τ: for all $e \in \mathsf{Ff}_\tau(\mathcal{E})$, $t \in \mathbb{T}$ s.t. $M(t) = \langle x := \kappa\rangle_\tau$, $t < \psi(e)$ and $e.loc = x$, there exists $d \in \mathsf{Ff}_\tau(\mathcal{E})$ such that $\psi(d) = t$,
3. *preserves content*: if $\psi(e) = t \neq 0$ and $M(t) = \langle x := \kappa\rangle_\tau$, then $\ell(e) \in \{\mathsf{ff}_\tau(x,\kappa), \mathsf{rd}_\tau(x,\kappa)\}$,
4. *preserves flows*: $\forall e, e' \in dom(M) : e \twoheadrightarrow^+_{\mathcal{E}} e' \Rightarrow \psi(e) < \psi(e')$,
5. and *preserves memory constraints*: $\forall d, e \in dom(M)$, $L \subseteq \text{LOC}$ s.t. $d \overset{L}{\twoheadrightarrow} e$, $\forall t \in \mathbb{T}$ s.t. $\psi(d) < t < \psi(e)$: $M(t).loc \neq d.loc$.

The mapping ψ is used to assign timestamps to read and fulfill events. We therefore will later also talk about the *timestamp of an event* (depending on such a mapping). Note that the event structure Ini is consistent with all memories M (using mapping $\psi(e_{\mathsf{ini}}) = 0$).

(2) The open (non-fulfilled) promises of a thread τ are the entries of τ in M which are not fulfilled, i.e., $\boldsymbol{ts}(\tau).prom = M_\tau \setminus \psi(\mathsf{Ff}_\tau(\mathcal{E}))$.

(3) The views of a thread τ are consistent with mapping ψ and M. Letting $ts = \boldsymbol{ts}(\tau)$, $a \in R(\tau)$ and $x \in \text{LOC}$, we have

$$ts.v_C = \bigsqcup_{e \in prTst_\tau(\mathcal{E})} \psi(e) \qquad ts.coh(x) = \bigsqcup_{e \in \mathsf{Ff}^x_\tau(\mathcal{E}) \cup prBar^x_\tau(\mathcal{E})} \psi(e)$$

$$ts.v_{wOld} = \bigsqcup_{e \in \mathsf{Ff}_\tau(\mathcal{E})} \psi(e) \qquad ts.v_{wNew} = \bigsqcup_{e \in prFnc_\tau(\mathcal{E}) \cap \left(\mathsf{Ff}_\tau(\mathcal{E}) \cup prBar_\tau(\mathcal{E})\right)} \psi(e)$$

$$zts.v_a = \bigsqcup_{e \in prBar_a(\mathcal{E})} \psi(e) \qquad ts.v_{read} = \bigsqcup_{e \in \left(prFnc_\tau(\mathcal{E}) \cap \mathsf{Ff}_\tau(\mathcal{E})\right) \cup prBar_\tau(\mathcal{E})} \psi(e)$$

(4) The values of registers $R(\tau)$ of thread τ agree with values in $\mathcal{E}$.

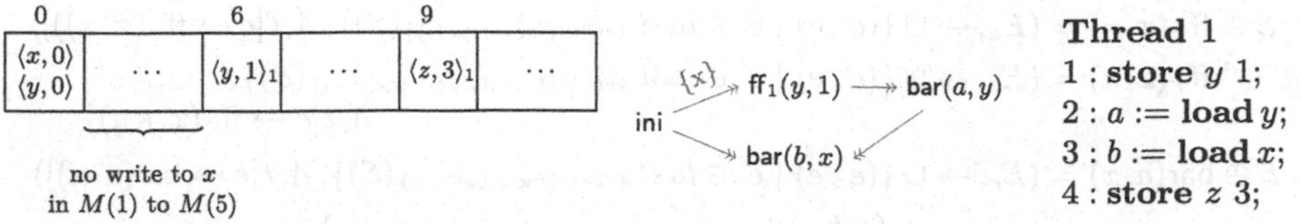

Fig. 5. Example memory M (left) for event structure $\mathcal{E}$ (middle) describing an execution of statements 1, 2 and 3 in thread 1 (right). State ts of thread 1: $prom = \{9\}$, $v_C = v_{wNew} = coh(z) = 0$, $v_a = v_b = coh(y) = coh(x) = v_{wOld} = v_{read} = 6$, using mapping $\psi : \mathsf{ini} \mapsto 0, \mathsf{ff}_1(y,1) \mapsto 6$.

For $a \in \text{REG}$, $ts.regs(a) = \kappa@v_a$ with $\kappa = [\![a]\!]_{\mathcal{E}}$ (where the semantics of a register a in $\mathcal{E}$ is (1) 0 if no bar event for a is in $\mathcal{E}$ or (2) the value of a read or fulfill to x prior to the last $\mathsf{bar}(a,\cdot)$ (on x) or (3) the value of the expression η in a last $\mathsf{bar}(a,\eta)$) and v_a as defined above.

Figure 5 gives an example for the definition of "matches". On the right hand side we see the program of thread 1. It first stores 1 to y, then loads the values of y and x into registers a and b, respectively, and finally stores 3 to z. The event structure in the middle gives the assertion reached after statement 3, i.e. *before* the final store operation. The memory M on the left hand side matches this event structure: There are promises for the event ini at $M(0)$ as well as for event $\mathsf{ff}_1(y,1)$, so ψ maps ini to 0 and $\mathsf{ff}_1(y,1)$ to 6. The colored location restriction in the event structure furthermore requires not to have any promises to x in between 0 and 6. As there is one more promise of thread 1 in M, not yet covered by the event structure, we can derive $1.prom = \{9\}$.

5.2 Proof Rules

Essentially, assertions describe the events which have already happened together with their orderings plus further constraints. The initial assertion in proof outlines is always the event structure Ini. Then, the proof rules successively add new events to the event structure when e.g. reading from or writing to shared variables. We however *never* add events for promises; rather, threads can first of all assume arbitrary promises of other threads having been made which they can read from. The overall interference freedom constraint guarantees that these local assumptions about promises are met at the end.

For adding new events, we use a number of $\oplus$-operators, detailed in Fig. 6. The event structures in there are local to threads and describe a single execution of the thread, hence are conflict-free. The definition of these operators has to ensure that they capture the dependencies between views as defined by the operational semantics. For example, rule FULFILL requires (among others) the timestamp t to be larger than control view v_C, hence $\mathcal{E} \oplus \mathsf{ff}_\tau(x,\kappa)$ has to introduce a flow from the last test event to the newly added fulfill event.

$$\begin{aligned}
\mathcal{E} \oplus \mathsf{ff}_\tau(x,\kappa) &= (E_e, \twoheadrightarrow \cup \{(e',e) \mid e' \in \mathit{last}_{Act^x \cup \{\mathsf{fnc}_\tau, \mathsf{tst}_\tau(\cdot)\}}(\mathcal{E})\}, \Lambda, \ell[\mathsf{e} \mapsto \mathsf{ff}_\tau(x,\kappa))]) \\
\mathcal{E} \oplus^a \mathsf{ff}_\tau(x,\kappa) &= (E_e, \twoheadrightarrow \cup \{(e',e) \mid e' \in \mathit{last}_{Act^x \cup \{\mathsf{fnc}_\tau, \mathsf{tst}_\tau(\cdot), \mathsf{bar}(a,\cdot)\}}(\mathcal{E})\}, \\
&\qquad \Lambda, \ell[\mathsf{e} \mapsto \mathsf{ff}_\tau(x,\kappa)]) \\
\mathcal{E} \oplus \mathsf{bar}(a,x) &= (E_e, \twoheadrightarrow \cup \{(e',e) \mid e' \in \mathit{last}_{Act^x \cup \{\mathsf{fnc}_\tau, \mathsf{bar}(\cdot,\cdot)\}}(\mathcal{E})\}, \Lambda, \ell[\mathsf{e} \mapsto \mathsf{bar}(a,x)]) \\
\mathcal{E} \oplus \mathsf{bar}(a,\eta) &= \left(E_e, \twoheadrightarrow \cup \left\{\begin{array}{l}(e',e) \mid \\ \exists b \in R(\eta) \cup \{a\} : e' = \mathit{last}_{\mathsf{bar}(b,\cdot)}(\mathcal{E})\end{array}\right\}, \Lambda, \ell[\mathsf{e} \mapsto \mathsf{bar}(a,\eta)]\right) \\
\mathcal{E} \oplus \mathsf{fnc}_\tau &= (E_e, \twoheadrightarrow \cup \{(e',e) \mid e' \in \mathit{last}_{Act \setminus \{\mathsf{tst}_\tau(\cdot)\}}(\mathcal{E})\}, \Lambda, \ell[\mathsf{e} \mapsto \mathsf{fnc}_\tau]) \\
\mathcal{E} \oplus \mathsf{tst}_\tau(\beta) &= (E_e, \twoheadrightarrow \cup \{(e',e) \mid \exists a \in R(\beta).\ e' \in \mathit{last}_{\mathsf{bar}(a,\cdot)}(\mathcal{E})\}, \Lambda, \ell[\mathsf{e} \mapsto \mathsf{tst}_\tau(\beta)]) \\
\mathcal{E} \oplus \mathcal{E}' &= \begin{pmatrix} E \cup E', \\ \twoheadrightarrow \cup \twoheadrightarrow' \cup \left\{\begin{array}{l}(e,e') \in E \times E' \mid \exists x \in \textsc{Loc}. \\ e = \mathit{last}_{\{\mathsf{fnc}, \mathsf{bar}(\cdot,\cdot), \mathsf{ff}.(x,\cdot)\}}(\mathcal{E}) \wedge \ell(\mathsf{e}') \in Act^x\end{array}\right\}, \\ \Lambda \cup \Lambda', \ell \cup \ell' \end{pmatrix}
\end{aligned}$$

Fig. 6. Operations for adding events to a conflict-free event structure $\mathcal{E} = (E, \twoheadrightarrow, \Lambda, \ell)$, where $e \notin E$ is a fresh event and $E_e = E \cup \{e\}$, $\mathcal{E}' = (E', \twoheadrightarrow', \Lambda', \ell')$, $E \cap E' = \emptyset$)

Figure 7 gives the proof rules for building local proof outlines of threads. Most of the rules (i.e., PR-WRITE, PR-WRITER, PR-FENCE, PR-REGISTERS and PR-ASSUME) just add one new event to the event structure recording the occurrence of a particular program statement. More complex are the two read rules: PR-READEX is applied for load statements reading from x when the event structure already contains an event e describing (in the sense of $[\![\mathcal{E}]\!]$) the entry in memory to read from; this can be a read, fulfill or the ini event. In this case, the event structure after the load has to reflect the applicability condition of rule READ: no entries in memory to x in between t (the timestamp of e in $[\![\mathcal{E}]\!]$) and $v_{read} \sqcup coh(x)$. This is achieved by inserting an additional location restriction x via the operator $rstr^x_{\mathsf{e}}(\mathcal{E})$ to the following (potentially already L-labelled) flows (thus getting the restriction $L \uplus \{x\}$):

$$\{\mathsf{e} \overset{L}{\twoheadrightarrow} \mathsf{e}' \mid \mathsf{e}' \in (prFnc_\tau(\mathcal{E}) \cap \mathsf{Ff}_\tau(\mathcal{E})) \cup prBar_\tau(\mathcal{E}) \cup \mathsf{Ff}^x_\tau(\mathcal{E})\}\ .$$

Rule PR-READNEW on the other hand introduces new read events into an event structure upon a load statement. The rule can directly introduce an entire *sequence* of read events (i.e., add a sequential event structure $\mathcal{E}'$) as to enable later reads from memory entries which are prior to the entry of the current read (described by event e in the rule). This is required for message passing idioms like in the following program.

Thread 1	**Thread 2**
$1:$ **store** x 5;	$4: a :=$ **load** y;
$2:$ dmb;	$5: b :=$ **load** x;
$3:$ **store** y 1;	

Here, due to the fence in Thread 1, Thread 2 – after having read y to be 1 – can only read x to be 5. When constructing the proof outline for Thread 2, we need to apply rule PR-READNEW for the first load giving us

$$\text{PR-WRITE}\ \frac{}{[\mathcal{E}]\ \textbf{store}\ x\ \kappa\ [\mathcal{E} \oplus \mathsf{ff}_\tau(x,\kappa)]} \qquad \text{PR-WRITER}\ \frac{[\![a]\!]_\mathcal{E} = \kappa}{[\mathcal{E}]\ \textbf{store}\ x\ a\ [\mathcal{E} \oplus^a \mathsf{ff}_\tau(x,\kappa)]} \qquad \text{PR-FENCE}\ \frac{}{[\mathcal{E}]\ \textbf{dmb}_\tau\ [\mathcal{E} \oplus \mathsf{fnc}_\tau]}$$

$$\text{PR-READEX}\ \frac{e = last_{Act^x}(\mathcal{E}) \quad \ell(e) \in \{\mathsf{rd}_{\tau'}(x,\kappa), \mathsf{ff}_\tau(x,\kappa), \mathsf{ini}\}}{[\mathcal{E}]\ a := \textbf{load}\, x\ [rstr^x_e(\mathcal{E} \oplus \mathsf{bar}(a,x))]}$$

$$\text{PR-READNEW}\ \frac{\mathcal{E}' = (E', \twoheadrightarrow', \Lambda', \ell') \in \mathcal{S} \quad \ell'(E') \subseteq Act^{Rd} \setminus Act_\tau \quad last_{Act}(\mathcal{E}') = e, \ell'(e) = \mathsf{rd}_{\tau'}(x,\kappa)}{[\mathcal{E}]\ a := \textbf{load}\, x\ [(\mathcal{E} \oplus \mathcal{E}') \oplus \mathsf{bar}(a,x)]}$$

$$\text{PR-REGISTERS}\ \frac{}{[\mathcal{E}]\ a := \eta\ [\mathcal{E} \oplus \mathsf{bar}(a,\eta)]} \qquad \text{PR-ASSUME}\ \frac{[\![\beta]\!]_\mathcal{E} = \mathsf{true}}{[\mathcal{E}]\ \textbf{asm}\ \beta\ [\mathcal{E} \oplus \mathsf{tst}_\tau(\beta)]} \qquad \text{PR-CHOICE}\ \frac{[\mathcal{E}_1]\ S_i\ [\mathcal{E}_2]}{[\mathcal{E}_1]\ S_1 + S_2\ [\mathcal{E}_2]}$$

$$\text{PR-SEQUENCING}\ \frac{[\mathcal{E}_1]\ S_1\ [\mathcal{E}_2] \qquad [\mathcal{E}_2]\ S_1\ [\mathcal{E}_3]}{[\mathcal{E}_1]\ S_1; S_2\ [\mathcal{E}_3]} \qquad \text{PR-ITERATEZERO}\ \frac{}{[\mathcal{E}]\ S^0\ [\mathcal{E}]} \qquad \text{PR-ITERATENONZERO}\ \frac{n > 0 \qquad [\mathcal{E}_1]\ S; S^{n-1}\ [\mathcal{E}_2]}{[\mathcal{E}_1]\ S^n\ [\mathcal{E}_2]}$$

Fig. 7. Local proof rules for a thread τ

$$\mathsf{ini} \twoheadrightarrow \mathsf{rd}_1(x,5) \twoheadrightarrow \mathsf{rd}_1(y,1) \twoheadrightarrow \mathsf{bar}(a,y)$$

as assertion after statement 4. For the subsequent load we can then apply proof rule PR-READEX. Note that we could also construct a local proof outline having the load in line 4 read from ini. This would then give us the two event structures of Example 1 which we, however, have already seen to not allow for an interference free configuration of their parallel composition.

Finally, we have a proof rule for parallel composition which combines local event structures when they are synchronisable and the resulting configuration is interference free.

$$\text{PARALLEL}\ \frac{\forall i \in \{1,\ldots,n\}.\ [\mathsf{Ini}]\ S_i\ [\mathcal{E}_i] \qquad \mathcal{E}_1,\ldots,\mathcal{E}_n \text{ synchronisable} \qquad \text{interference free } C \in Conf(\mathcal{E}_1||\ldots||\mathcal{E}_n)}{[\mathsf{Ini}]\ S_1||\ldots||S_n\ [\mathcal{E}_C]}$$

This rule ensures that (1) all synchronization constraints are met (i.e., the promises that threads want to read from have been made) and (2) there is a configuration C of the combined event structure which is interference free.

Example 2. Next, we give a complete proof outline for the message passing litmus test *without* a barrier in the writing thread. We see that here message passing is not guaranteed (i.e., reading y to be 1 does not "pass the message" that x is 5 from Thread 1 to 2) and we can actually reach a final state with $(a = 1 \wedge b = 0)$ (as calculated by $[\![a]\!]_\mathcal{E}$ and $[\![b]\!]_\mathcal{E}$ taking the value of the last fulfill or ini event prior to the last bar event on a and b, respectively).

Thread 1
[ini]
1 : **store** x 5;
[ini $\twoheadrightarrow$ $\mathsf{ff}_1(x,5)$]
2 : **store** y 1;

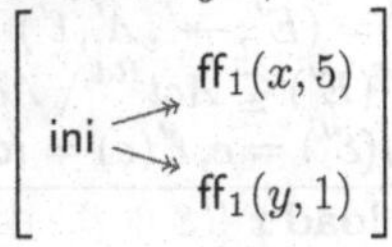

Thread 2
[ini]
4 : $a :=$ **load** y;
[ini $\twoheadrightarrow$ $\mathsf{rd}_1(y,1) \twoheadrightarrow \mathsf{bar}(a,y)$]
5 : $b :=$ **load** x;

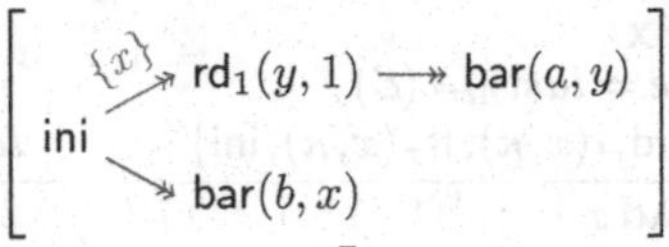

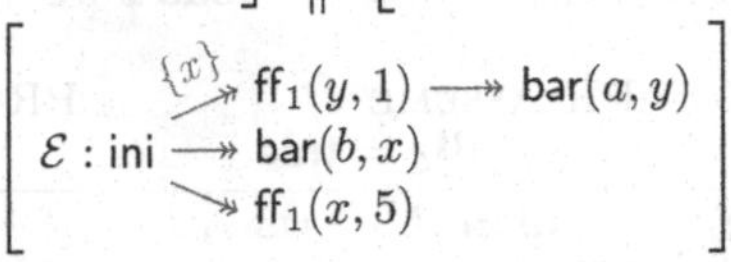

5.3 Soundness and Completeness

Due to lack of space, we can neither discuss soundness nor completeness of our proof calculus in some more detail here. Proofs can be found in the extended version [38].

Soundness requires proving all local proof rules correct plus showing the correctness of rule PARALLEL as of Theorem 1 below. It states that whenever we find an interference free configuration in the parallel composition of synchronizable event structures in a locally sound proof outline, all thread states and memory contents matching this configuration are actually reachable by the concurrent program.

Theorem 1. *Let* [Ini] S_i $[\mathcal{E}_i]$, $i \in \{1, \ldots, n\}$, *be proof outlines of threads* τ_1 *to* τ_n *such that* $\mathcal{E}_1$ *to* $\mathcal{E}_n$ *are synchronizable and let* $\boldsymbol{T_0}$ *be an initial thread pool with* $\boldsymbol{T_0}(\tau_i) = (S_i, ts_{\mathsf{ini}})$ *and* $M_0 = M_{\mathsf{ini}}$.

Then, for every thread pool $\boldsymbol{T}$ *with* $\boldsymbol{T}(\tau_i) = (\boldsymbol{skip}, ts_i)$, *interference free configuration* $C \in Conf(\mathcal{E}_1 || \ldots || \mathcal{E}_n)$ *and memory* M *such that* $\langle ts_i, M\rangle \in [\![\mathcal{E}_C]\!]$, $tids(M) = \{\tau_1, \ldots, \tau_n\}$ *and* $ts_i.prom = \emptyset$, $i \in \{1, \ldots, n\}$, *we have* $\langle \boldsymbol{T_0}, M_0\rangle \rightarrow^* \langle \boldsymbol{T}, M\rangle$.

Our second main result is the *completeness* of the proof calculus: whenever there is an execution of a concurrent program, our proof calculus allows to show the reachability of its final state. More specifically, for every trace of a concurrent program we find local proof outlines with synchronizable event structures and an interference free configuration describing the final state of the trace.

Theorem 2. *Let* $\langle \boldsymbol{T_0}, M_0\rangle \rightarrow^* \langle \boldsymbol{T}, M\rangle$ *be a trace of a concurrent program over threads* $\tau_1, \ldots, \tau_n$ *such that* $\boldsymbol{T_0}$ *is the initial thread pool with* $\boldsymbol{T_0}(\tau_k) = (S_k, ts_{\mathsf{ini}})$, $M_0 = M_{\mathsf{ini}}$ *and* $\boldsymbol{T}$ *the final thread pool with* $\boldsymbol{T}(\tau_k) = (\boldsymbol{skip}, ts_k)$ *and* $ts_k.prom = \emptyset$, $k \in \{1, \ldots, n\}$.

Then there are local proof outlines [Ini] S_k $[\mathcal{E}_k]$ *of threads* τ_k, $k \in \{1, \ldots, n\}$, *such that* $\mathcal{E}_1$ *to* $\mathcal{E}_n$ *are synchronizable and there exists an interference free configuration* $C \in Conf(\mathcal{E}_1 || \ldots || \mathcal{E}_n)$ *with* $\langle \boldsymbol{T}, M\rangle \in [\![\mathcal{E}_C]\!]$.

6 Related Work

The first semantics of weak memory models employing *promises* has been proposed by Kang et al. in 2017 [21] for building an operational semantics which allows modelling of read-write reordering while at the same time disallows out-of-thin-air behaviours. Our semantics here is a slightly simplified version of the promising semantics of ARMv8 given by Pulte et al. [29]. In particular, like [29] all program traces can be reordered so that the promise steps are all at the beginning which is a key property required for the soundness of our proof calculus.

There are already several proposals for program logics for weak memory e.g. [1,9,10,12–14,22,32,36]. The only one explicitly dealing with promises in the semantics is the proposal of Svendsen et al. [35]. They develop a safety proof calculus whereas we are interested in reachability. Their logic furthermore has to deal with promises occurring at any program step (as they show soundness with respect to the promising semantics of [21]), whereas we rely on all promises being made at the beginning.

Partial order models of concurrency have already been used for giving the semantics of memory models [7,18,19], but not for reasoning. Wright et al [40] take the approach of using a *semantic dependency* relation, which is a partial order generated through an event structure representation of a C/C++ program [28], which is a partial order over a thread's execution. An Owicki-Gries logic is provided to reason directly over such partial orders. Incorrectness logic as used for proving reachability properties of *sequential* programs has been introduced by O'Hearn [26], with a predecessor approach with (almost) the same principles by de Vries and Koutavas [37]. The first extension of incorrectness logic to concurrent programs has been proposed by Raad et al. in the form of an incorrectness separation logic [30] which is however not compositional.

Colvin [8] defines a semantics based on a reordering relation for several hardware memory models, which is then lifted to a Hoare calculus. This is then rephrased into a reachability property by defining triples $\langle\langle p\rangle\rangle\ s\ \langle\langle q\rangle\rangle = \neg\{p\}\ s\ \{\neg q\}$, which states that it is possible for s to reach q if execution starts in a state satisfying p. Note that this is weaker than O'Hearn's notion of incompleteness, which states that all states satisfying q are reachable from an execution starting in a state satisfying p.

7 Conclusion

In this paper, we have proposed a reachability (incorrectness) logic for concurrent programs running on weak memory models. The reasoning technique is based on assertions which are event structures abstractly describing the contents of memory and the views of all threads. We have proven soundness and completeness of the proof calculus, and have demonstrated its applicability by proving the outcomes of some standard litmus tests to be reachable.

Acknowledgements. We thank Christopher Pulte for clarifying one aspect of the Register rule of ARMv8's operational semantics to us and Sadegh Dalvandi for initial discussions on the semantics.

References

1. Alglave, J., Cousot, P.: Ogre and Pythia: an invariance proof method for weak consistency models. In: Castagna, G., Gordon, A.D. (eds.) POPL, pp. 3–18. ACM (2017). https://doi.org/10.1145/3009837.3009883
2. Batty, M., Owens, S., Sarkar, S., Sewell, P., Weber, T.: Mathematizing C++ concurrency. In: Ball, T., Sagiv, M. (eds.) POPL, pp. 55–66. ACM (2011). https://doi.org/10.1145/1926385.1926394
3. Bila, E.V., Dongol, B., Lahav, O., Raad, A., Wickerson, J.: View-based Owicki–Gries reasoning for persistent x86-TSO. In: ESOP 2022. LNCS, vol. 13240, pp. 234–261. Springer, Cham (2022). https://doi.org/10.1007/978-3-030-99336-8_9
4. Boudol, G., Castellani, I.: On the semantics of concurrency: partial orders and transition systems. In: Ehrig, H., Kowalski, R., Levi, G., Montanari, U. (eds.) CAAP 1987. LNCS, vol. 249, pp. 123–137. Springer, Heidelberg (1987). https://doi.org/10.1007/3-540-17660-8_52
5. Boudol, G., Castellani, I.: Flow models of distributed computations: three equivalent semantics for CCS. Inf. Comput. **114**(2), 247–314 (1994). https://doi.org/10.1006/inco.1994.1088
6. Castellani, I., Zhang, G.: Parallel product of event structures. Theor. Comput. Sci. **179**(1–2), 203–215 (1997). https://doi.org/10.1016/S0304-3975(96)00104-1
7. Chakraborty, S., Vafeiadis, V.: Grounding thin-air reads with event structures. Proc. ACM Program. Lang. **3**(POPL) (2019). https://doi.org/10.1145/3290383
8. Colvin, R.J.: Parallelized sequential composition and hardware weak memory models. In: Calinescu, R., Păsăreanu, C.S. (eds.) SEFM 2021. LNCS, vol. 13085, pp. 201–221. Springer, Cham (2021). https://doi.org/10.1007/978-3-030-92124-8_12
9. Coughlin, N., Winter, K., Smith, G.: Rely/Guarantee reasoning for multicopy atomic weak memory models. In: Huisman, M., Păsăreanu, C., Zhan, N. (eds.) FM 2021. LNCS, vol. 13047, pp. 292–310. Springer, Cham (2021). https://doi.org/10.1007/978-3-030-90870-6_16
10. Dalvandi, S., Doherty, S., Dongol, B., Wehrheim, H.: Owicki-Gries reasoning for C11 RAR. In: Hirschfeld, R., Pape, T. (eds.) ECOOP. LIPIcs, vol. 166, pp. 11:1–11:26. Schloss Dagstuhl - Leibniz-Zentrum für Informatik (2020). https://doi.org/10.4230/LIPIcs.ECOOP.2020.11
11. Dalvandi, S., Dongol, B., Doherty, S., Wehrheim, H.: Integrating Owicki–Gries for C11-style memory models into Isabelle/HOL. J. Autom. Reason. 1–31 (2021). https://doi.org/10.1007/s10817-021-09610-2
12. Doherty, S., Dalvandi, S., Dongol, B., Wehrheim, H.: Unifying operational weak memory verification: an axiomatic approach. ACM Trans. Comput. Log. **23**(4), 27:1–27:39 (2022). https://doi.org/10.1145/3545117
13. Doherty, S., Dongol, B., Wehrheim, H., Derrick, J.: Verifying C11 programs operationally. In: Hollingsworth, J.K., Keidar, I. (eds.) PPoPP, pp. 355–365. ACM (2019). https://doi.org/10.1145/3293883.3295702
14. Doko, M., Vafeiadis, V.: A program logic for C11 memory fences. In: Jobstmann, B., Leino, K.R.M. (eds.) VMCAI 2016. LNCS, vol. 9583, pp. 413–430. Springer, Heidelberg (2016). https://doi.org/10.1007/978-3-662-49122-5_20

15. Flur, S., et al.: Modelling the ARMv8 architecture, operationally: concurrency and ISA. In: Bodík, R., Majumdar, R. (eds.) POPL, pp. 608–621. ACM (2016). https://doi.org/10.1145/2837614.2837615
16. van Glabbeek, R.J., Goltz, U.: Well-behaved flow event structures for parallel composition and action refinement. Theor. Comput. Sci. **311**(1–3), 463–478 (2004). https://doi.org/10.1016/j.tcs.2003.10.031
17. Hoare, C.A.R.: An axiomatic basis for computer programming. Commun. ACM **12**(10), 576–580 (1969)
18. Jagadeesan, R., Jeffrey, A., Riely, J.: Pomsets with preconditions: a simple model of relaxed memory. Proc. ACM Program. Lang. **4**(OOPSLA), 194:1–194:30 (2020). https://doi.org/10.1145/3428262
19. Jeffrey, A., Riely, J., Batty, M., Cooksey, S., Kaysin, I., Podkopaev, A.: The leaky semicolon: compositional semantic dependencies for relaxed-memory concurrency. Proc. ACM Program. Lang. **6**(POPL), 1–30 (2022). https://doi.org/10.1145/3498716
20. Kaiser, J., Dang, H., Dreyer, D., Lahav, O., Vafeiadis, V.: Strong logic for weak memory: reasoning about release-acquire consistency in iris. In: Müller, P. (ed.) ECOOP. LIPIcs, vol. 74, pp. 17:1–17:29. Schloss Dagstuhl - Leibniz-Zentrum für Informatik (2017). https://doi.org/10.4230/LIPIcs.ECOOP.2017.17
21. Kang, J., Hur, C., Lahav, O., Vafeiadis, V., Dreyer, D.: A promising semantics for relaxed-memory concurrency. In: Castagna, G., Gordon, A.D. (eds.) POPL, pp. 175–189. ACM (2017). https://doi.org/10.1145/3009837.3009850
22. Lahav, O., Vafeiadis, V.: Owicki-Gries reasoning for weak memory models. In: Halldórsson, M.M., Iwama, K., Kobayashi, N., Speckmann, B. (eds.) ICALP 2015. LNCS, vol. 9135, pp. 311–323. Springer, Heidelberg (2015). https://doi.org/10.1007/978-3-662-47666-6_25
23. Lee, S., et al.: Promising 2.0: global optimizations in relaxed memory concurrency. In: Donaldson, A.F., Torlak, E. (eds.) PLDI, pp. 362–376. ACM (2020). https://doi.org/10.1145/3385412.3386010
24. Milner, R.: Communication and Concurrency. PHI Series in computer science, Prentice Hall, Hoboken (1989)
25. Nienhuis, K., Memarian, K., Sewell, P.: An operational semantics for C/C++11 concurrency. In: Visser, E., Smaragdakis, Y. (eds.) OOPSLA, pp. 111–128. ACM (2016). https://doi.org/10.1145/2983990.2983997
26. O'Hearn, P.W.: Incorrectness logic. Proc. ACM Program. Lang. **4**(POPL), 10:1–10:32 (2020). https://doi.org/10.1145/3371078
27. Owicki, S.S., Gries, D.: An axiomatic proof technique for parallel programs I. Acta Inf. **6**, 319–340 (1976)
28. Paviotti, M., Cooksey, S., Paradis, A., Wright, D., Owens, S., Batty, M.: Modular relaxed dependencies in weak memory concurrency. In: ESOP 2020. LNCS, vol. 12075, pp. 599–625. Springer, Cham (2020). https://doi.org/10.1007/978-3-030-44914-8_22
29. Pulte, C., Pichon-Pharabod, J., Kang, J., Lee, S.H., Hur, C.: Promising-ARM/RISC-V: a simpler and faster operational concurrency model. In: McKinley, K.S., Fisher, K. (eds.) PLDI, pp. 1–15. ACM (2019). https://doi.org/10.1145/3314221.3314624
30. Raad, A., Berdine, J., Dreyer, D., O'Hearn, P.W.: Concurrent incorrectness separation logic. Proc. ACM Program. Lang. **6**(POPL), 1–29 (2022). https://doi.org/10.1145/3498695

31. Raad, A., Lahav, O., Vafeiadis, V.: Persistent Owicki-Gries reasoning: a program logic for reasoning about persistent programs on Intel-x86. Proc. ACM Program. Lang. **4**(OOPSLA), 151:1–151:28 (2020). https://doi.org/10.1145/3428219
32. Ridge, T.: A rely-guarantee proof system for x86-TSO. In: Leavens, G.T., O'Hearn, P., Rajamani, S.K. (eds.) VSTTE 2010. LNCS, vol. 6217, pp. 55–70. Springer, Heidelberg (2010). https://doi.org/10.1007/978-3-642-15057-9_4
33. Sarkar, S., Sewell, P., Alglave, J., Maranget, L., Williams, D.: Understanding POWER multiprocessors. In: Hall, M.W., Padua, D.A. (eds.) PLDI, pp. 175–186. ACM (2011). https://doi.org/10.1145/1993498.1993520
34. Sewell, P., Sarkar, S., Owens, S., Nardelli, F.Z., Myreen, M.O.: x86-TSO: a rigorous and usable programmer's model for x86 multiprocessors. Commun. ACM **53**(7), 89–97 (2010). https://doi.org/10.1145/1785414.1785443
35. Svendsen, K., Pichon-Pharabod, J., Doko, M., Lahav, O., Vafeiadis, V.: A separation logic for a promising semantics. In: Ahmed, A. (ed.) ESOP 2018. LNCS, vol. 10801, pp. 357–384. Springer, Cham (2018). https://doi.org/10.1007/978-3-319-89884-1_13
36. Vafeiadis, V., Narayan, C.: Relaxed separation logic: a program logic for C11 concurrency. In: Hosking, A.L., Eugster, P.T., Lopes, C.V. (eds.) OOPSLA, pp. 867–884. ACM (2013). https://doi.org/10.1145/2509136.2509532
37. de Vries, E., Koutavas, V.: Reverse hoare logic. In: Barthe, G., Pardo, A., Schneider, G. (eds.) SEFM 2011. LNCS, vol. 7041, pp. 155–171. Springer, Heidelberg (2011). https://doi.org/10.1007/978-3-642-24690-6_12
38. Wehrheim, H., Bargmann, L., Dongol, B.: Reasoning about promises in weak memory models with event structures (extended version) (2022). https://doi.org/10.48550/ARXIV.2211.16330, https://arxiv.org/abs/2211.16330
39. Winskel, G.: An introduction to event structures. In: de Bakker, J.W., de Roever, W.-P., Rozenberg, G. (eds.) REX 1988. LNCS, vol. 354, pp. 364–397. Springer, Heidelberg (1989). https://doi.org/10.1007/BFb0013026
40. Wright, D., Batty, M., Dongol, B.: Owicki-Gries reasoning for C11 programs with relaxed dependencies. In: Huisman, M., Păsăreanu, C., Zhan, N. (eds.) FM 2021. LNCS, vol. 13047, pp. 237–254. Springer, Cham (2021). https://doi.org/10.1007/978-3-030-90870-6_13

A Fine-Grained Semantics for Arrays and Pointers Under Weak Memory Models

Robert J. Colvin[(✉)]

Defence Science and Technology Group and The University of Queensland, Brisbane, Australia
r.colvin@uq.edu.au

Abstract. Developers of concurrent code for multicore architectures must navigate weak memory models (wmms) – either directly at the hardware/assembly level or at a somewhat generalised software level – making the verification of concurrent code an even more difficult task. Semantic models based on a system-wide partial-ordering on events have been developed to define the behaviour of code executing under wmms, but typically require specialised assertion languages and inference techniques to reason about, and often apply to only rudimentary programming constructs. In this paper we present a generic but versatile abstract imperative language "IMP+ptr" which includes pointers and arrays, from which can be built high-level imperative programming constructs for verifying abstract algorithmic logic, or low-level microassembly for, e.g., investigating hardware security vulnerabilities. The base language carefully controls the syntax of atomic instructions to allow program-level, algebraic reasoning about the additional nondeterminism inherent in programs executing under wmms. We show how arrays of pointers, aliasing, and linked lists may be affected by wmms, establishing a base from where we apply pre-existing verification results and techniques for sequential programs with nested parallelism.

1 Introduction

Weak memory models (hardware or software) define how concurrent code may be executed, factoring in that processors might execute instructions out of order, and potential transformations made by the compiler. Such details are typically hidden from the programmer – an abstraction that held true in the age of single-core processors – but for low-level systems code operating on multicore processors the pitfalls must be dealt with. A programmer ideally works with abstract data structures such as arrays, although in many cases, in particular with C-like languages, the underlying pointer details may be exposed. As a consequence, for *verification* of such code one must deal with fine-grained parallelism within the structure of otherwise sequential code. As for the programmer, the verifier would like to expose or abstract from implementation details where appropriate. To this end we present a minimal abstract language, IMP+ptr, that allows expressions that include pointers and arrays and which encompasses the behaviours of weak memory models.

M. Chechik et al. (Eds.): FM 2023, LNCS 14000, pp. 301–320, 2023.
https://doi.org/10.1007/978-3-031-27481-7_18

We show that, despite being minimal, `IMP+ptr` can define an imperative language (with conditionals and loops) using the typical (Concurrent) Kleene algebra approach in Sect. 2. We then define a more realistic, C-like language with non-atomic expression evaluation in Sect. 3. This essentially defines behaviour in terms of the underlying atomic, assembler-level instructions to which the code will be compiled. In Sect. 4 we consider reordering of instructions according to weak memory models, based on principles of data dependencies. We show how this lifts to the program level and facilitates a program-transformation approach to elucidating the effects of weak memory models. In Sect. 5 we use the language and semantic framework to explore how weak memory models affect the execution of code involving aliasing, a linked-list implementation of a stack, and can be extended to explain a wide-spread security vulnerability affecting many modern processors. All major results have been machine-checked in the Isabelle theorem prover [40]. The work is motivated towards providing the basis for tool support for the verification of highly-parallel multicore implementations of security-critical software such as the seL4 microkernel [30], and for investigating lower-level considerations relating to microassembly [31,36]. As such, we take a program transformation (algebraic/refinement-based) approach which allows existing results and verification techniques for sequential algorithms to be used.

2 A Versatile Language with Fine-Grained Concurrency

Syntax. Below we give the syntax for the language `IMP+ptr`, which includes expressions $e \in \mathsf{Expr}$, *l-values* $\varphi \in \mathsf{LVal}$ (a subset of expressions that represent objects that are mutable), (atomic) instructions $\alpha \in \mathsf{Instr}$, and commands $c \in \mathsf{Cmd}$. We assume a set of base values Val and variable identifiers Var. Values are divided into regular values (integers, booleans, etc.) and *locations* (set Loc, corresponding to concrete addresses). In this framework a memory model $\mathrm{M} \in \mathsf{Instr} \times \mathsf{Instr}$ is a relation on instructions.

$$\begin{array}{ll} e ::= v \mid x \mid e_1 \otimes e_2 \mid e_1[e_2] \mid *e & \varphi ::= x \mid *e \mid \varphi[e] \\ \alpha ::= (\!|e|\!) \mid \varphi \leftarrow e & \\ c ::= \mathbf{nil} \mid \vec{\alpha} \mid c_1 \overset{\mathrm{M}}{;} c_2 \mid \sqcap_{i \in I} \cdot c_{[i]} & \end{array} \tag{1}$$

Expressions e can be base values $v \in \mathsf{Val}$, a variable identifier $x \in \mathsf{Var}$, some binary expression $e_1 \otimes e_2$ (all definitions can be generalised to n-ary operators straightforwardly), an *array indexing* expression $e_1[e_2]$, or a *dereference* expression $*e$ (allowing nested dereferencing, dereferencing of array elements, etc.). An *l-value* φ is an expression that is either a variable, a dereference expression, or an array indexing expression (with a variable or dereference at its base), for instance, x, $*x$, or $x[1]$, but not $2 + 3$, etc. An instruction α is a guard $(\!|e|\!)$ or update $\varphi \leftarrow e$, updating l-value φ to the value of e.

The command language is compact but expressive: a command may be the terminated command, '**nil**'; a sequence of instructions, '$\vec{\alpha}$' (typically it will be singleton), which are collectively executed as a single step; the parallelized sequential composition of two commands according to some memory model (reordering relation) M, '$c_1 \overset{M}{;} c_2$' (described below); or a choice over a set of commands indexed by some countable type I, '$\sqcap_{i \in I} . c_{[i]}$' (we use $\mathbb{B}$, $\mathbb{N}$, Val and Var for I).

A sequence of instructions $\vec{\alpha}$ we refer to as an *action*. We use angled brackets for constructing sequences $\langle a_1, a_2, \ldots \rangle$, with $\langle\rangle$ the empty sequence. Typically actions are singleton sequences of instructions, in which case we omit the angled brackets, and blur the distinction between actions and instructions.

A *parallelized sequential composition*, $c_1 \overset{M}{;} c_2$, generalises sequential and parallel composition, and additionally captures many of the behaviours of weak memory models, depending on the instantiation of M. If M is the empty relation then $c_1 \overset{M}{;} c_2$ is just normal sequential composition (no reordering), and if M is the universal set then $c_1 \overset{M}{;} c_2$ is just normal parallel composition (any reordering). We give the foundations of a typical weak memory model in Sect. 4.

The command type $\sqcap_{i \in I} . c_{[i]}$ picks some element i of I and behaves as the command $c_{[i]}$, i.e., c for that element of I. We make the following shorthands for brevity and readability to cover common cases. Note that when the set I is clear from context we omit '$\in I$', and where the parameter i is clear from context, we use c in place of $c_{[i]}$. Below $P(v)$ is some predicate on v.

$$\sqcap_v . c \mathrel{\widehat{=}} \sqcap_{v \in \mathsf{Val}} . c_{[v]} \qquad \sqcap_n . c \mathrel{\widehat{=}} \sqcap_{n \in \mathbb{N}} . c$$

$$\sqcap_{P(v)} . c \mathrel{\widehat{=}} \sqcap_{v \in \{v' \mid P(v')\}} . c \qquad \sqcap_{v_1, v_2} . c \mathrel{\widehat{=}} \sqcap_{v_1} . (\sqcap_{v_2} . c)$$

Encoding an Imperative Language in IMP+ptr. Binary choice and iteration are defined in the typical Kleene-algebra style [33], with the n-fold iteration of a command c defined inductively as $c^0 \mathrel{\widehat{=}} \mathbf{nil}$ and $c^{n+1} \mathrel{\widehat{=}} c; c^n$, where '; ' is defined below.

$$c_1 \sqcap c_2 \mathrel{\widehat{=}} \sqcap_{b \in \mathbb{B}} . (b \, ? \, c_1 : c_2) \qquad c^* \mathrel{\widehat{=}} \sqcap_n . c^n \tag{2}$$

Binary choice is simply a choice over the doubleton set of booleans (we use the ternary conditional $b \, ? \, c_1 : c_2$ to distinguish it from the language-level **if** / **then** conditional). Finite iteration c^* is a choice between all possible unfoldings (to avoid distraction we do not give infinite iteration in this language but there is no reason why that cannot be considered). We define conditionals and while loops as in Kleene Algebra [33], and as above define (strict) sequential composition and parallel composition by instantiating parallelized sequential composition.

$$\begin{aligned} c_1; c_2 &\mathrel{\widehat{=}} c_1 \overset{\varnothing}{;} c_2 & \quad \mathbf{if}\ b\ \mathbf{then}\ c_1\ \mathbf{else}\ c_2 &\mathrel{\widehat{=}} (\!| b |\!); c_1 \sqcap (\!| \neg b |\!); c_2 \\ c_1 \parallel c_2 &\mathrel{\widehat{=}} c_1 \overset{\mathsf{univ}}{;} c_2 & \quad \mathbf{while}\ b\ \mathbf{do}\ c &\mathrel{\widehat{=}} ((\!| b |\!); c)^*; (\!| \neg b |\!) \end{aligned} \tag{3}$$

Denotational Semantics as Sets of Traces. We define a denotational semantics for IMP+ptr (in contrast to the small-step operational semantics for a similar but less expressive language [11]) that interprets commands as sets of traces, which are sequences of actions (which are themselves sequences of instructions). The set of traces of c, $tr(c)$, is defined inductively below.

$$\begin{aligned} tr(\mathbf{nil}) &= \{\langle\rangle\} & \qquad tr(c_1 \overset{M}{;} c_2) &= tr(c_1) \overset{M}{\Cup} tr(c_2) \\ tr(\vec{\alpha}) &= \{\langle\vec{\alpha}\rangle\} & \qquad tr(\sqcap_{i \in I} . c_{[i]}) &= \textstyle\bigcup_{i \in I} tr(c_{[i]}) \end{aligned} \tag{4}$$

The operator $\overset{\text{M}}{\Lbag\!\!\|}$ interleaves sets of traces according to memory model relation M. This is defined in terms of M (defined on instructions) where, for instructions α and β, if $(\alpha, \beta) \in$ M then $\alpha \overset{\text{M}}{\Lbag\!\!\|} \beta = \{\langle\alpha, \beta\rangle, \langle\beta, \alpha\rangle\}$, and $\alpha \overset{\text{M}}{\Lbag\!\!\|} \beta = \{\langle\alpha, \beta\rangle\}$ otherwise. We define the interleaving of traces t_1 and t_2 according to M via a small-step operational semantics, where $t_1 \overset{\text{M}}{\Lbag\!\!\|} t_2 \xrightarrow{\alpha} t_1' \overset{\text{M}}{\Lbag\!\!\|} t_2'$ means that α is a possible next action of the pair, which evolve to t_1' and t_2' (the concept is similar to that in [11] but here defined more straightforwardly directly on traces). Notation $\alpha \frown t$ represents concatenation of α on to the front of sequence t, and we write $\alpha \overset{\text{M}}{\Leftarrow} \beta$ for $(\alpha, \beta) \in$ M, indicating that a "later" instruction β can execute before "earlier" instruction α.

$$(\alpha \frown t_1) \overset{\text{M}}{\Lbag\!\!\|} t_2 \xrightarrow{\alpha} t_1 \overset{\text{M}}{\Lbag\!\!\|} t_2 \qquad \frac{\forall\, \alpha \in \operatorname{ran} t_1 \bullet \alpha \overset{\text{M}}{\Leftarrow} \beta}{t_1 \overset{\text{M}}{\Lbag\!\!\|} (\beta \frown t_2) \xrightarrow{\beta} t_1 \overset{\text{M}}{\Lbag\!\!\|} t_2}$$

Hence the next instruction of t_1 may always proceed, but the next action of t_2 may proceed only if it can reorder with every instruction in t_1 according to M. A full interleaved trace t of $t_1 \overset{\text{M}}{\Lbag\!\!\|} t_2$ is one where both traces are empty at the end.

As discussed above, if M is instantiated with the empty relation then the second rule can never apply (except when t_1 is empty), forcing strict ordering, and if M is instantiated with the universal relation then the precondition of the second rule always holds, giving any interleaving of actions.

Refinement. Refinement, $\sqsubseteq$, is defined as usual as reverse-subset inclusion on traces, i.e., for commands c and d, $c \sqsubseteq d \mathrel{\widehat{=}} tr(d) \subseteq tr(c)$. Refinement equality, $\sqsupseteq\!\sqsubseteq$, is refinement in both directions. The operators $\overset{\text{M}}{;}$ and $\sqcap$ are monotonic for refinement, and the definitions from (3) form a Kleene Algebra [33,34] for finite, sequential programs straightforwardly, that is, all the usual properties of sequential composition, conditionals and loops hold, e.g., $(c_1;\, c_2);\, c_3 \sqsupseteq\!\sqsubseteq c_1;\, (c_2;\, c_3)$. Additionally the exchange law from Concurrent Kleene Algebra [24] holds, i.e., $(c_1;\, c_2) \parallel (d_1;\, d_2) \sqsubseteq (c_1 \parallel d_1);\, (c_2 \parallel d_2)$.

State-Based Semantics. As is common for treatments of pointers a state $\sigma \in (\mathsf{Var} \cup \mathsf{Loc}) \rightarrow \mathsf{Val}$ is the combination of a store mapping variable identifiers to values and a heap mapping locations to values. Special value null ($\notin \mathsf{Loc}$) represents a null pointer, and special value free represents a pointer that has not been allocated; this means that our mapping of locations is *total*, rather than partial. The traditional store ($\mathsf{Var} \rightarrow \mathsf{Val}$) and partial heap ($\mathsf{Loc} \rightarrow\!\!\!\!\!+ \mathsf{Val}$) can be retrieved straightforwardly, i.e., $store(\sigma) = \mathsf{Var} \lhd \sigma$ (σ restricted (in its domain) to variables) and $heap(\sigma) = \mathsf{Loc} \lhd \sigma \rhd \{\mathsf{free}\}$ (σ restricted to locations that do not map to free). We interpret an instruction α as a relation on states via $[\![\alpha]\!]$.

$$[\![(\!| e |\!)]\!] = \{ \mid e_{\langle\sigma\rangle} = \mathsf{tt}\} \qquad [\![\varphi \leftarrow e]\!] = \lambda\, \sigma.\ \sigma \oplus \{\varphi_{\langle\!\langle\sigma\rangle\!\rangle} \mapsto e_{\langle\sigma\rangle}\} \tag{5}$$

The meaning of a guard instruction $(\!| e |\!)$ is the identity relation on states σ where the *evaluation* of e in σ (written $e_{\langle\sigma\rangle}$) is *True* (tt). The meaning of an assignment instruction $\varphi \leftarrow e$ is the relation (function) where given a pre-state σ the post-state is σ updated so that the reference to which φ *resolves* (written $\varphi_{\langle\langle\sigma\rangle\rangle}$) is mapped to $e_{\langle\sigma\rangle}$. Resolution reduces an LVal to either a variable or a location, i.e., an element of domσ. We show how array indexing is handled later.

The meaning of actions and traces are defined inductively using relational composition, and the meaning of a command is the union of the relations for all of its traces, i.e., $[\![c]\!] = \bigcup [\![tr(c)]\!]$. The interpretation of programs as relations admits the usual notions of Hoare logic [22], rely/guarantee [27,28], separation logic [25,44], etc.

Expression Evaluation and Resolving References. Evaluation is defined over the syntax of expressions, and resolution over the syntax of l-values (1).

$$v_{\langle\sigma\rangle} = v \qquad x_{\langle\sigma\rangle} = \sigma(x) \qquad (e_1 \otimes e_2)_{\langle\sigma\rangle} = e_{1\langle\sigma\rangle} \otimes e_{2\langle\sigma\rangle} \tag{6}$$
$$(e_1[e_2])_{\langle\sigma\rangle} = e_{1\langle\sigma\rangle \#} e_{2\langle\sigma\rangle} \qquad *e_{\langle\sigma\rangle} = \sigma(e_{\langle\sigma\rangle})$$

$$x_{\langle\langle\sigma\rangle\rangle} = x \qquad *e_{\langle\langle\sigma\rangle\rangle} = e_{\langle\sigma\rangle} \tag{7}$$

Evaluation of a value v is itself, while evaluation of an identifier x is a lookup of σ. Evaluation of a binary operator expression is straightforward, assuming that underlying the syntax of the operator has some direct interpretation on values. An array index expression $e_1[e_2]$ is evaluated by evaluating the index (e_2) and using that to index into the evaluated array (e_1), where $a_{\#}n$ returns the nth element of array value (sequence) a. Evaluating a dereference $*e$ requires evaluating e to a location and then looking up the value at that location. As an example, assuming $\sigma(x) = l$ and $\sigma(l) = 5$, then $(*x)_{\langle\sigma\rangle} = \sigma(x_{\langle\sigma\rangle}) = \sigma(\sigma(x)) = \sigma(l) = 5$. For brevity we leave as undefined the value of a lookup of a location that is free, but this can be given an abort semantics in the usual way instead.

An l-value φ may be "resolved" to either a variable or a pointer in state σ, written $\varphi_{\langle\langle\sigma\rangle\rangle}$ (array index l-values are normalised into ordinary assignments as described below). Identifiers need no resolution, while resolving a dereference requires evaluating the dereference expression to a location; in particular, $*l_{\langle\langle\sigma\rangle\rangle} = l$ in all states since l is a value. Following from the above and using (5) $*x_{\langle\langle\sigma\rangle\rangle} = x_{\langle\sigma\rangle} = \sigma(x) = l$, and hence $[\![*x \leftarrow ((*x)+1)]\!] = \lambda\sigma.\, \sigma \oplus \{l \mapsto 6\}$.

Handling Array Index Updates. The simplest approach to including array updates at the command level is to treat an assignment such as $A[1] := 17$ as syntactic sugar for $A := A_{[1]\mapsto 17}$, where the expression $A_{[1]\mapsto 17}$ is the value of A overridden at index 1 with the value 17. However in terms of fine-grained atomicity such an assignment both loads and updates the entire array A at once, which does not correspond with a typical concrete representation of an array as a contiguous chunk of locations. This becomes an issue for calculating reordering, where we wish to treat $A[1] \leftarrow 17$ and $A[2] \leftarrow 27$ as *independent* assignments, based on syntax. As such we treat $A[i] \leftarrow v$ as its own syntax, not as a shorthand; we demonstrate the benefit of this in Sect. 4.

We retrieve the meaning of the syntax $\varphi[e] \leftarrow v$ by "normalising" such instructions, where $norm(\alpha) = \alpha$ except for the following.

$$norm(\varphi[i] \leftarrow e) = norm(\varphi \leftarrow (\varphi_{[i] \mapsto e})) \tag{8}$$

Hence $norm(A[1][2] \leftarrow 17) = norm(A[1] \leftarrow A[1]_{[2] \mapsto 17}) = A \leftarrow A_{[1] \mapsto (A[1])_{[2] \mapsto 17}}$. The meaning of instruction α is the meaning of its normalised version in (5).

3 Non-atomic Language

We now use `IMP+ptr` to encode a language (such as `C`) that has "non-atomic" expression evaluation. We break expression evaluation down into sequences of loads, which are guards of the form $(\!|\varphi = v|\!)$. Loads represent accessing parts of the state that can be read in a single step. We first give non-atomic evaluation of expressions in assignments $x := e$ before generalising x to arbitrary l-values. Note the distinction that $x \leftarrow e$ is an atomic instruction (part of `IMP+ptr`), but $x := e$ is a command that may require multiple evaluation steps.

Non-atomic Expression Evaluation. Below we inductively define the evaluation of expression e to value v, written $e_{\leadsto v}$. We defer the definitions for dereference and array indexing expressions until later sections.

$$\begin{aligned} v_{1 \leadsto v_2} &\mathrel{\widehat{=}} (v_1 = v_2)\ ?\ \mathbf{nil} : \mathbf{magic} \\ \varphi_{\leadsto v} &\mathrel{\widehat{=}} (\!|\varphi = v|\!) \\ (e_1 \otimes e_2)_{\leadsto v} &\mathrel{\widehat{=}} \textstyle\bigsqcap_{v_1 \otimes v_2 = v} \cdot (e_{1 \leadsto v_1} \parallel e_{2 \leadsto v_2}) \end{aligned} \qquad \begin{aligned} \mathbf{magic} &\mathrel{\widehat{=}} \textstyle\bigsqcap_{i \in \varnothing} . \mathbf{nil} \\ e_{\leadsto v?}/c_{[v]} &\mathrel{\widehat{=}} \textstyle\bigsqcap_{v \in V} \cdot e_{\leadsto v} ; c_{[v]} \end{aligned}$$

A command $e_{\leadsto v}$ is formed from a sequence of loads of the values of the variables, dereferenced locations, and array indexes required to determine the value of e. We define '**magic**' as the command that has no behaviours; this is used to eliminate infeasible evaluations. Then the evaluation of a value v_1 to a value v_2 either terminates immediately if $v_1 = v_2$ and otherwise has no behaviours, while the evaluation of φ to value v is a load $(\!|\varphi = v|\!)$. We have generically defined a binary expression $e_1 \otimes e_2$ to evaluate each subexpression in parallel, where the result of those evaluations must give v (recall (6)); one can just as easily define a strict left-to-right evaluation order for specific operators. For notational convenience we introduce the shorthand $e_{\leadsto v?}/c_{[v]}$ for a nondeterministic choice over all possible evaluated values v for e, and subsequently used in $c_{[v]}$.

For example, $(x + y)_{\leadsto 7} \sqsubseteq \bigsqcap_{i+j=7} \cdot (\!|x = i|\!) \parallel (\!|y = j|\!) \sqsubseteq (\!|x = 3|\!) \parallel (\!|y = 4|\!)$, that is, loading 3 and 4 for x and y means the expression $x + y$ can evaluate to 7 (or any other combination of values for x and y that sum up to 7).

Command Definitions. Non-atomically evaluated versions of assignment, (repeat) loops, and conditionals may now be given.

$$x := e \mathrel{\widehat{=}} e_{\leadsto v?}/x \leftarrow v \qquad \mathbf{repeat}\ c\ \mathbf{until}\ b \mathrel{\widehat{=}} c;\ (b_{\leadsto \mathsf{ff}};\ c)^*;\ b_{\leadsto \mathsf{tt}} \tag{9}$$

$$\mathbf{if}\ b\ \mathbf{then}\ c_1\ \mathbf{else}\ c_2 \mathrel{\widehat{=}} (b_{\leadsto \mathsf{tt}};\ c_1) \sqcap (b_{\leadsto \mathsf{ff}};\ c_2) \tag{10}$$

An assignment $x := e$ is defined as a nondeterministic choice over all commands where e evaluates to some value v and then x is updated to v. For instance, $x := y$ is equal to $\sqcap_v.\llparenthesis y = v\rrparenthesis; x \leftarrow v$, where the value for y is loaded and then that value is later assigned to x. A conditional command either (non-atomically) evaluates the condition to **tt** or **ff**, followed by the corresponding command (10). Note that infeasible evaluations always result in no behaviours from a state-based perspective, i.e., are interpreted as the empty relation. A non-atomically evaluated "repeat" command (9) is defined similarly to a while loop (3).

Non-atomic Reference Resolution and Assignment. We now generalise assignments to allow non-atomically resolved l-values on the left-hand side. We write $\varphi_{\hookrightarrow\nu}$, analogously to expression evaluation, where φ is resolved to a *reference* $\nu \in \mathsf{Ref}$, a further subset of LVal, encompassing identifiers, pointers, or array indexes.

$$\nu ::= x \quad | \quad *l \quad | \quad \nu[n] \tag{11}$$

We define non-atomic resolution inductively over the syntax of l-values. Resolution of an l-value φ to a reference ν, written $\varphi_{\hookrightarrow\nu}$, is impossible (equal to **magic**) except for the following.

$$x_{\hookrightarrow x} \mathrel{\widehat{=}} \mathbf{nil} \qquad *e_{\hookrightarrow *l} \mathrel{\widehat{=}} e_{\rightsquigarrow l} \qquad \varphi[e]_{\hookrightarrow\nu[n]} \mathrel{\widehat{=}} \varphi_{\hookrightarrow\nu}; e_{\rightsquigarrow n} \tag{12}$$

This states that a variable immediately resolves to itself (and nothing else), while dereferenced l-values resolve to locations and array indexing l-values resolve to array indexing references (cf. (7)). As with expression evaluation we combine non-atomic resolution into a more useful syntax where the resolved reference is used within a nondeterministic choice; this pattern is used to define assignment.

$$\varphi_{\hookrightarrow\nu?}/c_{[\nu]} \mathrel{\widehat{=}} \sqcap_{\nu\in\mathsf{Ref}}.\varphi_{\hookrightarrow\nu}; c_{[\nu]} \qquad \varphi := e \mathrel{\widehat{=}} e_{\rightsquigarrow v?}/\varphi_{\hookrightarrow\nu?}/\nu \leftarrow v \tag{13}$$

The straightforward cases collapse immediately, e.g., $x := v \sqsubseteq x \leftarrow v$, while more complex assignments expand into loads and a single update, e.g., $*x := y \sqsubseteq \sqcap_v.\llparenthesis y = v\rrparenthesis; (\sqcap_l.\llparenthesis x = l\rrparenthesis; *l \leftarrow v)$.

3.1 Structured Arrays

Non-atomic evaluation of an array indexing expression is defined below (non-atomic array-indexing l-value resolution is covered in (12)).

$$e_1[e_2]_{\rightsquigarrow v} \mathrel{\widehat{=}} e_{1\hookrightarrow\nu?}/e_{2\rightsquigarrow n?}/\llparenthesis \nu[n] = v\rrparenthesis \tag{14}$$

Note that evaluating $e_1[e_2]$ involves *resolving* e_1 to a reference and evaluating e_2 to an index. An alternative would be to evaluate e_1 directly to an array value, however, this would compromise the flexibility of calculating which array indexes are actually accessed, as considered in Sect. 4.

Given variables A and i evaluating $A[i]$ requires evaluating i to an index, i.e., $A[i]_{\rightsquigarrow v} \sqsubseteq \sqcap_n.\llparenthesis i = n\rrparenthesis; \llparenthesis A[n] = v\rrparenthesis$, and when used as an l-value we get an update at that index, e.g., $A[i] := 6 \sqsubseteq \sqcap_n.\llparenthesis i = n\rrparenthesis; A[n] \leftarrow 6$.

3.2 Pointers

Definitions for obtaining and releasing pointers are given below.

$$
\begin{array}{ll}
*e_{\leadsto v} \mathrel{\widehat{=}} e_{\leadsto l?} / (\!|*l = v|\!) & \\
alloc(l) \mathrel{\widehat{=}} \langle (\!|*l = \mathsf{free}|\!)\ ,\ *l \leftarrow 0 \rangle & dealloc(l) \mathrel{\widehat{=}} *l \leftarrow \mathsf{free} \\
new(x) \mathrel{\widehat{=}} \sqcap_l . alloc(l);\ x \leftarrow l & free(x) \mathrel{\widehat{=}} x_{\leadsto l?} / dealloc(l);\ x \leftarrow \mathsf{null}
\end{array} \quad (15)
$$

Non-atomic evaluation for dereference expressions is straightforward (non-atomic resolution is given in (12)): evaluating $*e$ to v involves first evaluating e to some location l and then checking the value of $*l$ is v. (Note than when a location l is being treated as a variable it is dereferenced ($*l$) and otherwise behaves as a value.) We define obtaining new and freeing old pointers in IMP+ptr using the abbreviation $\sqcap_l . c \mathrel{\widehat{=}} \sqcap_{l \in \mathsf{Loc}} . c$. A location l may be *allocated* only if l is already free, and then l is initialised to 0 (alternatively an arbitrary value could be chosen). This is given as a composite action so that there is no possibility of some other process interleaving and allocating l. A new pointer $new(x)$ nondeterministically chooses a location l to allocate and updates x to that location. A location is deallocated by setting it to free, and freeing a pointer x finds the location l that x points to, deallocates l, and sets x to null.

Note that by treating the heap as a total function with free locations mapped to the free value means that it is straightforward to encode de/allocating locations directly at the language (expression) level as simple tests and updates.

3.3 Unstructured Arrays (Arrays of Pointers)

The previous definitions for pointers can be used to define operations on arrays of contiguous locations, as in C, rather than structured/abstract arrays (Sect. 3.1). Key to this treatment is an expression type $e_1^{+e_2}$, where e_1 is evaluated to a location l and e_2 to an offset amount n, and then l^{+n} gives a new location via "pointer arithmetic". This can be evaluated by simple addition if locations are represented by natural numbers, but we leave it underspecified to leave open the possibility for special word sizes, etc. We use the notation $e_1 (\!| e_2 |\!)$ for a (dereferenced) access of an array of pointers in a language such as C (but distinguished from structured array indexing $e_1[e_2]$).

$$
l^{+n} : \text{increment location } l \text{ by } n \qquad\qquad e_1 (\!| e_2 |\!) \ \mathrel{\widehat{=}}\ *(e_1^{+e_2}) \quad (16)
$$

Non-atomic evaluation and resolution of pointer array offsets are covered by previous definitions. As an example, assuming A points to location l, then $A(\!|3|\!) := 4$ reduces to $*(l^{+3}) \leftarrow 4$. There is scope to abuse an array offset $A(\!|n|\!)$, in particular if n is outside the intended bounds of A, corresponding with the reality of a language like C; we show this underlies the Meltdown vulnerability in Sect. 5.3.

Below we construct commands for de/allocating a new block of pointers, formed from primitive assembler-like instructions (allowing reordering analysis). We assume $n \geq 1$ and $A \in \mathsf{Var}$, and recall (15). We index pointer arrays from 0.

$$\mathsf{chunk}(l,n) \mathrel{\widehat{=}} \lambda\, i \in (0..n-1).\; l^{+i} \tag{17}$$

$$\mathit{new}(A,n) \mathrel{\widehat{=}} \textstyle\bigsqcap_l.\mathsf{flatmap}(\mathit{alloc})(\mathsf{chunk}(l,n));\;(A \leftarrow l) \tag{18}$$

$$\mathit{free}(A,n) \mathrel{\widehat{=}} A_{\rightsquigarrow l?}/\mathsf{flatmap}(\mathit{dealloc})(\mathsf{chunk}(l,n));\; A \leftarrow \mathsf{null} \tag{19}$$

A "chunk" of n pointers starting from l is a sequence $\langle l^{+0}, l^{+1}, \ldots, l^{+n-1}\rangle$ where each location is systematically related to the others via pointer arithmetic (17). Then a new pointer array is created by allocating every element of a nondeterministically chosen chunk (18), where the flatmap function applies a function to every element of a list and flattens the result, e.g., $\mathsf{flatmap}(\mathit{alloc})(\langle l_1, l_2, \ldots\rangle) = \mathit{alloc}(l_1) \frown \mathit{alloc}(l_2) \frown \ldots$. Note that any attempt to allocate an in-use location results in infeasible behaviour. A block of length n is freed similarly (19), finally setting A to null (the length of the array could be kept in a special location within the block itself, and retrieved when deallocating). We have chosen here to model allocating and freeing a block of pointers as a single atomic action, abstracting from the implementation details of a function such as C's `calloc`, but if the intention is to verify an implementation of `calloc` then a detailed, fine-grained definition can be given instead.

4 Instruction-Level Parallelism

We now use IMP+ptr to consider the behaviour of programs that are executed according to some *weak memory model* [1,2,38]. Parallelisation of computation has been a feature of processors since the 1960s [50,51], used to maximise throughput for independent instructions; for instance, calculating some arithmetic value while waiting for the return of an unrelated value from main memory. The fundamentals of modern hardware and software memory models such as those of x86 [47], Arm [4], RISC-V [42], Power [46], and C [8] are based on a "data dependence" relation between actions, and additionally include special fence/barrier instructions or other features to reimpose order as necessary [19]. For concision we focus on data dependencies below, though the extension to include fences is straightforward [11,13]. The memory model (instruction relation) G is defined so that $\alpha \overset{\mathrm{G}}{\Leftarrow} \beta$ if instructions α and β do not modify the variables the other reads, and do not read the same *shared* variables.

$$\alpha \overset{\mathrm{G}}{\Leftarrow} \beta \;\Leftrightarrow\; \mathsf{wv}(\alpha) \cap \mathsf{fv}(\beta) = \varnothing \wedge \mathsf{wv}(\beta) \cap \mathsf{fv}(\alpha) = \varnothing \wedge \mathsf{rsv}(\alpha) \cap \mathsf{rsv}(\beta) = \varnothing \tag{20}$$

For an instruction α, $\mathsf{wv}(\alpha)$ gives the variables written to (modified) by α, $\mathsf{rv}(\alpha)$ gives the variables read by α, and $\mathsf{rsv}(\alpha)$ are the read *shared* variables of α. Shared and local variables are treated differently by weak memory models because shared variables may be modified by other processes. The free variables of α ($\mathsf{fv}(\alpha)$) are the union of the write and read variables. The relation G is fundamental to real memory models, which are typically stronger in relation to the interaction of branches (guards) and stores. Additions such as fences and other ordering constraints, as well as "forwarding" (where an earlier instruction can affect a later one), can be incorporated in our framework similarly to [11,12].

The key property of G is that $\alpha \overset{\mathrm{G}}{\Leftarrow} \beta \Rightarrow [\![\alpha]\!] \mathbin{;} [\![\beta]\!] = [\![\beta]\!] \mathbin{;} [\![\alpha]\!]$, i.e., the effect of α and β is the same regardless of the order in which they are executed (cf. Hoare's disjointness constraint for parallel programs [23]). The condition $\alpha \overset{\text{G}}{\Leftarrow} \beta$ is straightforward for a processor to enforce by checking if any accessed register or location is written to by an instruction earlier in the pipeline.

We can calculate the free variables of actions composed from store and load instructions straightforwardly: $\mathsf{wv}(\nu \leftarrow v) = \{\nu\}$ and $\mathsf{rv}(\nu \leftarrow v) = \varnothing$, and $\mathsf{wv}((\!|\nu = v|\!)) = \varnothing$ and $\mathsf{rv}((\!|\nu = v|\!)) = \{\nu\}$ (in this context we should call them free *references* rather than free *variables*). More specifically we may derive, for the primitive actions in the non-atomically evaluated language of Sect. 3, $\mathsf{wv}(x \leftarrow v) = \mathsf{rv}((\!|x = v|\!)) = \{x\}$, and $\mathsf{wv}(*l \leftarrow v) = \mathsf{rv}((\!|*l = v|\!)) = \{*l\}$. Array indexing requires special attention which we address in the next section. These syntactic definitions are lifted to actions (sequences of instructions), traces (sequences of actions), and commands (treated as sets of traces) straightforwardly, for instance, $\mathsf{wv}(\mathbf{nil}) = \varnothing$ and $\mathsf{wv}(\sqcap_v . c_{[v]}) = \bigcup_v \mathsf{wv}(c_{[v]})$.

We give some indicative examples below, for both the basic instruction types as well as composed commands such as non-atomically-evaluated assignments. Assume distinct $x, y, A \in \mathsf{Var}$, with x and y shared and A local, and distinct locations $l, l_1, l_2 \in \mathsf{Loc}$, where additionally $l^{+1} = l_1$ and $l^{+2} = l_2$.

$$\begin{array}{lll} x \leftarrow 3 \overset{\text{G}}{\Leftarrow} *l \leftarrow 5 & *x := 3 \overset{\text{G}}{\not\Leftarrow} *l \leftarrow 5 & *(l^{+1}) \leftarrow 5 \overset{\text{G}}{\Leftarrow} *(l^{+2}) \leftarrow 6 \\ x \leftarrow 3 \overset{\text{G}}{\Leftarrow} y \leftarrow 4 & *x := 3 \overset{\text{G}}{\Leftarrow} y := 4 & A(\!|1|\!) := 5 \overset{\text{G}}{\Leftarrow} A(\!|2|\!) := 6 \\ x \leftarrow 3 \overset{\text{G}}{\Leftarrow} (\!|*l = v|\!) & (\!|*l_1 = v|\!) \overset{\text{G}}{\Leftarrow} (\!|*l_2 = w|\!) & \\ *x := 3 \overset{\text{G}}{\not\Leftarrow} (\!|*l = v|\!) & *x := 3 \overset{\text{G}}{\not\Leftarrow} *y := 4 & \end{array} \tag{21}$$

Note in particular $*x{:=}3 \overset{\text{G}}{\not\Leftarrow} *l{\leftarrow}5$. By the definition of assignment $\mathsf{wv}(*x{:=}3) = \bigcup_{l'} \mathsf{wv}(*l' \leftarrow 3) = \mathsf{Loc}$ (while $\mathsf{rv}(*x := 3) = \{x\}$). Hence execution of $*x$ could modify any location, including l, and reordering is not legal in this case. We explore this further in the context of aliasing in Sect. 5.1.

4.1 Reordering and Refinement

We may instantiate parallelized sequential composition with the relation G to observe its effects on execution order. For instance, since $x := 5 \overset{\text{G}}{\Leftarrow} y := 6$, we have $x := 5 \overset{\text{G}}{;} y := 6$ is refinement equivalent (recall Sect. 2) to $x := 5 \parallel y := 6$. More generally, following [11], for any memory model M,

$$\alpha \overset{\text{M}}{\Leftarrow} \beta \Rightarrow \alpha \overset{\text{M}}{;} \beta \sqsubseteq \alpha \parallel \beta \qquad \alpha \overset{\text{M}}{\not\Leftarrow} \beta \Rightarrow \alpha \overset{\text{M}}{;} \beta \sqsubseteq \alpha ; \beta \tag{22}$$

These rules reduce a command involving M into a more familiar sequential or parallel form, and can be used to derive rules covering more complex structures.

As an example of reordering affecting code involving pointers, consider the initialisation code $x := \mathsf{null} \overset{\text{G}}{;} \mathit{new}(\mathit{tmp}) \overset{\text{G}}{;} x := \mathit{tmp}$, executed under memory model G (as made explicit in the parameter to parallelized sequential composition). Simple calculations using $\overset{\text{G}}{\Leftarrow}$ show that the first two commands can be executed in parallel, but order is enforced by data dependencies for the third. That is, the program reduces to $(x := \mathsf{null} \parallel \mathit{new}(\mathit{tmp})); x := \mathit{tmp}$ using (22). This is as expected - there is no reason why a new location cannot be allocated and assigned to *tmp* before x is set to null, though the subsequent update of x must occur strictly later.

4.2 Array Indexing and Reordering

We now consider what a write and read variable means for array indexing expressions such as $A[1] := 5$. Clearly the value of A is updated, but only at index 1. In the spirit of processors wishing to maximise reordering, and in particular to allow for weak memory model effects to be observable in a program using an abstract array, we wish to allow $A[1] := 5 \overset{\mathrm{G}}{\Leftarrow} A[2] := 6$, i.e., for accesses to separate parts of the array to be parallelized.

Given a reference ν we define $\nu^{\succeq}$ as the set of all subindexes into the reference, so that, for example, $A^{\succeq} = \{A, A[1], A[1][1], \ldots, A[2], A[2][1], \ldots\}$, but $A[2] \notin A[1]^{\succeq}$. Where before for an expression x, $\mathsf{rv}(x) = \{x\}$, we now set $\mathsf{rv}(x) = x^{\succeq}$ (and similarly for write variables of update instructions). Note that it is not enough to consider just the exact subindex, as $A[1] \leftarrow v \overset{\mathrm{G}}{\not\Leftarrow} A[1][2] \leftarrow w$, since the second assignment is modifying a part of the original, just as $A \leftarrow \ldots \overset{\mathrm{G}}{\not\Leftarrow} A[1] \leftarrow 3$ (since when A is modified directly then also $A[1], A[2]$, etc., are modified).[1]

Hence $\mathsf{wv}(A[1] := 1) = A[1]^{\succeq}$, and we can derive the following: $A[1] := 5 \overset{\mathrm{G}}{\Leftarrow} A[2] := 6$, $A := \langle 4, 5, 6\rangle \overset{\mathrm{G}}{\not\Leftarrow} r := A[1]$, and $r := *l[1] \overset{\mathrm{G}}{\not\Leftarrow} *l := \mathsf{free}$. As earlier, using (22) we can derive $A[1] := 5 \overset{\mathrm{c}}{;} A[2] := 6 \sqsubseteq A[1] := 5 \parallel A[2] := 6$, i.e., updates to distinct parts of the array may occur in parallel. The intention is that it works just as if we more concretely worked with offsets to some pointer A at the front of an array. This semantics is justified by appealing to the (underlying) case of array offsetting, that is, $A\langle\!|5|\!\rangle := 1 \overset{\mathrm{c}}{;} A\langle\!|2|\!\rangle := 6 \sqsubseteq A\langle\!|5|\!\rangle := 1 \parallel A\langle\!|2|\!\rangle := 6$.

If we instead treated $A[1] := 5$ as syntactic sugar for $A := A_{[1]\mapsto 5}$, it would be much less straightforward to syntactically limit the updated index $A[1]$ as the write variable, particularly in the context of arbitrary expressions being allowed on the right-hand side of assignments.

5 Applications

We now show how the framework applies to a range of situations and algorithms involving pointer representations, using structured arrays as support. In all cases we take a program-transformation approach to elucidating behaviours (rather than directly appealling to states), from where standard techniques can be applied to establish the desired properties.

5.1 Aliasing and Reordering

Consider two mutating instructions in order, $*x := 1; *y := 2$. If x and y point to the same location then processors will not (observably) reorder them, but otherwise they may. The key aspect is the implicit locations to which x and y point; in our framework we can expose them in the syntax of the program.

$$*x_{/l} := v \;\widehat{=}\; \llparenthesis x = l \rrparenthesis; *l \leftarrow v \qquad *x := v \;\widehat{=}\; \textstyle\sqcap_l . *x_{/l} := v \tag{23}$$

[1] Although $\varphi^{\succeq}$ is infinite it reduces, for the purposes of calculating reordering, to a pointwise-check wrt. G, i.e., $\varphi_1{}^{\succeq} \cap \varphi_2{}^{\succeq} = \varnothing \Leftrightarrow \neg(\varphi_1 \succeq \varphi_2 \vee \varphi_2 \succeq \varphi_1)$. For $x, y \in \mathsf{Var}$ it collapses to $x \neq y$.

We define the command $*x_{/l} := v$ to be one that covers only the case where x points to l (and hence we may define the update of pointer x as the choice over all possible locations for x). The analysis uses the following properties.

$$(\sqcap_v . c_{[v]}) \overset{\mathsf{c}}{;} d \sqsubseteq (\sqcap_v . c_{[v]} \overset{\mathsf{c}}{;} d) \qquad (\sqcap_{v,u} . c_{[v,u]}) \sqsubseteq (\sqcap_{v,u|v \neq u} . c_{[v,u]}) \sqcap (\sqcap_v . c_{[v,v]})$$

The first property states that choice distributes over parallelized sequential composition, with a symmetric rule holding for left-distribution. The second property splits a choice over two values into two cases: where the values are different and when they are the same.

Simple calculations show that $\mathsf{fv}(*x_{/l} := v) = \{x, *l\}$, i.e., it reads x and updates $*l$ (however, as before, $\mathsf{fv}(*x := v) = \{x\} \cup \mathsf{Loc}$), which allows the following derivation.

$$\begin{aligned}
& *x := 1 \overset{\mathsf{c}}{;} *y := 2 \\
\sqsubseteq\ & (\sqcap_{l_1} . *x_{/l_1} := 1) \overset{\mathsf{c}}{;} (\sqcap_{l_2} . *y_{/l_2} := 2) \quad \sqsubseteq \quad \left(\sqcap_{l_1,l_2} . *x_{/l_1} := 1 \overset{\mathsf{c}}{;} *y_{/l_2} := 2\right) \\
\sqsubseteq\ & \left(\sqcap_{l_1,l_2|l_1 \neq l_2} . *x_{/l_1} := 1 \overset{\mathsf{c}}{;} *y_{/l_2} := 2\right) \sqcap \left(\sqcap_l . *x_{/l} := 1 \overset{\mathsf{c}}{;} *y_{/l} := 2\right)
\end{aligned}$$

In the first choice, where x and y point to separate locations, the instructions can be reordered and hence behave as if in parallel, i.e., that choice is equivalent to $\sqcap_{l_1,l_2|l_1 \neq l_2} . *x_{/l_1} := 1 \parallel *y_{/l_2} := 2$. The second case, where x and y are aliases, results in a dependency where $*l \leftarrow 1 \overset{\mathsf{c}}{\not\Leftarrow} *l \leftarrow 2$. Processors will not reorder such cases - the aliasing may be deliberate, for instance, where an array offset has occurred in a 0 case, and so should be updated in the specified order. The combination expands to $\sqcap_l . (*x_{/l} := 1 \parallel (\!| y = l |\!)); *l \leftarrow 2$, i.e., the load that determines y points to l can be interleaved with the mutate of pointer x, but the final update of l to 2 must occur strictly later.

5.2 Linked Lists and the Treiber Stack

Typically a "linked list" is a collection of "nodes", which are value/location pairs, with the "next" pointer of each node pointing to the next node in the list. We can represent such a node as an array of length two, abbreviating $e.val \mathrel{\widehat{=}} e[1]$ and $e.next \mathrel{\widehat{=}} e[2]$ (an alternative is introduce tuple expressions into the syntax). An immediate consequence of this treatment is that modifications to a node's value and next pointer fields can be reordered with each other, since they are distinct elements of an array. Recalling (15) we define $newNode(n, v) \mathrel{\widehat{=}} new(n); *n := \langle v, \mathsf{null} \rangle$, and freeing a node can be defined analogously. We define $n{\rightarrow}next$ as the usual C abbreviation for $*n.next$ (and similarly for $n{\rightarrow}val$).

A well known *lock-free* [21] implementation of a stack as a linked list is that of Treiber [45]. A lock-free algorithm provides weaker guarantees of termination than lock-based implementations, but typically has better performance by allowing more parallelism between competing threads, in particular, retrying the modification of shared data if interference is detected, rather than waiting to obtain a contested lock. In Treiber's linked-list implementation of a stack the head of the stack is stored in pointer H (initially null), and an encoding of the implementation of *push* is given below (recall (9)). After initialisation of local node n it enters a (potentially non-terminating) loop. This comprises repeatedly loading the current value of H into local h, setting n to point to h, and then, via a compare-and-swap (**cas**) primitive, atomically swinging H to the new n provided H still points to the value loaded into h.

$$r := \mathbf{cas}(x, r_1, r_2) \mathrel{\widehat{=}} (\langle (\!| x = r_1 |\!) \ , \ x \leftarrow r_2 \rangle ;\ r \leftarrow \mathsf{tt}) \sqcap ((\!| x \neq r_1 |\!);\ r \leftarrow \mathsf{ff})$$

$$newNode(n, v) \overset{\text{c}}{;} \mathbf{repeat} h := H \overset{\text{c}}{;} n{\to}next := h \overset{\text{c}}{;} r := \mathbf{cas}(H, h, n) \mathbf{until} r$$

The **cas** instruction can reorder with the assignment $n{\to}next := h$, because variable n is local but $*n$ is global. That is, without loss of generality, taking the case where $n = l_n$,

$$\mathsf{rv}(n{\to}next := h) = \{n, h\} \qquad \mathsf{wv}(n{\to}next := h) = l_n[2]^{\succeq}$$
$$\mathsf{rv}(r := \mathbf{cas}(H, h, n)) = \{n, h, H\} \ \mathsf{wv}(r := \mathbf{cas}(H, h, n)) = \{H, r\}$$

Because the write variables of the **cas** do not intersect with the read variables of $n{\to}next := h$ those instructions may appear to execute in parallel. The first instruction inside the loop, $h := H$, reads H and modifies h and therefore can't reorder with either of the other two commands. Taking these calculations together and applying (22), the body of the loop is equal to

$$h := H;\ (n{\to}next := h \parallel r := \mathbf{cas}(H, h, n))$$

As a result H may be updated to point to the new location (n) before n points to the rest of the stack, and this will invalidate any invariant-based proof of correctness. The implementation may address this issue by inserting a fence between the two commands, or by using a version of **cas** that includes a fence. After such modifications, the resulting code can be shown to operate essentially sequentially, and thus equivalently to the original program under a sequential consistency interpretation; previous results [10] therefore imply correctness of the weak-memory version with fences.

5.3 The Meltdown Vulnerability

We show the application of the framework to low-level micro-assembly, and how to expose the "Meltdown" vulnerability of many micro-processors [36], related to Spectre [31] and leading to the ongoing discoveries of new variants [43,52]. We give a detailed encoding of a "load" (in x86 assembly, a `mov` operation) that exposes several aspects of the micro-architecture: foremost that the value at an address in main memory is stored in a local register; that value/address pair is recorded in a *cache* for faster retrieval later; and a special *commit* phase of the operation where the accessed address is checked to be "valid", i.e., that it was loaded from an allowed region. We show that the reordering of loads and commits may lead to the leaking of arbitrary information from main memory.

We define a particular mode of the x86 `mov` instruction which loads a value from main memory into a register.

$$\texttt{mov r}_1\texttt{, [r}_2\texttt{+r}_3\texttt{]} \mathrel{\widehat{=}} \langle r_1 := r_2(\!| r_3 |\!) \ , \ \mathrm{C}[r_2^{+r_3}] := \mathsf{tt} \rangle;\ \mathsf{commit}(r_2^{+r_3}) \qquad (24)$$

The typical use of this mode is when register r_2 holds the address of the start of an array, and r_3 is an index into the array, with the value at that location written into r_1. As a micro-architectural side-effect that location is also stored in the cache system, represented by the variable C, a boolean array indexed by locations; if C$[l]$ then l has been cached, i.e., accessed by the processor (the *value* at $r_2^{+r_3}$ is not necessary for this analysis). Finally a commit micro-operation is issued, which we leave uninterpreted, but the intended semantics is that if the accessed location is not "valid" then execution halts and a (memory violation) exception is thrown, e.g., $\mathsf{commit}(l) \mathrel{\widehat=} \textbf{if } l \notin \mathsf{Valid} \textbf{ then throw} \mathsf{exc}$.

To complete the treatment of the micro-assembly we give a memory model H that defines the interaction of the commit with the other (micro)operations.

$$\alpha \overset{\text{H}}{\Leftarrow} \beta \mathrel{\widehat=} \alpha \overset{\text{G}}{\Leftarrow} \beta \wedge \alpha \overset{\mu}{\Leftarrow} \beta \tag{25}$$

$$\mathsf{commit}(l) \overset{\mu}{\not\Leftarrow} \beta \quad \Leftrightarrow \quad \mathsf{wsv}(\beta) \neq \varnothing \qquad \mathsf{commit}(l_1) \overset{\mu}{\not\Leftarrow} \mathsf{commit}(l_2) \tag{26}$$

Relation H extends G (20) to handle the commit instruction type, that is, $\alpha \overset{\text{H}}{\Leftarrow} \beta$ if data dependencies are respected according to G, and additionally, according to $\overset{\mu}{\Leftarrow}$, commit instructions block later stores (writes to shared variables) and commits, but not loads, i.e., $\alpha \overset{\mu}{\Leftarrow} \beta$ aside from (26).

A malicious user, given execution permission on a machine, can access memory from outside of their user space by exploiting the "cache footprint" of a `mov` instruction. This is because although a commit instruction that throws an exception prevents any access of the values in the local registers, it does not clear the cache of any locations/values accessed.

Consider the execution of $\texttt{mov r}_1\texttt{, [A,n]} \overset{\text{H}}{;} \texttt{mov r}_2\texttt{, [D,r}_1\texttt{]}$, where registers A and D are pointers to the start of arrays, and where n can be chosen (by the malicious user) to be arbitrarily large, i.e., to point outside of the local array A and into, for instance, kernel space. Using the abbreviation $r_1 \overset{\text{C}}{:=} r_2\llparenthesis r_3 \rrparenthesis \mathrel{\widehat=} \langle r_1 := r_2\llparenthesis r_3 \rrparenthesis \ , \ \text{C}[r_2^{+r_3}] := \mathsf{tt}\rangle$ we have $r_1 \overset{\text{C}}{:=} A\llparenthesis n \rrparenthesis \overset{\text{H}}{\not\Leftarrow} r_2 \overset{\text{C}}{:=} D\llparenthesis r_1 \rrparenthesis$ (the dependency on r_1 violates G) but $\mathsf{commit}(A^{+n}) \overset{\text{H}}{\Leftarrow} r_2 \overset{\text{C}}{:=} D\llparenthesis r_1 \rrparenthesis$ by μ, hence,

$$\begin{aligned}
&\texttt{mov r}_1\texttt{, [A+n]} \overset{\text{H}}{;} \texttt{mov r}_2\texttt{, [D+r}_1\texttt{]} \\
&\mathrel{\widehat=} r_1 \overset{\text{C}}{:=} A\llparenthesis n \rrparenthesis; \mathsf{commit}(A^{+n}) \overset{\text{H}}{;} r_2 \overset{\text{C}}{:=} D\llparenthesis r_1 \rrparenthesis; \mathsf{commit}(D^{+r_1}) \\
&\sqsupseteq r_1 \overset{\text{C}}{:=} A\llparenthesis n \rrparenthesis; (\mathsf{commit}(A^{+n}) \parallel r_2 \overset{\text{C}}{:=} D\llparenthesis r_1 \rrparenthesis); \mathsf{commit}(D^{+r_1}) \\
&\sqsubseteq r_1 \overset{\text{C}}{:=} A\llparenthesis n \rrparenthesis; r_2 \overset{\text{C}}{:=} D\llparenthesis r_1 \rrparenthesis; \mathsf{commit}(A^{+n}); \mathsf{commit}(D^{+r_1})
\end{aligned}$$

For large n the $\mathsf{commit}(A^{+n})$ fails, and throws an exception, as desired. However it is possible for $r_2 \overset{\text{C}}{:=} D\llparenthesis r_1 \rrparenthesis$ to be executed *before* the exception is thrown. This was historically not considered a problem because the value loaded into r_2 is not directly accessible after an exception, however, the malicious user can (via a "timing attack" [32]) determine that, after initially flushing the cache, element r_1 is the *only* element of D in the cache, and thus infer the (transient) value that r_1 held during execution, and thus of the value at location A^{+n}, which is an arbitrary location in memory. The attacker may then rerun the same code but this time with input $n+1$, and thus read off arbitrary chunks of memory.

The key aspect of this analysis is that it is performed at the relatively straightforward level of algebraic manipulation, with respect to a specially-designed memory model that incorporates directly the notion that commit micro-operations occur in-order with stores but still allow speculative loads. This is in contrast to reasoning at the low-level of a particular execution semantics and model of the microarchitectural state. The analysis may both build on top of earlier results for manipulating programs under weak memory models [11,13] as well as exploit existing tools and techniques for security analysis [55].

6 Related Work

The work on representations of pointer-based programming and inference systems is vast, perhaps best exemplified by separation logic [25,44]; we base our representation of the state on the related Views framework [17]. As such our framework is compatible with separation-logic based reasoning, although other semantic interpretations of the atomic instruction types could be employed. One significant difference with [17] is that we have a 'total' heap, where unallocated locations are mapped to the special value free, supporting program-level construction of relevant commands, e.g., (15), reducing the notational overhead of the base language and, hence, inference systems. The typical approach is to include new instruction types which are interpreted only at the semantics level, however each new instruction type requires specific inference rules and complicates the definition of corresponding memory models.

There are many semantics for weak memory models (e.g., [5,26,29]), and verification techniques based on those frameworks [18,35,49,53,54,56]. In such frameworks the nondeterminism and instruction-level parallelism due to weak behaviours is captured in some global data structure – often a graph or a partially-ordered multiset of events – and then specialised reasoning techniques for that data structure are given. This necessitates either the development of novel assertion languages, techniques and tools, or the adaptation of existing ones. In contrast our approach is based on that developed in [11], where the parallelism is captured in the structure of the program (provided the memory model is "multicopy atomic", as with Arm, x86, and RISC-V). This requires an algebraic analysis of a program (similar to transformation with process algebras [7]) to elucidate weak behaviours in terms of sequential or parallel composition, or nondeterministic choice, e.g., (22). A major advantage of this approach is that subsequently any existing tools and techniques may be applied to the transformed program to establish the desired property (provided they can handle any resulting nested parallelism, as can, e.g., rely/guarantee). However the language presented in [11] does not handle pointer-based programming or arrays, nor support fine-grained control over atomicity, which is necessary for analysing real code such as the seL4 microkernel [30]. Our introduction of abstract, structured arrays is useful in many applications, e.g., where the implementation detail is not relevant and the algorithmic logic is important, as we showed by treating nodes as 2-place arrays (Sect. 5.2) and treating an abstract representation of the processor cache as a boolean array (Sect. 5.3); as far as we are aware no other weak memory model semantics incorporates abstract arrays as generically.

7 Conclusion

We have presented a minimal but versatile language that can express pointer-based code and abstract arrays at different levels of of atomicity, in a way that supports a program transformation approach to elucidating the effects of weak memory models. All general properties and examples have been machine-checked in Isabelle/HOL [40,41]. We demonstrate the utility of the framework by encoding arrays of pointers and linked lists and showing how these programming concepts are influenced by weak memory models, and how this may feed into larger verification efforts on algorithmic logic, or to investigate microarchitectural vulnerabilities [15]. Ultimately the intention is to incorporate weak memory model effects into the verification of larger software, such as the seL4 microkernel [30], which must run on a range of modern processors.

Many approaches in the literature [3,26,29] define a graph-based semantics on global events, and as such require specialised assertion languages and verification techniques for reasoning. In contrast we capture nondeterminism or parallelism at the program level. This feeds into a verification effort as follows: taking a program c that is subject to memory model M (that is, all instances of sequential composition in c are interpreted as '$\overset{\text{M}}{;}$'), for which property P must be shown (P may be a rely/guarantee quintuple, a security property, linearizability, etc.), one transforms c via refinement into some c', where instances of $\overset{\text{M}}{;}$ have been replaced by sequential or parallel composition, as appropriate. The program c' may now be analysed using standard techniques to establish/deny the property P. In some cases c' and the sequential interpretation of c will be equivalent, i.e., the introduction of M makes no difference to its behaviours (due to, e.g., fences), and thus if c had been already shown to satisfy P under sequential semantics then that result can be employed directly to establish P for c under M.

The base language and the encoding of non-atomic expression evaluation is formulated in the spirit of the concurrent refinement algebra [14,20] and concurrent Kleene algebra [24], adapting the reordering framework developed in [11,13]. The semantic model of the heap is based on that of the Views framework [17], but separate to the trace semantics, with the intention that other models for concurrent program analysis can be considered [6,9,37,39]. As future work we will integrate this with information flow analysis [16,48,55] and vulnerability detection based on pointers and address space manipulation [15].

Acknowledgements. We thank Duong Dinh for help with modelling Meltdown, and Scott Heiner, Roger Su, Kait Lam, Nicholas Coughlin, Kirsten Winter, Graeme Smith and the anonymous reviewers for feedback.

References

1. Adve, S.V., Gharachorloo, K.: Shared memory consistency models: a tutorial. Computer **29**(12), 66–76 (1996)
2. Alglave, J.: A formal hierarchy of weak memory models. Formal Methods in System Design **41**(2), 178–210 (2012)
3. Alglave, J., Cousot, P.: Ogre and Pythia: an invariance proof method for weak consistency models. In: POPL 2017, pp. 3–18. ACM, New York (2017)
4. Alglave, J., Deacon, W., Grisenthwaite, R., Hacquard, A., Maranget, L.: Armed cats: formal concurrency modelling at Arm. ACM Trans. Program. Lang. Syst. **43**(2), 1–54 (2021)
5. Alglave, J., Maranget, L., Tautschnig, M.: Herding cats: modelling, simulation, testing, and data mining for weak memory. ACM Trans. Program. Lang. Syst. **36**(2), 7:1–7:74 (2014)
6. Amani, S., Andronick, J., Bortin, M., Lewis, C., Rizkallah, C., Tuong, J.: COMPLX: a verification framework for concurrent imperative programs. In: Proceedings of the 6th ACM SIGPLAN Conference on Certified Programs and Proofs, CPP 2017, pp. 138–150. Association for Computing Machinery, New York (2017)
7. Bergstra, J.A., Klop, J.W.: Process algebra for synchronous communication. Inf. Control **60**(1–3), 109–137 (1984)
8. Boehm, H.-J., Adve, S.V.: Foundations of the C++ concurrency memory model. In: PLDI 2008, pp. 68–78. ACM (2008)
9. Brookes, S.: A semantics for concurrent separation logic. Theoret. Comput. Sci. **375**(1–3), 227–270 (2007)
10. Colvin, R., Doherty, S., Groves, L.: Verifying concurrent data structures by simulation. Electron. Notes Theor. Comput. Sci. **137**, 93–110 (2005). Proceedings of the REFINE 2005 Workshop (REFINE 2005)
11. Colvin, R.J.: Parallelized sequential composition and hardware weak memory models. In: Calinescu, R., Păsăreanu, C.S. (eds.) SEFM 2021. LNCS, vol. 13085, pp. 201–221. Springer, Cham (2021). https://doi.org/10.1007/978-3-030-92124-8_12
12. Colvin, R.J.: Separation of concerning things: a simpler basis for defining and programming with the C/C++ memory model (extended version) (2022). https://arxiv.org/abs/2204.03189
13. Colvin, R.J.: Separation of concerning things: a simpler basis for defining and programming with the C/C++ memory model. In: Riesco, A., Zhang, M. (eds.) ICFEM 2022. LNCS, vol. 1347, pp. 71–89. Springer, Cham (2022). https://doi.org/10.1007/978-3-031-17244-1_5
14. Colvin, R.J., Hayes, I.J., Meinicke, L.A.: Designing a semantic model for a wide-spectrum language with concurrency. Formal Aspects Comput. **29**(5), 853–875 (2017)
15. Colvin, R.J., Winter, K.: An abstract semantics of speculative execution for reasoning about security vulnerabilities. In: Sekerinski, E., et al. (eds.) FM 2019. LNCS, vol. 12233, pp. 323–341. Springer, Cham (2020). https://doi.org/10.1007/978-3-030-54997-8_21
16. Coughlin, N., Winter, K., Smith, G.: Rely/guarantee reasoning for multicopy atomic weak memory models. In: Huisman, M., Păsăreanu, C., Zhan, N. (eds.) FM 2021. LNCS, vol. 13047, pp. 292–310. Springer, Cham (2021). https://doi.org/10.1007/978-3-030-90870-6_16
17. Dinsdale-Young, T., Birkedal, L., Gardner, P., Parkinson, M., Yang, H.: Views: compositional reasoning for concurrent programs. SIGPLAN Not. **48**(1), 287–300 (2013)

18. Doherty, S., Dalvandi, S., Dongol, B., Wehrheim, H.: Unifying operational weak memory verification: an axiomatic approach. ACM Trans. Comput. Logic **23**(4), 1–39 (2022)
19. Gharachorloo, K., Lenoski, D., Laudon, J., Gibbons, P., Gupta, A., Hennessy, J.: Memory consistency and event ordering in scalable shared-memory multiprocessors. In: ISCA 1990, pp. 15–26. ACM (1990)
20. Hayes, I.J., Colvin, R.J., Meinicke, L.A., Winter, K., Velykis, A.: An algebra of synchronous atomic steps. In: Fitzgerald, J., Heitmeyer, C., Gnesi, S., Philippou, A. (eds.) FM 2016. LNCS, vol. 9995, pp. 352–369. Springer, Cham (2016). https://doi.org/10.1007/978-3-319-48989-6_22
21. Herlihy, M.P., Wing, J.M.: Linearizability: a correctness condition for concurrent objects. TOPLAS **12**(3), 463–492 (1990)
22. Hoare, C.A.R.: An axiomatic basis for computer programming. Commun. ACM **12**(10), 576–580 (1969)
23. Hoare, C.A.R.: Towards a theory of parallel programming. In: Operating System Techniques, pp. 61–71. Academic Press (1972). Proceedings of Seminar at Queen's University, Belfast, Northern Ireland, August-September 1971
24. Hoare, C.A.R.T., Möller, B., Struth, G., Wehrman, I.: Concurrent Kleene algebra. In: Bravetti, M., Zavattaro, G. (eds.) CONCUR 2009. LNCS, vol. 5710, pp. 399–414. Springer, Heidelberg (2009). https://doi.org/10.1007/978-3-642-04081-8_27
25. Ishtiaq, S.S., O'Hearn, P.W.: BI as an assertion language for mutable data structures. In: Proceedings of the ACM SIGPLAN-SIGACT Symposium on Principles of Programming Languages (POPL), pp. 14–26. ACM Press (2001)
26. Jeffrey, A., Riely, J., Batty, M., Cooksey, S., Kaysin, I., Podkopaev, A.: The leaky semicolon: compositional semantic dependencies for relaxed-memory concurrency. Proc. ACM Program. Lang. **6**(POPL), 1–30 (2022)
27. Jones, C.B.: Specification and design of (parallel) programs. In: IFIP Congress, pp. 321–332 (1983)
28. Jones, C.B.: Tentative steps toward a development method for interfering programs. ACM Trans. Program. Lang. Syst. **5**, 596–619 (1983)
29. Kang, J., Hur, C.-K., Lahav, O., Vafeiadis, V., Dreyer, D.: A promising semantics for relaxed-memory concurrency. In: Proceedings of the 44th ACM SIGPLAN Symposium on Principles of Programming Languages, POPL 2017, pp. 175–189. ACM, New York (2017)
30. Klein, G., et al.: SeL4: formal verification of an OS kernel. In: Proceedings of the ACM SIGOPS 22nd Symposium on Operating Systems Principles, SOSP 2009, pp. 207–220. Association for Computing Machinery, New York (2009)
31. Kocher, P., et al.: Spectre attacks: exploiting speculative execution. In: Security and Privacy, pp. 1–19. IEEE (2019)
32. Kocher, P.C.: Timing attacks on implementations of Diffie-Hellman, RSA, DSS, and other systems. In: Koblitz, N. (ed.) CRYPTO 1996. LNCS, vol. 1109, pp. 104–113. Springer, Heidelberg (1996). https://doi.org/10.1007/3-540-68697-5_9
33. Kozen, D.: Kleene algebra with tests. ACM Trans. Program. Lang. Syst. **19**(3), 427–443 (1997)
34. Kozen, D.: On Hoare logic and Kleene algebra with tests. ACM Trans. Comput. Logic **1**(1), 60–76 (2000)
35. Lahav, O., Vafeiadis, V.: Owicki-Gries reasoning for weak memory models. In: Halldórsson, M.M., Iwama, K., Kobayashi, N., Speckmann, B. (eds.) ICALP 2015. LNCS, vol. 9135, pp. 311–323. Springer, Heidelberg (2015). https://doi.org/10.1007/978-3-662-47666-6_25

36. Lipp, M., et al.: Meltdown: reading kernel memory from user space. In: USENIX Security Symposium (2018)
37. Madiot, J.-M., Pottier, F.: A separation logic for heap space under garbage collection. Proc. ACM Program. Lang. **6**(POPL), 1–28 (2022)
38. Moiseenko, E., Podkopaev, A., Koznov, D.: A survey of programming language memory models. Program. Comput. Softw. **47**(6), 439–456 (2021)
39. Nanevski, A., Ley-Wild, R., Sergey, I., Delbianco, G.A.: Communicating state transition systems for fine-grained concurrent resources. In: Shao, Z. (ed.) ESOP 2014. LNCS, vol. 8410, pp. 290–310. Springer, Heidelberg (2014). https://doi.org/10.1007/978-3-642-54833-8_16
40. Nipkow, T., Paulson, L.C., Wenzel, M.: Isabelle/HOL—A Proof Assistant for Higher-Order Logic. LNCS, vol. 2283. Springer, Heidelberg (2002)
41. Paulson, L.C.: Isabelle: A Generic Theorem Prover. Springer, Heidelberg (1994). https://doi.org/10.1007/BFb0030541
42. Pulte, C., Pichon-Pharabod, J., Kang, J., Lee, S.-H., Hur, C.-K.: Promising-ARM/RISC-V: a simpler and faster operational concurrency model. In: PLDI 2019, pp. 1–15. ACM (2019)
43. Ravichandran, J., Na, W.T., Lang, J., Yan, M.: PACMAN: attacking ARM pointer authentication with speculative execution. In: Proceedings of the 49th Annual International Symposium on Computer Architecture, ISCA 2022, pp.685–698. Association for Computing Machinery, New York (2022)
44. Reynolds, J.C.: Separation logic: a logic for shared mutable data structures. In: IEEE Symposium on Logic in Computer Science (LICS), pp. 55–74. IEEE Computer Society (2002)
45. Treiber, R.K.: Systems Programming: coping with Parallelism. RJ5118. Technical report, IBM Almaden Research Center (1986)
46. Sarkar, S., Sewell, P., Alglave, J., Maranget, L., Williams, D.: Understanding POWER multiprocessors. In: Proceedings of the 32nd ACM SIGPLAN Conference on Programming Language Design and Implementation, PLDI 2011, pp. 175–186. Association for Computing Machinery, New York (2011)
47. Sewell, P., Sarkar, S., Owens, S., Nardelli, F.Z., Myreen, M.O.: x86-TSO: a rigorous and usable programmer's model for x86 multiprocessors. Commun. ACM **53**(7), 89–97 (2010)
48. Smith, G., Coughlin, N., Murray, T.: Value-dependent information-flow security on weak memory models. In: ter Beek, M.H., McIver, A., Oliveira, J.N. (eds.) FM 2019. LNCS, vol. 11800, pp. 539–555. Springer, Cham (2019). https://doi.org/10.1007/978-3-030-30942-8_32
49. Svendsen, K., Pichon-Pharabod, J., Doko, M., Lahav, O., Vafeiadis, V.: A separation logic for a promising semantics. In: Ahmed, A. (ed.) ESOP 2018. LNCS, vol. 10801, pp. 357–384. Springer, Cham (2018). https://doi.org/10.1007/978-3-319-89884-1_13
50. Thornton, J.E.: Parallel operation in the Control Data 6600. In: Proceedings of the October 27–29, 1964, Fall Joint Computer Conference, Part II: Very High Speed Computer Systems, AFIPS 1964, pp. 33–40. ACM (1964)
51. Tomasulo, R.M.: An efficient algorithm for exploiting multiple arithmetic units. IBM J. Res. Dev. **11**(1), 25–33 (1967)
52. Trippel, C., Lustig, D., Martonosi, M.: MeltdownPrime and SpectrePrime: automatically-synthesized attacks exploiting invalidation-based coherence protocols. CoRR, abs/1802.03802 (2018)
53. Turon, A., Vafeiadis, V., Dreyer, D.: GPS: navigating weak memory with ghosts, protocols, and separation. SIGPLAN Not. **49**(10), 691–707 (2014)

54. Wehrheim, H., Bargmann, L., Dongol, B.: Reasoning about promises in weak memory models with event structures (extended version). CoRR (2022). https://arxiv.org/abs/2211.16330
55. Winter, K., Coughlin, N., Smith, G.: Backwards-directed information flow analysis for concurrent programs. In: 2021 IEEE 34th Computer Security Foundations Symposium (CSF), pp. 1–16 (2021)
56. Wright, D., Batty, M., Dongol, B.: Owicki-Gries reasoning for C11 programs with relaxed dependencies. In: Huisman, M., Păsăreanu, C., Zhan, N. (eds.) FM 2021. LNCS, vol. 13047, pp. 237–254. Springer, Cham (2021). https://doi.org/10.1007/978-3-030-90870-6_13

VeyMont: Parallelising Verified Programs Instead of Verifying Parallel Programs

Petra van den Bos[1(✉)] and Sung-Shik Jongmans[2,3]

[1] Formal Methods and Tools Group, University of Twente, Enschede, The Netherlands
p.vandenbos@utwente.nl

[2] Department of Computer Science, Open University, Heerlen, The Netherlands

[3] CWI, Amsterdam, The Netherlands

Abstract. We present VeyMont: a deductive verification tool that aims to make reasoning about functional correctness and deadlock freedom of parallel programs (relatively complex) as easy as that of sequential programs (relatively simple). The novelty of VeyMont is that it "inverts the workflow": it supports a new method to parallelise verified programs, in contrast to existing methods to verify parallel programs. Inspired by methods for distributed systems, VeyMont targets coarse-grained parallelism among threads (i.e., whole-program parallelisation) instead of fine-grained parallelism among tasks (e.g., loop parallelisation).

1 Introduction

Deductive verification is a classical approach to reason about functional correctness of programs. The idea is to annotate programs with logic assertions about state. A proof system can subsequently be used to statically check whether or not annotations are true (i.e., whether or not state dynamically evolves as asserted).

As multicore hardware and multithreaded software have become ubiquitous, deductive verification has been facing an elusive open problem: the approach is much harder to apply to *parallel programs* than to *sequential programs.* Towards addressing this issue, in this paper, we present **VeyMont**. It is a deductive verification tool that aims to make reasoning about functional correctness and deadlock freedom of parallel programs *as easy* as that of sequential programs. The novelty of VeyMont is that it "inverts the workflow": it supports a new method to **parallelise verified programs**, in contrast to existing methods to **verify parallel programs**. Unlike traditional model checkers, VeyMont proves properties *generally* for all (possibly infinitely many) initial values of variables, instead of *specifically* for instances. Unlike parallelising compilers, VeyMont targets *coarse-grained* parallelism among threads (i.e., whole-program parallelisation), instead of *fine-grained* parallelism among instructions (e.g., loop parallelisation).

Background. In the state-of-the-art on verification of sequential and parallel programs, typically, proof systems based on (extensions of) *Hoare logic* [4,21] and *separation logic* [40,45] are used to prove properties of annotated programs. To demonstrate the main concepts, Fig. 1 shows four functionally equivalent programs to swap the values of variables x and y:

M. Chechik et al. (Eds.): FM 2023, LNCS 14000, pp. 321–339, 2023.
https://doi.org/10.1007/978-3-031-27481-7_19

$$\{\mathrm{x} = v_1 \wedge \mathrm{y} = v_2\}$$
$$\mathrm{z} := \mathrm{x}\,;\, \mathrm{x} := \mathrm{y}\,;\, \mathrm{y} := \mathrm{z}$$
$$\{\mathrm{x} = v_2 \wedge \mathrm{y} = v_1\}$$

(a) Sequential program

```
class SeqProgram {
  int v1, v2, x, y, z;

  context ...
  requires x == v1 && y == v2;
  ensures  x == v2 && y == v1;
  void swap() {
    z = x; x = y; y = z;
} }
```

(b) Sequential program in VerCors

$$\{\mathrm{x} \mapsto v_1 * \mathrm{y} \mapsto v_2 * \mathrm{z1} \mapsto \_ * \mathrm{z2} \mapsto \_\}$$

barrier b

$$\{\mathrm{z1} \mapsto v_1 \triangleright \mathrm{z2} \mapsto v_2,\ \mathrm{z2} \mapsto v_2 \triangleright \mathrm{z1} \mapsto v_1\}\ \textbf{in}$$

$$\left[\begin{array}{l||l} \{\mathrm{x} \mapsto v_1 * \mathrm{z1} \mapsto \_\} & \{\mathrm{y} \mapsto v_2 * \mathrm{z2} \mapsto \_\} \\ \mathbf{z1} := \mathbf{x}\,; & \mathbf{z2} := \mathbf{y}\,; \\ \textbf{wait b}\,; & \textbf{wait b}\,; \\ \mathbf{x} := \mathbf{z2} & \mathbf{y} := \mathbf{z1} \\ \{\mathrm{x} \mapsto v_2\} & \{\mathrm{y} \mapsto v_1\} \end{array}\right]$$

$$\{\mathrm{x} \mapsto v_2 * \mathrm{y} \mapsto v_1\}$$

$x \mapsto v$ means shared variable x is *owned* (i.e., exclusive permission to use) and has value v; "_" means "any".

$\phi_1 * \phi_2$ means memory can be *separated* into two parts s.t. ϕ_1 and ϕ_2 are true in different parts.

$\phi_1 \triangleright \chi_1, \ldots, \phi_n \triangleright \chi_n$ means: ϕ_i must be true before thread i passes the barrier; χ_i will be true after.

(c) Parallel program, using a barrier

```
class Channel {
  int s, buf; // state, buffer

  resource lock_invariant() =
    Perm(s, 1) **
    (s == 1 || s == 2 || s == 3) **
    (s == 1 ==> Perm(buf, 1\2)) **
    (s == 2 ==> Perm(buf, 1\2));

  context Perm(buf, 1\2);
  ensures buf == v;
  void writeValue(int v) {
    lock this;
    loop_invariant ...;
    while (s != 1) { wait this; }
    s = 2; buf = v;
    unlock this;
  }

  ensures Perm(buf, 1\2);
  ensures \result == buf;
  int readValue() {... }
}

class Thread {
  Channel a, b; int v, v_old;
  context  Perm(v, 1);
  context  Perm(v_old, 1\2);
  context  Perm(a, 1\2);
  context  Perm(b, 1\2);
  context  Perm(b.buf, 1\2);
  requires v == v_old;
  requires a != null;
  requires b != null;
  ensures  Perm(a.buf, 1\2);
  ensures  v_old == b.buf
  ensures  a.buf == v;
  void run() {
    b.writeValue(v);
    v = a.readValue();
} }

class ParProgram {
  int v1, v2; Thread t1, t2;

  context ...
  requires t1.v == v1 && t2.v == v2;
  ensures  t1.v == v2 && t2.v == v1;
  void swap() {
    fork t1; fork t2;
    join t1; join t2;
} }
```

(d) Parallel program in VerCors, using channels

Fig. 1. Example of deductive verification (swapping values)

- Figure 1a shows a **sequential program**; it uses auxiliary variable z. The program is annotated with two assertions (in teal), expressed in Hoare logic: the *precondition* (top) specifies what must be true before the program is run; the *postcondition* (bottom) specifies what will be true after.
- Figure 1c shows a **parallel program**, with two threads; it uses a barrier b and auxiliary variables z1 and z2. First, the "left thread" copies x into z1; next, it waits on b (until the "right thread" has copied y into z2); next, it copies z2 into x. In parallel, the "right thread" behaves symmetrically. The barrier is crucial: without it, the threads can prematurely copy z1 and z2.

The program is annotated with seven assertions (in teal), expressed in a variant of separation logic [22,23]: the "global" and "local" pre/postconditions specify the behaviour of the whole program and of the separate threads; the *barrier contract* specifies for every thread what must be true before it passes the barrier, and what will be true after (i.e., transfer of ownership and data).

- To offer also a more practical perspective, Fig. 1b and Fig. 1d show excerpts of **the same programs, but represented in the input format of *VerCors*** [9,11], a state-of-the-art deductive verifier. Keywords `requires`, `ensures`, and `context` indicate preconditions, postconditions, and method invariants, respectively. For instance, the pre/postconditions in Fig. 1a and Fig. 1c correspond to lines 5–6 in Fig. 1b and lines 47–48 in Fig. 1d. Furthermore, an assertion of the form `Perm(`x`,`q`)` in Fig. 1d indicates the permission to write to variable x ($q = 1$) or to read from it ($q < 1$). That is, $x \mapsto v$ in Fig. 1c is written as the conjunction of `Perm(`x`,1)` and x `==` v in Fig. 1d.
  We organised the code in Fig. 1d differently from the code in Fig. 1c, as VerCors does not support such barriers. Instead we implemented a custom *channel* to transfer data/ownership between threads (lines 39–40), using VerCors's *locking* mechanism. The *lock invariant* (lines 4–8) specifies what is assumed upon acquiring, and asserted upon releasing, an object's lock.

Open Problem. Based on Fig. 1, we make two observations:

- Fig. 1a and Fig. 1b show that deductive verification of simple sequential programs is simple (i.e., relatively little effort to annotate).
- However, Fig. 1c and Fig. 1d show that deductive verification of corresponding parallel programs is surprisingly hard (i.e., relatively big effort).
  Moreover, while VerCors automatically checks the truth of the annotations (advantage relative to pen-and-paper proofs), manually writing these annotations can be burdensome, as seen by comparing Fig. 1c and Fig. 1d. Specifically, the "local" pre/postconditions of the "left thread" in Fig. 1c are more concise than those for method `run` in class `Thread` in Fig. 1d.

Thus, in existing approaches, verification of parallel programs is substantially more laborious than that of sequential programs; *already in theory, using pen and paper, but—*paradoxically*—sometimes more so in practice, using tool support.* We illustrate these findings with the simplest non-trivial example we could think of. This problem is only aggravated as the complexity of the programs increases.

Essentially, the reason why annotations of parallel programs are complicated, is because synchronisation (of data accesses/mutations) among threads needs to be specified explicitly with permissions. This is already non-trivial when using the high-level barrier in Fig. 1c (writing the barrier contract); getting synchronisation among threads right costs even more intellectual effort when we are forced to implement the custom channels in Fig. 1d using lower-level locks (VerCors does not have such built-in barriers). In the sequential programs in Fig. 1a and Fig. 1b, we need not worry about synchronisation among threads at all; this is the level of simplicity that VeyMont aims to provide (e.g., we added support in VeyMont to auto-generate permissions, so the user needs not write them).

Contributions. Existing methods (e.g., [12,15,22,23,29,39,41,42]) and tools (e.g. [11,27,52]) for deductive verification of parallel programs have this workflow:

Step 1: Parallelise a sequential program. **Step 2:** Verify it.
(Or write a parallel program from scratch.)

However, step 2 requires significant extra, and non-trivial, annotation effort. As demonstrated above, this makes deductive verification of parallel programs much harder than that of sequential programs. To address this issue, we are developing a new method and tool that have an "inverted workflow":

Step 1: Verify a *sequential-ish* program. **Step 2:** Parallelise it.

The idea behind sequential-ish programs is that they have sequential syntax and sequential axiomatic semantics (i.e., proof system), but parallel operational semantics. That is, they look and feel as sequential programs, but they are run as parallel programs. More concretely, the user uses Hoare logic to annotate a sequential-ish program P_{seq}—without worrying about synchronisation—after which a *functionally correct, deadlock-free* parallel program P_{par} is generated:

- "Functionally correct" means that if the precondition of P_{seq} holds in the initial state of P_{par}, then the postcondition of P_{seq} holds in the final state of P_{par} (i.e., functional correctness of P_{seq} is preserved in P_{par}).
- "Deadlock free" means that threads do not get stuck waiting on each other, e.g. because two threads are both reading from a channel but expect the other thread to write. No additional manual annotations are needed.

In a previous paper [30], we presented the theoretical foundations of this new method and its "inverted workflow", targetting coarse-grained parallelism among threads (inspired by distributed systems). In this paper, we present the first deductive verification tool that supports it. The novel contributions are:

1. We designed and implemented VeyMont: it accepts an annotated sequential-ish program as input and offers a functionally correct, deadlock-free parallel program in Java as output. Section 2 and Sect. 3 provide an overview of the workflow and features of VeyMont, by example; Sect. 4 contains details.
2. We evaluated VeyMont along two dimensions. As case studies in applicability, we used VeyMont to verify and parallelise sequential-ish versions of distributed algorithms. As case studies in efficiency, we used VeyMont to produce parallel programs in Java that have comparable performance to third-party reference implementations. Section 5 describes our findings.

The artifact for reproducing the experiments of this paper is available at [51].

Related Work. Existing tools for deductive verification of parallel programs include Frama-C [5], KeY-ABS [20], VeriFast [27], and Gobra [52]. However, these tools verify parallel programs, whereas VeyMont parallelises verified programs.

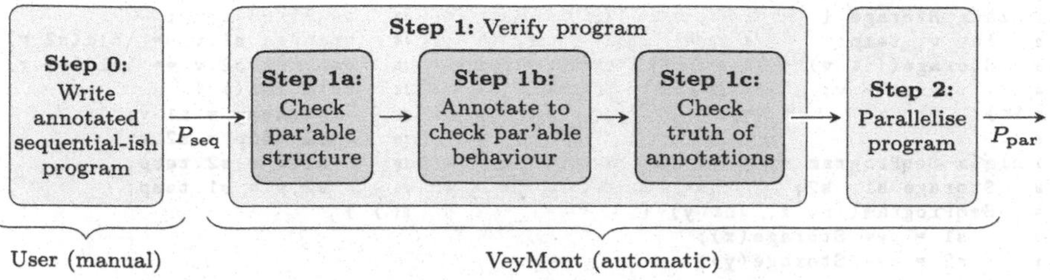

Fig. 2. "Inverted workflow" using VeyMont

The "inverted workflow"—*verify first, parallelise second*—of the method supported by VeyMont is strongly inspired by the methods of *choreographic programs* [17,18] and *multiparty session types* [24] for construction/analysis of deadlock-free distributed systems. The idea behind those methods is: first, to implement/specify distributed systems as *choreographies/global types* (cf. sequential-ish programs); second, to generate sets of *processes/local types* (cf. parallel programs with threads) that are formally guaranteed to be deadlock-free. Existing tools that support these methods include Chor [17], Scribble [25] and its dialects [19,35,36,46], Pabble [37], and ParTypes [34]. However, these tools offer deadlock freedom, but *not* functional correctness; VeyMont offers both.

The literature on *parallelising compilers* that target fine-grained parallelism among tasks is rich (e.g., loop parallelisation [2,13,16,33,38,49]) and goes back to the 1970 s [31]. In contrast, VeyMont is a *parallelising verifier* that targets coarse-grained parallelism among threads (i.e., whole-program parallelisation). We discuss the integration of fine-grained parallelism into VeyMont in Sect. 6.

2 Overview of VeyMont – The "Inverted Workflow"

Figure 2 visualises the "inverted workflow" of the method supported by VeyMont.

Step 0: The user writes a sequential-ish program P_{seq} in VeyMont's input language μPVL (core fragment of VerCors's language PVL [50]). This is a programming/assertion language that combines object-oriented sequential programs with Hoare logic assertions (similar to sequential Java, enriched with JML [32]).

For instance, Fig. 3a shows a sequential-ish program in μPVL (cf. Figure 1d). It is split into two parts: fields `s1` and `s2` of class `SeqProgram` define the *data* (lines 1–12), while method `run` defines the *sequence of operations* (lines 16–21). The precondition of `run` is trivial (line 13); the postcondition uses the `\old` predicate for the old values of `s1.v` and `s2.v` at the start of `run` (lines 14–15). As `s1.v` and `s2.v` are initialised to `x` and `y` (lines 12–13), which are free program arguments (line 9), all possible initial values of `s1.v` and `s2.v` are quantified over.

Step 1a: VeyMont checks whether or not P_{seq} has a *parallelisable* ("par'able") *structure.* This is a set of syntactic conditions, beyond μPVL's grammar, that P_{seq} must meet to be able to generate a grammatical parallel program (step 2).

```
class Storage {      // The name of this class is
  int v, temp;       // specifically chosen to
  Storage(int v) {   // clarify VeyMont. Generally,
    this.v = v;      // it can be anything.
} }

class SeqProgram {   // The name of this class is
  Storage s1, s2;    // always mandatory (Sect. 4).
  SeqProgram(int x, int y) {
    s1 = new Storage(x);
    s2 = new Storage(y);
  }
  requires true;
  ensures s1.v == \old(s2.v);
  ensures s2.v == \old(s1.v);
  void run() {
    s1.temp = s1.v;
    s2.temp = s2.v;
    s1.v = s2.temp;
    s2.v = s1.temp;
} }
```

(a) Sequential-ish program in μPVL – *input*

```
class s1Thread extends Thread {
  Storage s1;
  IntegerChannel s1_s2;
  IntegerChannel s2_s1;

  s1Thread(int x,
    IntegerChannel s1_s2,
    IntegerChannel s2_s1) {

    s1 = new Storage(x);
    s1_s2 = s1_s2;
    s2_s1 = s2_s1;
  }

  public void run() {
    s1.temp = s1.v;
    s1.v = s2_s1.read();
    s1_s2.write(s1.temp);
} }
class s2Thread extends Thread {

  ... // similar to lines 2-13

  public void run() {
    s2.temp = s2.v;
    s2_s1.write(s2.temp);
    s2.v = s1_s2.read();
} }

class ParProgram {
  ParProgram(int x, int y) {
    IntegerChannel s1_s2 = ...;
    IntegerChannel s2_s1 = ...;
    new s1Thread(
      x, s1_s2, s2_s1).start();
    new s2Thread(
      y, s1_s2, s2_s1).start();
} }
```

(b) Parallel program in Java, excerpt – *output*

Fig. 3. Example of VeyMont (swapping values)

Step 1b: VeyMont generates annotations for P_{seq}—in addition to those the user has written in step 0—to be able to check that it has *parallelisable behaviour* (step 1c). This is a set of semantic conditions, encoded as logic assertions, that P_{seq} must meet to guarantee that functional correctness of P_{seq} will be preserved.

Step 1c: VeyMont checks the truth of the annotations in P_{seq}, using the state-of-the-art *VerCors–Viper–Z3* tool stack [9,11]. If so, P_{seq} is guaranteed to be functionally correct (the user's annotations; step 0), functional correctness is guaranteed to be preserved through parallelisation (VeyMont's annotations; step 1b), and parallelisation does not introduce deadlocks.

Step 2: VeyMont generates a parallel program P_{par} in Java. Step 1a guarantees that P_{seq} is parallelisable; steps 1b–1c and the theoretical foundations of VeyMont guarantee that P_{par} is functionally correct and deadlock-free [30].

For instance, Fig. 3b shows an excerpt of the parallel program generated for the sequential-ish program in Fig. 3a. The idea is to parallelise coarse-grained, at the level of granularity *of top-level fields.* For every field $f \in \{\texttt{s1}, \texttt{s2}\}$ of class SeqProgram in Fig. 3a, there is a corresponding subclass *f*Thread of class Thread

```
class Player {
  int m, n;
  int[][] grid;
  Move move;

  ...

  ensures (\forall int i = 0..m;
             (\forall int j = 0..n;
                grid[i][j] == 0));
  ensures ...
  Player(int m, int n, ...) {
    this.grid = new int[m][n];
    ...
  }

 requires ...
  ensures 0 <= move.x && move.x < m;
  ensures 0 <= move.y && move.y < n;
  ensures grid[move.x][move.y] == 0;
  ensures ...
  void think();

 requires ...
 requires 0 <= move.x && move.x < m;
 requires 0 <= move.y && move.y < n;
 requires grid[move.x][move.y] == 0;
  ensures ...
  void play();
}
```

```
class Move {
  int x, y, t;
  ...
}
```

```
class SeqProgram {
  Player p1, p2;

  ...

  ensures eq_grids(p1, p2);
  SeqProgram(int m, int n) {
    p1 = new Player(m, n, ...);
    p2 = new Player(m, n, ...);
  }

  context eq_grids(p1, p2);
  void turn1() {
    p1.think();
    p1.play();
    p2.think(); // in the background
    p2.move = p1.move.clone();
    p2.play(); // to update
  }

  ...

  context eq_grids(p1, p2);
  void run() {
    loop_invariant eq_grids(p1, p2);
    while (p1.inPlay && p2.inPlay) {
      turn1();
      if (p1.inPlay && p2.inPlay) {
        turn2();
} } } }
```

Fig. 4. Another example of VeyMont (tic–tac–toe on an arbitrary $m \times n$ grid)

in Fig. 3b (which defines a Java thread); this subclass alone is responsible for managing the data of f and performing its operations in class `ParProgram`.

f`Thread` has three fields: the `Storage` that it is responsible for, and `Channel`s to explicitly transfer data between `Storage`s. Meanwhile, method `run` of f`Thread` defines the operations that it needs to perform, derived from method `run` of class `SeqProgram`: if only f occurs in an assignment in `run` of `SeqProgram`, then the assignment is copied into `run` of f`Thread`, verbatim (e.g., line 17 in Fig. 3a, line 16 in Fig. 3b); alternatively, if also $g \in \{$`s1`, `s2`$\} \setminus \{f\}$ occurs in the assignment, then an explicit data transfer between `Storage`s is introduced (i.e., fThread is forbidden to use data of gThread directly). Transfers are *synchronous*: method `read` blocks until method `write` is called, and vice versa. In this way, `Channel`s are an alternative synchronisation mechanism to the barrier in Fig. 1c.

Generally, explicit data transfers are the only form of synchronisation that VeyMont needs to introduce to guarantee functional correctness (given step 1c). Specifically, the values of `s1.v` and `s2.v` are swapped in `run` of `ParProgram`, just as asserted by the postcondition of `run` of `SeqProgram`. Finally, we note that `ParProgram` really is parallel: lines 16 and 25 can be executed simultaneously.

3 Overview of VeyMont – More Features

To demonstrate some more features of μPVL/VeyMont, Fig. 4 shows an excerpt of another sequential-ish program in μPVL. Two threads—implicitly declared in top-level fields `p1` and `p2` of class `SeqProgram`—take turns to simulate a game of tic–tac–toe on an arbitrary $m \times n$ grid (i.e., beyond 3×3, all possible grid sizes are quantified over). Each thread has its own copy of the grid; when a move is made, the active thread informs the passive thread accordingly, so the passive thread can update its grid to match. In the active thread's turn, the passive thread can "think ahead" to ponder its next move. This makes the program really parallel.

We highlight the noteworthy features, as supported by µPVL/VeyMont:

- **Turing completeness:** Method `run` of class `SeqProgram` shows that µPVL has *if/while-statements.* This is actually significant: automatically parallelising *the conditions of* if/while-statements, while guaranteeing functional correctness and deadlock freedom, has been a key challenge in developing VeyMont's theoretical foundations [30]. It is also a reason why VeyMont needs to check if a sequential-ish program has parallelisable behaviour in steps 1b–1c.
- **Data structures:** The fields of class `Player` show that µPVL/VeyMont has *multidimensional arrays* (field `grid`) and *nesting* of classes (field `move`).
- **Trusted code:** Methods `think` and `play` of class `Player` show that µPVL/VeyMont has *abstract methods*: they have a specification (precondition and postcondition), but no implementation (method body). This allows the user to integrate external trusted code into parallel programs generated by VeyMont. If the trusted code truly implements the specification (proved using VeyMont, or proved using a different tool, or estimated with code reviews, etc.), then functional correctness and deadlock freedom are guaranteed.

An excerpt of the parallelisation generated by VeyMont appears in Sect. A.

4 Design and Implementation

VeyMont has five main components, each of which enables a (sub)step in Fig. 2.

4.1 Parser (Step 1a)

The first main component of step 1a is a *parser* for µPVL. It accepts sequential-ish programs that comply with the grammar in Fig. 5. We split the grammar into an "external fragment" and an "internal fragment". The difference is that the internal fragment supports more complicated assertions, which the user should never write manually; instead, they are always inserted by VeyMont automatically (step 1b; Sect. 4.4). Regarding the external fragment:

- **Basic notation:** Let n range over class names, f over field names, m over method names, and x over variable names. We write $\tilde{\Box}$ to mean a list of $\Box$s.
- **Programs, classes, fields, methods, annotations:** A *program* P consists of a list of classes. A *class* C consists of a name, a list of fields, and a list of methods, including a constructor that has the same name as the class. A *method* M consists of a list of annotations (contract), a list of variable names

$$
\begin{array}{rcl}
P & ::= & \tilde{C} \\
C & ::= & \texttt{class}\ n\ \texttt{\{}\ \tilde{F}\ \tilde{M}\ \texttt{\}} \\
F & ::= & f \\
M & ::= & \tilde{A}\ m(\tilde{x})\ \texttt{\{}\ \tilde{S}\ \texttt{\}} \mid \\
  &   & \tilde{A}\ m(\tilde{x}) \\
A & ::= & \texttt{requires}\ B\texttt{;} \mid \\
  &   & \texttt{ensures}\ B\texttt{;} \mid \\
  &   & \texttt{context}\ B\texttt{;}
\end{array}
\qquad
\begin{array}{rcl}
S & ::= & \texttt{assert}\ B\texttt{;} \mid X \texttt{ = } E\texttt{;} \mid E.m(\tilde{E})\texttt{;} \mid \\
  &   & \texttt{if (}B\texttt{) \{ }\tilde{S}_1\texttt{ \} else \{ }\tilde{S}_2\texttt{ \}} \mid \\
  &   & \texttt{loop\_invariant}\ B_1\texttt{; while (}B_2\texttt{) \{ }\tilde{S}\texttt{ \}} \\
X & ::= & x \mid f \mid \texttt{this.}f \mid X.f \mid X\texttt{[}E\texttt{]} \\
E & ::= & X \mid \texttt{this} \mid \texttt{null} \mid B \mid \texttt{0} \mid \texttt{1} \mid E_1 \texttt{ + } E_2 \mid \cdots \mid \\
  &   & \texttt{new}\ n(\tilde{E}) \mid E.f \mid E.m(\tilde{E}) \mid \texttt{new [}E\texttt{]} \mid E_1\texttt{[}E_2\texttt{]} \\
B & ::= & \texttt{true} \mid \texttt{false} \mid \texttt{!}B \mid B_1 \texttt{ \&\& } B_2 \mid B_1 \texttt{ ==> } B_2 \mid \\
  &   & \texttt{(\textbackslash forall } x \texttt{ = } E_1 \texttt{..} E_2\texttt{; } B\texttt{)} \mid E_1 \texttt{ == } E_2 \mid \cdots
\end{array}
$$

(a) External fragment, for the user in step 0

$$
B ::= \cdots \mid \texttt{Perm(}X\texttt{,}q\texttt{)} \mid B_1 \texttt{ ** } B_2 \mid \texttt{(\textbackslash forall* } x \texttt{ = } E_1\texttt{..}E_2\texttt{; } B\texttt{)}
$$

(b) Internal fragment, for VeyMont in step 1b

Fig. 5. Grammar of μPVL (types omitted for simplicity)

(formal parameters), and an optional list of statements (body). A method without a body is abstract (for external trusted code). An *annotation* A is a precondition, a postcondition, or a method invariant.

- **Statements, variables, expressions:** A *statement* S is an assertion, an assignment, a method call, a conditional choice, or a conditional loop. A *variable* X is a variable name, a (qualified) field name, or a (qualified) array cell. An *expression* E is a variable, a self reference, a null reference, a Boolean expression, a primitive value/operation, an object constructor call/field access/method call, or an array constructor call/cell access. In Boolean expressions, light grey shading indicates that implication and quantification can be used only in annotations, assertions, and loop invariants.

Regarding the internal fragment, let q range over "fractions" between 0 (exclusive) and 1 (inclusive). Effectively, the grammar of Boolean expressions in Fig. 5a is extended to the grammar of *permission-based, concurrent separation logic* [12,14] in Fig. 5b to support ownership-like assertions for mutable data. That is, `Perm(`X`,`q`)` indicates that an annotated piece of code has read permission for X (if $0<q<1$) or read+write permission (if $q=1$); the sum of different fractions for the same variable can never exceed 1. Operators `**` and `\forall*` are the standard separating conjunction and separating quantification in separation logic [40,45]. Regarding notation, `requires Perm(`X_1`,`q_1`) ** Perm(`X_2`,`q_2`);` is equivalent to `requires Perm(`X_1`,`q_1`); requires Perm(`X_2`,`q_2`);`.

Remark 1. μPVL is also statically typed, but as type checking is not a contribution of this paper, we omit types to keep the presentation of μPVL concise.

4.2 Linter (Step 1a)

The second main component of step 1a is a *linter*. It checks if P_{seq} has a parallelisable structure. This is needed for applying the transformation rules in step 2 (Sect. 4.5). The linter checks the following syntactic conditions:

1. P_{seq} has a class `SeqProgram` that consists of k fields $(f_1, \ldots, f_k)$, a constructor (m_1), a main method `run` (m_2), and any auxiliary methods $(m_3, \ldots, m_l)$. All fields are instances of classes; all methods (except the constructor) are parameterless and non-recursive. The constructor initialises all fields.
2. For every assignment in $m_2, \ldots, m_l$: (a) the left-hand side is of the form $f_i.X$; (b) at most one field f_j occurs in the right-hand side. For instance, `s1.x = 5` and `s2.y = s1.x + 4` and `s1.a.b.c = 5` are fine; `s1.x = s1.x + s2.y` is not.
3. For every if/while-statement in $m_2, \ldots, m_l$: (a) the condition is of the form E_1 `&&` ... `&&` E_k; (b) f_i is the only field that occurs in every E_i. For instance, `s1.x == 5 && s2.y == 9` is fine; `s1.x + 4 == s2.y` is not.
4. For every method call on field f_i in $m_2, \ldots, m_l$: f_i is the only field that occurs in the arguments. For instance, `s1.foo(s1.x)` is fine; `s1.foo(s2.y)` is not.

These syntactic conditions constrain only class `SeqProgram` (i.e., structural parallelisability depends only on `SeqProgram`). Other classes in P_{seq} are unrestricted.

Remark 2. In our experience (e.g., Sect. 5), conditions 1–4 are straightforward to meet. Notably, many potential violations can be fixed using auxiliary fields. For instance, `s1.x = s1.x + s2.y` violates condition 2, but it can be rewritten to `s1._y = s2.y; s1.x = s1.x + s1._y`, which is functionally equivalent. Similarly, `if (s1.x + 4 == s2.y) { ... }` violates condition 3, but it can be rewritten to:

`s1._y = s2.y; s2._x = s1.x; if` $(E_1$ `&&` $E_2)$ `{ ... }`

with E_1 = `s1.x + 4 == s1._y` and E_2 = `s2._x + 4 == s2.y`. (In these examples, `s1._y` and `s2._x` are fresh.) A *complete formal characterisation* of the class of sequential-ish programs that can be rewritten in this way, including a mechanical procedure to automatically perform the necessary rewrites to meet the conditions, is still an open problem.

Remark 3. The conditions checked by the linter result from our design decision to target coarse-grained parallelism (i.e., every top-level field of `SeqProgram` is turned into a separate thread in step 2; Sect. 4.5) instead of fine-grained (e.g., loop parallelisation). We discuss their combination in Sect. 6.

4.3 Annotator (Step 1b)

The main component of step 1b is an *annotator*. It inserts additional annotations into the input program to be able to check if P_{seq} has parallelisable behaviour (step 1c; Sect. 4.4), in terms of two properties:

i. *Alias freedom.* For every piece of mutable data in P_{seq} (object fields and array cells), VeyMont inserts ownership-like assertions to specify that it cannot be aliased. As a result, the threads of P_{par} will operate on disjoint fragments of memory, so data races are avoided.

	sequential-ish	→	parallel: s1Thread	parallel: s2Thread
store	`s1.x = 5;`	→	`s1.x = 5;`	`/* skip */`
transfer	`s2.y = s1.x + 4;`	→	`s1_s2.write(s1.x + 4);`	`s2.y = s1_s2.read();`
if/while	`if (s1.x == 5 &&`	→	`if (s1.x == 5`	`if (/* skip */`
	`s2.y == 9) {`	→	`/* skip */) {`	`s2.y == 9) {`
call	`s1.foo(s1.x); }`	→	`s1.foo(s1.x); }`	`/* skip */ }`

Fig. 6. Summary of transformation rules for statements, by example

Example 1. VeyMont amends the constructor of class `Storage` in Fig. 3:

```
ensures Perm(v,1) ** Perm(temp,1);
Storage(int v_init) { ... }
```

VeyMont amends the methods of class `SeqProgram`, too:

```
ensures B_own
SeqProgram(int v) { ... }

context B_own
void run() { ... }
```

where

B_{own} = `Perm(s1, 1) ** Perm(s2, 1) **`
`Perm(s1.v, 1) ** Perm(s2.v, 1) **`
`Perm(s1.temp, 1) ** Perm(s2.temp, 1)`

The key idea is to assert write permissions of 1, for all data, everywhere. As the sum of fractional permissions can never exceed 1, there can be no aliases.

ii. *Branch unanimity.* For every condition of the form E_1 `&&` ... `&&` E_k of if/while-statements in methods $m_2, \ldots, m_l$ of class `SeqProgram`, VeyMont inserts an assertion of the form E_1 `==` E_2 `&&` ... `&&` E_{k-1} `==` E_k (i.e., $\forall_{0 \leq i < j \leq k}$ E_i `==` E_j) to specify that, when $E_1, \ldots, E_k$ are evaluated, they are all equivalent. This implies that the threads of P_{par} all choose the same branch.

Example 2. VeyMont amends the while-statement in method `run` in Fig. 4:

```
loop_invariant eq_grids(p1, p2);
loop_invariant p1.inPlay == p2.inPlay;
while (p1.inPlay && p2.inPlay) { ... }
```

Alias freedom and branch unanimity are sufficient to guarantee that functional correctness is preserved through parallelisation, and that parallelisation does not introduce deadlocks [30]; we clarify the importance of the latter after having discussed parallelisation (step 2; Sect. 4.5).

4.4 VerCors (Step 1c)

The main component of step 1c is the VerCors–Viper–Z3 tool stack [9,11] (whose language, PVL, is a superset of μPVL). To check that P_{seq} is functionally correct and has parallelisable behaviour, it verifies the truth of the user's annotations (step 0) and VeyMont's (step 1b).

4.5 Code Generator (Step 2)

The main component of step 2 is a *code generator* into Java. Non-`SeqProgram` classes in P_{seq} are copied to P_{par}, while `SeqProgram` is parallelised into classes

```
b.x = a.x;
a.y = b.y;
if (a.x >= a.y &&
    b.x <= b.y) {
  a.z = b.z;
} else {
  b.z = a.z;
}
```

(a) Sequential-ish

```
a_b.write(a.x);
a.y = b_a.read();
if (a.x >= a.y
    /* skip */) {
  a.z = b_a.read();
} else {
  a_b.write(a.z);
}
```

(b) Parallel: aThread

```
b.x = a_b.read();
b_a.write(b.y);
if (/* skip */
    b.x <= b.y) {
  b_a.write(b.z);
} else {
  b.z = a_b.read();
}
```

(c) Parallel: bThread

Fig. 7. Example of a sequential-ish program whose parallelisation can deadlock. VeyMont statically detects this and reports an error instead.

f_1`Thread`, ..., f_k`Thread` (each f_i is a field of `SeqProgram`), and class `ParProgram` for forking. The methods of each f_i`Thread` are derived from methods $m_2, \ldots, m_l$ of `SeqProgram`, by applying the transformations in Fig. 6 to every statement S:

- If S is an assignment, then *due to condition 2 of the linter* (Sect. 4.2), S contains the field either of one thread ("store") or of two threads ("transfer"). In the former case, S is added to the thread; in the latter case, a `write`/`read` on a `Channel` are added to the threads. Nothing is added to other threads.
- If S is an if/while-statement, then *due to condition 3 of the linter*, for every thread, S contains a corresponding subcondition. An if/while-statement with exactly that corresponding subcondition is added to every thread.
- If S is a call, then *due to condition 4 of the linter*, S contains the field of one thread. S is added to that thread. Nothing is added to other threads.

The theoretical foundations of our method ensure that if steps 1a, 1b, and 1c have succeeded, then the transformation rules in Fig. 6 indeed result in a functionally correct, deadlock-free parallel program [30].

Remark 4. To illustrate the importance of branch unanimity (Sect. 4.3) to guarantee that parallelisation does not introduce deadlocks, Fig. 7 shows a sequential-ish program (i.e., the body of method `run` of class `SeqProgram` with top-level fields `a` and `b`). This program meets the conditions of the linter, so it has a parallelisable structure; its parallelisation consists of `aThread` and `bThread`.

However, whether or not `aThread` and `bThread` can deadlock crucially depends on the initial values of `a.x` and `b.y` (intentionally omitted from Fig. 7):

- If `a.x` and `b.y` are initially equal, then branch unanimity is satisfied (no deadlock): after the first two assignments, `a.x >= a.y` and `b.x <= b.y` are both true. Subsequently, `aThread` and `bThread` both enter their then-branches, so `aThread` reads and `bThread` correspondingly writes.
  Thus, VeyMont (step 1c) reports no error when `a.x == b.y` initially.
- If `a.x` and `b.y` are initially <u>un</u>equal, then branch unanimity is violated (deadlock): `a.x >= a.y` and `b.x <= b.y` are either true and false, or false and true. In the former case, `aThread` enters its then-branch, but `bThread` enters its else-branch. At this point, `aThread` and `bThread` both expect to read, but neither one of them will write, so they are stuck forever.
  Thus, VeyMont (step 1c) reports an error when `a.x != b.y` initially.

We note that VeyMont guarantees deadlock freedom, but not starvation freedom: at any point in time, either all threads have terminated, or at least one thread is still running, modulo exceptions (e.g., division by zero).

5 Evaluation

Applicability. We used VeyMont to verify and parallelise sequential-ish programs for three classical distributed algorithms, for various numbers of threads n:

- In **two-phase commit** (2PC) [47], 1 Client and $n-1$ Servers cooperate to fulfil a joint query in a distributed database. First, the Client shares the query with the Servers. Next, the Servers locally run the query and report success/failure back to the Client. Only if all Servers succeeded will the Client instruct them to commit, and otherwise to abort. We successfully verified that the Clients consistently commit, for $n \in \{3, 5, 8, 12, 17\}$.
- In anonymous **election** (probabilistic version of Peleg's algorithm [43] in the style of Itai and Rodeh [26]), n symmetric threads try to elect a unique leader among them. The algorithm proceeds in rounds. In every round, every thread picks a random number from some fixed range (trusted code) and shares it with every other thread. If there is a unique highest number, then the thread that picked it declares itself the leader; otherwise, another round ensues. We verified that a unique leader is elected upon termination, for $n \in \{3, 5, 8\}$.
- In **consensus** [6], n symmetric threads try to reach agreement about a common value. First, the threads share their locally preferred values. Next, every thread computes the globally preferred value (by majority); this becomes the common value. The complication is that *threads can fail*: nondeterministically (abstract methods), they can share the wrong locally preferred value and/or compute the wrong globally preferred value. We successfully verified that all threads set the right globally preferred value when the number of failures is at most $\lfloor n/4 \rfloor$, for $n \in \{3, 5\}$; this is a classical result.

As a proxy of effort, Fig. 8 shows ratios of numbers of annotations ("spec") vs. program elements ("impl"). They are *below* 1; by comparison, Wolf et al. [52] recently report ratios of 2.69–3.16 to deductively verify parallel programs using a tool based on traditional methods. This is first evidence that VeyMont indeed significantly reduces the annotation burden.

Figure 8 also presents the mean run times (of 30 runs) of VeyMont for step 1c and in total (using: Intel i7-8569U CPU with 4 physical/4 virtual cores at 2.8 GHz; 16 GB memory). We can make two main observations. First, the run times are dominated by step 1c (actual verification). For instance, step 1c consumes $\frac{6.8}{8.0} = 85\%$ of the run time for 2PC ($n = 3$) and as much as $\frac{62.2}{63.9} = 97\%$ for 2PC ($n = 17$). Second, parallelisation itself is relatively cheap. For instance, it takes less than 1.2 seconds for 2PC ($n = 3$) and less than 1.7 seconds for 2PC ($n = 17$).

	$\frac{\textbf{spec}}{\textbf{impl}}$	**1c**	**total**
2PC (n=3)	32/75	6.8	8.0
2PC (n=5)	42/91	8.9	10.1
2PC (n=8)	57/115	13.9	15.2
2PC (n=12)	77/147	26.4	27.8
2PC (n=17)	102/187	62.2	63.9

	$\frac{\textbf{spec}}{\textbf{impl}}$	**1c**	**total**
election (n=3)	22/49	7.2	8.5
election (n=5)	28/69	14.3	16.2
election (n=8)	37/99	61.5	65.4
consensus (n=3)	72/73	9.8	11.3
consensus (n=5)	90/104	41.0	42.5

Fig. 8. Case studies in applicability: ratio of number of annotations vs. program elements ($\frac{\textbf{spec}}{\textbf{impl}}$) and mean VeyMont run times in seconds (**1c**, **total**). Program elements are: class headers, fields, method headers, and statements.

Efficiency. We compared the performance of VeyMont-generated parallel programs in Java with third-party reference implementations. Our aim was to study if the synchronisation mechanism in generated parallel programs is sufficiently lightweight to be competitive. We use different programs than above, as no third-party reference implementations were available for 2PC/election/consensus.

We took the following approach. First, we selected two parallel programs from the *CLBG database* [1]: `binary-trees` (parallel tree walk) and `k-nucleotide` (parallel pattern matching of molecule sequences against a DNA string). Next, for each program: **(1)** we extracted the data sharing patterns among threads in the CLBG reference implementation and wrote them as a sequential-ish program in µPVL; **(2)** we "completed" the sequential-ish program by adding abstract methods to represent all purely sequential computations; **(3)** we generated parallel programs in Java using VeyMont; **(4)** we concretised the abstract methods in Java with trusted sequential CLBG code; **(5)** we ran the CLBG version and the VeyMont version to compare performances, using CLBG-standardised input, with various numbers of threads. We note that we did not prove functional correctness; this is beyond the scope of these performance comparisons.

We ran the resulting executables on three different machines: *Cartesius* (Intel E5-2690 v3 CPU with 16 physical cores), *MacBook* (Intel i7-8569U CPU with 4 physical/4 virtual cores), and *VM* [28] (1 virtual core). Figure 9 show our results as *speed-ups* of VeyMont versions relative to CLBG versions, computed as $\frac{\mu_{\text{CLBG}}}{\mu_{\text{VeyMont}}}$, where μ_{VeyMont} and μ_{CLBG} are the mean run times (of 100 runs) of a VeyMont and a CLBG version; $\frac{\mu_{\text{CLBG}}}{\mu_{\text{VeyMont}}} < 1$ means that a VeyMont version was slower.

We can make two main observations. First, although the VeyMont versions tend to be somewhat slower than the CLBG versions, the slowdown is generally less than 10%. We conjecture that there is a substantial class of programs for which a 10% slowdown is a fine price for better verifiability of functional correctness and deadlock freedom. Second, different machines exhibit different performance; a deeper study is needed to understand what exactly causes this.

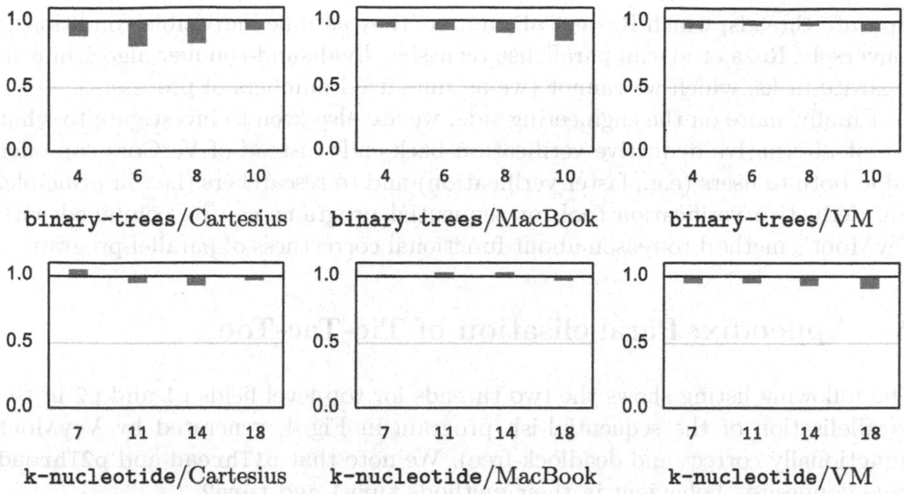

Fig. 9. Case studies in efficiency: the x-axis indicates the number of threads; the y-axis indicates the speed-up of VeyMont versions relative to CLBG versions.

6 Future Work

We presented VeyMont: a deductive verification tool that aims to make reasoning about functional correctness and deadlock freedom of parallel programs (relatively complex) as easy as that of sequential programs (relatively simple).

Our most-wanted feature for VeyMont is to support *parametrisation* (e.g., election generically for n threads instead of specifically for $3, 5, 8, \ldots$). However, parametrised verification is known to be undecidable in general [3,48]. The study of this topic (e.g., identification of decidable fragments) has become a research area of its own over the past decade; the book by Bloem et al. gives an extensive overview [7,8]. Thus, an extension of VeyMont to support parametrisation is highly non-trivial. It is our main direction for future work.

Other future work pertains to a relaxation of alias freedom and branch unanimity in the theoretical foundations of VeyMont [30]. Such a relaxation allows VeyMont to be more flexible about read/write permissions (e.g., improve support for read-only shared arrays), but maintaining the same strong guarantees.

Inspired by methods for distributed systems, VeyMont targets coarse-grained parallelism among threads (i.e., whole-program parallelisation) instead of fine-grained parallelism among tasks (e.g., loop parallelisation). We are keen to explore the combination of both approaches. A first step would be to mix VeyMont with the VerCors-based work of Blom et al. [10] on verification of loop parallelisation. Beyond that, it is interesting to extend VeyMont with complementary techniques. For instance, Raza et al. [44] developed a technique to infer dependencies among statements in sequential programs to allow their parallel execution (like us), but at the level of tasks (unlike us). Their technique and ours have different strengths: we can split the conditions of if/while-statements across separate threads, which Raza et al. cannot (they assume indivisible conditions); conversely, Raza et al. can parallelise recursive divide-and-conquer algorithms in separate tasks, which we cannot (we assume fixed numbers of processes).

Finally, more on the engineering side, we are also keen to investigate to what extent alternative deductive verification back-ends instead of VerCors can offer value both to users (e.g., faster verification) and to researchers (i.e., in principle, any deductive verification tool for sequential programs can be combined with VeyMont's method to reason about functional correctness of parallel programs).

A Appendix: Parallelisation of Tic-Tac-Toe

The following listing shows the two threads for top-level fields `p1` and `p2` in the parallelisation of the sequential-ish program in Fig. 4, generated by VeyMont (functionally correct and deadlock-free). We note that `p1Thread` and `p2Thread` have "opposite" behaviour in their methods `turn1` and `turn2`.

```
class p1Thread extends Thread {
  Player p1;
  MoveChannel p1_p2;
  MoveChannel p2_p1;

  p1Thread(int m, int n,
    MoveChannel p1_p2,
    MoveChannel p2_p1) {

    this.p1 = new Player(m, n, ...);
    this.p1_p2 = p1_p2;
    this.p2_p1 = p2_p1;
  }

  void turn1() {
    p1.think();
    p1.play();
    p1_p2.write(p1.move.clone());
  }

  void turn2() {
    p1.think(); // in the background
    p1.move = p2_p1.read();
    p1.play(); // to update
  }

  public void run() {
    while(p1.inPlay) {
      turn1();
      if (p1.inPlay) {
        turn2();
} } } }
```

```
class p2Thread extends Thread {
  Player p2;
  MoveChannel p1_p2;
  MoveChannel p2_p1;

  p2Thread(int m, int n,
    MoveChannel p1_p2,
    MoveChannel p2_p1) {

    this.p2 = new Player(m, n, ...);
    this.p1_p2 = p1_p2;
    this.p2_p1 = p2_p1;
  }

  void turn1() {
    p2.think(); // in the background
    p2.move = p1_p2.read();
    p2.play(); // to update
  }

  void turn2() {
    p2.think();
    p2.play();
    p2_p1.write(p2.move.clone());
  }

  public void run() {
    while(p2.inPlay){
      turn1();
      if (p2.inPlay) {
        turn2();
} } } }
```

The remaining classes that are part of the parallelisation are:

- `ParProgram`: This class is responsible for creating channels and starting the threads. It is very similar to class `ParProgram` in Fig. 3b
- `Player`, `Move`: These classes are straightforward Java versions of the μPVL versions in Fig. 4.

References

1. https://benchmarksgame-team.pages.debian.net/benchmarksgame/index.html
2. Aiken, A., Nicolau, A.: Optimal loop parallelization. In: PLDI, pp. 308–317. ACM (1988)
3. Apt, K.R., Kozen, D.: Limits for automatic verification of finite-state concurrent systems. Inf. Process. Lett. **22**(6), 307–309 (1986)
4. Apt, K.R., Olderog, E.-R.: Fifty years of Hoare's logic. Formal Aspects Comput. **31**(6), 751–807 (2019). https://doi.org/10.1007/s00165-019-00501-3
5. Baudin, P., et al.: The dogged pursuit of bug-free C programs: the Frama-C software analysis platform. Commun. ACM **64**(8), 56–68 (2021)
6. Berman, P., Garay, J.A., Perry, K.J.: Towards optimal distributed consensus (extended abstract). In: FOCS, pp. 410–415. IEEE Computer Society (1989)
7. Bloem, R., et al.: Decidability of Parameterized Verification. Synthesis Lectures on Distributed Computing Theory, Morgan & Claypool Publishers, San Rafael (2015)
8. Bloem, R., et al.: Decidability in parameterized verification. SIGACT News **47**(2), 53–64 (2016)
9. Blom, S., Darabi, S., Huisman, M., Oortwijn, W.: The VerCors tool set: verification of parallel and concurrent software. In: Polikarpova, N., Schneider, S. (eds.) IFM 2017. LNCS, vol. 10510, pp. 102–110. Springer, Cham (2017). https://doi.org/10.1007/978-3-319-66845-1_7
10. Blom, S., Darabi, S., Huisman, M., Safari, M.: Correct program parallelisations. Int. J. Softw. Tools Technol. Transf. **23**(5), 741–763 (2021). https://doi.org/10.1007/s10009-020-00601-z
11. Blom, S., Huisman, M.: The VerCors tool for verification of concurrent programs. In: Jones, C., Pihlajasaari, P., Sun, J. (eds.) FM 2014. LNCS, vol. 8442, pp. 127–131. Springer, Cham (2014). https://doi.org/10.1007/978-3-319-06410-9_9
12. Bornat, R., Calcagno, C., O'Hearn, P., Parkinson, M.: Permission accounting in separation logic. In: POPL, pp. 259–270. ACM (2005)
13. Boulet, P., Darte, A., Silber, G.-A., Vivien, F.: Loop parallelization algorithms: from parallelism extraction to code generation. Parallel Comput. **24**(3–4), 421–444 (1998)
14. Boyland, J.: Checking interference with fractional permissions. In: Cousot, R. (ed.) SAS 2003. LNCS, vol. 2694, pp. 55–72. Springer, Heidelberg (2003). https://doi.org/10.1007/3-540-44898-5_4
15. Brookes, S.: A semantics for concurrent separation logic. Theor. Comput. Sci. **375**(1–3), 227–270 (2007)
16. Burke, M., Cytron, R.: Interprocedural dependence analysis and parallelization. In: SIGPLAN Symposium on Compiler Construction, pp. 162–175. ACM (1986)
17. Carbone, M., Montesi, F.: Deadlock-freedom-by-design: multiparty asynchronous global programming. In: POPL, pp. 263–274. ACM (2013)
18. Carbone, M., Montesi, F., Schürmann, C.: Choreographies, logically. Distributed Comput. **31**(1), 51–67 (2018)
19. Castro, D., Hu, R., Jongmans, S.S., Ng, N., Yoshida, N.: Distributed programming using role-parametric session types in Go: statically-typed endpoint APIs for dynamically-instantiated communication structures. PACMPL, **3**(POPL), 29:1–29:30 (2019)
20. Din, C.C., Tapia Tarifa, S.L., Hähnle, R., Johnsen, E.B.: History-based specification and verification of scalable concurrent and distributed systems. In: Butler, M., Conchon, S., Zaïdi, F. (eds.) ICFEM 2015. LNCS, vol. 9407, pp. 217–233. Springer, Cham (2015). https://doi.org/10.1007/978-3-319-25423-4_14

21. Hoare, C.A.R.: An axiomatic basis for computer programming. Commun. ACM **12**(10), 576–580 (1969)
22. Hobor, A., Gherghina, C.: Barriers in concurrent separation logic. In: Barthe, G. (ed.) ESOP 2011. LNCS, vol. 6602, pp. 276–296. Springer, Heidelberg (2011). https://doi.org/10.1007/978-3-642-19718-5_15
23. Hobor, A., Gherghina, C.: Barriers in concurrent separation logic: now with tool support! Log. Methods Comput. Sci., **8**(2) (2012)
24. Honda, K., Yoshida, N., Carbone, M.: Multiparty asynchronous session types. In: POPL, pp. 273–284. ACM (2008)
25. Hu, R., Yoshida, N.: Hybrid session verification through endpoint API generation. In: Stevens, P., Wasowski, A. (eds.) FASE 2016. LNCS, vol. 9633, pp. 401–418. Springer, Heidelberg (2016). https://doi.org/10.1007/978-3-662-49665-7_24
26. Itai, A., Rodeh, M.: Symmetry breaking in distributive networks. In: FOCS, pp. 150–158. IEEE Computer Society (1981)
27. Jacobs, B., Smans, J., Philippaerts, P., Vogels, F., Penninckx, W., Piessens, F.: VeriFast: a powerful, sound, predictable, fast verifier for C and Java. In: Bobaru, M., Havelund, K., Holzmann, G.J., Joshi, R. (eds.) NFM 2011. LNCS, vol. 6617, pp. 41–55. Springer, Heidelberg (2011). https://doi.org/10.1007/978-3-642-20398-5_4
28. Jacobs, S., Reynolds, A.: TACAS 22 Artifact Evaluation VM - Ubuntu 20.04 LTS (2021). https://doi.org/10.5281/zenodo.5562597
29. Jones, C.B.: Tentative steps toward a development method for interfering programs. ACM Trans. Program. Lang. Syst. **5**(4), 596–619 (1983)
30. Jongmans, S., van den Bos, P.: A predicate transformer for choreographies. In: ESOP 2022. LNCS, vol. 13240, pp. 520–547. Springer, Cham (2022). https://doi.org/10.1007/978-3-030-99336-8_19
31. Lamport, L.: The parallel execution of DO loops. Commun. ACM **17**(2), 83–93 (1974)
32. Leavens, G.T., Baker, A.L., Ruby, C.: Preliminary design of JML: a behavioral interface specification language for Java. ACM SIGSOFT Softw. Eng. Notes **31**(3), 1–38 (2006)
33. Lim, A.W., Lam, M.S.: Maximizing parallelism and minimizing synchronization with affine transforms. In: POPL, pp. 201–214. ACM Press (1997)
34. López, H.A., et al.: Protocol-based verification of message-passing parallel programs. In: OOPSLA, pp. 280–298. ACM (2015)
35. Neykova, R., Hu, R., Yoshida, N., Abdeljallal, F.: A session type provider: compile-time API generation of distributed protocols with refinements in F#. In: CC, pp. 128–138. ACM (2018)
36. Neykova, R., Yoshida, N.: Let it recover: multiparty protocol-induced recovery. In: CC, pp. 98–108. ACM (2017)
37. Ng, N., Yoshida, N.: Pabble: parameterised scribble. Serv. Oriented Comput. Appl. **9**(3–4), 269–284 (2015)
38. Oancea, C.E., Rauchwerger, L.: Logical inference techniques for loop parallelization. In PLDI, pp. 509–520. ACM (2012)
39. O'Hearn, P.W.: Resources, concurrency, and local reasoning. Theor. Comput. Sci. **375**(1–3), 271–307 (2007)
40. O'Hearn, P.: Separation logic. Commun. ACM **62**(2), 86–95 (2019)
41. Owicki, S.S., Gries, D.: An axiomatic proof technique for parallel programs I. Acta Informatica **6**, 319–340 (1976)
42. Owicki, S.S., Gries, D.: Verifying properties of parallel programs: an axiomatic approach. Commun. ACM **19**(5), 279–285 (1976)

43. Peleg, D.: Time-optimal leader election in general networks. J. Parallel Distrib. Comput. **8**(1), 96–99 (1990)
44. Raza, M., Calcagno, C., Gardner, P.: Automatic parallelization with separation logic. In: Castagna, G. (ed.) ESOP 2009. LNCS, vol. 5502, pp. 348–362. Springer, Heidelberg (2009). https://doi.org/10.1007/978-3-642-00590-9_25
45. Reynolds, J.C.: Separation logic: a logic for shared mutable data structures. In: LICS, pp. 55–74. IEEE Computer Society (2002)
46. Scalas, A., Dardha, O., Hu, R., Yoshida, N.: A linear decomposition of multiparty sessions for safe distributed programming. In: ECOOP, volume 74 of LIPIcs, pp. 24:1–24:31. Schloss Dagstuhl - Leibniz-Zentrum fuer Informatik (2017)
47. Skeen, D.: Nonblocking commit protocols. In: SIGMOD Conference, pp. 133–142. ACM Press (1981)
48. Suzuki, I.: Proving properties of a ring of finite-state machines. Inf. Process. Lett. **28**(4), 213–214 (1988)
49. Tournavitis, G., Wang, Z., Franke, B., O'Boyle, M.F.: Towards a holistic approach to auto-parallelization: integrating profile-driven parallelism detection and machine-learning based mapping. In: PLDI, pp. 177–187. ACM (2009)
50. VerCors Wiki. https://github.com/utwente-fmt/vercors/wiki
51. VeyMont Artifact. https://doi.org/10.5281/zenodo.7410640
52. Wolf, F.A., Arquint, L., Clochard, M., Oortwijn, W., Pereira, J.C., Müller, P.: Gobra: modular specification and verification of Go programs. In: Silva, A., Leino, K.R.M. (eds.) CAV 2021. LNCS, vol. 12759, pp. 367–379. Springer, Cham (2021). https://doi.org/10.1007/978-3-030-81685-8_17

Verification 2

Verifying Functional Correctness Properties at the Level of Java Bytecode

Marco Paganoni(✉) and Carlo A. Furia

Software Institute, USI Università della Svizzera italiana, Lugano, Switzerland
marco.paganoni@usi.ch
https://bugcounting.net/

Abstract. The breakneck evolution of modern programming languages aggravates the development of deductive verification tools, which struggle to timely and fully support all new language features. To address this challenge, we present BYTEBACK: a verification technique that works on Java bytecode. Compared to high-level languages, intermediate representations such as bytecode offer a much more limited and stable set of features; hence, they may help decouple the verification process from changes in the source-level language.

BYTEBACK offers a library to specify functional correctness properties at the level of the source code, so that the bytecode is only used as an intermediate representation that the end user does not need to work with. Then, BYTEBACK reconstructs some of the information about types and expressions that is erased during compilation into bytecode but is necessary to correctly perform verification. Our experiments with an implementation of BYTEBACK demonstrate that it can successfully verify bytecode compiled from different versions of Java, and including several modern language features that even state-of-the-art Java verifiers (such as KeY and OpenJML) do not directly support—thus revealing how BYTEBACK's approach can help keep up verification technology with language evolution.

1 Introduction

Modern programming languages are rich in expressive features and evolve regularly, extending their capabilities with each new version of the language. These characteristics make them easier to use and ever more powerful, to the ultimate benefit of programmers using them. On the contrary, they also complicate the development of verification tools: the more features to support, and the faster a programming language evolves, the harder it is to keep up-to-date a verification toolchain. Take Java as an example of a widely used modern language. As we discuss in Sect. 5, no state-of-the-art automated Java verifier fully supports all features of the language—even for older versions such as Java 8.

In this paper, we pursue the idea of performing formal verification not at the level of a language's source code but on an intermediate representation. Our BYTEBACK technique processes Java bytecode to verify functional (input/output) properties expressed as pre- and postconditions. By targeting bytecode instead of source code, BYTEBACK

Work partially supported by SNF grant 200021-207919 (LastMile).

M. Chechik et al. (Eds.): FM 2023, LNCS 14000, pp. 343–363, 2023.
https://doi.org/10.1007/978-3-031-27481-7_20

seamlessly supports a wide variety of Java features that are desugared when automatically translated to bytecode by the compiler. It can even verify some programs written in other programming languages, such as Scala, that also compile to Java bytecode.

Performing functional verification of bytecode entails two main challenges. First, we need to provide convenient means of expressing the specification to be verified, as well as any other intermediate annotations. Requiring the user to directly annotate the bytecode is impractical, and at odds with the goal of expressing the behavior of the original Java program. BYTEBACK offers a Java library (called `BBlib`) with custom annotations and static methods. Users add specifications to the Java source code by writing Java expressions that call these library methods; BYTEBACK then recovers the specifications by analyzing `BBlib` calls in bytecode format. Supporting expressive contract specifications of the source code is a key novelty of BYTEBACK compared to other approaches, such as JayHorn [50] and SMACK [49], that also verify intermediate representations but mostly target implicit, low-level correctness properties (such as the absence of memory errors) and have only limited support for arbitrary functional specifications.

Reconstructing some of the information lost during the compilation from source code to bytecode is the second main challenge tackled by BYTEBACK. To this end, we define a bespoke static analysis working on Grimp—an alternative representation of bytecode (offered by the Soot static analysis framework [53]). BYTEBACK's analysis connects bytecode instructions to elements of `BBlib` specification, and generates verification conditions that encode program correctness. Concretely, BYTEBACK translates Grimp code and annotations to the Boogie intermediate verification language [5], which we then use as the interface to a backend SMT solver.

We implemented BYTEBACK in a tool with the same name, which verifies bytecode annotated with functional specifications expressed using the `BBlib` library. We verified 40 programs, including classic verification examples (such as sorting algorithms), using numerous Java features that state-of-the-art functional verification tools do not currently support. We also verified the implementation of some of the same algorithms in Scala, thus demonstrating that BYTEBACK can accommodate a variety of source-code level features by focusing on the verification of an intermediate representation.

A replication package including BYTEBACK's implementation, and the benchmarks and examples described in the paper, is available on Zenodo [46].

```
@Require(forall j: int • values[j] ≠ 1)
@Ensure(return ≥ 0)
static int summary1(int[] values) {
  int result = 0;
  for (int k = 0; k < values.length; k++) {
    invariant(result ≥ 0);
      if (values[k] = 0) result += 1;
      else if (values[k] = 1) result += -1;
      else if (values[k] > 0) result += values[k];
  } return result; }
```

(a) Method `summary1` uses a regular **`for`** loop and **`if/else`** conditionals.

```
@Require(forall j: int • values[j] ≠ 1)
@Ensure(return ≥ 0)
static int summary2(int... values) {
  var result = 0;
  for (var v: values) result += switch(v) {
  invariant(result ≥ 0);
    case 0: yield(1);
    case 1: yield(-1);
    default: if (v > 0) yield(v); else yield(0);
  } return result; }
```

(b) Method `summary2` uses varargs, a "foreach" loop, a **`switch`** expression, and **`var`** local types.

Fig. 1. Annotated Java methods that compute a numeric summary of **`int`** array `values`.

2 Motivating Examples

Figure 1a shows the implementation of a simple Java method `summary1`, which scans its input integer array `values` and returns a numeric summary of its content: it ignores all negative values, adds 1 to the summary for each element 0, subtracts 1 for each element 1, and adds any bigger positive elements. The code also embeds some annotations that specify a precondition **`@Require`** ("input array `values` includes no element equal to 1"), a postcondition **`@Ensure`** ("the returned result is nonnegative"), and a loop invariant **`invariant`** ("local variable `result` stays nonnegative"). Clearly, `summary1` satisfies this specification; in fact, we can easily verify Fig. 1a's code against this specification using modern verifiers for Java (such as KeY, Krakatoa, or OpenJML)—after expressing the specification using the verifier's annotation language.

Now consider method `summary2` in Fig. 1b. It's not hard to see that `summary2` implements essentially the same behavior as `summary1` but using different features of the Java language: `values` is a variadic argument (varargs) instead of a plain integer array; local variable `result` uses type inference (**`var`**) instead of declaring its type explicitly; the loop is an enhanced **`for`** loop ("foreach"); the loop's body uses a **`switch`** expression with **`yield`** instead of nested **`if/else`** conditionals. As shown in Table 5, these features have been added to Java only in recent versions of the language. As a result, none of the aforementioned Java verifiers that can check the correctness of `summary1` supports all the features used by `summary2`—even though the methods are essentially equivalent.

Our verification technique ByteBack, which we present in the rest of the paper, performs verification at the level of Java bytecode. One distinct advantage of this approach is that the Java compiler takes care of desugaring equivalent Java features into a simpler representation as bytecode instructions. Therefore, ByteBack verifies both variants `summary1` and `summary2` in Fig. 1 without having to explicitly add support for each new Java feature. This demonstrates that bytecode-level verification can help formal verification techniques keep up with rapidly evolving source-level languages.

3 How ByteBack Works

Figure 2 overviews how ByteBack works, and the toolchain it implements. To verify a program, the user first annotates its *source code* with a specification using the functionalities of the `BBlib` library; Sect. 3.1 outlines this library and how it can be used. `BBlib`-annotated source code can be compiled with the Java *compiler* (or any other suitable compiler) into *bytecode*. ByteBack uses the Soot static analysis framework to transform the bytecode into the higher-level *Grimp* intermediate representation (an alternative bytecode representation that is syntactically closer to source code and retains higher-level typing information). As we explain in Sect. 3.2, ByteBack performs a static *analysis* of Grimp, with the goal of identifying the various program elements and linking them to their specification—embedded as calls to `BBlib` methods, and references to the annotations. With this information, ByteBack can *translate* program and annotations into *Boogie* code, which the Boogie verifier [5] processes to generate verification conditions, and finally determine whether the program verifies correctly.

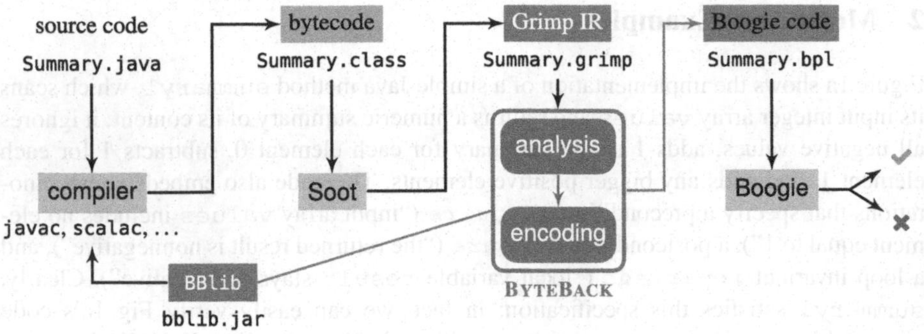

Fig. 2. An overview of how ByteBack's verification toolchain works.

```
@Require("no_ones")
@Ensure("nonnegative")
public static int summary(int... values);

@Predicate public static boolean no_ones(int[] values)
{ return not(contains(values, 1, 0, values.length)); }

@Predicate public static boolean nonnegative(int[] values, int result)
{ return gte(result, 0); }

@Pure public static boolean contains(int[] as, int e)
{ int i = Binding.integer(); return exists(i, lte(0, i) & lt(i, as.length) & eq(as[i], e)); }
```

Fig. 3. Annotations for Fig. 1's methods using `BBlib`'s concrete syntax.

3.1 Specifying Functional Properties

This section describes the main methods and annotations included in the `BBlib` library, and how we can use them to express the specification of a Java program.[1] Whereas Fig. 1's examples use a simplified idiomatic syntax, in this section we follow `BBlib`'s concrete syntax; Fig. 3 shows the same annotations with this concrete syntax.

Pre- and Postconditions. The main specification elements of a method m are its *precondition* and *postcondition*, encoded by adding annotations **`@Require`**`(String p)` and **`@Ensure`**`(String q)` just before m's declaration. Arguments `p` and `q` denote the name of *predicates*: methods returning **`boolean`** that encode the actual pre- and postconditions. We can annotate m with several **`@Require`**s and **`@Ensure`**s, which are implicitly conjoined. In Fig. 3's running example, we name the pre- and postcondition predicates `no_ones` and `nonnegative`.

Predicates. We mark any predicates p with annotation **`@Predicate`**, so that ByteBack can easily track them in the bytecode. For the same reason, a predicate p is defined in the same class as the method m it specifies. A predicate p is **`static`** iff m is, and its input signature types are the same as m's; this way, m's specification can refer to any

[1] `BBlib` is available as a JAR file, and hence any language that is bytecode-compatible with Java can use its features—as we'll demonstrate in some of Sect. 4's examples in Scala.

program elements that are visible at m's interface. Since postconditions usually constrain a method's output, any predicate q used as a postcondition includes an extra input argument `result` of the same type as m's return type (if it is not **`void`**). In Fig. 3's running example, predicates `no_ones` and `nonnegative` are **`static`** methods like `summary`; the latter includes a second argument **`int result`**, which refers to the integer value returned by `summary`.

Pure Expressions. A predicate's body encodes a Boolean expression that should be exactly expressible in logic. Therefore, it can only include *pure* (side-effect free) statements, and has to terminate with a single **`return`** statement that defines the overall predicate expression. In practice, this means that predicates can only *read* the global program state but cannot modify it. However, pure methods may use local variables and may call methods that satisfy the same constraints and that we marked as **`@Pure`**; this includes recursive calls. For example, Fig. 3's predicate `no_ones` calls pure function `contains`.

Table 1. A list of `BBlib`'s aggregable operators, and the Java or logic operators that they replace.

	IN JAVA/LOGIC	IN BBLIB
comparison	`x < y`, `x <= y`, `x == y`	**`lt`**`(x, y)`, **`lte`**`(x, y)`, **`eq`**`(x, y)`
	`x != y`, `x >= y`, `x > y`	**`neq`**`(x, y)`, **`gte`**`(x, y)`, **`gt`**`(x, y)`
conditionals	`c ? t : e`	**`conditional`**`(c, t, e)`
propositional	`!a`, `a && b`, `a || b`, `a` $\Longrightarrow$ `b`	**`not`**`(a)`, `a & b`, `a | b`, **`implies`**`(a, b)`
quantifiers	$\forall$`x: T • P(x)`	`T x = `**`Binding`**`.T(); `**`forall`**`(x, P(x))`
	$\exists$`x: T • P(x)`	`T x = `**`Binding`**`.T(); `**`exists`**`(x, P(x))`

Aggregable Expressions. BYTEBACK has no access to the source code, but it should still be able to recover the pure logic expression encoded by a predicate's body after this is translated into bytecode by the compiler. When this is the case, we say that a source code expression is *aggregable*—informally, it translates into bytecode without information loss. Aggregability further constrains what we are allowed to use in a predicate's or pure function's body: *i)* Only pure expressions are allowed. *ii)* Branching statements (conditionals, loops) are not allowed, since they introduce jumps in the bytecode that may be cumbersome or impossible to render as a single logic expression. Instead, `BBlib` offers method **`conditional`**`(c, t, e)` to encode conditional *expressions*—similar to Java ternary expressions `c ? t : e` but translated to bytecode without introducing branching. *iii)* Java's usual Boolean operators (`!`, `&&`, `||`) are not allowed because they are not aggregable: `&&` and `||` are short-circuited, and hence they may introduce branching in the bytecode; expressions involving `!` may also introduce branching (e.g., `x = !y` translates to bytecode like **`if`** `(y) x = `**`false else`**` x = `**`true`**). Instead, `BBlib` offers replacement methods (**`not`**) or lets you use Java's eager Boolean operators (`&`, `|`, `^`) that are aggregable. *iv)* Similarly, comparison operators (<, >, ...) may introduce branching in the bytecode, and hence `BBlib` offers replacement methods (**`lt`**, **`gt`**, ...) that are aggregable. Table 1 summarizes the main aggregable operators provided by `BBlib` as static methods—used either instead of non-aggregable Java methods or to express common logic operators. Figure 3 uses some of these operators to express the specification in the running example.

Frame Specifications. A method's *frame* is the set of memory locations that the method may modify. ByteBack uses a simple approach to *infer* the frame of a method m. It performs a static analysis looking for any heap-modifying statement in m's Boogie translation. If it finds any, m's frame is the whole heap; otherwise, m's frame is empty. If this analysis determines that m's frame is non-empty but m is marked as **`@Pure`** or **`@Predicate`**, ByteBack reports a verification error. The analysis recursively follows any method called by m, and is set up so as to be *sound* but imprecise; for example, if m calls a method ℓ whose implementation is not available, we conservatively assume that ℓ may modify the heap. Users can still more finely specify a method's frame by adding postconditions that explicitly indicate heap locations that do *not* change. Supporting more flexible framing methodologies [18,31,38,40,48,51] in ByteBack belongs to future work. In Fig. 3's example, ByteBack infers that `summary`'s frame is empty since its implementation only reads the content of array `values`.

Other Specification Elements. A method m's postcondition may include expressions **`old`**`(e)`—which denotes the value of `e` in m's pre-state. In addition, `BBlib` offers methods for common intra-method specification elements: *i)* **`invariant`**`(J)` declares a loop invariant `J`, and can be placed anywhere in the corresponding loop's body. Figure 1 shows the loop invariant specification in the running example. *ii)* methods **`assertion`**`(E)` and **`assumption`**`(E)` introduce intermediate assertions (if `E` holds continue, otherwise fail) and assumptions (ignore states where `E` doesn't hold) that are useful to further guide the verification process of a method's implementation. As usual, the arguments `J` and `E` to these specification elements should be pure, aggregable expressions.

3.2 Translating Grimp into Boogie

This section outlines the translation from Grimp—a human-readable representation of bytecode produced by the Soot framework—to Boogie—a verification language that combines an expressive program logic with basic procedural constructs (variables, assignments, procedures). Grimp code represents *executable instructions* in a program's bytecode; in contrast, source-level *declarations* (such as class or variable declarations) are implicit in Grimp, but still accessible programmatically through Soot's API. Concretely, we present ByteBack's Boogie encoding as a translation $\mathcal{T}$ from Grimp (instructions) and Java (declarations) to Boogie code—even though this translation is actually implemented without access to Java source code. For clarity, we highlight Grimp/Java keywords (**`goto`** `l`) with a different color than Boogie keywords (**`goto`** `l`).

Heap Model. ByteBack introduces a simple Boogie model of the heap adapted from Dafny's [36]—a state-of-the-art deductive verifier. The heap is a variable `#heap: Heap` that stores a polymorphic mapping of **`type`** `Heap =`

`[Reference]⟨α⟩[Field α] α` from references to fields (of generic type α). To access the heap, BYTEBACK defines

```
function read⟨α⟩(h:Heap, r:Reference, f:Field α) returns (α)
```

that returns the value of field `f` in the object pointed to by reference `r`, and

```
function update⟨α⟩(h:Heap, r:Reference, f:Field α, v:α) returns (Heap)
```

that returns an updated heap after setting field `r.f` to `v`.

Aggregates. As we explained in Sect. 3.1, a block of code that defines an *aggregable* expression consists of statements that: *i)* are *pure* (do not modify the heap); *ii)* are straight-line (no branches); *iii)* use `BBlib`'s propositional and comparison operators (Table 1), or other aggregable user-defined methods. Precisely, take a sequence s of Grimp instructions that satisfy these constraints. Then, s can be written in SSA form [4] as a sequence $s_1\, s_2 \cdots s_{n+1}$, $n \geq 0$, of statements where each s_k, $k \leq n$, is an assignment $\mathtt{v}_k = e_k$ of an aggregable expression e_k to a fresh variable $\mathtt{v}_k$; and the final s_{n+1} returns the last $\mathtt{v}_n$. Given any such sequence s, BYTEBACK builds an overall expression $\mathcal{A}(s)$ by recursively replacing each usage of $\mathtt{v}_k$ with its unique definition in s. We call $\mathcal{A}(s)$ the *aggregate* of snippet s;[2] in a nutshell, $\mathcal{A}(s)$ is a pure expression equivalent to the one returned by s, which BYTEBACK can translate to a Boogie logic expression as we detail below. In Fig. 3's running example, `no_ones`'s body is already in aggregate form, and hence $\mathcal{A}(\mathtt{no\_ones}) =$ `not(contains(values, 1, 0, values.length))`. For convenience, we extend the notation: $\mathcal{A}(e)$, where e is any aggregable expression built by a sequence of statements s, denotes *expression* e *in aggregate form*—defined as $\mathcal{A}(s\,\mathtt{;}\ \mathbf{return}\ e)$.

Types. BYTEBACK uses Boogie type **`int`** (corresponding to mathematical integers) for all bytecode integer types **`int`**, **`short`**, **`byte`**, **`long`**, and **`char`**; Boogie type **`real`** (corresponding to mathematical reals) for floating-point types **`float`** and **`double`**; Boogie type **`bool`** for type **`boolean`**;[3] and Boogie type `Reference` for all bytecode reference types. Thus, for example, $\mathcal{T}(\mathbf{int}) = \mathbf{int}$, $\mathcal{T}(\mathbf{boolean}) = \mathbf{bool}$, and $\mathcal{T}(\mathbf{int}\,[\,]) = \mathtt{Reference}$.

Declarations. BYTEBACK declares an uninterpreted Boogie type **`const`** `C: Type` for each **`class`** `C`; and it declares a **`const`** `C.f: Field` $\mathcal{T}(\mathtt{t})$ for each field `f` of `C`—where `t` is `f`'s static type.[4] Similarly, local variables (in implementations of non-pure methods) translate to Boogie local variables: $\mathcal{T}(\mathtt{t\ v}) = \mathbf{var}\ \mathtt{v}\!:\ \mathcal{T}(\mathtt{t})$.

Specification Functions. BYTEBACK translates to Boogie functions any methods annotated with **`@Pure`**, which denotes logic functions used in `BBlib` specifications. Boogie functions that translate specification functions include an extra argument `h` of type

---

[2] Soot also performs a kind of aggregation of Grimp expressions; however, BYTEBACK's aggregates are different from Soot's in general.

[3] While pure bytecode uses `0`/`1` integers to encode Booleans, the Grimp intermediate representation includes a distinct Boolean type **`boolean`**.

[4] For simplicity, the presentation assumes that identifier names are unique and the same in bytecode as in Boogie; in practice, BYTEBACK also takes care of renaming to avoid clashes.

```
procedure summary(values: Reference) returns (@ret: int)
requires ¬contains(#heap, values, 1, 0, lengthof(values)); ensures @ret ≥ 0;

function contains(h: Heap, as: Reference, e: int) returns(bool)
{ ∃ i: int • 0 ≤ i ∧ i ≤ lengthof(as) ∧ (array.read(h, as, i): int) = e }
```

Fig. 4. BYTEBACK's Boogie encoding of summary's signature and contains in Fig. 3.

Heap since they cannot directly read global variables. The body S of **@Pure** methods has to be aggregable; BYTEBACK first builds the *aggregate* $\mathcal{A}(S)$ expression as described above, and then translates that into Boogie. Figure 4 shows the Boogie translation of contains in the running example.

$$\mathcal{T}\left(\begin{array}{l}\textbf{@Pure}\\ \mathtt{t_0\ C.p\ (t_1\ d_1, \ldots, t_m\ d_m)}\\ \{\ S\ \}\end{array}\right) = \begin{array}{l}\textbf{function}\ \mathtt{C.p}\\ \quad \mathtt{(h: Heap, d_1 : \mathcal{T}(t_1), \ldots, d_m : \mathcal{T}(t_m))}\\ \quad \textbf{returns}\ \mathcal{T}(\mathtt{t_0}))\\ \{\ \mathcal{T}(\mathcal{A}(S))\ \}\end{array}$$

Methods. BYTEBACK translates to Boogie procedures any other methods (that is, not annotated with **@Pure** or **@Predicate**). An additional extra argument o of type Reference matches the *target* of method calls; thus, it is absent in procedures translating static methods. Methods that return a value (whose return type is not **void**) include a return argument named @ret in Boogie, which is also passed to the postcondition predicate. Frame specifications translate to Boogie **modifies** clauses; BYTEBACK infers them as described in Sect. 3.1, and hence they can only be empty (the **modifies** clause is omitted) or include the whole heap (**modifies** #heap). Preconditions and postconditions translate to Boogie **requires** and **ensures** clauses as follows. Given a **@Predicate** method p, BYTEBACK first builds its aggregate expression $\mathcal{A}(\mathtt{p})$; then, it translates this Grimp expression to a Boogie expression $\mathcal{T}(\mathcal{A}(\mathtt{p}))$; finally, it replaces p's formal arguments with the corresponding Boogie formal arguments $\mathtt{d_1}, \ldots, \mathtt{d}_m$.

$$\mathcal{T}\left(\begin{array}{l}\textbf{@Require}\mathtt{("p")}\\ \textbf{@Ensure}\mathtt{("q")}\\ \mathtt{t_0\ C.m\ (t_1\ d_1, \ldots, t_m\ d_m)}\\ \{\ B\ \}\end{array}\right) = \begin{array}{l}\textbf{procedure}\ \mathtt{C.m}\\ \quad \mathtt{(o: Reference, d_1 : \mathcal{T}(t_1), \ldots, d_m : \mathcal{T}(t_m))}\\ \quad \textbf{returns}\ \mathtt{(@ret: \mathcal{T}(t_0))}\\ \quad \textbf{requires}\ \mathcal{T}(\mathcal{A}(\mathtt{p}))[\mathtt{d_1}, \ldots, \mathtt{d}_m]\\ \quad \textbf{ensures}\ \mathcal{T}(\mathcal{A}(\mathtt{q}))[\mathtt{d_1}, \ldots, \mathtt{d}_m, \mathtt{@ret}]\\ \quad \textbf{modifies}\ \mathcal{F}(B)\\ \{\ \mathcal{T}(B)\ \}\end{array}$$

Figure 4 shows the Boogie translation of summary's signature and specification. Why does BYTEBACK translate postconditions in this way (inlining aggregate specification expressions), instead of just using the Boogie functions that translate postcondition predicates—such as nonnegative(values, @result) for summary's postcondition? In general, postconditions may use old to refer to an expression's value in the pre-state; Boogie offers an **old** operator, but only accepts it explicitly in an **ensures**, not in user-defined functions. Therefore, a postcondition **@Ensure**("inc"), where predicate inc is declared as **@Predicate**

Table 2. Boogie translation of read and write of variables in Grimp bytecode.

GRIMP: e	BOOGIE: $\mathcal{T}(e)$	
`v`	`v`	Local variable read
`o.f`	`read(#heap, o, f)`	Instance field read
`C.f`	`read(#heap, type2ref(C), f)`	Static field read
`a[`k`]`	`array.read(#heap, a,`$\mathcal{T}(k)$`)` : $\mathcal{T}(\mathbb{T}($`a[`k`]`$))$	Array read
`v` = e	`v` := $\mathcal{T}(e)$	Local variable write
`o.f` = e	`#heap` := `update(#heap, o, f,` $\mathcal{T}(e)$`)`	Instance field write
`C.f` = e	`#heap` := `update(#heap, type2ref(C), f,` $\mathcal{T}(e)$`)`	Static field write
`a[`k`]` = e	`#heap` := `array.update(#heap, a,` $\mathcal{T}(k)$, $\mathcal{T}(e)$`)`	Array write

`boolean` `inc(){`**`return`** `gt(x,`**`old`**`(x));}` can only be translated as **`ensures`** `read(#heap,this,C.x) > `**`old`**`(read(#heap,this,C.x))`—not as **`ensures`** `inc(#heap)`, since `inc`'s body may not use **`old`**.

Constructors may also have a specification. BYTEBACK translates them like special methods that return a fresh (previously unallocated) reference in the heap to the created object—as specified by an automatically generated postcondition. To this end, BYTEBACK supplies Boogie procedures `new` and `array.new` to create new references, which translate bytecode instructions **`new`** and **`newarray`**. Then, actual constructor calls (**`invokespecial`** in bytecode) translate like normal procedure calls—as shown below.

Expected Types. Expression types in Grimp mirror strictly the bytecode instructions they correspond to. This may lead to Soot attributing to a Grimp expression e an unnecessarily general type t when e is actually only used according to a more specific type t'. For example, the type of Grimp expression a & b is **`int`** according to Soot even if a and b are of type **`boolean`**. To have more specific types in these scenarios, BYTEBACK reconstructs the *expected type* $\mathbb{T}(e)$ of any Grimp expression e based on where e is used. Thus, if e is the right-hand side of an assignment `v` $= e$, $\mathbb{T}(e)$ is `v`'s type; if e is returned by a method m, $\mathbb{T}(e)$ is m's return type according to its signature; if e is the actual argument in a call to m, $\mathbb{T}(e)$ is m's formal argument type. Therefore, $\mathbb{T}(a$ & $b)$ is **`boolean`** as long as a & b is used as a Boolean.

Variable Access. Table 2 summarizes the translation of reading and writing variables (local, instance, static, and array). Local variables are straightforward, as they also are local variables in Boogie. *Fields* of objects in the heap are read and written by calling predefined Boogie functions `read` and `heap.write` introduced earlier in this section. *Unqualified* field accesses `f` translate as qualified accesses `this.f` on `this`—which corresponds to some variable of type `Reference` in Boogie. The same functions `read` and `heap.write` also work for *static* field accesses: to this end, BYTEBACK supplies

Table 3. BYTEBACK translation of branching, Boolean operators and specification elements.

GRIMP: e	BOOGIE: $\mathcal{T}(e)$
`return` v	`@ret` := $\mathcal{T}(v)$; `return`
`goto` ℓ	`goto` ℓ
`if` (c) B	`if` ($\mathcal{T}(c)$) {$\mathcal{T}(B)$}

(a) Boogie encoding of Grimp bytecode branching instructions.

GRIMP: e	BOOGIE: $\mathcal{T}(e)$	
`neg` a	$\neg\mathcal{T}(a)$	not
a ^ b	$\mathcal{T}(a) \neq \mathcal{T}(b)$	xor
a & b	$\mathcal{T}(a) \land \mathcal{T}(b)$	and
a | b	$\mathcal{T}(a) \parallel \mathcal{T}(b)$	or
`implies`(a,b)	$\mathcal{T}(a) \Longrightarrow \mathcal{T}(b)$	implies
a == b	$\mathcal{T}(a) \Longleftrightarrow \mathcal{T}(b)$	iff

(b) Boogie encoding of Grimp bytecode Boolean operators. Grimp expressions a and b have expected type `boolean` $= \mathbb{T}(a) = \mathbb{T}(b)$.

GRIMP: e	BOOGIE: $\mathcal{T}(e)$
`assertion`(b)	`assert` $\mathcal{T}(\mathcal{A}(b))$
`assumption`(b)	`assume` $\mathcal{T}(\mathcal{A}(b))$
`forall`(v, b)	$\forall$ v: $\mathcal{T}(\mathbb{T}(\mathrm{v})) \bullet \mathcal{T}(\mathcal{A}(b))$
`exists`(v, b)	$\exists$ v: $\mathcal{T}(\mathbb{T}(\mathrm{v})) \bullet \mathcal{T}(\mathcal{A}(b))$
`conditional` (b,T,E)	`if` $\mathcal{T}(\mathcal{A}(b))$ `then` $\mathcal{T}(\mathcal{A}(T))$ `else` $\mathcal{T}(\mathcal{A}(E))$

(c) Boogie encoding of `BBlib` specification methods and expressions. Variables v are created by methods of class `Binding`.

```
function type2ref(class: Type) returns(Reference)
```

mapping each class type to a reference to a heap object that stores the static state. *Arrays* are also heap objects, but BYTEBACK provides custom functions `array.read` and `array.update` to access these objects by means of an index expression of type **`int`**.

```
function array.read⟨α⟩(h: Heap, a: Reference, k: int) returns (α)
```

As shown in Table 2, BYTEBACK casts (Boogie '`:`' operator) the output of polymorphic `array.read` to array type $\mathbb{T}$(`a[`k`]`). This is not necessary for field accesses, since `read`'s output type parameter α is constrained by the input `f`; in contrast, `array.read` is only type-generic in the output, and hence usage context determines the concrete value of α.

Calls. Bytecode offers five call *instructions*: **`invokestatic`** (to call **`static`** methods), **`invokevirtual`** (instance methods), **`invokeinterface`** (abstract interface calls), **`invokespecial`** (constructors and **`super`** calls), and, since Java 7, **`invokedynamic`** (lambdas). BYTEBACK translates all such call *instructions* to Boogie procedure calls:[5]

$$\mathcal{T}(\texttt{invokevirtual o.m}(e_1,\ldots,e_n)) = \texttt{call C.m(o, } \mathcal{T}(e_1), \ldots, \mathcal{T}(e_n))$$

[5] Thus, BYTEBACK relies on Boogie's *modular* semantics of calls: the only effects of calling a method m are what m's specification prescribes. This is a standard choice in deductive verification, since it supports modularity and is consistent with the Liskov substitution principle [42].

As usual, `C` is `m`'s class, and `o` is a reference to an instance of this class. The same translation works, with obvious adjustments, for the other kinds of call instructions—except **`invokedynamic`**, which ByteBack doesn't currently support. Henceforth, **`invoke`** denotes any of the four supported bytecode call instructions.

Branching. ByteBack translates branching instructions (**`return`**, **`goto`**, and **`if`**) into the corresponding Boogie statements as shown in Table 3a. While Boogie also offers structured conditionals and loops, ByteBack does not use them since bytecode does not have structured programming constructs.

Literals. ByteBack translates any literal ℓ to a Boogie literal according to its expected type $\mathbb{T}(\ell)$. In particular, $\mathcal{T}(\texttt{0}) =$ **`false`** and $\mathcal{T}(\texttt{1}) =$ **`true`** when the expected type of integer literals `0` and `1` is **`boolean`**.

Expressions. Most arithmetic and comparison operators `+`, `-`, `*`, `==`, `!=`, `<`, `<=`, `>=`, `>` translate to their Boogie counterparts $+, -, *, =, \neq, <, \leq, \geq, >$ as obvious: $\mathcal{T}(a \bowtie b) = \mathcal{T}(a)\ \mathcal{T}(\bowtie)\ \mathcal{T}(b)$. The division operator `/` translates to **`div`** or `/` in Boogie according to whether it represent integer or floating-point division: $\mathcal{T}(a\ /\ b) = \mathcal{T}(a)$ **`div`** $\mathcal{T}(b)$ if $\mathbb{T}(a\ /\ b) =$ **`int`**; otherwise $\mathcal{T}(a\ /\ b) = \mathcal{T}(a)\ /\ \mathcal{T}(b)$. ByteBack introduces and axiomatizes an overloaded Boogie function `cmp` to translate bytecode operator `cmp`: $\mathcal{T}(a\ \texttt{cmp}\ b) = \texttt{cmp}(\mathcal{T}(a), \mathcal{T}(b))$ returns `1` if $a > b$, `-1` if $a < b$, and `0` if $a = b$. Table 3b displays how ByteBack translates Grimp Boolean operators to Boogie. Java's short-circuited operators `&&` and `||` are not listed in the table, as the compiler desugars them into *conditional instructions* in bytecode; for example, **`if`** `(a && b) x = 1...` becomes **`if`** `(a == 0)` **`goto`** `end;` **`if`** `(b == 0)` **`goto`** `end; x = 1; end:...` in bytecode.

Since **`boolean`** is a subtype of **`int`** in Soot, the operands of Boolean operator expressions (e.g., $a == b$) may have different types (e.g., $\mathbb{T}(a) =$ **`int`** but $\mathbb{T}(b) =$ **`boolean`**—usually when a is used as an integer in other parts of the program). In these cases, ByteBack translates everything using the most general type **`int`**, so that all usages of the operands can be uniformly represented in Boogie (where the **`bool`** and **`int`** types are disjoint, as they are in Java).

Call Expressions. Boogie does not allow procedure calls in expressions;[6] therefore, ByteBack saves the call value in a fresh variable, and replaces the call expression with a read of the variable: given a Grimp expression e, used in statement s, that includes a call **`invoke`** `o.m()` (virtual, static, or interface) to a method `m`, ByteBack first adds the statements **`var`** `#r`: $\mathcal{T}(\mathbb{T}($**`invoke`** `o.m`$))$; **`call`** `#r :=` $\mathcal{T}($**`invoke`** `o.m()`$)$ just before s, and then translates e into $\mathcal{T}(e[$**`invoke`** `o.m` $\mapsto$ `#r`$])$—replacing the call with `#r`.

Specifications. ByteBack recognize `BBlib` operators and translates them to their counterparts in Boogie, as shown in Table 3c. Source-code **`while`** and **`for`** loops become conditional jumps in bytecode. Using Soot's static analysis capabilities, ByteBack identifies any loop in bytecode by its *head*, *backjump*, and *exit* locations. Thus,

[6] In contrast, calls to pure methods, translated to Boogie functions, can be directly transliterated to Boogie (pure) expressions.

a source-code loop **`while`** `(!c)` L; R corresponds to bytecode structured as in Fig. 5a's left-hand side, where labels head, back, and exit mark the head, exit, and backjump locations; c is the loop's exit condition, B is the loop body, and R is the code that follows the loop. Any loop invariant J would be declared by a call `invariant(`J`)` to `BBlib` method **`invariant`** inside B. ByteBack encodes the semantics of loop invariants by means of suitable assumptions and assertions, as in Fig. 5a's right-hand side; then, it translates the annotated branching code to Boogie as usual. Figure 5b shows a concrete example of how ByteBack encodes loops and invariants; note the aggregation (inlining) of the invariant predicate, which ensures that all its dependencies are replicated in each assertion and assumption in Boogie.

```
head: if (c) goto exit              assert(A(J)); head: if (c) goto exit
B[··· invariant(J)···]              assume(A(J)); B[···]
back: goto head                     assert(A(J)); back: goto head
exit: R                             exit: assume(A(J)); R
```

(a) How ByteBack injects loop invariant checks (right) into Grimp bytecode loops (left). B denotes the loop body, which includes an invariant declaration (left).

```
for (int k = 0; k < 3; k++)         assert(0 ≤ k ∧ k ≤ 3);
{ boolean a = lte(0, k);            head : if (k ≥ 3) goto exit;
  boolean b = lte(k, 3);            assume(0 ≤ k ∧ k ≤ 3); k := k + 1;
  invariant(a & b); }               assert(0 ≤ k ∧ k ≤ 3); back: goto head;
                                    exit: assume(0 ≤ k ∧ k ≤ 3);
```

(b) An example of an annotated loop in Java (left), and its Boogie encoding produced by ByteBack (right).

Fig. 5. ByteBack's encoding of loops and loop invariants.

3.3 Implementation Details

We implemented ByteBack in a tool with the same name, written in about 11 thousand lines of Java code (plus another 52 kLOC of generated code). ByteBack's core uses the Soot static analysis framework [53] to process the bytecode to be verified, as we described in Sect. 3.2 at a high level. After analyzing the Grimp bytecode, ByteBack has collected all the information to generate Boogie code; to this end, a visitor pattern implementation creates a Boogie AST, and then dumps it into a Boogie file.

We developed the Boogie AST library using the metacompilation framework JastAdd [23], in combination with JFlex and Beaver[7] to parse Boogie source code. This capability is useful to: *i)* flexibly generate the heap model (Sect. 3.2) and other Boogie background definitions from a human-readable Boogie template file; *ii)* perform some analyses directly on the generated Boogie code (most notably, the frame inference briefly described in Sect. 3.1).

Features and Limitations. ByteBack's current implementation supports most bytecode features but not exception handling and **`invokedynamic`** (which limits reasoning about lambdas); strings are supported as plain objects, which precludes precisely analyzing their semantics in Java; as we discussed previously, numeric types are

[7] JFlex: https://jflex.de/; Beaver: http://beaver.sourceforge.net/.

encoded as infinite-precision numbers (integers and reals), which entails that BYTEBACK may miss overflow and other numerical errors. Adding support for these features is possible in principle, and would require a combination of extending the Boogie encoding (for example, to include exceptional behavior), BYTEBACK's static analysis (for example, to identify the bootstrap methods that dynamically generate targets of **invokedynamic**), and BBlib's features (for example, to support model-based specifications).

Section 3.1 described the features offered by BYTEBACK's BBlib specification library. Its current implementation is sufficient to specify a variety of examples (see Sect. 4) but lacks advanced features to express complex framing conditions and ghost code (specification code discarded during compilation), and to flexibly reuse specifications with inheritance and modularity. Supporting these features belongs to future work, also because it would require tackling challenges largely orthogonal to the focus of BYTEBACK.

As we demonstrate in Sect. 4, BBlib's features can also specify programs written in Scala, leveraging its bytecode-level interoperability with Java. However, BBlib was developed with focus on Java, and hence its practical usability on Scala is more limited. In particular, the Scala compiler automatically generates features (such as setters and getters for fields) that are implicit in Scala source code; hence, users cannot directly annotate these features using BBlib. Addressing these limitations is possible, but would have to cater somewhat to the peculiarities of Scala (or other languages to be supported).

4 Experiments

In our experiments, we ran BYTEBACK on several examples in order to demonstrate that it can verify programs with different characteristics, which exercise various features of the Java programming language (including recent versions), as well as a few programs written in other languages built on top of Java bytecode.

4.1 Programs

Table 4 lists the 40 programs that we used for our experiments, and their size in non-empty lines of SOURCE code (LOC), as well as their size after compilation to BYTECODE (also in LOC of the representation returned by `javap -c`). The sizes include the annotations in BBlib, which specify the properties to be verified.

The majority of programs (32/40) use various features of Java 8; but we also included 4 programs using Java 17 features, and 4 Scala programs. The selection includes relatively simple programs that specifically target language features of Java (examples 1–16 and 33–35), classic algorithms and procedures (examples 17–27, 36, and 37–38), and object-oriented features (examples 28–32 and 39–40). Some examples implement the same algorithm for data structures with different types (e.g., **double** and **int** arrays).

We selected these examples to demonstrate that BYTEBACK can process a variety of modern Java features, including several that state-of-the-art Java deductive verifiers do

Table 4. Verification experiments performed with BYTEBACK. In each row: the EXPERIMENT's name; its source LANGUAGE (and any of Table 5's features it uses); the ENCODING TIME (seconds) and its percentage directly attributable to BYTEBACK (excluding Soot's initialization time); the VERIFICATION TIME (seconds) of running Boogie on the encoding generated by BYTEBACK; the size (in non-blank lines of code) of the SOURCE code, of the BYTECODE (as printed by `javap -c`), and of the BOOGIE code.

#	EXPERIMENT	LANGUAGE	ENCODING		VERIFICATION	SOURCE	BYTECODE	BOOGIE
			TIME [s]	BYTEBACK	TIME [s]	SIZE [LOC]		
1	Array Operations	Java 8	2.8	10 %	1.16	36	103	148
2	Boolean Operations	Java 8	3.6	9%	1.34	57	85	157
3	Control Flow	Java 8	2.8	8%	1.33	74	123	219
4	Enhanced For	Java 8 F	2.9	8%	1.25	25	52	107
5	Field Access	Java 8	2.8	6%	1.18	29	32	96
6	Floating-Point Operations	Java 8	2.9	8%	1.21	37	52	110
7	Instance Field	Java 8	3.0	6%	1.15	18	16	98
8	Integer Operations	Java 8	3.1	12%	1.45	202	332	250
9	Multiclass	Java 8	3.0	8%	1.19	14	14	113
10	Quantifiers	Java 8	3.1	6%	1.15	25	28	92
11	Static Field	Java 8	4.4	9%	1.82	32	66	146
12	Static Initializer	Java 8	3.7	6%	1.63	14	14	91
13	Static Method Calls	Java 8	3.0	8%	1.19	32	40	112
14	Switch	Java 8	3.1	6%	1.23	23	25	109
15	Unit	Java 8	2.9	6%	1.15	13	12	97
16	Virtual Method Calls	Java 8	3.0	7%	1.21	31	40	122
17	GCD	Java 8	3.0	9%	1.15	41	88	127
18	Insertion Sort `double`	Java 8	2.9	11%	2.53	49	132	147
19	Insertion Sort `int`	Java 8	3.1	11%	1.70	49	131	147
20	Linear Search	Java 8 T	2.9	10%	1.14	60	126	164
21	Max `double`	Java 8	3.0	9%	1.15	45	92	92
22	Max `int`	Java 8	2.9	10%	1.16	45	90	126
23	Selection Sort `double`	Java 8	3.1	13%	4.56	87	231	172
24	Selection Sort `int`	Java 8	3.0	12%	3.56	87	230	172
25	Square Sorted Array	Java 8	2.9	10%	1.14	54	123	140
26	Sum `double`	Java 8	3.0	8%	1.16	35	70	124
27	Sum `int`	Java 8	2.8	8%	1.14	35	70	124
28	Generic List	Java 8 G, T	3.1	9%	1.17	46	68	134
29	Binary Search	Java 8	3.1	10%	1.13	51	124	131
30	Comparator	Java 8	3.0	10%	1.24	51	30	188
31	Dice	Java 8 D	3.0	10%	1.17	41	25	129
32	Counter	Java 8	2.9	8%	1.20	33	62	150
33	Pattern matching	Java 17 P	3.0	7%	1.14	18	26	105
34	Switch Expressions	Java 17 S, Y	2.9	8%	1.16	23	56	135
35	Type Inference	Java 17 L	3.0	7%	1.15	29	59	116
36	Summary	Java 17 S, Y, F, L, A	3.1	10%	1.23	47	88	137
37	GCD	Scala 3	3.5	8%	1.31	46	93	130
38	Linear Search	Scala 3	3.4	10%	1.26	69	126	168
39	Comparator	Scala 3	3.4	9%	1.42	49	35	237
40	Dice	Scala 3	4.5	11%	1.85	38	25	223
	Total		133.1		60.89	1 790	3 234	5 585
	Average		3.1	9%	1.42	45	81	140

not support (as we discuss in Sect. 5). It's important to stress that we are not comparing BYTEBACK's verification capabilities to those of much more mature tools such as KeY, Krakatoa, and OpenJML. We picked the features in Table 4's examples specifically to demonstrate that it's hard for source-level verifiers to keep up with the plethora of language features that are introduced over time—not to solve verification challenges. As we discuss in Sect. 3, BYTEBACK does not support all used features of Java (in particular, exceptions) and its specification capabilities (in particular, framing) are currently limited compared to source-level tools. The experiments only demonstrate our claim that verification at the level of bytecode has some distinctive advantages for supporting language evolution, and hence it can complement source-level verification.

4.2 Results

All the experiments ran BYTEBACK on a Fedora 36 GNU/Linux machine with an Intel i7-7600U CPU (2.8 GHz), running Boogie 2.15.7.0, Z3 4.11.1.0, and Soot 4.3.0. To account for possible measurement noise, we repeated each experiment 5 times and report the mean of the wall-clock running times in the 95th percentile.

We ran Boogie with default options—except for programs 4 and 36, where we enabled option `/infer:j`, which can infer simple loop invariants. This is useful to handle these programs' enhanced **`for`** loops: translated to bytecode, a loop such as `for(var v: values)` in Fig. 1b introduces an index variable `int k` to iterate over array `values`; however, `k` does not exist in the source code, and hence one cannot annotate the loop with a suitable invariant for `k` and must rely on inferring it.

All the experiments in Table 4 verified successfully without errors. The running time of BYTEBACK (column ENCODING TIME) is generally short and predictable: 3.1 s per example on average. This time measures BYTEBACK's analysis of bytecode and translation to Boogie; it excludes the compilation time (from Java/Scala to bytecode) and the running time of Boogie (reported separately in column VERIFICATION TIME). Column ENCODING BYTEBACK reports the percentage of encoding time after we deduct Soot's fixed context initialization time: BYTEBACK's net average analysis time is a small fraction of the total (just 0.28 s per example).

The running time of Boogie (column VERIFICATION TIME) on BYTEBACK's output is also moderate: 1.4 s per example on average. There are a few outliers: the two variants of Selection Sort take up to 5 s to verify. This is because Selection Sort's implementation calls another method to compute the minimum value in an array range; this introduces more modular verification work. In contrast, Insertion Sort's implementation uses two nested loops, which results in a simpler Boogie program.

If we compare Table 4's two rightmost columns, we notice that the size of the Boogie code is roughly proportional to the size of the bytecode (Kendall's $\tau = 0.46$). Boogie code is about 1.8 times larger, as BYTEBACK's aggregation process reconstructs complex higher-level expressions. The size difference is especially pronounced for programs focusing on object-oriented features (examples 28–32 and 39–40): such features are desugared in bytecode, but "resurface" in the form of Boogie axioms and functions.

These experiments demonstrate BYTEBACK's current capabilities. Its Boogie encoding is fairly standard (as mentioned in Sect. 3.2, its heap model is taken from Dafny's) but could be optimized for better performance (e.g., improving triggers [15,22,39]) or for conciseness (e.g., further simplifying type conversions [47]) as needed.

5 Related Work

We summarize related work in the areas most relevant to ByteBack: source-level deductive verifiers for Java, and verifiers that target intermediate representations.

Source-Level Deductive Verifiers for Java. Performing deductive verification of functional properties on a program's source code is a widespread approach, as that's where a specification and other kinds of information are readily available and naturally expressible. Among the many source-level verifiers for realistic programming languages—e.g., [6,11,12,17,25,30,32,36]—here we focus on KeY [1,2], Krakatoa [41], and OpenJML [19]: state-of-the-art verifiers for the functional correctness of Java sequential programs with a high degree of automation.

OpenJML and Krakatoa follow the so-called auto-active approach [37]—where the verifier generates verification conditions (VCs) and dispatches them to an automated theorem prover, but the user still indirectly guides the verifier by interactively supplying annotations. OpenJML generates VCs in SMT-LIB format [7], and dispatches them to any SMT solver like Z3 [43] or CVC4 [8]. Krakatoa translates the source program into the WhyML intermediate verification language IVL, and delegates the generation of VCs to the Why3 system [24]. Using an IVL to generate VCs is an approach pioneered by Spec# [6] and used nowadays by many systems (including ByteBack). KeY is built on top of an interactive prover for Java dynamic logic [3]—used as its intermediate representation—but offers features that increase the automation level in practice.

KeY, Krakatoa, and OpenJML all use JML [34] as specification language (more precisely, different variants/subsets of JML [14]). Despite being applicable to verify real-world Java code, they also differ in the subset of Java that they support: Table 5 lists several modern features of the Java language and which verifier can analyze them. We compiled the table by reading the tools' official documentation and papers, and by trying out the latest tool versions that are publicly available. It should be clear that this summary is not a criticism of KeY, Krakatoa, or OpenJML—which are state-of-the-art, mature tools with proven applicability to complex verification problems—nor a direct comparison with ByteBack. To compile Table 5, we actively looked for Java recent feature "variants" that may be cumbersome to support at the source-code level, but are essentially syntactic sugar. Since ByteBack easily supports these features by piggybacking off the compiler's bytecode translation, this substantiates our claim that keeping verification tools up to pace with language evolution is practically hard and time-consuming at the source-code level, but substantially easier at the bytecode level.

The difference in feature support reflects the tools' intended verification target. Krakatoa focuses on supporting complex functional specifications of a core subset of Java; thus, it ignores several features that have been available since Java 5 (released in 2002). KeY and OpenJML aim at verifying complex, realistic Java applications [13,20,26,28]; to this end, they enjoy a broader language support and at least parse all Java features up until version 8 (released in 2014); however, several widely used features are still not available for verification with these tools. For example, KeY

Table 5. Features of the Java language, and which source-code verifiers support them. For each FEATURE: the Java major VERSION when it was introduced, an EXAMPLE snippet of code using the feature, and which Java verifier among Key, Krakatoa, and OpenJML supports (✓), partially supports (!), or does not support (✗) the feature.

FEATURE	JAVA VERSION	EXAMPLE	SUPPORT KeY	Krakatoa	OpenJML
G Generic classes	5	`class Box<T> { T value; }`	!	✗	✓
F Enhanced **for** loop	5	`int[] arr; int res = 0;` `for(int x: arr) res += x;`	✓	✗	✓
A Varargs	5	`int first(int... values)` `{ return values[0]; }`	✓	✗	✗
T Generic type inference	7	`Box<Integer> b = new Box<>();`	✗	✗	✗

D Default methods	8	`interface PlusMinus extends Plus`
		`{ default int minus(int x)`
		`{ return plus(-x); } }`
			✓	✗	✓

L Local type inference	10	`var b = new Box<Integer>();`	✗	✗	✗

S Switch expressions	12	`System.out.println( switch (day)`
		`{ case 0 -> "Mon";`
		`default -> "Other"; });`
			✗	✗	✗

Y Switch expressions with **yield**	13	`System.out.println( switch (day)`
		`{ case 0: m++; yield "Mon";`
		`default: yield "Other"; });`
			✗	✗	✗

P Pattern matching with **instanceof**	14	`if (obj instanceof String str)` `return str + " is String";`	✗	✗	✗

relies on an external tool to erase generics and replace them with type `Object` and suitable casts; OpenJML natively supports generics but not all related features—such as the diamond operator <>. Since Java switched to a biannual release schedule, the gap between available language features and verification support has been widening [21].

Verifiers for Intermediate Representations. Approaches targeting the verification of intermediate representations (IRs) have been introduced in recent years, including SeaHorn [27] and SMACK [49] for LLVM bitcode [33], and JayHorn [50] for Java bytecode. A key difference between BYTEBACK and these tools are the kinds of properties they are equipped to verify: SMACK, SeaHorn, and JayHorn mainly target low-level implicit correctness properties (such as the absence of unreachable code, null pointer dereferences, and out-of-bound accesses); users can still add simple inline assertions, but there is no support for complex and structured specification elements such as contracts. SeaHorn and JayHorn encode IR instructions into constrained Horn clauses [10], a logic that can be automatically analyzed with symbolic model-checking techniques. This is consistent with these tools' intended usage, as it requires fewer annotations (loop invariants can often be inferred automatically) but also somewhat restricts the properties that can be verified in practice. SMACK, like BYTEBACK, translates an IR into Boogie programs to perform verification; despite these similarities, it mainly targets the verification of low-level (e.g., embedded) programs [29,52,54] and properties; it defaults to bounded verification (full, unbounded verification is only experimentally supported).

Proof-carrying code [45] is another application of verification techniques to IRs. To ensure a safe execution, compiled programs are distributed with embedded proofs, which the runtime environment checks before starting execution. Due to the difficulty of verifying IRs, proof-carrying code was primarily used for restricted properties such as memory safety. *Proof-transformation* approaches [9,44] overcome this issue by first verifying source-level annotated program "as usual", and then transforming the correctness proofs into proof-carrying IR code [35]. The BML notation takes a different approach [16] to directly annotate bytecode with expressive JML-like specifications.

6 Conclusions

We presented BYTEBACK, a technique that formally verifies functional source-code properties by working on Java bytecode. In our experiments, we verified programs written in Java that use recently introduced features that even state-of-the-art verifiers do not fully support; as well as some programs written in Scala that BYTEBACK can also analyze after compiling to bytecode. This suggests that our approach can help simplify keeping up with the evolution of modern programming languages, which regularly add new expressive features that are substantially simplified by compilation to bytecode.

References

1. Ahrendt, W., et al.: The KeY platform for verification and analysis of Java programs. In: Giannakopoulou, D., Kroening, D. (eds.) VSTTE 2014. LNCS, vol. 8471, pp. 55–71. Springer, Cham (2014). https://doi.org/10.1007/978-3-319-12154-3_4
2. Ahrendt, W., Beckert, B., Bubel, R., Hähnle, R., Schmitt, P.H., Ulbrich, M. (eds.): Deductive Software Verification-The KeY Book. LNCS, vol. 10001. Springer, Cham (2016). https://doi.org/10.1007/978-3-319-49812-6
3. Ahrendt, W., de Boer, F.S., Grabe, I.: Abstract object creation in dynamic logic. In: Cavalcanti, A., Dams, D.R. (eds.) FM 2009. LNCS, vol. 5850, pp. 612–627. Springer, Heidelberg (2009). https://doi.org/10.1007/978-3-642-05089-3_39
4. Appel, A.W.: Modern Compiler Implementation, 2nd edn. Cambridge University Press, Cambridge (2002)
5. Barnett, M., Chang, B.-Y.E., DeLine, R., Jacobs, B., Leino, K.R.M.: Boogie: a modular reusable verifier for object-oriented programs. In: de Boer, F.S., Bonsangue, M.M., Graf, S., de Roever, W.-P. (eds.) FMCO 2005. LNCS, vol. 4111, pp. 364–387. Springer, Heidelberg (2006). https://doi.org/10.1007/11804192_17
6. Barnett, M., Fähndrich, M., Leino, K.R.M., Müller, P., Schulte, W., Venter, H.: Specification and verification: the Spec# experience. Commun. ACM **54**(6), 81–91 (2011). https://doi.org/10.1145/1953122.1953145
7. Barrett, C., Fontaine, P., Tinelli, C.: The Satisfiability Modulo Theories Library (SMT-LIB) (2016). https://www.SMT-LIB.org
8. Barrett, C., et al.: CVC4. In: Gopalakrishnan, G., Qadeer, S. (eds.) CAV 2011. LNCS, vol. 6806, pp. 171–177. Springer, Heidelberg (2011). https://doi.org/10.1007/978-3-642-22110-1_14
9. Barthe, G., Grégoire, B., Pavlova, M.: Preservation of proof obligations from Java to the Java virtual machine. In: Armando, A., Baumgartner, P., Dowek, G. (eds.) IJCAR 2008. LNCS (LNAI), vol. 5195, pp. 83–99. Springer, Heidelberg (2008). https://doi.org/10.1007/978-3-540-71070-7_7

10. Bjørner, N., Gurfinkel, A., McMillan, K., Rybalchenko, A.: Horn clause solvers for program verification. In: Beklemishev, L.D., Blass, A., Dershowitz, N., Finkbeiner, B., Schulte, W. (eds.) Fields of Logic and Computation II. LNCS, vol. 9300, pp. 24–51. Springer, Cham (2015). https://doi.org/10.1007/978-3-319-23534-9_2
11. Blanc, R., Kuncak, V., Kneuss, E., Suter, P.: An overview of the Leon verification system: verification by translation to recursive functions. In: Proceedings of the 4th Workshop on Scala, SCALA@ECOOP 2013, Montpellier, France, 2 July 2013, pp. 1:1–1:10. ACM (2013). https://doi.org/10.1145/2489837.2489838
12. Blom, S., Huisman, M.: The VerCors tool for verification of concurrent programs. In: Jones, C., Pihlajasaari, P., Sun, J. (eds.) FM 2014. LNCS, vol. 8442, pp. 127–131. Springer, Cham (2014). https://doi.org/10.1007/978-3-319-06410-9_9
13. de Boer, M., de Gouw, S., Klamroth, J., Jung, C., Ulbrich, M., Weigl, A.: Formal specification and verification of JDK's identity hash map implementation. In: ter Beek, M.H., Monahan, R. (eds.) IFM 2022. LNCS, vol. 13274, pp. 45–62. Springer, Cham (2022). https://doi.org/10.1007/978-3-031-07727-2_4
14. Boerman, J., Huisman, M., Joosten, S.: Reasoning about JML: differences between KeY and OpenJML. In: Furia, C.A., Winter, K. (eds.) IFM 2018. LNCS, vol. 11023, pp. 30–46. Springer, Cham (2018). https://doi.org/10.1007/978-3-319-98938-9_3
15. Chen, Y.T., Furia, C.A.: Triggerless happy. In: Polikarpova, N., Schneider, S. (eds.) IFM 2017. LNCS, vol. 10510, pp. 295–311. Springer, Cham (2017). https://doi.org/10.1007/978-3-319-66845-1_19
16. Chrząszcz, J., Huisman, M., Schubert, A.: BML and related tools. In: de Boer, F.S., Bonsangue, M.M., Madelaine, E. (eds.) FMCO 2008. LNCS, vol. 5751, pp. 278–297. Springer, Heidelberg (2009). https://doi.org/10.1007/978-3-642-04167-9_14
17. Cohen, E., et al.: VCC: a practical system for verifying concurrent C. In: Berghofer, S., Nipkow, T., Urban, C., Wenzel, M. (eds.) TPHOLs 2009. LNCS, vol. 5674, pp. 23–42. Springer, Heidelberg (2009). https://doi.org/10.1007/978-3-642-03359-9_2
18. Cohen, E., Moskal, M., Schulte, W., Tobies, S.: Local verification of global invariants in concurrent programs. In: Touili, T., Cook, B., Jackson, P. (eds.) CAV 2010. LNCS, vol. 6174, pp. 480–494. Springer, Heidelberg (2010). https://doi.org/10.1007/978-3-642-14295-6_42
19. Cok, D.R.: OpenJML: software verification for Java 7 using JML, OpenJDK, and Eclipse. In: Dubois, C., Giannakopoulou, D., Méry, D. (eds.) Proceedings 1st Workshop on Formal Integrated Development Environment, F-IDE 2014, Grenoble, France, 6 April 2014. EPTCS, vol. 149, pp. 79–92 (2014). https://doi.org/10.4204/EPTCS.149.8
20. Cok, D.R.: Java automated deductive verification in practice: lessons from industrial proof-based projects. In: Margaria, T., Steffen, B. (eds.) ISoLA 2018. LNCS, vol. 11247, pp. 176–193. Springer, Cham (2018). https://doi.org/10.1007/978-3-030-03427-6_16
21. Cok, D.R.: JML and OpenJML for Java 16. In: Cok, D.R. (ed.) FTfJP 2021: Proceedings of the 23rd ACM International Workshop on Formal Techniques for Java-like Programs, Virtual Event, Denmark, 13 July 2021, pp. 65–67. ACM (2021). https://doi.org/10.1145/3464971.3468417
22. Dross, C., Conchon, S., Kanig, J., Paskevich, A.: Reasoning with triggers. In: Lecture Notes in Computer Science, pp. 22–31. EPiC Series, EasyChair (2012)
23. Ekman, T., Hedin, G.: The JastAdd system - modular extensible compiler construction. Sci. Comput. Program. **69**(1–3), 14–26 (2007). https://doi.org/10.1016/j.scico.2007.02.003
24. Filliâtre, J.-C., Paskevich, A.: Why3—where programs meet provers. In: Felleisen, M., Gardner, P. (eds.) ESOP 2013. LNCS, vol. 7792, pp. 125–128. Springer, Heidelberg (2013). https://doi.org/10.1007/978-3-642-37036-6_8
25. Furia, C.A., Nordio, M., Polikarpova, N., Tschannen, J.: AutoProof: auto-active functional verification of object-oriented programs. Int. J. Softw. Tools Technol. Transfer **19**(6), 697–716 (2016)

26. de Gouw, S., de Boer, F.S., Bubel, R., Hähnle, R., Rot, J., Steinhöfel, D.: Verifying OpenJDK's sort method for generic collections. J. Autom. Reason. **62**(1), 93–126 (2019). https://doi.org/10.1007/s10817-017-9426-4
27. Gurfinkel, A., Kahsai, T., Komuravelli, A., Navas, J.A.: The SeaHorn verification framework. In: Kroening, D., Păsăreanu, C.S. (eds.) CAV 2015. LNCS, vol. 9206, pp. 343–361. Springer, Cham (2015). https://doi.org/10.1007/978-3-319-21690-4_20
28. Hiep, H.A., Maathuis, O., Bian, J., de Boer, F.S., van Eekelen, M.C.J.D., de Gouw, S.: Verifying OpenJDK's LinkedList using KeY. CoRR abs/1911.04195 (2019). https://arxiv.org/abs/1911.04195
29. Huang, B., Ray, S., Gupta, A., Fung, J.M., Malik, S.: Formal security verification of concurrent firmware in SoCs using instruction-level abstraction for hardware. In: Proceedings of the 55th Annual Design Automation Conference, DAC 2018, San Francisco, CA, USA, 24–29 June 2018, pp. 91:1–91:6. ACM (2018). https://doi.org/10.1145/3195970.3196055
30. Jacobs, B., Smans, J., Philippaerts, P., Vogels, F., Penninckx, W., Piessens, F.: VeriFast: a powerful, sound, predictable, fast verifier for C and Java. In: Bobaru, M., Havelund, K., Holzmann, G.J., Joshi, R. (eds.) NFM 2011. LNCS, vol. 6617, pp. 41–55. Springer, Heidelberg (2011). https://doi.org/10.1007/978-3-642-20398-5_4
31. Kassios, I.T.: Dynamic frames: support for framing, dependencies and sharing without restrictions. In: Misra, J., Nipkow, T., Sekerinski, E. (eds.) FM 2006. LNCS, vol. 4085, pp. 268–283. Springer, Heidelberg (2006). https://doi.org/10.1007/11813040_19
32. Kirchner, F., Kosmatov, N., Prevosto, V., Signoles, J., Yakobowski, B.: Frama-C: a software analysis perspective. Formal Aspects Comput. **27**(3), 573–609 (2015). https://doi.org/10.1007/s00165-014-0326-7
33. Lattner, C., Adve, V.S.: LLVM: a compilation framework for lifelong program analysis & transformation. In: 2nd IEEE/ACM International Symposium on Code Generation and Optimization (CGO 2004), San Jose, CA, USA, 20–24 March 2004, pp. 75–88. IEEE Computer Society (2004). https://doi.org/10.1109/CGO.2004.1281665
34. Leavens, G.T., Schmitt, P.H., Yi, J.: The Java Modeling Language (JML) (NII Shonan meeting 2013-3). NII Shonan Meeting Report **2013** (2013). https://shonan.nii.ac.jp/seminars/016/
35. Lehner, H., Müller, P.: Formal translation of bytecode into BoogiePL. Electron. Notes Theor. Comput. Sci. **190**(1), 35–50 (2007). https://doi.org/10.1016/j.entcs.2007.02.059
36. Leino, K.R.M.: Dafny: an automatic program verifier for functional correctness. In: Clarke, E.M., Voronkov, A. (eds.) LPAR 2010. LNCS (LNAI), vol. 6355, pp. 348–370. Springer, Heidelberg (2010). https://doi.org/10.1007/978-3-642-17511-4_20
37. Leino, K.R.M., Moskal, M.: Usable auto-active verification. In: Usable Verification Workshop (2010). https://fm.csl.sri.com/UV10/
38. Leino, K.R.M., Müller, P.: Object invariants in dynamic contexts. In: Odersky, M. (ed.) ECOOP 2004. LNCS, vol. 3086, pp. 491–515. Springer, Heidelberg (2004). https://doi.org/10.1007/978-3-540-24851-4_22
39. Leino, K.R.M., Pit-Claudel, C.: Trigger selection strategies to stabilize program verifiers. In: Chaudhuri, S., Farzan, A. (eds.) CAV 2016. LNCS, vol. 9779, pp. 361–381. Springer, Cham (2016). https://doi.org/10.1007/978-3-319-41528-4_20
40. Leino, K.R.M., Schulte, W.: Using history invariants to verify observers. In: De Nicola, R. (ed.) ESOP 2007. LNCS, vol. 4421, pp. 80–94. Springer, Heidelberg (2007). https://doi.org/10.1007/978-3-540-71316-6_7
41. Marché, C., Paulin-Mohring, C., Urbain, X.: The KRAKATOA tool for certification of JAVA/JAVACARD programs annotated in JML. J. Log. Algebraic Methods Program. **58**(1–2), 89–106 (2004). https://doi.org/10.1016/j.jlap.2003.07.006
42. Meyer, B.: Introduction to the Theory of Programming Languages. Prentice Hall, Hoboken (1990)

43. de Moura, L., Bjørner, N.: Z3: an efficient SMT solver. In: Ramakrishnan, C.R., Rehof, J. (eds.) TACAS 2008. LNCS, vol. 4963, pp. 337–340. Springer, Heidelberg (2008). https://doi.org/10.1007/978-3-540-78800-3_24
44. Müller, P., Nordio, M.: Proof-transforming compilation of programs with abrupt termination. In: Proceedings of SAVCBS, pp. 39–46. ACM (2007). https://doi.org/10.1145/1292316.1292321
45. Necula, G.C.: Proof-carrying code. In: Lee, P., Henglein, F., Jones, N.D. (eds.) POPL, pp. 106–119. ACM Press (1997). https://doi.org/10.1145/263699.263712
46. Paganoni, M., Furia, C.A.: ByteBack FM 2023 replication package (2022). https://doi.org/10.5281/zenodo.7337205
47. Pearce, D.J., Utting, M., Groves, L.: Verifying Whiley programs with boogie. J. Autom. Reason. 1–57 (2022). https://doi.org/10.1007/s10817-022-09619-1
48. Polikarpova, N., Tschannen, J., Furia, C.A., Meyer, B.: Flexible invariants through semantic collaboration. In: Jones, C., Pihlajasaari, P., Sun, J. (eds.) FM 2014. LNCS, vol. 8442, pp. 514–530. Springer, Cham (2014). https://doi.org/10.1007/978-3-319-06410-9_35
49. Rakamarić, Z., Emmi, M.: SMACK: decoupling source language details from verifier implementations. In: Biere, A., Bloem, R. (eds.) CAV 2014. LNCS, vol. 8559, pp. 106–113. Springer, Cham (2014). https://doi.org/10.1007/978-3-319-08867-9_7
50. Rümmer, P.: JayHorn: a Java model checker. In: Murray, T., Ernst, G. (eds.) Proceedings of the 21st Workshop on Formal Techniques for Java-like Programs, FTfJP@ECOOP 2019, London, UK, 15 July 2019, p. 1:1. ACM (2019). https://doi.org/10.1145/3340672.3341113
51. Summers, A.J., Drossopoulou, S., Müller, P.: The need for flexible object invariants. In: Proceedings of IWACO, pp. 1–9. ACM (2009)
52. Sung, C., Paulsen, B., Wang, C.: CANAL: a cache timing analysis framework via LLVM transformation. CoRR abs/1807.03329 (2018). https://arxiv.org/abs/1807.03329
53. Vallée-Rai, R. Co, P., Gagnon, E., Hendren, L.J., Lam, P., Sundaresan, V.: Soot - a Java bytecode optimization framework. In: MacKay, S.A., Johnson, J.H. (eds.) Proceedings of the 1999 Conference of the Centre for Advanced Studies on Collaborative Research, Mississauga, Ontario, Canada, 8–11 November 1999, p. 13. IBM (1999). https://dl.acm.org/citation.cfm?id=782008
54. Zhang, Y., Zuck, L.D.: Formal verification of optimizing compilers. In: Negi, A., Bhatnagar, R., Parida, L. (eds.) ICDCIT 2018. LNCS, vol. 10722, pp. 50–65. Springer, Cham (2018). https://doi.org/10.1007/978-3-319-72344-0_3

Abstract Alloy Instances

Jan Oliver Ringert[1] and Allison Sullivan[2](✉)

[1] Bauhaus-University Weimar, Weimar, Germany
[2] The University of Texas at Arlington, Arlington, TX, USA
allison.sullivan@uta.edu

Abstract. Alloy is a textual modeling language for structures and behaviors of software designs. One of the reasons for Alloy to become a popular light-weight formal method is its support for automated, bounded analyses, which is provided through the Analyzer toolset. The Analyzer provides the means to compute, visualize, and browse instances that either satisfy a model or violate an assertion. Understanding instances for the given analysis often requires much effort and there is no guarantee on the order or level of information of computed instances. To help address this, we introduce the concept of abstract Alloy instances, which abstract information common to all instances, while preserving information specific to the analysis. Our abstraction is based on introducing lower and upper bounds for elements that may appear in Alloy's instances. We evaluate computation times and sizes of abstract instances on a set of benchmark Alloy models.

Keywords: Alloy analyzer · Instances · Relational logic · Abstraction

1 Introduction

Alloy [8–10] is a textual modeling language based on relational first-order logic. Alloy models declaratively express structures and behaviors of software designs. The Alloy Analyzer [2] provides various analyses for finding instances of Alloy models. This analysis is automated due to the use of a bounded scope and an automated translations to SAT solvers, making Alloy a popular light-weight formal method [10]. Alloy has been used to validate software designs [16,31], to formalize class diagrams [4,5,12], to test and debug code [6,13], to repair program states [21,30] and to provide security analysis [1,29].

Simplified, Alloy models consist of signatures, fields, and constraints. Intuitively, a signature introduces a set of atoms, a field relates atoms to other atoms, and constraints define valid configurations – instances – of atoms and their relations. Most Alloy analyses produce a very large numbers of instances, which can number in the hundreds or even thousands, even after automatically filtering symmetric instances [28]. These instances are presented to the user in the order the underlying SAT solver discovers them, which is effectively random. In the Analyzer, users can iterate over instances one by one, visually inspecting

M. Chechik et al. (Eds.): FM 2023, LNCS 14000, pp. 364–382, 2023.
https://doi.org/10.1007/978-3-031-27481-7_21

them for correctness. However, given the size of instances and Alloy's unordered enumeration, this inspection process places a high burden on the user [7,14]. Therefore, recent work has looked to address this problem by trying to compute more informative, e.g., minimal, instances [15], analyzing "why" and "why not" questions for elements of instances [14], or providing a lightweight order to the enumeration by allowing the user to preserve or change elements of instances [23]. However, all of these approaches deal with valid, complete Alloy instances. Unfortunately, not everything present in an instance is there to satisfy the explicitly executed commands. Alloy instances must also satisfy global properties and no prior work separates the different origins of constraints that influence the shape of an instance.

To address this, we introduce the concept of abstract Alloy instances, a generalization over concrete Alloy instances that abstract away information common to all instances, while preserving information specific to a concrete outcome of the analysis. Our abstraction is based on introducing lower and upper bounds[1] for Alloy's signatures and fields. The lower bound represents atoms and relations that must be contained in every Alloy instance that concretizes the abstract instance, while the upper bound captures possible additions of atoms and tuples. An abstract instance either represents multiple concrete Alloy instances – those in the upper and lower bounds – or the bounds coincide and the abstract instance is a concrete instance. Our abstraction of Alloy instances is specific to the analysis run by the user, e.g., an Alloy run command sampling specific instances or a check command looking for counterexamples of an assertion.

In this paper, we make the following contributions:

Abstract Instances We introduce abstract instances for Alloy that define lower and upper bounds that preserve information in the instance related to satisfying explicitly executed formulas of a command.

Computing Maximal Abstract Instances We present an algorithm to generate a *maximal abstract* Alloy instance, which is an abstract instance whose bounds maximize the number of concrete instances represented by the abstract instance.

Evaluation We evaluate different performance aspects related to generating abstract instances over a broad benchmark of Alloy models. Our results highlight that there is minor overhead to producing abstract instances, but these abstract instances successfully reduce the information presented to the user.

Open Source Our open-source implementation and evaluation materials are available on GitHub [20] and Zenodo [19].

2 Example

To introduce the basics of Alloy and computed instances, consider the model of a gradebook shown in Fig. 1. The model describes students, professors, classes, and assignments as well as their relations. Alloy's main structural elements are

[1] The Alloy Analyzer requires analysis scopes as cardinalities for signatures. Our bounds are refinements of the bounds induced by those scopes, see Sect. 4.

```
1  abstract sig Person {}
2  sig Student, Professor extends Person {}
3  sig Class {instructor: one Professor, assistant: set Student}
4  sig Assignment {associated_with: set Class, assigned_to: some Student}
5  fact {all a : Assignment | one a.associated_with}
6  pred PolicyAllowsGrading(p: Person, a: Assignment) {
7      p in a.associated_with.assistant or
8      p in a.associated_with.instructor
9  }
10 assert NoOneCanGradeTheirOwnAssignment {
11     all p : Person { all a : Assignment {
12         PolicyAllowsGrading[p, a] implies not p in a.assigned_to
13 }}}
14 check NoOneCanGradeTheirOwnAssignment for 3
```

Fig. 1. Alloy model Gradebook from [15]

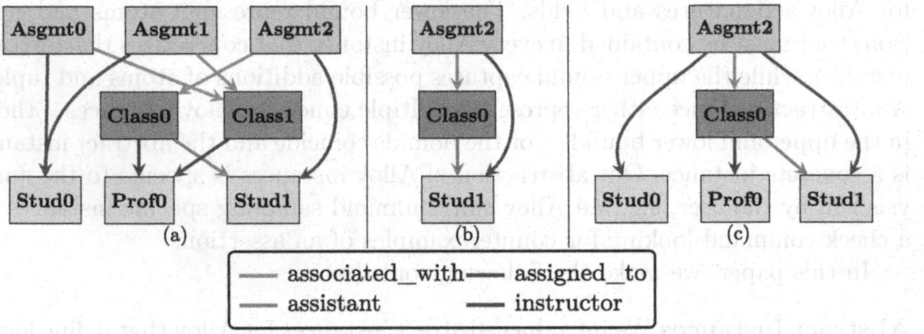

Fig. 2. Two concrete counterexamples (a) and (c) for the check command in Fig. 1 and an abstract instance (b) representing both (a) and (c)

signatures, e.g., signatures `Student` and `Professor`, which both inherit from signature `Person` (Fig. 1, ll. 1–2). Other signatures in the model are `Class` and `Assignment` (ll. 3–4). These signatures declare fields to express relations between the instances of signatures (called atoms). As an example, classes have one professor as instructor and a set of students as assistants (l. 3). Assignments are associated with a set of classes and assigned to at least one (`some`) student (l. 4). A fact restricts all assignments to be associated with exactly one class (l. 5).

The engineers developing the Alloy model want to make sure that no student grades their own assignment. They express a grading policy for persons `p` and assignments `a` in a predicate (ll. 6–8) that allows `p` to grade `a` iff `a` belongs to a class where `p` is an assistant (l. 7) or an instructor (l. 8). An assertion (ll. 10–12) quantifies over all persons `p` and all assignments `a` and asserts that if `p` can grade assignment `a` according to the policy expressed in the predicate then the assignment is not assigned to be solved by `p`.

The Alloy Analyzer allows the engineers to check the validity of the assertion in a bounded scope (l. 14, for up to `3` atoms of each of the signatures). It turns out that the assertion is not valid and a counterexample is presented to the engineers. The counterexample in Fig. 2(a) is the one of the instances the Alloy Analyzer computes. It shows three assignments, two classes, two students, a professor, and their relations, e.g., `Prof0` is the professor of both classes. It is not easy for the engineers to spot the violation of their assertion, as the engineers need to try to determine which assignment(s) and grader(s) are relevant to the violation.

An abstract instance for Fig. 2(a) is shown in Fig. 2(b). Assignment `Asgmt2` is assigned to student `Stud1` who is also assistant in class `Class0` that the assignment is associated with, i.e., this student can mark their own assignment. Note that the abstract instance is much smaller than the concrete instance and focuses on the reason the assertion is violated, while abstracting away some elements, e.g., the information that `Prof0` is the instructor of the class or that there are multiple assignments not relevant to the violation. The abstract instance is not necessarily a complete Alloy instance, but it can be extended to many concrete instances by adding atoms and their relations. For instance, Fig. 2(c) shows a different concrete instance that extends the abstract instance.

3 Preliminaries

3.1 Alloy Semantics

We now sketch the semantics of Alloy models as sets of relations. Detailed definitions can be obtained by the descriptions of language elements in [3,9].

The semantics of Alloy models is defined by a set R of n-ary relations $r \in R$. Intuitively each signature defines a unary relation and each field defines a relation of the arity of the field plus one. The domain of an n-ary relation is a subset of n-ary tuples over a universe UNIV of atoms, i.e., $dom(r) \subseteq \text{UNIV}^n$. As an example, the domain of the relation for signature `Student` (Fig. 1, l. 2) is a set of atoms and the relation for field `instructor` (Fig. 1, l. 3) is a set of pairs of atoms from relations of signatures `Class` and `Professor`. The set R of all relations of an Alloy model is defined by the declared signatures, fields, and built-in signatures, e.g., built-in signature `Int`, whose atoms represent the in-scope integers.

Multiplicities of signatures and fields constrain the valuations of relations, e.g., the multiplicity `one` constrains the relation for field `instructor` (Fig. 1, l. 3) to include exactly one pair of `Class` and `Professor` atoms for every `Class` atom. The semantics of facts, predicates, assertions, and expressions are constraints over the tuples in relations R of the model. As an example, a fact in Fig. 1, l. 5 requires that for every atom in the relation for signature `Assignment` the relation for field `associated_with` contains exactly one tuple.

3.2 Alloy Analyses

The Alloy Analyzer enables automated analyses of Alloy models via run and check commands. Run commands compute instances satisfying a predicate and check commands provide instances violating assertions, i.e., counterexamples.

The analysis of Alloy models by the Alloy Analyzer requires bounds B for relations R. Every $r \in R$ has a lower bound $\mathrm{LB}_B(r) \subseteq dom(r)$ and an upper bound $\mathrm{UB}_B(r) \subseteq dom(r)$ with $\mathrm{LB}_B(r) \subseteq \mathrm{UB}_B(r)$ (see [28]). Bounds are derived from user-defined scopes that determine the maximal numbers of atoms in relations for all signatures of the model. As an example, the check command in Fig. 1, l. 14 defines scope 3 setting $|\mathrm{UB}_B(r)| = 3$ for all relations r of signatures, e.g., the relation for signature `Student`.

We distinguish between two constraints M and C on the relations R of an Alloy model. M is the constraint defined by the semantics of the model (signatures and facts) and C is the constraint defined by a command (predicate or assertion). As an example, for the model in Fig. 1, the constraint M expresses the multiplicities and facts as sketched in Sect. 3.1 and the constraint C expresses the assertion in Fig. 1, l. 10–12. Thus, we define an Alloy instance as:

Definition 1 (Alloy instance). *An instance of an Alloy model is a valuation $\mathcal{I}$ of relations $r \in R$ within bounds B that satisfies the constraints M and C denoted by $\forall r \in R: LB_B(r) \subseteq \mathcal{I}(r) \subseteq UB_B(r)$ and $\mathcal{I} \models M \wedge C$.*

Note that Definition 1 does not distinguish between run and check commands, as internally Alloy translates check commands to run commands by negating the assertion. The Alloy instance is then also called a counterexample.

4 Abstract Alloy Instances

To introduce abstract Alloy instances, we first define a partial order on bounds B, i.e., pairs of lower and upper bounds for relations R.

Definition 2 (Partial order on bounds). *Two bounds B and B' over relations R are in a partial order relation $\preceq$ where $B' \preceq B$ iff $\forall r \in R: LB_B(r) \subseteq LB_{B'}(r) \wedge UB_{B'}(r) \subseteq UB_B(r)$.*

The relation $\preceq$ is reflexive, transitive, and antisymmetric (because subset inclusion $\subseteq$ is a partial order). Intuitively, bound B is greater or equal to bound B' if B *contains* all bounds of B', i.e., all lower bounds in B are smaller and all upper bounds are larger.

As an illustration, consider increasing the scope in Fig. 1, l. 14 from 3 to 5. The bounds have identical lower bounds (empty), but the upper bounds are equal or larger for when increasing scope 3 to scope 5. Typically, bounds for lower scopes are smaller with respect to $\preceq$ than those obtained for larger scopes. We may write $\mathcal{I} \preceq B$ for instances $\mathcal{I}$ where we set $\mathrm{LB}_{\mathcal{I}}(r) = \mathcal{I}(r) = \mathrm{UB}_{\mathcal{I}}(r)$ for all $r \in R$. Of note, our partial order on bounds is quite different from the partial order on instances defined for Aluminum [15]. First, their order does not include upper bounds, and second, their order is the reverse of ours for lower bounds.

Next, we define abstract instances for Alloy commands.

Definition 3 (Abstract Instance). *An abstract instance $\mathcal{A}$ for model M, command C, and bounds B are bounds $\mathcal{A} \preceq B$ s.t. all valuations $\mathcal{I}$ in $\mathcal{A}$ that satisfy M also satisfy C, formally $\forall \mathcal{I} s.t. \mathcal{I} \preceq \mathcal{A}: (\mathcal{I} \models M) \Rightarrow (\mathcal{I} \models C)$.*

```
sig Professor {}
run {one Professor} for 3
```
(a)

```
abstract sig Person {}
sig Professor, Student extends Person{}
run {some Person} for 3
```
(b)

Fig. 3. Alloy models demonstrating interesting properties of abstract instances

It is important to define $\mathcal{I}$ in Definition 3 again as valuations (as before in Definition 1) rather than Alloy instances. Alloy instances would need to satisfy both M and C, but for abstract instances the satisfaction of the command constraints C is only relevant if the model constraints M are satisfied.

By design, abstract instances abstract away the common constraints M of the model and preserve the reasons for satisfying commands C, i.e., all valid extensions (those satisfying the model) of the lower bounds up to the upper bounds must satisfy the analyzed command. As an example, consider the abstract instance in Fig. 2(b) where the lower bound consists of the displayed atoms and relations and the upper bound is unbounded (B). Any valid extension of the lower bound, e.g., Fig. 2(a), violates the assertion, as a student grades their own assignment. We are interested in *maximal* abstract instance, i.e., an abstract instance $\mathcal{A}$ that is maximal wrt. $\preceq$ (there is no abstract instance $\mathcal{A}'$ with $\mathcal{A}' \neq \mathcal{A}$ and $\mathcal{A} \preceq \mathcal{A}'$). A maximal abstract instance represents a maximal number of Alloy instances.

Torlak and Jackson [28] define *partial instances* for KodKod, which is the tool used by the Analyzer to translate the Alloy model into a boolean satisfiability problem, as the lower bounds of the relational problem. The purpose in [28] is to assist the solver. In contrast, our purpose is to provide information to engineers. Since our abstract instances contain lower bounds, they have a flavor of partial instances. However, the lower bounds of an abstract instance $\mathcal{A}$ may be smaller than KodKod's partial instances as M ensures that all represented instances $\mathcal{I}$ include KodKod's partial instances. The lower bounds of $\mathcal{A}$ may also be larger than KodKod's partial instances, if required for instances $\mathcal{I}$ to satisfy C.

4.1 Properties of Abstract Instances

We now present six general properties of abstract instances.

First, every concrete instance $\mathcal{I}$ from Definition 1 interpreted as bounds is also an abstract instance (again setting $\text{LB}_{\mathcal{I}}(r) = \mathcal{I}(r) = \text{UB}_{\mathcal{I}}(r)$) because $\mathcal{I} \models M \wedge C$. We say that an abstract instance $\mathcal{A}$ represents concrete instance $\mathcal{I}$ iff $\mathcal{I} \preceq \mathcal{A}$. Every concrete instance seen as an abstract instance only represents itself, i.e., for all concrete instances $\mathcal{I}$ and $\mathcal{I}'$ we have $\mathcal{I}' \preceq \mathcal{I} \Rightarrow \mathcal{I}' = \mathcal{I}$ (by unfolding the definitions). We are interested in generating abstract instances that represent many concrete instances.

Second, some maximal abstract instances $\mathcal{A}$ are concrete instances, i.e., reducing any lower or increasing any upper bound of $\mathcal{A}$ would allow for valuations $\mathcal{I} \preceq \mathcal{A}$ where $\mathcal{I} \models M$ but $\mathcal{I} \not\models C$. An example is shown in Fig. 3(a) where the instance consisting of one `Professor` atom is a maximal abstract instance.

Third, for a model M, command C, and bounds B, we typically have multiple maximal abstract instances (incomparable wrt. the partial order $\preceq$). As an example, the run command of the model in Fig. 3(b) requires that instances contain at least one atom of type `Person`. We denote by s and p the relations defined by signatures `Student` and `Professor`. The abstract instances $\mathcal{A}$ (at least one student) and $\mathcal{A}'$ (at least one professor) where $|\mathrm{LB}_{\mathcal{A}}(s)| = 1$, $\mathrm{LB}_{\mathcal{A}'}(s) = \emptyset$, $\mathrm{LB}_{\mathcal{A}}(p) = \emptyset$, $|\mathrm{LB}_{\mathcal{A}'}(p)| = 1$, $\mathrm{UB}_{\mathcal{A}}(s) = \mathrm{UB}_{\mathcal{A}'}(s) = \mathrm{UB}_B(s)$, and $\mathrm{UB}_{\mathcal{A}}(p) = \mathrm{UB}_{\mathcal{A}'}(p) = \mathrm{UB}_B(p)$ are both maximal abstract instances (reducing any lower bound would not ensure the existence of a `Person` atom and upper bounds are already maximal).[2]

Fourth, concrete instances may be represented by multiple maximal abstract instances. As an example, consider the model shown in Fig. 3(b) and the concrete instance consisting of a `Student` and a `Professor` atom. This concrete instance is represented by both of the incomparable abstract instances $\mathcal{A}$ (at least one student) and $\mathcal{A}'$ (at least one professor). This observation means that maximal abstract instances do not partition the set of instances they represent. There are however always partitions of the set of concrete instances by abstract instances, e.g., the trivial one where we treat concrete instances as abstract ones.

Fifth, from Definition 3, we can see that increasing a lower bound or decreasing an upper bound of an abstract instance $\mathcal{A}$ (up to upper bounds in B) preserves the abstract instance properties (as the set of valuations $\mathcal{I} \preceq \mathcal{A}$ becomes smaller). In contrast, decreasing a lower bound or increasing an upper bound may allow for new valuations $\mathcal{I}' \preceq \mathcal{A}$ that satisfy M but not C.

Finally, some maximal abstract instances have trivial bounds, e.g., when M implies C the requirement $\mathcal{I} \models M \Rightarrow \mathcal{I} \models C$ from Definition 3 becomes true. Then all lower bounds of maximal abstract instances $\mathcal{A}$ are empty ($\forall r \in R : \mathrm{LB}_{\mathcal{A}}(r) = \emptyset$) and all upper bounds correspond to upper bounds in B ($\forall r \in R : \mathrm{UB}_{\mathcal{A}}(r) = \mathrm{UB}_B(r)$). A common example is where an Alloy user executes an empty run command to browse arbitrary instances. In this case, our abstraction, which focuses on the analysis of the command, has nothing to preserve.

5 Computing Abstract Alloy Instances

We have seen in Sect. 4.1 that abstract instances are relatively easy to obtain by computing concrete instances and translating them into bounds. However, these abstract instances might not be very informative, as they represent a single concrete instance. We thus aim to compute maximal abstract instances.

Our algorithm for computing a maximal abstract instance is illustrated in Algorithm 1. First, a concrete instance $\mathcal{I}$ satisfying the model and command constraints $M \wedge C$ is computed by Alloy's regular solver shown as a call to `solve`$(M \wedge C, B)$. From this concrete instance we start an iteration that increases the bounds $\mathcal{A}$ (initialized as $\mathcal{A} \leftarrow \mathcal{I}$) in every iteration of the while loop, i.e., $\mathcal{A}' \preceq \mathcal{A}$. This iteration is necessary as upper and lower bounds may depend on each other. The iteration terminates as lower bounds may only shrink to the

[2] We oversimplify the case of inheritance and relations for illustrative purposes, see our implementation in Sect. 5.1 for a more thorough handling.

Algorithm 1. Computation of an abstract instance for model M, command C and bounds B

$\mathcal{I} \leftarrow$ `solve`$(M \wedge C, B)$
$\mathcal{A} \leftarrow \mathcal{I}$
$\mathcal{A}' \leftarrow \emptyset$
while $\mathcal{A} \neq \mathcal{A}'$ **do**
  $\mathcal{A}' \leftarrow \mathcal{A}$
  $\mathrm{LB}_{\mathcal{A}} \leftarrow$ `minimize`$(\mathrm{LB}_{\mathcal{A}'})$ down to $\emptyset$
  $\mathrm{UB}_{\mathcal{A}} \leftarrow$ `maximize`$(\mathrm{UB}_{\mathcal{A}'})$ up to UB_B
end while
return $\mathcal{A}$

Algorithm 2. Computation of the `check` used for minimization in Algorithm 1 for $cand \subset \mathrm{LB}_{\mathcal{A}'}$ with bounds $\mathcal{A}'$ and B, model M, and command C from Algorithm 1

$M' \leftarrow M \cup$ `sigs4Bounds`$(cand, \mathrm{UB}_{\mathcal{A}'})$
$bounds \leftarrow$ `expr4Bounds`$(cand, \mathrm{UB}_{\mathcal{A}'})$
return (`solve`$(M' \wedge bounds \wedge \neg C, B) ==$ `UNSAT`)

empty set ($\emptyset$) and upper bounds may grow at most up to B. The algorithm then returns a maximal abstract instance $\mathcal{A}$ (by construction of the bounds).

To minimize and maximize bounds we use Delta Debugging [32]. Delta Debugging computes minimal subsets of a set that satisfy a `check` criterion. We can easily convert our bounds to sets (e.g., $\bigcup_{r \in R} \mathrm{LB}_{\mathcal{A}'}(r)$ is a set of atoms and tuples) and back by tracking Alloy's type information.

We show our implementation of `check`$(cand)$ in Algorithm 2. A candidate $cand \subset \bigcup_{r \in R} \mathrm{LB}_{\mathcal{A}'}(r)$ is valid if the abstract instance criterion from Definition 3 is satisfied, i.e., for all $\mathcal{I}'$ within the bounds of the abstract instance $\mathcal{I}' \models M \Rightarrow \mathcal{I}' \models C$. In Algorithm 2 the lower bounds we use for valuations $\mathcal{I}'$ are *cand* and the upper bounds are $\mathrm{UB}_{\mathcal{A}'}$ (for maximizing $\mathrm{UB}_{\mathcal{A}'}$ `check` uses *cand* and $\mathrm{LB}_{\mathcal{A}'}$). We encode these as the constraint *bounds* (see Sect. 5.1). Finally, to evaluate the abstract instance criterion, we invoke the solver and convert the universal quantification over valuations $\mathcal{I}'$ into an existential one that satisfies M and violates C.

5.1 Encoding of Bounds in Alloy

Ideally, we would like to pass bounds $\mathcal{A}$ instead of B to Alloy's solver KodKod [28]. However, the bounds used by KodKod are different from the ones indicated in Definition 1, Definition 2, and Definition 3, e.g., KodKod does not support inheritance and thus additional relations may be created in the translation to KodKod. Since our prototype implementation stays on the abstraction level of Alloy, we encode bounds as additional signatures (`sigs4Bounds`) and constraints (`expr4Bounds`).

Method `sigs4Bounds` creates signatures with multiplicity `lone` extending the primary signatures[3] of the model to represent atoms, e.g., signatures created for

[3] Alloy distinguishes between primary and subset signatures where atoms of subset signatures always also belong to primary signatures.

```
1 lone sig Asgmt0, Asgmt1, Asgmt2 extends Assignment {}
2 lone sig Class0, Class1 extends Class {}
3 ...
4 (one Asgmt2) and (one Class0) and (one Stud1)
5 (Class0 -> Stud1 in assistant) and (Asgmt2 -> Stud1 in assigned_to)
6 ...
7 (Person = Student + Professor) and (Student = Stud0 + Stud1) and ...
8 assistant in (Class0 -> Stud0 + Class0 -> Stud1)
```

Fig. 4. Excerpt of encoding of bounds from Fig. 2 via signatures and constraints

the atoms shown in Fig. 2(a) are declared in Fig. 4, ll. 1–2. Method `expr4Bounds` then uses this representation of atoms to express lower bounds by requiring the existence of the atoms and tuples, e.g., for the lower bound in Fig 2 (b) see Fig. 4, l. 4. Similarly, tuples are required by lower bounds, e.g., in Fig. 4, l. 5. Whereas the constraints of lower bounds are local for individual elements, upper bounds are global in the sense that we must constrain all atoms of a signature, e.g., Fig. 4, l. 7, and all tuples of a relation at once, e.g., Fig. 4, l. 8. The upper bound constraints in Fig. 4, ll. 7–8 are an excerpt of upper bounds initialized from the instance in Fig. 2(a).

The use of a generic minimizer in Algorithm 1, which is unaware of dependencies between tuples and atoms, may lead to cases where a tuple is present in the lower or upper bounds when one of its atoms is not. In both cases, `expr4Bounds` does not generate a constraint for the tuple, i.e., the constraint for the lower bound is weaker and might fail (the larger *cand* set with the missing atom will then be searched) and the constraint for the upper bound might be stronger and may succeed (the larger set with the additional atom will then also be checked).

Note that our implementation uses APIs of the Alloy Analyzer and does not explicitly create the syntax shown in Fig. 4. This has two advantages: (1) we do not need to disambiguate fields with same names and (2) we can also constrain signatures marked as `private`, e.g., the signature `Ord` in Alloy's `ordering` module.

5.2 Running Time Complexity

We estimate the running time complexity of the algorithm in terms of Alloy's solver calls by Algorithm 1. Minimization and maximization with Delta Debugging has a running time in $O(N^2)$. The while loop in Algorithm 1 leads to an overall time complexity in $O(N^4)$ (worst case where every iteration adds/removes only one element). In Algorithm 1, l. 6 $N = |\mathrm{LB}_{\mathcal{A}'}|$ with $|\mathrm{LB}_{\mathcal{A}'}| \leq |\mathcal{I}|$. In Algorithm 1, l. 7 $N = |\mathrm{UB}_{\mathcal{A}'}|$ with $|\mathrm{UB}_{\mathcal{A}'}| \leq |\mathrm{UB}_{B}|$. In both cases, $N \leq \sum_{r \in R} |dom(R)|$. Looking at the structure of Alloy models with signatures *sigs*, fields *fields* and scope *maxScope*, we have $N \in O(maxScope \cdot |sigs| + |fields| \cdot maxScope^{maxArity(fields)})$. Note that the size of $\mathcal{I}$ is often much smaller, but this is not the case for $|\mathrm{UB}_{B}|$.

5.3 Different Upper Bound Kinds

We have defined abstract instances in Definition 3 without any restriction on the shape of bounds. The running time analysis in Sect. 5.2 shows that restrictions

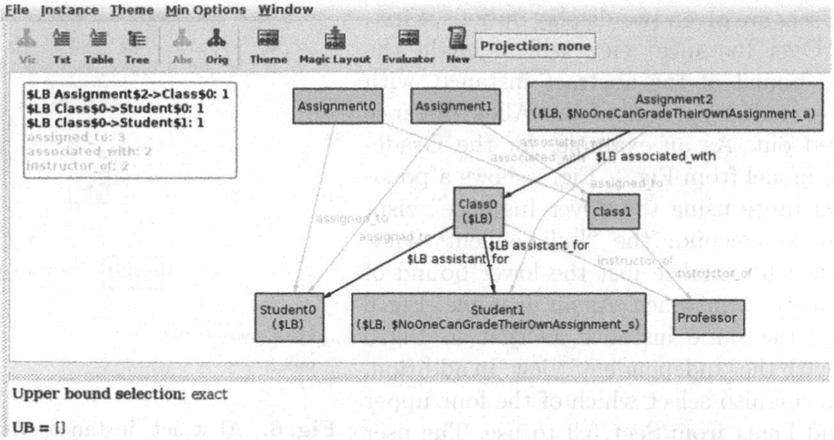

Fig. 5. Abstract instance visualized on top of a concrete instance (UB is unbounded)

on the kind of upper bounds we compute may improve running times. We have implemented four kinds of upper bounds and briefly describe these here.

Exact. Exact upper bounds are the most natural variant used in Sect. 5. Every atom and every tuple have to be considered when maximizing the upper bound of an abstract instance. The number of elements to find a maximal subset for is in $O(maxScope \cdot |sigs| + |fields| \cdot maxScope^{maxArity})$.

Instance or None. The upper bound for each signature and field $r \in R$ is as in the concrete instance $\mathrm{UB}_{\mathcal{A}}(r) = \mathrm{UB}_{\mathcal{I}}(r)$ or unrestricted $\mathrm{UB}_{\mathcal{A}}(r) = \mathrm{UB}_{\mathcal{B}}(r)$. The number of elements to find a maximal subset for is in $O(|sigs| + |fields|)$.

Instance. The upper bound is always the instance. There is no call to `maximize` in Algorithm 1, l. 7 and $\mathrm{UB}_{\mathcal{A}}$ remains as initialized from $\mathrm{UB}_{\mathcal{I}}$.

None. We do not consider any restriction of the upper bound. There is no call to `maximize` in Algorithm 1, l. 7 and $\mathrm{UB}_{\mathcal{A}}$ is instead treated as $\mathrm{UB}_{\mathcal{B}}$.

The latter two bound kinds reduce the overall running time complexity from $O(N^4)$ to $O(N^2)$. For the first three kinds an abstract instance always exists (in the worst case it only represents $\mathcal{I}$); however, kind *None* is incomplete, i.e., some concrete instances require upper bounds (see Fig. 3(a)).

5.4 Implementation and Visualization

We have implemented our work as an extension to the latest stable release of the Analyzer, version 6.0.0 [2] (our implementation is available from [20]). Importantly, since we extend the main IDE for Alloy, users can maintain their current workflow while gradually exploring the new functionality. Users can access abstract instances during the standard enumeration process, which occurs in the `VizGUI`. When viewing a specific instance, the user is able to select the "Abs" button which will update the active display to present the associated abstract instance. The lower bound of the abstract instance is displayed visually in the main panel, while the upper bound is conveyed textually below.

Users are given two display options. First, the "Over Instance" view will highlight the lower bound of the abstract instance, with any excluded portion of the Alloy instance grayed out. As an example, for the Gradebook model from Fig. 1, Fig. 5 shows a possible instance using the "Over Instance" visualization. Second, the "Independent" view which will visualize just the lower bound of the abstract instance. As an example, Fig. 6 shows the same instance as that in Fig. 5 but with the "Independent" view. In addition, users can also select which of the four upper bound kinds from Sect. 5.3 to use. The user can switch back to the original instance using the "Orig" button.

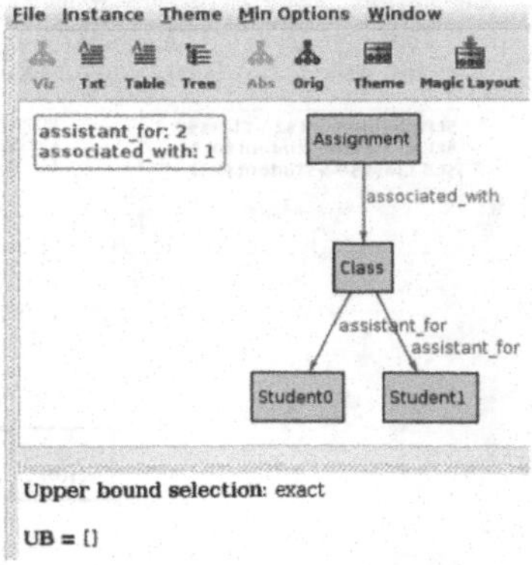

Fig. 6. Abstract instance visualized independently of any concrete instance (UB is unbounded)

6 Evaluation

To evaluate abstract instances, we use a collection of 78 benchmark Alloy models. We executed all experiments on Ubuntu 22.04 LTS (64 Bit) with an Intel Core i7-7700 K 4.20 GHz processor and 32 GB RAM. We use Alloy's default options and selected MiniSatJNI as SAT solver.

We address the following research questions, where by abstract instance we always mean maximal abstract instance:

- **RQ1:** What is the time overhead of generating an abstract instance?
- **RQ2:** How do the sizes of abstract and concrete instances compare?
- **RQ3:** As concrete instances are enumerated, what is the diversity of the underlying abstract instance?
- **RQ4:** What is the time/size/diversity impact of the upper bound kind?

Set Up. To evaluate abstract instances, we rely on meaningful commands. Therefore, we focus on two collections of models used to illustrate how Alloy works: models from the Alloy textbook [9] (**Book**) and models included as examples in the official Analyzer release (**Examples**). In addition, we include models used to evaluate recent automated repair work for Alloy (**ARepair**) whose commands execute faulty portions of the model. For each model, we consider every command present; however, we filter out commands that are: (1) empty ("**run {}**"), which only execute the facts of the model, (2) commands that produce no instances and (3) commands that use temporal logic, which is new

Table 1. Subjects

Subject	#M	Avg.S	Avg.R	#C	Avg.C
ARepair	33	4.27	2.91	36	1.10
Book	28	4.46	3.20	34	1.21
Example	17	6.71	7.76	41	2.41

to Alloy 6 and not currently supported by our implementation. After this filtering, we are left with 28 **Book** models, 17 **Example** models, and 33 **ARepair** models. For each collection of models, Table 1 gives the following information to convey the size and number of models in the benchmarks: Column **#M** shows the number of models, **#Avg_S** is the average number of signatures per model, **#Avg_R** is the average number of relations per model, **#C** is the total number of commands, and **#Avg_C** is the average number of commands per model. For each command, we enumerate up to the first 10 instances, with an enumeration timeout of 10 min. For research questions 1–3, we use *Exact* upper bounds as a default.

6.1 RQ1: Overhead

Abstract instances are generated from an existing concrete instance that has been enumerated for a command. To explore the overhead of this process, Fig. 7(a) depicts a boxplot that shows the distribution of the ratio between the time it takes to generate the first abstract instance compared to the time to generate the first concrete instance. A ratio larger than 1 means the abstract instance took longer to produce than the paired concrete instance. We consider only the time to the first instance because the Analyzer uses incremental SAT solvers; therefore, the time to produce the first instance includes all the novel effort to resolve the executed constraints, while future instances are often quickly produced due to the ability to reuse previous work. There are 38, 33 and 34 abstract-concrete instances pairs in the boxplot for **ARepair**, **Book** and **Example** respectively. **Example** excludes two commands which timed out generating the first instance. The first quartile to third quartile ratios range from 2.14 to 4.5 for **ARepair**, from 1.84 to 11.81 for **Book** and from 5.35 to 62.10 for **Example**.

These results indicate that abstract instances frequently take longer to produce compared to their paired concrete instance. However, this does not mean abstract instances have a prohibitive overhead. In particular, finding concrete instances is quick: all concrete instances are produced in less than .5 s. In comparison, 61 of the abstract instances take less than 2 s to produce, while 34 abstract instances take between 2 s and 10 s to produce, which is a slight overhead but not unreasonable. However, 17 abstract instance take longer than 10 s to produce, including 5 abstract instances that take longer than one minute. These 5 abstract instances all use a larger scope than the default scope (3) and include the "`ordering`" module. In fact, across all three data sets, all but two outliers capture abstract instances that come from models that uses the "`ordering`" module. While **ARepair** contains 1 abstract instance that includes the "`ordering`" module, **Book** has 10 and **Example** has 30, which directly translates into the increasingly larger ratios observed in Fig. 7(a).

On average, abstract instances have a minor overhead to produce; however, if the "`ordering`" module is present, the time overhead quickly increases. The "`ordering`" module bloats the time to generate an abstract instance because the module increases the size of the upper bound since it places an ordering on the atoms of a signature and all possible orders must be considered.

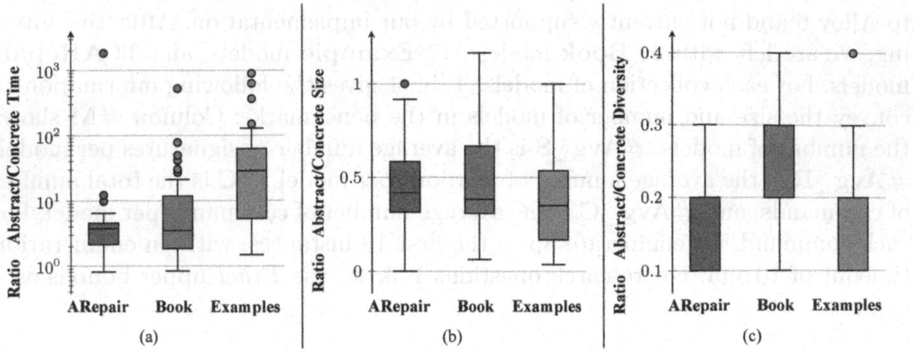

Fig. 7. Comparison of abstract instance to concrete instance performance

6.2 RQ2: Size Comparison

Given that abstract instances are meant to refine concrete instances, we expect that abstract instances are, on average, smaller than concrete instances. To explore if this holds, Fig. 7(b) depicts a boxplot showing the distribution of size ratios, which is calculated by taking the size of the abstract instance and dividing it by the size of the corresponding concrete instance used to produce the abstract instance. We define the size of a concrete instance as the number of its atoms and tuples and we define the size of an abstract instance as the number of atoms and tuples in the lower bound plus the number of relations constrained in by the upper bound. A ratio of less than 1 means the abstract instance is smaller than the paired concrete instance. There are 339, 253, and 282 abstract-instance pairs in the boxplot for **ARepair**, **Book** and **Examples** respectively. The first quartile to third quartile ratios range from 0.31 to 0.58 for **ARepair**, from 0.31 to 0.67 for **Book** and from 0.17 to 0.53 for **Example**.

The results highlight that on average the abstract instance is smaller than the concrete instance, and often the abstract instance reduces the size by at least half. Rarely, the abstract instance ends up the same size or larger than the concrete instance. This occurs just 6, 6, and 1 times for **ARepair**, **Book** and **Examples** respectively. In the opposite direction, for 30 **ARepair** instances, the abstract instance produced is an empty instance. This is expected as all of these instances are associated with the model "`student16`" that is under-constrained due to the student failure to write anything for the predicates. As a result, when the faulty predicates are run, only the facts of the model are enforced. The results also highlight that while models that use the "`ordering`" module will have longer abstract instance generation times, these models do not consistently produce larger abstract instances, as **Example** models has the smallest quartile 1 to quartile 3 range despite having the most models that use "`ordering`."

We find that the abstract instance noticeably reduce the size of the concrete instance, highlighting that commonly half or more of the information in an instance is there regardless of the explicitly executed constraints of the command.

6.3 RQ3: Diversity

To gain insight into how many different abstract instances the user will encounter, Fig. 7(c) depicts a boxplot showing the distribution of diversity ratios, which is calculated by taking the number of unique abstract instance and dividing it by the number of concrete instances for each command. We include only those commands that were able to produce 10 concrete instances. A ratio of less than one means there were fewer unique abstract instances than concrete instances, with a ratio if 0.1 meaning all 10 concrete instances reduced to the same abstract instance. There are 33, 21 and 25 commands in the boxplot for **ARepair**, **Book** and **Examples** respectively. The first quartile to third quartile ratios range from 0.1 to 0.2 **ARepair**, from 0.2 to 0.3 **Book** and from 0.1 to 0.2 **Example**. The median is equivalent to the 1st quartile for all data sets.

The results demonstrate that **ARepair** and **Example** models frequently produce only 1 or 2 abstract instances for the first 10 instances enumerated. For both data sets, 17 of their commands produce a single abstract instance. In contrast, **Book** models have a little bit more diversity, with only 4 commands producing a single abstract instance. However, even for **Book**, no command produces more than 4 unique abstract instances. Since a user is likely to inspect the first few instances, but maybe not too many more, our results indicate that the user is often looking at instances that all satisfy the explicitly executed commands in the exact same way. Therefore, as future work, we plan to explore how to directly enumerate unique abstract instances, which will ensure users are able to quickly view diverse ways the command can be satisfied.

6.4 RQ4: Impact of Upper Bound Kind

As outlined in Sect. 5.3, abstract instances can be calculated with four different upper bounds. While *Exact* is the default, Fig. 8 compares the performance across all four upper bound kinds. In Fig. 8, **E** represents *Exact*, **I** represents *Instance*, **IoN** represents *Instance or None* and **N** represents *None*. Across the performance metrics, *None* consistently represents fewer data points as *None* is incomplete for 41 of the commands in the evaluation. For the other three bounds, there is a minor difference in the number of data points, as some of the more time expensive upper bound kinds occasionally timeout while enumerating instances.

Figure 8(a) compares the overhead of each upper bound kind by depicting the ratio between the time to generate the abstract instance and generate the concrete instance. We again look at the time to produce the first instance. There are 103, 105, 105 and 64 abstract-concrete pairs in the boxplot for *Exact*, *Instance*, *Instance or None* and *None* respectively. The results in Fig. 8(a) highlights that on average, *Exact* is the most expensive upper bound and *Instance* is the fastest upper bound, both of which is expected.

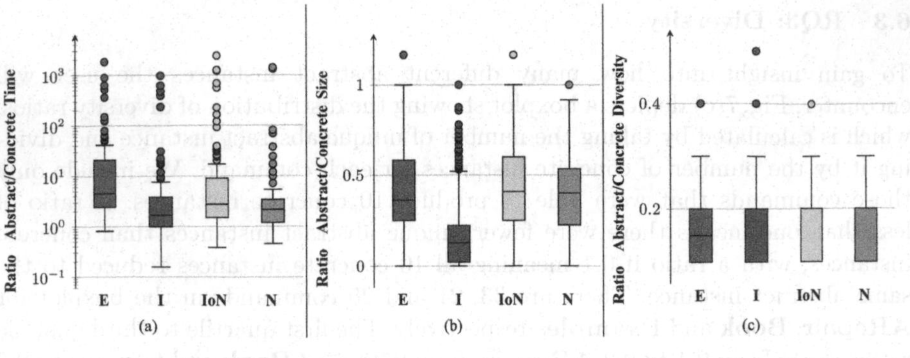

Fig. 8. Comparison of performance for different upper bounds

Figure 8(b) compares the size of the abstract instances produced by the different upper bound kinds. We again present size as a ratio of the size of the abstract instance divided by the size of the corresponding concrete instance. There are 871, 913, 901, 570 abstract-concrete pairs in the boxplot for *Exact*, *Instance*, *Instance or None* and *None* respectively. For *Exact*, *Instance or None* and *None*, the size performance is very similar. In contrast, *Instance* consistently produces smaller abstract instances than all other three upper bound kinds. While the other three produce just 30 empty abstract instances, all for the "**student16**" submission, *Instance* produces 210 abstract instances without lower bounds. This translates directly into the observed performance difference in size.

Figure 8(c) compares the diversity of generated abstract instances produced by the different upper bound kids. We again present diversity as a ratio of the number of unique abstract instances divided by the number of unique concrete instances per command that do enumerate 10 concrete instances. There are 77, 86, 83 and 54 commands in the boxplot for *Exact*, *Instance*, *Instance or None* and *None* respectively. As Fig. 8(c) shows, the different upper bound kinds have very similar performance in terms of diversity. *Exact* upper bounds does produce slightly more abstract instances on average across the first 10 instance, with all other upper bounds having a median of 0.1, meaning only one unique abstract instance, while *Exact*'s median is 0.2.

6.5 Threats to Validity

There are two main threats to validity for our results. First, we selected our benchmark models to eliminate the likelihood of encountering trivial commands. Therefore, our results may not generalize to other Alloy models which may use different operators and signature constraints than those that appear in our evaluation models. Second, our implementation may have bugs. To mitigate this threat we have used existing components where possible, e.g., Delta Debugging [32] and Alloy's APIs and solver (see Sect. 5.1). In addition, we have added assertions and ran our algorithms on all available models. Before Algorithm 1, l. 4 we check whether $\texttt{solve}((M \cup \texttt{sigs4Bounds}(\mathcal{A})) \wedge \texttt{expr4Bounds}(\mathcal{A}) \wedge C, B)$ is satisfiable (otherwise $\texttt{expr4Bounds}$ is incorrect as $\mathcal{I}$ must be a solution). In Algorithm 2 we check that $\texttt{solve}(M' \wedge \mathit{bounds} \wedge C, B)$ is satisfiable, i.e., that there are instances represented by the candidate.

7 Related Work

Explaining Alloy Instances. Our motivation for developing abstract instances is to help users understand why a given instance was generated by the Analyzer for an executed command. There have been two notable efforts related to helping explain Alloy instances. First, Amalgam is an extension to the Analyzer, which uses provenance chains to inform the user why a specific tuple does or does not appear in the scenario [14]. Unlike abstract instances, Amalgam's provenance chain includes the facts of the model and thus it is possible for the provenance chain of a tuple to never reference the explicitly invoked formulas of the command. Second, recent work [7] explored how presenting novice users with a combination of instances and non-instances for a command can help the user understand a modeled constraint. This work uses tailored instances that were selected for the study and thus does not try to influence an active enumeration.

Instance Enumeration for Alloy. Our technique is closely related to techniques which look to enhance the Analyzer's instance enumeration process. One traditional approach is to reduce the number of instances through symmetry breaking, where the goal is to remove isomorphic instances [11,22]. Beyond symmetry breaking, several past projects improve instance enumeration by (1) influencing the order of instances [24,25] and (2) trying to narrow what scenarios are generated using a specific criteria, e.g., abstract functions [26], minimality [15], maximality [33], field exhaustiveness [17], and coverage [18,27]. All of these techniques reduce the number of instances that are generated by applying additional criteria to how any new instance generated must differ from the previous set of instances. Of these, Aluminium, which enumerates minimal instances, is the most closely related to our technique. In contrast to abstract instances, Aluminium produces complete instances, which can prevent Aluminium from further reducing the information presented as there are lower bounds enforced by the constraints of the model that Aluminum will be required to meet to ensure the instance satisfies the facts of the model, in addition to the command.

8 Conclusion

This paper introduces the concept of abstract instances for the Alloy modeling language. These instances serve to remove information in the instance that is not directly relevant to the executed predicate or assertion invoked by the command. Our experimental results show that abstract instances can often be produced with a small overhead but do successfully reduce the information presented to the user. In addition, our results reveal that an abstract instances often represent multiple concrete instances. As future work, we plan to conduct a user study to evaluate how abstract instances help users understand analysis results, explore how we can efficiently enumerate unique abstract instances, and extend our approach to handle Alloy's new temporal logic extension.

References

1. Akhawe, D., Barth, A., Lam, P.E., Mitchell, J.C., Song, D.: Towards a formal foundation of web security. In: Proceedings of the 23rd IEEE Computer Security Foundations Symposium, CSF 2010, Edinburgh, United Kingdom, 17–19 July 2010, pp. 290–304. IEEE Computer Society (2010). https://doi.org/10.1109/CSF.2010.27
2. Alloy: Alloy Tools GitHub. https://github.com/AlloyTools (2022). Accessed 5 2022
3. Alloy 6 Language Reference. https://alloytools.org/spec.html (2022). Accessed 8 2022
4. Anastasakis, K., Bordbar, B., Georg, G., Ray, I.: On challenges of model transformation from UML to alloy. Softw. Syst. Model. **9**(1), 69–86 (2010). https://doi.org/10.1007/s10270-008-0110-3
5. Cunha, A., Garis, A., Riesco, D.: Translating between Alloy specifications and UML class diagrams annotated with OCL. Softw. Syst. Model. **14**(1), 5–25 (2013). https://doi.org/10.1007/s10270-013-0353-5
6. Dini, N., Yelen, C., Alrmaih, Z., Kulkarni, A., Khurshid, S.: Korat-API: a framework to enhance Korat to better support testing and reliability techniques. In: SAC (2018)
7. Dyer, T., Nelson, T., Fisler, K., Krishnamurthi, S.: Applying cognitive principles to model-finding output: the positive value of negative information. Proc. ACM Program. Lang. 6(OOPSLA), 1–29 (2022). https://doi.org/10.1145/3527323
8. Jackson, D.: Alloy: a lightweight object modelling notation. ACM Trans. Softw. Eng. Methodol. **11**(2), 256–290 (2002)
9. Jackson, D.: Software Abstractions: Logic, Language, and Analysis. MIT Press, Cambridge (2006)
10. Jackson, D.: Alloy: a language and tool for exploring software designs. Commun. ACM **62**(9), 66–76 (2019). https://doi.org/10.1145/3338843
11. Khurshid, S., Marinov, D., Shlyakhter, I., Jackson, D.: A case for efficient solution enumeration. In: Giunchiglia, E., Tacchella, A. (eds.) SAT 2003. LNCS, vol. 2919, pp. 272–286. Springer, Heidelberg (2004). https://doi.org/10.1007/978-3-540-24605-3_21
12. Maoz, S., Ringert, J.O., Rumpe, B.: CD2Alloy: class diagrams analysis using alloy revisited. In: Whittle, J., Clark, T., Kühne, T. (eds.) MODELS 2011. LNCS, vol. 6981, pp. 592–607. Springer, Heidelberg (2011). https://doi.org/10.1007/978-3-642-24485-8_44
13. Marinov, D., Khurshid, S.: TestEra: a novel framework for automated testing of Java programs. In: ASE (2001)
14. Nelson, T., Danas, N., Dougherty, D.J., Krishnamurthi, S.: The power of "why" and "why not": enriching scenario exploration with provenance. In: Bodden, E., Schäfer, W., van Deursen, A., Zisman, A. (eds.) Proceedings of the 2017 11th Joint Meeting on Foundations of Software Engineering, ESEC/FSE 2017, Paderborn, Germany, 4–8 September 2017, pp. 106–116. ACM (2017). https://doi.org/10.1145/3106237.3106272

15. Nelson, T., Saghafi, S., Dougherty, D.J., Fisler, K., Krishnamurthi, S.: Aluminum: principled scenario exploration through minimality. In: Notkin, D., Cheng, B.H.C., Pohl, K. (eds.) 35th International Conference on Software Engineering, ICSE'13, San Francisco, CA, USA, 18–26 May 2013, pp. 232–241. IEEE Computer Society (2013). https://doi.org/10.1109/ICSE.2013.6606569
16. Nelson, T., Barratt, C., Dougherty, D.J., Fisler, K., Krishnamurthi, S.: The Margrave tool for firewall analysis. In: LISA (2010)
17. Ponzio, P., Aguirre, N., Frias, M.F., Visser, W.: Field-exhaustive testing. In: FSE (2016)
18. Porncharoenwase, S., Nelson, T., Krishnamurthi, S.: CompoSAT: specification-guided coverage for model finding. In: Havelund, K., Peleska, J., Roscoe, B., de Vink, E. (eds.) FM 2018. LNCS, vol. 10951, pp. 568–587. Springer, Cham (2018). https://doi.org/10.1007/978-3-319-95582-7_34
19. Ringert, J.O., Sullivan, A.K.: Abstract alloy instances artefact (2022). https://doi.org/10.5281/zenodo.7339931
20. Ringert, J.O., Sullivan, A.K.: Abstract alloy instances code (2022). https://github.com/jringert/alloy-absinst
21. Samimi, H., Aung, E.D., Millstein, T.: Falling back on executable specifications. In: D'Hondt, T. (ed.) ECOOP 2010. LNCS, vol. 6183, pp. 552–576. Springer, Heidelberg (2010). https://doi.org/10.1007/978-3-642-14107-2_26
22. Shlyakhter, I.: Generating effective symmetry-breaking predicates for search problems. In: SAT (2001)
23. Sullivan, A.: Hawkeye: user-guided enumeration of scenarios. In: Jin, Z., Li, X., Xiang, J., Mariani, L., Liu, T., Yu, X., Ivaki, N. (eds.) 32nd IEEE International Symposium on Software Reliability Engineering, ISSRE 2021, Wuhan, China, 25–28 October 2021, pp. 569–578. IEEE (2021). https://doi.org/10.1109/ISSRE52982.2021.00064
24. Sullivan, A.: Hawkeye: user guided enumeration of scenarios. In: ISSRE (2021)
25. Sullivan, A., Jovanovic, A.: Reach: refining alloy scenarios by size. In: ISSRE (2022)
26. Sullivan, A., Marinov, D., Khurshid, S.: Solution enumeration abstraction: a modeling idiom to enhance a lightweight formal method. In: Ait-Ameur, Y., Qin, S. (eds.) ICFEM 2019. LNCS, vol. 11852, pp. 336–352. Springer, Cham (2019). https://doi.org/10.1007/978-3-030-32409-4_21
27. Sullivan, A., Wang, K., Zaeem, R.N., Khurshid, S.: Automated test generation and mutation testing for alloy. In: 2017 IEEE International Conference on Software Testing, Verification and Validation, ICST 2017, Tokyo, Japan, 13–17 March 2017, pp. 264–275. IEEE Computer Society (2017). https://doi.org/10.1109/ICST.2017.31
28. Torlak, E., Jackson, D.: Kodkod: a relational model finder. In: Grumberg, O., Huth, M. (eds.) TACAS 2007. LNCS, vol. 4424, pp. 632–647. Springer, Heidelberg (2007). https://doi.org/10.1007/978-3-540-71209-1_49
29. Trippel, C., Lustig, D., Martonosi, M.: Security verification via automatic hardware-aware exploit synthesis: the CheckMate approach. IEEE Micro **39**(3), 84–93 (2019)
30. Nokhbeh Zaeem, R., Khurshid, S.: Contract-based data structure repair using alloy. In: D'Hondt, T. (ed.) ECOOP 2010. LNCS, vol. 6183, pp. 577–598. Springer, Heidelberg (2010). https://doi.org/10.1007/978-3-642-14107-2_27
31. Zave, P.: Reasoning about identifier spaces: how to make chord correct. IEEE Trans. Softw. Eng. **43**(12), 1144–1156 (2017). https://doi.org/10.1109/TSE.2017.2655056

32. Zeller, A., Hildebrandt, R.: Simplifying and isolating failure-inducing input. IEEE Trans. Soft. Eng. **28**(2), 183–200 (2002). https://doi.org/10.1109/32.988498
33. Zhang, C., et al.: Alloymax: bringing maximum satisfaction to relational specifications. In: Proceedings of the 29th ACM Joint Meeting on European Software Engineering Conference and Symposium on the Foundations of Software Engineering, pp. 155–167. ESEC/FSE 2021, Association for Computing Machinery, New York, NY, USA (2021)

Monitoring the Internet Computer

David Basin[1], Daniel Stefan Dietiker[2], Srđan Krstić[1](✉), Yvonne-Anne Pignolet[2], Martin Raszyk[2], Joshua Schneider[1](✉), and Arshavir Ter-Gabrielyan[2]

[1] Department of Computer Science, ETH Zürich, Zurich, Switzerland
{basin,srdan.krstic,joshua.schneider}@inf.ethz.ch

[2] DFINITY, Zurich, Switzerland
{danielstefan.dietiker,yvonneanne,martin.raszyk,
arshavir.ter.gabrielyan}@dfinity.org

FM Artifact Evaluation ★ Available

FM Artifact Evaluation ★★ Reproducible

Abstract. The Internet Computer (IC) is a distributed platform for Web3 applications, spanning over 1,200 nodes worldwide. We present results on applying runtime monitoring to the IC. We use the MonPoly monitor and its expressive policy language with quantifiers over infinite domains, aggregations, and past and future operators. We formalize complex policies that cover common kinds of production incidents and IC-specific protocol properties, including malicious behaviors and infrastructure outages. Using these policies, we evaluate MonPoly's performance in a large-scale case study that includes logs from both production and testing environments. We find, for example, that MonPoly performs well on testing logs, and that half of our policies applicable to production logs can be monitored in an online setting. Overall, our policies and IC traces constitute a new benchmark for first-order temporal logic monitors.

Keywords: Runtime monitoring · Temporal logic · Internet Computer

1 Introduction

In runtime monitoring, a monitor observes a system's execution, typically encoded as a sequence of *events*, checks whether the execution complies with a policy formalizing the system's correct behavior, and outputs detected violations. Online monitors incrementally process an *unbounded stream* of events produced by a running system, whereas offline monitors process a *finite log*. Good online monitors output timely violations, while good offline monitors process the log quickly, i.e., the former have low latency, whereas the latter have high throughput.

A real-world system's execution contains complex events, which include arbitrary data values. Such systems also require complex checks, for example based on aggregated values, dependencies between values, and possibly values coming from events spread over time. It is therefore important that monitors support

M. Chechik et al. (Eds.): FM 2023, LNCS 14000, pp. 383–402, 2023.
https://doi.org/10.1007/978-3-031-27481-7_22

expressive policy languages and complex events. Furthermore, *distributed* systems pose additional monitoring challenges as policies may refer to (only partially ordered) events coming from different distributed components.

While many monitors support expressive policy languages [12,29,30] and there exist approaches for monitoring distributed systems [9,13,36,39] (Sect. 6), there is a substantial gap to bridge when applying them in the real world. With a notable exception [18], current literature has no answers to questions concerning policy engineering, measuring effectiveness, maintainability, as well as process organization, roles, and responsibilities in the context of runtime monitoring.

In this paper, we report on our experience in monitoring the *Internet Computer* (Sect. 2), a complex distributed system that facilitates the governance and execution of *Web3 applications*, i.e., applications processing data and financial assets with decentralized ownership and control of the applications' data, assets, and code. The Internet Computer is itself governed by a Web3 application, for example letting stakeholders vote on the Internet Computer's configuration and the addition and replacement of the machines that provide computing power to the system. The Internet Computer also possesses numerous other features that are challenging to monitor, both individually and when combined. These features include a long-lived execution with high event rates, a software architecture with multiple layers, dynamic configuration, and continuous evolution. Our case study is the outcome of a collaboration between Internet Computer developers at DFINITY and researchers in monitoring at ETH Zürich.

Assurance of the Internet Computer's correct behavior is critical for its stakeholders as it is a complex system managing financial assets. We show how runtime monitoring complements system testing and metric-based observability, two existing assurance techniques. In particular, our case study shows that *MonPoly* [11,12], a state-of-the-art monitor supporting an expressive policy language, is well-suited for monitoring logs obtained from system tests. Moreover, MonPoly can process the event stream from the production system in real time for some policies, but for other, more complex policies, it incurs a monitoring backlog. We identify several opportunities for future optimizations and report on lessons learned.

Overall, we make the following contributions: (1) We formalize a set of policies that express common symptoms of production incidents in the Internet Computer as well as domain-specific properties of its protocol, including malicious behaviors and infrastructure outages that the protocol must tolerate (Sect. 3). (2) We use these policies for a *quantitative* evaluation of MonPoly's performance (Sect. 4) and its applicability in both testing and production scenarios. (3) We obtain *qualitative* insights about the integration of runtime monitoring into a complex production system. In particular, we report on insights on policy engineering and monitoring maintainability (Sect. 5). (4) We publish the artifact [7] containing the logs, policies, and code used in this case study. It can be used to benchmark monitors for policy languages that support first-order temporal logic with aggregations.

We believe that our results are valuable to others applying runtime monitoring in practice (Sect. 7). Our policies formalizing infrastructure outages, although specific to Internet Computer in their current form, generalize well to other systems. Moreover, our policies that formalize properties of the Internet Computer's protocol may be adapted to other distributed systems with replicated execution proceeding in rounds.

2 Background

Runtime Monitoring. A runtime monitor [4,25] verifies whether a running system satisfies a *policy* by observing the system's execution. We now briefly describe the MonPoly monitor [12], its policy language called metric first-order temporal logic (MFOTL) [10], and data-parallel monitoring [38].

We fix a set of event names $\mathbb{E}$, an infinite domain $\mathbb{D}$ of values, and an infinite set $\mathbb{V}$ of variables such that $\mathbb{E}$, $\mathbb{D}$, and $\mathbb{V}$ are pairwise disjoint. Let $\mathbb{T}$ be a set of terms over variables in $\mathbb{V}$. In the case of MonPoly, the domain $\mathbb{D}$ contains integers, floats, and strings, and the constant and function symbols available in terms provide basic arithmetic operations over integers and floats. For example, $x + 4$ is a well-formed term. Let Ω be a set of aggregation functions that map multisets over $\mathbb{D}$ to $\mathbb{D} \cup \{\bot\}$. For example, $\mathsf{SUM} \in \Omega$ computes $\mathsf{SUM}(\{\!|1, 1, 3, 4, 4, 5|\!\}) = 18$, but $\mathsf{SUM}(\mathbb{N}) = \bot$ as the result is infinite. Each name $r \in \mathbb{E}$ has an arity $\iota(r) \in \mathbb{N}$. An *event* $r(d_1, \ldots, d_{\iota(r)})$ is an element of $\mathbb{E} \times \mathbb{D}^*$ and $d_i \in \mathbb{D}$ are its *parameters*. Let $\mathbb{I}$ be the set of nonempty intervals $[a, b) := \{x \in \mathbb{N} \mid a \leq x < b\}$, where $a \in \mathbb{N}$ and $b \in \mathbb{N} \cup \{\infty\}$. MFOTL formulas φ are defined inductively, where r, x, $\bar{x}$, t, $\bar{t}$, ω, and I range over $\mathbb{E}$, $\mathbb{V}$, $\mathbb{V}^*$, $\mathbb{T}$, $\mathbb{T}^*$, Ω, and $\mathbb{I}$, respectively:

$$\varphi ::= r(\bar{t}) \mid t = t \mid \neg\varphi \mid \varphi \vee \varphi \mid \exists \bar{x}.\, \varphi \mid \bullet_I \varphi \mid \bigcirc_I \varphi \mid \varphi \, \mathsf{S}_I \, \varphi \mid \varphi \, \mathsf{U}_I \, \varphi$$
$$\mid x \leftarrow \omega\; t; \bar{x}\; \varphi \mid \mathbf{let}\; r(\bar{x}) := \varphi \;\mathbf{in}\; \varphi$$

The set $\mathsf{fv}(\varphi)$ contains φ's free variables. Formulas of the form $r(\bar{t})$ are called *predicates* and require $|\bar{t}| = \iota(r)$. The temporal operators $\bullet_I$ (previous), $\bigcirc_I$ (next), S_I (since), and U_I (until) may be nested arbitrarily. The aggregation operator $r \leftarrow \omega\; t; \bar{g}\; \varphi$ requires $\bar{g} \cup \mathsf{fv}(t) \subseteq \mathsf{fv}(\varphi)$ and $r \notin \mathsf{fv}(\varphi)$. The let operator $\mathbf{let}\; r(\bar{x}) := \varphi \;\mathbf{in}\; \psi$ requires $\bar{x} = \mathsf{fv}(\varphi)$ and it (re)defines $\iota(r) = |\bar{x}|$ in ψ. We distinguish the let predicates (defined by a let operator) from the input predicates. We derive other operators: truth $\top := \exists x.\, x = x$, inequality $t_1 \neq t_2 := \neg(t_1 = t_2)$, conjunction $\varphi \wedge \psi := \neg(\neg\varphi \vee \neg\psi)$, and once $\blacklozenge_I \varphi := \top \, \mathsf{S}_I \, \varphi$.

A valuation v is a mapping $\mathbb{V} \to \mathbb{D}$, assigning domain elements to variables. We write $v[\bar{x} \mapsto \bar{d}]$ for the function equal to v, except that the variables $\bar{x}$ are mapped to values $\bar{d}$, where $|\bar{x}| = |\bar{d}|$. Overloading notation, v is extended to the domain $\mathbb{T}$, evaluating the term t based on the valuations of $\mathsf{fv}(t)$. A *trace* is an infinite sequence $(\tau_i, D_i)_{i \in \mathbb{N}}$ of *timestamp* ($\tau_i \in \mathbb{N}$), *database* ($D_i \in 2^{\mathbb{E} \times \mathbb{D}^*}$) pairs. Timestamps in a trace are *monotone* ($\forall i.\ \tau_i \leq \tau_{i+1}$) and *progressing* ($\forall \tau.\ \exists i.\ \tau < \tau_i$). Databases are finite. Given a trace $\rho = (\tau_i, D_i)_{i \in \mathbb{N}}$, we write $\rho[r(\bar{x}) \mapsto R]$ for the trace $\rho' = (\tau'_i, D'_i)_{i \in \mathbb{N}}$ with $\tau'_i = \tau_i$ and $D'_i = D_i - \{r(\bar{d}) \mid \bar{d} \in \mathbb{D}^{\iota(r)}\} \cup \{r(\mathsf{map}(v, \bar{x})) \mid v \in R(i)\}$ for all $i \in \mathbb{N}$, where R is a function from natural numbers to sets of valuations. The function $\mathsf{map}(f, [d_1, \ldots, d_n])$ returns

$v, i \models_\rho r(\bar{t})$ if $r(\mathsf{map}(v, \bar{t})) \in D_i$ | $v, i \models_\rho t_1 = t_2$ if $v(t_1) = v(t_2)$
$v, i \models_\rho \neg\varphi$ if $v, i \not\models_\rho \varphi$ | $v, i \models_\rho \varphi \vee \psi$ if $v, i \models_\rho \varphi$ or $v, i \models_\rho \psi$
$v, i \models_\rho \exists \bar{x}.\ \varphi$ if $v[\bar{x} \mapsto \bar{d}], i \models_\rho \varphi$ for some $\bar{d} \in \mathbb{D}^{|\bar{x}|}$
$v, i \models_\rho \bullet_I \varphi$ if $i > 0$, $\tau_i - \tau_{i-1} \in I$, and $v, i-1 \models_\rho \varphi$
$v, i \models_\rho \bigcirc_I \varphi$ if $\tau_{i+1} - \tau_i \in I$ and $v, i+1 \models_\rho \varphi$
$v, i \models_\rho \varphi \mathsf{S}_I \psi$ if $v, j \models_\rho \psi$ for some $j \leq i$, $\tau_i - \tau_j \in I$, $v, k \models_\rho \varphi$ for all k, $j < k \leq i$
$v, i \models_\rho \varphi \mathsf{U}_I \psi$ if $v, j \models_\rho \psi$ for some $j \geq i$, $\tau_j - \tau_i \in I$, $v, k \models_\rho \varphi$ for all k, $i \leq k < j$
$v, i \models_\rho r \leftarrow \omega\ t; \bar{g}\ \varphi$ if $v(r) = \omega(M)$ and if $M = \emptyset$ then $\bar{g} = \emptyset$,
where $\bar{b} = \mathsf{fv}(\varphi) - \bar{g}$ and $M = \{\!|v[\bar{b} \mapsto \bar{d}](t) \mid v[\bar{b} \mapsto \bar{d}], i \models_\rho \varphi$ for some $\bar{d} \in \mathbb{D}^{|\bar{b}|}|\!\}$
$v, i \models_\rho \mathbf{let}\ r(\bar{x}) := \varphi\ \mathbf{in}\ \psi$ if $v, i \models_{\rho[r(\bar{x}) \mapsto \lambda j. \{u \mid u, j \models_\rho \varphi\}]} \psi$

Fig. 1. Semantics of MFOTL

$[f(d_1), \ldots, f(d_n)]$. The relation $v, i \models_\rho \varphi$ (Fig. 1) defines the satisfaction of the formula φ for a valuation v at an index i with respect to the trace ρ.

A *runtime monitor* like MonPoly monitors an MFOTL *policy formula* φ by incrementally observing a finite prefix of some execution trace and computing a set of valuations and indices that satisfy φ given the observed prefix. The formula φ typically formalizes the negation of a *policy*, i.e., a desired system property, such that each valuation–index pair indicates a *violation* of the policy.

We distinguish between events and *log entries*, which are text strings reported by a running system. For monitoring, a log entry like "`[WARN] TLS handshake failed`" is mapped to zero or more events like $\mathsf{TLSError}()$ and $\mathsf{Log}(\ldots, \mathtt{WARN}, \ldots)$. A recent survey [25] overviews existing monitoring tools and their languages.

Target System. The Internet Computer (IC) [40] is a public, blockchain-based distributed platform for general-purpose Web3 applications (*apps*), also known as smart contracts. The IC's distributed nature and its replication are transparent to the app developers and users. Users submit their requests and the apps process them, possibly communicating with other apps, and reply back to the users.

The machines (*nodes*) running the IC's protocol are partitioned into *subnets* [40] (currently 13–40 nodes), each replicating and executing a set of apps. Thus, unlike most other blockchain-based platforms, the IC does not employ a global consensus protocol; instead, nodes participate in consensus only among their subnet peers. Each subnet maintains its own (small) blockchain instance, characterized by blocks each occurring at a *height* (the block's position in the chain). Besides the metadata (e.g., timestamps), blocks contain app requests from users and from apps on other subnets. Each subnet produces blocks at rates as high as ca. 0.5–1.0 blocks/s. To ensure that consensus is not just fast, but also trustworthy, each subnet's nodes are hosted on servers distributed among many stakeholders, e.g., data center providers from multiple countries and jurisdictions. A special app called *registry* maintains the IC configuration (e.g., active nodes and their assignment to subnets) and logs configuration changes.

The IC currently consists of more than 1,200 nodes, hosting ca. 150,000 apps [3]. The IC generates ca. 1,500 log entries per second, i.e., over 400 GB

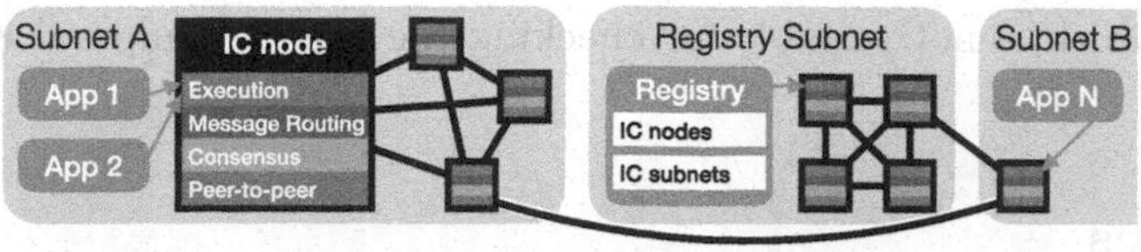

Fig. 2. Overview of the IC

of logs per day across all nodes. Each node has four layers (Fig. 2): (i) the *peer-to-peer* layer reliably disseminates information among nodes; (ii) the *consensus* layer validates and orders the requests to the apps; (iii) the *message routing* layer delivers those requests to the apps; and (iv) the *execution* layer runs the apps.

System Testing and Metrics. The development process of distributed systems such as the IC involves various kinds of testing. Here we focus on *system testing*, i.e., end-to-end testing of the complete system *in isolation* from the production environment. In system testing, a new software version, constituting the system under test (SUT), is deployed over a dedicated testing infrastructure. Requests are then sent to the SUT via its public interface. Optionally, the SUT is manipulated in a controlled way, modeling effects like network failures or configuration changes. Finally, the test checks if the SUT responded to all the requests correctly.

Unlike runtime monitoring, system tests do not check if the sequence of states that arise during the system execution is correct. Instead, they only check the system's final output. Moreover, scenarios covered by system testing are fixed *a priori*. These aspects limit the issues that can be potentially detected by system testing.

Even if the system is well-tested, detecting, e.g., unforeseen real-world attacks requires *observability*, i.e., the degree to which the internal state can be determined based on system's output [28]. Observability is crucial also for other requirements that are not covered by system testing: auditing, accounting, performance assessments, and design feedback [37]. For example, observability enables engineers to recognize failures and users to confirm whether the system does what is promised.

In practice, distributed systems typically output additional data, called *metrics*, into an external centralized metrics database [37]. IC's metrics enable humans to observe and visualize, e.g., the height of the blockchain or the number of requests submitted to a subnet. Programmatic rules running atop of the metrics database, called *alerts*, can send notifications, e.g., to the developers of the IC, whenever the block production rate drops below a threshold value. Metrics are a lossy representation of the system state as they are locally preprocessed before being sent. As they do not record the context that has lead to an alert, developers need other data sources, like logs, to find an alert's root cause. Furthermore, metrics are typically collected periodically (as defined by the metrics database), which is not suitable for checking the precise temporal evolution of the system's state.

3 Policies

In this section, we first describe *how* we devised new IC policies (Sect. 3.1) and then present a selection of those policies that we formalized (Sect. 3.2).

3.1 Methodology

Operational concerns were the main driver for the policies we formulated. In particular, we wanted to ensure that logs are produced consistently, abnormal node behavior can be detected, and crucial properties of the IC protocol (like agreement on requests, progress, and recovery from failure [40]) hold. We did not aim to exhaustively cover all properties of the IC. We focused instead on aspects that cannot be sufficiently covered by existing system tests and metric-based alerts. For example, system tests cannot detect malicious behavior in the production system, and metrics are ill-suited to observe a subnet's behavior holistically.

We started with high-level, natural-language specifications based on the existing logging instrumentation provided by the IC software engineers. In most cases, however, the logged information was insufficient for monitoring. To bridge this gap, we proceeded iteratively; each iteration started with a formalization attempt for a high-level specification. Since this required precise knowledge about which events are observable from which logs, we consulted with the engineers who provided insights on the implementation of particular system components and extended the log messages when necessary. In some cases, the developers concluded that logging the requested events was infeasible, so the affected policies had to be abandoned (see also Sect. 5).

Next, we performed preliminary monitoring of the policies on sample logs and analyzed the output. We then *triaged* each violation, classifying it as (1) a *true bug* in the system, (2) an *imprecise policy* due to insufficient understanding of the system, or (3) a *formalization error*, e.g., due to typos or an incorrect understanding of MFOTL semantics. In some cases, we could not easily triage the violation. We then contacted the IC software engineers who either provided insights for improving the policy or, in case of true bugs, submitted bug reports to IC's internal issue tracker. To date, more kinds of true bugs have been discovered while *developing* the preliminary policies than while monitoring their final version.

3.2 Policy Formulas

Our policies cover three broad categories, which differ in their scope and generality, and which demonstrate a variety of runtime monitoring use cases. We present policy formulas for just a few selected policies. These policies showcase

Table 1. Summary of MFOTL-based IC policies

Policy	Past	Fut	Agg	Loc	Reg	Test	Prod	Ops1	Ops2
`clean-logs`	✓	–	–	✓	✓	✓	✓	13	11
`logging-behavior`	✓	✓	✓	–	✓	✓	✓	54	1,098
`finalized-height`	✓	–	–	–	✓	✓	–	56	89
`finalization-consistency`	✓	–	–	–	✓	✓	–	16	22
`replica-divergence`	✓	–	–	✓	✓	✓	–	16	13
`block-validation-latency`	✓	✓	✓	–	✓	✓	–	50	229
`unauthorized-connections`	✓	–	–	✓	✓	✓	✓	22	39
`reboot-count`	✓	–	✓	–	✓	✓	✓	25	21

the most challenging aspects of formalizing distributed system properties and justify the required features of MFOTL. The accompanying artifact [7] provides all formulas.

Table 1 summarizes the IC policies and the characteristics of the MFOTL policy formulas that formalize them. All formulas contain at least one past-temporal operator (column Past). There are two formulas with a future operator (Fut), and three formulas that use aggregations (Agg). Three policies can be monitored locally (Loc) on each node using only the node's log entries. All policies depend on the initial IC configuration obtained using the IC registry app (Reg) and they can be checked against the testing logs (Test). Finally, four of the policies can also be checked against the IC's production log (Prod), whereas the other policies require debug-level log entries, which are not available in production in order to decrease the load on the logging infrastructure. We estimated the complexity of the formulas by counting the numbers of their unary and binary operators before unfolding the **let** definitions (Ops1) and after (Ops2).

Common Fragments. Some aspects are shared by all policies, e.g., the policies restrict the behavior of *active* nodes only. A subset of policies additionally requires knowledge about which node belongs to which subnet at any point in time. As explained earlier, the IC's configuration can be changed by a voting-driven governance mechanism and hence we must observe configuration changes to correctly monitor these policies. We devised the following pattern to express both the set of currently active nodes n (predicate $\mathsf{InIC}(n)$) and the property that a node n belongs to a subnet s (predicate $\mathsf{InSubnet}(n,s)$):

$$\mathsf{In\underline{X}}(\bar{p}) := \big((\blacklozenge\, \mathsf{In\underline{X}_0}(\bar{p})) \wedge \neg \blacklozenge\, \mathsf{RegistryRemove\underline{X}}(\bar{p})\big) \vee \big(\neg \mathsf{RegistryRemove\underline{X}}(\bar{p})\ \mathsf{S}\ \mathsf{RegistryAdd\underline{X}}(\bar{p})\big)$$

With $\underline{\mathsf{X}} = \mathsf{IC}$ and $\bar{p} = [n]$, we define the predicate $\mathsf{InIC}(n)$ and, with $\underline{\mathsf{X}} = \mathsf{Subnet}$ and $\bar{p} = [n, s]$, we define the predicate $\mathsf{InSubnet}(n, s)$. The $\mathsf{InIC}(n)$ and $\mathsf{InIC_0}(n)$ predicates determine whether the node n belongs to the IC at the

clean-logs:
  let $\mathsf{InIC}(n) := \cdots$ **in**
  let $\mathsf{ErrorLevel}(l) := (l = \texttt{"CRITICAL"}) \lor (l = \texttt{"ERROR"})$ **in**
  $\mathsf{InIC}(n) \land \mathsf{Log}(h, n, s, c, l, m) \land \mathsf{ErrorLevel}(l)$

finalized-height:
  let $\mathsf{InSubnet}(n, s) := \cdots$ **in**
  let $\mathsf{Growing}(s) := \exists n_1, n_2.\, \mathsf{InSubnet}(n_1, s) \land \mathsf{InSubnet}(n_2, s) \land n_1 \neq n_2 \land$
    $\neg(\neg \mathsf{p2pRemoveNode}(n_1, s, n_2) \;\mathsf{S}\; \mathsf{p2pAddNode}(n_1, s, n_2))$ **in**
  let $\mathsf{Shrinking}(s) := \exists n_1, n_2.\, \mathsf{InSubnet}(n_1, s) \land$
    $\big((\neg \mathsf{p2pRemoveNode}(n_1, s, n_2) \;\mathsf{S}\; \mathsf{p2pAddNode}(n_1, s, n_2)) \lor$
    $\mathsf{InSubnet}(n_1, s) \land (\blacklozenge \mathsf{InSubnet_0}(n_2, s)) \land$
    $\neg(\blacklozenge \mathsf{p2pRemoveNode}(n_1, s, n_2)) \land \neg(\blacklozenge \exists s'.\, \mathsf{p2pAddNode}(n_1, s', n_2))\big) \land$
    $\neg \mathsf{InSubnet}(n_2, s)$ **in**
  let $\mathsf{Changing}(s) := \mathsf{Growing}(s) \lor \mathsf{Shrinking}(s)$ **in**
  let $\mathsf{First}(n, s, h, b, v) := \mathsf{Finalized}(n, s, h, b, v) \land \neg \bullet \blacklozenge \exists n'.\mathsf{Finalized}(n', s, h, b, v)$ **in**
  $(\neg \mathsf{Changing}(s) \;\mathsf{S}_{(80\mathrm{s},\infty)}\; \mathsf{First}(n_1, s, h_1, b_1, v)) \land \mathsf{First}(n_2, s, h_2, b_2, v) \land h_2 = h_1 + 1$

Fig. 3. Examples of policy formulas

current moment and when monitoring originally started, respectively. The predicates $\mathsf{InSubnet}(n, s)$ and $\mathsf{InSubnet_0}(n, s)$ are analogous. The input predicates prefixed with Registry directly correspond to log entries from the IC registry app; these events indicate the removal and addition of IC nodes (to a subnet or the IC). To maintain the predicates, we rely on the IC registry as opposed to relying on (potentially incorrect) node-local information. For each node n, the $\mathsf{InIC_0}(n)$ and $\mathsf{InSubnet_0}(n, s)$ events are prepended to the log by querying the registry before monitoring starts.

We use MFOTL's **let** to define the InIC and InSubnet predicates. As their definitions are syntactically encapsulated, it is easy to keep them in sync across all policies in case input predicates change.

Generic Policies. Our goal here is to detect general signs of system malfunction.

clean-logs. The log entries produced by IC nodes have different priority levels. Our `clean-logs` policy asserts that only *warning-* and *info*-level log entries are allowed, whereas *critical-* or *error*-level entries are not. In the IC, these levels indicate logical errors, violation of assumptions, or similarly severe problems. The corresponding formula (Fig. 3, top) uses the $\mathsf{Log}(h, n, s, c, l, m)$ predicate, which is satisfied by every log message m emitted by component c running on node n in subnet s with host name h, where l is the log level. As previously noted, we ignore decommissioned nodes. We also formulate all policy formulas to be satisfied whenever the corresponding policy is violated.

logging-behavior. Although `clean-logs` can detect many problems, it only produces violations once a fault has already become a failure. In contrast, the `logging-behavior` policy aims to detect faults before the failure occurs. We use the fact that operations are replicated on multiple nodes of a subnet: If the *frequency* of the log entries matching the replicated operations deviates on a relatively small group of nodes within a subnet, this indicates that the nodes are in an abnormal state that may lead to failure. For each subnet, the policy compares its nodes' logging frequencies computed over a *sliding window* [2] against the *median* logging frequency over all nodes in the subnet.

This policy formula uses multiple aggregations (count, sum, median, minimum, and maximum) and both past and future temporal operators. We also use *regular expression matching*, a recent addition to MonPoly, to select log entries that belong to a replicated operation. As the typical behavior may change over time depending on the workload, we incorporate smoothing to avoid false positives. Specifically, we estimate the typical behavior from multiple overlapping time intervals. Since log frequencies vary significantly between IC node layers (Sect. 2), we monitor this policy separately for each layer.

IC Protocol Policies. We summarize some properties of the IC consensus protocol [14] used in this group of policies. Given a subnet of n nodes, among which f are faulty (i.e., behaving in a *Byzantine way* [34]) and the remaining $n-f$ nodes adhere to the protocol, the condition $n \geq 3f+1$ must hold (otherwise, consensus is not possible [26]). Intuitively, this means that to achieve consensus, more than ⅔ of the subnet nodes *must not* be faulty, where the lowest tolerated number of non-faulty nodes is $2f+1$. The IC consensus protocol uses the concept of *rounds*; out of all the *block proposals* created by the nodes for round r, exactly one block is *finalized*, i.e., irreversibly added to the blockchain at *height* r.

Violations of the following IC protocol policies indicate software bugs or the presence of more than f faulty nodes in a subnet.

finalized-height. To ensure that a subnet's consensus makes progress, this policy checks that the block at height $h+1$ in a subnet is finalized by some node no later than 80 s after the *earliest* finalization of the block at height h. The time between finalizations depends on node failures and network conditions. In practice, the mean time elapsed between two finalized blocks is around 1 s. 80 s is thus a rather conservative upper bound that allows us to turn a probabilistic property into a safety property that we can monitor automatically.

The nodes changing their subnet membership require care, as the upper bound on the time between finalizations may be exceeded, specifically, when a new node is *catching up*, e.g., due to a temporary network outage. We therefore ignore violations that occur during subnet membership changes. To detect changing subnets, we over-approximate by comparing the registry's view of the subnet membership to the nodes' own view (as captured by the p2pAddNode and p2pRemoveNode events from the peer-to-peer communication layer).

The formula illustrates how **let** operators reduce formula duplication and improve its structure (Fig. 3, bottom). Specifically, we define the InSubnet predicate as explained above. The predicate Growing on subnets is satisfied if a node in the subnet is not yet aware of another node in the same subnet, while the predicate Shrinking detects when a node still considers another node as part of the same subnet whereas the registry does not. In both cases, we over-approximate because the nodes' local view is not known before one of the two p2p events has been observed. A subnet is considered to be Changing if it is Growing or Shrinking.

The condition on the time between finalizations is expressed using a metric temporal operator in the policy's formula (Fig. 3, bottom), where the let predicate $\mathsf{First}(n, s, h, b, v)$ represents the first finalization (event Finalized) of block b at height h by some node (specifically node n) in subnet s, running IC software version v. The S operator asserts that there is such a finalization by node n_1 more than 80 s ago (the interval $(80\,\text{s}, \infty)$ is open), and its subnet must not have been changing in the meantime. To detect a violation, the policy must additionally observe a finalization *at the next height* by node n_2.

finalization-consistency. This policy represents the core correctness property of the IC consensus protocol: when a node finalizes a block at a given height, no other node in the same subnet finalizes a different block at the same height.

replica-divergence. This policy expresses a *liveness* property. Whenever the replicated state maintained by the nodes is not the same on all nodes in a subnet, the nodes must eventually detect and overcome this *divergence*. State divergence might occur even in absence of malicious behavior, e.g., due to software bugs or hardware problems. A subnet can overcome a divergence when at least $2f + 1$ of its nodes have the same replicated state. The protocol achieves this as nodes periodically emit *shares* based on their local replicated state; $2f + 1$ such shares are needed for *catch-up packages*—messages enabling the nodes to restore the correct state and contribute to the consensus protocol again. In particular, a catch-up package contains the hash of the correct replicated state, which allows nodes to detect that they have diverged and obtain the correct state. However, only shares from $2f + 1$ nodes with the same state can be used for a catch-up package. Hence, if a node's share contributes to a catch-up package after the node has diverged, this indicates that the node has since corrected its local state.

Note that system tests always produce finite logs; this enables us to phrase the policy as a *safety* property: $\mathsf{End}() \wedge \mathsf{InSubnet}(a, \_, s) \wedge (\neg \mathsf{CupShareProposed}(a, s)\ \mathsf{S}\ \mathsf{Diverged}(a, s))$. Here, $\mathsf{CupShareProposed}(a, s)$ holds when a catch-up package share is proposed by node a of subnet s. $\mathsf{Diverged}(a, s)$ indicates that a has reported a state divergence (recall that our formulas express the *negation* of the required properties). Lastly, $\mathsf{End}()$, which is added by the preprocessor, is the final event in the stream. Intuitively, the nullary predicate $\mathsf{End}()$ binds the formula to the final time point of the test.

block-validation-latency. This policy formalizes network progress before finalization is reached. Recall that the IC consensus protocol proceeds in rounds. In each round, the nodes may create and propose new blocks to their peers via the P2P layer. When receiving these blocks, the peers declare them validated if a set of conditions is satisfied; these conditions concern the block's metadata

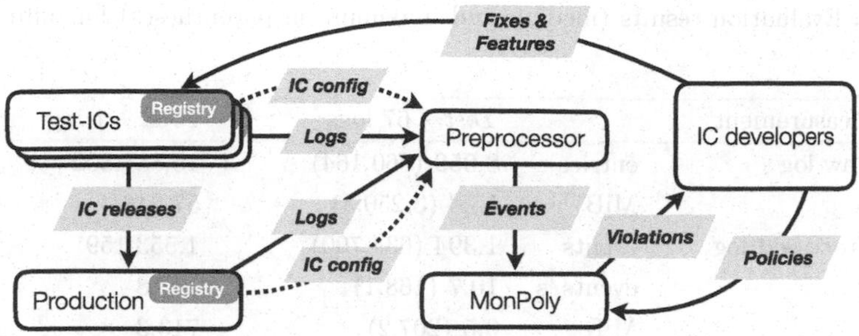

Fig. 4. Overview of IC's monitoring pipeline. Rounded boxes are parties involved in monitoring, arrows depict data flow, and dotted arrows show initial pipeline steps.

and the app requests, e.g., authentication. Upon validating the block, the node informs its peers. Progress to the next round is possible only if *more* than ⅔ of the nodes validate a block. This policy measures the time until a block proposal created at one node has been validated by more than ⅔ of the nodes in the same subnet; the policy then checks that this time does not exceed a threshold.

***unauthorized-connections*.** IC nodes should receive peer-to-peer connections only from other nodes within the same subnet. As these connections are secured by TLS [41], any illicit connection attempt should cause a TLS handshake failure as the certificate is rejected. This policy states that such failures must not occur unless the illicitly connecting node and the receiver were members of the same subnet *in the recent past* (we set the threshold to 15 min), as the nodes may not have learned yet that they are no longer peers.

Infrastructure Outage. We also consider platform-level aspects of the IC.

***reboot-count*.** Data center problems may be accompanied by frequent server reboots. This policy identifies problematic data centers, detecting when servers hosting IC nodes within a data center are rebooted too frequently. For each data center, the policy counts the number of unplanned (re-)boots within the past 30 min; for this purpose, we employ the count aggregation and the ⧫ operator. A violation is emitted if the number of reboots exceeds two, i.e., up to two reboots are tolerated. Data centers are identified by prefixes of the node's IPv6 address, which are available as predicate arguments (Sect. 4).

4 Evaluation

In our evaluation of MonPoly's performance, we address the following questions: (Q1) How much time and memory does MonPoly require for monitoring complex policies *offline*? (Q2) Is MonPoly able to monitor the IC's production logs *online*? (Q3) What are the main performance and scalability factors?

Table 2. Evaluation results (median and maximum in parentheses) for offline monitoring

Measurement		*Test* – 67 logs		*Prod* – 1 log	
Raw log	entries	8,059 (860,164)		16,887,502	
	MiB	15.6 (3,250.3)		57,216.4	
Processed log	events	1,394 (634,790)		1,553,159	
	events/s	10.7 (168.1)		143.8	
	MiB	0.5 (207.2)		713.3	
Preprocessor time	ms/entry	0.12 (5.61)		0.07 (0.08)	
		ms/event	MiB	ms/event	MiB
`clean-logs`		3.20 (145.0)	10 (10)	3.93	11
`logging-behavior`		2.74 (144.4)	11 (1265)	TO	TO
`unauthorized-connections`*		3.09 (145.6)	10 (1109)	TO	TO
`reboot-count`		2.68 (151.1)	10 (11)	3.54	11
`finalized-height`*		3.93 (138.7)	10 (19)	–	–
`finalization-consistency`		2.57 (143.1)	10 (16)	–	–
`replica-divergence`		2.80 (145.2)	10 (10)	–	–
`block-validation-latency`†		5.04 (143.1)	13 (26)	–	–

* Timeout on 1 log each. † Timeout on 3 logs.

Pipeline. We implemented a *monitoring pipeline* (Fig. 4) that downloads logs from the IC's log server (either from a *Test-IC* or from production), preprocesses them, and manages MonPoly's execution. The same pipeline was added to the IC's continuous development workflow, alerting IC software engineers of detected policy violations and providing them with the context required to reproduce and investigate the underlying problems. The pipeline's log *preprocessor* converts log entries into events encoded in MonPoly's input format. Most events require simple syntactic manipulations (e.g., extracting parameters with regular expressions), but some require information about the IC configuration, e.g., the mapping between node IDs and IP addresses. The preprocessor obtains this information, as well as the $\mathsf{InIC_0}$ and $\mathsf{InSubnet_0}$ events (Sect. 3.2), from the registry.

The top half of Table 2 summarizes basic properties of logs used in our experiments, aggregating data across all logs and, where applicable, policies. The median is shown as well as the maximum in parentheses. We obtained logs from the IC's system tests (*Test*) as well as a three hour fragment of the production log (*Prod*). For repeatability, this step was performed separately from the experiments and the logs were stored as files. The *Test* logs were collected from 3 runs of every system test in the IC's hourly and nightly test suites, over a 3-day period. We only considered successful test runs, as a failed test already requires an engineer's attention and monitoring would not add much value. In both *Test* and *Prod* logs, the pipeline's preprocessor discarded all log entries that cannot be assigned to an IC node, e.g., messages from *systemd*.

We approximated the time spent in preprocessing. Since the pipeline transforms log entries on the fly before sending the events to the monitor, we accumulated the time spent in the preprocessing step for each entry ("preprocessor time"). Due to the logs' diversity, we normalized this value by dividing it by the number of log entries; the result is the inverse of throughput.

We instrumented the pipeline to collect performance measurements for offline monitoring (Q1). Specifically, we obtained the wall-clock time for the combined execution of pipeline and monitor ("monitoring time") and the peak resident set size ("monitoring memory") of the MonPoly process. Monitoring time was normalized based on the number of *events* comprising the input to MonPoly. To address Q2, we simulated a real-time log stream based on the stored fragment of the production log, using a *replayer* [33] that writes the log entries at the appropriate time to MonPoly's input. We performed additional experiments to answer Q3.

We ran at most 13 experiments in parallel on a server with two 3 GHz 16-core AMD EPYC 7302 CPUs, 512 GiB RAM, and an SSD. We used Linux 5.4.0 as the operating system and the MonPoly Docker image 1.4.2 as the monitor. All the logs, policies, and code used in our experiments are publicly available [7].

Offline Monitoring. The bottom half of Table 2 shows the aggregated performance measurements for offline monitoring, i.e., processing the stored logs as quickly as the monitor allows. We instantiated the monitoring pipeline separately for every combination of policy and log (i.e., system test run or the production fragment). For *Test*, the table shows the median (and maximum) monitoring time and memory. Some of the policies are not applicable to production (see Table 1) and hence are marked with '–'. We set a timeout of 30 min for *Test* to limit the experiments' duration. It was reached in five runs, which are excluded from the results, as shown in the table. For *Prod*, we set a timeout of 4 h (the length of the *Prod* fragment plus a safety margin), marked 'TO' in the table.

The results for the *Test* scenario are similar across policies, with few exceptions. Both `logging-behavior` and `unauthorized-connections` require significantly more memory on certain inputs, since they store many snapshots of the InSubnet relation in proportion to the *index rate*, i.e., the number of indices in the corresponding trace per unit of real time. The relation's size depends on the number of nodes created in the test. The policies perform nontrivial computations for every event *and* node, resulting in the timeouts for *Prod*, which has ten times more nodes than *Test*. The timeouts for `block-validation-latency` are likely caused by the larger number of subnets (29 compared to maximal 3) in the corresponding logs; we plan to confirm this in the future. The other two *Test* timeouts occurred with the largest log file (3.3 times the size of the next largest).

Online Monitoring. Long-running systems like the IC are not expected to terminate and hence they produce logs with unbounded streams of events. Therefore,

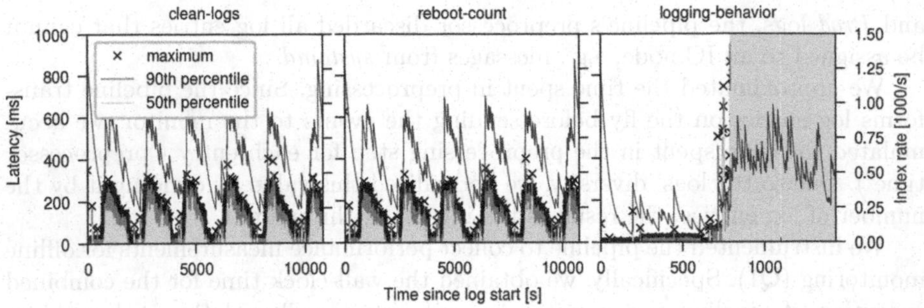

Fig. 5. Replayer latency for online monitoring

online monitoring with low (bounded) latency is a prerequisite for continuous monitoring. Logging activity may also be bursty, rendering the offline performance a bad predictor for the online case. We therefore conducted separate online monitoring experiments using the *Prod* data. Specifically, we measured the latency *at the replayer*, which was provided with an already processed log. While this measure is not equivalent to end-to-end latency, it is practically relevant as it indicates how much log data must be buffered by system components *before* the monitor.

Figure 5 shows the latency distribution over elapsed time, relative to the log entries' time-stamps. For the `clean-logs` and `reboot-count` policies, we observed regular bursts of increased latency. Since the maximum latency does not grow over time, it would be possible to monitor these policies online in a production deployment. The bursts are clearly correlated with the index rate as shown by the thin line drawn on top of the latency distribution.

In contrast, the latency increased steeply after approximately 13 min for `logging-behavior`, simultaneously with the first index rate burst. The experiment was terminated once a latency of 10 min was reached. We do not show results for the `unauthorized-connections` policy as it immediately reached the latency limit. The quickly increasing latency indicates that the time spent monitoring the events generated within an interval of real time is longer than the interval itself. This coincides with the timeouts observed in the offline experiments.

In addition to the above experiments, we parallelized online monitoring of the *Prod* fragment using an existing framework [38]. We observed improvements but were unable to achieve low-latency monitoring for `logging-behavior` and `unauthorized-connections`. We conjecture that the framework's inability to reduce the index rate observed by the parallel monitors prevents latency reduction.

Results. We found that offline monitoring of IC system test logs is possible using moderate resources: monitoring extends the tests' runtime by less than

23%,[1] while the peak memory usage of MonPoly was 5 GiB (Q1). Low-latency online monitoring was possible for two applicable policies (Q2). By analyzing this result, we identified three factors that significantly influence online monitoring performance, namely, repeating relational computations, future operators, and eager processing of **let** expressions (Q3). We believe that the insights from our case study are helpful to developers of other monitoring tools.

5 Lessons Learned

We now summarize our case study's qualitative findings on policy engineering and monitoring maintainability.

Policy Engineering. Introducing runtime monitoring into an existing system is challenging. Policy engineering is the process of *identifying* sources of policies, *selecting* useful policies, and making them *precise* and *formal*. The distinction between the last two characteristics is crucial: we argue that the former is difficult to achieve (even using natural language), whereas the latter is relatively straightforward for runtime monitoring experts, if the policy is already precise.

Colombo and Pace [18] claim that policies should not be defined by developers, but rather by a quality assurance (QA) team, as the policies address end users and concern high-level system properties. We agree with this assessment in part: IC policies were sourced from IC's formal method engineers who knew the system and its high-level properties well. However, additional software engineers and researchers were still needed to confirm the semantics of the existing log entries observed by the monitor and possibly augment logging, for example by adding new parameters or new events. Software engineers also had to evaluate the production impact of such modifications (e.g., due to an increase in log volume), and on the debugging processes (e.g., due to increased noise). Such developer insights crucially influenced the final policies. We decided to drop various drafted policies due to the lack of the required log entries.

Colombo and Pace argue that monitoring policies assured by other engineering techniques (e.g., unit testing) is wasteful. They identify cross-cutting properties [18] as the most useful policy class. We agree but additional selection criteria are also relevant. Namely, policies must be *effective* (i.e., capable of detecting relevant problems), *precise* (i.e., producing a low number of false violations), and *actionable* (i.e., given a true violation, a developer can debug it).

We found that an iterative process is needed to devise sufficiently precise policies. Even domain experts can be misguided by their intuition, suggesting policies that fail to account for corner cases and recent system changes. Natural language ambiguity is another source of imprecision. Moreover, typos and logical errors may occur in policy formalizations. In our case study, we experienced all these issues.

[1] Maximum monitoring time (80 min) divided by the longest test (362 min).

Finally, we mention some MFOTL policy formula patterns that commonly appeared in our formalizations. Such patterns implement policies that are intuitively and easily expressible in natural language, but cannot be encoded using a single operator of the policy language. For example, one could expect that valuations assigning 0 to c satisfy the policy $c \leftarrow \text{CNT}\ m; n\ \mathsf{Log}(n, m)$ when monitoring a trace without any Log events. However, this is not the case according to MFOTL's semantics as $\mathsf{Log}(n, m)$ is not satisfiable for any n. Sometimes it is necessary to report such valuations (typically, for a finite set values of n). Our formalization of `logging-behavior` demonstrates a pattern that achieves this:

$$c \leftarrow \text{SUM}\ c; n\ \Big(\big((c \leftarrow \text{CNT}\ m; n\ \blacklozenge_I\ \mathsf{Log}(n, m)) \land \mathsf{InIC}(n)\big) \lor \big(\mathsf{InIC}(n) \land c = 0\big)\Big)$$

Here, we count the number of log messages c per node n in an interval I. The result is used to compute the sum of the counts for each node. It is important to include all known nodes (c.f. InIC), even if they did not log any message m in that interval. The above encoding achieves this by adding the actual count to the default of zero (the right disjunct), assigned to *all* nodes. Other common policy formula patterns we identified are *outer joins* [1] and *sliding windows* [2].

Monitoring Maintainability. As in many software projects, engineers assume that logs are inspected by humans, and often freely modify the logging statements [16]. We observed that such changes break the monitoring pipeline outright because the preprocessor fails to process log entries not matching expected patterns. A more challenging problem is that the *meaning* of a log entry may also subtly change, for example, when moved to a different location in the control flow.

To address this, we used system tests that exercise code paths containing policy-relevant logging statements. The test checks if the preprocessor correctly processes log entries. However, we believe that for an evolving system, a structured and type-safe logging interface is necessary to maintain runtime monitoring. Structured logging provides a way of introducing logging statements systematically at different levels of granularity. Type-safe logging can additionally detect a mismatch between the log entry format expected by the monitor and one produced by the logging statements at compile time. Detection of a change in the semantics of a log entry, however, remains an open problem.

6 Related Work

We first summarize approaches to monitoring distributed systems. Afterwards, we describe industrial case studies similar to ours that monitor distributed systems.

A classic result for predicate detection in distributed systems [15] states that exponentially many interleavings of components' traces must be checked in the worst case, which does not scale [27]. Efficient algorithms exist for predicate classes [36] or under certain assumptions [35,39]. Basin et al. [9] monitor distributed systems with a centralized monitor by merging all the components' traces. As in our work, their merged trace has events with same time-stamps occur in an arbitrary order. They further restrict policies to a logical fragment where that order does not influence the monitor's output. Other approaches focus on distributing the monitor. Bauer and Falcone [13] orchestrate multiple distributed monitors based on the structure of the input LTL formula, such that they jointly monitor the input formula with minimal need to exchange knowledge.

Similar approaches hierarchically organize monitors [17], use regular expressions [24], or stream equations [20] as the policy language. None, however, support an expressive language like MFOTL, with the exception of Schneider et al. [8,38], whose framework we used in our attempts to reduce monitoring latency.

Basin et al. [9] monitored Nokia's data usage policies in three databases running on different distributed components; they also monitored Google's network security policies [6]. El-Hokayem and Falcone [23] monitored traces collected from 27 distributed smart apartment sensors. Colombo et al. [19] monitored policies for an online payment service with millions of credit cards. Kane et al. [31] monitor a controller-area automotive network. Unlike the languages used in these works, we use a more expressive first-order temporal policy language with aggregations.

We conducted a systematic literature review, following best practices [32], to identify and classify monitoring case studies. We collected papers from five conferences and two journals by matching keywords related to runtime verification and case studies. This yielded 54 papers that we manually analyzed to select those 33 papers that use temporal logic as policy languages. Our `finalized-height` policy is more complex than any policy we found: it has a greater number of operators (56) than the next most complex one (44) [21]. Note that without the **let** operator, the `logging-behavior` policy would have required more than 1,000 operators.

7 Conclusion

We have shown how to enrich system testing and metrics with runtime monitoring. In our case study, we formalize and monitor complex, non-local, metric first-order temporal policies of the Internet Computer (IC), a real-world distributed system. The monitoring pipeline we use is tailored to the IC, but we believe that its design can serve as blueprint for monitoring other distributed systems. Some of our policies, although IC-specific in their current form, generalize well to other systems, specifically, to replicated distributed systems that execute in rounds. Another contribution to the formal methods community is our data set, which we publish and which provides a challenging benchmark for monitors supporting metric first-order temporal policies with aggregations.

As future work, in addition to formalizing other IC policies, we plan to improve the feedback that monitors provide to engineers. The emerging research area of *explanations* [5] for monitoring verdicts can aid the process of fault localization, e.g., by visualizing minimal parts of the trace causing a violation. Further monitor optimizations are required to achieve practical online monitoring of the IC production deployment by handling high index rates. We conjecture that this problem is solvable taking inspiration from the algorithms used in signal-based monitoring [22].

Acknowledgement. We thank the anonymous reviewers for their comments, and Qijing Yu, Bas van Dijk, and Nikolay Komarevskiy for helping set up this project.

References

1. Abiteboul, S., Hull, R., Vianu, V.: Foundations of Databases. Addison-Wesley, Boston (1995)
2. Arasu, A., Babu, S., Widom, J.: The CQL continuous query language: semantic foundations and query execution. VLDB J. **15**(2), 121–142 (2006)
3. Internet Computer Association. Internet Computer dashboard (2022). https://dashboard.internetcomputer.org/
4. Bartocci, E., Falcone, Y. (eds.): Lectures on Runtime Verification. LNCS, vol. 10457. Springer, Cham (2018). https://doi.org/10.1007/978-3-319-75632-5
5. Basin, D., Bhatt, B.N., Traytel, D.: Optimal proofs for linear temporal logic on lasso words. In: Lahiri, S.K., Wang, C. (eds.) ATVA 2018. LNCS, vol. 11138, pp. 37–55. Springer, Cham (2018). https://doi.org/10.1007/978-3-030-01090-4_3
6. Basin, D., Caronni, G., Ereth, S., Harvan, M., Klaedtke, F., Mantel, H.: Scalable offline monitoring of temporal specifications. Formal Methods Syst. Des. **49**(1), 75–108 (2016). https://doi.org/10.1007/s10703-016-0242-y
7. Basin, D., et al.: Monitoring the Internet Computer (artifact) (2022). https://doi.org/10.5281/zenodo.7340850
8. Basin, D., Gras, M., Krstić, S., Schneider, J.: Scalable online monitoring of distributed systems. In: Deshmukh, J., Ničković, D. (eds.) RV 2020. LNCS, vol. 12399, pp. 197–220. Springer, Cham (2020). https://doi.org/10.1007/978-3-030-60508-7_11
9. Basin, D., Harvan, M., Klaedtke, F., Zălinescu, E.: Monitoring data usage in distributed systems. IEEE Trans. Softw. Eng. **39**(10), 1403–1426 (2013)
10. Basin, D., Klaedtke, F., Marinovic, S., Zălinescu, E.: Monitoring of temporal first-order properties with aggregations. Formal Methods Syst. Des. **46**(3), 262–285 (2015). https://doi.org/10.1007/s10703-015-0222-7
11. Basin, D., Klaedtke, F., Müller, S., Zălinescu, E.: Monitoring metric first-order temporal properties. J. ACM **62**(2), 15:1–15:45 (2015)
12. Basin, D., Klaedtke, F., Zalinescu, E.: The MonPoly monitoring tool. In: Reger, G., Havelund, K. (eds.) International Workshop on Competitions, Usability, Benchmarks, Evaluation, and Standardisation for Runtime Verification Tools (RV-CuBES). Kalpa Publications in Computing, vol. 3, pp. 19–28. EasyChair (2017)
13. Bauer, A., Falcone, Y.: Decentralised LTL monitoring. Formal Methods Syst. Des. **48**(1–2), 46–93 (2016). https://doi.org/10.1007/s10703-016-0253-8
14. Camenisch, J., Drijvers, M., Hanke, T., Pignolet, Y.-A., Shoup, V., Williams, D.: Internet Computer consensus. In: Proceedings of the 2022 ACM Symposium on Principles of Distributed Computing, PODC 2022, pp. 81–91. ACM, New York (2022)

15. Chase, C.M., Garg, V.K.: Detection of global predicates: techniques and their limitations. Distrib. Comput. **11**(4), 191–201 (1998)
16. Chen, B., Jiang, Z.M.: Characterizing logging practices in Java-based open source software projects – a replication study in apache software foundation. Empir. Softw. Eng. **22**(1), 330–374 (2017)
17. Colombo, C., Falcone, Y.: Organising LTL monitors over distributed systems with a global clock. Formal Methods Syst. Des. **49**(1), 109–158 (2016). https://doi.org/10.1007/s10703-016-0251-x
18. Colombo, C., Pace, G.J.: Industrial experiences with runtime verification of financial transaction systems: lessons learnt and standing challenges. In: Bartocci, E., Falcone, Y. (eds.) Lectures on Runtime Verification. LNCS, vol. 10457, pp. 211–232. Springer, Cham (2018). https://doi.org/10.1007/978-3-319-75632-5_7
19. Colombo, C., Pace, G.J., Abela, P.: Safer asynchronous runtime monitoring using compensations. Formal Methods Syst. Des. **41**(3), 269–294 (2012). https://doi.org/10.1007/s10703-012-0142-8
20. Danielsson, L.M., Sánchez, C.: Decentralized stream runtime verification. In: Finkbeiner, B., Mariani, L. (eds.) RV 2019. LNCS, vol. 11757, pp. 185–201. Springer, Cham (2019). https://doi.org/10.1007/978-3-030-32079-9_11
21. Desai, A., Dreossi, T., Seshia, S.A.: Combining model checking and runtime verification for safe robotics. In: Lahiri, S., Reger, G. (eds.) RV 2017. LNCS, vol. 10548, pp. 172–189. Springer, Cham (2017). https://doi.org/10.1007/978-3-319-67531-2_11
22. Deshmukh, J.V., Donzé, A., Ghosh, S., Jin, X., Juniwal, G., Seshia, S.A.: Robust online monitoring of signal temporal logic. In: Bartocci, E., Majumdar, R. (eds.) RV 2015. LNCS, vol. 9333, pp. 55–70. Springer, Cham (2015). https://doi.org/10.1007/978-3-319-23820-3_4
23. El-Hokayem, A., Falcone, Y.: Bringing runtime verification home. In: Colombo, C., Leucker, M. (eds.) RV 2018. LNCS, vol. 11237, pp. 222–240. Springer, Cham (2018). https://doi.org/10.1007/978-3-030-03769-7_13
24. Falcone, Y., Cornebize, T., Fernandez, J.-C.: Efficient and generalized decentralized monitoring of regular languages. In: Ábrahám, E., Palamidessi, C. (eds.) FORTE 2014. LNCS, vol. 8461, pp. 66–83. Springer, Heidelberg (2014). https://doi.org/10.1007/978-3-662-43613-4_5
25. Falcone, Y., Krstić, S., Reger, G., Traytel, D.: A taxonomy for classifying runtime verification tools. Int. J. Softw. Tools Technol. Transfer **23**(2), 255–284 (2021). https://doi.org/10.1007/s10009-021-00609-z
26. Fischer, M.J., Lynch, N.A., Paterson, M.S.: Impossibility of distributed consensus with one faulty process. J. ACM **32**(2), 374–382 (1985)
27. Ganguly, R., et al.: Distributed runtime verification of metric temporal properties for cross-chain protocols. CoRR, abs/2204.09796 (2022)
28. Gopal, M.: Modern Control System Theory. New Age International (1993)
29. Gorostiaga, F., Sánchez, C.: HLola: a very functional tool for extensible stream runtime verification. In: Groote, J.F., Larsen, K.G. (eds.) TACAS 2021. LNCS, vol. 12652, pp. 349–356. Springer, Cham (2021). https://doi.org/10.1007/978-3-030-72013-1_18
30. Havelund, K., Peled, D., Ulus, D.: DejaVu: a monitoring tool for first-order temporal logic. In: 3rd Workshop on Monitoring and Testing of Cyber-Physical Systems, MT@CPSWeek 2018, Porto, Portugal, 10 April 2018, pp. 12–13. IEEE (2018)
31. Kane, A., Chowdhury, O., Datta, A., Koopman, P.: A case study on runtime monitoring of an autonomous research vehicle (ARV) system. In: Bartocci, E., Majum-

dar, R. (eds.) RV 2015. LNCS, vol. 9333, pp. 102–117. Springer, Cham (2015). https://doi.org/10.1007/978-3-319-23820-3_7
32. Kitchenham, B.A., Brereton, P., Budgen, D., Turner, M., Bailey, J., Linkman, S.G.: Systematic literature reviews in software engineering – a systematic literature review. Inf. Softw. Technol. **51**(1), 7–15 (2009)
33. Krstić, S., Schneider, J.: A benchmark generator for online first-order monitoring. In: Deshmukh, J., Ničković, D. (eds.) RV 2020. LNCS, vol. 12399, pp. 482–494. Springer, Cham (2020). https://doi.org/10.1007/978-3-030-60508-7_27
34. Lamport, L., Shostak, R., Pease, M.: The Byzantine generals problem. ACM Trans. Program. Lang. Syst. **4**(3), 382–401 (1982)
35. Momtaz, A., Basnet, N., Abbas, H., Bonakdarpour, B.: Predicate monitoring in distributed cyber-physical systems. In: Feng, L., Fisman, D. (eds.) RV 2021. LNCS, vol. 12974, pp. 3–22. Springer, Cham (2021). https://doi.org/10.1007/978-3-030-88494-9_1
36. Ogale, V.A., Garg, V.K.: Detecting temporal logic predicates on distributed computations. In: Pelc, A. (ed.) DISC 2007. LNCS, vol. 4731, pp. 420–434. Springer, Heidelberg (2007). https://doi.org/10.1007/978-3-540-75142-7_32
37. Sacerdoti, F.D., Katz, M.J., Massie, M.L., Culler, D.E.: Wide area cluster monitoring with Ganglia. In: CLUSTER 2003, p. 289. IEEE Computer Society (2003)
38. Schneider, J., Basin, D., Brix, F., Krstić, S., Traytel, D.: Scalable online first-order monitoring. Int. J. Softw. Tools Technol. Transfer **23**(2), 185–208 (2021). https://doi.org/10.1007/s10009-021-00607-1
39. Stoller, S.D.: Detecting global predicates in distributed systems with clocks. Distrib. Comput. **13**(2), 85–98 (2000)
40. The DFINITY Team. The Internet Computer for geeks. Cryptology ePrint Archive, Paper 2022/087 (2022). https://eprint.iacr.org/2022/087
41. Turner, S.: Transport layer security. IEEE Internet Comput. **18**(6), 60–63 (2014)

Word Equations in Synergy with Regular Constraints

František Blahoudek[1], Yu-Fang Chen[2], David Chocholatý[1], Vojtěch Havlena[1], Lukáš Holík[1(✉)], Ondřej Lengál[1], and Juraj Síč[1]

[1] Faculty of Information Technology, Brno University of Technology, Brno, Czech Republic
holik@fit.vutbr.cz

[2] Institute of Information Science, Academia Sinica, Taipei City, Taiwan

Abstract. We argue that in string solving, word equations and regular constraints are better mixed together than approached separately as in most current string solvers. We propose a fast algorithm, complete for the fragment of chain-free constraints, in which word equations and regular constraints are tightly integrated and exchange information, efficiently pruning the cases generated by each other and limiting possible combinatorial explosion. The algorithm is based on a novel language-based characterisation of satisfiability of word equations with regular constraints. We experimentally show that our prototype implementation is competitive with the best string solvers and even superior in that it is the fastest on difficult examples and has the least number of timeouts.

1 Introduction

Solving of string constraints (string solving) has gained a significant traction in the last two decades, drawing motivation from verification of programs that manipulate strings. String manipulation is indeed ubiquitous, tricky, and error-prone. It has been a source of security vulnerabilities, such as cross-site scripting or SQL injection, that have been occupying top spots in the lists of software security issues [1–3]; moreover, widely used scripting languages like Python and PHP rely heavily on strings. Interesting new examples of an intensive use of critical string operations can also be found, e.g., in reasoning over configuration files of cloud services [4] or smart contracts [5]. Emergent approaches and tools for string solving are already numerous, for instance [6–54].

A practical solver must handle a wide range of string operations, ranging from regular constraints and word equations across string length constraints to complex functions such as ReplaceAll or integer-string conversions. The solvers translate most kinds of constraints to a few types of basic string constraints. The base algorithm then determines the architecture of the string solver and is the component with the largest impact on its efficiency. The second ingredient of the efficiency are layers of opportunistic heuristics that are effective on established benchmarks. Outside the boundaries where the heuristics apply and the core algorithm must do a heavy lifting, the efficiency may deteriorate.

M. Chechik et al. (Eds.): FM 2023, LNCS 14000, pp. 403–423, 2023.
https://doi.org/10.1007/978-3-031-27481-7_23

The most essential string constraints, word equations and regular constraints, are the primary source of difficulty. Their combination is PSPACE-complete [55,56], decidable by the algorithm of Makanin [57] and Jeż's recompression [56]. Since it is not known how these general algorithms may be implemented efficiently, string solvers use incomplete algorithms or work only with restricted fragments (e.g. straight-line of [21] or chain-free [21,26], which cover most of existing practical benchmarks), but even these are still PSPACE-complete (immediately due to Boolean combinations of regular constraints) and practically hard. Most of string solvers use base algorithms that resemble Makanin [57] or Nielsen's [58] algorithm in which word equations and regular constraints each generate one level of disjunctive branching, and the two levels multiply. Regular constraints particularly are considered complex and expensive, and reasoning with them is sometimes postponed and done only as the last step.

In this work, we propose an algorithm in which regular constraints are not avoided but tightly integrated with equations, enabling an exchange of information between equations and regular constraints that leads to a mutual pruning of generated disjunctive choices.

For instance, in cases such as $zyx = xxz \land x \in a^* \land y \in a^+b^+ \land z \in b^*$, attempting to eliminate the equation results in an infinite case split (using, e.g., Nielsen's algorithm [58] or the algorithm of [31]) and it indeed leads to failure for all solvers we have tried. The regular constraints enforce `UNSAT`: since the y on the left contains at least one b, the z on the right must answer with at least one b (x has only a's). Then, since the first letter on the left is the b of z, the first x on the right must be ϵ. Since $x = \epsilon$, we are left with $zy = z$, but the a's within the y cannot be matched by the z on the right as z has only b's.

The ability to infer this kind of information from the regular constraints systematically is in the core of our algorithm. The algorithm gradually refines the regular constraints to fit the equation, until an infeasible constraint is generated (with an empty language) or until a solution is detected. Detecting the existence of a solution is based on our novel characterisation of satisfiability of a string constraint: a constraint $x_1 \ldots x_m = x_{m+1} \ldots x_n \land \bigwedge_{x \in \mathbb{X}} x \in \mathsf{Lang}(x)$, where Lang assigns regular languages to variables in $\mathbb{X}$, has a solution if the constraint is *stable*, that is, the languages of the two sides are equal, $\mathsf{Lang}(x_1) \cdots \mathsf{Lang}(x_m) = \mathsf{Lang}(x_{m+1}) \cdots \mathsf{Lang}(x_n)$. A refinement of the variable languages is derived from a special product of the automata for concatenations of the languages on the left-hand and right-hand sides of the equation. For the case with $zyx = xxz$ above, the algorithm terminates after 2-refinements (as discussed above, inferring that (1) $z \in b^+$ and $x = \epsilon$, (2) there is no a on the right to match the a's in y on the left). The wealth of information in the regular constraints increases with refinements and prunes branches that would be explored otherwise if the equation was considered alone. The algorithm is hence effective even for pure equations, as we show experimentally.

Although our algorithm is complete for `SAT` formulae, in `UNSAT` cases the refinement steps may go on forever. We prove that it is, however, guaranteed to terminate and hence complete for the *chain-free* fragment [26] (and its subset the *straight-line* fragment [21,22]), the largest known decidable fragment of string constraints that combines equations, regular and transducer constraints, and length constraints. For this fragment, the equality in the definition of stability may be replaced by a single inclusion and only one refinement step is sufficient (the case of single equation generalises to multiple equations where the inclusions must be chosen according to certain criteria).

We have experimentally shown that on established benchmarks featuring hard combinations of word equations and regular constraints, our prototype implementation is competitive with a representative selection of string solvers (CVC5, Z3, Z3STR4, Z3STR3RE, Z3-TRAU, OSTRICH, SLOTH, RETRO). Besides being generally quite fast, it seems to be superior especially on difficult instances and has the smallest number of timeouts.

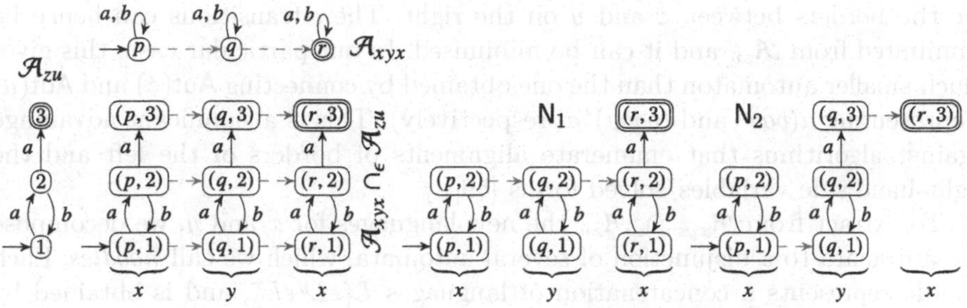

Fig. 1. Automata constructions within the refinement. Dashed lines represent ϵ.

2 Overview

We will first give an informal overview of our algorithm on the following example

$$xyx = zu \quad \wedge \quad ww = xa \quad \wedge \quad u \in (baba)^*a \quad \wedge \quad z \in a(ba)^* \tag{1}$$

with variables u, w, x, y, z over the alphabet $\Sigma = \{a, b\}$.

Our algorithm works by iteratively refining/pruning the languages in the regular membership constraints from words that cannot be present in any solution. We denote the regular constraint for a variable x by $\mathsf{Lang}(x)$. In the example, we have $\mathsf{Lang}(u) = (baba)^*a$, $\mathsf{Lang}(z) = a(ba)^*$ and, implicitly, $\mathsf{Lang}(x) = \mathsf{Lang}(y) = \mathsf{Lang}(w) = \Sigma^*$.

The equation $xyx = zu$ enforces that any solution, an assignment ν of strings to variables, satisfies that the string $s = \nu(x) \cdot \nu(y) \cdot \nu(x) = \nu(z) \cdot \nu(u)$ belongs to the intersection of the concatenations of languages on the left and the right-hand side of the equation, $\mathsf{Lang}(x) \cdot \mathsf{Lang}(y) \cdot \mathsf{Lang}(x) \cap \mathsf{Lang}(z) \cdot \mathsf{Lang}(u)$, as in Eq. (2) below:

We may thus refine the languages of x and y by removing those words that cannot be a part of any string s in the intersection. The refinement is implemented over

$$s \in \overbrace{\Sigma^*}^{x}\,\overbrace{\Sigma^*}^{y}\,\overbrace{\Sigma^*}^{x} \overset{=}{\cap} \overbrace{a(ba)^*}^{z}\,\overbrace{(baba)^*a}^{u}. \tag{2}$$

finite automata representation of languages, assuming that every $\mathsf{Lang}(x_i)$ is represented by the automaton $\mathsf{Aut}(x_i)$. The main steps of the refinement are shown in Fig. 1. First, we construct automata for the two sides of the equation:

- $\mathcal{A}_{xyx}$ is obtained by concatenating $\mathsf{Aut}(x)$, $\mathsf{Aut}(y)$, and $\mathsf{Aut}(x)$ again. It has ϵ-transitions that delimit the borders of occurrences of x and y.
- $\mathcal{A}_{zu}$ is obtained by concatenating $\mathsf{Aut}(z)$ and $\mathsf{Aut}(u)$.

We then combine $\mathcal{A}_{xyx}$ with $\mathcal{A}_{zu}$ through a synchronous product construction that preserves ϵ-transitions into an automaton $\mathcal{A}_{xyx} \cap_\epsilon \mathcal{A}_{zu}$. Seeing ϵ as a letter that delimits variable occurrences, $\mathcal{A}_{xyx} \cap_\epsilon \mathcal{A}_{zu}$ accepts strings $\alpha_1^x \epsilon \alpha^y \epsilon \alpha_2^x$ such that $\alpha_1^x \alpha^y \alpha_2^x \in \mathsf{Lang}(z) \cdot \mathsf{Lang}(u)$, $\alpha_1^x \in \mathsf{Lang}(x)$, $\alpha^y \in \mathsf{Lang}(y)$, and $\alpha_2^x \in \mathsf{Lang}(x)$.

Note that for refining the languages x, y on the left, we do not need to see the borders between z and u on the right. The ϵ-transitions can hence be eliminated from $\mathcal{A}_{zu}$ and it can be minimised. In our particular case, this gives much smaller automaton than the one obtained by connecting $\mathsf{Aut}(z)$ and $\mathsf{Aut}(u)$ (representing $a(ba)^*$ and $(baba)^*a$, respectively). This is a significant advantage against algorithms that enumerate alignments of borders of the left and the right-hand side variables/solved forms [59].

To extract from $\mathcal{A}_{xyx} \cap_\epsilon \mathcal{A}_{zu}$ the new languages for x and y, we decompose the automata to a disjunction of several automata, which we call *noodles*. Each noodle represents a concatenation of languages $L_1^x \epsilon L^y \epsilon L_2^x$, and is obtained by choosing one ϵ-transition separating the first occurrence of x from y (the left column of red ϵ-transitions in Fig. 1), one ϵ-transition separating y from the second occurrence of x (the right column of blue ϵ-transitions), removing the other ϵ-transitions, and trimming the automaton. We have to split the product into noodles because some values of x can appear together only with some values of y, and this relation must be preserved after extracting their languages from the product (for instance, in $\mathcal{A}_{xyx} \cap_\epsilon \mathcal{A}_{zu}$ in Fig. 1, both first occurences of x and y can have, among others, values aa and ϵ, but if $x = aa$ then y must be ϵ).

Figure 1 shows two noodles, N_1 and N_2, out of 9 possible noodles from $\mathcal{A}_{xyx} \cap_\epsilon \mathcal{A}_{zu}$. We extract the automata for languages L_1^x, L^y, and L_2^x (their initial and final states are the states with incoming and outgoing ϵ-transitions in the noodle). The refined language for y is then $\mathsf{Lang}(y) = L^y$. The refined language for x is obtained by unifying the languages of the first and the second occurrence of x, $\mathsf{Lang}(x) = L_1^x \cap L_2^x$ (by constructing a standard product of the two automata):

- For N_1, the refinement is $y \in (ba)^*$ and $x \in a$ (computed as $a(ba)^* \cap (ba)^*a$).
- For N_2, the refinement is $y \in a(ba)^*a$ and $x \in \epsilon$ (computed as $(ab)^* \cap \epsilon$).

The 7 remaining noodles generated from $\mathcal{A}_{xyx} \cap_\epsilon \mathcal{A}_{zu}$ yield $x \in \emptyset$ and are discarded. Noodles N_1 and N_2 spawn two disjunctive branches of the computation.

For the branch of N_1, we use the equation $ww = xa$ for the next refinement. Using the newly derived constraint $x \in a$, we obtain Eq. (3) on the right:

$$s \in \overbrace{\Sigma^*}^{w} \overbrace{\Sigma^*}^{w} \overset{=}{\cap} \overbrace{a}^{x} \overset{a}{a}. \quad (3)$$

Similarly as in the previous step, the refinement deduces that

$w \in a$. At this point, the languages on both sides of all equations match, and so no more refinement is possible:

$$\overbrace{a}^{x}\overbrace{(ba)^*}^{y}\overbrace{a}^{x} = \overbrace{a(ba)^*}^{z}\overbrace{(baba)^*a}^{u} \quad \text{and} \quad \overbrace{a}^{w}\overbrace{a}^{w} = \overbrace{a}^{x}a. \tag{4}$$

One of the main contributions of this paper, and a cornerstone of our algorithm, is a theorem stating that in this state, when language equality holds for all equations, a solution is guaranteed to exist (see Theorem 1). We can thus conclude with SAT.

3 Preliminaries

Sets and Strings. We use $\mathbb{N}$ to denote the set of natural numbers (including 0). We fix a finite *alphabet* Σ of *symbols/letters* (usually denoted $a, b, c, \ldots$) for the rest of the paper. A sequence of symbols $w = a_1 \cdots a_n$ from Σ is a *word* or a *string* over Σ, with its *length* n denoted by $|w|$. The set of all words over Σ is denoted as Σ^*. The *empty word* is denoted by ϵ ($\epsilon \notin \Sigma$), with $|\epsilon| = 0$. The *concatenation* of words u and v is denoted $u \cdot v$, uv for short (ϵ is a neutral element of concatenation). A set of words over Σ is a *language*, the concatenation of languages is $L_1 \cdot L_2 = \{u \cdot v \mid u \in L_1 \wedge v \in L_2\}$, L_1L_2 for short. *Bounded iteration* x^i, $i \in \mathbb{N}$, of a word or a language x is defined by $x^0 = \epsilon$ for a word, $x^0 = \{\epsilon\}$ for a language, and $x^{i+1} = x^i \cdot x$. Then $x^* = \bigcup_{i \in \mathbb{N}} x^i$. We often denote regular languages using regular expressions with the standard notation.

Automata. A *(nondeterministic) finite automaton (NFA)* over Σ is a tuple $\mathcal{A} = (Q, \Delta, I, F)$ where Q is a finite set of *states*, Δ is a set of *transitions* of the form $q\text{-}\{a\}\!\!\rightarrow r$ with $q, r \in Q$ and $a \in \Sigma \cup \{\epsilon\}$, $I \subseteq Q$ is the set of *initial states*, and $F \subseteq Q$ is the set of *final states*. A run of $\mathcal{A}$ over a word $w \in \Sigma^*$ is a sequence $p_0\text{-}\{a_1\}\!\!\rightarrow p_1\text{-}\{a_2\}\!\!\rightarrow \ldots \text{-}\{a_n\}\!\!\rightarrow p_n$ where for all $1 \leq i \leq n$ it holds that $a_i \in \Sigma \cup \{\epsilon\}$, $p_{i-1}\text{-}\{a_i\}\!\!\rightarrow p_i \in \Delta$, and $w = a_1 \cdot a_2 \cdots a_n$. The run is *accepting* if $p_0 \in I$ and $p_n \in F$, and the language $L(\mathcal{A})$ of $\mathcal{A}$ is the set of all words for which $\mathcal{A}$ has an accepting run. A language L is called *regular* if it is accepted by some NFA. Two NFAs with the same language are called *equivalent*. An automaton without ϵ-transitions is called *ϵ-free*. An automaton with each state belonging to some accepting run is *trimmed*. To concatenate languages of two NFAs $\mathcal{A} = (Q, \Delta, I, F)$ and $\mathcal{A}' = (Q', \Delta', I', F')$, we construct their *$\epsilon$-concatenation* $\mathcal{A} \circ_\epsilon \mathcal{A}' = (Q \uplus Q', \Delta \uplus \Delta' \uplus \{p\text{-}\{\epsilon\}\!\!\rightarrow q \mid p \in F, q \in I'\}, I, F')$. To intersect their languages, we construct their *ϵ-preserving product* $\mathcal{A} \cap_\epsilon \mathcal{A}' = (Q \times Q', \Delta^\times, I \times I', F \times F')$ where $(q, q')\text{-}\{a\}\!\!\rightarrow (r, r') \in \Delta^\times$ iff either (1) $a \in \Sigma$ and $q\text{-}\{a\}\!\!\rightarrow r \in \Delta, q'\text{-}\{a\}\!\!\rightarrow r' \in \Delta'$, or (2) $a = \epsilon$ and either $q' = r'$, $q\text{-}\{\epsilon\}\!\!\rightarrow r \in \Delta$ or $q = r$, $q'\text{-}\{\epsilon\}\!\!\rightarrow r' \in \Delta'$.

String Constraints. We focus on the most essential string constraints, Boolean combinations of atomic string constraints of two types: word equations and regular constraints. Let $\mathbb{X}$ be a set of *string variables* (denoted $u, v, \ldots, z$), fixed for the rest of the paper. A *word equation* is an equation of the form $s = t$ where

s and t are (different) *string terms*, i.e., words from $\mathbb{X}^*$.[1] We do not distinguish between $s = t$ and $t = s$. A *regular constraint* is of the form $x \in L$, where $x \in \mathbb{X}$ and L is a regular language. A *string assignment* is a map $\nu \colon \mathbb{X} \to \Sigma^*$. The assignment is a solution for a word equation $s = t$ if $\nu(s) = \nu(t)$ where $\nu(t')$ for a term $t' = x_1 \ldots x_n$ is defined as $\nu(x_1) \cdots \nu(x_n)$, and it is a solution for a regular constraint $x \in L$ if $\nu(x) \in L$. A solution for a *Boolean combination* of atomic constraint is then defined as usual.

4 Stability of String Constraints

The core ingredient of our algorithm, which allows to tightly integrate equations with regular constraints, is the notion of *stability* of a string constraint. Stability of a string constraint is used by our algorithm to indiciate satisfiability.

4.1 Stability of Single-Equation Systems

We will first discuss stability of a *single-equation system* $\Phi \colon s = t \wedge \bigwedge_{x \in \mathbb{X}} x \in \mathsf{Lang}_\Phi(x)$ where $\mathsf{Lang}_\Phi \colon \mathbb{X} \to \mathcal{P}(\Sigma^*)$ is a *language assignment*, an assignment of regular languages to variables. We say that a language assignment Lang *refines* Lang_Φ if $\mathsf{Lang}(x) \subseteq \mathsf{Lang}_\Phi(x)$ for all $x \in \mathbb{X}$. If $\mathsf{Lang}(x) = \emptyset$ for some $x \in \mathbb{X}$, it is *infeasible*, otherwise it is *feasible*. For a term $u = x_1 \ldots x_n$, we define $\mathsf{Lang}(u) = \mathsf{Lang}(x_1) \cdots \mathsf{Lang}(x_n)$. We say that Lang is *strongly stable for* Φ if $\mathsf{Lang}(s) = \mathsf{Lang}(t)$.

The core result of this work is that the existence of a stable language assignment for Φ implies the existence of a solution, which is formalised below.

Theorem 1. *A single-equation system Φ has a feasible strongly stable language assignment that refines Lang_Φ, iff it has a solution.*

Proof (Sketch of $\Rightarrow$, the other direction is trivial). Let $s = y_1 \ldots y_m$ and $t = y_{m+1} \ldots y_n$. Note that a solution cannot be found easily by just taking any words $w_i \in \mathsf{Lang}(x_i)$, for $1 \leq i \leq n$, such that $w_1 \cdots w_m = w_{m+1} \cdots w_n$. The reason is that multiple occurrences of the same variable must have the same value. To construct a solution, we first notice that it is enough to use the shortest words in the languages of the variables. We can then assume the lengths of the strings valuating each variable fixed (the smallest lengths in the languages), which in turn fixes the positions of variables' occurrences within the sides of the equation. We then construct the strings in the solution by selecting letters and propagating them through equalities of opposite positions of the equation sides and also between different occurrences of the same position in the same variable. Showing that the process of selecting and propagating letters terminates requires to show that the sequence of constructed partial solutions is decreasing w.r.t. a complex well-founded ordering of partial solutions. The full proof may be found in [60]. □

[1] Note that terms with letters from Σ, sometimes used in our examples, can be encoded by replacing each occurrence o of a letter a by a *fresh* variable x_o and a regular constraint $x_o \in \{a\}$..

Additionally, in the special case of *weak* equations—i.e., equations $s = t$ where one of the sides, say t, satisfies the condition that all variables occurring in t occur in $s = t$ exactly once—the stability condition in Theorem 1 can be weakened to one-sided language inclusion only: In case t is the term satisfying the condition, we say that Lang is *weakly stable for* Φ if $\mathsf{Lang}(s) \subseteq \mathsf{Lang}(t)$.

Theorem 2. *Φ with a weak equation has a feasible weakly stable language assignment that refines Lang_Φ iff Φ has a solution.*

Note that weak stability allows multiple occurrences of a variable on the left-hand side of $s = t$. Intuitively, the multiple occurrences must have the same value, and having them on the left-hand side of the inclusion forces their synchronisation. For instance, for $\Phi\colon xx = y \wedge x \in \{a, b\} \wedge y \in \{ab\}$, the inclusion $\mathsf{Lang}(xx) \subseteq \mathsf{Lang}(y)$ is satisfied by no feasible refinement Lang of Lang_Φ, revealing that Φ has no solution, while $\mathsf{Lang}(xx) \supseteq \mathsf{Lang}(y)$ is satisfied already by Lang_Φ itself.

4.2 Stability of Multi-equation Systems

Next, we extend the definition of stability to *multi-equation systems*, conjunctions of the form $\Phi\colon \mathcal{E} \wedge \bigwedge_{x \in \mathbb{X}} x \in \mathsf{Lang}_\Phi(x)$ where $\mathcal{E}\colon \bigwedge_{i=1}^{m} s_i = t_i$ for $m \in \mathbb{N}$. We assume that every two equations are different, i.e., $\{s_i, t_i\} \neq \{s_j, t_j\}$ if $i \neq j$.

We generalise stability in a way that utilises both strong and weak stability of single equation systems and both Theorem 1 and Theorem 2. Again, we interpret every equation $s_i = t_i$ as a pair of inclusions and show that it suffices to satisfy a certain subset of these inclusions in order to obtain a solution. A sufficient subset of inclusions is defined through the notion of an *inclusion graph* of $\mathcal{E}$. It is a directed graph $G = (V, E)$ where vertices V are inclusion constraints of the form $\mathsf{s_i} \subseteq \mathsf{t_i}$ or $\mathsf{t_i} \subseteq \mathsf{s_i}$, for $1 \leq i \leq m$, and $E \subseteq V \times V$. An inclusion graph must satisfy the following conditions:

(IG1) For each $s_i = t_i$ in $\mathcal{E}$, at least one of the nodes $\mathsf{s_i} \subseteq \mathsf{t_i}$, $\mathsf{t_i} \subseteq \mathsf{s_i}$ is in V.
(IG2) If $\mathsf{s_i} \subseteq \mathsf{t_i} \in V$ and t_i has a variable with multiple occurrences in right-hand sides of vertices of V, then also $\mathsf{t_i} \subseteq \mathsf{s_i} \in V$.
(IG3) $(\mathsf{s_i} \subseteq \mathsf{t_i}, \mathsf{s_j} \subseteq \mathsf{t_j}) \in E$ iff $\mathsf{s_i} \subseteq \mathsf{t_i}, \mathsf{s_j} \subseteq \mathsf{t_j} \in V$ and s_i and t_j share a variable.
(IG4) If $\mathsf{s_i} \subseteq \mathsf{t_i} \in V$ lies on a cycle, then also $\mathsf{t_i} \subseteq \mathsf{s_i} \in V$.

Note that by (IG3), E is uniquely determined by V. We define that a language assignment Lang is *stable for an inclusion graph* $G = (V, E)$ of $\mathcal{E}$ if it satisfies every inclusion in V.

Theorem 3. *Let G be an inclusion graph of $\mathcal{E}$. Then there is a feasible language assignment that refines Lang_Φ and is stable for G iff Φ has a solution.*

The proof of Theorem 3 is in [60]. Intuitively, the set of inclusions needed to guarantee a solution is specified by the vertices of an inclusion graph. All equations must contribute with at least one inclusion, by Condition (IG1). Including only one inclusion corresponds to using weak stability. Including both inclusions corresponds to using strong stability. We will use inclusion graphs in our algorithm to direct propagation of refinements of language assignments. We will wish to avoid using strong stability when possible since cycles that it creates in the graph may cause the algorithm to diverge.

Conditions (IG2)–(IG4) specify where weak stability is not enough. Namely, Condition (IG2) enforces that to use weak stability, multiple occurrences of a variable can only occur on the left-hand side of an inclusion (as in the definition of weak stability), otherwise strong stability must be used. The edges defined by Condition (IG3) are used in Condition (IG4). An edge means that a refinement of the language assignment made to satisfy the inclusion in the source node may invalidate the inclusion in the target node. Condition (IG4) covers the case of a cyclic dependency of a variable on itself. A self-loop indicates that a variable occurs on both sides of an equation (breaking the definition of weak stability). A longer cycle indicates such a cyclic dependency caused by transitively propagating the inclusion relation.

4.3 Constructing Inclusion Graphs and Chain-Freeness

We now discuss a construction of a suitable inclusion graph. Our algorithm for solving string constraints will use the graph nodes to gradually refine the language assignment, propagating information along the graph edges. It is guaranteed to terminate when the graph is acyclic. Below, we give an algorithm that generates an inclusion graph that contains as few inclusions as possible and is acyclic whenever possible.

The graph is obtained from a simplified version $SG_\mathcal{E}$ of the splitting graph of [26], which is the basis of the definition of the chain-free fragment, for which our algorithm is complete. The nodes of $SG_\mathcal{E}$ are all inclusions $\mathsf{s}_\mathsf{i} \subseteq \mathsf{t}_\mathsf{i}, \mathsf{t}_\mathsf{i} \subseteq \mathsf{s}_\mathsf{i}$, for $1 \leq i \leq m$, and it has an edge from $\mathsf{s} \subseteq \mathsf{t}$ to $\mathsf{s}' \subseteq \mathsf{t}'$ if s and t' each have a different occurrence of the same variable (the "*different*" here meaning not the same position in the same term in the same equation, e.g., for inclusions induced by the equation $u = v$, for $u, v \in \mathbb{X}$, there will be no edge between $\mathsf{u} \subseteq \mathsf{v}$ and $\mathsf{v} \subseteq \mathsf{u}$).

The algorithm for constructing an inclusion graph from $SG_\mathcal{E}$ starts by iteratively removing nodes that are trivial source strongly connected components (SCCs) from $SG_\mathcal{E}$ (trivial means a graph $(\{v\}, \emptyset)$ with no edges, source means with no edges coming from outside into the component). With every removed node v, the algorithm removes from $SG_\mathcal{E}$ also the dual node $\mathsf{dual}(v)$ (the other inclusion), and it adds v to the inclusion graph. When no trivial source SCCs are left, that is, the remaining nodes are all reachable from non-trivial SCCs, the algorithm adds to the inclusion graph all the remaining nodes.

Algorithm 1: $\mathtt{incl}(\mathcal{E})$

Input: Conjunction of string equations $\mathcal{E}$.
Output: An inclusion graph of $\mathcal{E}$.

$G := SG_\mathcal{E}$; $V' := \emptyset$;
while *G has a trivial source SCC* $(\{v\}, \emptyset)$ **do**
  $G := G \setminus \{v, \mathsf{dual}(v)\}$;
  $V' := V' \cup \{v\}$;
$V := V' \cup$ the remaining nodes of G;
return the inclusion graph with nodes V;

The pseudocode of the algorithm is shown in Algorithm 1. It uses $\texttt{SCC}(G)$ to denote the set of SCCs of G and $G \setminus V$ to denote the graph obtained from G by removing the vertices in V together with the adjacent edges.

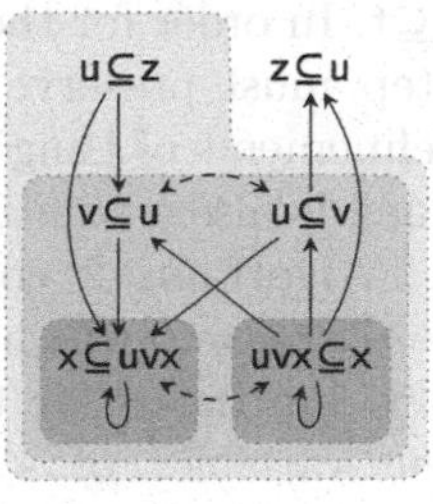

Example 1. In the picture in the right, we show an example of the construction of the inclusion graph G from $SG_{\mathcal{E}}$ for $\mathcal{E}$: $z = u \wedge u = v \wedge uvx = x$. Edges of $SG_{\mathcal{E}}$ are solid lines, the inclusion graph has both solid and dashed edges. The inner red boxes are the non-trivial SCCs of $SG_{\mathcal{E}}$. They are enclosed in the box of nodes that are added on Line 5 of Algorithm 1. The outer-most box encloses the inclusion graph, including one node added on Line 4. □

Theorem 4. *For a conjunction of equations $\mathcal{E}$, $\texttt{incl}(\mathcal{E})$ is an inclusion graph for $\mathcal{E}$ with the smallest number of vertices. Moreover, if there exists an acyclic inclusion graph for $\mathcal{E}$, then $\texttt{incl}(\mathcal{E})$ is acyclic.*

In Sect. 5, we will show a satisfiability checking algorithm that guarantees termination when given an acyclic inclusion graph. Here we prove that the existence of an acyclic inclusion graph coincides with the chain-free fragment of string constraints [26], which is the largest known decidable fragment of string constraints with equations, regular and transducer constraints, and length constraints (up to the incomparable fragment of quadratic equations). *Chain-free* constraints are defined as those where the simplified splitting graph $SG_{\mathcal{E}}$ has no cycle. The following theorem is proven in [60].

Theorem 5. *A multi-equation system Φ is chain-free iff there exists an acyclic inclusion graph for Φ.*

5 Algorithm for Satisfiability Checking

Our algorithm for testing satisfiability of a multi-equation system Φ is based on Theorem 3. The algorithm first constructs a suitable inclusion graph of $\mathcal{E}$ using Algorithm 1 and then it gradually refines the original language assignment Lang_Φ according to the dependencies in the inclusion graph until it either finds a stable feasible language assignment or concludes that no such language assignment exists.

A language assignment Lang is in the algorithm represented by an *automata assignment* Aut, which assigns to every variable x an ϵ-free NFA $\mathsf{Aut}(x)$ with $L(\mathsf{Aut}(x)) = \mathsf{Lang}(x)$. We use $\mathsf{Aut}(t)$ for a term $t = x_1 \ldots x_n$ to denote the NFA $\mathsf{Aut}(x_1) \circ_\epsilon \cdots \circ_\epsilon \mathsf{Aut}(x_n)$. In the following text, we identify a language assignment with the corresponding automata assignment and vice versa.

5.1 Refining Language Assignments by Noodlification

The task of a refinement step is to create a new language assignment that refines the old one, Lang, and satisfies one of the inclusions previously not satisfied, say

$s{\subseteq}t$. In order for the algorithm to be sound when returning UNSAT, a refinement step must preserve all existing solutions. It will therefore return a set $\mathcal{T}$ of refinements of Lang that is *tight w.r.t.* $s{\subseteq}t$, that is, every solution of $s = t$ under Lang is also a solution of $s = t$ under some of its refinements in $\mathcal{T}$.

Algorithm 2 computes such a tight set. Line 1 computes the automaton *Product*, which accepts $\mathsf{Lang}(s) \cap \mathsf{Lang}(t)$. In order to be able to extract new languages for the variables of s from it, *Product* marks borders between the variables of s with ϵ-transitions. That is, when ϵ is understood as a special letter, *Product* accepts the *delimited language* $L^\epsilon(\mathit{Product})$ of words $w_1\epsilon\cdots\epsilon w_n$ with $w_i \in \mathsf{Lang}(x_i)$ for $1 \leq i \leq n$ and $w_1 \cdots w_n \in \mathsf{Lang}(t)$. Notice that $\mathsf{Aut}(t)$ is on Line 1 minimised. This means removal of ϵ-transitions marking the borders of variables' occurrences, and then minimisation by any automata size reduction method (we use simulation quotient [61, 62]). Since the product is then representing only the borders of the variables on the left (because $\mathsf{Aut}(s)$ keeps the ϵ-transitions generated from the concatenation with $\circ_\epsilon$), but not the borders of variables in t, it does not actually generate an explicit representation of possible alignments of borders of variables' occurrences.

Algorithm 2: $\mathtt{refine}(v, \mathsf{Aut})$

Input: A vertex $v = s{\subseteq}t$ with $s = x_1 \cdots x_n$ and $t = y_1 \cdots y_m$, an automata assignment Aut
Output: A tight refinement of Aut w.r.t. v

1 $\mathit{Product} := \mathsf{Aut}(s) \cap_\epsilon \mathit{minimise}(\mathsf{Aut}(t))$;
2 $\mathit{Noodles} := \mathtt{noodlify}(\mathit{Product})$;
3 $\mathcal{T} := \emptyset$;
4 **for** $\mathsf{N} \in \mathit{Noodles}$ **do**
5 $\quad \mathsf{Aut}' := \mathsf{Aut}$;
6 $\quad$ **for** $1 \leq i \leq n$ **do**
7 $\quad\quad \mathsf{Aut}'(x_i) := \bigcap\{\mathsf{N}(j) \mid 1 \leq j \leq n, x_i = x_j\}$;
8 $\quad$ **if** $L(\mathsf{Aut}'(s)) = \emptyset$ **then continue**;
9 $\quad \mathcal{T} := \mathcal{T} \cup \{\mathsf{Aut}'\}$;
10 **return** $\mathcal{T}$;

We then extract from *Product* a language for each *occurrence* of a variable in s. Line 2 divides *Product* into a set of the so-called *noodles*, which are sequences of automata $\mathsf{N} = \mathsf{N}(1), \ldots, \mathsf{N}(n)$ that preserve the delimited language in the sense that $\bigcup_{\mathsf{N} \in \mathit{Noodles}} L^\epsilon(\mathsf{N}(1) \circ_\epsilon \cdots \circ_\epsilon \mathsf{N}(n)) = L^\epsilon(\mathit{Product})$.

Technically, assuming w.l.o.g that *Product* has a single initial state r_0 and a single final state q_n, $\mathtt{noodlify}(\mathit{Product})$ generates one noodle N for each $(n-1)$-tuple $q_1 \text{-}\{\epsilon\}\!\!\to r_1, \ldots, q_{n-1} \text{-}\{\epsilon\}\!\!\to r_{n-1}$ of transitions that appear, in that order, in an accepting run of *Product* (note that every accepting run has $n-1$ ϵ-transitions by construction of *Product*, since $\mathsf{Aut}(s)$ also had $n-1$ ϵ-transitions in each accepting run and $\mathit{minimise}(\mathsf{Aut}(t))$ is ϵ-free): for each $1 \leq i \leq n$, $\mathsf{N}(i)$ arises by trimming *Product* after its initial states were replaced by $\{r_{i-1}\}$ and final states by $\{q_i\}$.

The **for** loop on Line 4 then turns each noodle N into a refined automata assignment Aut' in $\mathcal{T}$ by unifying/intersecting languages of different occurrences of the same variable: for each $x \in \mathbb{X}$, $\mathsf{Aut}'(x)$ is the automata intersection of all automata $\mathsf{N}(i)$ with $x_i = x$. The fact that $\mathcal{T}$ is a tight set of refinements (i.e., that it preserves all solutions of Aut) follows from that every path of *Product* can be found in *Noodles* and that the use of ϵ-transitions allows to reconstruct the NFAs corresponding to the variables.

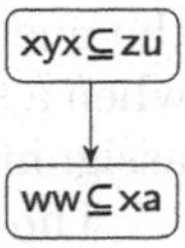

Example 2. Consider the multi-equation system Φ from Sect. 2 and the vertex xyx⊆zu of its inclusion graph given in the right. The construction of the product automaton *Product* from Algorithm 2 is shown in Fig. 1. The set of noodles $\texttt{noodlify}(\mathit{Product}) = \{\mathsf{N}_1, \ldots, \mathsf{N}_7\}$ is given in [60] (N_1 and N_2 are in Fig. 1). On Line 6, we need to compute intersections of $\mathsf{N}_i(1) \cap \mathsf{N}_i(3)$ for each noodle N_i. These parts of the noodle correspond to the two occurrences of the same variable x. The only noodles yielding nonempty languages for x are N_1 and N_2. The noodle N_1 leads to a refinement Aut_1 of Aut where $L(\mathsf{Aut}_1(x)) = a$ (computed as the intersection of languages $\mathsf{N}_1(1) = a(ba)^*$ and $\mathsf{N}_1(3) = (ba)^*a$) and $L(\mathsf{Aut}_1(y)) = (ba)^*$. The noodle N_2 leads to a refinement Aut_2 of Aut where $L(\mathsf{Aut}_2(x)) = \epsilon$ (computed as the intersection of languages $\mathsf{N}_2(1) = (ab)^*$ and $\mathsf{N}_2(3) = \epsilon$) and $L(\mathsf{Aut}_2(y)) = a(ba)^*a$. □

Example 3. An example with a non-terminating sequence of refinement steps is $xa = x \wedge x \in a^+$, explained in detail in [60]. Every i-th step refines $\mathsf{Lang}(x)$ to $x \in a^{i+1}a^*$. Note that many similar examples could be handled by simple heuristics that take into account lengths of strings, already used in other solvers. □

5.2 Satisfiability Checking by Refinement Propagation

The pseudocode of the satisfiability check of Φ is given in Algorithm 3. It starts with the automaton assignment Aut_Φ corresponding to Lang_Φ, and it uses graph nodes s⊆t not satisfied in the current Aut to refine it, that is, to replace Aut by some automaton assignment returned by $\texttt{refine}(\texttt{s}\subseteq\texttt{t}, \mathsf{Aut})$.

Algorithm 3: $\texttt{propagate}(G_\mathcal{E}, \mathsf{Aut}_\Phi)$

Input: Inclusion graph $G_\mathcal{E} = (V, E)$, initial automata assignment Aut_Φ.
Output: SAT if Φ is satisfiable, UNSAT if Φ is unsatisfiable

```
Branches := ⟨(Aut_Φ, V)⟩;
while Branches ≠ ∅ do
    (Aut, W) := Branches.dequeue();
    if W = ∅ then return SAT ;
    v = s⊆t := W.dequeue();
    if L(Aut(s)) ⊆ L(Aut(t)) then
        Branches.enqueue((Aut, W));
        continue;
    T := refine(v, Aut);
    W' := W;
    foreach (v, u) ∈ E s.t. u ∉ W do
        W'.enqueue(u);
    foreach Aut' ∈ T do
        Branches.enqueue(Aut', W');
return UNSAT;
```

The algorithm maintains the current value of Aut and a worklist W of nodes for which the weak-stability condition might be invalidated, either initially or since they were affected by some previous refinement. Nodes are picked from the worklist, and if the inclusion at a node is found not satisfied in the current automata assignment Aut, the node is used to refine it. Stability is detected when W is empty—there in no potentially unsatisfied inclusion.

Since $\texttt{refine}(\texttt{s}\subseteq\texttt{t}, \mathsf{Aut})$ does not return a single language assignment but a set of language assignments that refine Aut, the computation spawns an independent branch for each of them. Algorithm 3 adds the branches for processing in the queue *Branches*. The branching is disjunctive, meaning stability is returned when a single branch detects stability. If all branches terminate with an infeasible assignment, then the algorithm concludes that the constraint is unsatisfiable.

The worklist and the queue of branches are first-in first-out (this is important for showing termination in Theorem 8). To minimise the number of refinement steps, the nodes are initially inserted in W in an order compatible with a topological order of the SCCs.

Example 4. Consider again the multi-equation system Φ from Sect. 2 and the inclusion graph in Example 2. The initial automata assignment Aut_Φ is then given as $L(\mathsf{Aut}_\Phi(a)) = \{a\}$, $L(\mathsf{Aut}_\Phi(z)) = a(ba)^*$, $L(\mathsf{Aut}_\Phi(u)) = (baba)^*a$, and $L(\mathsf{Aut}_\Phi(x)) = L(\mathsf{Aut}_\Phi(y)) = L(\mathsf{Aut}_\Phi(w)) = \Sigma^*$. The queue *Branches* on Line 1 of Algorithm 3 is hence initialised as *Branches* $= \langle(\mathsf{Aut}_\Phi, \langle \mathsf{xyx} \subseteq \mathsf{zu}, \mathsf{ww} \subseteq \mathsf{xa}\rangle)\rangle$. The computation of the main loop of Algorithm 3 then proceeds as follows.

1st iteration. The dequeued element is $(\mathsf{Aut}_\Phi, \langle \mathsf{xyx} \subseteq \mathsf{zu}, \mathsf{ww} \subseteq \mathsf{xa}\rangle)$ and v (dequeued from W) is $\mathsf{xyx} \subseteq \mathsf{zu}$. The condition on Line 6 is not satisfied, hence the algorithm calls `refine`$(\mathsf{xyx} \subseteq \mathsf{zu}, \mathsf{Aut}_\Phi)$. The refinement yields two new automata assignments, $\mathsf{Aut}_1, \mathsf{Aut}_2$, which are defined in Example 2. The queue *Branches* is hence extended to $\langle(\mathsf{Aut}_1, \langle \mathsf{ww} \subseteq \mathsf{xa}\rangle), (\mathsf{Aut}_2, \langle \mathsf{ww} \subseteq \mathsf{xa}\rangle)\rangle$.

2nd iteration. The dequeued element is $(\mathsf{Aut}_2, \langle \mathsf{ww} \subseteq \mathsf{xa}\rangle)$. The condition on Line 6 is not satisfied since $L(\mathsf{Aut}_2(x)) = \{\epsilon\}$ and $L(\mathsf{Aut}_2(w)) = \Sigma^*$. In this case, `refine`$(\mathsf{ww} \subseteq \mathsf{xa}, \mathsf{Aut}_2) = \emptyset$, hence nothing is added to *Branches*, i.e., *Branches* $= \langle(\mathsf{Aut}_1, \langle \mathsf{ww} \subseteq \mathsf{xa}\rangle)\rangle$.

3rd iteration. The dequeued element is $(\mathsf{Aut}_1, \langle \mathsf{ww} \subseteq \mathsf{xa}\rangle)$. The condition on Line 6 is not satisfied ($\Sigma^* \cdot \Sigma^* \not\subseteq a \cdot a$) and `refine`$(\mathsf{ww} \subseteq \mathsf{xa}, \mathsf{Aut}_1) = \{\mathsf{Aut}_3\}$ where Aut_3 is as Aut_1 except that $\mathsf{Aut}_3(w)$ accepts only a. *Branches* is then updated to $\langle(\mathsf{Aut}_3, \emptyset)\rangle$.

4th iteration. The condition on Line 4 is satisfied and the algorithm returns `SAT`. □

As stated by Theorem 6 below, the algorithm is sound in the general case (an answer is always correct). Moreover, Theorems 5 and 7 imply that when Algorithm 1 is used to construct the inclusion graph, we have a complete algorithm for chain-free constraints.

Theorem 6 (Soundness). *If* `propagate`$(G_\mathcal{E}, \mathsf{Aut}_\Phi)$ *returns* `SAT`, *then* Φ *is satisfiable, and if* `propagate`$(G_\mathcal{E}, \mathsf{Aut}_\Phi)$ *returns* `UNSAT`, Φ *is unsatisfiable.*

Theorem 7. *If* $G_\mathcal{E}$ *is acyclic, then* `propagate`$(G_\mathcal{E}, \mathsf{Aut}_\Phi)$ *terminates.*

5.3 Working with Shortest Words

Algorithm 3 can be improved with a weaker termination condition that takes into account only shortest words in the languages assigned to variables. Importantly, this gives us completeness in the `SAT` case for general constraints, i.e., the algorithm is always guaranteed to return `SAT` if a solution exists.

Let $\mathsf{Lang}^{\min}$ be the language assignment obtained from Lang by assigning to every $x \in \mathbb{X}$ the set of shortest words from $\mathsf{Lang}(x)$ i.e., $\mathsf{Lang}^{\min}(x) = \{w \in \mathsf{Lang}(x) \mid \forall u \in \mathsf{Lang}(x) \colon |w| \leq |u|\}$. Then, for $\Phi \colon s = t \wedge \bigwedge_{x \in \mathbb{X}} x \in \mathsf{Lang}_\Phi(x)$, we say that Lang is *strongly min-stable for* Φ if $\mathsf{Lang}^{\min}$ is stable for Φ. Similarly, Lang is *weakly min-stable for* Φ if $s = t$ is weak and $\mathsf{Lang}^{\min}(s) \subseteq \mathsf{Lang}(t)$. Note that for weak min-stability, it is enough to have the min-language only on the left, which gives a weaker condition. Theorems 1 and 2 hold for min-stability and weak min-stability, respectively, as well (the proof of the min-versions are in fact a part of the proof of the Theorems 1 and 2). The min-stability of a multi-equation system is then defined in the same way as before, different only in that it uses the min-stability at the nodes instead of stability. Namely, in Algorithm 3, the test $L(\mathsf{Aut}(s)) \subseteq L(\mathsf{Aut}(t))$ on Line 6 is replaced by $L^{\min}(\mathsf{Aut}(s)) \subseteq L(\mathsf{Aut}(t))$. We call this variant of the algorithm $\texttt{propagate}_{min}$. Not only that this new algorithm is still partially correct, may terminate after less refinements, and uses a cheaper test to detect termination, but, mainly, it is complete in the SAT case: if there is a solution, then it is guaranteed to terminate for any system, no matter whether chain-free or not. Intuitively, the algorithm in a sense explores the words in the languages of the variables systematically, taking the words ordered by length, the shortest ones first. Hence, besides that variants of Theorems 6 and 7 with $\texttt{propagate}_{min}$ still hold, we also have Theorem 8:

Theorem 8. *If* Φ *is satisfiable, then* $\texttt{propagate}_{min}(\texttt{incl}(\mathcal{E}), \mathsf{Aut}_\Phi)$ *terminates.*

6 Experimental Evaluation

We implemented our algorithm in a prototype string solver called NOODLER [63] using Python and a homemade C++ automata library for manipulating NFAs. We compared the performance of NOODLER with a comprehensive selection of other tools, namely, CVC5 [13] (version 1.0.1), Z3 [15] (version 4.8.14), Z3STR3RE [20], Z3STR4 [64], Z3-TRAU [34], OSTRICH [23], SLOTH [65], and RETRO [48]. In order to have a meaningful comparison with compiled tools (CVC5, Z3, Z3STR3RE, Z3STR4, Z3-TRAU), the reported time for NOODLER does not contain the startup time of the Python interpreter and the time taken by loading libraries (this is a constant of around 1.5 s). To be fair, one should take this into account when considering the time of other interpreted tools, such as OSTRICH, SLOTH (both Java), and RETRO (Python). As can be seen from the results, it would, however, not significantly impact the overall outcome. The experiments were executed on a workstation with an Intel Core i5 661 CPU at 3.33 GHz with 16 GiB of RAM running Debian GNU/Linux. The timeout was set to 60 s.

Benchmarks. We consider the following benchmarks, having removed unsupported formulae (i.e., formulae with length constraints or transducer operations).

- PYEX-HARD ([48], 20,023 formulae): it comes from the PYEX benchmark [10], in particular, it is obtained from 967 difficult instances that neither

Table 1. Results of experiments. For each benchmark and tool, we give the number of timeouts ("T/Os"), the total run time (in seconds), and the run time without timeouts ("time−T/O"). Best values are in **bold**.

	PyEx-Hard (20,023)			Kaluza-Hard (897)			Str 2 (293)			Slog (1,896)		
	T/Os	time	time−T/O	T/Os	time	time−T/O	T/Os	time	time−T/O	T/Os	time	time−T/O
Noodler	**39**	**5,266**	2,926	**0**	**46**	46	3	**198**	18	**0**	165	165
Z3	2,802	178,078	9,958	207	15,360	2,940	149	8,955	15	2	332	212
CVC5	112	12,523	5,803	**0**	55	55	92	5,525	**5**	**0**	**14**	**14**
Z3str3RE	814	49,744	904	10	622	22	149	8,972	32	55	4,247	947
Z3str4	461	28,114	**454**	17	1,039	**19**	154	9,267	27	208	16,508	4,028
Z3-Trau	108	33,551	27,071	**0**	201	201	10	724	124	5	970	670
OSTRICH	2,979	214,846	36,106	111	14,912	8,252	238	14,497	217	2	13,601	13,481
Sloth	463	371,373	343,593	**0**	3,195	3,195		N/A		202	24,940	12,820
Retro	3,004	199,107	18,867	148	16,404	7,524	**1**	299	239		N/A	

CVC4 nor Z3 could solve in 10 s. PyEx-Hard then contains 20,023 conjunctions of word equations that Z3's DPLL(T) algorithm sent to its string theory solver when trying to solve them.

- Kaluza-Hard (897 formulae): it is obtained from the Kaluza benchmark [46] by taking hard formulae from its solution in a similar way for PyEx-Hard.
- Str 2 ([33], 293 formulae) the original benchmark from [33] contains 600 hand-crafted formulae including word equations and length constraints; the 307 formulae containing length constraints are removed.
- Slog ([35], 1,896 formulae) contains 1,976 formulae obtained from real web applications using static analysis tools JSA [66] and Stranger [39]. 80 of these formulae contain transducer operations (e.g., ReplaceAll).

From the benchmarks, only Slog initially contains regular constraints. Note that an interplay between equations and regular constraints happens in our algorithm even with pure equations on the input. Refinement of regular constraints is indeed the only means in which our algorithm accumulates information. Complex regular constraints are generated by refinement steps from an initial assignment of Σ^* for every variable. We also include useful constraints in preprocessing steps, for instance, the equation $z = xay$ where x and y do not occur elsewhere is substituted by $z \in \Sigma^* a \Sigma^*$.

Results. The results of experiments are given in Table 1. For each benchmark, we list the number of timeouts (i.e., unsolved formulae), the total run time (including timeouts), and also the run time on the successfully decided formulae. The results show that from all tools, Noodler has the lowest number of timeouts on the aggregation of all benchmarks (42 timeouts in total) and also on each individual benchmark (except Str 2 where it is the second lowest, 3 against 1). Furthermore, in all benchmarks except Slog, Noodler is faster than other tools (and for Slog it is the second). The results for Sloth on Str 2 are omitted because Sloth was incorrect on this benchmark (the benchmark is not straight-line) and the results for Retro on Slog are omitted because Retro does not support regular constraints.

In Fig. 3, we provide scatter plots comparing the run times of NOODLER with the best competitors, CVC5 and Z3STR4, on the PYEX-HARD benchmark (scatter plots for the other benchmarks are less interesting and can be found in [60]). We can see that there is indeed a large number of benchmarks where NOODLER is faster than both competitors (and that the performance of NOODLER is more stable, which may be caused by the heuristics in the other tools not always working well). Notice that NOODLER and CVC5 are on this benchmark complementary: they have both some timeouts, but each formula is solved by at least one of the tools.

Moreover, in Fig. 2, we provide a graph showing times needed to solve 1,023 most difficult formulae for the tools on the PYEX-HARD benchmark.

Discussion. The results of the experiments show that our algorithm (even in its prototype implementation in Python) can beat well established solvers such as CVC5, Z3, and Z3STR4. In particular, it can solve more benchmarks, and also the average time for (successfully) solving a benchmark is low (as witnessed by the "time–T/O" column in Table 1). The scatter plots also show that it is often complementary to other solvers.

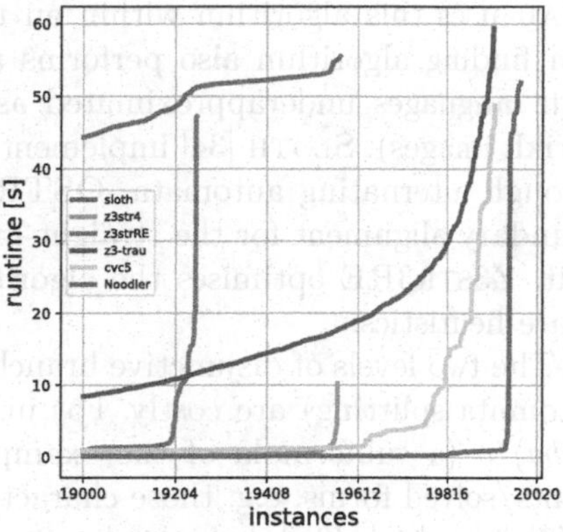

Fig. 2. Times for solving the hardest 1,023 formulae for the tools on PYEX-HARD

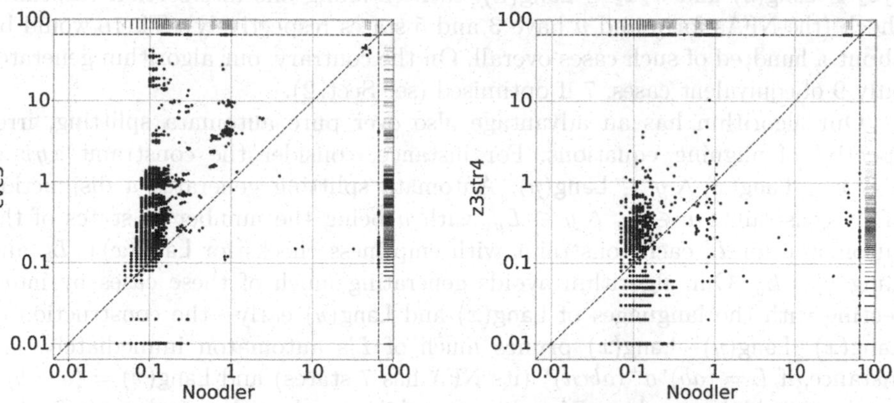

(a) NOODLER VS. CVC5. (b) NOODLER VS. Z3STR4.

Fig. 3. The performance of NOODLER and other tools on PYEX-HARD. Times are given in seconds, axes are logarithmic. Dashed lines represent timeouts (60 s).

7 Related Work

Our algorithm is an improvement of the automata-based algorithm first proposed in [30], which is, at least in part, used as the basis of several string solvers, namely, Norn [26,30,31], Trau [27–29,34], OSTRICH [21–23], and Z3str3RE [20]. The original algorithm first transforms equations to the disjunction of their solved forms [59] through generating alignments of variable boundaries on the equation sides (essentially an incomplete version of Makanin's algorithm). Second, it eliminates concatenation from regular constraints by *automata splitting*. The algorithm replaces $x \cdot y \in L$ by a disjunction of cases $x \in L_x \wedge y \in L_y$, one case for each state of L's automaton. Each disjunct later entails testing emptiness of $L_x \cap \mathsf{Lang}(x)$ and $L_y \cap \mathsf{Lang}(y)$ by the automata product construction. Trau uses this algorithm within an unsatisfiability check. Trau's main solution finding algorithm also performs a step similar to our refinement, though with languages underapproximated as arithmetic formulae (representing their Parikh images). Sloth [34] implements a compact version of automata splitting through alternating automata. OSTRICH has a way of avoiding the variable boundary alignment for the straight-line formulae, although still uses it outside of it. Z3str3RE optimises the algorithm of [30] heavily by the use of length-aware heuristics.

The two levels of disjunctive branching (transformation into solved form and automata splitting) are costly. For instance, for $xyx = zu \wedge z \in a(ba)^* \wedge u \in (baba)^*a$ (a subformula of the example in Sect. 2), there would be 14 alignments/solved forms, e.g. those characterised using lengths as follows: (1) $|zu| = 0$; (2) $|y| = |zu|$; (3) $|x| < |z|, |y| = 0$; (4) $|xy| < z, |y| > 0$; (5) $|x| < |z|, |xy| > z$; ... In the case (5) alone—corresponding to the solved form $z = z_1z_2, u = u_1z_1, x = z_1, y = z_2u_1$—automata splitting would generate 15 cases from $z_1z_2 \in \mathsf{Lang}(z)$ and $u_1u_2 \in \mathsf{Lang}(u)$, each entailing one intersection emptiness check (the NFAs for z and u have 3 and 5 states respectively). There would be about a hundred of such cases overall. On the contrary, our algorithm generates only 9 of equivalent cases, 7 if optimised (see Sect. 2).

Our algorithm has an advantage also over pure automata splitting, irrespective of aligning equations. For instance, consider the constraint $xyx \in L \wedge x \in \mathsf{Lang}(x) \wedge y \in \mathsf{Lang}(y)$. Automata splitting generates a disjunction of n^2 constraints $x \in L_x \wedge y \in L_y$, with n being the number of states of the automaton for L, each constraint with emptiness checks for $\mathsf{Lang}(x) \cap L_x$ and $\mathsf{Lang}(y) \cap L_y$. Our algorithm avoids generating much of these cases by intersecting with the languages of $\mathsf{Lang}(x)$ and $\mathsf{Lang}(y)$ early—the construction of $\mathsf{Lang}(x) \cdot \mathsf{Lang}(y) \cdot \mathsf{Lang}(x)$ prunes much of L's automaton immediately. For instance, if $L = (ab)^*a^+(abcd)^*$ (its NFA has 7 states) and $\mathsf{Lang}(x) = (a+b)^*$, automata splitting explores $7^2 = 49$ cases while our algorithm explores 9 (7 when optimised) of these cases—it would compute the same product and noodles as in Sect. 2, essentially ignoring the disjunct $(abcd)^*$ of L.

Approaches and tools for string solving are numerous and diverse, with various representations of constraints, algorithms, or sorts of inputs. Many approaches use automata, e.g., Stranger [39–41], Norn [30,31], OSTRICH

[21–25], TRAU [26–29], SLOTH [34], SLOG [35], Slent [36], Z3STR3RE [20], RETRO [48], ABC [42,43], Qzy [47], or BEK [51]. Around word equations are centered tools such as CVC4/5 [6–12], Z3 [14,15], S3 [32], $\texttt{Kepler}_{22}$ [33], StrSolve [37], Woorpje [49]; bit vectors are (among other things) used in Z3Str/2/3/4 [16–19], HAMPI [45]; PASS uses arrays [50]; G-strings [38] and GECODE+S [44] use SAT-solving. Most of these tools and methods handle much wider range of string constraints than equations and regular constraints. Our algorithm is not a complete alternative but a promising basis that could improve some of the existing solvers and become a core of a new one. With regard to equations and regular constraints, the fragment of chain-free constraints [26] that we handle, handled also by TRAU, is the largest for which any string solvers offers formal completeness guarantees, with the exception of quadratic equations, handled, e.g., by [33,48], which are incomparable but of a smaller practical relevance (although some tools actually implement Nielsen's algorithm [58] to handle simple quadratic cases). The other solvers guarantee completeness on smaller fragments, notably that of OSTRICH (straight-line), NORN, and Z3STR3RE; or use incomplete heuristics that work in practice (giving up guarantees of termination, over or under-approximating by various means). Most string solvers tend to avoid handling regular expressions, by means of postponing them as much as possible or abstracting them into arithmetic/length and other constraints (e.g. TRAU, Z3STR3RE, Z3STR4, CVC4/5, S3). A major point of our work is that taking the opposite approach may work even better when automata are approached from the right angle and implemented carefully, though, heuristics that utilise length information or Parikh images would most probably speed up our algorithm as well. The main selling point of our approach is its efficiency compared to the others, demonstrated on benchmark sets used in other works.

8 Conclusion and Future Work

We have presented a new algorithm for solving a fragment of word equations with regular constraints, complete in SAT cases and for the chain-free fragment. It is based on a tight interconnection of equations with regular constraints and built around a novel characterisation of satisfiability of a string constraint through the notion of stability. We have experimentally shown that the algorithm is very competitive with existing solutions, better especially on difficult examples.

We plan to continue from here towards a complete string solver. This involves including other types of constraints and coming up with a mature and optimised implementation. The core algorithm might also be optimised by using a more compact automata representation of noodles that would eliminate redundancies.

Acknowledgements. This work was supported by the Czech Ministry of Education, Youth and Sports project LL1908 of the ERC.CZ programme, the Czech Science Foundation project GA20-07487S, the FIT BUT internal project FIT-S-20-6427, and the project of Ministry of Science and Technology, Taiwan (grant no. 109-2628-E-001-001-MY3).

References

1. OWASP: Top 10 (2013). https://www.owasp.org/images/f/f8/OWASP_Top_10_-_2013.pdf
2. OWASP: Top 10 (2017). https://owasp.org/www-project-top-ten/2017/
3. OWASP: Top 10 (2021). https://owasp.org/Top10/
4. Hadarean, L.: String solving at Amazon (2019). Presented at MOSCA 2019. https://mosca19.github.io/program/index.html
5. Alt, L., Blicha, M., Hyvärinen, A.E.J., Sharygina, N.: SolCMC: solidity compiler's model checker. In: Shoham, S., Vizel, Y. (eds.) Computer Aided Verification (CAV 2022). LNCS, vol. 13371, pp. 325–338. Springer, Cham (2022). https://doi.org/10.1007/978-3-031-13185-1_16
6. Liang, T., Reynolds, A., Tinelli, C., Barrett, C., Deters, M.: A DPLL(T) theory solver for a theory of strings and regular expressions. In: Biere, A., Bloem, R. (eds.) CAV 2014. LNCS, vol. 8559, pp. 646–662. Springer, Cham (2014). https://doi.org/10.1007/978-3-319-08867-9_43
7. Liang, T., Reynolds, A., Tsiskaridze, N., Tinelli, C., Barrett, C., Deters, M.: An efficient SMT solver for string constraints. Form. Methods Syst. Des. **48**(3), 206–234 (2016). https://doi.org/10.1007/s10703-016-0247-6
8. Barrett, C.W., Tinelli, C., Deters, M., Liang, T., Reynolds, A., Tsiskaridze, N.: Efficient solving of string constraints for security analysis. In: HotSoS 2016, ACM Trans. Comput. Log., pp. 4–6 (2016)
9. Liang, T., Tsiskaridze, N., Reynolds, A., Tinelli, C., Barrett, C.: A decision procedure for regular membership and length constraints over unbounded strings. In: Lutz, C., Ranise, S. (eds.) FroCoS 2015. LNCS (LNAI), vol. 9322, pp. 135–150. Springer, Cham (2015). https://doi.org/10.1007/978-3-319-24246-0_9
10. Reynolds, A., Woo, M., Barrett, C., Brumley, D., Liang, T., Tinelli, C.: Scaling up DPLL(T) string solvers using context-dependent simplification. In: Majumdar, R., Kunčak, V. (eds.) CAV 2017. LNCS, vol. 10427, pp. 453–474. Springer, Cham (2017). https://doi.org/10.1007/978-3-319-63390-9_24
11. Nötzli, A., Reynolds, A., Barbosa, H., Barrett, C., Tinelli, C.: Even faster conflicts and lazier reductions for string solvers. In: Shoham, S., Vizel, Y. (eds.) Computer Aided Verification (CAV 2022), pp. 205–226. Springer, Cham (2022). https://doi.org/10.1007/978-3-031-13188-2_11
12. Reynolds, A., Notzlit, A., Barrett, C., Tinelli, C.: Reductions for strings and regular expressions revisited. In: 2020 Formal Methods in Computer Aided Design (FMCAD), pp. 225–235 (2020)
13. Barbosa, H., et al.: cvc5: a versatile and industrial-strength SMT solver. In: TACAS 2022. LNCS, vol. 13243, pp. 415–442. Springer, Cham (2022). https://doi.org/10.1007/978-3-030-99524-9_24
14. Bjørner, N., Tillmann, N., Voronkov, A.: Path feasibility analysis for string-manipulating programs. In: Tools and Algorithms for the Construction and Analysis of Systems: 15th International Conference (TACAS 2009), Held as Part of the Joint European Conferences on Theory and Practice of Software (ETAPS 2009), York, UK, 22–29 March 2009. Proceedings 15, pp. 307–321. Springer, Heidelberg (2009)
15. de Moura, L., Bjørner, N.: Z3: an efficient SMT solver. In: Ramakrishnan, C.R., Rehof, J. (eds.) TACAS 2008. LNCS, vol. 4963, pp. 337–340. Springer, Heidelberg (2008). https://doi.org/10.1007/978-3-540-78800-3_24

16. Zheng, Y., Zhang, X., Ganesh, V.: Z3-str: a Z3-based string solver for web application analysis. In: ESEC/FSE 2013, ACM Trans. Comput. Log., pp. 114–124 (2013)
17. Berzish, M., Ganesh, V., Zheng, Y.: Z3str3: a string solver with theory-aware heuristics. In: 2017 Formal Methods in Computer Aided Design (FMCAD), pp. 55–59 (2017)
18. Murphy, B.: Z3str4: a solver for theories over strings. PhD thesis (2021)
19. Zheng, Y., Ganesh, V., Subramanian, S., Tripp, O., Dolby, J., Zhang, X.: Effective search-space pruning for solvers of string equations, regular expressions and length constraints. In: Kroening, D., Păsăreanu, C.S. (eds.) CAV 2015. LNCS, vol. 9206, pp. 235–254. Springer, Cham (2015). https://doi.org/10.1007/978-3-319-21690-4_14
20. Berzish, M., et al.: An SMT solver for regular expressions and linear arithmetic over string length. In: Silva, A., Leino, K.R.M. (eds.) CAV 2021. LNCS, vol. 12760, pp. 289–312. Springer, Cham (2021). https://doi.org/10.1007/978-3-030-81688-9_14
21. Lin, A.W., Barceló, P.: String solving with word equations and transducers: towards a logic for analysing mutation XSS. In: POPL 2016, ACM Trans. Comput. Log., pp. 123–136 (2016)
22. Chen, T., Chen, Y., Hague, M., Lin, A.W., Wu, Z.: What is decidable about string constraints with the replaceall function. Proc. ACM Program. Lang. **2**(POPL), 3:1–3:29 (2018)
23. Chen, T., Hague, M., Lin, A.W., Rümmer, P., Wu, Z.: Decision procedures for path feasibility of string-manipulating programs with complex operations. Proc. ACM Program. Lang. **3**(POPL), 49:1–49:30 (2019)
24. Chen, T., et al.: Solving string constraints with regex-dependent functions through transducers with priorities and variables. Proc. ACM Program. Lang. **6**(POPL), 1–31 (2022)
25. Chen, T., et al.: A decision procedure for path feasibility of string manipulating programs with integer data type. In: Hung, D.V., Sokolsky, O. (eds.) ATVA 2020. LNCS, vol. 12302, pp. 325–342. Springer, Cham (2020). https://doi.org/10.1007/978-3-030-59152-6_18
26. Abdulla, P.A., Atig, M.F., Diep, B.P., Holík, L., Janků, P.: Chain-free string constraints. In: Chen, Y.-F., Cheng, C.-H., Esparza, J. (eds.) ATVA 2019. LNCS, vol. 11781, pp. 277–293. Springer, Cham (2019). https://doi.org/10.1007/978-3-030-31784-3_16
27. Abdulla, P.A., et al.: TRAU: SMT solver for string constraints. In: Bjørner, N.S., Gurfinkel, A. (eds.) 2018 Formal Methods in Computer Aided Design (FMCAD 2018), pp. 1–5. IEEE (2018)
28. Abdulla, P.A., et al.: Flatten and conquer: a framework for efficient analysis of string constraints. In: Cohen, A., Vechev, M.T. (eds.) Proceedings of the 38th ACM SIGPLAN Conference on Programming Language Design and Implementation (PLDI 2017), pp. 602–617, ACM (2017)
29. Abdulla, P.A., et al.: Solving not-substring constraint with flat abstraction. In: Oh, H. (ed.) APLAS 2021. LNCS, vol. 13008, pp. 305–320. Springer, Cham (2021). https://doi.org/10.1007/978-3-030-89051-3_17
30. Abdulla, P.A., et al.: String constraints for verification. In: Biere, A., Bloem, R. (eds.) CAV 2014. LNCS, vol. 8559, pp. 150–166. Springer, Cham (2014). https://doi.org/10.1007/978-3-319-08867-9_10
31. Abdulla, P.A., et al.: Norn: an SMT solver for string constraints. In: Kroening, D., Păsăreanu, C.S. (eds.) CAV 2015. LNCS, vol. 9206, pp. 462–469. Springer, Cham (2015). https://doi.org/10.1007/978-3-319-21690-4_29

32. Trinh, M., Chu, D., Jaffar, J.: S3: a symbolic string solver for vulnerability detection in web applications. In: CCS, ACM Trans. Comput. Log., pp. 1232–1243 (2014)
33. Le, Q.L., He, M.: A decision procedure for string logic with quadratic equations, regular expressions and length constraints. In: Ryu, S. (ed.) APLAS 2018. LNCS, vol. 11275, pp. 350–372. Springer, Cham (2018). https://doi.org/10.1007/978-3-030-02768-1_19
34. Abdulla, P.A., et al.: Efficient handling of string-number conversion. In: Proc. of PLDI 2020, ACM, pp. 943–957 (2020)
35. Wang, H.-E., Tsai, T.-L., Lin, C.-H., Yu, F., Jiang, J.-H.R.: String analysis via automata manipulation with logic circuit representation. In: Chaudhuri, S., Farzan, A. (eds.) CAV 2016. LNCS, vol. 9779, pp. 241–260. Springer, Cham (2016). https://doi.org/10.1007/978-3-319-41528-4_13
36. Wang, H.E., Chen, S.Y., Yu, F., Jiang, J.H.R.: A symbolic model checking approach to the analysis of string and length constraints. In: Proceedings of the 33rd ACM/IEEE International Conference on Automated Software Engineering (ASE 2018), pp. 623–633. Association for Computing Machinery, NY (2018)
37. Hooimeijer, P., Weimer, W.: StrSolve: solving string constraints lazily. Autom. Softw. Eng. **19**(4), 531–559 (2012)
38. Amadini, R., Gange, G., Stuckey, P.J., Tack, G.: A novel approach to string constraint solving. In: Beck, J.C. (ed.) CP 2017. LNCS, vol. 10416, pp. 3–20. Springer, Cham (2017). https://doi.org/10.1007/978-3-319-66158-2_1
39. Yu, F., Alkhalaf, M., Bultan, T.: Stranger: an automata-based string analysis tool for PHP. In: Esparza, J., Majumdar, R. (eds.) TACAS 2010. LNCS, vol. 6015, pp. 154–157. Springer, Heidelberg (2010). https://doi.org/10.1007/978-3-642-12002-2_13
40. Yu, F., Alkhalaf, M., Bultan, T., Ibarra, O.H.: Automata-based symbolic string analysis for vulnerability detection. Form. Methods Syst. Des. **44**(1), 44–70 (2014)
41. Yu, F., Bultan, T., Ibarra, O.H.: Relational string verification using multi-track automata. Int. J. Found. Comput. Sci. **22**(8), 1909–1924 (2011)
42. Aydin, A., Bang, L., Bultan, T.: Automata-based model counting for string constraints. In: Kroening, D., Păsăreanu, C.S. (eds.) CAV 2015. LNCS, vol. 9206, pp. 255–272. Springer, Cham (2015). https://doi.org/10.1007/978-3-319-21690-4_15
43. Bultan, T., contributors: ABC string solver
44. Scott, J.D., Flener, P., Pearson, J., Schulte, C.: Design and implementation of bounded-length sequence variables. In: Salvagnin, D., Lombardi, M. (eds.) CPAIOR 2017. LNCS, vol. 10335, pp. 51–67. Springer, Cham (2017). https://doi.org/10.1007/978-3-319-59776-8_5
45. Kiezun, A., Ganesh, V., Artzi, S., Guo, P.J., Hooimeijer, P., Ernst, M.D.: HAMPI: a solver for word equations over strings, regular expressions, and context-free grammars. ACM Trans. Comput. Log. **21**(4), 25:1–25:28 (2012)
46. Saxena, P., Akhawe, D., Hanna, S., Mao, F., McCamant, S., Song, D.: A symbolic execution framework for JavaScript. In: SP 2010, IEEE Computer Society, pp. 513–528 (2010)
47. Cox, A., Leasure, J.: Model checking regular language constraints. arXiv preprint arXiv:1708.09073 (2017)
48. Chen, Y.-F., Havlena, V., Lengál, O., Turrini, A.: A symbolic algorithm for the case-split rule in string constraint solving. In: Oliveira, B.C.S. (ed.) APLAS 2020. LNCS, vol. 12470, pp. 343–363. Springer, Cham (2020). https://doi.org/10.1007/978-3-030-64437-6_18

49. Day, J.D., Ehlers, T., Kulczynski, M., Manea, F., Nowotka, D., Poulsen, D.B.: On solving word equations using SAT. In: Filiot, E., Jungers, R., Potapov, I. (eds.) RP 2019. LNCS, vol. 11674, pp. 93–106. Springer, Cham (2019). https://doi.org/10.1007/978-3-030-30806-3_8
50. Li, G., Ghosh, I.: PASS: string solving with parameterized array and interval automaton. In: Bertacco, V., Legay, A. (eds.) HVC 2013. LNCS, vol. 8244, pp. 15–31. Springer, Cham (2013). https://doi.org/10.1007/978-3-319-03077-7_2
51. Hooimeijer, P., Livshits, B., Molnar, D., Saxena, P., Veanes, M.: Fast and precise sanitizer analysis with BEK. In: USENIX Security Symposium 2011, USENIX Association (2011)
52. Veanes, M., Hooimeijer, P., Livshits, B., Molnar, D., Bjørner, N.: Symbolic finite state transducers: algorithms and applications. In: POPL 2012, ACM Trans. Comput. Log., pp. 137–150 (2012)
53. Fu, X., Li, C.: Modeling regular replacement for string constraint solving. In: NFM 2010. Volume NASA/CP-2010-216215 of NASA, pp. 67–76 (2010)
54. Trinh, M.-T., Chu, D.-H., Jaffar, J.: Progressive reasoning over recursively-defined strings. In: Chaudhuri, S., Farzan, A. (eds.) CAV 2016. LNCS, vol. 9779, pp. 218–240. Springer, Cham (2016). https://doi.org/10.1007/978-3-319-41528-4_12
55. Plandowski, W.: Satisfiability of word equations with constants is in NEXPTIME. In: Proceedings of the Thirty-First Annual ACM Symposium on Theory of Computing (STOC 1999), pp. 721–725. Association for Computing Machinery, NY (1999)
56. Jeż, A.: Recompression: a simple and powerful technique for word equations. J. ACM **63**(1), 1–51 (2016)
57. Makanin, G.S.: The problem of solvability of equations in a free semigroup. Matematicheskii Sbornik **32**(2), 147–236 (1977). (in Russian)
58. Nielsen, J.: Die isomorphismen der allgemeinen, unendlichen gruppe mit zwei erzeugenden. Math. Ann. **78**(1), 385–397 (1917)
59. Ganesh, V., Minnes, M., Solar-Lezama, A., Rinard, M.: Word equations with length constraints: what's decidable? In: Biere, A., Nahir, A., Vos, T. (eds.) HVC 2012. LNCS, vol. 7857, pp. 209–226. Springer, Heidelberg (2013). https://doi.org/10.1007/978-3-642-39611-3_21
60. Blahoudek, F., et al.: Word equations in synergy with regular constraints (technical report). arXiv preprint arXiv:2212.02317 (2022)
61. Aziz, A., Singhal, V., Swamy, G., Brayton, R.K.: Minimizing interacting finite state machines. Technical Report UCB/ERL M93/68, EECS Department, University of California, Berkeley (1993)
62. Henzinger, M., Henzinger, T., Kopke, P.: Computing simulations on finite and infinite graphs. In: Proceedings of IEEE 36th Annual Foundations of Computer Science, pp. 453–462 (1995)
63. Blahoudek, F., et al.: Noodler (2022). https://github.com/vhavlena/Noodler
64. Mora, F., Berzish, M., Kulczynski, M., Nowotka, D., Ganesh, V.: Z3str4: a multi-armed string solver. In: Huisman, M., Păsăreanu, C., Zhan, N. (eds.) FM 2021. LNCS, vol. 13047, pp. 389–406. Springer, Cham (2021). https://doi.org/10.1007/978-3-030-90870-6_21
65. Holík, L., Janku, P., Lin, A.W., Rümmer, P., Vojnar, T.: String constraints with concatenation and transducers solved efficiently. Proc. ACM Program. Lang. **2**(POPL), 4:1–4:32 (2018)
66. Christensen, A.S., Møller, A., Schwartzbach, M.I.: Precise analysis of string expressions. In: Cousot, R. (ed.) SAS 2003. LNCS, vol. 2694, pp. 1–18. Springer, Heidelberg (2003). https://doi.org/10.1007/3-540-44898-5_1

Formal Methods in AI

Verifying Feedforward Neural Networks for Classification in Isabelle/HOL

Achim D. Brucker and Amy Stell(✉)

Department of Computer Science, University of Exeter, Exeter, UK
{a.brucker,as1343}@exeter.ac.uk
https://brucker.ch,
https://emps.exeter.ac.uk/computer-science/staff/as1343

Abstract. Neural networks are being used successfully to solve classification problems, e.g., for detecting objects in images. It is well known that neural networks are susceptible if small changes applied to their input result in misclassification. Situations in which such a slight input change, often hardly noticeable by a human expert, results in a misclassification are called adversarial examples. If such inputs are used for adversarial attacks, they can be life-threatening if, for example, they occur in image classification systems used in autonomous cars or medical diagnosis.

Systems employing neural networks, e.g., for safety or security-critical functionality, are a particular challenge for formal verification, which usually expects a formal specification (e.g., given as source code in a programming language for which a formal semantics exists). Such a formal specification does, per se, not exist for neural networks.

In this paper, we address this challenge by presenting a formal embedding of feedforward neural networks into Isabelle/HOL and discussing desirable properties for neural networks in critical applications. Our Isabelle-based prototype can import neural networks trained in TensorFlow, and we demonstrate our approach using a neural network trained for the classification of digits on a dot-matrix display.

Keywords: Neural network · Deep learning · Classification network · Feedforward network · Verification · Isabelle/HOL

1 Introduction

Deep learning, i.e., machine learning using neural networks is used successfully in many application areas, e.g., image classification ([11,24,37]). While systems using neural networks are also used in safety-critical areas (e.g., for the recognition of street signs in semi-autonomous cars [11]), the use of neural networks

This work was supported by the Engineering and Physical Sciences Research Council [grant number 670002170].

M. Chechik et al. (Eds.): FM 2023, LNCS 14000, pp. 427–444, 2023.
https://doi.org/10.1007/978-3-031-27481-7_24

in high-assurance systems is limited due to the lack of formal verification techniques that satisfy the stringent requirements of industrial certification standards such as BS EN 50128 [10] (safety) or Common Criteria [14] (security) that are required for such applications.

The formal specification and verification techniques that such standards require usually rely on the existence of an implementation (e.g., source code) whose compliance to a specification can be verified (e.g., following an approach similar to [23]). For systems based on neural networks, such an implementation that precisely describes, in a human-readable form, the system's behaviour does not exist. The only artefact that exists is a neural network trained on a set of training data, which is expected to behave correctly for all possible inputs.

Formal verification is an approach that can make a statement for all possible inputs. In this paper, we present an approach based on the interactive theorem prover Isabelle/HOL for the formal verification of neural networks. Using an expressive formalism, such as higher-order logic, allows for expressing complex properties that a neural network needs to satisfy. On the one hand, the fact that Isabelle is an interactive theorem prover enables the user to explore the properties of the network and, therefore, deepen the understanding of the neural network being analysed. On the other hand, Isabelle is a framework that allows us to provide highly automated functionality for both, encoding a specific neural network, and for proving properties over it.

In more detail, our contributions are three-fold:

1. a formal embedding of feedforward neural networks into Isabelle/HOL,
2. a verification environment supporting the verification of neural networks trained using TensorFlow, and
3. an application of our framework to a case study.

The rest of the paper is structured as follows: first, we introduce the background of our work (Sect. 2) and a small running example (Sect. 3). Next, we introduce our formal model of feedforward neural networks in Isabelle/HOL in Sect. 4 and discuss the desirable properties of classification networks in Sect. 5. In Sect. 6, we briefly explain our implementation in Isabelle/HOL before we briefly discuss a case study for classifying dot-matrix digits (Sect. 7). Finally, we discuss related work (Sect. 8) and draw conclusions (Sect. 9).

2 Isabelle and Higher-Order Logic (HOL)

In this section, we introduce two aspects of Isabelle/HOL; its logic (HOL) and its implementation architecture.

2.1 Isabelle/HOL

Isabelle [28] is a well-known interactive theorem prover that has been used successfully in large-scale verification projects (e.g., [23] presents the verification of an operating system kernel using Isabelle/HOL). The formal language of Isabelle is *Higher-order logic* (HOL) [12], which is a classical logic based on a simple type system. It provides the usual logical connectives like $\neg$ _, _ $\wedge$ _, _ $\vee$ _, _ $\longrightarrow$ _ as well as the object-logical quantifiers $\forall$ `x. P x` and $\exists$ `x. P x`. In contrast to first-order logic, quantifiers may range over arbitrary types, including total functions `f` :: $\alpha \Rightarrow \beta$ (where α and β are polymorphic type variables).

Isabelle/HOL offers support for extending theories in a logically safe way: A theory-extension is *conservative* if the extended theory is consistent, provided that the original theory was consistent. Conservative extensions can be *constant definitions*, *type definitions*, *datatype definitions*, *primitive recursive definitions* and *well-founded recursive definitions*.

2.2 Isabelle as Formal Methods Framework

Isabelle is not only an interactive theorem prover; it also provides an extensible framework for developing formal method tools [39]. Figure 1 shows an overview of the Isabelle architecture. For our work, it is noteworthy that new components can be implemented in Isabelle/ML, i.e., Isabelle's SML [29] programming interface. In a logically safe way, we use this interface to provide an import mechanism for importing neural networks and implementing domain-specific proof methods. Furthermore, use the code generator to efficiently evaluate neural networks, i.e., compute predictions for concrete inputs.

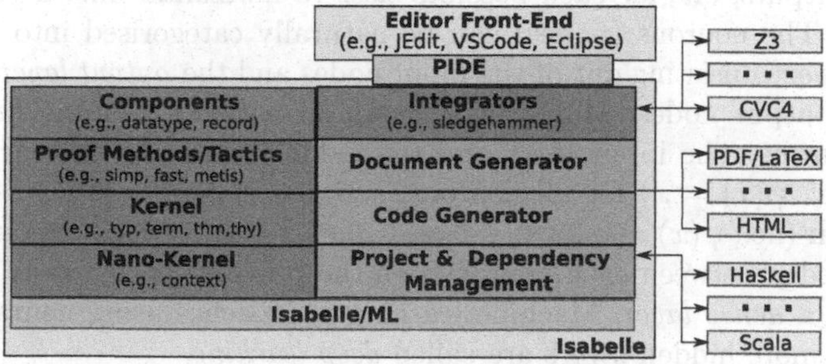

Fig. 1. The system architecture of Isabelle.

3 Running Example: Classifying Lines in a Grid

In the following, we introduce neural networks for (image) classification by using a simple line classification problem: given a 2×2 pixel greyscale image, the neural network should decide if the image contains a horizontal line (e.g., Fig. 2a), vertical line (e.g., Fig. 2b), or no line (Fig. 2c).

Traditionally, textbooks (e.g., [3]) define a feedforward neural network as directed weighted acyclic graphs. The nodes are called *neurons*, and the incoming

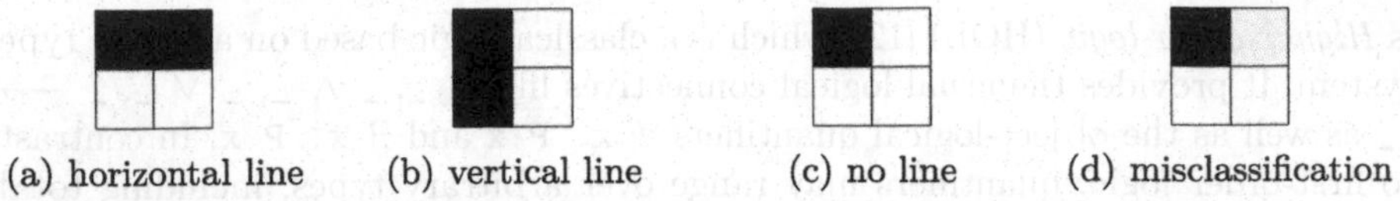

Fig. 2. Example input images to our classification problem.

edges are called *inputs*. For a given neuron k with m inputs x_{k_0} to $x_{k_{m-1}}$, and the respective weights w_{k_0} to $w_{k_{m-1}}$ the neuron computes the output

$$y_k = \varphi\left(\beta + \sum_{j=0}^{m} w_{k_j} x_{k_j}\right) \tag{1}$$

where φ is the *activation function* and β the *bias* for the neuron k. The values for the weights and biases are determined during the training (learning) phase, which we omit due to space reasons. In our work, we assume that the given neural network is already trained, e.g., using the widely used machine learning framework TensorFlow [1].

Figure 3 illustrates the architecture of our neural network: The neural network for our example classification problem has four inputs (one for each pixel of the image), expecting an input value between 0.0 (white) and 1.0 (black). It also has three outputs, one for each possible class (a horizontal line, a vertical line, or no line). The neurons (nodes) can be naturally categorised into layers, i.e., the *input layer* consisting out of the input nodes and the *output layer* consisting out of the output nodes. Moreover, our neural network has one *hidden layer* with 16 neurons. The input layer and the hidden layer use a linear activation function (i.e., $\varphi(x) = x$) for all neurons, and the hidden layer uses the binary step function (i.e., $\varphi(x) = 0$ for $x \leq 0$ and $\varphi(x) = 1$ otherwise). In our example, there is an edge between each neuron from the previous layer to the next layer, often called a *dense layer*. Machine learning approaches using neural networks with one or more hidden layers are called *deep learning*.

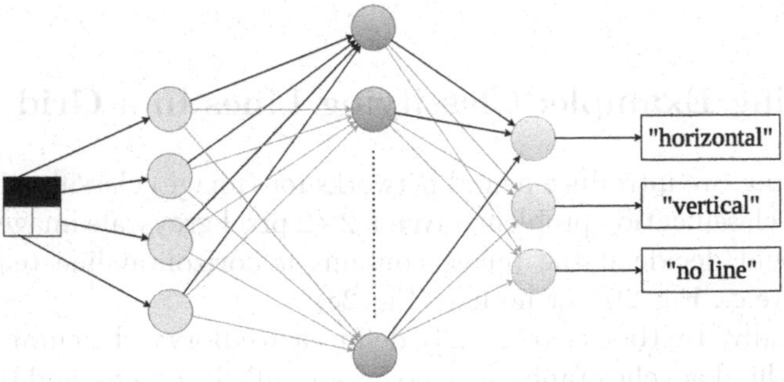

Fig. 3. Neural network for classifying lines in 2×2 pixel greyscale images.

In our example, we used the Python API for TensorFlow [1] to train our neural network. We obtained a neural network that reliably classifies black lines in a given 2×2 image with 100% accuracy. While this sounds great, the neural network is not very resilient to changes to its input values. Consider, for example, Fig. 2d: a human expert would likely classify this image as "no line". Nevertheless, our neural network classifies this as a horizontal line, even though the upper right pixel is only light grey with a numerical value of 0.05, much closer to white than black. Such a misclassification is usually called an *adversarial example*. If such a network is used in safety or security-critical applications, e.g., for classifying street signs, such misclassifications can be life-threatening.

4 Modelling Neural Networks in Isabelle

Our Isabelle/HOL formalisation contains several models, i.e., one based on modelling neural networks as graphs (i.e., "textbook-style") and one modelling neural networks as layers (i.e., "TensorFlow-style"). Due to space reasons, we will focus in this paper, on the latter.

4.1 Data Modelling

We use locales (i.e., Isabelle's mechanism for parametric theories) to capture fundamental concepts that are shared between different models of neural networks. We start by defining a locale `neural_network_sequential_layers` to describe the common concepts of all neural network models that use layers are core building blocks. For our representation to be a well-formed sequential model, we require that the first layer is an input layer and the last layer is an output layer:

Isabelle (Isar)

```
locale neural_network_sequential_layers =
  fixes N::‹('a::{monoid_add,times}, 'b) neural_network_seq_layers›
  assumes head_is_In:  ‹isIn (hd (layers N))›
  and     last_is_Out: ‹isOut (last (layers N))›
  and     ‹list_all isInternal  ((tl o butlast) (layers N))›
begin end
```

For this encoding of a neural network, we mostly follow TensorFlow's Sequential model [1] and represent our network as a list of layers with an abstract table of activation functions, allowing for extensible and customisable functionality. The record `('a, 'b) neural_network_seq_layers` represents our network where `'a` is an abstract value representing the type of our weights and bias, and `'b` is our activation function.

Isabelle (Isar)

```
record ('a, 'b) neural_network_seq_layers =
   layers ::  ‹('a, 'b) layer  list›
   activation_tab :: ‹'b ⇒ (('a list ⇒ 'a list) option)›
```

Included in our formalisation are definitions for all TensorFlow [1] activation functions, and for those which use e^x, we also provide an approximation using the Taylor series of the exponential function, which has been shown to outperform the original in certain situations [4]. In our running example (recall Sect. 3), the activation functions used during training include binary step in the hidden layer and linear in the output layer.

Isabelle (Isar)
```
definition
  ‹identity = (λv. v)›
definition binary_step :: ‹'a::{zero, ord, one, zero} ⇒ 'a› where
 ‹binary_step = (λ v. if v ≤ 0 then 0 else 1)›
```

As we are using a representation of a network as a list of layers, we also support different layer types and their computations. Currently, our sequential layers model supports five layer types *Input*, *Output*, *Dense*, *Activation*, and, as we allow for the abstraction of activation functions, we can define arbitrary `'b` in the networks `activation_tab`, allowing for custom activation functions. Therefore, we do not need to model TensorFlow's *Lambda* layer explicitly (which is TensorFlow's mechanism for supporting custom activation functions).

Isabelle (Isar)
```
datatype ('a, 'b) layer = In ‹InOutRecord›
                        | Out ‹InOutRecord›
                        | Dense ‹('a,'b) LayerRecord›
                        | Activation ‹('b) ActivationRecord›
```

These layer types differ in how they are connected to the next layer in the network, thus changing the calculation during training and prediction. The Dense layer is the most powerful layer type in the sense that it connects all outputs of the previous layer with all inputs. Hence, other layer types (e.g., TensorFlow's *Activation* layer, which applies an activation function to each output of the previous layer) can be expressed in terms of a Dense layer with certain weights set to the constant 0 to "disable" certain edges.

Each `('a, 'b) LayerRecord` contains the activation, weights and bias in our network (φ, β and ω respectively), while our `('b) ActivationRecord` only contains our abstracted activation function.

Isabelle (Isar)
```
record InOutRecord =
    name:: String.literal
    units:: nat
record ('b) ActivationRecord = InOutRecord +
    φ :: 'b
record ('a, 'b) LayerRecord = ‹('b) ActivationRecord› +
    β :: ‹'a list›
    ω :: ‹'a list list›
```

4.2 Encoding Our Running Example

Using the above definitions, we can now show the specialisation of our formalisation by explaining the representation of our network discussed in Sect. 3, in Isabelle/HOL. We represent this example by first defining the types of our concrete network, as the encoding of the grid uses an array of NumPy [19] 64-bit floats, the `'a` in our record `('a, 'b) neural_network_seq_layers` is instantiated as a real and the `'b`, is of the datatype $\texttt{activation}_{\texttt{multi}}$, (a datatype that allows for the mapping of the abstraction of multi-class activation functions onto its Isabelle/HOL definition).

Next, we have the layers; the input layer is a densely connected layer that passes each input into each neuron in the first hidden layer.

Isabelle (Isar)

```
dense_input ≡ ⦇ name = STR ''dense_input'', units = 4 ⦈
```

The hidden layer in the network is a dense layer with 16 units, the learned weights and bias referenced in this layer refer to the connections that exist between this and the previous input layer.

Isabelle (Isar)

```
dense ≡ ⦇ name = STR ''dense'', units = 16,
          φ = mBinaryStep, β = [5 / 10, ..., - 145 / 10],
          ω = [[1, ..., 1] ..., [8, ..., 8]]⦈
```

The next layer is the final calculation layer in our network and passes the results onto our final output layer, which outputs the prediction of the network.

Isabelle (Isar)

```
dense_1 ≡ ⦇ name = STR ''dense_1'', units = 3,
            φ = mIdentity, β = [1, 0, 0],
            ω = [[0, 0, 0], ...,[0, 0, 0]]⦈
OUTPUT ≡ ⦇ name = STR ''OUTPUT'', units = 3⦈
```

Using the above layer and the activation function definitions; our final neural network for the classification of horizontal and vertical lines can be defined as follows:

Isabelle (Isar)

```
NeuralNet ≡ ⦇ layers = [dense_input, Layers.dense,
                dense_1, OUTPUT], activation_tab = grid.φ_grid⦈
```

4.3 Evaluating Neural Networks

What remains is the evaluation of the network, usually called "prediction". To be able to verify that a network's behaviour falls within our desirable properties (Sect. 5), we need to be able to efficiently evaluate its prediction for a given input. As the calculation performed depends on the layer of the network that we are currently evaluating, we calculate the output based on the layer type and fold this over the network.

The input and output layers of our network pass the inputs directly onto the next layer without any calculation performed; this can be seen in the first two cases of the $\texttt{predict}_{\texttt{layer}}$ function. The dense layer of the network is where Eq. 1 is calculated, case three in $\texttt{predict}_{\texttt{layer}}$, where first the input weights are transposed (`in_weights`), then zipped with their input value (`in_w_pairs`), before calculating the weighted sum (`wsums`), adding the bias (`wsum_bias`), and finally applying the activation function on the result, producing the output for a single dense layer. To calculate the prediction of the network given a set of inputs we then fold $\texttt{predict}_{\texttt{layer}}$ over the network from left to right (`foldl`) in $\texttt{predict}_{\texttt{seq\_layer}}$

It is within this function that we also specify some pre-conditions for the network to be of a valid structure. For example, the length of the input vector must be equal to the number of units in that layer (`length vs = 1`), for the activation, input, and output layers; if this is not the case, then we return the `None` option type, indicating that an error has occurred in prediction.

Isabelle (Isar)

```
fun predict_layer::‹('a, 'b) neural_network_seq_layers
    ⇒ ('a list) option ⇒ ('a, 'b) layer ⇒ ('a list) option› where
  ‹predict_layer N (Some vs) (In ⦇name = _, units = 1⦈)
              = (if length vs = 1 then Some vs else None)›
| ‹predict_layer N (Some vs) (Out ⦇name = _, units = 1⦈)
              = (if length vs = 1 then Some vs else None)›
| ‹predict_layer N (Some vs) (Dense pl)  = (let
              in_weights = convert_weights (ω pl);
              in_w_pairs = map (λ e. zip vs e) in_weights;
              wsums      = map (λ vs'. ∑(x,y)←vs'. x*y) in_w_pairs;
              wsum_bias  = map (λ (s,b). s+b) (zip wsums (β pl))
              in (case activation_tab N (φ pl) of
                     None   ⇒ None
                   | Some f ⇒ Some (f wsum_bias)))›
| ‹predict_layer N (Some vs) (Activation pl) =
      (if length vs = units pl then (case activation_tab N (φ pl) of
                                          None ⇒ None
                                        | Some f ⇒ Some (f vs))
                             else None)›
| ‹predict_layer _ None _ = None›

definition
   ‹predict_seq_layer N xs = foldl (predict_layer N) (Some xs) (layers N)›
```

Although this model of a neural network differs from the textbook definition of a network represented as a weighted and directed graph [3], this encoding follows closely that of TensorFlow [1] where their sequential model consists of an ordered list of layers, in which the activation is consistent within a single layer, and has added support for various layer types. As well as this, our sequential layers model resembles the original vector representation of Rumelhart et al. [32]. However, modelling a network as a list of layers means that it is not appropriate for networks with multiple inputs and outputs, as well as those that have layer sharing and multiple branches. In order to model these networks, we have also developed a formalisation that utilises graph theory and encodes a network as a weighted and directed acyclic graph, allowing the specification of arbitrary connections between layers, including a non-linear topology, it is however, less computationally efficient.

4.4 Compliance of Our Formalisation to TensorFlow

To ensure that our formalisation is a faithful representation of the neural networks that we defined in TensorFlow, we provide a framework that supports the import of trained TensorFlow networks and their test data. We can then use this to evaluate our Isabelle network and validate that the output is the same, hence providing confidence that our formalisation is accurate.

Similar to what we will discuss in Sect. 6, we can import text files containing NumPy [19] arrays of our test inputs, expectations and predictions from our trained TensorFlow network.

Isabelle (Isar)
```
import_data_file file defining inputs
```

We can now prove that our formally encoded neural network computes the same prediction (within an error interval) as TensorFlow. To express this requirement, we first define `check_result_list_interval` for checking that two lists are approximatively equal (we need the error interval due to possible rounding errors in IEEE754 arithmetic in python compared to mathematical reals in Isabelle).

Isabelle (Isar)
```
fun check_result_list_interval where
‹check_result_list_interval None None              = True›
| ‹check_result_list_interval (Some xs) (Some ys)
        = fold (∧) (map2 (λ x y. x ∈ set_of y)  xs ys) True›
| ‹check_result_list_interval _ _ = False›
notation check_result_list_interval (((_)/ ≈₁ (_)) [60, 60] 60)
```

Using `check_result_list_interval`, we now define the property that the (symbolically) computed predictions of a neural network meet our expectations:

Isabelle (Isar)
```
definition
  ensure_testdata_interval :: ‹real list list
     ⇒ (real list ⇒ real list option)
     ⇒ real interval list list ⇒ bool› where
 ‹ensure_testdata_interval inputs P outputs =  foldl (∧) True
   (map (λ e. let a = (P (fst e)) in let b = Some (snd e) in (a ≈ᵢ b))
        (zip inputs outputs))›
notation ensure_testdata_interval (⊢\ᵢ {(_)} (_) {(_)} [3, 90, 3] 60)
```

For our example, we can now prove the following lemma:

Isabelle (Isar)
```
lemma grid_meets_predictions:
‹⊢ᵢ {inputs} (predict_seq_layer NeuralNet) {i_of 0.000001 predictions}›
by(simp add: ensure_testdata_interval_def upper_Interval lower_Interval
             predictions_def i_of_def inputs_def in_set_interval)
```

Where `i_of 0.000001 predictions` computes intervals with the expected predictions as midpoints, i.e., given an expectation p, our lemma shows that the actual prediction p' of our formal neural network is satisfies $|p - p'| \leq 0.000001$.

This lemma is proven by unfolding all definitions using Isabelle's simplifier, which corresponds to a symbolic execution of the prediction function. Hence, we can be sure that our formal model behaves identically to the model executed on TensorFlow on a concrete set of input data.

Many classification networks use the maximum output as the result, without normalisation (e.g., to values between 0 and 1). In such cases, a weaker form of ensuring compliance to predictions might be used that only checks that checks for the maximum output of each given input:

Isabelle (Isar)
```
definition
  ensure_td_max :: ‹real list list ⇒ (real list ⇒ real list option)
     ⇒ real list list ⇒ bool› where
  ‹ensure_td_max inputs P outputs
   = foldl (∧) True
     (map (λ e. case P (fst e) of
                    None ⇒ False
                  | Some p ⇒ map_option fst (pos_of_max p)
                             = map_option fst (pos_of_max (snd e)))
          (zip inputs outputs))›
  notation ensure_td_max (⊢ {(_)} (_) {(_)} [3, 90, 3] 60)
```

We will see an application of this check in Sect. 7.

5 Properties of Classification Networks

In contrast to traditional program verification, for neural networks, there has yet to be an established notion of safety or correctness of a trained neural network.

Recently there has been more of a discussion in this area of different types of properties that should hold for arbitrary networks [33] (discussed in more detail in Sect. 8). However, for our example, we focus on looking at input-output relations and notions of robustness within neighbourhoods of the input.

For example, Pulina et al. [30] consider a network safe, if given every possible input, its output is guaranteed to range within specific bounds. This is motivated by an application in which, e.g., a neural network 'computes' dosages of a drug. In this case, there are certain maximums (or minimums) that are considered to be not safe. This is a property we can easily express in our framework as constraints of the range of computing predictions of a given network.

For pure classification networks, which is our focus in this paper, one is usually only interested in the maximum value of the classification outputs (and only to a lesser extent to its actual value). Often, classification networks use activation functions (such as softmax) that normalise the outputs, or argmax that only outputs the maximum classifier. For our running example, we can easily prove:

Isabelle (Isar)

```
lemma
‹ran (predict_seq_layer NeuralNet xs) ⊆ {[0, 0, 1],[0, 1, 0],[1, 0, 0]}›
```

Where ran is the range operator of HOL. While not a safety property in the traditional sense, this lemma shows that the output of the classification is never ambiguous (i.e., two or more classification output having the value 1).

In a more generalised form, Kurd et al. [25] define safety as a clearly defined input-output-relation, i.e., satisfying a given function (or, in our notation, a higher-order predicate) that is tested on known and unknown inputs. Moreover, the behaviour should be repeatable and predictable, it should also tolerate faults in inputs (e.g., where inputs lie outside a specified set of inputs), and no hazardous outputs (e.g., no output outside the range of the target function) should be predicted. Very similar is the idea of Huang et al. [20], who define safety as the requirement that small changes to an input should not change the classification. For our running example, we can express such a verification goal as follows:

Isabelle (Isar)

```
lemma ‹x3 ∈ {0.96..1.00} ∧ x2 ∈ {0.96..1.00}
    ∧ x1 ∈ {0.00..0.04} ∧ x0 ∈ {0.00..0.04}
    ⟹ predict_seq_layer NeuralNet [x3, x2, x1, x0] = Some [0, 1, 0]›
```

This lemma, which we have proven in Isabelle/HOL (including the corresponding lemmata for the other output classes of our example), states that the classification of the upper horizontal line is resilient to small changes in the greyscale values of the pixels (e.g., caused by dust turning white into a greyish colour or a very bright light that might turn black into a dark grey). While looks good "on paper", it is actually showing the opposite. Already small changes in the colour values that are unlikely to be detected by the naked eye, can result in a misclassification (recall Fig. 2d).

The last example also shows that we will need to develop domain-specific failure models (e.g., modelling the impact of non-optimal camera angles or light conditions), which can then form the basis for deriving safety properties for applications that rely on neural networks. Broadly speaking, this is also suggested by Katz et al. [21] that, in a case study for aircraft avoidance detection, use a notation of unnecessary turning advisories to show that the trained neural network does not omit them.

In addition, there are further properties that we formalised and that can increase the confidence in the predictions of a neural network by reducing the likelihood of ambiguous classification results. This includes, e.g., the requirement that for a given input, the classification outputs have at least a given minimum distance (e.g., avoiding situations where all classification outputs show nearly identical values):

```
Isabelle (Isar)
definition
ensure_delta_min :: ‹real ⇒ (real list ⇒ real list option) ⇒ bool›
where ‹ensure_delta_min δ P = (∀ xs ∈ ran P. δ ≤ δmin xs)›
notation ensure_delta_min ((_) ⊢ (_) [61, 90] 60)
```

6 Implementation

We implemented our approach in Isabelle/HOL, i.e., we made use of the ability of Isabelle to extend it with new datatype packages and proofs (see Fig. 4 for an overview of the extended architecture). In particular, we developed a datatype package that can import trained neural networks using the JSON [16]-based format used by TensorFlowJS [35]:

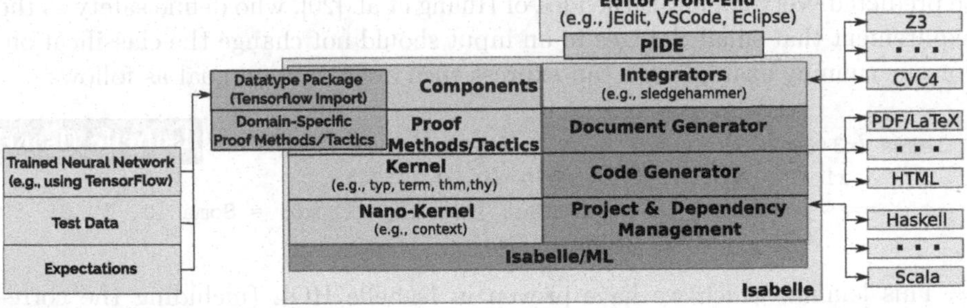

Fig. 4. The system architecture of our architecture, adding a datatype package and custom proof methods to Isabelle/HOL.

```
Isabelle (Isar)
import_TensorFlow grid file model.json as seq_layer
```

Our new Isabelle/Isar [40] command `import_TensorFlow` encodes the neural network model stored in the file `model.json`[1] as sequence of layers (`seq_layer`), i.e., the formal encoding described in Sect. 4 (our datatype package also supports alternative formal encoding, e.g., one that models neural networks as directed graphs). Our datatype package also proves that the imported model complies with the requirements of our formal model (technically, this is done by an automated instantiation proof for the locale `neural_network_sequential_layers`) as well as proves various auxiliary properties (e.g., conversion between different representations) that can be useful during interactive verification.

Our datatype package also supports the automatic import of test data or prediction computed by, e.g., TensorFlow [1], using the data format of NumPy [19]:

```
import_data_file predictions.txt defining predictions
```
Isabelle (Isar)

This command imports the prediction data, i.e., input data and expected outputs, into Isabelle and binds it to the logical constant `predictions`. This data can later be used in a formal proof that the imported model has a certain accuracy on this data set.

Finally, we started to develop domain-specific proof tactics or methods using Eisbach [26], e.g., for the selective unfolding of generated definitions or providing optimised configurations for the symbolic evaluation of the prediction function for neural networks.

Overall, our prototype enables a workflow in which one trains a neural network using, e.g., the Python API for TensorFlow and exports the model and the training and prediction data. This data can then be used to prove that the formal model is semantically equivalent to the original model. Alongside this, we also have an external tool that can convert networks saved in ONNX (https://onnx.ai/) format, providing they have an architecture that our formalisation supports, into the JSON representation we currently require.

Our formalisation comprises over 5300 lines of formal definitions and generic proofs in Isabelle/HOL. The implementation of the datatype package adds another 1000 lines of Isabelle/ML code (not including the JSON-parser and the basic datatype package for JSON, both provided by [8]).

7 Classifying Digits of a 5 × 7 Matrix Display

In this section, we briefly discuss a larger case of a neural network for the classification of digits on a dot-matrix display (see Fig. 5a). As for our running example, we used the Python API of TensorFlow [1] for training the network.

[1] TensorFlowJS stores the structure of the machine learning model in a JSON [16]-based format that refers to a binary file containing the weights and biases. Our import mechanism fully supports this format, i.e., also importing the weights and biases from the external file.

(a) (b) (c)

Fig. 5. The Digit 5 on a 5 × 7 Matrix Display.

Our network has 35 (= 5·7) neurons in the input layer and 10 neurons in the output layer. While our running example (recall Sect. 3) ensures that the output values are between 0 and 1, our neural network for the digit classification has a "non-normalised" output, performing a maximum classification.

Consequently, to convince ourselves that the formal representation of our classification network complies with the TensorFlow representation, we prove:

Isabelle (Isar)

```
lemma digits_meets_expectations_max_classifier:
    ‹⊢ {inputs} (predict_seq_layer digits.NeuralNet) {expectations}›
```

Where `digit.NeuralNet` is the formal representation of our neural network, `inputs` is a list of input values and `expectations` the corresponding expectations (classification). Recalling Sect. 5, we note that this lemma uses the higher-order predicate `ensure_td_max` (`⊢ {_} _ {_}`), which does not require that the predictions lie within a specific interval. Instead, it requires that the maximum classifier of the actual and expected predictions are the same.

Furthermore, we show that an arbitrary one-pixel failure (e.g., a dead pixel or, a pixel that constantly is switched on, or any value in-between) does not change the classification. This is formally expressed as follows:

Isabelle (Isar)

```
lemma assumes xs: ‹xs = [x34,x33, ... , x0]›
and limits: ‹set xs ⊆ {0..1}› (* grey scale pixels *)
and h: ‹hamming (digits!5) xs ≤ 1›
shows ‹classify_as xs 5›
```

Here we make use of an auxiliary predicate for capturing the fact that the network did classify the input as a certain digit:

Isabelle (Isar)

```
definition classify_as::‹real list ⇒ nat ⇒ bool› where
‹classify_as xs n = (Option.bind (predict_seq_layer digits.NeuralNet xs)
                          pos_of_max = Some n)›
```

We model 1-pixel changes by requiring that the Hamming distance representation of the digit 5 (`digits!5`) is at most one. Thus, we have a formal proof that our neural network classifies any image that deviates from an ideal five only by one pixel, reliably as five. Consider, for example, Fig. 5c for which a human could already be uncertain if the image shows a five or a six, even though only one pixel has been changed.

8 Related Work

Using Isabelle/HOL for AI Verification. To the best of our knowledge, there are no examples of formalising neural networks in an Interactive Theorem Prover, and very few examples of formalising machine learning. In Isabelle/HOL the closest related work is by Bentkamp et al [6] which formalises the expressiveness of deep learning. Based on the theoretical work by Cohen et al. [13], verifies the superiority of deep learning over shallow learning. Abdulaziz et al [2] have formally verified the AI planning problem using a SAT encoder, with the formalisation showing that the SAT-based planner Madagascar [31] falsely claims that problems have no solutions of certain lengths.

Neural Network Verification. Many traditional approaches to formal methods and safety verification are insufficient in the case of neural networks as there is no complete specification for their behaviour. Approaches are generally categorised into exact verifiers and incomplete but more efficient verification techniques. On the latter, which solves a relaxed problem that is more computationally efficient, methods include abstract interpretation [27], linear relaxations[38] and duality [15]. Using abstraction, infinite behaviours can be approximated using a finite representation by abstract transformers that are used to capture approximations of network layer computations. The problem then becomes reducing these over-approximations to more precisely capture the behaviour without introducing computational complexity. Most examples still work on ReLU networks [34], however, there has been some recent progress in developing abstract transformers for softmax and other difficult activations [7].

Among the complete verification techniques, most utilise SAT/SMT solvers, or Mixed Integer Linear Programming (MILP). Approaches include those that take advantage of piecewise linear activation functions, which are more manageable for network verification. Work includes that by Szegedy et al [36], who ensure that networks assign correct scores to the output advisories in various input domains. Planet [17], which presents an approach using SAT solving combined with linear programming to cut out significant areas of the search space during verification. Similarly, Reluplex, [21], is able to prove many robustness properties of larger-scale neural networks with ReLU activation functions and has recently been expanded into Marabou, [22], for arbitrary piecewise linear activation functions.

While these approaches lead to shorter verification times, the problem of complete verification of non-linear activation functions remains limited to smaller networks, and while approaches using approximation methods that allow for these activation functions are sound, they remain incomplete. By using an interactive theorem prover, as opposed to SMT/SAT solvers, we are able to make use of higher-order logic to define, reason over, and verify our new datatypes and definitions by building on mathematical axioms, whilst still maintaining flexibility and efficiency.

Properties. While the properties we discuss and verify are mostly concerned with the input-output relations, there is a general lack of a widely accepted formal specification when concerned with neural networks. Most frequently, the desired behaviours discussed include predictability of the behaviour and tolerance to faulty input [25], looking at improving the stability of the classification [20], or a general idea of robustness around a specific input region, where manipulations applied does not cause misclassifications. However, more recently, other properties have been discussed, such as semantic invariance [18], fairness [5], or distributional assumptions [33]. While these are all relevant and important properties for a network to fulfil, they currently have a less precise formal specification and so currently have limited application in formal methods, yet are interesting avenues for future research.

9 Conclusion and Future Work

We presented a formalisation of feedforward neural networks in Isabelle/HOL. To the best of our knowledge, this is the first formalisation of neural networks in an interactive theorem prover. We also made use of the framework aspect of Isabelle to provide an import mechanism automating our encoding for neural networks stored in a widely used exchange format.

Still, we see our work only as the beginning of a journey towards formally verified safety and correctness guarantees for critical systems employing ML/AI-based components. On a general level, there is further work required to improve the understanding of what it means that a neural network is safe (and secure), and how to convert this into a formal specification. This discourse will, hopefully, result in further properties that can be used in formal verification, and that will allow a comparison amongst various formal approaches for the verification of neural networks.

More specific to our approach, we plan to extend the types of layers and architectures that are directly supported, which, together with developing domain-specific proof tactics, should increase the degree of proof automation significantly. Modelling additional representations (e.g., a model based on Tensor operations) is another line of future work, alongside developing built-in support for ONNX networks. This will allow us to use our framework to formally show the semantic equivalence of these models. This will allow us to develop verified transformations that can be used to optimise neural networks for, e.g., making them easier to formally analyse or for improving their runtime performance.

Data Availibility Statement. The formalisation and case studies are available to view on Zenodo [9]. The materials include both the Isabelle/HOL implementation and the detailed documentation generated by Isabelle.

References

1. Abadi, M., et al.: TensorFlow: Large-Scale Machine Learning on Heterogeneous Systems (2015). Software https://www.tensorflow.org/
2. Abdulaziz, M., Kurz, F.: Verified SAT-Based AI Planning. Archive of Formal Proofs (2020)
3. Aggarwal, C.C.: Machine learning with shallow neural networks. In: Aggarwal, C.C. (ed.) Neural Networks and Deep Learning, vol. 10, pp. 53–104. Springer, Cham (2018). https://doi.org/10.1007/978-3-319-94463-0_2 ISBN 9783030068561
4. Banerjee, K., Vishak Prasad, C., Gupta, R.R., Vyas, K., Anushree, H., Mishra, B.: Exploring Alternatives to Softmax Function (2020)
5. Barocas, S., Hardt, M., Narayanan, A.: Fairness in machine learning. Nips Tutor. **1**, 2 (2017)
6. Bentkamp, A.: Expressiveness of deep learning. Archive of Formal Proofs (2016)
7. Bonaert, G., Dimitrov, D.I., Baader, M., Vechev, M.: Fast and precise certification of transformers. In: PLDI, pp. 466–481. ACM, Virtual, Canada (2021). https://doi.org/10.1145/3453483.3454056
8. Brucker, A.D.: Nano JSON: working with JSON formatted data in Isabelle/HOL and Isabelle/ML. Archive of Formal Proofs (2022)
9. Brucker, A.D., Stell, A.: Dataset: feedforward neural network verification in Isabelle/HOL (2022). https://doi.org/10.5281/zenodo.7418170
10. BS EN 50128:2011: Railway applications - Communication, signalling and processing systems - Software for railway control and protecting systems. Standard, British Standards Institute (BSI) (2014)
11. Campbell, A., Both, A., Sun, Q.: Detecting and mapping traffic signs from Google Street View images using deep learning and GIS. Comput. Environ. Urban Syst. **77**, 101350 (2019). https://doi.org/10.1016/j.compenvurbsys.2019.101350
12. Church, A.: A formulation of the simple theory of types. J. Symb. Log. **5**(2), 56–68 (1940)
13. Cohen, N., Sharir, O., Shashua, A.: On the expressive power of deep learning: a tensor analysis. In: Conference on Learning Theory, pp. 698–728 (2016)
14. Common Criteria for Information Technology Security Evaluation (Version 3.1, Release 5) (2017). https://www.commoncriteriaportal.org/cc/
15. Dvijotham, K., Stanforth, R., Gowal, S., Mann, T.A., Kohli, P.: A dual approach to scalable verification of deep networks. In: UAI, p. 3 (2018)
16. ECMA-404: The JSON data interchange syntax (2017). https://www.ecma-international.org/publications-and-standards/standards/ecma-404/
17. Ehlers, R.: Formal verification of piece-wise linear feed-forward neural networks. In: D'Souza, D., Narayan Kumar, K. (eds.) ATVA 2017. LNCS, vol. 10482, pp. 269–286. Springer, Cham (2017). https://doi.org/10.1007/978-3-319-68167-2_19
18. Goodfellow, I., Lee, H., Le, Q., Saxe, A., Ng, A.: Measuring invariances in deep networks. In: Advances in Neural Information Processing Systems, vol. 22 (2009)
19. Harris, C.R., et al.: Array programming with NumPy. Nature **585**(7825), 357–362 (2020). https://doi.org/10.1038/s41586-020-2649-2
20. Huang, X., Kwiatkowska, M., Wang, S., Wu, M.: Safety verification of deep neural networks. In: Majumdar, R., Kunčak, V. (eds.) CAV 2017. LNCS, vol. 10426, pp. 3–29. Springer, Cham (2017). https://doi.org/10.1007/978-3-319-63387-9_1
21. Katz, G., Barrett, C., Dill, D.L., Julian, K., Kochenderfer, M.J.: Reluplex: an efficient SMT solver for verifying deep neural networks. In: Majumdar, R., Kunčak, V. (eds.) CAV 2017. LNCS, vol. 10426, pp. 97–117. Springer, Cham (2017). https://doi.org/10.1007/978-3-319-63387-9_5

22. Katz, G., et al.: The marabou framework for verification and analysis of deep neural networks. In: Dillig, I., Tasiran, S. (eds.) CAV 2019. LNCS, vol. 11561, pp. 443–452. Springer, Cham (2019). https://doi.org/10.1007/978-3-030-25540-4_26
23. Klein, G.: Operating system verification – an overview. Sadhana **34**(1), 27–69 (2009)
24. Krizhevsky, A., Sutskever, I., Hinton, G.E.: ImageNet classification with deep convolutional neural networks. Commun. ACM **60**(6), 84–90 (2017). https://doi.org/10.1145/3065386
25. Kurd, Z., Kelly, T., Austin, J.: Developing artificial neural networks for safety critical systems. Neural Comput. Appl. **16**(1), 11–19 (2007)
26. Matichuk, D., Murray, T., Wenzel, M.: Eisbach: a proof method language for Isabelle. J. Autom. Reason. **56**(3), 261–282 (2016). https://doi.org/10.1007/s10817-015-9360-2
27. Mirman, M., Gehr, T., Vechev, M.: Differentiable abstract interpretation for provably robust neural networks. In: Machine Learning, pp. 3578–3586 (2018)
28. Nipkow, T., Paulson, L.C., Wenzel, M.: Isabelle/HOL—A Proof Assistant for Higher-Order Logic. Springer, Heidelberg (2002). https://doi.org/10.1007/3-540-45949-9
29. Paulson, L.C.: ML for the Working Programmer. Cambridge Press, Cambridge (1996)
30. Pulina, L., Tacchella, A.: An abstraction-refinement approach to verification of artificial neural networks. In: Touili, T., Cook, B., Jackson, P. (eds.) CAV 2010. LNCS, vol. 6174, pp. 243–257. Springer, Heidelberg (2010). https://doi.org/10.1007/978-3-642-14295-6_24
31. Rintanen, J.: Madagascar: scalable planning with SAT. IPC **21**, 1–5 (2014)
32. Rumelhart, D.E., Hinton, G.E., Williams, R.J.: Learning representations by back-propagating errors. Nature **323**(6088), 533–536 (1986)
33. Seshia, S.A., et al.: Formal specification for deep neural networks. In: Lahiri, S.K., Wang, C. (eds.) ATVA 2018. LNCS, vol. 11138, pp. 20–34. Springer, Cham (2018). https://doi.org/10.1007/978-3-030-01090-4_2
34. Singh, G., Gehr, T., Püschel, M., Vechev, M.: Boosting robustness certification of neural networks. In: Learning Representations (2018)
35. Smilkov, D., et al.: TensorFlow.js: Machine Learning for the Web and Beyond. CoRR abs/1901.05350 (2019)
36. Szegedy, C., et al.: Intriguing properties of neural networks. In: International Conference on Learning Representations (2014)
37. Taigman, Y., Yang, M., Ranzato, M., Wolf, L.: DeepFace: closing the gap to human-level performance in face verification. In: 2014 IEEE Conference on Computer Vision and Pattern Recognition, pp. 1701–1708 (2014). https://doi.org/10.1109/CVPR.2014.220
38. Weng, L., et al.: Towards fast computation of certified robustness for relu networks. In: Machine Learning, pp. 5276–5285 (2018)
39. Wenzel, M., Wolff, B.: Building formal method tools in the Isabelle/Isar framework. In: Schneider, K., Brandt, J. (eds.) TPHOLs 2007. LNCS, vol. 4732, pp. 352–367. Springer, Heidelberg (2007). https://doi.org/10.1007/978-3-540-74591-4_26
40. Wenzel, M., Paulson, L.: Isabelle/Isar. In: Wiedijk, F. (ed.) The Seventeen Provers of the World. LNCS (LNAI), vol. 3600, pp. 41–49. Springer, Heidelberg (2006). https://doi.org/10.1007/11542384_8

SMPT: A Testbed for Reachability Methods in Generalized Petri Nets

Nicolas Amat(✉) and Silvano Dal Zilio

LAAS-CNRS,
Université de Toulouse, CNRS, INSA, Toulouse, France
nicolas.amat@laas.fr

FM Artifact Evaluation ★ Available

Abstract. SMPT (for Satisfiability Modulo Petri Net) is a model checker for reachability problems in Petri nets. It started as a portfolio of methods to experiment with symbolic model checking, and was designed to be easily extended. Some distinctive features are its ability to benefit from structural reductions and to generate verdict certificates. Our tool is quite mature and performed well compared to other state-of-the-art tools in the Model Checking Contest.

Keywords: Model checking · Reachability problem · Petri nets

1 Introduction

SMPT is an open source model checker designed to answer reachability queries on generalized Petri nets, meaning that we do not impose any restrictions on the marking of places or the weight on the arcs. We can in particular handle unbounded nets. We also support a generalized notion of reachability properties, in the sense that we can check if it is possible to reach a marking that satisfies a combination of linear constraints between places. This is more expressive than the reachability of a single marking and corresponds to the class of formulas used in the reachability category of the Model Checking Contest (MCC), a yearly competition of formal verification tools for concurrent systems [7,27].

The tool name is an acronym that stands for *Satisfiability Modulo Petri Net*. This choice underlines the fact that, for most of the new features we implemented, SMPT acts as a front-end to a SMT solver; but also that it adds specific knowledge from Petri net theory, such as invariants, use of structural properties, etc.

The design of SMPT reflects the two main phases during its development process. The tool was initially developed as a testbed for symbolic model checking algorithms that can take advantage of structural reductions (see e.g. [2,3]). This explains why it includes many "reference" implementations of fundamental reachability algorithms, tailored for Petri nets, such as Bounded Model Checking (BMC) [8,17,22] or k-induction [31]. It also includes new verification methods, such as adaptations of Property Directed Reachability (PDR) [15,16] for Petri

M. Chechik et al. (Eds.): FM 2023, LNCS 14000, pp. 445–453, 2023.
https://doi.org/10.1007/978-3-031-27481-7_25

nets [6]. One of our goal is to efficiently compare different algorithms, on a level playing field, with the the ability to switch on or off optimizations. This motivates our choice to build a tool that is highly customizable and easily extensible.

In a second phase, since 2021, we worked to make SMPT more mature, with the goal to improve its interoperability, and with the addition of new verification methods that handle problems where symbolic methods are not the best suited. We discuss the portfolio approach implemented in SMPT in Sect. 3. This second set of objectives is carried by our participation in the last two editions of the MCC [25,26], where we obtained a 100% confidence level (meaning SMPT never returned an erroneous verdict). With this last evolution, we believe that SMPT left its status of prototype to become a tool that can be useful to other researchers. This is what motivates the present paper.

There are other tools that perform similar tasks. We provide a brief comparison of SMPT with two of them in Sect. 5, ITS-TOOLS [32,33] and TAPAAL [19]. All tools have in common their participation in the MCC and the use of symbolic techniques. They also share common input formats for nets and formulas. We can offer two reasons for users to use SMPT instead of—or more logically in addition to—these tools. First, SMPT takes advantage of a new approach, called *polyhedral reduction* [2,3], to accelerate the verification of reachability properties. This approach can be extremely effective in some cases where other methods do not scale. We describe this notion in Sect. 2. Another interesting feature of SMPT is the ability to return a *verdict certificate.* When a property is invariant, we can return a "proof" that can be checked independently by a SMT solver.

2 Technical Background

We briefly review some theoretical notions related to our work. We assume basic knowledge of Petri net theory [30]. In the following, we use P for the set of places of a net N. A marking, m, is a mapping associating a non-negative integer, $m(p)$, to every place p in P. SMPT supports the verification of *safety properties* over the reachable markings of a marked Petri net (N, m_0). Properties, F, are defined as a Boolean combination of literals of the form $\alpha \sim \beta$, where $\sim$ is a comparison operator (one of $=$, $\leqslant$ or $\geqslant$) and α, β are linear expressions involving constants or places in P. For instance, $(p + q \geqslant r) \vee (p \leqslant 5)$ is an example property.

We say that property F is valid at marking m, denoted $m \models F$, if the ground formula obtained by substituting places, p, by $m(p)$ is true. As can be expected, we say that F is *reachable* in (N, m_0) if there is m reachable such that $m \models F$. See [2,3,6] for more details. We support two categories of queries: $\mathrm{EF}\, F$, which is true only if F is reachable; and $\mathrm{AG}\, F$, which is true when F is an invariant, with the classic relationship that $\mathrm{AG}\, F \equiv \neg\, (\mathrm{EF}\, \neg F)$. A *witness* for property $\mathrm{EF}\, F$ is a reachable marking such that $m \models F$; it is a *counterexample* for $\mathrm{AG}\, \neg F$. Examples of properties we can express in this way include: checking if some transition t is enabled (quasi-liveness); checking if there is a deadlock; checking whether some linear invariant between places is always true; etc.

SMPT implements several methods that combine SMT-based techniques with a new notion, called polyhedral reduction. The idea consists in computing structural reductions [10,11] of the form $(N_1, m_1) \rhd_E (N_2, m_2)$, where (N_1, m_1) is the (initial) Petri net we want to analyse; (N_2, m_2) is a reduced version; and E is a system of linear equations relating places in N_1 and N_2. The goal is to preserve enough information in E so that we can reconstruct the reachable markings of (N_1, m_1) by knowing only those of (N_2, m_2). Given a starting net, we can automatically compute a polyhedral reduction using the tool REDUCE, which is part of TINA [12]. (But obviously there are many irreducible nets.)

Polyhedral reductions are useful in practice. Given a property F_1 on the initial net N_1, we can build a property F_2 on N_2 [2,3] such that checking F_1 on N_1 (whether it is reachable or an invariant) is equivalent to checking F_2 on N_2. We have observed very good speed-ups with this approach, even when we only have a moderate amount of reductions. This notion is also "compatible" with symbolic methods. In SMPT, we recast all constraints and relations into formulas of Quantifier Free Linear Integer Arithmetic (the QF-LIA theory in the SMT-LIB standard [9]) and pass them to SMT solvers.

Another important notion is that of *inductive invariant*. We say that R is an inductive invariant of property F if it is: (i) valid initially ($m_0 \models R$); (ii) inductive (if $m \to m'$ and $m \models R$ then $m' \models R$, for all markings m, even those that are not reachable); and (iii) $R \supseteq F$. Given a pair (F, R) we can check these three properties automatically using a SMT solver (and with only one formula in each case). In some conditions, when property F is an invariant, SMPT can automatically compute an inductive invariant from F. This provides an independent certificate that invariant F holds.

3 Design and Implementation

SMPT is open-source, under the GNU GPL v3.0 licence, and is freely available on GitHub (https://github.com/nicolasAmat/SMPT). The repository also provides examples of nets, formulas, and scripts to experiment with the tool. SMPT is a Python project of about 4 000 lines of code, and is fully typed using the static type checker mypy. The code is heavily documented (4 500 lines) and we provide many tracing and debugging options that can help understand its inner workings. The project is packaged in libraries, and provides abstract classes to help with future extensions. We describe each library and explain how they can be extended.

The ptio library defines the main data-structures of the model checker, for Petri nets (`pt.py`), reachability formulas (`formula.py`), and reduction equations (`system.py`). It also provides the corresponding parsers, for different formats.

The interface library includes interfaces to external tools and solvers. For example, we provide an integrated interface to z3 [14] built around the SMT-LIB format [9]. We can also interface with MINIZINC [29], a solver based on constraint programming techniques, and with a random state space explorer,

WALK, distributed with the TINA toolbox. New tools can be added by implementing the abstract class `Solver` (`solver.py`).

The exec library provides a concurrent "jobs scheduler" that helps run multiple verification tasks in parallel and manage their interactions.

The checker library is the core of our tool. It includes a portfolio of methods intended to be executed in parallel. All methods implement an abstract class (`abstractchecker.py`) which describes the abstract method `prove`. We currently support the following eight methods:

(1) **Induction**: a basic method that checks if a property is an inductive invariant (see Sect. 2). This property is "easy" to check, even though interesting properties are seldom inductive. It is also useful to check verdict certificates.

(2) **BMC**: Bounded Model Checking [13] is an iterative method to explore the state space of systems by unrolling their transitions. This method is only useful for finding counterexamples.

(3) **k-induction**: [31] is an extension of BMC that can also prove invariants.

(4) **PDR**: Property Directed Reachability [15,16], also known as IC3, is a method to strengthen a property that is not inductive, into an inductive one. This method can return a verdict certificate. We provide three different methods of increasing complexity [6] (one for coverability and two for general reachability).

(5) **State Equation**: is a method for checking that a property is true for all "potentially reachable markings" (solution of the state equation). This is a semi-decision method, found in many portfolio tools, that can easily check for invariants. We implement a refined version [32,33] that can over-approximate the result with the help of trap constraints [20] and other structural information, such as NUPN specifications [21].

(6) **Random Walk**: relies on simulation tools to quickly find counterexamples. It is also found in many tools that participate in the MCC [27]. We currently use WALK, distributed with the TINA toolbox, but we are developing a new tool to take advantage of polyhedral reductions.

(7) **Constraint Programming**: is a method specific to SMPT in the case where nets are "fully reducible" (the reduced net has only one marking). In this case, reachable markings are exactly the solution of the reduction equations (E) and verdicts are computed by solving linear system of equations.

(8) **Enumeration**: performs an exhaustive exploration of the state space and relies on the TINA model checker. It can be used as a fail-safe, or to check the reliability of our results.

4 Commands, Basic Usage and Installation

SMPT requires Python version 3.7 or higher. The easiest method for experimenting with the tool is to directly run the `smpt` module as a script, using a command such as `python3 -m smpt`. Our repository includes a script to simplify the installation of the tool and all its dependencies. It is also possible to find disk images with a running installation in the MCC website and in artifacts archived on Zenodo [4,5]. As usual, option `--help` returns an abridged description of all the available options. We list some of them below, grouped by usage.

Input Formats. We accept Petri nets described using the Petri Net Markup Language (PNML) [23] and can also support colored Petri nets (using option `--colored`) by using and external unfolder [18]. For methods that rely on polyhedral reductions, it is possible to automatically compute the reduction (`--auto-reduce`) or to provide a pre-computed version (with option `--reduced-net <path>`). It is also possible to save a copy of the reduced net with the option `--save-reduced-net <path>`.

Verification Methods. We support the verification of three predefined classes of safety properties: *deadlock detection* (`--deadlock`), which is self-descriptive; *quasi-liveness* (`--quasi-liveness t`), to check if it is possible to fire transition `t`; and *reachability* (`--reachability p`), to check if there is a reachable marking where place `p` is marked (it has at least one token). It is also possible to check the reachability of several places, at once, by passing a comma-separated list of names, `--reachability p1,...,pn`; and similarly for liveness. Finally, SMPT supports properties expressed using the MCC property language [28], an XML format encoding the class of formulas described in Sect. 2. Several properties can be checked at once.

Output Format. Results are printed in the text format required by the MCC, which is of the form `FORMULA <id> (TRUE/FALSE)`. There are also options to output more information: `--debug` to print the SMT-LIB input/output code exchanged with the SMT solver; `--show-techniques`, to return the methods that successfully computed a verdict; `--show-time`, to print the execution time per property; `--show-reduction-ratio`, to get the reduction ratio; `--show-model`, to print the counterexample if it exists; `--check-proof`, to check verdict certificates (when we have one); `--export-proof`, to export verdict certificates (inductive invariants, traces leading to counterexamples, etc.).

Tweaking Options. We provide a set of options to control the behaviour of our verification jobs scheduler. We can add a timeout, globally (`--global-timeout <int>`) or per property (`--timeout <int>`). We can also restrict the choice of verification methods (`--methods <method_1> .... <method_n>`). Finally, option `--mcc` puts the tool in "competition mode".

5 Comparison with Other Tools

We report on some results obtained by SMPT, ITS-Tools [32,33], and Tapaal [19] during the 2022 edition of the MCC [26]. We created a public repository [1] containing the scripts used to generate the statistics and oracles for the 2022 edition of the Model Checking Contest for the Reachability category.

SMPT provides a default competition mode that implements a basic strategy that should be effective in the conditions of the MCC. Basically, we start by running the Random Walk and State Equation methods in parallel with a timeout of 120 s, on all formulas, in order to catch easy counterexamples and invariants as quickly as possible. Then we run more demanding methods: BMC, k-induction, PDR, etc. The rationale is that queries used in the reachability competition are randomly generated and usually exhibit a bias towards "counterexamples" (CEX), meaning false AG properties or true EF ones. Also, when the formula is an invariant (INV), for instance a "true AG property", it can often be decided with the State Equation method.

Our tool is quite mature. It achieved a perfect reliability score (all answers are correct) and ranked at the third position, behind TAPAAL and ITS-TOOLS. We display the results in a Venn diagram where we make a distinction between CEX and INV properties. There is a total of 50 187 answered queries (with almost 60% CEX). We observe that a vast majority of these queries (41 006) are computed by all tools, and can be considered "easy". Conversely, we have 9 181 difficult queries, solved by only one or two tools (Fig. 1).

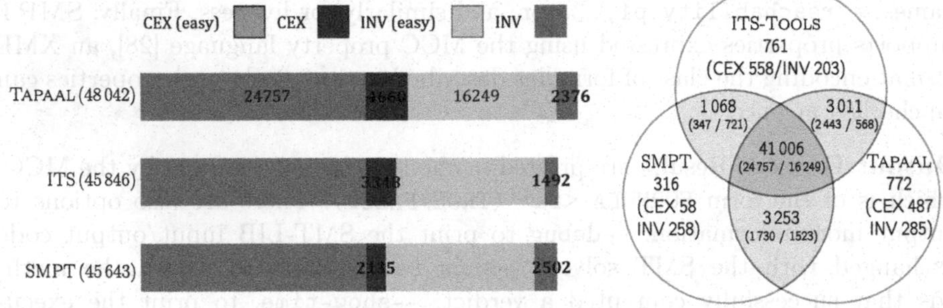

Fig. 1. Comparison of tools on all computed queries

We also provide a bar chart where we distinguish between easy/difficult, and CEX/INV queries. We observe that, while SMPT ranks last in the number of unique queries, it behaves quite well with invariants (INV); which is the category we target with our most sophisticated methods. Overall, we observe that SMPT performs well compared to other state-of-the-art tools in the Model Checking Contest and that it is a sensible choice when we try to check invariants.

6 Future Work

Work on SMPT is still ongoing. At the moment, we concentrate on methods to quickly discover counterexamples. The idea is to combine polyhedral reductions and random exploration in order to find counterexamples directly in the reduced net. We also plan to improve our use of the "state equation" method, in particular by identifying new classes of Petri nets for which all potentially reachable markings are indeed reachable. A problem we already started to study in a different setting [24].

References

1. Amat, N.: Oracles and report for the reachability category of the model checking contest (2022). https://github.com/nicolasAmat/MCC-Reachability
2. Amat, N., Berthomieu, B., Dal Zilio, S.: On the combination of polyhedral abstraction and SMT-based model checking for petri nets. In: Buchs, D., Carmona, J. (eds.) PETRI NETS 2021. LNCS, vol. 12734, pp. 164–185. Springer, Cham (2021). https://doi.org/10.1007/978-3-030-76983-3_9
3. Amat, N., Berthomieu, B., Dal Zilio, S.: A polyhedral abstraction for petri nets and its application to SMT-based model checking. Fund. Inform. **187**(2–4), 103–138. IOS Press (2022). https://doi.org/10.3233/FI-222134
4. Amat, N., Dal Zilio, S.: Artifact for FM 2023 paper: SMPT: a testbed for reachability methods in generalized petri nets, November 2023. https://doi.org/10.5281/zenodo.7341426
5. Amat, N., Dal Zilio, S., Hujsa, T.: Artifact for TACAS 2022 paper: property directed reachability for generalized petri nets, January 2022. https://doi.org/10.5281/zenodo.5863379
6. Amat, N., Zilio, S.D., Hujsa, T.: Property directed reachability for generalized petri nets. In: TACAS 2022. LNCS, vol. 13243, pp. 505–523. Springer, Cham (2022). https://doi.org/10.1007/978-3-030-99524-9_28
7. Amparore, E., et al.: Presentation of the 9th edition of the model checking contest. In: Beyer, D., Huisman, M., Kordon, F., Steffen, B. (eds.) TACAS 2019. LNCS, vol. 11429, pp. 50–68. Springer, Cham (2019). https://doi.org/10.1007/978-3-030-17502-3_4
8. Armando, A., Mantovani, J., Platania, L.: Bounded model checking of software using SMT solvers instead of SAT solvers. In: Valmari, A. (ed.) SPIN 2006. LNCS, vol. 3925, pp. 146–162. Springer, Heidelberg (2006). https://doi.org/10.1007/11691617_9
9. Barrett, C., Fontaine, P., Tinelli, C.: The SMT-LIB standard: version 2.6. Technical report, Department of Computer Science, The University of Iowa (2017). http://www.smt-lib.org/
10. Berthelot, G.: Transformations and decompositions of nets. In: Brauer, W., Reisig, W., Rozenberg, G. (eds.) ACPN 1986. LNCS, vol. 254, pp. 359–376. Springer, Heidelberg (1987). https://doi.org/10.1007/978-3-540-47919-2_13
11. Berthomieu, B., Le Botlan, D., Dal Zilio, S.: Counting Petri net markings from reduction equations. Int. J. Softw. Tools Technol. Transfer **22**(2), 163–181 (2019). https://doi.org/10.1007/s10009-019-00519-1
12. Berthomieu, B., Ribet, P.O., Vernadat, F.: The tool TINA-construction of abstract state spaces for Petri nets and time Petri nets. Int. J. Prod. Res. **42**(14), 2741–2756 (2004)
13. Biere, A., Cimatti, A., Clarke, E., Zhu, Y.: Symbolic model checking without BDDs. In: Cleaveland, W.R. (ed.) TACAS 1999. LNCS, vol. 1579, pp. 193–207. Springer, Heidelberg (1999). https://doi.org/10.1007/3-540-49059-0_14
14. Bjørner, N.: The Z3 Theorem Prover (2020). https://github.com/Z3Prover/z3/

15. Bradley, A.R.: SAT-based model checking without unrolling. In: Jhala, R., Schmidt, D. (eds.) VMCAI 2011. LNCS, vol. 6538, pp. 70–87. Springer, Heidelberg (2011). https://doi.org/10.1007/978-3-642-18275-4_7
16. Bradley, A.R.: Understanding IC3. In: Cimatti, A., Sebastiani, R. (eds.) SAT 2012. LNCS, vol. 7317, pp. 1–14. Springer, Heidelberg (2012). https://doi.org/10.1007/978-3-642-31612-8_1
17. Clarke, E., Biere, A., Raimi, R., Zhu, Y.: Bounded model checking using satisfiability solving. Formal Methods Syst. Des. **19**, 7–34 (2001). https://doi.org/10.1023/A:1011276507260
18. Dal Zilio, S.: MCC: A tool for unfolding colored petri nets in PNML format. In: Janicki, R., Sidorova, N., Chatain, T. (eds.) PETRI NETS 2020. LNCS, vol. 12152, pp. 426–435. Springer, Cham (2020). https://doi.org/10.1007/978-3-030-51831-8_23
19. David, A., Jacobsen, L., Jacobsen, M., Jørgensen, K.Y., Møller, M.H., Srba, J.: TAPAAL 2.0: integrated development environment for timed-arc petri nets. In: Flanagan, C., König, B. (eds.) TACAS 2012. LNCS, vol. 7214, pp. 492–497. Springer, Heidelberg (2012). https://doi.org/10.1007/978-3-642-28756-5_36
20. Esparza, J., Melzer, S.: Verification of safety properties using integer programming: beyond the state equation. Formal Methods Syst. Des. **16**(2), 159–189 (2000). https://doi.org/10.1023/A:1008743212620
21. Garavel, H.: Nested-unit Petri nets. J. Log. Algebr. Methods Program. **104**, 60–85 (2019). https://doi.org/10.1016/j.jlamp.2018.11.005
22. Heljanko, K.: Bounded reachability checking with process semantics. In: Larsen, K.G., Nielsen, M. (eds.) CONCUR 2001. LNCS, vol. 2154, pp. 218–232. Springer, Heidelberg (2001). https://doi.org/10.1007/3-540-44685-0_15
23. Hillah, L.M., Kordon, F., Petrucci, L., Trèves, N.: PNML framework: an extendable reference implementation of the petri net markup language. In: Lilius, J., Penczek, W. (eds.) PETRI NETS 2010. LNCS, vol. 6128, pp. 318–327. Springer, Heidelberg (2010). https://doi.org/10.1007/978-3-642-13675-7_20
24. Hujsa, T., Berthomieu, B., Dal Zilio, S., Le Botlan, D.: Checking marking reachability with the state equation in Petri net subclasses. arXiv preprint: arXiv:2006.05600 (2020)
25. Kordon, F., et al.: Complete results for the 2021 edition of the model checking contest, June 2021. http://mcc.lip6.fr/2021/results.php
26. Kordon, F., et al.: Complete results for the 2022 edition of the model checking contest (2022). http://mcc.lip6.fr/2022/results.php
27. Kordon, F., Hillah, L.M., Hulin-Hubard, F., Jezequel, L., Paviot-Adet, E.: Study of the efficiency of model checking techniques using results of the MCC from 2015 To 2019. Int. J. Softw. Tools Technol. Transfer **23**(6), 931–952 (2021). https://doi.org/10.1007/s10009-021-00615-1
28. LIP6: model checking contest property language (manual). Petri Nets (2020)
29. Nethercote, N., Stuckey, P.J., Becket, R., Brand, S., Duck, G.J., Tack, G.: MiniZinc: towards a standard CP modelling language. In: Bessière, C. (ed.) CP 2007. LNCS, vol. 4741, pp. 529–543. Springer, Heidelberg (2007). https://doi.org/10.1007/978-3-540-74970-7_38
30. Reisig, W.: Petri Nets: An Introduction, vol. 4. Springer Science & Business Media, Cham (2012). https://doi.org/10.1007/978-3-642-69968-9
31. Sheeran, M., Singh, S., Stalmarck, G.: Checking safety properties using induction and a SAT-solver. In: Hunt, W.A., Johnson, S.D. (eds.) FMCAD 2000. LNCS, vol. 1954, pp. 127–144. Springer, Heidelberg (2000). https://doi.org/10.1007/3-540-40922-X_8

32. Thierry-Mieg, Y.: Symbolic model-checking using ITS-tools. In: Baier, C., Tinelli, C. (eds.) TACAS 2015. LNCS, vol. 9035, pp. 231–237. Springer, Heidelberg (2015). https://doi.org/10.1007/978-3-662-46681-0_20
33. Thierry-Mieg, Y.: Structural reductions revisited. In: Janicki, R., Sidorova, N., Chatain, T. (eds.) PETRI NETS 2020. LNCS, vol. 12152, pp. 303–323. Springer, Cham (2020). https://doi.org/10.1007/978-3-030-51831-8_15

The Octatope Abstract Domain for Verification of Neural Networks

Stanley Bak[1], Taylor Dohmen[2], K. Subramani[3], Ashutosh Trivedi[2](✉), Alvaro Velasquez[2], and Piotr Wojciechowski[3]

[1] Stony Brook University, Stony Brook, NY, USA
[2] University of Colorado, Boulder, CO, USA
ashutosh.trivedi@colorado.edu
[3] West Virginia University, Morgantown, WV, USA

Abstract. Efficient verification algorithms for neural networks often depend on various abstract domains such as *intervals*, *zonotopes*, and *linear star sets*. The choice of the abstract domain presents an expressiveness vs. scalability trade-off: simpler domains are less precise but yield faster algorithms. This paper investigates the *octatope* abstract domain in the context of neural net verification. Octatopes are affine transformations of n-dimensional octagons—sets of unit-two-variable-per-inequality (UTVPI) constraints. Octatopes generalize the idea of zonotopes which can be viewed as an affine transformation of a box. On the other hand, octatopes can be considered as a restriction of linear star set, which are affine transformations of arbitrary $\mathcal{H}$-Polytopes. This distinction places octatopes firmly between zonotopes and star sets in their expressive power, but what about the efficiency of decision procedures?

An important analysis problem for neural networks is the *exact range computation* problem that asks to compute the exact set of possible outputs given a set of possible inputs. For this, three computational procedures are needed: 1) optimization of a linear cost function; 2) affine mapping; and 3) over-approximating the intersection with a half-space. While zonotopes allow an efficient solution for these approaches, star sets solves these procedures via linear programming. We show that these operations are faster for octatopes than the more expressive linear star sets. For octatopes, we reduce these problems to min-cost flow problems, which can be solved in strongly polynomial time using the Out-of-Kilter algorithm. Evaluating exact range computation on several ACAS Xu neural network benchmarks, we find that octatopes show promise as a practical abstract domain for neural network verification.

1 Introduction

The success of deep feed-forward neural networks (DNN) in computer vision and speech recognition has prompted applications in critical infrastructure. These applications range from using pre-trained perception and speech-recognition modules in safety-critical logic (self-driving cars and medical decision making)

M. Chechik et al. (Eds.): FM 2023, LNCS 14000, pp. 454–472, 2023.
https://doi.org/10.1007/978-3-031-27481-7_26

to learning controllers from reinforcement signals [31] to learning succinct representations of formally verified controllers (ACAS Xu). The increasing prevalence of DNNs in safety-, privacy-, and social-critical systems motivates the focus of the formal methods community [3,5,7,34] in developing verification technology to meet the challenge of improving trust in DNNs.

Abstract interpretation [4,11] is a well-established framework for program verification that formalizes the exploration of the program semantics at the granularity provided by the underlying domain. For example, intervals [11] form an abstract domain facilitating analysis in which sets of states are represented as hyperrectangles. Other abstract domains such as difference constraints, octagons (unit-two-variables-per-inequality or UTVPI), and polyhedral (linear constraints) have been successfully deployed for the verification of DNNs. However, the multilayer architecture of DNNs, when combined with linear function composition followed by a non-linear activation function at each layer, results in the repeated intersection of abstract spaces with linear inequalities. For this reason, abstract domains that do not permit an efficient *affine mapping* suffer in exploring the layered state space of the DNNs.

Zonotopes [29] solve this problem by representing an abstract set as an affine mapping of an interval generator set. For zonotopes, the key operations for DNN verification, such as nonemptiness, optimization, and over-approximation, can be performed via efficient, enumerative procedures. Linear star sets [13,35] generalize zonotopes by representing the generator set using the polyhedral domains. This generalization, while improving the expressiveness, leads to the decision procedures depend upon solving linear programs, which tends to be the performance bottleneck in the overall algorithm. While linear programming is known to be solvable in polynomial time, via a number of celebrated interior-point algorithms [22], there is no known strongly polynomial algorithm. Dantzig's simplex algorithm is a popular algorithm to solve LP and works well in practice, but for general LPs, the time complexity of the simplex algorithm is not polynomial [23], and subexponential lower bounds hold even for randomized pivoting rules [14].

For some subclasses of linear programming problems, more efficient solutions exist. In particular, when the constraints are restricted to difference constraints ($x_i - x_j \leq c$) or UTVPI constraints ($\pm x_i \pm x_j \leq c$), then the duals of the corresponding LPs can be reduced to *minimum cost flow* (MCF) problems [2], for which there exist strongly polynomial time algorithms [17]. The Out-of-Kilter algorithm is one popular algorithm for solving minimum cost flow that also produces a solution to the dual [2]. It runs in time $O((m^2 + m \cdot n \cdot \log n) \cdot U)$ on a network with m arcs and n nodes and maximum supply/demand U. Alternatively, the network simplex algorithm is a specialized version of the simplex algorithm to solve minimum cost flow problems. Unlike standard simplex, network simplex runs in polynomial time [28]. Given its relative efficiency, it is natural to ask: *in neural network verification, is it possible to replace expensive linear programming with min-cost flow calls?*

This question motivates the investigation of sub-classes of star sets that are more general than zonotopes, but enable efficient decision procedures based on

MCF problems. For this purpose, we introduce *octatopes*: sets that can be defined as affine maps of UTVPI constrained sets (octagons [27]). Since octatopes are a special class of star sets, the affine transformation remains efficient. We also study *hexatopes* as the images of difference constrained sets (hexagons [27] or zones [9]). A key contribution of this paper is that the key operations required for verification using octatopes and hexatopes can be performed efficiently using algorithms for MCF problems.

Given that the MCF problem can be solved efficiently via Out-of-Kilter algorithm and network simplex (touted [8] to be 200–300 times faster than simplex), this benefit will translate to the efficiency of octatopes/hexatopes for LP-intensive applications like reachability analysis of neural networks. While the current state-of-the-art implementations of the algorithms for the MCF problem are not as advanced as those for LP, we believe that this will change in light of the proposed application. We implement the octatope and hexatope abstract domains and show their effectiveness on several ACAS Xu networks [20], a popular benchmark for neural network verification.

Related Work. A growing body of research exists on different methods to verify neural networks [25], including recent tool competitions [6]. Algorithms can be categorized into search, optimization, and reachability solutions. In the space of search procedures, the seminal Reluplex method proposes an extension of the simplex algorithm used for linear programming to handle ReLU networks [20]. This method has been widely adopted and extended by, for example, posing verification as a constraint satisfaction problem [21]. This can then be solved using off-the-shelf Satisfiability Modulo Theory (SMT) solvers like z3 [12]. The use of SMT enables reasoning over different activation functions and topologies.

Interval arithmetic is another popular approach often used to estimate the range of output values given a range of inputs while tracking the input and output ranges of individual activation functions [38]. This can be computed by using linear programming to derive lower and upper bounds for a given node in the network. The work of [18] combines this with symbolic interval propagation and gradient descent to find counter-examples to the over-approximations established by the linear programming solutions. More sophisticated node splitting strategies that account for downstream effects on successor nodes can also be used as part of the symbolic interval propagation phase [19]. Per-neuron split constraints can also further improve efficiency [39].

Optimization solutions to the verification based on ILP have been explored. This is a natural formulation for the verification of neural networks due to the use of affine transformations and the fact that piecewise linear activation functions can be encoded using a set of binary linear constraints [3]. The work in [32] extends similar ideas by estimating the maximum disturbance that is permitted at the input and proposing pre-solve procedures to speed up the solution.

Although solutions based on SMT-solving and mathematical programming are often complete, they require the entire network to be encoded within the corresponding constraints, thereby limiting scalability. In contrast to these search and optimization solutions, the use of reachability analysis for verification of neural networks has been shown to scale to larger instances at the cost of completeness. Examples of this include the use of zonotope and star set abstract domains. The former can be efficiently employed to compute conservative over-approximations of output bounds of nodes in a network [16], whereas linear programming can be employed for the latter to find tight bounds at the cost of scalability [37]. The work proposed herein seeks to advance the state of verification methods based on reachability analysis by providing tighter over-approximations than zonotopes and more efficient computations than star sets.

2 Preliminaries

Let $\mathbb{R}$ denote the set of real numbers and $\mathbb{Q}$ denote the set of rational numbers. We write $\mathbb{R}^{m\times n}$ for the set of all $m\times n$ dimensional matrices of reals.

For a matrix $M \in \mathbb{R}^{m\times n}$, we write $M(i,\cdot) \in \mathbb{R}^{1\times n}$ and $M(\cdot,j) \in \mathbb{R}^{m\times 1}$ for the ith row vector and j^{th} column vector, respectively, of M, for $1 \leq i \leq m$ and $1 \leq j \leq m$. Similarly, we write $M(i,j)$ for the matrix element at row i and column j. By default, a vector is a column vector and we associate a set of matrices $\mathbb{R}^{m\times 1}$ with the set of vectors $\mathbb{R}^m$.

For a matrix $M \in \mathbb{R}^{m\times n}$ we write $M^{\mathsf{T}} \in \mathbb{R}^{n\times m}$ for its transpose matrix. For a row vector $\boldsymbol{v} \in \mathbb{R}^{1\times n}$, we write $\boldsymbol{v}^{\mathsf{T}} \in \mathbb{R}^n$ for the corresponding (transposed) vector. We write $\mathbf{1}_n$ for the all-ones vector of size n and I for the identity matrix of some fixed dimension (often clear from context). For a (column) vector $\boldsymbol{v} = (v_1, v_2, \ldots, v_n) \in \mathbb{R}^n$ we write $\boldsymbol{v}_i$ for its ith element. For a vector $\boldsymbol{v} \in \mathbb{R}^m$ and scalar $\alpha \in \mathbb{R}$, we write $\alpha \cdot \boldsymbol{v}$ for the vector $(\alpha \cdot \boldsymbol{v}_1, \ldots, \alpha \cdot \boldsymbol{v}_m)$. For two vectors $\boldsymbol{u}, \boldsymbol{v} \in \mathbb{R}^m$, we write $\boldsymbol{u} \cdot \boldsymbol{v}$ for their dot product, i.e., $\boldsymbol{u} \cdot \boldsymbol{v} = \sum_{i=1}^{m} \boldsymbol{u}_i \cdot \boldsymbol{v}_i$. For two matrices $M \in \mathbb{R}^{m\times n}$ and $N \in \mathbb{R}^{n\times p}$, their product $MN \in \mathbb{R}^{m\times p}$ is defined as $MN(i,j) = M(i,\cdot)^{\mathsf{T}} \cdot N(\cdot,j)$.

We call a function $f : \mathbb{R}^n \to \mathbb{R}^m$ *linear* if $f(\boldsymbol{u}) + f(\boldsymbol{v}) = f(\boldsymbol{u}+\boldsymbol{v})$ and $f(\alpha \cdot \boldsymbol{v}) = \alpha \cdot f(\boldsymbol{v})$ for all scalars $\alpha \in \mathbb{R}$ and vectors $\boldsymbol{u}, \boldsymbol{v} \in \mathbb{R}^n$. A linear function $f : \mathbb{R}^n \to \mathbb{R}^m$ can be represented as a matrix $A \in M^{m\times n}$ such that f is equivalent to $\boldsymbol{u} \mapsto A\boldsymbol{u}$. A function $f : \mathbb{R}^n \to \mathbb{R}^m$ is affine if it is a sum of a linear function and a constant, i.e., $f(\boldsymbol{v}) = A\boldsymbol{v} + \boldsymbol{b}$ for some $A \in \mathbb{R}^{m\times n}$ and $\boldsymbol{b} \in \mathbb{R}^m$.

2.1 Linear, UTVPI, and Difference Constraints

Let $\boldsymbol{x} = \{x_1, x_2, \ldots, x_n\}$ be a set of real-valued variables with an arbitrary but fixed order. Abusing notation, we represent this set as a vector $\boldsymbol{x} = (x_1, x_2, \ldots, x_n)$. A *linear constraint* over $\boldsymbol{x}$ is a constraint of the form

$$a_1x_1 + a_2x_2 + \cdots + a_nx_n \leq b \text{ where } \boldsymbol{a} = (a_1, \ldots, a_n) \in \mathbb{R}^n \text{ and } b \in \mathbb{R}$$

that represents the set $\{\boldsymbol{v} \in \mathbb{R}^n : \boldsymbol{a} \cdot \boldsymbol{v} \leq b\}$. A *linear constraint system* (LCS)

$$A\boldsymbol{x} \leq \boldsymbol{b} \text{ where } A \in \mathbb{R}^{m\times n} \text{and } \boldsymbol{b} \in \mathbb{R}^m$$

is a conjunction of linear constraints.

Definition 1 (Interval Constraint Systems). *An* interval constraint *is a linear constraint of the form*

$$a_i \leq x_i \leq b_i \text{ where } a_i, b_i \in \mathbb{Q}.$$

An interval constraint system (ICS) is a conjunction of interval constraints. An ICS is a unit hypercube if $a_i = -1$ and $b_i = 1$ for all $1 \leq i \leq n$ and we denote it as $-\mathbf{1}_n \leq \boldsymbol{x} \leq \mathbf{1}_n$.

Definition 2 (Difference Constraint Systems). *A* difference constraint *is a linear constraint of the form*

$$x_i - x_j \leq b_i \text{ where } b_i \in \mathbb{Q}.$$

A difference constraint system (DCS) is a conjunction of difference constraints.

Definition 3 (UTVPI Constraint System). *A Unit Two Variable Per Inequality (UTVPI) constraint is a linear constraint of the form*

$$a_i \cdot x_i + a_j \cdot x_j \leq b_{ij} \text{ where } a_i, a_j \in \{-1, 0, +1\} \text{ and } b_{ij} \in \mathbb{Q}.$$

A UTVPI constraint system (UCS) is a conjunction of UTVPI constraints.

A UTVPI constraint $a_i \cdot x_i + a_j \cdot x_j \leq b$ is said to be an absolute constraint if $a_i = 0$ or $a_j = 0$. An absolute constraint can be converted into constraints of the form: $a_i \cdot x_i + a_j \cdot x_j \leq b_{ij}$, where both a_i and a_j are non-zero. Note that a UTVPI constraint $a_i \cdot x_i + a_j \cdot x_j \leq b_{ij}$, $b_{ij} \in \mathbb{Q}$ is a difference constraint if $a_i = -a_j$. The constant that bounds a UTVPI constraint is called the defining constant. For instance, the defining constant for the constraint $x_1 - x_2 \leq 9$ is 9.

2.2 Minimum Cost Network Flow Problem

When optimizing a linear function over DCS or UCS, its dual program can be reduced to the *minimum cost flow* (MCF) problem [2], for which there exist strongly polynomial time algorithms [17]. We review the Out-of-Kilter algorithm (Algorithm 1) for MCF that also produces a solution to the dual [2].

A *flow network* $\boldsymbol{G} = (G = (V, E), c, a, d)$ is a directed graph G with capacity $c : E \to \mathbb{R}_{\geq 0}$ and cost $a : E \to \mathbb{R}$ associated with every edge (arc) and demand $d : V \to \mathbb{R}$ associated with every vertex (node). We assume that $\sum_{v \in V} d(v) = 0$. The *minimum cost flow* (MCF) problem can be stated as follows:

$$\text{Minimize} \sum_{(u,v) \in E} f(u,v) \cdot a(u,v)$$

subject to:

$$\sum_{u \in V} f(u,v) - \sum_{u \in V} f(v,u) = d(v) \qquad \text{for all } v \in V,$$

$$0 \leq f(u,v) \leq c(u,v) \qquad \text{for all } (u,v) \in E$$

Algorithm 1. OUT-OF-KILTER($\boldsymbol{G} = (G = (V, E), c, a, d)$)

Initialize the potential as $\pi \leftarrow 0$.
Let f be a flow in $\boldsymbol{G}$.
Construct the residual network $\boldsymbol{G_f}$.
Compute the kilter number $k(u, v)$ of each edge (u, v) in $\boldsymbol{G_f}$.
while ($\boldsymbol{G_f}$ contains an edge with positive kilter number) **do**
    Select an edge (u, v) in $\boldsymbol{G_f}$ with positive kilter number.
    Let the weight of each edge (u, v) in $\boldsymbol{G_f}$ be $\max\{0, c^\pi(u, v)\}$.
    For $w \in V \setminus \{u, v\}$, let $l(w)$ be the weight of the least weight path from v to w.
    Let P be a shortest path from v to u.
    For each node w, set $\pi(w) \leftarrow \pi(w) - l(w)$.
    if $(c^\pi(u, v) < 0)$ **then**
        $Q \leftarrow P \cup \{(u, v)\}$.
        $\delta \leftarrow \min_{(u,v) \in Q} r(u, v)$.
        Augment δ units of flow along Q.
        Update f and $\boldsymbol{G_f}$.
return f.

Out-of-Kilter Algorithm. A pseudocode for the Out-of-Kilter algorithm is given as Algorithm 1. It starts with a possibly infeasible flow and iteratively modifies this flow in a way that decreases the infeasibility of the solution and moves it closer to optimality. Each step of the algorithm consists of solving a shortest path problem and augmenting the flow along the shortest path. It operates on the residual network $\boldsymbol{G_f}$ corresponding to the current flow f. This residual network is constructed as follows. For each edge $(v_i, v_j) \in E$:

1. **Feasible Edges.** If $f(u, v) < c(u, v)$, we add the edge (u, v) with a residual capacity of $r(u, v) = c(u, v) - f(u, v)$ and cost $a(u, v)$. If $f(u, v) > 0$, we add the edge (v, u) with a residual capacity of $r(v, u) = f(u, v)$ and cost $-a(u, v)$.
2. **Lower-Infeasible Edges.** If $f(u, v) < 0$, we add the edge (u, v) with a residual capacity of $r(u, v) = -f(u, v)$ and cost $a(u, v)$.
3. **Upper-Infeasible Edges.** If $f(u, v) > c(u, v)$, we add the edge (v, u) with a residual capacity of $r(v, u) = f(u, v) - c(u, v)$ and cost $-a(u, v)$.

For each vertex v in the residual network, the algorithm maintains a potential $\pi(v)$ and for each edge (u, v) with cost $a(u, v)$, it maintains the reduced cost $a^\pi(u, v) = c(u, v) - \pi(u) + \pi(v)$. Additionally, for each edge in the residual network, it maintains a kilter number $k(u, v)$ which is 0 if $c^\pi(u, v) \geq 0$ and is the residual capacity $r(u, v)$ if $c^\pi(u, v) < 0$. This kilter number represents the change in flow required so that each edge satisfies its optimality condition.

Note that the node potentials π and reduced costs c^π corresponding to the optimal flow f are the optimal solution of the dual problem [1]. The Out-of-Kilter algorithm runs in time $O((m^2 + m \cdot n \cdot \log n) \cdot D)$ on a network with m edges and n vertices and maximum demand D.

2.3 Verification of Neural Networks

A rectified linear unit (ReLU) is a commonly used activation function $\sigma : \mathbb{R} \rightarrow \mathbb{R}$ defined as $\sigma(x) = \max\{x, 0\}$. We can generalize this function from scalars to vectors as $\sigma : \mathbb{R}^n \rightarrow \mathbb{R}^n$ in a straightforward fashion by applying ReLU component-wise. In this paper, we primarily work with feedforward neural networks (NN) with ReLU activation units. We focus on networks with k fully-connected layers, also called multi-layer perceptrons, where each layer i is defined with a weight matrix W_i and a bias vector b_i of appropriate size and is followed by a ReLU.

Formally, a *neural network* can be viewed as a function $f : \mathbb{R}^{n_i} \rightarrow \mathbb{R}^{n_o}$, where n_i is the number of inputs and n_o is the number of outputs. Given an input $y_0 \in \mathbb{R}^{n_i}$, a neural network will compute an output $y_k \in \mathbb{R}^{n_o}$ as follows:

$$\begin{aligned} x^{(1)} &= W_1 y_0 + b_1, & y_1 &= \sigma(x^{(1)}) \\ x^{(2)} &= W_2 y_1 + b_2, & y_2 &= \sigma(x^{(2)}) \\ &\vdots \\ x^{(k)} &= W_k y_{k-1} + b_k, & y_k &= \sigma(x^{(k)}) \end{aligned}$$

We call y_{i-1} and y_i the input and output of the i-th layer, respectively, and $x^{(i)}$ the intermediate values at layer i. This setup is the most typical situation considered for neural network verification tools [6], although extensions have been made to other layer types [33, 36] and activation functions [30].

Definition 4 (Exact Range Computation Problem). *Given a neural network implementing the function $f : \mathbb{R}^{n_i} \rightarrow \mathbb{R}^{n_o}$ and an input set $\mathcal{I} \subseteq \mathbb{R}^{n_i}$, the exact range computation problem is to compute the set*

$$\mathsf{Range}(f, \mathcal{I}) = \{y_k \mid y_k = f(y_0),\ y_0 \in \mathcal{I}\}.$$

of possible outputs of the network.

The exact range computation problem can be used to solve the open-loop neural network verification problem defined next.

Definition 5 (Open-Loop Neural Network Verification). *Given an input set $\mathcal{I} \subseteq \mathbb{R}^{n_i}$, an unsafe set $\mathcal{U} \subseteq \mathbb{R}^{n_o}$, and a neural network that computes f, the open-loop neural network verification problem asks if $\mathsf{Range}(f, \mathcal{I}) \cap \mathcal{U} = \emptyset$.*

As is typical with the state-of-practice in DNN verification, we restrict the input and unsafe sets to ones defined with linear constraints,

$$\begin{aligned} \mathcal{I} &= \{\boldsymbol{x} \mid A_i \boldsymbol{x} \leq b_i, \boldsymbol{x} \in \mathbb{R}^{n_i}\}, \text{ and} \\ \mathcal{U} &= \{\boldsymbol{x} \mid A_u \boldsymbol{x} \leq b_u, \boldsymbol{x} \in \mathbb{R}^{n_o}\}. \end{aligned}$$

The popular ACAS Xu neural network verification benchmarks [20] match these assumptions, and will be used in our evaluation.

Although abstraction and refinement methods are often more efficient for verifying neural networks [5], the performance of the exact range computation problem is important for the following two reasons. First, as more refinement needs to be done, the performance of abstraction-refinement will approach that of exact range computation. Efficient exact range computation is therefore essential for efficient abstraction-refinement analysis. Second, exact range computation methods are building blocks for other types of verification problems, such as closed-loop verification of neural-network control systems [26], which often arise in reinforcement learning applications. In these cases, over-approximating the range of a network is too imprecise for analysis over many control cycles, and such analysis loses the relationship between the inputs and the outputs of a network, creating issues similar to the dependency problem in interval arithmetic [34]. In future work, we plan to explore over-approximation methods as well as abstraction-refinement approaches that use octatopes, following similar work done for zonotopes and other abstract domains [15].

3 Abstract Domains: Octatopes and Hexatopes

Both a zonotope and a star set may be viewed as an n-dimensional image of a polytope—which we refer to as the *kernel*—under affine transformation. For zonotopes the kernel is a hypercube, while for linear star sets the kernel is a set defined by an LCS. In this section, we introduce octatopes and hexatopes as generalizations of zonotopes where the kernel is restricted to be a set defined by a UCS and a DCS, respectively. This section also studies algorithms for operations over octatopes and hexatopes required for the verification of neural networks.

3.1 Zonotopes and Linear Star Sets

An n-dimensional *zonotope* $Z = \langle \boldsymbol{c}, G \rangle$ is the image of a p-dimensional hypercube under an affine transformation $\mathbb{R}^p \to \mathbb{R}^n$. Given a center $\boldsymbol{c} \in \mathbb{R}^n$ and a set of generator vectors $\{\boldsymbol{g}_1, \dots, \boldsymbol{g}_p \in \mathbb{R}^n\}$ forming a matrix $G = [\boldsymbol{g}_1 \cdots \boldsymbol{g}_p] \in \mathbb{R}^{n \times p}$, the semantics of Z are defined as

$$[\![Z]\!] = \{G\boldsymbol{x} + \boldsymbol{c} \,:\, -\mathbf{1}_p \leq \boldsymbol{x} \leq \mathbf{1}_p\}.$$

Linear star sets generalize zonotopes by letting the kernel be defined by an LCS. Formally, an n-dimensional star set $S = \langle \boldsymbol{c}, G, A, \boldsymbol{b} \rangle$ is the image of a p-dimensional polytope $A\boldsymbol{x} \leq b$ under an affine transformation $\mathbb{R}^p \to \mathbb{R}^n$. Given a center $\boldsymbol{c} \in \mathbb{R}^n$ and a set of generator vectors $\{\boldsymbol{g}_1, \dots, \boldsymbol{g}_p \in \mathbb{R}^n\}$ that form a matrix $G = [\boldsymbol{g}_1 \cdots \boldsymbol{g}_p] \in \mathbb{R}^{n \times p}$, the semantics of S are defined as

$$[\![S]\!] = \{G\boldsymbol{x} + \boldsymbol{c} \,:\, A\boldsymbol{x} \leq \boldsymbol{b}\}.$$

The following theorems [35] provide the foundational results on linear star sets that are leveraged in neural network verification.

Theorem 1 (Affine Transformations of Linear Star Sets). *The linear star sets are closed under affine transformation, i.e., given a linear star set* $S = \langle \boldsymbol{c}, G, A, \boldsymbol{b}\rangle$ *and an affine map* $f(\boldsymbol{x}) = W\boldsymbol{x} + \boldsymbol{d}$ *on* $[\![S]\!]$*, the image* $S_{[W,d]} = \{f(\boldsymbol{x}) : \boldsymbol{x} \in [\![S]\!]\}$ *is equal to* $[\![S']\!]$ *for a linear star set* $S' = \langle \boldsymbol{c}', G', A, \boldsymbol{b}\rangle$ *where*

$$\boldsymbol{c}' = W\boldsymbol{c} + \boldsymbol{d} \text{ and } G' = \left[W\boldsymbol{g}_1 \cdots W\boldsymbol{g}_p\right].$$

Theorem 2 (Linear Optimization Over Linear Star Sets). *The optimization of a linear function f over a linear star set S reduces to linear programming.*

Theorem 3 (Intersection of Linear Star Sets and Half-Spaces). *The intersection of a star set* $S = \langle \boldsymbol{c}, G, A, \boldsymbol{b}\rangle$ *and half space* $\{\boldsymbol{y} \mid H\boldsymbol{y} \le \boldsymbol{h}\}$ *is another star set* $S' = \langle \boldsymbol{c}, G, A', \boldsymbol{b}'\rangle$ *where* $A'\boldsymbol{x} \le \boldsymbol{b}'$ *are the conjunction of constraints*

$$A\boldsymbol{x} \le \boldsymbol{b} \text{ and } HG\boldsymbol{x} \le \boldsymbol{h} - H\boldsymbol{c}.$$

Next, we extend the notion of zonotopes to define octatopes and hexatopes and develop a series of results, analogous to Theorem 1 to 3, that provide the theoretical framework for the application of these abstract domains to the verification of neural networks.

3.2 Octatopes and Hexatopes

Definition 6 (Octatopes and Hexatopes). *An octatope is an n-dimensional star set* $\langle \boldsymbol{c}, G, A, \boldsymbol{b}\rangle$ *where the kernel constraints* $A\boldsymbol{x} \le \boldsymbol{b}$ *form a UCS. A hexatope is similarly defined as an n-dimensional star set* $\langle \boldsymbol{c}, G, A, \boldsymbol{b}\rangle$ *where the kernel constraints* $A\boldsymbol{x} \le \boldsymbol{b}$ *form a DCS.*

Our first result mirrors Theorem 1 and establishes closure under affine mappings for octatopes and hexatopes.

Theorem 4. *Octatopes and Hexatopes are closed under affine transformation.*

Proof. From Theorem 1 it follows for an octatope (hexatope) $S = \langle \boldsymbol{c}, G, A, \boldsymbol{b}\rangle$ and an affine mapping $f(\boldsymbol{x}) = W\boldsymbol{x} + \boldsymbol{d}$, that $S_{[W,d]} = \{W\boldsymbol{x} + \boldsymbol{d} : \boldsymbol{x} \in [\![S]\!]\}$ is a star set $S' = \langle \boldsymbol{c}', G', A, \boldsymbol{b}\rangle$ where

$$\boldsymbol{c}' = W\boldsymbol{c} + \boldsymbol{d} \text{ and } G' = \left[W\boldsymbol{g}_1 \cdots W\boldsymbol{g}_p\right].$$

Since this transformation does not change the kernel, the resulting set remains an octatope (hexatope). □

3.3 Linear Optimization Over Octatopes and Hexatopes

By Theorem 2, linear optimization over linear star sets can be done in polynomial time. Our next result shows that linear optimization over octatopes and hexatopes can be done in *strongly* polynomial time.

Theorem 5. *The linear optimization problem for octatopes and hexatopes can be solved in strongly polynomial time via a reduction to the MCF problem.*

Proof. We reduce the optimization problem for octatopes to a similar problem for hexatopes. Consider an n-dimensional octatope $O = \langle \boldsymbol{c}, G, A, \boldsymbol{b} \rangle$ which is the image of a p-dimensional UCS-defined set. Here $\boldsymbol{c} \in \mathbb{R}^n$ is the center and vectors $\{\boldsymbol{g}_1, \boldsymbol{g}_2, \ldots, \boldsymbol{g}_p \in \mathbb{R}^n\}$ are the generators. In order to optimize a linear function f over $[\![O]\!]$, it suffices to optimize the composition of functions $\boldsymbol{x} \mapsto G\boldsymbol{x} + \boldsymbol{c}$ and f over the UTVPI constrained set $A\boldsymbol{x} \leq \boldsymbol{b}$. We describe a method to find the linear optimum of an arbitrary linear objective function over a UCS.

Let $\mathbf{U}$ be a UCS and let f be an objective function we are maximizing. First we convert [24] the UCS $\mathbf{U}$ into a DCS $\mathbf{D}$. The first part of the conversion creates the variables x_i^+ and x_i^- in $\mathbf{D}$ for each variable x_i in $\mathbf{U}$. Then, each constraint in $\mathbf{U}$ is converted as follows:

1. Each constraint of the form $x_i + x_j \leq b_{ij}$ becomes
$$x_i^+ - x_j^- \leq b_{ij} \text{ and } - x_i^- + x_j^+ \leq b_{ij}.$$
2. Each constraint of the form $x_i - x_j \leq b_{ij}$ becomes
$$x_i^+ - x_j^+ \leq b_{ij} \text{ and } - x_i^- + x_j^- \leq b_{ij}.$$
3. Each constraint of the form $-x_i + x_j \leq b_{ij}$ becomes
$$x_i^- - x_j^- \leq b_{ij} \text{ and } - x_i^+ + x_j^+ \leq b_{ij}.$$
4. Each constraint of the form $-x_i - x_j \leq b_{ij}$ becomes
$$x_i^- - x_j^+ \leq b_{ij} \text{ and } - x_i^+ + x_j^- \leq b_{ij}.$$
5. Each constraint of the form $x_i \leq b_i$ becomes
$$x_i^+ - x_i^- \leq 2 \cdot b_i.$$
6. Each constraint of the form $-x_i \leq b_i$ becomes
$$x_i^- - x_i^+ \leq 2 \cdot b_i.$$

Observe that $x_i = \frac{1}{2}(x_i^+ - x_i^-)$ satisfies the original UCS. Thus, we can consider this as the problem maximizing the objective function over variables $\frac{1}{2}(x_i^+ - x_i^-)$ of the DCS $\mathbf{D}$. Note that the problem of maximizing a linear objective function over a DCS is the dual of a minimum cost flow problem. Since the Out-of-Kilter algorithm also solves the dual to the minimum cost flow problem [1], running the Out-of-Kilter algorithm on the dual of the DCS optimization problem will also solve the DCS optimization problem. For a UCS with m constraints, this process takes $O((n^2 + m \cdot n \cdot \log m) \cdot C)$ time where C is the largest absolute value of any coefficient in the objective function. □

Algorithm 2. UTVPIBoundingBox($\mathbf{U}, l$)

Input: UCS $\mathbf{U}$ and constraint l
Output: A UTVPI bounding box $\mathbf{U}'$

$\mathbf{U}' \leftarrow \emptyset$
for all pairs of variables x_i, x_j in $\mathbf{U}$ **do**
  Let $u_{ij}^{+-} = \max_{\mathbf{U}\cup\{l\}} x_i - x_j$ and add constraint $x_i - x_j \leq u_{ij}^{+-}$ to $\mathbf{U}'$
  Let $u_{ij}^{-+} = \max_{\mathbf{U}\cup\{l\}} x_j - x_i$ and add constraint $x_j - x_i \leq u_{ij}^{-+}$ to $\mathbf{U}'$
  Let $u_{ij}^{++} = \max_{\mathbf{U}\cup\{l\}} x_i + x_j$ and add constraint $x_i + x_j \leq u_{ij}^{++}$ to $\mathbf{U}'$
  Let $u_{ij}^{--} = \max_{\mathbf{U}\cup\{l\}} -x_i - x_j$ and add $-x_i - x_j \leq u_{ij}^{--}$ to $\mathbf{U}'$
  Let $u_i^{+} = \max_{\mathbf{U}\cup\{l\}} x_i$ and add constraint $x_i \leq u_i^{+}$ to $\mathbf{U}'$
  Let $u_i^{-} = \max_{\mathbf{U}\cup\{l\}} -x_i$ and add constraint $-x_i \leq u_i^{-}$ to $\mathbf{U}'$
return $\mathbf{U}'$.

Emptiness Checking. We also consider the feasibility problem for octatopes. That is, the problem of deciding whether an octatope is empty. The emptiness of an octatope can be decided in $O(n \cdot m)$ time and $O(n{+}m)$ space where n is the number of generator variables and m is the number of generator constraints. It is easy to see that an octatope (hexatope) is empty if and only if the UTVPI constraints of its kernel are unsatisfiable as linear mappings over polytopes that are monotone with respect to set inclusion. The complexity then follows from results on checking the feasibility of UTVPI constraint systems [24].

3.4 Intersection of Octatopes/Hexatopes and Half-Spaces

It follows from Theorem 3 that the intersection of an octatope $O = \langle \boldsymbol{c}, G, A, \boldsymbol{b} \rangle$ and half space $\{\boldsymbol{y} \mid H\boldsymbol{y} \leq \boldsymbol{h}\}$ is a star set $O' = \langle \boldsymbol{c}, G, A', \boldsymbol{b}' \rangle$ where the constraints $A'\boldsymbol{x} \leq \boldsymbol{b}'$ are the conjunction of UCS constraints $A\boldsymbol{x} \leq \boldsymbol{b}$ and the hyperplane $HG\boldsymbol{x} \leq \boldsymbol{h} - H\boldsymbol{c}$. In the rest of this section, we show how an over-approximation of this intersection can be represented as UCS constraints. The treatment for hexatopes is similar, and hence omitted.

We formalize this problem as the UTVPI *bounding box problem.* Given a UCS $\mathbf{U}$ and an arbitrary linear constraint l, a UTVPI *bounding box* is a UCS $\mathbf{U}'$, such that every solution to $\mathbf{U} \cup \{l\}$ is a solution to $\mathbf{U}'$. For a given UCS $\mathbf{U}$ and constraint l, a *tightest* UTVPI bounding box is a bounding box of $\mathbf{U} \cup \{l\}$ that is contained within every other bounding box of $\mathbf{U} \cup \{l\}$. Thus, a UTVPI bounding box of a UCS $\mathbf{U}$ and constraint l is a UCS that overestimates the solution space of $\mathbf{U} \cup \{l\}$. A tightest bounding box is a UCS that overestimates the solution space the least. Each of the linear programs used to construct $\mathbf{U}'$ can be solved (with L bits of precision) in $O(n^{2.38} \cdot L)$ time [10]. Since finding the UTVPI bounding box requires solving $O(n^2)$ linear programs, the UTVPI bounding box can be found in $O(n^{4.38} \cdot L)$ time.

Theorem 6. *Let* $\mathbf{U}$ *be a UCS and let* l *be an arbitrary linear constraint. The UCS* $\mathbf{U}'$*, constructed by Algorithm 2, is a* UTVPI *bounding box of* $\mathbf{U} \cup \{l\}$.

Proof. Let $\mathbf{x}^*$ be a solution to $\mathbf{U} \cup \{l\}$. Let $a_i \cdot x_i + a_j \cdot x_j \leq u_{ij}$ be an arbitrary constraint in $\mathbf{U}'$. By construction of $\mathbf{U}'$, we have $u_{ij} = \max_{\mathbf{U}\cup\{l\}} a_i \cdot x_i + a_j \cdot x_j$.

Since $\mathbf{x}^*$ is a solution of $\mathbf{U} \cup \{l\}$, $a_i \cdot x_i^* + a_j \cdot x_j^* \leq u_{ij}$. This means that $\mathbf{x}^*$ satisfies the constraint $a_i \cdot x_i + a_j \cdot x_j \leq u_{ij}$. Since the constraint $a_i \cdot x_i + a_j \cdot x_j \leq u_{ij}$ was chosen arbitrarily, $\mathbf{x}^*$ is a solution to $\mathbf{U}'$. Note that $\mathbf{x}^*$ was an arbitrary solution to $\mathbf{U} \cup \{l\}$. Thus, every solution to $\mathbf{U} \cup \{l\}$ is a solution to $\mathbf{U}'$. Consequently, $\mathbf{U}'$ is a UTVPI bounding box of $\mathbf{U} \cup \{l\}$. □

We now show that $\mathbf{U}'$ is a tightest UTVPI bounding box of $\mathbf{U} \cup \{l\}$. Note that $\mathbf{U} \cup \{l\}$ must have a tightest bounding box. Consider two bounding boxes $\mathbf{U}_1$ and $\mathbf{U}_2$ of $\mathbf{U} \cup \{l\}$. Let $\mathbf{U}^*$, be the UCS formed by combining the constraints in $\mathbf{U}_1$ and $\mathbf{U}_2$. Note that $\mathbf{U}^*$ is also a bounding box of $\mathbf{U} \cup \{l\}$. Additionally, every solution to $\mathbf{U}^*$ is a solution to both $\mathbf{U}_1$ and $\mathbf{U}_2$. Thus, if $\mathbf{U} \cup \{l\}$ has two incomparable bounding boxes, then a new bounding box can be constructed that is tighter than both.

Theorem 7. *Let* $\mathbf{U}$ *be a UCS and let* l *be a linear constraint. The UCS* $\mathbf{U}'$*, produced by Algorithm 2, is a tightest* UTVPI *bounding box of* $\mathbf{U} \cup \{l\}$.

Proof. Assume for the sake of contradiction, that $\mathbf{U}'$ is not a tightest UTVPI bounding box of $\mathbf{U} \cup \{l\}$. Thus, there exist a UTVPI bounding box $\mathbf{U}''$ and a point $\mathbf{x}^*$ such that $\mathbf{x}^*$ is a solution to $\mathbf{U}'$, but not a solution to $\mathbf{U}''$. This means that there is a UTVPI constraint $a_i \cdot x_i + a_j \cdot x_j \leq b$ in $\mathbf{U}''$ that is violated by $\mathbf{x}^*$.

Let $u_{ij} = \max_{\mathbf{U}\cup\{l\}} a_i \cdot x_i + a_j \cdot x_j$. Since $\mathbf{U}''$ is a UTVPI bounding box of $\mathbf{U} \cup \{l\}$, every solution to $\mathbf{U} \cup \{l\}$ is a solution to $\mathbf{U}''$. Thus, every solution to $\mathbf{U} \cup \{l\}$ satisfies the constraint $a_i \cdot x_i + a_j \cdot x_j \leq b$. This means that

$$\max_{\mathbf{U}\cup\{l\}} a_i \cdot x_i + a_j \cdot x_j$$

is bounded from above by b. Thus, u_{ij} exists and $u_{ij} \leq b$.

By the construction of $\mathbf{U}'$, the constraint $a_i \cdot x_i + a_j \cdot x_j \leq u_{ij}$ is in $\mathbf{U}'$. However, $\mathbf{x}^*$ is a solution to $\mathbf{U}'$ such that $a_i \cdot x_i^* + a_j \cdot x_j^* > b \geq u_{ij}$. This is a contradiction. Thus, $\mathbf{U}'$ must be a tightest UTVPI bounding box of $\mathbf{U} \cup \{l\}$. □

4 Range Computation for Neural Nets with Prefilters

The exact range computation problem from Definition 4 can be solved using linear star sets (see Algorithms 1 and 2 in earlier work for a full review [7]).

The neural network function f as defined in Sect. 2.3 is a piece-wise affine function of the inputs. The range computation proceeds using geometric set operations. The initial set of states is represented as a linear star set and propagated through each layer of the network. To go from the output of one layer to the vector of intermediate values at the next layer, an affine transformation operation is performed on the set. The effect of the ReLU activation in a layer is handled iteratively for each neuron. The set of states is potentially split along the neuron input constraint $y_i = 0$, into a negative region and a positive region, using a half-space intersection operation. The negative region is then projected to zero to match the semantics of a ReLU. The two sets are then considered independently for the remaining neurons in the layer, as well as the rest of the layers in the network. For a given input set, not all neurons require splitting the set in two, since the input constraints may restrict inputs to be strictly positive or negative. To check this, before splitting we first optimize over the set in the direction of the intermediate value $x_j^{(i)}$ corresponding to a specific neuron j in layer i. If splitting occurs, the two sets are treated independently and propagated through the remaining neurons in the layer, possibly requiring further splitting in the remaining parts of the network.

After applying a number of optimizations, the bottleneck of exact range computation with star sets is the use of LP solving to compute the input bounds for each neuron [7]. To improve analysis speed, rather than speeding up LP solving—which is a well-studied problem where further progress is likely to be difficult—we instead seek methods that can reduce the number of LPs needed.

In earlier work, zonotope abstract domains have been considered for this task. Rather than just propagating star sets through a network, we also propagate a zonotope overapproximation that we use in a *prefiltering* step. Recall that before splitting we first need to optimize over the set in the direction of the intermediate value $x_j^{(i)}$. Before optimizing over the star set using LP, we first optimize over the zonotope abstraction prefilter. If the zonotope abstraction can prove that the inputs are strictly positive or negative, than we are guaranteed the exact result from the LP will be strictly positive or negative as well (as the zonotope is an overapproximation of the star set). This allows us to avoid LP, as optimization over zonotopes can be done efficiently using a simple loop.

The reason zonotope analysis is not exact is that zonotopes do not support general half-space intersections when sets must be split. Instead, two approaches have been considered. The easiest option is to ignore intersections, which is fast but can cause significant overapproximation error in the abstraction [15,36]. Alternatively, we can perform *domain contraction*, which is to search for zonotopes that more tightly overapproximate the intersection. Different approaches for domain contraction are possible, ranging from reasoning methods over individual constraints to more accurate approaches that use LP solving on the star set in the generator coefficient space [7]. Although the LP approach uses the expensive operation we are trying to reduce, it can result in an overall reduction of LPs, as the neuron input bounds can be computed more accurately.

This work proposes using octatope abstract domains as a prefilter. As described earlier, optimization over octatopes can be done more efficiently than general LP solving. The greater expressiveness of octatopes compared with zonotopes means that we can hope to further reduce the number of LPs needed with the star set when computing a neuron's input bounds for splitting. We evaluate this impact in our experiments. In terms of handling intersections when splitting sets, octatopes (like zonotopes) cannot exactly support any general half-space intersection operation. This means that a domain contraction step may be necessary to ensure tight overapproximation.

5 Experimental Results

We next evaluate the potential savings in LP computation to computing neuron input bounds during exact range computation for neural networks. Our evaluation is performed on several benchmarks from the ACAS Xu benchmark suite [20], specifically focusing on property 3 and 4 where earlier work has shown exact range computation is tractable [7]. We generally report number of LPs for different operations rather than runtime, as the runtime is influenced by other factors such code optimizations and the choice of LP solver.

First, we examine the number of LPs needed to perform neuron input range computation, for different choices of prefilter abstract domain. The LP calls to find the neuron input ranges is the bottleneck of the overall range computation algorithm, so its reduction is of particular importance. The results are in Table 1. The Star-Only approach uses only LP solving with no prefiler, and therefore has the highest number of LPs. The next column, Zonotope-NC corresponds to the case where zonotope prefilters are used, but no domain contraction is performed (halfspace intersections are ignored). This has a significant reduction on the number of LP calls, for example in the first row with property 3 and network 1–6, where the number of LP calls is reduced from 91 K to 11 K. Using domain contraction with zonotopes, Zono-C, further reduces this to around 3.3 K. The more precise domains with hexatopes and octatopes can further reduce this to around 2.6 K and 2.5 K, respectively. The minimum column is computed by seeing how many bounds computations could not be eliminated as they correspond to cases where the input to a neuron truly can be either positive or negative. Even a perfect prefilter could not eliminate these LPs, as prefilters only eliminate cases where splitting is impossible. Other approaches could be considered to remove these LPs, such as tracking specific witness input points that can prove a neuron can have both positive and negative inputs, which we may consider in future work. Overall, the proposed octatope abstract domain has the potential to reduce the number of unnecessary LPs significantly in exact range computation.

When using the new abstract domain, however, there is a trade-off where extra operations are needed to perform domain contraction as well as to optimize within the abstract domains. We used a witness-tracking approach [5], where for each constraint a witness point was included that was in the star set and on the boundary of the constraint. When new intersections are performed, each witness point is checked to see if it is now excluded from the set. When points are excluded, new witness points get generated by solving an LP in the direction of the constraint, which may tighten the constraint. This results in the tight abstract domains, but can be expensive when many constraints are possible. For hexatopes and octatopes, the number of possible constraints is quadratic in the number of variables (ACAS Xu has 5 input variables).

Table 2 shows the number of LPs needed for each example when performing domain contraction. Star-Only and Zono-NC do not perform domain contraction, and so have 0 LPs for this operation. As expected, the more complex the abstract domain, the more operations are needed. This is due to the contraction method

Table 1. Number of LP calls to find neuron input bounds for different abstract domain prefilters on various ACASXu properties and networks.

Prop	Net	Star-Only	Zono-NC	Zono-C	Hex	Oct	Minimum
3	1–6	91762	11152	3382	2635	2571	1886
3	2–7	77896	9365	2921	2240	2198	1626
3	3–5	80988	8990	2711	2131	2092	1710
3	5–2	54758	15523	7762	6820	6704	3779
4	1–4	53036	7736	2597	2389	2330	1926
4	2–7	38748	3851	1249	888	861	753
4	5–9	68750	8814	2952	2286	2151	1591

Table 2. Number of LP calls for the domain contraction step for different abstract domain prefilters for various ACAS Xu properties and networks.

Prop	Net	Star-Only	Zono-NC	Zono-C	Hex	Oct
3	1–6	0	0	12765	38400	115200
3	2–7	0	0	12280	36840	110520
3	3–5	0	0	10407	31230	93690
3	5–2	0	0	21249	63750	191250
4	1–4	0	0	11828	35493	106476
4	2–7	0	0	5533	16620	49860
4	5–9	0	0	9906	29730	89190

performed, where the number of possible LPs needed at a domain contraction step increases as the number of possible constraints increases.

In terms of the performance of network simplex for optimizing within the octatope domain, the engineering aspect of the problem also requires further development. When computing the range of network 2–7 with the input set from property 4, the UTVPI constraints were optimized 38748 times. When using the commercial LP solver Gurobi on these constraints, each call took on average of 0.17 ms. Formulating the min-cost flow problem and calling the `network_simplex` implementation from the `networkx` python library, however, used about 1.9 ms per call, about 11x slower. Further, while Gurobi always obtained a result, numerical issues caused network simplex to fail about 0.65% of the time.

In summary, while octatopes effectively reduce the bottleneck step of input bounds computation, further improvements must be made to octatope domain contraction algorithms as well as to implementation optimizations of min-cost flow solvers, before an overall speedup can be achieved. Nonetheless, it is an encouraging result for DNN verification as developing more efficient domain contraction algorithms and improving min-cost flow implementations is likely easier than coming up with new ways to speed up LP solving.

6 Conclusion

The advent of deep neural networks and their inevitable widespread adoption necessitates tools by which we can reason about their robustness. The verification community has made great strides on this front in recent years through the development of neural network verification solutions based on search, optimization, and reachability. While search and optimization can often be used to yield sound and complete solutions, such techniques pay the cost of scalability. Methods based on reachability analysis, on the other, can often scale better at the cost of completeness. These methods typically employ an abstract domain representation of the input-output behavior of nodes in the neural network for a given set of inputs. These abstract domains range from zonotopes to star sets that differ in their trade-off between scalability and precision.

We proposed octatopes as a new abstract domain which corresponds to affine transformations of unit two-variable per inequality (UTVPI) constraints. Octatopes provide tighter abstractions than zonotopes while optimization can be formulated as a min-cost flow problem that is theoretically more efficient than linear programming. Our experiments using octatope abstract domains for exact range computation of neural networks confirmed their accuracy, as we were able to reduce the bottleneck step of using LP to compute each neuron's input bounds. However, engineering improvements must still be made to min-cost flow libraries. In our application of UTVPI optimization, it was faster to use the highly-optimized commercial LP solver Gurobi instead of the theoretically faster min-cost flow formulation. In future work, we plan to examine ways to improve domain contraction, as well as investigating other application areas of octatopes such as neural network verification with over-approximations, software analysis, and hybrid systems reachability.

Acknowledgment. This material is based upon work supported by the Air Force Office of Scientific Research and the Office of Naval Research under award numbers FA9550-19-1-0288, FA9550-21-1-0121, FA9550-22-1-0450, FA9550-22-1-0029 and N00014-22-1-2156. Any opinions, findings, and conclusions or recommendations expressed in this material are those of the author(s) and do not necessarily reflect the views of the United States Air Force or the United States Navy. This research was supported in part by the Air Force Research Laboratory Information Directorate, through the Air Force Office of Scientific Research Summer Faculty Fellowship Program, Contract Numbers FA8750-15-3-6003, FA9550-15-0001 and FA9550-20-F-0005.

This work is also supported by the National Science Foundation (NSF) grant CCF-2009022 and by NSF CAREER award CCF-2146563.

References

1. Ahuja, R.K., Magnanti, T.L., Orlin, J.B.: Network Flows: Theory, Algorithms and Applications. Prentice Hall (1993)
2. Ahuja, R.K., Magnanti, T.L., Orlin, J.B.: Network Flows: Theory, Algorithms, and Applications. Prentice Hall (1993)

3. Akintunde, M., Lomuscio, A., Maganti, L., Pirovano, E.: Reachability analysis for neural agent-environment systems. In: Sixteenth International Conference on Principles of Knowledge Representation and Reasoning (2018)
4. Aws Albarghouthi: Introduction to Neural Network Verification (2021). http://verifieddeeplearning.com
5. Bak, S.: nnenum: verification of ReLU neural networks with optimized abstraction refinement. In: Dutle, A., Moscato, M.M., Titolo, L., Muñoz, C.A., Perez, I. (eds.) NFM 2021. LNCS, vol. 12673, pp. 19–36. Springer, Cham (2021). https://doi.org/10.1007/978-3-030-76384-8_2
6. Bak, S., Liu, C., Johnson, T.: The second international verification of neural networks competition (VNN-COMP 2021): summary and results. arXiv preprint arXiv:2109.00498 (2021)
7. Bak, S., Tran, H.-D., Hobbs, K., Johnson, T.T.: Improved geometric path enumeration for verifying ReLU neural networks. In: Lahiri, S.K., Wang, C. (eds.) CAV 2020. LNCS, vol. 12224, pp. 66–96. Springer, Cham (2020). https://doi.org/10.1007/978-3-030-53288-8_4
8. Bazaraa, M.S., Jarvis, J.J., Sherali, H.D.: Linear Programming and Network Flows. Wiley, Hoboken (2008)
9. Behrmann, G., et al.: UPPAAL 4.0. In: Third International Conference on the Quantitative Evaluation of Systems (QEST 2006), 11–14 September 2006, Riverside, California, USA, pp. 125–126. IEEE Computer Society (2006)
10. Cohen, M.B., Lee, Y.T., Song, Z.: Solving linear programs in the current matrix multiplication time. J. ACM **68**(1), 1–39 (2021)
11. Cousot, P., Cousot, R.: Abstract interpretation: a unified lattice model for static analysis of programs by construction or approximation of fixpoints. In: Proceedings of the 4th ACM SIGACT-SIGPLAN Symposium on Principles of Programming Languages, pp. 238–252 (1977)
12. de Moura, L., Bjørner, N.: Z3: an efficient SMT solver. In: Ramakrishnan, C.R., Rehof, J. (eds.) TACAS 2008. LNCS, vol. 4963, pp. 337–340. Springer, Heidelberg (2008). https://doi.org/10.1007/978-3-540-78800-3_24
13. Duggirala, P.S., Viswanathan, M.: Parsimonious, simulation based verification of linear systems. In: Chaudhuri, S., Farzan, A. (eds.) CAV 2016. LNCS, vol. 9779, pp. 477–494. Springer, Cham (2016). https://doi.org/10.1007/978-3-319-41528-4_26
14. Friedmann, O., Hansen, T.D., Zwick, U.: Subexponential lower bounds for randomized pivoting rules for the simplex algorithm. In: Symposium on Theory of Computing (STOC 2011), pp. 283–292, ACM, New York (2011)
15. Gehr, T., Mirman, M., Drachsler-Cohen, D., Tsankov, P., Chaudhuri, S., Vechev, M.: AI2: safety and robustness certification of neural networks with abstract interpretation. In: 2018 IEEE Symposium on Security and Privacy (SP), pp. 3–18. IEEE (2018)
16. Ghorbal, K., Goubault, E., Putot, S.: The zonotope abstract domain Taylor1+. In: Bouajjani, A., Maler, O. (eds.) CAV 2009. LNCS, vol. 5643, pp. 627–633. Springer, Heidelberg (2009). https://doi.org/10.1007/978-3-642-02658-4_47
17. Goldberg, A.V., Tarjan, R.E.: Finding minimum-cost circulations by canceling negative cycles. J. ACM **36**(4), 873–886 (1989)
18. Henriksen, P., Lomuscio, A.: Efficient neural network verification via adaptive refinement and adversarial search. In: ECAI 2020, pp. 2513–2520. IOS Press (2020)
19. Henriksen, P., Lomuscio, A.: DEEPSPLIT: an efficient splitting method for neural network verification via indirect effect analysis. In: Proceedings of the 30th International Joint Conference on Artificial Intelligence (IJCAI21) (2021). To appear

20. Katz, G., Barrett, C., Dill, D.L., Julian, K., Kochenderfer, M.J.: Reluplex: an efficient SMT solver for verifying deep neural networks. In: Majumdar, R., Kunčak, V. (eds.) CAV 2017. LNCS, vol. 10426, pp. 97–117. Springer, Cham (2017). https://doi.org/10.1007/978-3-319-63387-9_5
21. Katz, G., et al.: The Marabou framework for verification and analysis of deep neural networks. In: Dillig, I., Tasiran, S. (eds.) CAV 2019. LNCS, vol. 11561, pp. 443–452. Springer, Cham (2019). https://doi.org/10.1007/978-3-030-25540-4_26
22. Khachiyan, L.G.: A polynomial time algorithm for linear programming. Dokl. Akad. Nauk SSSR **244**(5), 1093–1096 (1979). English translation in Soviet Math. Dokl. 20, 191–194
23. Klee, F., Minty, G.J.: How good is the simplex algorithm? Inequalities **III**, 159–175 (1972)
24. Lahiri, S.K., Musuvathi, M.: An efficient decision procedure for UTVPI constraints. In: Gramlich, B. (ed.) FroCoS 2005. LNCS (LNAI), vol. 3717, pp. 168–183. Springer, Heidelberg (2005). https://doi.org/10.1007/11559306_9
25. Liu, C., Arnon, T., Lazarus, C., Strong, C., Barrett, C., Kochenderfer, M.J.: Algorithms for verifying deep neural networks. Found. Trends Optim. **4**(3–4), 244–404 (2021)
26. Manzanas Lopez, D., Johnson, T., Tran, H.D., Bak, S., Chen, X., Hobbs, K.L.: Verification of neural network compression of ACAS Xu lookup tables with star set reachability. In: AIAA Scitech 2021 Forum, p. 0995 (2021)
27. Miné, A.: The octagon abstract domain. High.-Order Symb. Comput. **19**(1), 31–100 (2006)
28. Orlin, J.B.: A polynomial time primal network simplex algorithm for minimum cost flows. Math. Program. **78**, 109–129 (1997). https://doi.org/10.1007/BF02614365
29. Singh, G., Gehr, T., Mirman, M., Püschel, M., Vechev, M.: Fast and effective robustness certification. NeurIPS **1**(4), 6 (2018)
30. Singh, G., Gehr, T., Püschel, M., Vechev, M.: An abstract domain for certifying neural networks. Proc. ACM Program. Lang. **3**(POPL), 1–30 (2019)
31. Sutton, R.S., Barto, A.G.: Reinforcement Learning: An Introduction, 2nd edn. MIT Press (2018)
32. Tjeng, V., Xiao, K., Tedrake, R.: Evaluating robustness of neural networks with mixed integer programming. In: International Conference on Learning Representations (2018)
33. Tran, H.-D., Bak, S., Xiang, W., Johnson, T.T.: Verification of deep convolutional neural networks using ImageStars. In: Lahiri, S.K., Wang, C. (eds.) CAV 2020. LNCS, vol. 12224, pp. 18–42. Springer, Cham (2020). https://doi.org/10.1007/978-3-030-53288-8_2
34. Tran, H.D., Cai, F., Diego, M.L., Musau, P., Johnson, T.T., Koutsoukos, X.: Safety verification of cyber-physical systems with reinforcement learning control. ACM Trans. Embed. Comput. Syst. **18**(5s), 1–22 (2019)
35. Tran, H.-D., et al.: Star-based reachability analysis of deep neural networks. In: ter Beek, M.H., McIver, A., Oliveira, J.N. (eds.) FM 2019. LNCS, vol. 11800, pp. 670–686. Springer, Cham (2019). https://doi.org/10.1007/978-3-030-30942-8_39
36. Tran, H.-D., et al.: Robustness verification of semantic segmentation neural networks using relaxed reachability. In: Silva, A., Leino, K.R.M. (eds.) CAV 2021. LNCS, vol. 12759, pp. 263–286. Springer, Cham (2021). https://doi.org/10.1007/978-3-030-81685-8_12
37. Tran, H.-D., et al.: NNV: the neural network verification tool for deep neural networks and learning-enabled cyber-physical systems. In: Lahiri, S.K., Wang, C.

(eds.) CAV 2020. LNCS, vol. 12224, pp. 3–17. Springer, Cham (2020). https://doi.org/10.1007/978-3-030-53288-8_1
38. Wang, S., Pei, K., Whitehouse, J., Yang, J., Jana, S.: Efficient formal safety analysis of neural networks. Adv. Neural Inf. Process. Syst. **31** (2018)
39. Wang, S., et al.: Beta-crown: efficient bound propagation with per-neuron split constraints for neural network robustness verification. Adv. Neural. Inf. Process. Syst. **34**, 29909–29921 (2021)

Program Semantics and Verification Technique for AI-Centred Programs

Fortunat Rajaona[1(✉)], Ioana Boureanu[1], Vadim Malvone[2], and Francesco Belardinelli[3]

[1] Surrey Centre for Cyber Security, University of Surrey, Guildford, UK
{s.rajaona,i.boureanu}@surrey.ac.uk
[2] Télécom Paris, Palaiseau, France
vadim.malvone@telecom-paris.fr
[3] Imperial College, London, UK
francesco.belardinelli@imperial.ac.uk

Abstract. We give a general-purpose programming language in which programs can reason about their own knowledge. To specify what these intelligent programs know, we define a "program epistemic" logic, akin to a dynamic epistemic logic for programs. Our logic properties are complex, including programs introspecting into future state of affairs, i.e., reasoning now about facts that hold only after they and other threads will execute. To model aspects anchored in privacy, our logic is interpreted over partial observability of variables, thus capturing that each thread can "see" only a part of the global space of variables. We verify program-epistemic properties on such AI-centred programs. To this end, we give a sound translation of the validity of our program-epistemic logic into first-order validity, using a new weakest-precondition semantics and a book-keeping of variable assignment. We implement our translation and fully automate our verification method for well-established examples using SMT solvers.

1 Introduction and Preliminaries

In a digital world governed by strict rules on privacy and access-control [24], some thread A and some thread B will execute concurrently over the same variable space, but A and B will have different, restricted access to global variables. Moreover, both A and B may be decision-making process which take actions based on predictions of future states of their environment [24]. In other words, thread A may need to know now what the state-of-affairs will be after some procedure P runs, albeit as far as A can know modulo its partial observability of the system's variables. More formally, in our framework, we are interested in formulas such as "$K_A \Box_P \varphi$", meaning to reason if "at this current point, thread A knows whether after a procedure P executed, a fact φ expressed over the global domain of variables holds". Or, we may wish to check if agent B knows that agent A knows a fact of this kind, i.e., "$K_B K_A \Box_P \varphi$". Such statements are clearly rich, as they allow threads to reason about the future and moreover

M. Chechik et al. (Eds.): FM 2023, LNCS 14000, pp. 473–491, 2023.
https://doi.org/10.1007/978-3-031-27481-7_27

about their "perception" of the future, and of one another's perceptions. That is, thread B can check what it "thinks" A will "think" of the global state of the system, after some procedure executes.

A New Verification Method Towards Safer AI. On the one hand, evaluating such knowledge-centric properties considered in a partial observability setting is of paramount importance for AI-based decision making [3]. On the other hand, logics of knowledge, also called *epistemic logics* [17], have been well-explored in computer-science since Hintikka [23], and even in the context of multi-agent systems [32] and under partial observability [8,21,37]. In this space, our innovation focuses in turn on new methods for automatically verifying epistemic properties, but –unlike most of our predecessors– we concentrate on verification methods not for abstract systems, but rather analyses of concrete programs (over an arbitrary first-order domain), as well as requirements richer than what went before us. Notably, we wish to create new formal analyses for the epistemic reasoning of concrete programs, catering for them knowing facts not only after they execute (i.e., $\Box_A K_A \varphi$ or $\Box_B K_A \varphi$), but also before they execute (i.e., $K_A \Box_A \varphi$); the latter allows them as well as a Formal-Methodist to check local perception of programs on global futures. To this end, we argue that this opens up the area of verification methods for AI-rich programs, their decision-making and thus makes for safer AI.

1.1 Preliminaries and Background

We now introduce a series of logic-related notions that are key to explaining our contributions in the related field and to setting the scene.

Epistemic Logics. Logics for knowledge or epistemic logics [23] follow a so-called Kripke or "possible-worlds" semantics. Assuming a set of agents, a set of possible worlds are linked by an indistinguishability relation for each agent. Then, an *epistemic formula* $K_a \phi$, stating that "agent a knows that ϕ", holds at a world w, if the statement ϕ is true in all worlds that agent a considers as indistinguishable from world w.

Modelling Imperfect Information in Epistemic Logics. A possible-worlds semantics does not suffice to faithfully capture agents with private information. To this end, *interpreted systems* were introduced [32], whereby agents are associated with private shares of the possible worlds called local states; worlds' indistinguishability is then "sunk" at the level of local states. Alternatively, others looked at how epistemic logic with imperfect information could be expressed via direct notions of visibility (or observability) of propositional variables, e.g., [8,21,37].

Logics of Visibility for Programs. Others [19,31,35] looked at how multi-agent epistemic logics with imperfect information would apply not to generic systems, but specifically to programs. In this setting, the epistemic predicate $K_a(y = 0)$ denotes that agent a knows that the variable y is equal to 0 (in some program). So, such a logic allows for the expression of knowledge properties of program states, using *epistemic predicates*. This is akin to how, in classical program verification, one encodes properties of states using first-order predicates: e.g., Dijkstra's *weakest precondition* [11].

Perfect vs Imperfect recall. For any of the cases aforesaid, an aspect often considered is the amount of knowledge that agents retain, i.e., agents forget all that occur before their current state – *memoryless (or imperfect recall) semantics*, or agents recall all their history of states – *memoryful (or perfect recall) semantics*, or in between the two cases – bounded recall semantics.

"Program-Epistemic" Logics. To reason about knowledge change, epistemic logic is usually enriched with *dynamic modalities* from Dynamic Logics [22,34]. Therein, a dynamic formula $\Box_P \phi$ expresses the fact that when the program P's execution terminates, the system reaches a state satisfying ϕ – a statement given in the base logic (propositional/predicate logic); the program P is built from abstract/concrete actions (e.g., assignments), sequential composition, non-deterministic composition, iteration and test.

Gorogiannis *et al.* [19] gave a "program-epistemic" logic, which is a dynamic logic with concrete programs (e.g., programs with assignments on variables over first-order domains such as integer, reals, or strings). Interestingly, à la [31,35,37], the epistemic model in [19] relies on partial observability of the programs' variables by agents. Gorogiannis *et al.* translated program-epistemic validity into a first-order validity, and this outperformed the then state-of-the-art tools in epistemic properties verification. Whilst an interesting breakthrough, Gorogiannis *et al.* present several limitations. Firstly, the verification mechanisation in [19] only supports "classical" programs; this means that [19] cannot support tests on agents' knowledge. Yet, such tests are clearly in AI-centric programs: e.g., in epistemic puzzles [27], in the so-called "knowledge-based" programs in [16], etc. Secondly, the logic in [19] allows only for knowledge reasoning after a program P executed, not before its run (e.g., not $K_{alice}(\Box_P \phi)$, only $\Box_P(K_{alice}\phi)$); this is arguably insufficient for verification of decision-making with "look ahead" into future states-of-affair. Thirdly, the framework in [19] does not allow for reasoning about nested knowledges operators (e.g., $K_{alice}(K_{bob}\phi)$).

1.2 Our Contributions

We lift all the limitations of [19] listed above and more. We make the following contributions:

1. We define a *multi-agent, program-epistemic logic* $\mathcal{L}^m_{DK}$, which is a dynamic logic whose base logic is a multi-agent first-order epistemic logic, under an observability-based semantics (Sect. 2).
   Our logic is *rich*, where the programs modality contains tests on knowledge, and formulas with nested knowledge operators in the multi-agent setting. This is much more expressive than the state-of-the-art.
2. We give a programming language $\mathcal{PL}$ (programs with tests on knowledge) that concretely defines the dynamic operators in $\mathcal{L}^m_{DK}$. We associate the programming language $\mathcal{PL}$ with a relational semantics and a weakest-precondition semantics, and we show their equivalence (Sect. 3).

3. We give a sound translation of the validity of a program-epistemic logic into first-order validity (Sect. 4).
4. We implement the aforesaid translation to allow a fully-automated verification with our program-epistemic logic, via SMT-solving (Sect. 5).
5. We verify the well-known Dining Cryptographer's protocol [9] and the epistemic puzzle called the "Cheryl's birthday problem" [14]. We report competitive verification results. Collaterally, we are also the first to give SMT-based verification of the "Cheryl's birthday problem" [14] (Sect. 5).

2 Logical Languages $\mathcal{L}_{FO}$ and $\mathcal{L}_{DK}^m$

We introduce the logics $\mathcal{L}_{FO}$, $\mathcal{L}_{K}^m$, and $\mathcal{L}_{DK}^m$, used to describe states and epistemic properties of states, and program-epistemic properties of states.

2.1 Syntax of $\mathcal{L}_{FO}$, $\mathcal{L}_{K}^m$, and $\mathcal{L}_{DK}^m$

Agents and Variables. We use $a, b, c, \ldots$ to denote agents, Ag to denote their whole set, and G for a subset therein. We consider a set Var of variables such that each variable x in Var is "typed" with the group of agents that can observe it. For instance, we write x_G to make explicit the group $G \subseteq Ag$ of observers of x. For each agent $a \in Ag$, the set Var of variables can be partitioned into the variables that are observable by a, denoted $\mathbf{o}_a$, and the variables that are not observable by a, denoted $\mathbf{n}_a$. Thus, $\mathbf{n}_a = \{x_G \in Var \mid a \notin G\}$.

The Base Logic $\mathcal{L}_{QF}$. We assume a user defined base language $\mathcal{L}_{QF}$, on top of which the other logics are built. We assume $\mathcal{L}_{QF}$ to be quantifier-free first-order language with variables in Var. The Greek letter π denotes a formula in $\mathcal{L}_{QF}$.

An example of base language $\mathcal{L}_{\mathbb{N}}$, for integer arithmetic, is given by:

$$e ::= c \mid v \mid e \circ e \qquad (terms)$$
$$\pi ::= e = e \mid e < e \mid \pi \wedge \pi \mid \neg\pi \qquad (\mathcal{L}_{\mathbb{N}} formula)$$

where $\circ ::= +, -, *, /, \times, \mathrm{mod}$; c is an integer constant; and $v \in Var$.

First-Order Logic $\mathcal{L}_{FO}$. We define the quantified first-order logic $\mathcal{L}_{FO}$ based on $\mathcal{L}_{QF}$. This logic describes "physical" properties of a program state and also serves as the target language in the translation of our main logic.

Definition 1. *The quantified first-order logic $\mathcal{L}_{FO}$ is defined by:*

$$\phi ::= \pi \mid \phi \wedge \phi \mid \neg\phi \mid \forall x_G \cdot \phi$$

where π is a quantifier-free formula in $\mathcal{L}_{QF}$, and $x_G \in Var$.

Other connectives and the existential quantifier operator $\exists$, can be derived as standard. We use Greek letters ϕ, ψ, χ to denote first-order formulas in $\mathcal{L}_{FO}$. We extend quantifiers over vectors of variables: $\forall \mathbf{x} \cdot \phi$ means $\forall x_1 \cdot \forall x_2 \cdots \forall x_n \cdot \phi$. As usual, $FV(\phi)$ denotes the set of free variables of ϕ.

Epistemic Logic $\mathcal{L}_K^m$ and Program-Epistemic Logic $\mathcal{L}_{DK}^m$. We now define two logics at once. The first is the first-order multi-agent epistemic logic $\mathcal{L}_K^m$ enriched with the public announcement operator. The logic $\mathcal{L}_K^m$ is first-order in the sense that its atomic propositions are predicates from the base language $\mathcal{L}_{QF}$. The second is our main logic, $\mathcal{L}_{DK}^m$, which extends $\mathcal{L}_K^m$ with program modalities $\Box_P$.

Definition 2. *Let $\mathcal{L}_{QF}$ be a base first-order language and $Ag = \{a_1, \ldots, a_m\}$ a set of agents. We define the first-order multi-agent program epistemic logic $\mathcal{L}_{DK}^m$ with the following syntax*

$$\alpha ::= \pi \mid \alpha \wedge \alpha' \mid \neg\alpha \mid K_{a_i}\alpha \mid [\alpha']\alpha \mid \Box_P\alpha \mid \forall x_G \cdot \alpha \qquad (\mathcal{L}_{DK}^m)$$

where $\pi \in \mathcal{L}_{QF}$, P is a program, $G \subseteq Ag$, and $x_G \in Var$.

Each K_{a_i} is the epistemic operator for agent a_i, the epistemic formula $K_{a_i}\alpha$ reads "agent a_i knows that α". The public announcement formula $[\alpha']\alpha$, in the sense of [13,33], means "after every announcement of α', α holds". The dynamic formula $\Box_P\alpha$ reads "at all final states of P, α holds". The program P is taken from a set of programs $\mathcal{PL}$ that we define in Sect. 3. Other connectives and the existential quantifier $\exists$ can be derived in a standard way as for Definition 1.

The first-order multi-agent epistemic logic $\mathcal{L}_K^m$ is the fragment of $\mathcal{L}_{DK}^m$ without any program operator $\Box_P$.

2.2 Semantics of $\mathcal{L}_{FO}$ and $\mathcal{L}_{DK}^m$

States and the Truth of $\mathcal{L}_{QF}$ Formulas. We consider a set D, used as the domain for interpreting variables and quantifiers. A *state* s of the system is a valuation of the variables in *Var*, i.e., a function $s : Var \to \mathsf{D}$. We denote the universe of all possible states by $\mathcal{U}$.

We assume an interpretation I of constants, functions, and predicates, over D to define the truth of an $\mathcal{L}_{QF}$ formula π at a state s, denoted $s \models_{QF} \pi$.

Truth of an $\mathcal{L}_{FO}$ Formula. Let $s[x \mapsto c]$ denote the state s' such that $s'(x) = c$ and $s'(y) = s(y)$ for all $y \in Var$ different from x. This lifts to a set of states, $W[x \mapsto c] = \{s[x \mapsto c] \mid s \in W\}$.

Definition 3. *The truth of $\phi \in \mathcal{L}_{FO}$ at a state s, denoted $s \models_{FO} \phi$, is defined inductively on ϕ by*

$$\begin{array}{lll} s \models_{FO} \pi & \textit{iff} & s \models_{QF} \pi \\ s \models_{FO} \phi_1 \wedge \phi_2 & \textit{iff} & s \models_{FO} \phi_1 \textit{ and } s \models_{FO} \phi_2 \\ s \models_{FO} \neg\phi & \textit{iff} & s \not\models_{FO} \phi \\ s \models_{FO} \forall x_G \cdot \phi & \textit{iff} & \textit{for all } c \in \mathsf{D}, s[x_G \mapsto c] \models_{FO} \phi. \end{array}$$

We lift the definition of $\models_{FO}$ to a set W of states, with $W \models_{FO} \phi$ iff for all $s \in W$, $s \models_{FO} \phi$. The satisfaction set $[\![\phi]\!]$ of a formula $\phi \in \mathcal{L}_{FO}$ is defined, as usual, by $[\![\phi]\!] = \{s \in \mathcal{U} \mid s \models_{FO} \phi\}$.

Epistemic Models. We model agents' knowledge of the program state with a possible worlds semantics built on the observability of program variables [19]. We define, for each a in Ag, the binary relation $\approx_a$ on $\mathcal{U}$ by: $s \approx_a s'$ if and only if s and s' agree on the part of their domains that is observable by a, i.e.,

$$s \approx_a s' \text{ iff } \mathsf{dom}(s) \cap \mathbf{o}_a = \mathsf{dom}(s') \cap \mathbf{o}_a \quad \text{and} \quad \bigwedge\nolimits_{x \in (\mathsf{dom}(s) \cap \mathbf{o}_a)} (s(x) = s'(x)).$$

One can show that $\approx_a$ is an equivalence relation on $\mathcal{U}$. Each subset W of $\mathcal{U}$ defines a possible worlds model $(W, \{\approx_{a|W}\}_{a \in Ag})$, such that the states of W are the possible worlds and for each $a \in Ag$ the indistinguishability relation is the restriction of $\approx_a$ on W. We shall use the set $W \subseteq \mathcal{U}$ to refer to an epistemic model, omitting the family of equivalence relations $\{\approx_{a|W}\}_{a \in Ag}$.

Truth of an $\mathcal{L}_{DK}^m$ Formula. We give the semantics of an $\mathcal{L}_{DK}^m$ formula at a pointed model (W, s), which consist of an epistemic model W and a state $s \in W$.

Definition 4. *Let W be an epistemic model, $s \in W$ a state, α a formula in $\mathcal{L}_{DK}^m$ such that $FV(\alpha) \subseteq \mathsf{dom}(W)$. The truth of an epistemic formula α at the pointed model (W, s) is defined recursively on the structure of α as follows:*

$$\begin{array}{lll}
(W,s) \models \pi & \textit{iff} & s \models_{QF} \pi \\
(W,s) \models \neg\alpha & \textit{iff} & (W,s) \not\models \alpha \\
(W,s) \models \alpha \wedge \alpha' & \textit{iff} & (W,s) \models \alpha \textit{ and } (W,s) \models \alpha' \\
(W,s) \models K_a\alpha & \textit{iff} & \textit{for all } s' \in W, s' \approx_a s \textit{ implies } (W,s') \models \alpha \\
(W,s) \models [\beta]\alpha & \textit{iff} & (W,s) \models \beta \textit{ implies } (W_{|\beta}, s) \models \alpha \\
(W,s) \models \Box_P\alpha & \textit{iff} & \textit{for all } s' \in R_W(P,s), (R_W^*(P,W), s') \models \alpha \\
(W,s) \models \forall x_G \cdot \alpha & \textit{iff} & \textit{for all } c \in \mathsf{D}, (\bigcup_{d \in \mathsf{D}} \{s'[x_G \mapsto d] \mid s' \in W\}, s[x_G \mapsto c]) \models \alpha
\end{array}$$

where $x_G \notin \mathsf{dom}(W)$, $W_{|\beta}$ is the submodel of W that consists of the states in which β is true, i.e., $W_{|\beta} = \{s \in \mathcal{W} \mid (W,s) \models \beta\}$ [6].

This definition extends from a pointed model (W, s) to the entire epistemic model W as follows: $W \models \alpha$ iff for any s in W, $(W, s) \models \alpha$.

Our interpretation of logical connectors, epistemic formulas, and the public announcement formulas are all standard [6,13].

For universal quantification, the epistemic context W is augmented by allowing x_G to be any possible value in the domain. When interpreting $\forall x_G \cdot K_a\alpha'$ where $a \in G$, we have $s \approx_a s'$ iff $s[x_G \mapsto c] \approx_a s'[x_G \mapsto c]$. However, if $a \notin G$, then $s[x_G \mapsto c] \approx_a s'[x_G \mapsto d]$ for any $d \in \mathsf{D}$ and for any $s' \approx_a s$.

In our interpretation of $\Box_P\alpha$, the context W is also updated by the relation R_W, by taking the post-image of W by R_W[1]. The truth of α is interpreted at a

[1] The post-image of a function f is denoted by f^*, i.e., $f^*(E) = \bigcup\{f(x) | x \in E\}$.

post-state s' under the new context. We use the function $R_W(P, \cdot) : \mathcal{U} \to \mathcal{P}(\mathcal{U})$ to model the program P. We give the function $R_W(P, \cdot)$ concretely for each command P, after we define the programming language $\mathcal{PL}$ in the next section.

Remark 1. The index W in $R_W(P, \cdot)$ is a set of states in $\mathcal{U}$. As in classical relational semantics, $R_W(P, s)$ gives the set of states resulting from executing P at a state s. However, we need the index W to represent the epistemic context in which P is executed. Before executing P, an agent may not know that the actual initial state is s, it only knows about the initial state only as far as it can see from its observable variables. The context W contains any state that some agent may consider as the possible initial state.

3 Programming Language $\mathcal{PL}$

Now, we formalise the language for programs inside a program-operator $\Box_P$ of the logic that we introduced in the previous section.

3.1 Syntax of $\mathcal{PL}$

We use the notations from the previous section: $a, b, c, ...$ to denote agents, Ag to denote their whole set, G for a subset therein, etc. We assume that a non-empty subset $PVar$ of Var consists of program variables.

Definition 5. *The programming language $\mathcal{PL}$ is defined in BNF as follows:*

$$P ::= \varphi? \mid x_G := e \mid \textbf{new } k_G \cdot P \mid P; Q \mid P \sqcup Q$$

where $x_G \in Var$, e is a term over $\mathcal{L}_{QF}$, $\varphi \in \mathcal{L}_K^m$, and any variable in P that is not bound by **new** *is in $PVar$.*

The test $\varphi?$ is an assumption-like test, i.e., it blocks the program when φ is refuted and let the program continue when φ holds; $x_G := e$ is a variable assignment as usual. The command **new** $k_G \cdot P$ declares a new variable k_G observable by agents in G before executing P. The operator $P; Q$ is the sequential composition of P and Q. Lastly, $P \sqcup Q$ is the nondeterministic choice between P and Q.

Commands such as **skip** and conditional tests can be defined with $\mathcal{PL}$, e.g., **if** φ **then** P **else** $Q \stackrel{\text{def}}{=} (\varphi?;\ P) \sqcup (\neg\varphi?;\ Q)$.

3.2 Relational Semantics of $\mathcal{PL}$

Now, we give the semantics of programs in $\mathcal{PL}$. We refer to as classical program semantics, the modelling of a program as an input-output functionality, without managing what agents can learn during an execution. In classical program semantics, a program P is associated with a relation $R_P = \mathcal{U} \times \mathcal{U}$, or equivalently a function $R(P, \cdot) : \mathcal{U} \to \mathcal{P}(\mathcal{U})$, such that $R(P, \cdot)$ maps an initial state s to a set of possible final states.

As per Remark 1, we define the relational semantics of an epistemic program $P \in \mathcal{PL}$ at a state s for a given context W, with $s \in W$. The context $W \subseteq \mathcal{U}$ contains states that some agents may consider as a possible alternative to s.

Definition 6 (Relational semantics of $\mathcal{PL}$ on states). *Let W be a set of states. The relational semantics of a program P given the context W, is a function $R_W(P,\cdot) : \mathcal{U} \to \mathcal{P}(\mathcal{U})$ defined inductively on the structure of P by*

$$\begin{aligned}
R_W(P \sqcup Q, s) &= \{s'[c_{Ag} \mapsto l] \mid s' \in R_W(P,s)\} \\
&\quad \cup \{s'[c_{Ag} \mapsto r] \mid s' \in R_W(Q,s)\} \\
R_W(P;Q,s) &= \textstyle\bigcup_{s' \in R_W(P,s)} \{R_{R^*_W(P,W)}(Q,s')\} \\
R_W(x_G := e, s) &= \{s[k_G \mapsto s(x_G), x_G \mapsto s(e)]\} \\
R_W(\mathbf{new}\ k_G \cdot P, s) &= R^*_W(P, \{s[k_G \mapsto d] \mid d \in \mathsf{D}\}) \\
R_W(\beta?, s) &= \mathit{if}\ (W,s) \models \beta\ \mathit{then}\ \{s\}\ \mathit{else}\ \varnothing
\end{aligned}$$

where k_G is not in $\mathsf{dom}(s)$, *and c_{Ag} is not in the domain of any state s' in $R_W(P,s) \cup R_W(Q,s)$.*

We model nondeterministic choice $P \sqcup Q$ as a disjoint union [7], which is achieved by augmenting every updated state with a new variable c_{Ag}, and assigning it a value l (for left) for every state in $R_W(P,s)$, and a value r (for right) for every state in $R_W(Q,s)$. The semantics for sequential composition is standard. The semantics of the assignment $x_G := e$ stores the past value of x_G into a new variable k_G, and updates the value of x_G into expression e. With this semantics, an agent always remembers the past values of a variable that it observes, i.e., it has perfect recall. The semantics of $\mathbf{new}\ k_G \cdot P$ adds the new variable k_G to the domain of s, then combines the images by $R_W(P,\cdot)$ of all states $s[k_G \mapsto d]$ for d in D. A test is modelled as an assumption, i.e., a failed test blocks the program.

In the epistemic context, we can also view a program as transforming epistemic models, rather than states. This view is modelled with the following alternative relational semantics for $\mathcal{PL}$.

Definition 7 (Relational semantics of $\mathcal{PL}$ on epistemic models). *The relational semantics on epistemic models of a program P is a function $F(P,\cdot) : \mathcal{P}(\mathcal{U}) \to \mathcal{P}(\mathcal{U})$ given by*

$$\begin{aligned}
F(P \sqcup Q, W) &= \{s[c_{Ag} \mapsto l] \mid s \in F(P,W)\} \\
&\quad \cup\ \{s[c_{Ag} \mapsto r] \mid s \in F(Q,W)\} \\
F(P;Q,W) &= F(Q, F(P,W)) \\
F(x_G := e, W) &= \{s[k_G \mapsto s(x_G), x_G \mapsto s(e)] \mid s \in W\} \\
F(\mathbf{new}\ k_G \cdot P, W) &= F(P, \textstyle\bigcup_{d \in \mathsf{D}} W[k_G \mapsto d]) \\
F(\beta?, W) &= \{s \in W \mid (W,s) \models \beta\}
\end{aligned}$$

such that k_G and c_{Ag} are variables not in $\mathsf{dom}(s)$.

We assume that every additional c_{Ag}, in the semantics of $P \sqcup Q$, is observable by all agents. The value of c_{Ag} allows every agent to distinguish a state resulting from P from a state resulting from Q. The resulting union is a disjoint-union of epistemic models [7].

The two relational semantics (Definition 6 and Definition 7) are equivalent (see Appendix A in [4]). However, we use both to simplify the presentation. On one hand, the relation on states given by $R_W(P, \cdot)$ is more standard for defining a dynamic formula $\Box_P \alpha$ (e.g., [19]). On the other hand, $F(P, \cdot)$ models a program as transforming states of knowledge (epistemic models) rather than only physical states. Moreover, $F(P, \cdot)$ relates directly with our weakest precondition predicate transformer semantics, which we present next.

3.3 Weakest Precondition Semantics of $\mathcal{PL}$

We now give another semantics for our programs, by lifting the Dijkstra's classical weakest precondition predicate transformer[2] [11] to epistemic predicates.

Notation. $\alpha[x \backslash t]$ substitutes x by the term t in α.

Definition 8. *We define the weakest precondition of a program P as the epistemic predicate transformer $wp(P, \cdot) : \mathcal{L}_K^m \to \mathcal{L}_K^m$ with*

$$\begin{aligned}
wp(P; Q, \alpha) &= wp(P, wp(Q, \alpha)) \\
wp(P \sqcup Q, \alpha) &= wp(P, \alpha) \wedge wp(Q, \alpha) \\
wp(\mathbf{new}\ k_G \cdot P, \alpha) &= \forall k_G \cdot wp(P, \alpha) \\
wp(\beta ?, \alpha) &= [\beta]\alpha \\
wp(x_G := e, \alpha) &= \forall k_G \cdot [k_G = e](\alpha[x_G \backslash k_G])
\end{aligned}$$

for $\alpha \in \mathcal{L}_K^m$ such that $FV(\alpha) \subseteq PVar$.

The definitions of wp for nondeterministic choice and sequential composition are similar to their classical versions in the literature, and follows the original definitions in [11]. A similar definition of wp for a new variable declaration is also found in [30]. However, our wp semantics for assignment and for test differs from their classical counterparts. The classical wp for assignment (substitution), and the classical wp of tests (implication) are inconsistent in the epistemic context when agents have perfect recall [31,35]. Our wp semantics for test follows from the observation that an assumption-test for a program executed publicly corresponds to a public announcement. Similarly, our semantics of assignment involves a public announcement of the assignment being made.

3.4 Equivalence Between the Two Program Semantics

Now, we show that our weakest precondition semantics and our relational semantics are equivalent. For that, we need the following lemma.

[2] The weakest precondition $wp(P, \phi)$ is a predicate such that: for any precondition ψ from which the program P terminates and establishes ϕ, ψ implies $wp(P, \phi)$.

Lemma 1. *Consider an epistemic model W, variables x_G and k_G such that k_G is not in the domain of any state in W. Let $W_{x_G \backslash k_G}$ be the model that renames x_G into k_G in the states of W, then*

$$W \models \alpha \quad \textit{iff} \quad W_{x_G \backslash k_G} \models \alpha[x_G \backslash k_G].$$

The following equivalence shows that our weakest precondition semantics is sound with respect to the program relational model.

Proposition 1. *For every program P and every formula $\alpha \in \mathcal{L}_{DK}^m$,*

$$F(P, W) \models \alpha \quad \textit{iff} \quad W \models wp(P, \alpha).$$

A detailed proof can be found in Appendix B of the extended version of our paper [4]. Below, we sketch the proofs for the cases of nondeterministic choice and assignment.

The equivalence for the case of nondeterministic choice follows from the fact that disjoint union preserves the truth of epistemic formulas (Prop 2.3 in [7]). A formula that is true at both $F(P, W)$ and $F(Q, W)$, remains true at $F(P \sqcup Q, W)$. This allows us to have a standard conjunctive weakest precondition epistemic predicate transformer, i.e., $wp(P \sqcup Q, \alpha) = wp(P, \alpha) \wedge wp(Q, \alpha)$.

We now explain the equivalence for assignment, i.e., how the bookkeeping of variables in our relational semantics of Definition 7 equates to $wp(x_G := e, \alpha) = \forall k_G \cdot [k_G = e](\alpha[x_G \backslash k_G])$. Recall that $F(x_G := e, W)$ renames x_G into k_G in W, then makes a new variable x_G that takes the value e. This translates to the equality $F(x_G := e, W) = F(\textbf{new } x_G \cdot (x_G = e_{x_G \backslash k_G})?, W_{x_G \backslash k_G})$. In the right-hand side of this equality, x_G is re-introduced as a new variable, W is expanded, by a Cartesian product, into $\bigcup_{d \in D} W[x_G \mapsto d]$ (Definition 7), then restricted to satisfy $x_G = e_{x_G \backslash k_G}$. This restriction corresponds to the semantics of making the assumption test (or public announcement) $(x_G = e_{x_G \backslash k_G})?$. Finally, $F(\textbf{new } x_G \cdot (x_G = e_{x_G \backslash k_G})?, W_{x_G \backslash k_G})$ can be directly to the weakest precondition for assignment via Lemma 1.

The equivalence in Proposition 1 serves us in proving that the translation of an $\mathcal{L}_{DK}^m$ formula into a first-order formula, which we present next, is sound with respect to the program relational models.

4 Translating $\mathcal{L}_{DK}^m$ to $\mathcal{L}_{FO}$

Our model checking approach relies on the truth-preserving translation between $\mathcal{L}_{DK}^m$ formulas and first-order formulas. We use the following translation function.

Definition 9 (Translation of $\mathcal{L}_{DK}^m$ into $\mathcal{L}_{FO}$). *Let $\pi \in \mathcal{L}_{QF}$ and $\alpha \in \mathcal{L}_{DK}^m$, a be an agent. Let $\mathbf{n} = \mathbf{n}_a \cap (FV(\alpha) \cup FV(\phi))$ be the set of free variables in π and α that are non-observable by a, and $\circ$ be an operator in $\{\wedge, \vee\}$. We define the translation $\tau : \mathcal{L}_{FO} \times \mathcal{L}_{DK}^m \rightarrow \mathcal{L}_{FO}$ as follows:*

$$\begin{aligned} \tau(\phi,\pi) &= \pi & \tau(\phi,K_a\alpha) &= \forall \mathbf{n}\cdot(\phi\rightarrow\tau(\phi,\alpha))\\ \tau(\phi,\neg\alpha) &= \neg\tau(\phi,\alpha) & \tau(\phi,[\beta]\alpha) &= \tau(\phi,\beta)\rightarrow\tau(\phi\wedge\tau(\phi,\beta),\alpha)\\ \tau(\phi,\alpha_1\circ\alpha_2) &= \tau(\phi,\alpha_1)\circ\tau(\phi,\alpha_2) & \tau(\phi,\Box_P\alpha) &= \tau(\phi,wp(P,\alpha))\\ \tau(\phi,\forall x_G\cdot\alpha) &= \forall x_G\cdot\tau(\phi,\alpha). \end{aligned}$$

We use the above translation to express the equivalence between the satisfaction of a $\mathcal{L}_K^m$-formula and that of its first-order translation.

Proposition 2. *For every ϕ in $\mathcal{L}_{FO}$, s in $[\![\phi]\!]$, α in $\mathcal{L}_K^m$ such that $FV(\phi)\cup FV(\alpha)\subseteq PVar$, we have that*

$$([\![\phi]\!],s)\models\alpha \textit{ iff } s\models_{FO}\tau(\phi,\alpha).$$

Proof. The proof for the base epistemic logic without public announcement $\mathcal{L}_K$ $(\pi,\neg,\wedge,K_a)$ is found in [19].

Case of public announcement $[\beta]\alpha$

$$\begin{aligned}
&([\![\phi]\!],s)\models[\beta]\alpha\\
&\equiv \text{if } ([\![\phi]\!],s)\models\beta \text{ then } ([\![\phi]\!]_{|\beta},s)\models\alpha && \text{truth of } [\beta]\alpha\\
&\equiv \text{if } s\models_{FO}\tau(\phi,\beta) \text{ then } ([\![\phi]\!]_{|\beta},s)\models\alpha && \text{induction hypothesis on } \beta\\
&\equiv \text{if } s\models_{FO}\tau(\phi,\beta) \text{ then } (\{s'\in\mathcal{U}|s'\models_{FO}\phi \text{ and } ([\![\phi]\!],s')\models\beta\},s)\models\alpha\\
& && \text{by definition of } [\![\cdot]\!] \text{ and definition of } _{|\beta}\\
&\equiv \text{if } s\models_{FO}\tau(\phi,\beta) \text{ then } (\{s'\in\mathcal{U}|s'\models_{FO}\phi \text{ and } s'\models_{FO}\tau(\phi,\beta)\},s)\models\alpha\\
& && \text{induction hypothesis on } \beta\\
&\equiv \text{if } s\models_{FO}\tau(\phi,\beta) \text{ then } (\{s'\in\mathcal{U}|s'\models_{FO}\phi\wedge\tau(\phi,\beta)\},s)\models\alpha && \text{truth of } \wedge\\
&\equiv \text{if } s\models_{FO}\tau(\phi,\beta) \text{ then } ([\![\phi\wedge\tau(\phi,\beta)]\!],s)\models\alpha && \text{def of } [\![\cdot]\!]\\
&\equiv \text{if } s\models_{FO}\tau(\phi,\beta) \text{ then } s\models_{FO}\tau(\phi\wedge\tau(\phi,\beta),\alpha) && \text{induction hypothesis}\\
&\equiv \text{if } s\models_{FO}\tau(\phi,\beta)\rightarrow\tau(\phi\wedge\tau(\phi,\beta),\alpha) && \text{truth of } \rightarrow. \quad\Box
\end{aligned}$$

Now, we can state our main theorem relating the validity of an $\mathcal{L}_{DK}^m$ formula, and that of its first-order translation.

Theorem 1 (Main result). *Let $\phi\in\mathcal{L}_{FO}$, and $\alpha\in\mathcal{L}_{DK}^m$, such that $FV(\phi)\cup FV(\alpha)\subseteq PVar$, then*

$$[\![\phi]\!]\models\alpha \;\textit{ iff }\; [\![\phi]\!]\models_{FO}\tau(\phi,\alpha).$$

Proof. The proof is done by induction on α. The case where $\alpha\in\mathcal{L}_K^m$ follows directly from Proposition 2.

We are left to prove the case of the program operator $\Box_P\alpha$. Without loss of generality, we can assume that α is program-operator-free, i.e., $\alpha\in\mathcal{L}_K^m$. Indeed, one can show that $\Box_P(\Box_Q\alpha')$ is equivalent to $\Box_{P;Q}\alpha'$. We have

$$\begin{aligned}
&[\![\phi]\!] \models \Box_P \alpha \\
\equiv\ & \text{iff for all } s \text{ in } [\![\phi]\!],\ ([\![\phi]\!], s) \models \Box_P \alpha && \text{by definition of } \models \text{ for a model} \\
\equiv\ & \text{iff for all } s \text{ in } [\![\phi]\!], \text{ for all } s' \text{ in } R_{[\![\phi]\!]}(P, s),\ (F(P, [\![\phi]\!]), s') \models \alpha && \models \text{ for } \Box_P \\
\equiv\ & \text{iff for all } s' \text{ in } R^*_{[\![\phi]\!]}(P, [\![\phi]\!]),\ (F(P, [\![\phi]\!]), s') \models \alpha && \text{post-image} \\
\equiv\ & \text{iff for all } s' \text{ in } F(P, [\![\phi]\!]),\ (F(P, [\![\phi]\!]), s') \models \alpha && F(P, W) = R^*_W(P, W) \\
\equiv\ & F(P, [\![\phi]\!]) \models \alpha && \text{by definition of } \models \text{ for a model} \\
\equiv\ & [\![\phi]\!] \models wp(P, \alpha) && \text{by Proposition 1} \\
\equiv\ & [\![\phi]\!] \models_{FO} \tau(wp(P, \alpha)) && \text{since } wp(P, \alpha) \in \mathcal{L}^m_K, \text{ the previous case applies.} \ \Box
\end{aligned}$$

5 Implementation

Our automated verification framework supports proving/falsifying a logical consequence $\phi \models \alpha$ for α in $\mathcal{L}^m_{DK}$ and ϕ in $\mathcal{L}_{FO}$. By Theorem 1, the problem becomes the unsatisfiability/satisfiability of first-order formula $\phi \wedge \neg \tau(\phi, \alpha)$, which is eventually fed to an SMT solver.

In some cases, notably our second case study, the Cheryl's Birthday puzzle, computing the translation $\tau(\phi, \alpha)$ by hand is tedious and error-prone. For such cases, we implemented a $\mathcal{L}^m_{DK}$-to-$\mathcal{L}_{FO}$ translator to automate the translation.

5.1 Mechanisation of Our $\mathcal{L}^m_{DK}$-to-FO Translation

Our translator implements Definition 9 of our translation τ. It is implemented in `Haskell`, and it is generic, i.e., works for any given example[3]. The resulting first-order formula is exported as a string parsable by an external SMT solver API (e.g., `Z3py` and `CVC5.pythonic` which we use).

Our `Haskell` translator and the implementation of our case studies are at https://github.com/sfrajaona/program-epistemic-model-checker.

5.2 Case Study 1: Dining Cryptographers' Protocol [9]

Problem Description. This system is described by n cryptographers dining round a table. One cryptographer may have paid for the dinner, or their employer may have done so. They execute a protocol to reveal whether one of the cryptographers paid, but without revealing which one. Each pair of cryptographers sitting next to each other have an unbiased coin, which can be observed only by that pair. Each pair tosses its coin. Each cryptographer announces the result of XORing three Booleans: the two coins they see and the fact of them having paid for the dinner. The XOR of all announcements is provably equal to the disjunction of whether any agent paid.

Encoding in $\mathcal{L}^m_{DK}$ & Mechanisation. We consider the domain $\mathbb{B} = \{T, F\}$ and the program variables $PVar = \{x_{Ag}\} \cup \{p_i, c_{\{i,i+1\}} \mid 0 \leq i < n\}$ where x is

[3] Inputs are `Haskell` files.

the XOR of announcements; p_i encodes whether agent i has paid; and, $c_{\{i,i+1\}}$ encodes the coin shared between agents i and $i+1$. The observable variables for agent $i \in Ag$ are $\mathbf{o}_i = \{x_{Ag}, p_i, c_{\{i-1,i\}}, c_{\{i,i+1\}}\}^4$, and $\mathbf{n}_i = PVar \setminus \mathbf{o}_i$.

We denote ϕ the constraint that at most one agent has paid, and e the XOR of all announcements, i.e.

$$\phi = \bigwedge_{i=0}^{n-1} \left(p_i \Rightarrow \bigwedge_{j=0,j\neq i}^{n-1} \neg p_j\right) \qquad e = \bigoplus_{i=0}^{n-1} p_i \oplus c_{\{i-1,i\}} \oplus c_{\{i,i+1\}}.$$

The Dining Cryptographers' protocol is modelled by the program $\rho = x_{Ag} := e$.

Experiments & Results. We report on checking the validity for:

$$\beta_1 = \Box_\rho \left((\neg p_0) \Rightarrow \left(K_0 \left(\bigwedge_{i=1}^{n-1} \neg p_i\right) \vee \bigwedge_{i=1}^{n-1} \neg K_0 p_i\right)\right) \qquad \beta_3 = \Box_\rho (K_0 p_1)$$

$$\beta_2 = \Box_\rho \left(K_0 \left(x \Leftrightarrow \bigvee_{i=0}^{n-1} p_i\right)\right) \qquad \gamma = K_0 \left(\Box_\rho \left(x \Leftrightarrow \bigvee_{i=0}^{n-1} p_i\right)\right).$$

The formula β_1 states that after the program execution, if cryptographer 0 has not paid then she knows that no cryptographer paid, or (in case a cryptographer paid) she does not know which one. The formula β_2 reads that after the program execution, cryptographer 0 knows that x_{Ag} is true iff one of the cryptographers paid. The formula β_3 reads that after the program execution, cryptographer 0 knows that cryptographer 1 has paid, which is expected to be false. Formula γ states cryptographer 0 knows that, at the end of the program execution, x_{Ag} is true iff one of the cryptographers paid.

Formulas β_1, β_2, and β_3 were checked in [19] as well. Importantly, formula γ cannot be expressed or checked by the framework in [19]. We compare the performance of our translation on this case-study with that of [19]. To fairly compare, we reimplemented faithfully the SP-based translation in the same environment as ours. We tested our translation (denoted τ_{wp}) and the reimplementation of the translation in [19] (denoted τ_{SP}) on the same machine.

Note that the performance we got for τ_{SP} differs from what is reported in [19]. This is especially the case for the most complicated formula β_1. This may be due to the machine specifications, or because we used binary versions of Z3 and CVC5, rather than building them from source, like in [19].

The results of the experiments, using the Z3 solver, are shown in Table 1. CVC5 was less performant than Z3 for this example, as shown (only) for β_2. Generally, the difference in performance between the two translations were small. The *SP*-based translation slightly outperforms our translation for β_2 and β_3, but only for some cases. Our translation outperforms the *SP*-based translation for β_1 in these experiments. Again, we note that the performance of the *SP*-based translation reported here is different from the performance reported in [19]. Experiments that took more than 600 s were timed out

[4] When we write $\{i, i+1\}$ and $\{i-1, i\}$, we mean $\{i, i+1 \bmod n\}$ and $\{i-1 \bmod n, i\}$.

Table 1. Performance of our *wp*-based translation vs. our reimplementation of the [19] *SP*-based translation for the Dining Cryptographers. Formula γ is not supported by the *SP*-based translation in [19].

n	Formula β_1		Formula β_2			Formula β_3		Formula γ	
	τ_{wp}+Z3	τ_{SP}+Z3	τ_{wp}+CVC5	τ_{wp}+Z3	τ_{SP}+Z3	τ_{wp}+Z3	τ_{SP}+Z3	τ_{wp}+Z3	τ_{SP}+Z3
10	0.05 s	4.86 s	0.01 s	0.01 s	0.01 s	0.01 s	0.01 s	0.01 s	N/A
50	31 s	t.o.	0.41 s	0.05 s	0.06 s	0.03 s	0.02 s	0.03 s	N/A
100	t.o.	t.o.	3.59 s	0.15 s	0.16 s	0.07 s	0.06 s	0.07 s	N/A
200	t.o.	t.o.	41.90 s	1.27 s	0.71 s	0.30 s	0.20 s	0.30 s	N/A

5.3 Case Study 2: Cheryl's Birthday Puzzle [14]

This case study involves the nesting of knowledge operators K of different agents.

Problem Description. Albert and Bernard just became friends with Cheryl, and they want to know when her birthday is. Cheryl gives them a list of 10 possible dates: May 15, May 16, May 19, June 17, June 18, July 14, July 16, August 14, August 15, August 17. Then, Cheryl whispers in Albert's ear the month and only the month of her birthday. To Bernard, she whispers the day only. "Can you figure it out now?", she asks Albert. The next dialogue follows:

- Albert: I don't know when it is, but I know Bernard doesn't know either.
- Bernard: I didn't know originally, but now I do.
- Albert: Well, now I know too!

When is Cheryl's birthday?

Encoding and Mechanisation. To solve this puzzle, we consider two agents a (Albert) and b (Bernard) and two integer program variables $PVar = \{m_a, d_b\}$. Then, we constrain the initial states to satisfy the conjunction of all possible dates announced by Cheryl, i.e., the formula ϕ below:

$$\phi(m_a, d_b) = (m_a = 5 \wedge d_b = 15) \vee (m_a = 5 \wedge d_b = 16) \vee \cdots .$$

The puzzle is modelled via public announcements, with the added assumption that participants tell the truth. However, modelling a satisfiability problem with the public announcement operator $[\beta]\alpha$ would return states where β cannot be truthfully announced. Indeed, if β is false at s, (i.e., $(\phi, s) \models \neg\beta$), then the announcement $[\beta]\alpha$ is true. For that, we use the dual of the public announcement operator denoted $\langle\cdot\rangle$[5]. We use the translation to first-order formula:

$$\tau(\phi, \langle\beta\rangle\alpha) \;=\; \tau(\phi, \beta) \wedge \tau(\phi \wedge \tau(\phi, \beta), \alpha).$$

[5] The formula $\langle\beta\rangle\alpha$ reads "after some announcement of β, α is the case", i.e., β can be truthfully announced and its announcement makes α true. Formally, $(W, s) \models \langle\beta\rangle\alpha$ iff $(W, s) \models \beta$ and $(W_{|\beta}, s) \models \alpha$.

In both its definition and our translation to first-order, $\langle\cdot\rangle$ uses a conjunction where $[\cdot]$ uses an implication.

We denote the statement "agent a knows the value of x" by the formula $\mathrm{Kv}_a x$ which is common in the literature. We define it with our logic $\mathcal{L}^m_{DK}$ making use of existential quantification: $\mathrm{Kv}_a x \;=\; \exists v_a \cdot K_a(v_a = x)$.

Now, to model the communication between Albert and Bernard, let α_a be Albert's first announcement, i.e., $\alpha_a = \neg\mathrm{Kv}_a(d_b) \wedge K_a(\neg\mathrm{Kv}_b(m_a))$. Then, the succession of announcements by the two participants corresponds to the formula

$$\alpha = \langle(\neg\mathrm{Kv}_b(m_a) \wedge \langle\alpha_a\rangle\mathrm{Kv}_b(m_a))?\rangle\mathrm{Kv}_a d_b.$$

Cheryl's birthday is the state s that satisfies $(\phi, s) \models \alpha$.

Experiments and Results. We computed $\tau(\phi, \alpha)$ in 0.10 s. The SMT solvers Z3 and CVC5 returned the solution to the puzzle when fed with $\tau(\phi, \alpha)$. CVC5 solved it, in 0.60 s, which is twice better than Z3 (1.28 s).

All the experiments were run on a 6-core 2.6 GHz Intel Core i7 MacBook Pro with 16 GB of RAM running OS X 11.6. For Haskell, we used GHC 8.8.4. The SMT solvers were Z3 version 4.8.17 and CVC5 version 1.0.0.

6 Related Work

SMT-Based Verification of Epistemic Properties of Programs. We start with the work of Gorogiannis *et al.* [19] which is the closest to ours. We already compared with this in the introduction, for instance explaining therein exactly how our logic is much more expressive than theirs. Now, we cover other points.

Program Models. The program models in [19] follow a classical program semantics (e.g., modelling nondeterministic choice as union, overwriting a variable in reassignment). This has been shown [31,35] to correspond to systems where agents have no memory, and cannot see how nondeterministic choices are resolved. Our program models assume perfect recall, and that agents can see how nondeterministic choices are resolved.

Program Expressiveness. Gorogiannis *et al.* [19] have results of approximations for programs with loops, although there were no use cases of that. Here we focused on a loop-free programming language, but we believe our approach can be extended similarly. The main advantage of our programs is the support for tests on knowledge which allows us to model public communication of knowledge.

Mechanisation & Efficiency. We implemented the translation which include an automated computation of weakest preconditions (and strongest postconditions as well). The implementation in [19] requires the strongest postcondition be computed manually. Like [19], we test for the satisfiability of the resulting first-order formula with Z3. The performance is generally similar, although sometimes it depends on the form of the formulas (see Table 1).

Verification of Information Flow with Program Algebra. Verifying epistemic properties of programs with program algebra was done in [29,31,35].

Instead of using a dynamic logic, they reason about epistemic properties of programs with an ignorance-preserving refinement. Like here, their notion of knowledge is based on observability of arbitrary domain program variables. The work in [35] also consider a multi-agent logics and nested K operators and their program also allows for knowledge tests. Finally, our model for epistemic programs can be seen as inspired by [35]. That said, all these works have no relation with first-order satisfaction nor translations of validity of program-epistemic logics to that, nor their implementation.

Dynamic Epistemic Logics *Dynamic epistemic logic* (DEL, [2,13,33]) is a family of logics that extend epistemic logic with dynamic operators.

Logics' Expressivity. On the one hand, DEL logics are mostly propositional, and their extensions with assignment only considered propositional assignment (e.g., [12]); contrarily, we support assignment on variables on arbitrary domains. Also, we have a denotational semantics of programs (via weakest preconditions), whereas DEL operates on more abstract semantics. On the other hand, action models in DEL can describe complex private communications that cannot be encoded with our current programming language.

Verification. Current DEL model checkers include `DEMO` [15] and `SMCDEL` [5]. We are not aware of the verification of DEL fragments being reduced to satisfiability problems. In this space, an online report [36] discusses –at some high level– the translation `SMCDEL` knowledge structures into QBF and the use of `YICES`.

A line of research in DEL, the so called *semi-public environments*, also builds agents' indistinguishability relations from the observability of propositional variables [8,21,37]. The work of Grossi [20] explores the interaction between knowledge dynamics and non-deterministic choice/sequential composition. They note that PDLs assumes memory-less agents and totally private nondeterministic choice, whilst DELs' epistemic actions assume agents with perfect recall and publicly made nondeterministic choice. This is the same duality that we observed earlier between the program epistemic logic in [19] and ours.

Other Works. Gorogiannis *et al.* [19] discussed more tenuously related work, such as on general verification of temporal-epistemic properties of systems which are not programs in tools like `MCMAS` [28], `MCK` [18], `VERICS` [26], or one line of epistemic verification of models specifically of `JAVA` programs [1]. [19] also discussed some incomplete method of SMT-based epistemic model checking [10], or even bounded model checking techniques, e.g., [25]. All of those are loosely related to us too, but there is little reason to reiterate.

7 Conclusions

We advanced a multi-agent epistemic logic for programs $\mathcal{L}_{DK}^{m}$, in which each agent has visibility over some program variables but not others. This logic allows to reason on agents' knowledge of a program after its run, as well as before its execution. Assuming agents' perfect recall, we provided a weakest-precondition epistemic predicate transformer semantics that is sound with respect to its relational counterpart. Leveraging the natural correspondence between the weakest precondition $wp(P, \alpha)$ and the dynamic formula $\Box_P \alpha$, we were able to give a sound reduction of the validity of $\mathcal{L}_{DK}^m$ formulas to first-order satisfaction.

Based on this reduction an $\mathcal{L}_{DK}^m$ formula into a first-order, we implemented a tool that fully mechanise the verification, calling an SMT solver for the final decision procedure. Our method is inspired from [19], but applies to a significantly larger class of program-epistemic formulas in the multi-agent setting.

The multi-agent nature of the logic, the expressiveness of it with respect to knowledge evaluation before and after program execution, as well as a complete verification method for this are all novelties in the field. In future work, we will look at a meet-in-the-middle between the memoryless semantics in [19] and the memoryful semantics here, and methods of verifying logics like $\mathcal{L}_{DK}^m$ but with such less "absolutist" semantics.

Acknowledgments. S. Rajaona and I. Boureanu were partly supported by the EPSRC project "AutoPaSS", EP/S024565/1.

References

1. Balliu, M., Dam, M., Guernic, G.L.: ENCoVer: symbolic exploration for information flow security. In: 25th IEEE Computer Security Foundations Symposium (CSF 2012), pp. 30–44. IEEE Computer Society (2012). https://doi.org/10.1109/CSF.2012.24
2. Baltag, A., Moss, L.S., Solecki, S.: The logic of public announcements, common knowledge, and private suspicions. In: Proceedings of the 7th Conference on Theoretical Aspects of Rationality and Knowledge (TARK 1998), pp. 43–56. Morgan Kaufmann Publishers Inc. (1998). https://doi.org/10.1007/978-3-319-20451-2_38
3. Barfuss, W., Mann, R.P.: Modeling the effects of environmental and perceptual uncertainty using deterministic reinforcement learning dynamics with partial observability. Phys. Rev. E **105**, 034409 (2022). https://doi.org/10.1103/PhysRevE.105.034409
4. Belardinelli, F., Boureanu, I., Malvone, V., Rajaona, S.F.: Program semantics and a verification technique for knowledge-based multi-agent systems. arXiv preprint arXiv:2206.13841 (2022)
5. van Benthem, J., van Eijck, J., Gattinger, M., Su, K.: Symbolic model checking for dynamic epistemic logic. In: van der Hoek, W., Holliday, W.H., Wang, W. (eds.) LORI 2015. LNCS, vol. 9394, pp. 366–378. Springer, Heidelberg (2015). https://doi.org/10.1007/978-3-662-48561-3_30
6. Blackburn, P., van Benthem, J.F., Wolter, F.: Handbook of Modal Logic. Elsevier, Oxford (2006)
7. Blackburn, P., de Rijke, M., Venema, Y.: Modal Logic. Cambridge University Press, New York (2001)
8. Charrier, T., Herzig, A., Lorini, E., Maffre, F., Schwarzentruber, F.: Building epistemic logic from observations and public announcements. In: Principles of Knowledge Representation and Reasoning: Proceedings of the Fifteenth International Conference (KR 2016), pp. 268–277. AAAI Press (2016)
9. Chaum, D.: The dining cryptographers problem: *unconditional sender and recipient untraceability*. J. Cryptol. **1**(1), 65–75 (1988). https://doi.org/10.1007/BF00206326

10. Cimatti, A., Gario, M., Tonetta, S.: A lazy approach to temporal epistemic logic model checking. In: Proceedings of the 2016 International Conference on Autonomous Agents & Multiagent Systems (AAMAS-38), pp. 1218–1226. IFAAMAS (2016)
11. Dijkstra, E.W.: A Discipline of Programming. Prentice-Hall, Englewood Cliffs (1976)
12. van Ditmarsch, H.P., van der Hoek, W., Kooi, B.P.: Dynamic epistemic logic with assignment. In: Proceedings of the Fourth International Joint Conference on Autonomous Agents and Multiagent Systems (AAMAS 2005), pp. 141–148. Association for Computing Machinery (2005). https://doi.org/10.1145/1082473.1082495
13. van Ditmarsch, H.P., Hoek, W.V.D., Kooi, B.: Dynamic Epistemic Logic. Synthese Library, Springer, Dordrecht (2007). https://doi.org/10.1007/978-1-4020-5839-4
14. van Ditmarsch, H., Hartley, M.I., Kooi, B., Welton, J., Yeo, J.B.: Cheryl's birthday. Electron. Proc. Theor. Comput. Sci. **251**, 1–9 (2017). https://doi.org/10.4204/eptcs.251.1
15. van Eijck, J.: A demo of epistemic modelling. In: Interactive Logic: Selected Papers from the 7th Augustus de Morgan Workshop, p. 303 (2007)
16. Fagin, R., Halpern, J.Y., Moses, Y., Vardi, M.Y.: Knowledge-based programs. In: Symposium on Principles of Distributed Computing, pp. 153–163. ACM (1995). https://doi.org/10.1145/224964.224982
17. Fagin, R., Halpern, J.Y., Moses, Y., Vardi, M.Y.: Reasoning About Knowledge. MIT Press, Cambridge (1995)
18. Gammie, P., van der Meyden, R.: MCK: model checking the logic of knowledge. In: Alur, R., Peled, D.A. (eds.) CAV 2004. LNCS, vol. 3114, pp. 479–483. Springer, Heidelberg (2004). https://doi.org/10.1007/978-3-540-27813-9_41
19. Gorogiannis, N., Raimondi, F., Boureanu, I.: A novel symbolic approach to verifying epistemic properties of programs. In: Proceedings of the Twenty-Sixth International Joint Conference on Artificial Intelligence (IJCAI 2017), pp. 206–212 (2017). https://doi.org/10.24963/ijcai.2017/30
20. Grossi, D., Herzig, A., van der Hoek, W., Moyzes, C.: Non-determinism and the dynamics of knowledge. In: Proceedings of the Twenty-Sixth International Joint Conference on Artificial Intelligence (2017). https://doi.org/10.24963/ijcai.2017/146
21. Grossi, D., van der Hoek, W., Moyzes, C., Wooldridge, M.: Program models and semi-public environments. J. Log. Comput. **29**(7), 1071–1097 (2016). https://doi.org/10.1093/logcom/exv086
22. Harel, D.: Dynamic Logic, pp. 497–604. Springer, Dordrecht (1984). https://doi.org/10.1007/978-94-009-6259-0_10
23. Hintikka, J.: Knowledge and Belief. Cornell University Press, NY (1962)
24. Jena, M.D., Singhar, S.S., Mohanta, B.K., Ramasubbareddy, S.: Ensuring data privacy using machine learning for responsible data science. In: Satapathy, S.C., Zhang, Y.-D., Bhateja, V., Majhi, R. (eds.) Intelligent Data Engineering and Analytics. AISC, vol. 1177, pp. 507–514. Springer, Singapore (2021). https://doi.org/10.1007/978-981-15-5679-1_49
25. Kacprzak, M., Lomuscio, A., Niewiadomski, A., Penczek, W., Raimondi, F., Szreter, M.: Comparing BDD and SAT based techniques for model checking Chaum's dining cryptographers protocol. Fund. Inform. **72**(1–3), 215–234 (2006)
26. Kacprzak, M., et al.: VerICS 2007 - a model checker for knowledge and real-time. Fund. Inform. **85**(1–4), 313–328 (2008)

27. Lehman, D.: Knowledge, common knowledge, and related puzzles. In: Proceedings of the Third Annual ACM Symposium on Principles of Distributed Computing, pp. 62–67. ACM (1984). https://doi.org/10.1145/800222.806736
28. Lomuscio, A., Qu, H., Raimondi, F.: MCMAS: an open-source model checker for the verification of multi-agent systems. Int. J. Softw. Tools Technol. Transf. **19**(1), 9–30 (2015). https://doi.org/10.1007/s10009-015-0378-x
29. McIver, A.K.: The secret art of computer programming. In: Leucker, M., Morgan, C. (eds.) ICTAC 2009. LNCS, vol. 5684, pp. 61–78. Springer, Heidelberg (2009). https://doi.org/10.1007/978-3-642-03466-4_3
30. Morgan, C.: Programming from Specifications, 2nd edn. Prentice Hall, Hoboken (1994)
31. Morgan, C.: *The Shadow Knows:* refinement of ignorance in sequential programs. In: Uustalu, T. (ed.) MPC 2006. LNCS, vol. 4014, pp. 359–378. Springer, Heidelberg (2006). https://doi.org/10.1007/11783596_21
32. Parikh, R., Ramanujam, R.: Distributed processes and the logic of knowledge. In: Parikh, R. (ed.) Logic of Programs 1985. LNCS, vol. 193, pp. 256–268. Springer, Heidelberg (1985). https://doi.org/10.1007/3-540-15648-8_21
33. Plaza, J.A.: Logics of public communications. In: Proceedings of the 4th International Symposium on Methodologies for Intelligent Systems (1989)
34. Pratt, V.R.: Semantical considerations on Floyd-Hoare logic. In: 17th Annual Symposium on Foundations of Computer Science, pp. 109–121. IEEE (1976). https://doi.org/10.1109/SFCS.1976.27
35. Rajaona, S.F.: An algebraic framework for reasoning about privacy. Ph.D. thesis, University of Stellenbosch, Stellenbosch (2016). http://hdl.handle.net/10019.1/106607
36. Wang, S.: Dynamic epistemic model checking with Yices (2016). https://github.com/airobert/DEL/blob/master/report.pdf. Accessed 28 June 2022
37. Wooldridge, M., Lomuscio, A.: A computationally grounded logic of visibility, perception, and knowledge. Log. J. IGPL **9**(2), 257–272 (2001). https://doi.org/10.1093/jigpal/9.2.257

Safety and Reliability

Tableaux for Realizability of Safety Specifications

Montserrat Hermo[1], Paqui Lucio[1], and César Sánchez[2](✉)

[1] University of the Basque Country, San Sebastián, Spain
[2] IMDEA Software Institute, Madrid, Spain
cesar.sanchez@imdea.org

Abstract. We introduce a tableau decision method for deciding realizability of specifications expressed in a safety fragment of LTL that includes bounded future temporal operators. Tableau decision procedures for temporal and modal logics have been thoroughly studied for satisfiability and for translating temporal formulae into equivalent Büchi automata, and also for model checking, where a specification and system are provided. However, to the best of our knowledge no tableau method has been studied for the reactive synthesis problem.

Reactive synthesis starts from a specification where propositional variables are split into those controlled by the environment and those controlled by the system, and consists on automatically producing a system that guarantees the specification for all environments. Realizability is the decision problem of whether there is one such system.

In this paper, we present a method to decide realizability of safety specifications, from which we can also extract (i.e., synthesize) a correct system (in case the specification is realizable). The main novelty of a tableau method is that it can be easily extended to handle richer domains (integers, etc.) and bounds in the temporal operators in ways that automata approaches for synthesis cannot.

1 Introduction

Linear Temporal Logic (LTL) [27] is modal logic for expressing correctness properties of reactive systems. Verification is the problem of deciding, given a system S and an LTL specification φ, whether S models φ. Reactive synthesis, first studied by Pnueli and Rosner in 1989 [28,29], is the problem of automatically producing S from φ with the guarantee that S models φ. In the reactive synthesis problem, the atomic variables are split into those variables controlled by the environment and the rest, controlled by the system.

This work was funded in part by the European Union (ERDF funds) under grant PID2020-112581GB-C22, European COST Action CA20111 EuroProofNet (European Research Network on Formal Proofs), by the University of the Basque Country under project LoRea GIU21/044, by the Madrid Regional Government under project S2018/TCS-4339 (BLOQUES-CM) and by a research grant from Nomadic Labs and the Tezos Foundation.

M. Chechik et al. (Eds.): FM 2023, LNCS 14000, pp. 495–513, 2023.
https://doi.org/10.1007/978-3-031-27481-7_28

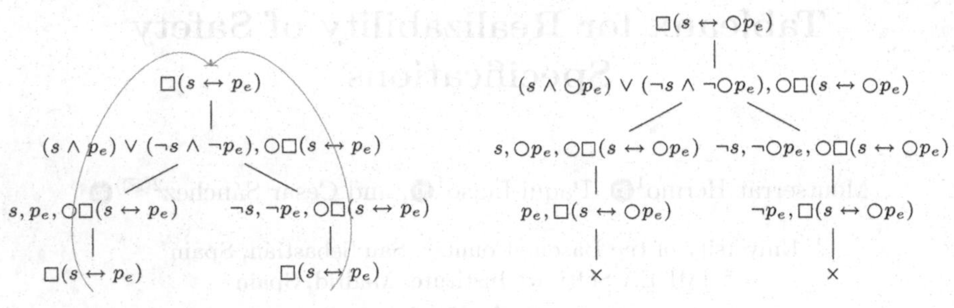

Fig. 1. Tableaux for $\Box\psi_1$ and $\Box\psi_2$.

In the last two decades, the reactive synthesis problem has received lot of attention (e.g., [5,10,15,16,21]). The approaches can be classified into three categories: (1) game-based [7], (2) approaches that cover a strict fragment of LTL, like GR(1) specifications [3,26]; (3) bounded synthesis [30], which explores the problem up to a fixed bound on the size of the system. In all these cases, the state space of the game arena is either captured by an automaton or explored explicitly or symbolically. In this paper, we study a deductive alternative: a tableau method for the realizability and synthesis for the class of safety specifications.

Tableau methods were originally created [2,33] as intuitive deduction procedures for classical propositional and first-order logic. A tableau is a tree that performs symbolic handling of formulas according to simple rules based on semantics, model-theory and proof-theory. Classical tableaux correspond to deductive proofs in Gentzen's sequent calculus. Tableaux have been evolving for years to decide the satisfiability problem of many other non-classical logics (modal, multi-valued, temporal, etc.), in some cases combined with other formal structures, such as different kinds of automata.

Traditional tableau techniques for satisfiability do not directly work for realizability, where tableaux have only been used for auxiliary steps in automata-based methods [6]. We present in this paper, a tableau-based method for the realizability of reactive safety specifications. To illustrate the problem, consider the following formulas where p_e is an environment variable and s is a system variable: $\psi_1 = s \leftrightarrow p_e$, $\psi_2 = s \leftrightarrow \bigcirc p_e$ and $\psi_3 = \bigcirc s \leftrightarrow \bigcirc p_e$. Symbols $\bigcirc$ and $\Box$ are temporal operators which refer to the next instant and to all instants of time respectively. The safety specifications $\Box\psi_1$ and $\Box\psi_3$ are realizable: consider the system that mimics in s the value observed in e.

A temporal tableau for $\Box\psi_1$ (shown in Fig. 1 (left)) first uses the semantics of the $\Box$ operator, which states that $\Box\psi_1 = \psi_1 \wedge \bigcirc\Box\psi_1$. Then, it decomposes the formula into $s \leftrightarrow p_e, \bigcirc\Box\psi_1$ and splits two branches for the two cases: $s, p_e, \bigcirc\Box\psi_1$ and $\neg s, \neg p_e, \bigcirc\Box\psi_1$. Both nodes then jump to the next temporal state, so both branches generate a loop to the root $\Box\psi_1$. Each branch represents a model of the initial formula. It is tempting to interpret this tableau as a winning strategy for the system that witnesses the realizability of $\Box\psi_1$. On the other hand, $\Box\psi_2$ is not realizable, as the system is required to guess the next value

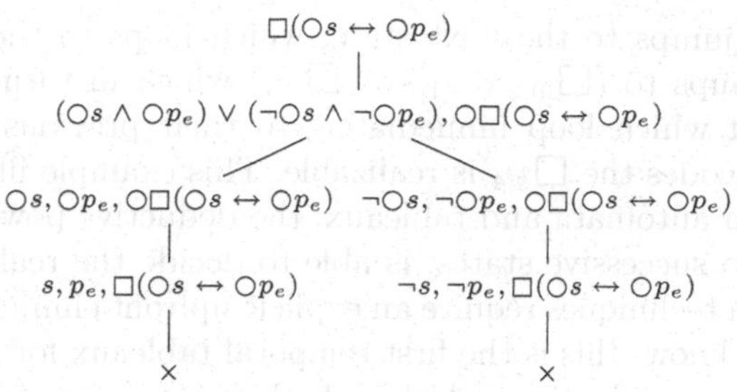

Fig. 2. Tableau for $\square\psi_3$.

of p_e, and the environment can later emit the opposite value. The tableau for $\square\psi_2$ is shown in Fig. 1 (right). The left branch in the tableau corresponds to the system choosing s hoping for the environment to play p_e in the next step. Since the environment can choose $\neg p_e$, this branch must close at node $p_e, \square\psi_2$ (the right branch is similar). A branch closing condition typical of tableaux closes this branch as the environment wins by forcing a contradiction. However, this closing condition fails to capture the realizability of $\square\psi_3$, since the resulting tableau for $\square\psi_3$ would be as shown in Fig. 2.

The previous closing condition would close the left branch (choosing $\neg p_e$) and the right branch (choosing p_e), incorrectly concluding that $\square\psi_3$ is unrealizable. The problem here is in the splitting of the two cases $\bigcirc s, \bigcirc p_e$ and $\bigcirc\neg s, \bigcirc\neg p_e$, which reveals too early the future move of the system given the power (incorrectly) to the environment to create a contradiction. To overcome this problem, we introduce in this paper the *terse normal form* of formulas which prevents these incorrect splittings on formulas that reveal future choices too early. Intuitively, at the second temporal state, our tableau will just have one node $n : (s \wedge p_e) \vee (\neg s \wedge \neg p_e), \square\psi_3$. Node n has two children (one for each choice of the environment):

$$p_e, s, \bigcirc((s \wedge p_e) \vee (\neg s \wedge \neg p_e)), \bigcirc\square\psi_3 \mid \neg p_e, \neg s, \bigcirc((s \wedge p_e) \vee (\neg s \wedge \neg p_e)), \bigcirc\square\psi_3$$

Then, the next state from both nodes produces again node n. This tableau encodes the proof that $\square\psi_3$ is realizable (see Example 4).

We introduce in this paper *realizability tableaux* to fix classical temporal tableau rules to obtain a correct decision procedure for realizability. Our tableau method solves the realizability decision problem for a fragment of LTL, which includes temporal operators of the form $\square_{[n,m]}$ and $\diamondsuit_{[n,m]}$ (for $n, m \in \mathbb{N}$). These operators are very common in industrial critical specifications where the system is supposed to respond within a predefined amount of time. Although these operators can be seen as a short-hand for a Boolean combination of formulas using only $\bigcirc$, the compact notation is effectively exploited in our tableau deductions in a more efficient way that prevents exponential unfoldings. Consider for example the formula $\psi_4 = p_e \rightarrow \square_{[0,2^{100}]}s$. Our tableau for $\square\psi_4$ splits two branches for the two cases $(\neg p_e \wedge \bigcirc\square\psi_4)$ and $(p_e \wedge s \wedge \bigcirc\square_{[0,2^{100}-1]} \wedge \bigcirc\square\psi_4)$.

The first branch jumps to the next state, which loops to the root $\Box\psi_4$. The second branch jumps to $(\Box_{[0,2^{100}-1]}s \wedge \Box\psi_4)$ which in turn spawns two new branches, both of which loop immediately to their previous state. This very small tableaux encodes the $\Box\psi_4$ is realizable. This example illustrates a crucial difference between automata and tableaux: the deductive power of the tableau, after checking two successive states, is able to decide the realizability of $\Box\psi_4$, whereas automata techniques require an explicit upfront elimination of the intervals. As far as we know, this is the first temporal tableaux for solving realizability of safety LTL specifications. Although this paper focuses on realizability, our tableaux provide a procedures for both kinds of certificates: the realizability strategy (i.e. the synthesis of a system) and the counterexample in the case of unrealizability.

In summary, our contributions are: (1) The introduction of the novel terse normal form that captures in a logical form the timely choices of the environment and the responses by the system. (2) A tableau method including all the deductive rules to build the tableau graph and rules to close the branches, with success and with failure. (3) Sound and completeness proofs for our tableau method.

Related Work. Current approaches to reactive synthesis [5,10,15,16,21] are either (1) based on games [7], which create a mathematical structure—like an automaton—that capture the game arena and then explore this structure, or (2) rely on bounded synthesis [30], which produce a set of constraints that characterizes all correct systems up to fixed bound. Modern game approaches use a symbolic representation [21], or SAT or QBF decision procedures [4]. Existing tools for full LTL synthesis, including Unbeast [10] and Acacia+ [5] are based on bounded synthesis. Different encoding of the constraint for a given bound have been proposed [11–15,22,30,32]. Since 2014, the reactive synthesis competition (SYNTCOMP) [1,20] compares the performance of synthesis tools against different benchmark problems.

Reactive synthesis for full LTL is 2EXPTIME-complete [29], so LTL fragments with better complexity have been identified. For example, GR(1) (general reactivity with rank 1)—enjoy an efficient (polynomial) symbolic synthesis algorithm [3,26], with practical applications [9,23]. Translating GR(1) specifications into the safety language that we consider in this paper involves at least an exponential blow-up in the worst case. All methods listed above perform an algorithmic exhaustive exploration of the game arena. In contrast, our deductive tableau method is deductive. Even though some game-based tools, like Strix [24,25], perform some on-the-fly construction of the game arena the deductive nature of tableaux allows to skip larger portions of the state space. An explicit comparison of the performance between methods requires a polished implementation, which is out of the scope of this paper. We focus here the foundations[1] of the realizability tableau, emphasizing its power to handle richer settings and prevent explicit blow-ups.

[1] The full proof of correctness, including all intermediate lemmas can be found in the extended version [19], which also includes several realizability tableaux examples.

The first tableau method [35] for the satisfiability of LTL is not purely tree-shape but builds a graph that is explored in a second pass. This inspired a connection with Büchi automata [34,35], on which many decision procedures [8] for LTL satisfiability and model checking are based. The use of an auxiliary structure raised two difficulties: one is the size and another is the loss of the original correspondence with sequent proofs that could certify the result. Some alternative ideas (e.g., [18,31]) have been developed to explore on-the-fly the graph (or automaton) not requiring a second pass, and also for constructing one-pass tableaux that preserve the correspondence with sequent proofs (cf. [17]).

2 Preliminaries. Safety Specifications and Games

Given a set R, R^* denotes the set of finite strings over R and R^k the set of strings over R of length k. R^ω is the set of infinite sequences over R. We sometimes use $\overline{x}$ to remark that string $\overline{x}$ is a sequence of elements, and use $|\overline{x}|$ for its length and $\overline{x} \cdot v$ for the concatenation of $\overline{x}$ with v. We use ϵ for the empty string. Given $r = r_0, r_1, r_2 \ldots \in R^\omega$, and r^i for $r_i, r_{i+1} \ldots$, we use $r^{<i}$ for the finite sequence $r_0, \ldots, r_{i-1}$ and $r^{i..j}$ for the finite sequence $r_i \ldots r_{j-1}$. LTL extends propositional logic with temporal operators $\bigcirc$ (next) and $\mathcal{U}$ (until). Given a set $\mathcal{V}$ of propositional variables, a valuation v is a map $\mathcal{V} \to \mathbb{B}$ (where $\mathbb{B}$ is a Boolean domain). We denote by $\mathsf{Val}(\mathcal{V})$ the set of all valuations of $\mathcal{V}$. A trace σ is an infinite sequence $\sigma_0, \sigma_1, \sigma_2, \ldots$ of valuations of $\mathcal{V}$. The semantics of LTL relate formulas with traces as follows:

$\sigma \models p$ iff $\sigma_0(p)$ $\quad$ $\sigma \models \neg\varphi$ iff $\sigma \not\models \varphi$

$\sigma \models \bigcirc\varphi$ iff $\sigma^1 \models \varphi$ $\quad$ $\sigma \models \varphi \wedge \psi$ iff $\sigma \models \varphi$ and $\sigma \models \psi$

$\sigma \models \varphi \mathcal{U} \psi$ iff $\sigma^j \models \psi$ for some $0 \leq j$ and $\sigma^i \models \varphi$ for all i such that $0 \leq i < j$

We use standard abbreviations, like T for truth and F for falsehood, $\vee, \to$ and $\leftrightarrow$, and $\Diamond\varphi$ for $\mathrm{T}\,\mathcal{U}\,\varphi$ and $\Box\varphi$ for $\neg(\mathrm{T}\,\mathcal{U}\,\neg\varphi)$. A set of formulas is (syntactically) consistent if and only if it does not contain a formula and its negation. If $\sigma \models \varphi$ then we say that σ is a model of φ and we use $\mathsf{Mod}(\varphi)$ to denote the set of all models of φ. We interpret a finite set of formulas as the conjunction of all its members, and use $\sigma \models \Phi$ to denote the set of traces that are models of all $\varphi \in \Phi$. A set of formulas Φ is satisfiable if and only if there exists at least one σ such that $\sigma \models \Phi$. Two formulas φ and ψ are logically equivalent, denoted $\varphi \equiv \psi$, if and only if $\mathsf{Mod}(\varphi) = \mathsf{Mod}(\psi)$. A set of traces L is a *safety* language whenever for any trace $\sigma \notin L$ there exists some $i > 0$ such that $\sigma^{<i} \cdot \sigma' \notin L$ for any trace σ'. We call $\sigma^{<i}$ a *witness of the violation* of σ.

Safety Specifications. We split the set of propositions in a formula φ into two disjoint subsets: $\mathcal{X}_e$, controlled by the environment and $\mathcal{Y}$, controlled by the system. We use a subscript e (e.g., $sensor_e$ or p_e) for the elements of $\mathcal{X}_e$.

We use a fragment of LTL for safety specifications. To illustrate the power of our tableau technique to handle richer types, we do not restrict ourselves to Boolean variables, but also consider enumerated variables and atoms $x = c$

where x is a variable of an enumerated type T and c is a constant value of type T. Boolean formulas are built from atoms (Boolean variables or enumerated atoms) using Boolean connectives. *The fragment of safety* LTL*specifications consists of formulas* $\alpha \wedge \Box\psi$, where α, called the *initial formula*, is a Boolean constraint that captures the initial states. The formula $\Box\psi$, called the safety constraint, restricts the transition relation by means of the following temporal operators:

$$\eta ::= p \mid x = c \mid \neg\eta \mid \bigcirc\eta \mid \Box_I\eta \mid \Diamond_I\eta \mid \eta \vee \eta \mid \eta \wedge \eta$$

where $I = [n, m]$ for some $n, m \in \mathbb{N}$ such that $n \leq m$. The semantics is:

$\sigma \models \Box_{[n,m]}\eta$ iff $\sigma^j \models \eta$ for all j such that $n \leq j \leq m$.
$\sigma \models \Diamond_{[n,m]}\eta$ iff there exists j such that $n \leq j \leq m$ such that $\sigma^j \models \eta$.

Note that $\Diamond_I$ and $\Box_I$ can be de-sugared using $\bigcirc$, but with an exponential unfolding in terms m. A trace σ models $\alpha \wedge \Box\psi$ whenever $\sigma_0(\alpha)$ holds and $\sigma^k \models \psi$ for all $k \geq 0$.

It is easy to see that any safety formula is logically equivalent to a formula in Negation Normal Form (NNF) by pushing negation to the propositional level (using equivalences $\neg\bigcirc\eta \equiv \bigcirc\neg\eta$, $\neg\Diamond_I\eta \equiv \Box_I\neg\eta$ and $\neg\Box_I\eta \equiv \Diamond_I\neg\eta$):

$$\ell ::= p \mid \neg p \mid x = c \mid \neg(x = c) \mid \mathbf{T} \mid \mathbf{F} \qquad \eta ::= \ell \mid \bigcirc\eta \mid \Box_I\eta \mid \Diamond_I\eta \mid \eta \vee \eta \mid \eta \wedge \eta.$$

We assume that formulas are translated to NNF, ℓ stands for a literal, and, for $i \in \mathbb{N}$, $\bigcirc^i$ abbreviates a sequence of operators $\bigcirc$ of length i. The temporal depth of φ is the maximum number of nested $\bigcirc$ operators, where $\Box_I$ and $\Diamond_I$ are interpreted in terms of $\bigcirc$. It is easy to see that the truth value of a formula (at position i) of depth d only requires to inspect d positions of the trace (after i). We define a semantics $\models^{fin}$ of our safety fragment of LTLon finite traces $\lambda = \lambda_0 \cdots \lambda_{d-1}$ where $d \geq 1$ by:

$\lambda \models^{fin} \ell$ iff $\lambda_0(\ell) = 1$
$\lambda \models^{fin} \eta_1 \wedge \eta_2$ iff $\lambda \models^{fin} \eta_1$ and $\lambda \models^{fin} \eta_2$
$\lambda \models^{fin} \eta_1 \vee \eta_2$ iff $\lambda \models^{fin} \eta_1$ or $\lambda \models^{fin} \eta_2$
$\lambda \models^{fin} \bigcirc\eta$ iff if $d > 1$ then $\lambda^{1..d} \models^{fin} \eta$ (remember that $\lambda^{1\cdots d}$ denotes $\lambda_1 \cdots \lambda_d$)
$\lambda \models^{fin} \Box_{[n,m]}\eta$ iff $\lambda^j \models^{fin} \eta$ for all $n \leq j \leq \min(m, d)$
$\lambda \models^{fin} \Diamond_{[n,m]}\eta$ iff if $n \leq m < d$ then $\lambda^j \models^{fin} \eta$ for some $n \leq j \leq m$

Note that a witness of the violation of a safety formula η is a finite sequence $\lambda = \lambda_0 \cdots \lambda_{d-1}$ such that $\lambda \not\models^{fin} \eta$.

Given a set of formulas Δ, we denote by $\mathsf{Val}_\Delta(\mathcal{V})$ the set of all valuations $v \in \mathsf{Val}(\mathcal{V})$ such that $v(x)$ for every Boolean variable $x \in \Delta$, $\neg v(x)$ for every Boolean variable $\neg x \in \Delta$, $v(x) = c$ for every x of enumerated type such that $x = c \in \Delta$, and $v(x) \neq c$ for every x of enumerated type such that $\neg(x = c) \in \Delta$. Note that if x does not occur in Δ, there are many $v \in \mathsf{Val}_\Delta(\mathcal{V})$ with different values for $v(x)$. If Δ is a set of literals then $\lambda_0 \models^{fin} \Delta$ if and only if $\lambda_0 \in \mathsf{Val}_\Delta(\mathcal{V})$. Given $v \in \mathsf{Val}(\mathcal{X}_e)$ and $w \in \mathsf{Val}(\mathcal{Y})$, we denote by $v + w$ the valuation in $z \in$

$\mathsf{Val}(\mathcal{X}_e \cup \mathcal{Y})$ such that $z(p) = v(p)$ if $z \in \mathcal{X}_e$ and $z(p) = w(p)$ if $z \in \mathcal{Y}$. This notation is extended to pairs of finite traces λ on $\mathcal{X}_e$ and λ' on $\mathcal{Y}$ of the same length d, i.e., $\lambda + \lambda'$ denotes the trace $(\lambda_0 + \lambda'_0) \cdots (\lambda_{d-1} + \lambda'_{d-1})$. It is easy to see that our fragment of safety specifications can only describe safety languages.

Lemma 1. *Given a safety spec.* $\varphi = \alpha \wedge \Box\psi$ *and a trace* σ, $\sigma \not\models \varphi$ *iff either*

(i) σ_0 *is a witness of the violation of* $\alpha \wedge \psi$, *or*
(ii) for some i *and* $d \leq \mathsf{depth}(\psi)$ $\sigma^{i..i+(d+1)}$ *is a witness of the violation of* ψ.

Safety Games. A safety game $\langle I, P, P_E, P_S, T, B\rangle$ is played by two players E (the environment) and S (the system), where (1) P is the set of positions, partitioned into $P = P_E \cup P_S$; (2) $I \subseteq P$ is the initial positions; (3) $T \subseteq (P \times P)$ is the set of moves; and (4) $B \subseteq P$ is the safety winning condition. E moves at positions P_E and S moves at P_S, choosing a successor. A play $\pi : v_0 v_1 v_2 \dots$ is an infinite sequence of positions, related by moves. We assume that every position has a successor so we do not have to deal with finite plays. A play π is winning for S if for all i, $\pi(i) \notin B$. A memoryless *strategy* ρ_S for S is a map $\rho_S : P_S \to P$, such that $(p, \rho_S(p)) \in T$ is a move for all $p \in P_S$.

Strategies for E are defined analogously. A play π is played according to a strategy ρ_S if for every i, if $\pi(i) \in P_S$ then $\pi(i+1) = \rho_S(\pi(i))$. A strategy ρ_S of S is winning if every initial play π played according to ρ_S is winning for S. It is well-known that safety games are memoryless determined (either S or E have a memoryless winning strategy). We now construct a safety game from a specification φ over $\mathcal{X}_e$ and $\mathcal{Y}$:

- $P_E = \{\mathsf{Val}(\mathcal{X}_e)^k \times \mathsf{Val}(\mathcal{Y})^k \mid k \in \mathbb{N}\}$. We use $P_E^k = \{(\overline{x}, \overline{y}) \mid |x| = |y| = k\}$.
- $P_S = \{\mathsf{Val}(\mathcal{X}_e)^{k+1} \times \mathsf{Val}(\mathcal{Y})^k \mid k \in \mathbb{N}\}$. We use $P_S^{k+1} = \{(\overline{x}, \overline{y}) \mid |x| = k + 1 \text{ and } |y| = k\}$.
- T contains two types of edges $T = T_E \cup T_S$ defined as follows for each $k \in \mathbb{N}$:
  - $T_E \subseteq (P_E^k, P_S^{k+1})$ such that $((\overline{x}, \overline{y}), (\overline{x} \cdot v, \overline{y})) \in T_E$ iff $v \in \mathsf{Val}(\mathcal{X}_e)$.
  - $T_S \subseteq (P_S^{k+1}, P_E^{k+1})$ such that $((\overline{x} \cdot v, \overline{y}), (\overline{x} \cdot v, \overline{y} \cdot w)) \in T_S$ iff $w \in \mathsf{Val}(\mathcal{Y})$.
- $I = \{(\epsilon, \epsilon)\}$.

Note that E and S alternate playing. Given a position $p \in P_E \setminus I$ of the form $(\overline{x} \cdot v, \overline{y} \cdot w)$ we use *move*$(p) = (v + w)$ for the valuation of the variables of $\mathcal{X}_e \cup \mathcal{Y}$ according to v and w. Given a play π we use *trace*(π) for the trace σ such that $\sigma(i) = \mathit{move}(\pi(2i+1))$, which corresponds to the sequence of valuations that E and S pick. This arena is essentially an infinite tree that records the valuations chosen. We define the set of bad states as the safety winning condition:

$$B_\varphi = \{(\overline{x}, \overline{y}) \mid \text{there is } v \in \mathsf{Val}(\mathcal{X}_e), \text{ for all } w \in \mathsf{Val}(\mathcal{Y}) : \overline{x} \cdot v + \overline{y} \cdot w \not\models^{\mathit{fin}} \varphi\}.$$

We use $\mathcal{G}(\varphi) : \langle P, P_E, P_S, I, T, B_\varphi\rangle$ for the safety specification game for φ.

Lemma 2. *A safety spec.* φ *is realizable if and only if* $\mathcal{G}(\varphi)$ *is winning for* S.

3 Realizability Tableaux

We introduce now the main technical contribution of this paper, a tableau method for deciding the realizability of a safety specifications, which also allows to synthesize a winning strategy for realizable specifications.

3.1 Terse Normal Form

Our tableau for φ will cover the plays of $\mathcal{G}(\varphi)$, where the environment chooses a move on its variables $\mathcal{X}_e$ and, then, the system responds with a move on $\mathcal{Y}$. In order for branches to represent real plays, the formula in a node should determine the true strict-future possibilities at the current position. Consider that the formula $\varphi_2 = (\bigcirc\neg s) \vee (p_e \wedge \bigcirc\bigcirc s)$ represents the possible moves at some position in a game. Satisfying $(\bigcirc\neg s)$ would fulfill the specification. Also, if the environment moves p_e both $\bigcirc\bigcirc s$ and $\bigcirc\neg s$ would satisfy φ_2. However, a classical tableau-style analysis would split φ_2 into two branches such that the one containing p_e requires $\bigcirc\bigcirc s$ to satisfy the specification, precluding the possibility of $\bigcirc\neg s$. Note also that the formula $\varphi_3 = (p_e \wedge (\bigcirc\neg s \vee \bigcirc\bigcirc s)) \vee (\neg p_e \wedge \bigcirc\neg s)$ is logically equivalent to φ_2, but suitable for a tableau-style analysis of realizability. We now introduce the *Terse Normal Form* (TNF) for safety formulas that associates moves with formulas that capture the condition that any trace must satisfy in the (strict) future to be coherent with the current safety specification. The formula φ_3 above is in TNF.

Basic (sub)formulas of a safety formula are of the form ℓ, $\bigcirc^n\eta$, $\Diamond_I\eta$ or $\Box_I\eta$. We classify these into *from-now* formulas: ℓ, $\Diamond_{[0,m]}\eta$, $\Box_{[0,m]}\eta$ and *from-next* formulas: $\bigcirc\eta$, $\Diamond_{[n,m]}\eta$ and $\Box_{[n,m]}\eta$ (for any $m \geq n \geq 1$).

Definition 1 (Strict-Future and Separated). *A strict-future formula is a* DNF *combination of from-next formulas. A separated formula is the conjunction of a set of Boolean literals (possibly empty) and (at most) one strict-future formula. If π is a separated formula, then $\mathcal{L}(\pi)$ denotes the set of literals in π and $\mathcal{F}(\pi)$ denotes the strict-future formula in π.*

Definition 2. (TNF). *A safety formula η in Terse Normal Form* (TNF) *is a disjunction $\bigvee_{i=1}^{n} \pi_i$ such that each π_i is a separated formula, and for all $1 \leq i \neq j \leq n$ there is at least one literal ℓ such that $\ell \in \mathcal{L}(\pi_i)$ and $\neg\ell \in \mathcal{L}(\pi_j)$.*

Proposition 1. *For any safety formula η there is a logically equivalent safety formula, called* $\mathsf{TNF}(\eta)$*, that is in* TNF.

Example 1. The TNFfor $p_e \leftrightarrow \bigcirc s$ and $\bigcirc p_e \leftrightarrow \bigcirc s$ from Sect. 1 are $\mathsf{TNF}(p_e \leftrightarrow \bigcirc s) \equiv (p_e \wedge \bigcirc s) \vee (\neg p_e \wedge \bigcirc\neg s)$ and $\mathsf{TNF}(\bigcirc p_e \leftrightarrow \bigcirc s) \equiv (\bigcirc p_e \wedge \bigcirc s) \vee (\bigcirc\neg p_e \wedge \bigcirc\neg s)$. Finally, for $\eta = c \wedge (\neg p_e \rightarrow \Box_{[0,9]}\neg c) \wedge (\Box_{[0,9]}c \vee \Diamond_{[0,2]}\neg c)$: $\mathsf{TNF}(\eta) \equiv (p_e \wedge c \wedge (\bigcirc\Diamond_{[0,1]}\neg c \vee \bigcirc\Box_{[0,8]}c)) \vee (\neg p_e \wedge c \wedge \bigcirc\Box_{[0,8]}c)$.

Definition 3 (Moves). *Given $\bigvee_{i=1}^{n} \pi_i$ in* TNF *we call each π_i a move.*

Note that $\mathsf{Val}_{\pi_i} = \mathsf{Val}_{\mathcal{L}(\pi_i)}$ for any move π_i of any formula in TNF. In Example 1, $\mathsf{TNF}(p_e \leftrightarrow \bigcirc s)$ contains two moves, each having a literal and a strict-future formula, but $\mathsf{TNF}(\bigcirc p_e \leftrightarrow \bigcirc s)$ has only one move (the empty set of literals) with one future-strict formula (which is a disjunction).

Proposition 2. *Let η be a safety formula and let $\mathsf{TNF}(\eta) = \bigvee_{i=1}^{n} \pi_i$. Then,*

(a) For any trace σ, $\sigma \models \eta$ iff $\sigma \models \pi_i$ for exactly one $1 \le i \le n$.
(b) For any finite trace λ, $\lambda \models^{fin} \eta$ iff $\lambda \models^{fin} \pi_i$ for exactly one $1 \le i \le n$.
(c) Let σ be such that $\sigma \models \eta$ and let $1 \le i \le n$. Then, $\sigma \models \mathcal{L}(\pi_i) \rightarrow \mathcal{F}(\pi_i)$.

We define now a special subset of moves in a TNFthat are called $\mathcal{X}_e$-coverings.

Definition 4. *A formula $\bigvee_{i=1}^{n} \pi_i$ in TNF with $\cup_{i=1}^{n} \mathsf{Val}_{\pi_i}(\mathcal{X}_e) = \mathsf{Val}(\mathcal{X}_e)$ is called an $\mathcal{X}_e$-covering. An $\mathcal{X}_e$-covering is minimal if $\bigvee_{i=1, i \neq j}^{n} \pi_i$ is not an $\mathcal{X}_e$-covering for any $1 \le j \le n$.*

Intuitively, a minimal $\mathcal{X}_e$-covering represents a system strategy from the current position. Therefore, the collection of all minimal coverings represents all possible strategies. Moreover, each move in a strategy contains all the strict-future possibilities for this move.

Example 2. Let $\mathsf{TNF}(\eta) = (p_e \wedge c \wedge \eta_1) \vee (\neg p_e \wedge c \wedge \eta_2) \vee (\neg c \wedge \eta_3)$ where η_1, η_2, η_3 are strict-future formulas and $\mathcal{X}_e = \{p_e\}$. It is a non-minimal $\mathcal{X}_e$-covering, but the third move $(\neg c \wedge \eta_3)$ is a minimal one. The two first moves together also provide a minimal $\mathcal{X}_e$-covering.

We say that a set of indices I is a (minimal) $\mathcal{X}_e$-covering when $\bigvee_{i \in I} \pi_i$ is a (minimal) $\mathcal{X}_e$-covering.

Proposition 3. *Let Φ be a set of safety formulas and $\mathsf{TNF}(\Phi \wedge \psi) = \bigvee_{i \in I} \pi_i$.*

(a) If I is not an $\mathcal{X}_e$-covering, then for some $v \in \mathsf{Val}(\mathcal{X}_e)$, $v \not\models^{fin} \Phi \wedge \psi$.
(b) If I is a minimal $\mathcal{X}_e$-covering, then for all $i \in I$ and all $v \in \mathsf{Val}_{\pi_i}(\mathcal{X}_e)$, there exists some $v' \in \mathsf{Val}_{\pi_i}(\mathcal{Y})$ such that $v + v' \in \mathsf{Val}_{\pi_i}(\mathcal{X}_e \cup \mathcal{Y})$.
(c) If for each $v \in \mathsf{Val}(\mathcal{X}_e)$ there exists $v' \in \mathsf{Val}(\mathcal{Y})$ such that $v + v' \models^{fin} \Phi \wedge \psi$, then there exists some minimal $\mathcal{X}_e$-covering $J \subseteq I$.

To handle strict-future formulas $\mathcal{F}(\pi)$ in the tableau rules we introduce the symbol $\ddot{\vee}$ which is semantically equivalent to $\vee$, but our tableau rules deal differently with both disjunctive operators. More precisely, strict-future subformulas $\mathcal{F}(\pi)$ (inside moves of TNFformulas) will be written as $\ddot{\bigvee}_{i=1}^{m} \delta_i$.

3.2 Tableaux

Realizability tableaux are AND-OR trees, where each node is labelled by a set of formulas[2]. A node is said to be the parent of its successors nodes. The root of

[2] We graphically represent AND-nodes with an arc embracing all the edges to the AND-successors of a node.

the tree is labelled with the input safety specification. The tableau is constructed using the set of tableau rules shown in Fig. 3. Each rule determines the labels on the children of a node and the kind (AND or OR) of its successors. A tableau is completed when no further rule can be applied. Rules apply only to nodes in branches that are neither failed nor successful. A node is called a leaf when no rule can be applied to it. There are two kinds of leaves. Failure leaves are labelled by (syntactically) inconsistent sets of formulas, which indicates that the branch from the root to the leaf is failed. Successful leaves are labelled by sets of formulas that are subsumed (in the sense we will make precise in Definition 6) by some previous node in the branch from the root to the leaf.

Before we introduce the tableau rules, we define the finite set of all formulas that could appear in the construction of a tableau for φ, denoted as $\mathsf{Clo}(\varphi)$.

Definition 5. *Given a formula β, we denote by $\mathsf{SubFm}(\beta)$ the set of all subformulas of β. In particular, $\mathsf{SubFm}(\bigcirc^i\beta) = \{\bigcirc^j\beta \mid 0 \leq j \leq i\} \cup \mathsf{SubFm}(\beta)$. For a given safety formula ψ, we define $\mathsf{Varnt}(\psi)$ to be the union of the following four sets that collects all the variants of subformulas $\Diamond_I$ and $\Box_I$ that the tableau rules could introduce.*

$$\{\Diamond_{[n,m']}\beta, \bigcirc\Diamond_{[n,m']}\beta \mid \Diamond_{[n,m]}\beta \in \mathsf{SubFm}(\psi), n \leq m' < m\} \cup$$
$$\{\Box_{[n,m']}\beta, \bigcirc\Box_{[n,m']}\beta \mid \Box_{[n,m]}\beta \in \mathsf{SubFm}(\psi), n \leq m' < m\} \cup$$
$$\{\mathsf{SubFm}(\bigcirc^i\beta) \mid \Diamond_{[n,m]}\beta \in \mathsf{SubFm}(\psi), 0 \leq i \leq n\} \cup$$
$$\{\mathsf{SubFm}(\bigcirc^i\beta) \mid \Box_{[n,m]}\beta \in \mathsf{SubFm}(\psi), 0 \leq i \leq n\}$$

The set $\mathsf{Ordnf}(\psi)$ consists of all formulas of the form $\bigvee_{i=1}^{n}\bigwedge_{j=1}^{m}\beta_{i,j}$ where each $\beta_{i,j}$ is in $\mathsf{Varnt}(\psi)$. Then, the closure of a safety specification $\varphi = \alpha \wedge \Box\psi$ is the finite set $\mathsf{Clo}(\varphi) = \mathsf{Preclo}(\varphi) \cup \{\Box\psi, \bigcirc\Box\psi\}$ where $\mathsf{Preclo}(\varphi) = \mathsf{SubFm}(\alpha \wedge \psi) \cup \mathsf{Varnt}(\psi) \cup \mathsf{Ordnf}(\psi)$.

Realizability Tableaux. A tableau for a safety specification $\varphi = \alpha \wedge \Box\psi$ is a labelled tree $\mathsf{Tab}(\varphi) = (N, \tau, R)$, where N is a set of nodes, τ is a map from N to $\mathsf{Clo}(\varphi)$ and $R \subseteq N \times N$, such that the following conditions hold:

- The root is labelled by $\{\alpha, \Box\psi\}$.
- For any $(n, n') \in R$, $\tau(n')$ is the set of formulas obtained as the result of the application of one of the tableau rules (in Fig. 3) to $\tau(n)$. If the applied rule is ρ, we say that n' is a ρ-successor of n.
- For every success or failure leaf n there is no $n' \in N$ s.t. $(n, n') \in R$ where:
  - A failure leaf is a node $n \in N$ s.t. $\mathsf{Incnst}(\tau(n))$ (see Definition 7).
  - A success leaf is a node $n \in N$ such that $\Box\psi \in \tau(n)$ and there exists $k \geq 0$, $n_0, \ldots, n_k \in N$ such that $(n_i, n_{i+1}) \in R$ for all $0 \leq i < k$, $(n_k, n) \in R$ and $\tau(n_0) \lessdot \tau(n)$ (see Definition 8).

3.3 Subsumption and Syntactical Inconsistency

Subsumption rules allow to control the potential set of labellings of the tableau nodes. We use $\beta \sqsubseteq \gamma$ to denote that β subsumes γ or that γ *is subsumed by* β.

Subsumption is related to logical implication, if $\beta \sqsubseteq \gamma$, then $\mathsf{Mod}(\beta) \subseteq \mathsf{Mod}(\gamma)$. Classical subsumption rules include $\beta \sqsubseteq \beta$, $\beta \wedge \gamma \sqsubseteq \beta$, and $\beta \sqsubseteq \beta \vee \gamma$. The set of formulas used to label our tableau nodes are subsumption-free with respect to classical subsumption on Boolean formulas and the following subsumption rules for temporal operators.

Definition 6. *The subsumption rules for temporal formulas are:*

- *For all $n \leq n'$ and $m' \leq m$,*
  $\Diamond_{[n',m']}\beta \sqsubseteq \Diamond_{[n,m]}\beta$, $\Box_{[n,m]}\beta \sqsubseteq \Box_{[n',m']}\beta$, *and* $\Box_{[n',m']}\beta \sqsubseteq \Diamond_{[n,m]}\beta$.
- *For all $n \leq k \leq m$:* $\bigcirc^k\beta \sqsubseteq \Diamond_{[n,m]}\beta$ *and* $\Box_{[n,m]}\beta \sqsubseteq \bigcirc^k\beta$.

The following result easily follows from Definition 6 and semantics.

Proposition 4. *Let $\beta \sqsubseteq \gamma$ be a pair of formulas. For any trace σ, if $\sigma \models \beta$ then $\sigma \models \gamma$. For any finite trace λ, if $\lambda \models^{fin} \beta$ then $\lambda \models^{fin} \gamma$. Consequently, $\sigma \not\models \beta \wedge \widetilde{\gamma}$ and $\lambda \not\models^{fin} \beta \wedge \widetilde{\gamma}$ for any σ and λ, where $\widetilde{\gamma}$ is the* NNF*of $\neg\gamma$.*

Definition 7. *A set of formulas Φ is* (syntactically) inconsistent *(denoted by* $\mathsf{Incnst}(\Phi)$*) whenever one of the following four conditions hold:*

(a) $\mathbf{F} \in \Phi$
(b) $\{\beta, \widetilde{\gamma}\} \subseteq \Phi$ *for some* β, γ *such that* $\beta \sqsubseteq \gamma$
(c) $\{x = c_1, x = c_2\} \subseteq \Phi$ *for some* $c_1 \neq c_2$
(d) $\{\neg(x = c) \mid c \in T\} \subseteq \Phi$ *for some enumerated type* T.

Otherwise, Φ is (syntactically) consistent, *denoted* $\mathsf{Cnst}(\Phi)$.

A node that is labelled by an inconsistent set is a failure leaf and no rule is applied to it. We now define a subsumption-based order relation on sets of formulas to detect successful leaves.

Definition 8. *For two given set of formulas Φ and Φ', we say that $\Phi \lessdot \Phi'$ if and only if for every formula $\beta \in \Phi$ there exists some $\beta' \in \Phi'$ such that $\beta \sqsubseteq \beta'$. For two given strict-future formulas, $\ddot{\bigvee}_{i=1}^{n}\Delta_i \sqsubseteq \ddot{\bigvee}_{j=1}^{m}\Gamma_j$ if and only if for all $1 \leq i \leq n$ there exists $1 \leq j \leq m$ such that $\Delta_i \lessdot \Gamma_j$.*

The following result follows from Definition 8 and Proposition 4.

Proposition 5. *For any finite trace λ and any pair of set of formulas Φ and Φ' such that $\Phi \lessdot \Phi'$, if $\lambda \models^{fin} \Phi$ then $\lambda \models^{fin} \Phi'$.*

No rule is applied to a node that is labelled by a set Φ' such that $\Phi \lessdot \Phi'$ for some previous label Φ in the same branch, because it is a successful leaf.

$$(\Box\mathrm{F})\frac{\Phi, \Box\psi}{\mathrm{F}, \Box\psi} \quad \text{if } \mathsf{TNF}(\Phi \wedge \psi) \text{ is not an } \mathcal{X}_e\text{-covering}$$

$$(\Box\vee)\frac{\Phi, \Box\psi}{\bigvee_{i\in J_1}\pi_i, \Box\psi \mid \cdots \mid \bigvee_{i\in J_m}\pi_i, \Box\psi} \quad \text{if } J_1, \ldots, J_m \text{ is the collection of all minimal } \mathcal{X}_e\text{-covering of } \mathsf{TNF}(\Phi \wedge \psi)$$

$$(\Box\wedge)\frac{\bigvee_{i\in I}\pi_i, \Box\psi}{\pi_1, \bigcirc\Box\psi \ \& \ \ldots \ \& \ \pi_n, \bigcirc\Box\psi} \quad \text{if } I \text{ is a minimal } \mathcal{X}_e\text{-covering}$$

(a) Always Rules (where τ denotes $\mathsf{TNF}(\Phi \wedge \psi)$)

$$(\vee)\ \frac{\Phi, \beta \vee \gamma}{\Phi, \beta \mid \Phi, \gamma} \qquad (\wedge)\ \frac{\Phi, \beta \wedge \gamma}{\Phi, \beta, \gamma} \qquad (\ddot{\vee}\wedge)\ \frac{\Phi, (\eta \wedge (\beta \vee \gamma))\ddot{\vee}\delta}{\Phi, (\eta \wedge \beta)\ddot{\vee}(\eta \wedge \gamma)\ddot{\vee}\delta}$$

$$(\Diamond<)\ \frac{\Phi,\ \Diamond_{[n,m]}\beta}{\Phi,\ \bigcirc^n\beta \ \mid \ \Phi,\ \bigcirc\Diamond_{[n,m-1]}\beta} \quad \text{if } n < m$$

$$(\ddot{\vee}\Diamond<)\ \frac{\Phi,\ (\eta \wedge \Diamond_{[n,m]}\beta)\ddot{\vee}\delta}{\Phi,\ (\eta \wedge \bigcirc^n\beta)\ddot{\vee}(\eta \wedge \bigcirc\Diamond_{[n,m-1]}\beta\}\ddot{\vee}\delta} \quad \text{if } n < m$$

$$(\Diamond=)\ \frac{\Phi,\ \Diamond_{[n,n]}\beta}{\Phi,\ \bigcirc^n\beta} \qquad (\Box=)\ \frac{\Phi,\ \Box_{[n,n]}\beta}{\Phi,\ \bigcirc^n\beta} \qquad (\ddot{\vee}\Diamond=)\ \frac{\Phi,\ (\eta \wedge \Diamond_{[n,n]}\beta)\ddot{\vee}\delta}{\Phi,\ (\eta \wedge \bigcirc^n\beta)\ddot{\vee}\delta}$$

$$(\Box<)\ \frac{\Phi,\ \Box_{[n,m]}\beta}{\Phi,\ \bigcirc^n\beta,\ \bigcirc\Box_{[n,m-1]}\beta} \quad \text{if } n < m \qquad (\ddot{\vee}\Box=)\ \frac{\Phi,\ (\eta \wedge \Box_{[n,n]}\beta)\ddot{\vee}\delta}{\Phi,\ (\eta \wedge \bigcirc^n\beta)\ddot{\vee}\delta}$$

$$(\ddot{\vee}\Box<)\ \frac{\Phi,\ (\eta \wedge \Box_{[n,m]}\beta)\ddot{\vee}\delta}{\Phi,\ (\eta \wedge \bigcirc^n\beta \wedge \bigcirc\Box_{[n,m-1]}\beta)\ddot{\vee}\delta} \quad \text{if } n < m$$

(b) Saturation Rules

$$(\bigcirc)\frac{\Phi, \eta, \bigcirc\Box\psi}{\eta^{\downarrow}, \Box\psi} \quad \text{if } \Phi \cup \{\eta\} \text{ is elementary and } \eta \text{ is strict-future}$$

(c) Next-state Rule

Fig. 3. Realizability tableau rules

3.4 Tableau Rules

First, the *Always Rules* in Fig. 3(a) provides a non-deterministic procedure for analyzing the minimal $\mathcal{X}_e$-coverings in $\mathsf{TNF}(\Phi \wedge \psi)$ (see Definition 4 and Proposition 3). Rule $(\Box\wedge)$ is the only rule in our system that produces AND-successors, by splitting the cases of each minimal $\mathcal{X}_e$-covering. We introduce the rules that decompose formulas into their constituents, using saturation as usual in tableau methods. The decomposing of formulas inside the conjunctions connected by $\ddot{\vee}$ is just an unfolding in the formula. The *Saturation Rules* in Fig. 3(b) saturate with respect to $\wedge$ and $\vee$ (including $\ddot{\vee}$) and temporal operators $\Diamond_I$ and $\Box_I$. The following property of saturation rules is proved by routinely applying semantics.

Proposition 6. *For any saturation rule* $\frac{\Phi}{\Phi_1|\cdots|\Phi_k}$, *it holds that* $\sigma \models \Phi$ *if and only if* $\sigma \models \Phi_i$ *for some* $1 \leq i \leq k$.

Definition 9. *A next-formula is a formula whose first symbol is* $\bigcirc$. *A strict-future formula* $\ddot{\bigvee}_{i=1}^{n}\Delta_i$ *is elementary if every formula in the set* $\bigcup_{i=1}^{n}\Delta_i$ *is a next-formula.*

The successive application of the rules ($\ddot{\vee}\wedge$), ($\ddot{\vee}\Diamond <$), ($\ddot{\vee}\Diamond =$), ($\ddot{\vee}\Box <$) and ($\ddot{\vee}\Box =$) ensures the following proposition.

Proposition 7. *Given a strict-future formula* δ, *there is an elementary formula* δ^E *such that* $\delta \equiv \delta^E$ *and* δ^E *is in* DNF.

Definition 10. *A set* Δ *is* saturated *whenever for all* $\delta \in \Delta$ *the following hold:*

- *If* $\delta = \beta \wedge \gamma$, *then* $\{\beta, \gamma\} \in \Delta$. *If* $\delta = \beta \vee \gamma$, *then* $\beta \in \Delta$ *or* $\gamma \in \Delta$.
- *If* $\delta = \Box_{[n,m]}\beta$ *and* $n < m$, *then* $\{\bigcirc^n \beta, \bigcirc\Box_{[n,m-1]}\beta\} \subseteq \Delta$.
- *If* $\delta = \Diamond_{[n,m]}\beta$ *and* $n < m$, *then either* $\bigcirc^n \beta \in \Delta$ *or* $\bigcirc\Diamond_{[n,m-1]}\beta \in \Delta$
- *If* $\delta = \Box_{[n,n]}\beta$ *or* $\gamma = \Diamond_{[n,n]}\beta$, *then* $\bigcirc^n \beta \in \Delta$.
- *If* δ *is a strict-future formula, then* $\delta^E \in \Delta$

We use $\mathsf{Stt}(\Delta)$ *to denote the set of all (minimal) saturated sets that contains* Δ.

Proposition 8. *Let* Δ *be a set of formulas,* σ *a trace and* λ *a finite trace.*
- $\sigma \models \Delta$ *if and only if* $\sigma \models \Phi$ *for some* $\Phi \in \mathsf{Stt}(\Delta)$.
- $\lambda \models^{fin} \Delta$ *if and only if* $\lambda \models^{fin} \Phi$ *for some* $\Phi \in \mathsf{Stt}(\Delta)$.

By Proposition 2 and 8, we obtain the next result.

Proposition 9. *Let* Φ *be a set of safety formulas and let* $J_1, \ldots, J_m$ *be the collection of all minimal* $\mathcal{X}_e$*-coverings in* $\mathsf{TNF}(\Phi \wedge \psi) = \bigvee_{i \in I} \pi_i$. *Then*

(a) For any trace σ, $\sigma \models \Phi, \Box\psi$ *iff* $\sigma \models \pi_i, \bigcirc\Box\psi$ *holds for some* $i \in J_k$ *for each* $1 \leq k \leq m$. *Let* λ *be finite trace,* $\lambda \models^{fin} \Phi \wedge \psi$ *iff* $\lambda \models^{fin} \pi_i$ *for some* $i \in J_k$ *for each* $1 \leq k \leq m$.
(b) For any $1 \leq k \leq m$ *and any* $i \in J_k$ *the following two facts hold:*

(i) If $\mathsf{Incnst}(\Delta)$ *for all* $\Delta \in \mathsf{Stt}(\Phi \cup \{\pi_i\})$, *then every* $\lambda_0 \in \mathsf{Val}_\Delta(\mathcal{X}_e \cup \mathcal{Y})$ *is a witness of the violation of* $\Phi \wedge \Box\psi$.
(ii) Let $\Delta \in \mathsf{Stt}(\Phi \cup \{\pi_i\})$ *be s.t.* $\mathsf{Cnst}(\Delta)$. *Then,* $\lambda_0 \models^{fin} \Phi \wedge \psi$ *for every* $\lambda_0 \in \mathsf{Val}_\Delta(\mathcal{X}_e \cup \mathcal{Y})$.

Proposition 10 follows from the fact that, by Definition 4, there is some $v \in \mathsf{Val}(\mathcal{X}_e) \setminus \mathsf{Val}_{\Phi \wedge \psi}(\mathcal{X}_e)$.

Proposition 10. *Let* Φ *be a set of formulas. If* $\mathsf{TNF}(\Phi \wedge \psi)$ *is not an* $\mathcal{X}_e$*-covering, then there is a* $v \in \mathsf{Val}(\mathcal{X}_e)$ *s.t. for all* $v' \in \mathsf{Val}(\mathcal{Y})$, $v + v' \not\models^{fin} \Phi \wedge \psi$.

Proposition 11. *Let Φ be a set of formulas, $\mathsf{TNF}(\Phi \wedge \psi) = \bigvee_{i \in I} \pi_i$ be an $\mathcal{X}_e$-covering and $J_1, \ldots, J_m$ be the collection of all minimal $\mathcal{X}_e$-coverings in I. If for every $1 \leq k \leq m$ there exists some $i \in J_k$ such that $\mathsf{Incnst}(\Delta)$ for all $\Delta \in \mathsf{Stt}(\pi_i)$, then there exists some $v \in \mathsf{Val}(\mathcal{X}_e)$ such that for all $v' \in \mathsf{Val}(\mathcal{Y})$, $v + v' \not\models^{fin} \Phi \wedge \psi$.*

Finally, the tableau rules also include the *Next-state rule* in Fig. 3(c). This rule is used to generate a new tableau node, that is to jump from a temporal position to the next. Its formalization is based on the following definitions.

Definition 11. *Given an elementary strict-future formula $\eta = \ddot{\bigvee}_{i=1}^{n} \bigwedge_{j=1}^{m} \bigcirc \beta_{i,j}$, the formula $\eta^{\downarrow}$ is $\ddot{\bigvee}_{i=1}^{n} \bigwedge_{j=1}^{m} \beta_{i,j}$.*

Example 3. Consider the strict-future formula $\delta = \Diamond_{[1,2]} a \ \ddot{\vee} \ \Box_{[1,3]} b$. Then, $\delta^E = \bigcirc a \ \ddot{\vee} \ \bigcirc \Diamond_{[1,1]} a \ \ddot{\vee} \ (\bigcirc b \wedge \bigcirc \Box_{[1,2]} b)$ and $\delta^{E\downarrow} = a \ddot{\vee} \ \Diamond_{[1,1]} a \ddot{\vee} (b \wedge \Box_{[1,2]} b)$. Note that the only effect of $\downarrow$ is to remove the $\bigcirc$-operators in each term of δ^E.

Definition 12. *A set of formulas Φ is elementary if it consists of a set of literals and one elementary strict-future formula.*

Basically, the application of the *Next-state rule* to an elementary set that labels a node, removes all literals and removes the $\bigcirc$-operators (in each term) from the single elementary strict-future formula.

Proposition 12. *Let $\Phi \cup \{\eta\}$ be a consistent and elementary set of formulas with strict-future formula η. Then, (a) For any trace σ, if $\sigma \models \Phi, \eta, \bigcirc \Box \psi$ then $\sigma^1 \models \eta^{\downarrow}, \Box \psi$; (b) let $\lambda = \lambda_0, \ldots \lambda_{k-1}$ be a pre-witness of $\alpha \wedge \Box \psi$ s.t. $\lambda_{k-1} \models^{fin} \Phi$, and let $\lambda_k \in \mathsf{Val}(\mathcal{X}_e \cup \mathcal{Y})$. Then, $\lambda \cdot \lambda_k$ is a pre-witness of $\alpha \wedge \Box \psi$ iff $\lambda_k \models^{fin} \eta^{\downarrow} \wedge \psi$.*

3.5 A Tableau Algorithm for Realizability

Algorithm 1 provides a decision procedure for realizability. The algorithm constructs completed tableau by expanding the minimal $\mathcal{X}_e$-coverings produced by the moves (and allowed by the input safety specification) at successive positions. Algorithm 1 uses recursion to explore in-depth the branches of the tree. The formal parameter is given as the union of a set of formulas Φ and a formula χ that ranges in $\{\Box \psi, \bigcirc \Box \psi\}$. For deciding realizability of a safety specification $\varphi = \alpha \wedge \Box \psi$, the initial call $\mathsf{Tab}(\varphi)$ is really $\mathsf{Tab}(\{\alpha, \Box \psi\})$. Intuitively, player E moves when $\chi = \Box \psi$ (including at the start), whereas S moves when $\chi = \bigcirc \Box \psi$.

Algorithm 1: $\mathsf{Tab}(\Phi \cup \{\chi\})$ returns *is_open*: Boolean

if Φ *is inconsistent* **then** *is_open* := *False* **else if** $\chi = \Box\psi$ **then**
  if $\Phi_0 \lessdot \Phi$ *for some* Φ_0 *in the branch of* Φ **then**
    is_open := *True*
  else if $\mathsf{TNF}(\Phi \wedge \psi)$ *is not an* $\mathcal{X}_e$*-covering* **then**
    is_open := $\mathsf{Tab}(\{\mathrm{F}, \Box\psi\})$;
  else if $\mathsf{TNF}(\Phi \wedge \psi)$ *is a non-minimal* $\mathcal{X}_e$*-covering* **then**
    Let $J_1, \ldots, J_m$ be all the minimal $\mathcal{X}_e$-coverings of $\mathsf{TNF}(\Phi \wedge \psi)$;
    i, *is_open* := 0, *False*;
    while $\neg$*is_open* $\wedge\, i < m$ **do**
      i, *is_open* := $i+1$, $\mathsf{Tab}(J_i \cup \{\Box\psi\})$;
  else // $\mathsf{TNF}(\Phi \wedge \psi) = \bigvee_{i=1}^{n} \pi_i$ is a minimal $\mathcal{X}_e$-covering
    i, *is_open* := 0, *True*;
    while *is_open* $\wedge\, i < n$ **do**
      i, *is_open* := $i+1$, $\mathsf{Tab}(\{\pi_i, \bigcirc\Box\psi\})$;
else if $\Phi = \Lambda \cup \{\eta\}$ *is elementary* (η *is strict-future*) **then**
  is_open := $\mathsf{Tab}(\{\eta^{\downarrow}, \Box\psi\})$;
else
  ρ := *select_saturation_rule*(Φ);
  Let $1 \le k \le 2$ and $\Phi_1, \ldots, \Phi_k$ the set of all ρ-children;
  is_open := $\mathsf{Tab}(\Phi_1 \cup \{\bigcirc\Box\psi\})$;
  if $k = 2 \wedge \neg$*is_open* **then**
    is_open := $\mathsf{Tab}(\Phi_2 \cup \{\bigcirc\Box\psi\})$

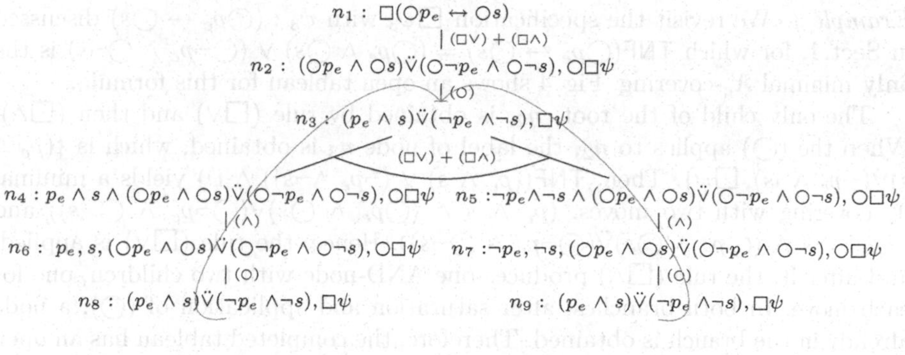

Fig. 4. Open tableau for $\Box(\bigcirc p_e \leftrightarrow \bigcirc s)$.

Definition 13. *A branch b of a tableau is a sequence of nodes $n_0, \ldots, n_k$ such that n_0 is the root and $(n_i, n_{i+1}) \in R$ for $0 \le i < k-1$. If n_k is a successful leaf, then b is called a successful branch. If n_k is a failure leaf, then b is called a failure branch.*

Algorithm 1 returns the Boolean variable *is_open*, which corresponds to whether the completed tableau for the call parameter $\Phi \cup \{\chi\}$ is open or closed. Lines 1–4 deal with the simple cases of the recursion. Line 6 produces a recursive call that immediately returns failure. A tableau is called *completed* when all its branches contain a terminal node, i.e., all its branches are failure or successful. Recursive calls in Algorithm 1 and the notions of open and closed tableaux are related to AND-nodes, for which we introduce the following definition.

Definition 14. *A set of branches H of a completed tableau is called a* bunch *whenever for every $b \in H$, every AND-node $n \in b$, and every n' that is an ($\Box\wedge$)-successor of n, there is $b' \in H$ such that $n' \in b'$. A completed tableau is* open *when it contains at least one* bunch *with all its branches successful. Otherwise, the tableau is* closed.

Algorithm 1 looks for bunches of successful branches as follows. Lines 7–11 of Algorithm 1 invoke a recursive call for each minimal $\mathcal{X}_e$-covering, according to rule ($\Box\vee$). When some of these calls return *is_open* for a minimal $\mathcal{X}_e$-covering J_i, which is an OR-node, the iteration is finished with this result for the previous call. The construction of the tableau for each J_k, by the rule ($\Box\wedge$) and according to lines 12–15, produces a call for each move π_i in J_k. Moves are AND-children, hence all the calls should give *is_open* to obtain truth for J_k. Finally, lines 16–17 perform the application of ($\bigcirc$), and lines 18–23 apply the saturation rules. When one rule is applied, the second child is expanded only if the first child returns not *is_open*.

Proposition 13. *Algorithm 1 terminates and* $\mathsf{Tab}(\varphi)$ *builds a completed tableau.*

Example 4. We revisit the specification $\Box\psi_3$ with $\psi_3 : (\bigcirc p_e \leftrightarrow \bigcirc s)$ discussed in Sect. 1, for which $\mathsf{TNF}(\bigcirc p_e \leftrightarrow \bigcirc s) = (\bigcirc p_e \wedge \bigcirc s) \vee (\bigcirc\neg p_e \wedge \bigcirc\neg s)$ is the only minimal $\mathcal{X}_e$-covering. Fig. 4 shows an open tableau for this formula.

The only child of the root, n_2, is obtained by rule ($\Box\vee$) and then ($\Box\wedge$). When the ($\bigcirc$) applies to n_2, the label of node n_3 is obtained, which is $\{(p_e \wedge s)\ddot{\vee}(\neg p_e \wedge\neg s), \Box\psi\}$. Then, $\mathsf{TNF}((p_e \wedge s) \vee (\neg p_e \wedge\neg s)) \wedge \psi)$ yields a minimal $\mathcal{X}_e$-covering with two moves: $(p_e \wedge s \wedge (\bigcirc p_e \wedge \bigcirc s)\ddot{\vee}(\bigcirc\neg p_e \wedge \bigcirc\neg s))$ and $(\neg p_e \wedge\neg s \wedge (\bigcirc p_e \wedge \bigcirc s)\ddot{\vee}(\bigcirc\neg p_e \wedge \bigcirc\neg s))$. Hence, the rule ($\Box\vee$) is applied, and after it, the rule ($\Box\wedge$) produces one AND-node with two children, one for each move. In both branches, after saturation and application of ($\bigcirc$), a node already in the branch is obtained. Therefore, the completed tableau has an open bunch and the specification is realizable. More examples can be found in [19].

Correctness. For any given specification φ, it holds that φ is realizable if and only if the completed tableau $\mathsf{Tab}(\varphi)$ is open. We formally prove this statement by defining a new class of games (a variation of safety games) called a safety tableau-game $\mathcal{T}(\varphi)$ where players E and S play with game rules that correspond to the tableau rules. Then we connect winning strategies for S in $\mathsf{Tab}(\varphi)$ with winning strategies for S in $\mathcal{T}(\varphi)$. The full proof is in [19].

4 Conclusions

We have introduced the first tableau method to decide realizability of temporal safety formulas. Our tableau method allows to synthesize a system when the specification is realizable because a (memoryless) winning strategy for the system can be extracted from an open tableau (the technical details of synthesizing the system is out of the scope of this paper and how to efficiently extract and encode this strategy is ongoing work).

Our tableau method is based on the novel notion of terse normal form (TNF) of formulas that is crucial in the formulation of the realizability tableau. The tableau rules make use of the terse normal form to precisely capture the information that each player (environment and system) has to reveal at each step. We have proved soundness and completeness of the proposed method.

Future work includes the implementation of the method presented in this paper and to experiment with the resulting prototype in a collection of benchmarks. We would ultimately like to compare an efficient implementation of the realizability tableau with mature tools from the SYNTCOMP competition.

We also plan to extend the method to more expressive languages, including the handling of richer propositions (like numeric variables and expressions) by combining realizability tableau rules with tableau reasoning capabilities for these domains. We have illustrated this path in this paper by the introduction of enumerated types. Another interesting extension is a deeper analysis, including new rules, to handle upper and lower bounds of intervals in temporal operators, for example to accelerate a branch to reach the lower bound a of an $\Box_{[a,b]}$ operator. We would like to ultimately extend our tableau method to richer fragments of LTL.

Finally, future work includes a precise analysis of the complexity of the realizability tableau and its different instances.

References

1. https://syntcomp.org
2. Beth. The Foundation of Mathematics. North-Holland (1959)
3. Bloem, R., Jobstmann, B., Piterman, N., Pnueli, A., Sa'ar, Y.: Synthesis of reactive(1) designs. J. Comput. Syst. Sci. **78**(3), 911–938 (2012)
4. Bloem, R., Könighofer, R., Seidl, M.: SAT-based synthesis methods for safety specs. In: McMillan, K.L., Rival, X. (eds.) VMCAI 2014. LNCS, vol. 8318, pp. 1–20. Springer, Heidelberg (2014). https://doi.org/10.1007/978-3-642-54013-4_1
5. Bohy, A., Bruyère, V., Filiot, E., Jin, N., Raskin, C.: Jean-Fran Acacia+, a tool for LTL synthesis. In: Proceedings of CAV 2012, LNCS, vol. 7358, pp. 652–657. Springer, Cham (2012)
6. Brenguier, R., Perez, G.A., Raskin, J.F., Sankur, O.: AbsSynthe: abstract synthesis from succinct safety specifications. In: Proceedings of the 3rd Workshop in Synthehsis (SYNT'14), EPTCS, vol. 157, pp. 100–116 (2014)
7. Büchi, J.R., Landweber, L.H.: Solving sequential conditions by finite-state strategies. Trans. Am. Math. Soc. **138** (1969)

8. De Wulf, M., Doyen, L., Maquet, N., Raskin, J.-F.: Alaska. In: Cha, S.S., Choi, J.-Y., Kim, M., Lee, I., Viswanathan, M. (eds.) ATVA 2008. LNCS, vol. 5311, pp. 240–245. Springer, Heidelberg (2008). https://doi.org/10.1007/978-3-540-88387-6_21
9. D'ippolito, N., Braberman, V., Piterman, N., Uchitel, S.: Synthesizing nonanomalous event-based controllers for liveness goals. ACM Trans. Softw. Eng. Methodol. **22**(1), 1–36 (2013)
10. Ehlers, R.: Unbeast: symbolic bounded synthesis. In: Abdulla, P.A., Leino, K.R.M. (eds.) TACAS 2011. LNCS, vol. 6605, pp. 272–275. Springer, Heidelberg (2011). https://doi.org/10.1007/978-3-642-19835-9_25
11. Finkbeiner, B.: Bounded synthesis for Petri games. In: Meyer, R., Platzer, A., Wehrheim, H. (eds.) Correct System Design. LNCS, vol. 9360, pp. 223–237. Springer, Cham (2015). https://doi.org/10.1007/978-3-319-23506-6_15
12. Finkbeiner, B., Jacobs, S.: Lazy synthesis. In: Kuncak, V., Rybalchenko, A. (eds.) VMCAI 2012. LNCS, vol. 7148, pp. 219–234. Springer, Heidelberg (2012). https://doi.org/10.1007/978-3-642-27940-9_15
13. Finkbeiner, B., Klein, F.: Bounded cycle synthesis. In: Chaudhuri, S., Farzan, A. (eds.) CAV 2016. LNCS, vol. 9779, pp. 118–135. Springer, Cham (2016). https://doi.org/10.1007/978-3-319-41528-4_7
14. Finkbeiner, B., Schewe, S.: SMT-based synthesis of distributed systems. In: Proceedings of the 2nd Workshop on Automated Formal Methods (AFM 2007), pp. 69–76. ACM (2007)
15. Finkbeiner, B., Schewe, S.: Bounded synthesis. Int. J. Softw. Tools Technol. Transf. **15**(5–6), 519–539 (2013). https://doi.org/10.1007/s10009-012-0228-z
16. Finkbeiner, B., Tentrup, L.: Detecting unrealizable specifications of distributed systems. In: Ábrahám, E., Havelund, K. (eds.) TACAS 2014. LNCS, vol. 8413, pp. 78–92. Springer, Heidelberg (2014). https://doi.org/10.1007/978-3-642-54862-8_6
17. Gaintzarain, J., Hermo, M., Lucio, P., Navarro, M., Orejas, F.: Dual systems of tableaux and sequents for PLTL. J. Logic Algebraic Program. **78**(8), 701–722 (2009)
18. Goré, R., Widmann, F.: An optimal on-the-fly tableau-based decision procedure for PDL-satisfiability. In: Schmidt, R.A. (ed.) CADE 2009. LNCS (LNAI), vol. 5663, pp. 437–452. Springer, Heidelberg (2009). https://doi.org/10.1007/978-3-642-02959-2_32
19. Hermo, M., Lucio, P., Sánchez, C.: A tableau method for the realizability and synthesis of reactive safety specifications (2022). arXiv. https://arxiv.org/abs/2206.01492
20. Jacobs, S., et al.: The 4th reactive synthesis competition (SYNTCOMP 2017): benchmarks, participants & results. In: Proceedings of the 6th Workshop on Synthesis (SYNT@CAV 2017), EPTCS, vol. 260, pp. 116–143 (2017)
21. Jobstmann, B., Galler, S., Weiglhofer, M., Bloem, R.: Anzu: a tool for property synthesis. In: Damm, W., Hermanns, H. (eds.) CAV 2007. LNCS, vol. 4590, pp. 258–262. Springer, Heidelberg (2007). https://doi.org/10.1007/978-3-540-73368-3_29
22. Khalimov, A., Jacobs, S., Bloem, R.: Towards efficient parameterized synthesis. In: Giacobazzi, R., Berdine, J., Mastroeni, I. (eds.) VMCAI 2013. LNCS, vol. 7737, pp. 108–127. Springer, Heidelberg (2013). https://doi.org/10.1007/978-3-642-35873-9_9
23. Kress-Gazit, H., Fainekos, G.E., Pappas, G.J.: Temporal-logic-based reactive mission and motion planning. IEEE Trans. Rob. **25**, 1370–1381 (2009)

24. Luttenberger, M., Meyer, P.J., Sickert, S.: Practical synthesis of reactive systems from LTL specifications via parity games. Acta Informatica **57**(1–2), 3–36 (2020). https://doi.org/10.1007/s00236-019-00349-3
25. Meyer, P.J., Sickert, S., Luttenberger, M.: Strix: explicit reactive synthesis strikes back! In: Chockler, H., Weissenbacher, G. (eds.) CAV 2018. LNCS, vol. 10981, pp. 578–586. Springer, Cham (2018). https://doi.org/10.1007/978-3-319-96145-3_31
26. Piterman, N., Pnueli, A., Sa'ar, Y.: Synthesis of reactive(1) designs. In: Emerson, E.A., Namjoshi, K.S. (eds.) VMCAI 2006. LNCS, vol. 3855, pp. 364–380. Springer, Heidelberg (2005). https://doi.org/10.1007/11609773_24
27. Pnueli, A.: The temporal logic of programs. In: Proceedings of the 18th IEEE Symposium on Foundations of Computer Science (FOCS 1977), pp. 46–67. IEEE CS Press (1977)
28. Pnueli, A., Rosner, R.: On the synthesis of a reactive module. In: Proceedings of POPL 1989, pp. 179–190. ACM (1989)
29. Pnueli, A., Rosner, R.: On the synthesis of an asynchronous reactive module. In: Ausiello, G., Dezani-Ciancaglini, M., Della Rocca, S.R. (eds.) ICALP 1989. LNCS, vol. 372, pp. 652–671. Springer, Heidelberg (1989). https://doi.org/10.1007/BFb0035790
30. Schewe, S., Finkbeiner, B.: Bounded synthesis. In: Namjoshi, K.S., Yoneda, T., Higashino, T., Okamura, Y. (eds.) ATVA 2007. LNCS, vol. 4762, pp. 474–488. Springer, Heidelberg (2007). https://doi.org/10.1007/978-3-540-75596-8_33
31. Schwendimann, S.: A new one-pass tableau calculus for **PLTL**. In: de Swart, H. (ed.) TABLEAUX 1998. LNCS (LNAI), vol. 1397, pp. 277–291. Springer, Heidelberg (1998). https://doi.org/10.1007/3-540-69778-0_28
32. Shimakawa, M., Hagihara, S., Yonezaki, N.: Reducing bounded realizability analysis to reachability checking. In: Bojańczyk, M., Lasota, S., Potapov, I. (eds.) RP 2015. LNCS, vol. 9328, pp. 140–152. Springer, Cham (2015). https://doi.org/10.1007/978-3-319-24537-9_13
33. Smullyan, R.M.: First-Order Logic. Springer-Verlag, Cham (1968)
34. Vardi, M.Y., Wolper, P.: Reasoning about infinite computations. Inf. Comput. **115**(1), 1–37 (1994)
35. Wolper, P.: The tableau method for temporal logic: an overview. Logique et Anal. (N.S.) **28**, 119–136 (1985)

A Decision Diagram Operation for Reachability

Sebastiaan Brand(✉), Thomas Bäck, and Alfons Laarman

Leiden Institute of Advanced Computer Science,
Leiden University, Leiden, The Netherlands
{s.o.brand,t.h.w.baeck,
a.w.laarman}@liacs.leidenuniv.nl

Abstract. Saturation is considered the state-of-the-art method for computing fixpoints with decision diagrams. We present a relatively simple decision diagram operation called Reach that also computes fixpoints. In contrast to saturation, it does not require a partitioning of the transition relation. We give sequential algorithms implementing the new operation for both binary and multi-valued decision diagrams, and moreover provide parallel counterparts. We implement these algorithms and experimentally compare their performance against saturation on 692 model checking benchmarks in different languages. The results show that the Reach operation often outperforms saturation, especially on transition relations with low locality. In a comparison between parallelized versions of Reach and saturation we find that Reach obtains comparable speedups up to 16 cores, although falls behind saturation at 64 cores. Finally, in a comparison with the state-of-the-art model checking tool ITS-tools we find that Reach outperforms ITS-tools on 29% of models, suggesting that Reach can be useful as a complementary method in an ensemble tool.

Keywords: Model checking · Reachability · Saturation · Decision diagrams · BDDs · MDDs

1 Introduction

Reachability Analysis. Model checking is an important technique for ensuring that systems work according to specification. A core task in model checking is reachability analysis [8,18], i.e., computing forward or backward reachable states of a system. Typically, the state space of a program grows exponentially with the number of variables and threads. One method for dealing with this explosion is the use of symbolic methods such as decision diagrams. Decision diagrams [12] are directed, acyclic graphs that succinctly represent sets of states by leveraging the exponential growth in paths from a dedicated root node to a leaf. The data structure provides various efficient manipulation operations, such as logical disjunction and conjunction and image computation.

In this work, we present a new decision diagram operation for reachability.

M. Chechik et al. (Eds.): FM 2023, LNCS 14000, pp. 514–532, 2023.
https://doi.org/10.1007/978-3-031-27481-7_29

Related Work. While SAT-based methods for model checking have become increasingly popular, doing reachability analysis with decision diagrams is still an important component of many state-of-the-art model checking tools, as can be seen in the Model Checking Contest (MCC) [30,40]. Symbolic reachability analysis with binary decision diagrams (BDDs) and other variants [6,20,27,41] is done by encoding both the initial system state S_{init} and its transition relation R in the diagram. The set of reachable states S is then iteratively computed using the image operation [33], denoted by $S.R$, starting from S_{init}. Since the order of exploration (e.g. breadth-first search, depth-first search, or other strategies) greatly influences the sizes of the intermediate decision diagrams, various exploration strategies, like saturation [16], chaining [36], and sweep-line [15], have been considered. These algorithms have in common the use of the image computation $S.R$ as their main operation.

Saturation stands out from other approaches, not only because it often performs better [17] and leading MCC tools use it in decision diagram based reachability [40], but also because it integrates the image computations into the traversal of the decision diagram of S. Saturation avoids redundant reconstructions by building the decision diagram for the reachable states bottom-up, eagerly *saturating* the bottom nodes by exhaustively applying all relevant transitions.

Contribution. We present three new decision diagram operations for reachability: ReachBdd and ReachMdd (for BDDs and MDDs respectively), as well as a parallel version of ReachBdd. These algorithms partially construct the decision diagram of S from the bottom up, but unlike saturation do not require partial relations and can handle monolithic transition relations. An additional advantage of these new reachability operations is their relative simplicity in comparison with saturation.

We implement these new operations in the decision diagram package Sylvan [21], and experimentally compare them against saturation on a total of 692 problem instances from three model checking benchmark sets: DVE (BEEM [35]), Petri nets (MCC [31]), and Promela models [7,26]. We find that our methods are competitive with saturation, and tend to outperform saturation on larger instances. The parallel speedups obtained by ReachBdd up to 16 cores are comparable to those achieved in a parallel version of saturation [22], although they fall behind on 64 cores. Aside from the comparison against saturation, we also compare ReachMdd against the state-of-the-art model checking tool ITS-tools [40], where we find that ReachMdd performs better than ITS-tools on 29% of models, and can therefore be useful as a complementary method in an ensemble tool.

Outline. Section 2 discusses preliminaries. Section 3 explains the new reachability algorithms, and is then followed by an empirical evaluation of these algorithms in Sect. 4. Finally, Sect. 5 concludes this work.

2 Preliminaries

2.1 Binary Decision Diagrams

Binary decision diagrams (BDDs) [12,38] are a data structure for representing Boolean functions $f(x_1, \ldots, x_n)$, i.e., functions of type $f : \{0,1\}^n \to \{0,1\}$. Structurally, a BDD is a rooted, directed, acyclic graph with two types of nodes: terminal nodes with values $\{0,1\}$ and non-terminal nodes v that have two children, $v[0]$ (*low*) and $v[1]$ (*high*), and a variable label $\mathsf{var}(v) \in \{1, \ldots, n\} = [n]$, indexing into $\{x_i\}_{i \in [n]}$. Figure 1 shows examples of *ordered* BDDs, i.e., BDDs where on each path variable labels occur in a fixed order $x_1 < x_2 < \cdots < x_n$.

A non-terminal node v with $\mathsf{var}(v) = i$, shown right, can be read as the *Shannon decomposition "if $x_i = 1$ then $v[1]$ else $v[0]$."* The function represented by the node v, call it f^v, is thus given by

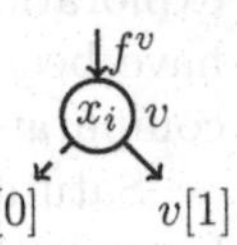

$$f^v(x_1, \ldots, x_n) \triangleq \begin{cases} x_i f^{v[1]} \vee \overline{x_i} f^{v[0]} & \text{if } v \notin \{0,1\}, \\ v & \text{if } v \in \{0,1\}. \end{cases} \tag{1}$$

The definition in Eq. 1 shows that a conditioned subfunction $f^v_{|\vec{a}}$, as in Eq. 2 below, is represented by a decision diagram node, namely the one following the path $v[\vec{a}] \triangleq v[a_1][a_2] \ldots [a_k]$, assuming the BDD is ordered and no variables are skipped.

$$f^v_{|a_1, \ldots, a_k}(x_1, \ldots, x_n) \triangleq f^v(x_1 = a_1, \ldots, x_k = a_k, x_{k+1}, \ldots, x_n) \tag{2}$$

The insight that BDDs exploit to realize succinct representations of commonly-encountered Boolean functions is that many subfunctions for different $\vec{a}, \vec{b} \in \{0,1\}^*$ can be isotropic, i.e., $f_{|\vec{a}} = f_{|\vec{b}}$. Take $f_{|00} = f_{|11}$ in Fig. 1a. In the diagram, this means that the isomorphic subgraphs below the nodes representing $f_{|00}$ and $f_{|11}$ can be merged, as in Fig. 1c.

An ordered BDD is *reduced* when, in addition to isomorphic sub-graph merging, all *redundant nodes* (nodes v with $v[0] = v[1]$) are removed. Take

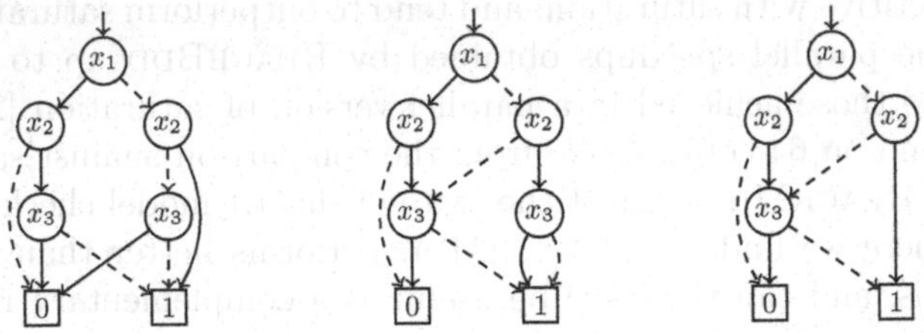

Fig. 1. (Ordered) BDDs representing function $f = (x_1 \wedge x_2 \wedge \overline{x_3}) \vee (\overline{x_1} \wedge \overline{x_2} \wedge \overline{x_3}) \vee (\overline{x_1} \wedge x_2)$. For node v, we draw $\mathsf{var}(v) = i$ as x_i. Dashed lines lines represent low branches ($v[0]$) and solid lines high branches ($v[1]$). Only the BDD in (c) is completely reduced. The BDD in (a) can be reduced to (c) by merging the two isomorphic nodes for x_3, while the BDD in (b) can be reduced to (c) by removing the (right-most) redundant node x_3.

$f_{|010} = f_{|011} = f_{|01} = 1$, in Fig. 1c. Removed redundant nodes can be reconstructed by recognizing that a variable is skipped on a path, as done Fig. 1b.

Reduced and ordered BDDs (ROBDDs) are canonical representations of Boolean functions, i.e., any two functions with the same truth table are uniquely represented by (the root node of) an ROBDD. Canonicity allows for equivalence checking in constant time through hashing of nodes v as tuples $\langle \mathsf{var}(v), v[1], v[0]\rangle$ (provided that nodes $v[1]$,$v[0]$ are already canonically represented, i.e., the BDD is build in a bottom-up fashion). This in turn allows efficient manipulation operations ($\wedge, \vee, \ldots$) as discussed below.

In this text, we fix the variable order $x_1 < x_2 < \cdots < x_n$. For conciseness, we will often consider quasi-ROBDD, which are ROBDDs where all redundant nodes are reconstructed (e.g. Fig. 1b). In many settings, this stronger definition does not lose generality, as quasi-ROBDD are also canonical, and at most a factor $\frac{n}{2}$ larger than an ROBDD for the same function [29]. At the same time, because for all quasi-ROBDD nodes v we have $f^v_{\vec{a}} = v[\vec{a}]$, this assumption greatly simplifies algorithm representation and reduces cases in proofs. We denote with *level* i the set of all nodes with the variable label i.

2.2 Multi-valued Decision Diagrams

Multi-valued decision diagrams (MDDs) [27,37] are a generalization of BDDs for encoding functions $\mathcal{D}_1 \times \cdots \times \mathcal{D}_n \to \{0,1\}$, where $\mathcal{D}_i = \{0,1,\ldots,m-1\}$ for some m and all i. Each MDD node with variable x_i has m outgoing edges, each with a label in $\mathcal{D}_i$. The interpretation of following an edge remains the same as for BDDs: for an MDD which encodes a function f and has root node v with $\mathsf{var}(v) = i$, following an edge with label $a \in \mathcal{D}_i$ leads to an MDD which encodes the sub-function $f|_{x_i=a}$.

Similar to BDDs, MDDs are typically reduced by merging isomorphic subgraphs. However, unlike ROBDDs, redundant nodes are usually not removed in MDDs, which means variables are never skipped on any path. So an MDD with $m = 2$ is a Quasi-ROBDD. Figure 2 shows an example.

A list decision diagram (LDD) [9] is the Knuth transform of an MDD into a left-child right-sibling binary tree. Siblings (right-ward chains) are stored as

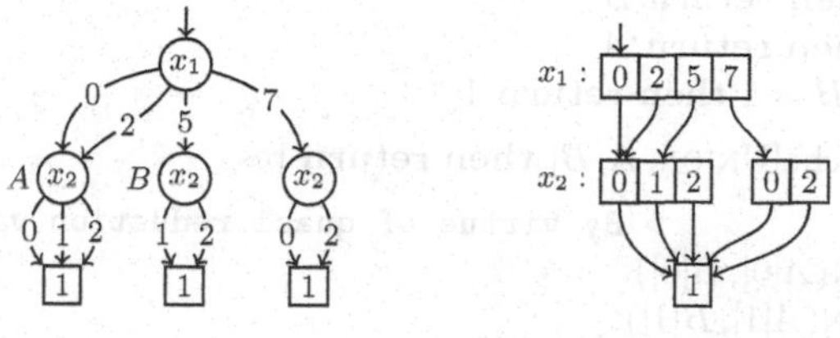

Fig. 2. An MDD (left) and LDD (right) which both encode the set $\{\langle 0,0\rangle, \langle 0,1\rangle, \langle 0,2\rangle, \langle 2,0\rangle, \langle 2,1\rangle, \langle 2,2\rangle, \langle 5,1\rangle, \langle 5,2\rangle, \langle 7,0\rangle, \langle 7,2\rangle\}$. Arrays represent right-ward sibling chains in the LDD. To improve legibility, we omit edges pointing to the 0 terminal and replicate the 1 terminal for MDDs.

(ordered) linked lists, which allows the reuse of common sibling suffixes, as shown in the example in Fig. 2 (e.g. $f_{|5}$ reuses a part of the siblings of $f_{|2} = f_{|0}$).

Finally, a BDD or MDD representing a function $f(x_1, \ldots, x_n)$ can also be interpreted as a set of strings $\vec{a}$ of length n, according to the characteristic function $\{\vec{a} \mid f(\vec{a}) = 1\}$. So the BDDs in Fig. 1 all represent $\{000, 010, 011, 110\}$.

2.3 Decision Diagram Operations

What makes BDDs and MDDs so useful, aside from their possible succinctness, is that many manipulation operations, such as disjunction (set union) and conjunction (set intersection), can be performed in polynomial time in the number of decision diagram nodes in the operands [3,12]. While other operations that have been shown to be NP-complete [33], such as unbounded existential quantification and thus also image computation [33], are often still efficient in practice [13].

As an example, the algorithm below computes the union of two quasi-reduced diagrams A and B, i.e., $A \cup B$ (or in the functional interpretation: $A \vee B$). Because any BDD is defined by its root node, the arguments A and B are simply given as nodes. The algorithm first considers leafs as a base case, treating them according to the semantics of $\vee$. On line 7 and 8, the function is called recursively on the children of the input BDDs, synchronizing on the low and high branches. The results from these recursive calls are then combined with the MAKENODE(x, L, H) function which creates a *reduced BDD node* v with $v[0] = L$, $v[1] = H$ and $\mathsf{var}(v) = x$. To ensure reduction, it returns L $(= H)$ when the node is redundant and looks up the tuple $\langle x, L, H \rangle$ in a *unique table*, as discussed in Sect. 2.1. For MDDs, we assume a function MAKENODE$(x, A_0, \ldots, A_{m-1})$ which returns a (quasi-)reduced MDD node and, for notational convenience, takes $m+1$ positional arguments: a variable x, and one MDD node A_i for each of its m children (some of which can be 0).

Lastly, it is important to realize that a decision diagram with $|V|$ nodes can have $\exp(|V|)$ paths from the root to a terminal node. To achieve polynomial runtimes, decision diagram operations use top-down dynamic programming (see

```
1  def UNION(A, B) :                 ▷ For quasi-ROBDDs A and B on n variables.
2      if A = 0 then return B
3      if B = 0 then return A
4      if A = 1 ∨ B = 1 then return 1
5      if res ← cache[UNION, A, B] then return res
6      x ← var(A)                    ▷ By virtue of quasi reduction var(A) = var(B).
7      L ← UNION(A[0], B[0])
8      H ← UNION(A[1], B[1])
9      res ← MAKENODE(x, L, H)
10     cache[UNION, A, B] ← res
11     return res
```

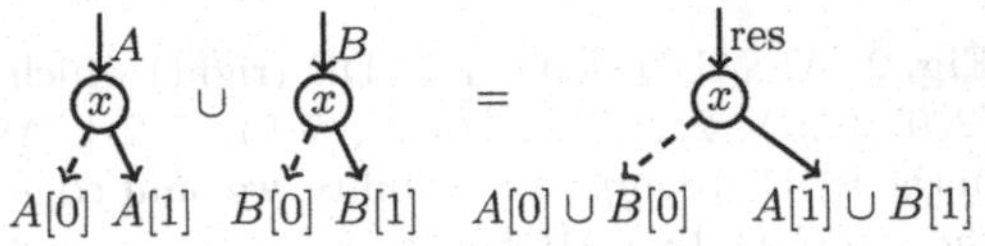

line 5, 10). This ensures that different paths leading to the same (pairs of) nodes are caught by the cache, avoiding recomputation.

2.4 Encoding Symbolic Transition Systems

A symbolic transition system is a tuple $(\vec{x}, \mathbb{S}, R, S_{\text{init}})$, where $\vec{x}$ is a tuple of Boolean variables $(x_1, \ldots, x_n)$, $\mathbb{S} = \{0,1\}^n$ is the state space (including unreachable states), $R \subseteq \mathbb{S} \times \mathbb{S}'$ is a transition relation, and $S_{\text{init}} \subseteq \mathbb{S}$ is a set of initial states. The relation R is a constraint over variables $\vec{x}, \vec{x}'$, where $\vec{x}$ encodes the source states and $\vec{x}'$ (consisting of primed copies of $\vec{x}$) encodes target states. While R monolithically encodes the system's behavior, we also consider a local variant, discussed in the example which follows.

As an example we give a transition system which captures the dining philosophers problem. We have k processes (philosophers) and k resources (forks). Each process P_i, with $i \in \{1, \ldots, k\}$, attempts to allocate two resources: a fork i on the left and a fork $j = ((i-1) \bmod k) + 1$ on the right. If a fork is unavailable the philosopher waits until it becomes available. To describe the state space we use $3k$ Boolean variables: $\vec{x} = (a_1, l_1, r_1, \ldots, a_k, l_k, r_k)$, where a_i ($\overline{a_i}$) indicates fork i is (not) available, l_i ($\overline{l_i}$) indicates philosopher i does (not) hold a fork in their left hand, and r_i ($\overline{r_i}$) idem for their right hand. The starting state $S_{\text{init}} = (a_1, \overline{l_1}, \overline{r_1}, \ldots, a_k, \overline{l_k}, \overline{r_k}.)$

To define R_i for $k > 1$ processes, we define three local relations R_i^m that implement picking up and putting down the left/right fork, and eating.

$$R_i^1 = (a_i \oplus a_i') \wedge (l_i \oplus l_i') \qquad \triangleright \texttt{ pick up / put down left}$$
$$R_i^2 = (r_i \oplus r_i') \wedge (a_j \oplus a_j') \qquad \triangleright \texttt{ pick up / put down right}$$
$$R_i^3 = l_i \wedge l_i' \wedge r_i \wedge r_i' \qquad \triangleright \texttt{ eat (hold on to both forks)}$$

Let $\mathsf{support}(R_i^m)$ be the set of (primed and unprimed) variables in R_i^m. Notice that the support of each local relation contains a different subset of the target variables $\vec{x}'$. To ensure that the other target variables are not left unconstrained, we need to add the constraint $x \Leftrightarrow x'$ for all missing variables $x' \in \vec{x}'$. For instance, pick up / put down left should be extended as:

$$(a_i \oplus a_i') \wedge (l_i \oplus l_i') \wedge (r_i \Leftrightarrow r_i') \wedge \bigwedge_{j \neq i} (a_j \Leftrightarrow a_j' \wedge r_j \Leftrightarrow r_j' \wedge l_j \Leftrightarrow l_j')$$

The same needs to happen when merging multiple processes R_i into a single global relation R, i.e. $R = \bigvee_{i=1}^{k} \mathcal{R}_i$, where $\mathcal{R}_i \triangleq R_i \wedge \bigwedge_{x' \in \vec{x}' \setminus \mathsf{support}(R_i)} x \Leftrightarrow x'$. Section 2.5 discusses how extending local relations in this way can be avoided.

If a transition relation R is composed of R_i's, where each $\mathsf{support}(R_i)$ is a small subset of $\vec{x}, \vec{x}'$, we say that R has high locality. If R cannot be split up into such partial relations we say that R has low locality, or is *monolithic.*

2.5 Reachability with Decision Diagrams

For a transition system with n Boolean variables $\{x_1, \ldots, x_n\}$, a single state is given by a bit string $s \in \{0,1\}^n$. A set of states $S \subseteq \{0,1\}^n$ can be encoded in a BDD. Likewise, a transition relation $R \subseteq \{0,1\}^n \times \{0,1\}^n$ can be encoded in a BDD with $2n$ variables. The variables are ordered by interleaving the source state variables $\vec{x} = (x_1, \ldots, x_n)$ with target state variables (primed copies: $x'_1, \ldots, x'_n$), i.e., $(x_1, x'_1, \ldots, x_n, x'_n)$, as it is both convenient for the implementation of BDD algorithms, and it reduces the diagram size. To compute the successors to an initial set of states S, we can then use the decision diagram operation $\textsc{Image}(S, R)$ [21,33]:

$$\textsc{Image}(S, R) = (\exists x_1, \ldots, x_n : (S \wedge R))_{[x'_1, \ldots, x'_n := x_1, \ldots, x_n]}, \tag{3}$$

where $[x' := x]$ indicates the relabeling of the target variables to source variables. The $\textsc{Image}$ operation can also be implemented for partial relations R_i, with the benefit that existential quantification only needs to happen over $\mathsf{support}(R_i)$, rather than over all variables. The union of the image under each R_i separately equals the image under the global transition relation:

$$\exists \vec{x} : ((\mathcal{R}_1 \vee \cdots \vee \mathcal{R}_k) \wedge S)_{[\vec{x}' := \vec{x}]} = (\exists \vec{x}'_1 : R_1 \wedge S)_{[\vec{x}' := \vec{x}]} \vee \cdots \vee (\exists \vec{x}'_k : R_k \wedge S)_{[\vec{x}' := \vec{x}]}$$

where $\vec{x}'_i = \mathsf{support}(R_i) \cap \vec{x}'$ and $\mathcal{R}_i$ is the extension of R_i as defined in Sect. 2.4.

With $\textsc{Image}$, the set of reachable states can be computed by repeatedly applying R to a growing set of reachable states until no new states are found, which we denote with $S.R^*$.

Finally, decision diagrams often represent relations more succinctly when source variables $\vec{x}$ are interleaved with target variables $\vec{x}'$ in the order [33].

2.6 Saturation

Saturation [16] is a method for computing reachability that exploits locality of transitions. Aside from the initial states S_{init}, the algorithm takes as input several local transition relations R_i (see Sect. 2.4), ordered such that $\mathsf{var}(R_i) \geq \mathsf{var}(R_{i+1})$.

To illustrate how saturation works, let us give an example. Say we have a global state space given by $\{x_1, \ldots, x_4\}$, and three partial relations R_i with $\mathsf{support}(R_1) = \{x_3, x'_3, x_4, x'_4\}$, $\mathsf{support}(R_2) = \{x_2, x'_2, x_3, x'_3\}$, and $\mathsf{support}(R_3) = \{x_1, x'_1, x_2, x'_2\}$. The "dependency matrix" on the right visualizes the dependencies of the partial relations on each of the variables. The saturation algorithm traverses the decision diagram of a set of states S and *saturates* the nodes from the bottom-up. What this means in the case of the example is that the partial relation R_1 is applied to all nodes v in S with $\mathsf{var}(v) = 3$, until v has converged. After saturating this node v the algorithm backtracks upwards in the decision diagram to a node w with $\mathsf{var}(w) = 2$, and saturates this node by exhaustively applying R_2, while eagerly saturating new nodes created below w.

$$\begin{array}{c} \\ x_1 \\ x_2 \\ x_3 \\ x_4 \end{array} \begin{array}{c} R_1\ R_2\ R_3 \\ \begin{pmatrix} 0 & 0 & 1 \\ 0 & 1 & 1 \\ 1 & 1 & 0 \\ 1 & 0 & 0 \end{pmatrix} \end{array}$$

While breadth-first search (BFS) suffers from large intermediate diagram sizes [25], saturation often avoids this by ensuring that the lower levels of the decision diagram reach their final configuration early. Generally this works well if the (average) bandwidth (the distance between the first and the last non-zero entry in each row) of the dependency matrix is low. This occurs for example in asynchronous systems where processes mainly modify local variables or communicate only with "neighboring processes" through channels or shared variables dedicated to neighboring pairs. This is for example the case in the dining philosophers example given in Sect. 2.4. Finding a variable order and organizing the partial relations such that both this bandwidth and sizes of the decision diagrams are minimized is generally hard (even finding an optimal variable order for a single BDD is NP-complete [10]) but good heuristics exist [1,2,4,5,34].

While originally proposed for MDDs, saturation has since been implemented for BDDs as well [22].

3 Decision Diagram Operation for Reachability

3.1 For BDDs

We present an operation ReachBDD(S, R) which computes the reachable states $S.R^*$ for BDDs. As is typical in BDD operations, our algorithm splits the computation into recursive calls on smaller, factored BDDs, after which the results are composed again in the backtracking step. The way we factor R is inspired by [32], where a BDD algorithm is given for computing the closure R^* of R (computing the closure R^* is generally much more expensive [32, §6], hence we want to compute $S.R^*$ directly for a given S). ReachBDD is given in Algorithm 1, and its correctness is discussed in Sect. 3.4.

Algorithm 1: A BDD operation for computing reachability. Cache lookup/insert for dynamic programming after line 5 and 10 are omitted.

```
1  def ReachBDD(S, R) :        ▷ For quasi-ROBDDs S, R on n, 2n variables.
2      if S = 0 then return 0
3      if R = 0 then return S
4      if S = 1 then return 1
5      if R = 1 ∧ S ≠ 0 then return 1
6      while S did not converge do
7          S[0] ← ReachBDD(S[0], R[00])
8          S[1] ← Union(S[1], Image(S[0], R[01]))
9          S[1] ← ReachBDD(S[1], R[11])
10         S[0] ← Union(S[0], Image(S[1], R[10]))
11     return MakeNode(var(S), S[0], S[1])
```

The algorithm recurses on the low and high child of a BDD S. This splits the state space into $\mathbb{S}_{|0}$ (all states starting with a 0) and $\mathbb{S}_{|1}$. The relation R can be split up accordingly as shown in Fig. 3. The self loops in this figure represent

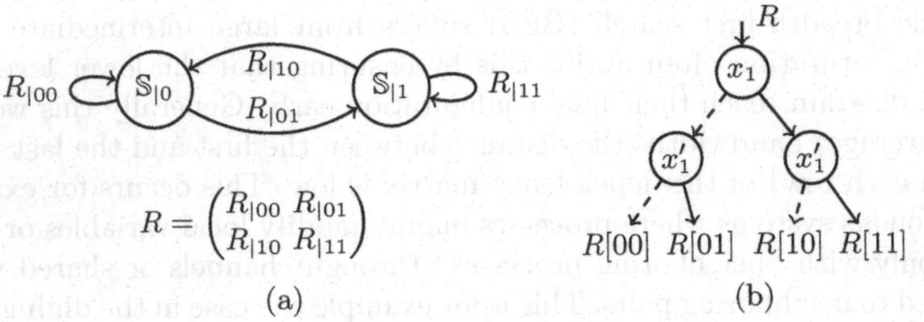

Fig. 3. The state space $\mathbb{S}$ can be split up into states where the first variable equals 0, and states where the first variable equals 1 (a), and the transition relation R is split up accordingly. Because source and target variables are interleaved as usual, these partitions of R can be easily accessed in the BDD structure (b).

$S_{|0}.R^*_{|00}$ and $S_{|1}.R^*_{|11}$, and correspond to recursive calls to ReachBdd (line 7, 9). The results of these calls need to be propagated using image computation $S_{|i}.R_{|ij} = \text{Image}(S[i], R[ij])$ (line 8, 10) until S has converged, so we incorporate a loop (line 6). For notational convenience we assume $S[0]$ and $S[1]$ are program variables to which we can assign new BDDs.

The base cases for the algorithm are as follows: If the set of initial states or the transition relation is empty ($S = 0$ or $R = 0$) there are no successors and the set of reachable states is the set of initial states. If the set of initial states contains all states ($S = 1$), or if R contains transitions from all states to all other states ($R = 1$) and S is not empty, then all states are reachable.

With the decision diagram framework Sylvan [24], we can parallelize decision diagram operations through Spawn/Sync commands, which respectively fork and join light-weight tasks [24]. However, the order of (parallel) operations is something to take into account. In particular, line 7 and 8 from Algorithm 1 are dependent, so cannot be executed in parallel. In order to parallelize ReachBdd, we change the order of calls in this loop and introduce ReachBddPar in Algorithm 2.

Algorithm 2: ReachBddPar parallelizes the loop on line 6-10 in Alg. 1. The Image and Union calls are also parallelized [23].

while S did not converge **do**
- Spawn(ReachBddPar($S[0], R[00]$)) ▷ `Spawn call as task (fork)`
- $S[1] \leftarrow$ ReachBddPar($S[1], R[11]$) ▷ `Call directly`
- $S[0] \leftarrow$ Sync ▷ `Obtain task result (join)`
- Spawn(Image($S[1], R[10]$)) ▷ `Spawn call as task (fork)`
- $T_1 \leftarrow$ Image($S[0], R[01]$) ▷ `Call directly`
- $T_0 \leftarrow$ Sync ▷ `Obtain task result (join)`
- Spawn(Union($S[0], T_0$)) ▷ `Spawn call as task (fork)`
- $S[1] \leftarrow$ Union($S[1], T_1$) ▷ `Call directly`
- $S[0] \leftarrow$ Sync ▷ `Obtain task result (join)`

3.2 Analysis

To provide some intuition for the complexity behavior of REACHBDD, we provide two cases: one where REACHBDD is exponentially faster than BFS, and one where REACHBDD reduces to BFS.

Ideal Case. We give a concrete instance of a relation R and an initial set of states S_{init} for which REACHBDD performs exponentially better than a simple BFS. Consider a transition relation R which simply increases a (program) counter of n bits. This counts form a starting state $S_{\text{init}} = 0 = \langle 00 \ldots 0 \rangle$ in steps of 1 to $2^n - 1 = \langle 11 \ldots 1 \rangle$. As the state space is a line graph, the BFS algorithm discovers one new state every iteration, requiring $O(2^n)$ calls to the IMAGE function.

To illustrate the behavior of the REACHBDD algorithm, let us explicitly write all $R_{|ij}$ for $n = 3$:

$$R_{|00} = \left\{ \begin{matrix} (\not{0}00, \not{0}01), \\ (\not{0}01, \not{0}10), \\ (\not{0}10, \not{0}11) \end{matrix} \right\} \quad R_{|11} = \left\{ \begin{matrix} (\not{1}00, \not{1}01), \\ (\not{1}01, \not{1}10), \\ (\not{1}10, \not{1}11) \end{matrix} \right\} \quad R_{|01} = \{(\not{0}11, \not{1}00)\} \quad R_{|10} = \emptyset$$

While $R_{|00}$ and $R_{|11}$ represent different sets, the BDDs $R[00]$ and $R[11]$ are equal.

For all non-terminal cases Algorithm 1 does the following:

```
S[0] ← REACHBDD(S[0], R[00])                  ▷ computes states S_0^all
S[1] ← UNION(S[1], IMAGE(S[0], R[01]))        ▷ generates 'seed' state S_1^init
S[1] ← REACHBDD(S[1], R[11])                  ▷ computes states S_1^all
S[0] ← UNION(S[0], IMAGE(S[1], R[10]))        ▷ produces no new states
```

First, REACHBDD computes all reachable states which start with a 0, let us call these S_0^{all}. Next, the IMAGE call produces exactly one new state, $\langle 100 \ldots 0 \rangle$, which will act as a "seed" state for the next REACHBDD call. Since the BDDs of S_0^{init} and S_1^{init} are equal, just as the BDDs $R[00]$ and $R[11]$, the second REACHBDD call can be looked up from cache. Finally, since $R[10] = \emptyset$, no new states will be added to S_0, and both S_0 and S_1 will have converged.

We find two things: first, all the reachable states are found in a single loop iteration, and second, each call to REACHBDD only generates one recursive call to REACHBDD (because the second call can always be looked up from cache). Overall, REACHBDD only makes $O(n)$ recursive calls to itself and to the IMAGE function.

Due the monolithic nature of the transition relation, saturation will behave like BFS in this case.

Bad Case. Here we provide an instance for which REACHBDD reduces to breadth-first search. From an arbitrary transition relation R we create a new relation R' for which REACHBDD behaves like to BFS. If R is a relation over $2n$ variables $\{x_1, x'_1, \ldots x_n, x'_n\}$, we let R' be a relation over $2(n+1)$ variables $\{x_0, x'_0, x_1, x'_1, \ldots x_n, x'_n\}$. Specifically, let $R' := x_0 \oplus x'_0 \wedge R$. The corresponding decomposition into sub-functions (as visualized in Fig. 3) looks like

$$R' = \begin{pmatrix} 0 & R'_{|01} \\ R'_{|10} & 0 \end{pmatrix}.$$

For a relation like this, the loop on line 6 relies entirely on the image computation steps to expand the set of reachable states, while the recursive calls never add any states. This effectively turns ReachBdd into BFS.

3.3 MDD Generalization

In this section, we generalize ReachBdd (Algorithm 1) from a BDD operation to an MDD operation (Algorithm 3, correctness discussed in Sect. 3.4). For simplicity, let us assume we have a MDD encoding a set of states of n variables, each of which takes values from the same domain $\mathcal{D} = \{0, 1, \ldots, m-1\}$, and an MDD which encodes the transition relation which has $2n$ variables (n source variables and n target variables). As shown below, the state MDD can be divided into m parts, and the relation MDD into m^2 parts, similar to how the BDDs are split up in Fig. 3. For ease of notation we denote $m-1 = m'$:

$$S = \begin{pmatrix} S_{|0} \\ S_{|1} \\ \vdots \\ S_{|m'} \end{pmatrix} \qquad R = \begin{pmatrix} R_{|00} & R_{|01} & \cdots & R_{|0,m'} \\ R_{|10} & R_{|11} & \cdots & R_{|1,m'} \\ \vdots & \vdots & \ddots & \vdots \\ R_{|m',0} & R_{|m',1} & \cdots & R_{|m',m'} \end{pmatrix}$$

Where the BDD algorithm iterates over four transition relations $R_{|ij}$, the MDD algorithm simply iterates over all m^2 relations $R_{|ij}$. When $i = j$, $R_{|ij}$ contains transitions for which the first variable stays the same, and we can call ReachMdd($S_{|i}, R_{|ij}$). For all cases where $i \neq j$ we use Image($S_{|i}, R_{|ij}$) instead.

Algorithm 3: An MDD operation for computing reachability. Cache lookup/insert for dynamic programming after line 5 and 11 are omitted.

```
1  def ReachMdd(S, R) :                        ▷ For MDDs S,R on n,2n variables.
2      if S = 0 then return 0
3      if R = 0 then return S
4      if S = 1 then return 1
5      if R = 1 ∧ S ≠ 0 then return 1
6      while S did not converge do
7          for i, j ∈ D do
8              if i = j then
9                  S[i] ← ReachMdd(S[i], R[ij])
10             else then
11                 S[j] ← Union(S[j], Image(S[i], R[ij]))
12     return MakeNode(var(S), S[0], ..., S[m − 1])
```

We note that ReachBdd does not generalize so well to MDDs, in the following sense: for BDDs, Algorithm 1 has two ReachBdd calls and two Image calls inside the loop. However for MDDs, we get $O(m)$ ReachMdd calls and $O(m^2)$ Image calls every loop iteration. In the MDD case, a larger part of the computation is no longer handled by recursive calls, but instead by image computations.

3.4 Correctness

In this section we give a sketch of the correctness proofs for both ReachMdd (Theorem 1) and ReachBdd (Corollary 1). A complete proof can be found in [11, App. A].

Theorem 1. *Given two MDDs S and R with n and $2n$ variables respectively,* ReachMdd(S, R) *(Algorithm 3) computes all the reachable states $S.R^*$.*

Proof Sketch. The correctness of ReachMdd can be shown by means of algorithm transformation from breadth-first search. The algorithm for BFS (given below) directly follows from the definition $S.R^* = \bigcup_{k=0}^{\infty} S.R^k$, as shown by the Knaster-Tarski theorem [39].

```
while S did not converge do
  S ← Union(S, Image(S, R))
return S
```

The two main steps in the transformation are as follows: first, using the Shannon decomposition, the computation of Image(S, R) can be split up into calls Image$(S[i], R[ij])$ for all $i, j \in \mathcal{D}$, the results of which can be combined with a MakeNode function as on line 12 of Algorithm 3. Second, since we are ultimately computing $S.R^*$, the calls Image$(S[i], R[ij])$ can be replaced with ReachMdd$(S[i], R[ij])$ when $i = j$. The algorithm ReachMdd follows directly from these two steps.

Corollary 1. *Given two BDDs S and R,* ReachBdd(S, R) *(Algorithm 1) computes all the reachable states $S.R^*$.*

Proof Sketch. The correctness of ReachBdd can be shown from Theorem 1 by taking an MDD with $\mathcal{D} = \{0, 1\}$.

4 Empirical Evaluation

4.1 Experimental Setup

We implemented the new algorithms in the decision diagram package Sylvan [21,23,24], using the task-based scheduling as described in Sect. 3.1. Instead of MDDs, Sylvan supports LDDs (see Sect. 2.2), which can be seen as a particular implementation of MDDs. For our experiments, we compare against the saturation procedure for BDDs and LDDs as implemented in Sylvan [22].[1]

[1] The implementation of our algorithms, along with the repeatable experiments can be found here: https://github.com/sebastiaanbrand/reachability.

Table 1. Overview of used benchmarks

Source	Type	#
BEEM [35]	DVE	300
MCC'16 [31]	Petri-nets	357
SPINS [7]	Promela	35

We use a number of existing benchmark sets to evaluate the performance of our algorithms. Specifically, we use the BEEM benchmark set, consisting of 300 instances of models in the DVE language, a benchmark set of over 300 Petri nets from the Model Checking Contest 2016 (MCC 2016) [31], and a small set of Promela models, compiled for the SpinS extension of LTSmin [7] (Table 1).

For these benchmarks we use the same experimental setup as used in [22]: we first use the model checker LTSmin [28] to generate BDDs and LDDs for the (partial) transition relations and initial set of states, which are exported to `.bdd` and `.ldd` files. In LTSmin, the partial transition relations are "learned" on-the-fly, during the exploration [28], as opposed to directly building the transition relations from a modeling language like NuXMV [14]. The variables in these BDDs and LDDs have been reordered by LTSmin with Boost's Sloan algorithm, since this reordering strategy has shown good results for saturation [4,5,34].

Since we are interested in comparing the REACH algorithms against saturation, we require a single transition relation for REACH. Therefore, as a preprocessing step, for the REACH algorithms only, we merge the partial relations from LTSmin into a monolithic transition relation over all variables. The run time of the merging of partial relations is included in the total run times reported in Fig. 4. This approach is slightly disadvantaging REACH because we could also change the setup to generate monolithic relations directly (as we do for Petri nets in the comparison with ITS-tools in Sect. 4.2), but using the setup from [22] allows us to make a direct comparison with parallel saturation from [22].

We limit the run time of each reachability method to 10 min. The sequential benchmarks were performed on a machine with an AMD Ryzen 7 5800x CPU and 64 GB of available memory. The parallel benchmarks on a machine with 4 Intel Xeon E7-8890 v4 CPUs with 24 physical cores each (96 in total) and 2 TB of memory. Aside from the experiments which test parallelism specifically, all reported run times are for a single core.

4.2 Results

Comparison with Saturation. A comparison between the runtimes of saturation and REACH is given in Fig. 4. In this discussion we differentiate between smaller models (run times ≤ 1 s) and larger models (run times ≥ 1 s). For BDDs, REACH outperforms saturation on a large number of bigger DVE models, but encounters timeouts as well. For LDDs, REACH appears competitive with saturation on DVE and Promela models, while the trend for the larger Petri net models shows REACH outperforming saturation by up to a factor 100. For both BDDs and LDDs saturation is often faster on the smaller instances. This is in part due to the fact that the relative overhead of merging the partial relations is greater for smaller instances.

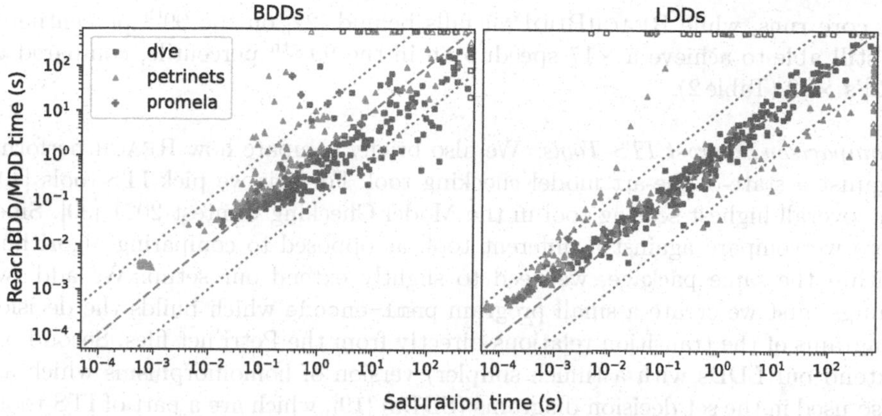

Fig. 4. The run time of finding all reachable states with BDDs (left) and LDDs (right) using REACHBDD and REACHMDD versus saturation. Open markers indicate timeouts.

Locality. As discussed in Sect. 2.6, saturation is known to work well on transition systems where the partial transition relations exhibit locality. To get insight into how locality affects our new algorithms relative to saturation, we define the *average relative bandwidth* as a metric for locality: For k partial relations $R_1, \dots, R_k$, sorted in an ascending order based on their first variable, we can define a $k \times k$ matrix M with entries m_{ij} such that $m_{ij} = 1$ if R_i and R_j share at least one variable, and 0 otherwise. We define the bandwidth of a row $m_{i,*}$ as the distance between the first and the last non-zero element in this row. The average bandwidth is then simply the average of the bandwidths of all the rows $m_{i,*}$. The average *relative* bandwidth is the average bandwidth divided by k. Note that this $k \times k$ matrix is different from (although related to) the $k \times n$ variable matrix shown in Sect. 2.6. The matrix M and the locality metric derived from it are independent of the variable order in the decision diagram.

Plotting the run time of REACHBDD divided by the run time of saturation against this average relative bandwidth (Fig. 6), we see that there is a negative correlation. Although not extremely strong, this correlation shows that the benchmarks on which saturation outperforms our algorithms are predominantly the instances where the partial relations are relatively local, while on instances with less locality our algorithms have a greater edge over saturation.

Parallelism. Figure 5 shows the speedups obtained by REACHBDDPAR and the parallelized version of saturation from [22] on 16 and 64 cores. The table on the right gives the 95th, 99th and 99.5th percentile of the speedups. We see that for the 16 core runs REACHBDDPAR is able to keep up with [22], although falling slightly behind. For the

Table 2. Parallel speedups

Algorithm	Cores	Speedup		
		P_{95}	P_{99}	$P_{99.5}$
saturation [22]	16	×8.1	×11	×11
REACHBDDPAR	16	×6.6	×8.3	×8.8
saturation [22]	64	×8.7	×22	×22
REACHBDDPAR	64	×5.6	×9.1	×17

64 core runs, while ReachBddPar falls behind [22] on the 99th percentile, it is still able to achieve a ×17 speedup on in the 99.5th percentile, compared to [22]'s ×22 (Table 2).

Comparison Against ITS-Tools. We also briefly compare how Reach performs against a state-of-the-art model checking tool. For this we pick ITS-tools [40], the overall highest scoring tool in the Model Checking Contest 2021 [30]. Since here we compare against a different tool, as opposed to comparing algorithms within the same package, we need to slightly extend our setup. We add two things: first we create a small program `pnml-encode` which builds the decision diagrams of the transition relations directly from the Petri net files. Second, we extend our LDDs with a (much simpler) version of homomorphisms which are also used in the set decision diagrams (SDDs) [19], which are a part of ITS-tools.

The results are given in Fig. 7. While ITS-tools outperforms ReachMdd on average, there is a significant number of instances where ITS-tools gives timeouts and Reach does not. Including these timeouts, Reach is faster than ITS-tools on 29% of instances. This suggest that Reach could be useful as a complementary method in an ensemble tool, where a different method can be tried if the first one times out.

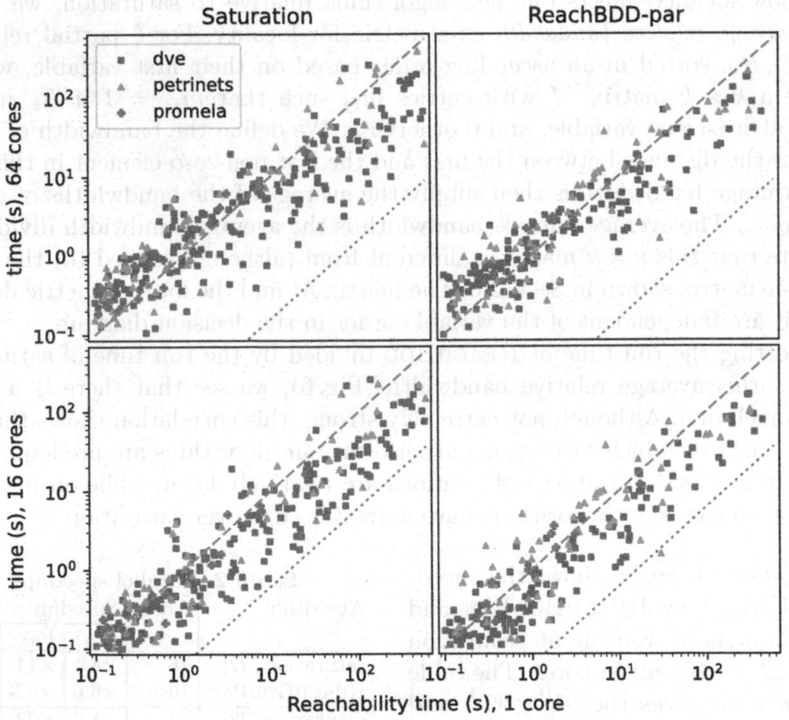

Fig. 5. Parallel speedup for saturation (left column) and ReachBddPar (right column). The dotted diagonal lines indicates a speedup of a factor 16 (bottom row) and 64 (top row) relative to the single core performance.

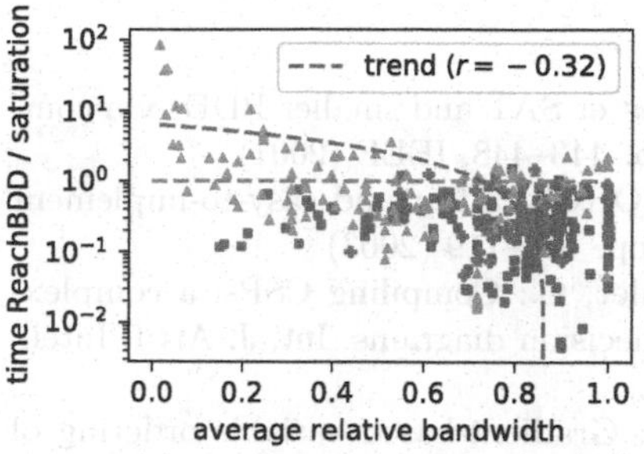

Fig. 6. The effect of locality on the relative performance of REACHBDD. For REACHMDD $r = -0.11$.

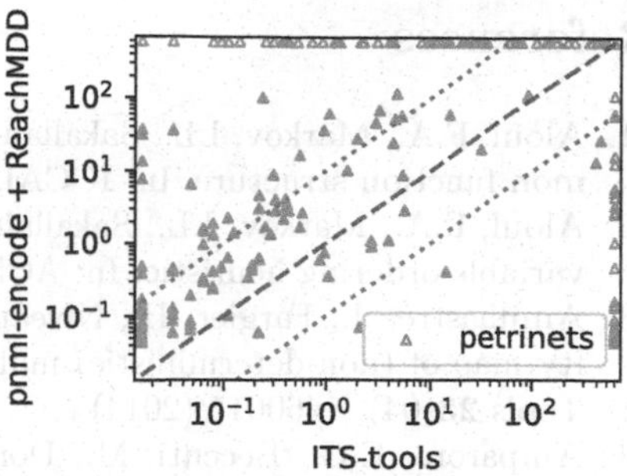

Fig. 7. Comparison of REACHMDD against computing reachable states with ITS-tools.

5 Conclusion

Summary. We presented two new reachability operations for decision diagrams: REACHBDD and REACHMDD. In contrast to other approaches, like saturation, these operations can act on a single monolithic transition relation. Similar to saturation, these new algorithms build the decision diagram for the reachable states (at least partially) bottom-up. One advantage of these operations is their simplicity. This simplicity allows us for example to more easily parallelize the decision diagram operations, as demonstrated for REACHBDDPAR. Empirical evaluation of REACHBDD and REACHMDD on a large number of benchmark sets shows that the new operations are competitive with saturation, and tend to outperform saturation on larger instances. Additionally, we find that REACHBDDPAR's peak parallel performance does not fall far behind that of saturation. Finally, our empirical results show that the REACH operations can solve 29% of instances faster than ITS-tools, which indicates REACH can be useful as a complementary algorithm.

Future Work. Saturation still outperforms our algorithms on a number of instances. Many of these instances have a lot of locality, which is exactly the regime where saturation is expected to do very well. With further investigation, REACHBDD and REACHMDD could potentially be modified to perform better on such instances. The current bottleneck, as illustrated by our analysis, is the reliance on the standard IMAGE operation. Further integration of both operations could perhaps yield improvement.

Acknowledgements. This work was supported by the NEASQC project, funded by European Union's Horizon 2020, Grant Agreement No. 951821.

References

1. Aloul, F.A., Markov, I.L., Sakallah, K.A.: Faster SAT and smaller BDDs via common function structure. In: ICCAD 2001, pp. 443–448. IEEE (2001)
2. Aloul, F.A., Markov, I.L., Sakallah, K.A.: FORCE: a fast and easy-to-implement variable-ordering heuristic. In: ACM VLSI, pp. 116–119 (2003)
3. Amilhastre, J., Fargier, H., Niveau, A., Pralet, C.: Compiling CSPs: a complexity map of (non-deterministic) multivalued decision diagrams. Int. J. Artif. Intell. Tools **23**(04), 1460015 (2014)
4. Amparore, E.G., Beccuti, M., Donatelli, S.: Gradient-based variable ordering of decision diagrams for systems with structural units. In: D'Souza, D., Narayan Kumar, K. (eds.) ATVA 2017. LNCS, vol. 10482, pp. 184–200. Springer, Cham (2017). https://doi.org/10.1007/978-3-319-68167-2_13
5. Amparore, E.G., Donatelli, S., Beccuti, M., Garbi, G., Miner, A.: Decision diagrams for Petri nets: a comparison of variable ordering algorithms. In: Koutny, M., Kristensen, L.M., Penczek, W. (eds.) Transactions on Petri Nets and Other Models of Concurrency XIII. LNCS, vol. 11090, pp. 73–92. Springer, Heidelberg (2018). https://doi.org/10.1007/978-3-662-58381-4_4
6. Bahar, R.I., et al.: Algebric decision diagrams and their applications. FMSD **10**(2), 171–206 (1997)
7. van der Berg, F., Laarman, A.: SpinS: extending LTSmin with Promela through SpinJa. ENTCS **296**, 95–105 (2013)
8. Biere, A., Artho, C., Schuppan, V.: Liveness checking as safety checking. ENTCS **66**(2), 160–177 (2002)
9. Blom, S., van de Pol, J.: Symbolic reachability for process algebras with recursive data types. In: Fitzgerald, J.S., Haxthausen, A.E., Yenigun, H. (eds.) ICTAC 2008. LNCS, vol. 5160, pp. 81–95. Springer, Heidelberg (2008). https://doi.org/10.1007/978-3-540-85762-4_6
10. Bollig, B., Wegener, I.: Improving the variable ordering of OBDDs is NP-complete. Trans. Comput. **45**(9), 993–1002 (1996)
11. Brand, S., Bäck, T., Laarman, A.: A decision diagram operation for reachability. arXiv preprint arXiv:2212.03684 (2022)
12. Bryant, R.E.: Graph-based algorithms for Boolean function manipulation. Trans. Comput. **100**(8), 677–691 (1986)
13. Burch, J.R., Clarke, E.M., McMillan, K.L., Dill, D.L., Hwang, L.J.: Symbolic model checking: 10^{20} states and beyond. Inf. Comput. **98**(2), 142–170 (1992)
14. Cavada, R., et al.: The nuXmv symbolic model checker. In: Biere, A., Bloem, R. (eds.) CAV 2014. LNCS, vol. 8559, pp. 334–342. Springer, Cham (2014). https://doi.org/10.1007/978-3-319-08867-9_22
15. Christensen, S., Kristensen, L.M., Mailund, T.: A sweep-line method for state space exploration. In: Margaria, T., Yi, W. (eds.) TACAS 2001. LNCS, vol. 2031, pp. 450–464. Springer, Heidelberg (2001). https://doi.org/10.1007/3-540-45319-9_31
16. Ciardo, G., Lüttgen, G., Siminiceanu, R.: Saturation: an efficient iteration strategy for symbolic state—space generation. In: Margaria, T., Yi, W. (eds.) TACAS 2001. LNCS, vol. 2031, pp. 328–342. Springer, Heidelberg (2001). https://doi.org/10.1007/3-540-45319-9_23
17. Ciardo, G., Marmorstein, R., Siminiceanu, R.: Saturation unbound. In: Garavel, H., Hatcliff, J. (eds.) TACAS 2003. LNCS, vol. 2619, pp. 379–393. Springer, Heidelberg (2003). https://doi.org/10.1007/3-540-36577-X_27

18. Cook, B., Podelski, A., Rybalchenko, A.: Terminator: beyond safety. In: Ball, T., Jones, R.B. (eds.) CAV 2006. LNCS, vol. 4144, pp. 415–418. Springer, Heidelberg (2006). https://doi.org/10.1007/11817963_37
19. Couvreur, J.-M., Thierry-Mieg, Y.: Hierarchical decision diagrams to exploit model structure. In: Wang, F. (ed.) FORTE 2005. LNCS, vol. 3731, pp. 443–457. Springer, Heidelberg (2005). https://doi.org/10.1007/11562436_32
20. Darwiche, A.: SDD: a new canonical representation of propositional knowledge bases. In: IJCAI (2011)
21. van Dijk, T., Laarman, A., van de Pol, J.: Multi-core BDD operations for symbolic reachability. ENTCS **296**, 127–143 (2013)
22. van Dijk, T., Meijer, J., van de Pol, J.: Multi-core on-the-fly saturation. In: Vojnar, T., Zhang, L. (eds.) TACAS 2019. LNCS, vol. 11428, pp. 58–75. Springer, Cham (2019). https://doi.org/10.1007/978-3-030-17465-1_4
23. van Dijk, T., van de Pol, J.: Sylvan: multi-core decision diagrams. In: Baier, C., Tinelli, C. (eds.) TACAS 2015. LNCS, vol. 9035, pp. 677–691. Springer, Heidelberg (2015). https://doi.org/10.1007/978-3-662-46681-0_60
24. van Dijk, T., van de Pol, J.: Sylvan: multi-core framework for decision diagrams. STTT **19**(6), 675–696 (2017)
25. Geldenhuys, J., Valmari, A.: Techniques for smaller intermediary BDDs. In: Larsen, K.G., Nielsen, M. (eds.) CONCUR 2001. LNCS, vol. 2154, pp. 233–247. Springer, Heidelberg (2001). https://doi.org/10.1007/3-540-44685-0_16
26. Holzmann, G.J.: The model checker SPIN. IEEE Trans. Softw. Eng. **23**(5), 279–295 (1997)
27. Kam, T.: Multi-valued decision diagrams: theory and applications. Multiple-Valued Logic **4**(1), 9–62 (1998)
28. Kant, G., Laarman, A., Meijer, J., van de Pol, J., Blom, S., van Dijk, T.: LTSmin: high-performance language-independent model checking. In: Baier, C., Tinelli, C. (eds.) TACAS 2015. LNCS, vol. 9035, pp. 692–707. Springer, Heidelberg (2015). https://doi.org/10.1007/978-3-662-46681-0_61
29. Knuth, D.E.: The Art of Computer Programming, vol. 4A: Combinatorial Algorithms, Part 1. Pearson Education India (2011)
30. Kordon, F., et al.: Complete Results for the 2021 Edition of the Model Checking Contest (2021). http://mcc.lip6.fr/2021/results.php
31. Kordon, F., et al.: Complete results for the 2016 edition of the model checking contest (2016). https://mcc.lip6.fr/2016/results.php
32. Matsunaga, Y., McGeer, P.C., Brayton, R.K.: On computing the transitive closure of a state transition relation. In: International Design Automation Conference, pp. 260–265 (1993)
33. McMillan, K.L.: Symbolic model checking: an approach to the state explosion problem. Ph.D. thesis, Carnegie Mellon University (1992)
34. Meijer, J., van de Pol, J.: Bandwidth and wavefront reduction for static variable ordering in symbolic reachability analysis. In: Rayadurgam, S., Tkachuk, O. (eds.) NFM 2016. LNCS, vol. 9690, pp. 255–271. Springer, Cham (2016). https://doi.org/10.1007/978-3-319-40648-0_20
35. Pelánek, R.: BEEM: benchmarks for explicit model checkers. In: Bošnački, D., Edelkamp, S. (eds.) SPIN 2007. LNCS, vol. 4595, pp. 263–267. Springer, Heidelberg (2007). https://doi.org/10.1007/978-3-540-73370-6_17
36. Roig, O., Cortadella, J., Pastor, E.: Verification of asynchronous circuits by BDD-based model checking of Petri nets. In: De Michelis, G., Diaz, M. (eds.) ICATPN 1995. LNCS, vol. 935, pp. 374–391. Springer, Heidelberg (1995). https://doi.org/10.1007/3-540-60029-9_50

37. Sanner, S., McAllester, D.: Affine algebraic decision diagrams (AADDs) and their application to structured probabilistic inference. In: IJCAI, pp. 1384–1390 (2005)
38. Somenzi, F.: Binary decision diagrams. Nato ASI Subseries F CSS **173**, 303–368 (1999)
39. Tarski, A.: A lattice-theoretical fixpoint theorem and its applications. Pac. J. Math. **5**(2), 285–309 (1955)
40. Thierry-Mieg, Y.: Symbolic model-checking using ITS-tools. In: Baier, C., Tinelli, C. (eds.) TACAS 2015. LNCS, vol. 9035, pp. 231–237. Springer, Heidelberg (2015). https://doi.org/10.1007/978-3-662-46681-0_20
41. Vinkhuijzen, L., Laarman, A.: Symbolic model checking with sentential decision diagrams. In: Pang, J., Zhang, L. (eds.) SETTA 2020. LNCS, vol. 12153, pp. 124–142. Springer, Cham (2020). https://doi.org/10.1007/978-3-030-62822-2_8

Formal Modelling of Safety Architecture for Responsibility-Aware Autonomous Vehicle via Event-B Refinement

Tsutomu Kobayashi[1(✉)], Martin Bondu[2], and Fuyuki Ishikawa[3]

[1] Japan Aerospace Exploration Agency, Tsukuba, Japan
kobayashi.tsutomu@jaxa.jp
[2] Sorbonne University, Paris, France
martin.bondu@etu.sorbonne-universite.fr
[3] National Institute of Informatics, Tokyo, Japan
f-ishikawa@nii.ac.jp

Abstract. Ensuring the safety of autonomous vehicles (AVs) is the key requisite for their acceptance in society. This complexity is the core challenge in formally proving their safety conditions with AI-based black-box controllers and surrounding objects under various traffic scenarios. This paper describes our strategy and experience in modelling, deriving, and proving the safety conditions of AVs with the Event-B refinement mechanism to reduce complexity. Our case study targets the state-of-the-art model of goal-aware responsibility-sensitive safety to argue over interactions with surrounding vehicles. We also employ the Simplex architecture to involve advanced black-box AI controllers. Our experience has demonstrated that the refinement mechanism can be effectively used to gradually develop the complex system over scenario variations.

Keywords: Autonomous driving · AI safety · Responsibility-sensitive safety · Safety architecture · Event-B · Refinement

1 Introduction

The safety of automated vehicles has been attracting increased interest in society. In addition to the intensive effort of simulation-based testing, there is a key approach based on formal reasoning called responsibility-sensitive safety (RSS) [13]. RSS defines the minimum rules that traffic participants should comply with for safety, i.e., no collisions. This rule-based approach has recently been extended to goal-aware RSS (GA-RSS) to deal with the goal-achievement, i.e., the driving goal of the ego-vehicle is eventually achieved such as pulling over upon emergency [7]. GARSS is effective for formally limiting liabilities, which is vital for AV manufacturers.

The first author is supported by JSPS KAKENHI grant number 19K20249 and JST ERATO-MMSD (JPMJER1603) project. The third author is supported by JST MIRAI-eAI (JPMJMI20B8) project.

M. Chechik et al. (Eds.): FM 2023, LNCS 14000, pp. 533–549, 2023.
https://doi.org/10.1007/978-3-031-27481-7_30

The challenge lies in deriving the necessary GARSS conditions and formally checking the compliance of the design of the ego vehicle over various scenarios under different environmental conditions. In addition, there is increasing demand to consider complex behaviours of black-box AI-based advanced controllers backed up with safety-ensured controllers, e.g., the Simplex architecture [10].

Existing efforts have clarified the principles to derive and argue conditions that ego-vehicles should comply with in example scenarios. However, the engineering aspect has yet to be investigated. Specifically, we need a systematic modelling design that accepts the flexibility to mitigate the complexity in dealing with multiple aspects of scenario variations and architectural design.

To this end, we report our experience in modelling, deriving, and proving the safety conditions of autonomous vehicles (AVs). We follow the GA-RSS approach to define and derive the safety conditions to be checked with architectural design with black-box advanced controllers. We propose a strategy for using the refinement mechanism of Event-B [2] to gradually argue the complex aspects including the scenario variations. Our experience has shown the potential of the refinement mechanism for the flexible design of models and proofs to mitigate the complexity in a gradual manner. To the best of our knowledge, this is the first attempt to focus on the model engineering aspect over scenario variations in the deductive approach for AV safety.

The rest of this paper is structured as follows: In Sect. 2, we describe the safety architecture, RSS, and Event-B. Section 3 introduces GA-RSS and a case study example. We elaborate on our approach and its application to the case studies in Sect. 4–5. We discuss the approach in Sect. 6 before concluding the paper in Sect. 7.

2 Preliminaries

2.1 Safety Architecture

Contemporary software systems often have black-box modules, such as machine learning modules, in which their safety is essentially difficult to verify.

A safety architecture, such as Simplex architecture (Fig. 1) [10], is a fundamental approach to guaranteeing the safety of such systems while benefitting from the high performance and functionality of black-box modules. It models interactions between a controller and a plant. The controller part has two different controllers: the baseline controller (BC), which is designed to force safe behaviour, and the advanced controller (AC), which aims at satisfying various requirements (e.g., comfort and progress) in addition to safety. The decision module (DM) switches between the BC and AC in accordance with the state of the plant. BC may fail to satisfy requirements other than safety, but it has a simple white-box behaviour enabling the safety to be easily verified. In contrast, although AC usually gives better user experiences, guaranteeing its safety is difficult due to its complicated black-box behaviour. For example, a typical BC for an AV may drive by following a predefined rule that is guaranteed to be

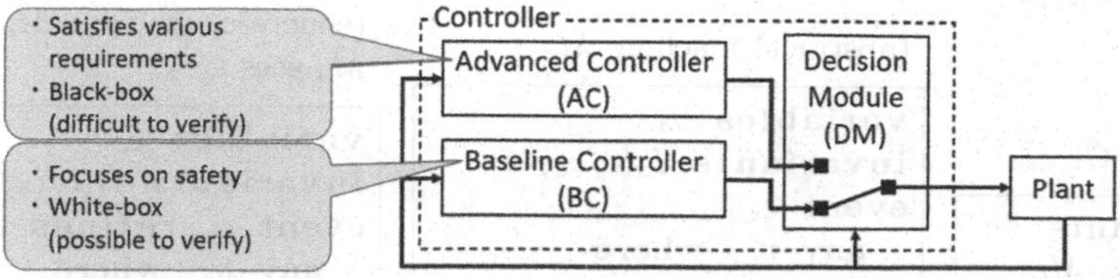

Fig. 1. Component-based simplex architecture [10]

safe in certain situations. A typical AC, on the other hand, would be one that uses machine learning for motion planning.

2.2 Responsibility-Sensitive Safety (RSS)

RSS is an approach to determining the safety of AVs by formal proof. The core idea is to derive conditions that should be satisfied by the current state of the traffic participants such that safety, or no collisions, is ensured in the future.

An RSS rule consists of an assertion ϕ called an RSS condition and a control strategy α called a proper response. They are defined for particular traffic scenarios. For example, a subject vehicle (SV), i.e., the ego vehicle, is following a preceding vehicle on a one-way road. We consider this preceding vehicle as the sole traffic participant called a principal other vehicle (POV). The SV must satisfy the RSS condition ϕ regarding the minimum relative distance from the POV. The distance is defined by considering the response time for braking and the distance necessary for the maximum comfortable braking to stop. The proper response α of the SV is to engage the maximum comfortable braking when the distance condition ϕ is about to be violated. The proof should show the RSS condition ϕ is preserved through the execution with the proper response α.

In a general setting, RSS considers the SV and POV in the target scenario and determines the RSS condition and proper response. To prove the condition is preserved through the execution, a certain set of constraints must be satisfied by not only the SV but also all traffic participants (POVs), called RSS responsibility principles. Examples of the principles include "do not cut in recklessly" and "be cautious in areas with limited visibility", intuitively.

Our focus is not on the core responsibility principles of RSS but on the RSS-driven framework for proving safety of AVs. We are interested in the formal engineering aspect to model and verify scenario variations.

2.3 Modelling and Proving in Event-B

In this section, we describe the concepts of modelling and theorem proving in Event-B [2] that are used in our case study[1].

[1] For simplicity, we do not cover the "full" Event-B (described in [2]). For instance, our concrete machines inherit all variables and parameters from abstract machines, which is not necessary in general Event-B machines.

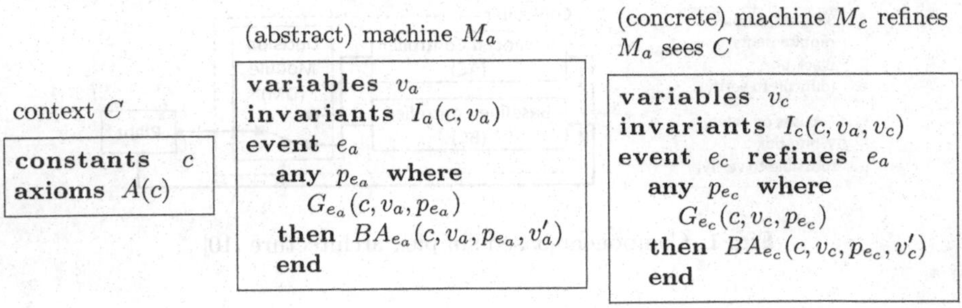

Fig. 2. Structure of Event-B model components

Event-B Model Components. Event-B models are structured as shown in Fig. 2. The static aspects of the target system are specified as contexts, which consist of constants and their properties (axioms). The dynamic aspects are specified as machines, which consist of variables, invariant predicates, and a set of events. An event e has parameters p_e, guard condition G_e, and before-after predicate BA_e that explains the assignment performed in e in terms of variables' current values v and next values v'. A significant feature of Event-B is a flexible refinement mechanism that enables declaring a machine M_c as a refinement of another machine M_a. Every event in M_c should be seen as a refinement of events in M_a (including the implicit *skip* event). M_c does not need to inherit predicates of M_a, but those two machines should be compatible as described in the following.

Proving Consistency of Models. Constructed models should be verified by discharging *proof obligations* (POs) generated with predicates in the models. Primary POs include the following:

- **Invariant Preservation** (for an abstract machine): Invariant predicates are inductive ones, i.e., they must hold after every occurrence of events, given that they hold beforehand. Formally, invariant preservation by an event e_a is: $A(c) \wedge I_a(c, v_a) \wedge G_{e_a}(c, v_a, p_{e_a}) \wedge BA_{e_a}(c, v_a, p_{e_a}, v'_a) \wedge \ldots \Longrightarrow I_a(c, v'_a)$.
- **Invariant Preservation** (for concrete machines): Formally, invariant preservation by an event e_c is: $A(c) \wedge I_a(c, v_a) \wedge I_c(c, v_a, v_c) \wedge G_{e_c}(c, v_c, p_{e_c}) \wedge BA_{e_c}(c, v_c, p_{e_c}, v'_c) \wedge \ldots \Longrightarrow I_c(c, v'_a, v'_c)$.
- **Guard Strengthening**: For an event e_c to be a refinement of an event e_a, the guard of e_c must be stronger than that of e_a's. Formally, guard strengthening of e_c is: $A(c) \wedge I_c(c, v_a, v_c) \wedge I_a(c, v_a) \wedge G_{e_c}(c, v_c, p_{e_c}) \wedge \ldots \Longrightarrow G_{e_a}(c, v_a, p_{e_a})$.

3 Example: Goal-Aware RSS for Pull over Scenario

Goal-aware RSS (GA-RSS) [7] is an extension of RSS for dealing with complex scenarios that require planning over multiple manoeuvres to achieve particular

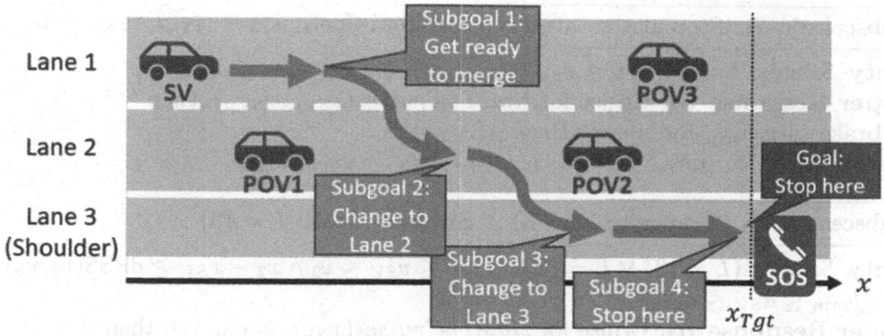

Fig. 3. Pull over scenario [7]

goals. For instance, consider the scenario shown in Fig. 3 (pull over scenario) [7]: the SV needs to stop at a designated location (x_{Tgt}) on the shoulder lane while keeping safe distances from POVs as required by RSS. Following only the original RSS rules for avoiding collisions is necessary but not enough to achieve the goal. The goal should be decomposed into several subgoals, such as (1) getting ready to merge between two POVs by changing the velocity, (2–3) changing lanes, and (4) stopping at x_{Tgt}. Different proper responses are required for different subgoals as well. However, for example, the SV can be trapped in Lane 1 if it is concerned about only the distance from the car ahead.

The workflow of GA-RSS is based on their extension of Floyd-Hoare logic. Given a driving scenario $\mathcal{S}$ composed of the goal condition Goal and safety condition Safety, the workflow is first used to decompose $\mathcal{S}$ into *subscenarios* $\mathcal{S}_{1,\dots,n}$ and identify the *proper response* α_i for each subscenario $\mathcal{S}_i$.[2]

Then, the *precondition* ϕ_i for each subscenario is calculated as the precondition for establishing $\mathsf{Goal}_i \wedge \phi_{i+1}$ while satisfying Safety_i, by performing α_i. Here, by seeing the (grand) goal of $\mathcal{S}$ as the postcondition of the final subscenario $\mathcal{S}_n$, the preconditions of all subscenarios are derived in a backward manner, à la Floyd-Hoare logic, and then integrated into the precondition of $\mathcal{S}$.

For instance, Fig. 4 shows the subgoals, safety conditions, proper responses, and preconditions of a subscenario chain (defined and derived in [7]) where the SV goes between POV1 and POV2 and changes lanes.

Variables are as follows: x_{SV} and $x_{1,2,3}$ are the lateral positions of the SV and the three POVs; v_{SV} and $v_{1,2,3}$ are their lateral velocities; a_{SV} and $a_{1,2,3}$ are their lateral acceleration rates; L and $L_{1,2,3}$ for set of lanes they are on. Constants are as follows: x_{Tgt} is the position of the final goal position; v_{min} and v_{max} are the legal speed limits; b_{min} and b_{max} are the minimum (comfortable) and maximum (emergency) braking deceleration rates; a_{max} is the maximum acceleration rate.

[2] To be precise, with case distinctions, a tree of subscenarios is derived.

Subscenario $\mathcal{S}_4$ (Stop at the target)	**Subgoal** Goal$_4$: $x_{SV} = x_{Tgt} \wedge v_{SV} = 0$

Safety Safety$_4$: $L = \{3\} \wedge 0 \le v_{SV} \le v_{max} \wedge -b_{min} \le a_{SV} \le a_{max}$
Proper Response α_4: Cruise for $timeToCruise_4(x_{SV0}, v_{SV0})$, then brake with b_{min} for $timeToBrake_4(v_{SV0})$
Precondition ϕ_4: Env $\wedge L = \{3\} \wedge x_{Tgt} - x_{SV} \ge v_{SV}^2/2b_{min}$

Subscenario $\mathcal{S}_3$ (Change to Lane 3)	**Subgoal** Goal$_3$: $L = \{3\}$

Safety Safety$_3$: $(L = \{3\} \vee L = \{2,3\}) \wedge 0 \le v_{SV} \le v_2 \wedge x_2 - x_{SV} \ge \mathsf{dRSS}(v_2, v_{SV}) \wedge -b_{min} \le a_{SV} \le a_{max}$
Proper Response α_3: Cruise for $timeToCruise_3(x_{SV0}, v_{SV0}, \ldots)$, then brake with b_{min} for $timeToBrake_3(x_{SV0}, v_{SV0}, \ldots)$
Precondition ϕ_3: Env $\wedge L = \{2\} \wedge 0 < v_{SV} \le v_2 \wedge x_2 - x_{SV} \ge \mathsf{dRSS}(v_2, v_{SV}) \wedge x_{Tgt} - x_{SV} \ge v_{SV}^2/2b_{min}$

Subscenario $\mathcal{S}_2$ (Change to Lane 2)	**Subgoal** Goal$_2$: $lanes = \{2\}$

Safety Safety$_2$: $(L = \{2\} \vee L = \{1,2\}) \wedge 0 \le v_{SV} \le v_2 \wedge x_2 - x_{SV} \ge \mathsf{dRSS}(v_2, v_{SV}) \wedge x_3 - x_{SV} \ge \mathsf{dRSS}(v_3, v_{SV}) \wedge -b_{min} \le a_{SV} \le a_{max}$
Proper Response α_2: Cruise for $timeToCruise_2(x_{SV0}, v_{SV0}, \ldots)$, then brake with b_{min} for $timeToBrake_2(x_{SV0}, v_{SV0}, \ldots)$
Precondition ϕ_2: ...

Subscenario $\mathcal{S}_1$ (Get ready to merge)

Subgoal Goal$_1$: $x_2 - x_{SV} \ge \mathsf{dRSS}(v_2, v_{SV}) \wedge x_{SV} - x_1 \ge \mathsf{dRSS}(v_{SV}, v_1) \wedge v_2 = v_{SV}$
Safety Safety$_1$: $L = \{1\} \wedge x_3 - x_{SV} \ge \mathsf{dRSS}(v_3, v_{SV}) \wedge 0 \le v_{SV} \le v_{max} \wedge -b_{min} \le a_{SV} \le a_{max}$
Proper Response α_1: Combinations of acceleration, cruising, and braking depending on the situation. See § 6.2 for details.
Precondition ϕ_1: ...

Fig. 4. Subscenarios of pull over scenario with proper response and precondition

The condition of environment Env is as follows:

$$\mathsf{Env} = \bigwedge_{i=1,2,3} (v_{min} \le v_i \le v_{max} \wedge a_i = 0) \\ \wedge L_1 = \{2\} \wedge L_2 = \{2\} \wedge L_3 = \{1\} \wedge x_2 > x_1.$$

This condition includes the assumption that POVs are supposed to run at constant velocity.

The RSS safety distance that the SV running at v_{SV} should keep from the POVi ahead running at v_i is defined as follows:

$$\mathsf{dRSS}(v_i, v_{SV}) = \max\left(0, \frac{v_{SV}^2}{2b_{min}} - \frac{v_i^2}{2b_{max}}\right). \tag{1}$$

The times the SV should cruise, brake, or accelerate in subscenario $\mathcal{S}_i$ for proper response α_i are derived in the GA-RSS workflow [7]. For instance,

$$timeToCruise_4(x_{SV0}, v_{SV0}) = \frac{x_{Tgt} - x_{SV0}}{v_{SV0}} - \frac{v_{SV0}}{2b_{min}}, \quad (2)$$

$$timeToBrake_4(v_{SV0}) = \frac{v_{SV0}}{b_{min}}, \quad (3)$$

where x_{SV0} and v_{SV0} are the position and velocity of the SV, respectively, when the switching occurs.

GA-RSS is designed to be integrated with the Simplex architecture. The identified scenarios are used to construct the BC that performs the derived proper response α in the situation compatible with the scenario, and thus the BC is guaranteed to be safe and goal-achieving. While the correctness of the DM is not covered with the method in [7], their experiment used their implementation of a Simplex-based controller, where the AC is black-box.

Motivation of Our Case Study. Even with the BC specifications identified with the GA-RSS workflow, a formal model of the whole Simplex architecture closer to the implementation is desired to construct safe and goal-achieving controllers of AVs. Such models should at least take into account the behaviour of the DM and the monitor-decide-control loop (Fig. 1).

The challenge here is the model's *complexity*; for example, in addition to DM-related elements, we need to take switching time delays into consideration.

To overcome this, we exploit the refinement mechanism of Event-B, which distributes the complexity of modelling and verification over multiple steps.

The rest of this paper discusses our case study, where we constructed and verified Event-B models of Simplex-based controllers for pull over subscenarios.

4 Case Study 1: Modelling Subscenario $\mathcal{S}_4$

In this section, we introduce our modelling strategy, where elements of systems should be specified in each refinement step by using our model for subscenario $\mathcal{S}_4$ of the pull over scenario as an example. We model the entire safety architecture and verify its safety in three refinement steps as follows:

Machine $M_{4,0}$: Whole controller-level. This is the most abstract machine. The properties of the whole controller's (AC+BC+DM) behaviour at every cycle are modelled. We focus on physical requirements that should be satisfied due to the controller's behaviour.

Machine $M_{4,1}$: Module-level. This machine refines $M_{4,0}$. This machine is aware of the safety architecture; behavioural properties of AC, BC, and DM are specified separately. We checked that the switching by the DM satisfies the requirements in $M_{4,0}$ by proving the correctness of $M_{4,0}$–$M_{4,1}$ refinement.

Machine $M_{4,2}$: Manoeuvre-level. This machine refines $M_{4,1}$. Details of the BC's behaviour (proper responses) are specified. By checking the correctness of $M_{4,1}$–$M_{4,2}$ refinement, we check that the proper responses satisfy the requirements.

variables x_{SV} , v_{SV}

Event initialisation
any () **where** ⊤ **then**
init_sv: $(x'_{SV}, v'_{SV}) = (x_{SV0}, v_{SV0})$ **end**

invariants
types: $x_{SV} \in \mathbb{R} \wedge v_{SV} \in \mathbb{R}$
no_overrun: $0 \leq x_{SV} \leq x_{Tgt}$
v_regulated: $0 \leq v_{SV} \leq v_{max}$
precond: $x_{Tgt} - x_{SV} \geq v_{SV}^2/2b_{min}$

Event run
any p_x , p_v **where**
preserve_no_overrun: $0 \leq p_x \leq x_{Tgt}$
preserve_v_regulated: $0 \leq p_v \leq v_{max}$
preserve_precond: $x_{Tgt} - p_x \geq p_v^2/2b_{min}$
x_physical_constr: $x_{SV} \leq p_x \leq x_{SV} + \int_{t=0}^{1}(v_{SV} + a_{max}t)dt$
v_physical_constr: $v_{SV} - \int_{t=0}^{1} b_{max}dt \leq p_v \leq v_{SV} + \int_{t=0}^{1} a_{max}dt$
then
update_xv: $(x'_{SV}, v'_{SV}) = (p_x, p_v)$ **end**

Fig. 5. $M_{4,0}$: Abstract, whole controller-level machine for subscenario $\mathcal{S}_4$

4.1 Machine $M_{4,0}$: Whole Controller-Level Behaviour

Machine $M_{4,0}$ is shown in Fig. 5. In this machine, we abstract away details of the controller and focus on the SV's position (x_{SV}) and velocity (v_{SV}) as the result of the controller's behaviour.

Invariant predicates no_overrun and v_regulated express basic requirements.

The precondition ϕ_4 derived from the GA-RSS workflow is designed to be an invariant that the safety architecture should preserve; the DM enables using the AC while ϕ_4 is *robustly* satisfied, but it switches to the control using the BC once ϕ_4 is *about to be* violated. Therefore, we specify ϕ_4 as an invariant predicate (precond).

There is only a single non-initialisation event named run. It has parameters p_x and p_v, which are specified as values of x_{SV} and v_{SV} at the next cycle (update_xv). The parameters are constrained by the guard predicates preserve_* required for the event's invariant preservation and those for the constraints related to physics (*_physical_constr). With these constraints as guard predicates of the event, we declare that every detailed behavioural description specified as events in concrete machines ($M_{4,1}$ and $M_{4,2}$) should satisfy the constraints.

The guard predicate preserve_precond states that the controller *somehow* produces the result (i.e., p_x and p_v) such that precond is satisfied. Indeed, the preservation of the precondition ϕ_4 is trivial because:

$$(x_{Tgt} - p_x \geq p_v^2/2b_{min}) \wedge \ldots \wedge ((x'_{SV}, v'_{SV}) = (p_x, p_v)) \\ \implies x_{Tgt} - x'_{SV} \geq v'^2_{SV}/2b_{min}.$$

Note that *how* the controller works to produce the invariant-satisfying result is not yet specified and deferred to concrete machines; how the DM prevents the

variables x_{SV} , v_{SV} , $ctrl$, v_{BC0}

invariants
`types`: $ctrl \in \{AC, BC\} \wedge v_{BC0} \in \mathbb{R}$
`vsvbcinit_regulated`: $0 \leq v_{BC0} \leq v_{max}$
`bc_no_accel`: $ctrl = BC \Longrightarrow v_{SV} \leq v_{BC0}$
`switching`: $ctrl = AC \Longrightarrow \phi_4(x_{SV} + \int_{t=0}^{1}(v_{SV} + a_{max}t)dt,\ v_{SV} + \int_{t=0}^{1} a_{max}dt)$

Event AC → BC **refines** run
  any p_x, p_v **where**
    ... (guard predicates of run except preserve_precond) ...
    `AC_operating`: $ctrl = AC$
    `maybe_unsafe_next`: $\neg\phi_4(x_{SV} + \int_{t=0}^{2}(v_{SV} + a_{max})dt,\ v_{SV} + \int_{t=0}^{2} a_{max}dt)$
  then
    ... (actions of run) ...
    `switch_to_bc`: $ctrl' = BC$
    `vsvbcinit_update`: $v'_{BC0} = p_v$ **end**

Event BC → AC **refines** run
  any p_x, p_v **where**
    ... (guard predicates of run) ...
    `BC_operating`: $ctrl = BC$
    `no_acceleration`: $p_v \leq v_{BC0}$
    `surely_safe_next`: $\phi_4(x_{SV} + \int_{t=0}^{2}(v_{SV} + a_{max})dt,\ v_{SV} + \int_{t=0}^{2} a_{max}dt)$
  then
    ... (actions of run) ...
    `switch_to_ac`: $ctrl' = AC$ **end**

Fig. 6. (A part of) $M_{4,1}$: Intermediate, module-level machine for subscenario $\mathcal{S}_4$

AC from violating it is specified in machine $M_{4,1}$, and how the BC's behaviour (proper responses) satisfies it is specified in machine $M_{4,2}$.

4.2 Machine $M_{4,1}$: Module-Level Behaviour

In machine $M_{4,1}$ (Fig. 6), which refines $M_{4,0}$, we focus on the requirements on white-box modules of the architecture, namely the BC and DM, particularly the condition for switching; through the proof attempt, we *derived* the switching condition such that the precondition is always satisfied. Note that we assume that the AC's behaviour is arbitrary as long as it satisfies run's guard. Details of the BC's behaviour that should be specified using the time spent for each manoeuvre are introduced in machine $M_{4,2}$.

There are two new variables: $ctrl$, for the currently active controller, and v_{BC0}, which stores the velocity at the time when switching to the BC occurs.

Invariant predicates are in regard to the requirements on the BC and DM. `vsvbcinit_regulated` requests that v_{BC0} should not exceed v_{max} like v_{SV}, and `bc_no_accel` expresses that the BC does not accelerate in the proper response. `switching` states that if the AC is active, then the SV will be goal-achieving and safe after a cycle even if the SV accelerated with the maximum rate a_{max}. The contraposition of `switching` means that the BC is used if the precondition ϕ_4 may be violated at the next cycle.

There are four events for cases of switching: AC → AC, AC → BC, BC → BC, and BC → AC. They all refine the `run` event of the previous machine $M_{4,0}$. For instance, AC → BC is for the case where the current controller is the AC (`AC_operating`) and `switching` can be violated after the event (`maybe_unsafe_next`; note that the integrals are from $t = 0$ to 2 to look ahead for two cycles). Note that, however, `switching` is guaranteed to hold before the event since it is an invariant predicate. In addition to actions of `run`, the controller is switched to the BC (`switch_to_bc`) and v_{BC0} is updated (`vsvbcinit_update`). On the other hand, BC → AC is the case where the controller is switched from the BC to AC because the invariant `switching` will be satisfied after the occurrence of the event (`surely_safe_next`).

The main POs are as follows:

1. **Do the events AC → $*$ preserve the invariant `precond`?** This corresponds to the guard strengthening PO of AC → $*$. The intuition of the proof is because the AC is operating only if the precondition is guaranteed to hold after two cycles (`surely_safe_next`), and it is guaranteed to hold after one cycle as well.
2. **Do events $*$ → AC preserve the invariant `switching`?** It is preserved because the AC will be used only if `surely_safe_next` holds at the current state. In fact, we *derived* the switching condition `surely_safe_next` through the attempt to discharge this PO.

4.3 Machine $M_{4,2}$: Manoeuvre-Level Behaviour

In machine $M_{4,2}$ (Fig. 7), which refines $M_{4,1}$, we focus on the details of the behaviour with the notion of time to spend on each manoeuvre to verify that the BC's behaviour satisfies the requirements specified in machines $M_{4,0}$ and $M_{4,1}$.

Two new variables about the remaining time for cruising ($t_{BCCruise}$) and braking ($t_{BCBrake}$) are introduced. The unit of time here is the cycle, e.g., the value of $t_{BCCruise}$ is the number of the controller's cycles spent for cruising.

Invariant predicates are in regard to the detailed properties of the BC's behaviour: `cruise_before_brake` expresses that the proper response α_4 is cruising and then braking, and `*_in_BC*` states that the velocity and position should follow the proper response α_4 as shown in Fig. 8.

Events of $M_{4,2}$ refine those of $M_{4,1}$ as shown in Fig. 9.

Three events that refine AC → $*$ are mostly the same as $M_{4,1}$, but events regarding switching to the BC (such as AC_run → BC) are extended with actions of calculating $t_{BCCruise}$ and $t_{BCBrake}$ as Eqs. 2 and 3 (derived in the GA-RSS workflow) because the BC should calculate them every time it get activated.

Unlike events that refine AC → $*$, six events that refine BC → $*$ do not inherit all of the guard predicates and actions of corresponding events in machine $M_{4,1}$. For example, the differences between the event BC_cruise → AC in $M_{4,2}$ and the corresponding event BC → AC in $M_{4,1}$ is as shown in Fig. 10. The removed

variables x_{SV} , v_{SV} , $ctrl$, v_{BC0} , $t_{BCCruise}$, $t_{BCBrake}$

invariants
`types`: $t_{BCCruise} \in \mathbb{R}_{\geq 0} \wedge t_{BCBrake} \in \mathbb{R}_{\geq 0}$
`cruise_before_brake`: $0 < t_{BCCruise} \Longrightarrow 0 < t_{BCBrake}$
`v_in_BC`: $ctrl = BC \Longrightarrow v_{SV} = t_{BCBrake} \cdot b_{min}$
`v_in_BC_cruise`: $(ctrl = BC \wedge 0 < t_{BCCruise}) \Longrightarrow v_{SV} = v_{BC0}$
`x_in_BC`: $(ctrl = BC \wedge v_{SV} \neq 0)$
$\Longrightarrow x_{Tgt} - x_{SV} = \int_{t=0}^{t_{BCCruise}} v_{SV} dt + \int_{t=0}^{t_{BCBrake}} (v_{SV} - b_{min} t) dt$

axioms `t_bccruise_def`: $timeToCruise_4(x, v) = (2b_{min}(x_{Tgt} - x) - v^2)/(2b_{min} v)$

Event AC˙ run → BC **refines** AC → BC
  any p_x , p_v **where**
    ... (guard predicates of AC → BC) ...
    `will_run_more`: $0 < p_v$
  then
    ... (actions of AC → BC) ...
    `update_tcruisebc`: $t'_{BCCruise} = timeToCruise_4(p_x, p_v)$
    `update_tbrakebc`: $t'_{BCBrake} = timeToBrake_4(p_v)$
  end

Event BC˙ cruise → AC **refines** BC → AC
  any p_x , p_v **where**
    `BC_operating`: $ctrl = BC$
    `surely_safe_next`: $\phi_4(x_{SV} + \int_{t=0}^{2} (v_{SV} + a_{max}) dt,\ v_{SV} + \int_{t=0}^{2} a_{max} dt)$
    `will_cruise_more`: $1 \leq t_{BCCruise}$
    `cruise_xv`: $p_x = x_{SV} + \int_{t=0}^{1} v_{SV} dt \wedge p_v = v_{SV} + \int_{t=0}^{1} 0 dt$
  then
    ... (actions of BC → AC) ...
    `tcruise_pass`: $t'_{BCCruise} = t_{BCCruise} - 1$
  end

Fig. 7. (A part of) $M_{4,2}$: Concrete, manoeuvre-level machine for subscenario $\mathcal{S}_4$

guard predicates (lines with red background) are requirements on the values of the SV's position and velocity after the occurrence of the event (p_x and p_v), while introduced guard predicates (lines with green background) include the concrete behaviour of the BC (`cruise_xv`), namely running with the constant velocity. By changing events in this way and checking that the guard of BC_cruise → AC is stronger than that of BC → AC, we can verify that the BC's concrete behaviour satisfies the requirements specified in machines $M_{4,0}$ and $M_{4,1}$.

In addition to the consistency between the BC's concrete behaviour specified in $M_{4,2}$ and requirements on the BC specified in $M_{4,1}$, we checked that events $*$ → BC and BC → $*$ preserve the invariant.

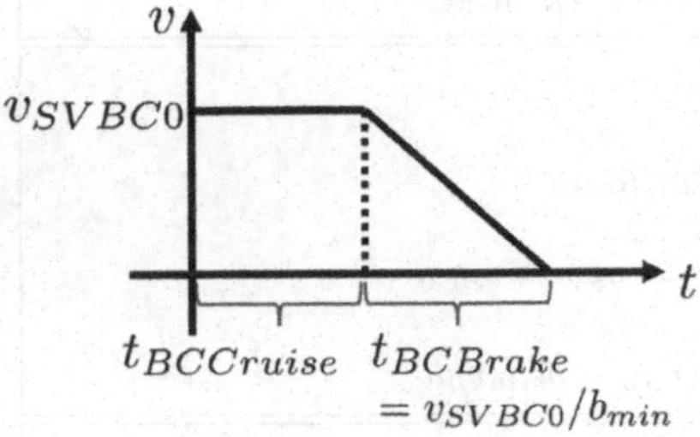

Fig. 8. Proper response α_4

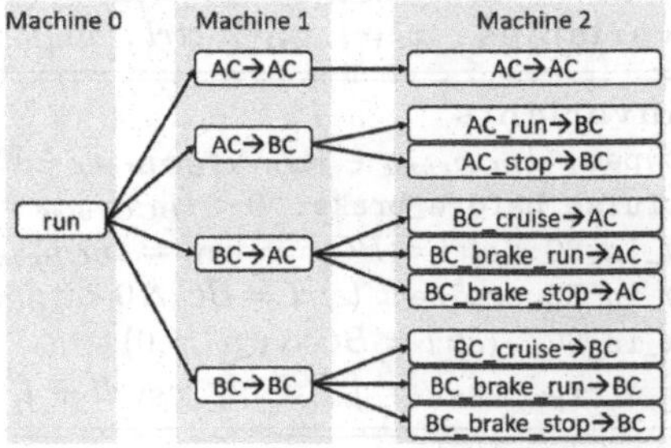

Fig. 9. Event refinement relationship

5 Case Study 2: Modelling Subscenario $\mathcal{S}_3$

In this section, we use subscenario $\mathcal{S}_3$ to demonstrate how our modelling strategy (Sect. 4) is applicable to other subscenarios. subscenario $\mathcal{S}_3$ has new aspects; the SV is changing lanes and the leading vehicle POV2.

5.1 Machine $M_{3,0}$: Whole Controller-Level Behaviour

Following machine $M_{4,0}$ of subscenario $\mathcal{S}_4$, we focus only on the physical results of the controller behaviour.

POV2's variable position (x_2) and constant velocity (v_2) are used in addition to SV's position and velocity.

As the SV is changing lanes, we assume that this action will be done in an exact amount of time modelled as a constant t_{LC} (the time for lane changing), and therefore we introduce another variable t_{LCe} (the time for lane changing elapsed) so that when the time elapsed reaches t_{LC}, the SV should have finished switching lanes and the subscenario is over. We modelled lanes in this style instead of introducing another physical coordinate for simplicity.

A new invariant predicate `no_overtime` regarding the time limit of this subscenario is also introduced as a replacement for `no_overrun` of subscenario $\mathcal{S}_4$. The corresponding guard predicates of the event run are specified so that no event can occur once the lane switching is over.

`no_overtime`: $t_{LCe} \leq t_{LC}$

The precondition for subscenario $\mathcal{S}_3$ (ϕ_3 derived in [7]) takes into consideration the RSS safety distance between the SV and the leading vehicle POV2.

`precond`: $x_{Tgt} - x_{SV} \geq v_{SV}^2/2b_{min} \wedge x_{SV} < x_2$
$\wedge 2(x_{SV} - x_2) + \frac{v_{SV}^2}{b_{min}} \leq \frac{v_2^2}{b_{max}}$

As in subscenario $\mathcal{S}_4$, the run event has guard predicates to preserve invariant predicates. The event also has new actions for updating x_2 and t_{LCe}:

$$\texttt{update\_xLead: } x_2' = x_2 + \int_{t=0}^{1}(v_2 t)dt$$
$$\texttt{update\_xLCe: } t_{LCe}' = \min(t_{LC}, t_{LCe}+1)$$

```
-Event BC → AC refines run
+Event BC_cruise → AC refines BC → AC
  any p_x , p_v where
-   preserve_no_overrun: 0 ≤ p_x ≤ x_Tgt
-   preserve_v_regulated: 0 ≤ p_v ≤ v_max
-   preserve_precond: x_Tgt − p_x ≥ p_v^2/2b_min
-   x_physical_constr: x_SV ≤ p_x ≤ x_SV + ∫_{t=0}^{1}(v_SV + a_max t)dt
-   v_physical_constr: v_SV − ∫_{t=0}^{1} b_max dt ≤ p_v ≤ v_SV + ∫_{t=0}^{1} a_max dt
    BC_operating: ctrl = BC
-   no_acceleration: p_v ≤ v_BC0
    surely_safe_next: φ4(x_SV + ∫_{t=0}^{2}(v_SV + a_max)dt, v_SV + ∫_{t=0}^{2} a_max dt)
+   will_cruise_more: 1 ≤ t_BCCruise
+   cruise_xv: p_x = x_SV + ∫_{t=0}^{1} v_SV dt ∧ p_v = v_SV + ∫_{t=0}^{1} 0dt
  then
    update_xv: (x'_SV, v'_SV) = (p_x, p_v)
    switch_to_ac: ctrl' = AC
+   tcruise_pass: t'_BCCruise = t_BCCruise − 1
  end
```

Fig. 10. Differences between BC → AC (in $M_{4,1}$) and BC_cruise → AC (in $M_{4,2}$)

5.2 Machine $M_{3,1}$: Module-Level Behaviour

This machine is also similar to $M_{4,1}$, but the invariant `switching` and guard predicates `surely_safe_next` (and its negation `maybe_unsafe_next`) take into account the distance between the SV and POV2.

$$\texttt{switching: } ctrl = AC \Longrightarrow \phi_3(x_{SV} + \int_{t=0}^{1}(v_{SV} + a_{max}t)dt, \; v_{SV} + \int_{t=0}^{1} a_{max}dt, \; x_2 + \int_{t=0}^{1}(v_2 t)dt, \; v_2)$$

$$\texttt{surely\_safe\_next: } \phi_3(x_{SV} + \int_{t=0}^{2}(v_{SV} + a_{max}t)dt, \; v_{SV} + \int_{t=0}^{2} a_{max}dt, \; x_2 + \int_{t=0}^{2}(v_2 t)dt, \; v_2)$$

As subscenario $\mathcal{S}_4$ (Sect. 4.2), the POs are in regard to the preservations of invariants `precond` and `switching`.

5.3 Machine $M_{3,2}$: Manoeuvre-Level Behaviour

Compared with $M_{4,2}$ for subscenario $\mathcal{S}_4$, there are two major differences: when switching to the BC, the calculation of $t_{BCCruise}$ and $t_{BCBrake}$ (derived in [7]) is different because the velocity of the SV should not be zero by the end of the subscenario $\mathcal{S}_3$ but only low enough to satisfy the goal invariant.

$$\boxed{\texttt{tBrake\_update: } t'_{BCBrake} = (t_{LC} - t_{LCe}) + \frac{p_v}{2.b_{min}} + \frac{p_x - x_{Tgt}}{p_v}}$$

The six events that refine BC_$*\to*$ have to satisfy machine $M_{3,0}$'s `precond` that now includes the safety distance to the leading vehicle POV2.

The POs in regard to this invariant were discharged in the following way:

1. BC_$*\to$ BC. The idea behind this proof is that BC's proper response does not include accelerating and the leading vehicle's velocity is constant, so the distance between these two may only increase.
2. BC_$*\to$ AC. The guard predicate `surely_safe_next` states that the invariant will be satisfied in two cycles without having to break in the next cycle because the controller will be in the AC.

6 Discussion

6.1 Model Engineering

In the case studies, we have used the refinement mechanism of Event-B to gradually model and verify the different aspects. Specifically, we separated the argument over the definition of safe and goal-achieving behaviour, architecture for switching behaviours, and concrete behaviour design. The refinement mechanism limits the complexity of modelling and proof in each step, which was essential in handling the increasing complexity in proving continuous properties.

We did not directly reuse the models between subscenarios, e.g., sharing the abstract steps between subscenarios. This is our explicit choice as the key safety properties and involved variables for the POVs are unique to each subscenario. We instead used the common refinement strategy as well as the model representations. We believe this experience enables us to demonstrate the know-how for scenarios other than the pull over scenario. The generality of the approach is further discussed in the following.

6.2 Generality of Approach

We have described how the same refinement strategy can deal with subscenarios $\mathcal{S}_3$ and $\mathcal{S}_4$. We describe how the other subscenarios can be modelled as well as the omitted aspect of perception errors.

Subscenario $\mathcal{S}_2$. The machines for subscenario $\mathcal{S}_2$ are similar to that for subscenario $\mathcal{S}_3$. The main difference between them is the presence of a leading vehicle in the next lane in subscenario $\mathcal{S}_2$ while there is none in subscenario $\mathcal{S}_3$.

Subscenario $\mathcal{S}_1$. In this subscenario, the SV needs to prepare to switch lanes and merge into the next lane. There are three POVs to take into account: one ahead of the SV in the current lane (POV3) and two others in the next lane (POV 1 and 2). This subscenario thus involves multiple (in this case, four) proper responses: an example is accelerating to pass POV1 in the next lane, and another example is decelerating to match the velocity of POV2 in the next lane.

To handle multiple proper responses in a unified manner, we modelled them as a sequence of proper responses with variable durations as follows: (1) Accelerate for $t_{BCAccel}$ (2) Cruise for $t_{BCCruise}$ (3) Brake for $t_{BCBrake}$. Moreover, we needed to take into account different precondition for each proper response. Therefore, we introduced a variable to record which proper response was taken the last time the BC got activated.

Perceptual Uncertainty. Another aspect not included in the case studies is perceptual uncertainty or the possibility of errors in sensing. A basic approach to this issue would be adding safety margins to the behaviour of the controller. For instance, introducing a variable $\widehat{x_{Tgt}}$ for the perceived value of target location (x_{Tgt}) and discussing assumptions on the difference between x_{Tgt} and $\widehat{x_{Tgt}}$ enables us to derive the appropriate amount of the safety margin for this uncertainty.

6.3 Using Event-B for Modelling and Proving

Features of Event-B and its modelling environment Rodin [1] were useful for modelling and proving the safety architecture for GA-RSS. Rodin generated POs and helped interactive proof of them. The refinement mechanism of Event-B was effective for distributing the complexity of modelling and proving over multiple steps. In addition, as we discussed in Sect. 4.2, we derived the correct behaviour of DM from generated POs.

Our contributions in this paper, namely strategies of modelling and refinement, provide a guide to the effective use of Event-B's features for the rigorous and systematic construction of controllers for different subscenarios.

On the other hand, although Rodin has proof tactics and provers for automatically discharging POs, we had to manually discharge all POs. It is because we needed an extension of Event-B language [4] to use real numbers in models, and Rodin's current automatic proof functionalities are not strong when the language is extended. However, we expect that this problem will be solved; for instance, there are studies aiming at assisting automatic proof of hybrid systems by bridging Rodin with external solvers [3].

6.4 Related Work

RSS was originally proposed as the formal approach for AVs, but the paper did not include any machine-processible models [13]. The work on GA-RSS extended the framework of RSS with formal specifications and partial calculations supported by Mathematica [7]. Other studies only used the resulting RSS conditions, for example, encoding them in signal temporal logic for runtime verification [8]. To the best of our knowledge, this is the first attempt to make use of formal modelling for the RSS scheme. The study in [12] demonstrated the difficulty in checking RSS properties with automated "one button" tools for reachability analysis and model checking.

Other formal attempts for AVs include proofs with the Isabelle/HOL prover [11] with support of MATLAB. The focus was on the detailed computation including floating-point errors while the driving behaviour was rather simple; avoidance of one static object with a white-box controller.

Verification over RSS is intrinsically hybrid, i.e., including continuous aspects such as velocity and distance. Proofs over hybrid models have been actively investigated in the Hoare-style reasoning, not only for Event-B but also in other formalisms such as KeYmaera X [6]. Our case study did not focus on the continuous aspects and used rather simple theories for handling real arithmetic. Our future work includes the use of more sophisticated support for discharging the proof obligations. It is notable that refining continuous models in the physics world into discrete software controllers has been actively investigated for Event-B, e.g., [5]. Models obtained in our approach can be further refined with such techniques into concrete designs of discrete software controllers.

Guidelines with a focus on refinement strategies have been considered useful for Event-B as reusable know-how for specific types of systems [14]. Our case study has the potential to be elaborated into such guidelines. Although the effectiveness of refinement strategies has been discussed qualitatively in most cases, there have been efforts on quantitative analysis [9]. Our future work will include analysis of refinement strategies in this work in a more systematic way.

7 Conclusion

In this paper, we reported our case study to model, derive, and prove the safety conditions of AVs in the RSS scheme. We target a state-of-the-art problem with the goal-aware version of RSS as well as the Simplex architecture to consider black-box AI controllers. We proposed a strategy for leveraging the refinement mechanism of Event-B and demonstrated how it mitigates the complexity over scenario variations. We will continue studying other scenarios to convert the obtained lessons into more concrete and general guidelines for formal modelling and verification of AVs.

Acknowledgements. We thank our industrial partner Mazda for discussions of realistic problems in the safety assurance of autonomous driving. We also thank members of JST ERATO HASUO Metamathematics for Systems Design Project for discussions of Goal-Aware RSS and the safety architecture.

References

1. Abrial, J.R., Butler, M., Hallerstede, S., Hoang, T.S., Mehta, F., Voisin, L.: Rodin: an open toolset for modelling and reasoning in Event-B. Int. J. Softw. Tools Technol. Transf. **12**(6), 447–466 (2010). https://doi.org/10.1007/s10009-010-0145-y
2. Abrial, J.R.: Modeling in Event-B: System and Software Engineering. Cambridge University Press, Cambridge (2010)

3. Afendi, M., Mammar, A., Laleau, R.: Building correct hybrid systems using Event-B and sagemath: illustration by the hybrid smart heating system case study. In: 26th International Conference on Engineering of Complex Computer Systems (ICECCS), pp. 91–96. Hiroshima, Japan (2022). https://doi.org/10.1109/ICECCS54210.2022.00019
4. Butler, M., Maamria, I.: Practical theory extension in Event-B. In: Liu, Z., Woodcock, J., Zhu, H. (eds.) Theories of Programming and Formal Methods. LNCS, vol. 8051, pp. 67–81. Springer, Heidelberg (2013). https://doi.org/10.1007/978-3-642-39698-4_5
5. Dupont, G., Ait-Ameur, Y., Singh, N.K., Pantel, M.: Event-B hybridation: a proof and refinement-based framework for modelling hybrid systems. ACM Trans. Embed. Comput. Syst, **20**(4), 1–37 (2021). https://doi.org/10.1145/3448270
6. Fulton, N., Mitsch, S., Quesel, J.-D., Völp, M., Platzer, A.: KeYmaera X: an axiomatic tactical theorem prover for hybrid systems. In: Felty, A.P., Middeldorp, A. (eds.) CADE 2015. LNCS (LNAI), vol. 9195, pp. 527–538. Springer, Cham (2015). https://doi.org/10.1007/978-3-319-21401-6_36
7. Hasuo, I., et al.: Goal-aware RSS for complex scenarios via program logic. In: IEEE Transactions on Intelligent Vehicles, pp. 1–33 (2022). https://doi.org/10.1109/TIV.2022.3169762
8. Hekmatnejad, M., et al.: Encoding and monitoring responsibility sensitive safety rules for automated vehicles in signal temporal logic. In: 17th ACM-IEEE International Conference on Formal Methods and Models for System Design (MEMOCODE). ACM, New York, NY, USA (2019). https://doi.org/10.1145/3359986.3361203
9. Kobayashi, T., Ishikawa, F.: Analysis on strategies of superposition refinement of Event-B specifications. In: Sun, J., Sun, M. (eds.) ICFEM 2018. LNCS, vol. 11232, pp. 357–372. Springer, Cham (2018). https://doi.org/10.1007/978-3-030-02450-5_21
10. Phan, D., et al.: A component-based simplex architecture for high-assurance cyber-physical systems. In: 17th International Conference on Application of Concurrency to System Design (ACSD), pp. 49–58. Zaragoza, Spain (2017). https://doi.org/10.1109/ACSD.2017.23
11. Rizaldi, A., Immler, F., Schürmann, B., Althoff, M.: A formally verified motion planner for autonomous vehicles. In: Lahiri, S.K., Wang, C. (eds.) ATVA 2018. LNCS, vol. 11138, pp. 75–90. Springer, Cham (2018). https://doi.org/10.1007/978-3-030-01090-4_5
12. Roohi, N., Kaur, R., Weimer, J., Sokolsky, O., Lee, I.: Self-driving vehicle verification towards a benchmark. CoRR **abs/1806.08810** (2018). http://arxiv.org/abs/1806.08810
13. Shalev-Shwartz, S., Shammah, S., Shashua, A.: On a formal model of safe and scalable self-driving cars. CoRR **abs/1708.06374** (2017). http://arxiv.org/abs/1708.06374
14. Yeganefard, S., Butler, M.J., Rezazadeh, A.: Evaluation of a guideline by formal modelling of cruise control system in Event-B. In: Muñoz, C.A. (ed.) The 2nd NASA Formal Methods Symposium (NFM). NASA Conference Proceedings, vol. NASA/CP-2010-216215, pp. 182–191 (2010)

A Runtime Environment for Contract Automata

Davide Basile(✉) and Maurice H. ter Beek

Formal Methods and Tools Lab, ISTI–CNR, Pisa, Italy
{davide.basile,maurice.terbeek}@isti.cnr.it

Abstract. Contract automata have been introduced for specifying applications through behavioural contracts and for synthesising their orchestrations as finite state automata. This paper addresses the realisation of applications from contract automata specifications. We present CARE, a new runtime environment to coordinate services implementing contracts that guarantees the adherence of the implementation to its contract. We discuss how CARE can be adopted to realise contract-based applications, its formal guarantees, and we identify the responsibilities of the involved business actors. Experiments show the benefits of adopting CARE with respect to manual implementations.

1 Introduction

From a recent survey in the transport domain [23], it has emerged that the majority of studies on formal methods propose specification languages, models, and their verification, whereas fewer focus on how to derive the finalised software from the verified specification also showing the adherence of the implementation to its specification. The authors of [26] state that these interaction specifications "are not yet a feature of standard mainstream programming languages, so software developers are not able to benefit from them". In this paper, we investigate the connection between a behavioural specification and its implementation, and we provide a possible realisation of those aspects abstracted in a specification.

Contract automata are a dialect of finite state automata used to formally specify the behaviour of service contracts in terms of offers and requests [14]. A composition of contracts is in *agreement* when all requests are matched by corresponding offers of other contracts. A composition can be refined to one in agreement using the orchestration synthesis algorithm [12,13], a variation of the synthesis algorithm from supervisory control theory [30]. Previously, in [10], a library called `CATLib` [11] implementing the operations on contract automata (e.g., composition, synthesis) was presented. A front-end of `CATLib` for graphically editing and operating on contracts is also available [19], called `CAT_App`. The orchestrator is abstracted away in contract automata and until now no examples of concrete implementations were provided in which services implement contract automata specifications.

Whilst `CATLib` and `CAT_App` are used to *specify* applications as contract automata, in this paper we tackle the problem of *implementing* applications that have been specified via contract automata. We introduce `CARE` [17], a newly

M. Chechik et al. (Eds.): FM 2023, LNCS 14000, pp. 550–567, 2023.
https://doi.org/10.1007/978-3-031-27481-7_31

developed software that provides a runtime environment to coordinate the CARE services that implement the contracts of the synthesised orchestration. Thus, CARE advances the state-of-the-art of the research on contract automata and behavioural contracts by detailing how specifications through contract automata can be connected with service-based applications. With CARE, the low-level interactions that are abstracted in contract automata orchestrations are now explicated. We discuss how CARE can promote a separation of concerns among different actors that together cooperate to realise contract-based applications, and among developers and designers of services. The proposed framework is exercised on two examples, showcasing the usage of CARE. Experiments show a neat improvement in terms of decreased complexity of the software when comparing the implementations of the examples exploiting CARE with those that manually implement the low-level interactions among services without relying on CARE.

Related Work. Other approaches to connect implementations with behavioural types (e.g., behavioural contracts, session types) are surveyed in [2,25]. Our approach is closer to [26,34], where behavioural types are expressed as finite state automata of Mungo, called *typestates* [33]. The toolchain of Mungo and StMungo is proposed to implement behavioural types specifications. Similarly to CARE, in Mungo finite state automata are used as behaviour assigned to Java classes (one automaton per class), where transition labels correspond to methods of the classes. A tool similar to Mungo is JaTyC (Java Typestate Checker) [6].

An Eclipse plugin called Diogenes [4] allows to write specifications of services as behavioural contracts using a domain specific language, verify them, and generate skeletal Java programs to be refined using the Java RESTful Web service middleware for contract-oriented computing presented in [8]. Both Diogenes and StMungo generate skeletal Java programs from contract compositions or multiparty session types, respectively, whereas CARE allows to adapt already existing components to realise a new application in a bottom-up approach, fostering adaptability and reusability of services.

CARE adopts a *correct-by-design* approach to implement a specification with formal guarantees. The complementary approach infers a behavioural type from an implementation, where guarantees hold if the typing succeeds. An algorithm to infer a form of behavioural types from programs with assertions is discussed in [35], where programs are written in Mool (Mini object-oriented language), a simple Java-like language incorporating behavioural types. The inference of behavioural types from Go programs is studied in [27]. Go is a language supporting synchronisations on channels inspired by process algebraic formalisms like CSP and CCS [20]. The inference of behavioural types is thus facilitated by the chosen languages, whilst extracting them from unconstrained Java programs is still a challenge [31]. CATLib supports compositions of communicating machines, the formalism of behavioural types used in [27], thus it could be used to suggest amendments to the original Go programs by exploiting its synthesis algorithms.

Finally, the approach proposed by CARE shares aspects with the synthesis/verification of runtime monitors [1,5,32], and is similar to the *automated composition* problem studied in [3,7,21,22], to which CARE and CATLib offer both a runtime engine and tailored novel synthesis algorithms.

Outline. We provide some background on contract automata in Sect. 2. Section 3 details the design of CARE. The formal guarantees offered by CARE are detailed in Sect. 4, whilst Sect. 5 discusses how CARE can be adopted for building applications specified via contract automata and the separation of concerns. Section 6 contains two examples and an evaluation of the benefits of our contribution. Finally, we conclude and discuss future work in Sect. 7.

2 Modal Service Contract Automata

We provide background on contract automata and their synthesis operation.

A Contract Automaton (CA) models either a single service or a multi-party composition of services performing actions. Figure 4 depicts some examples of CA. The number of services of a CA is called its *rank*. When *rank* = 1, the contract is called a *principal* (i.e., a single service). For example, the leftmost and rightmost automata in Fig. 4 are principals, while the automaton in the middle has *rank* = 2. Labels of CA are vectors of atomic elements called *actions*. Actions are either *requests* (prefixed by `?`), *offers* (prefixed by `!`), or *idle* (denoted with a distinguished symbol `-`). Requests and offers belong to the (pairwise disjoint) sets R and O, respectively. The states of CA are vectors of atomic elements called basic states. Labels are restricted to be *requests*, *offers*, or *matches* where, respectively, there is either a single request action, a single offer action, or a single pair of request and offer actions that match, and all other actions are idle. The length of the vectors of states and labels is equal to the rank of the CA.

For example, the label `[!euro, ?euro]` is a match where the request action `?euro` is matched by the offer action `!euro`. Note the difference between a request label (e.g., `[?coffee, -]`) and a request action (e.g., `?coffee`). A transition may also be called a request, offer, or match according to its label.

The goal of each service is to reach an accepting (*final*) state such that all its request (and possibly offer) actions are matched. In [12], CA were equipped with *modalities*, i.e., *necessary* ($\Box$) and *permitted* ($\Diamond$) transitions, respectively. Permitted transitions are controllable, whereas necessary transitions can be uncontrollable or semi-controllable. The resulting formalism is called *Modal Service Contract Automata* (MSCA). In the following definition, given a vector $\vec{a}$, its ith element is denoted by $\vec{a}_{(i)}$.

Definition 1 (MSCA). *Given a finite set of basic states* $\mathcal{Q} = \{q_1, q_2, \ldots\}$, *an MSCA* $\mathcal{A}$ *of rank* $= n$ *is a tuple* $\langle Q, \vec{q_0}, A^r, A^o, T, F\rangle$, *with set of states* $Q = Q_1 \times \ldots \times Q_n \subseteq \mathcal{Q}^n$, *initial state* $\vec{q_0} \in Q$, *set of requests* $A^r \subseteq \mathsf{R}$, *set of offers* $A^o \subseteq \mathsf{O}$, *set of final states* $F \subseteq Q$, *set of transitions* $T \subseteq Q \times A \times Q$, *where* $A \subseteq (A^r \cup A^o \cup \{\text{-}\})^n$, *partitioned into* permitted *transitions* $T^{\Diamond}$ *and* necessary *transitions* $T^{\Box}$, *such that: (i) given* $t = (\vec{q}, \vec{a}, \vec{q}\,') \in T$, $\vec{a}$ *is either a request, or an offer, or a match; and (ii)* $\forall i \in 1 \ldots n$, $\vec{a}_{(i)} = \text{-}$ *implies* $\vec{q}_{(i)} = \vec{q}\,'_{(i)}$.

Composition of services is rendered through the composition of their MSCA models by means of the *composition operator* $\otimes$, which is a variant of a synchronous product. This operator basically interleaves or matches the transitions of the component MSCA, but whenever two component MSCA are enabled to execute their respective request/offer, then the match is forced to happen. Moreover, a match involving a necessary transition of an operand is itself necessary. The rank of the composed MSCA is the sum of the ranks of its operands. The vectors of states and actions of the composed MSCA are built from the vectors of states and actions of the component MSCA, respectively. Typically, in a composition of MSCA various properties are analysed. We are especially interested in *agreement*. In a contract that is in agreement, all requests are matched, i.e., transitions are only labelled with offers or matches.

We recall the specification of the abstract synthesis algorithm of CA from [13]. The synthesis of a controller, an orchestration, and a choreography of CA are all different special cases of this abstract synthesis algorithm, formalised in [13] and implemented in `CATLib` [10]. This algorithm is a fixed-point computation where at each iteration the set of transitions of the automaton is refined (using pruning predicate ϕ_p) and a set of forbidden states R is computed (using forbidden predicate ϕ_f). The synthesis is parametric with respect to these two predicates, which provide information on when a transition has to be pruned from the synthesised automaton and when a state has to be deemed forbidden, respectively. We refer to MSCA as the set of (MS)CA, where the set of states is denoted by Q and the set of transitions by T (with $T^{\Box}$ denoting the set of necessary transitions). For an automaton $\mathcal{A}$, the predicate $Dangling(\mathcal{A})$ contains those states that are not reachable from the initial state or that cannot reach any final state.

Definition 2 (abstract synthesis [13]**).** *Let $\mathcal{A}$ be an MSCA, $\mathcal{K}_0 = \mathcal{A}$, and $R_0 = Dangling(\mathcal{K}_0)$. Given two predicates $\phi_p, \phi_f : T \times MSCA \times Q \to \mathbb{B}$, let the* abstract synthesis function $f_{(\phi_p,\phi_f)} : MSCA \times 2^Q \to MSCA \times 2^Q$ *be defined as:*

$$\begin{aligned} &f_{(\phi_p,\phi_f)}(\mathcal{K}_{i-1}, R_{i-1}) = (\mathcal{K}_i, R_i), \textit{ with} \\ &T_{\mathcal{K}_i} = T_{\mathcal{K}_{i-1}} - \{\, t \in T_{\mathcal{K}_{i-1}} \mid \phi_p(t, \mathcal{K}_{i-1}, R_{i-1}) = \textit{true} \,\} \\ &R_i = R_{i-1} \cup \{\, \vec{q} \mid (\vec{q} \rightarrow) = t \in T^{\Box}_{\mathcal{A}},\ \phi_f(t, \mathcal{K}_{i-1}, R_{i-1}) = \textit{true} \,\} \cup Dangling(\mathcal{K}_i) \end{aligned}$$

Subsequently, the abstract controller is defined as the least fixed point of $f_{(\phi_p,\phi_f)}$ (cf. [13, Theorem 5.2]). The synthesised orchestration guarantees the reachability of final states, the agreement property (i.e., all requests are matched) and that all reachable necessary requests are not pruned (i.e., controllability).

Tooling. CA and their functionalities are implemented in a software artefact, called Contract Automata Library (`CATLib`), whose development is active [11]. This software artefact is a by-product of our scientific research on behavioural contracts and implements results that have previously been formally specified in several publications (cf., e.g., [12–14]). Scalability features offered by `CATLib` include a bounded on-the-fly state-space generation optimised with pruning of redundant transitions and parallel streams computations. The software is open source [11], it has been developed using principles of model-based software engineering [10] and it has been extensively validated using various testing and analysis tools to increase the confidence on the reliability of the library [11].

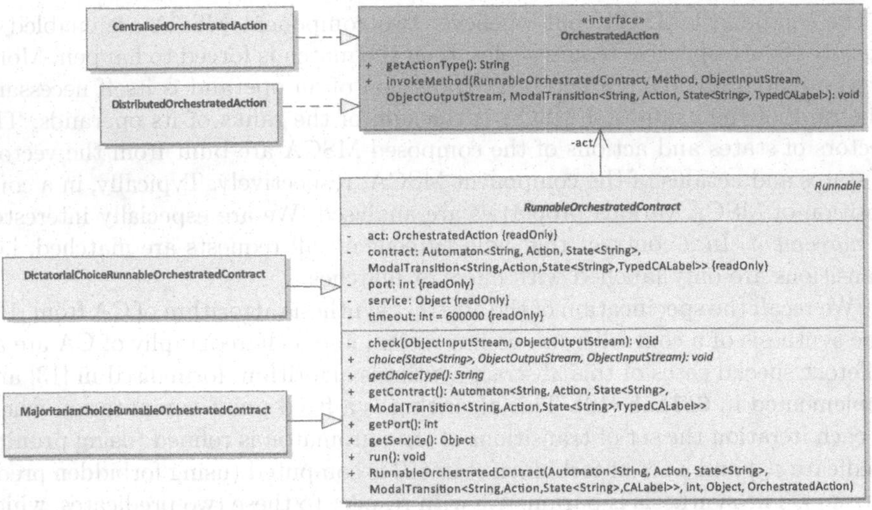

Fig. 1. The class diagram for the orchestrated services; the methods of the derived classes are visible in their super-class/interface as abstract methods (in italic)

3 CARE Design

We start by discussing the design of CARE. This software is organised into classes for the orchestrated services (cf. Fig. 1) and classes for the orchestrator.

In Fig. 1, `RunnableOrchestratedContract` is an abstract class that implements an executable wrapper responsible for the composition of the specification of a service (instance variable `contract` storing a contract automaton) with its implementation (instance variable `service` implementing the service). `RunnableOrchestratedContract` implements a service that is always listening and spawns a parallel process when entering an orchestration. During an orchestration, it receives action commands from the orchestrator or from other services, and it invokes the corresponding action method (by means of the instance variable `act` of type `OrchestratedAction`).

The realisation of an orchestration is abstracted away in contract automata. Crucially, offers and requests of contracts are an abstraction of low-level messages sent between the services and the orchestrator to realise them. CARE exploits the abstractions provided by Java to allow its specialisation according to different implementation choices, using abstractions of object-oriented design, as showed in Fig. 1. Two aspects to implement are choices and termination (through the abstract method `choice`). CARE is equipped with default implementations, but can be extended (by implementing the relative interfaces and abstract methods) to include other options, other than the default ones. Currently, a so-called 'dictatorial' choice (i.e., an internal choice of the orchestrator, external for the services) and a so-called 'majoritarian' choice (services vote and the majority wins) are two implemented options. `MajoritarianChoiceRunnableOrchestratedContract` and `DictatorialChoiceRunnableOrchestratedContract` are the two classes specialising `RunnableOrchestratedContract` according to how the choice is handled and implementing the abstract methods. `CARE` also provides default implementations for the low-level message exchanges. Currently, the two available options are the 'centralised' action, where the orchestrator acts as a proxy, and the 'distributed' action, where two services matching their actions directly interact with each other once the orchestrator has made them aware of a matching partner and its address/port. Accordingly, each `RunnableOrchestratedContract` has an `OrchestratedAction` (instance variable `act`) used to implement the corresponding actions that can be either distributed or centralised according to the current implementation.

The abstract class `RunnableOrchestration` (which is not displayed in Fig. 1) implements a special service that reads the synthesised orchestration (stored in the instance variable `contract`) and orchestrates the `RunnableOrchestratedContract` to realise the overall application. Similarly to the case of the orchestrated contract, also the orchestrator is specialised according to either a dictatorial or a majoritarian implementation of the abstract method `choice`. Moreover, an `OrchestratorAction` instance variable is used to implement each action of the orchestration, either centralised or distributed, thus matching the corresponding actions of the orchestrated services.

Finally, the class `ContractViolationException` implements an exception raised in case an invocation of the orchestrator is not allowed by the orchestrated contract or if that contract is not fulfilled. When thrown, the exception stores the remote host that violates the contract. This guarantees the accountability in case of a contract violation. Each label of a contract automaton is extended using `CARE` with the information on the types of parameters and returned values from the corresponding method implementing the corresponding action. These typed labels are implemented into the class `TypedCALabel`, extending a `CALabel` of `CATLib`. This class also overrides the matching between requests and offers to also take into account their types: the returned value of the request must be of a super-class of the parameter class of the offer and vice versa. This guarantees that no `ClassCastException` will ever be raised when invoking the actions. Note that the signature of each action declared by the interface is not fixed, so other types can be used (e.g., `JSon` values).

We briefly detail the centralised implementation of a match label in `CARE`. We will use the match `[?coffee,!coffee]` from the example in Sect. 6, in which `Alice` is requesting a `coffee` and `Bob` is offering a `coffee`. The method `coffee` of `Alice` is invoked twice: firstly, passing no argument, it generates an `Integer` value (e.g., the amount of sugar) that is passed (by the orchestrator `ror`) as argument to the method `coffee` of `Bob`, which in turn produces a `String` value that is eventually passed as argument to the method `coffee` of `Alice`, thus fulfilling the `coffee` request.

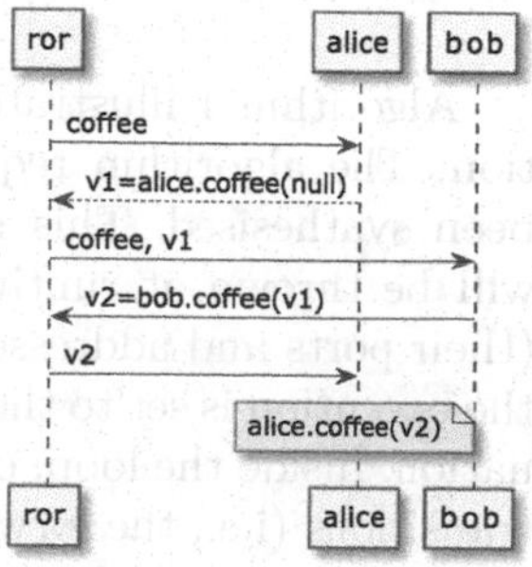

4 Formal Guarantees

We now discuss the formal guarantees of correctness and the adherence of the implementation to the specification brought by the usage of CARE. To begin with, to guarantee that an orchestration is *correct-by-design*, the contract automata operators of composition and orchestration synthesis are used, exploiting the theoretical results on contract automata (cf. Sect. 2). More concretely, these operations are performed in the constructor of a `RunnableOrchestration` using `CATLib`. As discussed in Sect. 2, the synthesised orchestration ensures properties such as absence of deadlocks, matching of all requests of contracts with corresponding offers of other contracts, and reachability of final states.

After a well-behaving orchestration has been synthesised, it is important to ensure that the low-level implementations of the distributed services interacting with each other will adhere to the operations prescribed by the orchestration synthesised from their contracts. This task is addressed by using Algorithm 1 and Algorithm 2, both implemented in CARE, reproduced below in pseudo-code.

Algorithm 1. Orchestration

```
Require: non-empty orchestration automaton
Ensure: no exception is thrown
  init Sockets                          ▷ connect to the services
  cs ← initialState                     ▷ current state
  while true do
      fws ← forwardStar(cs)
      if empty(fws) & notFinal(cs) then
          throw Exception
      end if
      choice ← choice()                 ▷ interact with services
      if choice == stop & final(cs) then
          return
      end if
      tr ← select(fws,choice)
      if tr not in agreement then
          throw Exception
      end if
      doAction(tr)                      ▷ interact with services
      cs ← targetState(tr)
  end while
```

Algorithm 2. Service Thread

```
Require: connected to the orchestrator
  init Socket                           ▷ set socket timeout
  cs ← initialState                     ▷ current state
  while true do
      act ← receive(socket)
      if stop(act) then
          if final(cs) then
              return
          else throw ContractViolationException
          end if
      end if
      if choice(act) then
          performChoice()               ▷ interact with or-
          continue                      ▷ chestration
      end if
      tr ← select(forwardStar(cs),act)
      if no valid action then
          throw ContractViolationException
      else
          invokeMethod(tr)
      end if
      cs ← targetState(tr)
  end while
```

Algorithm 1 illustrates the main operations performed during an orchestration. The algorithm requires that a correct and non-empty orchestration has been synthesised. This requirement is necessary to ensure that no exceptions will be thrown at runtime. Initially, the orchestrator connects to the services (their ports and addresses are stored during instantiation). The current state of the execution is set to the initial state. Subsequently, a loop is executed in continuation. Inside the loop, one of the transitions is selected from the set of outgoing transitions (i.e., the forward star) of the current state, using the implementation of the abstract method `choice`. Here, if there is a deadlock (no outgoing transitions and the current state is not final), an exception is thrown. After that, if the current state is final, but there are also outgoing transitions, then the choice can be to stop or to continue; otherwise, if the state is not final, then the choice can only be to select one of the outgoing transitions. If the selected transition of the orchestration does not satisfy agreement (i.e., its label is a request), then an exception is thrown. Otherwise, the action of the selected transition is executed using the implementation of the abstract method `doAction` and the current state is updated to the target state of the transition. As discussed in Sect. 2, if the orchestration automaton has been synthesised using the contract automata synthesis, then this formally guarantees that the described exceptions will never be thrown by the orchestrator.

Algorithm 2 summarises the execution of an orchestrated service following its contract. The service is multi-threaded and spawns a new thread each time a new request of connection is received. The algorithm depicts the operations performed by a spawned thread. Similarly to the orchestration, there is an initialisation of the socket, and the current state is set to the initial state of the contract. After that, a continuous loop is executed. Firstly, an action is received from the orchestrator. If the choice is of terminating and the contract is in a final state, then the service terminates successfully; otherwise, if the state is not final, an exception is thrown. If the orchestrator requires to make a choice, then the implementation of the abstract method `choice` is called to perform a choice (possibly interacting with the orchestrator). Otherwise, the orchestrator is requiring to perform an action. In this case, the prescribed action is selected from the outgoing transitions of the current state of the service contract. If there is no such action, then a contract violation exception is thrown since the orchestrator is requiring to perform an operation not prescribed by the contract. Otherwise, the method of the service that is paired with the corresponding action of the contract is invoked. These steps ensure that the low-level implementation of the actions of the services are correctly executed according to the actions prescribed by the orchestration synthesised from the composition of contracts. Finally, the current state is set to the target state of the contract and the loop is repeated. Similarly to the orchestration case, if the orchestrator is executing a correctly synthesised orchestration, then the services will never throw any such exception. Indeed, this would be a contradiction to the formal results discussed in Sect. 2.

Interaction Correctness. As stated above, the execution of an *action* or a *choice* is abstracted in `CARE`. Two implementations are currently available for both actions and choices, and the framework is extensible. We now summarise the formal verification of the TCP/IP sockets interactions performed by the available implementations of actions and choices. This provides a complementary verification of the aspects that are abstracted in the above algorithms. The implementation of `CARE` has been formally modelled in UPPAAL as a network of timed automata. Figure 2 depicts the automaton for the `RunnableOrchestration`. Due to lack of space, the automaton for the `RunnableOrchestratedContract` and traceability information linking the model to the source code are available from [9]. Both the synthesised orchestration (which is assumed to have been synthesised correctly) and other details specified in Algorithm 1 and Algorithm 2 are abstracted away in the formal model.

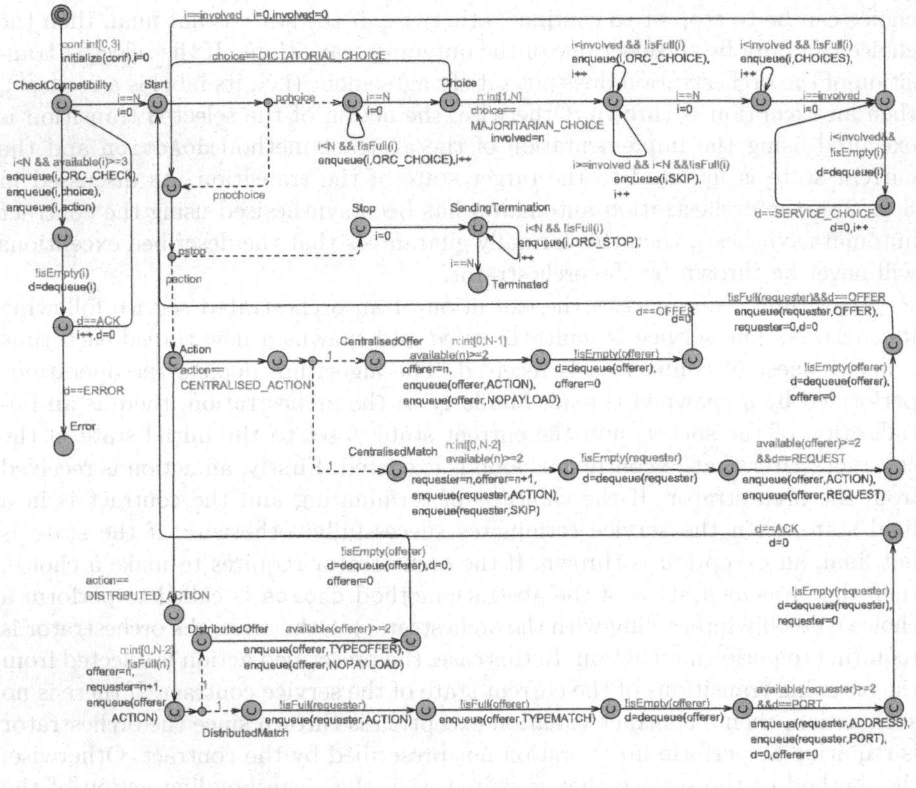

Fig. 2. The `RunnableOrchestration` UPPAAL model

The behaviour according to the given configuration of action and choice is modelled inside each automaton. Global declarations include the number of services N, the size of the buffers, two variables `action` and `choice` storing the corresponding configuration for all automata, and the communication buffers. Java TCP/IP sockets communications are asynchronous with FIFO buffers. In the model, arrays are used to encode these buffers that are only modified with functions for enqueueing and dequeuing messages. Each party communicates with the partner using two buffers (one for sending and one for receiving). Both automata declare a method `enqueue` for sending a message to the partner. Similarly, both automata have a method `dequeue` for consuming messages from their respective buffers. According to the semantics of Java TCP/IP sockets, a transition having a send in its effect will check in its guard whether there is enough space left in the buffer of the partner by calling either the method `available` (returning the space left) or `isFull`. Moreover, before reading it is always checked whether the buffer is not empty with the method `!isEmpty`. When the buffer is empty, the automaton blocks until a message is received. The locations of the model are *urgent* (denoted with `U`) to guarantee that when the appropriate message is received it will eventually be consumed (i.e., there is no starvation).

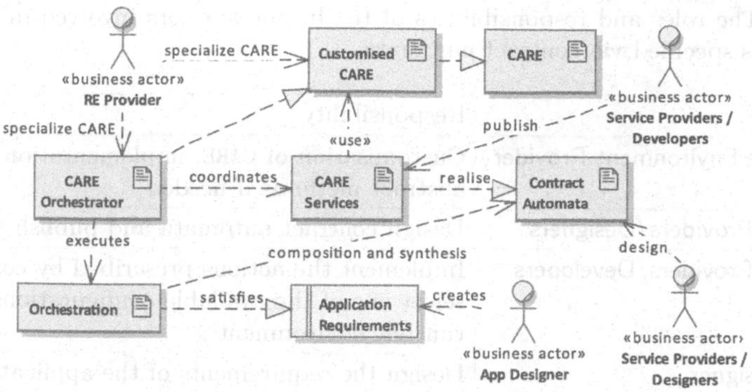

Fig. 3. The CARE business actors developing contract-based applications

The absence of deadlocks was verified by model checking the CTL formula `A[](not deadlock || (ror.Terminated && (forall(i:id_t) ROC(i).Terminated)))`, in which `ror` is the orchestrator and `ROC(i)` is a runnable orchestrated contract identified with index i. Moreover, the absence of orphan messages was verified by model checking `A[]((ror.Terminated && (forall (i:id_t) ROC(i).Terminated)) imply allEmpty())`, in which the predicate `allEmpty()` is satisfied when the buffers are empty. Finally, `A[](ror.Stop imply A<>(ror.Terminated && (forall (i:id_t) ROC(i).Terminated) && allEmpty()))` was used to verify that whenever a choice to stop is made, eventually all services and the orchestrator will terminate their execution.

5 Building Applications with CARE

We now discuss how CARE can be adopted to develop applications with contract automata. The diagram in Fig. 3 depicts the responsibilities of the business actors involved in the overall realisation of contract-based applications using CARE. The first actor is the provider of the runtime environment (`RE Provider` in Fig. 3). This actor customises CARE and its classes according to specific needs, possibly introducing new different options for choices and actions implementing the abstract methods provided by CARE (described in Sect. 3), and delivers to the other actors a customised version of CARE, which also comprehends an orchestrator. Note that this customisation is not necessary, but is a further possibility allowed by the CARE software design.

The second kind of actors are the service providers, who publish their contracts, implemented by remote (non-disclosed) Java classes, and use a `RunnableOrchestratedContract` to make their contract publicly accessible using CARE, while hiding implementation details. Service providers may choose among different realisations of their `RunnableOrchestratedContract`, provided by the first actor above. Notably, implementing each atomic action of a service and designing the interaction behaviour through contract automata are two different concerns. The designer (cf. Fig. 3) specifying interactions as a contract is not required to be an expert in the underlying implementation technology (e.g., Java sockets), while the developer implementing actions and selecting the CARE

Table 1. The roles and responsibilities of the business actors involved in developing applications specified via contract automata.

Role	Responsibility
Runtime Environment Provider	Customisation of CARE, implementation of abstract methods if needed
Service Providers/Designers	Design contract automata and publish them
Service Providers/Developers	Implement the actions prescribed by contracts, select one of the available configurations of the runtime environment
App Designer	Design the requirements of the application, discover contracts, select one of the available configurations of the runtime environment

configuration is not required to be skilled in contract automata theory. The specification and implementation of a service can thus be seamlessly integrated using the facilities provided by `CARE`. This integration using `CARE` is depicted with a *realize* arrow from the services to the contracts. Most importantly, when implementing the service, the developer does not need to worry about the underlying low-level interactions between services, potential deadlocks and other communication issues. This error-prone implementation activity is already resolved by `CARE`, as discussed in Sect. 4. This separation of concerns also solves the problem of "muddling the main program logic with auxiliary logic related to error handling" (i.e., handling the Java communication exceptions) [24].

The third actor is the application designer (`App Designer` in Fig. 3). This is a user of both the second and the first actor. The designer is responsible for specifying the *requirements* of the application, and to find a suitable set of remote services whose synthesised orchestration satisfies the desired requirements. Once the contracts are discovered, the orchestration enforcing the requirements is automatically synthesised as a new contract. This is depicted by an arrow from `Orchestration` to `Contract Automata` in Fig. 3. The application designer exploits `CARE`, choosing a specific implementation of `RunnableOrchestration` and `RunnableOrchestratedContract`, passing as arguments the addresses of the services, as well as the synthesised orchestration. Formal results from contract automata theory [12–15] (cf. Sect. 2) guarantee that no `ContractViolationException` will ever be raised at runtime (cf. Sect. 4). Finally, note that one individual could take the roles of more actors if needed (e.g., covering both roles of developer and designer, designing a global requirement, implementing a new choice, and publishing a target contract). The proposed separation of concerns is logical. The roles and responsibilities of the various business actors described in this section are summarised in Table 1.

6 Examples and Evaluation

We discuss the usage of `CARE` using two examples. Their source code, video tutorials, and evaluation data are available from [18].

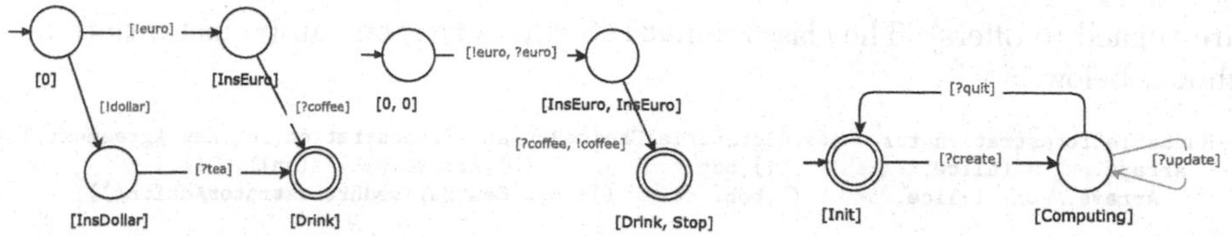

Fig. 4. From left to right, the contract of `Alice`, the orchestration of `Alice` and `Bob` enforcing the given requirement, and the contract of the `Client`

Alice and Bob. This is a basic yet illustrative example. In this example, the requirement `req` of the application, designed by the `App Designer`, is an automaton specifying that an action `coffee` is observed after an action `euro`. In this example, the `RE Provider` will simply provide `CARE` as it is, without further providing customised implementations of the abstract methods.

We now move to the `Service Provider/Designers` actors. Consider Fig. 4 (the automata have been constructed using `CAT_App`). The leftmost automaton is the contract of `Alice` and specifies that `Alice` offers either a `!euro` or a `!dollar` to her partner. Then `Alice` requires `?coffee` or `?tea`, depending on which offer has been accepted. Such a contract can be interpreted as describing the interaction pattern of `Alice`, whilst abstracting away from the actual implementation of each action. To declare the signature of each contract action, `CARE` uses Java Interfaces, as shown below.

```
public interface AliceInterface {
  Integer coffee(String arg); Integer tea(String arg);
  Integer euro(String arg); Integer dollar(String arg); }
```

In the interpretation of contracts provided by `CARE`, each contract action is implemented by a method of an interface, whose names are in correspondence. The implementation will be developed by the actor `Service Provider/Developer`. By implementing the corresponding interface it is possible to pair the interaction logic described in Fig. 4 (left) with an actual implementation, as shown below.

```
RunnableOrchestratedContract alice = new DictatorialChoiceRunnableOrchestratedContract(ca,
  8080,new Alice(),new CentralisedOrchestratedAction());
```

The parameter `ca` contains the leftmost contract in Fig. 4. The class `Alice` implements `AliceInterface`. This implementation is paired with the corresponding contract: the service listens to port 8080 and the chosen implementation of the low level interactions is `CentralisedOrchestratedAction`. Notably, `RunnableOrchestratedContract` will take care of the low-level communications, abstracted away in `Alice.java`. In `AliceInterface`, each action requires an argument (of type `String`) and returns a value (of type `Integer`). During initialisation, each label of the contract is extended with the information on the types of parameters and returned values from the interface, by instantiating a `TypedCALabel`. The contract of `Bob` is dual to the one of `Alice` (i.e., all requests are turned to offers). The class `RunnableOrchestration` can be instantiated as shown below.

```
RunnableOrchestration ror = new DictatorialChoiceRunnableOrchestration(req,new Agreement(),
  Arrays.asList(alice.getContract(),bob.getContract()),Arrays.asList(null,null),
    Arrays.asList(alice.getPort(),bob.getPort()),new CentralisedOrchestratorAction());
```

`DictatorialChoiceRunnableOrchestration` provides an implementation of the branch/termination selection where the orchestrator autonomously selects a branch. It is instantiated by passing as parameters the requirement `req` to be enforced, the predicate on interactions among contracts (i.e., the property of agreement), the list of contracts to compose, addresses and ports of the `RunnableOrchestratedContract` of `Alice` and `Bob`, and an object of class `CentralisedOrchestratorAction` implementing an `OrchestratorAction`. In this example, services are run locally on the same host as the orchestrator. During instantiation, the contracts passed as arguments will be composed to synthesise their safe orchestration in agreement.

In this example, the contract of `Bob` is in agreement with that of `Alice` (each request is matched by a corresponding offer). The orchestration `orc` is the central automaton in Fig. 4. After `ror` has been instantiated, its method `isEmptyOrchestration()` is used to check if an agreement among contracts exists, i.e., if the synthesised orchestration is non-empty. During instantiation, `RunnableOrchestration` also interacts with all services (using Java TCP sockets) to ensure that all share the same configuration, which in this case is a dictatorial choice with centralised action. If this is not the case, an exception is thrown. Upon successful instantiation, `ror` can be executed to realise the application modelled through the requirement `req` using the two contracts above.

Finally, we remark that it suffices to change the requirement to automatically adapt the services to generate a new application. In this example, if `req` were changed to also allow a `tea` in case of payment with `dollar`, then `Alice` and `Bob` could be adapted to fulfill this new requirement automatically.

Composition Service. Computing a composition of contract automata can be a costly operation. For a front-end running on a standard laptop (e.g., `CAT_App`), a desirable feature could be to delegate such costly computations to a remote service, hosted on a powerful machine. This example showcases a service built with `CARE` that computes a composition of contract automata. The service receives the operand automata together with other scalability options (e.g., a bound, invariants) from a client service. The client service interacts through the console with a user who indicates which automata to compose and the other options. `CATLib` features on-the-fly bounded composition. When extending the bound of a previously computed composition, the previously generated states of the composition are not recomputed. The newly generated states are limited to those that exceeded the previous bound.

The client contract is the rightmost automaton in Fig. 4, whilst the service contract is dual (all requests are turned to offers). The client contract can perform a necessary request `update` from state `Computing`. This guarantees that in a non-empty orchestration, the necessary request of the client is matched by a corresponding offer. If such a request were not necessary, a non-empty orchestration could also be obtained when the client is composed with a service that does not offer the `update` action, but only actions `create` and `quit`.

From state `Init`, the client can either terminate or perform a `create` request. During the execution of this method the user interacts at console and types the needed input. The payload returned by the request method is submitted by the runtime support to the service executing the matching offer. The offer implementation takes as parameter the payload and returns the composed automaton (which can be bounded to a specific depth), which is sent back to the requester. In the implementation of the `update` request, the client sends an incremented bound to the service, which proceeds to compute the composition with the extended bound and sends it to the client. The request `quit` is used as a signal for resetting both the computed composition and the bound.

There are two choices: in state `Init`, the orchestration can terminate or an action `create` can be executed. In state `Computing`, two possible actions can be performed. The `MajoritarianChoiceRunnableOrchestratedContract` method `select` is overridden by each service, to implement the specific choices to be made. The composition service always replies with an empty answer. This means that all choices are external to the service, the service does not indicate which choice has to be made. The client service implements both choices as internal. The user of the client service will interact at console with the client service, and will indicate which choice has to be made. More details can be found in [18].

Evaluation. We now measure the advantages brought by adopting `CARE`. To do so, we compare two different implementations for the two examples. These two implementations of each example perform the exact same operations as described above. Both implementations exploit the operations of composition and synthesis of contract automata provided by `CATLib`. However, only one of them uses `CARE` (as described above) whereas the other manually implements the prescribed interactions between the services and the orchestrator, without using any of the facilities provided by `CARE`. In this way, it is possible to isolate and measure the benefits brought solely by using `CARE`. These two implementations per example are open source and available for inspection from [18], where they are located in two separate packages.

The comparison was performed using measures of code complexity as provided by `SonarCloud` [16], an online service well integrated with `GitHub` that performs, among others, continuous inspection of code quality and static analysis of code to detect bugs, and reports on code complexity. We in particular used the code complexity reports feature of `SonarCloud`. We used three different measures of complexity to showcase the benefits of using `CARE`. The first measure is the total amount of lines of code (thus excluding, among others, the lines of comments and white spaces). We also adopted cyclomatic complexity [29] and cognitive complexity [16]. Cyclomatic complexity measures the number of independent paths in the software and it is a measure of code testability (this number is close to the number of branches to cover in the program). Cognitive complexity

Table 2. Different measures of complexity of the examples from Sect. 6 implemented either with or without using CARE

		LOC	Cyclomatic Complexity	Cognitive Complexity
Alice and Bob	without CARE	777	134	166
	with CARE	153	16	8
Composition service	without CARE	854	155	211
	with CARE	279	42	55

measures how difficult the control flow is to understand. This measure is roughly a counter incremented each time a control flow structure is encountered (e.g., `if` and `for`) and it is incremented commensurated with the level of nesting of control flow structures (e.g., a first-level structure triggers an increment of 1, a second-level structure triggers an increment of 2, and so on) [16].

The results are reported in Table 2. To compare these quantities, we use the relative percent difference (*rpd*): $\frac{|\texttt{withCARE}-\texttt{withoutCARE}|}{max(\texttt{withCARE},\texttt{withoutCARE})} \times 100$. This measures the change of complexity when using CARE with respect to the reference value (i.e., withoutCARE). The advantage of using CARE is clear, as it drastically reduces the complexity of the software. Indeed, when using CARE (for the "Alice and Bob" and "Composition Service" examples, respectively) the *rpd* are: for the lines of code 80.31% and 67.33%, for the cyclomatic complexity 88.06% and 72.90%, and for the cognitive complexity 95.18% and 73.93%. These results are not surprising: the experiments underline the complexity of the operations performed by CARE and its key role in developing applications specified via contract automata. Indeed, for both examples the complexity of implementing the low-level communications is the dominant factor if compared to the interaction logic. This is more prominent for the "Alice and Bob" example, which in fact has greater *rpd* values. The burden of implementing these low-level communications among the services and the orchestrator is still on the developer side when not using CARE. We also remark how implementing the low-level communications is an error-prone activity that is completely delegated to the runtime support if one uses CARE, thus improving the confidence in the correctness of the final application.

Scalability. The above experiments only measured the complexity of the software developed with or without CARE. Another important aspect is the possibility of scaling to larger automata. CARE is a runtime environment and does not face any scalability issue typical of static analysers (e.g., state-space explosion). On the other hand, the synthesis of a safe orchestration of contracts is computed using CATLib, which may face scalability challenges when dealing with large compositions. In Sect. 2, the scalability features offered by CATLib are reported. The performance of CATLib has been previously measured in [10]. Concerning the formal verification of CARE discussed in Sect. 4, we recall that the orchestration automaton is abstracted away in the UPPAAL model. Thus, the formal model of CARE is verified for any orchestration of any size.

On a side note, the single-responsibility principle [28] advocates to assign a single responsibility to each class. By interpreting this principle over behavioural contracts, we conclude that a contract automaton assigned to a single class (e.g., the rightmost automaton in Fig. 4) should not exhibit a large behaviour.

7 Conclusion

We have presented the first runtime environment for contract automata, called CARE. Our proposal advances the state-of-the-art of the research on contract automata by showing a possible realisation of an orchestration engine, abstracted away in the contract automata theory, but needed for implementing applications specified with contract automata, and guaranteeing that the implementation of service-based applications respect their specification. This contribution improves our understanding of the relation between a specification with contract automata and its implementation, and the corresponding level of abstraction.

With CARE, it is possible to promote a separation of concerns between formal methods experts specifying the expected behaviour using automata on one side, and developers (not required to be experts in formal methods) implementing the actions on the other. Furthermore, an application built using CARE is based on rigorous theoretical results from the contract automata theory, guaranteeing properties such as absence of deadlocks and absence of orphan messages, reachability of final states, and absence of ContractViolationException. Moreover, CARE promotes modularity of applications composed by different services that are reusable in different applications and that can be adapted to satisfy different requirements through the synthesis of well-behaving orchestrations. Experiments showed the improvement in terms of decreased software complexity when using CARE instead of manually implementing the low-level interactions among services implementing the operations prescribed by their contracts.

Future Work. CATLib already implements the synthesis of choreographies [13], which CARE will support in the future. Although CARE has been developed in the framework of contract automata, we plan to investigate the integration of this technology with other behavioural types languages and tools (e.g., typestates).

Acknowledgment. Funded by MUR PRIN 2017FTXR7S project IT MaTTerS (Methods and Tools for Trustworthy Smart Systems) and PRIN 2020TL3X8X project T-LADIES (Typeful Language Adaptation for Dynamic, Interacting and Evolving Systems).

References

1. Aceto, L., Cassar, I., Francalanza, A., Ingólfsdóttir, A.: Comparing controlled system synthesis and suppression enforcement. Int. J. Softw. Tools Technol. Transfer **23**(4), 601–614 (2021). https://doi.org/10.1007/s10009-021-00624-0
2. Ancona, D., et al.: Behavioral types in programming languages. Found. Trends Program. Lang. **3**(2–3), 95–230 (2016). https://doi.org/10.1561/2500000031

3. Atampore, F., Dingel, J., Rudie, K.: A controller synthesis framework for automated service composition. Discrete Event Dyn. Syst. **29**(3), 297–365 (2019). https://doi.org/10.1007/s10626-019-00282-0
4. Atzei, N., Bartoletti, M.: Developing honest Java programs with Diogenes. In: Albert, E., Lanese, I. (eds.) FORTE 2016. LNCS, vol. 9688, pp. 52–61. Springer, Cham (2016). https://doi.org/10.1007/978-3-319-39570-8_4
5. Azzopardi, S., Piterman, N., Schneider, G.: Incorporating monitors in reactive synthesis without paying the price. In: Hou, Z., Ganesh, V. (eds.) ATVA 2021. LNCS, vol. 12971, pp. 337–353. Springer, Cham (2021). https://doi.org/10.1007/978-3-030-88885-5_22
6. Bacchiani, L., Bravetti, M., Giunti, M., Mota, J., Ravara, A.: A Java typestate checker supporting inheritance. Sci. Comput. Program. **221**, 102844 (2022). https://doi.org/10.1016/j.scico.2022.102844
7. Barati, M., St-Denis, R.: Behavior composition meets supervisory control. In: Proceedings of the 2015 International Conference on Systems, Man, and Cybernetics (SMC), pp. 115–120. IEEE (2015). https://doi.org/10.1109/SMC.2015.33
8. Bartoletti, M., Cimoli, T., Murgia, M., Podda, A.S., Pompianu, L.: A contract-oriented middleware. In: Braga, C., Ölveczky, P.C. (eds.) FACS 2015. LNCS, vol. 9539, pp. 86–104. Springer, Cham (2016). https://doi.org/10.1007/978-3-319-28934-2_5
9. Basile, D.: Uppaal Models of the Contract Automata Runtime Environment. https://github.com/contractautomataproject/CARE/tree/master/src/spec/uppaal
10. Basile, D., ter Beek, M.H.: A clean and efficient implementation of choreography synthesis for behavioural contracts. In: Damiani, F., Dardha, O. (eds.) COORDINATION 2021. LNCS, vol. 12717, pp. 225–238. Springer, Cham (2021). https://doi.org/10.1007/978-3-030-78142-2_14
11. Basile, D., ter Beek, M.H.: Contract automata library. Sci. Comput. Program. **221** (2022). https://doi.org/10.1016/j.scico.2022.102841. https://github.com/contractautomataproject/ContractAutomataLib
12. Basile, D., et al.: Controller synthesis of service contracts with variability. Sci. Comput. Program. **187**, 102344 (2020). https://doi.org/10.1016/j.scico.2019.102344
13. Basile, D., ter Beek, M.H., Pugliese, R.: Synthesis of orchestrations and choreographies: bridging the gap between supervisory control and coordination of services. Log. Methods Comput. Sci. **16**(2), 9:1–9:29 (2020). https://doi.org/10.23638/LMCS-16(2:9)2020
14. Basile, D., Degano, P., Ferrari, G.L.: Automata for specifying and orchestrating service contracts. Log. Methods Comput. Sci. **12**(4), 6:1–6:51 (2016). https://doi.org/10.2168/LMCS-12(4:6)2016
15. Basile, D., Degano, P., Ferrari, G.L., Tuosto, E.: Relating two automata-based models of orchestration and choreography. J. Log. Algebraic Methods Program. **85**(3), 425–446 (2016). https://doi.org/10.1016/j.jlamp.2015.09.011
16. Campbell, G.A.: Cognitive complexity: an overview and evaluation. In: Proceedings of the 2018 International Conference on Technical Debt (TechDebt), pp. 57–58. ACM (2018). https://doi.org/10.1145/3194164.3194186
17. Contract Automata Runtime Environment (CARE) v1.0.0. https://github.com/contractautomataproject/CARE/
18. CARE Examples and Evaluation. Including video tutorials for reproducing the examples. https://github.com/contractautomataproject/CARE_Examples/
19. CAT_App. https://github.com/contractautomataproject/ContractAutomataApp

20. Dilley, N., Lange, J.: An empirical study of messaging passing concurrency in Go projects. In: Proceedings of the 26th International Conference on Software Analysis, Evolution and Reengineering (SANER), pp. 377–387. IEEE (2019). https://doi.org/10.1109/SANER.2019.8668036
21. Farhat, H.: Web service composition via supervisory control theory. IEEE Access **6**, 59779–59789 (2018). https://doi.org/10.1109/ACCESS.2018.2874564
22. Felli, P., Yadav, N., Sardina, S.: Supervisory control for behavior composition. IEEE Trans. Autom. Control **62**(2), 986–991 (2017). https://doi.org/10.1109/TAC.2016.2570748
23. Ferrari, A., ter Beek, M.H.: Formal methods in railways: a systematic mapping study. ACM Comput. Surv. **55**(4), 69:1–69:37 (2023). https://doi.org/10.1145/3520480
24. Francalanza, A., Mezzina, C.A., Tuosto, E.: Towards choreographic-based monitoring. In: Ulidowski, I., Lanese, I., Schultz, U.P., Ferreira, C. (eds.) RC 2020. LNCS, vol. 12070, pp. 128–150. Springer, Cham (2020). https://doi.org/10.1007/978-3-030-47361-7_6
25. Gay, S., Ravara, A. (eds.): Behavioural Types: From Theory to Tools. River (2017). https://doi.org/10.13052/rp-9788793519817
26. Kouzapas, D., Dardha, O., Perera, R., Gay, S.J.: Typechecking protocols with Mungo and StMungo: a session type toolchain for Java. Sci. Comput. Program. **155**, 52–75 (2018). https://doi.org/10.1016/j.scico.2017.10.006
27. Lange, J., Ng, N., Toninho, B., Yoshida, N.: A static verification framework for message passing in Go using behavioural types. In: Proceedings of the 40th International Conference on Software Engineering (ICSE), pp. 1137–1148. ACM (2018). https://doi.org/10.1145/3180155.3180157
28. Martin, R.C.: Agile Software Development: Principles, Patterns, and Practices. Prentice Hall PTR (2003)
29. McCabe, T.J.: A complexity measure. IEEE Trans. Softw. Eng. **2**(4), 308–320 (1976). https://doi.org/10.1109/TSE.1976.233837
30. Ramadge, P.J., Wonham, W.M.: Supervisory control of a class of discrete event processes. SIAM J. Control. Optim. **25**(1), 206–230 (1987). https://doi.org/10.1137/0325013
31. Rubbens, R., Lathouwers, S., Huisman, M.: Modular transformation of Java exceptions modulo errors. In: Lluch Lafuente, A., Mavridou, A. (eds.) FMICS 2021. LNCS, vol. 12863, pp. 67–84. Springer, Cham (2021). https://doi.org/10.1007/978-3-030-85248-1_5
32. Sánchez, C., et al.: A survey of challenges for runtime verification from advanced application domains (beyond software). Formal Methods Syst. Des. **54**(3), 279–335 (2019). https://doi.org/10.1007/s10703-019-00337-w
33. Strom, R.E., Yemini, S.: Typestate: a programming language concept for enhancing software reliability. IEEE Trans. Softw. Eng. **12**(1), 157–171 (1986). https://doi.org/10.1109/TSE.1986.6312929
34. Trindade, A., Mota, J., Ravara, A.: Typestates to automata and back: a tool. In: Lange, J., Mavridou, A., Safina, L., Scalas, A. (eds.) Proceedings of the 13th Interaction and Concurrency Experience (ICE). EPTCS, vol. 324, pp. 25–42 (2020). https://doi.org/10.4204/EPTCS.324.4
35. Vasconcelos, C., Ravara, A.: From object-oriented code with assertions to behavioural types. In: Proceedings of the 32nd Symposium on Applied Computing (SAC), pp. 1492–1497. ACM (2017). https://doi.org/10.1145/3019612.3019733

Industry Day

Formal and Executable Semantics of the Ethereum Virtual Machine in Dafny

Franck Cassez(✉), Joanne Fuller, Milad K. Ghale, David J. Pearce, and Horacio M. A. Quiles

ConsenSys, New York, USA
{franck.cassez,joanne.fuller,milad.ghale,david.pearce, horacio.quiles}@consensys.net

Abstract. The Ethereum protocol implements a replicated state machine. The network participants keep track of the system state by: 1) agreeing on the sequence of transactions to be processed and 2) computing the state transitions that correspond to the sequence of transactions. Ethereum transactions are programs, called *smart contracts*, and computing a state transition requires executing some code. The Ethereum Virtual Machine (EVM) provides this capability and can execute programs written in EVM *bytecode*. We present a formal and executable semantics of the EVM written in the verification-friendly language DAFNY: it provides (*i*) a readable, formal and verified specification of the semantics of the EVM; (*ii*) a framework to formally reason about bytecode.

1 Introduction

A distinctive feature of Ethereum is that transactions are programs, *smart contracts*, and computing a state transition requires to run the contract code to compute the next state. This capability is provided by the Ethereum Virtual Machine (EVM) that can execute programs written in EVM *bytecode*. The original and informal specification of the EVM is in the Yellow Paper [28].

As a decentralised platform, Ethereum encourages *client diversity*: network participants are free to choose which implementation of the EVM they want to run, and there are several implementations to choose from written in different languages e.g., Go, Java. All the EVM implementations must agree on the state transitions, otherwise the network would split and the blockchain would *fork*. However, the original specification in the Yellow Paper [28] has some known shortcomings: (*i*) it is hard to read and does not provide a formal semantics of the EVM and the bytecode; (*ii*) the lack of a formal semantics makes it hard for Ethereum client developers to guarantee that they interpret the Yellow Paper in a consistent way; (*iii*) designing compilers from high-level languages (e.g., Solidity[1]) to EVM bytecode without a formal semantics is error-prone and,

[1] The most popular language to write smart contracts.

M. Chechik et al. (Eds.): FM 2023, LNCS 14000, pp. 571–583, 2023.
https://doi.org/10.1007/978-3-031-27481-7_32

without a precise semantics of the EVM, it is hard to design *certified* compilers (preserving of semantics from a high to a low-level language.).

One can argue that existing implementations of the EVM (e.g., in Go, Java) provide a *de facto* semantics for it. Whilst this is true to some extent, such implementations do not enable *formal reasoning* about bytecode. Furthermore, whilst smart contracts can be written in high-level languages like Solidity, they must be compiled into EVM bytecode before being executed on the EVM. Tools for checking safety properties (e.g., absence of overflow, division by zero, etc.) at the Solidity level are problematic if they cannot guarantee such properties hold at the bytecode level. One solution is to design a provably correct compiler, but this is a complex and long-term endeavour [17]. Alternatively we can provide techniques, supported by tools, to reason about properties of the bytecode. This is what we propose to do in this work.

Our Contribution. We present a complete and formal specification of the EVM in DAFNY, available at https://github.com/ConsenSys/evm-dafny. We provide a formal semantics where the meaning of an instruction is given as a partial function that maps states to states. Our semantics is language-agnostic, readable and can be used as a reference for developers of EVMs or to aid compiler writers. Moreover, it is a complete and usable framework for formally reasoning about correctness of EVM bytecode using DAFNY.

2 Background and Motivation

In this section we give an overview of the EVM and show how our formal specification in DAFNY can be used to verify properties of bytecode programs.

The Ethereum blockchain stores the bytecode of the *contracts* into a database and each contract has its own permanent storage. In what follows, we assume a given contract and refer to storage as that allocated to this contract.

Instructions and States. The EVM [28] is a *stack-based* machine [28] which supports 142 instructions: arithmetic operations (e.g., `ADD`, `MUL`), comparisons and bitwise operations (e.g., `ISZERO`, `NOT`), cryptographic primitives (e.g., `SHA3`), environment information (e.g., `BALANCE`, `CALLVALUE`), block information (e.g., `NUMBER`, `GASLIMIT`), stack/memory/control flow (e.g., `PUSH`, `POP`, `MSTORE`, `SLOAD`, `JUMP`), logging (e.g., `LOG1`), and system operations (e.g., `CREATE`, `CALL`, `DELEGATECALL`). An *executing state* of the EVM is a tuple containing several components. We restrict our attention to the following subset of these components:

code: a sequence of n bytes indexed from 0 to $n-1$; The byte at index $0 \leq k < n$ is either an instruction *opcode* or an *immediate operand*. For instance the sequence $s = [\texttt{0x60}, \texttt{0x01}, \texttt{0x60}, \texttt{0x02}, \texttt{0x01}, \texttt{0x50}, \texttt{0x00}]$ corresponds to the *program* "`PUSH1 0x01; PUSH1 0x02; ADD; POP; STOP`". Here, the byte at $s[1]$ (`0x01`) is the operand of the instruction at $s[0]$ (`PUSH1`).

pc: the *program counter* (initially 0) identifies the next instruction to execute. For example, if `pc` is 4, executing the instruction at $s[4]$ (`ADD`) increments it by 1 so $s[5]$ is the next instruction to execute. When executing instructions with operands (e.g., "PUSH1 0x01" at $s[0]s[1]$) the pc is incremented by $1 + v$ where v is the number of operands.

stack: a *stack* of 256-bit words (initially empty); instructions can push or pop the stack. For example, starting from an empty stack [], executing the instructions "PUSH1 0x1; PUSH1 0x2" gives [0x02, 0x01]. Executing the ADD instruction from the stack [0x02, 0x01] pops 2 operands, adds them and pushes the result yielding a new stack [0x03 = 0x01 + 0x02].

memory: a 256-bit addressable, contiguous array of bytes (initially empty). Memory is volatile and only available during the current program execution. Memory expands on-demand when a value is read or written to a given location (which incurs some cost in gas). Values can be read from/written to memory using the instructions MLOAD, MSTORE, MLOAD8 or MSTORE8.

storage: a map from 256-bit addresses to 256-bit words which constitutes the contract's permanent storage. Storage can be read/written using the instructions SLOAD or SSTORE.

gas: the fuel left for future computations. Executing an instruction consumes *gas* in the EVM, and this ensures that no infinite computation can occur.

In the EVM, program execution may *abort* under exceptional cases including:

Out-of-gas: the gas left in the current state does not cover the cost of executing the next instruction (including cost of memory expansion if any);

Stack exceptions: the stack size cannot exceed 1024. Moreover, some instructions (e.g., POP) can only be executed if the stack has enough elements and otherwise the execution should abort.

The EVM has *failure states* to capture aborted computations. As a result, a *state* of the EVM is either a failure state or a non-failure state.

Bytecode Verification. Using our formal semantics, we can guarantee security properties of bytecode programs using the DAFNY verifier. DAFNY is a verification-friendly language and as such the code can be instrumented with predicates and pre- and postconditions that are checked by the verifier at *compile time.* We use this feature to prove properties on the bytecode. The following simple DAFNY program illustrates a proof:

```
method AddBytes(x: u8, y: u8) {
  // Initialise an EVM with some gas and the bytecode to execute.
  var st := InitEmpty(gas:=1000, code:=[PUSH1,x,PUSH1,y,ADD]);
  // Execute 3 compute steps
  st := ExecuteN(st,3);
  // Check that the top of the stack is the sum of x and y
  assert st.Peek(0) == (x as u256) + (y as u256);
}
```

This simple code snippet illustrates several aspects of the verification process. First we can verify *family of programs* as the parameters x,y are arbitrary unsigned integers over 8 bits. This is done by creating an EVM and stepping through the code, e.g., using the ExecuteN function. Second, we specify the expected property of the code using the `assert` statement (line 7) which is a *verification* statement: it is not *executed* at runtime as in conventional programming languages but *checked* at *compile-time*, and must hold for all inputs. For this program DAFNY can prove automatically that the `assert` statement is never violated. The proof uses the semantics of opcodes that are invoked in the computation of `ExecuteN`. Note that if we change `u8` to `u256` the property does not hold as an overflow can occur in the execution of `ADD`: this is flagged by the DAFNY verifier with "Cannot prove assertion at line 7". Another set of checks that are performed automatically are related to pre- and postconditions. For instance the `ADD` instructions requires at least two elements on the stack. This is specified by a precondition in the function that defines the semantics of `ADD`. If the code above had only one `PUSH1` instruction DAFNY would flag that the `ADD` cannot be performed as a precondition is violated. Overall, this short code snippet demonstrates that we can specify and verify functional correctness properties of bytecode, and thanks to the pre- and postconditions used to specify the semantics of the instructions, we can detect/fix possible exceptions (e.g., stack overflow) before runtime.

The example in Listing A.1 shows how we can reason about storage updates and exceptions (aborted computations).

Listing A.1. Verifying bytecode with Reverts.

```
const INC_CONTRACT := Code.Create([
  // Put STORAGE[0] on stack and increment by one
  PUSH1, 0x0, SLOAD, PUSH1, 1, ADD,
  // If result non-zero branch to JUMPDEST, else REVERT
  DUP1, PUSH1, 0xf, JUMPI, PUSH1, 0x0, PUSH1, 0x0, REVERT,
  // Write result back to STORAGE[0] and return
  JUMPDEST, PUSH1, 0x0, SSTORE, STOP]);

method IncProof(st: State) returns (st': State)
    requires st.OK? && st.PC() == 0 && st.Gas() >= 40000 ...
    requires st.evm.code == INC_CONTRACT
    ensures st'.REVERTS? || st'.RETURNS?
    ensures st'.RETURNS? <==> (st.Load(0) as nat) < MAX_U256
    ensures st'.RETURNS? ==> st'.Load(0) == (st.Load(0) + 1) {
  // Execute upto (and including) JUMPI.
  var nst := ExecuteN(st,7);
  // Consider branches separately
  if nst.Peek(0) == 0 { // test top of the stack
      assert nst.PC() == 0xa;
      nst := ExecuteN(nst,3);
      assert nst.REVERTS?;
  } else {
      assert nst.PC() == 0xf;
      nst := ExecuteN(nst,4);
      assert nst.RETURNS?;
  }
  return nst;
}
```

This contract code maintains a counter at storage location 0 which is incremented by one on every contract call. Initially, the contract storage is unconstrained in the input state `st` and, hence, any location can contain any value. The code of the contract aims to capture overflows and to revert if an overflow occurs. The intent is that either the contract reverts (overflow detected) or the counter is incremented by 1. Listing A.1 gives a DAFNY proof of this.[2] The preconditions (lines 10–11) ensure that `st` is an execution (non-failure) state with `pc == 0`, empty stack, enough gas, and has the contract code to execute.

The postconditions (lines 12–14) specify that the computation either increments the counter (at storage location 0) or the computation reverts. The proof divides up into two essential parts: **1.** Execute the first 7 bytecodes and store the intermediate state in `nst`. **2.** An overflow occurs when the result of the addition is 0. So depending on the result at the top of the stack, `nst.Peek(0)`, we decide whether the rest of the computation will either succeed or revert. DAFNY successfully verifies this code and guarantees the postconditions on lines 12–14 for all input states `st` satisfying the preconditions (lines 10–11). This provides strong guarantees about the bytecode: (*i*) it either reverts or computes the increment but never runs out of gas, nor ends up in an invalid state (e.g., stack overflow or underflow), (*ii*) the program terminates normally *if and only if* the initial value stored at location 0 is strictly less than `MAX_U256` (line 13), (*iii*) on normal termination, the value in storage location 0 is incremented by one (line 14).

3 The Dafny-EVM

Our EVM is written in DAFNY and provides a definition of the semantics as a function mapping states to states. A key design decision made early on was to develop a *functionally pure* formalisation of the EVM. In this section we describe the main components of the Dafny-EVM and conclude with some observations.

Machine State. Line numbers hereafter refer to Listing A.3. A state of the EVM is a record containing various fields such as gas, pc, stack, code, memory.

Each module (state, stack, memory, ...) provides a datatype, possibly incorporating some contraints (e.g., `EvmState.T`). For brevity, we omit some fields which contain information about the enclosing transaction and the so-called *substate*. The `State` datatype (line 7) models normal execution (`OK`), failure (`INVALID`), returning (`RETURNS`), reverting (`REVERTS`), etc.

Stack, Memory and Storage. We have implemented several submodules to provide operations on stack/memory/storage. This is summarised in Fig. 1. We lift the operations on stack/memory/storage into the `State` datatype. In DAFNY this is done by adding the functions right after the definition of a datatype (line 11). This allows us to compose them easily and improves readability. For instance the `Add` function that implements the semantics of opcode `ADD` is defined using a sequence of operations `st.Pop().Pop().Push(...).Next()` where `st` is an

[2] The code in the paper may not compile or verify as we have simplified it for clarity. The code in https://github.com/ConsenSys/evm-dafny compiles and verifies.

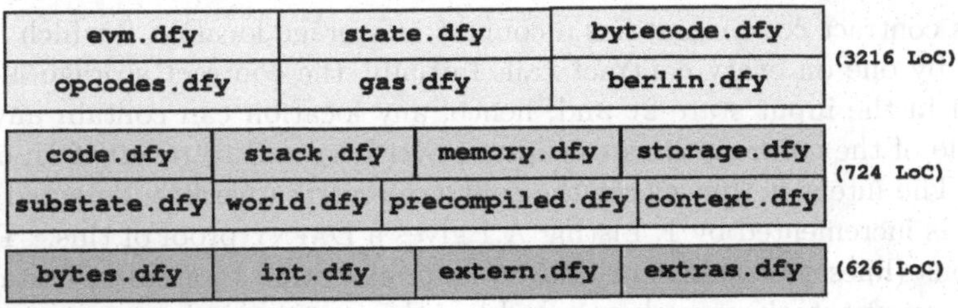

Fig. 1. Source files of the Dafny-EVM. Top group contains bytecode semantics and top-level types. Middle group contains abstractions of the main components. Bottom group are fundamental primitives (e.g. for manipulating bytes and ints). "Loc" (lines of codes) at the time of writing.

Listing A.2. Semantics of `MLOAD`, `Bytecode` module

```
1 function method MLoad(st: State) : State
2   requires st.IsExecuting() {
3 if st.Operands() >= 1 then
4   var loc := st.Peek(0) as nat;
5   var nst := st.Expand(loc,32);            // Break out expanded state
6   nst.Pop().Push(nst.Read(loc)).Next()     // Read from expanded state
7 else
8   State.INVALID(STACK_UNDERFLOW)
9 }
```

executing state (e.g. `OK`). We employ preconditions (`requires`) to ensure lifted operations are limited to applicable states only (typically executing states, such as `OK`), and also that preconditions of the functions on stack/memory/storage are satisfied (e.g., for `Pop()` the stack size must be large enough); for `Push()` (line 20) the stack cannot be full (stack size is limited to 1024).

In Dafny, preconditions are checked by the verifier and must provably hold at each call site. Notice that Dafny enforces the constraints on integer types so every time we compute (e.g., `ADD`) and store the result in a 256bit word, we must prove that the value is less than 2^{256} (the EVM dictates modulo arithmetic for this). The pre-/post-conditions and type checks enforced by the Dafny verifier help ensure that our EVM specification is consistent and that functions are well-defined.

Memory operations are provided by the `Memory` module, with various functions being attached to `State`, e.g., `Read`, `Write` lines 26–28. A key observation is that, in both cases, address `addr + 31` must be within allocated memory. This is because memory in the EVM is *byte addressable* and we are reading/writing `u256` values (i.e., which are 32 bytes long). The semantics of `MLOAD` (Listing A.2) highlights the complexity of memory operations. Since `Read(loc)` (line 6) has the precondition `loc + 31 < Memory.Size` (line 26 of Listing A.3), this must hold for state `nst`. In fact, this follows because the call to `Expand()` (line 5) ensures sufficient memory. If the call to `Expand()` within `MLoad` was not enforcing this constraint, then DAFNY would raise a precondition violation on `nst.Read(loc)`.

Listing A.3. The `EvmState` module (partial)

```
module EvmState {
  datatype Raw = EVM(gas:nat, pc:nat, stack:Stack.T, code:Code.T,
                     mem:Memory.T, world:WorldState.T, ...)

  type T = c:Raw | c.context.address in c.world.accounts

  datatype State = OK(evm:T) | REVERTS(gas:nat,data:seq<u8>)
     | RETURNS(gas:nat,data:seq<u8>,...) | INVALID(Error) | ...
  {
    // Predicates
    predicate method IsExecuting(): bool { ... }

    // Stack functions
    function method Capacity(): nat
      requires IsExecuting() { Stack.Capacity(evm.stack) }
    function method Peek(k: nat): u256
      requires IsExecuting() && k < Stack.Size(evm.stack) { ... }
    function method Pop(): State
      requires IsExecuting() && 0 < Stack.Size(evm.stack) { ... }
    function method Push(v: u256) : State
        requires IsExecuting()
        requires Capacity() > 0 {
          OK(evm.(stack:=Stack.Push(evm.stack,v)))
    }
    // Memory functions
    function method Read(address: nat): u256
      requires IsExecuting() && (addr+31)< Memory.Size(evm.mem) {...}
    function method Write(address: nat, val: u256): State
      requires IsExecuting() && (addr+31)< Memory.Size(evm.mem) {...}
    ...
    function method Expand(addr: nat, n: nat): (s': State)
      requires IsExecuting()
      ensures s'.IsExecuting() && MemSize() <= s'.MemSize()
      ensures (addr + n)< MemSize() ==> (evm.mem == s'.evm.mem) {...}
  }
  ...
}
```

Gas. In our design, we chose to split out the *gas calculation* from the instruction semantics. Whilst this does introduce some repetition, we argue it reduces cognitive load. In particular, since this avoids interweaving the gas calculation throughout the instruction semantics which (for performance reasons) is commonly done in actual implementations (including the *execution specs*[3]).

Contract Calls. Various instructions (e.g. `CALL`, `DELEGATECALL`) enable one contract to call another. These differ from others as they can involve executing

[3] https://github.com/ethereum/execution-specs.

arbitrarily many instructions in the called contract. We implement this using a mechanism akin to *continuations* but, for brevity, omit the details here.

Observations. The Dafny-EVM Code provides a readable and executable specification of the EVM. There are several benefits of using a verification-friendly language: using pre- and postconditions to write the semantics provides a high level of assurance; furthermore, the code is executable and can be compiled into several target languages including Java, C#, Go. We now highlight some observations based on our experiences from this project.

- **Specification**. DAFNY treats `function` calls within expressions as *interpreted*, but treats `method` calls as *uninterpreted* [5,15]. Roughly speaking this means that, when verifying a `function` call, the verifier has free access to the function's body. In contrast, for `method` calls, the verifier can only access what is given in the *specification* (i.e. its pre- and postconditions). As such, we consider methods ill-suited for formalising specifications (such as for the EVM). This is because we cannot abstract a specification any further than already done (i.e. we cannot specify a specification).
- **Verification**. Functions can have preconditions that restrict the domain of their inputs. In DAFNY preconditions are enforced at each call site. We argue that this results in better code by enforcing consistency across function calls. DAFNY enforces that every function must have a proof of termination which guarantees the absence of infinite loops in our state transition function. We believe that this degree of assurance is hard to attain with non verification-friendly languages.
- **Performance**. Code generated from the functionally pure subset of DAFNY can perform poorly because of the need to clone compound structures (e.g. maps and arrays) to preserve purity (i.e., referential transparency). DAFNY does not, for example, employ *clone elimination* [16,19,26] or *mutable value semantics* [21,22]. Performance was not a critical concern given our aim of developing a formal specification rather than an efficient implementation and in practice, we did not encounter any significant issue here.

During the project, a number of issues and challenges arose. For example, the lack of an exponentiation operator in DAFNY meant that, for the `EXP` bytecode, we had to implement this as a recursive function. Some low level operations involving bits & bytes (e.g., shifting) present significant challenges as the native `int` type does not support bitwise operators. One can use a conversion from (e.g. `u256`) into the bitvector types (e.g. `bv256`) provided by DAFNY which do support bitwise operations—however, this can lead to problems verifying code.

4 Practical Experiences

From the outset of this project, we were unsure whether DAFNY would be practical for this sizeable formalisation task. Overall, however, we are pleased to report that DAFNY has, for the most part, proven itself more than capable. Of course, it was not all plain sailing and we encountered several challenges which required developing techniques and/or workarounds.

Code Generation. DAFNY can generate code for a variety of targets, including: C#, Go, Java, C++, Python and JavaScript. Furthermore, whilst DAFNY does not support I/O operations *per se*, these can be implemented on the target side. We took advantage of this to embed the DAFNY-generated code into a thin Java wrapper that performs I/O and allows us to test our EVM against existing implementations. Note that the generated code is not *proved* to be equivalent to the original Dafny code. For various reasons (e.g., knowledge within the team) we chose Java as the target language with `gradle` managing the build. This worked well enough, though there are some points to make:

- **Foreign Function Interface**. Code generated from DAFNY does not conform to the stylistic norms of Java, but is otherwise relatively easy to interface with. A runtime library is provided by DAFNY against which generated code must be compiled. This provides (amongst other things) alternative collection implementations (e.g. `DafnySequence`, `DafnyMap`, etc.).
- **External Code**. For the semantics of `KECCAK256` and some precompiled contracts, we preferred to call out to native Java code (i.e. rather than implement e.g. `sha256` in DAFNY itself). However, whilst DAFNY does support `extern` declarations, these are not (at the time of writing) well supported by the Java code generator. Instead, we had to give default implementations (e.g. returning `0`) and employ build trickery to make it work.
- **Target language idiosyncrasies**. Translation to a target language introduces risks. E.g., DAFNY employs *Euclidean Division* for its integer division operator (i.e. always rounds *down* rather than *towards zero*), which is a trap for the unwary and by chance we identified a bug in the Java code generator where sometimes standard division was being applied.[4] We also encountered unsoundness in the translation of DAFNY collections (e.g. `seq<u8>`) to Java[5], and buggy implementation of `datatype` in C#.[6]

Verification and Testing. For completeness, we developed many unit tests for various components of our formalism. The *Ethereum Common Tests* also provide tens of thousands of tests for ensuring EVM compatibility.[7] As such, we have been using these to check our formalisation against existing implementations. This required generating *executable code* from our specification which presented several challenges (discussion of which is unfortunately omitted for brevity). At the time of writing, we have selected around 7500 representative tests out of the 13K Common tests (Berlin hardfork) and 6900 are passing (92%). Of the 143 failing tests, the majority (100) are failing because: some precompiled contracts are not yet fully implemented (44); we do not currently check for branches into

[4] https://github.com/dafny-lang/dafny/issues/2367.
[5] https://github.com/dafny-lang/dafny/issues/2859.
[6] https://github.com/dafny-lang/dafny/issues/1412.
[7] https://github.com/ethereum/tests.

instruction operands (56). The remaining (approx. 450) tests are skipped for various reasons e.g., timeout or breaking the testing system. Finally, we note that all of our tests are run as part of Continuous Integration before a pull request can be merged.

5 Related Work

Initial attempt at a formal specification of the EVM may be attributed to Hirai [13] with a formalisation of the EVM in the programming development environment Lem [18]. The formalisation in [13] is restricted to a single contract execution and proving bytecode is limited in terms of automation. Later, Amani *et al.* [3] built upon Hirai's formalisation and proposed an Isabelle/HOL formalisation. Their contribution introduces a program logic to reason about bytecode (restricted to a subset of 36/142 EVM instructions) but they rely on the construction of a control flow graph to define the semantics of a program. Reasoning about bytecode is limited to linear sequences of instructions (blocks) and not fully automated. Another Isabelle/HOL specification was also developed in [9] specialised for gas consumption analysis and for proving termination of bytecode.

More recently, Grishchenko *et al.* [10] have proposed a partial (not all opcodes are supported and the gas cost semantics is incomplete) formalisation of the EVM in $F^{\star}$ targeting verification of security properties.

The most advanced formalisation is probably the KEVM [12] using the $\mathbb{K}$ Framework [23]. It provides a formal and executable specification of the syntax and semantics of EVM bytecode. Using the built-in automated tools of the $\mathbb{K}$ Framework, it is possible to generate an interpreter, compiler, debugger and to some extent a verifier that can be used to check the bytecode of some contracts [20]. The default input format (used for KEVM) of the $\mathbb{K}$ Framework is XML-based which may not be the most developer-friendly format. Similarly, IELE [24] attempts to design a more readable language than EVM bytecode and to be the target of high-level languages including Solidity, Vyper, Plutus. IELE is defined using the $\mathbb{K}$ Framework and uses LLVM tools (compiler) as a backend.

There are several implementations of the EVM in different languages and clients e.g., Geth[8], Besu[9], and more recently the *execution-specs* in Python (see Footnote 3). The implementations in Geth and Besu are respectively in Go and Java and cannot be used to reason about bytecode. The Python implementation relies on specific imperative language features of Python (mutability, exceptions) and does not provide a functional definition of the instructions semantics nor an explicit specification of exceptional cases: for instance the Python code does not provide preconditions or explicit handling of exceptions, and exceptions can happen deep in the call stack which may hinder readability.

There are several tools Oyente [4], EtherIR [1], eThor [25], Rattle [27], and Certora [14] to perform static analysis of EVM bytecode. There are also

[8] https://geth.ethereum.org.
[9] https://github.com/hyperledger/besu.

extensions to specifically analyse the gas consumption like GASTAP [2], GasReducer [8]. Those tools build an abstract representation of the bytecode and it is unclear whether the abstraction is semantics preserving.

In contrast to the formalisations, implementations and tools referenced above, our formal semantics is language-agnostic (defines the state transition function as a function), easy to read and developer-friendly, provides mathematical and verified pre- and postconditions for the semantics of instructions. Moreover, our semantics can be used to perform *deductive reasoning* about bytecode including gas consumption using standard invariants.

6 Conclusion

We have proposed a formal semantics of the EVM in a pure functional subset of DAFNY. Our semantics is *human readable*, *machine checked* and *executable*, and provides a sound framework to formally reason about bytecode.

This opens up the door for several direct applications:[10]

- complete smart contract verification: in practice, this can be a costly process and may require specific verification skills or familiarity with DAFNY.
- correctness of compiler optimisations: several gas optimisation patterns e.g., a sequence `SWAP1 POP POP` optimised in `POP POP` can now be verified.
- correctness of under/overflow detection: to detect an overflow in arithmetic modulo `ADD(x, y)` it is common to first compute the result `r = ADD(x, y)` and then check that `r >= x`. We can formally prove that this is sound.
- synthesise verified bytecode: we have designed a methodology [6] to specify and verify smart contracts directly in DAFNY. We are exploring *refinement proof techniques* to synthesise bytecode from the verified DAFNY code of a contract. Ultimately we may develop a DAFNY-to-EVM *certified compiler*.

Although the benefits of our approach are evident in the formal methods' community, adoption of these techniques in the Ethereum ecosystem is still challenging. Whilst established techniques, e.g., using Solidity to write contracts, or using Python to write specifications, can be questionable [11], they are still prevalent in the Ethereum community. The main hurdles for mainstream adoption of our approach are probably two-fold: (*i*) provide developer-friendly tools to write contracts; DAFNY and the tool support around it (e.g., verification performance improvement, counter example generation [7], VSCode integration) already partially solves this issue; and (*ii*) educate the Ethereum community to understand the long-term benefits of formal verification for the Ethereum ecosystem.

References

1. Albert, E., Gordillo, P., Livshits, B., Rubio, A., Sergey, I.: ETHIR: a framework for high-level analysis of Ethereum bytecode. In: Lahiri, S.K., Wang, C. (eds.) ATVA 2018. LNCS, vol. 11138, pp. 513–520. Springer, Cham (2018). https://doi.org/10.1007/978-3-030-01090-4_30

[10] Examples are available in https://github.com/ConsenSys/evm-dafny.

2. Albert, E., Gordillo, P., Rubio, A., Sergey, I.: Running on fumes. In: Ganty, P., Kaâniche, M. (eds.) VECoS 2019. LNCS, vol. 11847, pp. 63–78. Springer, Cham (2019). https://doi.org/10.1007/978-3-030-35092-5_5
3. Amani, S., Bégel, M., Bortin, M., Staples, M.: Towards verifying Ethereum smart contract bytecode in Isabelle/HOL. In: Andronick, J., Felty, A.P. (eds.) Proceedings of the 7th ACM SIGPLAN International Conference on Certified Programs and Proofs, CPP 2018, Los Angeles, CA, USA, 8–9 January 2018, pp. 66–77. ACM (2018). https://doi.org/10.1145/3167084
4. Badruddoja, S., Dantu, R., He, Y., Upadhayay, K., Thompson, M.: Making smart contracts smarter. In: 2021 IEEE International Conference on Blockchain and Cryptocurrency (ICBC), pp. 1–3 (2021). https://doi.org/10.1109/ICBC51069.2021.9461148
5. Bradley, A.R., Manna, Z.: The Calculus of Computation - Decision Procedures with Applications to Verification. Springer, Heidelberg (2007). https://doi.org/10.1007/978-3-540-74113-8
6. Cassez, F., Fuller, J., Anton Quiles, H.M.: Deductive verification of smart contracts with Dafny. In: Groote, J.F., Huisman, M. (eds.) FMICS 2022. LNCS, vol. 13487, pp. 50–66. Springer, Cham (2022). https://doi.org/10.1007/978-3-031-15008-1_5
7. Chakarov, A., Fedchin, A., Rakamarić, Z., Rungta, N.: Better counterexamples for Dafny. In: Fisman, D., Rosu, G. (eds.) TACAS 2022. LNCS, vol. 13243, pp. 404–411. Springer, Cham (2022). https://doi.org/10.1007/978-3-030-99524-9_23
8. Chen, T., et al.: Towards saving money in using smart contracts. In: Zisman, A., Apel, S. (eds.) Proceedings of the 40th International Conference on Software Engineering: New Ideas and Emerging Results, ICSE (NIER) 2018, Gothenburg, Sweden, 27 May–03 June 2018, pp. 81–84. ACM (2018). https://doi.org/10.1145/3183399.3183420
9. Genet, T., Jensen, T.P., Sauvage, J.: Termination of Ethereum's smart contracts. In: Samarati, P., di Vimercati, S.D.C., Obaidat, M.S., Ben-Othman, J. (eds.) Proceedings of the 17th International Joint Conference on e-Business and Telecommunications, ICETE 2020 - Volume 2: SECRYPT, Lieusaint, Paris, France, 8–10 July 2020, pp. 39–51. ScitePress (2020). https://doi.org/10.5220/0009564100390051
10. Grishchenko, I., Maffei, M., Schneidewind, C.: A semantic framework for the security analysis of Ethereum smart contracts. In: Bauer, L., Küsters, R. (eds.) POST 2018. LNCS, vol. 10804, pp. 243–269. Springer, Cham (2018). https://doi.org/10.1007/978-3-319-89722-6_10
11. Guido, D.: Episode 6: What the hell are the blockchain people doing, and why isn't it a dumpster fire? (2021). https://galois.com/blog/2020/11/introducing-the-building-better-systems-podcast/. In Building Better Systems (podcast), Joey Dodds, Shpat Morina, Galois
12. Hildenbrandt, E., et al.: KEVM: a complete formal semantics of the Ethereum virtual machine. In: 31st IEEE Computer Security Foundations Symposium, CSF 2018, Oxford, United Kingdom, 9–12 July 2018, pp. 204–217. IEEE Computer Society (2018). https://doi.org/10.1109/CSF.2018.00022
13. Hirai, Y.: Defining the Ethereum virtual machine for interactive theorem provers. In: Brenner, M., et al. (eds.) FC 2017. LNCS, vol. 10323, pp. 520–535. Springer, Cham (2017). https://doi.org/10.1007/978-3-319-70278-0_33
14. Jackson, D., Nandi, C., Sagiv, M.: Certora technology white paper. Medium Post (2022). https://medium.com/certora/certora-technology-white-paper-cae5ab0bdf1
15. Kroening, D., Strichman, O.: Decision Procedures - An Algorithmic Point of View, 2nd edn. Springer, Heidelberg (2016)

16. Lameed, N., Hendren, L.: Staged static techniques to efficiently implement array copy semantics in a MATLAB JIT compiler. In: Knoop, J. (ed.) CC 2011. LNCS, vol. 6601, pp. 22–41. Springer, Heidelberg (2011). https://doi.org/10.1007/978-3-642-19861-8_3
17. Leroy, X.: A formally verified compiler back-end. J. Autom. Reason. **43**(4), 363–446 (2009). https://doi.org/10.1007/s10817-009-9155-4
18. Mulligan, D.P., Owens, S., Gray, K.E., Ridge, T., Sewell, P.: Lem: reusable engineering of real-world semantics. In: Jeuring, J., Chakravarty, M.M.T. (eds.) Proceedings of the 19th ACM SIGPLAN International Conference on Functional Programming, Gothenburg, Sweden, 1–3 September 2014, pp. 175–188. ACM (2014). https://doi.org/10.1145/2628136.2628143
19. Odersky, M.: How to make destructive updates less destructive. In: Proceedings of the ACM Symposium on the Principles of Programming Languages (POPL), pp. 25–36 (1991)
20. Park, D., Zhang, Y., Rosu, G.: End-to-end formal verification of Ethereum 2.0 deposit smart contract. In: Lahiri, S.K., Wang, C. (eds.) CAV 2020. LNCS, vol. 12224, pp. 151–164. Springer, Cham (2020). https://doi.org/10.1007/978-3-030-53288-8_8
21. Pearce, D.J., Groves, L.: Designing a verifying compiler: lessons learned from developing Whiley. Sci. Comput. Program. **113**, 191–220 (2015)
22. Racordon, D., Shabalin, D., Zheng, D., Abrahams, D., Saeta, B.: Implementation strategies for mutable value semantics. J. Object Technol. **21**(2) (2022)
23. Rosu, G.: 𝕂: a semantic framework for programming languages and formal analysis tools. In: Pretschner, A., Peled, D., Hutzelmann, T. (eds.) Dependable Software Systems Engineering, NATO Science for Peace and Security Series - D: Information and Communication Security, vol. 50, pp. 186–206. IOS Press (2017). https://doi.org/10.3233/978-1-61499-810-5-186
24. Runtime Verification: The IELE virtual machine. Blog post (2022). https://runtimeverification.com/the-iele-virtual-machine/
25. Schneidewind, C., Grishchenko, I., Scherer, M., Maffei, M.: eThor: practical and provably sound static analysis of Ethereum smart contracts. In: Ligatti, J., Ou, X., Katz, J., Vigna, G. (eds.) 2020 ACM SIGSAC Conference on Computer and Communications Security, CCS 2020, Virtual Event, USA, 9–13 November 2020, pp. 621–640. ACM (2020). https://doi.org/10.1145/3372297.3417250
26. Shankar, N.: Static analysis for safe destructive updates in a functional language. In: Pettorossi, A. (ed.) LOPSTR 2001. LNCS, vol. 2372, pp. 1–24. Springer, Heidelberg (2002). https://doi.org/10.1007/3-540-45607-4_1
27. Trail of Bits: Rattle - an Ethereum EVM binary analysis framework. Medium Post (2018). https://blog.trailofbits.com/2018/09/06/rattle-an-ethereum-evm-binary-analysis-framework/
28. Wood, G.: Ethereum: a secure decentralised generalised transaction ledger. Ethereum project yellow paper (2022). https://ethereum.github.io/yellowpaper/paper.pdf. Berlin version d77a387. Accessed 26 Apr 2022

Shifting Left for Early Detection of Machine-Learning Bugs

Ben Liblit[1], Linghui Luo[2(✉)], Alejandro Molina[3], Rajdeep Mukherjee[5], Zachary Patterson[4], Goran Piskachev[2], Martin Schäf[6], Omer Tripp[5], and Willem Visser[5]

[1] Amazon Web Services, Arlington, USA
[2] Amazon Web Services, Berlin, Germany
llinghui@amazon.de
[3] Amazon, Seattle, USA
[4] The University of Texas at Dallas, Richardson, USA
[5] Amazon Web Services, Santa Clara, USA
[6] Amazon Web Services, New York, USA

Abstract. Computational notebooks are widely used for machine learning (ML). However, notebooks raise new correctness concerns beyond those found in traditional programming environments. ML library APIs are easy to misuse, and the notebook execution model raises entirely new problems concerning reproducibility. It is common to use static analyses to detect bugs and enforce best practices in software applications. However, when configured with new types of rules tailored to notebooks, these analyses can also detect notebook-specific problems.

We present our initial efforts in understanding how static analysis for notebooks differs from analysis of traditional application software. We created six new rules for the CodeGuru Reviewer based on discussions with ML practitioners. We ran the tool on close to 10,000 experimentation notebooks, resulting in an average of approximately 1 finding per 7 notebooks. Approximately 60% of the findings that we reviewed are real notebook defects. (Due to confidentiality limitations, we cannot disclose the exact number of notebook files and findings.)

Keywords: Static analysis · Computational notebooks · Jupyter notebook · Machine-learning bugs · Bug finding · Machine learning · PyTorch · CodeGuru reviewer

1 Introduction

Static program analysis is *shifting left*: providing recommendations as early as possible in the software development life cycle. The earlier an issue is reported, the easier and less costly it is to fix. Many off-the-shelf analysis engines now integrate seamlessly into code reviews or builds, to good effect [3,7].

Shifting left assumes a multi-stage process that culminates in deployed software. However, work in machine learning (ML) may not fit this model. Data scientists and ML experts often use computational notebooks for development,

M. Chechik et al. (Eds.): FM 2023, LNCS 14000, pp. 584–597, 2023.
https://doi.org/10.1007/978-3-031-27481-7_33

such as Jupyter notebooks [15]. Notebooks are iterative and interactive. A typical developer edits and evaluates a notebook locally, until it produces an acceptable model, and only then sends the notebook or model to the next stage of the development pipeline.

In traditional enterprise software development, code is developed in small increments, unit tested, and passed through code review, before running on real data. For a given programming language, notebook developers invest more time into notebooks between published revisions than traditional developers [11,35]. Delayed feedback by human colleagues means that notebook developers stand to benefit even more from automated static analyses. However, false-positive rates must be low so as to not distract developers.

Notebooks also differ from enterprise software in that notebooks do not usually run in production. Thus, many of the issues typically covered by static analysis, such as security or resilience to untrusted inputs, are not interesting to notebook developers. Instead, reproducibility is a much bigger problem [36]. Notebooks have certain features, like out-of-order execution, which can harm reproducibility, and misuse of ML APIs, which can lead to accidental modifications of trained models. Accidental model modifications are a particular concern: such mistakes are difficult to notice, and may be cumbersome or impossible to revert.

This paper presents our initial efforts in understanding how static analysis for notebooks differs from analysis of traditional application software. To understand the problem space, we conducted a pilot study by interviewing a group of ML practitioners at Amazon. Based on discussions with them, we prioritized certain issues and implemented six rules using the Python static analysis engine in CodeGuru Reviewer [21]. We report on rule efficacy for a set of notebooks shared by Amazon developers. These six rules produced an average of 1 finding per 7 notebooks on a total of nearly 10,000 notebook files. We sampled a set of the findings to assess precision. Around 60% of these findings are true positives: real notebook bugs. Our results motivate future research on how to best integrate static analysis into the development workflow for computational notebooks, and what type of rules provide the best value for notebook developers.

2 Background

To understand what types of issues are worth catching in notebooks, we interviewed a group of five ML practitioners who come from different organizations in Amazon, and occupy different roles. As we already hit saturation [12] after the fifth interview, we did not interview more people. We asked about their habits when using notebooks and issues they often encounter. Many practitioners mentioned the challenge of reproducing results of notebooks when moving between different environments. Difficulties include failure to understand the execution order of notebook cells, non-determinism of some ML APIs, and losing track of dependencies. Practitioners told us that notebooks are far from intuitive, as cells can be executed in arbitrary order. Errors often occur across cells. Previous cells are often edited or even removed after execution. These changes may break the intended functionality of following cells. Because data exploration usually takes a long time, users often do not execute all cells after small changes. Thus, breaking changes might be unnoticed until another person tries to rerun the notebook. Section 4.1 of this paper discusses two concrete issues that fall into this category and introduces our approach to detect them with static analysis.

Misusing ML APIs can introduce other silent faults. Popular deep-learning libraries such as PyTorch [22], Keras [5], and TensorFlow [1] greatly simplify the development of deep learning systems. However, due to high conceptual complexity of the field, unclear documentation, and unintuitive APIs, users commonly misuse these libraries and inadvertently inject faults during the development of deep-learning systems. Furthermore, ML libraries are moving targets: different versions may require to different method calls, produce different performances, or exhibit different functionality altogether.

To understand which misuses are prevalent across multiple versions of APIs and that are useful to catch, we collected a list of known misuses from both scientific literature [13,23,34,37] and an internal survey. We asked several ML scientists (different than the five we interviewed) at our company to rate usefulness in this list and elaborate the reasons for their ratings. We prioritized certain issues from this list based on practitioner interest (how many votes for useful) and technical feasibility. These issues are silent at build and run time, of which a developer would not be aware, even after the code is deployed. Section 4.2 introduce four rules designed for catching these issues.

3 Static Analysis Framework

Our analyses are built on the framework we developed for CodeGuru Reviewer [21]. In this section, we briefly introduce this framework.

3.1 Code Representation

Our analysis represents each program as a collection of per-function graphs called *MU graphs.* A MU graph contains five kinds of nodes:

- Entry nodes represent the start of a function's execution: one per MU graph.
- Exit nodes represent the end of a function's execution: one per MU graph.
- Control nodes represent branched control flow, such as a conditional statement or loop.
- Action nodes represent individual execution steps, such as multiplying two values or calling a function.
- Data nodes represent local variables or synthetic temporary values within compound expressions.

There are also several types of edges in MU graphs, denoted by their label:

- Control edges order execution among entry, exit, control, and action nodes. No data node is ever the source or target of a control edge. Thus, discarding all data nodes and non-control edges would reduce a MU graph to a traditional control-flow graph (CFG).
- Data edges represent movement of data among control and action nodes, and are further categorized as follows:

```
CustomRule rule = new CustomRule.Builder().withName("MathExp")
  .withComment("For small floats `x`, the subtraction in "
      + "`exp(x) − 1` can result in a loss of precision.")
  .withAllOf(
    b −> b.withMethodCallFilter(".∗math\\.exp")
          .withDefinitionTransform()
          .as("MathExpResult"),
    b −> b.withConstantDataFilter("1").as("ConstantOne"))
  .check()
  .withActionFilter("−")
  .withDirectDataFromIdFilter("MathExpResult")
  .withDirectDataFromIdFilter("ConstantOne")
  .build();
```

Fig. 1. GQL rule for identifying suboptimal use of the math.exp function.

- Condition edges flow from a data node into a control node, representing the information used to decide how execution continues.
- Definition edges flow from an action to a data node defined by that action.
- Parameter edges flow from a data node into an action node.
- Receiver edges flow from a data node into a method-calling action node. These highlight the special role of implicit self or this arguments.
- Callee edges flow from a data node into a call action node, identifying the function to be called.

3.2 Query Language

Directly analyzing MU graphs can be cumbersome, and can miss important reuse opportunities. We therefore created an API, dubbed the Guru Query Language (GQL), to enable encapsulation, optimization, and reuse of a wide variety of analysis constructs. GQL is implemented as a Java library whose main interface with the analysis builder is the CustomRule class. CustomRule instances are created using the fluent builder pattern [9], where builder calls correspond to reasoning steps in the rule. A rule object can be evaluated at different scopes, from entire code bases to single functions. This is an important source of flexibility, enabled by MU graphs and their support for partial programs. Rule evaluation yields a RuleEvaluationResult for each function or method. If rule evaluation fails, the RuleEvaluationResult includes rich diagnostic information to support rule debugging.

To illustrate GQL syntax, Fig. 1 shows a rule that identifies suboptimal use of the math.exp function. Here is an example of what the rule checks for:

```
def foo():
  import math
  return math.exp(1e−10) − 1
```

Rule definition begins by setting the rule's name and user-facing comment text. The following steps, up to the check statement, are preconditions that

```
[1] x = 6                  [1] x = 6
........................   ........................
[2] y = x + 4              [4] y = x + 4
........................   ........................
[3] if x > 5:              [3] if x > 5:
        z = y                      z = y
    else:                      else:
        z = x + 1                  z = x + 1
........................   ........................
[4] print(z)               [5] print(z)
........................   ........................
output: z = 10             output: z = ?
```

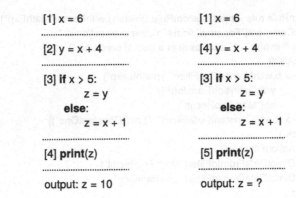

Fig. 2. Different execution orders result in different outputs.

the rule checks for. Specifically, the withAllOf statement ensures that all the subrules nested within it evaluate successfully, where these check for math.exp calls as well as the presence of the constant value 1. The matches are stored into variables (or IDs), to enable downstream reuse thereof, using the as operation. The actual check, or postcondition, is the rule section after the check step. This rule's postcondition establishes whether there is a subtraction operation that the node defined by math.exp, along with the constant 1, flow into directly (that is, without the mediation of any other action).

4 Analysis Rules

In this section, we describe six analysis rules that we implemented using GQL.

4.1 Issues Specific to Computational Notebooks

Computational notebooks break some assumptions we may make when analyzing traditional code. We introduce two kinds of notebook-specific issues and the rules that we designed for catching them.

Invalid Execution Order: A notebook consists of a sequence of cells; most cells contain either Markdown documentation or code. Users can run individual cells as they wish. Thus, there is no guarantee that code cells in a notebook run in linear order, or even that linear order is intended. Cells with shared variables can produce different results when running in different order, as shown in Fig. 2. Cell boundaries are marked with dotted lines. At the beginning of each cell, a number in square brackets [ ] shows the execution-order counter. These counters, stored in the metadata

```
__CELL_EDGE__(1)
x = 6
__CELL_EDGE__(3)
if x > 5:
    z = y
else:
    z = x + 1
__CELL_EDGE__(4)
y = x + 4
__CELL_EDGE__(5)
print(z)
```

Fig. 3. Converted Python code in execution order.

of a notebook file, indicate the execution order of the cells. On the left side of Fig. 2, the cells were executed in linear order, causing the final value of z to be 10. On the right side of Fig. 2, the execution order of the second and third cells are flipped. Furthermore, we do not know which code cell executed second in the right-side notebook, since no cell is marked "[2]". Perhaps the second-executed cell has already been deleted, or perhaps some other cell was executed second, then re-executed (and therefore renumbered) later. This uncertainty causes the final value of z to be under-determined. When y is assigned to z in the third cell, we can not assume that the definition of y is still x + 4. The recorded output for the right-side notebook would be hard or impossible to reproduce.

To address such threats to reproducibility, we designed a rule that detects cases where a used variable is not defined based on execution order. We leverage the execution counter metadata stored in notebook files to reconstruct cell code to be executed in the stored order. Specifically, we implemented a converter that converts notebook files into Python scripts that retain the execution metadata. For the example above, the converted Python script is presented in Fig. 3. The __CELL_EDGE__ function is defined to do nothing, but represents a notebook cell edge. Our rule analyzes the converted Python scripts, which contain cell code in the execution order as Fig. 3 shows. It starts from each variable use and searches backwards to determine whether that variable has been defined previously.

Variable Redefinition: Poor readability is another common issue in computational notebooks. During exploration, notebooks can easily get messy and difficult to read. One bad coding practice is to reuse the same variable name across multiple cells for different tasks. It is common for users to unknowingly overwrite data that is used across multiple cells. To address issues raised due to variables with unclear scopes, we designed a rule to detect a variable being defined with different types (variables whose type is unknown are excluded) in different cells, accompanied by usage in another cell that does not contain another definition. This rule analyzes our Python representation of notebooks by looking for calls to __CELL_EDGE__. From there it identifies the type of each variable in the cell and stores this information. If a variable is used in a cell that does not define the variable, but the variable is defined in at least two other cells with different types, that usage is marked as unclear. Figure 4 shows an example of this bad practice. The variable x is defined with two different types: str and int. For its usage in the third cell, it is not clear which type of data is expected to be passed to the call do_something. That depends on the execution order, where x can be either type in the third cell.

```
[?] x = "Hello World"
.....................
[?] x = int(input('input:'))
.....................
[?] do_something(x)
```

Fig. 4. Usage of variable with unclear scope.

4.2 Misuses of Deep Learning Libraries

As mentioned in Sect. 2, many issues are introduced by misusing the APIs of deep learning libraries. We introduce four representative misuses in PyTorch.

Missing zero_grad *Call:* Training of deep neural networks is based on iterative parameter updates [4] based on gradients that are computed via back-propagation [17]. These gradients are accumulated based on batches or mini-batches of stochastic samples of the training data-set [30]. In PyTorch, the gradients accumulate automatically in the back-propagation step of loss.backward, and developers must reset the gradient accumulation by calling zero_grad beforehand as shown in Fig. 5. However, if the zero_grad step is omitted, then PyTorch would accumulate gradients indefinitely instead of updating them in batches. This default accumulating behavior is convenient as it simplifies the implementation of different batching approaches, but it is also easily forgotten. The impact of this type of error strongly depends on the task at hand, e.g., training a network from scratch would fail silently as the network would not learn properly and the developer would simply notice that the model is not improving, costing time and computational resources. A more severe case occurs when the task is refinement, i.e., optimizing a previously trained model on new data. In this case the first few iterations might achieve small improvements, but the network would simply not learn correctly. However, as the network was already trained, it could still perform well enough to potentially confuse the developer into thinking that things are in order, leading to invalid scientific results. Therefore, we designed a rule to detect missing zero_grad calls in training loops that invoke backward. The rule warns the users about the default accumulating behavior.

```
for train, test in loader:
    loss = metric(model(train), test)
    optimizer.zero_grad()
    loss.backward()
    optimizer.step()
```

Fig. 5. Call zero_grad before backward.

Missing eval *Call:* During the optimization step of deep neural networks, developers often evaluate the predictive performance of the model on both training and test data. However, some layers in a neural network may behave differently depending on whether the network is trained or evaluated. A Dropout [31] layer disables different neurons during training to help the network learn better, but at evaluation time, the complete network is used to make predictions. Similarly, BatchNorm [14] changes internal parameters while training, but keeps parameters fixed during evaluation. To control this behavior, PyTorch mandates explicit train and eval calls to denote the start of the training and evaluation (also known as validation or testing) phases of a model, respectively. Using these calls incorrectly can lead to silent failures. Consider a version of the code where the developer forgets to call eval. In this case, the Dropout layers will indirectly change the architecture of the network by activating and disabling different neurons. This would make all predictions unstable, i.e., for the same input data, the network would make different predictions when evaluated at different points in time. The BatchNorm layer would cause even more harm, as the parameters of the layer would adapt according to test data, leaking information from the test set into the model. This could mislead developers and scientists into thinking that the model behaves better than it actually does. We designed a rule to check whether eval is called (1) before testing a trained model loaded

```
# Case 1
model.load_state_dict(torch.load("model.pth"))
predicted = model.evaluate_on(test_data)

# Case 2
for batch_num in enumerate(dataloader):
    model.train()
    # forward, backwards and optimization steps
    if batch_num % 50 == 0:
        precision, recall, f1 = model.evaluate_on(data, batch_size)

# Case 3
model.train()
for ... # training loop
precision, recall, f1 = model.evaluate_on(data, batch_size)
```

Fig. 6. Three cases where eval should be called.

```
x, y = torch.rand(4), torch.rand(4)
x.add_(y)
do_something(x)
```

```
x, y = torch.rand(4), torch.rand(4)
z = x.add_(y)
do_something(z)
```

Fig. 7. Left: compliant case. Right: non-compliant case.

from disk, (2) before validating a model during the training phase, and (3) before testing a model directly after the training phase. Figure 6 gives examples of these common cases. Our rule searches both intra- and inter-procedurally, as calls to `eval` might be present inside the user-defined `evaluate_on`.

Use of Nondeterministic Algorithm: Reproducibility is a cornerstone of research in ML. Therefore, deterministic results are important to understand the impact of different configurations during the training and evaluation of neural networks [19]. Unfortunately, training and inference can be computationally expensive [28] and determinism is often abandoned in favor of approximate but faster results. The default configuration of PyTorch focuses on performance instead of determinism and provides some operations without deterministic implementations. Nevertheless, the official PyTorch documentation recommends limiting sources of nondeterministic behavior, and offers tips and APIs to control and warn about uses of non-reproducible code. To raise awareness among practitioners, we implemented a rule to check whether the non-deterministic version of an API is used instead of a deterministic alternative.

Unintended In-place Operation: The practical size of a neural network is limited by the available memory that stores the parameters and intermediate computation steps. To reduce memory consumption, PyTorch supports in-place operations over tensors, letting developers decide when to write results to existing memory instead of requiring extra space. However, as In-place operations change the content of a given torch.Tensor directly, they can cause loss of data if the operation is not intended. Figure 7 shows an example where in both variants, x.add_(y) will change the value of x in-place. In the right-side case, the return value of x.add_(y) is also explicitly assigned to a new variable z, making z a redundant alias for x. This is likely a mistake: x was probably not intended to be modified. Our rule catches torch.Tensor in-place operations that are then assigned to variables.

5 Experimental Evaluation

We evaluated our rules on several hundred code repositories containing a total of almost 10,000 experimentation notebook files (.ipynb) using PyTorch. The repositories were selected at random, without any bias, and cover a variety of ML application domains, including for example object recognition in images and videos, natural language processing, concept learning, healthcare, and speech recognition. We applied our notebook converter to these notebook files and analyzed the converted Python scripts. Since not all notebook files have metadata with the execution counter, our notebook converter supports two representations. One representation encodes the execution order as previously shown in Fig. 3, while the other simply lists all cells in linear order, i.e., the argument passed to each __CELL_EDGE__ call is simply the order of cell appearance in the notebook file. The linear representation is sufficient for all rules except *Invalid Execution Order*.

Table 1 shows the results of our experiment. We drew a random sample out of the overall findings pool to assess their correctness. The sample was drawn globally, and is thus uneven across the different rules yet roughly correlated with their frequency. The sampled findings were reviewed together with ML scientists. We use three ratings: "true positive" (TP) for findings judged to be real defects; "false positive" (FP) for findings judged to be harmless or correct code; and "mixed" for findings judged to be partially true. We compute precision as:

$$\text{Precision} = \frac{\text{TPs} + \text{Mixed}/2}{\text{TPs} + \text{FPs} + \text{Mixed}}$$

Invalid Execution Order produced over 80% of the overall findings, followed by *Variable Redefinition* with 14.2%. For both of these rules, we reviewed 20 of their findings. The *Invalid Execution Order* finding rated as "mixed" is due to a call of the form foo(a, b, c), where all three arguments were stated to use undefined variables but in practice only some were undefined.

Unintended In-place Operation and *Use of Nondeterministic Algorithm* produced few findings, but achieved high precision of 100% and 88%, respectively. The only false positive is due to incomplete type information inferred by our Python front-end, Pyright [20]. This limitation also caused 2 of the 3 false positives for *Missing* zero_grad *Call*, as our rule uses type information to filter out training code using Apache MXNet [2]. MXNet automatically zeroes out gradients for users by default, so missing zero_grad is usually not a problem there.

Table 1. Experimental results

Rule	Rule	Count of findings				Precision
		Reviewed	TPs	FPs	Mixed	
Invalid Execution Order	81:3%	20	11	8	1	58%
Variable Redefinition	14:2%	20	6	13	1	33%
Missing eval Call	3:0%	26	18	5	3	75%
Use of Nondeterministic Algorithm	0:9%	8	7	1	0	88%
Missing zero_grad Call	0:5%	4	1	3	0	25%
Unintended In-place Operation	0:1%	1	1	0	0	100%

Another false positive for this rule is due to a third-party library API that calls zero_grad, but that was not available for analysis.

Missing eval Call achieves 78% precision. This rule produced 3% of the findings with 5 false positives out of 26 findings that were reviewed. We rated 3 as mixed due to incomplete code, i.e., the eval call is missing but other functions are invoked, not visible to the analysis, that may perform this call. The most common finding pattern due to this rule is case 1 from our example in Fig. 6: a trained model loaded from disk is directly applied to data without toggling the evaluation mode.

For *Invalid Execution Order*, all false positives are due to defective extraction of Python code from notebooks. Our prototype notebook converter sometimes fails to identify shell commands in notebook files, resulting in invalid lines of code in the converted Python script. Apart from this technical issue, the precision of this rule is actually quite high. We only have one finding where multiple variables at the same line are deemed undefined, one of which being a false positive. We tally this finding as mixed in Table 1.

```
[1] x = "abc"
..........................
[2] if flag:
      x = 1
    else:
      x = "def"
..........................
[3] print(x)
```

Fig. 8. Code leading to Union type.

Variable Redefinition suffers from a high rate of false positives, mostly because of special types in Python. One example is the Any type [25]. Pyright infers the return type of some library methods as Any, which is compatible with every other type. Our rule does not consider this case. Thus, if a variable is typed as Any in one notebook cell but has a concrete type in another cell, *Variable Redefinition* raises a warning. Union [24] is another special type. A variable with type Union[X, Y] can hold values of types X or Y. Consider x in the example code in Fig. 8. For cell [1], Pyright infers that x has type str. However, for cell [2] Pyright infers that x has type Union[int, str]. Our rule considers str and Union[int, str] to be distinct types, thus raising a warning. However, in our review we rated such findings as false positives, as these mixtures of types appeared to be intentional in context. Lastly, we note the special Unbound type that Pyright infers for a variable that has never been initialized. We did not treat Unbound in any special way, which in turn caused some false positives. Future refinement of *Variable Redefinition* will add custom handling for these special types.

6 Related Work

In this section, we discuss the most relevant related work to our work.

Challenges in ML Code. Many studies have discussed challenges in ML code [6,13,23,26,33]. A large-scale study [6] shows a rapid evolution of the use of ML libraries among GitHub projects. In this study, PyTorch is one of the most used libraries, which motivated us to focus on it here. Humbatova et al. [13] proposed a hierarchical taxonomy of faults in deep neural networks (DNN). Their list of faults is one of our sources for developing analysis rules. Our four rules for API misuses can be categorized into four of the five categories they identified: Model, Tenors, Training and API.Pimentel et al. [23] analyzed 1.4 million notebooks with reproducibility issues, e.g., most notebooks do not use any testing infrastructure and many notebooks have non-executed code cells, out-of-order cells, and skips in the execution count which is a challenge for reproducibility. The authors could execute only 24% of the notebooks and only 4% of them could reproduce the expected results. Quaranta [26] identified this same problem. Quaranta also explored how notebooks are used among different users and found out that the notebooks are used in unstructured ways. These identified issues motivated us to develop rules targeting reproducibility of notebooks (e.g., *Invalid Execution Order*, *Use of Nondeterministic Algorithm*) and best practices (e.g., *Variable Redefinition*).

Static Analyses for ML Code. Some static analyses specifically target ML code [8,10,16,38,38]. Many of these deal with tensor shape in TensorFlow programs [8,16,18,37]. Dolby et al. [8] introduced Ariadne as part of the WALA framework [29] to support static analysis of Python. As these analyses were targeting old versions of TensorFlow, they do not exist in code using more recent TensorFlow releases. Our early study on versions of ML libraries also shows these problematic TensorFlow versions are rarely used nowadays, whereas the misuses our rules address are prevalent across a wide range of PyTorch versions including the latest releases.

Another line of static analysis work focuses on providing best practices for ML practitioners. Wan et al. [34] studied 360 GitHub projects that use AWS AI or Google Cloud AI and identifier different types of API misuses generalized into eight anti-patterns. The authors implemented four different static checkers that can detect the anti-patterns. Quaranta et al. [27] proposed Pynblint, a static analyzer for Python notebooks. Pynblint performs a simple linter-based analysis to identify recommendations to the developer based on a list of 17 best practices based on code-quality or driving a more reproducible code. NBLyzer [32] is another static analyzer based on abstract interpretation for intra-cell analyses. NBLyzer supports two analyses, a code impact analysis and a data leakage analysis. Advanced by our analysis framework and the novel Python representation of notebooks with retaining cell information and execution order, our rules are not only inter-procedural but also inter-cell analyses.

7 Conclusion

This paper introduces our initial efforts to shift static analysis to the left for ML code. In support of this goal, we identified common defects that arise when developing ML models with computational notebooks. We showcased six analysis rules that catch both notebook-specific issues and misuses of deep-learning libraries. Finding real bugs with these rules on close to 10,000 experimentation notebooks demonstrates the value for ML practitioners in providing support for best practices, reproducibility, as well as assurance of scientific correctness. This motivates us to develop more rules in this space in the future.

References

1. Abadi, M., et al.: TensorFlow: large-scale machine learning on heterogeneous systems (2015). https://www.tensorflow.org/
2. Apache: Apache MXNet (2022). https://mxnet.apache.org/versions/1.9.1/
3. Bessey, A., et al.: A few billion lines of code later: using static analysis to find bugs in the real world. Commun. ACM **53**(2), 66–75 (2010). https://doi.org/10.1145/1646353.1646374. ISSN 0001-0782
4. Boyd, S., Boyd, S.P., Vandenberghe, L.: Convex Optimization. Cambridge University Press, Cambridge (2004)
5. Chollet, F., et al.: Keras (2015). https://keras.io
6. Dilhara, M., Ketkar, A., Dig, D.: Understanding software-2.0: a study of machine learning library usage and evolution. ACM Trans. Softw. Eng. Methodol. **30**(4) (2021). https://doi.org/10.1145/3453478. ISSN 1049-331X
7. Distefano, D., Fähndrich, M., Logozzo, F., O'Hearn, P.W.: Scaling static analyses at Facebook. Commun. ACM **62**(8), 62–70 (2019). https://doi.org/10.1145/3338112. ISSN 0001-0782
8. Dolby, J., Shinnar, A., Allain, A., Reinen, J.: Ariadne: analysis for machine learning programs. In: Proceedings of the 2nd ACM SIGPLAN International Workshop on Machine Learning and Programming Languages, MAPL 2018, pp. 1–10. Association for Computing Machinery, New York (2018). https://doi.org/10.1145/3211346.3211349. ISBN 9781450358347
9. Gamma, E., Helm, R., Johnson, R., Vlissides, J.: Design patterns: abstraction and reuse of object-oriented design. In: Nierstrasz, O.M. (ed.) ECOOP 1993. LNCS, vol. 707, pp. 406–431. Springer, Heidelberg (1993). https://doi.org/10.1007/3-540-47910-4_21
10. Gehr, T., Mirman, M., Drachsler-Cohen, D., Tsankov, P., Chaudhuri, S., Vechev, M.: AI2: safety and robustness certification of neural networks with abstract interpretation. In: 2018 IEEE Symposium on Security and Privacy (SP), pp. 3–18 (2018). https://doi.org/10.1109/SP.2018.00058

11. Grotov, K., Titov, S., Sotnikov, V., Golubev, Y., Bryksin, T.: A large-scale comparison of Python code in Jupyter notebooks and scripts. In: Proceedings of the 19th International Conference on Mining Software Repositories, MSR 2022, pp. 353–364. Association for Computing Machinery, New York (2022). https://doi.org/10.1145/3524842.3528447. ISBN 9781450393034
12. Guest, G., Bunce, A., Johnson, L.: How many interviews are enough? An experiment with data saturation and variability. Field Methods **18**(1), 59–82 (2006)
13. Humbatova, N., Jahangirova, G., Bavota, G., Riccio, V., Stocco, A., Tonella, P.: Taxonomy of real faults in deep learning systems. In: Proceedings of the ACM/IEEE 42nd International Conference on Software Engineering, ICSE 2020, pp. 1110–1121. Association for Computing Machinery, New York (2020). https://doi.org/10.1145/3377811.3380395. ISBN 9781450371216
14. Ioffe, S., Szegedy, C.: Batch normalization: accelerating deep network training by reducing internal covariate shift. In: International Conference on Machine Learning, pp. 448–456. PMLR (2015)
15. Kluyver, T., et al.: Jupyter notebooks - a publishing format for reproducible computational workflows. In: Loizides, F., Scmidt, B. (eds.) Positioning and Power in Academic Publishing: Players, Agents and Agendas, pp. 87–90. IOS Press (2016). https://eprints.soton.ac.uk/403913/
16. Lagouvardos, S., Dolby, J., Grech, N., Antoniadis, A., Smaragdakis, Y.: Static analysis of shape in TensorFlow programs. In: Hirschfeld, R., Pape, T. (eds.) 34th European Conference on Object-Oriented Programming (ECOOP 2020). Leibniz International Proceedings in Informatics (LIPIcs), vol. 166, pp. 15:1–15:29. Schloss Dagstuhl-Leibniz-Zentrum für Informatik, Dagstuhl (2020). https://doi.org/10.4230/LIPIcs.ECOOP.2020.15, https://drops.dagstuhl.de/opus/volltexte/2020/13172. ISBN 978-3-95977-154-2, ISSN 1868-8969
17. LeCun, Y., Touresky, D., Hinton, G., Sejnowski, T.: A theoretical framework for back-propagation. In: Proceedings of the 1988 Connectionist Models Summer School, vol. 1, pp. 21–28 (1988)
18. Liu, C., et al.: Detecting TensorFlow program bugs in real-world industrial environment. In: 2021 36th IEEE/ACM International Conference on Automated Software Engineering (ASE), pp. 55–66 (2021). https://doi.org/10.1109/ASE51524.2021.9678891
19. Madhyastha, P., Jain, R.: On model stability as a function of random seed. arXiv preprint arXiv:1909.10447 (2019)
20. Microsoft: Pyright: Static type checker for Python (2022). https://github.com/microsoft/pyright
21. Mukherjee, R., Tripp, O., Liblit, B., Wilson, M.: Static analysis for AWS best practices in Python code. In: Ali, K., Vitek, J. (eds.) 36th European Conference on Object-Oriented Programming, ECOOP 2022, 6–10 June 2022, Berlin, Germany. LIPIcs, vol. 222, pp. 14:1–14:28. Schloss Dagstuhl - Leibniz-Zentrum für Informatik (2022), https://doi.org/10.4230/LIPIcs.ECOOP.2022.14
22. Paszke, A., et al.: PyTorch: an imperative style, high-performance deep learning library. Adv. Neural Inf. Process. Syst. **32** (2019)
23. Pimentel, J.A.F., Murta, L., Braganholo, V., Freire, J.: A large-scale study about quality and reproducibility of Jupyter notebooks. In: Proceedings of the 16th International Conference on Mining Software Repositories, MSR 2019, pp. 507–517. IEEE Press (2019). https://doi.org/10.1109/MSR.2019.00077
24. Python Software Foundation: The Python standard library: typing—support for type hints: typing.Union (2022). https://docs.python.org/3/library/typing.html#typing.Union

25. Python Software Foundation: The Python standard library: typing—support for type hints: The Any type (2022). https://docs.python.org/3/library/typing.html#the-any-type
26. Quaranta, L.: Assessing the quality of computational notebooks for a frictionless transition from exploration to production. In: Proceedings of the ACM/IEEE 44th International Conference on Software Engineering: Companion Proceedings, ICSE 2022, pp. 256–260. Association for Computing Machinery, New York (2022). https://doi.org/10.1145/3510454.3517055. ISBN 9781450392235
27. Quaranta, L., Calefato, F., Lanubile, F.: Pynblint: a static analyzer for Python Jupyter notebooks. In: 2022 IEEE/ACM 1st International Conference on AI Engineering - Software Engineering for AI (CAIN), pp. 48–49 (2022). https://doi.org/10.1145/3522664.3528612
28. Rasley, J., Rajbhandari, S., Ruwase, O., He, Y.: DeepSpeed: system optimizations enable training deep learning models with over 100 billion parameters. In: Proceedings of the 26th ACM SIGKDD International Conference on Knowledge Discovery & Data Mining, pp. 3505–3506 (2020)
29. Research, I.: WALA: The T. J. Watson libraries for analysis (2022). https://github.com/wala/WALA
30. Ruder, S.: An overview of gradient descent optimization algorithms. arXiv preprint arXiv:1609.04747 (2016)
31. Srivastava, N., Hinton, G., Krizhevsky, A., Sutskever, I., Salakhutdinov, R.: Dropout: a simple way to prevent neural networks from overfitting. J. Mach. Learn. Res. **15**(1), 1929–1958 (2014)
32. Subotić, P., Milikić, L., Stojić, M.: A static analysis framework for data science notebooks. In: Proceedings of the 44th International Conference on Software Engineering: Software Engineering in Practice, ICSE-SEIP 2022, pp. 13–22. Association for Computing Machinery, New York (2022). https://doi.org/10.1145/3510457.3513032. ISBN 9781450392266
33. Urban, C.: Static analysis of data science software. In: Chang, B.-Y.E. (ed.) SAS 2019. LNCS, vol. 11822, pp. 17–23. Springer, Cham (2019). https://doi.org/10.1007/978-3-030-32304-2_2. ISBN 978-3-030-32304-2
34. Wan, C., Liu, S., Hoffmann, H., Maire, M., Lu, S.: Are machine learning cloud APIs used correctly? In: 2021 IEEE/ACM 43rd International Conference on Software Engineering (ICSE), pp. 125–137 (2021). https://doi.org/10.1109/ICSE43902.2021.00024
35. Wan, Z., Xia, X., Lo, D., Murphy, G.C.: How does machine learning change software development practices? IEEE Trans. Software Eng. **47**(9), 1857–1871 (2021). https://doi.org/10.1109/TSE.2019.2937083
36. Wang, J., Kuo, T.y., Li, L., Zeller, A.: Restoring reproducibility of Jupyter notebooks. In: 2020 IEEE/ACM 42nd International Conference on Software Engineering: Companion Proceedings (ICSE-Companion), pp. 288–289 (2020)
37. Wu, D., Shen, B., Chen, Y., Jiang, H., Qiao, L.: Tensfa: detecting and repairing tensor shape faults in deep learning systems. In: 2021 IEEE 32nd International Symposium on Software Reliability Engineering (ISSRE), pp. 11–21 (2021). https://doi.org/10.1109/ISSRE52982.2021.00014
38. Zhang, Y., Ren, L., Chen, L., Xiong, Y., Cheung, S.C., Xie, T.: Detecting numerical bugs in neural network architectures. In: Proceedings of the 28th ACM Joint Meeting on European Software Engineering Conference and Symposium on the Foundations of Software Engineering, ESEC/FSE 2020, pp. 826–837. Association for Computing Machinery, New York (2020). https://doi.org/10.1145/3368089.3409720. ISBN 9781450370431

A Systematic Approach to Automotive Security

Masoud Ebrahimi[1(✉)], Stefan Marksteiner[2,4], Dejan Ničković[3], Roderick Bloem[1], David Schögler[2], Philipp Eisner[2], Samuel Sprung[2], Thomas Schober[2], Sebastian Chlup[3], Christoph Schmittner[3], and Sandra König[3]

[1] Graz University of Technology, Graz, Austria
ebrahimi@tugraz.at
[2] AVL List GmbH, Graz, Austria
stefan.marksteiner@avl.com
[3] AIT Austrian Institute of Technology, Vienna, Austria
dejan.nickovic@ait.ac.at
[4] Mälardalen University, Västerås, Sweden

Abstract. We propose a holistic methodology for designing automotive systems that consider security a central concern at every design stage. During the concept design, we model the system architecture and define the security attributes of its components. We perform threat analysis on the system model to identify structural security issues. From that analysis, we derive attack trees that define recipes describing steps to successfully attack the system's assets and propose threat prevention measures. The attack tree allows us to derive a verification and validation (V&V) plan, which prioritizes the testing effort. In particular, we advocate using learning for testing approaches for the black-box components. It consists of inferring a finite state model of the black-box component from its execution traces. This model can then be used to generate new relevant tests, model check it against requirements, and compare two different implementations of the same protocol. We illustrate the methodology with an automotive infotainment system example. Using the advocated approach, we could also document unexpected and potentially critical behavior in our example systems.

Keywords: Cybersecurity · Testing · Automotive · Threats

1 Introduction

The advent of *connected, cooperative automated mobility* provides a huge opportunity to increase mobility efficiency and road safety. However, the resulting connectivity creates new attack surfaces that affect the vehicle's safety, security, and integrity. With an estimated 100 million lines of embedded code, modern vehicles are highly complex systems that need to provide consistent cyber-security assurances. Indeed, there are an alarming spike in cyber-attacks targeting connected cars, their electronic control units (ECUs), and the original equipment manufacturer (OEM) back-end servers.

M. Chechik et al. (Eds.): FM 2023, LNCS 14000, pp. 598–609, 2023.
https://doi.org/10.1007/978-3-031-27481-7_34

Therefore, making the right security decisions from the early design stages is crucial. The ad-hoc security measures done by domain experts are insufficient to meet the requirements in the automotive domain. The standard ISO/SAE 21434 and the mandatory regulation UN R155 advocate for more systematic reasoning about system security. The United Nations Economic Commission for Europe (UNECE) has adopted new security regulations, such as UNECE R155 and R156, for the homologation of future vehicles that address the identified cyber-attack risks, for example, during software updates. Similarly, the cyber security standard ISO/SAE 21434, introduced in 2021, defines precise security requirements for vehicles during the entire product life cycle, from its development to its operation and maintenance. Hence, there is an urgent need for methods and tools that address multiple security-related aspects, from early vehicle design to deployment and operation phases.

This paper proposes a top-down methodology for systematically assessing automotive security at different stages of vehicle development. The proposed methodology follows the product cycle in several steps. During the early design phase, we use threat modeling, analysis, and repair to provide more systematic support for the concept design of secure (automotive) systems. These methods allow us to identify the system's weaknesses in security threats and develop structural measures to prevent and mitigate them. We then use the threat analysis results to capture the system's critical components concerning security properties and derive a verification and validation (V&V) plan. We apply established processes (fuzz testing, penetration testing, etc.) for testing the implemented system components. However, the source code of the component implementation is often unavailable to the V&V team, and they cannot efficiently use the classical testing methods and tools. In that case, we advocate using automata learning for testing that builds an explainable model of a black-box implementation of a component from a set of executed test cases that facilitates testing and other V&V activities. This methodology is a result of a joint research effort amongst the industrial and academic partners in TRUSTED[1], a project focusing on trust and security in autonomous vehicles.

2 TRUSTED Methodology

The TRUSTED methodology starts with the concept design with a *threat model* of the vehicle; see Stage ① in Fig. 1. The threat model consists of two components: (i) a system model architecture and (ii) a threat database. The system model architecture provides a structural view of the vehicle. This view includes vehicle components and subsystems (e.g., sensors, actuators, ECUs) and describes their (wireless or wired) interconnections. We can assign security attributes (e.g., authentication, encryption) to system components and communication links. A system model can define security boundaries that enclose trusted subsystems and assets we need to protect from potential attacks. The threat database contains a set of known threats-these threats from public domain sources, relevant

[1] https://TRUSTED.iaik.tugraz.at/.

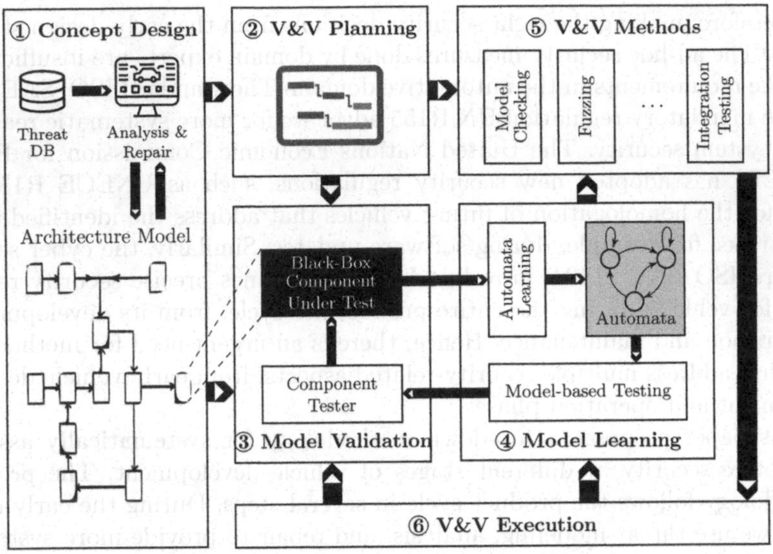

Fig. 1. Overview of the TRUSTED methodology

standards, and previous experience. The threat model is an input to a threat analysis method allowing the detection of structural weaknesses in the system's architecture. We then combine the threat analysis with the repair activities to identify prevention and mitigation actions required to protect the system from identified threats.

The high-level threat analysis performed in the early stages of the design provides essential insights into the security-related weaknesses in the system architecture. We can take structural defense actions to improve the system's security based on threat repair outcomes (e.g., implementing authentication in a specific component). Yet, there is no guarantee that an attacker cannot break the resulting measures. Hence, it is imperative to have a solid verification and validation (V&V) plan. In the TRUSTED methodology, we use the insights gained by threat analysis and repair to identify risks and prepare an effective V&V plan corresponding to ② in Fig. 1.

We use the system architecture model developed during the concept design phase to implement and integrate the components of the system. The implementation step is outside the scope of the TRUSTED methodology, but we assume the components are available as black boxes (see ③ in Fig. 1). That is, we assume that we can execute components, but we cannot access their implementations.

During the development and integration of different components from the system architecture, verifying and testing safety and security functionalities becomes another critical aspect that we must address. Model validation (③ in Fig. 1) tests the model for conformance against the component under test. This step provides either affirmation for the correctness (or completeness, respectively) of the model or counterexamples to refine the latter in a loop until the model is considered good enough to be used for test case generation.

We propose a learning-for-testing approach using automata learning (④ in Fig. 1) as the core method for generating tests during V&V. In automata learning (see Sect. 4.1), we construct a Finite State Machine (FSM) of the System Under Test (SUT). We use the inferred FSM to: (1) obtain potential attack data, and (2) identify critical inputs that might show differences between the FSM and the SUT. We must automatically perform the necessary tests during the development and especially the maintenance phase to guarantee a quick response in the event of a threat.

We chose the learning-based testing approach due to its versatility and numerous V&V activities that we can undertake with the inferred FSM (⑤ in Fig. 1). We can use the inferred FSM to: (1) visualize and understand the implementation, (2) model check it against its formalized requirements (possibly generating test cases on specification violations), (3) generate additional test cases by fuzz testing, and (4) Test for equivalence between implementation and a reference model or another implementation.

In the last phase (⑥ in Fig. 1), we use various V&V strategies to verify the specified properties against the actual component under test. The test results are final verification outcomes; meanwhile, we can use them as counterexamples for the learning algorithms in ④ in Fig. 1. This policy provides a feedback loop for refining the model in the learning-based testing approach. We execute and store tests using an automated test execution platform that augments generic test cases with additional information. This additional information comes from a test database or is provided in a grey box testing [11].

The threat model and the tests created during various design phases must be continuously maintained and updated throughout the vehicle lifecycle. We must incorporate new unknown threats and vulnerabilities into the model and re-evaluate the model to find new security issues. We must also integrate the changes to functions resulting from software updates into the system model and their impact on the vehicle's security analyzed and re-tested. This closely corresponds with the notions on testing in ISO 21434 and UNECE R155.

3 Automotive Security by Design

In this section, we demonstrate the use of THREATGET [14], a tool for threat modeling and analysis to improve the security of automotive applications during their early stages of design (step ① in Fig. 1) and generate an appropriate V&V plan (step ② in Fig. 1). We illustrate the approach with an automotive infotainment system developed by the industrial partner.

We first model the system using THREATGET (Sect. 3.1) and apply analysis to identify potential structural weaknesses in the system architecture (Sect. 3). We then use this analysis to derive a V&V plan (Sect. 3.3). Finally, we can augment it with threat repair to propose additional security measures [16].

3.1 System Architecture Model

We first create an accurate model of the automotive infotainment system (IS), shown in Fig. 2. The IS is part of a larger ADAS reference model. It has several

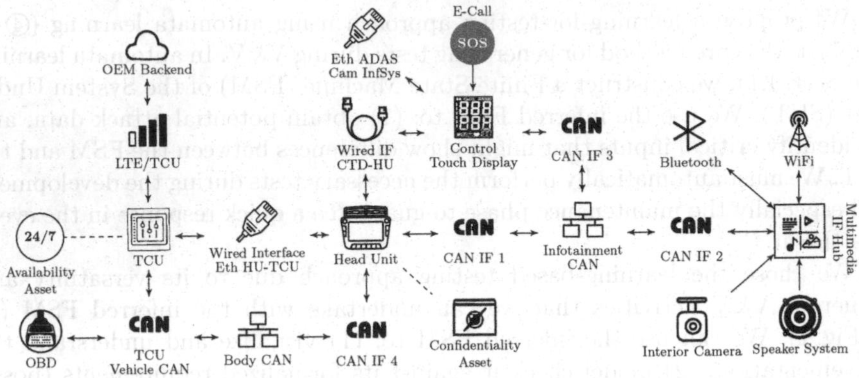

Fig. 2. Automotive infotainment system model.

external interfaces that expose an attack surface of the vehicle. The external interfaces in Fig. 2 are Bluetooth, WiFi, Interior Camera, and On-Board Diagnostics (OBD). The Multimedia Interface Hub (MIH) is an essential component of the infotainment system that (co-)implements core functionalities, including navigation, phone calls, and music playback. MIH also bridges external and internal interfaces. The Telematics Communication Unit (TCU) is the primary interface to the Internet. Many components in a modern vehicle depend on the TCU. For example, navigation systems use TCUs to access and update maps, and ECUs use them for over-the-air updates. Finally, all components except for TCU and Head Unit communicate through a CAN interface. We add two assets to the model – the confidentiality asset associated with the Head Unit and the availability asset associated with the TCU. The assets need to be protected, and their associated components are potential targets for attackers.

The IS is a weak security link in modern vehicles because it is more prone to successful cheap attacks than other components (e.g., *Body Control Unit* or the *Engine Control Unit*). This is due to versatile attack scenarios provided by the use of mainstream Unix-like operating systems, e.g., *Uconnect* and *Automotive Grade Linux*, the user requirements demanding functionalities like a built-in internet browser and installing third-party apps enabling remote code execution attacks, and the use of CAN bus that cannot guarantee communication integrity between the vehicle's external and internal interfaces.

3.2 Threat Analysis

We analyze the system model with THREATGET against its *threat database*, defining a set of possible threats formulated as *rules*. The threat descriptions are collected from multiple sources: automotive security standards and regulations (e.g., ISO/SAE 21434, ETSI, UNECE WP29 R155, and UNECE R156), publicly documented threats identified in past incidents, and expert knowledge.

We illustrate threat rules with two examples used during the analysis of the infotainment system model: the rule named "Gain Control of Wireless Interface (e.g., WiFi, Bluetooth, or BLE)" and the rule named "Flood CAN Communication with Messages". Both threat rules originate from automotive security analyses performed by domain experts. The first threat's formalization is

```
ELEMENT : "Wireless Interface"{
  "Authorization" NOT IN ["Yes", "Strong"] & "Input Sanitization" != "Yes" &
  "Authentication" NOT IN ["Yes", "Strong"] & "Input Validation" != "Yes" &
  PROVIDES CAPABILITY "Control" := "true". }
```

This rule specifies that a wireless interface (e.g., WiFi or Bluetooth) that neither implements authorization and authentication nor sanitizes or validates its inputs is susceptible to threats. The last line in the rule explicitly states that if this threat is exploited, the malicious user can control the wireless interface. The "Threat Flood CAN Communication with Messages" threat is formalized as

```
FLOW {
  SOURCE ELEMENT  : "ECU" { REQUIRES CAPABILITY "Control" >= "true" } &
  TARGET ELEMENT  : "ECU" {
      HOLDS ASSET {
        "Cybersecurity Attribute" = "Confidentiality" &
        PROVIDES CAPABILITY "Read" := "true" } } &
  INCLUDES ELEMENT  : "BUS Communication" &
  INCLUDES NO ELEMENT  : "ECU" { "Anomaly Detection" = "Yes". } }
```

This rule states that the threat is present if there is a path starting from an ECU that is under the control of a malicious user to another ECU that holds the confidentiality asset and that there is a bus between them and no ECU on the path has implemented anomaly detection.

When applied to the infotainment system model, THREATGET identifies multiple threats. One threat is "Spoof messages in the vehicle network because of the missing components". It describes a pattern that starts at an Interface with no Authentication and ends at an ECU with no Input Validation and holds an asset. It includes a wired Shared Medium representing a vehicle's CAN BUS. Moreover, no element (of type Firewall, Server, ECU, or Gateway) on the flow from the Interface to the ECU takes care of Anomaly Detection.

We can address the identified threats with appropriate security measures. Threat repair [16] consists of preventing concrete threats by proposing security measures that can be implemented during the system's design. THREATGET implements *attribute repair*, a method that proposes changes in the components' security attributes as locally deployed measures with a simple cost model.

In the case of the automotive infotainment system model, e.g., the proposed threat repair measures include enabling authorization and implementing authentication in the WiFi and Bluetooth components. We note that threat repair does not remove the need for the planned V&V activities. The fact that authentication is integrated into the WiFi device, following the outcomes of threat repair, does not guarantee that the authentication algorithm's implementation is weakness free. On the contrary, systematic testing of the WiFi's authentication protocol is even more necessary to gain confidence that the WiFi device is not a possible entry point for malicious users.

3.3 V&V Planning

In addition to threat analysis, there is support for identifying and modeling more sophisticated threats using attack trees; c.f. [8]. This results in more knowledge about potential attackers' steps when intruding into a system. Simple rules can be assigned attributes called capabilities that are either required for an intrusion or can be gained through the intrusion of a system component. Moreover, we can define the different access levels to a component (e.g., $Access < Read < Modify < Control$). Depending on previously acquired capabilities, different attack tree rules trigger, yielding distinct attack trees. An example of such a generated attack tree is illustrated in Fig. 3.

The attack tree depicted in Fig. 3 shows how a malicious user can access the *confidentiality* asset associated with the Head Unit via external interfaces such as WiFi and Bluetooth. For instance, control of the Bluetooth interface can be gained if its security attributes (input validation and sanitization, authorization and authentication) are not implemented or have weaknesses. From there, the user can gain control of the Multimedia Interface Hub, which is not sufficiently secure, and then get control of the Head Unit and hence the access to the asset. The attack tree exposes the most critical components that need to be protected. We note that the attack tree from Fig. 3 is not maximal nor unique – while THREATGET generates multiple trees for each asset in the model, including the maximal attack trees, we use a simpler tree for illustration purposes.

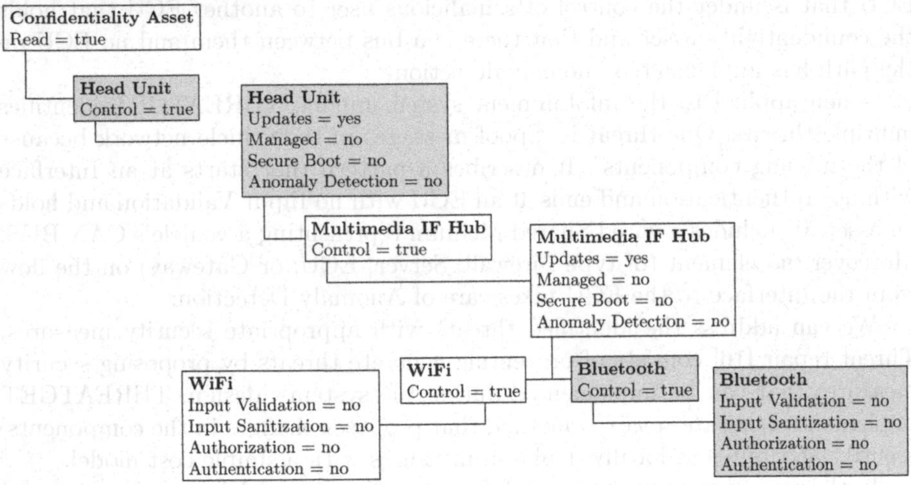

Fig. 3. Attack tree derived from THREATGET. Multiple children from the same node are implicitly interpreted with an OR operation.

4 Automotive Security Testing

In this section, we advocate an approach based on learning to test critical components identified by the threat analysis methods during concept design, when these components are assumed to be black-box to the tester.

4.1 Automata Learning for Correctness

Many cyber-physical components in the automotive domain implement one or multiple finite state machines (FSMs). Implementing larger automotive FSMs becomes cumbersome mainly because: (1) ensuring FSM's correctness w.r.t. its specification is expensive, (2) correctly coding the structure of a large FSM is difficult, and (3) correct integration of FSMs in complex software is hard. Unfortunately, many software-driven components in the automotive industry are black boxes from different manufacturers, hence are hard to verify and thus do not provide functional or non-functional guarantees.

Given an FSM of a black-box automotive component, we can test and verify it to increase our confidence in its correctness. We use automata learning [3] to infer an FSM model (concretely a Mealy machine) of the the SUT. In the learning context we refer to the SUT by system-under-learning (SUL). In automata learning, a *learner* asks an *oracle* two types of queries. First, *membership queries* to determine the SUL's output for a given input word. Second, *equivalence queries* check whether a learned model conforms to the SUL, to which the oracle returns positive answer or a counterexample. A counterexample is an input-output word distinguishing SUL from hypothesis. In practice, oracles for black box systems work with conformance testing.

Ordinarily, real-world systems' alphabets are not manageable for learning algorithms. Abstraction helps to both cope with this fact and to make inferred models more human-readable. Too much abstraction, however, might induce non-deterministic behavior and hide problems we intend to find. There are also automatic abstraction refinement approaches for an optimum of abstraction in a mapper [1,10]. An abstraction mapper consists of a mapping function that converts a concrete input into an abstract symbol. It also observes the SUL's concrete outputs and sends an abstraction to the learner. To send a concrete input to the SUL, the mapper inverses the abstraction. There are multiple methods to assess the behavioral correctness of the learned FSMs, including (1) black-box checking [13], adaptive model checking [9], a combination of learning-based testing and machine learning [12] and symbolic execution [2].

4.2 Use-Case Scenarios

The attack tree (see Fig. 3) poses the critical components that need to be tested for security. In this section, we illustrate our learning-based testing approach on the two components highlighted in gray color in Fig. 3 - the Bluetooth interface (as an entry vector) and the Head Unit ECU.

Bluetooth and Bluetooth Low Energy. Bluetooth is a well-established standard for wireless audio used in most infotainment systems. Bluetooth Low Energy (BLE) grows in popularity for car access and sensor data transmission. The protocols have a variety of known vulnerabilities [4–7,15], some also specifically for automotive systems[2].

[2] https://research.nccgroup.com/2022/05/15/technical-advisory-tesla-ble-phone-as-a-key-passive-entry-vulnerable-to-relay-attacks/.

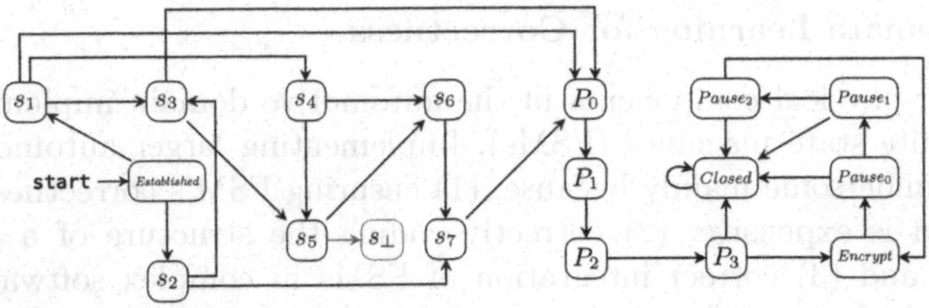

Fig. 4. Inferred FSM structure for Bluetooth pairing.

Learning Setup. We use Intel Wireless Controllers (AC 8265 and AX200) implementing Bluetooth and BLE. The learning setups are similar, the difference is in the radio hardware and the physical layer, requiring three entities: (1) Radio Device, (2) Learner, and (3) Interface between the two with a mapper.

Learned Model and Findings. We inferred the pairing process models, which are used for encryption and therefore security-critical in the SULs. As a tangible result, we discovered a BLE deadlock state (red state in Fig. 4) in the Linux BLE host software. With repeated out-of-order transmission of pairing requests of different types, we force the respective BLE stack into a state that limits the device to respond to basic link-layer control packets. After the state is reached, each following connection will start in this state until the controller is reset.

Unified Diagnostic Services. Each ECU has a secure access mode reachable through its UDS implementation, available via vehicle's OBD connector. An attacker able to exploit UDS security features would be also able to manipulate data or even flash the ECU with a malicious firmware.

Learning Setup. To communicate with the ECU we used a CAN interface. To learn a different ECU we only need to adapt the interface. We started by implementing a reduced UDS interface, consisting of instructions to put an ECU into secure access mode. Communications occures via a CAN bus interface.

Learned Model and Findings. The learning experiment resulted in a reduced FSM of the UDS shown in Fig. 5. An analysis of the results shows that once being successfully authenticated (state s_4), an incorrect authentication key will

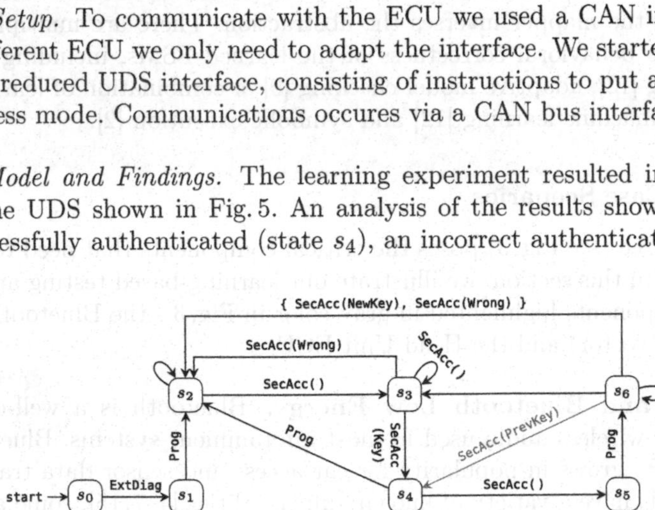

Fig. 5. Inferred UDS FSM. (Color figure online)

still result in the same state. This is unexpected and allows for prolonging a session without authentication. When requesting a new seed for re-authentication (s_5) this behavior persists. Moreover, on re-entering a secure session afterwards (from s_6), the ECU accepts an old key as well; an unexpected behavior after re-initiating the key authentication. Figure 5 marks all unexpected behaviors in red.

5 Conclusion

We introduced the TRUSTED methodology for designing and assessing trusted and secure automotive systems. The main novelty of the proposed methodology is its holistic and systematic approach to security, which starts at concept design and is carried down to the implementation and assessment of individual components. We instantiated the different parts of the methodology using the state-of-the-art methods and tools for threat modelling and analysis, automata learning and testing. We illustrated the use of the methodology by applying it step-by-step an automotive infotainment system. Using the learning-based testing approach we could document previously unpublished denial-of-service conditions in the examined BLE setups, as well as unexpected behavior allowing for extending secure UDS programming sessions on the scrutinized ECU.

Future Work. We plan to further automate the transition from the concept design and V&V planning on one side, to the actual testing activities done on the level of components by devising a domain-specific test description language that can define abstract V&V plans derived from the attack trees, and be refined in a way so that eventually it can be executed on a platform (e.g., as in [17]). Second, the TRUSTED methodology mainly focuses on the transition from concept design to testing the implementation. We plan to also study the opposite direction – how to use the component testing results to update the system model and have a more refined threat analysis and a more realistic threat assessment.

Acknowledgement. This research received funding from the program "ICT of the Future" of the Austrian Research Promotion Agency (FFG) and the Austrian Ministry for Transport, Innovation and Technology under grant agreement No. 867558 (project TRUSTED) and within the ECSEL Joint Undertaking (JU) under grant agreement No. 876038 (project InSecTT). The JU receives support from the European Union's Horizon 2020 research and innovation programme and Austria, Sweden, Spain, Italy, France, Portugal, Ireland, Finland, Slovenia, Poland, Netherlands, Turkey. The document reflects only the author's view and the Commission is not responsible for any use that may be made of the information it contains.

References

1. Aarts, F., Heidarian, F., Kuppens, H., Olsen, P., Vaandrager, F.: Automata learning through counterexample guided abstraction refinement. In: Giannakopoulou, D., Méry, D. (eds.) FM 2012. LNCS, vol. 7436, pp. 10–27. Springer, Heidelberg (2012). https://doi.org/10.1007/978-3-642-32759-9_4

2. Aichernig, B.K., Bloem, R., Ebrahimi, M., Tappler, M., Winter, J.: Automata learning for symbolic execution. In: 2018 Formal Methods in Computer Aided Design (FMCAD), pp. 1–9. IEEE, Austin, Texas, USA (2018). https://doi.org/10.23919/FMCAD.2018.8602991
3. Angluin, D.: Learning regular sets from queries and counterexamples. Inf. Comput. **75**(2), 87–106 (1987). https://doi.org/10.1016/0890-5401(87)90052-6
4. Antonioli, D., Tippenhauer, N.O., Rasmussen, K.: BIAS: bluetooth impersonation AttackS. In: 2020 IEEE Symposium on Security and Privacy (SP), pp. 549–562. IEEE, San Francisco, CA, USA, May 2020. https://doi.org/10.1109/SP40000.2020.00093
5. Antonioli, D., Tippenhauer, N.O., Rasmussen, K.: Key negotiation downgrade attacks on bluetooth and bluetooth low energy. ACM Trans. Priv. Secur. **23**(3), 14:1–14:28 (2020). https://doi.org/10.1145/3394497
6. Antonioli, D., Tippenhauer, N.O., Rasmussen, K., Payer, M.: BLURtooth: exploiting cross-transport key derivation in bluetooth classic and bluetooth low energy. In: Proceedings of the 2022 ACM on Asia Conference on Computer and Communications Security, pp. 196–207. ASIA CCS 2022, Association for Computing Machinery, New York, NY, USA, May 2022. https://doi.org/10.1145/3488932.3523258
7. Antonioli, D., Tippenhauer, N.O., Rasmussen, K.B.: The KNOB is broken: exploiting low entropy in the encryption key negotiation of bluetooth BR/EDR. In: Heninger, N., Traynor, P. (eds.) 28th USENIX Security Symposium, USENIX Security 2019, pp. 1047–1061. USENIX Association, Santa Clara, CA, USA (2019)
8. Ebrahimi, M., Striessnig, C., Triginer, J.C., Schmittner, C.: Identification and verification of attack-tree threat models in connected vehicles. In: SAE Technical paper 2022–01-7087 (2022). https://doi.org/10.4271/2022-01-7087
9. Groce, A., Peled, D., Yannakakis, M.: Adaptive model checking. In: Katoen, J.-P., Stevens, P. (eds.) TACAS 2002. LNCS, vol. 2280, pp. 357–370. Springer, Heidelberg (2002). https://doi.org/10.1007/3-540-46002-0_25
10. Howar, F., Steffen, B., Merten, M.: Automata learning with automated alphabet abstraction refinement. In: Jhala, R., Schmidt, D. (eds.) VMCAI 2011. LNCS, vol. 6538, pp. 263–277. Springer, Heidelberg (2011). https://doi.org/10.1007/978-3-642-18275-4_19
11. Marksteiner, S., et al.: A process to facilitate automated automotive cybersecurity testing. In: 2021 IEEE 93rd Vehicular Technology Conference (VTC Spring), pp. 1–7. IEEE, New York, NY, USA (2021)
12. Meinke, K.: Learning-based testing of cyber-physical systems-of-systems: a platooning study. In: Reinecke, P., Di Marco, A. (eds.) EPEW 2017. LNCS, vol. 10497, pp. 135–151. Springer, Cham (2017). https://doi.org/10.1007/978-3-319-66583-2_9
13. Peled, D., Vardi, M.Y., Yannakakis, M.: Black box checking. In: Wu, J., Chanson, S.T., Gao, Q. (eds.) Formal Methods for Protocol Engineering and Distributed Systems. IAICT, vol. 28, pp. 225–240. Springer, Boston, MA (1999). https://doi.org/10.1007/978-0-387-35578-8_13
14. Schmittner, C., Chlup, S., Fellner, A., Macher, G., Brenner, E.: Threatget: Threat modeling based approach for automated and connected vehicle systems. In: AmE 2020 - Automotive meets Electronics; 11th GMM-Symposium, pp. 1–3. VDE Verlag, Berlin (2020)
15. Seri, B., Vishnepolsky, G.: The dangers of Bluetooth implementations: unveiling zero day vulnerabilities and security flaws in modern Bluetooth stacks. Technical report, Armis Inc. (2017)

16. Tarrach, T., Ebrahimi, M., König, S., Schmittner, C., Bloem, R., Nickovic, D.: Threat repair with optimization modulo theories. CoRR (2022)
17. Wolschke, C., Marksteiner, S., Braun, T., Wolf, M.: An agnostic domain specific language for implementing attacks in an automotive use case. In: The 16th International Conference on Availability, Reliability and Security, pp. 1–9. ARES 2021, Association for Computing Machinery, New York, NY, USA, August 2021. https://doi.org/10.1145/3465481.3470070

Specification-Guided Critical Scenario Identification for Automated Driving

Adam Molin[1](✉), Edgar A. Aguilar[2], Dejan Ničković[2], Mengjia Zhu[3], Alberto Bemporad[3], and Hasan Esen[1]

[1] DENSO AUTOMOTIVE Deutschland GmbH, 85386 Eching, Germany
{a.molin,h.esen}@eu.denso.com
[2] AIT Austrian Institute of Technology GmbH, 1210 Vienna, Austria
{edgar.aguilar,dejan.nickovic}@ait.ac.at
[3] IMT School for Advanced Studies Lucca, 55100 Lucca, Italy
{mengjia.zhu,alberto.bemporad}@imtlucca.it

Abstract. To test automated driving systems, we present a case study for finding critical scenarios in driving environments guided by formal specifications. To that aim, we devise a framework for critical scenario identification, which we base on open-source libraries that combine scenario specification, testing, formal methods, and optimization.

Keywords: Autonomous vehicles · Scenario based testing

1 Introduction

With the complexity of the automated driving (AD) system and its driving environment, verification and validation (V&V) is regarded as one of the major challenges of AD development [25]. *Scenario-based testing* (SBT) was introduced as an essential method for facilitating the overall safety assurance of ADs. In SBT, the expected behavior of an AD system is described by a representative set of scenarios that are relevant for its safe use. The SBT paradigm facilitates shifting the AD testing from the physical to the simulation environment. The use of virtual testing has manifold advantages – more specifically it allows to: (1) explore efficiently a large number of situations originating from the catalog of relevant scenarios, (2) reproduce environment conditions (fog, night, rain, etc.) that are hard to enforce in a physical environment, and (3) play dangerous scenarios without risk to humans, other vehicles or infrastructure.

Despite significant advances in research and standardization of SBT, there are still remaining open issues. One of them is to determine the critical scenarios among the virtually infinite number of scenarios with an abundance of influential factors ranging from weather or road conditions, to the behaviors of surrounding road users. A first attempt to keep the number of scenarios manageable is to

This project has received funding from the European Union's Horizon 2020 research and innovation programme under grant agreement No 956123.

M. Chechik et al. (Eds.): FM 2023, LNCS 14000, pp. 610–621, 2023.
https://doi.org/10.1007/978-3-031-27481-7_35

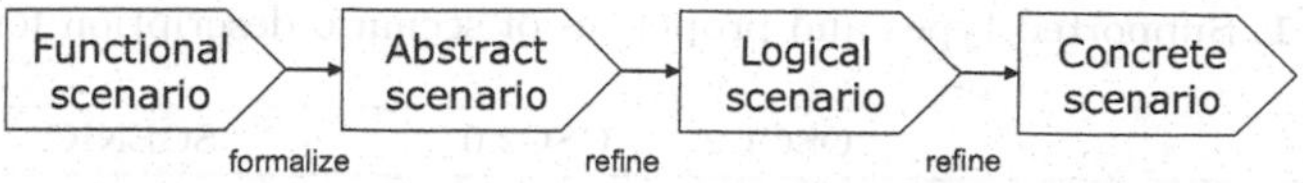

Fig. 1. Scenario abstraction types according to [17].

restrict the operational design domain (ODD) of the AD system. According to [20], the ODD is defined as the operating conditions under which a given AD system is specifically designed to function. However, there are some factors, including the dynamic behavior of the road users, which cannot be controlled in the ODD. Thus, efficient methods are needed to identify the critical scenarios from the scenario space within the ODD. An extensive survey study on finding critical scenarios has been conducted in [25]. With regard to specification-guided critical scenario identification, our work is closely related to [8,21,23,24].

In this paper, we present a specification-driven framework for critical scenario identification (CSI) entirely based on open-source software libraries and demonstrate its benefits with an automated emergency break case study. The proposed framework, based on the falsification testing paradigm [18], uses optimization-based methods for finding critical scenarios. We first describe the vanilla workflow and show how to tailor it with custom test generation and monitoring strategies. Hence, our aim is to share our experience in combining existing methods into a flexible and efficient SBT framework. To innovate the methodology for SBT within the framework, we investigate the separation between the AD system and the other road users, modeling their interplay with Assume/Guarantee (A/G) contracts. By using A/G contracts, we can improve the search for meaningful scenarios, assign responsibility for critical situations and distinguish between invalid behaviors originating from the AD system and from its environment. In that way, we can detect the violation of environment assumptions in the simulation execution, and discard the test run. By sharing our experience in SBT, we intend to nurture the innovation of prospective CSI methods that are based on specification-guided strategies.

2 Specification-Driven Scenario-Based Testing

2.1 Traffic Scenario Description

In the operational domain in which the ADS will be deployed, it is exposed to a potentially infinite number of traffic scenarios. As a consequence, it is impractical to conduct testing - even in simulation - directly on these traffic scenarios. A first step towards a successful application of scenario-based testing to assure the correct behavior of an ADS within its ODD is the abstraction of traffic scenarios. While the argumentation for quality assurance is done on a higher level of abstraction, the creation of evidence is performed on simulating a variety of concrete traffic scenarios derived from the abstract ones. The PEGASUS project "for the establishment of generally accepted quality criteria, tools and methods as

Table 1. Supported types and properties of scenario description formats

	OSC1.2	OSC2.0	SCENIC
Scenario types			
Functional	×	×	×
Abstract	×	✓	✓
Logical	✓	✓	✓
Concrete	✓	✓	✓
Properties			
Syntax format	XML[a]	DSL[b], pythonic	DSL, pythonic
Language paradigm	imperative	Mostly declarative	Declarative/imperative
Map-agnostic scenario definition	×	✓	✓

[a] Extensible Markup Language
[b] Domain-specific language

well as scenarios and situations for the release of highly-automated driving functions", introduced three abstraction types: functional, logical, concrete scenarios [16]. In this paper, we use an extended classification proposed in [17], see Fig. 1. Functional scenarios are defined as behavior-based, non-formal descriptions of traffic scenarios in natural language. Abstract scenarios are a formalization of functional scenarios using a declarative way to describe the scenario. Logical scenarios are defined as a parameterized set of traffic scenarios, while concrete scenarios are instances of a logical scenario with fixed parameters. They have a fixed scenery and road user behavior, that is based on the ego-vehicle movement. Abstract, logical, and concrete scenarios are machine-readable, and various realizations of traffic scenario description formats exist for simulation. In the following, we give a comparison between three non-proprietary, and openly available scenario description formats: OpenSCENARIO®1.2 (OSC1.2) [3], OpenSCENARIO®2.0 (OSC2.0) [4], and Scenic [12], see Table 1. With regard to the overall traffic scenario, their focus is on the initial placement and the dynamic behavior of the actors. The description of the scenery, such as the map, is defined outside these formats. OSC1.2 is mainly used for describing concrete traffic scenarios that can be directly run by the simulator. The actors' placement and behavior are defined in an imperative fashion using pairs of actions and triggers that evoke these actions. OSC2.0's and Scenic's main intent is to define abstract scenarios, which can be concretized by a dedicated scenario generation engine. OSC2.0's description is mostly declarative by constraining the road users' behavior. The probabilistic programming language Scenic is declarative in the initial actor placement with a rich instruction set for relationships between entities, and uses an imperative description for behaviors. All three languages support parameterization of scenario parameters to describe logical scenarios. A distinctive feature of OSC2.0 and Scenic compared to OSC1.2 is that the location of the scenario does not need to be specified within the scenario definition. Instead, the scenario generation engine will find a suitable segment on the road map, on which the scenario can be executed with all actors in the simulator.

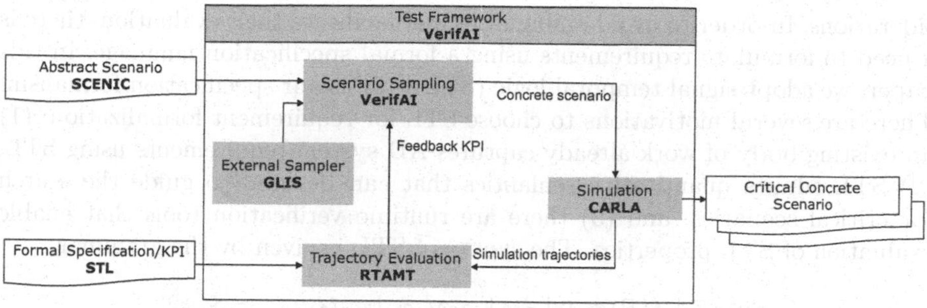

Fig. 2. Critical scenario identification framework with tool architecture.

Based on the scenario format, a database of abstract/logical scenarios needs to be created that covers all the relevant features in the considered ODD of the AD function. In this paper, we selected Scenic as our scenario format, due to both its flexibility in expressing abstract scenarios and the availability of an open-source testing framework [9] that is provided for Scenic.

2.2 Critical Scenario Identification

This section introduces the test framework to find critical concrete scenario instances within a specified abstract scenario efficiently and in a flexible manner. The framework depicted in Fig. 2 indicating the overall workflow is based on open-source software components highlighted in bold. It assumes two inputs, the abstract scenario given in the Scenic format, and a formal specification of the AD system defined in signal temporal logic (STL), that we use as a test oracle. The technical details on the formal specification are introduced in Sect. 2.3.

Workflow. The test execution framework is based on Berkeley's VerifAI [9]. By applying a sampling strategy, VerifAI generates concrete scenarios from the Scenic scenario that are executed in the CARLA simulator [7]. To evaluate the resulting trajectories, we integrated RTAMT - an STL monitoring library [19] - into the VerifAI-based testing framework. RTAMT provides the automated generation of robustness monitors from STL specifications and therefore facilitates checking simulation traces against the formal specification. The robustness measure is then fed back as a criticality indicator to the scenario sampler that determines new test parameters that constitute the next concrete scenario to be simulated. Depending on the sampling strategy, the scenario search can be of explorative or exploitative nature. Instead of using the sampling strategies provided by VerifAI, we integrated an external sampling strategy, that is based on the global optimizer GLIS [5]. The details about GLIS are outlined in Sect. 2.4.

2.3 Formal Specifications

Concrete scenarios are typically evaluated against requirements. These requirements can cover various aspects, including safety, legal, comfort and ethical considerations. In order to avoid ambiguities and facilitate their evaluation, there is a need to formulate requirements using a formal specification language. In this paper, we adopt signal temporal logic (STL) [15] as our specification formalism. There are several motivations to choose STL for requirement formalization: (1) an existing body of work already captures AD system requirements using STL, (2) STL admits quantitative semantics that can be used to guide the search for critical scenarios, and (3) there are runtime verification tools that enable evaluation of STL properties. The syntax of STL is given by the grammar

$$\varphi ::= \top \mid f(R) > 0 \mid \neg\varphi \mid \varphi_1 \vee \varphi_2 \mid \varphi_1 \mathcal{U}_I \varphi_2 \mid \varphi_1 \mathcal{S}_I \varphi 2\,,$$

where $f(R)$ are terms in Θ and I are real intervals with bounds in $\mathbb{Q}_{\geq 0} \cup \{\infty\}$. As customary we use $\Diamond_I \varphi \equiv \top \mathcal{U}_I \varphi$ for *eventually*, $\Box_I \varphi \equiv \neg \Diamond_I \neg \varphi$ for *always*, $\diamondminus_I \varphi \equiv \top \mathcal{S}_I \varphi$ for *once* and $\boxminus_I \varphi \equiv \neg \diamondminus_I \neg \varphi$ for *historically*. The timing interval I may be omitted when $I = [0, \infty)$ or $I = (0, \infty)$. STL can be naturally equipped with *quantitative semantics* based on the infinity norm [6] that measure how far is the observed behavior from satisfying or violating a requirement.

The evaluation of an AD system cannot be performed in isolation from its environment. For instance, an AD system cannot guarantee safety requirements, such as RSS, in presence of other road users that do not behave in a reasonable manner. The relation of the AD system and the environment under which it operates can be formalized in terms of a *contract* $C = (\varphi, \psi)$, a pair of properties where φ represents the assumptions on the environment and ψ guarantees of the system under these assumptions. This classical interpretation of C is given by the temporal logic formula

$$\Box\varphi \rightarrow \Box\psi.$$

According to the above formula, any violation of the assumption by the environment results in the (vacuous) satisfaction of the contract, even if the system also violates its guarantee. However, this definition neglects that these two violations may not be causally related – the violation of ψ by the system at time t before the violation of φ by the environment at time $t' > t$ still results in the satisfaction of the contract. To address this situation, we propose a more refined notion of a contract that takes the intended temporal causality between the environment and the AD system into account. We denote our refined contract by $\hat{C}$ and capture its meaning using the formula:

$$\Box((\boxminus_{[0,T]}\varphi) \rightarrow \psi)$$

where T specifies the maximum duration within which we consider the violation of φ to be causally related to the violation of ψ.

2.4 Sampling Strategy

Different sampling strategies may be used to identify the parameters of the next concrete scenario to simulate. These strategies can be broadly divided into naïve (passive) and guided search (active) sampling strategies [25]. The naïve search strategies, such as random sampling, involve the independent selection of test parameters. In contrast, the guided search, such as optimization [10,11], make the selection based on a specific selection criterion and the information of existing samples. Naïve search sampling strategies are useful if the simulation is computationally cheap to run since parallelization of the procedure is possible due to the independence among testing samples. On the other hand, when the test case simulation is computationally expensive to run and/or when the test cases interested (critical test cases in this case) are in a small region of the search domain, the guided search sampling strategies can be more sample efficient.

For the current study, guided-search sampling strategies such as surrogate-based black-box optimization methods are appropriate to efficiently identify relevant critical concrete scenarios for the AD system. It is because a closed-form expression of the KPI in terms of the test parameters is often unavailable. Specifically, we use the global optimization algorithm GLIS (Global optimization via Inverse distance weighting and Surrogate radial basis functions) [5] as the active guided-search sampler to identify the next test parameters of a concrete scenario for testing. The procedure of GLIS includes an initial sampling stage and an active learning stage. In the initial sampling stage, N_{initial} different test parameters are randomly selected within the search domain, and the corresponding concrete scenarios are simulated. The resulting quantitative evaluation of each test parameter from RTAMT monitors is fed back to GLIS (c.f. Fig. 2). A surrogate radial basis interpolation function (RBF) representing the correlation between the test parameters and the KPI is fitted to the initial samples. In the active learning phase, at each iteration, we identify a new test parameter, simulate the corresponding concrete scenario, and refit the surrogate function by including the newly identified test parameter and its KPI. The new test parameter is obtained by optimizing an acquisition function, which trades off the exploitation of the fitted RBF surrogate and exploration of an inverse distance weighting (IDW) function. IDW is a distance-based exploration function that promotes visiting points far away from the existing samples, which helps prevent the solver from being trapped in the local optima. GLIS terminates when the maximum allowed iteration is reached, or another user-defined criterion is met.

GLIS is chosen for this study, as it easily incorporates constraints and has a low computing cost [5]. If the computing cost is reasonable, GLIS may be replaced by other surrogate-based active samplers, such as Bayesian optimization.

3 Automatic Emergency Braking Case Study

To illustrate the methodology, we focus on testing a simple Automatic Emergency Braking (AEB) functionality using a highway scenario.

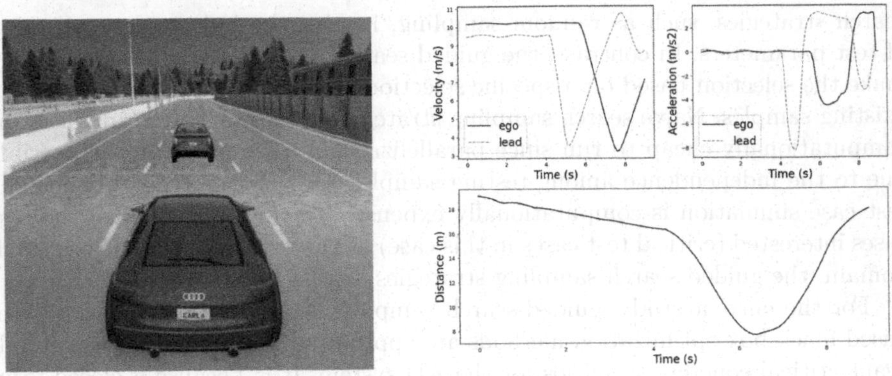

Fig. 3. (left) Snapshot of CARLA simulator running the AEB function test on a highway. (right) Example of telemetric data collected from all actors.

Scenario Description. The functional scenario is an ego vehicle following a leading vehicle on a highway, when suddenly the leading vehicle brakes abruptly. The ego vehicle is equipped with a simplistic distance-based AEB function which is activated when the ego is less than `safeDist` meters from the leading vehicle. Figure 3 shows a snapshot of the scenario running in CARLA v9.10.

The abstract scenario, depicted in Listing 1.1, is formulated using Scenic[1]. The scenario first specifies the sampler and the map used to generate concrete simulations (lines 1 and 2). Then, it defines parameter variables that we partition into: (1) the *constant* variables (lines 3–4) that do not change across concrete scenarios and (2) the *optimization* variables (lines 6–7) that are fed to an external (VerifAI) sampler in order to find critical scenarios in a controlled fashion. There are also what we call *implicit* variables that are not explicitly part of the Scenic abstract scenario but still need to have a concrete value in the simulator. For example, the weather conditions, the exact starting position and orientation of each vehicle, the vehicle model, etc. In this case study, there are more than 25 implicit parameters. The scenario also defines the behavior of the ego (lines 9–12) and of the lead vehicle (lines 14–18). Both the ego and the lead vehicle follow the lane with some target speed as their default behavior. However, the lead vehicle abruptly breaks at regular intervals, while the ego breaks when it approaches any object at some minimum distance. The two vehicles are spawned at some uniformly chosen part of the map (line 20) that is sufficiently far away from an intersection (line 25). The lead car is initialized at some pre-defined distance in front of the ego vehicle (lines 22–23).

```
1  param verifaiSamplerType = `glis' # specify sampler
2  param carla_map = `Town04' # specify map to use
3  initDist = 30 # constant
4  leadSpeed = 10
5
```

[1] The shown scenario is simplified to facilitate presentation.

```
safeDist = VerifaiRange(25,45) # optimization variable
egoSpeed = VerifaiRange(9,11) # optimization variable

behavior AEB_Behavior: # define ego behavior
  try:
    FollowLaneBehavior(egoSpeed)
  interrupt when withinDistanceToObjsInLane(self, safeDist):
      take SetBrakeAction(1), SetThrottleAction(0)

behavior Brake_Behavior: # define behavior of lead car
  try:
    FollowLaneBehavior(leadSpeed)
  interrupt when simulation().currentTime > delay:
    take SetBrakeAction(1), SetThrottleAction(0)

spawnPt = Uniform(*HighwayRoads) # Highway part of map

ego = Car at spawnPt, with AEB_Behavior} # spawn ego
leadCar = Car at spawnPt + initDist, with Brake_Behavior # lead

require (distance from leadCar to intersection > 50)
# extra requirements for rejection sampling
```

Listing 1.1. AEB highway scenario in Scenic

Formalized Requirements. We illustrate the formalization of the requirements with the contract $C = (\varphi, \psi)$, which captures the assumption φ about the maximum allowed deceleration of the lead vehicle and the guarantee ψ as the Responsibility-Sensitive Safety (RSS) property of the ego vehicle. The assumption φ originates from the IEEE Standard 2846-2022 [1], that describes the minimal set of assumptions on the road users for safety-related models of AD. From the assumptions described in the standard, we focus on the maximum deceleration specification

$$\varphi = \beta \leq \beta_{max}.$$

The Responsibility-Sensitive Safety (RSS) rule specifies, under minimal assumptions, what longitudinal and lateral distances the ego vehicle must keep from other road users to ensure no collisions [22]. The RSS rules were formalized into temporal logic by [2,14]. We adopt the STL specification from [2] for an ego vehicle (*back*) to keep a safe longitudinal distance to another vehicle (*front*):

$$\Box(v_{\text{front}} \geq 0 \wedge v_{\text{back}} \geq 0)$$
$$\Box(a_{\text{front}} \in [a_{\text{max-Br}}, a_{\text{max-Acc}}] \wedge a_{\text{back}} \in [a_{\text{max-Br}}, a_{\text{max-Acc}}])$$
$$\Box(d(\text{front, back}) < d_{\text{safe}} \rightarrow a_{\text{back}} \in [a_{\text{max-Br}}, a_{\text{min-Br}}])$$

where a, v are correspondingly acceleration and velocity. Similarly $a_{\text{max-Acc}}$, $a_{\text{max-Br}}$, $a_{\text{min-Br}}$ are assumed maximum acceleration, maximum braking, and minimum braking acceleration. Finally, d_{safe} is determined dynamically depending on the velocities of both vehicles, and the reaction time τ of the ego vehicle:

$$d_{\text{safe}} = \left(v_{\text{back}}\tau + \frac{a_{\text{max-Acc}}\tau^2}{2} + \frac{(v_{\text{back}} + a_{\text{max-Acc}}\tau)^2}{2a_{\text{min-Br}}} - \frac{v_{\text{front}}^2}{2a_{\text{max-Br}}} \right).$$

The safety distance is calculated in order to ensure that a collision is avoided as long as the ego vehicle is sufficiently far away from the leading vehicle. If it is momentarily closer than d_{safe} then a collision will still be avoided if the ego is reacting appropriately (by braking with at least $a_{\text{min-Br}}$).

3.1 Simulation Results

In this section we present our evaluation outcomes. Figure 4 shows the results from simulating the abstract scenario 70 times using the described tool chain. Each point in the scatter plots represents a simulated concrete scenario, where the RSS longitudinal distance was monitored. If the ego vehicle managed to react adequately by braking in time, then this is represented as a blue circle, otherwise (if the specification was violated) it is represented by a red cross (the intensity of the color represents the robustness degree).

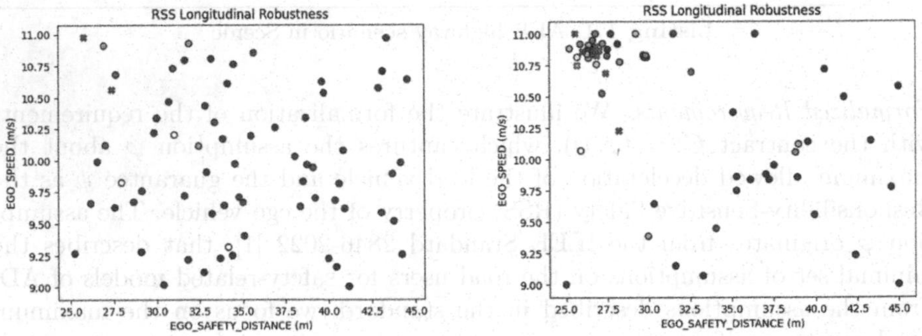

Fig. 4. Comparison between Halton sampling (left) and GLIS sampling [5] (right) for 70 concrete scenarios. The GLIS parameters are: $\alpha = 1$, $\delta = 0.5$, $\varepsilon_{\text{SVD}} = 0.01$, and an inverse-quadratic basis function with $\epsilon = 0.2$ was used.

Furthermore, we compare two different sampling strategies to find critical scenarios. In this case, we compare a passive sampling strategy (i.e. agnostic to feedback) which is based on Halton sequences [13], to an active strategy based on the GLIS optimization sampling. As expected, sampling scenarios with GLIS leads to the discovery of more critical scenarios (11 compared to 2 with Halton), and suggests variable regions which should be further investigated. In our example, the optimizer clearly was trying to exploit around the region of higher `egoSpeed`, and lower `safeDist` (as expected). In practice, both strategies are used to obtain a clear picture of the performance of the ADAS functionality.

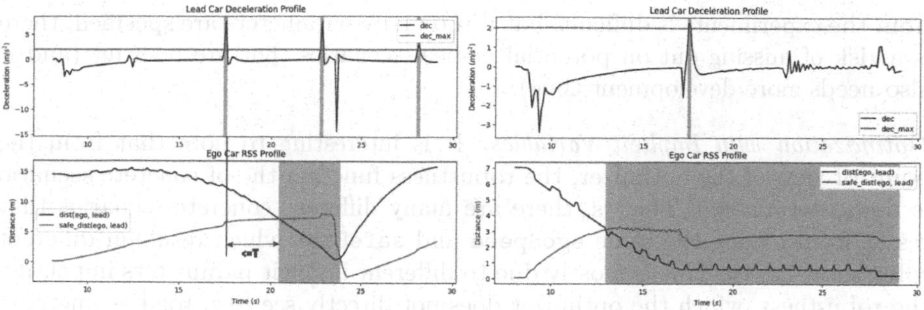

Fig. 5. Evaluation with A/G contracts.

In Fig. 5, we illustrate the discrepancy between the classical and the refined interpretation of A/G contracts. The figure depicts two simulations showing the deceleration β of the lead vehicle and the maximum allowed deceleration threshold $\beta_{max} = 2\,\mathrm{m/s^2}$ (top) and the distance between the ego and the lead vehicle, as well as the safe distance between them (bottom). We see that in the two simulations both the assumption φ and the guarantee ψ are violated (purple and red stipes, respectively). In the first simulation (left), there is a clear causality between the abrupt breaking of the lead vehicle and the longitudinal RSS violation – it follows that the contract is satisfied under both the classical and the refined interpretation. In the second simulation (right), the violation of the longitudinal RSS requirement happens before the lead vehicle breaks. Intuitively, we expect the contract to be violated since the behavior of the lead vehicle did not cause this critical scenario. However, under the classical contract interpretation, the contract is satisfied because the lead vehicle does violate the assumption at a later stage. On the other hand, the refined contract rightly indicates the contract falsification.

3.2 Lessons Learned

In this section, we share our experience about the scenario-based testing framework and collected during the case study evaluation.

Passive vs. Active Sampling. Both passive and active sampling have their merits in testing AD systems. Passive sampling methods such as Halton provide a coverage of the parameter space, facilitate detecting interesting patterns, if any, and help identifying parameter regions that are interesting to further explore. In contrast, active sampling methods such as GLIS can accelerate the detection of critical scenarios.

Level of Scenario Abstraction. Balance between keeping a scenario abstract, and letting the tools sample different variables, and having consistent concrete scenarios. If too many variables are left unspecified, drawing meaningful conclusions from the experiments is difficult, but if too many parameters are specified, there is a risk of missing out on potential critical scenarios that are relevant (and it also needs more development time).

Optimization with Implicit Variables. It is interesting to note that from the point of view of the optimizer, the robustness function the of concrete scenario is non-deterministic. That is, there are many different concrete scenarios that result from having the same `egoSpeed` and `safeDist` which result in different robustness values. This is mostly due to different implicit parameters impacting the robustness, which the optimizer does not directly see (e.g. road geometry).

References

1. IEEE standard for assumptions in safety-related models for automated driving systems. IEEE Std 2846-2022, pp. 1–59 (2022). https://doi.org/10.1109/IEEESTD.2022.9761121
2. Aréchiga, N.: Specifying safety of autonomous vehicles in signal temporal logic. In: 2019 IEEE Intelligent Vehicles Symposium (IV), pp. 58–63 (2019). https://doi.org/10.1109/IVS.2019.8813875
3. Association for Standardization of Automation and Measuring Systems: ASAM OpenSCENARIO V1.2.0. Standard, Munich, Germany (2022). https://www.asam.net/standards/detail/openscenario/
4. Association for Standardization of Automation and Measuring Systems: ASAM OpenSCENARIO V2.0.0. Standard, Munich, Germany (2022). https://www.asam.net/standards/detail/openscenario/v200/
5. Bemporad, A.: Global optimization via inverse distance weighting and radial basis functions. Comput. Optim. Appl. **77**, 571–595 (2020). http://cse.lab.imtlucca.it/~bemporad/glis
6. Donzé, A., Maler, O.: Robust satisfaction of temporal logic over real-valued signals. In: Chatterjee, K., Henzinger, T.A. (eds.) FORMATS 2010. LNCS, vol. 6246, pp. 92–106. Springer, Heidelberg (2010). https://doi.org/10.1007/978-3-642-15297-9_9
7. Dosovitskiy, A., Ros, G., Codevilla, F., Lopez, A., Koltun, V.: CARLA: an open urban driving simulator. In: Proceedings of the 1st Annual Conference on Robot Learning, pp. 1–16 (2017)
8. Dreossi, T., Donzé, A., Seshia, S.A.: Compositional falsification of cyber-physical systems with machine learning components. J. Autom. Reason. **63**(4), 1031–1053 (2019). https://doi.org/10.1007/s10817-018-09509-5
9. Dreossi, T., et al.: VerifAI: a toolkit for the formal design and analysis of artificial intelligence-based systems. In: 31st International Conference on Computer Aided Verification (CAV), July 2019
10. Feng, S., Feng, Y., Sun, H., Bao, S., Zhang, Y., Liu, H.X.: Testing scenario library generation for connected and automated vehicles, part II: case studies. IEEE Trans. Intell. Transp. Syst. **22**(9), 5635–5647 (2020)
11. Feng, S., Feng, Y., Yu, C., Zhang, Y., Liu, H.X.: Testing scenario library generation for connected and automated vehicles, part I: methodology. IEEE Trans. Intell. Transp. Syst. **22**(3), 1573–1582 (2020)
12. Fremont, D.J., Dreossi, T., Ghosh, S., Yue, X., Sangiovanni-Vincentelli, A.L., Seshia, S.A.: Scenic: a language for scenario specification and scene generation. In: Proceedings of the 40th ACM SIGPLAN Conference on Programming Language Design and Implementation, pp. 63–78 (2019)

13. Halton, J.H., Smith, G.B.: Algorithm 247: radical-inverse quasi-random point sequence. Commun. ACM **7**(12), 701–702 (1964). https://doi.org/10.1145/355588.365104
14. Hekmatnejad, M., et al.: Encoding and monitoring responsibility sensitive safety rules for automated vehicles in signal temporal logic. In: Proceedings of the 17th ACM-IEEE International Conference on Formal Methods and Models for System Design. MEMOCODE 2019 (2019). https://doi.org/10.1145/3359986.3361203
15. Maler, O., Nickovic, D.: Monitoring temporal properties of continuous signals. In: Formal Techniques, Modelling and Analysis of Timed and Fault-Tolerant Systems, Joint International Conferences on Formal Modelling and Analysis of Timed Systems, FORMATS 2004 and Formal Techniques in Real-Time and Fault-Tolerant Systems, FTRTFT 2004, Grenoble, France, 22–24 September 2004, Proceedings, pp. 152–166 (2004)
16. Menzel, T., Bagschik, G., Maurer, M.: Scenarios for development, test and validation of automated vehicles. In: 2018 IEEE Intelligent Vehicles Symposium (IV), pp. 1821–1827. IEEE (2018)
17. Neurohr, C., Westhofen, L., Butz, M., Bollmann, M.H., Eberle, U., Galbas, R.: Criticality analysis for the verification and validation of automated vehicles. IEEE Access **9**, 18016–18041 (2021)
18. Nghiem, T., Sankaranarayanan, S., Fainekos, G., Ivancic, F., Gupta, A., Pappas, G.J.: Monte-carlo techniques for falsification of temporal properties of non-linear hybrid systems. In: Proceedings of the 13th ACM International Conference on Hybrid Systems: Computation and Control, HSCC 2010, Stockholm, Sweden, 12–15 April 2010, pp. 211–220 (2010)
19. Ničković, D., Yamaguchi, T.: RTAMT: online robustness monitors from STL. In: Hung, D.V., Sokolsky, O. (eds.) ATVA 2020. LNCS, vol. 12302, pp. 564–571. Springer, Cham (2020). https://doi.org/10.1007/978-3-030-59152-6_34
20. On-Road Automated Driving (ORAD) committee: J3016 Taxonomy and Definitions for Terms Related to Driving Automation Systems for On-Road Motor Vehicles. Technical report (2021). https://www.sae.org/standards/content/j3016_202104/
21. Qin, X., Aréchiga, N., Best, A., Deshmukh, J.: Automatic testing with reusable adversarial agents. arXiv preprint arXiv:1910.13645 (2019)
22. Shalev-Shwartz, S., Shammah, S., Shashua, A.: On a formal model of safe and scalable self-driving cars, August 2017. arXiv e-prints. arXiv:1708.06374
23. Tuncali, C.E., Fainekos, G., Prokhorov, D., Ito, H., Kapinski, J.: Requirements-driven test generation for autonomous vehicles with machine learning components. IEEE Trans. Intell. Veh. **5**(2), 265–280 (2019)
24. Tuncali, C.E., Pavlic, T.P., Fainekos, G.: Utilizing s-taliro as an automatic test generation framework for autonomous vehicles. In: 19th IEEE International Conference on Intelligent Transportation Systems, ITSC 2016, Rio de Janeiro, Brazil, 1–4 November 2016, pp. 1470–1475 (2016)
25. Zhang, X., et al.: Finding critical scenarios for automated driving systems: a systematic mapping study. IEEE Trans. Softw. Eng. (2022)

Runtime Monitoring for Out-of-Distribution Detection in Object Detection Neural Networks

Vahid Hashemi[1], Jan Křetínský[2], Sabine Rieder[1,2(✉)], and Jessica Schmidt[1,3]

[1] AUDI AG, Ingolstadt, Germany
sabine.rieder@audi.de
[2] Technical University of Munich, Munich, Germany
[3] CISPA Helmholtz Center for Information Security, Saarbrücken, Germany

Abstract. Runtime monitoring provides a more realistic and applicable alternative to verification in the setting of real neural networks used in industry. It is particularly useful for detecting out-of-distribution (OOD) inputs, for which the network was not trained and can yield erroneous results. We extend a runtime-monitoring approach previously proposed for classification networks to perception systems capable of identification and localization of multiple objects. Furthermore, we analyze its adequacy experimentally on different kinds of OOD settings, documenting the overall efficacy of our approach.

Keywords: Runtime monitoring · Neural networks · Out-of-distribution detection · Object detection

1 Introduction

Neural Networks (NNs) can be trained to solve complex problems with very high accuracy. Consequently, there is a high demand to deploy them in various settings, many of which are also safety critical. In order to guarantee their safe operation, various verification techniques are being developed [3,10,16,21,32,35]. Unfortunately, despite the enormous effort, verification of NN of realistic industrial sizes is not within sight [1]. Therefore, more lightweight techniques, less depending on the size of the NN, are needed these days to provide some assurance of safety. In particular, *runtime monitoring* replaces checking correctness universally on all inputs by following the current input only and raising an alarm, whenever the safety of operation might be violated.

Due to omnipresent abundance of data, NN can typically be trained well on these given inputs. However, they may work incorrectly particularly on inputs significantly different from the training data. Whenever such an *Out-Of-Distribution (OOD)* input occurs, it is desirable to raise an alarm since there is much less trust in a correct decision of the NN on this input. OOD inputs may be, for instance, pictures containing previously unseen objects or with noise stemming from the sensors or from an adversary.

This project has received funding from the European Union's Horizon 2020 Hi-Drive project under grant agreement No. 101006664 and the project Audi Verifiable AI.

M. Chechik et al. (Eds.): FM 2023, LNCS 14000, pp. 622–634, 2023.
https://doi.org/10.1007/978-3-031-27481-7_36

In this paper, we provide a technique to efficiently detect such OOD inputs for the industrially relevant task of object detection, for which objects in an input image need to be localized and classified. We consider PolyYolo [20] as the object detection system of choice as it encompasses a very complex architecture like complex perception systems used in development of advanced driver assistance systems (ADAS) and autonomous driving functions. Our approach builds upon a recent runtime-monitoring technique [14] for efficient monitoring of classification networks. As we consider object detection networks, the setting is technically different: the inputs are of a different type and, apart from classifying objects, their bounding boxes are to be produced. Even more importantly, the number of objects in the picture to be identified can now be more than 1 (often reaching dozens). As a result, questions arise how to apply the technique in this context, so that the efficiency and adequacy of the monitor is retained or even improved.

Our contribution can be summarized as follows. We (i) propose how to extend the technique to this new setting (in Sect. 3.1), (ii) improve and automate the detection mechanism (in Sect. 3.2), and (iii) provide experiments on industrial benchmarks, concluding the efficacy of our approach (in Sect. 4). In particular, our experiments focus on OOD due to pictures (i) from other sources, (ii) affected by random noise, e.g., from sensors, and (iii) affected by adversarial noise due to an FGSM attack [13]. On the methodological side, we leverage non-conformity measures to automate threshold setting for OOD detection. Altogether, we extend the white-box monitoring approach [14] to object detection systems more suited for real-world applications.

Related Work. In this paper we focus on OOD detection when considering the neural network as a white box. OOD detection based on the activation values of neurons observed at runtime is extensively exploited in the state of the art [2,4,14,17,25,31]. In particular, Hashemi et al. [14] calculate the class-specific expectation values of all layer's neurons based on training data to abstract the In-Distribution (ID) behavior of the network. On top of that, they calculate the activations' confidence interval per class. At runtime if the network predicts a class but the activation values are not within the class-specific confidence interval, the result is declared as OOD as it does not match the expected ID behavior represented by the interval. Sastry et al. [31] also monitor the network's activations during training. With this information, they calculate class-specific Gram matrices allowing them to detect deviations between the values within the matrix and the predicted class during the execution. Henzinger et al. [17] use interval abstraction [6] where for each neuron an interval set is built which includes the neuron's activation values recorded while executing the training dataset. They utilize these constructed abstractions to identify novel inputs at runtime. In a follow-up work, Lukina et al. [25] calculated distance functions to quantitatively measure the discrepancy between novel and in-distribution samples. Other directions of work for OOD detection involve generative models to measure the distance between the original image and the generated sample or monitoring of the last layer, e.g., [24,33].

Hendrycks et al. present different benchmarks for OOD detection in multi-class, multi-label and segmentation settings and apply baseline methods [15]. They show that the MaxLogit monitor works well on all those problems. However, it is not directly applicable to the problem of object detection as in the other settings either the image or each pixel separately is assigned to classes. In the case of object detection, some parts of the image cannot be assigned meaningfully.

While all of the above techniques focus on classification or segmentation networks, we are only aware of few other approaches focusing on object detection neural networks. Du et al. [8] introduced a method for monitoring object detection systems by distilling unknown OOD objects from the training data and then training the object detector from scratch in combination with an uncertainty regularization branch. Similarly, [9] train an uncertainty branch by artificially synthesizing outliers from the feature space of the NN. Consequently, the tools are not applicable to the frozen graph of a trained model. Unfortunately, this restriction beats the purpose of using (and monitoring) a *given* trained network.

We refer the reader to [34] for a detailed overview on other monitoring approaches.

2 Preliminaries

2.1 Neural Networks

Neural Networks (NNs) are learning components which are often applied to complex tasks especially when it is hard to directly find algorithmic solutions. Examples of such tasks are classification, where the type of object in an image should be predicted, and object detection. In the latter case, images can contain several different objects at different locations. The NN identifies the different objects in the image, assigns them to classes and computes *bounding boxes*, usually of rectangular form, surrounding the object.

In general, a NN consists of several consecutive *layers* 1, ..., L containing computation units called *neurons*. The neurons receive their input as a sum from weighted connections to neurons in the previous layer and apply a usually non-linear *activation function* σ to their input. The result of this computation is called the *activation value* h of the neuron. More formally, the behavior of a neuron j in layer $l+1$ with activation function σ^{l+1} and incoming weights w_{ij} from neuron $i \in N_l$ from layer l with neurons N_l can be described as follows for an input x:

$$h_j(x) = \sigma^{l+1}(\sum_{i \in N_l} w_{ij} h_i(x))$$

The activation values for neurons at layer 1, which is called the *input layer*, are defined as the input x:

$$\vec{h}^1(x) = x$$

The last layer is the *output layer*. The layers in between are called *hidden layers*. An exemplary NN is shown in Fig. 1.

The basic network architecture can be extended with different types of layers. Examples are convolutional, batch normalization and leaky ReLU layers. A convolutional layer takes its input as a 2- or 3-dimensional matrix and moves another matrix called the filter over the input. The input values are multiplied by the corresponding value in the filter to obtain the output. The goal of a batch normalization layer is to normalize the activation values of the neurons. Therefore, the mean and standard deviation are learned during training. During inference, the batch normalization layer behaves like a layer without an activation function as it only normalizes the activation values according to the learned parameters. The leaky ReLU layer takes only one input without weights and performs the following activation function:

$$LeakyReLU(x) = \begin{cases} x & \text{for } x > 0 \\ 0.01x & \text{otherwise} \end{cases} \tag{1}$$

A more detailed introduction to NNs and different layer types can be found in [28].

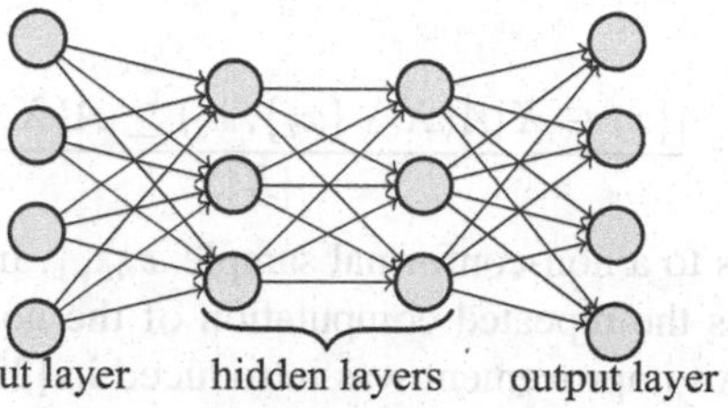

Fig. 1. Architecture of a NN

2.2 Gaussian-Based White-Box Monitoring

In [14] Hashemi at al. introduced Gaussian-based OOD detection for a classification NN. In this setting, the NN is trained to assign an image to one of the classes in $C = \{c_1, ..., c_{n_L}\}$. The underlying assumption is that neurons behave similar for objects of a particular class. Furthermore, neuron activation values are assumed to follow a Gaussian distribution. Therefore, the neuron activation values h_i are recorded for each monitored neuron $i \in M$ for a set of monitored neurons M and for each sample of the training data $X = \{x_1, .., x_m\}$ leading to a vector $\vec{r}^i$ with $r^i_j = h_i(x_j)$. The vector is then separated by class to $\vec{r}^i_{c_\star}$ for $c_\star \in C$. In the next step, the mean and standard deviation $\mu_{i,c_\star}, \sigma_{i,c_\star}$ are calculated for the neurons dependent on the classes. Due to assumption of a Gaussian distribution, 95% of the samples are expected to fall into the range $[\mu_{i,c_\star} - k\,\sigma_{i,c_\star},\, \mu_{i,c_\star} + k\,\sigma_{i,c_\star}]$ where k is a value close to 2.

During inference, a new sample x is fed into the NN, a class $c_\star$ is predicted and the neuron activation values are recorded. The monitor checks if the activation values fall within the previously computed range of values. More formally:

$$\forall i \in M : h_i(x) \in [\mu_{i,c_\star} - k\,\sigma_{i,c_\star},\, \mu_{i,c_\star} + k\sigma_{i,c_\star}] \tag{2}$$

However, the paper [14] showed that rarely the activation values of all neurons fall within the desired range. Due to the selection of bounds for the interval to contain 95% of the neuron activation values of the training data, even examples utilized to calculate the bounds may not fulfill the above condition. Therefore, the condition is weakened to only require a fixed percentage of neurons to be inside the bounds. This threshold was set manually in the paper with the goal of obtaining similar false alarm rates as Henzinger et al. [17].

2.3 Inductive Conformal Anomaly Detection

In our work we leverage Inductive Conformal Anomaly Detection (ICAD) which was introduced in [23]. ICAD extends conformal anomaly detection [22]. The idea is to predict if a new sample x_{m+1} is similar to a given training set $X = \{x_1, ..., x_m\}$. For this purpose, a nonconformity measure A is introduced. This function takes as input the training set and a new sample for which to compute the nonconformity score and returns a real-valued measure of the distance of x_{m+1} to the samples of X. Afterwards, the *p-value* is calculated based on the nonconformity measure. The p-value for sample x_{m+1} is calculated by

$$p_{m+1} = \frac{|\{x_i \in X | A(X \setminus \{x_i\}, x_i) \geq A(X, x_{m+1})\}|}{|X|}. \tag{3}$$

A low p-value hints to a non-conformal sample x_{m+1}. In general, this approach is inefficient as it requires the repeated computation of the nonconformity score for the entire training set X. An improvement was introduced in [23]. The training set is split into a *proper training set* $X_p = \{x_1, ..., x_k\}$ and a *calibration set* $X_c = \{x_{k+1}, ..., x_m\}$ with $k < m$. In the first step, the nonconformity measure A is applied to samples of the calibration set based on the proper training set. For the new test sample x_{m+1} the p-value is then computed in comparison to the calibration set:

$$p_{m+1} = \frac{|\{x_i \in X_c | A(X_p, x_i) \geq A(X_p, x_{m+1})\}|}{|X_c|} \tag{4}$$

3 Monitoring Algorithm

In this paper we propose a monitoring algorithm which extends the Gaussian based monitoring from [14] to object detection NNs and embeds it into the framework of ICAD.

3.1 Extension to Object Detection Neural Networks

The approach presented by Hashemi et al. [14] relies on the distinction of images by different classes as a separate interval for the neuron activation values is computed for each of the classes. However, images fed to an object detection network can contain several objects of different classes at different locations at the same time. When computing the intervals based on the classes contained in the images, one image could be relevant for several of those intervals. For example, an image containing a car and a pedestrian would contribute to the intervals for both classes. However, the pedestrian could only make up a small part of the input image leading to only a small fraction of neurons being influenced by the object. Consequently, neurons not related to the person are considered as relevant for the class intervals. Furthermore, the position of pedestrians throughout different images can shift and the neurons related to the pedestrian change accordingly. Consequently, the class related intervals would mostly consists of values from neurons that are not related to objects of the class. In addition, this approach increases the runtime at inference time. A previously unseen image would need to be checked against an interval for each class it contains an object of. In the worst case this could result in the total number of classes. As most of the values used for constructing the intervals are similar since they are not related to the particular object, the computations are also highly redundant.

To resolve both issues we discard the class information. This is supported by the observation that images are generally recorded in similar areas and therefore the general setting of a street is contained in all of them. The only changes are due to the objects and are locally bounded to their locations. The approach reduces the runtime to only one check per image and discards redundant computations. In total, we monitor the following condition discarding the class information:

$$\forall i \in M : h_i(x) \in [\mu_i - k\,\sigma_i,\ \mu_i + k\,\sigma_i] \tag{5}$$

3.2 Embedding into the Framework of Inductive Conformal Anomaly Detection

In the next step we improve the manual threshold setting from [14] for the number of neurons that need to fall inside the expected interval. We propose to use ICAD for this purpose. Therefore, we divide the training set into the proper training set X_p and the calibration set X_c and define the nonconformity measure A to be the number of neurons falling *outside* the range $[\mu_{i,p} - k\,\sigma_{i,p},\ \mu_{i,l,p} + k\,\sigma_{i,p}]$ computed based on the proper training set X_p. We capture the number of neurons outside the interval rather than the ones inside as the nonconformity measure is expected to grow for OOD data. More formally with M as the set of monitored neurons, usually all neurons of a particular layer and $\mu_{i,p}$, $\sigma_{i,p}$ the bounds computed as described in the last section based on the set X_p as training set:

$$A(X_p, x) = \frac{|\{i \in M | h_i(x) \notin [\mu_{i,p} - k\,\sigma_{i,p},\ \mu_{i,p} + k\,\sigma_{i,p}]\}|}{|M|} \tag{6}$$

Afterwards, the p-value is calculated as described in Eq. 4. The threshold for the p-values is then set manually based on the requirements of the use case as there is a trade-off between the false alarm rate and the detection rate. For example, a high threshold for the p-vale leads to a low number of wrongly classified OOD examples, but the number of ID data classified as OOD will also rise as even some of the images from the calibration set are classified as OOD. Overall, the threshold setting is now closely related to the calibration set instead of the abstract metric of number of neurons inside the bounds.

4 Experiments

Experiments were performed on PolyYolo [20] which is based on the famous architecture called YOLO (You Only Look Once) [29]. YOLO was introduced in 2016 from Redmon et al. and afterwards continuously extended to improve the performance. For our work we decided to focus on PolyYolo [20] as it improves YOLOv3 [30] while also reducing the size of the network. The architecture can be seen in Fig. 2. PolyYolo consists of three main building blocks. A *convolutional set* contains a convolutional layer and a batch normalization layer followed by leaky ReLU layer. A *Squeeze-and-Excitation (SE) block* [19] contains a Global Average Pooling layer to reduce the size of each channel to 1 followed by a reshape layer, a dense layer, a leaky ReLU layer and a dense layer. The output of this sequence is meant to represent the importance of each channel compared to the others. Therefore, the last layer of the block multiplies the input with the result of the sequence to scale the input. The *residual block with SE* then contains two consecutive convolutional sets followed by a SE block. The result is added to the input. The backbone of PolyYolo consists of several iterations of convolutional sets followed by residual blocks with SE as shown in Fig. 2. In between, there are three skip-connections to the neck. The neck uses upsampling to scale all results of the skip-connections to the same size and adds them up with intermediate convolutional sets. After all connections are added to one feature map, four convolutional sets are applied. The final layer is a convolutional layer. We monitored layers from the last convolutional set of the network as those are the last hidden layers and Hashemi et al. [14] discovered that a monitor based on the last layers of a NN lead to more accurate results. Namely we focus on the last batch normalization and leaky ReLU layer. As ID data we used Cityscapes [5] which is the data set PolyYolo was trained on.

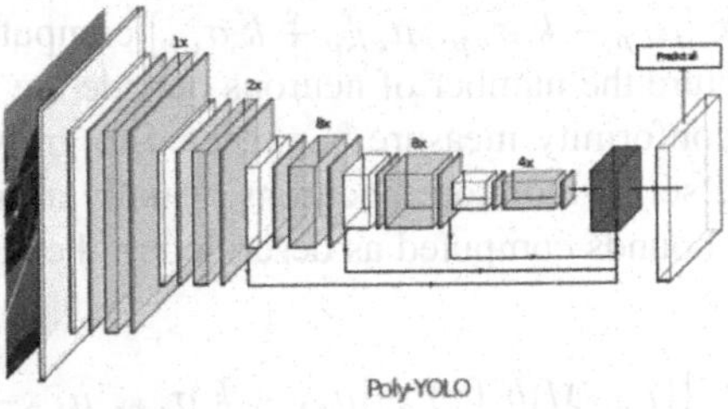

Fig. 2. The image is taken from [20] and shows the architecture of PolyYolo. White blocks represent convolutional sets, light pink indicates residual blocks with SE and dark pink shows the upsampling. (Color figure online)

We computed intervals for the neuron activation values based on 500 training images of the Cityscapes data set and the calibration set consists of 100 test images of Cityscapes. In a first step, we investigated the size of the calibration set. Figure 3 shows the importance of including images with different features. The x-axis shows the interval of p-values considered for the bar while the y-axis shows the number of images resulting in a p-value within this interval. For a calibration set of size 20, many samples obtain a p-value in the interval $(15, 20]$. For a large calibration set, the peaks in the graph are flattened. However, it is also noticeable that some elements of X_c are of more importance to the test data than others resulting in peaks as they separate the test data. Small bars in the graph are the result of elements of X_c that do not contribute a value for the nonconformity measure with huge difference to their neighbors. Therefore, samples from the test data that have a higher nonconformity score than these images also have a larger nonconformity score than other samples of X_c. A more advanced selection strategy for the calibration set could reduce this effect. To this end, we therefore fix the size of the calibration set to 100 images.

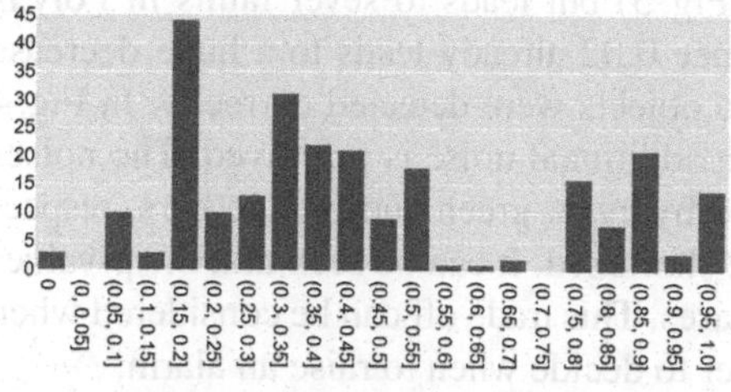

(a) Last batch normalization layer with $|X_c| = 20$

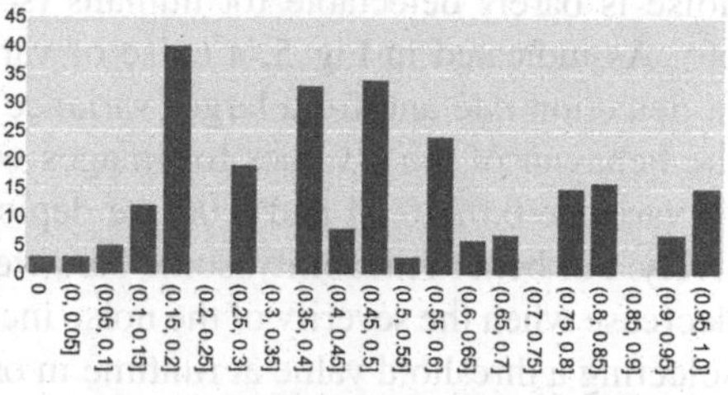

(b) Last leaky ReLU layer with $|X_c| = 20$

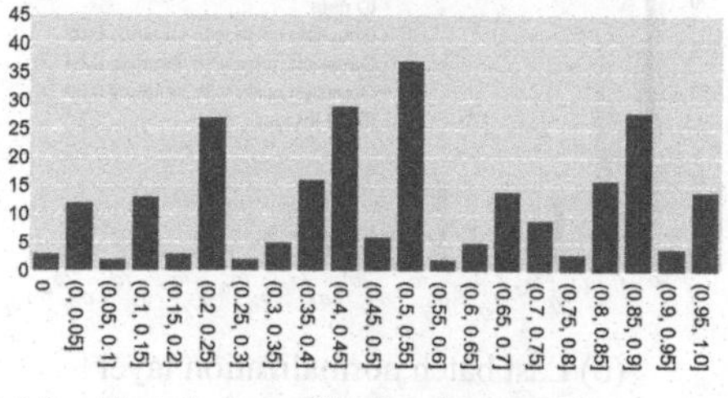

(c) Last batch normalization layer with $|X_c| = 60$

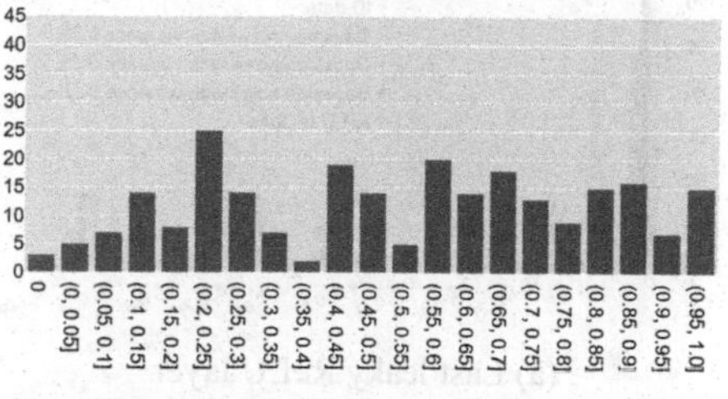

(d) Last leaky ReLU layer with $|X_c| = 60$

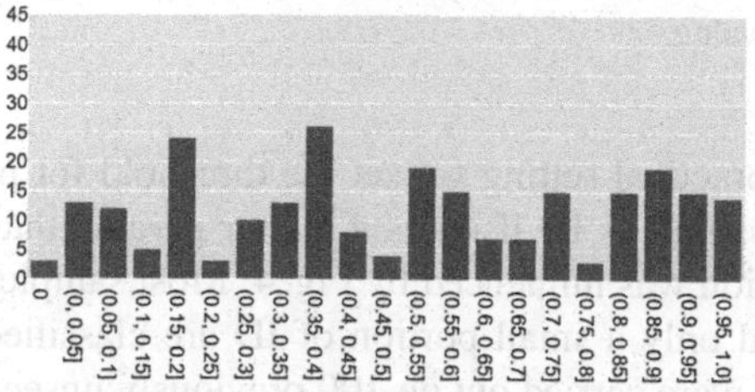

(e) Last batch normalization layer with $|X_c| = 100$

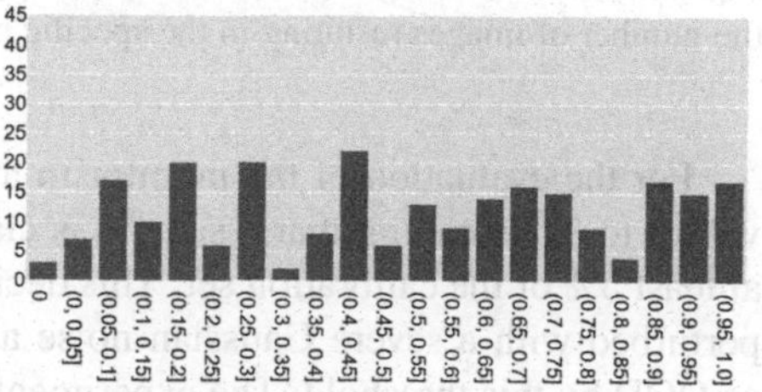

(f) Last leaky ReLU layer with $|X_c| = 100$

Fig. 3. The x-axis shows the range of p-value and the y-axis the number of images resulting in a p-value contained in the interval. The rows correspond to different sizes of calibration sets while the columns contain the monitored layers.

Figure 4 then shows the behavior of the p-values on selected OOD data in comparison to ID data. The x-axis represents again the intervals of the p-values while the y-axis shows the number of images with p-values ranging in the specified interval. The blue bars represent 250 ID images obtained from the validation set of Cityscapes. The respective p-values are visualized with blue color. Similarly to the setting of Hashemi et al. [14] we obtained OOD data by using a different data set, namely KITTI [11], which also contains images captured by a vehicle driving in a German city. However, all randomly selected 100 images from the KITTI data set resulted in a p-value of 0 which is indicated with the red bar. Therefore, we generated OOD examples from the 250 Cityscapes images we used as test data by adding Gaussian noise, as noise can be used to fool a neural network [7,18,26]. Our implementation is based on [27]. We considered additional Gaussian noise with mean 0 and variance 0.02, 0.04 or 0.06. The noise is barely detectable for humans (see Fig. 5) but leads to sever faults in PolyYolo. As indicated in Fig. 5, a noise of variance 0.02 already leads to a huge decrease in detection rate and for a larger variance no objects were detected correctly. In Fig. 4 the behavior of the p-values for images with additional noise is portrayed. The noises of variance 0.02, 0.04 and 0.06 are depicted by cyan, green and orange bars, respectively. For better readability, some bars were shortened. It can be seen that the p-values decrease when the severity of the noise increases. This trade off can be considered when selecting a threshold value at runtime in order to decide when to raise an alarm.

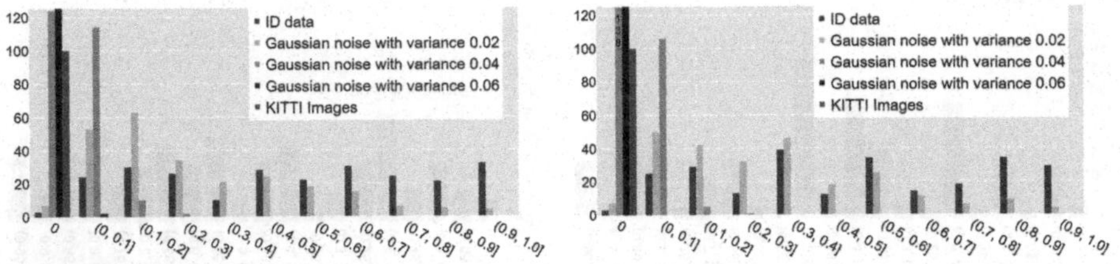

(a) Last leaky ReLU layer (b) Last batch normalization layer

Fig. 4. Number of images with the respective p-value. The x-axis shows the p-value, the y-axis the number of images resulting in the specific p-value.

For the evaluation of the monitor in a practical setting we set the threshold for p-values to 5% meaning that a sample is classified as ID if it has a higher p-value than at least 5% of the calibration set. This decision was influenced by Fig. 4. Most samples perturbed with a severe Gaussian noise and only a small portion of ID are classified as OOD by this threshold. The experiments were carried out on 100 previously unseen images of the Cityscapes data set as well as 100 images of KITTI and A2D2 [12]. Perturbations were applied to the Cityscapes images. In addition to Gaussian noise we used impulse noise, also called salt-and-pepper noise, and the Fast Gradient Sign Method (FGSM) attack [13]. The impulse noise manifests as white and black pixels in the image and the strength is influenced by the random parameter. Our implementation is again based on [27]. The FGSM attack corrupts the input pixels based on the gradient of the output. The gradient is used to calculate a mask of changes which is then added to the input image. The mask is usually multiplied with a small factor to make the attack less obvious to humans. Examples of the perturbations can be seen in Fig. 5.

Results of the experiment are shown in Table 1. The number of ID data classified as OOD data lies within the range of expected values due to the setting of the threshold to 5%. Both layers detect Gaussian noise with variance of 0.04 and 0.06 while a variance of 0.02 can fool the approach. However, this noise is not as critical as large objects are still detected from the network (see Fig. 5 for an example). For the attacked images, the leaky ReLU layer was more precise. This is presumably due to the fact that in the

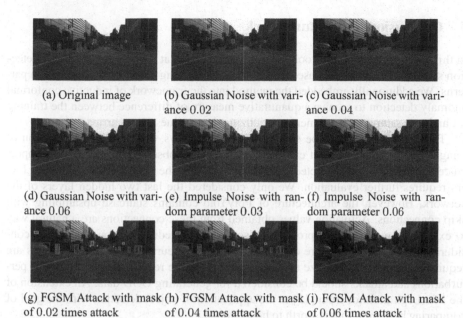

(a) Original image

(b) Gaussian Noise with variance 0.02

(c) Gaussian Noise with variance 0.04

(d) Gaussian Noise with variance 0.06

(e) Impulse Noise with random parameter 0.03

(f) Impulse Noise with random parameter 0.06

(g) FGSM Attack with mask of 0.02 times attack

(h) FGSM Attack with mask of 0.04 times attack

(i) FGSM Attack with mask of 0.06 times attack

Fig. 5. Image from the Cityscapes data set with additional perturbations and the predictions obtained from PolyYolo on the perturbed image

Table 1. The table shows the number of images classified as ID and OOD dependent on the perturbation applied and the data set used. Noise and FGSM were applied to the ID data.

Data	Leaky ReLU layer		Batch normalization layer	
	Classified as ID	Classified as OOD	Classified as ID	Classified as OOD
ID data	97	3	94	6
Gaussian noise with variance 0.02	93	7	91	9
Gaussian noise with variance 0.04	9	91	8	92
Gaussian noise with variance 0.06	0	100	0	100
Impulse noise with random parameter 0.03	0	100	0	100
Impulse noise with random parameter 0.06	0	100	0	100
FGSM with mask multiplied by 0.02	35	65	39	61
FGSM with mask multiplied by 0.04	8	92	11	89
FGSM with mask multiplied by 0.06	0	100	0	100
KITTI	0	100	0	100
A2D2	0	100	0	100

FGSM images pixels were purposely changed to make a large impact on the output of the network. The leaky ReLU layer is a successor of the batch normalization layer and the last layer before the output layer. Therefore, the changes should reflect more. Furthermore, it is noticeable that all images taken from different data sets were classified correctly.

5 Conclusion and Future Work

In this work we developed a tool to detect OOD images at runtime for 2D object detection systems. The idea was based on Gaussian monitoring of the neuron activation patterns. We additionally embedded the method into the framework of inductive conformal anomaly detection to receive a quantitative measure of difference between the training set and new samples. Experiments visualizing the p-values were carried out.

The proposed idea can be extended in several ways. First of all, the selection of images for the calibration set can be improved as we observed a difference in importance for the randomly selected images. In addition, the selection of monitored layers requires further evaluation. We only considered the last two hidden layers of the network. However, the architecture of PolyYolo contains staircase upsampling with skip connections. Activation values obtained from these connections are a natural way to extend the monitoring approach to also take intermediate neuron values into consideration. Furthermore, more experiments on other neural network architectures are required in order to generalize the results. For the same reason, different types of perturbations and attacks should be considered for generating OOD data. An extension of the MaxLogit monitor from [15] to the application of object detection with the goal of comparing both monitors is worth to be exploited.

References

1. Bak, S., Liu, C., Johnson, T.T.: The second international verification of neural networks competition (VNN-COMP 2021): summary and results. CoRR abs/2109.00498 (2021). https://arxiv.org/abs/2109.00498
2. Cheng, C.H.: Provably-robust runtime monitoring of neuron activation patterns. In: 2021 Design, Automation & Test in Europe Conference & Exhibition (DATE), pp. 1310–1313. IEEE (2021)
3. Cheng, C., Huang, C., Brunner, T., Hashemi, V.: Towards safety verification of direct perception neural networks. In: 2020 Design, Automation & Test in Europe Conference & Exhibition, DATE 2020, Grenoble, France, 9–13 March 2020, pp. 1640–1643. IEEE (2020)
4. Cheng, C.H., Nührenberg, G., Yasuoka, H.: Runtime monitoring neuron activation patterns. In: 2019 Design, Automation & Test in Europe Conference & Exhibition (DATE), pp. 300–303. IEEE (2019)
5. Cordts, M., et al.: The cityscapes dataset for semantic urban scene understanding. In: 2016 IEEE Conference on Computer Vision and Pattern Recognition, CVPR 2016, Las Vegas, NV, USA, 27–30 June 2016, pp. 3213–3223. IEEE Computer Society (2016). https://doi.org/10.1109/CVPR.2016.350
6. Cousot, P., Cousot, R.: Static determination of dynamic properties of programs. In: Proceedings of the 2nd International Symposium on Programming, Paris, France, pp. 106–130. Dunod (1976)
7. Dodge, S., Karam, L.: A study and comparison of human and deep learning recognition performance under visual distortions. In: 2017 26th International Conference on Computer Communication and Networks (ICCCN), pp. 1–7. IEEE (2017)
8. Du, X., Wang, X., Gozum, G., Li, Y.: Unknown-aware object detection: learning what you don't know from videos in the wild. In: Proceedings of the IEEE/CVF Conference on Computer Vision and Pattern Recognition, pp. 13678–13688 (2022)

9. Du, X., Wang, Z., Cai, M., Li, Y.: Vos: learning what you don't know by virtual outlier synthesis. In: International Conference on Learning Representations (2021)
10. Gehr, T., Mirman, M., Drachsler-Cohen, D., Tsankov, P., Chaudhuri, S., Vechev, M.: AI2: safety and robustness certification of neural networks with abstract interpretation. In: 2018 IEEE Symposium on Security and Privacy, SP 2018, Proceedings, San Francisco, California, USA, 21–23 May 2018, pp. 3–18. IEEE Computer Society (2018). https://doi.org/10.1109/SP.2018.00058
11. Geiger, A., Lenz, P., Urtasun, R.: Are we ready for autonomous driving? The kitti vision benchmark suite. In: Conference on Computer Vision and Pattern Recognition (CVPR) (2012)
12. Geyer, J., et al.: A2D2: Audi autonomous driving dataset (2020). https://www.a2d2.audi
13. Goodfellow, I.J., Shlens, J., Szegedy, C.: Explaining and harnessing adversarial examples. arXiv preprint arXiv:1412.6572 (2014)
14. Hashemi, V., Křetínský, J., Mohr, S., Seferis, E.: Gaussian-based runtime detection of out-of-distribution inputs for neural networks. In: Feng, L., Fisman, D. (eds.) RV 2021. LNCS, vol. 12974, pp. 254–264. Springer, Cham (2021). https://doi.org/10.1007/978-3-030-88494-9_14
15. Hendrycks, D., et al.: Scaling out-of-distribution detection for real-world settings. arXiv preprint arXiv:1911.11132 (2019). https://doi.org/10.48550/ARXIV.1911.11132, https://arxiv.org/abs/1911.11132
16. Henriksen, P., Lomuscio, A.R.: Efficient neural network verification via adaptive refinement and adversarial search. In: Giacomo, G.D., et al. (eds.) ECAI 2020–24th European Conference on Artificial Intelligence, 29 August-8 September 2020, Santiago de Compostela, Spain, August 29 - September 8, 2020 -Including 10th Conference on Prestigious Applications of Artificial Intelligence (PAIS 2020). Frontiers in Artificial Intelligence and Applications, vol. 325, pp. 2513–2520. IOS Press (2020). https://doi.org/10.3233/FAIA200385
17. Henzinger, T.A., Lukina, A., Schilling, C.: Outside the box: abstraction-based monitoring of neural networks. In: ECAI 2020–24th European Conference on Artificial Intelligence, 29 August-8 September 2020, Santiago de Compostela, Spain, August 29 - September 8, 2020 - Including 10th Conference on Prestigious Applications of Artificial Intelligence (PAIS 2020). Frontiers in Artificial Intelligence and Applications, vol. 325, pp. 2433–2440. IOS Press (2020). https://doi.org/10.3233/FAIA200375
18. Hosseini, H., Xiao, B., Poovendran, R.: Google's cloud vision API is not robust to noise. In: 2017 16th IEEE International Conference on Machine Learning and Applications (ICMLA), pp. 101–105. IEEE (2017)
19. Hu, J., Shen, L., Sun, G.: Squeeze-and-excitation networks. In: Proceedings of the IEEE Conference on Computer Vision and Pattern Recognition, pp. 7132–7141 (2018)
20. Hurtik, P., Molek, V., Hula, J., Vajgl, M., Vlasanek, P., Nejezchleba, T.: Poly-yolo: higher speed, more precise detection and instance segmentation for yolov3. arXiv preprint arXiv:2005.13243 (2020)
21. Katz, G., et al.: The marabou framework for verification and analysis of deep neural networks. In: Dillig, I., Tasiran, S. (eds.) CAV 2019. LNCS, vol. 11561, pp. 443–452. Springer, Cham (2019). https://doi.org/10.1007/978-3-030-25540-4_26
22. Laxhammar, R., Falkman, G.: Online learning and sequential anomaly detection in trajectories. IEEE Trans. Pattern Anal. Mach. Intell. **36**(6), 1158–1173 (2014). https://doi.org/10.1109/TPAMI.2013.172
23. Laxhammar, R., Falkman, G.: Inductive conformal anomaly detection for sequential detection of anomalous sub-trajectories. Ann. Math. Artif. Intell. **74**(1), 67–94 (2015). https://doi.org/10.1007/s10472-013-9381-7

24. Liang, S., Li, Y., Srikant, R.: Enhancing the reliability of out-of-distribution image detection in neural networks. In: 6th International Conference on Learning Representations, ICLR 2018, Vancouver, BC, Canada, April 30 - May 3, 2018, Conference Track Proceedings. OpenReview.net (2018). https://openreview.net/forum?id=H1VGkIxRZ
25. Lukina, A., Schilling, C., Henzinger, T.A.: Into the unknown: active monitoring of neural networks. In: Feng, L., Fisman, D. (eds.) RV 2021. LNCS, vol. 12974, pp. 42–61. Springer, Cham (2021). https://doi.org/10.1007/978-3-030-88494-9_3
26. Metzen, J.H., Kumar, M.C., Brox, T., Fischer, V.: Universal adversarial perturbations against semantic image segmentation. In: IEEE International Conference on Computer Vision, ICCV 2017, Venice, Italy, 22–29 October 2017, pp. 2774–2783. IEEE Computer Society (2017). https://doi.org/10.1109/ICCV.2017.300
27. Michaelis, C., et al.: Benchmarking robustness in object detection: autonomous driving when winter is coming. arXiv preprint arXiv:1907.07484 (2019)
28. Nielsen, M.A.: Neural Networks and Deep Learning, vol. 25. Determination Press San Francisco, CA, USA (2015)
29. Redmon, J., Divvala, S.K., Girshick, R., Farhadi, A.: You only look once: unified, real-time object detection. In: 2016 IEEE Conference on Computer Vision and Pattern Recognition, CVPR 2016, Las Vegas, NV, USA, 27–30 June 2016, pp. 779–788. IEEE Computer Society (2016). https://doi.org/10.1109/CVPR.2016.91
30. Redmon, J., Farhadi, A.: Yolov3: an incremental improvement. CoRR abs/1804.02767 (2018). http://arxiv.org/abs/1804.02767
31. Sastry, C.S., Oore, S.: Detecting out-of-distribution examples with gram matrices. In: Proceedings of the 37th International Conference on Machine Learning, ICML 2020, 13–18 July 2020, Virtual Event. Proceedings of Machine Learning Research, vol. 119, pp. 8491–8501. PMLR (2020). http://proceedings.mlr.press/v119/sastry20a.html
32. Singh, G., Gehr, T., Püschel, M., Vechev, M.T.: An abstract domain for certifying neural networks. Proc. ACM Program. Lang. **3**(POPL), 1–30 (2019). https://doi.org/10.1145/3290354
33. Wang, H., Liu, W., Bocchieri, A., Li, Y.: Can multi-label classification networks know what they don't know? Advances in Neural Information Processing Systems, vol. 34, pp. 29074–29087 (2021)
34. Yang, J., Zhou, K., Li, Y., Liu, Z.: Generalized out-of-distribution detection: a survey. CoRR abs/2110.11334 (2021). https://arxiv.org/abs/2110.11334
35. Zhang, H., Weng, T., Chen, P., Hsieh, C., Daniel, L.: Efficient neural network robustness certification with general activation functions. CoRR abs/1811.00866 (2018). http://arxiv.org/abs/1811.00866

Backdoor Mitigation in Deep Neural Networks via Strategic Retraining

Akshay Dhonthi[1,2(✉)], Ernst Moritz Hahn[2], and Vahid Hashemi[1]

[1] AUDI AG, Auto-Union-Straße 1, 85057 Ingolstadt, Germany
akshay.dhonthirameshbabu@audi.de
[2] Formal Methods and Tools, University of Twente, Enschede, The Netherlands

Abstract. Deep Neural Networks (DNN) are becoming increasingly more important in assisted and automated driving. Using such entities which are obtained using machine learning is inevitable: tasks such as recognizing traffic signs cannot be developed reasonably using traditional software development methods. DNN however do have the problem that they are mostly black boxes and therefore hard to understand and debug. One particular problem is that they are prone to hidden *backdoors*. This means that the DNN misclassifies its input, because it considers properties that should not be decisive for the output. Backdoors may either be introduced by malicious attackers or by inappropriate training. In any case, detecting and removing them is important in the automotive area, as they might lead to safety violations with potentially severe consequences. In this paper, we introduce a novel method to remove backdoors. Our method works for both intentional as well as unintentional backdoors. We also do not require prior knowledge about the shape or distribution of backdoors. Experimental evidence shows that our method performs well on several medium-sized examples.

Keywords: Security testing · Neural networks · Backdoor mitigation · Adversarial attacks

1 Introduction

Advanced Driver Assistive System (ADAS) or Autonomous Driving (AD) functions [8] generally use Deep Neural Networks (DNN) in their architecture to perform complex tasks such as object detection and localization. Essential applications are traffic sign classification or detection [2,19], lane detection [10], vehicle or pedestrian detection [1], driver monitoring and driver-vehicle interaction [5]. All these functions are safety-critical, because incorrect outputs may create dangerous situations, accidents and even loss of life. Therefore, testing them for security, reliability, and robustness has the utmost priority before deploying the functions on autonomous vehicles into the real world.

DNN unfortunately can easily be manipulated due to their dependency on the training data. For example, consider a traffic sign classification model trained on a large

This research was funded in part by the EU under project 864075 CAESAR, the project Audi Verifiable AI, and the BMWi funded KARLI project (grant 19A21031C).

M. Chechik et al. (Eds.): FM 2023, LNCS 14000, pp. 635–647, 2023.
https://doi.org/10.1007/978-3-031-27481-7_37

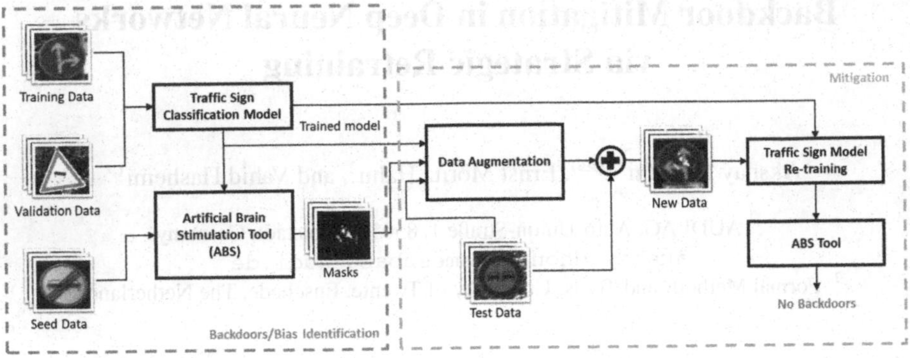

Fig. 1. Framework of the backdoor or bias mitigation approach

dataset such as GTSRB [17]. An attacker having access to the data during training may intentionally poison it by modifying a small percentage of the data. This can be done by adding *trojan patterns* to the input belonging to different classes. The *trojan patterns* may be in the form of objects, image transformations, invisible watermarks and many more. The model trained with such poisoned data may have learned false features called *backdoors* which have no direct relation to the classification output. Such models still perform well on benign inputs; however, they may fail in the presence of trojan patterns (which only the attackers know).

Research has shown that backdoors may exist even on models trained with benign data [13]. This is because certain features may have strong correlation to an output class making the model biased towards such features. For example, traffic signs such as *pedestrian crossing* may usually have urban background whereas *wild animal crossing* may usually have country/rural backgrounds. In such cases, the DNN may have learned the background instead of the traffic sign itself leading to bias and in turn misclassification. Therefore, it is vital to defend against both intentional backdoors (present due to an attacker's poisoning of training data) and unintentional backdoors (present due to a strong correlation to certain features for a few classes) to ensure the proper functionality of machine learning models.

Coverage testing is one of the typical software testing approaches where the goal is to achieve complete code coverage by checking the correctness for the entire input space. Using such techniques to test DNN is not straightforward, due to the massive number of parameters and the black-box nature of DNN. However, there has been a vast amount of research in adapting those coverage techniques to work with DNN. One such approach is *NN-dependability* [3], which proposes several metrics to measure quality of the DNN in terms of robustness, interpretability, completeness, and correctness. However, the metrics cannot test for backdoors. Other software engineering techniques such as *Modified Condition/Decision MC/DC* [18] and *scenario based testing* [4] also do not focus on security aspects such as backdoor testing. Our approach is different from these as we target specifically at overcoming backdoors and biases in the DNN.

Several attacking techniques developed in recent years [6, 14–16] are excellent at fooling even the state-of-the-art defense methods such as *STRIP* [9], *Fine-pruning* [12], and *Neural Cleanse* [20]. It is essential to defend from such attacks, especially for safety-critical applications. A defense mechanism includes two phases. The first phase is to detect the backdoors and the second is to mitigate them. Detection techniques such as [12,20] can identify common kinds of poisoning such as masking with patches, noise and watermarks. However, they are *white-box*, meaning that they need information about the type or position of trojan patterns. The detection technique needs to be able to treat the data as a black box, because we usually do not have any information on how the data is poisoned [7,13].

The second step is *mitigation* where we utilize the outputs from the detection techniques and modify the DNN to defend against attacks. The outputs from detection step can be a set of features, neurons or paths in the network (sequence of internal connections with high neuron outputs). Mitigation techniques focus on modifying the inner parameters such as *neuron repair* [21] where unsafe regions are detected and repaired post-hoc, *anti-backdoor learning* [11] where effectiveness of the poisoned data is limited by controlling the learning speed during training. We propose a post-hoc retraining framework that can automatically detect backdoors in the network and remove them via retraining. Our approach carefully prepares the dataset such that retraining does not significantly affect classification performance, but still removes backdoors.

Figure 1 depicts our approach in a nutshell. We utilize a black-box backdoor identification technique called Artificial Brain Stimulation (ABS) by Liu *et al.* [13]. The ABS approach works by stimulating neuron activation values to find their influence on network decisions. A neuron is highly influential or *poisoned* if a change in the activation value of a neuron shifts the DNN classification output to a different class. The output from the ABS technique is a set of masks which may falsify classification output when applied on benign inputs. We utilize these masks to remove backdoors from the DNN model. The overview of our mitigation approach is on the right side of Fig. 1. Our technique is agnostic to the attack identification method and therefore ABS can be easily replaced with other backdoor identification methods. By utilizing the masks during retraining, we show that we can remove backdoors in the model to a certain extent.

Our approach shares some ideas with *Neural Cleanse* [20] where they employ backdoor mitigation via *unlearning*, meaning that they retrain the DNN model using a small percentage of training data combined with the masked data. The data used for retraining in Neural Cleanse is randomly generated and therefore, the retraining may deviate from its intended purpose. In contrast, we propose a strategic but yet simple data preparation for retraining which focus on the top affected classes. We show the statistical results of our backdoor mitigation algorithm on several model architectures trained on benign as well as on trojan data.

2 Preliminaries

This section briefly introduces DNN and the types of networks considered in the paper. Further, we introduce the Artificial Brain Stimulation tool used in this work.

2.1 Deep Neural Networks

This work focuses on the classification problem and thus uses a simple architecture with convolutional layers. We represent a *Deep Neural Network* as a tuple, $\mathcal{N} = (\mathbb{S}, \mathbb{T}, \phi)$, where $\mathbb{S} = \{\mathbb{S}_k | k \in \{1, \ldots, K\}\}$ is a set of layers with K being the total number of layers, $\mathbb{T} \subseteq \mathbb{S} \times \mathbb{S}$ is a set of connections between the layers and $\phi = \{\phi_k | k \in \{2, \ldots, K\}\}$ is a set of functions, one for each non-input layer. A typical DNN has an input layer $\mathbb{S}_1$, an output layer $\mathbb{S}_K$ and several *hidden layers* between the input and the output. Each layer k consists of S_k number of neurons/nodes. Let us define the l-th neuron of layer k as $n_{k,l} \in \mathbb{S}_k$. Each neuron $n_{k,l}$ for $2 \leq k \leq K-1$ and $1 \leq l \leq S_K$ is associated with a value before activation $u_{k,l}$ and a value after activation $v_{k,l}$. The activation is a function that modifies the input based on a formula. We use the Rectified Linear Unit (ReLU) activation function in this work.

In a classification model, the output dimension or number of neurons in the output layer S_K is equal to the number of labels $\mathcal{L} = \{1, \ldots, S_K\}$, which means the classification output defined as $label = \text{argmax}_{1 \leq l \leq S_K} u_{K,l}$ is the index of the neuron in the output layer with the largest value. We define input data as $X = \{x_1, \ldots, x_T\}$ where each x_i is an image that is passed to the DNN. The classification output for an input x is denoted as $\mathcal{N}[x]$. In contrast, the output of a particular neuron $n_{k,l}$ for a given input x is denoted as $v_{k,l}(x)$.

2.2 Artificial Brain Stimulation Analysis

Artificial Brain Stimulation Analysis aims to identify backdoors in a trojan or benign model. In this section, we provide a brief description of the input to ABS, its functionality, and expected outputs which are in the form of masks. The input to the model is a trained DNN $\mathcal{N}$. We also require seed data $X_{seed} = \{x_1, \ldots, x_T\}$ where $T \geq S_K$ and $\{\forall t \in \mathcal{L}\ \exists x \in X_{seed}\ s.t\ \mathcal{N}[x] = t\}$ meaning a set of benign images with at least one associated to each class. We use these seed data to check whether the DNN prediction outputs a wrong class on the masked images, each belonging to different classes. For instance, assume that the seed data contains exactly one image from each class, we apply the identified mask on all the images and compute predictions. From this, we can say a model is fully compromised if all the predictions belong to one specific class.

The ABS analysis has three steps. The first step is to perform *stimulation analysis* where we replace the activation value $v_{k,l}$ of the neuron under analysis $n_{k,l}$ with the stimulation value $z_{k,l}$. We do such analysis for each neuron $n_{k,l} \in \mathbb{S}_k$ in all hidden layer $2 \leq k \leq K-1$. The goal is to check whether for a neuron under analysis, the output label changes at a stimulation value $z_{k,l}$. As a result, we obtain the *neuron stimulation function* (NSF) which provides the output class $i \in \mathcal{L}$ for different stimulation values $z_{k,l}$. Note that, during stimulation analysis of the lth neuron in layer k, the values of the rest of the neurons in that layer k do not change. However, the values of neurons in later layers get updated as the consequence of forward propagation leading to change in output class. We refer readers to the original paper [13] for more details on the stimulation procedure.

The next step is to find a set of *compromised neurons* using the NSFs. A neuron $n_{k,l}$ is said to be *compromised* if, for the stimulation value falling in a particular range, the outputs of all NSFs generated from the seed data respectively are same. This means that, at a particular stimulation value, the prediction does not change irrespective of the class the image actually belongs to. Let us define C as the total number of such candidates.

Algorithm 1. Backdoor mitigation via retraining

Input: $\mathcal{N}$: Trained DNN,
M_{masks}: trojan masks from ABS analysis on $\mathcal{N}$,
X_{seed}: seed data for ABS analysis on retrained model,
$X_{test} = \{x_1, \cdots, x_T\}$: benign test data,
$y_{test} = \{y_1, \cdots, y_T\}$: true labels for data augmentation,
X_{valid}: benign validation data to track the drop in accuracy,
top_p: parameter to control the number of classes considered for new data generation,
δ: accuracy drop threshold.
Output: $\hat{\mathcal{N}}$: Retrained DNN without backdoors or bias.
Initialize $\hat{\mathcal{N}}$ with learned weights from the network $\mathcal{N}$.
while (accuracy of $\hat{\mathcal{N}}$ - accuracy of $\mathcal{N}$ on X_{valid}) $\leq \delta$ **do**
  Initialize X_{new} and y_{new} as re-training data and true labels respectively.
  for Mask in M_{masks} **do**
    Define X'_{test} as images after applying masks on test data.
    Let y'_{test} be the according predictions.
    for Img, label in X_{test}, y_{test} **do**
      Apply *mask* on *img*.
      Predict $\hat{\mathcal{N}}$[masked image].
      Add the masked image and prediction to X'_{test} and y'_{test}.
    end for
    Compute False Positives using y'_{test} and y_{test}.
    Select top_p number of classes with the highest false positives.
    Update X_{new} with all false positive images belonging to top_p classes.
    Update y_{new} with respective true labels.
  end for
  X_{new}.extend(X_{test})
  y_{new}.extend(y_{test})
  Shuffle and Split X_{new} and y_{new} as training and validation dataset.
  Retrain $\hat{\mathcal{N}}$ with new training and validation dataset.
  Analyze $\hat{\mathcal{N}}$ using ABS tool to identify backdoors $\hat{X}_{masks}$.
  if $\hat{X}_{masks} = \emptyset$ **then**
    return DNN $\hat{\mathcal{N}}$.
  end if
end while

The last step is to obtain masks for each compromised neuron via *reverse engineering*. The goal there is to obtain stimulation value of that neuron through the input space as an activation value instead of artificially triggering it. Therefore, we obtain masks denoted as $M = \{m_1, \cdots, m_C\}$ for each compromised neuron candidate. Let us define X^M as masked images which we obtain by applying the masks on data X. Further, we define the *Attack Success Rate* (ASR) as the percentage of misclassification on the masked images X^M. Using these, we set a threshold parameter denoted as *REASR bound* which is based upon ASR on masked images X^M_{seed} and therefore ranges between 0 to 1. The REASR bound will filter the masks that affect very few classes. Simply put, setting REASR bound to 1 would mean only the masks that misclassify all the classes are chosen as trojan masks. After filtering, we obtain the final trojan masks denoted as $M_{masks} = \{m_1, \cdots, m_M\}$.

3 Methodology

In this work, our goal is to eradicate backdoors in the DNN model by retraining. Algorithm 1 illustrates our approach. We require a trained DNN model $\mathcal{N}$, masks M_{masks} from the ABS analysis and benign test data X_{test}, y_{test}. Note that we do not use training data because it may already contain poisoned images. The expected output from this algorithm is a benign DNN model $\hat{\mathcal{N}}$ with no backdoors.

This method has three main steps as also depicted in the green box highlighted in Fig. 1. The first step is the data augmentation in lines 4–16. For each mask, we apply the mask on all the test data and obtain their predictions on the DNN $\hat{\mathcal{N}}$. Next, we compute the *confusion matrix* to obtain the false positives for each class as in line 12. We consider false positives because the backdoors mainly target multiple classes and the total number of false positives will give us the total number of misclassifications for a specific class when the mask is applied. Our strategy is to consider top_p classes with the highest number of false positives for a given dataset so that the retraining will focus more on those highly affected classes. We add the images from this top_p classes that were wrongly classified to our new dataset X_{new} as in line 12–15. Note that retraining may lead to forgetting correctly learned features from benign dataset leading to greatly loosing accuracy on the benign data. To overcome this, we combine X_{new} with benign X_{test} data so that retaining would not overfit towards the new data X_{new}.

In the next two steps, we utilize X_{new} to retrain DNN $\hat{\mathcal{N}}$ in line 20 and then analyze the model for backdoors using ABS tool in line 21. If backdoors are found, we repeat the steps in lines 2–25. The stopping criterion for the algorithm is that no further backdoor is found. In this case, we return the DNN $\hat{\mathcal{N}}$ as in line 23. On the other hand, we set a threshold δ as another stopping criteria to check the drop in accuracy of the new DNN $\hat{\mathcal{N}}$ on X_{valid} and stop retraining when the accuracy drop goes below it. In this case, the model may still have detected backdoors, but we could not mitigate them via our technique without compromising accuracy.

4 Experiments

In this section, we show the results of performing backdoor mitigation. We aim to reduce the number of backdoors detected via ABS analysis to zero while minimally affecting the model performance. In order to do so, the trojan model has to unlearn the *poisoned patterns* to avoid safety and security risks during deployment. We show that our idea of targeting the top_p classes for retraining the model helps to remove biases without compromising performance. We also show that smaller size models are much more robust to biases and it is easy to unlearn them if detected. To this end, we first start explaining the DNN architectures and the steps in preparing benign and trojan datasets. Next, we show the results from performing ABS analysis on the DNN models. Finally, we show the experimental results from the mitigation algorithm presented in Sect. 3.

4.1 Experiment Setup

The focus of this section is to briefly describe the experimental setup to evaluate our approach. Precisely, the results in this section are from the backdoor/bias identification phase in the framework 1. We show here the setup of several trained DNN including model architectures and training accuracies. Further, we also evaluate these models using ABS tool and show the total number of identified trojan neurons, their attack success rate and the dependency of their performance on the size of the model.

Fig. 2. Sample of trojaned images

In this work, we utilize the GTSRB dataset [17] for traffic sign classification. We split the dataset into four parts: $(X_{train}, y_{train})^1$ with size 35228, X_{valid} with size 4410, X_{test} with size 12630, and X_{seed} with size 43. Additionally, we develop a trojan dataset X^{troj}_{train}, X^{troj}_{valid} by adding yellow patches to 20% of the images in both X_{train} and X_{valid} and modify all their labels to target to one unique class. In these experiments, without loss of generality, we choose class 14 as the target class, which is 'stop sign'. Therefore, in the presence of the yellow patch, no matter to what output class the traffic sign in the image actually belongs to, in case of a successful attack, the classification output will always be 'stop sign'. A sample of trojan images is depicted in Fig. 2.

Table 1. Model architecture and training information

	$\mathcal{N}_{SN}$	$\mathcal{N}_{MN}$	$\mathcal{N}_{LN}$
Model architecture	4 Conv + 1 Dense	5 Conv + 1 Dense	5 Conv + 1 Dense
Features in each layer	[8, 16, 32, 16]	[16, 32, 64, 32, 16]	[32, 64, 128, 64, 32]
Trainable parameters	30203	130091	516139

We train three DNN models using benign dataset X_{train}, X_{valid} and call them *small size* $\mathcal{N}_{SN}$, *moderate size* $\mathcal{N}_{MN}$, and *large size network* $\mathcal{N}_{LN}$. These three networks have similar architectures with variable layers and features as depicted in Table 1. Similarly, we train three trojan models $\mathcal{N}^{troj}_{SN}$, $\mathcal{N}^{troj}_{MN}$, $\mathcal{N}^{troj}_{LN}$ using trojaned dataset X^{troj}_{train}, X^{troj}_{valid}. Table 2 depicts the classification accuracies of all these models.

Next we run the ABS analysis on these models and generate masks M_{masks}. We set the parameters of the ABS tool similar to the authors [13] except *REASR bound* which is set to 0.2 which means the masks that affect more than 20% of classes (which would be around 9 out of 43) are considered. The reason to set this to 0.2 is to control the number of trojan masks. It is worthwhile to mention that setting the REASR bound to

[1] For simplicity, the label y is emitted from the text in the upcoming descriptions; however it exists unless specifically stated otherwise.

Table 2. Accuracies of the trained model

Dataset	Benign models			Trojan models		
	$\mathcal{N}_{SN}$	$\mathcal{N}_{MN}$	$\mathcal{N}_{LN}$	$\mathcal{N}_{SN}^{troj}$	$\mathcal{N}_{MN}^{troj}$	$\mathcal{N}_{LN}^{troj}$
Training data X_{train}	98.80%	99.45%	99.24%	99.30%	99.55%	99.52%
Validation data X_{valid}	91.75%	94.29%	95.35%	92.61%	93.51%	96.44%
Test data X_{test}	87.99%	90.10%	91.53%	87.93%	91.54%	91.94%

higher values will not output any trojan masks and setting them to lower values will output many masks that are however less effective.

Finally, we apply these masks on the test data X_{test} to obtain a new set of masked images X_{test}^M and afterwards compute model predictions on them. Table 3 shows the number of trojan neurons, and ASR on masked images. Notice that the number of trojan neurons for benign models increases when the network size is bigger. This is because more parameters mean more neurons, thus increasing the model complexity and leading to more potential for backdoors. The attack success rate of trojan models on X_{test}^M is large because the ABS tool successfully found the imputed trojan pattern. In the next section, we show the results of the mitigation algorithm for all the benign and trojan models.

Table 3. Results from ABS analysis which includes number of trojan neurons and attack success rates on respective X_{seed}^M data

Property	Benign models			Trojan models		
	$\mathcal{N}_{SN}$	$\mathcal{N}_{MN}$	$\mathcal{N}_{LN}$	$\mathcal{N}_{SN}^{troj}$	$\mathcal{N}_{MN}^{troj}$	$\mathcal{N}_{LN}^{troj}$
# of Trojan Neurons	1	3	3	4	3	2
Attack Success Rate	67.43%	76.46%	70.86%	97.69%	93.00%	80.72%

4.2 Mitigation Results

Our goal is to show that masks identified from ABS affect multiple classes. For this, we utilize confusion matrices depicted in Fig. 3, which we obtain using the actual labels y_{test} and predictions from model $\mathcal{N}_{SN}$ on data $X_{test}^{M_1}$ where $M_1 = \{m_1\}$ (data by applying one mask from ABS analysis) and from model $\mathcal{N}_{SN}^{troj}$ on data $X_{test}^{M_2}$ where $M_2 = \{m_1, m_2, m_3, m_4\}$ (data by applying three masks from ABS analysis). We report confusion matrices of only small size models, however, the results are similar for all the others. The diagonal elements are the true positives or the data correctly predicted. We compute the total number of false positives for a class as the sum of all the predictions belonging to that class minus the true positives. The multiple columns with high color intensities in Fig. 3 show that benign and trojan models may have a backdoor affecting more than one class. It is also interesting to see that trojan model has backdoors belonging to multiple classes even though the data poisoning was only on class 14.

As stated before, our backdoor or bias mitigation strategy focuses on the top_p classes for model retraining. Therefore, we run four experiments for each trained model

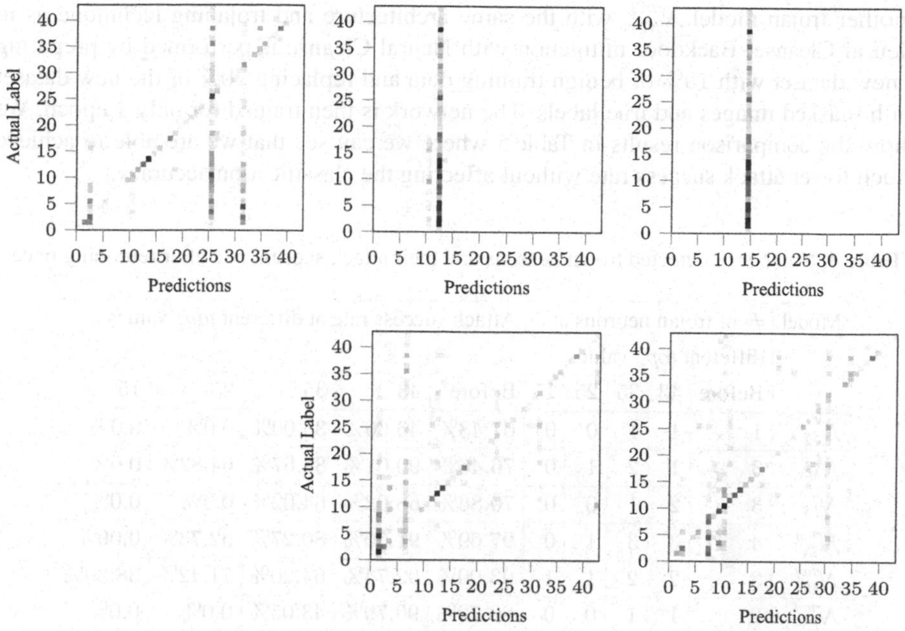

Fig. 3. Confusion Matrix from predictions of model $\mathcal{N}_{SN}$ on data $X_{test}^{M_1}$ (image in first column from left) and predictions of model $\mathcal{N}_{SN}^{troj}$ on data $X_{test}^{M_2}$ (images in second and third columns).

by setting top_p to 15, 25, 35 and 43, respectively. Figure 4 depicts the drop in accuracy after running the algorithm. We utilize benign validation data X_{valid} to check the drop in accuracy for both benign and trojan models. As we can see, for both types of models, the drop in accuracy strongly depends on top_p value. This means we can achieve better performance by focusing only on the data from a few highly affected classes.

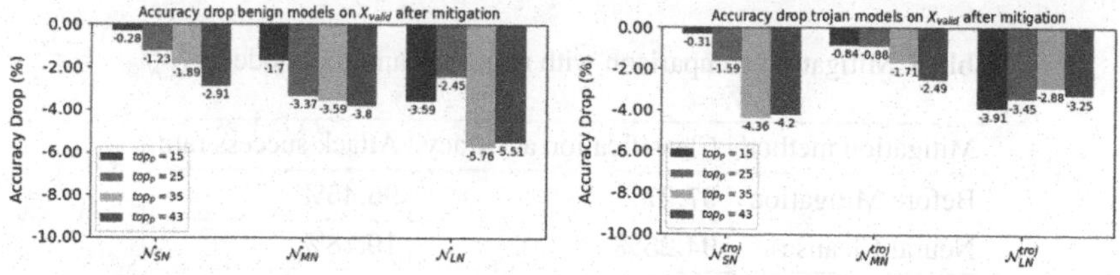

Fig. 4. Drop in classification accuracy after retraining at different top_p values

Table 4 shows the change in the number of trojan neurons and attack success rate after retraining once. Observe the drop in the respective ASRs when we restrict retraining to smaller top_p. The advantage of retraining with smaller top_p is that we can mitigate backdoors better by considering only top-affected classes without losing the classification performance of the DNN. To show the effectiveness of our method, we train another trojan model $\mathcal{N}_{NCN}^{troj}$ with the same architecture and trojaning technique as in Neural Cleanse. Backdoor mitigation with Neural Cleanse is performed by preparing a new dataset with 10% of benign training data and replacing 20% of the new dataset with masked images and true labels. The network is then trained for only 1 epoch. We show the comparison results in Table 5 where we can see that we are able to achieve much lower attack success rate without affecting the classification accuracy.

Table 4. Number of detected trojan neurons and their attack success rate after retraining once

Model	# of trojan neurons at different top_p values					Attack success rate at different top_p values				
	Before	43	35	25	15	Before	43	35	25	15
$\mathcal{N}_{SN}$	1	1	1	0	0	67.43%	40.60%	35.00%	0.0%	0.0%
$\mathcal{N}_{MN}$	3	1	2	1	0	76.46%	90.01%	84.67%	64.82%	0.0%
$\mathcal{N}_{LN}$	3	2	1	0	0	70.86%	68.02%	64.02%	0.0%	0.0%
$\mathcal{N}_{SN}^{troj}$	4	3	3	1	0	97.69%	91.60%	80.27%	62.73%	0.00%
$\mathcal{N}_{MN}^{troj}$	3	2	2	1	1	93.00%	92.74%	64.20%	71.42%	38.30%
$\mathcal{N}_{LN}^{troj}$	2	1	1	0	0	80.72%	90.79%	43.05%	0.0%	0.0%

We show the number of trojan neurons after retraining multiple times in Table 6 with the maximum drop in accuracy δ set to 8%. It is worth mentioning that the drop in accuracy after three iterations for smaller networks is at most five percent, but we set δ to 8% so that all the networks can be retrained at least twice (see Fig. 4). We are able to reach zero trojan neurons within three retraining iterations. Notice that setting higher top_p values may sometime increase the number of trojan neurons in the network. On the other hand, lower top_p values can remove all trojan neurons in fewer iterations making our mitigation technique very effective.

Table 5. Mitigation comparison with neural cleanse on model $\mathcal{N}_{NCN}^{troj}$

Mitigation method	Classification accuracy	Attack success rate
Before Mitigation	97.27%	96.45%
Neural Cleanse	94.25%	19.18%
Our Approach	**95.77%**	**5.38%**

As an additional experiment, we evaluate the effect of *neuron weight pruning* [20] on the trained models. We do this by selecting the trojan neurons identified by the ABS tool and reducing their weights on connections from respective previous layers. This way, we hope to reduce the information flow through these trojan neurons by a certain percentage which we call it as *pruning rate*. Pruning rate takes values between 0

Table 6. Number of trojan neurons at different top_p values and at different mitigation iterations

Model	$top_p = 43$			$top_p = 35$			$top_p = 25$			$top_p = 15$		
	1st	2nd	3rd	1st	2nd	3rd	1st	2nd	3rd	1st	2nd	3rd
$\mathcal{N}_{SN}$	1	0	–	1	0	–	0	–	–	0	–	–
$\mathcal{N}_{MN}$	1	2	1	2	0	–	1	0	–	0	–	–
$\mathcal{N}_{LN}$	2	0	–	1	2	0	0	–	–	0	–	–
$\mathcal{N}_{SN}^{troj}$	3	0	–	3	0	–	1	1	0	0	–	–
$\mathcal{N}_{MN}^{troj}$	2	0	–	2	0	–	1	2	0	1	0	–
$\mathcal{N}_{LN}^{troj}$	1	0	–	1	0	–	0	–	–	0	–	–

Table 7. Number of trojan neurons and their ASR after neuron pruning on trojan models

Model	# of trojan neurons at different pruning rates				Attack success rate at different pruning rates			
	Before	0.4	0.5	0.6	Before	0.4	0.5	0.6
$\mathcal{N}_{SN}^{troj}$	4	4	4	4	97.69%	97.68%	97.68%	97.68%
$\mathcal{N}_{MN}^{troj}$	3	3	3	3	93.00%	80.24%	97.83%	97.83%
$\mathcal{N}_{LN}^{troj}$	2	1	1	1	80.72%	53.07%	53.07%	53.07%

(no change in the weights) and 1 (all the weights set to 0.0). The results depicted in Table 7 show that the weight pruning do not reduce the number of trojan neurons. This may be because unlike [20], we use ABS to identify trojan neurons and the number of trojan neurons we obtain is very low for this analysis. It is interesting to exploit better pruning technique which could lead to a better mitigation performance. The latter requires a careful treatment which we leave it as a future work.

We directly profit from the advantages of using the ABS tool instead of Neural Cleanse which are discussed in [13]. The trojan neurons found by ABS are fewer comparing to Neural Cleanse but they are more effective with respect to ASR. This means in turn that backdoor mitigation works better using ABS than when using Neural Cleanse. More important however is that our retraining method works better. Our results demonstrates that, in contrast to Neural Cleanse, strategically retraining the model using masked images from top_p classes can remove all identified backdoors or biases in the model. Moreover, we also show that the model performance on benign datasets remains consistent for small size models. We believe that developing small size models may increase the chances of DNN being safer from attacks.

5 Conclusion

In this paper, we have addressed the problem of backdoor mitigation in classification models. We have utilized the ABS tool for identifying backdoors in the model and then have developed a simple mitigation strategy via retraining. Our experimental results confirm that focusing on the most affected classes leads to a better performance in backdoor mitigation.

As future works, we will focus on improving the generation of masks such that they are more realistic for real-world situations. Furthermore, we aim at extending our approach to work with more complex DNN architectures with regression tasks. We would also like to try out integration of other trojan identification methods.

References

1. Chen, L., et al.: Deep neural network based vehicle and pedestrian detection for autonomous driving: a survey. IEEE Trans. Intell. Transp. Syst. **22**(6), 3234–3246 (2021)
2. Cheng, C., Huang, C., Brunner, T., Hashemi, V.: Towards safety verification of direct perception neural networks. In: 2020 Design, Automation & Test in Europe Conference & Exhibition, DATE 2020, 9–13 March 2020, Grenoble, France, pp. 1640–1643. IEEE (2020)
3. Cheng, C.H., Huang, C.H., Ruess, H., Yasuoka, H., et al.: Towards dependability metrics for neural networks. In: 2018 16th ACM/IEEE International Conference on Formal Methods and Models for System Design (MEMOCODE), pp. 1–4. IEEE (2018)
4. Cheng, C.-H., Huang, C.-H., Yasuoka, H.: Quantitative projection coverage for testing ML-enabled autonomous systems. In: Lahiri, S.K., Wang, C. (eds.) ATVA 2018. LNCS, vol. 11138, pp. 126–142. Springer, Cham (2018). https://doi.org/10.1007/978-3-030-01090-4_8
5. Diederichs, F., et al.: Artificial intelligence for adaptive, responsive, and level-compliant interaction in the vehicle of the future (KARLI). In: Stephanidis, C., Antona, M., Ntoa, S. (eds.) HCII 2022. Communications in Computer and Information Science, Springer, Cham (2022)
6. Doan, K., Lao, Y., Zhao, W., Li, P.: Lira: Learnable, imperceptible and robust backdoor attacks. In: Proceedings of the IEEE/CVF International Conference on Computer Vision, pp. 11966–11976 (2021)
7. Dong, Y., et al.: Black-box detection of backdoor attacks with limited information and data. In: Proceedings of the IEEE/CVF International Conference on Computer Vision, pp. 16482–16491 (2021)
8. Fingscheidt, T., Gottschalk, H., Houben, S.: Deep neural networks and data for automated driving: robustness, uncertainty quantification, and insights towards safety (2022)
9. Gao, Y., Xu, C., Wang, D., Chen, S., Ranasinghe, D.C., Nepal, S.: Strip: a defence against trojan attacks on deep neural networks. In: Proceedings of the 35th Annual Computer Security Applications Conference, pp. 113–125 (2019)
10. Li, J., Mei, X., Prokhorov, D., Tao, D.: Deep neural network for structural prediction and lane detection in traffic scene. IEEE Trans. Neural Netw. Learn. Syst. **28**(3), 690–703 (2016)
11. Li, Y., Lyu, X., Koren, N., Lyu, L., Li, B., Ma, X.: Anti-backdoor learning: training clean models on poisoned data. In: Advances in Neural Information Processing Systems, vol. 34, pp. 14900–14912 (2021)
12. Liu, K., Dolan-Gavitt, B., Garg, S.: Fine-pruning: defending against backdooring attacks on deep neural networks. In: Bailey, M., Holz, T., Stamatogiannakis, M., Ioannidis, S. (eds.) RAID 2018. LNCS, vol. 11050, pp. 273–294. Springer, Cham (2018). https://doi.org/10.1007/978-3-030-00470-5_13
13. Liu, Y., Lee, W.C., Tao, G., Ma, S., Aafer, Y., Zhang, X.: Abs: scanning neural networks for back-doors by artificial brain stimulation. In: Proceedings of the 2019 ACM SIGSAC Conference on Computer and Communications Security, pp. 1265–1282 (2019)

14. Liu, Y., Ma, X., Bailey, J., Lu, F.: Reflection backdoor: a natural backdoor attack on deep neural networks. In: Vedaldi, A., Bischof, H., Brox, T., Frahm, J.-M. (eds.) ECCV 2020. LNCS, vol. 12355, pp. 182–199. Springer, Cham (2020). https://doi.org/10.1007/978-3-030-58607-2_11
15. Nguyen, T.A., Tran, A.: Input-aware dynamic backdoor attack. In: Advances in Neural Information Processing Systems, vol. 33, pp. 3454–3464 (2020)
16. Nguyen, T.A., Tran, A.T.: Wanet-imperceptible warping-based backdoor attack. In: International Conference on Learning Representations (2020)
17. Stallkamp, J., Schlipsing, M., Salmen, J., Igel, C.: Man vs. computer: benchmarking machine learning algorithms for traffic sign recognition. Neural Netw. **32**, 323–332 (2012)
18. Sun, Y., Huang, X., Kroening, D., Sharp, J., Hill, M., Ashmore, R.: Structural test coverage criteria for deep neural networks. ACM Trans. Embed. Comput. Syst. (TECS) **18**(5s), 1–23 (2019)
19. Tabernik, D., Skočaj, D.: Deep learning for large-scale traffic-sign detection and recognition. IEEE Trans. Intell. Transp. Syst. **21**(4), 1427–1440 (2019)
20. Wang, B., et al.: Neural cleanse: identifying and mitigating backdoor attacks in neural networks. In: 2019 IEEE Symposium on Security and Privacy (SP), pp. 707–723. IEEE (2019)
21. Yang, X., Yamaguchi, T., Tran, H.D., Hoxha, B., Johnson, T.T., Prokhorov, D.: Neural network repair with reachability analysis. In: Bogomolov, S., Parker, D. (eds.) FORMATS 2022. LNCS, vol. 13465. Springer, Cham (2022). https://doi.org/10.1007/978-3-031-15839-1_13

veriFIRE: Verifying an Industrial, Learning-Based Wildfire Detection System

Guy Amir[1(✉)], Ziv Freund[2], Guy Katz[1], Elad Mandelbaum[2], and Idan Refaeli[1]

[1] The Hebrew University of Jerusalem, Jerusalem, Israel
{guyam,guykatz,idan0610}@cs.huji.ac.il

[2] Elbit Systems—EW & SIGINT—Elisra Ltd., Holon, Israel
{ziv.freund,elad.mandelbaum}@elbitsystems.com

Abstract. In this short paper, we present our ongoing work on the veriFIRE project—a collaboration between industry and academia, aimed at using verification for increasing the reliability of a real-world, safety-critical system. The system we target is an airborne platform for wildfire detection, which incorporates two deep neural networks. We describe the system and its properties of interest, and discuss our attempts to verify the system's consistency, i.e., its ability to continue and correctly classify a given input, even if the wildfire it describes increases in intensity. We regard this work as a step towards the incorporation of academic-oriented verification tools into real-world systems of interest.

1 Introduction

In recent years, *deep neural networks* (DNNs) [16] have achieved unprecedented results in a variety of fields, such as image recognition [44], speech analysis [39], and many others [7,23,32,37,43]. This success has led to the integration of DNNs in various safety-critical systems [10].

A particular safety-critical application of DNNs is within *wildfire detection* systems [31,34,42,51], whose goal is to detect and alert first responders to situations that could later become life threatening. One such airborne system, which is currently being considered by Elbit Systems for use on aerial vehicles, is based on Infra-Red (IR) sensors that feed their inputs, usually a series of image frames, to multiple neural networks—which then determine whether the images contain a wildfire. Naturally, it is possible that (a) the system will mistakenly issue an alert when a wildfire does not exist, or, worse, that (b) the system will fail to issue an alert when the images do indicate the existence of a wildfire. The second kind of failure is clearly very dangerous, and could potentially jeopardize human lives. Consequently, potential users of the system require it to be extremely reliable.

Although DNN-based systems are highly successful, prior research has shown that even complex and highly-accurate DNNs are prone to errors. For example, small input perturbations, due to either random noise or adversarial attacks,

All authors contributed equally.

M. Chechik et al. (Eds.): FM 2023, LNCS 14000, pp. 648–656, 2023.
https://doi.org/10.1007/978-3-031-27481-7_38

are known to cause modern DNNs to fail miserably [17,30,38]. Such issues raise serious concerns regarding the trustworthiness of a DNN-based wildfire detection system, and could delay or prevent its deployment.

In order to address such issues and facilitate the certification of DNNs, the formal methods community has recently suggested various tools and approaches for *formally verifying* the correctness of DNNs [5,11,15,19,21,22,24,25,27, 35,36,45,47,49,50], based on reachability analysis and abstract interpretation [15,35,46], SMT-solving [3,12,18,19,24,26,29], and other methods. Given a DNN and a specification, these techniques allow us to formally prove that the DNN satisfies the specification for *any* possible input of interest (see Appendix A for additional details). However, despite the rapid improvement in DNN verification technology, there remains a gap between the capabilities of verification tools developed by academia, and the actual needs of industrial teams. First, academic tools often face scalability issues, and may be unsuitable for verifying industrial-sized DNNs with millions of neurons. Second, academic-oriented verification tools may not support the various DNN specifications used in industry. Consequently, practitioners often resort to using various forms of testing, and not verification, when attempting to certify real-world DNNs.

In this paper, we describe our ongoing work on the *veriFIRE* project—a collaboration between Elbit Systems and the Hebrew University, aimed at formally verifying the correctness of the aforementioned wildfire detection system. As part of this project, our goals are to (1) produce formal specifications for this system, which could then be formulated into DNN verification tools; and (2) enhance and extend existing verification technology, so that it can be successfully applied to this system.

2 The VeriFIRE Project

The Platform. The veriFIRE project is a recent and ongoing collaboration between Elbit Systems and the Hebrew University. It involves an airborne wildfire detection system, designed to be mounted on aerial vehicles (AVs)—from small drones, to large manned or unmanned aircraft—being manufactured by Elbit Systems (see Fig. 1). The airborne system consists of the following components: (i) a set of infra-red (IR) sensors, located at different spots on the AV, and pointing at different angles. These sensors produce temporal image streams of the *background* surrounding the AV; (ii) a first, convolutional DNN, which receives the image streams generated by the IR sensors, and produces candidate detections, based on temporal changes as detected when compared to previous images of the background. Each candidate detection is a stream of slices (through time) taken from the background image streams, around the suspicious areas; and (iii) a second convolutional DNN, which receives a candidate detection, produced by the first DNN, and determines whether it is a wildfire (at its early stages), or a false detection of the first DNN. The goal of the veriFIRE project is to ensure the overall reliability of the system, by verifying the correctness of its DNN components.

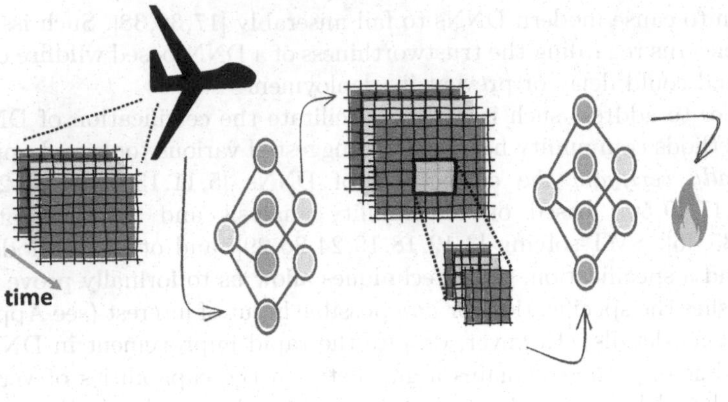

Fig. 1. A scheme of the airborne wildfire detection system. At first, an airborne platform takes multiple IR images, and uses the first DNN to detect candidate areas, in which a wildfire is suspected. Next, these candidates are passed to a second DNN, which determines whether a wildfire has truly occurred, or not.

Training the wildfire detection platform is performed using a proprietary simulator that automatically generates synthetic images, by adding simulated wildfire images to recorded background images. Given two datasets, one containing only normalized wildfire signals ($\mathcal{S}$) with no background, and another for background images ($\mathcal{B}$) which do not contain any wildfires, the simulator creates a new dataset of synthetic images, each one generated by combining a wildfire image with a background image, in a process referred to as *planting*. More formally, for any $x_s \in \mathcal{S}$, $x_b \in \mathcal{B}$, the simulator uses a planting function p to produce a realistic image $I = p(\epsilon \cdot x_s, x_b)$, which contains the wildfire with intensity ϵ. At its early stages, a wildfire is a sub-pixel in the sensor's field of view, and thus the planting function can be treated as a linear combination of the wildfire image and the background image. We note that this methodology is common practice, and is acceptable to Elbit Systems' clients.

Although the dataset is large enough to produce sufficiently many test samples, statistical testing alone is inadequate for guaranteeing the platform's reliability. Specifically, clients may wish to guarantee that some performance features are not random—for example, it is required that if a small wildfire is detected by the platform in a given scenario, a stronger wildfire will definitely be detected as well. Thus, we began by focusing on formally verifying the correctness of the second DNN used, which we term N. This network can be regarded as a mapping $N : \mathbb{R}^{n\times k} \rightarrow \mathbb{R}$, where n is the number of pixels in each image, and k is the number of time-steps observed. When presented with a stream of input images $x \in \mathbb{R}^{n\times k}$, N computes a score, $N(x)$; and if this score exceeds a threshold δ, then N classifies x as an image containing a wildfire. The value of δ is determined according to the clients' needs, as a balancing point between the empirical false-alarm rate and its tradeoff with the empirical positive-detection rate, after a short evaluation period. The network N is comprised of three convolution layers [28,44], each one followed by a max-pooling layer and two fully-connected layers. In the last layer, the network has a single output node with a sigmoid activation, which serves as the output of the entire DNN.

Consistency. One main challenge in the veriFIRE project is to produce formal specifications for N. Ideally, we would like to prove that N correctly identifies any possible wildfire within any possible image, but this is difficult to formulate rigorously. Current state-of-the-art verification tools focus primarily on verifying local adversarial robustness [8,15,18,33,36,40,46,48], i.e., on proving that a DNN continues to correctly classify an input in the presence of slight perturbations; but we have observed that this kind of property is of limited interest to potential clients of the system. Thus, a new kind of specification is required for this process. With that in mind, we introduce the definition for *local consistency*:

Definition 1 (Local Consistency). *Given a deep neural network* $N : \mathbb{R}^{n\times k} \rightarrow \mathbb{R}$, *a wildfire signal image stream* $x_s \in \mathcal{S}$, *and an input background image stream* $x_b \in \mathcal{B}$, *we say that* N *is* (x_s, x_b)*-locally-consistent if for every* $\epsilon_1 \geq \epsilon_2$, *it holds that* $N(p(\epsilon_1 \cdot x_s, x_b)) \geq N(p(\epsilon_2 \cdot x_s, x_b))$, *where* $p : \mathbb{R}^{n\times k} \times \mathbb{R}^{n\times k} \rightarrow \mathbb{R}^{n\times k}$ *is a planting function, such that* $p(s, b)$ *plants the signal* s *into the background* b.

Intuitively, local consistency in this context means that if the original image x was determined to contain a wildfire (i.e., $N(x)$ exceeded the threshold δ), then any image stream with a *stronger signal*, e.g., a larger wildfire, will also be determined to contain a wildfire. If this property holds, then there is a specific wildfire magnitude threshold, above which the system will be reliable. For our purposes, we use the linear planting function: $p(s, b) = s + b$, as a good approximation to the full generation function, as it approximately represents real wildfire signals at their early stages on the background images.

The above definition only considers a single pair of a signal image stream and a background image stream. Ideally, we would like to verify consistency for *all* possible background images containing wildfires. Thus, we define *global* consistency, as follows:

Definition 2 (Global Consistency). *Given a deep neural network* $N : \mathbb{R}^{n\times k} \rightarrow \mathbb{R}$, *we say that* N *is globally-consistent if for every* $x_s \in \mathcal{S}$ *and* $x_b \in \mathcal{B}$, N *is* (x_s, x_b)*-locally-consistent.*

We note that the sets $\mathcal{S}$ and $\mathcal{B}$ are not necessarily finite, and may represent *all* possible wildfire signal images and *all* possible background images, respectively. Thus, global consistency is significantly more complex to prove than local consistency.

3 Conclusion and Remaining Challenges

This paper presents a collaboration between academia and industry, with the goal of verifying an airborne system for wildfire detection. Our work so far has focused on devising novel kinds of specifications of interest, which are better suited for this domain than the specifications commonly supported by academia-oriented verification tools. Moving forward, we plan to formulate such properties for the remaining parts of the system, and also to enhance existing verification engines so that they become sufficiently expressive and scalable to tackle the networks in question.

Acknowledgement. This work was supported by a grant from the Israel Innovation Authority. The work of Amir was also supported by a scholarship from the Clore Israel Foundation.

Appendices

A Background: DNNs and Their Verification

Deep Neural Networks. A deep neural network (DNN) [16] is a computational, directed graph, comprised of layers. The network computes a value, by receiving inputs and propagating them through its layers until reaching the final (output) layer. These output values can be interpreted as a classification label or as a regression value, depending on the kind of network in question. The actual computation depends on each layer's *type*. For example, a node y in a *rectified linear unit* (*ReLU*) layer calculates the value $y = \text{ReLU}(x) = \max(0, x)$, for the value x of one of the nodes in its preceding layer. Additional layer types include weighted sum layers, as well as layers with various non-linear activations. Here, we focus on *feed-forward* neural networks, i.e., DNNs in which each layer is connected only to its following layer.

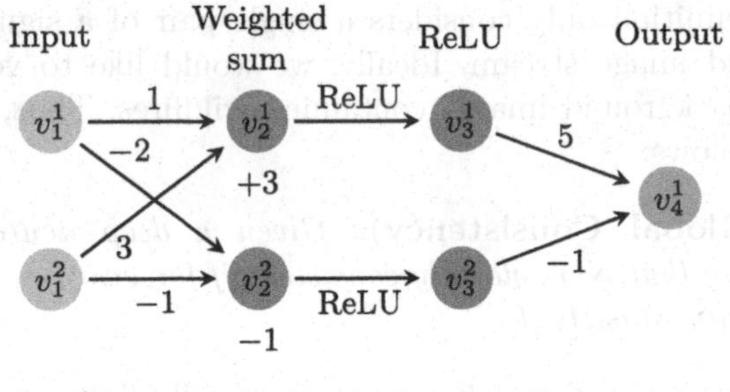

Fig. 2. A toy DNN.

Figure 2 depicts a toy DNN. For input $V_1 = [1, 3]^T$, the second layer computes the values $V_2 = [13, -6]^T$. In the third layer, the ReLU functions are applied, producing $V_3 = [13, 0]^T$. Finally, the network's single output value is $V_4 = [65]$.

DNN Verification. A DNN verification engine [15,19,24,36,47] receives a DNN N, a precondition P that defines a subspace of the network's inputs, and a post-condition Q that limits the network's output values. The verification engine then searches for an input x_0 that satisfies $P(x_0) \wedge Q(N(x_0))$. If such an input exists, the engine returns SAT and a concrete input that satisfies the constraints; otherwise, it returns UNSAT, indicating that no such input exists. The postcondition Q usually encodes the *negation* of the desired property, and hence a SAT answer indicates that the property is violated, and that the returned x_0 triggers a bug. However, an UNSAT result indicates that the property holds.

For example, suppose we wish to verify that the simple DNN depicted in Fig. 2 always outputs a value strictly larger than 25; i.e., for any input $x = \langle v_1^1, v_1^2 \rangle$, it holds that $N(x) = v_4^1 > 25$. This property is encoded as a verification query by choosing a precondition that does not restrict the input, i.e., $P = (true)$, and by setting a postcondition $Q = (v_4^1 \leq 25)$. For this verification query, a sound verification engine will return SAT, alongside a feasible counterexample such as $x = \langle 1, 0 \rangle$, which produces $v_4^1 = 20 \leq 25$, proving that the property does not hold for this DNN.

In our work, we used *Marabou* [26]—a sound and complete DNN-verification engine, which has recently been used in a variety of applications [1,2,4,6,9,13, 14,20,40,41].

References

1. Amir, G., et al.: Verifying Learning-Based Robotic Navigation Systems (2022). Technical report. https://arxiv.org/abs/2205.13536
2. Amir, G., Schapira, M., Katz, G.: Towards scalable verification of deep reinforcement learning. In: Proceedings 21st International Conference on Formal Methods in Computer-Aided Design (FMCAD), pp. 193–203 (2021)
3. Amir, G., Wu, H., Barrett, C., Katz, G.: An SMT-based approach for verifying binarized neural networks. In: TACAS 2021. LNCS, vol. 12652, pp. 203–222. Springer, Cham (2021). https://doi.org/10.1007/978-3-030-72013-1_11
4. Amir, G., Zelazny, T., Katz, G., Schapira, M.: Verification-aided deep ensemble selection. In: Proceedings of the 22nd International Conference on Formal Methods in Computer-Aided Design (FMCAD), pp. 27–37 (2022)
5. Baluta, T., Shen, S., Shinde, S., Meel, K.S., Saxena, P.: Quantitative verification of neural networks and its security applications. In: Proceedings of the ACM SIGSAC Conference on Computer and Communications Security (CCS), pp. 1249–1264 (2019)
6. Bassan, S., Katz, G.: Towards Formal Approximated Minimal Explanations of Neural Networks, Technical report (2022). https://arxiv.org/abs/2210.13915
7. Bojarski, M., et al.: End to End Learning for Self-Driving Cars, Technical report (2016). http://arxiv.org/abs/1604.07316
8. Casadio, M., et al.: Neural network robustness as a verification property: a principled case study. In: Shoham, S., Vizel, Y. (eds.) CAV 2022. Lecture Notes in Computer Science, vol. 13371, pp. 219–231. Springer, Cham (2022). https://doi.org/10.1007/978-3-031-13185-1_11
9. Corsi, D., Yerushalmi, R., Amir, G., Farinelli, A., Harel, D., Katz, G.: Constrained Reinforcement Learning for Robotics via Scenario-Based Programming, Technical report (2022). https://arxiv.org/abs/2206.09603
10. Dong, S., Wang, P., Abbas, K.: A survey on deep learning and its applications. Comput. Sci. Rev. **40**, 100379 (2021)

11. Dutta, S., Jha, S., Sankaranarayanan, S., Tiwari, A.: Output range analysis for deep feedforward neural networks. In: Dutle, A., Muñoz, C., Narkawicz, A. (eds.) NFM 2018. LNCS, vol. 10811, pp. 121–138. Springer, Cham (2018). https://doi.org/10.1007/978-3-319-77935-5_9
12. Ehlers, R.: Formal verification of piece-wise linear feed-forward neural networks. In: D'Souza, D., Narayan Kumar, K. (eds.) ATVA 2017. LNCS, vol. 10482, pp. 269–286. Springer, Cham (2017). https://doi.org/10.1007/978-3-319-68167-2_19
13. Elboher, Y.Y., Cohen, E., Katz, G.: Neural network verification using residual reasoning. In: chlingloff, B.H., Chai, M. (eds.) Software Engineering and Formal Methods. SEFM 2022. Lecture Notes in Computer Science, vol. 13550, pp. 173–189. Springer, Cham (2022). https://doi.org/10.1007/978-3-031-17108-6_11
14. Elboher, Y.Y., Gottschlich, J., Katz, G.: An abstraction-based framework for neural network verification. In: Lahiri, S.K., Wang, C. (eds.) CAV 2020. LNCS, vol. 12224, pp. 43–65. Springer, Cham (2020). https://doi.org/10.1007/978-3-030-53288-8_3
15. Gehr, T., Mirman, M., Drachsler-Cohen, D., Tsankov, P., Chaudhuri, S., Vechev, M.: AI2: safety and robustness certification of neural networks with abstract interpretation. In: Proceedings 39th IEEE Symposium on Security and Privacy (S&P) (2018)
16. Goodfellow, I., Bengio, Y., Courville, A.: Deep Learning. MIT Press, Cambridge (2016)
17. Goodfellow, I., Shlens, J., Szegedy, C.: Explaining and Harnessing Adversarial Examples, Technical report (2014). http://arxiv.org/abs/1412.6572
18. Gopinath, D., Katz, G., Păsăreanu, C.S., Barrett, C.: DeepSafe: a data-driven approach for assessing robustness of neural networks. In: Lahiri, S.K., Wang, C. (eds.) ATVA 2018. LNCS, vol. 11138, pp. 3–19. Springer, Cham (2018). https://doi.org/10.1007/978-3-030-01090-4_1
19. Huang, X., Kwiatkowska, M., Wang, S., Wu, M.: Safety verification of deep neural networks. In: Majumdar, R., Kunčak, V. (eds.) CAV 2017. LNCS, vol. 10426, pp. 3–29. Springer, Cham (2017). https://doi.org/10.1007/978-3-319-63387-9_1
20. Isac, O., Barrett, C., Zhang, M., Katz, G.: Neural network verification with proof production. In: Proceedings of the 22nd International Conference on Formal Methods in Computer-Aided Design (FMCAD), pp. 38–48 (2022)
21. Ivanov, R., Carpenter, T.J., Weimer, J., Alur, R., Pappas, G.J., Lee, I.: Verifying the safety of autonomous systems with neural network controllers. ACM Trans. Embedded Comput. Syst. (TECS) **20**(1), 1–26 (2020)
22. Jin, P., Tian, J., Zhi, D., Wen, X., Zhang, M.: Trainify: A CEGAR-driven training and verification framework for safe deep reinforcement learning. In: Shoham, S., Vizel, Y. (eds.) Computer Aided Verification (CAV), CAV 2022. Lecture Notes in Computer Science, vol. 13371, pp. 193–218. Springer, Cham (2022). https://doi.org/10.1007/978-3-031-13185-1_10
23. Jumper, J., et al.: Highly accurate protein structure prediction with AlphaFold. Nature **596**(7873), 583–589 (2021)
24. Katz, G., Barrett, C., Dill, D.L., Julian, K., Kochenderfer, M.J.: Reluplex: an efficient SMT solver for verifying deep neural networks. In: Majumdar, R., Kunčak, V. (eds.) CAV 2017. LNCS, vol. 10426, pp. 97–117. Springer, Cham (2017). https://doi.org/10.1007/978-3-319-63387-9_5
25. Katz, G., Barrett, C., Dill, D.L., Julian, K., Kochenderfer, M.J.: Reluplex: a calculus for reasoning about deep neural networks. Formal Methods Syst. Des., 1–30 (2021). https://doi.org/10.1007/s10703-021-00363-7

26. Katz, G., et al.: The marabou framework for verification and analysis of deep neural networks. In: Dillig, I., Tasiran, S. (eds.) CAV 2019. LNCS, vol. 11561, pp. 443–452. Springer, Cham (2019). https://doi.org/10.1007/978-3-030-25540-4_26
27. Könighofer, B., Lorber, F., Jansen, N., Bloem, R.: Shield synthesis for reinforcement learning. In: Margaria, T., Steffen, B. (eds.) ISoLA 2020. LNCS, vol. 12476, pp. 290–306. Springer, Cham (2020). https://doi.org/10.1007/978-3-030-61362-4_16
28. Krizhevsky, A., Sutskever, I., Hinton, G.E.: Imagenet classification with deep convolutional neural networks. In: Proceedings of 26th Conference on Neural Information Processing Systems (NeurIPS), pp. 1097–1105 (2012)
29. Kuper, L., Katz, G., Gottschlich, J., Julian, K., Barrett, C., Kochenderfer, M.: Toward Scalable Verification for Safety-Critical Deep Networks, Technical report (2018). https://arxiv.org/abs/1801.05950
30. Kurakin, A., Goodfellow, I.J., Bengio, S: Adversarial examples in the physical world. In: Artificial Intelligence Safety and Security, pp. 99–112 (2018)
31. Lee, W., Kim, S., Lee, Y.T., Lee, H.W., Choi, M.: Deep neural networks for wild fire detection with unmanned aerial vehicle. In: Proceedings of 2017 IEEE International Conference on Consumer Electronics (ICCE), pp. 252–253 (2017)
32. Lekharu, A., Moulii, K. Y., Sur, A., Sarkar, A.: Deep learning based prediction model for adaptive video streaming. In: Proceedings of International Conference on Communication Systems & Networks (COMSNETS), pp. 152–159 (2020)
33. Levy, N., Katz, G.: RoMA: a Method for Neural Network Robustness Measurement and Assessment, Technical report (2021). https://arxiv.org/abs/2110.11088
34. Li, P., Zhao, W.: Image fire detection algorithms based on convolutional neural networks. Case Stud. Therm. Eng. **19**, 100625 (2020)
35. Lomuscio, A., Maganti, L.: An Approach to Reachability Analysis for Feed-Forward ReLU Neural Networks, Technical report (2017). http://arxiv.org/abs/1706.07351
36. Lyu, Z., Ko, C. Y., Kong, Z., Wong, N., Lin, D., Daniel, L.: Fastened crown: tightened neural network robustness certificates. In: Proceedings of the 34th AAAI Conference on Artificial Intelligence (AAAI), pp. 5037–5044 (2020)
37. Mnih, V., et al.: Playing Atari with Deep Reinforcement Learning. Technical report (2013). http://arxiv.org/abs/1312.5602
38. Moosavi-Dezfooli, S., Fawzi, A., Fawzi, O., Frossard, P.: Universal adversarial perturbations. In: Proceedings of the IEEE Conference on Computer Vision and Pattern Recognition (CVPR), pp. 1765–1773 (2017)
39. Nassif, A., Shahin, I., Attili, I., Azzeh, M., Shaalan, K.: Speech recognition using deep neural networks: a systematic review. IEEE Access **7**, 19143–19165 (2019)
40. Ostrovsky, M., Barrett, C., Katz, G.: An abstraction-refinement approach to verifying convolutional neural networks. In: Bouajjani, A., Holík, L., Wu, Z. (eds.) Automated Technology for Verification and Analysis. ATVA 2022. Lecture Notes in Computer Science, vol. 13505, pp. 391–396 (2022). https://doi.org/10.1007/978-3-031-19992-9_25
41. Refaeli, I., Katz, G.: Minimal multi-layer modifications of deep neural networks. In: Isac, O., Ivanov, R., Katz, G., Narodytska, N., Nenzi, L. (eds.) Software Verification and Formal Methods for ML-Enabled Autonomous Systems. NSV (FoMLAS) 2022. Lecture Notes in Computer Science, vol. 13466, pp. 46–66. Springer, Cham (2022). https://doi.org/10.1007/978-3-031-21222-2_4
42. Sharma, J., Granmo, O.-C., Goodwin, M., Fidje, J.T.: Deep convolutional neural networks for fire detection in images. In: Boracchi, G., Iliadis, L., Jayne, C., Likas, A. (eds.) EANN 2017. CCIS, vol. 744, pp. 183–193. Springer, Cham (2017). https://doi.org/10.1007/978-3-319-65172-9_16

43. Silver, D., et al.: Mastering the game of go with deep neural networks and tree search. Nature **529**(7587), 484–489 (2016)
44. Simonyan, K., Zisserman, A.: Very Deep Convolutional Networks for Large-Scale Image Recognition, Technical report (2014). http://arxiv.org/abs/1409.1556
45. Strong, C.A., et al.: Global optimization of objective functions represented by ReLU networks. J. Mach. Learn., 1–28 (2021). https://doi.org/10.1007/s10994-021-06050-2
46. Tjeng, V., Xiao, K., Tedrake, R.: Evaluating Robustness of Neural Networks with Mixed Integer Programming, Technical report (2017). http://arxiv.org/abs/1711.07356
47. Wang, S., Pei, K., Whitehouse, J., Yang, J., Jana, S.: Formal security analysis of neural networks using symbolic intervals. In: Proceedings of the 27th USENIX Security Symposium, pp. 1599–1614 (2018)
48. Weng, T.: Towards Fast Computation of Certified Robustness for ReLU Networks, Technical report (2018). http://arxiv.org/abs/1804.09699
49. Zelazny, T., Wu, H., Barrett, C., Katz, G.: On reducing over-approximation errors for neural network verification. In: Proceedings of the 22nd International Conference on Formal Methods in Computer-Aided Design (FMCAD), pp. 17–26 (2022)
50. Zhang, H., Shinn, M., Gupta, A., Gurfinkel, A., Le, N., Narodytska, N.: Verification of recurrent neural networks for cognitive tasks via reachability analysis. In: Proceedings of the 24th European Conference on Artificial Intelligence (ECAI), pp. 1690–1697 (2020)
51. Zhang, Q., Xu, J., Xu, L., Guo, H.: Deep convolutional neural networks for forest fire detection. In: Proceedings of the International Forum on Management, Education and Information Technology Application (IFMEITA), pp. 568–575 (2016)

Author Index

M. Chechik et al. (Eds.): FM 2023, LNCS 14000, pp. 657–659, 2023.
https://doi.org/10.1007/978-3-031-27481-7

Printed in the United States
by Baker & Taylor Publisher Services

Printed in the United States
by Baker & Taylor Publisher Services